Michael Scammell is the editor of *Russia's Other Writers*, an anthology of *Samizdat*, *Soviet Unofficial Art* and *From under the Rubble*, a collection of essays by Solzhenitsyn and others. He has also translated extensively from Russian, including works by Tolstoy, Dostoyevsky, Nabokov, Solzhenitsyn, Bukovsky and Marchenko.

MICHAEL SCAMMELL

Solzhenitsyn
A Biography

PALADIN
GRAFTON BOOKS
A Division of the Collins Publishing Group

LONDON GLASGOW
TORONTO SYDNEY AUCKLAND

Paladin
Grafton Books
A Division of the Collins Publishing Group
8 Grafton Street, London W1X 3LA

Published in Paladin Books 1986

First published in Great Britain by
Hutchinson & Co (Publishers) Ltd 1985

Copyright © Michael Scammell 1984

ISBN 0-586-08538-6

Printed and bound in Great Britain by
Collins, Glasgow

Set in Garamond

The following works have been consulted in the preparation of
this biography:

August 1914. Translated by Michael Glenny, copyright 1972,
Bodley Head. *Cancer Ward.* Translated by Nicholas Bethell
and David Burg, copyright 1969, Bodley Head. *The First Cirle.*
Translated by Thomas Whitney, copyright 1968, Wm Collins. *The
Gulag Archipelago.* Vol. 1. Translated by Thomas Whitney,
copyright 1975, Wm Collins. *The Gulag Archipelago.* Vol. 2.
Translated by Thomas Whitney, copyright 1975, Wm Collins. *The
Gulag Archipelago.* Vol. 3. Translated by Harry Willetts, copyright
1979, Wm Collins. *The Oak and the Calf.* Translated by Harry
Willetts, copyright 1979, Wm Collins. *Prussian Nights.* Translated
by Robert Conquest, copyright 1977, Wm Collins. *Stories and Prose
Poems.* Translated by Michael Glenny, copyright 1971,
Bodley Head.

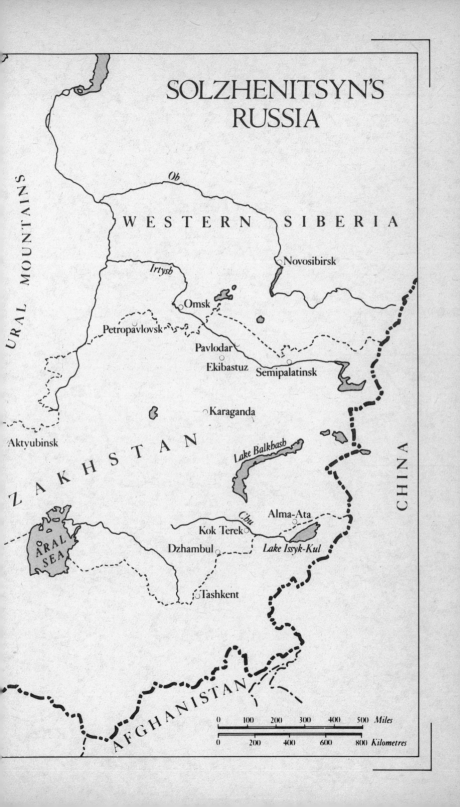

Solzhenitsyn speaks from another tradition and this, for me, is impressive: his voice is not modern but ancient. It is an ancientness tempered in the modern world. His ancientness is that of the old Russian Christianity, but it is a Christianity that has passed through the central experience of our century—the dehumanization of the totalitarian concentration camps—and has emerged intact and strengthened. If history is the testing ground, Solzhenitsyn has passed the test. His example is not intellectual or political or even, in the current sense of the word, moral. We have to use an even older word, a word that still retains a religious overtone—a hint of death and sacrifice: *witness*. In a century of false testimonies, a writer becomes the witness to man.

—Octavio Paz, "Polvos de aquellos lodos"
(Dust after Mud), *Plural*, no. 30 (March 1974)

Rien ne vous tue un homme comme d'être obligé de représenter un pays.

—Jacques Vache, letter to André Breton

CONTENTS

PREFACE

Writing the biography of a living man is sufficiently hazardous an undertaking as to call for some explanation. The very word "biography" provokes expectations of candour and disclosure that are often precluded when one writes about a contemporary. It is simply not feasible to exercise that close scrutiny of private emotions, subconscious desires, and deep-seated motives that are the stock-in-trade of the post-Freudian biographer. Nor is it possible to inspect any but a tiny fraction of the letters and private papers that can throw light into obscure corners of the subject's life. It is a story that is still continuing and therefore incomplete: there is always the possibility that some new event, some new work, or some new revelation will occur to modify or perhaps transform our perception of what has gone before. Or that the subject may turn, in old age, to reveal a facet of his character that had been completely unremarked till then. For these reasons, the present work aspires to being little more than a biographical chronicle, a portrait "from the outside," relying less on psychological analysis than on an examination of the biographical and historical facts available to me.

This simple caveat would apply to the biography of any contemporary, and the adjustment the reader needed to make would not be very great. But there are special problems encountered in writing about a person who has lived the greater part of his life in the Soviet Union that immensely complicate the task of the biographer and that the reader needs to understand to avoid certain types of frustration. Though these problems are general, they take on an extra dimension in the case of such a controversial figure as Alexander Solzhenitsyn.

The first great difficulty to be contended with is that for sixty-five years the Soviet government has laboured systematically to destroy all notions of objective truth. This is not at first sight surprising: nowhere and at no time have governments been addicted to the truth. But nowhere in the modern world has such a prolonged and determined assault been carried out by so powerful a government, and nowhere is the divorce between observable reality and the picture of that reality presented by the authorities greater and more striking than in the Soviet Union. The ferocity of this assault has a dual purpose: to distort or destroy the individual's perception of reality, and to conquer that perception and remould it according to the government's wishes. But since the exigencies of politics are inevitably short-term and changeable, whereas reality and our perception of it are (or should be) long-term and more or less durable, there is a permanent conflict between observable reality and the need to distort it, which leads to such demonstrable Soviet absurdities as doctored photographs of the changing leadership, where faces are erased one by one, or the distribution of substitute pages for the Large Soviet Encyclopedia, to be pasted in over articles about individuals who have fallen into disgrace.

One will not find Solzhenitsyn in that or any other Soviet reference work today, for in his case, the Soviet mania for rewriting history has reached absurd heights. At the time of his literary debut (with Khrushchev's express approval), he was hailed as "a true helper of the Party" and "a writer with a rare talent" in the tradition of Tolstoy. In printing the bare facts of his biography, the newspapers emphasized his distinguished war record and played down the facts of his imprisonment and exile, pointing out that he had suffered from "groundless political accusations" from which he had since been exculpated. A year later he was nominated for the Soviet Union's most prestigious literary award, the Lenin Prize, and only narrowly missed winning it. When the attitude of the authorities began to change, so did "history." Solzhenitsyn became "a mediocre writer with an exaggerated view of his own importance," who had "abandoned his conscience" and was socially dangerous. This later escalated to "corrupt self-seeker" and "internal émigré, alien and hostile to the entire life of the Soviet people," and culminated in accusations that he had "surrendered to the Germans," had "fought with Vlasov against Soviet forces," and had even "worked for the Gestapo." More recently, since being expelled from the USSR, he has been accused of having worked (from the beginning of his career) for the CIA.

Much of this is patently absurd and can be dismissed as the inevitable consequence of the fluctuations of the Party line. But it also presents some special problems, not all of which can be overcome by even the most assiduous biographer, especially if he is working in the West. For example, one is obliged to resort to Soviet sources, while knowing that little credence can be given to printed information without a careful verification of the facts. But they cannot be simply discounted or "reversed" either, for they quite often turn out to be correct, or correct in part. Generally speaking, working in a subject area affected by Soviet propaganda is like working in a mighty blast of wind. You learn to lean into it in order to stay upright, but there is an ever-present danger that you will lean too far—and, if the wind should stop blowing for a moment, fall flat on your face.

Another problem that cannot be wished away is the difficulty of access to places and sources. The Soviet Union, as Solzhenitsyn has graphically shown, is still run more or less along the lines of a giant concentration camp. The borders are sealed, foreign visitors are grudgingly admitted under the most stringent conditions, and travel is restricted to a tiny proportion of the country. To understand what this means for the foreign biographer, one should try to imagine writing the biography of a Hemingway or a Graham Greene while restricted to travelling within a radius of twenty-five miles of the capital cities of the countries in which they lived and along rigidly defined corridors to specified resorts and places of interest, but with no access to their birthplaces and the various towns or villages in which they lived and were brought up, or to the people who might have known them during their formative years. In my own case, even these restricted possibilities have been closed to me since 1973, when I was detained at Moscow airport, my notes on dissident writers confiscated as contraband, and my activities used as a pretext to vilify the Soviet writer Lydia Chukovskaya.

Unfortunately, the problem of access to sources that this creates cannot be resolved simply by staying away and communicating at a distance. The Soviet mails are closely watched, and telephones are often tapped: it takes more than ordinary courage and ingenuity for a Soviet citizen to communicate with a foreigner. Worse still, many of Solzhenitsyn's friends and relatives in the Soviet Union—or even those who simply supplied him with information for his books—have been subjected to systematic harassment and their lives made unbearable. The official campaign to discredit Solzhenitsyn has also scored some notable successes. Two of the closest friends of his childhood and youth, Nikolai Vitkevich and the now deceased Kirill Simonyan, were induced to speak out against him after his expulsion. His aged aunt, Irina Shcherbak, was persuaded to part with some of her memoirs and make disparaging remarks about Solzhenitsyn's family in her dotage. And the natural grief and resentment of his first wife, Natalia Reshetovskaya, after her acrimonious divorce from her husband, were exploited by the authorities when they obtained her memoirs, carefully edited them, and published them in a tendentious and distorted form.

Partly as a result of this unremitting pressure—and partly because it answered to certain psychological imperatives—Solzhenitsyn made it a rule, while still in the Soviet Union, to maintain an almost complete silence about his past, and when he did release certain facts, to do so only when he regarded them as "safe" or when they furthered his struggle with the authorities. In this sense, the facts of his biography became a weapon in that struggle, to be described or passed over depending on where the advantage lay. This emerged with great clarity from Solzhenitsyn's revealing (but also misleading) memoir, *The Oak and the Calf*, where one was struck by the abundance of military metaphors employed in the narrative. His life was described in terms of constant attack and retreat, bridgeheads, flanking movements, cavalry charges, and artillery bombardments. There was little room (or desire) for objective analysis and dispassionate debate, and the biographer who tries to follow him is in danger of being swept off his feet. After his expulsion to the West, Solzhenitsyn did not significantly change his attitude to these matters and still attempted to exercise some control over discussion of his biography; but, of course, the immediate danger to himself had receded and the intensity of his concern was somewhat diminished.

In the light of these obstacles, it is natural to ask whether the attempt is worth making at all and what the attitude of Solzhenitsyn himself is to such an enterprise. There have been a number of attempts to write his biography before, most notably by David Burg and George Feifer in 1970. At that time Solzhenitsyn was still in the Soviet Union, and his struggle to manage the facts of his biography was at its height. After initially seeming to favour their plan, he turned against them and denounced them, pronouncing an anathema on biographies of him generally that has maintained its force to this day. Burg and Feifer went ahead and published their book in 1972. It was an adequate summary of what was known at that time and certainly did not cause Solzhenitsyn any harm, but it suffered from the crippling limitations that applied to anyone writing about Solzhenitsyn's past as early as 1972, and inevitably was padded with speculation and superfluous detail.

Since then, the situation has changed considerably. In 1971 Solzhenitsyn published *August 1914*, with much information about his mother and his mother's family, and rather less about his father's family. After this came an attempt by the Soviet authorities to exploit this information for their own ends, to which Solzhenitsyn replied with further details in a series of interviews with Western correspondents. Then came the three volumes of *The Gulag Archipelago*, containing many pages and even chapters of autobiography; *The Oak and the Calf*, which is all autobiography; and more recently the publication of Solzhenitsyn's early plays in Russian, in which there is again a significant autobiographical element. Meanwhile, two of his closest associates from his labour-camp years, Lev Kopelev and Dimitri Panin, have emigrated to the West and published memoirs that cover their time spent with Solzhenitsyn; and Natalia Reshetovskaya's memoirs, though captured and doctored by the Soviet authorities, contain a mass of valuable information, especially when juxtaposed with some of the other sources just mentioned.

There is thus no comparison now with the situation as it obtained when Solzhenitsyn was still in the Soviet Union, but the key to writing a successful biography has nevertheless lain, all along, in his attitude and his willingness to co-operate. Without that willingness, many key sources, even in the West, would still refuse to talk. Fortunately, Solzhenitsyn's attitude to a biography did change after his arrival in the West, though not at once, not without considerable misgivings and hesitations, and not without regrets after the work had started.

The detailed reasons why this happened would take too long to describe here. Suffice it to say that my interest in writing Solzhenitsyn's biography dates back to 1970, that is, to the time when Burg and Feifer were writing theirs. I did in fact make a beginning but, owing to a lack of first-hand material, ran into serious difficulties and abandoned it. By 1974, when Solzhenitsyn was expelled, I was in regular contact with Solzhenitsyn's Swiss lawyer, Dr Heeb, and had been able to carry out one or two little services for Solzhenitsyn at Heeb's request. In February 1974, when Solzhenitsyn's expulsion took place, I was in New York revising the American translation of volume 1 of *The Gulag Archipelago*. This naturally gave me what racing fans would call an inside track with Solzhenitsyn. We did not meet until the autumn of 1974, and when we did, I mentioned the idea of a biography and requested his co-operation.

His response was affable but guarded. An early draft I showed him reminded him, he wrote, of looking at his reflection in a puddle across which "a strong breeze was blowing." His likeness was there, but almost unrecognizable. I urged that the best way to put an end to (mostly Soviet) misrepresentations of his life was to allow a reliable and accurate biography to appear, and pointed out that this could be done only with his approval and help. Solzhenitsyn felt that it was possible only if it were to be an authorized biography, but authorization would require unstinted attention and concentration on his part, and he was not prepared to divert time from other projects that were precious to him. The discussion, mainly by letter, extended over many months. I was unhappy with the concept of authorization, since it implied a degree of supervision to which I was unwilling to commit myself and which would compromise the book's independence. On the other hand, I understood that it was difficult for Solzhenitsyn to abandon his all-or-nothing position, because it expressed the logic of his entire career in the Soviet Union and reflected psychological drives that could not lightly be set aside. Eventually, we agreed on a compromise more English than Russian: I was free to ask what questions I liked, and Solzhenitsyn would reply at whatever length and in whatever detail he thought fit.

In practice, this meant a visit to his house in Vermont (in the strictest secrecy) in the summer of 1977, and a stay there of one week, during which time I questioned him for one to three hours each day after his writing was finished. Solzhenitsyn showed me his juvenilia and some early works, placed certain letters and documents at my disposal, and allowed me to browse through and question him on his photograph albums. He allowed me to interview his second wife, Natalia Svetlova, and authorized me to interview one or two close friends and a relative by marriage, Veronica Stein (a cousin of his first wife). After our initial interviews, I continued to send Solzhenitsyn supplementary questions by letter, and he would send brief answers, but this procedure did not suit Solzhenitsyn's temperament or work habits, and he cut it short in 1979. The termination of relations was friendly but final and is important to an understanding of some of what follows. Occa-

sionally, the most precise and detailed data will be accompanied by speculation about the surrounding events, which produces an unfortunate impression
of imprecision. This stems from the impossibility, since 1979, of obtaining
direct answers from Solzhenitsyn to even the simplest questions of fact, often
in cases where alternative sources of information are not available. (Perhaps
I should add that 95 per cent of the information Solzhenitsyn gave me concerned his ancestry and early life up to the age of thirty-seven, when he
returned to central Russia from exile.)

Fortunately, this impediment was mitigated at a late stage in my work
by a most unexpected development. In 1982 I received a message that Solzhenitsyn's first wife, Natalia Reshetovskaya, who lives in Moscow, had learned
of the biography I was writing and was anxious for me to hear her side of the
story of her relations with Solzhenitsyn. She felt that she had been unfairly
maligned by Solzhenitsyn in his memoir and in certain of his public statements and wished to vindicate herself and rehabilitate her reputation. Moreover, she now realized and regretted, it seems, the way in which the Soviet
authorities had manipulated her memoirs, and therefore had this additional
reason for wishing to set the record straight. As a result, I entered into correspondence with her, and between March 1982 and May 1983 she sent me
a series of letters touching upon her relationship with her former husband,
together with some excerpts from her rewritten memoirs. She willingly
answered the various questions I put to her, including many concerning
uncontroversial aspects of her early life with Solzhenitsyn. It was not and is
not my intention to take sides in the often bitter quarrel between them, but
to try and give a fair account of their joint life and their parting and to show
how this important relationship affected Solzhenitsyn's work and public
actions. In the perhaps controversial and undoubtedly painful matter of
Reshetovskaya's attempted suicide in 1970, I should make it clear that I received
a circumstantial account of this episode from "both sides" (first from Solzhenitsyn's side via his cousin-in-law, and then from Reshetovskaya) and that
the accounts matched in every important detail.

I do not expect my biography to be anything other than controversial,
at least among those in whom Solzhenitsyn's work evokes strong emotions.
In a flash of insight concerning my possible treatment of her problems with
her former husband, Reshetovskaya once wrote that "you will probably end
up pleasing neither side"—which is all too likely an outcome (and will probably extend to political matters no less than personal ones). Solzhenitsyn's is
a personality that is writ uncommonly large. It would be idle to deny that he
is a man with substantial faults, as well as with some towering virtues. Some
have called him a saint, a prophet, a political visionary, a living literary classic. Others think him a megalomaniac, a monster of egotism, and a literary
mediocrity. At one time one almost never heard a word against him; he was
lionized and idolized. Since then the pendulum has swung back again, and
he is now more often denounced as embittered or ignored as irrelevant.

Insofar as the swing of the pendulum has been a reaction against excessive and often insincere adulation, it is healthy and to be welcomed, and it is no part of my intention to "redress the balance." My aim has been not to act as advocate or judge, but to illuminate and explain a quintessential Russian and a major figure of our era. This figure indisputably merits close study in his own right, but there is more to it than that. It would be a pity, in my view, if controversy over Solzhenitsyn's personality and opinions were to cloud our understanding of that society and that political order from which he sprang, for it has definitely been part of my plan to examine that society through the prism of one exceptional man's life and career.

That is important for two reasons. In the first place, it is impossible to understand Solzhenitsyn without grasping the nature of the society in which he was born and lived, and the price he paid for achieving what he did. Secondly, that society also merits study. One is aware that millions of words have been spilled already on the subject of the Russian Revolution, the Bolshevik *putsch*, the Leninist experiment, and the society that resulted from them. Solzhenitsyn himself has added significantly and invaluably to their volume, and he continues to do so. Yet the debate is far from concluded. By its restitution of medieval and in some respects barbarous social and political forms and their continuance into the fourth quarter of the twentieth century, the Soviet state defies all logic. Is this a temporary aberration of European culture (though much less temporary than the similar phenomenon of nazism) or the beginning of the end, the start of a general collapse of our civilization into barbarism?

Whatever the case, it seems to me of vital importance to come to grips with this phenomenon and understand it. It is the question of the age. And Solzhenitsyn, in his life and career, with all his faults and failings, has dramatized it with a force and consistency unprecedented since Lenin first posed it in 1917. To study this life, therefore, is also to study the question.

Leonia, New Jersey
July 1983

ACKNOWLEDGEMENTS

The writing of this biography would not have been possible without the co-operation of Alexander Solzhenitsyn, who first discussed the project with me in Zurich in 1974 and kindly invited me to spend a week at his house in Vermont in the summer of 1977. I am extremely grateful to him for this unique indulgence and for the wise tolerance of his decision not to require a sight of the finished product. I am similarly grateful to Natalia Solzhenitsyn for consenting to be interviewed and for generously answering my supplementary questions by letter until our correspondence ended in 1979. Another rich source of information on Solzhenitsyn's life between his return from internal exile and his expulsion to the West was Solzhenitsyn's cousin by marriage, Veronica Stein (together with her husband, Yuri), for whose self-less assistance I am also grateful; and in the final stages of writing this book, I received invaluable assistance, by letter, from Solzhenitsyn's first wife, Natalia Reshetovskaya, who showed me some chapters from her revised memoirs and willingly answered every question I put to her.

Among the many people who have been friends or associates of Solzhenitsyn at one time or another and who answered questions or supplied me with information, I would particularly like to thank Irina Alberti, Heinrich Böll, Claude Durand, Efim Etkind, Alexander Gorlov, Dr Fritz Heeb, Per Hegge, Peretz Hertzenberg, Lev Kopelev, Naum Korzhavin, Vladimir Maximov, Zhores Medvedev, Victor Nekrasov, Raisa Orlova, Dimitri Panin, Maria Rozanova, the late Janis Sapiets, the late Father Alexander Schmemann, Andrei Sinyavsky, Nikita Struve, and Sigmund Widmer.

Others who contributed to this book with help or information and whom I would like to thank include Mikhail Agursky, Bayara Aroutunova, Mark

Bonham Carter, Nicholas Bethell, Vladimir Bukovsky, Valeri Chalidze, Paul Fritz, Alexander Ginzburg, the late Evgenia Ginzburg, Michael Glenny, Xenia Howard Johnson, Alexis Klimoff, Edward Kline, Winthrop Knowlton, Oskar Krause, Frances Lindley, Pavel Litvinov, Dr Emil Luboshitz, Dr Eva Martin, Galina Nekrasova, Petr Pašek, Boris Sachs, Raissa Scriabine, Maria Slonim, Victor Sparre, Dieter Steiner, Vladimir Voinovich, Anna Voloshina, Thomas Whitney, Irina Zholkovskaya, and Ilya Zilberberg.

I should like to acknowledge the patient assistance and encouragement of the various editors who watched over this book—William Weatherby (whose idea it was), Philippa Harrison, James Cochrane, and Starling Lawrence—and especially the unobtrusive erudition of my copy editor, Otto Sonntag, whose innumerable improvements are invisible to anyone but myself. My thanks also go to Dr Michael Nicholson, formerly of the University of Lancaster and now at Oxford University, the most selfless and encyclopaedically informed of Solzhenitsyn scholars, who read the entire book in manuscript form and offered me all kinds of invaluable advice and information; to the eagle-eyed and similarly well informed Dr Martin Dewhirst of Glasgow University, who also read the manuscript; and to Tatyana Litvinova, who read and commented on most of that part of the book that deals with Solzhenitsyn's life inside the Soviet Union. I am indebted more than I can say to Natalia Lusin of Columbia University, New York, for reading and commenting on the entire manuscript, for compiling the source notes and bibliography, and for helping to see the book through the final stages of its preparation for the press.

The many typists who worked on the manuscript during its author's wanderings include Jean Dick, Anne Pattinson, Nancy Boensch, Patrick Merla, Christopher Packard, and Batya Harlow. I should like to thank Sara Hassan and the rest of the staff at the Radio Liberty library, in New York, for their cheerful assistance in tracking down information; Alan Levy for permission to quote from an unpublished article on Solzhenitsyn's stay in Zurich; Anwar Khan for assistance in reproducing some photographs; and my bank manager, Geoffrey Clark, for keeping me solvent as I overran deadline after deadline.

I am grateful to the W. Averell Harriman Institute for the Advanced Study of the Soviet Union (formerly the Russian Institute), at Columbia University, for an appointment as a senior visiting fellow in 1981–83; to the New York Institute for the Humanities for making me a visiting scholar in 1981–82 and a fellow in 1982–84; and to the Rockefeller Foundation, in New York, and the Arts Council of Great Britain, for financial assistance while I was writing this book.

I cannot omit the customary, and in this case richly deserved, thanks to my patient and understanding wife, Erika, for her unswerving support over an unduly long period of literary gestation (not to speak of her assistance with typing and other chores); and to my long-suffering children, Catherine, Stephen, Lesley, and Ingrid, who will now have to find a new subject for their unfilial jokes.

SOLZHENITSYN

I

OUT OF CHAOS
AND SUFFERING

I F GOD PRESIDED over the birth of Alexander Solzhenitsyn, he was lavish
with appropriate omens, for the child was born into an atmosphere of
chaos and suffering that rivalled anything he was to experience in his later
life. Six months before his birth his young father had died in excruciating
pain from wounds received in a hunting accident. His grief-stricken, pregnant mother had rejoined her family in a nearby summer resort, only to find
herself in the thick of the pitched battle that was then raging between Reds
and Whites in Russia's Civil War. In Petrograd and Moscow, Lenin and his
small band of Bolsheviks were fighting ferociously to consolidate their *coup
d'état*, and the whole of Russia was awash with blood.

Solzhenitsyn was born on 11 December 1918 in his uncle's villa in Kislovodsk, a fashionable spa in the Caucasus Mountains, in southern Russia.
His dead father, Isaaki Solzhenitsyn, would have been twenty-seven years
old at the time of his son's birth. His mother, Taissia Solzhenitsyn, was
twenty-three.

The Solzhenitsyn family was not special enough to have kept track of
its ancestry. A supposed forebear, Philip Solzhenitsyn, is known to have
been living in a free colony of peasants outside the town of Bobrov, in the
central Russian province of Voronezh, at the time of Peter the Great. In
1698, enraged by some routine act of rebelliousness, Peter had ordered the
colony to be burnt to the ground and had forced its inhabitants to move
elsewhere. About a hundred years later another Solzhenitsyn, Alexander's
great-great-grandfather, was convicted of having participated in another peasant
rebellion in Voronezh and was exiled to the just conquered virgin lands in
the south—a traditional method of colonizing new territory at that time.

There was thus a tradition of stubbornness and independence in the family, which was to stand them in good stead when they were sent to the newly created province of Stavropol, a wedge of territory on a low plateau between the Caucasus Mountains and the Caspian Plain. To the north and south were the two major "hosts," as they were called, of the Kuban and Terek Cossacks,* who had helped conquer these territories and been installed here by Catherine the Great to secure the new frontiers. There were some Cossacks in Stavropol, too, but not many, for this area had been reserved by the crown. The chief colonists were the so-called *inogorodniye*, or "outsiders," the somewhat contemptuous name applied by Cossacks to non-Cossack Russians and subsequently adopted by the latter as a normal mode of description. The Solzhenitsyns were non-Cossack Russians, or "outsiders."

The land they found in Stavropol Province was less fertile than in the lush valleys of the Kuban and Terek rivers, but there was plenty of it. According to Solzhenitsyn himself, the Solzhenitsyns and their fellows "were let loose in the wild steppe country beyond the Kuma River, where they lived in harmony, with land in such abundance that they didn't have to divide it up in strips. They sowed where they ploughed, sheared sheep where their carts took them, and put down roots."[1]

Of the next generation of Solzhenitsyns we know nothing, except the name of the Voronezh rebel's son and Solzhenitsyn's great-grandfather, Efim, which survives in the patronymic of Solzhenitsyn's grandfather, Semyon Efimovich. But with Grandfather Semyon we enter the second half of the nineteenth century and the era of photography. A sole surviving faded snapshot shows him standing, tall and self-consciously erect, in a field of corn, gazing firmly into the camera lens. Balding, with bristling Victorian mustaches and a full beard, and wearing a striped shirt, cravat, waistcoat, and jacket, he looks the very picture of a self-confident yeoman farmer.

The village where they lived was known locally as Sablia, after the many-branched shallow stream that flowed through it in winter (in summer it was usually dry), though it is now marked on the map as Sablinskoye. It was a typical south Russian settlement, consisting of a single main street lined with adobe houses, each with its own yard and kitchen garden at the back and outbuildings for the livestock. By the 1880s it had a parish church and a parish school and was a posting stage on the broad, muddy road that wound its way from the town of Stavropol, the provincial capital, to Georgievsk, forty miles away, in the foothills of the Caucasus Mountains. There was little to distinguish this place, except perhaps the view of the distant mountains, which had so captivated Lev Tolstoy when he drove through here in 1851 on his way to join the Terek Cossacks. Early one morning, he writes, he was stunned by these "gleaming white colossi with their delicate silhouettes and the distinct contours of their summits etched against the distant sky."[2] It is pleasant to think of Solzhenitsyn's literary model and hero passing this way

*The Cossacks of southern Russia generally took their name from the river along which they settled. The Kuban and the Terek were the principal rivers of the North Caucasus.

some 70 years before his disciple's birth, when the Solzhenitsyns still toiled at the plough. Did Solzhenitsyn think of that when, 120 years later, he devoted the opening pages of *August 1914* to an evocation of that same mountain scenery (and was there an element of competition in that opening)?

The Solzhenitsyn farm was about six miles east of Sablia and consisted of a low clay farmhouse and a cluster of outbuildings standing in the midst of the open steppe, surrounded by fields. This isolation was a distinctive feature of the Russian South. In the North, the vast majority of the peasants were serfs or share-croppers, living on their owners' land and paying tribute in the form of goods, taxes, or labour. There the land was managed collectively, divided into strips and allocated on a family basis, under a feudal system whose iniquities were to provide much of the fuel for the Revolution when it eventually came. In the South, with land available in such abundance, independence was the rule, the peasants either owning or leasing large parcels of land and working as individual farmers. This bred an entirely different spirit from that prevailing in the North and was to leave its mark on Solzhenitsyn, too.

Semyon, Solzhenitsyn's grandfather, worked the farm with the help of his elder sons. He married twice. By his first wife, Pelageya, he had three sons and two daughters, and by his second, Marfa, a son and a daughter. The gap between their ages was considerable. Konstantin, the eldest of the first three sons, was over twenty when the youngest, Isaaki, was born. The middle son was Vasily, and in between came the two daughters, Evdokia and Anastasia. Marfa's two children, considerably younger than Isaaki, were Ilya and Maria.[3]

Solzhenitsyn maintains that his paternal grandfather was not particularly rich and that several pairs of oxen and horses for ploughing, a dozen cows, and a couple of hundred sheep were the sum total of his disposable wealth. And it seems that he employed no hired labourers, so that his land could not have been particularly extensive. But after Semyon's remarriage to Marfa, a rift appears to have opened up between Semyon and the two older sons. Marfa, according to Solzhenitsyn, was "energetic and greedy," anxious to take over the family property for herself and her two children, and Konstantin and Vasily were sufficiently well off to move away and buy farms of their own. Meanwhile, the two daughters, Evdokia and Anastasia, were married and moved to the neighbouring villages of Kursavka and Nagutskoye.*

Solzhenitsyn's father, Isaaki, who was born on 6 June 1891 (Old Style),† had been just a child when his mother died and was replaced by an unwelcome stepmother. Solzhenitsyn believes that he felt his orphanhood keenly, but he was set apart from his older brothers and sisters in another way, too—

---

*Coincidentally the birthplace of Yuri Andropov.
† Until the Revolution, Russia adhered to the Julian calendar, which was thirteen days behind the Gregorian calendar, used in Europe and most of the rest of the world. Isaaki was born on 19 May according to the Gregorian calendar.

he was the first and only one of the family to receive a proper education. Whereas the others had merely attended the local parish school, before joining their father on the farm, Isaaki had gone on to secondary school and then to the unheard-of heights of a gymnasium in Pyatigorsk, the biggest of the Caucasian mountain spas. It had not been accomplished without a struggle. Semyon saw no reason why his third son shouldn't do exactly as the first two had done and join him on the land. For a whole year he had refused to yield to Isaaki's demands for a proper schooling, while Isaaki marked time on the farm. But in the end Isaaki's stubbornness had won through, and he went to Pyatigorsk. After four years at the gymnasium the whole process was repeated, and another year passed before Isaaki was allowed by his disgruntled and sceptical father to go on to university. This was in 1911, when Isaaki was twenty.

He went first to the University of Kharkov, in the Ukraine. In *August 1914* Solzhenitsyn tells a story of Isaaki's being refused admission because his first name, the Orthodox Christian "Isaaki," was confused with the Jewish "Isaak," which would have made him subject to the limitations on university admissions for the Jews. Solzhenitsyn heard this story from a distant relative, but he now believes it to be mistaken. It seems to be true, however, that Isaaki's peasant name, which he had been given in honour of the obscure saint Isaac the Dalmatian, on whose name-day he was born, struck university ears as outlandish and quaint and was already old-fashioned in the central parts of Russia. But Kharkov, in any case, did not suit Isaaki very well. The gymnasium in Pyatigorsk had been of a very high intellectual standard, whereas this newly opened provincial university, whose only virtue was that it was cheap and fairly close to home, was mediocre. The following year, in 1912, overcoming any residual opposition from his father, Isaaki transferred to the University of Moscow.

He was now at the top of the educational ladder and began to enter fully into the intellectual life of the time. In the short period of ten years, he had made the leap from peasant to membership in the metropolitan intelligentsia. Yet it was not plain sailing. Sensitive to his origins and loyal to his roots, Isaaki was torn by the conflict between the pull of his peasant past and his hopes for a brilliant future. His ambition, like that of generations of scholarship boys before and since, was somehow to link these two worlds of past and future, to be a bridge between them and perhaps to narrow the gap for future generations. But the task was uphill, and human nature, as he found it in himself and others, unregenerate.

According to Solzhenitsyn's description of his father in *August 1914*, Isaaki was very attached to his native village and always returned to work on the family farm during his vacations. But he grew increasingly estranged from his roots as his education progressed, and he was teased by the villagers for his city clothes and his *narodnik*, or "populist,"* opinions. He regarded

---

*The Russian populists were utopian socialists who took their inspiration from Proudhon and their name from the Russian *narod*, meaning "people." They were influential in the 1870s and 1880s. Herzen was a forerunner and Mikhailovsky their chief theoretician.

himself as "someone who had received an education in order to use it for the benefit of the people and who would go back to the people with the book, the word, and with love."

The two intellectual movements that appear to have influenced the idealistic Isaaki the most (and that were to be not without influence on Solzhenitsyn himself) were populism and Tolstoyanism,* both of which were well past their peak by 1912 and would have been regarded as distinctly old-fashioned in Moscow. The populists had long since been supplanted in the public esteem by the anarchists, the anarchists by the Socialist Revolutionaries and increasingly by the Social Democrats, which was the innocuous-sounding official name of what was in effect the Communist Party. Earlier that same year, in fact, in Prague, a then obscure lawyer by the name of Vladimir Ulyanov (alias Lenin) had taken over the leadership of the Social Democratic Party and was laying the foundations of a tightly knit conspiratorial group that had taken the name of Bolsheviks. And shortly afterwards the Party was joined by a lapsed seminarist named Iosif Dzhugashvili (alias Stalin), whose views on revolutionary development far outstripped, in their ruthlessness, the theories of the fierce-sounding Socialist Revolutionaries and anarchists.

When war broke out between Russia and Germany, on 1 August 1914, Isaaki was holidaying on the family farm in the south and helping his father in the fields. Two manifestos declaring war on Germany and Austria were read aloud in the Sablia village church and then posted in the church square. A commission of local worthies was appointed to deal with requisitions. Sablia's horses were rounded up and handed over to the district centre for use as remounts by local detachments of the Cossack cavalry. But when the time came for the villagers to be recruited, they were sent to the infantry, for Russian "outsiders" could not be admitted to the exclusive Cossack regiments.

The Solzhenitsyn brothers escaped the recruiters' attention completely. Konstantin was too old. Vasily was passed over because he had several fingers missing from one hand. Isaaki was excused because he was a student. And their stepbrother, Ilya, was too young. Rather surprisingly, in the light of his Tolstoyan and pacifist views, Isaaki decided to enlist. Whether this was the fruit of impulse, reinforced by the wave of patriotic feeling that swept the country after the declaration of war, or whether it was in response to some deeper imperative in Isaaki's nature, we do not know. But his decision was to make a lasting impression on Solzhenitsyn when he subsequently learned of it, and it was with the story of his father's enlistment that Solzhenitsyn opened *August 1914* and his epic on the fate of twentieth-century Russia.

Within a month of the declaration of war, Isaaki was in Moscow. Having completed an officer-training course at the Sergiev School of Heavy Artillery, he was dispatched to the front to commence his service with Field

---

*Tolstoyanism was an ill-defined philosophico-religious movement inspired by Tolstoy's ideas about nonresistance to violence and the need for a kind of agrarian socialism in Russia.

Marshal Bryusov's First Grenadier Artillery Brigade. Little is known of his wartime career, except that he served for part of the time as an artillery look-out and was mentioned in dispatches for having personally rescued several boxes of ammunition from a fire started by enemy shells. He ended the war with three medals, including the George and Anna crosses.[4]

There was also the episode of his election to the Brigade Soviet of Sol-diers' Deputies. In February 1917 the February Revolution had led not only to the abdication of the tsar and the setting up of a provisional government to call a general election and elect a constitutent assembly but also to the establishment of a popular assembly known as the Petrograd Soviet (the word *soviet* in Russian simply means "council," but it had acquired new meaning during the abortive revolution of 1905, when a famous workers' "soviet" had arisen spontaneously in St Petersburg out of the general strike committee and temporarily wielded power). The most significant single act of the Petro-grad Soviet was the handing down, in March 1917, of "Order No. 1," which stipulated that soldiers should be allowed to keep possession of their arms when not on active service, that they should form their own councils, or "soviets," to elect delegates to the national Soviet in Petrograd, and that they should carry out only those orders that had been issued or approved by the Petrograd Soviet (except while on duty).

The main thrust of Order No. 1 was against the traditional draconian discipline of the tsarist army and the despotic privileges of an entrenched officer caste. These had already led to widespread demoralization and mass desertions, which Order No. 1 merely intensified. But the situation was complicated by the fact that the Russian army in wartime had hundreds of thousands of volunteer officers (of whom Isaaki was one) who were remote from the career officers and their code. Isaaki Solzhenitsyn apparently sym-pathized with his soldiers and the introduction of the soviets and allowed himself to be elected as a deputy.[5]

It was at about this time that he made the acquaintance of Taissia Za-kharovna Shcherbak in Moscow. Taissia, the daughter of a wealthy land-owner of Ukrainian origin, was also from the South. Her father's estate was in the same region of the North Caucasus as the Solzhenitsyn farm—near Armavir, in the Cossack Kuban, just north of Stavropol. Like Isaaki, Taissia had attended boarding-school in Pyatigorsk and must even have been there at the same time as he, though the two had never met. Later she studied at the exclusive Andreyeva Gymnasium, in Rostov-on-Don, and in 1912 had moved to the Golitsyn Academy of Agriculture, in Moscow. Isaaki had gone on a brief leave to Moscow in the spring of 1917 and met Taissia at some kind of student celebration. It seems to have been a genuine instance of that time-honoured romantic formula of love at first sight. Isaaki was able to remain in the capital for only a few days, and it is not clear whether he made any further visits to Moscow, yet a mere four months later, in August 1917, the pair were married at the Belorussian front, in a special ceremony conducted by the brigade chaplain. Taissia returned to Moscow and Isaaki continued his service.

In October 1917* the Bolsheviks carried out their coup. The Petrograd Soviet had called the First All-Russian Congress of Soviets in June and was due to hold a second congress at the end of October. On the night before the congress opened, Lenin ordered a *coup d'état*, took over the congress, announced the dissolution of the Provisional Government, and established the Bolshevik-dominated Council of People's Commissars to rule the country—ostensibly until the Constituent Assembly could be elected. In November, when the eagerly awaited elections took place (the first and last fully free elections in the entire history of Russia), the Bolsheviks came out the second-largest party, with 24 per cent of the vote. They had no intention of listening to the wishes of the electorate, however, and when the Constituent Assembly met the following January, they first attempted to dominate it and then, having failed, ordered the executive committee of the Congress of Soviets to dissolve it. The assembly never met again.

An important aim of Lenin's was to sign a separate peace treaty with the Germans, but the German demands were so exorbitant that not even he could swallow them at the time. The war therefore dragged on through the winter of 1917. Russian morale was at an all-time low, with revolution raging not only behind the lines but within the armed forces as well, and with mass desertions, the Russian army was in no condition to fight back. The Germans easily advanced to the Black Sea in the south and almost to Petrograd in the north. In February 1918 the Russians sued for peace and in March signed the Treaty of Brest-Litovsk, ceding Finland, the Baltic states, and large areas of the Ukraine to the enemy.

Isaaki remained at his post to the bitter end, setting an example of patriotism and devotion to duty that subsequently became a byword in the Solzhenitsyn family and deeply influenced his son's attitudes twenty years later, when faced with another world war. But in March, after Brest-Litovsk, Isaaki abandoned his unit and made his way south to join Taissia. She had left Moscow shortly after the October coup and was now staying with her family in the Caucasian resort of Kislovodsk.

Kislovodsk at this time was also under a Soviet administration, whose aims and style sat rather oddly with the character of the place. Kislovodsk was a typical nineteenth-century spa, famous for its Narzan mineral waters, luxuriant vegetation and associations with high society. Perched in a narrow glen, the most romantic, inaccessible, and exclusive of that cluster of elegant summer resorts at the northern tip of the Caucasus Mountains, it frankly proclaimed its dedication to the epicurean delights of taking the waters, strolling in the shade of its celebrated poplar avenue, gaming in the casino, or simply gossiping in the pump room of the Narzan Gallery. It was a monument to the idle pleasures of the rich, whose sumptuous villas were scattered picturesquely on the lower slopes of the mountainside, and the new town "Soviet" was hard put to find a role for itself. During the early months of 1917 it chose

* According to the Old Style Russian calendar (see note p. 27), hence the name October Revolution. Since the calendar reform of 1918, the Revolution has been celebrated on 7 November each year.

to adopt a more or less neutral posture, neither condoning the old ways nor, other than in rhetoric, condemning them, while the struggle for power in the country raged elsewhere.

Taissia was staying with her wealthy elder brother, Roman Shcherbak, and his wife, Irina, in their summer villa on Sheremetyev Street. Life here was still luxurious, and Isaaki was made doubly welcome as an officer and Taissia's husband. He was introduced to Taissia's parents, Zakhar and Evdokia Shcherbak, who had recently been forced off their estate near Armavir by a local Bolshevik rising and had come to Kislovodsk to await events. Here also was Taissia's elder sister, Maria, who lived nearby in Tolstoy Street with her husband, a landowner named Afanasy Karpushin, with whom Zakhar and Evdokia were staying.[6]

Isaaki did not remain there long. It seems that he found the idleness and luxury of Kislovodsk irksome after the rigours of the front. They offended against his belief in the simple life. And it is possible that there were also political differences between them. His father- and mother-in-law were shocked and embittered by the violent sequestration of their estate. Roman, Irina, and the Karpushins must have been of like mind (presumably Karpushin had lost his estate as well), but Isaaki, with strong sympathies for the new Soviet regime, may well have taken a different view, or at the very least have remained uncommitted until the situation grew clearer. At all events, after observing the necessary formalities, he made his excuses, left Kislovodsk, taking an already pregnant Taissia with him, and travelled the sixty-odd miles eastwards to his father's farm in Sablia. It was there, a few weeks later, after a bare three months of married life with Taissia, that he suffered his tragic accident.[7]

The exact circumstances of the accident are shrouded in obscurity. It seems that on 8 June 1918 Isaaki went hunting for small game with a friend on the flat, prairie-like steppe around the farm. They were travelling in a horse-drawn cart. At one point Isaaki stood up in the stationary cart to disembowel a freshly shot hare, and in a moment of carelessness leaned his cocked shotgun against the cart's side. The horse started, as if bitten by a fly. The cart gave a jerk, and the shotgun fell and exploded, peppering Isaaki's chest and abdomen with shot.

They immediately returned to the farm, and from there Isaaki was driven, still in the cart, via Sablia to the town of Georgievsk, some forty miles southwest. It was that same dirt road that Tolstoy had once travelled, and it was not much changed either, being pitted with those ruts and potholes that have been the hallmark of Russian provincial roads since time immemorial. The unsprung cart was obliged to proceed at a funereal pace to minimize the wounded man's sufferings—every lurch, every jolt, sent a spasm of agonizing pain coursing through his body—and it took them twenty-four hours to cover the forty miles to Georgievsk.

Isaaki was admitted to the hospital without delay and speedily operated on. But conditions in Georgievsk at this time were already beginning to suffer from the effects of the Civil War. Essential services were breaking down. Professional standards and discipline were poor. The operation was hasty and slapdash, not all the shot was removed (nor the wad, which had entered his chest as well), and the after-care was perfunctory. The wounds turned septic, and within a week Isaaki was dead. The date was 15 June 1918. Isaaki was four days short of his twenty-eighth birthday.

Taissia, who had accompanied her husband in the cart and watched him die, was ill-equipped to bear the shock of this sudden widowhood. Vivacious, sensitive, and delicate, she had led a life that till now was cosseted and carefree, shielded by the great wealth of her father and the loving attention that had been her birthright as the youngest and most gifted of his three children. Four happy years at boarding-school had been followed by four more at Moscow University, a romantic whirlwind marriage to a handsome young officer, and finally the promise of a child to bless their union. But now, her young officer was dead, and the child would be born fatherless at a moment when Russia was in the throes of an unprecedented cataclysm.

Fortunately, she was not entirely alone—she had already summoned her brother, Roman, and her sister-in-law, Irina, from Kislovodsk. Irina was Taissia's closest female relative. Only seventeen when married off by a sick and dying father to the wealthy Roman Shcherbak, Irina was eleven years younger than her husband and only six years older than Taissia, to whom she felt drawn at once. Her marriage had not been a great success, and she had taken refuge in the consolations of religion and art. She was a woman of firm principles and strongly held convictions, tenacious and dedicated, the ideal companion in a crisis; and she and Roman had answered Taissia's call with alacrity.

She had arrived in time to see Isaaki die, and in old age, when memory was failing, she claimed to recall his dying words to her: "Take care of my son. I am sure I am going to have a son."[8] Whether these words were actually spoken is not clear—there seems to have been a tradition in the family that Isaaki was convinced his child would be a son—and if they were, they were more probably addressed to Taissia than to her sister-in-law. However, Irina was to take as passionate an interest in her nephew's upbringing as she had earlier in Taissia's, and her subsequent influence on Solzhenitsyn was to be both permanent and deep. Her recollection (uttered long years after Taissia's death) therefore has a certain retrospective logic to it, but cannot be taken literally.

Georgievsk was only fifty miles from Kislovodsk, and after burying Isaaki in the town cemetery, Taissia returned with Roman and Irina to the tree-shaded villa on Sheremetyev Street. By now the residents of Kislovodsk had little stomach for the pleasures of spa life, for the situation in the town, as in the rest of Russia, had deteriorated dramatically. Having secured their position in central Russia, the Bolsheviks had launched a major offensive in the south, immediately after the signing of the peace treaty with Germany. Rostov had been recaptured from the White Volunteer Army, and Bolshevik forces overran both the Don Cossack capital of Novocherkassk and the Kuban Cossack capital of Ekaterinodar, the main centres of White resistance. The North Caucasus, it seemed, was about to be incorporated into the freshly proclaimed Soviet state. At the same time, a new and harsher form of Bolshevik power was returning to those parts of the Caucasus already in pro-Bolshevik hands, including the mountain resorts.

Nikolai Zernov, who was living in the neighbouring resort of Essentuki at the time, twelve miles from Kislovodsk, has described the second Bolshevik takeover in his reminiscences. On 10 March 1918, he writes, a battered old lorry flying the red flag had crawled into the main square and ground to a halt. It was filled to overflowing with a motley assortment of armed men "of indeterminate origin and nationality," but none of them local, who leapt out and proclaimed the resort "an inalienable part of the Soviet Socialist Republic," after which they repaired to the Metropole Hotel, expelled its residents, and settled in. A small group of curious onlookers, including Zernov, had "listened to this declaration in silence before dispersing to their homes."[9]

On the surface, life had not changed much at first. The shops had stayed open, the schools had continued to teach, and people had gone about their business much as before. But the Civil War and the struggle for power, combined with the ruthless insistence by both sides on an all-or-nothing policy in every aspect of the struggle, had opened a Pandora's box of bitterness, resentments, hatreds, and revenge, so that, beneath the surface, changes had begun at once. The first sign had been the institution of sweeping searches of all the houses of the better-off inhabitants, ostensibly in quest of weapons but in reality extending much wider than that. According to Zernov, "gangs of rampaging and frequently drunk Bolsheviks went round bursting into houses, demanding all weapons, confiscating gold and valuables, and looking for supplies of food." This was followed by the imposition of compulsory financial levies, which frequently took no account of the victim's ability to pay and were backed by threats of arrest if the money was not forthcoming. Finally, to reinforce these methods, the new authorities rounded up the most prominent local citizens and announced that they would be held as hostages against the good conduct of the town's inhabitants and the payment of the levies. These hostages were removed to the administrative centre of Pyatigorsk, and it was assumed that they would return to their homes when sufficient money had been collected. Suddenly, however, the walls of the town were festooned with ill-printed proclamations declaring that all the hostages had been "liquidated" as a consequence of the class struggle and as "enemies of the people." The shock to the populace, writes Zernov, was indescribable.

It is difficult to convey to anyone who hasn't experienced it the feelings of a man who falls into the category of individuals earmarked for liquidation in the interests of achieving . . . the Communist utopia. In such cases death is not a punishment for some particular action. It is an inevitable consequence of the victim's social origin. . . . In times to come the systematic destruction of "parasites" and "enemies of the people" as a daily occurrence in the Communist countries was to blunt the conscience of mankind, but in 1918 these "sacramental" murders, which were meant to signify "a leap from the world of necessity into the realm of freedom," according to Marx, were a totally new phenomenon and had a shattering impact on us.[10]

In Kislovodsk the situation was, if anything, worse than in Essentuki, for it had become the temporary headquarters of the commander-in-chief of the Revolutionary Army of the North Caucasus, Avtonomov, who installed himself in a luxurious armoured train at the Kislovodsk terminus. The large Bolshevik garrison behaved pretty much as it pleased in the town and surrounding district. The garrison commander, a former coach driver named Sorokin, was aided in his terrorization of the populace by the chairman of the Kislovodsk Town Soviet, Tulenev, a former fitter, who not only loathed the local bourgeoisie but was also at daggers drawn with the moderate Avtonomov and opposed him at every turn. After a few weeks in Kislovodsk, Avtonomov moved north and was recalled to Moscow on charges of plotting against the Soviet regime, while the town was virtually taken over by two new commissars, Axelrode and Gay. The latter had a strikingly beautiful wife, Xenia, a former singer and dancer who was particularly fond of throwing grand parties, at which she would appear decked out in the extravagant jewellery extorted from hostages in exchange for sparing their lives. Those who refused, or couldn't pay, were executed in the cellars of a neighbouring villa.[11]

This was the situation into which the pregnant Taissia was plunged at the beginning of June 1918. She had little choice of where to go. She had known her husband's family for only a few weeks, and there was no question of staying on the somewhat primitive Solzhenitsyn farm in the later stages of her pregnancy. Her father's estate near Armavir was still occupied by revolutionary forces, and her entire family was still holed up in Kislovodsk. Because of their great wealth, they were naturally in a precarious position. Together with Kislovodsk's other prominent families, they went in daily fear of their lives, staying indoors as much as possible and making the sign of the cross over their closed shutters each night in the hope that this might ward off the search parties. But it didn't. One night a gang of armed men burst into the house and took Roman away as a hostage. There was a certain irony in this, since of all the Shcherbaks, Roman was the most liberal and most sympathetic to the Revolution. A lifelong admirer of the later Tolstoy and of Maxim Gorky, he was, despite his conspicuous wealth, a fervent opponent of tsarism and a firm advocate of social and political change. For his captors this was irrelevant—he was the class enemy, whatever his political views. He was taken immediately to Pyatigorsk, thrown into a cell, and condemned to death.

The intrepid Irina refused to be cowed by this blow. Gathering together as much jewellery and money as she could, she followed him to the Bolshevik headquarters in Pyatigorsk. For a young woman this was no easy thing to do. Zernov's sister Sophia had gone on a similar errand that summer in Pyatigorsk, running the gauntlet of jeering, undisciplined guards and confronting a young commissar who not only had the power of life and death over her but was also known for his taste for young women. She had emerged unscathed, as did Irina in her turn. Combining eloquence with bribery, she was able to purchase Roman's release.[12]

Meanwhile, events in Kislovodsk were being watched from a different vantage point by Colonel A. G. Shkuro, a retired Cossack officer who had only recently returned from fighting in the First World War. Shkuro was a prominent Kuban Cossack who had distinguished himself in the war by his bravery and his uncharacteristically democratic handling of his subordinates. Unlike most Cossack officers, he had no monarchist sympathies and was wholeheartedly in favour of the February Revolution, the Provisional Government, and the Constituent Assembly. He had even welcomed the establishment of Soviet power, and at one point had been invited to join the Bolsheviks by Avtonomov, but had declined (it is possible that their meeting had something to do with Avtonomov's subsequent recall to Moscow and fall from grace). He preferred for the moment to sit on the sidelines.[13]

By the early summer of 1918 the situation all over the North Caucasus was chaotic.[14] The high tide of enthusiasm for Soviet power that had engulfed most of the Kuban, Stavropol Province, and the mountain resorts in early 1918 was already receding. In the South, whatever the position might have been in central Russia, the proportion of political idealists and convinced socialists to thugs and adventurers in the Bolshevik ranks was very small, and the latter's terroristic policies had disgusted and alienated nine-tenths of the population, especially after Lenin's proclamation of the "Red Terror." Shkuro was well aware of the mutinous feelings these policies had engendered among the Cossacks, for he had a wide network of friends and informants in the villages on the strength of his wartime reputation. In May 1918 he formed a guerrilla army and raised a Cossack rebellion. Soon the entire region was ablaze with civil war. The rebellion centred at first on the mainly Cossack village of Soldatsko-Alexandrovskoye, about a dozen miles east of the Solzhenitsyn farm at Sablia, before spreading to other areas. Around Sablia itself, however, the villages were more mixed, with Russian colonists outnumbering the Cossacks. These, though not siding with the Soviets, appear to have remained neutral and uncommitted.

Meanwhile, the tide was turning against the Soviets in the rest of the North Caucasus. Rostov had fallen to the Volunteer Army in May. In June there had been a White officers' rising in Stavropol that led to bloody street fighting but ended in failure. In July, the town finally fell to the Volunteers, and a White administration was installed. In the same month Red forces abandoned Armavir, where the Shcherbaks had their estate, and in August they were forced out of the Kuban capital of Ekaterinodar. During the next three months the fighting raged back and forth over the countryside, many towns and villages being repeatedly taken and retaken by either side. For the long-suffering civilian populace, the consequences were catastrophic. Each side, upon occupying a fresh village or town, would attempt to identify its adversaries there, relying on denunciations for its information. The supposed ringleaders would be shot or hanged, causing ripples of hatred and vengefulness to run through their families and friends, and an uneasy calm would be imposed until the next battle. When the opposing side prevailed, the whole sequence would be repeated in reverse. On top of this, both sides fought for much of the time in guerrilla style, with all the gratuitous violence that that form of warfare brings in the form of ambushes, lightning raids, requisitions, and the taking of hostages.

Unfortunately, we have no information about the Solzhenitsyn family during this violent period. We may speculate that Semyon and his sons, as reasonably prosperous and successful peasants, would not have been attracted to the doctrines of the Bolsheviks, who deliberately espoused the cause of the landless labourers and the poorest peasants and incited them against their brethren. On the other hand, the White opposition was primarily, though not exclusively, Cossack led, so it is possible that the Solzhenitsyns, as non-Cossacks, found themselves somewhere in the middle. In the existing histories of the period, the village of Sablia figures neither as a Bolshevik nor as a White stronghold and was the site of no notable battles.

In September 1918 Shkuro's Cossack partisans invaded Kislovodsk, took three thousand prisoners, and executed the local Bolshevik leaders, including Alexander Gay and his wife, Xenia. Xenia, according to Zernov, demanded permission to smoke a last cigarette before coolly ascending the gallows. Her defiant last words were "Us today, you tomorrow!"[15]*

The truth of these words was already being illustrated in neighbouring Pyatigorsk, which still had not fallen to the Whites. On the night of 18 September, while Shkuro was executing Red prisoners in Kislovodsk, a Polish Bolshevik named Andziewski cut off the heads of 155 hostages by the light of specially kindled fires. A few days later, Shkuro was forced to withdraw from Kislovodsk and the Reds took over again, bringing another harvest of executions, but at the end of December Shkuro launched a fresh offensive on the mountain resorts and this time was successful. On 5 January 1919 he captured Pyatigorsk and Essentuki, and one day later, Kislovodsk.

> On 6 January I arrived in Kislovodsk and was given a tumultuous welcome by the populace, which had suffered grievously under the Bolshevik regime. The town had also suffered. Many houses had been pillaged, and the celebrated poplar avenue had been cut down. The Red butchers had slaughtered hundreds of the townsfolk with sword and bullet. Since it was Epiphany there was the Blessing of the Waters and a thanksgiving mass, after which I held a parade of my troops.[16]

---

*This slogan, reversed, was to become a favourite saying in Soviet labour camps: "You today, me tomorrow"—meaning you will die today (or may you die today), and I will die tomorrow (or, with luck, never).

Is it fanciful to suppose that the Shcherbaks attended that thanksgiving mass, in the beautiful church of St Panteleimon on the hill overlooking Irina's dacha? Zakhar and Evdokia were outstandingly pious believers in the old tradition of Russian Orthodoxy, and Irina had been devout from childhood. As for Taissia, on this occasion she had particular reason to thank the Lord. Less than three weeks previously, on 11 December 1918, amid the chaos and the carnage, she had given birth to a son. She named him Alexander, and he was christened in that selfsame church on the hill.

2

CHILDHOOD

TAISSIA WAS, WITH the possible exception of Roman, the least religious member of the Shcherbak family. Although raised by her parents in an atmosphere of old-fashioned piety and devotion (her aunt Ashkelaya was a nun), later to be reinforced by the arrival of the devout Irina in their household, she seemed to have had all of this knocked out of her by her progressive boarding-school in Rostov. Morning and evening genuflections before the icon in her room had given way to amused contempt for the rituals of an abandoned cult, and holidays at home had become an embarrassing bore, involving, as they did, repeated family excursions to church and the strict observance of all religious fast-days and holidays. Later, as a student in Moscow, she had willingly followed the prevailing university trends of atheism and anticlericalism, delighted with this opportunity to slough off her provincial intellectual baggage. But now, amid the heightened terrors and apocalyptic fears engendered by the Civil War, she found herself, like so many others, turning back to the church again. "The atmosphere created in the Caucasian resorts," writes Zernov, "encouraged our religious enthusiasm. . . . It seemed to us that Russia was on the eve of a spiritual renaissance, that the church, purified by her suffering, would reveal to a penitent people the radiant lineaments of our Saviour, and teach Russians how to found their lives on brotherly love." No doubt, Taissia partook of these emotions when she attended church herself. Father Alexei, the resident priest at St Panteleimon's, was famous throughout the region for the fervency of his prayer, his religious message a balm to the strife-torn and war-weary inhabitants of battered Kislovodsk.[1]

The entire region, and indeed most of the Caucasus, was for the time being firmly in the hands of the Whites. The Volunteer Army, led by General Denikin, soon began to press northwards to Moscow. With Admiral Kolchak advancing through Siberia, it began to look as if the Red forces would be rolled back and the Bolsheviks defeated. So, at least, it appeared to the people in southern Russia and also, at last, to Russia's former allies in the war, who belatedly sent expeditionary forces, munitions, and supplies.

As a consequence of these changes the Shcherbak family reshuffled itself. Zakhar and Evdokia left Maria's house to return to their estate near Armavir, while Taissia and the infant Solzhenitsyn moved in with Maria to take their place. Maria was less educated than Taissia, having gone straight from boarding-school, at the age of seventeen, to be married to Karpushin. Karpushin had died of typhus the preceding year, however, and so Maria was all alone. A comparatively simple soul, generous and kind-hearted, she welcomed them with open arms, and it was here, on aptly named Tolstoy Street, that Solzhenitsyn was to spend the first six years of his life.[2]

By the summer of 1919 the White armies of Denikin and General Wrangel had penetrated as far north as Orel and Saratov and were poised to strike at Moscow, a mere two hundred miles away. The entire South and East were in their grasp, and it seemed only a matter of time before the Bolsheviks would be overcome and the old order restored. But appearances were highly deceptive. Just as the old Russia had not so much been conquered as it had simply collapsed from inertia, incompetence, and corruption, so the Civil War was not so much won by the Reds as lost by the Whites, who had absolutely nothing new to offer. On the contrary, all the vices of the old regime had survived on their territory and been magnified by them. Shkuro, when he met the leaders of the Volunteer Army, was appalled by their ignorance and dismayed by their blind arrogance and lofty disdain for the common people. Denikin and his generals made no secret of their contempt for the democratic reforms of the February Revolution and short-lived Constituent Assembly, nor did they hide their determination to restore the tsar and the tsarist regime. And in the field their local commanders proved every bit as savage and ferocious as those of the Reds. In the town of Stavropol, for instance, General Uvarov instituted a policy of mass executions of peasants and workers as reprisals for former Red successes, while in the surrounding countryside General Pokrovsky conducted mass hangings in every village he came to, making no attempt to establish or prove the guilt of his victims. In this way the Whites were but a mirror image of the Reds, the extremes overcame the middle, and the stage was set for a war of devastation and attrition that would decimate the innocent population.

In purely military terms, too, the Whites proved unequal to their task. By the end of the summer the Red Cossack cavalry, led by Budenny and Dumenko, had stemmed the White advance, blocking their way to Moscow and driving them south again. This Red offensive continued all through the autumn and winter, and by February 1920 they had reoccupied Rostov and driven the Whites back into the Caucasus, onto the territory whence they had started out.

Conditions in the South during these last, bitter phases of the Civil War were appalling. One of the many English officers fighting with the British Expeditionary Force there, Captain H. N. H. Williamson, later described in his book how the whole countryside had been laid waste by the see-saw fighting and how the stations and the villages grew shabbier with every visit he made to them. Windows were boarded up, the hammer and sickle had been scrawled on some of the houses and the doors daubed with red paint during the last Red occupation, and machine-gun bullets had marked the facades. "The posters with their slogans—applicable to both Reds and Whites, 'War to the Finish' and 'Death Is Better Than Slavery'—grew more tattered every time I saw them."³ Williamson noted the breakdown of agriculture, the shortage of food owing to the harsh requisitions policy of both Reds and Whites, and the ever-growing menace of typhus, which raged unchecked over thousands of square miles of southern Russia. "The disease had spread like wildfire and whole trainloads of people perished unattended or froze to death because they were too weak to help themselves. Their bodies, frozen stiff like logs, were dumped alongside the track, stripped of boots and clothing, which only passed on the disease to the healthy who removed them."⁴ This epidemic took a heavy toll of the Solzhenitsyn family, carrying away both of Solzhenitsyn's paternal grandparents, Semyon and Marfa, his uncle Vasily, and his aunt Anastasia.⁵

In March 1920 the White resistance finally collapsed, and the rump of the Volunteer Army was evacuated from Novorossiisk by the British. Throughout the Caucasus there was a wave of revenge killing, and in Armavir there was a veritable pogrom by the Reds. Zakhar and Evdokia were obliged to abandon their estate for the second and last time and flee back to Kislovodsk, taking with them a few sticks of furniture and whatever movables they could transport. There they moved in once more with Maria, Taissia, and the infant Solzhenitsyn.

Bolshevik rule now came to the Caucasus to stay, and with it the policy of "War Communism" that had already been instituted in the rest of Russia. In the countryside this meant the forcible expropriation of all landowners, the establishment of "committees of poor peasants" to confiscate produce from the better-off ones, and the unleashing of armed food detachments from the towns to requisition grain and other foodstuffs. At the same time, all business and industry was nationalized and a system of barter introduced in place of private trade. The results, here as elsewhere, were catastrophic. The already ravaged and pillaged agricultural system simply collapsed, all trade and industry came to a halt, and only a flourishing black market and increasingly savage requisitions prevented a famine of epidemic proportions.

Throughout the first year of Bolshevik rule the Shcherbaks remained marooned in their mountain resort of Kislovodsk. In the winter of 1920, like everyone else, they had virtually starved, selling off their furniture and possessions at derisory prices to buy food. The infant Solzhenitsyn was presumably secure and oblivious of these hardships. Many years later he was to recall the reassuring icon that hung in one corner of his room, suspended in the angle between wall and ceiling and tilted downwards so that its holy face seemed to be gazing directly at him. At night the candle in front of it would flicker and shudder. And at that magic moment between waking and sleeping, the radiant visage seemed to detach itself and float out over his bed, like a true guardian angel. In the mornings, instructed by his grandmother Evdokia, he would kneel before the icon and recite his prayers.[6]

Only rarely did the outer chaos impinge on his world. His earliest memory of it comes from one of his regular visits to St Panteleimon in 1921, when he was nearly three.

> I remember I was in church. There were lots of people, candles, vestments. I was with my mother, then something happened: the service was brusquely interrupted. I wanted a better view, so my mother held me up at arm's length and I looked over the heads of the crowd. I saw, filing arrogantly down the central aisle of the nave, the sugar-loaf "Budenny" hats of Soviet soldiers. It was the period when the government was confiscating church property all over Russia.[7]

In most respects, life for the small boy was the same as for any other child. But not for Taissia. By the winter of 1921 her resources had run out. Maria had just remarried, this time choosing an enormously tall and affable ex-guardsman by the name of Fyodor Garin. Garin had three children of his own from a former marriage, two girls and a boy, and although he and Maria were happy to have Taissia and Solzhenitsyn stay on, the house was now somewhat crowded. Zakhar and Evdokia were also living there again and had nowhere to go. Besides, there was no work for Taissia in Kislovodsk. Judging that Alexander was old enough to stand a temporary separation and that he would be well looked after by Maria, Taissia moved to the large seaport and regional centre of Rostov-on-Don, where, with some difficulty, she successfully took a course in shorthand and typing and found a post as a secretary. Almost at the same time, Roman and Irina abandoned the villa on Sheremetyev Street and moved a short way down the railway line to the quiet hamlet of Minutka. In their case the move was dictated by prudence. There were too many people in Kislovodsk who knew of Roman's former arrest and miraculous release, and the chances were that the new Bolshevik administration might choose to settle old scores. For Roman and Irina, as "socially alien" elements, it was the first of a long and exhausting series of moves to forestall "revolutionary revenge."

Solzhenitsyn spent the next two and a half years living with his Aunt Maria (or "Marusia," as he called her), his new uncle, and his three new cousins, with whom he played throughout the winter months, spending his summers with Irina and Roman ("Auntie Ira and Uncle Romasha") in Minutka. But in 1924 Maria's villa was confiscated. She and Garin decided to move to Georgievsk and with what remained of Maria's money bought a small adobe house, which they divided into two. One large, self-contained room was for the use of Zakhar and Evdokia, and the rest for themselves. The old couple, however, found it difficult to settle. Zakhar, in particular, was drawn back to his old estate near Armavir, and although it was out of the question for him to reoccupy it, he and Evdokia moved for a while to the nearby village of Gulkevichi, where Zakhar had many relations. There they lived with one of his cousins and were supported by gifts of food from the family and from some of Zakhar's former employees.

Solzhenitsyn, now five, did not go with his aunt Maria to Georgievsk. Roman and Irina were also moving—to Novocherkassk, the Don Cossack capital, a couple of hundred miles to the north, not far from Rostov. Having established themselves there in the autumn of 1924, they returned to collect the boy and take him back with them by train on the eve of his sixth birthday. In some later verse, he was to recall this first journey of his, the long train ride, the mysterious drive after dark down the snowbound Kreshchensky Boulevard in Novocherkassk, and the strange sights and sounds of a large town. He also wrote vividly of a church procession at midnight being jeered by hostile students, an interesting prefiguration of his story "The Easter Procession," describing a similar scene in Peredelkino forty years later. A few days after his arrival in Novocherkassk, he was taken to Rostov to be reunited with his mother.[8]

There is a posed picture of him at the age of six, taken just after his arrival in Rostov, showing a stocky boy in a striped smock holding a toy popgun in the "present arms" position. The face is broad, round, and intelligent, with a high forehead and closely cropped hair, but what most captures the attention is the alert gaze of the eyes and the expressive mobility of the brows above them. Yet the studied smartness of this studio photograph is also a little misleading, for apparently there was much of the unlicked urchin about him when he first arrived from Kislovodsk. Preoccupied with the greater cares of her new family and difficult living conditions, Aunt Maria had given him a free rein in Kislovodsk, while his troubled grandparents had had distractions of their own. From Grandfather Zakhar, a Ukrainian peasant by birth (despite his later wealth), and from Maria, he had acquired a distinct Ukrainian accent that has remained with him to the present day. Even now he speaks with a soft, guttural southern *g*—"like Brezhnev," as he jokingly remarked on one occasion[9]—and tends to slip dialect words into his speech when he is not paying attention. The Ukrainian dimension has remained important to him: "Ukrainian and Russian are intermingled in my blood, in my heart, and in my thoughts," he was to write in volume 3 of *The Gulag Archipelago*.[10]

Somewhat surprisingly, he took to the city of Rostov at once, perhaps because it displayed some of the colour, variety, and liveliness that were still missing from Kislovodsk. By now the New Economic Policy (NEP)* had

---

* The New Economic Policy was introduced by Lenin in March 1921 to cope with a disastrous drop in the popularity of the Bolshevik government and with a rising tension in the country, symbolized by the Kronstadt Rebellion in Petrograd the preceding month. The policy allowed for the controlled and limited admission of market forces into the economy and was designed above all to placate a hostile peasantry.

been in force for nearly three years and in that time had transformed the conditions of everyday life. As the rigours of War Communism receded and normal trade relations were resumed, food became more plentiful in the shops, consumer goods began to reappear, and everyday life reverted to a simulacrum of what it had been before the Revolution.

This was particularly felt and noticed in Rostov. Throughout its history the city had been noted as a prosperous trading centre, important both as an outlet for the rich agricultural produce of southern Russia and as a magnet for goods and investment from the wealthy countries of western Europe. The English writer Stephen Graham has written that in 1911 the main street of Rostov was "an 'emporium' of steam-ploughs, harvesting machines, threshing machines, cranes, fire engines, butter factory machinery and the rest, all imported from abroad." And every other kind of import was on display, from "Tottenham Court Road furniture, Sheffield cutlery," English and German clothes to "Persian rugs, Caucasian silks, and Turkish fruits and sweetmeats."[11] The picturesqueness of its position on the steep right bank of the Don, with its crowded terraces tumbling down the hill to the broad, shallow harbour, was also a great attraction. Another English writer, Rhoda Power, who was there as a governess during the First World War, wrote that it reminded her of a Cubist picture: "It seemed to be all higgledy-piggledy, a jumble of vivid colours, domes and oddly shaped houses."[12] Visitors noted the cosmopolitan population characteristic of a flourishing southern port, its large communities of Cossacks, Jews, Greeks, and, above all, Armenians, who had been settled here by Catherine the Great and had built their distinctive quarter of Nakhichevan, on the eastern outskirts of the city. The spirit of Rostov was spontaneous, independent, democratic, mercantile, competitive, and pleasure-loving. No wonder it had become the centre of southern resistance to the Boshevik coup and had earned itself the nickname of "White Guard City" during the Civil War.

Of course, there could be no return to those halcyon pre-war days, but the memory of them was still fresh, and hopes had been raised by the liberal policies of the NEP. In his unpublished autobiographical poem, *The Way*,* Solzhenitsyn was later to evoke the atmosphere of these early childhood years. Old Rostov, he wrote, seemed to be coming back to life. There were Greek and Italian ships in the harbour, and a brisk trade revived in grain, cattle, wool, and fish. Horse cabbies vied with motor cars on the roads, church bells continued to ring out each morning, the streets and parks had not yet been renamed for revolutionary leaders, and "all that seemed to have happened"

---

* The title of this poem seems to have undergone some changes. It was originally called *Enthusiasts' Highway (Shosse entuziastov)*, an ironic reference to the Soviet renaming of the old Vladimir High Road, famous as the starting-point in Moscow for convicts being transported to Siberia, to symbolize the inauguration of a new (convictless) era. Solzhenitsyn then changed the title to *Dorozhen'ka*, meaning literally "The Way," but with derisive overtones that cannot be compactly conveyed in an English translation. Judging by a note in *Vestnik*, no. 117, it appears that he may now prefer the original title once more.

was that the pre-revolutionary sign of "Duma"* had been exchanged for a new one saying "Soviets."[13]

Solzhenitsyn has sometimes given the impression that he did not care for Rostov. In a number of interviews he has played down his association with the city, partly, perhaps, because of his later estrangement from it and partly, one suspects, to divert attention from relatives and family friends who still live there. It is true that he does not much care for the people, whom he has said he finds too boisterous and volatile for his own conservative tastes. Nor does he care for their colourful southern dialect, which holds no charms for him as a writer. But of the city itself he was exceedingly fond, as he later showed in his descriptions of it in *The Way* and above all in the scene in *August 1914*, in which Xenia Tomchak's heart is said "always to beat faster" whenever she returned to Rostov. "Sadovaya Street was fresh and clean in the deep shade of the trees as it climbed the hill towards Dolomanovsky. . . . The trams . . . had long arms with runners instead of hoop-shaped pick-ups, there were special cars for summertime with airy, open sides. . . . Typical, too, were the special mobile lattice-work bridges, arc-shaped with handrails, which were placed across flooded streets in the southern rainstorms and were kept on the pavements when the weather was dry. From Nikolsky Street onwards the Bolshaya Sadovaya straightened out and ran like a mile-long arrow to the city limits at the suburb of Nakhichevan."[14] In writing these pages, Solzhenitsyn had had the sights and sounds of his own childhood in mind, and he later said, "To this very day I love its stones."[15]

Taissia's motives for moving to Rostov must have been mixed. Since it was by far the largest city in the North Caucasus, it was simply an easier place in which to find a job. It was also easier for her, as a "social alien" under the new system, to melt into the multitude and not stand out too much, which was impossible in the small provincial town of Kislovodsk. Thirdly, it was still not too far from Kislovodsk, which meant that she was able to stay in touch with her family and her son until he was able to rejoin her. The alternative of Moscow, which was the only other city in which she had friends, was too remote and forbidding, and in the still-chaotic conditions of 1921, threatened a permanent, if involuntary, separation. Fortunately, the happiest years of her childhood had been spent at a boarding school in Rostov, and the family of the headmistress of the school that she had attended was in many ways dearer to her than her own.

The family in question were the Andreyevs, whom Solzhenitsyn has described in some detail in *August 1914* under the name of Kharitonov. The mild-mannered father, Nikolai, had been a school inspector, but the real power in the family was his wife, Alexandra Fyodorovna, who had owned and run an exclusive gymnasium for young ladies on the corner of Staro-

---

* The name of one of two assemblies forming the Russian parliament from 1905 to 1917. The Duma was elected under a limited franchise and had severely restricted powers until February 1917 (Old Style). After the February Revolution it acted as the effective government of Russia until the Bolshevik takeover in October.

pochtovaya and Nikolayevsky streets behind the cathedral in the old quarter of Rostov. Taissia had come there in exactly the same circumstances as described for Xenia Tomchak in *August 1914*, brought by her wealthy father Zakhar, and virtually dumped on the headmistress's doorstep with a plea that she be taken in. In those days Taissia had been a homespun country girl, pious and naïve, but Mme Andreyeva's progressive school and household had transformed her into a poised and sophisticated young lady, showing hardly a trace of her former awkwardness.

Solzhenitsyn still possesses one of those charming old composite photographs that schools used to distribute in the tranquil days before the First World War, showing Taissia's graduation class of 1911–12. Two medallions at the top enclose portraits of Mme Andreyeva and her husband, followed by thirteen rectangular photographs of the teachers, including a priest wearing a surplice and a heavy cross. Then come thirty-six oval portraits of thirty-six well-groomed young ladies, wearing high-buttoned black school dresses with wide starched lace collars resting on their shoulders. A few of them are wearing cloaks, including Taissia, who is turned three-quarters to face the camera, a mischievous half-smile on her round face, her hair hanging in unruly ringlets. In another year, as a student in Moscow, her transformation was to be complete. A touch of superciliousness hovers about the pretty plump face that regards us from another photograph, a confident self-possession perfectly expressed by the ostrich feather in the showy hat and the expensive tailored coat.

The portrait of Mme Andreyeva on the graduation photograph depicts a grey-haired and severe-looking elderly lady wearing an intimidating pince-nez, whose formidable personality is barely confined by the constricting circle of girlish faces. Despite her liberal political views—allowing her, among other things, freely to admit Jews to her school at a time when anti-Semitism was at its height and actively encouraged in a city like Rostov—she ruled her establishment like an absolute monarch. Taissia had been admitted to her home as a paying guest, and there, too, Andreyeva was unbending. For Taissia she "was not 'Mama' but 'the headmistress.' To the end of her days she would be the headmistress . . . meeting her was always slightly awe-inspiring and one could never argue with her or contradict anything she said."[16]

Taissia had done extremely well in Mme Andreyeva's school, coming out at the top of the class in her final year and winning the annual gold medal for the best pupil. From there she had gone straight to Moscow and had become a close friend of Mme Andreyeva's daughter, Evgenia—Zhenia for short. Zhenia was four years older than Taissia and had gone to study in Moscow in the same year that Taissia arrived in Rostov—Taissia had taken Zhenia's room. And when she went to Moscow herself, she became enmeshed in the drama of Zhenia's marriage to an "unsuitable" husband, a young engineer by the name of Vladimir Fedorovsky. The truth of the matter was that Zhenia had fallen head over heels in love with Fedorovsky, become pregnant by him, and married him in a cloud of disapproval from her imperious mother, who deplored not only the indecent circumstances of the betrothal but also the social disgrace of linking her ancient family with the fortunes of an unknown upstart. The whole thing is described with some humour in *August 1914*, where Fedorovsky appears as Filomatinsky. Taissia's role as a go-between during her frequent visits to Mme Andreyeva in Rostov is also portrayed there, as is the ultimate reconciliation brought about by the upheavals of the World War, the Revolution, and the Civil War.

By 1921, when Taissia arrived in Rostov from Kislovodsk, the school had been confiscated and closed down by the new Soviet authorities, and the Andreyevs were under a cloud as "social aliens," like Taissia herself. Mme Andreyeva's two sons had fought for the White Volunteer Army during the Civil War and had never returned. But the situation was saved by the formerly despised son-in-law, who was now a successful engineer working for the new regime. Through him the Andreyevs had managed to retain their large, comfortable flat attached to the former school and were still living there when the young Solzhenitsyn arrived in 1924. He can still remember its welcoming rooms and broad balcony overlooking a narrow sidestreet. In 1926 they were deprived of this flat, but moved to equally spacious quarters in a solid building adjoining the ornate edifice of one of Rostov's former banks on Sredni Prospekt.[17]

Taissia herself managed, after great difficulty, to find some accommodation close by, in the region of Nikolsky Lane, but it was nothing like the Fedorovskys', and her life was hard in the extreme, for it was decidedly difficult for her to obtain any kind of work. As the daughter of a wealthy landowner (although her inheritance had been confiscated and she was now as penniless as anyone else), she was automatically suspect. The official policy was not to employ such people at all if it could be avoided, or else to assign them to the most menial, poorly paid, and insecure positions possible. Taissia did everything she could to conceal her shameful origins. On one occasion she asked her son to help her bury his father's three medals, lest it be discovered that he had been an officer during the First World War. Photographs of his father in uniform also had to be concealed, and on the endless probing questionnaires that had to be completed at every turn, Taissia took to describing her husband's former status as *sluzhashchi*, or office worker, as distinct from the superior *rabochi*, or manual worker. The category of "officer" would have cut her off irrevocably not only from work but also from the all-important ration card.

She was enabled to get her first job—as a shorthand typist with Melstroi, a large building combine specializing in the construction of grain mills—thanks to a recommendation from the chief engineer there, Alexander Arkhangorodsky (described under his correct surname in *August 1914*,), whose daughter, Lyuba, had been Taissia's best friend at the Andreyeva gymnasium. Arkhangorodsky, an assimilated Jew, had been highly successful even before the Revolution, and on the grounds of his former wealth and prestige might equally have fallen into the disgraced category of "social alien." But the early post-revolutionary situation was more complicated than that. As a Jew, Arkhangorodsky counted as a member of a formerly despised minority that had identified itself particularly closely with the Revolution and was singled out for preferential treatment. Secondly, he had been known for his liberal and progressive views even before the Revolution. Thirdly and most importantly, he was a skilled engineer, indispensable to the reconstruction and continued smooth running of industry, a member of the professional group that was deliberately being wooed and pampered by the new Soviet authorities. Like Vladimir Fedorovsky, Arkhangorodsky was a member of virtually the only elite to weather the Revolution with its former status more or less intact, an elite that was particularly numerous and strong in Rostov, with its industrial tradition. It was thanks to their patronage and friendship that Taissia was able to survive at all.

Unfortunately, someone who knew Taissia's background informed on her, and she was soon dismissed. Worse still, her papers were officially marked to fix her lowly status, which meant that she was automatically barred from the large number of well-paid and reserved jobs that had been spawned by the post-revolutionary bureaucracy, together with access to the privileged food and clothing supplies that usually went with them, and was also looked upon with suspicion by employers in the non-reserved sectors. Feeling vulnerable and exposed *vis-à-vis* the vast state apparatus, they were reluctant to hire and embarrassingly eager to fire her, often as the result of a denunciation. What usually happened was that she would be called into the director's office, told of the problem created by the revelation of her social origins, and invited to resign. This happened about half a dozen times in all, and each time Taissia had to trail from office to office in search of new work.*

An immediate consequence of this inability to obtain an officially approved post was that she was automatically disqualified from applying for an officially controlled room or flat, which, since 90 per cent of the housing sector had been nationalized, excluded her from normal accommodation. Furthermore, there was a built-in catch, in that rents in the tiny private sector were incomparably higher, so that Taissia was squeezed between the inexorable pressures of an artificially enforced low income and an equally artificially enforced high expenditure.

With great difficulty she eventually found a rickety, weather-boarded shack in a narrow cul-de-sac in the centre of town. It consisted of a single large room and scullery, measuring about twelve feet by nine, with loose boards and a leaky tin roof through which the wind whistled in winter and the water dripped when it rained or snowed. There was no drainage or plumbing. Water had to be fetched from a standpipe about 150 yards away, and all slops had to be carried out and emptied by hand. The shack was one of about half a dozen surrounding a tumbledown yard, which had rubble

* It is not clear how often Taissia lost her job or for how long she remained without work, but eventually she seems to have obtained more settled employment, perhaps with Arkhangorodsky's help again.

heaped in the corners and was criss-crossed by washing lines strung between a handful of stunted trees. Taissia and Solzhenitsyn lived there for twelve years, from 1924 to 1936.

Taissia was obliged to spend extremely long hours at her various jobs and often brought work home as well to supplement her meagre income. At some point she began to get more or less regular work as a conference stenographer, but since many of the conferences took place in the evenings, it meant spending even longer hours away from home.[18] Her long hours meant that the housework often had to be done late at night. Water for the laundry had to be boiled on a tiny Primus stove in their draughty, unheated scullery, which was freezing cold in winter, and Solzhenitsyn regularly fell asleep to the sound of his mother scrubbing and splashing at their zinc tub. As soon as he was old enough, he, too, helped with the chores, fetching water, carrying out the slops, and doing the shopping after school. He still has vivid memories of standing in endless queues for bread and other commodities.

Taissia was ill-equipped for this strenuous and precarious existence. She was basically a soft-hearted person, naïve and impractical and unsuited to the tough, scheming world of the young Soviet republic. She had been raised in luxury, and was now disoriented and disheartened, in constant doubt about what to do next or what was best for herself and her son, and worn down by incessant labour. An internal-passport picture of this period tells the whole story. Gone is the plump, slightly mocking face of the well-to-do young lady with an ostrich feather in her hat. In its place we find the lined and careworn face of an exhausted drudge, the forehead corrugated, the brows knitted, the lips tightly compressed. Her hair (now streaked with grey) is badly cut in a frizzy utility style reminiscent of British factory women of the war years, and her entire expression is suffused with repressed pain and defeat. In less than ten years she had aged twenty.

An example of Taissia's characteristic gullibility and helplessness was her abortive attempt at this time to acquire a decent home. Although she had sold most of her possessions in Kislovodsk, she had managed to hang on to one precious heirloom—her grand piano. In 1927 an order was issued for the demolition of their shack, and she resolved to sell the piano and apply the proceeds to the purchase of a four-roomed co-operative flat. She duly completed the sale and deposited the money with the co-operative, having been informed that the flats would be ready in two years. Two years passed, then three, four, five, and still no flat was offered her. Initially the construction was postponed. Then, when the first lot of flats had been built, someone bribed the co-operative to give them Taissia's flat in her place. She was promised another, at a later date, but nothing came of it, and eventually she requested her money back. More time passed, and by the time the co-operative repaid her, inflation had reduced the money's value to less than half, so that there was no longer any question of buying a flat with it. Her only stroke of good fortune—if good fortune it be—was that the demolition order was never acted upon and that she was able to continue living in her tumbledown shack.[19]

In these circumstances it might have been wiser for Taissia to remarry—she was precisely the sort of woman who needed a strong companion in life. And it seems there was no shortage of suitors. But in this, too, her fastidious and vacillating character told against her. She could never make up her mind. Above all, she feared for the well-being of her son, in whom she worshipped the image and memory of her dead husband. Solzhenitsyn possessed his father's fair hair and blue eyes (Taissia's hair and eyes were brown), and she kept Isaaki's memory alive by calling her son by his father's unconventional nickname, Sanya—or Sanyechka—instead of the more usual "Sasha."* In later years Solzhenitsyn came to feel that his mother's failure to remarry had been a needless sacrifice and an error, not only for her own sake but for his as well: "When I was older and able to grasp the full significance of this sacrifice, I concluded it was a mistake, since I believe no harm is done to children by their having a strict father."[20]

One effect of this orphanhood was to lead the son to idealize his dead father. Taissia told him all she knew, especially about Isaaki's heroism during the war, but her own knowledge was scant enough. Out of the fifteen months she had known him, Isaaki had spent twelve on active service, and she had been cut off from Isaaki's family by his death and the Civil War. The deaths of Semyon, Vasily, and Anastasia Solzhenitsyn in 1919 meant that only Evdokia and Konstantin were left of Isaaki's immediate family, not counting his estranged stepmother and her two children, and that there was thus virtually no one on that side with whom she could communicate any more. The only way to make it up to the son was to take him to his father's grave, and Taissia and Solzhenitsyn made regular pilgrimages to Georgievsk until 1931. The great void of his father's early life had therefore to be filled by the son's imagination, which appears to have been obsessed by the subject in childhood and has remained haunted by it ever since. Today as he labours at his vast epic on the Revolution, in Vermont, it is his father's portraits that stand guard on his writing desk. In one of them the youthful Isaaki, wearing his high-buttoned school uniform, has his peaked cap tilted at a rakish angle, revealing tufts of unruly hair sticking out to front and sides. The pose and expression are challenging but are belied by the soulful eyes and irresolute mouth, framed by a bushy beard. In the second and possibly later photograph the cap has been removed, the long hair is carefully parted on the right side, the beard has shrunk to a neatly trimmed goatee, and the high, broad forehead serves to emphasize the thoughtful look in those sensitive eyes. Here, nurtured in the author's imagination for half a century, is the hero of his latest series of novels, the prototype of his fictional reincarnation as Isaaki Lazhenitsyn in *August 1914*.

---

*The usual diminutives of Alexander are Sasha or Shura. Taissia seems to have preferred Sanyechka to Sanya in addressing her son. It was she who, when registering his birth, decided that his patronymic should be Isayevich rather than the more clumsy (but literally correct) Isaaki-yevich.

Another effect of Solzhenitsyn's fatherlessness was to encourage precocity. As the only male in the household, living alone with a doting mother, he grew to early independence and maturity, a process that was hastened by his increasing assumption of responsibility for household and other chores. Taissia's vacillations developed in him a strong and imperious will, which was exercised all the more fully in the absence of paternal authority. Indeed, impatience of authority, whether in the shape of parent, teachers, senior officers, prison guards, the Writers' Union, the Soviet government, or of anyone but God Himself, was to become a leitmotiv of his career and determine his adult life. And with it went a rare practical energy, in which he differed as much as could possibly be from his own father and mother and which, like his will-power, harked back a generation, to his maternal grandfather.

Grandfather Zakhar was in effect the only man in the family. I had no father, so grandfather somehow took his place. I loved them dearly, Zakhar and Evdokia. I didn't visit them all that often, but they weren't remote from me at all. Grandma was a woman of rare goodness and kindness. But granddad was a man of exceptional energy, and had a drastic temper. In certain respects I take after him in my character. I got all my energy from him, for example, because papa was a completely different sort of person. Papa was a soft, lyrical, philosophical man, very soft. So my energy comes from my grandfather.[21]

Solzhenitsyn's early independence and self-sufficiency often took the form of solitariness and self-absorption. Though happy enough to play adventure games and hide-and-seek with the other boys in the yard, he was inclined to retire early from the fray and seek refuge in a book. Similarly, he spent his first two summer holidays from school away from Rostov with Zakhar and Evdokia in Gulkevichi, and whereas he has the fondest memories of scampering among the houses with the village children, still more fondly does he recall the strange peace of the countryside and the delights of communing with nature. Whatever the company and whatever the game, he invariably withdrew after a certain period in order to be alone, occupying himself with childhood hobbies and personal projects or pottering about the house.

His solitariness was fostered by frequent long visits to other relatives as well. For his mother it was both a financial and a psychological relief to be able to send him to stay with other members of the family. After the two holidays with his grandparents, he went most of the time to Roman and Irina, who in 1927 left Novocherkassk and bought a house in Yeisk, a small fishing town about forty miles from Rostov on the shores of the Sea of Azov. In Yeisk, Solzhenitsyn used to wander round the harbour or go swimming on his own and was able to indulge his increasingly voracious appetite for reading. Irina had a first-class library, which she had miraculously preserved throughout all her peregrinations. Here Solzhenitsyn read Pushkin, Gogol, Tolstoy, Dostoyevsky, Turgenev, and most of the Russian classics. Many of the books he read again and again, starting at an unusually early age. He claims to have read *War and Peace*, for example, at the age of ten, and to have reread it several times in the course of ensuing summers. It seems to have been during this period that the figure of Tolstoy became embedded in his imagination as the archetypal Russian writer. Irina also presented him with a copy of Vladimir Dahl's famous collection of Russian proverbs, though it wasn't until much later that Dahl came to occupy as prominent a place in Solzhenitsyn's literary pantheon as Tolstoy himself. Other authors who made an impression on him at this time were Shakespeare, Schiller, and particularly Dickens. Another favourite was Jack London, an enormously popular author in Russia both before and after the Revolution, whom Solzhenitsyn first discovered in the supplement to one of the Rostov newspapers. Half a lifetime later, on his first visit to the United States, he was to pay homage to his childhood hero by seeking out London's home in California and making a brief pilgrimage.

Irina encouraged him in his reading and did her best to foster his love of literature. From the very day of his birth, it seems, in her house in Kislovodsk, she had regarded him as being somehow in her special charge. Childless herself, she bestowed on him all the love and affection that might otherwise have gone to her own children, and he in turn came to love his "Auntie Ira" with a tenderness and loyalty that fully reciprocated her own. Uncle Roman, on the other hand, though familiar to him from early childhood, struck him as being a remote and unattractive figure.[22]

In every writer's biography it is possible to pick out one or two individuals who had a decisive influence on the writer's imagination, particularly at an early age, either by virtue of their own adventures, which they then recounted to the child, or by the tales they told of others, whether real or invented. In Solzhenitsyn's case we can point to Aunt Irina as such an influence.* Profoundly conservative and patriotic, with her imagination forcibly turned to the past by the cataclysm of the Revolution, she regaled her nephew during the long summer holidays with stories of olden times, and especially with stories of his immediate forebears.

The tale she had to tell was redolent of a bygone era, like those faded sepia photographs from an Edwardian snapshot album in which we find overdressed people frozen in stiff poses, sitting bolt upright in outlandish motor cars, or grouped in the foreground of milky landscapes at a season that seems always to have been high summer. It was a vanished age, never to return, but its features sank deep into the boy's imagination, to be re-created in his mature works half a century later.

The family she told him of was his mother's family, the Shcherbaks. Like the Solzhenitsyns, they were of peasant stock and knew even less of their origins. Above all it was the story of Solzhenitsyn's grandfather, the

---

* Solzhenitsyn's first wife, Natalia Reshetovskaya, disputes this and is of the opinion that Solzhenitsyn invented Irina's influence on his childhood after meeting her again in the 1950s and 1960s.

energetic Zakhar Shcherbak, who seems to have been one of the most extraordinary men in southern Russia. Zakhar had been born in 1858 in Tavria, in the southern Ukraine. After a mere year and a half of schooling, he had worked as a shepherd boy until about 1870, when his entire family migrated to the North Caucasus in search of work. They settled just south of the Kuban, not far from the Solzhenitsyn farm, and worked as hired labourers. After ten years or so, Zakhar was given a dozen sheep, a cow, and a handful of piglets by a grateful employer and urged to make a start on his own. He quickly showed uncommon energy and industry. By dint of hard work and shrewd dealing, he built up a substantial holding and amassed a fair sum of capital. He also met and married Evdokia Ilyinichna, the daughter of a village blacksmith. She appears to have been a pious woman, who insisted on a strict observance of all the religious holidays, and she bore Zakhar nine children, of whom six died in a single week from an epidemic of scarlet fever. This act of God only served to intensify her religious devotion.

Zakhar's success as a farmer led to the rapid accumulation of real wealth, and sometime during the 1880s he moved 150 miles north-west to the district of Armavir in the Kuban, among Ukrainians like himself. About ten miles from Armavir, at a place called Kubanskaya Stantsia between the Vladikavkaz Railway line and the river Kuban, he bought a large piece of land, which he transformed into a sumptuous estate with a luxurious house and an elaborate park. A grand two-storey mansion was erected, with a wrought-iron balcony running around the entire first floor, and the windows were equipped with shutters and venetian blinds against the heat. Piped water was supplied through four separate systems from four separate sources, and electricity was provided by a diesel generator. After the house came the park, which Solzhenitsyn later described in *August 1914*, with its avenues of balsam and pyramid poplars, its pond for swimming in, its orchard, its vineyard, its Moorish garden, herb garden, and rose garden, "and a lawn of emerald-green English rye-grass alongside the drive, which was cut with lawn-mowers."[23]

In the central provinces of Russia, country estates like this were a familiar part of the scene, but they were mostly hereditary, going back, in many cases, for centuries, and were often dilapidated. Down here in the Kuban, by contrast, there were few hereditary estates, and those that existed had been there for less than a hundred years. The Cossacks, who owned most of the land, were by temperament restless and disinclined to dig deep roots. Their *stanitsas*, even when they grew to twenty or thirty thousand inhabitants, remained overgrown villages, with unpaved streets and a bare minimum of public buildings. When the richer Cossacks built estates, they traditionally had an informal, impermanent air about them. And in almost all cases their organization and appearance reflected the prevailing Russian taste for disorder and cheerful anarchism in their surroundings.

In *August 1914* Solzhenitsyn has drawn an affectionate portrait of his uncouth and unlettered, yet dynamic and remarkable, grandfather. By the turn of the present century, Shcherbak was farming fifty-five hundred acres and had twenty thousand sheep. The home farm alone, with its outbuildings and kitchen gardens, took up fifty acres. And on this land he liked to use the most modern "progressive" methods, modelling himself on the German colonists who were particularly numerous in the North Caucasus and were famous for their industry, efficiency, and unbelievably high productivity. As a result he was spectacularly successful. And yet he could not escape his origins. His life was an exotic mixture of ostentatious consumption and patriarchal custom. The interior of the big house was lavishly decorated to match the exterior, with imitation-walnut panelling, a wealth of heavy Victorian furniture, and all the appurtenances of gracious living. There were ten indoor and ten outdoor servants, including a butler, cooks, serving maids, a chauffeur (at first for the "Russo-Baltic carriage" that Zakhar purchased in a fit of enthusiasm for the latest technology, later for his Mercedes), and a coachman for his more conventional horse-drawn carriages. There were dozens of other employees—a bailiff, an accountant, clerks, stewards, foremen, storekeepers, grooms, herdsmen, mechanics, gardeners, labourers, and, after the disturbances occasioned by the 1905 revolution, four armed Cossacks to guard the estate. Yet domestically his life remained little touched by his wealth. Scorning his modern bedroom, he had constructed a special room leading off his wife's, without a door to the outside because he was terrified of draughts and insisted on sleeping warm. To this end he also installed a tiled bunk beside a traditional upright stove in his room and slept there in winter in the fashion of generations of Russian peasants before him.

All this and more Irina must have told her nephew, widening his eyes with her tales of wealth and luxury. She herself had married into the family as a rich woman in her own right. Her father, an ex-soldier, was also a self-made man. Childless for most of his life, he had fallen madly in love with a younger woman when already old and had taken the unorthodox and scandalous step of bribing the bishop of Stavropol with forty thousand rubles for permission to divorce and remarry. Irina was the only child of this second union, and at the age of seventeen, when her father was already dying, had been married off to Roman Shcherbak straight from boarding-school. It was not a love match. Her own opinion had never been asked. But she had been too obedient a child, and the patriarchal traditions of the Kuban were too strong, for her to think of resisting.

Roman Shcherbak, Zakhar's only son, was by far the eldest of the three children who survived the scarlet-fever epidemic. He affected the style of an English country gentleman, complete with tweeds and patent-leather boots, and sometime after his marriage acquired that ultimate in English status symbols, a white Rolls-Royce, said to be one of only nine Rolls-Royces in the whole of Russia. He cultivated an English sang-froid, maintaining a cold reserve in company and striving for a pedantic meticulousness in questions of honour and financial probity. Like Solzhenitsyn's father, Isaaki, he was something of a Tolstoyan in domestic politics and, somewhat incongruously for a rich man, an admirer of Maxim Gorky and his woolly brand of natural socialism, preferring it to the "English" party of the Constitutional Democrats.

Irina was finer-spun than her husband and in-laws, with interests in literature and the arts that they were unable to share, and had sought solace in helping to plan the furnishings of the big house and introducing some style and taste into her immediate surroundings. She had an aristocratic hobby: shooting. In her handbag she carried a small Browning automatic, and an English-made lady's shotgun hung on the wall of her room. But more important to her than these pursuits was her devotion to religion. Christianity, and particularly the mysteries of the Gospels, appealed to her imagination, and the stately rituals of the Orthodox liturgy, rich in sight and sound, strongly affected her appreciation of beauty. In this devotion she was fortunate to find common ground with her pious mother-in-law, Evdokia, so that the multiple fasts and acts of worship indulged in by the elder Shcherbaks did not cause her any of the hardship that they caused the worldly Roman. She found it comforting to have an icon in virtually every room, and reassuring to go down on her knees before her bed each night. Moreover, there was another dimension to her faith that took her, strictly speaking, beyond the bounds of Christianity. According to Solzhenitsyn, she was a firm believer in the transmigration of souls and felt that certain concepts of Eastern religion were a beautiful complement to Christian beliefs. She did not find them in any way contradictory; they were merely alternative manifestations of beauty.[24]

Solzhenitsyn appears to have come deeply under the spell of his intrepid and romantic aunt. By the time she had moved to Yeisk, the anti-religious fanaticism of the immediate post-revolutionary years had begun to abate, and she was once again an avid communicant at the local church. Solzhenitsyn, at a loose end for much of his time in this sleepy little town, generally accompanied her during the holidays and was much thrown into his aunt's company. She taught him the true beauty and meaning of the rituals of the Russian Orthodox church, emphasizing its ancient traditions and continuity. She showed him its importance for Russian history, demonstrating how the history of the church was inextricably intertwined with the history of the nation; and she instilled into the boy a patriotic love of the past and a firm faith in the greatness and sacred destiny of the Russian people.

Irina thus supplied him with a sense of tradition, of family, and of roots that was otherwise severely attenuated. Freudians would say that one of the most serious effects of fatherlessness is the production of a sense of disorientation and an early identity crisis, particularly in the case of an only child and a son. The search for a masculine model is frustrated, and the boy is obliged to cast about for a substitute. It was no wonder, perhaps, that Solzhenitsyn was so attracted by the example of his virile grandfather, and his imagination fired by the stories of his colourful aunt. Consciousness of a glorious family past was an essential source of pride to him, one that could be freely indulged in and enjoyed in the backwater of Yeisk, whereas in Rostov it had to be treated as a shameful secret and a stigma to be concealed.

Irina's simultaneous and eloquent praise of the Russian past must also have forged a link between these things in the boy's mind: his family's former success had coincided with Russia's greatness. Patriotic pride fused with family pride in repairing his wounded sense of self.

Irina was not alone in staunching the wound: there were also the Fedorovskys. Zhenia and Vladimir Fedorovsky were Taissia's oldest and closest friends in Rostov. It was with them that she habitually spent most of her free time and to whom she turned for assistance and advice, and it was to them that she appealed to keep an eye on her son when she was unavoidably absent from home. Since she was away at work most of the day and often collecting or delivering additional work in the evenings, Solzhenitsyn would generally go there after school and wait for his mother to arrive.[25]

Apart from the loss of the school and the disappearance of Zhenia's two brothers during the Civil War, the Andreyevs and Fedorovskys had come through the Revolution quite well. Their new flat, on Sredni Prospekt, with its spacious, high-ceilinged rooms and wide balcony overlooking a secluded courtyard, was as big and solid and comfortable as the one they had been evicted from. For Solzhenitsyn it was a home from home. The Fedorovsky family, especially in the early years, was his own family too, and the entire bustling establishment offered a striking and welcome contrast to the forbidding and lonely hovel off Nikolsky Lane.

Solzhenitsyn's playmates were Zhenia's two children, Mikhail and Irina—Misha and Lialia, to their friends. Misha was about a year older than Solzhenitsyn and Lialia four years older, but in childhood the three of them were inseparable, playing endless games together. A particular interest when the boys were about ten and eleven was the composition of their own illustrated newspapers and journals, which became a positive craze and drew in some of Lialia's friends as well.

Taissia's old headmistress, Mme Andreyeva, was still alive when Solzhenitsyn started going there, and he remembers her, in her seventies, sitting stern and aloof in one corner of the drawing room, playing games of patience. But the person who made the deepest impression on him was her once-despised son-in-law and Misha's father, Vladimir Fedorovsky. Fedorovsky was the epitome of what was in early Soviet times called a *spets*, a technical specialist or expert whose field was some aspect of technology or engineering. His own speciality was mining engineering, and his particular subject was the relatively new field of underground combustion, a technique whereby coal was to be ignited directly underground, without excavation, and the resulting gas piped off automatically. Such a technique naturally held potent attractions for Soviet technocrats still dazzled by the vision of speedy industrialization, and Fedorovsky benefited enormously from the industrial mystique of those years. He also had a teaching post in the Faculty of Steam Engineering at the University of Rostov, as a result of which his circle included not only practising engineers and mining consultants but also teachers, theoreticians, students, and young graduates.

Fedorovsky was a tremendously busy and hard-working man. A photograph in Solzhenitsyn's possession shows him sitting at his drawing board, thin and dapper, his hair parted almost in the middle, his sinewy hands resting in front of him, with a thoughtful, slightly melancholy expression on his face. He had a habitual stoop, carrying one shoulder higher than the other as he walked, and used a pince-nez for reading. On normal evenings he would disappear after dinner through the frosted-glass door of his study and continue working until late into the night, but on Saturdays and holidays the Fedorovskys would throw a family party, where he would be the life and soul as a host. Plenty of visitors came, there would be card games, charades, someone would play the piano for dancing, and there was lots to eat and drink. On other occasions there were late dinner parties at which Fedorovsky and his friends would discuss politics and international affairs, art and literature, as well as engineering and business matters. The children were allowed to stay up on these occasions, and Solzhenitsyn has tried to re-create something of their atmosphere in the closing chapters of *August 1914*. He would drink in as much conversation as he could, but the moment inevitably came when he and the Fedorovsky children would be banished to bed and would have to listen to the sounds of continuing merriment through the closed door of their room.

Solzhenitsyn later recalled these happy times in chapter 1 of his autobiographical poem, *The Way*:

> Now it seems a fairy tale—
> That friendly, liberal home of theirs,
> Where friend and stranger were at ease,
> Where all took part in noisy table talk
> And ate and drank whate'er they pleased.

Their house was always open to him, and he spent "half his childhood" there, like a "second son," acquiring a brother and a sister in the process.

In later years Solzhenitsyn himself opted for physics and mathematics as a means of making a living, and he was to spend a large part of his life in the company of scientists and engineers. Some of them became close friends, and his books, articles, and interviews are studded with expressions of warmth for their calling. In his mother's immediate circle there were three engineers: Vladimir Fedorovsky, Alexander Arkhangorodsky, and Boris Ostrovsky (whose son, Misha, was also a playmate of Solzhenitsyn's). But it was above all the Fedorovskys who kindled this glow in him, and it was childhood memories of those convivial conversations around the dinner table that stood behind the moving tribute he paid in volume 1 of *The Gulag Archipelago:*

> Engineer! It so happens that I was brought up in an engineering milieu, and I can remember the engineers of the twenties perfectly—that candidly luminous intellect, that unrestrained and inoffensive humour, that freedom and breadth of thought, the ease with which they moved from one field of engineering to another,

or in general from technical subjects to current affairs and art. And they were so
well educated, with such good taste. Their Russian was excellent, rhythmical
and correct, and devoid of popular slang. Some played an instrument, others
painted, and one and all had the stamp of spiritual nobility on their faces.[26]

A notable feature of these conversations was the political freedom with
which everybody spoke. At that point in the twenties, after the introduction
of the New Economic Policy, the ideological rigours of War Communism
had been considerably relaxed and there was a definite lightening of the
atmosphere. To many it began to seem as if the harsh years of the Civil War
and its aftermath had been nothing but a bad dream. Soviet society was
reverting to more and more of the practices of the past, and the rupture of
the Revolution began to seem less drastic than it had formerly appeared.
Time was to show that this relaxation was an illusion, that it was basically a
question of consolidating before making the next leap forward. But in the
twenties this was not at all clear, and the mood among people like the Fedorovskys was one of private optimism and confidence.

Solzhenitsyn recalls that members of his own family, too, used to express
themselves with complete freedom in his presence. He was never sent out of
the room when the conversation turned to "difficult" subjects, nor was he
kept from the truth about the difficulties of the immediate past. On the contrary, his mother and Irina frequently dwelt on the horrors of the Civil War
and the way the family had suffered. He knew all about the family friends
who had been arrested or killed, of his uncle Roman's temporary detention
and death sentence and Irina's bold intervention, of the confiscation of his
grandfather's estate, the searches and reprisals in Kislovodsk, Roman and
Irina's enforced flight and subsequent peregrinations in search of a refuge.
"Everyone, of course, was anti-Bolshevik in the circle in which I grew up,"
he later remarked, and this had important psychological consequences: "The
political, religious, and social upbringing I received at home differed tremendously from the surrounding Soviet world. And for that reason I was slow
in coming to terms with that Soviet world."[27]

Discussing the same subject on another occasion Solzhenitsyn commented:

The fact that they used to say everything at home and never shielded me from
anything decided my destiny. Generally speaking . . . if you want to know the
pivotal point of my life, you have to understand that I received such a charge of
social tension in childhood that it pushed everything else to one side and diminished it. . . . I even constructed out of this a totally false picture of life for
myself. I used to maintain, for example, that a man's personal life was on the
whole secondary and of little importance to him. Whether it was this way or
that, good or bad, was not important. The main thing was how he created his
public life. I had to live through dozens of years before I discovered that this was
false. . . . And for this I have been frequently and cruelly punished in life. But
that's the way I am and was, because inside me I bore this social tension—on the

one hand they used to tell me everything at home, and on the other they used to work on our minds at school. Those were militant times, not like today. . . . And we used to listen with such wide eyes to the exploits of the Reds, wave flags, beat drums, blow trumpets. . . . "We'll complete the Revolution." . . . And so this collision between two worlds gave birth to such social tension within me that it somehow defined the path I was to follow for the rest of my life. . . . Even now it is that same social tension that drives me on.[28]

3

FAREWELL TO
THE OLD WORLD

THE COLLISION BETWEEN the two worlds of family and society came to a head for Solzhenitsyn when he was between the ages of eleven and fourteen, coinciding with his puberty. He was at that stage when the bonds of childhood and his ties to the past were in any case certain to be loosened. Writing of this period later in *The Gulag Archipelago*, with reference to the Fedorovskys and their friends, he recalled that "from the beginning of the thirties I started to lose touch with this circle";[1] and in a whole variety of ways he began to move away from the scenes and influences of his early years. It was, in fact, a time of rapid change, both for Solzhenitsyn and for the society in which he lived.

In his own case, the situation was complicated by his particular psychological needs. The lack of a father had been partially compensated for by a deep love of family and tradition, internalized in the form of loyalty to the past and its values. With the onset of puberty, normal feelings of rebellion and disenchantment compelled him to seek alternative role models, but so great was his attachment to the past that the process of adaptation was of necessity painful and intense. At the same time there was the hitherto unnoticed ambivalence of his relations with his lonely mother. Unconsciously called upon to play the roles of both son and husband, he needed now to assert his independence of her and break away. He was therefore ripe for new experiences, and it was only natural that he should begin to reach out from the family circle and involve himself more in society at large.

The forms and direction that this involvement assumed were, of course, influenced by the general development of Soviet society as a whole, which at this time was experiencing its own crisis. The end of the twenties and the beginning of the thirties marked a watershed in Soviet history, after which things were never the same again. Indeed, this "third revolution," as it has sometimes been called, wrought a transformation in Russia almost as great as that wrought by the October Revolution itself.

None of this was apparent at the outset. The honeymoon of the New Economic Policy had created the illusion of a return to pre-revolutionary ways—society seemed to be growing both more prosperous and more relaxed. But beneath the surface political developments were moving in the opposite direction. By 1928 Stalin had emerged the clear victor in the power struggle that had broken out in the Party after the death of Lenin. He had eliminated Trotsky, Kamenev, and Zinoviev as rivals and intimidated all the rest, and was ready to assert his power.

The numerically tiny Communist Party had meanwhile strengthened its grip on the country. At the time of Lenin's death, it had had less than half a million members. By 1928 this figure had more than doubled, and it continued to grow rapidly in the early thirties. These new members were young and malleable, dependent on Stalin and the Party Secretariat for favours and advancement. They were also poorly educated—less than 1 per cent had received any higher education—and were dependent on specialists like Fedorovsky to run government and industry. But the Party held all political power firmly in its hands and created two special instruments to assist its rule. One was psychological and propagandistic: the cult of Lenin, inaugurated by Stalin with the construction of the Lenin Mausoleum in Red Square and the installation in it of Lenin's embalmed body. Stalin ordered millions of portraits of Lenin to be printed, together with booklets of his sayings, all of which were distributed to a superstitious, semi-literate population to lay the foundations of a new faith to replace the old. These were to be the icons and prayer-books of the new "church." The second instrument was older and more practical: the secret police. Secret-police forces had existed before, of course, notably in tsarist Russia, but there had been nothing anywhere to equal the Soviet Cheka,* set up by Lenin as a "temporary" measure in the early days of the Revolution. Endowed with the essential power of summary execution without trial, the Cheka had been the chief instrument of Lenin's "Red Terror," itself an innovation in European history. At the end of the Civil War this fearsome body was renamed the GPU ("State Political Directorate"), and in 1923 it became the OGPU ("Unified State Political Directorate") and was brought under closer Party control, but it remained a virtual state within a state and proved itself indispensable to continuing Communist rule. By the mid-twenties the OGPU had established an efficient nation-wide network of organized terror, while the concentration or "labour" camps, first opened in 1919 to house the victims of that terror, were fast becoming an integral part of the economy.

In 1928 came Stalin's "third revolution." With it he abolished the New

---

*An abbreviation of *Chrezvychainaya kommissiya* (Extraordinary Commission for Combating Counter-revolution, Sabotage, and Speculation).

Economic Policy and called for an almost total forcible collectivization of the peasantry, with the aim of extorting sufficient funds to finance a vast expansion of heavy industry. At the same time the kulaks, or rich peasants, were to be "liquidated" as a class, and all private trading, on however small a scale, abolished. The consequences of this draconian policy were not immediately apparent, and it was only in the early thirties that they were eventually worked out in terms of mass purges, famine, deportations, the mushrooming of the labour camps, and the mobilization of the entire population for Stalin's "great leap forward."

The young Solzhenitsyn could have been no more than dimly aware of these developments in his early years, except insofar as they were palely reflected in the life of the school—only later did the true pattern of events become clear to him. The school he attended was the former Pokrovsky College, a high-class gymnasium in Soborny Lane not far from the Bolshaya Sadovaya, the main street that ran through the centre of town. After the Civil War it had been renamed for Zinoviev, but for a long while was still referred to as the "Malevich Gymnasium," for the popular and talented headmaster, Vladimir Malevich, who had directed the school before the Revolution and was able to remain for several years afterwards. In the general opinion it was the best school in Rostov.

Solzhenitsyn arrived there in 1926, at the age of seven, still wearing round his neck the cross that he had worn since infancy, and became an instant favourite with his first teacher, Elena Belgorodtseva (who was known to have icons hanging in her home, as did Solzhenitsyn's mother). Belgorodtseva taught all subjects to the junior classes. Solzhenitsyn adored her,* despite her reputation for old-fashioned strictness, and soon went to the top of the class. But higher up in the school he ran into some difficulties. It was a period of great educational upheaval and experimentation, when the schools were being repeatedly reorganized, and the students had to adjust as best they could.

Malevich, for instance, at the head of the school, was an outstanding teacher, as were most of the other instructors who had survived the Revolution, but they were not considered politically "reliable" by the Soviet authorities, and by about 1930 the majority of them had been removed. A typical case was that of the mathematics teacher, Nikolai Chefranov, an inspiring pedagogue who was eased out for political reasons having nothing whatsoever to do with mathematics but who managed to obtain an alternative post at the technical college, where the rules were less strictly applied. He even managed to get reinstated at the Malevich school much later, but after a term was obliged to leave once more. He was one of the Solzhenitsyn's favourite teachers and deeply influenced him. It was because of Chefranov, said Solzhenitsyn, that he later decided to take up mathematics. Malevich himself

---

* According to a reliable source that does not wish to be identified, Solzhenitsyn later collected information with a view to writing a story about her, but the story has never appeared.

was forced out of the school in 1930.[2]*

One of the first school reforms to be introduced after the end of the Civil War had been the abolition of examinations. This was done partly for ideological reasons—examinations were an expression of bourgeois elitism—and partly for practical ones: it was easier for the horny-handed sons of toil and Party favourites to get their certificates if there was no independent verification of results. Soon after Solzhenitsyn arrived in school, this practice was replaced by the "brigade system" of education. "Brigades" of seven to ten pupils were formed to study together and pass the examinations collectively, each pupil in the brigade being responsible for a good performance in a particular subject. But this, too, led to chaos and "complete idling, just as in American schools today,"[3] as Solzhenitsyn later remarked. Another problem was textbooks. The old books were regarded as ideologically harmful, but it was a long time before suitable new ones could be produced.

> When I was in the middle classes, we didn't have any standard textbooks at all. We were taught from random newspaper articles or specially printed brochures and pamphlets. And then, one day, a decision was taken to establish regular textbooks that would be used on a permanent basis and remain the same from year to year. By the time of my last three years at school, the system had been strengthened and had settled down, and the teaching was very good.[4]

Another feature of the schools after the Revolution was the virtual abolition of history as a subject and the increasing attention paid to propaganda and ideological training in its stead. The Bolsheviks had been pioneers in the imaginative and effective use of propaganda, and they quickly perceived the advantages of catching people young and of commencing their indoctrination at a tender age. It was particularly important for a revolutionary government that demanded a complete and apocalyptic rupture with the past, in the name of building a new society. In such circumstances their hopes were pinned on the youth, for the adult population was past "re-education" in any fundamental sense. And this was an additional reason why the old teachers and textbooks had to be withdrawn and replaced by "revolutionary" ones.

In the case of the schoolchildren of the twenties and early thirties, the new policies were on the whole successful. The myth of the Revolution triumphant, of the fierce, ultimately successful struggle of the underprivileged to throw off the yoke of their cruel oppressors, had tremendous appeal for the imaginations of the young. It was Robin Hood on a mass scale and with a happy ending. As Solzhenitsyn has noted, those were militant times. It was tremendous fun to parade through the streets, waving red flags, beating drums, and singing revolutionary songs to whip up emotions and stir the masses. Here was a new opium to replace the old—and to distract questioning minds from the drabness and misery of everyday life.

* It seems that Malevich was eventually arrested in 1937 or 1938 and sent to the labour camps, and that Solzhenitsyn may have sought him out and interviewed him when he was collecting material for *The Gulag Archipelago*.

Solzhenitsyn was as stirred as most of his schoolfellows by this revolutionary rhetoric, and at the age of twelve, in 1930, he took a decisive step away from his early training and beliefs by joining the Young Pioneers. The Young Pioneers were the junior wing of the Communist Party's youth movement, the Komsomol, founded in 1918. In a sense they were a sort of Soviet equivalent of the Boy Scouts, except that they had no independence and were financed and controlled by the Party. They were also ubiquitous—an official, integral part of every school, and a potent instrument of indoctrination. Joining them was not complicated. On the contrary, it was part of the genius of the builders of the Soviet system to take over so many of the paraphernalia and simulacra of normal "bourgeois" society, and only behind the scenes to link them with an imperceptible but unbreakable web of hidden controls, so that every lever could ultimately be pulled by the Party. This was gradually accomplished with the trade unions, professional associations, cultural groups, social clubs, and eventually even with sports clubs, as well as with the youth organizations, and always with great success. From the point of view of the children, you joined the Young Pioneers in order to be with your friends, go to camp, learn to tie knots, sing rousing songs, parade on public holidays and to have the right to wear the Pioneer's red tie and red badge, with its five logs (representing the five continents) ablaze in the fire of world revolution. As another writer has pointed out more recently, there was nothing to it: "When you were old enough you became a Young Pioneer, then a member of the Komsomol, and then a member of the Party. It was as simple as that. That was what happened to everybody, just as you moved regularly from class to class."[5] But the songs you sang, the occasions you marched on, and the speeches you listened to were carefully selected and prepared—very much as in the Boy Scouts, except that the organization preparing and controlling these events controlled everything else as well.

Solzhenitsyn had come to the idea of joining the Young Pioneers rather reluctantly at first, and only under a certain amount of pressure. At the age of ten he had had the cross ripped from his neck by jeering Pioneers, and for over a year he was held up to ridicule at school meetings and told that he ought to join.[6] He was used to regarding himself as "different" from the other children and to standing somewhat apart, but eventually the need to conform proved greater than his urge for a difficult independence. But it was not a simple matter, for the cross-currents in the school were rather complex. It would appear that the principal activists in the Pioneer and Komsomol movements, at least in Rostov, were Jewish children, whose parents had been systematically discriminated against under the tsarist regime. They were naturally enthusiastic about the new order, but the fact of their nationality endowed their hostility to Solzhenitsyn's cross with a certain ambiguity. This emerged in another incident that Solzhenitsyn became involved in soon after he had joined the Pioneers.

A routine scuffle took place one day between two boys in his class, Valeri Nikolsky and Dimitri Shtitelman, in the course of which they exchanged insults and Nikolsky called Shtitelman a "Russky slob."* Solzhenitsyn, sitting nearby, witnessed the scene, but when Shtitelman accused Nikolsky of anti-Semitism, Solzhenitsyn refused to support him, on the grounds that "everybody has the right to say what he likes." After this he, too, was accused of anti-Semitism[7] and arraigned before a special meeting of the Young Pioneers. The incident must have rankled with Solzhenitsyn, for years later he introduced it into *The First Circle* in the form of a flashback in the mind of Adam Roitman, a major in the MVD,† who recalls a scene from his childhood. In this scene the Solzhenitsyn figure is called Oleg Rozhdestvensky, a "pale thin boy who was top of his class, never talked about politics and had joined the Pioneers with obvious reluctance." Rozhdestvensky has been observed attending church with his mother and wearing a cross round his neck, but his principal crime is to declare in the class-room one day that "everybody has the right to say what he thinks," and when a Jewish boy challenges him ("Nikola called me a 'dirty Yid'—is that all right too?") to reply that "everybody has the right to *say* what he likes." As a result, he is denounced at a Pioneers' meeting (one after another "the twelve-year-old Robespierres got up in front of the whole school and denounced this accomplice of anti-Semites") and expelled from the Pioneers, which could possibly lead to his expulsion from the school. Roitman, one of the Jewish boys who made up "about half of the class in that southern town," is portrayed in the novel as Rozhdestvensky's "social accuser," responsible for reading out the charges.[8]

Six months before these painful events, there had occurred another incident that would have sunk into oblivion, had it not, on the one hand, resulted in a lifelong and highly visible physical scar and, on the other, later become the subject of ingenious and scurrilous inventions on the part of his enemies.

The incident occurred on 9 September 1930, when Solzhenitsyn was eleven. He and another boy, Alexander Kagan, were wrestling in the class-room for possession of a sheath knife when Kagan snatched it from Solzhenitsyn and accidentally pricked a nerve in the latter's hand. Solzhenitsyn felt dizzy, and started out for the cloakroom in order to put his hand under the tap. After a step or two, he fainted and fell, striking his brow on the stone doorpost and inflicting a deep gash. His companions picked him up and carried him to the cloakroom, where they bathed his forehead in cold water. They then took him to the out-patients' department of the local hospital to have his wound stitched and dressed, but the cut on his forehead was crudely cobbled, turned septic, and had to be reopened and restitched. Solzhenitsyn was obliged to spend over a month in bed before it was completely healed.[9]

One result of this boyish prank was the scar on his right temple that has remained prominent to the present day. Another was a henceforth recurrent tendency to faint when experiencing physical pain—a peculiarity that was to prove highly embarrassing in the army: on at least one occasion he was to

---

* An approximate translation of the original insult, which was based on a popular term of abuse used by Ukrainians about Russians.

† *Ministerstvo vnutrennikh del* (the Ministry of the Interior).

faint while being vaccinated. Perhaps the most curious consequence of this episode, however, was the use to which it was put by the Soviet authorities nearly half a century later in its campaign to discredit Solzhenitsyn. In 1975, after the appearance in the West of *The Gulag Archipelago*, a series of publications appeared in which the acquisition of the scar was attributed to all sorts of character deficiencies. According to one version, Solzhenitsyn fainted in a fit of rage after having been reprimanded by his class teacher Alexander Bershadsky, and thus cut his forehead. According to another, the scar was caused by Solzhenitsyn's anti-Semitism. Instead of having wrestled with Kagan for the knife, Solzhenitsyn was said to have called Kagan a "Yid" and to have fallen against the doorpost as a result of being punched.*

The latter version obviously owed something to the Shtitelman incident (and may even have been inspired by Solzhenitsyn's description of the incident in *The First Circle*). It also incorporated expulsion as the probable punishment for this crime, but according to Solzhenitsyn, the only real threat of expulsion he ever experienced occurred some two years later, when he, Kagan, and a third boy skipped classes to play soccer, and Solzhenitsyn subsequently hid the class register behind a cupboard to conceal from the director of studies the number of black marks he had against his name. On this occasion it was Bershadsky who threatened Solzhenitsyn with expulsion, and only the entreaties of the rest of the class (especially the girls) persuaded him to relent.[10]

During the early thirties a number of other events contributed to the loosening of Solzhenitsyn's ties with his family and the world of his childhood, symbolically underlining, as it were, the larger changes that were taking place all around him. In 1930 Roman and Irina ran out of the possessions and money that had sustained them since the Civil War, and they were obliged to give up their comfortable house in Yeisk and move to a flat. At the same time Roman took his first job—as a driver for a local enterprise. That summer, instead of going to Irina and Roman as usual during the holidays, Solzhenitsyn went with his mother to Georgievsk to visit Aunt Maria and her family. Grandfather Zakhar and Grandmother Evdokia were there, having recently moved back from Gulkevichi, and their situation was pitiful. Zakhar, with no money, no work, and no prospects, was but a pale shadow of his former self, though still capable of violent rages against the present regime and their confiscation of his property, whereas Evdokia was silent and resigned.

While in Georgievsk, Taissia and Solzhenitsyn made their last visit to his father's grave in the little churchyard there. Afterwards, Taissia took him for his first and only childhood trip to his father's birthplace, Sablia, forty miles to the east. Grandfather Semyon was no longer there, of course. Two aunts and an uncle had died (his step-aunt, Maria, at the end of the twenties

---

*These versions were published (after Solzhenitsyn's expulsion from the Soviet Union) by his first wife, Natalia Reshetovskaya, by his former school friend Kirill Simonyan (who, despite being at the same school, had not witnessed the incident), and by the Czech writer Tomáš Řezáč, who wrote a scurrilous "biography" of Solzhenitsyn in 1978.

after a long illness). Another aunt, Evdokia, had moved away, and only Uncle Konstantin and Solzhenitsyn's step-uncle, Ilya, were left in the village. Konstantin had inherited a part of the family farm, and Solzhenitsyn later recalled travelling across the wide, dusty plain to get there. The simple farmhouse was made of reddish-brown adobe and consisted of a single spacious living-room and one somewhat smaller bedroom, with various barns, stables, and outbuildings attached to it. His uncle's sheep, as he recalled, simply wandered over the open steppe, although there were special pens for them in winter.

Mother and son's visit was brief, as much a farewell as greeting, leaving no strong impressions on the young Solzhenitsyn. Within a few months both Konstantin and Ilya were to be declared kulaks* and deported to Siberia under Stalin's forced collectivization policies. A few years later, in 1933 or 1934, the cemetery in Georgievsk where his father lay buried was flattened to make way for a sports stadium. It was to be nearly thirty years, after his own deportation to Siberia and spell in the labour camps, before Solzhenitsyn was able to return to these parts, and by then the already tenuous links with his father's family had been stretched almost to vanishing-point.[11]

That same winter of 1930, not long after their trip to Georgievsk and Sablia, Taissia and Solzhenitsyn had a visit from Grandfather Zakhar. Such visits were a rare occurrence, for their hovel was too cramped to accommodate guests, and anyone who stayed was obliged to sleep on the floor. Zakhar, though now seventy-two, was not deterred by this. Despite the tribulations he had endured since the confiscation of his estate, which included recurrent harassment and repeated questioning by the Soviet authorities, he remained an imposing figure of a man, and had clung defiantly to the old customs and manner of dress. With his shaven head, big purple nose, and luxuriant moustaches, and clad in riding boots and an old-fashioned hip-length waisted coat, he looked what he was—an anachronism—in the now drab and down-at-heel city of Rostov. On this occasion, after stamping into Taissia's tiny shack, he sank down in one corner and began to leaf through the pages of the bible he was carrying, loudly bewailing his useless existence and cursing the new regime that had deprived him not only of his possessions but also of all purpose in life. Like many of the older generation, he still clung to the belief, twelve years after the Revolution, that the Bolsheviks would one day be defeated or disappear and that life would return to normal. Above all he was deeply concerned about the fate of his estate and anxious that it should be properly cared for, so that he could hand it on, he said, to the young Solzhenitsyn, his only grandchild, to carry on his work. Roman, Zakhar's son and natural heir, had no children of his own, and Zakhar regarded Roman as unfit to run a large estate.

As the old man continued to maunder on in this fashion, talking half to

---

*The name applied first to rich, then to moderately well-off, and eventually to almost all independent peasants who showed hostility to collectivization. *Kulak* is also the Russian word for "fist."

himself and half to his daughter and grandson, Solzhenitsyn went over to commiserate with him and comfort him. He had been taught at school about the evils of property, and he assured his grandfather that there was no cause for distress. "Don't worry about it, granddad. I don't want your estate anyway. I would have refused it on principle."[12]

Early next morning, while Taissia and Solzhenitsyn were still sleeping, Zakhar crept away to go to church. Soon afterwards mother and son were awakened by the thunderous kicking of boots against the door. Two OGPU agents in sugar-loaf hats and sheepskin coats burst into the room and demanded to see Zakhar. He was wanted for questioning, they said, in connection with the hoarding of gold. They were there as a result of Stalin's celebrated campaign to extort gold from private businessmen and traders—from those who had been in business before the Revolution and from those who had been active only during the New Economic Policy. Apparently, the OGPU agents had followed Zakhar from Georgievsk, where he had been twice detained and questioned on the subject of gold, and were astonished not to find him at home. They turned on Taissia, abusing her as a "class enemy" and demanding that she hand over any money, gold, or other valuables that she had in her possession. She said she had none, whereupon they threatened her with imprisonment and asked her to sign a statement swearing that she had no gold in the house, on pain of immediate arrest if their search proved she had lied. Taissia asked whether the statement included wedding rings. The agents nodded. When she handed them her own ring, they insisted on having her dead husband's ring too. Taissia fetched it and then signed the statement.

At that moment Zakhar returned from church. The police agents jeered at him, and said that they had come for his gold. Ignoring them, Zakhar fell to his knees before the icon in the corner and commenced to pray. The agents cursed him, hauled him to his feet, and conducted a thorough body search, but found nothing. After a further stream of curses they stamped out, threatening to catch him on some future occasion.

Zakhar returned to Georgievsk. Two months later, in February 1931, his wife, Evdokia, died. Unable to attend the funeral, Taissia arranged a memorial mass for her mother in Rostov Cathedral. This called for considerable courage, for church-goers were now regularly spied on and denounced to the authorities. Often enough, they lost their jobs as well. For Taissia, however, the death of her mother was an exceptional event, and she duly held the service and attended with her son. Fortunately, she escaped retribution, but Solzhenitsyn was reported to the headmaster by one of his schoolfellows and was reprimanded for conduct unbecoming to a Young Pioneer.

The following year, in 1932, Zakhar died too. The circumstances of his death were somewhat mysterious, and Taissia and Solzhenitsyn remained unaware of it for some time afterwards. It seems that, grief-stricken after the death of his wife, Zakhar had wandered back to the district where his estate was, in the vicinity of Armavir. He continued to be pursued by the OGPU, who were convinced he had a secret hoard of gold, and finally, half-maddened by their taunts and bullying, he is said to have hung a rough wooden cross round his neck, like a beggar, and gone to the OGPU headquarters in Armavir. "You have stolen all my money and possessions," he said, "so now you can take me into your jail and keep me." Whether they put him into the cells or not, whether he collapsed or died in some other way, nobody seemed to know. The news took a long time to filter through to Taissia, and all she was able to do upon hearing it was conduct another memorial service at Rostov Cathedral.[13]

Solzhenitsyn's connections with childhood were being irrevocably snapped in other ways too. One evening in March 1932, with the thawing slush still on the ground, he ran round on one of his usual visits to the Fedorovskys. He was brought up short at the gate by an unusual sight. Thin, tight-lipped, stooping Vladimir Fedorovsky, the nearest thing he had had to a father, was being escorted through the yard by two strangers to a waiting saloon car. In his hand he held a small white parcel tied up with string. He got into the car and was driven away. Solzhenitsyn rushed into the flat and was met with a scene of utter devastation. Drawers and cupboards had been violently emptied onto the floor, rugs and carpets had been torn up and tossed aside, books and ornaments had been scattered everywhere. The whole flat had been turned upside down in a search by OGPU agents that had lasted twenty-four hours.[14]

This was Solzhenitsyn's first direct encounter with the brutalities of an actual arrest. He was aware, in a generalized way, of some of the activities of the OGPU and had experienced their summary treatment of his mother and grandfather. But never, till now, had he seen the claws so nakedly unsheathed. The memory of what he witnessed on that grey March evening surely informs the vivid description of a typical arrest that appears in the opening pages of The Gulag Archipelago.

> [Arrest] is a sharp ringing in the middle of the night or a rude knocking at the door. The insolent entrance of unwiped jackboots worn by the unsleeping agents of the secret police. It is the cowed and frightened witness who follows them in. . . .
>
> The traditional arrest also includes the gathering up by trembling hands of soap and towel for the victim, a change of underwear, and something to eat—nobody knows what is needed or what is allowed, or what it is best to wear. . . .
>
> The traditional arrest also means . . . an alien, brutal crushing force raging unchecked in your home for hours and hours. It means a smashing, a ripping open, a tearing and a pulling down from the walls, a hurling onto the floor of the contents of desks and drawers, an emptying out, a scattering and a ripping—and a piling of mountains of possessions on the floor and their crunch beneath jackboots. . . .
>
> And for those left behind after the arrest, it is the long tail of a life turned upside down and gutted. And attempts to deliver food parcels. And voices barking back at you through the grilles: "No one here by that name!"[15]

The scene depicted in that last paragraph was familiar to Solzhenitsyn from a different source. To get to his home from school, he was obliged to walk down Nikolsky Lane, which ran along one side of the enormous building that had been taken over as the OGPU prison in the centre of Rostov. The back entrance to the prison was situated in the lane and was permanently marked by a long and dismal line of silent women waiting to make inquiries or to hand in food parcels.[16]

One of the four massive wings that made up the prison faced the main boulevard, the Bolshaya Sadovaya (later Engels Street—the OGPU prison was at No. 33) next to the university, its ironclad gates patrolled by sentries in kepis, who chased away any idlers. In a later poem Solzhenitsyn described how its basements used to run out under the pavement, lit by opaque pavement lights set into the asphalt. These basements contained dungeons, so that passers-by were actually walking over the heads of the prisoners incarcerated there. He also described how one day a man appeared in one of the usually blank windows of the top floor of the prison block, clambered out onto the sill, leapt, and hurtled onto the roadway below, where he smashed to pieces. His body was hastily removed by the sentries and the blood washed away with hose-pipes, but everyone knew what had happened.[17]

There were also the columns of prisoners marched through the streets from time to time under armed guard, accompanied by the chilling shouts of the escort commander: "One step out of line and I'll give the order to shoot or sabre you down!" As a boy, Solzhenitsyn saw and knew these things too, and yet he could not grasp their meaning. He was not old enough; he did not have the necessary experience to interpret what he saw around him, and he went with the crowd. Only much later, after his odyssey through Soviet prisons and camps, did he appreciate the true significance of this prison and these columns. Only then could he write, in *The Gulag Archipelago*, his brilliant evocation of that secret "fourth dimension" of prison, lurking behind the usual three, of which not only children but also so many adults were blissfully unaware until they discovered it for themselves.[18]

It turned out that Vladimir Fedorovsky was a late victim of the campaign against the "wrecker-engineers," who had been condemned at the Shakhty trial in 1928 and in the trial of the "Industrial Party" two years later.* These trials, coinciding with the end of the New Economic Policy, had signalled the ending of the ten-year alliance between the Communist Party and the non-Communist specialists, and the inauguration of an era of rigid Party discipline. Throughout the twenties the Party had needed the specialists in order to survive, although the specialists were free-thinking and

---

*Shakhty was a city in the Caucasus not too far from Rostov, where the secret police claimed to have uncovered a vast sabotage network run by veteran engineers. No evidence was produced, other than confessions extracted under torture, but eleven people were sentenced to death, of whom five were executed. It was the first Stalinist show trial. The "Industrial Party" trial was centred on the city of Kuibyshev; it alleged the existence of a similar network of saboteurs organized into a party led by Professor Ramzin. Again the only evidence was that of forced confessions, and again death sentences were passed down, although this time none were carried out (on the other hand, forty-eight officials were said to have been executed before the trial began). The "Industrial Party" was also accused of working for Western capitalist interests.

hard to control. Now, with the rising of a new generation of Communist-educated engineers more amenable to taking orders, the "bourgeois specialists" had become expendable and could be dealt with. The pretext was the introduction of Stalin's First Five-Year Plan. Many of the targets in this plan were impossibly high. The "bourgeois specialists," as responsible experts, advised the Party that the plan was too ambitious and the targets unattainable. But instead of being listened to, they were accused of sabotage and put on trial for treason. These were the first of Stalin's great series of show trials, in which forced confessions and rigged evidence were employed to secure conviction. Professor L. K. Ramzin, for instance, a former Bolshevik and star witness at the "Industrial Party" trial, claimed to have established an opposition party among the engineers with over two thousand members. At the conclusion of the trial, he and seven alleged accomplices were sentenced to long terms of imprisonment, leaving behind a fertile soil for the continuation of investigations to find the remaining 1,992. These continued for some years in an atmosphere of increasing mistrust, even after Ramzin himself had been released and rehabilitated following a suspiciously short time in jail.

Vladimir Fedorovsky's crime, it transpired, was to have among his possessions a photograph of an engineers' congress in which both he and Ramzin appeared. This was the sole evidence turned up by the twenty-four-hour search. It was not sufficient for him to be put on trial, and he was released after a year's detention and interrogation, but he was completely broken in health and spirits and never got his old job back again. He lived on more or less aimlessly for another ten years and died in 1943 in Tashkent.

Meanwhile, fresh disasters struck the Fedorovskys after Vladimir's arrest. Literally within days his mother-in-law, Taissia's old headmistress, Mme Andreyeva, was struck by paralysis and died after a short illness. Soon afterwards Solzhenitsyn's childhood friend Misha was involved in a skating accident, in which he fell and banged his head. He contracted meningitis and within a short time was also dead. A pall of grief settled over the household. Solzhenitsyn and Taissia continued to call, but Solzhenitsyn fancied he could read a silent reproach in Zhenia's eyes for his survival, while her own precious son was dead. And in truth there was little for him to do there now that his childhood playmate had gone. The place of happy refuge had become a house of mourning.

As for Lialia, Misha's sister, she was four years older than Solzhenitsyn and at an age when the difference between them was most marked. The long-legged blonde with the tousled hair, who had shared all his games and secrets, was now a young woman. There had been a brief period when he was infatuated with her, hanging round the desk where she painted watercolours, with her little vase of lilies of the valley and three ornamental elephants. He had been intoxicated by her scent, the rustle of her dresses and her femininity. But with increasing maturity Lialia had tired of their games and Solzhenitsyn's dogged chivalry. At school she had heeded the siren voices of Party propaganda and rejected her upbringing and early ties. Soon her passionate idealism would transform her into an equally passionate Communist, and she married a man who was to become one of the leading Party officials of the city of Rostov.[19]

By about 1934 Solzhenitsyn had more or less broken out of his childhood environment and entered upon a new phase of existence, in which he would take a greater and always eager part in the larger life of his school and his circle of adolescent friends. Paradoxically, his active engagement with social questions and with official Soviet ideology came just at the time when the last drops of idealism were being squeezed out of the Party and when Stalin was feeling his way towards establishing the most complete police state the world had yet known. But this development was masked not only from the outside world but also from the bulk of the population of the Soviet Union itself, let alone from its young people. For the moment their idealism remained intact, and it was to be a full twenty years before the truth became clear to more than a few, by which time Solzhenitsyn would have discovered it for himself by the hardest possible path. Meanwhile, he shared the optimism and hopes of those around him.

4

WRITER AND COMMUNIST

ONE OF THE abiding images that has come down to us of Solzhenitsyn's youth is that of deprivation and poverty. Lev Kopelev, his close friend in later life, once pointed out that the origin of Ivan Denisovich's celebrated thrift in Solzhenitsyn's first published story was to be sought not simply in the author's labour-camp experiences but also in his straitened and hungry childhood, which had left an indelible mark on his character.[1] Thrift, economy, modesty of material demands, and indifference to comfort came naturally to him and have remained a permanent feature of his way of life even in his present affluence. Solzhenitsyn once had occasion to confirm this when asked by a French interviewer, "What sensations are rekindled in your mind when you think of your childhood?" He replied:

> Hardships. I'm afraid the word won't mean much to you for all your experience of the war and the Nazis, especially as it doesn't apply to my childhood alone. Things were no better when I became an adult. Up to the age of forty I knew nothing but a kind of dignified destitution. From the end of 1918, the year I was born, until 1941, I didn't know what a house was. We lived in huts which were constantly assailed by the cold. Never enough fuel to keep us warm. No water in the room where we lived—we had to go out and fetch it some distance away. A pair of shoes or a suit of clothes had to last for several years. As for the food, don't mention it. After the starvation of the 1930s, ordinary shortages were a minor evil. In some mysterious way, all these things struck me as more or less normal.[2]

This perception of "normality" was quite natural. All children accept the world as they find it and regard their childhood as normal, at least until experience teaches them otherwise. And in one sense this poverty and hunger *was* normal in the Soviet thirties, for Stalin's First Five-Year Plan, with its forced collectivization of the peasantry and its forced industrialization, ensured that the bulk of the population would go hungry throughout most of their lives.

Collectivization was the result of a tangle of motives on Stalin's part, but a principal cause had been the winding up of the New Economic Policy in 1928 and the replacement of a free market for foodstuffs by requisitions and coercion. The peasants, deprived of any economic incentives, responded by cutting production, and it was this that persuaded Stalin to push through his "revolution from above" and take over the land. Not unexpectedly, force was necessary nearly everywhere, for the peasants fought tooth and nail to defend their holdings. Their very support for the Revolution had been bought by promises of land; now, twelve years later, they were being asked—and forced— to give it up again. Stalin in turn placed the mark of "counter-revolution" on the kulaks and stretched the meaning of the word to include not only rich peasants but any peasant who was moderately successful or well-to-do, while other innocent victims were accused of being "kulak-minded" (*podkulachniki*). In the end it made little difference, for all who opposed the collectivization in any way were herded off to Siberia, either to swell the growing numbers in the labour camps or simply to be let loose in the Arctic tundra to fend for themselves or die.

The full consequences are incalculable, but the immediate result was a terrible famine—"the only case in history of a purely man-made famine," as Robert Conquest has pointed out in his book on this period, *The Great Terror*.[3] Estimates of the number of Soviet citizens who died vary from the figure of three and a half million submitted to Stalin by the OGPU at the time to an estimate of five to six million computed by a League of Nations report in 1946. An almost equal number were deported to Siberia. It was an event unique in the annals of Europe, the greatest catastrophe of modern times apart from the Nazi Holocaust, to which it fully bears comparison. At the same time, it was Stalin's first major exercise in large-scale deception, both at home and abroad. The few contemporary reports that leaked out were quickly denounced and mainly disbelieved. At home a frightened population was kept in ignorance, while those in the cities knew only that there was a serious, inexplicable famine, without drought and without war, and that the wise course was not to inquire into it too closely.

The inhabitants of Rostov could not fail to be aware of what was happening. As the commercial centre for a rich agricultural region, and as a leading producer of tractors and agricultural machinery for that region, Rostov had numerous links with the countryside, and news was bound to filter through. The Cossacks of the Kuban, where Zakhar's estate had been, rebelled so violently that they had to be put down through the personal intervention of Lazar Kaganovich, head of the Party's Central Control Commission. A correspondent of the London *Times*, Iverach McDonald, who travelled through the North Caucasus at this time, later described how "the fields were untilled;

men had been taken away after resisting the collectivization drive; children came whimpering to the train for bread."[4]

Stalin, for his part, was instantly ready with plausible explanations for the abuses. They were the work of "over-zealous" officials, or the result of "wrecking" on the part of the kulaks and other "class enemies," or the machinations of foreign powers and the supporters of counter-revolution—of anything, in fact, other than the policies that had caused them. Methods might sometimes be wrong, but policies never. The press was under total Party control and thoroughly censored, and all links with foreign sources of information were deliberately broken off, for this was the year in which the Iron Curtain was first lowered. Not even the adult population was aware of the enormity of what was happening to them.

To Taissia and Solzhenitsyn's endemic difficulties of trying to live on one small salary was now added a general situation of widespread shortages and hunger. Long queues for bread and other necessities of life became more prevalent than they had ever been before. Private hardship was paralleled by public hardship, private suffering by general suffering. Another resident of Rostov at this time recalls the enormous difficulty one had in buying any sort of clothing. To get a pair of shoes, for instance, could mean queuing for up to six months. The normal method was to go to the shop where the arrival of a consignment of shoes was announced and to queue for a number, which lasted for one day. If the queue lasted longer, you were obliged to return every day and get a new number, and if you missed a day, you were struck off the list. When the consignment arrived (usually without warning), you queued again in numerical order until you were able, if lucky, to buy your shoes.

The same person remembers another typical Rostov incident. A barrel of paraffin on two wheels was being pulled through the streets one day, and word got about that it was for sale. People rushed to fetch cans and pails and fell in behind it, or turned in their tracks and followed it just to keep their places in the queue. In next to no time the man with the barrel found himself at the head of a vast procession that grew longer and longer as it twisted and turned from street to street. Nobody knew whether the paraffin was really for sale or not, and the delivery man either could not or would not say. And so the crowd followed him, a latter-day Piper of Hamelin, in silent hope. It was no longer icons and sacred relics that attracted processions in the streets, but barrels of paraffin on wheels.[5]

Solzhenitsyn's penury merged with the public penury, and had both practical and psychological consequences. Practically, the biggest problem was clothing. Apart from having to queue all the time, he could scarcely afford what was available, and his clothes, though neat, were often shabby and threadbare. Unforeseen accidents could occur to make the situation worse. On one occasion he sat on some ink on a chair and came away with a spot on the seat of his trousers. The ink resolutely resisted all attempts to wash it out, and he was obliged to continue wearing the trousers for two more years before he could afford another pair.

Psychologically, the effects were more impalpable. As the top educational establishment in Rostov, the Malevich school had a number of children from families suddenly impoverished and now suffering discrimination, like the Solzhenitsyns, the "exes," as they were picturesquely called, meaning the ex-professional people and ex-bourgeoisie. But they were the exception, rather than the rule. The majority came from families that had survived socially and economically, like the Fedorovskys, or from those of the new Party functionaries and proletarian elite. These latter were the new Soviet aristocracy, already beginning to be well dressed and well fed. Shortages meant nothing to them, for they had their own, reserved commissaries where they could obtain virtually anything they liked—entry being carefully restricted to those with the right Party cards. Those who suffered worst under this system were the genuine workers and minor office employees, because members of the former bourgeoisie and intelligentsia could at least sell their possessions—the new aristocrats were the eager buyers. And until they ran out, there was at least a cushion against the general austerity. But apart from her grand piano, Taissia soon had nothing left. Solzhenitsyn was therefore excluded from popular pastimes like skating, because he could never afford the blades or the special boots to go with them. Another sport he longed to try was tennis, and he recalls how he used to press his nose to the wire in his youth, watching those unattainable white-clad figures leaping about the court, and yearn to be able to join them. Neither the special clothes nor the racquets were remotely within his means, let alone the opportunity to join the club.[6]

These social tensions, combined with a sensitivity about his fatherlessness and a simmering sense of shame over his class origins, seem to have fuelled a driving ambition and a rage to excel that showed themselves in Solzhenitsyn from an exceptionally early age. As a young child he had decided that he wanted to become one of three things: a general, a priest, or a writer. At school he was always an outstanding pupil, equally good at arts and at science subjects; like his mother before him, he was invariably top of his class. And his mother, indeed, played no small role in his education, constantly encouraging him with her love and devotion, admiring his progress, and helping him with his school work in every way she could. As a consequence, he shone at just about everything he touched. Natalia Reshetovskaya was once told by a former classmate of Solzhenitsyn's that the one thing he seemed to be poor at was drawing, but by stubbornly applying himself to the problem over many months, he overcame his deficiency and began to obtain excellent marks in that subject as well.

Fortunately, Solzhenitsyn's scholastic excellence did not turn him into a prig or cut him off from the other pupils. He was one of a number of outstandingly clever children attracted to the school by its reputation (it was well known as the favourite school of the "exes"), and he became close friends with three of the most talented pupils in his class: Nikolai Vitkevich, Kirill Simonyan, and Lydia Ezherets. He and the two other boys soon referred to themselves jokingly as "The Three Musketeers" and were inseparable throughout most of their school years and at university.

Kirill Simonyan, an Armenian from Nakhichevan, arrived in Solzhenitsyn's school in 1930. His father had been a wealthy businessman who had
extensive links abroad, especially in Persia, and who spoke many languages.
Apparently, he had been able to continue with his business activities until
the end of the New Economic Policy, in 1928, but had then fled to Persia to
escape persecution, crossing the border on foot and leaving Kirill, nine, his
sister, Nadezhda, five, and their mother to look after themselves. His mother
was summoned by the GPU for questioning, but nothing worse followed
and she was allowed to return to her family. Mrs Simonyan was thrown back
on her own resources and was even more helpless than Taissia, for she suffered from emphysema and her health was too fragile to permit her to work.
The Armenian community, however, was very close-knit. Friends and relations rallied round, and the family was ultimately able to manage reasonably
well for those times.[7]

Many things drew the two boys together: the secret shame of their fathers'
pasts, their present fatherlessness, their poverty (Kirill, his sister, and mother
lived in a single room on Dmitrievskaya Street; their courtyard, with its
overhanging iron balconies and an iron staircase, looked even grimmer and
more run-down than the Solzhenitsyns' cul-de-sac). And they had a common
interest in the arts. Kirill was a sensitive, dreamy boy with a passion for
music. Indeed, his whole family was gifted musically. His sister, Nadezhda,
went on to become a well-known composer (she wrote the score for that
exquisite Soviet period film *The Lady with the Little Dog*, based on the Chekhov story), and Kirill himself, despite a hearing defect, was a pianist of some
accomplishment. In the summers, he insisted on taking Solzhenitsyn to free
concerts in the park, and explained the principles of music to him. Kirill was
also interested in the occult and, when his mother was out, used to organize
seances, which seemed to Solzhenitsyn to establish genuine contact with the
other world. He recounted his dreams to Solzhenitsyn, discussed their meaning, and had a mystical bent that intrigued and fascinated Solzhenitsyn, much
as Irina's mysticism had fascinated him earlier. But with such interests and
with his dark-skinned, soulful good looks, he struck the other boys as effem-
inate. His mane of black hair, heavy black brows, dark eyes, prominent
Armenian nose, and wide mobile mouth made him almost too handsome for
his own good, and he had a way of carrying a handkerchief in his hand or of
grimacing theatrically that inevitably led to much teasing. He was dubbed
"Kirilla" or "Kirochka" and sometimes imitated, but apparently without mal-
ice. In early adolescence, when he suddenly grew much taller than the others, he earned the nickname of "Ostrich," a name that stuck with him into
manhood.[8]

Solzhenitsyn also had a nickname at school: the "Walrus," given to him
because of his love of the cold. A preference for winter and cold weather was
to become an enduring trait. The autobiographical Gleb Nerzhin in *The First
Circle* strips to the waist in midwinter before sawing some firewood: "Picking
up handfuls [of snow], he rubbed it vigorously over his chest, back, and
sides. All through winter he rubbed himself down to the waist with snow."[9]

And Solzhenitsyn's later choice of Vermont as a place to settle in the United States was dictated by its climate and by his preference for cold winters and cool summers. "Walrus" is a common Russian nickname for such lovers of cold weather.

As Musketeers, Kirill evidently was "Aramis" and Solzhenitsyn "Athos." The third musketeer, "Porthos," was Nikolai Vitkevich—Koka to his friends. Like Solzhenitsyn, Nikolai was an orphan. His father, a civil servant in tsarist times, had died during the Civil War, and Nikolai was an only son. Nikolai's mother, Antonina Vitkevich, was a tough, resilient woman, determined to make her way in the world. She had joined the Party, remaining a staunch member of it till the end of her days, and this had enabled her, as a shorthand typist, to work for "sensitive" Party and government institutions, where the pay was better and some privileges were available. She had also tried re-marrying. In 1930 her second husband, a Daghestanian Moslem, had taken her and Nikolai to Daghestan with him, where they had lived in semi-oriental fashion and Nikolai had attended a Moslem school. But in 1934 the stepfather had died, and Nikolai and his mother had returned to Rostov.

Nikolai was Solzhenitsyn's oldest and closest friend. The two had met at school as early as 1928, when both were nine, but it was only after Nikolai returned from Daghestan that their friendship really blossomed. If Kirill's character was lyrical and unstable, Nikolai's seems to have been the opposite: dour, down to earth, determined, independent. Photographs of him reveal a stocky, broad-shouldered youth with a short neck and bullet-like head. The mouth is set in an obstinate line, the eyes look stubborn and somehow abstracted as well, as if his thoughts were turned in on himself. He was far less extroverted than Solzhenitsyn or Kirill, but seems to have held his own in their common pursuits.

The other close school friend who deserves mention at this stage is Lydia Ezherets (known to her friends as Lida). Lydia came from a highly cultivated Jewish family that was very prominent in Rostov during the inter-war years. Her father, Dr Alexander Ezherets, was head of the main Rostov polyclinic and director of the Regional Health Board for the Black Sea coast, an exceedingly popular and influential man. Lydia seems to have resembled him in that she, too, was popular and was esteemed for her outstandingly generous and unselfish character. Solzhenitsyn remembers her as a kind, gentle, loveable girl who was never known to lose her temper or quarrel with anyone. Others, who met her in later life, invariably recall her intelligence, sensitivity, and willingness to help.

The principal bond that drew these friends together was their common love of literature. Neither Kirill, in later life, nor Natalia Reshetovskaya (in her edited memoirs) is an entirely reliable witness in these matters, but Kirill's words, as quoted by Reshetovskaya, on the subject of their enthusiasm and their relations with their literature teacher, Anastasia Grünau, have the ring of truth to them.

We wrote essays on Shakespeare, Byron, and Pushkin, consulting a mass of out-of-school sources and each trying to outdo the other. Gradually it became clear that the best at this were Lida Ezherets, Sanya Solzhenitsyn, and myself.

At first we wrote very bad, very imitative poetry, until Anastasia Sergeyevna suggested we try writing a novel together. At the same time we started producing a satirical magazine in which we wrote poems, epigrams on one another and even on the teachers, which they then marked as "witty," "not witty," "witty but tactless," and so on.

In the ninth and tenth classes, we added to this an infatuation with the theatre. We organized a drama club and rehearsed plays by Ostrovsky, Chekhov, and Rostand. We had ready-made characters in our class for all possible roles.[10]

This picture of the friends' literary activities at school was later confirmed by Solzhenitsyn in a supplement to *The Oak and the Calf*. The joint novel was dubbed "the novel of the three madmen" and was written rather in the manner of the old parlour game of truth and consequences: each person would take it in turn to write a chapter, starting from whatever had gone before but without indicating how the plot should develop further.[11] Solzhenitsyn retained a great affection for Anastasia Grünau and in later life, when already famous, made a point of visiting her in Moscow. It appears that he never forgot her lessons in his favourite subject and the love for literature that she helped instil in him.[12]

Kirill was as passionate about literature as Solzhenitsyn, and while still at school the two of them wrote reams of verse that they dispatched to various writers for comment. Usually their letters went unanswered, but on one occasion Leonid Timofeyev wrote back with a detailed and very negative criticism of their efforts. After that they approached a local poet called Cato for instruction and were encouraged to submit their work to a Rostov literary magazine, *The Hammer*, but nothing came of that either. Solzhenitsyn later felt that Kirill had had it in him to develop into a capable and perhaps outstanding writer (Anastasia Grünau actually thought him the more talented of the two), but Kirill gradually lost heart, and after taking a medical degree he abandoned writing altogether (except for medical books). Lydia, too, had literary ambitions, and it was usually to her flat (her father being comparatively wealthy and their flat sumptuous by Soviet standards) that the friends went to read and discuss their works. Of the entire group, she was the only one to take a degree in literature and end up teaching it, becoming a specialist in German literature and writing a certain amount of academic criticism. Nikolai Vitkevich was more interested in politics and philosophy than in literature proper and took little part in these exercises.[13]

Solzhenitsyn's love of amateur theatricals led to his toying at one stage with the idea of becoming a professional actor. Rostov was particularly well off for theatres at this time. The city's Bolshoi Theatre company had just moved into a sumptuous new glass-and-concrete theatre complex designed by the celebrated architect A. V. Shchuko, the man responsible for the Lenin Mausoleum in Red Square. The huge central block, flanked by two satellite wings, had so enraged Rostov's citizens with its modernity and expense that it had been ironically dubbed "the tractor," in honour of Rostov's best-known manufacture, but it was a vital centre of theatrical life, particularly after the arrival there of the Moscow director Yuri Zavadsky. Zavadsky, a famous actor-manager who had worked with Stanislavsky and Nemirovich-Danchenko, was formerly the director of the Red Army Theatre in Moscow, but in 1936, as a result of a routine artistic purge, he was accused of "an excessive preoccupation with aestheticism," of pursuing "falsely understood ideas of novelty and innovation" (though some said that Nemirovich-Danchenko's jealousy was at the root of the matter), and banished to Rostov.

Perhaps fascinated by Zavadsky's reputation, Solzhenitsyn began attending his youth studio, which was jammed with enthusiastic applicants eager to get in. He passed most of the two-part entrance examination without difficulty and was praised by Zavadsky for his comic talent, but Zavadsky tested his voice by the simple expedient of getting him to call out to Kirill some distance away and pronounced his vocal cords too weak. He retained a lifelong fascination with the theatre that was subsequently to issue in four stage plays, two film scripts, and a decidedly dramatic approach to prose fiction. He also conceived a passion for recitation, which in later life took the form of reading from his works. At the height of his fame in Moscow, he liked nothing better than to read to a private gathering of admirers and friends, always with gusto and verve, if not always with the requisite dramatic effect. Later, after his deportation to the West, in 1974, one of his first acts was to issue a gramophone recording of himself reading the text of his long narrative poem *Prussian Nights*.

Even had his voice not failed, it is doubtful, in retrospect, whether Solzhenitsyn would have taken the final step of entering the theatre, for his overriding passion was literature, and of his three possible choices for a vocation, that of becoming a writer quickly became uppermost in his mind. The first stirrings of this ambition had occurred as early as the age of nine. The very statement of it invites a sceptical response. How many people have written childish poems and stories when they were nine, only to forget and dismiss them later, even if they returned to writing? But Solzhenitsyn's juvenilia have survived intact and confirm beyond doubt that he did begin to write systematically and at unusual length from the age of nine and that he continued writing single-mindedly, without a break, through adolescence, youth, and early manhood into what we now know as his literary maturity. Throughout these early years the qualities that stand out in his writing, apart from a natural but not unduly precocious talent, are application, energy, and stamina—not unimportant attributes of a writer possessed of such vaulting ambition.[14]

The first series of juvenilia dates from the winter of 1928–29. The first story in it, begun in 1928, is "Pirates," written in large, rounded handwriting on the backs of invoices and other blanks from Melstroi, where his mother had worked. This is followed by "The Blue Arrow" (alternatively titled

"V.V.," for the initials of the main hero) on tiny sheets of office paper and by the astonishingly long "Science Fiction Story," both written in 1929. The science fiction was evidently intended for some journal that Solzhenitsyn was planning at the time, either on his own or jointly with Misha and Lialia Fedorovskaya. The first journal to have survived intact, however, is the ambitiously named *Twentieth Century*, with its no less ambitious subtitle: "On the Meaning of the Twentieth Century." The journal was neatly printed in handwritten capital letters, contained illustrations, verse, jokes, and stories, all by Solzhenitsyn, and featured a long serial, "The Last Pirate," whose subject matter hardly fitted the journal's grandiose aspirations but which ran in no fewer than twenty separate numbers.

There seems then to have been a slight pause until January 1932, when the thirteen-year-old tyro launched a new journal, *The Literary Gazette*. This one was in school exercise books (paper no longer being in such short supply), ran for two years, and devoted much of its space to a long play, *The Banquet*, a comedy in two acts. It also contained another science-fiction adventure entitled "Rays." Meanwhile Solzhenitsyn was trying new genres outside his journals. In 1934 he wrote *Mikhail Snegov*, described as "a novel" on the exercise book cover and "a tale" *(povest)* inside. Not surprisingly, its eponymous hero was an actor. Simultaneously, he wrote a great deal of verse, collected in one volume as *Verse 1932–36* and later as *Juvenile Verse*, a miscellany of jokes, epigrams, and "especially intimate poems," some of them the fruit, no doubt, of those class activities referred to by Kirill Simonyan. Solzhenitsyn also collected a number of his early stories together under the common title of *The Fateful Tragedy*. An interesting detail, for lovers of coincidence and omens (of whom Solzhenitsyn is one), is that the heroine of one of the stories, "The Money Box," was named Alia Svetlova, prefiguring not only the surname but also the affectionate nickname of Solzhenitsyn's second and present wife, Natalia Svetlova.

Solzhenitsyn's efforts were well known within the family and led on one occasion to his being drawn to the attention of Maxim Gorky. It happened as follows. His uncle Roman worshipped Gorky as an even greater writer than Tolstoy. There was a certain irony in this, for Roman himself was a typical Gorky anti-hero—a rich merchant's son attracted by progressive ideas, but with patriarchal ways that were hopelessly at odds with contemporary society. Gorky repeatedly reviled and lampooned such characters in his endless novels devoted to merchant families, and was repaid by their applause and adoration. At the end of the twenties, Gorky developed a theory that anyone at all could become a writer, if only he was given the right amount of encouragement and opportunity. As a result, people started sending him things to read from all over Russia. At about this time, in 1932 or 1933, Solzhenitsyn sent Roman and Irina a long letter about a trip he had made to the Black Sea coast with the Young Pioneers, describing the sights he had seen and his impressions. His uncle and aunt were so impressed that they sent a copy to Maxim Gorky. Some time later a reply duly arrived signed by one of Gorky's secretaries voicing approval and encouragement: yes, the young author definitely had it in him to become a writer.[15]

Of a somewhat different character from the early stories and verse, and of more interest for his biography, are what Solzhenitsyn called his *Cycling Notes*, composed in the autumn of 1937 to describe a month's tour of the Caucasus in July and August in the company of six friends.

Solzhenitsyn had acquired his bicycle in somewhat unorthodox fashion. In 1936, during his last year at school, he had been nominated by the headmaster for some sort of civic prize for outstanding pupils. The award of the prize was usually a formality once the nominations were in, but for some reason Solzhenitsyn's name was missing from the published list, and his school went without a prize-winner. His nomination had been blocked on account of his social background. The headmaster was incensed and kicked up a tremendous fuss, demanding that the injustice be righted. The officials concerned said it was too late to alter the prize-winners, but consented to award Solzhenitsyn a bicycle as an extraordinary consolation prize. The headmaster was supplied with a sum of money for Solzhenitsyn and a letter to be presented to the main city sports shop. In return for the letter and the money, a bicycle would be provided.

For Solzhenitsyn this was better than a normal prize. Bicycles were a rare luxury in those days, and he would never have been able to afford one on his own. When he arrived at the sports shop with the letter, he was informed that there was a terrible shortage but that they would tip him off before the next consignment arrived so that he could come to the shop the night before and be first in the queue.

When the tip-off came, Solzhenitsyn informed Kirill and Nikolai, and all three of them went to the shop at closing time the night before. During the evening and night they were joined by dozens of others, until a crowd of about 150 people was waiting outside the shop. Some policemen tried to disperse it, but without success. The following morning the three musketeers were the first into the shop and had the pick of the bicycles. Thereafter cycling became a favourite hobby, and their next three summers were devoted to touring holidays.

Their first trip, in 1937, consisted of a tour of the famous Georgian military highway, leading through the most scenic and spectacular passes of the Caucasus Mountains to Tbilisi. Five boys and two girls loaded their cycles onto the train and travelled to the town of Ordzhonikidze (named for Stalin's fellow Georgian revolutionary, the late commissar for heavy industry) and cycled into the mountains from there.

Solzhenitsyn's notes on the journey are contained in three school exercise books grandiloquently labelled "My Travels, Volume IV, Books 1, 2, and 3." They begin in unpromising schoolboy fashion, facetious, self-conscious, full of private jokes and satirical descriptions. Surprisingly quickly, however, the facetiousness drops away and yields to genuinely infectious high spirits and good humour. Some of the cameo scenes and dialogue are extremely funny, including a description of a series of punctures and other mishaps in the pouring rain when the group was on its way to visit Stalin's birthplace at Gori.

The young Solzhenitsyn waxed indignant over the Georgians' arrogant discrimination against women, and was jealous of their easy southern charm. The Georgian men, he found, exhibited an insufferably patronizing attitude towards Russian women, regarding them as easy conquests and therefore of easy virtue—an interesting replica of Mediterranean men's attitudes to northern women well west of the Caucasus. Indignation of a different kind was provoked by a TB sanatorium: "Two things cause tuberculosis—poverty and the impotence of medicine. The Revolution has liquidated poverty. Medicine, why are you lagging behind? Tear these unfortunates from death's grasping paws!" The glib optimism and shallow rhetoric echoed the trite motto on the exercise book's cover: "We shall have excellent and numerous cadres in industry, agriculture, transport, and the army—our country will be invincible (Stalin)."

Much the most interesting parts of the *Cycling Notes* are the lyrical digressions. Being well read, Solzhenitsyn could not resist noting the places that Pushkin, Lermontov, and Tolstoy—all of whom had been influenced by the Russian cult of the Caucasus—had visited there. In Tbilisi he visited the grave of "that radiant genius, that pride of the Russian nation," Alexander Griboyedov,* which provoked him to the following thoughts:

> I love graveyards! . . . Sitting in a graveyard you involuntarily cast your mind back over all your past life, your past actions, and your plans for the future. And here you do not lie to yourself as you do so often in life, because you feel as if all those people sleeping the sleep of peace around you were somehow still present, and you were conversing with them. Sitting in a graveyard you momentarily rise above your daily ambitions, cares and emotions—you rise for an instant even above yourself. And then, when you leave the graveyard, you become yourself again and subside into the morass of daily trivia, and only the rarest of individuals is able to leap from that morass onto the firm ground of immortality.

Was he one of those "rarest of individuals"? He dares not put the question, but a jocular aside refers to it indirectly: "What is life if it isn't sheer daring? To dare! To dare! The winner is he who dares all!"

Elsewhere he touches on the nature of the notes and his reasons for writing them. He is now firmly back in Rostov.

> I am writing them in the very thick of preparing for the examinations. All evening I have been ploughing my way through the mounds of mathematical computations, and every few minutes I look at my watch—when will it be ten o'clock? Ten arrives and I throw aside my boring textbooks. . . . Why do people have to

---

*Griboyedov's masterpiece, *Woe from Wit* (1822–23), a verse comedy in the manner of Molière, was one of Solzhenitsyn's favourite plays. As a student he used to declaim passages from it when taking part in readings.

go to lectures? Having discarded the textbooks, I take something from my drawer and hastily begin writing. . . . I write for half an hour, an hour, no more, and already feel a sense of relief, and no mathematics can spoil my mood any longer. . . .

But is it worth writing with no reader in mind? Yes. Romain Rolland's advice is that you should write without a care for the future of your work. He is right. Anyone who writes with an eye to what the press, critics, and other people are likely to think is nothing better than a dauber, or a concocter of thin literary gruel.

In another place, the young author muses on whether to finish his notes or not. He is obviously having some difficulty in sticking to them through the autumn examination period. But looking back over his long experience as a writer, he recalls an episode in "childhood" when writing adventure stories. Wearying of the endless episodes of one particular adventure, he had abandoned it, taken a fresh sheet of paper, and written at the top, "Novel, Part One, Chapter One." Struck dumb by the magnitude of the enterprise, he had then remained immobile, pen poised over paper, for what seemed an age before writing: "The Kara-Kum desert is very extensive," only to fall into a trance once more and become lost in his thoughts. This must not happen again, he resolves. He must learn from previous experience and finish at all costs, even if the notes never find a reader besides himself.

From this busy period dates Solzhenitsyn's first attempt at a longer work. On 18 November 1936, when not quite eighteen, he resolved to write "a big novel about the Revolution," on the face of it a more modest and realistic aim than his childish ambition to understand the meaning of the twentieth century, but wholly in the same spirit. He quickly realized that it was impossible to do justice to the Revolution without taking the First World War into account, yet if he attempted to describe the whole war he would never reach the Revolution. He therefore decided to study some of the war's military campaigns and became increasingly fascinated by the defeat of General Samsonov at the Battle of Tannenberg, in East Prussia. It struck him that this was a kind of key to the entire progress of the war. Samsonov personified many of the best qualities of the Russian character and represented the very best aspects of Russian patriotism and Russian generalship. On the other hand he was at the mercy of corrupt and stupid superiors and of a decaying court, and was defeated as much by Russian incompetence as by the efficiency of the German military machine.

Solzhenitsyn spent the first three months of 1937 intensively studying this campaign in the Rostov libraries, an experience he was later to evoke in *Prussian Nights*.

> In the dark cathedral gloom
> Of one or another reading room
> I shared with none my boyish grief,
> I bent over the yellow pages

Of those ageing maps and plans,
Till little circles, dots, and arrows
Came alive beneath my hands,
Now as a fire-fight in the marshes,
Now as a tumult in the night:
Thirst. Hunger. August. Heat.[16]

The following year he drafted a plan for an immense epic novel (in scope, if not in theme, modelled on Tolstoy's *War and Peace*) in multiple volumes and parts, which he provisionally labelled *R-17* (its principal subject being the Revolution of 1917). Solzhenitsyn intended to approach the subject from his then-Communist point of view. As he later wrote in *The Gulag Archipelago*, "I had somehow known from childhood that my objective was the history of the Russian Revolution and that nothing else had any relevance for me. And to understand the Revolution I needed nothing but Marxism. I hacked away all else that adhered to it and turned my back on it."[17] The novel's hero, Olkhovsky (who became Lenartovich in *August 1914*), was intended to be an idealistic Communist.* In 1937 and 1938 Solzhenitsyn drafted the first few chapters of part 1 of his novel under the provisional title, "Russians in the Advance Guard," and also sketched in a scene between Olkhovsky and Severtsev (later Vorotyntsev) for a chapter entitled "Black on Red." Thirty years later, when writing *August 1914*, he was able to take from it not only source material but also some scenes that he hardly needed to change at all.

By the time Solzhenitsyn started his novel, he had entered the university. It was usual at this time for students to have to take an entrance examination and to submit their social credentials for scrutiny. Thanks to his record of straight 5s in school, however, Solzhenitsyn was accepted without an examination, and his scholastic record averted too close a scrutiny of his social origins. On the endless questionnaires that had now become a feature of life in the Soviet Union (permitting a degree of bureaucratic control that meshed perfectly with the requirements of the security organs), Solzhenitsyn invariably wrote "office worker" when describing his father's former occupation. "I could never tell anyone that he had been an officer in the Russian army, because that was considered a disgrace."[18]

Somewhat surprisingly, Solzhenitsyn chose to take a degree in physics and mathematics rather than in literature, but there were sound reasons for this. His secret ambition had been to go to Moscow and study literature there, but concern for his mother held him back. Worn down by years of exhaustion and overwork, the struggle to make ends meet, and the cold and damp of their unheated shack, she had contracted tuberculosis and was no longer robust enough to contemplate such a move. Furthermore, in 1934 the

* According to Natalia Reshetovskaya, Solzhenitsyn's novel was intended to show "the complete triumph of the Revolution on a global scale." She herself was to be the prototype for a character called Lucy Olkhovskaya, presumably Olkhovsky's wife or sister.

Solzhenitsyns had finally been able to move from their hovel in the cul-de-sac (via some temporary accommodation) into a converted stable at 39 Voroshilov Prospekt (formerly the Bolshoi Prospekt). Its two rooms were no bigger than their old ones, but at least it was drier and warmer, and Taissia was thankful to have the security of better quarters.

It would seem that by the mid to late thirties Taissia's situation with regard to work had somewhat improved. She was no longer chased from job to job, and she had begun to obtain occasional evening work as a stenographer at official conferences, which was extremely well paid when one could get it. A younger colleague, Anna Voloshina, who used to be responsible for hiring stenographers for these conferences, has described Taissia as tall and thin during this period, her brown hair already streaked with grey (she was not much over forty at the time), and almost invariably dressed in an "English blouse," with a severe high collar, and wearing a black or dark grey skirt. She never wore jewellery. According to Voloshina, Taissia was universally acknowledged to be far and away the best stenographer among them (she was, of course, nearly twenty years older than the others), with an impeccable knowledge of Russian and very good speeds. She was also a work-horse, and never complained, as a result of which the younger girls used to take advantage of her by arriving late when it was their turn to take over a shift. On the one occasion when Voloshina remonstrated with her for being so patient, Taissia smiled and said, "The time will come, Anna dear, when life will teach you to avoid any sort of quarrel." Taissia rarely smiled. Her reserve and self-control were absolute, and she spoke only when spoken to. She almost never talked about her home life or her son, except in generalities, and the only subject that Voloshina heard her discuss, apart from work, was music, which Taissia said soothed her and calmed her nerves.

As the tuberculosis advanced, towards the end of the thirties, it became more difficult for Taissia to take on extra work. Solzhenitsyn later recalled her sometimes dragging herself out of bed, even when her temperature was over a hundred and she had a certificate from the doctor, to go and look for work at conferences. She did it, he said, because she felt she had to earn the extra money for his sake and to see that he was well looked after. And yet, this was at a period when he was growing away from her and beginning to escape from her all-embracing but sometimes stifling care. There were some difficult scenes. She would weep and say that he no longer shared his thoughts with her, that she could not keep up with his new ideas—and no doubt she was made uneasy by his growing involvement with the Komsomol. But there was no question of his leaving home. It would have broken her heart, and he put the idea completely aside.[19]

To study literature in Rostov, however, was not an attractive prospect. As befitted an industrial port and manufacturing centre, the subjects in which the local university was strongest were shipbuilding, engineering, chemistry, physics, geology, and the applied sciences. Literature was not taught at all at the faculty level, but only in a *pedinstitut*, or teacher training college, whose function was to prepare students for teaching in secondary schools, and Solzhenitsyn was not interested in that at all.

> I had no desire to become a teacher of literature, because I had too many complex ideas of my own, and I simply wasn't interested in retailing crude, simplified nuggets of information to children in school. Teaching mathematics, however, was much more interesting. I didn't have any particular ambitions in the field of science, but I found it came easy to me, very easy, so I decided it would be better for me to become a mathematician and keep literature as a consolation of the spirit. And it was the right thing to do.[20]

In the event, none of the three musketeers took up literature at the university level. Kirill, growing disillusioned with his literary efforts, opted for chemistry and a year later switched to medicine. Nikolai also studied chemistry, and only Lydia went into the *pedinstitut* to study German literature.

Solzhenitsyn continued to shine at the university, receiving top marks in all his examinations, and in his middle years acquired a new interest—Marxism-Leninism. Like most of his friends, he had passed easily and automatically from the Young Pioneers to the Komsomol in his tenth and final year at school, when he was seventeen. Academically outstanding students were assiduously wooed by the Party authorities and given every encouragement to play a strong role in the youth organization. But for Solzhenitsyn it could be no empty formality. Earnest and intense by nature, he was incapable of doing things by halves, and he threw himself into the study of Party doctrine with an enthusiasm and energy typical of his eager spirit.

> You know, by the end of my school years a Soviet education had won me over, and so I joined the Komsomol. Later, during my years at the university, I spent a lot of time studying dialectical materialism, not only as part of my courses but in my spare time as well. Then and later . . . I read an enormous amount about it and got completely carried away. I was absolutely sincerely enthralled by it over a period of several years.[21]

How did it happen that the grandson of a millionaire, the son of a tsarist officer, brought up to revere the Russian patriarchal past and virtually weaned on stories of Red atrocities during the Civil War, could be so carried away by this seemingly alien doctrine? Perhaps it had to do with the fact that the grandson had known no wealth himself; he had experienced only poverty and hardships. His officer father had been of left-liberal sympathies, and both his grandfathers had at one time laboured in the fields as peasants, so the distance between them was not so very great—only two generations. There had also been a change in the times. As Solzhenitsyn later pointed out in an interview, a great psychological difference separated the Soviet 1920s and 1930s: "The old world wasn't remote between 1920 and 1925. Everyone remembered how it had been. No one dared pass judgement, but everyone was still making comparisons and almost everyone realized that the truly totalitarian regime was the one that had just been set up." By the thirties, however, the situation had been transformed.

> A new generation had grown up. Its members had no personal memories of the preceding period, so they accepted the interpretation placed upon it by their Komsomol instructors. . . . During those years Russia underwent a kind of retrogressive development. It was a stupendous change. . . .
>   Many of the older generation remained silent, and the rest died in one camp or another. The Party had become our father and we, the children, obeyed. So when I was leaving school and embarking on my time at university, I made a choice: I banished all my memories, all my childhood misgivings. I was a Communist. The world would be what we made of it.[22]

Like orphaned Russia, the orphans of the Revolution and Civil War had found a new father. The tsar-father of Irina's tales was gone for good and had been replaced by a new protector, all-wise and all-compassionate, whose words betrayed a Georgian accent and whose faithful right hand was the Party. When asked what it was that had particularly attracted him to communism, Solzhenitsyn replied that it was "undoubtedly . . . justice. I thought it might be born of this marriage between the tragedy of our age and our own desires."[23]

It seems that Solzhenitsyn put aside his memories of the arrest and temporary disappearance of Vladimir Fedorovsky, of the vicissitudes of Nikolai Chefranov and other teachers at his school, and looked at life in a new way. There were still awkward facts to cope with, of course. In 1937, during his first year at the university, some senior students were arrested and disappeared, and a few of the professors were said to have disappeared as well. There was Professor Trifonov, scurrying down the corridors and never stopping in answer to a call—"we later discovered that he had already *done time*, and each time his name was shouted he had visions of the secret police."[24] Another of his university teachers, Professor Mordukhai-Boltovskoi (described in *The First Circle* as Goryainov-Shakhovskoi), a famous mathematician whose son had taught Solzhenitsyn geology for a time at the Malevich school, was temporarily removed from the university during a clean-up. Mordukhai-Boltovskoi was celebrated for his haughty indifference to Party dogma and was the subject of innumerable popular stories. On one occasion, according to Solzhenitsyn, while lecturing on his favourite subject of Newton, he was sent up a note which said, "Marx wrote that Newton was a materialist, yet you say he was an idealist." To which the professor replied, "I can only say that Marx was wrong. Newton believed in God, like every other great scientist." On another occasion, just when he was getting into trouble, his students told him that there was an attack on him in the wall newspaper.* "My

---

* Wall newspapers were (and are) a revered relic of post-revolutionary days, when the Bolsheviks had pasted their news sheets on walls for the masses to read. The texts were often simplified and accompanied by expressive graphics to hammer home the desired message to people who were unaccustomed to buying and reading newspapers, and propaganda was a major element in

nanny told me never to read what was written on walls," he replied.[25]

Mordukhai-Boltovskoi was saved from the GPU prison by his age, his reputation, and allegedly by the personal intervention of Kalinin, chairman of the Central Executive Committee of the USSR, to whom he turned for help (it was rumoured that Kalinin's father had been a serf of the professor's father).* As a result he was reprieved and transferred to the *pedinstitut*, but most others were not so lucky. In the mid-thirties Solzhenitsyn himself narrowly escaped arrest when standing in a bread queue. The people in the queue were accused of being "saboteurs" and "sowing panic" among the public by suggesting there was a bread shortage. Fortunately, someone interceded for him and he was released.[26]

Yet all this was somehow perceived as being, if not normal, then more or less inevitable. The arrests and purges were nation-wide and affected everyone high and low, from the top Party leaders in Moscow down to the humblest workers and peasants in the small towns and countryside. The logic of the campaign of terror set in motion by collectivization and forced industrialization had assumed a momentum of its own. Then came the Kirov murder in 1934, the trial of Kamenev and Zinoviev in 1935, the Old Bolsheviks trial in 1936, the trial of Pyatakov and Radek in 1937, the trial of Rykov and Bukharin in 1938,† and on and on, right up to the Second World War. Soviet society was turned upside down and remade in Stalin's image.

Meanwhile, the newspapers were full of detailed descriptions of the trials, with gloating accounts of the defendants' confessions and sycophantic praise of the "eternal vigilance" of the secret police. There was strident propaganda about alleged "enemies of the people," "ideological sabotage," and all the other cunning slogans of the time. Pavlik Morozov, who achieved immortality by denouncing his father to the secret police, was held up as a model for Soviet youth, and armies of Party spokesmen were mobilized to lecture to the students on why the purges were necessary and to brainwash them into acceptance. The lecturers' efforts were directed above all at the brightest students and the leaders of the Komsomol, who were being groomed for the future leadership of the Party. Among the latter, a specially privileged place was reserved for the "October children"—children born during or just after the Revolution. These constituted the first wholly Soviet generation in existence. Given that "being defines consciousness" (according to Marx), great hopes were placed in them as the first of the "new Soviet men," an entirely new breed that would take over the Revolution and raise it to new heights.

them. The idea persisted in two different forms. Copies of national newspapers like *Pravda* and *Izvestia* continued to be hung in special showcases for the public to read, and all institutions, including university departments, were required to publish their own wall newspapers, in which internal notes, news, and announcements were carried in addition to party propaganda.

* Another rumour held that Kalinin was the illegitimate son of Mordukhai-Boltovskoi's father, and therefore the professor's half-brother.

† These prominent Bolsheviks were all actual or potential rivals of Stalin, who perceived them as threats to his supremacy. Their systematic elimination meant the elimination of any possible challenge to his rule.

Solzhenitsyn was an "October child," gaily marching through Rostov to the sound of martial music. He and his Komsomol friends knew of the arrests yet managed somehow to brush them aside as a temporary but necessary phenomenon, essential to the success of the Revolution. Looking back on it all after his imprisonment, Solzhenitsyn exclaimed over "the astonishing swinishness of egotistical youth. . . . We had no sense of living in the midst of a plague, that people were dropping all around us, that a plague was in progress. It's amazing, but we didn't realize it."[27]

In this respect Solzhenitsyn was generally no better and no worse than the mass of his contemporaries. Young, enthusiastic, and idealistic, anxious to win the approval of his teachers and ambitious to succeed in his studies, he found it easy to look the other way, cocooned as he was in that self-regarding world of scholarship that is characteristic of universities everywhere. "I was borne along on the tide," he later told one of his interviewers about this period, although "I had forgotten nothing."[28]

And yet, perhaps he *was* different after all, for he does seem to have seen through Stalin and to have taken a dislike to him from an unusually early age. There is an eloquent and much-quoted passage in *The First Circle* describing the reactions of the autobiographical hero, Gleb Nerzhin, to the events of the thirties. Nerzhin, too, is described as having spent his childhood and youth in Rostov and as having been carried away on the current of the times. Yet he notices some things that others don't.

> Gleb had grown up without once having read any children's books, but he had been only twelve when he unfolded the enormous pages of *Izvestia*, which obscured him from top to toe, and read there of the trial of the "saboteur engineers." And at once he had disbelieved it. He didn't know why; he couldn't give a rational explanation for it. But it was as plain as a pikestaff to him that the whole thing was lies, lies, lies. There were engineers in many of the families he knew, and it was unthinkable that such people could be committing sabotage instead of working honourably. . . .
>
> Was it because his ear was still young, or perhaps because he read more than just the newspapers, that he could detect so clearly the hypocrisy in all that inordinate, gushing adulation of just one man, always one man? For if this man was everything, did that mean the rest were all nothing? Gleb recoiled from such an idea and was unable to follow the crowd.[29]

There is, of course, a fictional sharpening here, an idealization of the writer's past (Nerzhin is said to have guessed the truth of Kirov's murder, which seems unlikely) that gilds experience. But Nerzhin's underlying psychology is a convincing reflection of Solzhenitsyn's own, and the distaste for Stalin undoubtedly began early and ran deep.*

---

* A Rostov contemporary of Solzhenitsyn's informs me that it was not unlikely that he guessed the truth of Kirov's murder—it was the common opinion among families that had been part of the middle or upper classes before the Revolution. On the other hand, Solzhenitsyn himself has written that, because of his ideological commitment during the thirties, he did not understand the significance of Stalin's purges and that Kirill Simonyan grasped it better.

For most of the time these misgivings were suppressed or pushed to the back of his mind. In the universal atmosphere of suspicion and mistrust, there were few people he could reveal them to, except his closest friends. But his doubts did surface briefly again in response to an episode that he later described in *The Gulag Archipelago*.

In the autumn of 1938 all student members of the Komsomol were summoned to the Komsomol District Committee headquarters and handed a set of questionnaires to fill out. No explanation was offered, but the students quickly discovered that they were application forms for entry to one of the training colleges of the NKVD.* They were not surprised. The year before, they had been asked to fill out application forms for the air force, and they took it for granted that as members of the elite they would be offered the pick of the jobs available. Solzhenitsyn and his friends had easily resisted the air force, but this time the pressure was more insistent. After all, the NKVD had undergone an enormous expansion and was working flat out under Stalin (few outside its ranks realized that it, too, was losing members to the jails and camps). It was also one of the highest-paid and best-regarded jobs then available, carrying privileges far beyond the reach of most of the students, who had little reason to connect it with arrests and torture. "How were we to know about the arrests," writes Solzhenitsyn in *The Gulag Archipelago*, "and why should we think of them? The fact that all the regional Party leaders had been replaced didn't concern us at all. Two or three professors had been arrested, but so what? It wasn't them we went dancing with, and exams would be all the easier to pass for their loss. We twenty-year-olds marched in the column of the October children, and as the Revolution's children, we looked forward to a glittering future."[30]

However, when the test came, Solzhenitsyn held back.

It isn't easy to define the exact nature of that inner intuition, not founded on any rational argument, that prompted our refusal to enter the NKVD training college. It certainly didn't derive from the lectures on historical materialism we had attended: from them it was clear that the struggle against the internal enemy was a crucial battlefront and a glorious mission. It also contradicted our material interests: at that time our provincial university could promise us nothing more than a village school in the back of beyond and a miserable pittance for a salary, whereas the NKVD college dangled before us special rations and double or triple pay. Our feelings could not be put into words (even if we had found the words we would have been too frightened to say them to one another). The opposition came not from our heads but from somewhere inside our breasts. People may shout at you from all sides, "You must!" and your own head may also say, "You

* *Narodny kommissariat vnutrennikh del* (the People's Commissariat for Internal Affairs), which in those days was also responsible for recruitment to the secret police. The name of the police force itself had been changed in 1922 from Cheka to GPU (State Political Administration) and in 1923 to OGPU (General State Political Administration), at which time it had been removed from the control of the NKVD and made into an independent ministry. In 1934, however, the two had been merged again and the name OGPU abolished.

must!" but the breast recoiled: "I won't, I feel sick! Do what you want without me, I want no part of it."[31]

He was a Marxist, a Leninist, a Communist, but to become a secret police-man was asking too much of him. And yet, as he wrote in the same place, "if they had really put the pressure on us, I think they would have broken us all." He had come a long way since removing the cross from around his neck.

5

MARRIAGE

In most respects Solzhenitsyn and his friends were models of Soviet youth. Soviet ideals during this period were embodied in the "literature of the Five-Year Plan" and in the classics of communism, whose authors had been canonized by the recent introduction of "socialist realism" as the country's approved artistic doctrine. Much of this literature was devoted to the period of the Revolution and Civil War. Novels like *Cement*, *The Iron Flood*, *The Rout*, *Chapayev*, and *How the Steel Was Tempered* portrayed "positive heroes" with all the military virtues of courage, iron self-discipline, severity with subordinates, dedication to the cause, and loyalty to the collective, coupled with unfailing optimism and faith in a better future. In civilian life (which was increasingly being forced into a semi-military pattern), these virtues were transmuted into concepts of total self-abnegation, the sacrifice of personal comforts and family life to the furtherance of the Communist cause and an almost monastic dedication to a life of sustained study or toil. The supreme vices in this religiose world view were frivolity, detachment, scepticism, sophistication, worldliness, balance. The supreme virtues were sincerity, loyalty, commitment, simplicity, and total identification with the Communist cause.

Of course, not everyone was expected to succeed in meeting these standards. Although everything possible was done to get the "right" people to join the Komsomol and the Party, the idea of party organizations as exclusive, sacred brotherhoods was also propagated, and entry was made to seem formally more difficult than it really was. The idea of Party-minded behaviour was one to which all sensible mortals aspired—and had to be seen to aspire—but though many were called, few could be chosen. This was convenient, among other things, for the periodic conducting of "purges," whose punitive purpose was masked by the requirement of ideological purity.

Solzhenitsyn and his friends were heavily imbued with this puritanical Party spirit and seem in many respects to have been as straitlaced a bunch of youngsters as you could hope to find anywhere. Out of school and university their first inclination was to head not for the cafe or sports field but for the library and reading-room, where they crammed the prescribed texts and vied with one another in doctrinal erudition. Their evenings would be spent in Komsomol clubrooms, organizing meetings, writing up the Komsomol wall newspapers, and holding political discussions, rather than down on the main boulevard (now named Engels Street), where the rest of Rostov youth congregated to promenade and ogle the girls in normal southern fashion. Indeed, girls and their romantic possibilities seem to have occupied a very small part of the boys' attention, as Solzhenitsyn later recalled in his autobiographical poem:

> A book, a desk, you opposite me—
> And nobody else in the world exists!
> . . . .
> And no regrets for this curious
> Wineless, girl-less, bachelor youth of ours.[1]

The "you" was Nikolai Vitkevich, to whom Solzhenitsyn found himself particularly drawn during their university years. What united them was their passionate interest in politics and philosophy, and especially Marxism. While all members of the group took these things seriously, Solzhenitsyn and Vitkevich stood out from the rest for the depth of their commitment, the intensity of their faith, the strength of their resolve to participate, and their dynamic activism. Long evenings in the library were devoted to reading Hegel, Marx, Engels, Lenin. They strove to master the technicalities of philosophy, politics, economics, and history and to apply their learning to the Soviet political scene. Very soon they concluded that Stalin was an idol with feet of clay. They despised not only his ruthless political opportunism and dictatorial one-man rule but also his personal uncouthness, his heavily accented Russian, and his poor command of the language in his writings—"indigestible kasha," as Solzhenitsyn later characterized them. It was distrust of Stalin that had made Solzhenitsyn alert to the hollowness of the show trials; and the secret of their mutual detestation of Stalin served to increase the friends' intimacy, for in the atmosphere of the time such thoughts could be breathed only in the narrowest and safest of inner circles.

Their enthusiasm for Lenin, on the other hand, knew no bounds. They eagerly devoured his every word, not to speak of the flood of memoirs and reminiscences of his life that was spilling off the presses, with Stalin's encouragement, as part of the booming Lenin cult. It is not surprisng that Solzhenitsyn's early fascination with Lenin should have taken later literary shape in his epic on the Revolution. *Lenin in Zurich* was the fruit not only of his fortuitous exile and later studies there but also of these early meditations, though Lenin, like the fictional Lenartovich, was also to make the transition from positive to negative hero in the course of a prolonged literary gestation period. One of the private jokes that the two friends indulged in at this time was that if Lenin were to be resurrected and returned to the Soviet Union, he would immediately be arrested. "Back to Leninism and Leninist norms" was their slogan some twenty years before Khrushchev was to make it fashionable, for they seriously believed that Stalin, and Stalin alone, was responsible for the negative aspects of Soviet life and that the only way to correct them was to restore the "Lenin line."

Their zeal for self-improvement reached into other spheres as well. In their last year at school, the three musketeers enrolled for English classes at the evening institute (Solzhenitsyn's mother, Taissia, also enrolled, in the hope of improving her qualifications and earning more money). Solzhenitsyn passed with good marks and subsequently earned some pocket-money by doing technical translations in his spare time. He tried his hand at some literary texts as an exercise in style, and did the same from German, but no longer remembers what they were.

The culmination of their scholarly ambitions came as a result of Solzhenitsyn's suggestion that they enrol as external students at the Moscow Institute of Philosophy, Literature, and History (MIFLI), the top institution in the country for the study of the humanities. Solzhenitsyn, who had not lost his old yearning for Moscow, seems to have felt that in this way he would be able to make some contact with the country's best scholars and measure himself against the best students from elsewhere. He was like Gleb Nerzhin in *The First Circle:*

> Young Gleb was growing up in the city. Success was showered on him from the cornucopia of science. He noticed that he was agile of mind but that there were others with minds even more agile than his and whose vast store of knowledge was overpowering. . . . He reasoned that the only people of any consequence were those who carried in their heads the legacy of world culture: encyclopedists, scholars versed in antiquity, devotees of the fine art—versatile men with a multifaceted education. These were the elect and one must belong to them.[2]

The three friends decided that the best time to enrol would be in the summer of 1939, so that their first year at the institute would coincide with their final year of university studies. Solzhenitsyn chose to study literature, Nikolai opted for philosophy, and Kirill decided on comparative literature. In this system the external students received their instruction by post, sent in their answers to questions also by post, and twice a year, during the winter and summer vacations, travelled to Moscow to attend a special course of lectures and be examined on the work of the preceding six months. The content of the courses and the examinations were exactly the same as for residential students, and the diploma they received would be equal in academic value.

In the summer of 1939, at the age of twenty, Solzhenitsyn made his first journey north to the capital to register at MIFLI. He and Nikolai had already resolved to take advantage of this visit to see a little more of central Russia, and after completing the formalities and listening to some introductory lectures, they made their way to Kazan on the river Volga and bought themselves an ancient *budarka*—a species of primitive dug-out with high boarded gunwales peculiar to that river and region. In this cumbersome craft they set out for a three-week camping trip through the heartland of Russia, using the Volga as their route. Their "equipment" was minimal. By night they slept on straw in the bottom of the boat, and by day they either rowed or drifted downstream, stopping from time to time to light a campfire and cook a meal or to visit a place of particular interest.[3]

For both of them it seems to have been a high point in their friendship, a sealing of that mystical bond that flourishes between ardent young men in the early years of their maturity. Characteristically, the larger part of their luggage was made up of books. Stimulated by the first lectures at MIFLI and their latest researches, they had passionate discussions on the nature of the state, Lenin's intentions before his early death, Stalin's mistakes, and the future prospects of communism. But it was not just a life of the mind—they responded just as receptively to the physical stimuli of their journey down the great river. Solzhenitsyn was deeply impressed by the scenery of this part of Russia and felt the first stirrings of dissatisfaction with the hot, dusty, featureless South. Here, he felt, was the real Russia, and here he was on the broad mother of Russian rivers, with its high, rocky bank to the east and its low, marshy meadows stretching away to the west, so much hymned in Russian literature and folklore. He drank in its sights and sounds: steamers, launches, tugs, and barges sailing up and down, old men and boys fishing from the banks, primeval virgin forest alternating with grassy steppe, wild flowers and wild strawberries, mushrooms and fruits, with the occasional glimpse of a grey dome or a cluster of houses lying farther back. Awaking sometimes in the chilly dawn, dusted with hoar-frost, they would leap naked into the Volga to swim, then race and wrestle on the shore to get dry and warm, revelling in the solitude and their youthful strength and vitality.[4]

The enchantment of this voyage was to remain with Solzhenitsyn for the rest of his life, but other experiences along the way disturbed and saddened him. The two friends had with them a basic supply of dry biscuits and potatoes, expecting to augment it with food purchased from villages on the way. But the Russian village, about which they had read so much in the Russian classics, had undergone a dramatic transformation since the days of Turgenev, Tolstoy, and Chekhov, a transformation that was later to be described in Solzhenitsyn's autobiographical poem, *The Way*. When the two friends enter a village in chapter 1 of the poem, they find only a shabby travesty of a village there, with decaying, dilapidated houses and a general air of desolation and neglect. Loudspeakers blare trite propaganda jingles, and the *selpo*, or village consumer co-operative, displays row upon row of forlornly empty shelves. Passing a fly-blown copy of *Pravda* enclosed in a glass case on the wall, the friends enter the village "tea-shop," filled with alcohol fumes and the smoke of hand-rolled cigarettes. "No tea," they are told by the man behind the counter and are offered vodka instead, which they refuse. All they can find in the way of food is a bucketful of apples, which they purchase for a few copecks.

The village had been devastated by collectivization, but they were too young and too loyal to grasp the true reasons for the desolation, just as they missed the significance of certain odd adventures that befell them on the way. At a place called Krasnaya Glinka one evening, while moored by the bank, they were suddenly surrounded by a platoon of armed guards and tracker dogs. The guards were searching for a pair of escapees and had mistaken the two boys for their quarry. With a volley of curses they ordered the bewildered students to move on, before they dashed away in further pursuit. On another occasion the boys passed an open launch crammed with prisoners handcuffed to one another, who smiled strangely diffidently at them as they passed; and near Zhiguli they saw crowds of ragged men with picks and shovels digging foundations for a power station. They were unprepared for these things and unable to make much sense of them, so they soon faded from memory—"untypical" incidents, like the nocturnal arrests in Rostov, that were hardly to be connected with their philosophical objections to Stalinism.

In Kuibyshev the friends sold their dug-out for 200 rubles, only 25 rubles less than they had paid for it, and congratulated themselves on a bargain voyage. But they still had to get themselves back to Rostov. They were loaded down with gear from their camping holiday, and on top of everything else, Nikolai had bought a big, old-fashioned loudspeaker cone, without a cabinet, to take back with him—they were unobtainable at home. Casting one glance at the enormous crowds waiting to be allowed onto the platform at Kuibyshev, Solzhenitsyn hit on a scheme for boarding the train first. He picked up the loudspeaker cone, marched importantly to the staff entrance, pointed at the cone, and motioned to the railwaywoman on duty to let them through: "I'll just put this on board and then I'm finished." Taken in by his confidence, she let him through, and he was able to grab two luggage racks, on which they slept all the way home.[5] This incident was to inspire the last scene in *Cancer Ward*, in which Oleg Kostoglotov employs a similar trick to secure himself a luggage rack and rides off to an unknown destination. They returned well pleased with themselves and eager to start on their fourth and final year at the university.

Solzhenitsyn had an additional reason to be pleased at returning to Rostov, unknown to Nikolai. In fact, the existence of this secret between them may have been a source of embarrassment. For Solzhenitsyn had recently decided to abandon his "girl-less bachelor youth" and become engaged. The girl in question was a close friend of Nikolai's, and it appears that Nikolai's own feelings towards her, insofar as they could be divined beneath his imperturbable exterior, were by no means neutral.

It had been at the beginning of their first year in the university that Nikolai had introduced Solzhenitsyn to his new friend, a full-lipped, chest-nut-haired, self-confident girl named Natalia Reshetovskaya. In her memoirs Reshetovskaya has described this first meeting of theirs, in September 1936, as follows: "A tall, skinny youth came bounding up the staircase two steps at a time. He explained that he was attending some lectures in our chemistry department. His speech was extremely rapid, and everything else about him seemed rapid and headlong. His features, too, were very mobile."[6] He had made an impression on her, and Solzhenitsyn, for his part, had noticed her too, though he later remarked that he had been able to see only half her face at the time: the other half was obscured by an enormous apple.

Natalia was soon drawn closer into the circle of the three musketeers, and in November she invited them to her home for a party. She was an excellent pianist, and Solzhenitsyn took the opportunity to praise her playing as he poured water from a jug for her to wash her hands before supper. Ten days later there was a second party, given by Liulia Oster, another student friend, at which Solzhenitsyn again paid her a great deal of attention. Look-ing back on this evening twenty years later, he recalled that this was the evening "when I fell utterly and irrevocably in love with you: the party at Liulia's, you in a white silk dress and I (playing a game, joking, but also in earnest) on my knees before you. The next day was a holiday—I walked along the Pushkin Boulevard head over heels in love."[7]

Solzhenitsyn did not voice his feelings at the time, perhaps out of loyalty to Nikolai. Nikolai sat next to her at chemistry lectures, shared notes with her, taught her to play chess and ride a bicycle. On the boys' first cycling tour of the Caucasus, it was Nikolai who had written letters to Natalia. But in the winter of 1937 the scales had tipped decisively in Solzhenitsyn's favour. The university started a course of dancing classes, and the only members of their group to sign up were Solzhenitsyn and Natalia. Naturally, they became dancing partners and subsequently went as a pair to the theatre, cinema, and parties.

In the summer of 1938, on 2 July, Solzhenitsyn had made his first pro-posal. Natalia was taken aback and did not know what to say. Her concept of love and marriage seems to have been the conventional one of an over-whelming romantic passion, absorbing the entire personality and blotting out the rest of the world. Was that what she felt for Solzhenitsyn? "My life was so varied in those days that it seemed Sanya could not take the place of everything else, even though he already meant a great deal to me. For me the world did not consist of him alone."[8] Her first reaction was to draw back, which led to a period of coolness between them. But separation was also unendurable, and they were quickly reconciled again, though he was still without an answer to his question.

Natalia's family and social circumstances were very similar to Solzhen-itsyn's. Like him and his friends a virtual orphan (someone should one day write a thesis on the impact of orphanhood on Soviet society after the Revolution), she was three-quarters Cossack, with a touch of the Turk, to judge by her maternal grandfather's surname—Turkin. Turkin, a Don Cossack, had married a Polish Catholic who subsequently converted to Orthodoxy and opened a music school in the Don Cossack "capital" of Novocherkassk. Their daughter (and Natalia's mother) Maria married a well-to-do young Cossack named Alexei Reshetovsky, whose family was very prominent in Novocherkassk. Both families were members of the educated stratum that formed the backbone of the bureaucratic and service class of Cossackdom before the Revolution. More parochial and patriarchal, less liberal and cosmopolitan, than the intellectuals of Moscow or even Rostov, they nonetheless took a serious interest in politics and the arts and sought a liberal education for their children. Maria as well as her two sisters had been to the university in Moscow.

Natalia was her parents' only surviving child. Before her there had been twins, but they had been born prematurely and had died in infancy. Her father, Alexei, had served as a Cossack officer in the First World War and had fought on the side of the Whites during the Civil War. After the Whites' defeat in November 1919, he had fled abroad with the remnants of the Volunteer Army. Natalia had been ten months old at the time and had never known her father—in this her experience was identical with Solzhenitsyn's.

Had it not been for her tiny baby and the sudden illness and death of her widowed mother, Maria Reshetovskaya would probably have followed her husband abroad—she was a strong-willed, capable, and energetic woman who would have had no qualms about making the journey. But she had felt that her first duty was to her family, and so she had stayed in Novocherkassk until it was too late. From then on, she had been obliged to make her own way in the world. Luckily, she had already worked as a private tutor before the war, and for some years she was able to teach, notably in a reform school in Rostov, where she had moved at the beginning of the twenties. In time she had retrained as a bookkeeper. Meanwhile, she had been joined in Rostov by her former husband's three unmarried sisters—Alexandra ("Shura"), Nina, and Manya.[9]

When Solzhenitsyn met Natalia, he had thus found her living in a flat with four middle-aged ladies, three of them maiden aunts. Naturally, she was the darling of this all-female ménage, always in the centre of the spotlight and the object of much fuss and attention. Her mother and aunts looked after the shopping, cooking, and housework and liked to pamper her whenever they could. Aunt Nina in particular used to sew her pretty dresses and accessories, so that in the austere world of the Soviet thirties, Natalia stood out as exceptionally well-groomed and well-dressed. But she was not emptyheaded. She had inherited the family talent for music (her mother was musical too) and spent long hours every week practising the piano. Aunt Nina and her mother were both well-read, and her mother wrote children's verse and stories in her spare time (and sometimes children's plays that she and the aunts would perform with Natalia). Aunt Nina, in addition, had for many years been a schoolmistress of the traditional kind, and was apt to remind Natalia to sit and stand straight (as a child Natalia had been obliged to walk with a ruler down her back to keep it erect), mind her manners, eat properly, and behave like a young lady.[10]

Solzhenitsyn was evidently much attracted by the elegance, femininity, and social poise of Natalia and her family, but she was not the only eligible girl on his horizon at this time. There was another girl, nicknamed "Little Gipsy," to whom he wrote poems and about whom he later wrote a short story (also called "Little Gipsy"), though none of these works were ever published.[11] He still has a photograph of her in his family album—a pretty, smiling face with brushed-back dark hair and brooding eyes. Other photographs show him dancing with her at a student picnic in April 1938—well after the date when he is supposed to have fallen in love with Natalia—to music from a hand-wound gramophone nestling in the grass, and posing with his arm round her for a group picture at the same spot. In both photographs he appears to be holding her more tightly than she would like, and she is inclining her head away smilingly, as if to say, you think you've got me, but you haven't. Recently, after the problems of his first marriage, Solzhenitsyn was tempted to muse on whether he would have done better to marry the little gipsy. She was evidently simpler and more direct than Natalia Reshetovskaya. But it is by no means certain that she would have agreed, at least if the evidence of the photographs is to be believed: Solzhenitsyn appears keener than she does.

In the end it was Natalia he gave his preference to, and it is not difficult to imagine why. She was physically beautiful and knew how to dress to make the most of her charms. She had social graces and good manners, qualities to which the young would-be revolutionary was by no means indifferent. Her talent for music and her interest in the arts coincided with his views on what a wife should be like. And last but not least, Natalia seems to have been happy to play up to his high-flown literary airs, flattered and intrigued by his seductive fantasies about their future life together, and only too eager to fulfill the roles he allotted her in his imagination. This romantic image of "the writer's wife and inspiration" and their conflicting interpretations of what it meant were to feature prominently in the drama of their final rupture and divorce thirty years later. In her memoirs, written after that episode in a spirit of self-vindication, she captures some of that pink haze through which both seem to have viewed their relationship: "That very same evening Sanya decided to write a historical novel. And the following day, when he was mulling over his project, I appeared to him as one of the heroines, to bear the lilting name of Lucy Olkhovskaya."[12]

Solzhenitsyn undoubtedly had plans for her in real life, and like all his schemes they were quite clear and definite. After one of several lovers' tiffs, he wrote her a long letter about them, and also about some of the problems that might arise to get in the way. According to Reshetovskaya:

He wrote that he could not conceive of me in the future other than as his wife, On the other hand, he feared that this might interfere with his main goal in life. To achieve the success he wanted, and which he counted on, he had to finish MIFLI as quickly as possible after graduating from the university. Meanwhile, I had to finish the conservatory. This in itself would make rigorous demands on our time. But "time could be jeopardized" by the myriad trivia that were an inevitable part of family life. These trivia could ruin us before we had a chance to "spread our wings." Time! This one word summed up the basic obstacle to our immediate marriage. Sanya could see no way out of this dilemma, and that was why he, too, was suffering.[13]

Reshetovskaya mentions one other obstacle that tormented Solzhenitsyn at this time: the "pleasant unpleasant consequence" of having a child. His views on this were quite uncompromising—and have remained so to this day, as he explained in 1977.

I never wanted to have children. I realized that they would be a distraction. To have small children when you are in your twenties and thirties is to have serious demands made upon you and takes away a part of your life. Because you yourself haven't accomplished anything yet, but you've got to start putting things into your children, you've got to devote all your strength and endeavours to them, that's quite clear. . . . In my youth I was terribly afraid of having a child, and that made me very careful. And later I never wanted children either.[14]

It was as if marriage, for the young Solzhenitsyn, was almost a chore, an inevitable hurdle that somehow had to be taken in one's stride, without causing too much distraction, before resuming one's momentum. And indeed, that is how it worked out.

The decision to marry was taken in the spring of 1939, shortly before Solzhenitsyn's departure for Moscow to study at MIFLI, on the understanding that the wedding would take place one year later. One of the reasons for this delay may have been Solzhenitsyn's plea for time—he obviously had no intention of changing his ways or his work patterns for the sake of marriage and was apparently hoping to accomplish the matter with as little disruption to his plans as possible. Another reason was economic. Neither of them had money to rent a separate room or a flat; and there was no extra space in their respective homes and no immediate prospect of any change. They might, of course, have chosen to marry and live apart, especially since they both took the old-fashioned view (Natalia more strongly than Solzhenitsyn) that intimacy before marriage was out of the question, but the idea seems to have struck both of them as untenable.

And so they remained a conventional courting couple throughout the winter of 1939–40, or rather, not quite conventional, as Natalia later indicated in her memoirs, where she offers an intriguing glimpse of Solzhenitsyn's eccentric wooing. Obsessed with his studies and the need not to waste a single precious minute, he would invariably set the time for their meetings

at 10 p.m.—the hour when the library closed. It was not unknown for Nikolai Vitkevich, his vanquished rival, to come into the reading-room at five to
ten and announce to Solzhenitsyn, "Natasha's downstairs. Aren't you going
to go down to her?" "Not yet. I've got five more minutes to go." On their
way to the theatre or a concert, Solzhenitsyn would invariably take out a set
of index cards and ask her to test him on historical dates, Latin vocabulary,
or some other subject he was studying. Standing at the trolleybus stop, waiting for a meal, or queuing to get in somewhere, he would get the cards out
again, anxious to make the most of every available scrap of time.[15]

The marriage eventually took place on 27 April 1940, when they were
both still only twenty-one years old, a spare, informal affair without fuss or
ceremony. On a warm, windy spring day, they simply went to the city registry office and registered their marriage, informing not a soul. The only incident to enliven the occasion occurred when they signed the register. The pen
provided for this purpose was an ancient quill. Natalia dipped it in the inkwell
with a vigorous flourish, but caught the nib on the side as she attempted to
withdraw it. The pen flew out of her hand, somersaulted in mid-air and
landed on Solzhenitsyn's forehead, depositing a large blot. "It was an omen,"
he said, not altogether jokingly, when describing the incident years later.[16]
On that same day he gave his bride a signed photograph of himself with an
inscription on the back: "Will you, under all circumstances, love the man to
whom you once joined your life?"[17]

The honeymoon was to be spent that summer in Moscow. A few days
after the ceremony, Natalia, together with Nikolai and some of the other
chemistry students, departed for Moscow to do some practical work at the
National Institute for Science and Research. Solzhenitsyn was to follow on
18 June in order to take the half-yearly MIFLI examinations. After that they
would have their honeymoon and inform their families of the marriage.

In Moscow, Natalia stayed with Veronica Turkina, an aunt who was
living with her fourteen-year-old daughter, also Veronica, on Patriarch's Ponds
in the suburbs. Solzhenitsyn, when he arrived, stayed in one of the MIFLI
hostels in the city suburbs. Their marriage was still a secret, and they could
meet only in the intervals between her study sessions and his examinations,
or during evenings and weekends, using their time to tour Moscow and see
the sights, or go strolling and boating in the Moscow parks. The younger
Veronica, who now lives in America, remembers them as an earnest, somewhat humourless and strait-laced provincial couple. Solzhenitsyn, tall and
thin, with a mop of fair hair flying in the wind, wore his shirt hanging outside his trousers and struck her as self-absorbed, impatient, and brusque,
with little time or attention to spare for a pigtailed schoolgirl. Natalia, by
contrast, was charming and attentive, genuinely delighted to be in Moscow
and to be making the acquaintance of an aunt and cousin whom she was
seeing for the first time. Maria, her mother, had talked endlessly and with
great admiration about her Moscow relations, and she was delighted to be
among them.

The younger Veronica was particularly impressed with Natalia's extensive collection of dresses, blouses, and skirts, all made for her by her aunts. Natalia's delight in dressing up and looking her best was infectious. At twenty-one she was indeed in the full bloom of womanhood, freshly married, intensely happy, and sparkling with vitality and high spirits. A studio photograph taken of the young couple shows how pretty she was, with her soft round face, apple cheeks, full lips, and those high cheekbones that are the hallmark of Slavonic beauty. A soft silk blouse, open at the neck, added to her allure.

The cloudless bliss of these weeks in Moscow was temporarily marred when Natalia caught a chill and found her neck glands painfully swollen. Advice was sought from another relative, Elizaveta Polkovnikova, a doctor and neuropathologist, who immediately pronounced the illness serious—too serious to be dealt with in a normal Soviet hospital, where the treatment would be slapdash and unreliable. Nor did she want to upset Natalia's mother with the rigmarole of form-filling that hospital admission entailed. She therefore cleared an entire room of furniture, turned it into an impromptu operating theatre, and used her influence to persuade a surgeon to come and operate *in situ*. He removed the offending glands while Solzhenitsyn sat nervously in the adjoining room. The whole operation was highly irregular, of course, but not untypical of what could be achieved by people with influence in the right quarters.[18]

The member of the family who made the deepest impression on Solzhenitsyn and Natalia was Natalia's uncle, Valentin Turkin, a distinguished film historian and critic, and one of the founders of the Moscow Institute of Cinematography, where he held the first chair in script-writing. He had separated from Veronica four months after the birth of their daughter and now lived a short distance away with his second wife. Turkin fascinated the provincial Solzhenitsyn with his metropolitan sophistication and ready erudition, while Natalia, who had heard all about her famous uncle from her mother, was awed and flattered to be able to spend time in his company.

Turkin had a dacha in the district of Tarusa, a favourite country resort of Moscow's intellectuals, about seventy miles south of the capital. He habitually spent the summer there and suggested to the young couple that they might find this a congenial spot in which to pass their honeymoon. They gladly accepted the suggestion and found themselves a modest cabin on the fringe of the forest, into which they moved in July. Tarusa was filled in the summer season with members of the Moscow intelligentsia, especially from the film and theatre worlds, and Solzhenitsyn was amazed by the opulence in which they lived. Trunk-loads of bacon, sugar, and coffee beans had been shipped down from Moscow, together with cases of wine and vodka. There were barrels of paraffin for the cooking stoves, larders were lavishly stocked with every sort of delicacy, and basement iceboxes were filled to bursting with imported fresh meat, fruit, and vegetables, in stark contrast to the empty village co-operative shop and the forlorn market, where limp mushrooms were the only vegetable you could buy.

Echoes of this privileged life-style were to find their way many years later into Solzhenitsyn's first published play, *Candle in the Wind*, in which the character of the epicurean music professor, Maurice Craig, is based on Turkin and in which the external details of Craig's relations with his first wife and his estranged daughter mirror those between Turkin and the two Veronicas. There is a description of Tarusa in *The Way* as well, evoking the leisurely life of the summer visitors, their Chekhovian garden parties, the tinkle of tea glasses on shaded verandas, the nostalgic twanging of guitars, and endless indolent conversations about the theatre, cinema, and literature.

The Solzhenitsyns' cabin was more spartan than the comfortable dachas of the Moscow intellectuals and was situated at the very edge of the settlement, among the trees. As hard-up young students, they were obliged to do their own shopping in the shabby market and fly-blown village shop, which did not allow for much variety. Natalia, wearing a brand-new, dazzlingly white apron, fumblingly prepared their frugal meals on a traditional peasant stove, savouring the unaccustomed role of housewife and cook. Solzhenitsyn, characteristically, was preoccupied with his MIFLI syllabus, which he was studying in advance of the coming term, breaking off occasionally to read his wife snippets from *War and Peace* or the poems of Esenin. His particular preoccupation at this time was history, especially the reforms of Peter the Great, which did not appeal to him at all. He later wrote in *The Way* about his feelings towards Peter and his attitude to the reforms:

> It's obvious—PROGRESS! But I'm a heretic:
> By what right was our country spurred into line?
> Let's make a note, I'll call it the *Swedish thesis:*
> "Was the cost of Poltava truly justified?"
> Two hundred years of conquest, conquest, conquest,
> Destruction and strife, wars with their endless ruin—
> Yet the Swedes we crushed on the Vorskla
> Have grown fat as capons.[19]

Was this Irina's teaching coming back to haunt him? Lovers of the old Russian way of life and the traditional forms of the Russian church had never forgiven Peter his brutal treatment of them. Solzhenitsyn was now a Marxist, presumably an atheist, and the Marxists endorsed Peter's reforms, but Solzhenitsyn's antipathy to Peter was deep-rooted and was to stay with him throughout his life.

In addition to history, Solzhenitsyn was still much preoccupied with Marxism—he must be one of the few bridegrooms in history to have taken *Das Kapital* on his honeymoon (and to have read it). Awaking drowsily in the mornings to find the space in the bed beside her empty, Natalia would shuffle out onto the veranda to see her spouse head down over an annotated copy of Marx's masterpiece. In *The Way* Solzhenitsyn evokes his bride's understandable perplexity at his neglect of her, but remarks that he could not help it. His faith in Marxism was burning brighter than ever. He and his friends were "Dukhobors* . . . rebels . . . apostles . . . Bolsheviks . . . And I? I believe to the marrow of my bones. I suffer no doubts, no hesitations—life is crystal clear to me." And later he added, striking an unexpected Mayakovskian note, "It is History's Sorrow, the Grief of our Era, that I carry about with me like an anathema."[20]

Solzhenitsyn was helped in getting through his reading programme by a bout of malaria, which kept him indoors for much of the time or restricted him to the shade. Unlike the other holiday-makers, he and Natalia neither sunbathed nor swam in the nearby river Oka. Perhaps it was the illness that persuaded them to extend their stay in Tarusa into the early autumn, when the leaves were beginning to turn yellow. For Solzhenitsyn this central-Russian countryside was a revelation, confirming the shock of recognition he had experienced on his trip down the Volga and intensifying his vivid impression that he had been "born in the wrong place" (but had now "found himself"). From Tarusa, Natalia informed her family of her marriage. Solzhenitsyn had already written his mother from Moscow, and Taissia had informed the rest of the family. Solzhenitsyn's two aunts, Irina and Maria in Georgievsk, were shocked by the secrecy of the marriage. Since it had not taken place in church, they flatly refused to recognize it, and that response only served to increase Solzhenitsyn's sense of alienation from his relatives. It may also explain Irina's curious reference to Natalia as a "mistress," in her interview with *Stern* magazine in 1971, although she there links it, somewhat illogically, with the idea of wives who did not join their husbands in exile. Another person who appears to have been upset by the news was Nikolai, who had not been let into the secret before and whose own hopes were now dashed forever.[21]

On the rail journey back to Rostov there occurred an incident that Solzhenitsyn would have forgotten had his later life turned out differently. Their train halted in a siding next to another that didn't look quite right—neither a passenger train like theirs nor a freight train either. Peering through his window he caught a glimpse of compartments crowded with shaven-headed troglodytes looking as if they had come from a different planet. Their eyes were deep-sunken, their faces distorted, their features looked semi-human, and they gazed back at him with such brazen insolence that he was obliged to avert his eyes. They were convicts being transported from one labour camp to another, but Solzhenitsyn knew nothing of such things at twenty-one. The train started again and they disappeared. The whole thing had lasted only a minute or two.[22] Like the incidents on the Volga, it quickly faded to the back of his mind, only to be recalled long afterwards, when he himself had changed trains (and places).

Now that they were officially man and wife, Solzhenitsyn and Natalia

* Literally "spirit wrestlers," a schismatic sect that first appeared in the Orthodox church in the eighteenth century and achieved great prominence in the closing years of the nineteenth century when their cause was espoused by Tolstoy. Many of them subsequently emigrated to Canada.

at last moved in together. They found a room on Chekhov Lane. Their life there has been described by Natalia in her memoirs.

> The room we found on Chekhov Lane was small but comfortable, even though we had to put up with a cantankerous landlady. It was convenient because we lived quite close to my mother and aunts and to Sanya's mother. Also, his two favourite reading-rooms were nearby, the so-called "Heavy" (Institute of Heavy Industry) and the "Thinky" (Party Education Club), the latter so named because he found it a particularly fruitful place in which to think.
>
> During the first year of our marriage . . . we were both frantically busy. After an early breakfast, we would run to the university, or, if there were no classes, Sanya would leave for the library, while I stayed at home to prepare for my last special subjects or write reports on my course work.
>
> On weekdays we would meet later, at my mother's home, where we had lunch on the dot of three. Lunch was supposed to be exactly on time, not a minute late. If it was nonetheless delayed, Sanya would take out his familiar little cards and get me to test him.
>
> After lunch, I would sit down at the piano, while my husband ran off to the reading-room again. Back home he would continue studying, often enough until two in the morning, until he gave himself a headache. . . . [23]

Relations between Solzhenitsyn's and Natalia's mothers seem to have been quite close during this period. Taissia had gone to see Maria Reshetovskaya immediately after receiving Solzhenitsyn's letter from Moscow informing her of the marriage, and the two of them had talked for four hours on that first occasion. They had much in common as widows struggling to bring up only children, and it turned out that Maria knew Taissia's birthplace; she had once worked as a private tutor for a wealthy horse-breeder called Nikolenko, who had been a neighbour of the Shcherbaks in the Kuban. The two women continued to visit one another after the young couple came back from Moscow, and took turns in feeding them, for neither of the newly-weds was prepared to cook.

During this last year at the university, Solzhenitsyn was considerably better off than in previous years; he had been awarded one of the newly instituted Stalin scholarships for outstanding achievement.* Only three were given to the Faculty of Physics and Mathematics (and only four more in the entire university), and they carried a stipend two and a half times greater than the usual grant. They were a reward not only for academic performance (Solzhenitsyn had straight 5s) but also for social and political activism in the Komsomol.

Solzhenitsyn's most notable achievement in this field was his success in editing the students' wall newspaper and in transforming it from a dull propaganda sheet into an immensely popular and eagerly read publication. At the University of Rostov responsibility for the wall newspapers was assigned

---

* It was presumably the increased income from the Stalin scholarship that enabled Solzhenitsyn and Natalia to marry.

to the appropriate Party or Komsomol committee, and over the years they had become meaningless rehearsals of ritual propaganda. They were usually left on the walls for months at a time, until they became wrinkled and yellowed and covered by cobwebs. Changes were made twice a year, on 1 May and 7 November (the anniversary of the October Revolution), but even when they were fresh they did not attract much notice.

Bursting with enthusiasm, commitment, and above all literary talent, Solzhenitsyn was determined to change all that. He gathered round himself a group of enthusiastic Komsomol activists and introduced the idea of changing the wall newspaper every week, instead of every six months. Each Monday a fresh newspaper was hung up on the wall. Real reporting of faculty and student activities was begun, and there was a large humour section pulling the legs of students and faculty members alike. Every Monday crowds of staff and students would gather round to read the latest news and find out who were the targets this week. Solzhenitsyn kept it up for a whole year. It was a considerable strain on top of his double degree course and his writing, but he seems to have borne the burden gladly and to have much appreciated the praise the newspaper drew both from the establishment and from fellow students.[24]*

In every respect he seemed on the threshold of a brilliant career. Already a junior member of the local establishment, he could expect an easy transition from Komsomol to full Party membership, with all the privileges that went with it. As an outstanding student, he could look forward to the pick of the best jobs available (it must have been about now that he was invited to apply for training with the security police, who dwelt at the very heart of the Soviet political system). He surely felt he had the world at his feet.

And yet, though he seemed outwardly orthodox and a model example of the "October generation," glad to march in the street parades and willing to participate in the ballyhoo of Party gatherings, this picture contained hidden flaws, hidden currents flowing in quite a different direction. For instance, his passionate belief in Marxism-Leninism and his ardent idealism were already fast becoming anachronisms in Soviet society. The time for revolutionary optimism had been the twenties. By the late thirties, within the Party, Stalin had crushed this spirit almost out of existence and ushered in a general attitude of cynicism, opportunism, and bureaucratic conservatism. To be a genuine Marxist revolutionary was already to be out of step, as both Solzhenitsyn and Vitkevich had sensed in their hostility to Stalin. But they were not experienced enough to suspect the true depth of the corruption of Soviet society or to realize the true danger they were in when they put their heads together, as students, to draw up not only a plan for future action within the Party but also—ultimate heresy—a political programme. They believed, in their innocence, that it was still a matter of argument and persuasion, that the country's course could be altered by rational debate. They hoped to turn the

* It appears that at the height of Solzhenitsyn's success, perhaps after he won the Stalin scholarship, he was the subject of a short film.

Party back to Leninist purity, and they plotted how to do this. Fortunately they showed their projects to no one—their dreams remained private to themselves—but they were headed, had they known it, in quite a different direction from what they supposed.

In the realm of work and a career, Solzhenitsyn also proved himself a kind of misfit. A first-class degree in mathematics and physics opened innumerable avenues to him, particularly in Stalin's beloved industrial sector. But he had already decided that he would not take that path, and when the choice had to be made, he was to opt for the modest post of a village schoolteacher, in preference to the glittering prizes that were within his reach.

What he truly held dear were his MIFLI studies and the secret occupation that really set him apart—his writing—though Solzhenitsyn seems to have conceived of his career in entirely orthodox terms. If he kept his activities secret and was afraid to reveal them to any but intimate friends, it was the hesitancy of the tyro and the bashfulness of the beginner that held him back. His literary idols were the standard Soviet models—Maxim Gorky, Lev Tolstoy, and the classical realists of the nineteenth century. His planned historical epic would show the triumph of the Russian Revolution, just as Tolstoy's epic had shown the triumph of Russian arms. But to become a writer you first had to write something worthwhile. There was no straight career path from university to a seat in the Writers' Union.

At the time of his marriage Solzhenitsyn seems to have been as much absorbed in his philosophical and political studies as in his writing. The only known fruits of these studies is one exercise book labelled *Remarks on Dialectical Materialism and Art*, whereas some purely political notes that he made at this time have since disappeared. Among the stories he was occupied with were "The Little Gipsy," inspired by the girl of that nickname, which he wrote in 1938; "The Nikolayevskys," written in 1939; "The River Pointsmen," apparently based on his experiences during his voyage down the Volga, written in 1940; and "Mission Abroad," a conventional tale about a Soviet diplomat outwitting bourgeois statesmen in Western Europe, which was completed in February 1941. He also wrote quite a bit of poetry that found its way into the exercise books containing his *Juvenile Verse*.[25]

In June 1941, having completed his physics and mathematics degree at the University of Rostov, Solzhenitsyn travelled to Moscow once more to take his second-year examinations at MIFLI. According to Reshetovskaya, he still nursed his old dream of living there: "Sanya drew alluring pictures for his wife of how things were going to be. They would work for the coming year in a village school (he would study village customs at the same time) and then they would try to move to Moscow. He would finish MIFLI, she would study at the Moscow Conservatory."[26] Quite how this fitted in with Solzhenitsyn's obligations to his mother is not clear. Possibly, he counted on taking her with them, although her tuberculosis was fairly advanced by now (in December 1940 she had been to the Crimea for treatment). But get to Moscow he must, particularly after his first, intoxicating experiences of it last year and this. He also associated his desire to go there with problems he was experiencing in his writing.

> If [my mother] had gone to Moscow, my youth would have been spent there and things would have been very different. Rostov, of course, delayed my linguistic development, because the language in Rostov is horrible. It was impossible to acquire proper Russian there. It was by a miracle and thanks to my own hard work that I eventually learnt it. . . . When I first began writing as a boy, I experienced great difficulties with the language. I felt that somehow it was all stiff and unmalleable in my hands. It was too clumsy.[27]

Not for the last time Solzhenitsyn's plans were shattered by external events. On the very day of his arrival in Moscow, on 22 June 1941, war was declared between the Soviet Union and Germany. MIFLI was thrown into a state of total confusion, and all thought of examinations was abandoned. Many students went straight home to fetch their draft cards and volunteered on the spot. Solzhenitsyn also rushed to the recruitment office in Moscow, but his card was in Rostov and the bureaucrats were adamant: he must return to Rostov and enlist there. He went to the station, but in the panic and confusion sown by the declaration of war, the railways were in pandemonium. It was several days before he could get onto a train going south, and even then the journey was insufferably slow.

In Rostov he made a second attempt to enlist, indicating his father's old service, the artillery, as the branch of the army in which he desired to serve. But again he was turned away. Thanks to a disorder in the groin that had gone undetected in infancy and never been corrected, he suffered from an abdominal disability that had resulted in a classification of "limited fitness" at his army medical. This disability, though it was later to be one of the causes of his cancer and to threaten his very life, was sufficiently slight at the time as to be hardly noticeable to him, but it was enough to secure him a certificate of disqualification.[28]

He was told to go home and wait for a proper enlistment notice. It never arrived, and after a few weeks of mounting impatience Solzhenitsyn returned to the recruiting office and tried again. But again he was rebuffed—nobody dared disobey the regulations. Seething with frustration, Solzhenitsyn was obliged to return home. It was particularly galling to be rejected at such a time. Virtually all his fellow university graduates had enlisted and had been dispatched for training. Nikolai had gone to an officer-training school and looked all set for a promising military career. Solzhenitsyn, moreover, had not the slightest doubt as to the justice of this war or the necessity of fighting it. Both his patriotic upbringing and his studies in dialectical materialism led to the same inescapable conclusion: this was a just war, Russia was the victim of aggression, her adversary was at once her historic enemy, intent on Russia's humiliation and dismemberment, and the standard-bearer of fascism, communism's mortal enemy.[29] He was equally confident what the result would be. As he later wrote in *The Gulag Archipelago*, "Not for a moment, from the

day the war began, did I doubt that we would conquer the Germans."[30]
Only a year previously, on his honeymoon, he had written an ode on this
very theme, prefiguring a world-wide conflagration and the role that he and
his friends would play in it.

> We were not born to be happy.
> The sick world writhes in pain.
> Inexpressible turbulence looms
> To engulf us! War impends!!
>
> On the eve of this awesome convulsion
> Let them tell us the naked truth,
> The way Vladimir Ilyich Lenin
> Told our fathers sans fear sans ruth:
>
> "Our foe's no coward, not weak, not stupid!"
> He who lies to us is no friend.
> We will die!! Upon our dead bodies
> The Revolution will ascend!!!
>
> From the whirlwind of October
> A generation sprang to life.
> That others may flourish and prosper
> It must make the supreme sacrifice. . . . [31]

The supreme sacrifice was as far away as ever when, in September 1941,
Solzhenitsyn was obliged to move to the Cossack settlement of Morozovsk,
about 180 miles north-east of Rostov and half-way to Stalingrad, to begin
work as a village schoolteacher. His subjects were mathematics and astronomy. Natalia was to teach chemistry and the foundations of Darwinism in
the same village school.

His old urge to make a study of village customs was now pushed aside
by anxiety over the course of the war. The Germans continued to advance
rapidly on all fronts and soon were within hailing distance of Rostov. "Every
day," Solzhenitsyn later wrote of this autumn, "new train-loads of refugees
stopped at the station, on their way to Stalingrad. Refugees filled the market-
place with rumours, terrors, 100-ruble notes that were burning holes in their
pockets and then moved on. They named towns that had surrendered and
that the Informburo, frightened to tell people the truth, would continue to
keep quiet about for some time to come." Nameless fear and disquiet overcame them "like invisible clouds stealing over the milky sky to smother the
small and defenceless moon," and news of the war dominated their lives more
than ever.[32]

Another sombre chord was struck by their chance meeting with some
neighbours in the house where they rented rooms, a childless middle-aged
couple called the Bronevitskys. Despite his obvious intelligence and excellent
qualifications, Bronevitsky inexplicably occupied a lowly post in some local

building enterprise, while his wife worked as a bookkeeper; but the mystery was clarified when, in answer to Solzhenitsyn's cautious questions, Bronevitsky told him his story. It turned out that he was one of the thousands of engineers who had been arrested during the thirties and sent to the newly opened labour camps. He had been in all sorts of prisons and camps but dwelt with passion on only one—the camp of Dzhezkazgan, where the water had been poisoned by copper, the air by industrial fumes, and the life of the prisoners by indiscriminate brutality and murder. His present wife had come out to Dzhezkazgan when a mere slip of a girl to marry him, and then, by some miracle, he had been released. Since their internal passports were marked to show their special status, they were now barred from living in towns and had found refuge in this benighted rural settlement.

The Solzhenitsyns were intrigued by this story but also totally baffled. They did not regard it as significant or typical; it did not shock them or arouse their indignation. When the Bronevitskys in turn asked them about their lives in Rostov, all they could think to tell them about was their school and university studies, dances, amateur theatricals, sporting contests, and so on. The Bronevitskys' questions about arrests and repressions struck them as odd, and they had nothing to say on the subject.

Solzhenitsyn also noticed that when the Bronevitskys discussed the progress of the war, they referred to towns not as having been "surrendered" to the Germans but as "taken," which did not jibe with his own patriotic sentiments at all, just as the Bronevitskys' idiosyncratic view of Soviet society was far removed from his and Natalia's. But none of this disturbed their friendship, and Solzhenitsyn's response was one of slightly incredulous curiosity and interest rather than condemnation. Later, during his army service, he was to try to write a story about this unusual couple, and later still, when he arrived in the camps, he was to meditate once more on their fate and perceive their lives from a vastly altered point of view.[33]

Meanwhile, the German victories merely increased his impatience at his enforced inaction and sharpened his keenness to enlist. In mid-October, the war took a dramatic turn for the worse. Moscow was threatened, the German advance looked irresistible, and on 16 October the Soviet authorities mobilized all available reserves. In the district of Morozovsk virtually every able-bodied man in the place was called to the local recruitment centre, together with all the available horses and carts. Solzhenitsyn went too. Years later he wrote to Natalia, "How difficult it was to leave home on that day . . . but it was only that day that my life began. We never know at the time what is happening to us."[34]

Indeed not. Least of all did he suspect, leaving for war at the age of twenty-two, that it would be fully fifteen years before he returned from that journey.

6

FIGHTING FOR
THE FATHERLAND

SOLZHENITSYN'S MILITARY CAREER began as farce and ended in tragedy.
It began with the seventy-fourth Horse-drawn Transport Battalion of the Stalingrad Army Command, based on the river Buzuluk about 150 miles north-west of Stalingrad. His unit consisted for the most part of elderly and in some cases ailing Don Cossacks from the district of Morozovsk; they had been passed over in earlier mobilizations as too old to serve but now found themselves swept up in a last-ditch scraping of the barrel to strengthen the Soviet rear. To his vast disgust and embarrassment, Solzhenitsyn was pressed into service as a cart-driver and groom, jobs for which he had not the slightest qualification or aptitude. He barely knew one end of a horse from another and quickly became the butt of veteran Cossacks born to the saddle. His sergeant particularly disliked this supercilious young schoolteacher, who had had the effrontery to arrive at the barracks clutching a brief-case, and took every opportunity to humiliate him in front of the others. On one occasion he ordered Solzhenitsyn to pasture all ninety of his platoon's horses alone. Unable even to sit on a horse, Solzhenitsyn knew that once out on the open steppe, he would be powerless to prevent the herd from bolting, and was forced to beg the sergeant to change the punishment to something else. He was set to mucking out the stables, a job with which he soon became extremely familiar.

It was his experiences here that Solzhenitsyn later recalled in *The First Circle*, when he made Gleb Nerzhin ruminate on that favourite abstraction of Russian intellectuals—"the people."

When the war broke out, Nerzhin . . . found himself serving as a driver in a horse-drawn transport unit in the rear, where, dying of shame, clumsy, and awkward, he was obliged to pursue horses around the corral and attempt to head them off or jump on their backs. He had no idea how to ride, he had no idea how to handle harness or a pitchfork, and even the very nails used to bend beneath his hammer, as though in silent mockery of his chronic hamfistedness. And the more desperate his plight became, the louder grew the guffaws of that great unwashed . . . people.[1]

As the weeks and months went by, Solzhenitsyn got to know the horses better and even learned to ride bareback. The Cossacks became reconciled to him. Life was easy, with no drill, no weapons to look after, and no military training of any kind. His evenings were free, he even found time to read. But nothing could compensate for his profound chagrin at being forcibly confined to the rear. On 25 December 1941, he wrote to Natalia, "Today I was shovelling manure and remembered that it was my name-day, which couldn't be more appropriate." And in another letter, characteristically: "One cannot become a great Russian writer, living in the Russia of 1941–43, without having been at the front."[2]

From the very day of his arrival in Buzuluk, his overriding preoccupation was how to get to the front. He wrote application after application, appealed personally to his commanding officer, and sought advice on how to achieve his aim from any superior who would listen. It was all to no avail. But after nearly six months of this frustration, his luck changed. In March 1942 the new commissar* who arrived to join Solzhenitsyn's battalion turned out to be a former student of mathematics at Rostov University. He was sympathetic to Solzhenitsyn's complaints and remembered that he was required to send some sort of packet to the headquarters of the Thirteenth Military District in Stalingrad. He offered to let Solzhenitsyn take it. Once he was there, it would be up to Solzhenitsyn to make inquiries on his own and try to get himself accepted in some capacity.

Solzhenitsyn was delighted and reported to battalion headquarters the next day. His rudimentary groom's uniform, consisting of the stained khaki smock and fustian trousers that had been issued to him upon mobilization, was regarded as totally unsuitable for visiting Stalingrad, and he was hastily kitted out with a regular private's uniform and a voluminous greatcoat, which suited his brief-case better. While waiting outside the office to be given the packet, he attracted the attention of a young tank-corps lieutenant who had been wounded in battle and had somehow ended up in Buzuluk for treatment and convalescence. He explained to Solzhenitsyn that for some reason he was being prevented by the battalion commander from sending a dispatch to Stalingrad reporting his whereabouts, and asked him whether he would take an additional packet and hand it in to the cadre department at headquarters. Solzhenitsyn agreed and on 25 March set off with two packets in his brief-

*Every large unit in the Soviet army had dual leadership: a military commander and a political commissar. The commissars were officially described as the "representatives of the Party and government in the Red Army"; they were charged with watching over the troops' morale and were exclusively responsible for questions of security, political instruction, and the maintenance of a "correct" ideological view of the war's progress.

case. That evening he paid a surprise visit to Natalia in Morozovsk and spent the night there, before departing the next day for Stalingrad to complete his mission. The officers in the cadre department were amazed to hear about the tank lieutenant and peppered Solzhenitsyn with questions. Such was the chaos provoked by the Russian retreat that communications had been badly disrupted. They had had no idea of the lieutenant's whereabouts and were delighted to have news of him.

Taking advantage of their goodwill, Solzhenitsyn asked the officers whether they could direct him to the cadre department for the artillery. A captain pointed the way, and Solzhenitsyn decided to barge straight in and try his luck. He told them he had a university degree and wanted to join the artillery. His mind was inalterably fixed on the artillery, because of his father's example and because he felt that his mathematical training suited him for it.* To his relief, the staff in the artillery-cadre office did not seem affronted by this direct assault, or even unduly surprised. After examining his papers, they informed him that they would post him to a course for battery commanders due to begin shortly in the town of Semyonov. Within days, Solzhenitsyn, great coat, and brief-case (containing the necessary papers) were on their way to the training college.[3]

Travelling in war-torn Russia in the spring of 1942 was a nightmare. The German armies had advanced nearly a thousand miles into Russian territory and were holding a line stretching from Rzhev in the north to the Crimea in the south. Their soldiers had fought in the suburbs of Leningrad and Moscow; their advance units had penetrated to the Black Sea and were threatening Rostov (they had already occupied the city briefly in November 1941 but had been driven out again after a week) and were bunching in the south to commence the great push against Stalingrad. Communications had been seriously dislocated both by the cutting off of numerous road and rail routes and by the hundreds of thousands of refugees and retreating troops streaming eastwards.

It took Solzhenitsyn more than two weeks to travel the few hundred miles to Semyonov, and something of what he saw and experienced on that journey was later incorporated into his short story (written in 1962) "Incident at Krechetovka Station." The story is set a few months earlier, in October 1941, during a period of torrential rain that temporarily halted the German advance. At that time Solzhenitsyn was still in Morozovsk, and the scenes of hungry retreating soldiers and marauding refugees in the story appear to reflect what he had seen during those panicky weeks when Moscow itself seemed about to fall and he destined to remain a civilian indefinitely. Lieutenant Zotov, the story's hero, is shown in charge of transport arrangements at a small provincial station in the region of Voronezh, about 300 miles south of Moscow, not far behind the shifting Russian front line, through which thousands of soldiers are pouring as they retreat eastwards.

---

*Tolstoy, as a matter of interest, was also a lieutenant in the artillery.

Solzhenitsyn portrays Zotov very much as he himself was at that time, overwhelmed by the bold spirits of men who had been under fire and self-consciously envious of their front-line experience. "He was shy of them. . . . He was ashamed of his position as commander of a unit at the rear. He envied them and was even prepared, he thought, to adopt some of their unscrupulousness, if only he could have known battles, been under fire, and made difficult river crossings, just as they had." Solzhenitsyn endows Zotov with his own desperate concern for the safety and honour of his country and an idealistic urge to sacrifice himself for it. And he lends Zotov his consternation at the Soviet Union's disastrous start to the war.

> The progress of the war was so weirdly incomprehensible to him that Zotov felt like howling aloud in sheer despair. It was impossible to establish the line of the front from the bulletins put out by the Informburo, you couldn't tell who had Kharkov or who held Kaluga. . . . But . . . why was the war going this way? Not only was no revolution taking place in Europe, and not only had we failed to break through with minor losses against any possible combination of aggressors, but it was now a question of how much longer things were going to go on like this. . . . was Moscow to be surrendered? Not only was he frightened to ask such a question aloud (to ask aloud was dangerous), but he even dreaded asking it of himself, although, in fact, despite all his efforts to the contrary, he could think of nothing else.[4]

The true subject of "Krechetovka" is not the war but Stalinism, and the handing over of an innocent man to the NKVD on mere suspicion. But it does deal indirectly with the causes for the poor Soviet military performance, commencing with the 1937–39 purge of the Red Army, proceeding to its deliberate politicization by the introduction of the political commissars, and ending with Stalin's personal ineptitude and inadequacies as commander-in-chief. By the time Solzhenitsyn was on his way to training school, it was an open secret that the Soviet armies, despite their superiority in numbers, had collapsed ignominiously in the face of the German onslaught. The air force, with a numerical superiority of five to one in aircraft, had been destroyed on the ground. Only outside Moscow and Leningrad had a real stand been taken, and even then most of the government had abandoned the capital in panic; the siege of Leningrad was to result in nearly a million Soviet citizens dying of starvation. Solzhenitsyn, already hostile to Stalin in peace-time, was quick to perceive his hand in the country's unpreparedness and poor military performance; and though the colours are undoubtedly laid on more thickly in "Krechetovka" than they were perceived by him at the time, there is little doubt that this new evidence of Stalin's ineptitude added to his growing reserve of contempt for Lenin's successor. Similarly, he was disgusted by Stalin's bombast about a "revolution in Europe" and the Soviet Union's ability to repel "any combination of aggressors," as well as by the cult of adulation and sycophancy that made it a crime "even to harbour such thoughts." As he wrote in "Krechetovka," "It was defamatory, it was an insult to the omniscient and omnipotent Father and Teacher—who was always at his post, who foresaw everything and would be sure to take all the necessary measures in time, who would not permit it."[5]

Arriving at last in Semyonov, Solzhenitsyn joined the course for artillery officers. It was being run by the Leningrad Military Academy, and since it had a large mathematical component, he found he could follow it quite well. But in other respects he was totally at a loss. It turned out that the course was intended for second lieutenants and captains who had completed their military training and already been appointed to command batteries. Solzhenitsyn, by contrast, was still a raw recruit who had had no basic training whatsoever. He didn't even know how to salute his superiors properly, while they, for their part, were astounded to discover a private among them. When summoned to see his commanding officer, Solzhenitsyn discovered that the CO suspected some kind of trick, fearing that he had been sent by security to report on the school. Fortunately, he managed to persuade the CO that it was a blunder on the part of the Stalingrad cadre office, and the CO consented to send him to a proper officer-training school. It was obvious that Solzhenitsyn fully grasped the technical aspects of the course, and it never occurred to the CO to question him as to how he had missed the proper training in the first place.

Solzhenitsyn was dispatched to the Third Leningrad Artillery School, in Kostroma, about two hundred miles north-east of Moscow, for an accelerated training course for artillery officers. He was still wearing the shabby greatcoat that had been issued to him in the transport battalion and clutching his battered brief-case, which, according to Solzhenitsyn, struck his new commanding officer as so funny that he burst out laughing. "Who the hell are you?" he demanded of this dishevelled new arrival. "I'm a schoolteacher, sir," replied Solzhenitsyn, "and I've come to join the artillery." After asking some further questions, the CO told him that it was too late to put him through a conventional officer-training course but that courses were about to begin for a new and specialized branch of the artillery for which his mathematical skills ideally suited him: instrumental reconnaissance. It was a technique for plotting the position of enemy guns by registering and analysing their sound waves. The information was passed to the regular artillery, which set its targets accordingly.[6]

It was now the end of April 1942 and the crash-course in instrumental reconnaissance was to last three months, combining basic military training with detailed technical instruction. Like millions of raw trainees before and since, Solzhenitsyn found the draconian discipline, physical privations, and psychological pressures of military school utterly bewildering and exhausting. He later described them in *The Gulag Archepelago*.

> We were permanently hungry in that school and kept our eyes skinned to see where we might scrounge an extra bite to eat, and jealously watched one another to see who else might have wangled something. What we feared most of all was getting slung out before we got our stars (if you failed the course, you were sent

to the Battle of Stalingrad). And they trained us like wild young beasts: the idea was to make us so mean that we would later take it all out on other people. We never got enough sleep, because after lights out, as a punishment, they would force us to go through our entire drill routine under the watchful eyes of a sergeant. Or in the middle of the night the entire squad would be rooted out of bed and lined up before one dirty boot: all right, get cleaning, you bastard, and the rest can stand there until it shines like a new pin.[7]

This gratuitous discipline and relentless attention to trivialities seem to have infuriated Solzhenitsyn, who stubbornly refused to be cowed and insistently tried to carve out snatches of time for his own interests, for writing up his diary, and for reading. His brief-case full of books was a badge of defiance and at one point called down the ire of his commanding officer, who termed it a "student self-indulgence" and ordered him to keep it out of sight.

Naturally, the trainees were not allowed out of camp, except for a weekly visit to the bath-house in Kostroma and for manoeuvres in the surrounding countryside. The latter were eagerly awaited as a change and a relief from the relentless daily training routines, and Solzhenitsyn found himself curiously drawn to the bleak landscape of northern Russia. The region around Kostroma was an agriculturally poor one, and the surrounding villages had an abandoned and dilapidated air to them, yet Solzhenitsyn found their atmosphere of desolation and decrepitude oddly compelling. It was his first experience of the Far North, and he found that in many ways it moved him more deeply even than the green woods and meadows of the centre. It appealed to his ascetic side, to a subconscious fascination with austerity, sacrifice, and hardships, and it perhaps echoed, in a superficial way, the deprivations he was undergoing at the training school.

The course turned out to be longer than three months, and it was the end of October 1942 before Solzhenitsyn passed out and was awarded his first lieutenant's stars. "In passionate anticipation of those stars, we had worked at developing a tiger-like stride and a rasping voice of command," he later recalled in *The Gulag Archipelago*. "I remember that it was right after finishing the officer-training school that I experienced the 'joy of simplification,' of being a military man and not having to think about things for myself. I experienced the joy of immersing myself in the business of doing exactly what everyone else did, which was 'the done thing' in our military circles."[8] Solzhenitsyn had been licked into shape, and within a few days he wrote to his wife.

My dear Natashenka,
I am writing in terrible haste from the Kostroma station. The graduation order has just been read out to us. Half of me is dressed in uniform, the rest of the outfitting comes tomorrow. All accounts are squared with Kostroma.
Your lieutenant.[9]

Natalia received this letter not in Morozovsk, where Solzhenitsyn had last seen her on his way to Semyonov, but in Kazakhstan, in Central Asia,

in a place called Taldy-Kurgan, whither she and her mother had been evacuated. Soon after their last meeting, the school in Morozovsk had been closed
and Natalia had returned to her mother in Rostov, where she had started
working as a laboratory technician at the university. In July 1942 the Germans had begun their big push eastwards to the Volga and southwards into
the Caucasus, and on 28 July Rostov had fallen again. The evacuation of the
city had been a terrible mess. Despite intensive German artillery bombardments, one of which had destroyed Natalia's laboratory and another her and
Solzhenitsyn's old one-room flat on Chekhov Lane, the authorities seemed to
be taken quite unawares, and they abandoned the city in panic. On hearing
the news of an evacuation, the people simply rushed into the street and stood
around in bewildered crowds, listening to the loudspeakers. Then followed
a mad scramble across the river Don to safety, but the military were in such
a hurry to blow up the bridges that only 10 per cent of the population managed to get across in time. Natalia and her mother were among the lucky
ones, catching one of the last trains out of the city and crossing the river in
the midst of a violent thunderstorm. Taissia Solzhenitsyn was with them and
travelled to Georgievsk to stay with Maria and her husband. Roman and
Irina were already there. They had moved into Zakhar and Evdokia's old
room at the start of the war, when their flat in Nalchik was bombed.

Natalia and her mother stayed with her mother's sister in Kislovodsk
for a while, but when it became clear that the Germans were overrunning
the entire North Caucasus, they decided to move on. On 6 August, Natalia,
her mother, her aunt, and her cousin walked from Pyatigorsk to Nalchik,
whence they were able to take a train to Baku and a ferry across the Caspian
Sea to safety. Lydia Ezherets and Kirill Simonyan, who was still finishing
his medical studies and had not been called into the army, followed an almost
identical route to Central Asia but did not meet Natalia at any point.

From July to September, while all this was going on, Solzhenitsyn had
lost touch with his wife. She had scribbled him notes from various places,
but he had been unable to reply because she was constantly on the move.
When they finally re-established contact, he wrote how worried he had been
for her safety and how helpless he had felt at not being able to do anything
for her. He was concerned about their few belongings and above all about
the manuscripts, notebooks, and literary exercises that he had left in her care.
"I am even afraid to ask what you have managed to preserve. Just what could
you have salvaged when you had to travel on foot all the way to Nalchik?"[10]
He also inquired after the whereabouts of his MIFLI records. After all, he
planned to return to his studies when all the fighting was over—not even a
world war was going to deflect him from his chosen path in life.

Meanwhile, his heart continued to burn for Russian losses and the Russian retreat. Throughout the summer of 1942 the Germans had continued to
make major gains. As early as May they had overrun the Crimea, except for
Sebastopol, and had captured Kharkov in a pitched battle whose loss was
clearly the fault of Stalin, although every effort was made by the Soviet

authorities to keep the matter quiet. After the German capture of Rostov in July, Solzhenitsyn wrote to Natalia, he had felt an irresistible urge to abandon his training course and request a transfer to the southern front to fight for his native city, but of course it was out of the question: until his training was finished, he was useless to anyone. In August he had had fresh cause for concern when the Germans swept into the Caucasus, overrunning the Kuban and Stavropol Province, arriving in Pyatigorsk and Kislovodsk on 21 August, and advancing as far as Vladikavkaz in the south. Their new territory included Georgievsk, where his mother and the rest of the family were living, and he had no means of knowing how they were. By the beginning of September, the Germans had crossed the Don, and they were now fighting in the very suburbs of Stalingrad. Yet, according to Reshetovskaya, it was precisely in October 1942, when the Soviet Union was on its knees and Stalingrad hung in the balance, that Solzhenitsyn wrote her an amazingly optimistic and prescient letter, expressing his hopes for a Russian victory.

> The summer and autumn campaign is coming to a close. What are the results? Stalin will summarize them shortly in his speech. But it can be said already: Russian fortitude is immense! For two summers Hitler has been trying to topple this boulder with the hands of all Europe. But he has not succeeded. Nor will he succeed in another two summers.
>
> What will this winter bring us? If our army finds it possible to repeat the advance of last year—moving from Stalingrad in the direction of Rostov—the results could be colossal. The recapture of Rostov would be a suitable prize in itself for the entire winter campaign—for the Fritzes on the Don, for the Fritzes in the Caucasus, for the Fritzes in Berlin.[11]

In early November, Solzhenitsyn was posted to Saransk, in central Russia, a town that he characterized to Natalia as "three little houses in a flat field."[12] He was at once appointed deputy commander of a sound-ranging battery in the 796th Autonomous Artillery Reconnaissance Battalion, which was just then being formed, but soon afterwards the battalion was re-formed as part of a larger reorganization of the Soviet army as a whole. Every battery was split in half and reconstituted as two batteries, each with its own commander, so that within months of becoming an officer Solzhenitsyn had his own command. On 13 February 1943 the battalion left Saransk by rail not for the southern front, as Solzhenitsyn had hoped, but for the Far North, arriving a week or two later in Ostashkov, midway between Rzhev and Novgorod. From there they moved slowly westwards to a line following the river Lovat just south of Staraya Russa on Lake Ilmen and encamped in the forest, waiting for orders to advance. Solzhenitsyn was keyed up at the prospect of seeing some active service at last, but his hopes were dashed. Six weeks went by without a murmur. Then, in April 1943, they entrained once more and were transferred four hundred miles south-east to a point just east of Orel, where they dug in on the river Neruch.

He was able to ease some of his frustration during these months by plunging into writing. Ever since his call-up, he had been filling his note-books and diaries. As a groom in the transport battalion, he had listened to the language of the Cossacks and admired their simple Russian speech, find-ing it much more attractive than Rostov slang. Then, in Saransk he had begun a short story called "The Lieutenant," loosely based on some of his experiences. In Staraya Russa he had completed and revised it, giving it to one of his soldiers to copy out for him. He now had a folding wooden chair and field table as part of his equipment and took every opportunity, during intervals between his other duties, to set it up in his dug-out, or outside if the weather was nice, and get on with his writing. A surviving photograph from this period shows him sitting—slightly self-consciously—at this table in a clearing in the forest, wearing his greatcoat and fur cap, a holstered revolver on his hip, posing with his pencil poised over a book. "The ideas are simply crowding onto my pen," he wrote to Natalia, "I feel an incredible urge to write." Soon he had ideas for two more short stories and had thought of "a wonderful third variant" of "The Lieutenant." He was also stimulated by an unexpected piece of news from Natalia: during the German occupation of Morozovsk, their old neighbour Bronevitsky had been appointed mayor. Solzhenitsyn was at first upset by this information, but then it struck him as a wonderful subject for a story. "I already had such a theme in mind," he wrote to Natalia, "but I needed a real live human being for it! What are such people like?" He urged Natalia to find out as much as she could for him, and soon afterwards commenced a story with the Chekhovian title "In the Town of M."[13]

While in Saransk, Solzhenitsyn had learned of the German retreat from the Caucasus and on 12 January 1943 had sent a telegram to his mother, but it was only now, four months later, that he finally discovered what had become of her. Soon after the arrival of the Germans in Georgievsk the preceding October, Taissia had moved back to Rostov, only to find their converted stable in ruins and her few sticks of furniture destroyed. She had rented a room on the fourth floor somewhere, again without running water or heat-ing, and had been obliged to struggle up four floors with buckets of water and firewood. There was little to eat in the devastated and occupied city, it was freezing cold throughout the winter, and she had been struck down by a severe attack of tuberculosis, forcing her to return to Maria in Georgievsk. All this Solzhenitsyn now learned, at the end of May, from her letter. Her handwriting was so weak and spidery that he barely recognized it, and he upbraided himself for not having guessed the true cause of her long silence. He had been worried for her on account of the bombing and shelling and the German occupation, but "for some reason I never expected it from that direc-tion, from the tuberculosis," he afterwards wrote to Natalia. "Somehow I forgot to expect it."[14]

Encamped on the river Neruch near the small town of Novosil, Sol-zhenitsyn now had the opportunity to study a fresh part of the Russian coun-tryside. This, too, was a poor region, low-lying, swampy and dotted with woods. Its agricultural resources had been modest at the best of times, but having been twice fought over—once during the German advance and again during their retreat—it was shattered beyond belief. Houses, trees, whole villages, had been flattened by bombs, shells, and caterpillar tracks. Roads and fields had been ploughed into a soupy porridge, and Solzhenitsyn could still hear the thump of both sides' artillery as he surveyed the desolate scene. Yet Russia, prostrate and ravished, filled him with still more tender love for her sad resignation and beauty. As he wrote in *The Way*:

> It was May. Fresh from the swamps of Lake Ilmen,
> We came to Orel, to the sunny banks of the Neruch.
> Turgenev country, abandoned, wild, overgrown.
> Not a grain of rye. No crops. Not a vegetable patch.
> Over tough black peasant bread baked out of vetch,
> I at last understood that one word—*homeland*.[15]

During this enforced lull at Orel, Solzhenitsyn was able to correspond freely with Natalia, who had found work as a schoolteacher in Taldy-Kurgan and was settling down happily to life as an evacuee. He was also able to exchange letters with Lydia and Kirill, who had moved from Central Asia to Moscow (Kirill had recently joined the medical corps). But he had completely lost touch with the friend who meant most to him—Nikolai Vitkevich. When Nikolai had gone off to officer-training school, leaving Solzhenitsyn behind in Rostov, he had promised to write, and when Solzhenitsyn was in Morozovsk, Nikolai had sent him the number and address of his regiment, and they had corresponded. This had continued while Solzhenitsyn was with the Cossacks at Buzuluk, but after that they had lost one another. Solzhenitsyn had been totally absorbed by his officer-training course and first-command, and Nikolai, an infantry officer, had been moving from place to place with the ebb and flow of battle. One day in May, however, a sergeant in Solzhenitsyn's battalion casually mentioned that he had just returned from visiting such and such a regiment in a neighbouring sector of the front. Solzhenitsyn pricked up his ears—it was Nikolai's regiment. Having asked the sergeant for directions, Solzhenitsyn at once set off in a captured Opel Blitz acquired by his unit, and a short time afterwards was directed to where he would find Lieutenant Vitkevich.

The two friends were amazed and overjoyed to find themselves neighbours on the same front—their two units had been brought here as part of the Soviet build-up for the attack on Orel. Throughout the next two months, they met regularly, Solzhenitsyn visiting Nikolai's unit in his Opel and Nikolai returning the visits on horseback. In Solzhenitsyn's battalion there was a photographic platoon responsible for photographing the German trenches and gun emplacements. It also specialized in taking unofficial snapshots of battalion members, and on one of these we find the two friends arm in arm on the occasion of Koka's first visit.

The most significant consequence of their unexpected reunion was that the two friends immediately resumed the political discussions that they had begun in Rostov. Each had a mountain of fresh experiences to bring to these discussions, and each had developed his thinking considerably in the intervening years. There was also an important formal difference between them. Koka, perhaps influenced by his mother's example, had succumbed to the immense pressure put on all Soviet officers to join the Party and had allowed himself to be recruited. Solzhenitsyn, faithful to his non-joining instincts, had resisted the pressure and was one of only two officers out of the thirty in his battalion who had refused to join. In all other respects, however, the friends found that their thinking had developed along remarkably similar lines and that they were politically and emotionally closer than ever before. "Like the two halves of a single walnut," as Solzhenitsyn later wrote in *The Way*.[16] Days and nights of feverish debate and exhilarating speculation culminated in the joint drafting of a political manifesto, "Resolution No. 1," which, in the best Marxist tradition, contained both an analysis of prevailing conditions and a programme for action and change.

It was, Solzhenitsyn said later, a "Leninist document."

> Koka and I had moved a very long way forward. What we did in essence was to found a kind of new political party. We wrote our . . . Resolution No. 1. There was a descriptive introduction in which we characterized the Soviet regime as having all the attributes of feudalism and exploiting all our lives. . . . Then we described its influence on economics, how it stifled economic development, how it stifled literature and culture and our everyday lives. We said that it had to be fought against and that it was impossible to undertake all these tasks without forming an organization. This was our final point: an organization was absolutely essential. That is, we were saying in effect that we needed to create a new party.[17]

Leninist or not, it was an astonishing document to compile after so many years of the cult of Stalin. It is true that Stalin's stock had slumped as a result of the disastrous first year and a half of the war, that the generals and military leaders had been sharing the limelight during those eighteen months, and that the cult of the omnipotent leader had abated somewhat. But this dip in his reputation was strictly relative. There was no conceivable rival in sight, or group of rivals, and no obvious nucleus of something that could grow into an opposition. Moreover, through the victory at Stalingrad, for which Stalin was already beginning to take personal credit, he had re-established his position as the all-wise commander-in-chief of the armed forces and the indispensable leader of the nation, and a new wave of adulation was already beginning to flood the press and colour the military communiqués. To attempt to stand out against such an irresistible tide was suicide if done openly. Fortunately, the two subalterns were not in a position to do more than set out the terms of their disagreement with the system and bide their time. This they did, solemnly copying out the text of "Resolution No. 1" and swearing to carry it on their persons throughout their military service. Nikolai stored his copy in his gas-mask holder and Solzhenitsyn his in his map-case, which had now replaced his brief-case as the repository of his most intimate papers.

Their political naïvety was paralleled, in Solzhenitsyn's case, by the naïve relish he still took in his new-found independence as a commissioned officer and in the joys of military life. Just as he had been innocently shocked by the senseless rigours of the officer-training school, so now he was innocently thrilled by the vistas of freedom open to him. In a letter to Natalia, he wrote humorously and at some length about a new hair-style he was experimenting with. He took up smoking: "If it helps me to write, why should I give it up? What's your opinion?" And he sampled the hitherto unknown pleasures of the free vodka ration: "Imagine, it makes me quite merry, even a single tot. I always knock it back in a single gulp!" However, he was not going to let himself be carried away: "Still, to hell with it! I'm not going to drink it every day, it's bad for you. I'll swap it for sugar."[18]

Solzhenitsyn's series of meetings with Nikolai and the suspenseful wait on the river Neruch ended in early July with the launching of the great German attack on the Kursk salient, which was to be the turning point of the war on the eastern front. The two friends met for the last time on 9 July 1943, when fighting had already begun, and stayed up the whole night in Solzhenitsyn's dug-out before Nikolai returned to his unit. Two days later the battle for Orel erupted, and the two of them were swept into action.

The Orel battle was the final phase in the titanic struggle between the Germans and the Russians for supremacy on the eastern front. Since their defeat at Stalingrad the Germans had been pushed out of the Caucasus and westwards from the Volga as far as the Ukraine. Solzhenitsyn's prophecy of the preceding year had been fulfilled: Rostov had been liberated in February, and the Russians had advanced as far as a line running south from Orel and Kursk to just east of the river Donets. But Hitler's aim was to deliver a death-blow to Russian preparations for a fresh summer offensive westwards and to take revenge for Stalingrad. No fewer than seventeen panzer divisions and eighteen infantry divisions were committed to the final onslaught, in which the Germans confidently expected to smash through the Russian lines. The Russians, however, had also built up colossal forces in the area. Their trenches and defensive fortifications stretched back to a depth of sixty miles behind the front. For months they had been concentrating their troops and armaments here. The first set-piece tank battle lasted for three weeks and ended in a stalemate. The Germans had failed to capture Kursk, the object of their offensive, and had hardly moved the front forward at all. But they still held Orel, and the battle there lasted another three weeks. For Solzhenitsyn it was his first taste of battle conditions. His unit was part of the central front, commanded by General Rokossovsky, and on 5 August, after three weeks of continuous fighting, he entered Orel with the victorious Russian army. Ten days later, on 15 August, Solzhenitsyn was awarded the Order of the Patriotic War, second class, and promoted to first lieutenant.

A curious feature of this battle was the exaltedly patriotic and nationalistic terms in which it was interpreted by the Soviet government and presented to the fighting forces. Already in 1941, to lift morale against the Germans, Stalin had invoked the myths of Holy Russia and of its heroic struggles in the Middle Ages against the Tartars and the Teutonic knights. In 1942 he had suddenly granted favours to the Orthodox church and eased the persecution of believers. After the fall of Rostov the status of the political commissars had been downgraded and that of the purely military commanders enhanced. Special medals had been struck for officers only, named for famous Russian military figures of the past: the Orders of Suvorov, Kutuzov, and Alexander Nevsky. After Stalingrad, gold braid and epaulettes had been reintroduced for the first time since the Revolution, and the status of officers as a class was returned to something approximating what it had been under the tsars. All this was designed to emphasize the traditional Russian character of the war that was being fought in defence of the homeland, to stress continuity with the past, to improve the morale of the army, and to draw on reserves of patriotism that were deeper and stronger than mere loyalty to Soviet institutions and the Communist state.

About many of these reforms Solzhenitsyn was sceptical, perceiving cynical manipulation and calculating deceit on the part of Stalin, but the patriotic chord was one he responded to, and doubtless he shared many of the sentiments voiced by the Red Army newspaper, *Red Star*, at the start of the battle.

> Our fathers and forefathers made every sacrifice to save their Russia, their homeland. Our people will never forget Minin and Pozharsky, Suvorov and Kutuzov, and the Russian partisans of 1812. We are proud to think that the blood of our glorious ancestors is flowing in our veins, and we shall be worthy of them. . . . [19]

Another interesting feature is that the Battle of Orel inaugurated what was to become a regular tradition of victory salutes in Moscow. The announcement was made on 5 August by Stalin, and that night, twelve artillery salvoes from 120 guns marked the second great Soviet victory of the war.

In the ensuing weeks the Russian army chased the Germans westward towards the river Dnieper. Solzhenitsyn and his battery were continuously in action, Solzhenitsyn exulting in the strenuous demands of leadership and the tumult of battle. This he had yearned for during that first, wasted year of the war; this was the goal for which all his training had prepared him. In the small town of Starodub, west of Orel, they paused for a few days to take a rest. On one of his walks Solzhenitsyn stumbled across the town library, which had been badly neglected under the German occupation. Its books had all tumbled off the shelves and lay in heaps on the floor. Having sought permission from the local commander, he requisitioned a couple of dozen volumes of Russian and Soviet works for his battery and instituted a novel scheme of readings from them. [20]

The immediate purpose of the readings was utilitarian—to keep his men awake at their posts. The battery had six separate listening posts, widely separated and positioned as far forward as possible, and connected to a central switchboard by telephone wires. The posts had to be manned round the clock, which meant there was lots of time to kill, particularly when the German artillery was quiet or retreating. At the same time the telephones made it particularly suitable for Solzhenitsyn to carry out his plan, which was simply to have the switchboard operator read extracts from the books to the men on the other end of the telephone lines. It was uplifting and educational, and in the course of it he made some interesting discoveries. His old favourite, Lev Tolstoy, was very popular with the soldiers. They particularly enjoyed *War and Peace* for the accuracy with which it communicated the flavour of life at the front and the feel of battle. And they liked Tolstoy's merciless exposure of the pomp and puffery of the top brass and his satirical attacks on the officers. But the overwhelming favourite, it turned out, was *Vasily Tyorkin*, Alexander Tvardovsky's earthy mock-epic, written in imitation of Russian folk rhymes, about a simple Russian soldier of that name.* Solzhenitsyn expressed his own opinion of *Tyorkin* and its creator in a letter home to Natalia.

> I recently came across the first truthful (in my sense) book about the war—*Vasily Tyorkin* by Tvardovsky. If you read the poem carefully you can find many things that no one has ever touched on before. Generally speaking, Tvardovsky is one of the best Soviet poets (if not the best). One day I must get a letter off to him expressing my appreciation.[21]

There was little time for fan letters, however, in the months that lay ahead. Throughout the autumn and winter of 1943, the Soviet forces moved implacably westward, driving the Germans before them. At the river Dnieper the Germans attempted to establish a fortified line, the Hagen line, from behind which they hoped to stem the Soviet advance. But Hitler had weakened his forces by withdrawing several divisions for transfer to Italy, and they were forced to retreat before the Hagen line was properly ready. The first Russian breach of the Dnieper came in the autumn in the region of Kiev. On the central front, where Solzhenitsyn's battalion was operating, they did not get across until February 1944, having performed a forced march to get there before the ice melted. The Germans made a stand, however, and they were forced back across the Dnieper again and obliged to retreat rapidly south-east in the direction of Gomel. From Gomel they marched westward once more and crossed the Dnieper for the third and last time, in March 1944, near the small town of Zhlobin, where they dug themselves in. Solzhenitsyn had been blooded and had won his first spurs; now there would be a long rest, while the Soviet army consolidated for the next big push towards Germany.

---

* Tvardovsky's long poem appeared in instalments throughout the war and was completed only in 1946.

7

ARREST

SOLZHENITSYN TOOK ADVANTAGE of the pause at Zhlobin to get back to his writing, recording his impressions of the recent fighting in his diaries and continuing work on some stories. Apart from "The Lieutenant" and "In the Town of M," he had more or less completed two more stories, "Letter No. 254" and "A Woman's Tale," and was working on another, called "The Orchard." He also sketched out a novel about the war to be called *The Sixth Course*—the hero, an ex-student, had completed five years at the university (like Solzhenitsyn himself) before embarking on his "sixth course" in the army.[1]

Solzhenitsyn's single-mindedness about his writing was now greater than ever before. He complained in his letters to Natalia and Nikolai that his duties took "too much time" and that the continuous fighting hindered him from getting down to his "main work." The war was wonderful in terms of the experience it afforded him and as a source of material for his books, if only it wouldn't get in the way. That quality of detachment and dispassionate analysis of one's surroundings that is the writer's hallmark was already developed in him to a remarkable degree. Everything and anything was grist to his mill—the landscape, the weather, the lives of his soldiers, their stories about home and the front, the fighting, the movements and manoeuvres of the army, his glimpses of what life had been like under the German occupation. Everything went into the diary or the stories. He also found time to worry about what had happened to his earlier work:

Darling, where are my *Cycling Notes?* And where is the plan for *Russians in the Advance Guard* and the first few chapters (on large white sheets of paper)? They

must be with you—aren't they? And the sketch for the chapter "Black on Red."
. . . Don't tell me they're lost?

When Natalia was able to reassure him that everything was safe, he was
filled with relief and gratitude: "Thank you enormously for saving the three
short stories for me—this is one of the most graphic expressions of your love,
which I shall never forget. After all, you were on foot and you had to carry
this on you."[2]

He was equally concerned with how much progress he was making in
his chosen profession. Already in 1941 he had sent three of his early stories,
"Mission Abroad," "The River Pointsmen," and "The Nikolayevskys" to
two Soviet writers whom he admired—the novelist Konstantin Fedin and
the novelist and playwright Boris Lavrenev. But because of the war he had
never received a reply from either of them. Now he was in touch with Kirill
and with Lydia Ezherets, who were together in Moscow. Lydia was studying
for a post-graduate degree in German literature at the university, and she
suggested that she try and get in touch with the two writers again and show
them some of Solzhenitsyn's more recent work, as well as remind them of
the old stories. Solzhenitsyn sent off a batch of new stories for her to forward, torn between foreboding (if they should say he had no talent, "I'll tear
my heart out of my breast, I'll stamp out fifteen years of my life")[3] and
anxious hopes for a positive response.

Correspondence with Natalia, Lydia, and Kirill offered him a temporary escape from the rigours of life at the front and reminded him of their
carefree years as students together in Rostov and of their half-serious plans
for the five of them—Nikolai, Kirill, Lydia, Natalia, and himself—to get
together after the war and found an informal "commune," where they would
study and write and debate politics together. It also reminded him of how
long it had been since he had seen any of them except Nikolai. Natalia,
especially, had been away in distant Kazakhstan for a year and a half now; it
was exactly two years since he had seen her in Morozovsk, on his way to
Stalingrad. Now that Rostov had been liberated, he could not understand
why Natalia and her mother did not return at once. Natalia had written that
she was enjoying her life as a schoolteacher in Taldy-Kurgan and feared that
it would be difficult to find anything as good in Rostov. But eventually she
bowed to his wishes and announced that she was making preparations to
return in March.

Learning that their battalion was due to remain in Zhlobin for another
month at least, Solzhenitsyn persuaded his commanding officer to allow him
to take a ten-day leave in March 1944 to visit his wife and friends. Such leave
from the front was irregular, but the battalion was a small, independent unit
whose commander had wide powers, and it was not difficult to get the necessary travel warrant endorsed with the obligatory rubber stamp. Solzhenitsyn went first to Moscow, where he had a joyful reunion with Lydia and
Kirill. Lydia's father had moved from Rostov to Moscow at the beginning of

the war to become chief doctor of the well-known government sanatorium in Barvikha, in the Moscow suburbs, and had found Kirill a comfortable position there—Kirill was now a captain in the medical corps. When Solzhenitsyn arrived, the sanatorium was being used as a rest home for the top military brass. Marshal Rokossovsky, Solzhenitsyn's commander-in-chief, had only just left, and on Lydia's father's instructions Solzhenitsyn was given the luxury suite that Rokossovsky had just vacated.[4]

Solzhenitsyn had not seen Kirill or Lydia since their university days, and with Kirill sat up all night to exchange news. Kirill did not share Solzhenitsyn's political enthusiasms. He was more pessimistic about Marxism in general, and although he disliked Stalin as much as Solzhenitsyn and Nikolai did, he was not much interested in "Resolution No. 1" and their plans for world revolution. But he still had literary ambitions and looked forward to the time, after the war, when they could all be together again—this time in Moscow—and could work on parallel lines. As for Solzhenitsyn's stories sent from the front, Lydia still had no news from Fedin or Lavrenev.

From Moscow, Solzhenitsyn made his way painfully slowly by train to Rostov, only to find that Natalia and her mother had not yet arrived. Maria Reshetovskaya had fallen ill in Kazakhstan on the very day designated for their departure, and they had been delayed in Taldy-Kurgan. When they did return, they too travelled via Moscow, stopping with Veronica Turkina for two weeks. Natalia's mother had not been in Moscow since 1913, when she was a schoolgirl. There was a tearful reunion with her brother, Valentin, and she succeeded in arranging a reconciliation between Valentin and his daughter, the younger Veronica, who had never seen her father. While in Moscow, Natalia also went to visit Lydia and Kirill, learned of Solzhenitsyn's recent visit, and heard, among other things, that Lavrenev had just been in touch with Lydia about the stories. His immediate comment had been: "The stories are nice, I like them."[5] And he wrote that he had submitted them to the monthly literary magazine *Znamya* (The Banner) for publication.

Natalia sent Solzhenitsyn a postcard about Lavrenev's positive response and soon afterwards travelled back to Rostov, where she found two letters waiting for her. The first had been written at the time of his leave. He wrote of the terrible difficulties he had had in travelling about the country and of his disappointment at not finding her there when he arrived. But he had an ingenious and unorthodox plan to make up for their missing one another: he would get her some forged army papers that would enable her to travel to Zhlobin and spend some time with his unit. She was to prepare herself for the journey and await the arrival of a sergeant he would send to her.

The second letter was in answer to her Moscow postcard. His response to the news from Lavrenev was guarded: "I was pleased by Lavrenev's opinion. I will wait for a more detailed account from Lydia or from Lavrenev himself. But I was surprised by his promise to submit them for publication. I hadn't expected or thought of such a thing."

He also had one piece of devastating news to communicate.

Mama has died. I am left with all the good she did for me and all the bad I did to her. No one wrote to me about her death. A money order came back marked that the addressee was deceased. Apparently she died in March.[6]

He later learned that she had died as long ago as 17 January 1944, but the letter from his aunts had taken over two months to reach him. There had been no money to pay for a grave-digger, and she had been laid in the same grave as his uncle Roman, who had died just two weeks earlier, from a neglected stomach ulcer.

We can only imagine Solzhenitsyn's feelings on learning of the death of his mother. He must have felt frustrated at being so far away and so helpless to do anything. And naturally he experienced that involuntary sense of guilt we all seem to feel when a loved one dies, especially a mother. This emerges clearly from his letter. He later resented Natalia's publication of the letter in her memoirs, particularly since she insinuated that he had neglected his mother, and a wrangle developed between them over the way he had distributed his officer's pay. Throughout his army service he had divided it between his mother and his wife, but it seems that for most of the time he had sent the larger share to Natalia in Kazakhstan, a smaller sum going to Taissia in Georgievsk. Only towards the end of Taissia's life, shortly before she died, had he realized quite how poverty-stricken and desperate she was, and by then it was too late. Her dreadful end, in sickness and penury, a thousand miles away, was bound to leave him with painful memories.[7]

Natalia, meanwhile, was vastly excited at the prospect of seeing her husband again and waited eagerly in Rostov for the summons to join him at the front. It came early one morning at three. Sergeant Ilya Solomin, from Solzhenitsyn's battery, arrived bearing a tunic, a wide leather belt, epaulettes, and a dark-grey beret to wear, together with a faked Red Army pass and a faked travel warrant. The two of them set out the next evening for Moscow, where they stayed with the Turkins overnight. The jolly sergeant praised his dashing commander and told tales of life at the front. A few days later they arrived at the trenches outside Zhlobin.

It was May 1944. The weather was unseasonably cold, but Solzhenitsyn's battalion had been dug in for over a month and had made itself comfortable, with a complex network of trenches for every eventuality, including one trench with a bath-house. The fighting and the front line had moved westwards, leaving an atmosphere of almost festive peace behind the lines, an impression that was confirmed for Natalia when she was invited to the battalion commander's trench for a leisurely glass of vodka upon her arrival.

Solzhenitsyn seems to have hoped that once Natalia had arrived and got used to life at the front, she would agree to stay with him. This would certainly have been irregular, but not exceptionally so, for Natalia could have been taken onto the battalion strength officially. Several women were there already, working mainly as nurses and orderlies. Some had established themselves legally, but many others had arrived unofficially, in order to be with their menfolk, while other women had simply been picked up along the way.

The battalion commander, for instance, had his wife living with him. His deputy, the political commissar, was living with the battalion medical officer, who owed her position to him, and the adjutant was also living with a woman he had met at the front.[8]

Solzhenitsyn was too faithful and fastidious (and perhaps too prudish) to try to pick up a woman along the way, but he missed an intimate female presence every bit as much as his comrades did and was desperately anxious to keep Natalia with him. It seems he had romantic visions of their working side by side throughout the war (perhaps, at the back of his mind, he was influenced by the memory of his father's wedding at the front). He arranged for Natalia to work in his calculating platoon, sitting at the switchboard and plotting gun positions and distances from the sound-ranging tapes. In their spare time he taught her to fire a pistol and read aloud to her from *The Sixth Course* (he also read to her from *The Life of Matvei Kozhemyakin*, by Maxim Gorky, whom, according to Reshetovskaya, he then regarded as "the greatest writer").[9] She started to make fair copies of two of his stories to save him from having to ask one of the soldiers to do it. They also told one another in detail about their experiences of the past two years and discussed their plans for the future, when the war would be over. But the idyll was not to be. Natalia had led too sheltered an existence to take easily to the rough life of the front, the coarse food (and language), and the deprivations of the trenches. She disliked the demands of discipline and naturally saw her husband in quite a different light from his brother officers and subordinates. One serio-comic point of friction between them was her refusal to stand at attention whenever Solzhenitsyn entered the trench where she was working. It was normal practice for soldiers to stand when their battery commander entered, but Natalia found the idea of standing for her husband ridiculous. But from his point of view, her refusal undermined the unit's discipline: How could he expect everyone else to stand if she remained seated?[10]

There were many such clashes over military routine. More ominously, they found that both had changed considerably over the preceding two years (their separation had lasted twice as long as their marriage) and that their views diverged alarmingly on a number of issues. One such issue was Solzhenitsyn's continuing distaste for the idea of having children, a subject that he was to return to, in a letter (September 1944), after Natalia's return to Rostov.

> When you were with me at the front you once said to me: I cannot imagine our future life together if we don't have a child. Practically anyone is capable of producing a child and bringing it up. But to write a history of the post-October years as a work of art is something that perhaps I alone can do, and even then only by dividing my work with Koka, and perhaps with somebody else. That's how much this work is beyond the brain, body, and life of one person! . . . You and almost everyone else think of the future in terms of your personal life and happiness. But the only terms in which I can think are: What can I do for Leninism? How can I arrange my life for that?[11]

Their time together at the front had turned out to be more of a strain than a pleasure, and their relationship less enchanting when deprived of the romantic haze lent by distance. Solzhenitsyn was wholly absorbed by his military duties and the demands of writing about the front, while Natalia sought the cosy exclusivity of their former life in Rostov, which did little to enhance the military efficiency of the battery. His commander, drawing the necessary inferences, called Natalia aside and informed her that she could stay for three weeks, but no longer, because he could not take responsibility for an extended stay. He also informed her that the battalion was soon to lose its autonomous status and to be merged with a brigade under the command of a Colonel Zakhar Travkin, which would make it much more difficult for him to take his own decisions. Travkin was known to dislike having women in the front line. Almost with relief, therefore, husband and wife agreed to say goodbye. Natalia told Solzhenitsyn that she had seen an announcement in the newspaper inviting applications for post-graduate work in chemistry at Moscow University, and asked whether she should apply. Solzhenitsyn said yes; it seemed a good first step towards the realization of their post-war plans, for he still cherished his dream of living and working in Moscow. But nothing came of the application, and later that year Natalia took work at Rostov University as a temporary laboratory assistant.

In June 1944 Solzhenitsyn was promoted to captain. That same month the Soviet army launched its formidable assault on Belorussia. Solzhenitsyn's battery of sixty men, now part of Travkin's brigade and Rokossovsky's Second Belorussian Front, was in the thick of it: north-west to Bobruisk, almost as far north as Minsk, then westward across Belorussia to Baranovichi and triumphantly into Poland following a line midway between Bialystok and Warsaw. As always, Solzhenitsyn carried his notebook at the ready, although for the first nine days of the advance he barely had time to jot down even the most fleeting impressions. He was fascinated by the figure of their political commissar, Major Arseny Pashkin, who fought just as bravely as the military men around him and subordinated his political duties to more urgent military tasks. Solzhenitsyn observed him closely and made plans to include him in the design of his novel on the war.

I'm sketching in more and more new details of Pashkin—oh, when will I be able to sit down to write *The Sixth Course?* I will write it so magnificently! Especially now, when the battle of Orel-Kursk stands out in such bold relief and can be seen so vividly through the prism of the year 1944.[12]

He made a point of going into as many small towns as he could along the way to discover what life had been like under the German occupation. Initially, he had done this to assist in the writing of his story about Bronevitsky, "In the Town of M," but even after it was finished he continued to be fascinated by the phenomenon of occupation and the population's psychological reactions to it. In Starodub, where he obtained the library books, he discovered that the occupying troops had been Hungarians and that they had enjoyed great popularity among the local women. The latter had gone to the station and unashamedly sobbed their eyes out to see the occupiers go, according to a local cobbler who told Solzhenitsyn the story, saying that they had shown far more distress on that occasion than "when they had seen their husbands off to war."[13]

Solzhenitsyn strove to understand the feelings of the people in the occupied territories, and especially of the collaborators among them. Their treachery repelled him, and he shared the general emotions of indignation and disgust, so sedulously stoked by Soviet propaganda, over their defection to the enemy. But the writer in him could not be satisfied by these stock responses, nor could he participate in the rituals of revenge. In Starodub he had been a reluctant witness of the operations of an NKVD tribunal, which had moved in on the heels of the advancing Soviet army and immediately set about "purging" the local population, with all the usual paraphernalia of informers, denunciations, exemplary punishments, and so on. Back in Novosil, he had been invited by his commanding officer to attend the exemplary public execution of a pair of collaborators. The execution was conducted as a deliberately festive occasion, attended by crowds of officers, soldiers, nurses, and women and girls from nearby villages. It was to be followed by much eating and drinking and music, and the CO invited Solzhenitsyn to stay the night and find himself a woman, but Solzhenitsyn had declined and returned alone to his dug-out.

A more complex issue was the position of those Russians who had actively gone over to the other side and were fighting with the Germans—ostensibly, after 1943, under the leadership of General Vlasov. Solzhenitsyn had first heard about them while waiting to go into battle at Orel, when he had stumbled across some faded and weathered leaflets blowing about in the long grass, with a portrait of General Vlasov on them. They announced the formation, in 1942, of some sort of "Russian Committee," whose aim, with the help of the Germans, was to form a non-Communist Russian state and overthrow Stalin. He later wrote about them in *The Way*.

> In rain-pocked leaflets it was proposed
> That we *surrender* without a fight.
> How stillborn seemed their brazen pose,
> Reeking of German might.
> Written by an alien hand without grief
> —By Russians? No, that beggared belief.[14]

The leaflets were pitifully unconvincing, but in the battle for Orel Solzhenitsyn discovered that there were Russians fighting on the other side, and not in the least unconvincingly. On the contrary, having so much to lose from defeat, they fought more ferociously and tenaciously than the Germans and were extremely hard to overcome. Later that year, in December, when taking part in the storming of the Dnieper fortified line, Solzhenitsyn learned

that it was Russians again who were dug in south of Kursk in the snow, and
it took several days of desperate fighting to dislodge them.

The reason for their desperate courage was not far to seek. Although
most of them had been starved into joining the Germans, although a few
held hopes of being able to topple Stalin and get rid of Communism, and
although they were less pro-Nazi than anti-Communist (they had been
repeatedly tricked and exploited by the German high command), they were
traitors to their homeland, and as such could expect no mercy.

Furthermore, the rituals of revenge had been elaborately worked out by
Stalin and the leaders of the secret police. Traitors and collaborators were to
be given short shrift as an example to the rest of the population and the still-
occupied areas. When he arrived in Bobruisk at the start of the Belorussian
offensive, Solzhenitsyn had witnessed an example of the drastic punishments
that awaited the ex-Vlasovites. It was a scene that burned itself into his memory as a symbol of this entire pitiless policy towards the occupied areas and
towards Russians who were guilty, or suspected of being guilty, of collaboration with the enemy.

> I am ashamed to recall an incident I observed during our mopping up . . . after
> the Bobruisk encirclement. I was walking along the highway among a welter of
> wrecked and overturned German cars and scattered piles of booty, when from a
> shallow depression, in which a number of cars and wagons had become stuck
> and buried in the mud, and whence the smoke from bonfires of booty was rising
> into the air, with German cart-horses wandering aimlessly back and forth, I
> heard a cry for help: "Captain, sir! Captain, sir!" I was being appealed to in pure
> Russian by a prisoner in German breeches, naked from the waist up, with blood
> all over his face, chest, shoulders, and back, who was being driven along by a
> mounted security sergeant with liberal blows of his whip and by spurring his
> horse into him. He kept lashing the naked body again and again with his whip,
> preventing him from turning round or crying for help, driving him and whipping
> him, raising ever new crimson welts on his skin.[15]

Such moments were like bad dreams punctuating the more prosaic,
everyday reality of the military advance westwards. For most of the time
Solzhenitsyn was absorbed in the problems of commanding his battery and
in providing adequate leadership, tasks in which, to judge from the testimonial offered by one of his fellow officers, Captain Melnikov, at the time of
his rehabilitation, he was distinctly successful. According to that testimonial,
Solzhenitsyn "fought courageously on several fronts, repeatedly displayed
personal heroism, and inspired the devotion of the section he commanded.
Solzhenitsyn's section was the best in the unit for discipline and battle effec-
tiveness."[16]

Solzhenitsyn was noted for the strict discipline he maintained in his
unit, which was yet one more reason why Natalia's insubordinate behaviour
had so irritated him. He revelled in his rank and enjoyed to the full the
perquisites and privileges of an officer in the Soviet army, where the gulf

between commissioned and other ranks, despite the smoke-screen of contra-dictory propaganda, was far greater than in the Western armies (it had been deliberately widened by Stalin after Stalingrad). In *The Way* Solzhenitsyn reflected on the enormous enjoyment he had derived from his rank, the naïve pride he took in his epaulettes, his leather belt and shoulder-straps, his immaculately pressed uniform, his polished boots, the clink of spurs, and all the outward trappings of being an officer. Filled with sheer animal joy by the consciousness of his youth and power, he would stride and strut and issue orders, the abstracted studious youth of two years ago now having been transformed into a bold and jaunty leader. He also reflected on some of the effects of this pride and these privileges, recalling the way he had been pam-pered by his men and the power, even of life and death, that he had over them. Later, in *The Gulag Archipelago*, he recapitulated these ideas about his past and saw his actions in a much more sombre light, excoriating himself for his youthful hubris and rhetorically inflating his sins to underline his subsequent contrition.[17]

Yet Solzhenitsyn was little different from any of his fellow officers in his everyday behaviour, unless it was precisely in these qualities of thought-fulness and occasional self-doubt that were of a piece with his detachment and analytical disposition. And he was always on close and friendly terms with his subordinates. Of the two lieutenants under him, he was fondest of Lieutenant Ovsyannikov, in charge of the line-laying platoon, an open-faced Russian peasant boy with a quiff of flaxen hair, a broad nose, and unswerving blue eyes: "At the front there was no one closer to me than he. Throughout half the war we ate out of the same mess tin. Even under fire we would gulp down our food betweeen explosions so the stew wouldn't get cold. He was a peasant lad with a clean soul and a view of life so unsullied that neither officer-training school nor his commission had spoiled him to any degree."[18] Ovsyannikov, according to Solzhenitsyn's account, was a simple fellow who believed everything he read in the newspapers, swallowed Stalin's propa-ganda whole, and allowed himself to be convinced that the Germans were dumb mercenaries and peasants who had no equipment and hardly knew how to fight. Only harsh experience taught him otherwise, but even then he never questioned the sources of the false information or the motives of those dishing it out. Solzhenitsyn was fascinated by Ovsyannikov's naïve candour and filled a notebook with his tales. Ovsyannikov told him about collectivi-zation and the famine that had followed it—to Ovsyannikov they had seemed like natural and inevitable disasters that the Russian heart, clothed in a spe-cial armour, could and should endure without protest.

Solzhenitsyn's other platoon commander (Lieutenant Yevlashin in *The Way*), who used to read the books over the telephone to the listening posts, interested him less, but he was very fond of his sergeant, Ilya Solomin, a convivial young fellow whose versatility and reliability he greatly prized. It was the trusty Solomin who had gone to fetch Natalia from Rostov. Solomin was a Jew from Minsk whose whole family had been killed by the Germans when they occupied it. He had hoped to return there on the march through

Belorussia to try to discover what had happened, but their unit turned west before coming to Minsk. Another man who interested Solzhenitsyn was the soldier he called Ilya Turich* in *The Way*, who was quite the opposite of the other Ilya: he was extremely reserved and rarely spoke unless spoken to. It turned out that his mother had been a Socialist Revolutionary exiled to the Urals after the Revolution. His father had been a peasant sent to Moscow to intercede for his village with the new Soviet government. He had later fought on the Soviet side in the Civil War but had been too outspoken in his criticisms at an open meeting and had himself been exiled to the Urals, where he met and married Ilya's mother. All of these men Solzhenitsyn observed and questioned closely, writing up what they told him in his notebooks and war diaries and storing it as material for his future works.

By the end of 1944 Solzhenitsyn and his battery had crossed the border into Poland and were encamped on the river Narev south-east of Belostok (then Bialystok). It was here that he learned of Lavrenev's letter to Lydia containing his full appreciation of Solzhenitsyn's stories, and got Lydia's own letter about it. Lavrenev had read the new stories and had remembered the old ones from 1941. The former, he said, had displayed the author's "rudimentary skill in putting his thoughts and observations into literary form," no more. But now he felt that "the author has traversed a long path, he has matured, and it is now possible to start to speak about real literary productions." He added, "I have no doubt about the author's aptitude for literary work, and I believe that in the calm conditions that will prevail after the war, when he can devote himself totally to the work which he evidently loves, the author will be able to achieve success."[19]

This was encouraging but still enigmatic. He still spoke in terms of literary "promise" and of "future" successes rather than of actual achievement. Yet on receipt of the stories Lavrenev had immediately submitted them to *Znamya*. *Znamya*'s editors had rejected them, saying that they were not their sort of stories: "Their sort" were more heroic, more positive, and more orthodox. "The Lieutenant," was about a professional army lieutenant on active service being saved by the actions of a reserve lieutenant, which contradicted the accepted roles of professional and reserve soldiers. Similarly, "In the Town of M" made too much effort to understand the motives of the collaborators, instead of simply projecting the black and white figures of conventional war propaganda. Perhaps it was this unorthodoxy that had led Lavrenev to tone down his enthusiasm? Fedin, meanwhile, had not responded at all to the stories Lydia had sent him.

All of this Solzhenitsyn reported to Natalia in a letter in December 1944. Their correspondence had continued steadily since she had left his unit six months beforehand and returned to Rostov, but the strain of their meeting and the revelation of the differences that had grown up between them had left an unpleasant after-taste that affected many of their letters. Solzhenitsyn, in particular, had begun to doubt their suitability for one another and at one

---

* His true identity is not known.

point wrote a long letter enumerating Natalia's shortcomings and voicing his many misgivings. Then he was stricken with remorse and tried to make amends: "My last letters probably filled you with depression. Put all those grand theories far, far away from you, or else burn them. Let none of it disturb you." And in response to her reproaches, feeling that he hadn't expressed himself properly, he wrote, "You complain that I seldom write to you. The truth is, my dear, that I write to you not seldom but badly." The problem was, he explained, that for two people to understand one another while separated they had to develop similarly, along the same path and more or less at the same speed. He was aware that all his life he had developed "painfully one-sidedly" and tended to go forward by fits and starts, first in one direction and then another. He was no longer sure in which direction life was pulling him. More and more his literary plans were being "captured, swept up, sucked in, and carried away by Politics."[20]

Yet there was one person who answered all his requirements in every respect: Nikolai Vitkevich, "the one person in the world" who could send him a letter even after a year's silence and it wouldn't make any difference, for they were "like two trains travelling side by side at the same speed, and you could step from one to the other while they were still moving."[21] But something seemed to be the matter with Nikolai of late. In the early months after their meetings at Novosil, they had exchanged several letters on the subject of "Resolution No. 1." At one point Nikolai had seemed to be changing his mind about Stalin—whom they referred to derogatorily in their letters as the *pakhan*, or "big shot," or as "the moustachioed one"—and suggested that he might not be so bad as they had thought; but in that case, replied Solzhenitsyn, what conclusions should they draw about "Vovka"?* Was he to blame for the mess the country was in? Surely not. On another occasion, in early April, Solzhenitsyn had written to Nikolai about his recent leave to Moscow and Rostov, and his chance meeting on the train to Rostov with an apparent sympathizer: "From his very first words I saw that he was one of us! And he has a friend who thinks exactly the same way. $5 + 2 = 7$!" This was the naval lieutenant Leonid Vlasov, and Solzhenitsyn corresponded with him for a while. But it turned out that Vlasov, although sharing Solzhenitsyn's and Nikolai's views on the sorry state of Soviet society, did not place the blame for this on Stalin, and later wrote a letter to Solzhenitsyn in which he contradicted him: "No, Sanya, I've thought about it a lot, and I've come to the conclusion that Stalin is a great man and has never been wrong about anything. He is our sun!"[22]

The two friends, however, remained in close agreement. Their meetings in Novosil they now referred to jokingly as "the conference of the big two," parodying the recent conference of the "big three" in Tehran. They discussed the necessity of setting up their own organization to carry out "future joint practical activities in the party political sphere," of seeking the support

* A playful diminutive of the name Vladimir (i.e., meaning Lenin).

of intellectual, literary, and university circles for their political programme and of winning influential individuals over to their point of view. All this they jocularly referred to as the "war after the war," and indeed the whole correspondence was conducted half in the solemn, clotted jargon of dialectical materialism and half in the language of facetious schoolboy exaggeration.[23] The most curious thing of all was that this thinly disguised vein of facetiousness was the only concession they made to the existence of the military censors. Nikolai had told Solzhenitsyn as early as 1944 that the censors were inexperienced, feather-brained girls who had been assigned to this job for lack of anything more suitable and that they were looking only for military information—philosophical and political subjects did not interest them. Presumably the very frankness and unbuttoned simplicity of life at the front had also dulled their memory of what conditions had been like before the war, and had blunted the alertness that had been second nature then. Whatever the reason, Solzhenitsyn seems to have had no explanation for the fact that he was now receiving fewer and fewer letters from Nikolai, while Nikolai began complaining to Natalia that he was receiving fewer letters from Solzhenitsyn. It got so bad that Solzhenitsyn sent a letter to Nikolai via Natalia in Rostov, to which Nikolai responded, "Dear Natasha, I have received Sanya's letter from you. Only he is capable of such things. He's only 90 miles away, yet he sends his letters via Rostov."[24] That December, having learned Nikolai's whereabouts, Solzhenitsyn made preparations to visit him during the lull before the big Soviet offensive into East Prussia, but a fellow officer returned late from leave, and Solzhenitsyn was unable to get away.

In the second week of January 1945, the Russians launched their offensive, an offensive that everyone knew was destined to end in Berlin. Solzhenitsyn, who had recently been awarded his fourth star, was awake before dawn on the appointed day to receive a special packet delivered from headquarters. The packet contained a bundle of leaflets for the soldiers bearing Marshal Rokossovsky's famous message to his troops: "Soldiers, sergeants, officers, and generals! Today at 5 a.m. we commence our great last offensive. Germany lies before us! One more blow and the enemy will collapse, and immortal victory will crown our divisions!"[25] There had been other messages too. Stalin had announced that once the Soviet forces entered Germany, "everything was allowed." They were to wreak vengeance for all that Russia had suffered during the war, exacting an eye for an eye and a tooth for a tooth. Nothing was forbidden, and special norms were laid down for how much plunder was permitted to the different ranks, beginning with ten pounds for each private soldier, and on up to tons for the senior officers. Political commissars and Party officials held special meetings with the troops to drive the message home. Till now the soldiers had had to make do with vodka and girls as their only reward, but fat, prosperous Germany lay ahead of them, a prize for all their past exertions and the incentive for one last, mighty push.

Solzhenitsyn was repelled by this naked incitement to cruelty and greed. He lectured his battery on the need to show moderation and self-control, insisted that the ten-pound limit for booty would be rigidly adhered to, and inwardly prayed that his men would show dignity and restraint. Looking back on this moment in *The Way* he composed an imaginary speech to his men recapitulating his hopes and his fears on the eve of this violent incursion into "Europe."

> Display a sense of honour and pride
> In the presence of those Europeans.
> Remember, in a Europe now petrified,
> Where Russians are not such frequent guests,
> Our every act, by thousands multiplied,
> Will become a legend. They will forgive us,
> As they'd forgive us looking like beggars,
> Our tattered elbows, our stinking leggings,
> If we keep our heads, take a responsible stand,
> Act the proud sons of a magnanimous land.
> . . . .
> . . . be it only fleetingly, in flashes,
> Let us show these haughty, well-fed men
> That we will never let Russia, even though leprous,
> Be brought by foreigners into contempt.[26]

Once started, the Polish offensive unfolded with immense speed. The collapsing German armies retreated as fast as they could in the direction of home, or else were surrounded and captured. Solzhenitsyn dashed off a quick note to Natalia: "Today we have *begun*, we are off and starting to march. I am replying on the run. I have wrapped up the farthest listening-post and am waiting for the all clear. The last mail suddenly showered on me—like three handshakes, like three wishes for life and victory—three letters: yours, Lydia's, and Ostrich's. And for five (!) hours I couldn't open a single one of them—you can imagine from this what's happening here."[27] Solzhenitsyn's regiment, commanded by Travkin (now a brigadier-general), swung north into East Prussia, in the direction of Königsberg. To his delight, he found himself in the very region in which General Samsonov had fought and been defeated in the First World War (and where his father had also been), and even passed through some of the towns and villages he had attempted to describe in 1936 in his planned series of novels. Like Samsonov thirty years beforehand, he entered the town of Neidenburg when it was in flames—set ablaze by exulting Russian troops on the rampage. "Am tramping through East Prussia for the second day—a hell of a lot of impressions," he wrote to Natalia. And again: "Am sitting not far from the forest where Olkhovsky and Severtsev were surrounded!"*[28]

In East Prussia, even more than in the battle for Orel or the drive across Belorussia, Solzhenitsyn was able to get a first-hand, inside view of what it was like to fight as part of a large army on the move, and to get a feel for the

* I.e., characters in *The Sixth Course*.

thrusts, feints, and manoeuvres of major military units—experiences that were to be drawn upon for the battle scenes in *August 1914* (it helped that he was now moving across the same terrain). Yet this headlong advance carried its own risks, as when Solzhenitsyn and his battery suddenly found themselves cut off from the rest of their battalion and virtually surrounded by the enemy. The incident occurred on the night of 26 January 1945, near the village of Dietrichsdorf.[29] Solzhenitsyn's battery had been stationed in an abandoned country mansion on the outskirts of the village, and his men were in the process of setting up listening-posts in the silent countryside when they discovered that the woods were full of German and Vlasovite infantrymen. The Germans had been left behind the Russian lines in the general retreat and had abandoned their heavy guns and their vehicles in favour of a quick march back to rejoin their main force, and in this way had stumbled upon, and virtually surrounded, Solzhenitsyn's battery.

When Solzhenitsyn reported this development to battalion headquarters he was not believed: it was thought impossible for there to be a German attack without the thump of howitzers and the roar of lorries and tanks. But Solzhenitsyn's information was quickly confirmed when his link with headquarters was cut. There remained two paths back to where the battalion artillery was stationed. Solzhenitsyn sent the bulk of his technical equipment along the one he judged safer, in the care of one subaltern and Solomin, and himself, with Ovsyannikov, took the rest of the men along the other. Both groups returned safely, but in going back to rescue the lorry with his field kitchen, which had got bogged down in the snow, Solzhenitsyn (now accompanied by Commissar Pashkin) came under heavy rifle fire, and they and their companions were forced to scatter into the woods to escape. Solzhenitsyn later wrote that his main impression of that night was one of a kind of weightlessness, a sense of "having merely visited this world, rather than being attached to it, of my body feeling strangely light and having been lent to me for just a while." There was a "sharpness of sensation that was not born of fear, but a rarer sharpness that comes when you swallow danger and when scenes of your past life go rushing through your head."

Such experiences were the very stuff of war and were to inform the action passages in both *Prussian Nights* and *August 1914*. Solzhenitsyn's sensations in coming under fire, and his long, roundabout trek through the woods—after his battalion had scattered—to rejoin his men, were recalled especially in *August 1914*, in the episode in which Vorotyntsev and a group of soldiers are themselves cut off and have to make a long march through the forest to return to safety.*

Other experiences of these weeks were to leave a bitterer taste in his mouth and to arouse more complex emotions, notably the behaviour of the victorious Soviet troops in Prussia. Egged on by their commanders and political commissars, they raged through the neat and orderly Prussian country-

---

*It is interesting that the fictional episode parallels Solzhenitsyn's experiences in East Prussia right down to the detail of the soldiers being obliged to carry a dead body with them.

side like the avenging hordes of Genghis Khan. Whole towns and villages were fired and burnt to the ground. Houses, churches, shops, offices, schools, and the unfortunate population were picked clean of anything that could be moved and carried away as plunder, and anything that couldn't be moved was smashed or burnt. In *Prussian Nights* Solzhenitsyn has described this crazy, drunken rampage of the Russian army through Prussia, combining incidents that he himself witnessed with ones later related to him by his prison-camp friend Lev Kopelev, who served on the same front. His ambivalent feelings come through with great clarity.

> Well, land, industrious and proud,
> Blaze and smoke and flame away.
> Amid the violence of the crowd
> In my heart no vengeance calls.
> I'll not fire one stick of kindling,
> Nor will I quench your flaming halls.
> Untouched I'll leave you. I'll be off
> Like Pilate when he washed his hands.
> Between us there is Samsonov,
> Between us many a cross there stands
> Of whitened Russian bones. For strange
> Feelings rule my soul tonight.
> I've know you now for all these years . . .
> Long since a premonition rose,
> Ostpreussen! that our paths would cross.
> Back home beneath the dust of years
> Secret archives hold unseen
> What your arrogance thrust up
> In the towers of Hohenstein . . .
> I nursed inside me till I filled
> With muffled shouting, all the pain,
> And all the shame of that campaign.[30]

Ambivalence about the cruelty and looting and the unnamed hero's half-hearted involvement in the pillaging are the principal theme of *Prussian Nights*, which sets out to show the corrupting influence of victory in war and of an unbridled lust for vengeance. Solzhenitsyn was not immune from temptation either, although his looting was selective, idiosyncratic, and not directed towards enriching himself. In eastern Poland he had acquired a useful library of rare or unobtainable Russian books, including many from the period of the Revolution and the early twenties that were now banned in the Soviet Union. Mere possession of these books was technically a crime, but it was simple enough to conceal them in the hurly-burly of war. Solzhenitsyn had stored them in an empty howitzer case that he carried in his captured Opel.

But in *Prussian Nights* he describes a moment when sheer greed took possession of him too—in a German post office—at the sight of gleaming piles of good-quality paper, bundles of Faber and Koh-i-noor pencils, and heaps of paper clips, drawing pins, labels, folders, scissors—riches beyond the dreams of avarice in the shabby, pinched, and poverty-stricken Soviet Union of the thirties and forties, where the paper was spongy and crumbling, the pens scratchy, the ink watery, and the pencils prone to snap at the first pressure.

On another occasion Solzhenitsyn chanced upon a mill. The miller was not there, but Solzhenitsyn discovered that the miller had been an amateur writer; in his study there were several manuscripts, including an unfinished critical essay on Dostoyevsky (an apologetic letter from a German publisher praised the essay, but said the times were unpropitious for publishing work on a Russian writer). Solzhenitsyn was particularly interested by a book in the miller's library that dealt with the First World War and that was illustrated with small photographs of the main protagonists. The book itself was of no value, but he cut out the portraits that interested him. They were all postage-stamp size and included pictures of Tsar Nicholas II, the German and Russian generals of the time—Ludendorff, Hindenburg, Samsonov, Brusilov, and so on—and some of the Soviet revolutionary leaders, including Lenin and Trotsky. He stowed them in his suitcase and moved on.

There was something else about the advance into Prussia that disturbed him, and that was the sight of columns of Russian prisoners of war, recently released from German captivity, marching back towards the Soviet Union— "the only people who looked sorrowful when all around were rejoicing," as he wrote in *The Gulag Archipelago*. "I was stunned by their dejection, although I didn't understand the cause of it at the time. I left my car and went over to those people voluntarily forming up in columns. (Why columns? Why had they lined up in ranks? After all, nobody was forcing them; prisoners of war from all the other nations were making their own way home as scattered individuals. But ours wanted to appear as submissive as possible in their return home.) But I was prevented by my captain's epaulettes from learning the true cause of their sadness, and there was no time to stop and inquire further."[31]

Solzhenitsyn still found time to write to his friends and to Natalia, but relations between husband and wife remained strained and continued to reflect the differences that had emerged between them on her visit to the trenches. He was still evidently disturbed by some of the arguments they had had.

In the spring of 1944 I saw how egotistical your love still was, how full of prejudices you still were about family life. . . . You imagine our future as an uninterrupted life together, with accumulating furniture, a cosy flat, regular visits by guests, evenings at the theatre. . . . It is quite likely that none of this will happen. We may lead a restless life, moving from place to place. Things will be acquired and be discarded just as easily again.

Everything depends on you. I love you, I love nobody else. But just as a train cannot depart from the rails by a single millimetre without crashing, so it is with me—I cannot swerve for an instant from my path.

At the moment you love only me, which means, in the final analysis, that you love me for your own sake, for the satisfaction of your own needs.[32]

There again was that image of a train implacably proceeding in a pre-determined direction. In her book Natalia Reshetovskaya writes that the main issue between them was still whether or not to have children. Commenting on this in a conversation on the subject much later, Solzhenitsyn was adamant that he had been right.

> Of course, having children is an important part of life. But I was so wound up—my path was like that of a piston. . . . Everything's important, yes, every side of life has its importance, but at the same time I would have lost my momentum and my kinetic energy. Take a stone. Of course, it flies over nice, attractive places, but it begins to falter, so to speak, if it begins to fall, and loses its energy. . . . But it's got to fly on and on . . . and that was the whole point with me. I had been born as a wound up spring, and the spring then started to unwind. . . .[33]

In his postscript to Natalia, Solzhenitsyn complained yet again about Nikolai's silence: "No letters from Koka, but I see that General Kolpakchi is heading straight for Berlin."[34]

Three days after Solzhenitsyn's visit to the miller's house, on 9 February 1945, in the village of Wormdit, just east of Königsberg, one of his subalterns took a telephone call from brigade headquarters and informed him that he was to report at once to Brigadier-General Travkin. What happened next has been described by Solzhenitsyn in *The Gulag Archipelago*. As he entered the brigadier-general's office, he noticed a group of officers standing in one corner of the room but recognized only one of them, the brigade's political commissar. Travkin ordered Solzhenitsyn to step forward and hand over his revolver. Solzhenitsyn removed the revolver with its strap and gave it to Travkin, who slowly wound the leather strap round and round the butt before placing it in his desk drawer. Then Travkin said gravely to Solzhenitsyn in a low voice:

"All right, you must go now."

Uncomprehendingly, Solzhenitsyn thought the general must be referring to some special mission he had been selected for.

"Yes, yes," repeated Travkin in the silence, "it is time for you to go somewhere."

At that moment two officers from among the group in the corner stepped forward and shouted:

"You're under arrest!"

They were from Smersh, the Soviet counter-espionage service.* Solzhenitsyn could manage only a feeble question.

"Me? What for?"

Instead of answering, they ripped his epaulettes from his shoulders and the star from his cap, removed his belt, snatched the map-case from his hands, and began to march him from the room.

"Solzhenitsyn, come back here," barked Travkin.

---

*Smersh was an acronym for *smert' shpionam*—"death to spies."

Solzhenitsyn broke away from his escort and turned back towards the brigadier-general.

"Have you," said Travkin meaningfully, "a friend on the First Ukrainian Front?"

"That's against regulations! You have no right!" shouted the two Smersh officers, a captain and a colonel, confident, as counter-intelligence officers, of their right to shout at a general. The remaining officers, serving members of the brigade, shrank back in their corner.

Solzhenitsyn understood instantly that the reference was to Nikolai and that this was a warning. He also realized why he had been receiving so few letters from Nikolai. They had been intercepted and read.

The angry counter-intelligence men prepared once more to lead Solzhenitsyn away, but the general slowly rose to his feet behind his desk, leaned across it, and ostentatiously shook Solzhenitsyn by the hand.

"I wish you happiness, Captain!"[35]

8

AN ENEMY OF
THE TOILING MASSES

THE SHOCK OF this sudden and wholly unexpected arrest completely unnerved Solzhenitsyn. He was stunned, mortified, and bewildered and felt, like so many before him, that there must have been some mistake. If so, he would sort it out at Smersh headquarters. Travkin, at least, had shown his good opinion of him—Solzhenitsyn would treasure his handshake for the rest of his life. "That handshake," he later said, "was the most courageous act I witnessed throughout the war."[1] It was courageous because his very arrest proclaimed Solzhenitsyn "an enemy of the people" or, rather, "an enemy of the toiling masses," as the formula ran in those days. There was no question of him being found innocent. "We never make mistakes" was the proud boast of the Soviet security organs, meaning not that mistakes were never made but simply that they were never admitted. Travkin must have been aware of this, but Solzhenitsyn was still a naïve "rabbit" and later admitted in his description of this moment in *The Gulag Archipelago* that he was more concerned with appearances: How was he to make his way through the telephone operator's room and keep his dignity, with his insignia torn off and his cap denuded of its officer's star?

The Smersh men were unconcerned with such niceties. German shells were thudding into the ground less than two hundred yards away, and they were frightened. Ilya Solomin had been ordered to bring Solzhenitsyn's personal belongings in his suitcase, but when the sergeant arrived, there was no chance to speak to him or to exchange glances. Solzhenitsyn noted with gratitude that Solomin had not brought the howitzer case with the banned books; and he later discovered that Ilya had saved some of his personal notes and Natalia's letters, and returned them to Natalia.

Solzhenitsyn was driven to the brigade Smersh headquarters, where he was searched and the contents of his case were examined. A list was made of all confiscated items, except for a small scarlet cigarette-case that he had once looted from a German and that was now pocketed by one of his captors. The suitcase was handed back to him and he was handcuffed and ordered to get back into the car. Solzhenitsyn has noted that after the first shock had passed, he felt strangely detached and light-headed. Once more a part of his brain seemed to drift out of his head and float alongside him, contemplating his situation from outside. As the car raced along the asphalt road through the night, its headlights picking out the now-familiar features of the German countryside, he experienced a flash of fantastic hope and exhilaration: Perhaps he was being taken straight to Moscow to see the leaders in the Kremlin, perhaps even to Stalin himself? How much more sensible than talking to these counter-intelligence dolts. There he would explain everything, explode the tired myths of the present system, and convince them that his was the best programme for future development.[2]

He was brought down to earth when he suddenly noticed they were going the wrong way—towards Passarg, where the German army was encamped. He hesitated whether to tell them, and decided he should, but they were suspicious. They stopped the car. Suddenly there was an explosion. The Germans had started shelling them. In the flat countryside their lights could be seen for miles. They jumped back into the car and drove back the way they had come. Sheepishly, the major held out the map to Solzhenitsyn and asked him to navigate: counter-intelligence officers were not taught to read maps. He also offered him his cigarette-case back and invited him to light up. Obediently, Solzhenitsyn took the maps and directed them to the jail.

The forty-sixth Army Smersh headquarters was situated in a former vicarage in the small Prussian town of Osterode. Solzhenitsyn's clothing and suitcase were searched once more, his suitcase was sealed, and his cigarette-case was again confiscated by the major, who accused Solzhenitsyn of having concealed it from him. Solzhenitsyn was taken down into the cellar, where three other prisoners were already lying on some straw on the floor. There was barely room to stretch out, and the bodies were packed tightly together, but Solzhenitsyn was obliged to squeeze in, and he spent a restless night, burning with shame at the indignity of it all. Up till now he had felt that perhaps his officer's status would save him. But the concrete cellar quickly put an end to that dream—his fellow prisoners were all officers too—and there were fresh humiliations to follow. The next morning, having been joined by a fifth prisoner, they were ordered upstairs by a blustering sergeant-major. A circle of machine-gunners stood in the yard guarding a path that led behind the barn. It was a latrine call, and the prisoners were obliged to squat and defecate in a yard already littered with human faeces, and under the gaze of the grim guards with their machine-guns cocked.

Later that day Solzhenitsyn was lined up with seven other prisoners and marched from the army counter-intelligence headquarters in Osterode to the front headquarters in Brodnitz.* All except one of his companions were returned prisoners of war, with the letters *SU* painted crudely on their backs by their former German captors. Having survived months or years of German captivity, they were suspected of treason and were being herded back into Russia for security checks and investigation. The eighth prisoner, marching beside Solzhenitsyn, was a German civilian of about fifty. Still clinging to his officer's privileges, Solzhenitsyn insisted that the German carry his suitcase for him, which the German did until he started to drop from exhaustion. The case was then carried by each of the other seven in turn, who were all privates.

It was forty-five miles to Brodnitz, and it took them two days to walk the whole way, with one stop overnight. The weather was cold, damp, and changeable, with sudden squalls of snow that drenched them to the skin and chilled them to the marrow. At one point they met a long string of empty horse-drawn carts going the other way, being driven by Russian soldiers. It was a transport unit like the one Solzhenitsyn had served in at the beginning of the war. The cart-drivers quickly noticed Solzhenitsyn's tailored greatcoat and gleaming gold buttons, which contrasted vividly with the shapeless, mud-stained coats of the former prisoners of war, and concluded that he must be a captured Vlasov officer. "Vlasovite bastard! Shoot the rat!" they jeered as they passed by, adding a variety of mother oaths. Disconcerted and mortified, Solzhenitsyn smiled back at them, trying to make them understand that he was not really a traitor. On the contrary, he felt that he was on their side: "I smiled in pride that I had been arrested not for stealing, or for treason, or desertion, but because with the power of reason I had penetrated Stalin's evil secrets. I smiled at the thought that I wanted, and might still be able, to effect some small remedies and changes in our Russian life." But his smiles only made things worse and brought fiercer insults from the jeering cart-drivers.[3]

In Brodnitz the prisoners were placed in cells while a decision was taken about where to send them. Solzhenitsyn remained there three days and heard his first tales about the new underworld he had entered—about the interrogations and the beatings, about the deceptions and tricks practised by the investigators, about the fact that once you were arrested there was no hope, that no one was ever released, and about the "tenners" (ten-year sentences) automatically handed out by the military tribunals. It was all new, and he scarcely believed it could apply to him. After three days he was taken out and escorted to the station by a Smersh lieutenant and two sergeants. The sergeants were loaded with two heavy suitcases apiece, as well as their automatic rifles, and he was told that their destination was Moscow. The suitcases were stuffed with war booty—not theirs, but belonging to their superior officers, who were exploiting this opportunity to get their trophies safely back to Moscow.

* Now Brodnica, in western Poland.

The first part of the journey, from Brodnitz to Bialystok and thence to the Soviet border, was made on the platform of a flat railway wagon, on which they were totally exposed to the snow, rain, and icy winds of February. Three-quarters of the train consisted of similar wagons packed tight with Russian women and girls who had been rounded up in the occupied territories and were being sent back to the Soviet Union to be tried as collaborators. Also on the train was a handful of regular soldiers going home on leave, including four women who had boarded in Brodnitz. At the Soviet border the train was stopped for border formalities. The "collaborators" were locked in a barn preparatory to being questioned by Smersh officers on their activities in the occupied zones, while Solzhenitsyn and his guards paced the platform waiting for the next train east. They were not bothered by the frontier police, for they had Smersh passes to Moscow, the very sight of which acted like magic on the local bureaucrats. They then caught a normal passenger train to Minsk, where they transferred to the Minsk–Moscow Express and were able to travel in some comfort. By this time Solzhenitsyn was on familiar "thou" terms with the officer in charge of his escort and friendly with the sergeants too. To make things easier all round they agreed to pretend that he wasn't under arrest at all—he still had his officer's greatcoat on, and the lack of epaulettes merely gave him a devil-may-care, fresh-from-the-front appearance. The lieutenant even treated him to vodka and allowed him to walk up and down the train, but always with one of the three as escort: they took turns guarding him at night throughout the four-day journey.[4]

Once again Solzhenitsyn had regained a precarious foothold in the normal, respectable society that he had always inhabited until now, but his glimpses of the nether world that yawned beneath his feet had filled him with foreboding. In *The Way* he later compared this ignominious return to Russia with that of the nineteenth-century poet and friend of Pushkin—William Küchelbecker—who was later banished to Siberia for his part in the Decembrist conspiracy.*

> I am riding like Küchelbecker
> To be questioned by hirelings of the tsar,
> My escorts those very same gendarmes—
> Like the poet, I too am right.

Like Küchelbecker he was riding from west to east, from Europe to Muscovy, which was more Asiatic than European, and like Küchelbecker he went unresistingly, as if having half expected such a thing to happen.

*The Decembrists were a group of aristocratic officers who organized a rebellion in December 1825, on the death of Tsar Alexander I, in an attempt to install Alexander's brother Constantine on the throne in place of his chosen younger brother, Nicholas. Their hope was that the more liberal Constantine would promulgate an enlightened constitution for Russia limiting the monarch's powers and enshrining the rule of law. Constantine had already refused the throne and supported the installation of Nicholas, who promptly crushed the rebellion by force, executed the ringleaders, imprisoned others, and exiled considerable numbers to Siberia. Küchelbecker spent the last twenty years of his life first in prison and then in Siberian exile.

We have been slaves from time immemorial,
We love our submissive state.
That's why destiny drives us—
Europe to Asia expresses our fate.[5]*

This refusal to resist, this willing acceptance of his lot and his inability to cry out and protest even in the Minsk–Moscow express, even in the crowded Moscow metro when he eventually arrived there, was later to strike Solzhenitsyn as astonishing and became a metaphor for the attitude of the entire Soviet people. But at the time there was little chance of his conceiving such an idea, let alone putting it into practice. He was a loyal citizen, a believer (however distrustful of Stalin), still faithful to the system and convinced that there were peaceful and democratic ways of bringing about a change. His arrest was a mistake, a nightmarish slip that would be put right when he got to Moscow. And he knew that if he did cry out and make a fuss, nobody could do anything about it, nobody would believe him. In fact, the one small action he did attempt ended in failure. The four servicewomen on leave had also boarded the Moscow express. Their presence reminded him of his earlier concern for Natalia and gave him an idea. He went and sat by them, singled out the youngest and most attractive one, and struck up a conversation with her. The girl responded to Solzhenitsyn's advances and soon the others leaned away, leaving them to their tête-à-tête. When he judged the moment right, Solzhenitsyn leaned forward and in a transparent code informed her that he was under arrest. He then whispered "Rostov Sredny 27, Reshetovskaya"— Natalia's address—and asked the girl to memorize it and pass the message on. But the girl was outraged and turned away. The guard, observing her from afar, concluded cheerfully that Solzhenitsyn had made a different sort of proposition and that the girl had refused.

In Moscow, Solzhenitsyn found himself pressed into the role of guide once again. The Smersh men had never been in Moscow before and had no idea where to go. He led them down into the metro from the Belorussian Station and conducted them—himself—to the seat of the NKGB, the Lubyanka.[6] The Lubyanka was the most famed and feared of all Moscow's many prisons and one of the three (the others were Butyrki and Lefortovo) that specialized in political prisoners. Unlike the others, it had not been built as a prison. It had been the headquarters of the pre-revolutionary insurance company Rossia and was noted for the fine architecture of its public rooms and the opulence of its furnishings—attributes to which the leaders of the Cheka-GPU-OGPU-NKVD-NKGB were by no means indifferent. Solzhenitsyn arrived there on 20 February 1945.

The procedures for receiving new prisoners at the Lubyanka were immutable, having been worked out and perfected over the twenty-five years

* Solzhenitsyn later published a long extract from *The Way* in the Paris *Vestnik RKbD*, no. 117 (1976), describing his arrival on the Soviet frontier and his thoughts at the time, but this stanza was omitted.

of Soviet rule. They have been described so many times by westerners and Russians that the very words "Lubyanka," "interrogation," "KGB," "political prisoner," "purge," have become common currency, bogeys with which to frighten children and to which adults tend to become indifferent, preferring to forget the evil reality that lies behind them. But Solzhenitsyn did not forget, and nowhere have they been better described than in the closing pages of *The First Circle*, where Innokenti Volodin's treatment recapitulates Solzhenitsyn's experiences exactly.[7]

Basing ourselves on *The First Circle*, we can say with some confidence that Solzhenitsyn was led downstairs and thrown into a tiny windowless cell to which the Russians have attached the English name of "box." The box was so small that it was impossible to lie down in it. The sole furniture was a table and stool, filling almost the entire floor space, and when Solzhenitsyn sat down, there was no room even to straighten his legs. The walls were green to shoulder height and then white, dazzling his eyes with the reflected light from a mesh-covered 200-watt bulb in the high ceiling. The door was about four inches thick and had a judas-hole in it. The outside cover was regularly slid back every minute or so for a solitary eye to peer in at him. Apart from that, he was unable to hear a sound, except for the occasional click of a lock in the distance as other cells were opened or closed.

Suddenly the door was unlocked and the cell invaded by a man in a grey overall, who brusquely demanded to know his name. He was ordered to go to another room, strip off his clothes and drop them on the floor. When Solzhenitsyn was naked, the man stepped up to him, told him to open his mouth, say "ah" and put his tongue in the roof of his mouth. He then thrust his fingers into Solzhenitsyn's mouth and thoroughly explored his cheeks. Next he pulled down his lower eyelids and peered inside, jerked Solzhenitsyn's head back so that the light shone into his nostrils, poked his fingers into Solzhenitsyn's ears, and ordered him to splay his fingers and raise his arms to make sure everything was clear. All this was done without a word of explanation. The man maintained a stony indifference to the prisoner and did not permit himself the slightest human expression. Solzhenitsyn was then obliged to take hold of his penis, turn the foreskin back, lift it to the left and the right, then to spread his legs as far apart as they would go, bend over, take his buttocks in each hand and pull them apart, while the man inspected him. Finally, he had to stand and squat repeatedly until the man was satisfied.

When the body search was over, Solzhenitsyn was motioned to sit on a stool, his teeth chattering from the cold. The man in the grey overall then went to his pile of clothes on the floor and began to pinch and prod them and hold them up to the light, article by article. Underpants, vest, socks—piece by piece he pinched all the seams and folds before throwing them at Solzhenitsyn's feet and telling him to put them on. Picking up Solzhenitsyn's boots, he contemptuously shook out the little pieces of broken pencil that Solzhenitsyn had attempted to conceal in them, took out a jack-knife, thrust it between the soles, and pierced the heels with a marlinspike. When he reached Solzhenitsyn's tunic, he carefully ripped off all the gold braid and piping, cut off the buttons and button loops, and ripped open the lining to feel inside. Solzhenitsyn's trousers lost their buttons, too, and had their seams and pleats minutely explored. Finally came the tailored greatcoat, which had its lining slit open and its kapok stuffing pulled about, and his rubber galoshes, which the warder bent and twisted in every possible direction to make sure nothing was concealed in them.

All this lasted about an hour. When it was over, the man scooped up the pencils, the ripped-off braid and piping, and Solzhenitsyn's suspenders and braces and left without a word. Solzhenitsyn's precious captain's uniform was in rags, his greatcoat had all its stuffing sticking out, and his boots were full of holes; worst of all, he had no means of keeping his trousers up. In answer to his protest, the departing warder merely barked something about string and slammed the door. Stage one of his induction into the Lubyanka was complete, leaving him with feelings of disorientation and bewilderment that were later described in *The First Circle*.

> When he had thought beforehand about being arrested he had had a mental picture of a pitiless duel of wits. He had been inwardly tensed up, prepared for some sort of lofty struggle to defend his ideas and his future. But he had never suspected that it would all be so simple, so banal, and so inexorable. These people who dealt with him in the Lubyanka, men of lowly rank and intelligence, were indifferent to his individuality and to the reasons for his being there. On the other hand they were minutely attentive to details that he had never thought of before and in which he was unable to offer any resistance. But what possible meaning could resistance have and what would be the use? At every step, for a different reason, they demanded of him things that were the merest trifles in comparison with the great battle that lay ahead of him, and there was no point at all in kicking up a fuss about such matters. But taken all together, the methodical indirectness of the procedure was such as utterly to break the prisoner's will.[8]

But this procedure represented only a beginning of the Lubyanka's ritual. No sooner had Solzhenitsyn gathered his composure than the cell door opened again to admit another warder, this time in an off-white overall. Solzhenitsyn was ordered to take off his clothes again and sit on the stool. Suddenly he felt an iron grip on the back of his neck and some sort of cold vibrating machine being pressed against his head. Without a word the warder shaved Solzhenitsyn's head from back to front, from side to side, until he was as bald as a coot. Then he shaved his armpits and his pubic hair. Picking up his bag and his clippers, the warder let himself out of the cell as wordlessly and as casually as he had come. After a short pause there came a medical examination, for which Solzhenitsyn was obliged to strip once more and answer questions about VD, syphilis, leprosy, and other diseases.

The inexorable, consistent, and mechanical application of these procedures expressed the very essence of the Lubyanka system. Its primary purpose was purely practical, for the robotlike functionaries working at this level were exclusively concerned to see that the reception system worked efficiently and could be applied to all without distinction. But it also had a symbolic dimension that affected the prisoner psychologically. "The free man's habit of thinking about the consequences before acting quickly atrophied," wrote Solzhenitsyn later, for these procedures turned him into an object and "lulled [him] into a stupor, depriving him of his common sense and the will to resist."[9] Other practices reinforced this disposition. Not long after returning to his box, Solzhenitsyn was taken out again and led to the bathroom, where he was obliged to strip yet again and take a shower. When he emerged, his clothes had disappeared: they were being sterilized in the so-called fryer before they came back—limp, crumpled, and scorching hot. He was issued with shapeless prison underwear that didn't fit and a tiny square of Turkish towelling to dry himself on. From the bathroom he was taken back to his box, then out again and down endless corridors to another room, where he was photographed in profile and full face and had his fingerprints registered on a file-card that bore the legend "to be preserved forever." Then he was returned to his box again. Each time he left his box or entered another one, he had to recite the same mechanical litany—surname, name and patronymic, date of birth, and place of birth; and everywhere he went, the warder who was leading him would click his tongue loudly as if calling a dog. The point of this, Solzhenitsyn soon found out, was to warn other warders with prisoners of their approach (in some prisons they tapped their keys on their belt-buckles), for it was a rigid rule that prisoners should never meet, and if two should chance to approach one another from opposite directions, one would be roughly pushed into one of the plywood booths that lined the corridors at intervals especially for this purpose, and be commanded to stand there with his face to the wall.

It was late at night by the time these formalities had been completed. Solzhenitsyn was enervated but was not allowed to sleep. Every time he tried to curl up on the floor or lean his head on the table, he was roused by a warder and ordered to stay awake. At last he was told to put on his clothes and was led out of his box, along corridors, into a yard, down some stairs, and eventually into another wing, which he later learned was the interrogation block. He was taken up to the fourth floor in a lift and put into another box, which he at first took for his new home, but was then led out once again, after reciting the usual litany, and locked in a somewhat bigger one, measuring about ten feet by five.

This was the biggest box that Solzhenitsyn had yet seen. It had a stool, a table, and a wooden bench fastened to the wall, long enough to sleep on. Soon after his arrival the door opened, and instead of being called out, he was handed a red-checked mattress, a sheet, pillow, pillowslip, and blanket and was told he could lie down. Exhausted, he got into bed and tried to sleep. Almost before he had had time to close his eyes, the door burst open with a crash and the warder stormed in. He was supposed to sleep with his arms outside the blanket. It sounded simple, but proved to be a fiendishly difficult thing to do. He tossed and turned, burning with humiliation for the hundredth time that night. The light from the 200-watt bulb bored through his lids, his arms grew cold and stiff on top of the blanket, and he fell into a fitful and restless sleep. He did not know it, but he was now ready for the investigation.

The crucial period of a Soviet investigation is the first few days, when the prisoner is bewildered and disoriented and at the mercy of his investigator. In Solzhenitsyn's case, this period lasted for four days and nights, during which time he was deprived of sleep. This deprivation was not total, but since it was strictly forbidden to sleep after 6 a.m., the technique was simply to arrange for most of the interrogating to take place at night. As another ex-prisoner has pointed out, the result of this treatment was that you felt yourself on a knife-edge. Although exhausted by lack of sleep, you never knew when you would be summoned again, so that even when you lay down for a while, you involuntarily kept one ear cocked for the warder's footsteps, and every time a neighbouring door banged or a key grated in a lock, you automatically started awake, convinced that your turn had come. When it did come, the interrogation usually lasted until dawn, so that by the time you returned to your cell it was too late to sleep anyway.

By all accounts, deprivation of sleep was the very mildest of the techniques in use at the Lubyanka at that time and was virtually taken for granted by the investigators. It was applied universally, and only "recalcitrant" prisoners were subjected to physical ill-treatment and torture. James Allan, an Englishman who had escaped to Russia from the Germans during the war, was flung into the Lubyanka as a suspected spy and beaten with rubber truncheons to make him confess.[10] Worse than the Lubyanka was Lefortovo Prison, specializing in brutal forms of solitary confinement, and for really difficult cases there was Sukhanovka, where prisoners were made to stand motionless for days at a time and kept without sleep for months, as well as being physically tortured.*

Solzhenitsyn knew little of this when he was first marched down the endless corridors by a tongue-clicking warder and into the presence of Captain I. I. Ezepov, his investigator. Ezepov's office was large and imposing, one of the swankier rooms of the Rossia Insurance Company, with an enormously high ceiling. On one wall hung a thirteen-foot-high, full-length portrait of Stalin, before which Ezepov would stand theatrically, invoking the leader's name in moments of high stress and patriotic fervour. It was particularly ironic, in view of the nature of Solzhenitsyn's political views, that an icon of none other than the great leader should gaze down on him as he was being interrogated.

The charges were now read out to Solzhenitsyn, and he learned that he

---

* Sukhanovka has been graphically described in a book by an American citizen who was kidnapped in the street and taken there: Alexander Dolgun, with Patrick Watson, *Alexander Dolgun's Story* (London and New York, 1975).

was accused of anti-Soviet propaganda under Article 58 of the criminal code, paragraph 10, and of founding a hostile organization under paragraph 11.* As he quickly discovered, his case did not present any special difficulties to the investigator. Apart from possessing copies of all correspondence between Solzhenitsyn, Nikolai, Natalia, Kirill, and Lydia from April 1944 to February 1945, Ezepov now had a copy of "Resolution No. 1" from Solzhenitsyn's map-case, with its unambiguously stated intention to organize a new party and attract support for it. There were also the numerous derogatory references to Stalin in the letters. Still in a state of shock from the succession of humiliations he had endured, and numbed by lack of sleep, Solzhenitsyn must have listened with a mixture of stunned fascination and blank disbelief as the interrogator swiftly refashioned this material into a smooth conspiracy for the overthrow of the Soviet regime. His instinct, he later wrote, was to deny it all, to resist this distortion of his and Nikolai's intentions, and to "correct" the investigator's interpretation of them. He pointed out that they were loyal citizens, anxious only to reform and improve the system, not to overthrow it, invoked Lenin, and explained that there was nothing subversive or traitorous in what they had planned. What he did not realize was that the man facing him was a cynical *apparatchik*, indifferent to claims of truth or humanity alike, and that the system of "justice" that had him in its grip was the same. Despite his misty awareness of the arrests, trials, and purges, Solzhenitsyn had believed, like millions of his fellow countrymen, that an ultimately benign government was striving to achieve justice, equality, brotherhood, and all those other ideals for which the Revolution had allegedly been carried out. Even now, when presented with direct evidence to the contrary, he could not bring himself to change his mind. And so, apart from all his other disadvantages, he suffered from the psychological disability of being taken completely unawares and having to re-examine and readjust attitudes and habits that had been fifteen years in the making.

* Article 58, paragraph 10, part 2, read as follows: "Propaganda or agitation containing an appeal to overthrow, undermine, or weaken the Soviet regime or to commit individual counter-revolutionary crimes, and also the preparation, distribution, or conservation of literature of this nature, shall be punishable by deprivation of liberty for a period of not less than six months. Similar actions undertaken under conditions of mass unrest or involving the exploitation of the religious or national prejudices of the masses, or under conditions of war, or in localities placed under martial law, are punishable by the measures of social defence laid down in Article 58, section 2, of the Criminal Code." Paragraph 11 read as follows: "Any type of organizational activity directed towards the preparation or commission of crimes dealt with in the present chapter, and also participation in an organization formed for the preparation or commission of such crimes, shall be punishable by the measures of social defence laid down in the relevant sections of the present chapter." The "measures of social defence" prescribed in a case like Solzhenitsyn's were summed up as follows: "The supreme measure of social defence is death by shooting or the declaration of the accused to be an enemy of the toiling masses, whereby his property shall be confiscated, he shall be deprived of citizenship of his union republic and therefore of the USSR itself and be banished beyond the borders of the USSR forever. In extenuating circumstances a reduction of sentence is permitted to not less than three years' deprivation of liberty and the confiscation of all or part of his property."

He was particularly disarmed, it seems, by the cynical manner in which his testimony was manipulated and distorted. All criminal investigations begin with the police or investigating authority marshalling the evidence for a crime and then seeking to substantiate it, either with further evidence from witnesses or with testimony by the accused. The Soviet judicial organs, however, had introduced a number of novelties into this traditional scheme, with a view to increasing the rate of conviction and securing a 100 per cent record. The purpose of the investigation was not to ascertain whether or not the alleged crime had been committed or, if committed, whether or not by the accused, but simply to build a plausible case for finding the accused guilty. From this flowed a number of consequences. Only evidence that confirmed the allegations was sought and recorded—all evidence to the contrary was ignored. Since it was often difficult to collect any evidence at all, confessions were assigned a major role in Soviet judicial practice, and sufficient ill-treatment and torture could persuade a defendant to sign almost anything. All evidence and confessions were clothed in tendentious language favourable to the prosecution's case. This was facilitated by the rule that all evidence had to be written down by the investigator, including the testimony or "confession" of the accused. These depositions constitute the famous "protocols" (the word the Russians use for them) that always loom so large in Soviet political trials. But although the investigator has to write the protocols down, the prisoner (or witness) must still sign each one as a correct record, and it is then he discovers that whenever he has used the word "meeting," it turns up in the protocol as "criminal gathering"; "views" are invariably "anti-Soviet views"; to give someone something to read is to "distribute anti-Soviet material", and to do anything in concert with anyone else is to form an "organization" (usually "anti-Soviet"). Similarly, there can be no grey areas or vaguenesses in protocols. If the defendant doesn't deny something outright, but attempts to fudge the answer with a "sort of," "perhaps," "I don't know," "I'm not sure," or "I've forgotten," he is recorded as saying "yes," and the questions are almost invariably leading ones, presented in biased formulations that are hard to deny without committing oneself to an outright lie, which most innocent individuals are reluctant to do. Another factor is that although the charges are read to the defendant, he usually has no means of checking them himself or of seeking advice. Copies of the criminal code are rarely on sale in the Soviet Union—it counts as a semi-secret document. Nor is he allowed any legal representation during the investigation, so that he hasn't the faintest idea what his rights might be. Even if, as in post-Stalinist times, he later has the benefit of a defence counsel, such counsel must invariably be approved by the KGB, is quite often chosen by the KGB, and just as often works for the KGB, in other words, for the prosecuting organs. Finally, in Stalin's day, everything possible was done to convince the prisoner of his guilt even before the investigation began: his possessions were confiscated, his head was shaven, he was put on convict's rations, and was treated like a criminal from the very moment of his arrest, all of which was designed to reinforce the weight of the prosecution.

Solzhenitsyn discovered a great deal of this through painful experience during his first few days in the Lubyanka, but not enough to enable him to deal with Captain Ezepov on equal terms; and it quickly became clear that Solzhenitsyn's conviction under Article 58, paragraph 10, was virtually assured. What interested Ezepov more were the charges under paragraph 11—forming an organization—and his questions were directed towards establishing the number of people Solzhenitsyn might have recruited to it. This could mean only Natalia, Kirill, and Lydia, since Nikolai was already as deeply implicated as Solzhenitsyn by their exchange of letters. Nikolai was also carrying a copy of "Resolution No. 1," though Solzhenitsyn had no idea whether Nikolai, too, had been arrested. But anxiety over the fate of Nikolai, his wife, and his friends was yet one more worry to add to the others that were tormenting him. Their letters all lay on the investigator's desk, together with his own.[11]

Fortunately Ezepov seemed quite pleased with Solzhenitsyn's initial spirit of co-operation, and after only four days allowed him to be transferred from solitary confinement to a normal investigation cell. It was just after bedtime on the fourth day when the warder came to wake him again. Expecting yet another call for interrogation, Solzhenitsyn kept his head on the pillow as long as he could but was surprised to be told to gather up his things and take them with him. Walking on tiptoe, the guard led him silently along a series of corridors to Cell 67, unlocked the door, and told him to enter. There were three other prisoners inside, all asleep on their metal cots.

> At the sound of the door opening, all three started and raised their heads for an instant. They, too, were waiting to see which of them was being called for interrogation. And those three heads lifted in alarm, those three unshaven, crumpled, pale faces seemed to me so human, so dear, that I stood there hugging my mattress and smiled with happiness. And they also smiled. And what a forgotten expression that was—after only one week!

In *The Gulag Archipelago*, where this scene appears, Solzhenitsyn has explained the emotional significance of this first reunion with his fellow men after the ordeal of arrest, imprisonment, and interrogation.

> Of all the cells you've been in, your first cell is a very special one, the place where you first encountered others like yourself, doomed to the same fate. All your life you will remember it with an emotion that can only be compared to memories of your first love. And those people with whom you shared the floor and air of that stone cubicle during the days when you rethought your entire life will later be recalled by you as members of your own family.[12]

Solzhenitsyn at once responded to the warmth of human company and began to exchange information with his new acquaintances, a procedure that continued for as long as it took for his trestle bed to be delivered and set up and his bedding arranged upon it. He was then silenced by the oldest man in the cell and reminded that every moment of sleep was precious to them. Nearly an hour of sleep time had passed already, and nobody knew which of them might be called out for interrogation later that night. But the real joy of his first cell and its exceptional interest and importance for his later life derived not merely from the warmth of personal contact but even more from what he heard and learned from the other people in the cell. It was to be the start of his true education, an education that developed slowly and painfully at first and was to continue throughout his entire term in prisons, camps, and exile, and that eventually changed his life. It was here that the first cracks developed in his hitherto impregnable Marxist faith, cracks that had been started by his encounters with his interrogator and that were now to be widened—but not too far—by his companions in the cell.

The first to attract his sympathy and interest was the old man who had shushed him on his arrival, Anatoly Ilyich Fastenko. It turned out that Fastenko was that revered phenomenon, a genuine Old Bolshevik.* He had been arrested under the tsarist regime as long ago as 1904, had participated in the revolution of 1905, served eight years' hard labour, gone into exile, escaped from exile and fled abroad, travelled to Canada and the United States, and finally returned to Russia after the October Revolution. It was the classic odyssey of the genuine revolutionary. But what interested Solzhenitsyn most of all was that Fastenko had personally known Lenin and had worked in the Bolshevik school at Longjumeau. Solzhenitsyn pressed him for anecdotes and impressions of the great man and was utterly bewildered to find Fastenko cool and non-committal on this subject. Indifference to such a colossus, the founder of the Soviet state, bordered on sacrilege, an outrage soon compounded by another form of sacrilege of which Fastenko was not the perpetrator but the object. His patronymic, Ilyich, was the same as Lenin's. It was (and is) common practice in the Soviet Union to refer to Lenin by his patronymic alone, implying affection and respect in about equal measure. Solzhenitsyn was therefore appalled to hear his new cell-mates addressing Fastenko as "Ilyich," especially when it came to such comments as "Ilyich, it's your turn to take out the piss bucket."

Solzhenitsyn was fascinated by Fastenko's stories of his revolutionary exploits in tsarist times but was surprised and disappointed to learn that after the Revolution he had opted for a lowly job on *Pravda* and had more or less dissociated himself from the new revolutionary government. And when Fastenko recounted how the private society formed by men who had done hard labour under the tsar was disbanded in the thirties and how he had been arrested for "terrorism" for possessing an ancient pistol, Solzhenitsyn interpreted these things as yet further proof of the evils of Stalinism and evidence of the way in which Stalin had perverted the course of the Revolution. Fa-

*Old Bolsheviks were those men and women who had been members of the Bolshevik Party before the Revolution. The Society of Old Bolsheviks, to which many of them belonged, had been dissolved in 1935, and Old Bolsheviks suffered heavily in Stalin's purges of 1937–39.

stenko, for some reason, did not endorse Solzhenitsyn's conclusions, and a slight coolness developed between them. "Thou shalt not make unto thee any graven image," Fastenko said to Solzhenitsyn apropos of Lenin, and on another occasion he cautioned him, as a mathematician, to remember Descartes's maxim "Question everything," reminding him that "everything" meant what it said. Learning that Gorky was one of Solzhenitsyn's favourite authors, he advised him to read not the novels but *Untimely Thoughts;** and from among the Marxist classics he recommended Plekhanov, especially his *One Year in the Motherland*.†

Second only to Fastenko in interest (and eventually to come before him in Solzhenitsyn's affections) was a middle-aged Estonian lawyer named Arnold Susi. Unlike Fastenko, who represented a type familiar to Solzhenitsyn from his reading and his knowledge of revolutionary history, Susi was something quite new to him: an educated European. It was some time before the two of them came together. Susi, with his grave, reserved air and gentle manners, was not an obvious partner for the impulsive young officer with his Russian directness and front-line asperity. Having studied at the University of Petrograd, he spoke fluent Russian, in addition to his native Estonian, and was equally fluent in German and English. In Estonia between the wars he had been a leading barrister (known affectionately as "golden-tongued") and passionately interested in politics. Prisoners in cells, as opposed to boxes, were permitted twenty minutes' exercise every day, and during these brief walks Solzhenitsyn invariably tried to pair off with Susi and talk politics, since this was the one place where they could not be overheard by the inevitable stool-pigeon in each cell. And he learned of a whole new dimension in life.

> From childhood on I had somehow known that my objective was the history of the Russian Revolution and that nothing else concerned me. To understand the Revolution, I had long needed nothing besides Marxism. I cut away everything else involved and turned my back on it. But now fate had brought me together with Susi. He breathed a completely different sort of air, and he talked to me enthusiastically about his own world, and that world was Estonia and democracy. And although it had never occurred to me before to take an interest in Estonia—still less in bourgeois democracy—I listened and listened to his loving stories about the twenty free years of that reticent, hardworking, small nation of big men with their slow, solid ways. I listened to the principles of the Estonian constitution drawn from the best European experience and how it had been worked out by their single-chamber parliament of a hundred deputies. And although I didn't know why, I began to be attracted by it all and to store it all away as part of my experience.[13]

*Gorky's "heretical" musings on the Bolsheviks and culture first appeared in the Petrograd newspaper *Novaya Zhizn'* (New Life) from May 1917 to July 1918. They were never republished in the Soviet Union but were reprinted in the West.
†Georgi Plekhanov, the "father" of Russian Marxism, died in Finland in 1918 deeply disappointed with the Russian Revolution. His *God na rodine* (One Year in the Motherland), an account of the events of 1917–18, was published posthumously in Paris (two volumes) in 1924.

The third cell-mate, Georgi Kramarenko, was the cell's stool-pigeon, whose job it was to report to the investigators on what the other prisoners were saying, how they reacted to their interrogation sessions, whether their mood was buoyant or depressed, and on anything else that could be of help to the investigators in breaking the prisoners' morale. This role was not acknowledged, of course. All sorts of subterfuges were used to enable Kramarenko to be called out and questioned, and Kramarenko denied his role vigorously when pressed. Solzhenitsyn was interested to find that he developed an instant distrust and dislike of the man at their first encounter and that his worst suspicions were subsequently confirmed. He also learned that at least one stool-pigeon was present in every cell—this was to prove the rule throughout his prison career—and that they could usually be spotted by their disposition to cadge, by the indulgent treatment they received from the authorities, and by a general air of deceitfulness and insincerity.

Not long after Solzhenitsyn's arrival in Cell 67, the authorities added a fifth inmate who also contributed to his education, though in a sense contrary to Fastenko and Susi. This was Leonid Z (Solzhenitsyn omits the full name from his account in *The Gulag Archipelago*), an engineer and the son of a peasant who had experienced a meteoric rise through Soviet society as a result of past reforms in education and who owed his all to the Soviet system, of which he was an outstanding product. Here was a living example of what the Revolution had been about. From barefoot peasant lad he had risen to become chief engineer of vast construction projects around Moscow and then, automatically exempted from military service, had been transferred to the rear, to Alma-Ata, where he had supervised even bigger projects, many of which had been carried out by convicts from the labour camps. In Alma-Ata he had lived like a king, as much hot money passing through his hands as through those of any Western profiteer or capitalist speculator. He had "uncorked," as he put it, over 290 women—he had kept careful count of them and boasted endlessly to his new cell-mates—and had flung his weight about with the abandon of a robber baron. But he had been careless. He had told a few questionable jokes, been loose with his opinions, and, worst of all, had crossed the secret police by refusing to supply free materials for a public prosecutor's dacha. Arrested under Article 58, he had collapsed like an over-inflated balloon. In the cell he ceaselessly bewailed his fate, forecast that he was doomed to be shot, and repeatedly burst into tears. Not even the white bread, butter, red caviar, veal, and sturgeon that his wife periodically brought him in food parcels could lift his depression, and to his cell-mates he appeared utterly crushed.

Solzhenitsyn understood well enough that there were plenty of barefoot peasant lads who had not only done well out of the Revolution but had become splendid citizens with all the civic virtues. You could not generalize from single examples. Nevertheless, just as Fastenko was his first Old Bolshevik, and Susi his first European democrat, so Leonid Z was the first example he had seen of a real Soviet businessman (and Kramarenko the first example of a Soviet stool-pigeon). Two for the system and two against, and there was little doubt as to which he preferred. As he later wrote, "for the first time in my life I was learning to look at things through a magnifying glass." He had also noticed that "as each of us had been arrested, everything in our world had switched places, a 180-degree shift in our concepts had occurred." [14] In fact, he had a long way to go before he completed the 180 degrees, but the path he had entered upon in the Lubyanka was to take him there in the end.

9

TWO ARE AN
ORGANIZATION

T HE REGIMEN IN the investigation cells was more humane than that in
the boxes, and Solzhenitsyn has described in *The Gulag Archipelago*
how the presence of fellow prisoners made it richer in incident than the
oppressive monotony of solitary confinement. The prisoners were still obliged
to sleep beneath a blinding 200-watt bulb at night, with their arms outside
the blankets, resorting to handkerchiefs over their faces and towels wrapped
round their arms to mitigate the worst effects of these regulations. Reveille
was at six o'clock sharp, and no mercy was shown to the prisoner who failed
to leap from his bed without an instant's delay, even if he had been up most
of the night under interrogation. Punishments for this and other infringements ranged from immediate removal to a punishment cell, on reduced rations,
to deprivation of library or exercise privileges for the entire cell. The two
hours from six to eight in the morning were spent in total silence and immobility—it was an offence to doze off for a single second. All that interrupted
the monotony of these two dreary hours between sleep and waking was the
toilet break. Solzhenitsyn has described the routine in part 1 of *The Gulag
Archipelago.*

> Then you formed up in single file, hands behind your backs, and the appointed
> bearer led the file, carrying the two-gallon tin slop-pail with a lid on it chest high
> before him. When you reached your goal you were locked in again, each having
> first been handed a scrap of paper the size of two railway tickets.[1]

Breakfast was at eight o'clock and consisted of a mug of tea, two lumps
of sugar, and a pound of bread. Solzhenitsyn particularly remembered the
bread.

That pound of unrisen wet bread, with its swamplike soggy dough, made half of potato flour was our *crutch* and the main event of the day. Life had begun! The day had begun—this was when it really began! Each of us had myriad problems: Had he correctly apportioned his ration the day before? Should he cut it with a thread? Or greedily break it into lumps? Or nip off pieces bit by bit? Wait for the tea or pile in straight away? Leave some for supper or only for lunch? And how much?[2]

At the 9 a.m. roll-call, each of the cells was visited by the duty lieutenant. Traditionally, this was the moment when the prisoners had a right to make complaints or requests. Solzhenitsyn quickly found out that complaints were a waste of time—they were rejected out of hand and never went further than the lieutenant. Requests for medical treatment and the like were almost equally useless. The medical treatment available in the Lubyanka was primitive, brutal, and hard to obtain. As often as not, it left you worse than before, for its purpose was not to mitigate the effects of sleeplessness, over-exhaustion, starvation, or beatings, but simply to reassure the prison authorities that the prisoner was still not in danger of dying. A common experience was for a man recovering consciousness after a beating or incarceration in an unheated punishment cell to find the prison doctor bending over him, saying, "All right, you can continue." And it was these same doctors who signed the death certificates with false diagnoses of the causes of death.

Another formal right was that of twice a month writing petitions. These petitions are a peculiar feature of the Soviet penal system and appear to be a vestige of the old tsarist custom of allowing prisoners to appeal to the higher powers for mercy, when it was both a safety valve and a tacit admission of the injustice of much penal practice. In the Soviet period this right became as vestigial as the emu's wings and serves no useful purpose, yet it persisted throughout Stalin's time and continues to the present day. When you made a petition you were taken out of your cell and locked in a box, where you were given a tiny piece of poor-quality paper measuring four inches by three, a wooden pen with a broken nib, and an ink-well containing watered-down ink. The pen would barely write, the paper was as porous as blotting paper, and there was little chance of producing anything legible (nor was there room to write a proper message). Nevertheless, most prisoners, including Solzhenitsyn, went through with this farcical procedure, especially in the early stages of their investigation, when they believed in pardons and did not accept or realize that their fate had been determined in advance, or suspect that these petitions invariably ended up on the desk of their investigator. For the latter they were useful evidence of the prisoner's state of mind, his hopes and perhaps his fears, and made a valuable addition to his dossier.

The day's activities began after the nine o'clock inspection. Sometimes the prisoners were called for interrogation at this time, particularly if their case was going smoothly. If it wasn't, they would be kept up all night or transferred to Lefortovo for harsher treatment, which is what happened to Leonid Z when he became stubborn and refused to sign the investigator's versions of his depositions. Otherwise, the prisoners could play chess, indulge in the endless conversations and the telling of anecdotes that Solzhenitsyn so loved, or read books from the Lubyanka library, which turned out to be a great surprise.

> The Lubyanka library was unique. In all probability it had been assembled out of confiscated private libraries. The bibliophiles who had collected these books had already rendered up their souls to God. But the main thing was that while the security service had been busy censoring and emasculating all the nation's libraries for decades, it had forgotten to dig in its own bosom, and here, in the beast's lair, one could read Zamyatin, Pilnyak, Panteleimon Romanov, and any volume at all of the complete works of Merezhkovsky.[3]*

The prisoners were allowed to order one book every ten days. They frequently failed to get the book of their choice, for the librarian doled out the books like so many hunks of bread, concerned only to see that they all got one book apiece, regardless of its title or contents. Nevertheless, they received plenty to interest them, and by swapping around had enough, in a cell of five, to keep themselves more or less continuously in reading matter until the next order became possible.

Immediately before lunch the prisoners were let out for their twenty minutes of exercise. Those on the fourth and fifth floors, where Solzhenitsyn was, were taken up onto the roof of the Lubyanka and allowed to walk in a concrete yard surrounded by high concrete walls. They were accompanied by an unarmed warder, and an armed guard manned the watch-tower that overlooked the yard. The prisoners were ordered to line up in pairs, keep their hands behind their backs, and stay silent, but they usually contrived to talk among themselves in whispers. It was here that Solzhenitsyn learned about Estonian democracy from Susi, and here that he spent some of his happiest moments in the Lubyanka, out in the fresh air and away from the claustrophobic atmosphere of the cell, with its constant reminders of his helplessness and humiliation. Here, too, he could see the sun for the first time since his arrival in Moscow and hear the distant honking of the traffic far below on Dzerzhinsky Square, a reminder that somewhere out there life still proceeded normally.

At one o'clock they were served lunch—a ladle of soup and a ladle of thin, fatless gruel, each dumped onto a flat aluminium plate. If they had saved some of their bread ration, it could now be eaten with the soup. If not, the soup and the gruel were gone in a trice, so that in the early days they were hardly aware that they had eaten anything. But "then, if you managed to get it under control, your stomach shrank and adapted itself to this meagreness, and the miserable Lubyanka slops became just right."[4] There followed a two-hour rest period during which, if they were not called out for

---

*I.e., censored authors. It was also in the Lubyanka that Solzhenitsyn first read Dos Passos (once condemned in the Soviet Union for decadent formalism).

interrogation, the prisoners were allowed to lie on their bunks and read. Strictly speaking, it was still forbidden to sleep, but they usually contrived to doze with a book propped in front of them. "Supper" was at 4 p.m.— another ladle of gruel—and then there were six hours to lights out, which was the favourite period for discussions, arguments, stories, debates.

In mid-March a sixth prisoner was added to the five in Cell 67, and since it was now too small for them, all six were transferred to a larger cell in another wing: Cell No. 53. Here the ceiling was enormously high—sixteen and a half feet—and an almost full-length window was set in one wall, although four-fifths of it were blocked on the outside by a riveted steel sheet known colloquially as a muzzle. Muzzles were (and still are) a standard fitting in Soviet jails, blocking off all but a tiny patch of window and sky and serving to make electric light necessary day and night.

The new arrival in the cell, Yuri Y, turned out to be a Soviet officer who had spent two years in captivity in a German death camp and had survived by becoming the camp artist. He told Solzhenitsyn that while there he had learnt the reason for the particularly inhuman treatment of Russian prisoners of war—as opposed to the Poles, Yugoslavs, Norwegians, and Englishmen that he saw—in the German camps. It was because the Soviet Union had refused to recognize the Hague Convention on war prisoners and therefore neither accepted any obligations in its treatment of enemy prisoners nor imposed any to protect its own. In Stalin's eyes a prisoner of war was a traitor: Red Army soldiers were expected to fight on or die, but never to surrender. Nor did the USSR recognize the International Red Cross. Therefore, while the prisoners of other nationalities were more or less decently fed and allowed to receive food parcels, the Russians starved and were allowed to die like dogs. Yuri Y had been transformed by his experiences from a Soviet patriot (his father had been a high-ranking officer in the revolutionary forces) into an ardent anti-Communist and had allowed himself to be recruited into the Vlasov army, thinking, like many of its members, that he was going to be allowed to fight for the liberation of his homeland from the Communist yoke. But the Germans had deceived and cheated the Russians who joined their side. Towards the end of the war, Yuri was contacted by a Soviet agent who promised him a free pardon if he would go over to the Soviet side and give them information about a spy school that he had helped to organize. After much vacillating, Yuri accepted, crossed the lines, and told Soviet counter-intelligence all he knew, only to be cheated once again and flung into the Lubyanka.

Yuri was almost the same age as Solzhenitsyn, and Solzhenitsyn was much attracted by his frank and open personality. Their education and military experiences had in many ways been similar, and they spoke the same language. But Solzhenitsyn's patriotism and his burning conviction that the war against the Germans was utterly right could not be reconciled with Yuri's apparent treachery. Here was a living example of those Vlasovites whose leaflets had so disgusted him at the front, and although Solzhenitsyn was beginning dimly to understand something of their motives and although he found Yuri personally attractive, he was nonetheless alienated by his views.

> In all, Yuri spent three weeks in our cell. I argued with him throughout those three weeks. I said that our Revolution was magnificent and just, that only its 1929 distortion was horrible. He looked at me pityingly and compressed his lips. . . . I said that there had been a long period in our country when all our major affairs were conducted exclusively by utterly dedicated men of high principle. He said they were all cut from the same cloth as Stalin from the very beginning. (We agreed that Stalin was a bandit.) I praised Gorky to the skies: what a genius, what a wonderfully correct point of view, what an artist! Yuri parried: a pathetic, boring creature who had invented himself and all his characters—his books were complete fairy tales. Lev Tolstoy was the tsar of our literature.[5]

Yuri soon departed and was replaced by another newcomer, whose story eclipsed anything Solzhenitsyn had heard up to now. The new prisoner, a thin young man with a pale, innocent-looking face, dressed in a cheap blue suit and blue cap, quietly announced, in answer to questions, that he had been arrested for writing a proclamation to the Russian people. When asked why he had written it, he confided shyly that he was none other than the Emperor Mikhail Romanov. Solzhenitsyn was electrified—he had never expected to meet an emperor in the Lubyanka.

Victor Alexeyevich Belov, which was his real name, was a former chauffeur who had worked at the Kremlin for a while and had been a driver to Khrushchev* as well as to Marshal Blyukher and other bigwigs. Solzhenitsyn listened raptly to his tales of life at the top, his descriptions of the way the Kremlin leaders led a closed, secret life of their own, eating and drinking lavishly at private banquets, moving in a magic circle of government dachas, reserved shops filled with every kind of delicacy and modern consumer goods, official limousines, being cradled in the lap of luxury and privilege. Only Khrushchev, said Victor, had any sort of egalitarian principles and treated his chauffeur as a friend. But the key event in Victor's life had occurred in 1943 when a venerable old man with a white beard had visited him and his mother at home, had crossed himself before their icon, and had said to Victor gravely, "Hail, Mikhail, God gives you his blessing!" The old man, it turned out, had visited Victor's mother once before, in 1916, when Victor was a year old, and had predicted a great and mysterious future for him, saying also that he would return. And here he was back again. Victor's mother had almost fainted with the shock, while the old man instructed Victor to prepare for his destiny. In 1953 there would be a change of rule, and Victor would become emperor of all the Russians.

Solzhenitsyn and his cell-mates barely knew whether to laugh or cry when they heard Victor's breathless tale, but his patent simplicity, guileless-

---

* This was presumably between 1935 and 1938, when Khrushchev was secretary of the Moscow District Party Committee. Marshal Blyukher, commander of the Soviet Army of the Far East after the Revolution, was executed by Stalin in 1939.

ness, and conviction commanded respect and forebade mockery. Victor had been instructed to start gathering his forces in 1948, but, fired by the old man's words, he had been impatient to begin earlier. He was then working in the People's Commissariat for the Oil Industry in Moscow, and in the autumn of 1943 he wrote his first proclamation, which he showed to four fellow workers. A year later, when working as a mechanic in a car depot, he wrote another proclamation and showed it to ten fellow workers, and also to two girls. The workers apparently approved of it, and, like the first four, they kept his secret. But the two girls informed on him, and soon afterwards he was picked up by the police and brought to the Lubyanka.

Victor's story got a mixed reception from the members of Cell 53 (a number that gave Victor a distinct *frisson*—it was the year of his predicted accession to the throne). Kramarenko, the cell stool-pigeon, at once found a pretext to visit his investigator and denounce the workers who had failed to inform on Victor. Fastenko, though far from a monarchist, seized on the workers' approval as evidence of mutinous feelings among the proletariat. Leonid Z, the engineer, found the whole thing preposterous and took great delight in teasing Victor, just as the investigators began to do when news of Victor's claim spread through the Lubyanka. Solzhenitsyn also found the story far-fetched, but he was much impressed by Victor's stories of high life in the Kremlin and the wretched conditions of his fellow workers. He wasn't sure how much to believe, but here was material on Soviet life such as he had never dreamed of acquiring, or had had any chance to acquire, up till now. His sense that his real education was only now beginning was strengthened. And he also began to get a feel for that Arabian Nights quality of prison life, and the endless stories that the prisoners told about themselves and others, like so many Scheherazades, to while away the time. Not even the most fantastic tales could be neglected or dismissed out of hand, and in many cases, as in that of the "Emperor Mikhail," the fantastic stories were the ones that told him most. What fascinating adventures they heard, what wonderful conversations they conducted on their causes and meaning:

> Oh, the weightless Lubyanka evenings!. . . . What light, free thoughts! It was as though we had been lifted up to the heights of Sinai, and there the truth manifested itself to us from out of the fire. Was it not of this that Pushkin dreamed? "I want to live so as to think and suffer." And there we suffered, and we thought, and there was nothing else in our lives.[6]

Solzhenitsyn had been released from solitary confinement and allowed into a communal cell as a mark of favour for his co-operative attitude during the investigator's initial assault, but it transpired that Captain Ezepov was far from finished with him. The charge against him under Article 58, paragraph 10 (anti-Soviet agitation), was, it seems, taken as proved, but there remained the question of paragraph 11 (forming an anti-Soviet organization), and Ezepov now turned to the various letters that had passed between Solzhenitsyn and Nikolai, and between the two of them and Natalia, Lydia and Kirill.

Phrases that had seemed quite innocent when dashed off at the front in the jocular tone they had adopted now acquired an entirely different resonance when issuing from Ezepov's mouth: "conference of the big two," "the war after the war," the need for a "new organization," a "party of five plus two." Ezepov had also gone through the papers found in Solzhenitsyn's suitcase, read copies of the war stories that he had sent to Lydia (that had failed to appeal to *Znamya* because of their unorthodoxy), and come across the postage-stamp-size portraits that Solzhenitsyn had cut from the Prussian miller's book about the First World War. Putting aside the Hindenburgs and Ludendorffs, Ezepov had retained only two: "Tell me, Solzhenitsyn, why were you carrying portraits of Nicholas II and Trotsky in your suitcase?"

Solzhenitsyn's confession of his own guilt was not enough, it seemed, to satisfy the suspicions aroused in Ezepov by the picture Ezepov had conjured up of a hardened counter-revolutionary with secret dreams of sabotage. His friends must have been deeply involved as well. If this was what they wrote about in their letters, what did they talk about when they met? And what happened at the meetings referred to in the letters? He insisted that in giving his answers, Solzhenitsyn should go back as far as 1940, to the time when the friends were still at the university in Rostov.[7]

Solzhenitsyn's first thought had been to say that he had forgotten everything, but this threw the investigator into a rage and brought forth dark threats of shooting or physical ill-treatment. Besides, Ezepov had the letters in front of him, so that the pretext of forgetfulness didn't seem very convincing. Solzhenitsyn pretended that he and his friends had discussed nothing but the weather and sport and similar trivialities, but again the letters contradicted him: they were too serious, too circumstantial, and too specific to allow him to wriggle off the hook in that way. He would have to think of something else. But what?

His dilemma in approaching this problem was threefold. In the first place, he had no idea whether the others had been arrested, and if they had, he had no idea what they might be saying. In Nikolai's case he was fairly sure that arrest must have taken place, but the fates of Kirill, Lydia, and Natalia were completely unknown. Ezepov deliberately kept him in suspense, implying that the others were bound to be arrested and that confrontations would be arranged, at which his evidence would be compared with theirs for its veracity. Secondly, of the three others, Kirill was most at risk: his father had fled the country illegally, and he had generally been the most outspoken in his student criticisms of Soviet society, although in his letters he had been more reticent than either Solzhenitsyn or Nikolai. Thirdly, and most importantly, Solzhenitsyn was worried about his front-line diaries and notebooks. These, too, were in Ezepov's possession and were crammed with stories and descriptions of life at the front, many told to him by men in his unit or by others he had happened to meet in the course of his military service.* The stories were totally frank about military life at the front, describing it with unvarnished directness and illustrating complexities of motive and response that were far removed from the stereotypes of Stalinist propaganda. With his zeal for completeness and accuracy, Solzhenitsyn had not only noted them down in voluminous detail but had named the people who told him these stories, the dates when they told him and the dates when the incidents had occurred. He had also noted down stories of collectivization and famine in the villages, of shortages and miserable living conditions in the towns, each time with the name of his informant. These diaries lay like a time bomb ticking away among the documents and papers lying on Ezepov's desk, and he could hear it ticking in his mind as he duelled with his investigator. They were a permanent reminder of the havoc that could still be created among his innocent army comrades if their stories were discovered and read.

From Ezepov's lines of questioning, Solzhenitsyn deduced that the investigator had not yet read the diaries. This was partly because they weren't necessary to the main case against him—they looked as if they would add little to the charge of starting an organization, which was now the main object of Ezepov's questions—and partly the result of sheer laziness on Ezepov's part: the diaries consisted of four notebooks of small format, written in faded pencil in the tiny, cramped handwriting that Solzhenitsyn had developed in order to cram a maximum of information onto every page. They were crumpled and moisture stained, and to read them demanded the sort of effort and concentration that Ezepov was loth to apply, particularly in such an easy case. Congenitally idle, he was quite content to do a botched job so long as it served the immediate purpose, and he was corrupted by his knowledge of the protection that the security service enjoyed. He it was whom Solzhenitsyn later described in *The Gulag Archipelago* as ringing his wife to apologize that he would not be returning home for the night, since he had an important interrogation to carry out, and then ringing his mistress to say he would come in an hour or so—all this in the presence of the despised prisoner.

Solzhenitsyn could not be sure that Ezepov wouldn't take it into his head to investigate the diaries, and he still did not know what the others might be saying. For that was the whole point of the investigation—to keep him in suspense, to remind him of his solitariness, to deceive him, and to trap him into unwary admissions. Finding pure negation no use, he resolved that his task must be to draw all suspicion and attention away from his war diaries and to interpret the letters and conversations that interested the investigator in such a way as to make them seem innocent and harmless, the inconsequential babbling of callow students. It seemed a good idea at the time. "The idea flashes through your mind . . . that you ought to come as close as you can to the truth of what was actually said—of course rounding off the sharp edges and skipping the dangerous parts. After all, people say that when

---

*One of these was the story that Leonid Vlasov had told him in the train to Rostov in 1944 and that became the nucleus of "Incident at Krechetovka Station."

you lie you should always stay as close to the truth as possible." Later, tempered by long years in prison and camps and hardened by his encounters with the KGB, Solzhenitsyn realized that this had not been such a good idea: "You wanted to outsmart your investigator! You have a quick, ingenious mind. You are an intellectual. And you outsmarted yourself!"[8] Solzhenitsyn likened his psychological reactions to those of Raskolnikov in *Crime and Punishment*:

> Out of my inexperience—and who was there to teach us otherwise?—I repeated the mistake described by Dostoyevsky. Porfiry Petrovich says to Raskolnikov, "I don't need to bother myself with finding an explanation for all this. You're an intellectual and you'll explain the whole thing to me neatly yourself, so that it all adds up." And he was quite right. I was amazed when I read it afterwards in jail. All they need to say to you if you're an intellectual is, "All right, explain to me yourself where you got your views from." And you start to think, "How can I explain it all so that he believes me and leaves me alone?" And off you go with your explanations.[9]

Keeping as close as he could to their actual conversations, Solzhenitsyn attempted to portray everything in the letters as if he and his friends had been completely loyal. For instance, on one occasion they had complained about the introduction of tuition fees for higher education.* Yes, said Solzhenitsyn, it was true they had been discontented, but only because this represented a step away from egalitarianism and Communist ideals. Were they also dissatisfied with the reduction in piece-work rates? Yes, they were, because they felt this measure was unfair to the workers. Collectivization? Well, yes, but they had criticized it only because they wanted it to be even more successful than hitherto. On other occasions he attributed their discontent to youthful inexperience, egotism, and insufficient understanding of the intentions of the Party. But it was of little avail, because the investigator was interested only in evidence that confirmed the group's guilt, not in testimony that contradicted it, and he wrote everything down in his own special language: ". . . tried to create an illegal organization. . . . From 1940 onwards he conducted systematic anti-Soviet agitation . . . worked out plans for effecting a forcible change in the policy of the Party and state, and maliciously slandered Stalin."[10]

It was a typical "beginner's" mistake, as Solzhenitsyn ruefully admitted in later years, yet he succeeded in his immediate aims. Neither Natalia, Kirill, nor Lydia was arrested or even called in for questioning, and no case was started against them. As for the diaries, in the fourth month of his investigation "all my notebooks were cast into the hellish maw of the Lubyanka furnace, where they burst into flames—the red pyre of one more novel that had perished in Russia—and flew out of the highest chimney in black butter-

---

*This was a quite common theme in those days. Panin, in his memoirs, tells the story of a former student called Anechka who was jailed for allegedly complaining about the introduction of fees and writes that many innocent people went to the camps on similar charges.

flies of soot."[11] In this way, he later said, "I lost my novel about the war."[12] Soon afterwards he was requested to sign a document confirming that the notebooks had been burnt as being of no relevance to the case against him. For once he did so gladly.

The investigation and the war were both drawing to a close. Shortly before 1 May 1945, the black-out shade was removed from the exposed corner of the window in their high-ceilinged cell. That evening it was uncannily quiet in the Lubyanka. The investigators all seemed to be out and no one was taken for interrogation. The only sign of normality was the sound of a prisoner being taken from his cell and into a nearby box, where for some reason he was noisily beaten up by the warders. On 2 May the prisoners heard a thirty-gun salute being fired. That signalled the capture of Berlin, if only they had known it. On 9 May there was another thirty-gun salute followed later by a forty-gun salute. That meant the capture of Prague and the end of the war in Europe. Again the investigators were all away, joining in the wild celebrations that engulfed the Moscow streets that day. A Western eyewitness has described the scene as follows.

> May 9 was an unforgettable day in Moscow. The spontaneous joy of the two or three million people who thronged the Red Square that evening—and the Moscow River embankments, and Gorki Street, all the way up to the Belorussian Station—was of a quality and a depth I had never yet seen in Moscow before. They danced and sang in the streets; every soldier and officer was hugged and kissed; outside the US Embassy the crowds shouted "Hurray for Roosevelt!" (even though he had died a month before); they were so happy they did not even have to get drunk, and under the tolerant gaze of the militia, young men even urinated against the walls of the Moskva Hotel, flooding the wide pavement. Nothing like *this* had ever happened in Moscow before. For once, Moscow had thrown all reserve and restraint to the winds. The fireworks display that evening was the most spectacular I have ever seen.[13]

Solzhenitsyn saw the fireworks through the bars of his cell. He who had fought his way across the Ukraine, Belorussia, Poland, and East Prussia for three battle-filled years before his arrest, who had been on active service in Orel when Stalin decreed the first victory salute, was filled with emotion at the thought of final victory. The Lubyanka, however, though packed with soldiers and ex–prisoners of war who had been arrested at the front, was as silent as the grave. All they could see were snatches of the fireworks and the searchlight beams in the sky, just visible above the muzzle that covered their window. The only other sign that something unusual had occurred was the simultaneous delivery of lunch and supper: two ladles of gruel instead of one, and a ladle of soup, something that generally occurred only on national holidays. In all other respects the day was absolutely normal; the security police and the Lubyanka continued to function faultlessly. The prisoners were allowed *their* turn to urinate at—as usual—precisely 6 p.m.

A week or two later, Solzhenitsyn was summoned to see Lieutenant-

Colonel Kotov, the prosecutor in charge of supervising his case. According to the law, the prosecutor was supposed to review the investigation as it proceeded and to check that it was being conducted correctly. He was also required to ask the prisoner what complaints he had about the investigation and whether his legal rights had in any way been infringed. But the prosecutors held their appointments only on the approval of the security police, whose performance they were supposed to be assessing, and therefore the interview was a pure formality.

> Kotov, a calm, well-fed, impersonal blond man, neither malevolent nor benevolent but entirely neutral, sat behind his desk and yawningly examined my dossier for the first time. He spent fifteen minutes acquainting himself with it while I watched. . . . Finally he raised his indifferent eyes to look at the wall and lazily asked if I had anything I wanted to add to my testimony.[14]

Solzhenitsyn sensed the hopelessness of trying to influence this man in any way. Nonetheless, he raised the question of his charge under paragraph 11 of Article 58, in addition to paragraph 10, that is, of setting up an anti-Soviet group or organization. After all, only two of them were involved, and this hardly constituted an organization. Kotov listened to him in silence, leafed through the dossier again, weighing up the consequences of causing a hitch in the procedure at this late stage of the case, then sighed, spread his hands, and said, "What is there to say? One person is a person, but two persons are . . . people."[15]

Not long after this, Solzhenitsyn was summoned to the same room again for a final session with his investigator. According to Article 206 of the criminal-procedure code, the prisoner was required to read through his earlier depositions, and any other testimony in the case, and sign to the effect that he had read and agreed them. Captain Ezepov pushed the thick file across the desk to Solzhenitsyn and invited him to open it. Almost at once Solzhenitsyn's eyes fell on the printed text inside the front cover. According to the criminal-procedure code, he had had all sorts of rights that he had never known about, including the right to complain about the conduct of the interrogation and to have his complaints recorded and included with the documents in his case. His gorge rose and his indignation boiled when he saw copies of his letters accompanied by wildly slanted interpretations of their meaning, together with the depositions in Ezepov's handwriting, with their distorting language and tendentious implications. Finally, there was the preposterous accusation of forming an organization.

Solzhenitsyn said hesitantly that he would refuse to sign because the investigation had been conducted improperly. Ezepov was unmoved and suggested that in that case they should begin all over again. He uttered some threat about sending Solzhenitsyn to the place where collaborators were held and made as if to reach for the file. But that didn't seem to be the right solution either.

Begin all over again? It seemed to me easier to die than to begin all over again. Ahead of me was the promise of at least some sort of life. . . . And then, what about that place where they kept the collaborators? Anyway, I had better not annoy him, for that would affect the tone in which he phrased the final indict-ment.

And so I signed. I signed it complete with paragraph 11, whose significance I didn't then understand. All they said was that it wouldn't add to my sentence.[16]

With the investigation completed, Solzhenitsyn was at last removed from the Lubyanka and transferred to another Moscow prison, Butyrki, to await the pleasure of the "organs." It was a wrench to leave his friends in Cell 53. As he had discovered from his first arrival in a communal cell, no one could be closer or dearer to you than a cell-mate, a comrade in the extremes of adversity like yourself. At the back of his mind, behind all the misery, the scorching humiliation, the indignation, and the resentment that occupied most of his waking thoughts, there had also been kindled a tiny glow of pride that at least he had been *here* in the Soviet Union's most celebrated and most important political prison, had seen with his own eyes and walked with his own feet the cells and boxes and corridors and investigation rooms of the world-famous Lubyanka, which had swallowed and consigned to oblivion so many outstanding Soviet citizens. It was true that he was as yet only dimly aware of the significance of what he had seen, but the memories would stay with him forever.

When he arrived in Butyrki, at the end of June 1945, Solzhenitsyn regarded himself as a veteran, yet his education was only just beginning. His cell was three times as large as the one he had left in the Lubyanka, with more than three times as many inmates in it. The vast majority turned out to be returned prisoners of war, Russian peasants and workers who had been carried off to Germany to work as labourers there, or members of the Vlasov forces. The stories that Yuri Y had told him about life in the German camps or about fighting alongside the Germans were now repeated in a hundred variations. Solzhenitsyn was stunned. He recalled the tattered Vlasov leaflets he had read at Orel and in Belorussia, the collaborator he had seen being horsewhippped through the streets near Bobruisk, the last-ditch stand of the Vlasovites in East Prussia, and the distaste and disdain he had felt for these contemptible traitors. He also remembered the returning columns of pris-oners of war, obediently lined up and submissive to their Smersh guards, and the six with the letters *SU* on their backs who had marched with him for two days and a night to Brodnitz immediately after his arrest. Was it because he himself had been taken for a Vlasovite by the jeering cart-drivers that he now felt such an urge to identify with them and to understand them? Once again he heard how the Soviet prisoners of war had been renounced by their rulers and how some of them had allowed themselves to be recruited into a so-called Russian army fighting on the side of the Germans, while others had stuck it out as prisoners of war only to find themselves equally rejected upon their return home. The truth was that Stalin made almost no distinction between them. Anyone who had had real experience of Western Europe, whether inside a camp or out of it, was regarded as a potential danger and a security risk, for Stalin feared the comparisons that would be made with home. He also feared that free-thinking officers and men who had mixed with the British, American, and French forces might bring home the Decembrist virus that the victorious Russians had returned with from Paris a hundred years beforehand, after the Napoleonic Wars. If a poor, benighted soldier had spent his entire time in a death camp and by a miracle survived, that, too, was nourishment for Stalin's paranoia: if you survived the death camps, there must be something fishy about you; you *must* have collaborated. All this and more, Solzhenitsyn heard from the men around him in Butyrki, and he now came to realize the justice of Yuri Y's strictures, so much so that when an elderly Russian worker whom he otherwise admired began to curse the "traitors" in their cell, it was he, together with two other young lads, who defended them from the old man's ire.

Another world that opened up to Solzhenitsyn's fascinated gaze in Butyrki was that of the Russian *émigrés*, thousands of whom had been overrun by Soviet troops in Western Europe or had been unjustifiably handed over to Stalin by the Allies on the pretext that they were traitors. Now they were in Soviet jails awaiting sentence.

> It was just like a dream, the resurrection of buried history. The weighty tomes on the Civil War had long since been completed and their covers shut tight. The causes for which people fought in it had been decided. The chronology of its events had been set down in textbooks. The leaders of the White movement were, it appeared, no longer our contemporaries on earth, but mere ghosts of a past that had melted away. The Russian *émigrés* had been more cruelly dispersed than the tribes of Israel. And, in our Soviet imagination, if they were still dragging out their lives somewhere, it was as pianists in stinking little restaurants, as lackeys, laundresses, beggars, morphine and cocaine addicts, and as virtual corpses.[17]

Yet now Solzhenitsyn went to a medical examination with Captain Borshch and Colonel Mariushkin, both veterans of that same tsarist army in which his father had fought in the First World War. Later these men had fought on the side of the Whites and left with the retreating Volunteer Army; since then they had lived out their lives peacefully in Western Europe, only to be cruelly and unjustly returned. Among the other prisoners in his cell was a Colonel Yasevich, also a veteran of the Civil War, and a young *émigré*, Igor Tronko, who was Solzhenitsyn's peer but had left Russia with his parents while still a baby. From these men Solzhenitsyn obtained a picture of the Russian emigration totally different from that prevailing in the Soviet Union—a picture of decent, sober, self-disciplined, and for the most part impoverished people, clinging with dignity to their language, culture, and customs and imbued with a spontaneous love of the motherland that was all the more touching in the face of the hatred with which the motherland regarded them. Nor were they all dyed-in-the wool reactionaries, especially not the young people like Igor, who had reacted against the conservative views of their parents and were eager to give the Soviet government the benefit of every doubt.

Through the windows of Butyrki Prison they could still hear the sound of the post-war celebrations. Brass bands seemed to be parading the streets almost every other day, and on 22 June 1945, the fourth anniversary of the beginning of the war, there was an enormous victory parade in Red Square. The prisoners heard about it on the grape-vine, and heard it with mixed feelings. They shared the pride and relief of their countrymen at the victory over the Germans, but they were prevented from showing it and were excluded from the celebrations. Yet they desperately wanted to join in, to belong— and to be released from their misery, almost at any price.

Some of this longing took the form of a craving to know their sentences. If only it were all over and they at least had the certainty of knowing what lay in store for them. They dreamed of being sent to the wide-open spaces of southern Siberia, where the climate was mild and they could lose themselves in nature. "In the end, that spring, even the most stubborn of us wanted forgiveness and were ready to yield a great deal in return for just a little more life." Or, more poignantly, they dreamed of an amnesty.

> The spring itself sounded a summons to mercy. It was the spring that marked the ending of such an enormous war! We saw that millions of us prisoners were flowing in and knew that millions more would greet us in the camps. It just couldn't be that so many people were to be held in prison after the greatest victory in the world. They were only holding us now to teach us a lesson, so we wouldn't forget. Of course, there was bound to be a great amnesty, and we would soon be released.[18]

The prison was rife with rumours of amnesty. Even the date was repeatedly predicted. One day, upon entering the lavender vestibule of the Butyrki baths, Solzhenitsyn and his cell-mates read, high on the wall and written in soap, a graffito announcing what they had all been waiting for: "Hurray! Amnesty on July 17!" In fact the anonymous scribe was ten days off—the amnesty came early, on 7 July 1945. But not as expected. It was to apply only to criminal prisoners, to deserters, and to just a small number of political prisoners—to that tiny percentage of those charged under Article 58 who had been sentenced to less than three years. But nobody had seen the text yet, and so the prison remained thick with rumours.

Three weeks later, on 27 July 1945, Solzhenitsyn and a prisoner named Valentin, from Kiev, were called out of their cell after breakfast. Their cell-mates noisily ribbed them and assured them they were being amnestied. They were even asked to take out messages and to send in food parcels. Of course it was all nonsense. "Perhaps you honestly didn't believe it, perhaps you wouldn't allow yourself to believe it, you tried to brush it aside with jokes, but flaming pincers hotter than anything else on earth suddenly seized your heart: What if it were true?"

They were taken with about twenty other men to the bath-house, then led through Butyrki's interior courtyard with its emerald garden. The green of the trees seemed unbearably bright to Solzhenitsyn. "Never had my eyes seen the green of the leaves with such intensity as they did that spring! And never in my life had I seen anything closer to God's paradise than that little Butyrki garden, which took no more than thirty seconds to cross on the asphalt path."[19] The prisoners were locked into a spacious box known colloquially as "the station," since it was used mainly for prisoners' arrivals and departures, and left without explanation. By now they were on tenterhooks, but did not dare voice their hopes aloud. It turned out that none of them had done anything very serious and that they were all cases for the so-called Special Board of the NKVD.

After three hours of suspense the door was suddenly opened and the first prisoner summoned, a thirty-five-year-old bookkeeper. Within minutes he was back again, and the next one was called. What was the verdict? The bookkeeper looked crushed: five years. Then the next prisoner returned, a hysterical giggle on his lips: fifteen years.

Eventually it was Solzhenitsyn's turn. He was led into an equally large box next door. It was the famous "frisking box," where all new prisoners were searched on arrival. It had a number of empty rough-hewn tables in it and space for up to twenty prisoners to be searched at a time, but now the only person there was a neat, black-haired NKVD major sitting at a small table on the far side with a table lamp on it. There was no one else and no "board," just this one solitary officer. The major gestured to Solzhenitsyn to sit down, asked his name, then leafed through a pile of typed documents on one side of the table and pulled out a sheet about half the size of a normal piece of typing paper. In a bored voice he read out the bureaucratic formula of Solzhenitsyn's sentence, then turned the paper over and at once began to write a statement on the back confirming that it had been read to the defendant. Solzhenitsyn understood that he had been sentenced to eight years, but it was all so flat and boring and all over so quickly that he could barely take it in. How had he been sentenced? When? By whom? Was there to be no hearing, no trial, no "due process"? It was a crucial turning-point in his life, yet no one seemed to be interested. He writes that he wanted to linger over it, to savour the gravity of the moment, and when the major pushed the sheet face down to him to sign, he said, "No, I have to read it for myself." "Do you really think I would deceive you?" retorted the major lazily, but nonetheless invited him to go ahead and read it.

The small piece of paper in Solzhenitsyn's hand wasn't even the original, but a carbon copy. It was dated 7 July 1945, the very day of the amnesty that did not affect him—the date of his official "trial." The document did not waste words. On the left it said, "Heard: The charges against—(name, date and place of birth)." On the right it said, "Resolved: To award—(name) for anti-Soviet agitation and attempting to found an anti-Soviet organization 8 (eight) years in corrective labour camps." And at the bottom it said, "Copy verified. Secretary." The blanks had been filled in with Solzhenitsyn's personal details, and that was all. It looked like an invoice or a chit for obtaining office supplies. Solzhenitsyn says that he looked at it and tried to summon up an air of solemnity. For form's sake he said, "But this is terrible. Eight years! What for?" But his words sounded unconvincing—both he and the major could hear their falsity. The major was now in a hurry. "Sign there," he said, pointing to the paper. Solzhenitsyn signed but still said, "In that case, allow me to write an appeal here and now. The sentence is unjust." The major nodded: "When the time comes, you can." And the waiting warder hurried him out.[20]

IO

FIRST STEPS IN

THE ARCHIPELAGO

T HE TIME WOULD never come for Solzhenitsyn to lodge an appeal against his sentence by the Special Board. No appeal was possible, if only because the board figured neither in the Soviet criminal code nor in the constitution. It was as if, from the point of view of criminal procedure, it didn't exist at all, and since it was not part of the visible judicial system and had no judicial organs above or below it, there was simply no mechanism for appealing against its sentences.

In part 1 of *The Gulag Archipelago*, for which Solzhenitsyn drew extensively on his memories of his first months in prison, he traces the concept of such a special board all the way back to Catherine the Great and points out that there was a regular tradition in Russia of condemning individuals to exile or imprisonment on the whim of the tsar or powerful officials. Like many tsarist injustices, these instances of extra-judicial repression were random and capricious, affecting numerous individuals in an arbitrary way, but they had not been erected into a system affecting millions. This occurred only with the "troikas" of the GPU, established after the Revolution expressly to bypass the courts and carry on the work of the revolutionary tribunals. And these in turn gave way to the Special Board, which Stalin set up in 1934, immediately after the Kirov murder.* Ironically, its establishment coincided with the abolition of the old OGPU and the latter's replacement by the NKVD, a move intended to signify a liberalization of political conditions and the reform of the secret police. The OGPU had become so synonymous with

---

*Sergei Kirov, first secretary of the Party in Leningrad, was murdered on 1 December 1934 while working in his office. It is generally believed that Stalin was responsible because he feared Kirov's popularity, but the full story has never been told in the Soviet Union and Stalin's involvement never admitted.

police terror and the unprecedented brutality of collectivization that it was deemed prudent to replace it with something else. A thorough reorganization of the Soviet judicial structure was also carried through, with the avowed aim of unifying the system of justice under the NKVD and of providing, it was alleged, greater guarantees for the rights of the individual. In the midst of this reforming zeal the setting up of the Special Board was practically overlooked and seemed to come as a kind of administrative afterthought. There were no fanfares at the time, and little was said about it. But typically for Soviet political practice, it turned out to be one of those Stalinist innovations that made nonsense of all the pretty paper guarantees in the Soviet criminal code and completely contradicted its ostensible intentions.

From the very beginning the board's powers had been ill defined. The main proviso was that the Special Board could try "socially dangerous persons" without recourse to the courts, which meant that, after the investigation had been completed, cases were invariably heard *in absentia*, the accused having no right either to appear in person or to be represented by a lawyer. In other words, it was a purely administrative procedure.

Exactly who these socially dangerous persons were was left up to the secret police to decide, and this was the source of the abuses. In *The Gulag Archipelago* Solzhenitsyn lists the main categories of "crime" dealt with by the Special Board (they were known colloquially as "alphabet articles," to distinguish them from the numbered articles of the criminal code): ASA, Anti-Soviet Agitation; CRA, Counter-revolutionary Activities; SE, Suspicion of Espionage; CLSE, Contacts Leading to Suspicion of Espionage; and so on, right down to SDE (Socially Dangerous Element) and even MF (Member of Family—of an accused person). The punishments handed out by the board consisted mainly of terms in the labour camps and internal exile, and these ranged from periods of five to ten, twenty, and even twenty-five years, with execution a possibility during the latter part of the war. As the wave of purges mounted throughout the thirties, the Special Board had increased in importance and expanded its work, until, under the pressure of numbers, it turned into a simple rubber-stamping machine. The sheer arbitrariness of its operations and its true character were revealed in 1965, some time after it had been abolished, when a Soviet legal journal admitted that the Special Board had usually dealt with the cases for which there was insufficient evidence to secure a conviction even in a Soviet court.[1]

Two other peculiarities of the Special Board should be mentioned. Whereas men and women who had been sentenced by the courts were generally (although not invariably) released at the conclusion of their sentences, Special Board victims were usually re-sentenced by administrative decree to a further period of imprisonment, or else to internal exile under police surveillance. Secondly, the Special Board operated in complete secrecy. Its membership was never divulged, and it was responsible only to the minister of internal affairs and to Stalin (which was an additional reason why there was no appeal).

When he returned to the "station" after being told his punishment, Solzhenitsyn found that a sense of suppressed hysteria was beginning to spread among prisoners who already knew their fate. Not only could they not muster the solemnity that seemed appropriate to the moment but they were like chastised schoolboys returning one by one from the headmaster's study, only to break into giggles when the worst was over and they were all together again. Prisoners departed and returned, departed and returned, and somehow the entire absurdity of this mechanical bureaucratic routine was translated into tension-releasing laughter. Only the bookkeeper remained subdued, yet he had the lightest sentence of all. The next lightest sentence was Solzhenitsyn's, while most of the others got ten years. Here and there some of the prisoners still talked of amnesty and said that Stalin was just trying to scare them. But the voices were less confident than before, and in their heart of hearts most of the prisoners knew that their reckoning had come. The laughter was simply a way of purging the emotions and preparing themselves for the ordeals ahead.

Before the next step, they were all made to take another bath, although it was only a matter of hours since they had had one. Solzhenitsyn's companion Valentin, cheerful and making the best of it, tried to be reassuring: "Well, never mind, we're still young and we'll survive. The main thing is not to make any more mistakes. When we get to the camp, we'll keep mum with everybody, so they don't slap another sentence on us. We'll work honestly and keep our mouths shut."[2] When they had all dried themselves and dressed, they were led to the Butyrki church. But their purpose was not to pray. The church had been converted to more practical uses. Its great height had been divided into three storeys, and each storey contained several cells. Solzhenitsyn was pushed into the south-east cell, an enormous square room holding two hundred prisoners. There were bunks for less than half this number, and the rest slept on the tiled floor, either directly beneath the bunks or in the aisles, in a great, seething mass of arms, legs, kitbags, cases, sacks, and other receptacles. There were no books or chess sets in this cell, the muzzles on the windows were makeshift, cobbled together out of unplaned boards, and the dented aluminum bowls and splintered wooden spoons were handed out before each meal and collected up again afterwards. All this was because the church cells were only temporary—prisoners came here in transit, after being sentenced and before space could be found for them at their next port of call.

> The church cells had their own special atmosphere: it trembled from the first draughts of future transit prisons, from the distant breeze of the Arctic camps. In the church cells you celebrated the rite of adjustment—to the fact that your sentence had been pronounced and it was no joke, and to the fact that no matter how cruel this new era of your life was going to be, your brain had to digest and accept it. This was very hard to do.
>
> And here there were no permanent cell-mates, such as you had had in the investigation cells and who became like a family to you. Day and night, people were brought in and taken away singly and by tens, and as a result the prisoners

were kept constantly on the move along the floor and the bunks, and it was rare to lie next to any one neighbour for more than two nights.[3]

Solzhenitsyn was made extremely uncomfortable by this constant movement and missed the camaraderie of his first five months of imprisonment. His only friends were two young Moscow intellectuals. He had met one of them, Boris Gammerov, in Butyrki before, and had had many discussions with him on politics and literature. Gammerov's father had been killed in the great purge of 1937.* Gammerov himself had joined an anti-tank unit during the Second World War while he was still very young, had been wounded in the lung and had been invalided out of the army with TB. After that he had enrolled in the biology department of Moscow University, begun to write poetry, and joined a students' discussion circle, which is what got him into trouble and led to his arrest. The other man, Georgi Ingal, was from the same discussion group. Ingal was evidently a gifted writer, a pupil of the influential historical novelist and critic Yuri Tynyanov, and already a candidate member of the Writers' Union despite his comparative youth. He had almost finished a novel about Debussy. But Tynyanov, a former member of the controversial "Formalist" school of criticism,† had undergone considerable persecution in his time and at his funeral in 1943, Ingal had made a grave-side speech in which he referred to Tynyanov's tribulations in unambiguous terms. This had contributed to his ultimate downfall, in the spring of 1945, and to his sentence of eight years.

At earlier meetings Gammerov had surprised Solzhenitsyn by vehemently expressing his belief in God and taking Solzhenitsyn to task for some disdainful remarks on the subject of religious belief. Solzhenitsyn had been startled that one so young, born in 1923, could be a Christian when he himself, born and baptized a Christian when Christianity was still universal in Russia, had long since lost his faith and declared his atheism. Now Gammerov and Ingal assailed Solzhenitsyn together.

This conflict was very hard for me. I was extremely attached at the time to that view of the world that is incapable of admitting any new fact or of appraising any new opinion until it can find some ready-made label for it, whether it is the "vacillating hypocrisy of the petty bourgeoisie" or the "militant nihilism of the declassified intelligentsia."[4]

---

* The great purge is the name usually given to Stalin's mass murders and the mass terror inflicted on the Soviet population in the years 1937–39. Its origins go back to 1934 (and even to the collectivization of 1929–30), but it is generally agreed to have reached its height during and after 1937. Robert Conquest's book *The Great Terror* is devoted to this subject, as is, in large part, Solzhenitsyn's *The Gulag Archipelago*.

† The Formalists were prominent in Russia from just before the First World War until the 1930s; they were so named because they denied the importance of social content in literature and concentrated on its formal and aesthetic qualities. They were heavily criticized and extensively victimized after about 1930, when many lost their jobs and were prevented from publishing their work.

They didn't attack Marx as such, but they did attack Solzhenitsyn's literary idol, Lev Tolstoy. Tolstoy, they said, had been totally wrong in his rejection of church and state, he had been foolish to preach that every individual should combine mental and physical work in equal measure, and he had misunderstood history when claiming that it could not be influenced and directed by strong individuals. If that were the case, how could one account for Stalin?

The attack on Tolstoy was hard for Solzhenitsyn to accept, but bolstered by the ghastly example of Stalin, it was equally difficult to resist, and Solzhenitsyn was forced to reconsider his former ideas. There were other surprises too. They praised Pasternak to the skies, reciting his verse by heart. Solzhenitsyn had read only one volume of Pasternak's verse, *My Sister, Life*, and had disliked it, finding it "precious, arcane, and far removed from simple human concerns."[5] But when the two young men recited Lieutenant Schmidt's last speech at his trial (from Pasternak's long poem "Lieutenant Schmidt"), he saw a new side of him and conceded his admiration.*

What struck him most of all about these young men was their fierce disdain for Stalin's regime and their cool, even proud, acceptance of their sentences. It seemed that emotionally they had completely cut themselves off from Stalin's Russia and somehow found their presence here inevitable. For Solzhenitsyn such detachment was impossible. Try as he might, he felt bound to this society, even responsible for it in certain ways. The best years of his youth had been dedicated to it. Society itself had recently thrust him away, had rejected and crushed him, and he was learning new aspects of its character every day, but still it wasn't enough. The umbilical cord still bound him not only to Mother Russia, which he had always adored, but also to Soviet Russia and the paternal Party, whose ultimate magnanimity and justness he still did not doubt.

It was one source of enormous relief to him that on the conclusion of his investigation and his move to Butyrki he had been given the right to receive parcels. In the harsh conditions of Soviet jails, this right was invaluable—a regular supply of basic foodstuffs and a few items of warm clothing could make all the difference between near-death from starvation or hypothermia and an existence that was just tolerable. More important, it gave him an opportunity to inform his family of the bare facts of his survival and whereabouts.

Solzhenitsyn could only guess at the consternation that his sudden disappearance must have caused. Natalia's first inkling that something was wrong had not come until March 1945, a whole month after his arrest, when one of her postcards was returned marked, "Addressee has left unit." What could that mean? Natalia immediately wrote again and sent separate letters to Pashkin and Sergeant Solomin. Lydia Ezherets also wrote to Pashkin and to Captain Melnikov. Their first thought was that Solzhenitsyn must have been

---

*My Sister, Life, Pasternak's third book of poetry, had appeared in 1922 and immediately consolidated his reputation as one of post-revolutionary Russia's best young poets. "Lieutenant Schmidt" was published in 1927 in Pasternak's book *The Year 1905*.

killed in action, but Kirill, now a captain in the medical corps and recently posted to East Prussia himself, had disabused them of that idea: "Our army is not so delicately trained as to conceal from families the truth about the fallen. If anything had happened to Sanya, the situation would have been written on the letter: 'wounded—or killed—on such and such a date.' "[6] A month passed, during which Natalia did not know whether to hope or to mourn. Neither she, nor her mother and aunts, nor Lydia and the two Veronicas in Moscow could explain this total silence. In the second week of April, Solomin had replied to her letter with a guarded note not to Natalia but to Natalia's mother:

> Circumstances are now such that I must write to you. You are interested, of course, in Sanya's fate, why he hasn't written to you and what has happened to him. . . . He has been recalled from our unit. Where and for what reason I cannot tell you now. All I know is that he is alive and well, but nothing more, and also that nothing bad will happen to him. . . . Please do not worry and help Natasha.[7]

This reassured them that Solzhenitsyn was not dead, but why had Solomin written to Natalia's mother, whom he had met only once, rather than to Natalia herself, whom he had escorted to the front in 1944 and whom he knew much better? And why should Natalia's mother have to "help" her? All this only deepened the mystery.

Soon afterwards Antonina Vitkevich began to complain that she, too, was not receiving any letters from Nikolai, and Nikolai's letters to Natalia also ceased. "Why both of them?" asked Nikolai's grandmother one day, on learning of the news.

After another month of waiting, Natalia received a second letter from Ilya Solomin. This time he was a little more explicit.

> His departure was sudden . . . we didn't have a chance to talk to one another, that's why you shouldn't be surprised if he wasn't able to tell you anything. . . . Don't expect any letters from him, because he's in no position to write to you. And don't make any inquiries either, at best it's hopeless. . . .[8]

Solomin was still unable to say anything directly for fear that the censors might be reading his letters, and since he had no idea of the reason for Solzhenitsyn's arrest, he, too, might be in danger. It took considerable courage to write to Natalia at all. Solzhenitsyn's superior officers didn't reply to her letters.

Permission to receive parcels was granted to Solzhenitsyn in late June. Upon being asked to give the name and address of the person to whom notification should be sent, he decided that Natalia's aunt Veronica would be the most practical, since she lived in Moscow. Veronica received a printed card informing her, out of the blue, that "permission has been granted to you to deliver parcels to the Prisoner Solzhenitsyn, A.I." This was the first news the family had received in six months of the fact of Solzhenitsyn's arrest, and the address on the card was Butyrki Prison. Veronica at once dispatched a telegram to Natalia in Rostov: "Sanya alive well details later." Two days later, on 27 June, she sent another telegram, asking Natalia to come to Moscow or to book a long-distance telephone call. Natalia booked the call and endured agonies during the several hours she was obliged to wait for a line. Finally, she heard Veronica's voice on the other end of the telephone: "I took him a parcel today." At last she knew for sure. After the first telegram she had hoped that perhaps he had been sent on some sort of secret assignment. But now she knew without a doubt: her husband had been arrested and was in jail in Moscow.[9]

It was not possible for Natalia to pack her bags and leave for Moscow on the instant. She still had her job in the Rostov University laboratory, and she was studying to take the entrance examinations for admission to a postgraduate degree course in chemistry. But the summer term was drawing to an end, and a stroke of luck came her way. Her post-graduate supervisor, Professor Trifonov, was moving to the University of Kazan to become chairman of the department there, and he offered her three choices: to go to Kazan with him, to move to the Polytechnical Institute in her home town of Novocherkassk, where she would have a suitable supervisor, or to take on the more difficult task of gaining entrance to Moscow University. For reasons then unknown to Professor Trifonov, Natalia took the third possibility and immediately began preparations to go to Moscow and be interviewed for admission. The head of the Department of Physical Chemistry in Moscow, Professor Frost, had taught one of Natalia's Rostov professors when he had studied there, and her chances seemed reasonably good.

To be near her husband and, if possible, to visit him in jail was the immediate goal that beckoned her, but there were subsidiary reasons why the move to Moscow was attractive. Solzhenitsyn and Natalia were quite well known in university and Party circles in Rostov. He had been an outstanding student and Komsomol member, and she had worked in two different university departments, acquiring many friends among the faculty members. During the war she had eagerly responded to friendly inquiries about his progress, had boasted of his battle experiences and medals, and had even read extracts from his letters to some of her friends and colleagues. Everyone knew of his disappearance, and throughout the spring and early summer she had been bombarded with sympathetic requests for news of him. But now the situation looked entirely different. The war was almost won, only Japan still held out against the allies, and it was clear that, contrary to the universal hopes and the half-made promises, an era of ideological rigour was on the way again. Prisoners of war were failing to return to Rostov from captivity, many front-line soldiers were also missing, not all of them in action, and the press gave great prominence to official reprisals being inflicted on those who had collaborated with the German occupiers and to the need for vigilance in the reclaimed territories. Rostov itself had been occupied by the Germans for a while, and Rostov's citizens knew what turmoil that had created. So Natalia realized that to be known as the wife of a political prisoner would almost certainly put an end to her career in Rostov. Not only would she not be able to continue with her post-graduate studies but she would also be condemned to the life of a third-class citizen (fortunately, she was oblivious of the fact that she also ran the risk of arrest under the "MF" article—member of the family of a convicted man). There was no reason to jeopardize her entire career unnecessarily. She informed her colleagues that Solzhenitsyn had been reported missing in action, and after paying three times the normal price for an air ticket, she flew to Moscow at the end of June.

In three weeks Natalia visited Professor Frost in the chemistry department, was refused admission and was recommended to try Professor Kobozev, visited Kobozev, read his works, went to the Ministry of Higher Education to investigate the procedures for a transfer, applied to the assistant dean of the Chemistry Faculty, and finally, on 18 July, got Kobozev's permission to transfer and be supervised by him. She had won her first battle; she would be coming to Moscow. Meanwhile she extracted what meagre news she could from Aunt Veronica, with whom she was staying, about Veronica's delivery of a parcel to Butyrki, and made arrangements to deliver a second one herself. This meant making inquiries at the information department of the NKVD on Kuznetsky Most, then going in person to the prison on Novoslobodskaya Street and queuing up with the other wives and mothers. She had become like those women whom the young Solzhenitsyn had passed and barely noticed fifteen years ago outside the OGPU prison in Rostov.

Natalia also found time to go and see Lydia and compare notes about Nikolai and Solzhenitsyn and their correspondence. Lydia had achieved her ambition of marrying her childhood sweetheart, Kirill—the wedding had taken place in 1944, just before he left for the front—and Kirill was now back again. The two of them shared Natalia's grief and discussed what might have been the cause of Solzhenitsyn's and Nikolai's arrest. Lydia also went with her to the grim fortress of Butyrki, helped her prepare the first couple of parcels, and tried to assuage her anxieties. Then it was time for Natalia to dash back to Rostov to take her post-graduate examinations before the autumn term began. On these depended success or failure in her plan to move to Moscow. Before she left, she jotted a quick note to her mother.

> Dear Mamochka! Nothing new. Maybe that's what I'll return to Rostov with. Yesterday I sent off the second parcel. In addition to some food, I sent underwear, a towel, socks, and some handkerchiefs. Don't forget to register me at the canteen and hand in my work card to the university.[10]

She paid a last visit to the information department on Kuznetsky Most, where they told her that Solzhenitsyn had been sentenced to eight years. Would she be able to write letters? Yes. Unlike vast numbers of political prisoners, he had the right to write and receive a limited number of letters each year, but only when it had been resolved what labour camp to send him to.

A decision on this was now imminent, and in the first days of August, as Natalia travelled south to take her examinations, Solzhenitsyn was transferred to the Krasnaya Presnya transit prison in another part of Moscow.

Krasnaya Presnya is another jail that has been much described in the annals of the Gulag.* A vast overcrowded warren of a building whose cells seem to have been permanently bursting at the seams, Krasnaya Presnya was at the very hub of of the labour-camp system, a hive that not only served as the launching point for almost all new recruits to the Gulag's army of labourers but was also the central terminus through which they all passed when being moved from one part of the archipelago to another. Just as the Soviet empire's railway lines all lead to Moscow, so do the communication channels of the Gulag Archipelago all lead to Krasnaya Presnya; and there are few ex–labour-camp prisoners who have not been there at one time or another.

Krasnaya Presnya differed from Butyrki in fundamental ways and contributed greatly to Solzhenitsyn's education. In Butyrki all the inmates had been political prisoners charged with disloyalty to the Soviet regime. They were neither thieves, nor embezzlers, nor thugs, nor murderers, but had been jailed for their thoughts, their words, or on the simple presumption of unreliability. They were comparatively fresh from the outside world and had come trailing habits of courtesy, consideration, decency, respect for others, and a sense of responsibility. Upon finding themselves together in communal cells, the politicals had quickly struck up friendships and a sense of solidarity. Similarly, the "enemy" had been easy to spot and identify—warders, investigators, police officials. Within the cells, only the stool-pigeons stood out as belonging to the other side, and they, too, were easily recognized. But Krasnaya Presnya was entirely different. Here there were all kinds of prisoners, from timid, newly convicted, political "rabbits," still wet behind the ears, to hardened criminals with fifteen or twenty years of jail behind them, for whom Gulag was their life and their element. When taken together, the politicals may have been a majority, especially in the first years after the war, but they were demoralized, shocked, naïve, and inexperienced in the ways of the criminal world, and above all they were new arrivals and in transit, whereas the criminals were permanent, occupied all the positions of petty power in the prison, and virtually ran the place. Solzhenitsyn was to stumble across them very quickly. "From your very first steps in the transit prison you notice that here you are not in the hands of the warders or of officers with stars on their shoulders, who at least minimally observe some kind of written law. Here you are in the hands of the prison 'trusties.' "[11]

The trusties made no secret of their corruption and their greed for the

* Gulag stands for *Glavnoye upravleniye lagerei* (Main Administration of the Camps). Solzhenitsyn appears to have been the first to use it as an independent noun.

prisoners' meagre possessions, which was dispiriting enough to Solzhenitsyn and his fellow politicals, but other unpleasant surprises were to follow. Having been unloaded from the prison van in which they had been transported from Butyrki, they were ordered to squat on the ground in the prison yard, beneath the cell windows. The windows were barred with muzzles, which prevented them from seeing in, but from inside they heard hoarse, friendly voices shouting to them: "Hey, fellows! There's a rule here that when they search you, they take away everything loose, like tea and tobacco. So if you've got any, toss it in through the window and we'll give it back to you later."[12] These friendly voices were in such stark contrast to the curses and shouting of the armed guards that the new arrivals enthusiastically gave up their tobacco pouches and packets of sugar, only to discover, much later, that they had been fooled. Their new "friends" denied all knowledge of tobacco or sugar, and of the invitations to leave it with them.

A sign of the special status that awaited politicals from now on in the prisons and camps was the insulting designation of "Mister Fascist." "Mister" was derogatory because it harked back to a pre-revolutionary form of address, pre-dating the revolutionary "comrade." "Comrade" was applied not only to Party members but to anyone who accepted—or, more importantly, was accepted by—the Soviet system. It meant you were a "Soviet man," one of us, one of ours, whereas "mister" indicated that you were socially alien—either a throwback to the pre-revolutionary bourgeoisie, or a class enemy (or both). "Comrade" was not allowed to be used as a form of address to political prisoners (nor to any other prisoners, for that matter), nor were the politicals allowed to use this hallowed word in addressing others. They were invariably known mockingly as "mister" or more formally as "citizen." The very utterance of either word by a security officer was equivalent to saying, "You are under arrest." From the very moment that Solzhenitsyn's epaulettes had been torn off, he had been no longer "comrade" but "mister" or "citizen." Similarly, prisoners were obliged to address members of the NKVD and the prison administration as "citizen" but never as "comrade."

"Fascist" was a reference to the large numbers of alleged collaborators and returned prisoners of war who were now filling the jails. No one could be presumed to be more socially alien or hostile to the Soviet system than a Fascist, and therefore it was judged particularly appropriate—and humiliating—to call all political prisoners by this name. The criminal prisoners were actually encouraged to employ this terminology and were repeatedly assured by the prison authorities that they were the superior and more favoured class. They were still "comrades" in all but name and were therefore to be given positions of privilege and trust. This not only coincided with Soviet theories of criminality, according to which political nonconformity was a graver crime than social deviancy, but conveniently enabled the authorities to inflict an additional punishment on the politicals by placing them at the criminals' mercy.

Solzhenitsyn was only dimly aware of these ramifications when he arrived in Krasnaya Presnya, but its effects were immediately apparent not only in the episode of the tobacco and the reception procedures but also upon his assignment to a cell. He and Valentin were thrust into a cell that was smaller than the Butyrki church cells, yet had over a hundred prisoners in it. All the two-tiered bunks were full, but most of the asphalt floor beneath the bunks was free, and so were the aisles between the bunks. The normal procedure in cells of this kind was for the newcomers to start on the floor next to the stinking latrine tank, then work their way round the cell beneath the bunks before graduating to the lower tier and working their way round again, until finally, if they were lucky, they got to the privileged top tier and reached the windows. The speed and manner in which they moved depended on the numbers that were taken out and put in each day, for the prisoners in a transit prison were constantly on the move. Solzhenitsyn and Valentin, thankful for having arrived among their fellow prisoners at last, crawled under two bunks where the floor was free. The bunks were very low, and they had to inch in on their bellies. Luckily, their personal belongings had been handed to the prison store for safe-keeping until their destination was decided, and they had with them only knapsacks containing lard, sugar, and bread that they had received in parcels from their families. These, however, were more than enough to cause their undoing.

> We were going to lie there quietly and talk quietly. Not a chance! In the semi-darkness, with a wordless rustling, some "juveniles" started to creep up on us from all sides and on all fours, like big rats. They were still boys, some no more than twelve years old, but the criminal code accepted them too. They had already been "processed" under the thieves' law and were continuing their apprentice-ship with the thieves here. They had been unleashed on us. They leapt on us from all sides, and six pairs of hands wrenched from under us and stripped us of all our wealth. And all this took place in total silence, to the sound of sinister sniffing. And we were trapped—we couldn't get up, we couldn't move. It took no more than a minute for them to seize our bundles. . . . They were gone. We lay there feeling stupid. We had given up our food without a fight. And we could go on lying there now, but that was utterly impossible. Creeping out awkwardly, backsides first, we got up from under the bunks.[13]

The young criminals had been sent by their gang-leader, a hardened professional crook who occupied the top bunk next to the window, with his cronies on either side of him. Solzhenitsyn's stolen victuals now lay on the bunk before him. Resenting his humiliation, Solzhenitsyn went over to where the thief sat looking triumphantly down at him. His instinct, as he later described the scene in *The Gulag Archipelago*, was to leap up and grab his food back, or punch the thief on the nose, or at least grab one of those grinning urchins and punish him for the brazen robbery. But he did not dare. The gang-leader was both bigger and stronger than he and had plenty of friends to help him. From his scarred and deformed face it was obvious he would show no mercy in a fight. And it was unclear who made up the grey mass of prisoners lying motionless on the lower bunks. To save face and preserve some sense of honour, Solzhenitsyn protested indignantly that if the thieves were going to take their food, they might at least give him and Valentin a place on the bunks in exchange. It was a lame response and an ignoble one, as Solzhenitsyn later realized ("for many years thereafter I blushed every time I remembered it"),[14] for it played directly into the thieves' hands, acknowledging their power over him and acquiescing in their lawless rule. The gang-leader readily agreed to Solzhenitsyn's request and ordered two other prisoners to vacate the lower bunks by the window and move onto the floor. Solzhenitsyn and Valentin thus accelerated their progress round the cell at the expense of two other politicals, and were bitterly reproached for it later that night.

Krasnaya Presnya marked a new stage in Solzhenitsyn's education. In East Prussia he had thought there could be nothing worse than huddling four abreast in a freezing-cold concrete cellar, or marching for two days through icy winds and rain. In the Lubyanka he had discovered solitary confinement and the mental agonies of interrogation. In Butyrki he had had his hopes raised and dashed by false rumours of an amnesty, had heard himself finally condemned to eight years in the camps, and had slept on the floor in a cell with two hundred people in it. At each stage he had been stunned by the ferocity of the blows and the unexpected direction from which they had come, and at each stage his numbed brain had told him that the worst was now over and that things were bound to get better. And at each stage he had been deceived. Was there a logic to it, or was there none? Perhaps it was Solzhenitsyn's optimism that made the blows seem progressively worse: his irrepressible hopes invariably rose after each new trial, only to be cut down again by the following one, and then to bob back again, until the next blow came and felled them once more. And yet even here, in retrospect, he came to look upon the bright side of his vicissitudes. "Even for the greenhorn," he later wrote, "whom the transit prison cracks open and shells, like a nut, it is very, very necessary. It gives him some gradual preparation for the labour camps. Such a transition in one leap would be more than the heart could bear. His consciousness would be incapable of orienting itself in that murk. It has to be done gradually."[15]

Krasnaya Presnya, however, was qualitatively different from anything he had experienced before. In leaving Butyrki, he had cast off from the mainland and was already on one of the subsidiary islands of the archipelago. Here the distant draughts from the labour camps, which had barely ruffled the air of the Butyrki church cells, began to blow in a stiff breeze, one that struck a distinct chill into the heart despite the summer heat.

It was from Krasnaya Presnya that Solzhenitsyn was allowed to write his first letter to Natalia, a procedure he was later to describe in *The Gulag Archipelago*. It was

the first unfamiliar words home of a man who had been thoroughly ploughed by the investigation. At home they still remembered him as he had been before, but he would never be the same again—and suddenly this would flash out from one of the crooked lines. Crooked because, although letters were allowed from the transit prison and there was a post-box in the yard, it was impossible to lay hands on paper or pencil, and you had no means of sharpening it anyway. However, you could always smooth out a tobacco wrapper or a sugar packet, and someone in the cell was bound to have a pencil, and so the lines would go down in an indecipherable scrawl, determining the family's future in harmony or discord.[16]

Solzhenitsyn had already exchanged brief letters with Veronica following the delivery of her first parcel. Above all he was desperate for news of the others: Where were Kirill and Lydia, what did she know of Nikolai? "Reply to me, if only briefly, telling me the essential points. . . . For ten days I've been impatiently waiting for news . . . I pray from the bottom of my heart that Nikolai and Kirill avoided my fate." He had also received Natalia's first letter written to Krasnaya Presnya after being informed of the address from Moscow by Lydia. "What indescribable joy I derived from the sheets of paper written in your own hand," he wrote to Natalia; "in this way I learned that you are alive, healthy and free. . . . To this day I don't know whether or not 'sir' has shared my fate."[17] "Sir" was a transparent reference to Nikolai. Throughout his investigation Solzhenitsyn had half expected to be confronted with Nikolai, or at least with Nikolai's evidence, and perhaps with the others too, but it seemed that no confrontations had been necessary—the case was not serious enough and Ezepov not thorough enough for that. As a result Solzhenitsyn still did not know what had happened to his friends. He was overjoyed to learn that his wife was well and unharmed; and from the absence of any hints to the contrary in her letter, he deduced that the same was true of Kirill and Lydia.

Judging from the letters to Natalia that she later quoted in her book, he now regretted the last, irritable letters he had written her from East Prussia, and felt exaggeratedly repentant and ashamed. How could he have behaved that way towards her? She was his "beautiful wife," who from the depths of his present degradation seemed infinitely alluring and desirable. He mentioned to her the rumours of an amnesty, still persistent enough to be believed, and wrote with characteristic optimism that he was confident he wouldn't have to serve his full eight years. But if by chance he was proved wrong, he would feel bound to grant her "complete personal freedom" throughout the time he was away. In theory, at least, he shared the sentiments he later put into the mouth of the autobiographical Gleb Nerzhin in *The First Circle*: "My darling, for four years of war you waited for me—don't curse that you waited in vain: now it will be ten more years. All my life I will remember our brief happiness like a shaft of sunlight. But you should feel free from now on. There is no need for your life to be ruined as well. Marry again."[18]

The future looked dark and uncertain from his Krasnaya Presnya cell, but still he experienced an irrepressible urge to discuss it, just as he had liked to do in his letters from the front. Only now the picture had changed. Instead of a life in the thick of politics and literature in Moscow or Leningrad, he dreamed of getting away from it all. Those conversations in the Butyrki church cell about the joys of a quiet country life somewhere in Siberia reflected a whole new approach to life. After his return, he wrote Natalia, they would go to live in some "remote, but thriving, well-provisioned, and picturesque village," perhaps in Siberia, perhaps down in the Kuban where his grandfather had lived, or on the river Don or the Volga.[19] They would both take up teaching again, and in the summer holidays make tourist visits to Moscow, to Leningrad, to Rostov. Above all, it seemed, he now craved a peaceful life, close to nature, far from places where "accidents" might happen, like the one that had got him into his present mess. Six months of prison had knocked the stuffing out of him. He wanted nothing more than to crawl into a quiet corner where he could lick his wounds and be left alone.

11

TO THE NEW
JERUSALEM

HERE WAS LITTLE chance of Solzhenitsyn's realizing his dream of a quiet life within the confines of Krasnaya Presnya. Not only was he being subjected to the first rigours of the Gulag but the occupants of the cell were constantly being turned upside down, subtracted from, added to, stirred and mixed in new combinations. There was the same assortment of interesting individuals as before, with fascinating lives and unbelievable stories to tell, but there was no time to get to know them properly or hear them out. In the Butyrki church cell he had bumped into a co-defendant of the "Emperor Mikhail"; into a participant in the Austrian *Schutzbund* rebellion of 1934, most of whose members, he learned, had, after taking refuge in the Soviet Union, been sent to the labour camps in the great purge of 1937; and into a certain Lieutenant Vladimirescu, who calmly announced that he was a Rumanian spy. It was not as it had been in the investigation cells, however, where you had time to get to know the other prisoners. In the transit cells you had to snatch what information you could, before you or your companion were moved on. On the other hand, you gained from the desperate candour and openness with which everyone in the transit prison spoke. As Solzhenitsyn put it in *The Gulag Archipelago*, "You were refreshed and aired by the incessant traffic back and forth, by the comings and goings of dozens and hundreds of people, by the frankness of their stories and conversations . . . and you became more lucid, you began to understand better what was happening to you, to your people and even to the world. One eccentric in the cell could open up worlds to you that you would never be able to read about in any book."[1]

In Krasnaya Presnya there were dozens of such eccentrics, but the prisoner who made the deepest impression on Solzhenitsyn was a "special-assignment prisoner" who spent only two nights there and by chance slept in a neighbouring bunk. This prisoner was a labour-camp veteran, a "true son of Gulag," as veterans were called, who had served years and years in all parts of the archipelago. He owed his status to the fact that he had been officially designated a construction specialist and had a chit in his dossier indicating that he was to be used on no other form of work. To obtain this status was a great achievement in the labour camps and meant that he was exonerated from "general duties," a term that Solzhenitsyn still did not understand. But the price of that achievement was written on his face, whose dominant expression was one of cruelty and determination. "I did not then realize," Solzhenitsyn later wrote in *The Gulag Archipelago*, "that this precise expression was a national characteristic of the denizens of the Gulag islands. Persons with soft, accommodating expressions quickly died out on the islands."

The veteran, like a revered professor, was quickly surrounded by a group of novices demanding to know what awaited them in the camps. And, like a professor, he read them a lecture.

From your first step in the camp, everyone will try to deceive and rob you. Trust no one but yourself. . . . The law there is the law of the jungle. There never was and never will be any *justice* in Gulag. . . . And above all, avoid "general duties" like the plague. Avoid them from the very outset. If you land up on general duties on your first day, you're lost, lost forever![2]

There it was again, "general duties." What did it mean? The professor patiently explained that general duties referred to the basic labouring in each camp, at which 80 to 90 percent of the prisoners slogged away. The work was so gruelling, the norms set so high, and the food so meagre that the vast majority of prisoners on general duties sooner or later subsided into scavenging and died of exhaustion and malnutrition. That was the reason the professional thieves did their utmost not to leave Krasnaya Presnya or, if they did, to get for themselves the trusties' jobs assisting the administration. They above all knew what awaited them in the camps. But could this concept of general duties be squared with Valentin's vow to "work honestly" in the camps?

Solzhenitsyn was to try a form of general duties rather sooner than he had anticipated: the heat and stench in his Krasnaya Presnya cell were unbearable. Its two windows faced south, and the sheet-metal muzzles, preventing the entry of all except a trickle of fresh air, heated up in the August sun and roasted the people inside. Stripped to their underwear, braving the unbiquitous bedbugs, the hundred-odd prisoners sweltered and writhed in helpless immobility, praying to be called out and sent on to their next assignment. For this reason, when the call came for volunteers to go down to the Moscow River and unload timber, Solzhenitsyn was among them, grateful for the chance to spend the day in the fresh air. The work consisted of shifting balks of timber from one spot to another on one of the wharves, and Solzhenitsyn was appalled to discover that none of them had the strength left to do the work very quickly. Nevertheless, they earned an extra three and a half ounces of bread per day and barely noticed the watch-towers with armed guards and the high fence that surrounded the wharf. Evidently a proper camp was in formation here, and the Krasnaya Presnya prisoners were just a temporary expedient.

It was while they were being marched back from the wharf that Veronica Turkina caught a glimpse of Solzhenitsyn in one of the columns, the first sight that any of the family had had of him since his arrest. She wrote at once to Natalia, disguising her message by feminizing Solzhenitsyn's name and striking an exaggeratedly cheerful note to dispel Natalia's gloom. "Saw Shurochka* just once. She was returning with friends from her job of unloading timber on the Moscow River. She looks marvellous. She is suntanned, energetic, cheerful, smiling from ear to ear, teeth sparkling! I'm very glad she's in good spirits."[3] Solzhenitsyn was later to use this incident in *The First Circle*, attributing the chance encounter to Gleb Nerzhin's wife, Nadia, instead of her aunt, and describing his own appearance as "sallow and emaciated," like that of the other skinny prisoners in the column.[4]

Meanwhile, Natalia had received Solzhenitsyn's letter from Krasnaya Presnya, four tightly crammed pages written in hard pencil in the minuscule handwriting that Solzhenitsyn had perfected for his notes at the front, and folded into a tiny triangle. She had completed her summer chemistry examinations in Rostov and was preparing to go to Moscow in the hope of seeing him. But getting there was no easy matter, for first she had to show good reason why she needed to travel, so that she could get a permit to leave her place of residence, and then she had to obtain a ticket, which meant joining endless queues or offering a bribe.

While she was making these preparations she received another letter from Veronica, dated 24 August. Her aunt wrote that the last time she had tried to deliver a parcel to Solzhenitsyn she had been informed by the Krasnaya Presnya office that he was no longer there. They refused at first to inform her of where he had been moved, and it was only several days later that they had consented to reveal his destination.

> It's the absolute truth that you were born under a lucky star! Natasha, my darling, how many envious eyes were fixed on me yesterday. You can rest easy. Every Sunday you will be going from Moscow to Novy Ierusalim. It's a holiday spot set in wonderful countryside. It used to be called the "Russian Switzerland." There you will be able to see him.[5]

Novy Ierusalim—"New Jerusalem," a pregnant name for a corrective labour camp—and set in the "Russian Switzerland." What more promising place for the fledgeling convicts to take their first faltering steps on an island

* The usual diminutive of Alexandra—in this case a device for not referring directly to Alexander.

of the archipelago? Solzhenitsyn and sixty other politicals were transported there on 14 August 1945, in the back of two open lorries, squatting on the floor so as to be invisible to inquisitive onlookers. To their surprise, they found the streets and houses decked with flags—it was the day of final victory over Japan. The Second World War had at last come to an end.

Within a short time they arrived at their destination in New Jerusalem. "The Fascists have arrived! The Fascists have arrived!" was the cry that greeted them as they climbed down from the backs of the lorries and stretched their stiff limbs. The district of Zvenigorod, where the camp was situated, was only thirty miles west of Moscow, and the ride had taken no more than an hour, but thanks to the long-windedness of the Krasnaya Presnya discharge procedures, the endless formalities and the inefficiency of the transport arrangements, it was nearly sunset by the time they arrived. They were at once surrounded by inquisitive prisoners and asked the usual questions about where they were from, whether they were "Fascists" (political prisoners) or criminals, and so on, before being left alone to go through the seemingly interminable admission procedures.

At first glance the camp struck them as attractive and even cosy. The freshness and greenness of the surrounding landscape dazzled their eyes, accustomed for so many months to the drabness of a city prison. Through the loosely interwoven strands of barbed wire, they could see the gentle hills of Zvenigorod, dotted with unkempt cottages and tumbledown hamlets; the sprawling informality of the Russian countryside seemed to extend right through the wire to the ramshackle barns and sheds that housed the camp canteen, bath-house, stores, latrines, and other services. Even the white, two-storey brickworks, with its tall chimney, which was the centre-piece of the camp, the stone barracks for the men, and the wooden barrack, with an attic perched on the top, for the women, were momentarily perceived by them as endearingly familiar and normal.

They were led to the living compound, an area about two hundred yards square and fenced off from the work compound by barbed wire, with a guardhouse between the two. It was late. They still had to queue up to hand in their belongings to the stores. Solzhenitsyn waited obediently, handed in his suitcase, and remained with only what he stood up in. Then they were taken to the stone barracks to see their new quarters, where the impression of cosiness was quickly dissipated.

The cavernous barrack rooms were totally devoid of furniture, except for row upon row of some curious sleeping structures known in camp jargon as "wagonettes." Each wagonette consisted of two vertical steel posts standing about six feet apart on shaky legs, with two crossbars sticking out to either side like a double T, one at knee height and the other at about the height of a man's shoulders. Across these bars and holding the whole thing together were bare boards fixed to form four narrow bunks, two above and two below. There was no bedding of any kind, not even a straw mattress (let alone a pillow). Each prisoner was obliged to lie directly on the bare boards in whatever clothes he was wearing. He dared not remove his boots—or anything else—for the next morning they would be gone; and in any case there was nowhere to put them. In the mornings, when the prisoners filed out, the barrack room was left as clean as a whistle. Not a rag, not even a piece of fluff, was left to show that any humans had been there.

But the feature of the wagonettes that was to upset Solzhenitsyn the most, and make his life on them a misery, was their chronic instability. Every time a prisoner climbed onto one of the four bunks, or climbed down again, or turned over, the whole structure wobbled and trembled, so that the other three occupants would be shaken out of their sleep. Solzhenitsyn detested them, for they left him with no control over the most precious hours in a prisoner's day and deprived him of his last vestige of privacy.[6]

Not surprisingly, he slept badly that first night. The boards were excruciatingly narrow and uncomfortable, he could not get used to the itchy feeling of sleeping in his clothes and boots, and he was painfully conscious of the other three bodies tossing and turning on their joint wagonette. His mind was also full of apprehension. He recalled the insistent words of the special-assignment veteran: whatever you do, keep off general duties! Yet how was it to be done? Barely an hour had gone by before one member of their transport entered and announced that he had been put in charge of maintenance work in the compound. Another had been given permission to open a barber's shop for the free workers at the brickworks. A third had run into an old friend who had fixed him up in the planning section. All good jobs, but there was a limited number of them available. What should he do? To whom should he turn? Did it require bribes, or was there some other way? What was for the best?

The next morning he was woken at a quarter past four by the loud ringing of a bell and the shouts of the guards. Time for the first shift to get up. Stiff and shivering, still drunk with sleep, not wishing to wash and not needing to dress, Solzhenitsyn stumbled blindly to the canteen. "Everyone was pushing and shoving and knew exactly what he wanted. Some were racing to get their bread, others to collect their gruel. And you staggered about like a lunatic, unable to make out under the dim lights and in the steam from the gruel where to go for the one or the other."[7] At length he obtained his pound and a quarter of soggy bread and dipped his spoon into his bowl, only to discover a meatless, saltless, fatless, evil-smelling nettle soup that made his stomach heave and his head swim. Lifting his eyes to the wall opposite, he saw through the gloom a big red slogan so beloved of Soviet administration: "Whoever does not work does not eat!"

After breakfast the newcomers were lined up, counted, and marched to the work compound, escorted by armed guards and trained Alsatians baying and straining at the leash. It was 6 a.m. and just beginning to get light. To keep them busy, they were ordered to move a pile of rubbish from one spot to another by wheel- and hand-barrow. The work was obviously meaningless, and Solzhenitsyn took every opportunity to stop and chat with Boris

Gammerov and Georgi Ingal. To take their minds off their work, they talked about their favourite subject—literature. Ingal described Tynyanov's funeral to Solzhenitsyn and informed him that he regarded himself as Tynyanov's pupil in the writing of historical novels. This led to an interesting clash of opinion, which Solzhenitsyn later described in *The Gulag Archipelago*.

> We argued about historical novels—ought people to write them? After all, a historical novel deals with things the author never saw. Burdened by remoteness and the ripeness of his own era, the author can try to convince himself as much as he likes that he has thoroughly *comprehended*, but nonetheless he is never able to *enter into it* properly, which means, surely, that a historical novel is an invention?[8]

That question mark presumably indicates the gap through which Solzhenitsyn squeezed when he came to start on his own series of historical novels. He would later argue that he lived close enough in time, and knew enough eyewitnesses, to make *August 1914* and its successors different in kind from the usual run of historical novels, and in this there is some truth. On the other hand, the break between tsarist and Soviet Russia was so radical and so complete that he could never recapture that pre-revolutionary world with the same authority as he has the Soviet one, a circumstance that later led to some fierce polemics concerning the authenticity of *August 1914*.

One by one the new arrivals were called in to be given their permanent assignments. Ingal had already met someone with influence and been given a job as a bookkeeper. Gammerov, true to his disdain for the authorities and refusal to treat with them in any way, proudly accepted general duties. Soon it was Solzhenitsyn's turn. He had already thought about how to make an impression and keep off the dreaded general duties, and had carefully put on his full officer's uniform (minus the epaulettes): tunic buttoned up to the neck; broad officer's belt; riding breeches; and patent-leather riding boots. When he entered the director's office, according to Solzhenitsyn's account of the meeting, his clothes had the desired effect.

> "Officer?" guessed the director.
> "Yes, sir!"
> "Any experience with men?"
> "Yes."
> "What unit did you command?"
> "An artillery battalion." (I lied on impulse, a battery seemed too small to me.)
> He looked at me, half-trusting and half-doubting.
> "But can you manage here? It's hard here."
> "I think I'll manage," I said.
> . . . He frowned and thought for a moment . . .
> "All right. You can be shift foreman in the clay-pit."[9]

Solzhenitsyn was triumphant. He had avoided general duties at the very outset. Another former officer, named Akimov, was also appointed shift

foreman, and the two of them strolled off together. They agreed that the
director had seemed unduly hesitant in giving them the job and could not
fathom why. After all, there were only twenty men in each shift and both
had commanded larger numbers than that in the army.

Work in the camp was carried out round the clock, in three shifts. The
morning shift began at six and ended at two, the afternoon shift ran from
two to ten, and the night shift from ten to six. Solzhenitsyn was assigned the
morning shift, and during the first day or so seemed to be getting into the
swing of it. But after a day or two he was confronted, shortly before his shift
was due to end, with a new brigade of workers, a punishment brigade, consisting entirely of professional crooks who had just been released from the
camp lock-up after threatening to cut the camp commandant's throat. They
had been brought to the clay-pit because it was the heaviest and most difficult
work, but instead of picking up their shovels and bending their backs, they
simply sprawled on the ground and commenced sunbathing. Solzhenitsyn
went over to them and curtly ordered them to start work. He was met with
laughter and a volley of obscenities. He would have liked to stand his ground,
but his experiences in Krasnaya Presnya had already taught him that it was
dangerous to meddle with criminals. Enraged and confused, he beat a prudent retreat. Soon afterwards his shift came to an end, and he was replaced
by Akimov; and later that day he learned of the sequel to his encounter.
Akimov had started by approaching the thieves in exactly the same way as
Solzhenitsyn. He had more to lose, however, with a whole shift ahead of
him, and had therefore pressed the thieves much harder. When they still
refused, he had reported them to the supervisor, an engineer by the name of
Olga Matronina, but she had simply ordered Akimov to force the thieves to
work. Akimov had returned to the clay-pit and tried again, and on this occasion the crooks had chased him into a distant corner, knocked him down,
and smashed his kidneys with a crowbar. Akimov was carried off to hospital
and never seen again.

Fortunately, there were no more confrontations between Solzhenitsyn
and the thieves, but his life was little the better for that, for he immediately
came into conflict with the brigade leader on his shift, a prisoner who was
neither a political nor a professional criminal, but a man convicted of a civil
offence. He was a Muscovite named Barinov, a veteran of the clay-pit who
knew the work through and through and whose main aim in life was to shield
his men from the worst rigours of the camp and fulfil the norms as efficiently
and painlessly as possible. Later in his camp career Solzhenitsyn came to
admire such far-sighted brigade leaders and later still immortalized one of
them in the person of Tiurin in *A Day in the Life of Ivan Denisovich*. But in
New Jerusalem he still identified with authority and insisted on his right to
give Barinov orders, just as he would have done in the army. Barinov did not
try to resist Solzhenitsyn or to beat him up; he simply made a complete and
utter fool of him. The work in the clay-pit consisted of digging the raw clay
from the ground with shovels, filling wagons with it, and rolling the wagons

to the wet-pressing plant, where the clay was pressed into bricks. The wagons had to be pushed on tracks that ran along the floor of shallow ravines where the clay had already been dug out, then hauled out of the pit with the help of a mechanized winch and pushed again over flat ground to the plant. These wagons proved to be Barinov's weapon. Whenever something went wrong with one of them, Barinov would ostentatiously call Solzhenitsyn over and ask him for instructions on how to put it right. Or he would ask for guidance on where to lay the tracks next, or on how to repair the winch if it broke down, all the time aware that he knew the answers perfectly well and Solzhenitsyn didn't. Alternatively, if Solzhenitsyn gave orders for certain things to be done, Barinov would invariably discover reasons why they couldn't and would demonstrate them to Solzhenitsyn in front of the other men. In the end Solzhenitsyn was forced to abandon the unequal struggle. His spirit was numbed; he felt utterly bewildered and helpless. Krasnaya Presnya, Butyrki—even the Lubyanka—had been nothing like this. It was still true, it seemed, that every new step he took was worse than the one before. How long would it go on? He was soon grateful to let Barinov have his way in everything, and every morning as he entered the clay-pit, dreading the day ahead, he would pray only to be left alone and not to be bothered by Barinov.

Unfortunately for Solzhenitsyn, another pair of eyes was watching him as well—that of Olga Matronina. Matronina, although technically a political prisoner (her husband, a Party member, had been shot during the thirties, and she had got eight years as a member of the family), was an even more fiercely loyal Communist than Solzhenitsyn, and absolutely dedicated to the system. Her consuming goal in life was to maximize brick production just as in any normal enterprise, regardless of the fact that the work-force consisted of half-starved convicts working in abominable conditions with out-of-date equipment (or, in some cases, with none at all). As she had recently written in a petition to Kalinin, the president of the Soviet Union, "my long sentence has not broken my will in the struggle on behalf of Soviet power and Soviet industry."

Matronina was chief of the wet-pressing plant, to which the clay-pit was attached, and one day she announced that the number of wagon-loads per shift was to be doubled—just like that. Solzhenitsyn regarded himself as essentially on her side but on this occasion made no attempt to comply. He simply did not see how his starving and exhausted men could possibly double a production norm that was already beyond their strength, and he did not understand that the task of a foreman was precisely to *make* them double it at all costs. That was the price of his privileged position on the side of the camp authorities, and of his better rations, which he now received from a different hatch in the canteen. And that was the promise that his Soviet officer's uniform had seemed to make to the director and Matronina when he had pleaded for the job. Confronted by his failure, Matronina was implacable and roasted him in front of Barinov and the men—to Barinov's vast satisfaction. A day or two later, Solzhenitsyn seized the opportunity to go to Matronina and humbly beg to be taken on as a ledger clerk in the plant, but she roasted him again. If she needed a ledger-clerk, she said, she had plenty of girls available for the job. What were needed were "production commanders," and she sent him back to the clay-pit.

The following day Solzhenitsyn was informed that the post of foreman had been abolished. Barinov was to be placed in charge of the morning shift, and Solzhenitsyn was to be put on general duties, under Barinov, digging clay. "Give him a crow bar and don't take your eyes off him. See he loads six wagons a shift. Make him sweat![10] was Matronina's parting shot to Barinov.

Solzhenitsyn's rise and fall had been uncommonly swift, in the best tradition of the labour camps. Either you adapted quickly and were saved, or you failed to adapt and were subjected to all the rigours that the labour-camp regime had to offer, which could quickly end in your demise if you were unlucky. But besides the physical privations, there was the mental anguish. One of the things that stands out in Solzhenitsyn's descriptions of New Jerusalem in *The Gulag Archipelago* is the vivid recollection of his white-hot indignation and outrage over the sheer bovine stupidity of the camp arrangements. For instance, members of the three shifts at the brickworks were mixed together in the barrack rooms. This meant that there was contin-ual noise and movement. No sooner had the morning shift had supper and returned to their rooms for the night than the members of the night shift began to get up from their bunks and prepare to go outside. Soon after they left, the afternoon shift would return and crowd into the rooms, boisterous and talkative now that work was over. Finally, well after midnight, it would fall quiet at last, but at four-fifteen it was time to get up again, and it was the morning shift's turn to disturb the others. Worse still, at each changeover the wagonettes would be set creaking and shaking, and the bright electric light was kept on all the time.

The day was also organized in such a way that the prisoners were kept constantly at the beck and call of their overseers, yet at the same time forced to stand around unoccupied for long periods at a stretch. In addition to per-forming the cumbersome rituals of washing and eating, they had to queue twice a day at the stores, once to hand in their belongings in the morning and once to get them out again in the early evening. There was also the daily roll-call.

> Everyone in the compound had to form up in ranks while an illiterate guard with a plywood board in his hand went round, continually licking his pencil, corru-gating his forehead with mental strain and whispering to himself. He counted the ranks several times over, then went round every building to check, leaving the prisoners standing there. Sometimes he made a mistake in his sums or got mixed up over how many were in the lock-up. And this senseless waste of time went on, if you were lucky, for an hour and sometimes for an hour and a half.[11]

What is interesting here is the sense of outrage and frustration that still burned so deeply in Solzhenitsyn twenty years afterwards, when he was writing *The Gulag Archipelago*. It was partly the irritation of an intellectual confronted by the mindless procedures of any cumbersome control system—anyone who has done military service will recognize his frustration—but the level of intolerance of it was highly personal to him. As he writes in *The Gulag Archipelago*, a sense of time is not very highly developed in the Russian people—and was totally alien to labour-camp prisoners; but to anyone who possessed it (Solzhenitsyn was one of the very, very few) these endless delays were agonizing. Ingal and Gammerov got round them by standing on parade with closed eyes and composing verse or prose, or letters home, in their heads. And in general they coped better with the pressures of camp life, although they were younger and had less front-line experience than Solzhenitsyn. Georgi Ingal, whose physical work was easy, insisted on underlining his creative freedom and independence by refusing to sleep during the first half of each night and sitting up on his bunk writing. Boris Gammerov, whose independence had been expressed in his willing acceptance of general duties, was too exhausted to emulate him but still led an active mental life, debating with the other two and composing verse. But Solzhenitsyn was too confused and depressed to keep up with them. He did write to Natalia asking her to send him paper, pencils, pens, ink, and some English textbooks, since he had resolved to revise and improve his English as an antidote to camp depression, but he found the obscenities of the morning parade and the din of the barrack room too intrusive to contemplate any creative work, and the effort of composition was totally beyond him. His will-power had been sapped by his ambivalence about the camp authorities, his instinctive urge still to "belong" and be accepted as "one of them." He was bewildered and disoriented. When he wrote to Natalia, he complained of "spiritual fatigue" and a head clogged with a "viscous jumble of dullness." He had no clear idea of what was for the best or what he should try to do next.

His vacillation became even more marked after he was summoned one day for an interview with a young NKVD lieutenant. In fact, the lieutenant did not interview him but simply invited Solzhenitsyn to write his autobiography.

After the investigation depositions, in which I had only spat all over myself, after the humiliation of the prison vans and transit cells, after the armed guards and prison warders, after the thieves and trusties had refused to see in me a former captain of our glorious Red Army, here I sat behind a desk, not being pressed by anyone at all, beneath the benign gaze of this friendly lieutenant, and wrote at just the right length and in thick ink on excellent smooth paper, such as you did not get in the camps, that I had been a captain, that I had commanded a battery, and that I had been awarded such and such medals. And thanks to the very fact of writing, it seemed to me that I was getting back my own personality, my "I." (Yes, my epistemological subjective "I"! . . .) And the lieutenant, reading through my autobiography, was completely satisfied. "So you're a Soviet man, is that right?" Yes, of course it was right, why not? How agreeable it was to rise from the dust and ashes and become a Soviet man again—it was one half of freedom![12]

That dream of freedom still burned bright in Solzhenitsyn's imagination, and he was still hoping for an amnesty. The 7 July amnesty had been only slowly put into operation, and it was not until his arrival in New Jerusalem that he discovered its terms and saw how it was working. Releases from New Jerusalem had begun only with the arrival of the "Fascists," for the new work-force was needed to take the place of the old. Solzhenitsyn then discovered that it was only professional thieves and civil offenders who were to benefit from the July amnesty—he himself witnessed dozens of them being released from New Jerusalem and returning to Moscow. Nevertheless, it did not seem possible that the amnesty would or could stop there. Rumour said that now that the war was well and truly finished with the victory over Japan, Stalin would "take account of the victory" and declare a second amnesty expressly for political prisoners. It was even said that the amnesty had been prepared and lay on Stalin's desk ready for his signature but that he was away on holiday (Solzhenitsyn later incorporated this rumour into his play *The Tenderfoot and the Tart*). "The basic hope," wrote Solzhenitsyn to Natalia, "is for an amnesty for those convicted under Article 58. I still think that this will happen."[13]

One result of this farcically partial amnesty was the appearance all over the camp of giant slogans: "For this broad amnesty let us thank our dear Party and government by doubling productivity." Another was a shortage of manpower with which to achieve this doubling. Solzhenitsyn was switched for a time from the clay-pit to Matronina's pressing plant. There he was able to observe Matronina queening it over the several dozen women prisoners who worked eight-hour shifts (without a break) at conveyor belts carrying the newly pressed clay bricks. Solzhenitsyn's job was to manhandle wagons loaded with 120 wet bricks stacked on shelves from one end of the conveyor belt, where they were loaded by two girls, along rails to the drying chambers. The wagons were top-heavy and the wooden kiln floors were rotting and full of holes. Solzhenitsyn frequently stumbled and fell while trying to line up the wagons and drop the shelves onto racks in the chambers. "There was probably supposed to be some kind of ventilation in the chambers, but it was no longer working, and while I struggled with my mistakes in positioning the shelves (I used to get them crooked, they got stuck, wouldn't settle on the racks, and wet bricks would rain down on my head), I gulped in carbon fumes which burned my windpipe."[14]

He was almost relieved when ordered back to the clay-pit again, where he teamed up with Boris Gammerov. They had been transferred because the amnesty was reducing the ranks of the digging brigades once more. The shift norm for each worker was six wagons of clay (eight cubic yards) filled and pushed by hand to the winch—sixteen cubic yards for two people. But the most they could manage was six and a half yards between them: less than half the norm. And that was in dry weather. Boris still had shrapnel in his lung, and his TB was getting worse. Solzhenitsyn's arms felt as if they were dropping off. "The work-loads of an unskilled labourer are beyond my strength," he wrote to Natalia. "I curse my physical underdevelopment."[15]

A few days later it began to rain. Autumn was setting in, and the rain went on and on, neither turning into a downpour nor completely stopping. "In New Jerusalem for some reason they did not even issue us with padded jackets, and there in the red clay-pit, beneath that monotonous drizzle, we wallowed and caked our army greatcoats, which by the end of the third day had already absorbed a pail of water each. Nor did the camp issue any foot-wear, and we were rotting our last front-line boots in the wet clay."[16] Sol-zhenitsyn resolved to get rid of his tunic and cavalry trousers for a while and packed them away in his suitcase in the store, applying to the quartermaster for some patched and faded camp rags in their place—oblivious, for the moment, of the symbolic importance of this change. But it still didn't help. He and Gammerov tried to keep up their spirits by talking about Chekhov and Vladimir Solovyov* (whom Solzhenitsyn had not then read) and by tell-ing jokes, but the norm became even more unattainable in the squelching mud. They were put on punishment rations: three ladles of nettle broth and one of thin gruel a day, and less than a pound of bread. And still the rain fell.

> The clay-pit had become drenched, and we were well and truly stuck in it. No matter how much clay you picked up on your shovel and no matter how much you banged it on the side of the wagon, the clay would not drop off. Each time we had to reach over and push the clay off the shovel into the car. And then we realized that we had merely been doing extra work. We put aside our shovels and began simply to scoop up the squelching clay from beneath our feet and toss it into the wagon.[17]

Just before two o'clock and the end of the shift, Matronina appeared on the edge of the clay-pit and could be seen gesturing to the brigade leader as she walked around and pointed out certain spots: she was giving orders for the prisoners to be kept in the pit until their norms had been fulfilled. The afternoon dragged on. "Our hands had grown numb from the cold clay, and by this time we couldn't even throw anything into the wagon. We left this futile occupation, climbed up to the grass, sat down there, bent our heads, and pulled the collars of our coats up over the backs of our necks. From the side we looked like two reddish stones in a field."[18] Soon everyone had left the pit, and the wagons stood abandoned, some of them turned on their sides. Gammerov and Solzhenitsyn picked up their shovels and dragged their way over to the foot of Matronina's pressing plant, where they huddled in the dust beneath a brick vault. Not far away some other prisoners were dig-ging into a heap of coal, picking out some greyish black lumps and eating

---

*A religious philosopher and poet of the latter half of the nineteenth century who propounded the union of all Christian churches and who combined liberal political views with a profound belief in the importance of mystical revelation. He has recently become popular with Russian intellectuals opposed to the Soviet political system.

them. Solzhenitsyn asked what they were. He was told it was "sea-clay." It had no nutritional value, but it didn't do any harm either. It simply made the men feel full, as if they had eaten a good meal.

Right up to nightfall they were kept at the clay-pit, but no one fulfilled his norm. Matronina cursed and ordered that they be kept out all night. But there were no lights in the work compound and it was too big a risk. Some-one might escape. The men were rounded up and herded back to the living compound by armed guards and baying dogs. They gulped down their two ladles of nettle soup—one for lunch and one for supper—to the dim light from two paraffin lamps flickering in the canteen, then lay down as they were, soaking wet and muddy, on their polished wooden boards. For three nights now they had slept in sopping-wet clothing. There were no facilities for drying anything, and it was cold from the draughts.

Solzhenitsyn felt at a lower ebb than he could ever remember: exhausted, rain-sodden, cold, drained of all hope. And tomorrow would be the same, and every day after that: Six wagons of red clay, three scoops of black gruel. "We had felt that we were growing weaker in prison, but here it went much quicker. There was already a sort of ringing in our heads. We were on the brink of that pleasant lassitude when it would be easier to yield than to fight back."[19]

He understood that the archipelago was more brutal than he had ever realized, more merciless even than the special-assignment prisoner had pre-dicted. He had made his bid to escape general duties and had failed. He still had nearly eight years to serve, yet he already felt he had one foot in the grave, and the future seemed an utter blank to him. He had completed exactly three weeks of his sentence.

12

LIFE AMONG
THE TRUSTIES

Reprieve from the clay-pits of New Jerusalem came suddenly and unexpectedly, on 9 September 1945, when all the prisoners were told to collect their belongings from the store and to stand by for transfer: the camp was to be emptied to make way for a contingent of German prisoners of war. To his great relief, Solzhenitsyn was not sent on one of the distant convoys to the Urals, Central Asia, or Siberia that he had heard so much about, but was transferred back to Moscow—to Kaluga Gate, on the south side of the city.

As usual, the parading and roll-calls at either end seemed interminable, and again it was night before the Kaluga Gate contingent arrived at their destination. Shocked and frightened by his experiences on general duties at New Jerusalem, and with the words of the Krasnaya Presnya veteran still ringing in his ears, Solzhenitsyn was determined to avoid a repetition of his recent ordeal at all costs. The commander of Kaluga Gate, Lieutenant Nevezhin, was on hand at the guardhouse to inspect and question new arrivals. When he came to Solzhenitsyn, who had specially dressed up in his cavalry breeches and officer's topcoat for the occasion, Solzhenitsyn announced boldly that he was a "norm setter." It was a word he had first come across in the camp, and he had no idea what it meant, but he hoped it had something to do with mathematics. Nevezhin asked Solzhenitsyn a few questions; he appears to have been impressed by his willingness to please, because the following day Solzhenitsyn's name was missing from the list of those sent out to do general duties, and two days later he found himself appointed to the unimaginably exalted post of production superintendent, a new job specially created for him, that placed him in charge of all the brigade leaders, the work allocator, and most of the trusties in the camp.

This was higher than he had dared dream, and it carried with it the privilege of sleeping in one of two special rooms set aside for the production trusties. This room, on the third floor, was for six people only. It had single bunks instead of shuddering wagonettes, bedside tables shared between two people, and a hotplate on which to cook food brought in from outside. During the day the room was locked, so there was no necessity to queue twice a day at the stores, and life was more comfortable than anything he had known since his arrest.

The company in the room was also rather special: two generals, a doctor, an engineer—and only one peasant, though even he had once been chairman of a village Soviet. Solzhenitsyn looked and listened and learned—his education was continuing.

Of the two generals, much the grander was the air-force major-general Alexander Beliayev, who worked as assistant to the norm setter. As production superintendent, Solzhenitsyn was senior to Beliayev in the camp hierarchy, but, like everybody else in camp, he still deferred to Beliayev and called him "general" (an almost unique instance of a man's informally retaining his former rank in the labour camps) and treated him with the exaggerated respect that seemed to be universally accorded him at Kaluga Gate. This was because Beliayev himself insisted on it. Solzhenitsyn encountered him for the first time in the construction office when he approached the general for a light, thinking that the latter would offer him his cigarette to light from. But not at all. Beliayev removed his cigarette from his mouth, took an expensive lighter from his pocket, and placed it ostentatiously on the desk for Solzhenitsyn to use. Subsequently, Solzhenitsyn noticed that this was typical of Beliayev's whole attitude: "He stood out from the grey-black, lice-ridden prisoners' ranks not only by his height and handsome figure but also by his particular air of not being present. Even when lined up with all the others and without moving a muscle, he was able to demonstrate that he had no connection whatever with the teeming camp rabble around him and that until his dying day he would never understand how he had come to find himself among them."[1]

Beliayev never entered the camp canteen, boasting that he didn't know where the door was. Every day at 1 p.m., when the prisoners returned to their living quarters from the work compound, Beliayev's wife would punctually present herself at the camp guardhouse and hand over a freshly cooked hot meal for him, stored in an expensive vacuum container. This he ate in their room every day, together with a portion of his bread ration, which was brought to him by the peasant, Prokhorov. Even then he could not resist cutting a thin slice off all six sides of his piece of bread to ensure that his mouth touched nothing that had been handled by the other prisoners.

The other general, Pavel Zinoviev, had been a general in the MVD, which meant he had once been responsible for administering the prisons and camps. Indeed he still wore the same bluish grey uniform of his captors, with its azure piping so familiar to, and detested by, the other prisoners, and remarks that he dropped made it clear that in the past he had personally supervised prisoners working on construction projects. He, too, shunned the camp canteen and had all his food brought to him by his wife and daughter, who lived not far from the camp, but they were poorer than Beliayev's wife, and therefore, in addition to the bread, he made Prokhorov bring him his soup and gruel from the canteen, which he reheated over the hotplate.

Zinoviev was milder mannered than the blustering Beliayev, but he had a sharp tongue and felt his present humiliation much more keenly than the air-force general did. Both had been jailed for corruption and embezzlement, but whereas Beliayev had not had his personal property confiscated, Zinoviev had lost half of his, and this, too, filled him with resentment. Solzhenitsyn observed the two of them with fascination and not without a certain sympathy, though their arrogance and obvious contempt for everyone around them precluded real friendship. He was also happy to tolerate their mild despotism after the bruising rigours of New Jerusalem.

The doctor in the room, Dr Pravdin, a neuropathologist in his former life and now chief of the camp medical section, had been imprisoned, like Solzhenitsyn, under Article 58, for anti-Soviet agitation and propaganda, and like Solzhenitsyn had been sentenced to eight years. He was a big, distinguished-looking man of about seventy, with a mop of silvery hair that he had been able to preserve from shaving by a special dispensation. Yet he seemed to Solzhenitsyn to be as timid as a rabbit and to have "the naïvety of a backward child. . . . He believed that we had all been imprisoned only temporarily, as a kind of joke, and that a magnificent and generous amnesty was being prepared so that we would value freedom all the more and be eternally grateful to the Organs for this lesson."[2] Not surprisingly, Pravdin was diligent in his efforts to please the camp administration and consequently not in the least concerned for the medical standards by which he had lived all his life. The medical section's task, as he saw it, was simply to rubber-stamp the administration's neglect of the prisoners.

The two remaining inhabitants of the room were most unpopular with the generals, who did everything in their power to get rid of them. One of them, Orachevsky, had been an engineering instructor and had been jailed for five years for "smiling" while reading *Pravda* and for passing a negative comment when asked to fill in a political report on someone. Orachevsky was taciturn and seldom joined the endless conversations in the room, which were invariably led by the generals, but what fascinated Solzhenitsyn about him was his passionate devotion to his work.

The other odd man out was the peasant Prokhorov, who was unacceptable to the generals because of his coarseness and rude simplicity, although formally speaking he was the leader of the production trusties' brigade and had to deal with the camp authorities on their behalf. He was a peasant of vast experience and had been jailed for doling out too many ration coupons to his starving villagers when re-elected chairman of the village Soviet (having held this position before the war) after the German occupation and retreat. He was also the first of many independent-minded peasant figures that Solzhenitsyn came to admire in the camps, and Solzhenitsyn opposed the generals' request for his removal.

> What I immediately liked about him was this: in bringing Zinoviev his mess tins and Beliayev his bread, Prokhorov was never servile and never produced a false smile or an empty word. . . . He needed a great deal of food to nourish his big worker's body. For the sake of the general's gruel and broth, he patiently endured his humiliating position. He knew they despised him here, but did not suck up to them either. He could see through the lot of us as if we were naked, but the time had not come to voice his opinion. I felt about Prokhorov that he was founded on bedrock, that much in our people rests on shoulders like his. He was in no hurry to smile at anyone, his gaze was sullen, but he wouldn't stab you in the back either.[3]

Solzhenitsyn's reign as production superintendent at Kaluga Gate was ignominiously brief. Less than a week after his appointment, Lieutenant Nevezhin was removed from the post of commandant, for stealing building materials. In itself, such stealing was neither unusual nor exceptionable among the officers and administrative staff—it went on constantly. And the prisoners were bribed and blackmailed into helping too. But Nevezhin was insatiable, so that in the end his superior could ignore it no longer. He was replaced by a Lieutenant Mironov, who quickly found Solzhenitsyn too naïve to supervise the other prisoners. Instead of increasing their quotas and extracting maximum labour for minimum reward, he had been too much on their side, insisting on the observation of the safety regulations and the supply of proper tools and materials, and had only hindered those who were determined to "get things done" at any price. From production superintendent he was kicked all the way down to general duties, but even now he retained a modicum of luck. As a mark of indulgence he was put into the painting brigade, which was one of the easier brigades, and he was allowed to retain his place in the trusties' room, since his replacement as superintendent already had a bunk in the other room set aside for trusties.

It was about now that he had his first, long-awaited meeting with Natalia. It had taken her some weeks to settle her affairs in Rostov, obtain the necessary permission to change her place of residence, get a permit to travel, and buy a train ticket, and she was quite surprised, on arrival in Moscow, to be met by Veronica with news of her husband's move to Kaluga Gate—she had imagined him to be still in New Jerusalem. The following day she made her way to the camp, whose situation Solzhenitsyn later described in The First Circle.

> Kaluga Street was a broad, busy thoroughfare with a steady flow of limousines, occasionally with diplomatic number-plates. Buses and trolleybuses stopped by the end of the railings enclosing Neskuchny Park, where the camp guardhouse

stood, looking like the entrance to a normal building site. High up on the unfinished structure swarmed some people in dirty, tattered clothing, but all building
workers looked like that and none of the passers-by guessed that these were
convicts.[4]

Unfortunately, neither Solzhenitsyn nor Natalia has described their
meeting in any detail. In her edited memoirs Natalia passes over it very
quickly, recording how she entered the guardhouse and waited alone in an
empty low-ceilinged room, with wooden benches around the walls, for Solzhenitsyn to be summoned. "I heard the sound of steps. There in the doorway stood my husband smiling at me! He held his cap in his hands, revealing
his shaven head." They were not alone—a guard was present throughout the
meeting—but it must have been a highly emotional occasion for both of them.
Natalia indicates that Solzhenitsyn was still contrite about his last letters
from East Prussia and again asked her forgiveness for the harshness of some
of his expressions. "The former Sanya had not known how to stop to consider the pain he might be causing others," she writes in her memoirs, "but
there was something about the new Sanya that already made him more sensitive to the beat of another's heart. He wanted to cross out the lines in his
old letters that had offended me."[5] Solzhenitsyn has confirmed that this was
how he felt, and in *The First Circle* he shows Gleb Nerzhin similarly chastened and softened by his experiences: "He had become gentler, he kissed
his wife's hand, he watched for the glint in her eyes; while with her he was
no longer in jail. The ruthlessness of camp life . . . had altered him."[6]

In the novel, Solzhenitsyn conflates their many meetings at Kaluga Gate
and raises the theme of a possible legal separation between husband and wife,
and it seems that he did on several occasions repeat the assurances first given
in his letter to Natalia from Krasnaya Presnya—that she should feel free to
divorce him and seek her happiness elsewhere. But she interpreted this at
first as a *desire*, on his part, to get rid of her, and so, on the heels of the East
Prussian misunderstanding, came a new misunderstanding to muddy their
relationship and lead to endless self-doubt and questioning. It was all exaggerated, of course, by their artificial separation, but Natalia soon made it
clear that she still loved her husband and had not the slightest intention of
taking advantage of his offer, while he made no secret of his immense relief
at her decision. His arrest and imprisonment, and the grief and despair inflicted
on both of them, had brought them closer together than at any other time
since their wedding. Natalia swore to remain faithful and to wait for him all
the eight years of his sentence, and he, filled with confusion, guilt, and foreboding, fervently prayed that he, too, would be able to keep faith and that it
would be less than eight years until the day of their reunion.

To tell the truth, despite his retrospective disdain for Dr Pravdin, he
was also hoping for an amnesty. At first the prisoners thought it would come
at the time of the November holidays, on the anniversary of the Revolution,
as an act of clemency by Stalin to mark the complete end of the war and the

victory over Japan. But November 1945 came and went, and nothing happened. In December, Matyushin, the camp artist, was released as a result of the July amnesty. Matyushin had originally been sentenced to only three years, had served four and a half years, and had secured his release only as the result of a long-drawn-out campaign of petitioning. Nevertheless, it seemed like an omen. His charge had been a political one—Article 58, paragraph 1B—and the July amnesty was being put into effect so slowly and haphazardly that the prisoners still hoped against hope that it might somehow be extended to all politicals. One day during this period Solzhenitsyn climbed to the top of the block of flats they were building, to the eighth floor, and looked out over Moscow.

> Over to one side were the Sparrow Hills, still open and clear. The future Lenin Prospekt was still in the planning stage and hadn't yet been built. Kanatchikova Dacha [the lunatic asylum] could be seen in its pristine original state. On the other side could be seen the cupolas of the Novodevichi Nunnery, the hulk of the Frunze Academy, and—far, far away, in a violet haze beyond the bustling streets, the Kremlin, where all they had to do was sign the amnesty that had been prepared for us.
>
> To us, the doomed, this world appeared tempting in its riches and glory as it lay virtually at our feet, yet forever unattainable.[7]

Remembering his earlier dream of getting away from it all and seeking refuge in some distant corner of the country, Solzhenitsyn turned his thoughts to exile as an alternative to amnesty and petitioned the Supreme Soviet to commute his eight years' imprisonment to exile for life to any part of the country it chose (he didn't then realize that his sentence included exile anyway). But no reply came, and by March 1946 he was dreaming of an amnesty again. "I am 100 per cent sure," he wrote to Natalia, "and am still convinced that the amnesty was prepared in the autumn of 1945, and that it was approved in principle by our government. But then for some reason it was postponed." As late as May 1946 he and his comrades were still hoping that an amnesty would be proclaimed to mark the first anniversary of victory over the Germans, as emerged in another letter to Natalia. "Today we were full of expectation. Although there were conflicting rumours about the ninth, still there is a possibility during the week or two following the ninth. Such weariness has descended upon us all as if the newspapers had actually promised it for today."[8]

Not long after Solzhenitsyn's demotion to the painting brigade, General Beliayev was moved to Butyrki and Solzhenitsyn was able to slip into his job as assistant norm setter. Once more he was a legitimate occupant of the trusties' room and needed no longer to go in fear of expulsion. He also took this opportunity to revert to his officer's tunic, cavalry breeches, and patent-leather boots, all of which he had earlier put aside for ragged overalls when joining the painter's brigade. He was pleased to be made a trusty again, proud of his officer's clothing and more anxious than ever to make a good impression on the authorities. And once again he succeeded better than he had imagined.

Proof of his success came with a visit to the trusties' room one evening by one of the camp guards, a young man named Senin. Senin was a fourth-year student at Moscow University who earned extra money by working for the MVD in his spare time. He was apparently ashamed of his secret occupation, for he invariably arrived and left in civilian clothes and changed in the guardhouse. And "Senin" was not his proper name. There was nothing unusual in Senin's visits. He fancied himself an intellectual and liked to visit the trusties' room to discuss the latest films he had seen or to talk about literature. On this occasion, however, after chatting inconsequentially for a while, he secretly signalled Solzhenitsyn to leave the room. A few minutes later, Senin followed him out and instructed him to go to the security officer's room.

This seemed like bad news. Being summoned to see the security officer usually meant a new case was being prepared against you, or that you were being called to give evidence in someone else's case. Either way it was an unpleasant business. But his immediate fears were quickly put to rest. The security officer had a small, cosily furnished room "that didn't seem to be a part of Gulag at all." It contained a desk, a sofa, and a radio playing some familiar classical music. As Solzhenitsyn later described it in *The Gulag Archipelago:* "I instantly softened: somewhere life still went on! My God, we had already got used to the idea of taking our own life for normal, yet somewhere it still went on, out there. . . ."[9] Instead of barking at him, the security officer was courteousness itself. How was Solzhenitsyn feeling? What did he think of camp life? Was he comfortable in the trusties' room? Solzhenitsyn answered briefly and non-committally, until they came to the crucial question.

"Well, after everything that has happened to you, after everything you have experienced, have you remained a Soviet man?"

Solzhenitsyn knew what lay behind those words. "Soviet" didn't just mean "Russian" or a citizen of the Soviet Union. "Soviet" in this context meant you supported the Soviet system. He hesitated and replied that the Special Board had itself pronounced him "anti-Soviet" with its sentence. But the security officer waved that aside. Everybody knew the Special Board was a rubber stamp. Its verdict didn't count in what they were discussing now. The main thing was: How did Solzhenitsyn feel? Had he changed or become embittered? After all, he had been Soviet in his youth, the officer knew from his autobiography. (Solzhenitsyn now understood why he had been asked to write his autobiography in New Jerusalem. It had led to nothing at the time, but had found its way into his dossier, had accompanied him to Kaluga Gate, and was being taken up again by the ever-vigilant "organs.") He had been a Soviet officer, and was still proud to wear his uniform around the camp. He was also desperately keen for an amnesty, and had petitioned the authorities for exile, so he still believed in the justice and mercy of the system, still had faith in the authorities—did he not?

Sensing a threat behind this smooth recitation of his former virtue, Solzhenitsyn hastened to assure the officer that he was not embittered and was still a socialist; and of course he was still Soviet. This was evidently what the officer had been waiting to hear. They could talk as two Soviet people. They shared the same ideology and had common goals. "We must act in unity. You help us and we will help you."

Solzhenitsyn felt trapped by this and wondered where it was leading. The officer lost no time in explaining. Solzhenitsyn was the ideal person to help him keep in touch with what was going on in the camp. He could choose to overhear certain conversations and report their contents to him. Solzhenitsyn demurred and claimed to suffer from a bad memory, but the officer became threatening. Did Solzhenitsyn want to go back to general duties or be sent to Siberia? For two hours and more, according to Solzhenitsyn's account of the matter, they circled back and forth around this central point, the security officer striving to convince him that it was in his own interests, while Solzhenitsyn stonewalled and tried to find a way of retreating from his commitment to behave like a "Soviet man."

It was well past the time for lights out in the rooms when the officer switched his attack. He had heard from Senin, he said, that Solzhenitsyn was hostile to the professional crooks and thieves. Was that so? Solzhenitsyn confirmed that it was. He had hated them from the day he first set eyes on them and had already had several serious clashes with them. Well then, said the officer, surely Solzhenitsyn was not in favour of criminals' escaping from the camp? What if a bunch of them got out and robbed or raped his wife on the street while she was making her way home from her institute? She was young and pretty, wasn't she, and all alone with her husband locked up in the camps? Surely she, and others like her, should be protected from such things? Solzhenitsyn writes that he still wondered what the security officer was leading up to, but felt a sense of relief at having found some common ground at last. Yes, they should be protected from thugs, and he could agree to that with a clear conscience. In that case, said the security officer, surely Solzhenitsyn wouldn't refuse to report to him any plans he heard for the thieves to escape? Solzhenitsyn hesitated. The idea of reporting to any security officer was repugnant to him but at least it applied only to the hated criminals. He hardly ever mixed with them, so it was most unlikely he would have anything to report. And the threat of Siberia would be lifted. Reluctantly, he agreed to the officer's suggestion.

As if by magic the security officer produced a sheet of paper for Solzhenitsyn to sign: "Pledge. I the undersigned pledge to report to the camp security officer any escapes planned by prisoners. . . ." Solzhenitsyn resisted. He had not said all prisoners, only the crooks. And he preferred not to sign his name. But the security officer was adamant. What difference did it make if Solzhenitsyn was truly "one of us"? They both knew that it really meant only the criminals. In the end, he had to sign the pledge, as well as another pledge never to disclose the contents of this first pledge. And as a final humiliation, the security officer insisted that Solzhenitsyn choose a pseudonym, for all informers had to have a pseudonym for their denunciations; it was an essential part of the system. For once, Solzhenitsyn's literary inventiveness failed him, and it was left to the security officer to suggest "Vetrov." Vetrov it became, and Solzhenitsyn duly signed the form with his new name.

This episode marked the nadir of Solzhenitsyn's camp career and indeed the nadir of his life. He was to know far worse physical deprivations, he was to endure far greater psychological pressures, and he was to come within an ace of death on at least two later occasions, but never was he to sink morally or spiritually lower than in this confrontation with the security officer at Kaluga Gate. Yet, as he has shown in *The Gulag Archipelago*, such a confrontation was almost inevitable in the light of his early behaviour in the camps. The entire thrust of his ambition in New Jerusalem and at Kaluga Gate (and also at Krasnaya Presnya) had been to "get on," to rise to the top, to become a part of the camps' ruling elite and occupy a position of trust, just as he had strained every nerve to become an officer. And he had been prepared to do almost anything to keep away from the dreaded general duties, which the benighted mass of the prisoners ended up performing, thus hastening the day when they went to the wall. To this end he had flaunted his uniform, his ability to command, and his loyalty to the system, showing himself pathetically eager to please; and at the same time, nursing his bruised ego and sense of personal outrage over his ill-fortune, he had pleaded and petitioned for mercy.

On the other hand, we can salute his courage in confessing this ignominy nearly thirty years later. As he said after publishing volume 2 of *The Gulag Archipelago*, he had revealed in it worse things about himself than his enemies could have ever dreamt he would do. Indeed, we owe most of what we know of his inglorious first years in the camps to his own revelations scattered through the various parts of *The Gulag Archipelago* and a few other works. It is possible that he has even darkened the image in places, for *The Gulag Archipelago* is, among other things, a summons to the Russian people to repent their sins, and Solzhenitsyn attempted to lead the way by conspicuously displaying some of his own. In his rage to atone, he may have exaggerated at times. On balance, however, the picture does not seem overdrawn. The self-portrait that Solzhenitsyn sketches is essentially confirmed by what Natalia Reshetovskaya has told us of him at this period, and by what we know of his later psychology and development.

In the short term, it would appear, Solzhenitsyn's pledge made little difference to him. He continued to work as assistant norm setter, and Senin periodically pumped him for information. Since Solzhenitsyn never seemed to have anything to report, Senin urged him to give information on his workmates or anything else that he knew, but Solzhenitsyn fell back on the narrow terms of his commitment and said that it applied only to thieves and escapes, and nothing more.

Meanwhile, he was becoming more closely acquainted with other aspects of camp life and the complexity of the hierarchy that governed it. In effect, there were three hierarchies, one consisting of the camp guards and administration, another of the free personnel supervising the construction work—none of whom was a prisoner—and a third of the trusties and other prisoners with positions of responsibility in the day-to-day running of the camp. These hierarchies did not mix at the upper and lower ends of the three scales, but in the middle, the free personnel and the prisoners worked very closely together and were virtually indistinguishable, with the crucial difference, of course, that the free workers went home at the end of the working day.

At the top of the heap was the camp commandant, first Lieutenant Nevezhin and later Lieutenant Mironov, answerable to the Ministry of Internal Affairs (MVD). Beneath him came the armed guards, who looked after the physical security of the camp, and the warders, responsible for the day-to-day supervision of the prisoners, both of whom also worked for the MVD. Somewhat to one side and in many ways more powerful than the commandant was the security officer, who was responsible for security matters, for the behaviour of the political prisoners, and for ensuring ideological conformity. He worked for the secret police (now known as the NKGB)* and was a law unto himself. Parallel with this hierarchy and subordinate to it was the construction hierarchy, consisting of the chief engineer, responsible for overseeing the entire building project and guaranteeing that the architect's plans were carried out, the works manager in charge of all the construction workers, and specialist foremen for all the main building trades: bricklaying, joinery, plumbing, electrical work, and plastering. There was also a group of individual free workers who worked as tractor drivers, excavator drivers, dispatch clerks, firemen, and so on.

The prisoners' hierarchy was headed by the so-called compound trusties, those who worked most closely with the construction personnel and held the most confidential positions: chief bookkeeper, stock-room clerk, work allocator. Their job was to assist the works manager in making the project pay its way. Since they controlled the quotas and the deployment of the prisoners' labour, they played a key role in determining how and by whom the camp was run. Of course, the compound trusties could not move openly against the commandant and his MVD personnel, against the security officer, or against the works manager and chief engineer, but they could influence them heavily in their decisions and sometimes, by virtue of their control over output, could effectively dictate some of those decisions insofar as they affected the other prisoners. For instance, Lieutenant Mironov had dismissed Solzhenitsyn from his job as production superintendent without their intervention, but it was the compound trusties who, a short time afterwards, ousted Solzhenitsyn's successor, Vasily Pavlov, and installed in the post their own preferred nominee, Alexander K. Shortly after that they removed Solzhenitsyn from his job as assistant norm setter and got him put back onto

* *Narodny kommissariat gosudarstvennoi bezopasnosti* (People's Commissariat for State Security). The security apparatus had been separated from the NKVD once more and renamed in 1941.

general duties, with the result that he was expelled from the production trusties' room and consigned to the wagonettes in the big barrack room.

There was one other privilege, particularly valuable in a camp where men and women mixed, that the compound trusties exercised to the full, and that was control over the women. The life of a woman could quickly be made insupportable in the camps: she was more vulnerable than a man to the hard physical labour of general duties and to such humiliations as the intimate body searches, the shaving of pubic hair, the bathing in front of male orderlies, all of which oppressed her psychologically and intensified her physical deprivation. Furthermore, women were in short supply, so that the pressure from trusties to show them favours and ultimately to climb into bed with them was intense and unavoidable. There was at Kaluga Gate one girl in particular who made an impression on Solzhenitsyn. She was a former lieutenant and a sniper in the army, and according to Solzhenitsyn she was "like a princess in a fairytale: crimson lips, the bearing of a swan, jet-black locks." The chief bookkeeper, a fat Jew named Isaak Bershader, whom she could hardly bear to look at, resolved to have her for his mistress. For weeks he laid siege to her, made sure she was kept on the heaviest forms of general duties, persuaded the warders to victimize her on petty charges, and threatened her with a transport to Siberia, all the while making no secret of his objective. In the end she capitulated: "One evening," writes Solzhenitsyn, "in a twilight pale from the snow and the sky, I myself saw how she flitted like a shadow from the women's barracks and with lowered head knocked on the greedy Bershader's store-room door. After that she was well taken care of in the camp compound."[10]

The production trusties were a rung lower on the prisoners' ladder, although the most senior of them, the production superintendent, had a great deal of power if he chose to wield it. Alexander K, the energetic thirty-five-year-old engineer who succeeded Vasily Pavlov in the job, was very fond of tyrannizing those under his control. "He was one of those prisoners whose actions put more fear into the inmates than the Archipelago's inveterate bosses: once he had got you by the throat, he would never let go or relax his grip. He got the rations reduced . . . visits banned and transports increased—anything to squeeze more out of the prisoners. And both the camp commandant and the construction chiefs were equally pleased with him."[11] The production trusties included the norm setter and his assistant, various minor office staff, and, most importantly, the brigade leaders.

As at New Jerusalem, Solzhenitsyn noticed that from the ordinary prisoners' point of view, these were the key figures. The brigade leaders were the ones who haggled over the quotas with their various superiors. If they were good, they attempted at all costs to shield their men from the worst rigours of the camp, to protect them from the arbitrary punishments of the commandant and his warders, the exorbitant demands of the production trusties, and the even worse corruption and tyranny of the compound trusties. Their role was a heroic one, and the well-being of the majority of the prisoners absolutely depended on them. Fortunately, they had considerable room for manoeuvre, because in a sense the rest of the camp depended on them. Solzhenitsyn had experienced this at New Jerusalem with Barinov. It was Barinov who decided how many wagons the prisoners should load and who saw that they obtained what little pay they were due,* and there had been little that Solzhenitsyn could do, as foreman, to shift him.

After his relegation from norm setting to general duties, Solzhenitsyn was able to observe the relations between the prisoners and the foremen from below. Fyodor Muravyov, the joinery foreman, was a drunkard and a fool. He would sign almost any work voucher the brigade leader put in front of him and was incapable of distinuishing good work from bad, which of course was very much to the prisoners' advantage—it was often impossible to fulfil the quotas if the work was done properly (and if the quotas were not fulfilled, their already skimpy rations would be cut still further). The brigade leader, as the one responsible for the quotas and therefore for how much the prisoners received to eat, was thus the only trusty who was able to carry out his work without detriment to the ordinary labourers.

Lastly, there were the "service trusties"—the storekeeper, clerks, nurses, cooks, breadcutters, canteen staff, bath attendants, cleaners, and the doctor, dentist, and barber. All these were prisoners too, but since their work was privileged and much easier than that in the construction brigades, it was apportioned by either the compound trusties or the production superintendent, who naturally reserved it for their favourites and for those prisoners prepared to pay for it in some way or another. Many of them were women, and the form of payment was explicit, as with the woman lieutenant subjugated by Bershader. In other instances it meant willingness to pay bribes, usually in the form of tea, tobacco, or clothing, or to connive at and take an active part in the widespread stealing that was endemic to the camps.

Solzhenitsyn was too naïve and inexperienced to make much headway in the complex web of power bargaining and corruption that prevailed in the camp. While not devoid of ruthlessness when his innermost goals were at stake, he did not possess that naked drive for power at all costs that was the recipe for success in the camps, and so he was a failure as a production supervisor, a failure as an assistant norm setter, and even, from the authorities' point of view, a failure as an informer as well. If he was to survive in the camps, it would have to be by cunning, and it was here at Kaluga Gate that he began to develop a talent for craftiness that was to become second nature in the years ahead. In a sense, his deal with the security officer had marked the first step along this road. By agreeing to inform, he had ingratiated himself with the authorities, but seems never to have intended to act on the agreement. He was also determined to stay on the side of power if he could,

*The remuneration of labour-camp prisoners varied according to place and time. Generally speaking, it was impossible, in the forties, to earn more than about twenty-five rubles a month, but that depended on 100 per cent fulfilment of the "norm," or quota, which was generally set too high. Most prisoners earned at best a handful of rubles, at worst nothing at all.

and indeed, throughout his stay at Kaluga Gate, was able to remain on the fringes of the trusty aristocracy even after being expelled from the production trusties' room.

One aspect of this drive for social acceptability was his participation in the amateur theatricals staged in the camp's cultural and educational section (CES). These cultural and educational sections were a throwback to early post-revolutionary times, when "corrective labour" was still an ideal and not just a threat, and they had been intended to assist in the "correction" of criminals through propaganda and ideologically approved cultural activities. During the thirties the early idealism had been stripped away, but the sections had remained and continued to exist as a sort of shadow of their former selves. This was the place, for instance, where you obtained pen and paper with which to write letters home or petitions to the government for clemency. The CES was also responsible for censoring and distributing incoming letters to the prisoners and for emptying the brown boxes into which the petitions were posted. The CES housed the library, if one existed, or the few books that were allowed in the camp, as well as whatever newspapers were allowed. It was the place where artists could go to get materials and paint their pictures—artists were much prized in the camps and occupied a highly privileged position, since they could provide the officers and guards with pictures to take home. At Kaluga Gate they also stencilled rugs,* which the guards paid for in commodities and sold outside. And the CES organized periodic concerts and theatrical performances, most of which were staged in the camp canteen after supper.

Solzhenitsyn gravitated to this section soon after his arrival at Kaluga Gate—it was the one place where he could go in the evenings to get away from the endless, boring conversations of Beliayev and Zinoviev and talk about something more elevated and interesting. It was also the one place where the men prisoners were allowed to mix with the women prisoners on equal terms, where they could rehearse together and put on concerts and plays.

There were specially printed collections of plays labelled "for performance only in Gulag"—plays that were ideologically innocuous but so ill-written and ridiculous that they would have been laughed off the stage elsewhere. Solzhenitsyn managed, after great difficulty in finding a copy, to stage a performance of Chekhov's *The Proposal*, and he gave a number of dramatic readings, just as he had done as a schoolboy and student (indeed, the whole thing was reminiscent of his Komsomol activities in Rostov). On one occasion he accidentally aroused the ire of the officer in charge by reading a monologue of Chatsky's from Griboyedov's celebrated play, *Woe from Wit*. It had been a favourite of Solzhenitsyn's for a long time, and he writes that in his enthusiasm he overlooked its topical satirical content. Here in the

* This may have been the inspiration for the scene in *A Day in the Life of Ivan Denisovich* in which Ivan Denisovich learns with distaste that his fellow villagers have abandoned agricultural and craft pursuits for stencilling and selling cheap rugs.

camp it took on quite a different resonance. "Who are the judges?" it began, and included the line "Their hostility to a free life was implacable." When Solzhenitsyn reached the couplet "Where, oh where are the fatherland's fathers? Is it not these men loaded with plunder?" the section chief exploded and ordered him off the stage.[12]

Solzhenitsyn was soothed and diverted by his theatrical activities. Not only did they give him the opportunity to move around the camp compound freely for a couple of hours in the evenings but they also offered him an imaginative refuge from the repellent world of everyday camp life. Having been convicted partly on the grounds of what he had written, he dared not have many books in his room or show an overt interest in literature. If he took a book to read while waiting for the endless roll-calls to be finished, he took care to see that it was a textbook on physics. The cultural and educational section was therefore an oasis, and the books and plays that he was able to handle there gave him the strength to carry on at his general duties.

At some point during these activities, he heard of the existence of whole theatrical troupes of prisoners in Gulag, whose members were freed from general duties in order to rehearse and perform their plays full-time, and he clutched at this straw as yet another possible means of ensuring his survival. Gulag actors were trusties of a sort, but at least their privileges did not depend on deceiving or persecuting others. As it happened, there was a long tradition of theatre companies in Gulag. In the thirties already, senior MVD officers had indulged themselves by forming such groups and had vied with one another to collect the best actors and actresses from various prisons and camps and outshine one another, much as nineteenth-century Russian landowners had done with their serf theatres. Now, in the post-war period, every Gulag region had its own "professional" theatre troupe, and the Moscow region had several, one of which unexpectedly came to Kaluga Gate.*

Solzhenitsyn was fascinated. "What a strange sensation! To watch a performance of professional convict actors in a camp canteen! Laughter, smiles, singing, white dresses, black frock coats. . . ."[13] He quickly got to know an elderly Latvian couple who played leading parts in the troupe, Oswald and Isolde Glazunov. Oswald had been a pupil of Vakhtangov and had later performed in Riga during the German occupation, together with his wife, a dancer. For this they had been charged with treason and sentenced to ten years. Isolde also danced at Kaluga Gate, despite her advanced years, but Solzhenitsyn heard that soon afterwards she was separated from her husband and sent away on a camp transport, while he was forced to stay behind. Such were the immutable, cruel laws of the Gulag: not even membership in a theatre group was a guarantee against sudden transfers, punishment cells, reduced rations, or any of the thousand shocks to which the prisoner was arbitrarily subjected.

Solzhenitsyn also became friendly with Glazunov's "spiritual daughter,"

* Varlam Shalamov, in his *Kolyma Tales* (New York and London, 1980), has a story about an actor in one of the camp theatres ("Esperanto").

Nina, the leading actress in the troupe, who turned out, like Solzhenitsyn, to have attended the Moscow Institute of Philosophy, Literature, and History and to have studied under the same art history professor. It is not clear to what degree Solzhenitsyn was attracted to her physically but she already had a lover in the troupe, a former dancer from the Bolshoi ballet. Solzhenitsyn was desperately keen to join the troupe as well, but his hopes were in vain.

> Despite all my efforts, I did not succeed in becoming a member of the ensemble. Soon afterwards they left Kaluga Gate and I lost sight of them. . . . I remained there in the modest little amateur group with Anechka Breslavskaya, Shurochka Ostretsova, and Lyova. I now look back upon my participation in it as a mark of my spiritual immaturity and a humiliation. The worthless Lieutenant Mironov, if he found no other distractions in Moscow of a Sunday evening, could arrive at the camp tipsy and give the orders: "I want a concert in ten minutes!" And the actors could be roused from bed or dragged away from the camp hotplate . . . and in a trice we would be singing and prancing about and performing on a brilliantly lit stage before an empty hall, with only the arrogant, doltish lieutenant and a trio of guards for an audience.[14]

Perhaps the pill was sweetened for Solzhenitsyn by the chance it gave him to be near Anya Breslavskaya, with whom, it appears, he fell in love at Kaluga Gate. He later informed Natalia that this was the only time he was unfaithful to her throughout the fourteen years of his army service, imprisonment, and exile.[15] Anya is portrayed as Lyuba Negnevitskaya in *The Tenderfoot and the Tart*, which, in its first variant (as *The Republic of Labour*), was dedicated to her.*

As spring gave way to summer, life at Kaluga Gate became somewhat pleasanter. There was no longer the biting cold of the Russian winter to contend with, and the prisoners no longer needed to tear down partitions and plunder rafters and joists with which to stoke up their fires. Solzhenitsyn laboured ten hours a day at laying parquet floors and found himself reasonably able to cope with his moderate form of general duties, but the rations were meagre, and not even Natalia's twice-weekly parcels could stave off his growing hunger and lassitude. Meanwhile, the threat of a sudden transport to a harsher climate and harder work still hung over him.

Suddenly, on the morning of 18 July 1946, he was summoned from the ranks at morning roll-call and told not to go to work with the others. All the guard could tell him in answer to his questions was that he should report to

---

* The question of what to call this play in English is problematical. Solzhenitsyn's Russian title *Olen' i shalashovka* is based on camp slang. *Olen'* (literally "deer") means a camp novice, and *shalashovka* (derived from *shalash*, meaning a rough hunter's cabin or bivouac) means a woman prisoner who agrees to sleep with a trusty or with trusties in exchange for food and privileges—not quite a whore, more a tart or a tramp. The published English title *The Love-girl and the Innocent* seems to me to catch none of this raciness. Alternative titles proposed, besides mine, include *The Paragon and the Paramour*, *The Greenborn and the Camp-whore*, *The Greenborn and the Shackereen*, and even *The Reindeer and the Little Tent*.

the guardhouse "with his belongings" and that he was being moved from Kaluga Gate on special instructions from the Ministry of the Interior. As his brigade disappeared into the work compound, Solzhenitsyn was surrounded by the compound trusties, who animatedly discussed this unusual event. Some predicted a new case against him and a new sentence. Others said the opposite—that he would be amnestied and set free. Solzhenitsyn's hopes soared. Was it possible that his petitions had been answered at last, that his optimism had not been unfounded? Or was he destined to have his sentence doubled and to spend the rest of his life in the camps, as had happened to several prisoners he knew?[16]

He had almost forgotten that six months earlier all the prisoners at Kaluga Gate had been required to fill out Gulag registration forms under a new ordinance. Among other things, the form had asked for the prisoner's profession. Solzhenitsyn had realized that in the camps the answer to this question could be decisive. Many of the cons had gone for the main Gulag specialities, putting themselves down as "bakers," "barbers," "cooks," and "tailors," regardless of their occupations in real life outside. Solzhenitsyn followed the same principle but built instead on his training in mathematics and physics. He had recently acquired a book on the exploding of the first American atom bomb—a translation of an American government report on the subject— which he had been able to keep and read for a few days, and he knew that atomic energy was a top priority in Soviet science. He had therefore listed his occupation as "atomic physicist" in the hope that it would catch some official's eye. He had heard rumours that in some part of the Gulag there existed special camps where prisoners who had been engineers, technologists, and scientists were put to work in their own specialities and led a privileged life, with easier conditions, better living quarters, and decent rations. Like the other prisoners at Kaluga Gate, he had never met a former resident of one of these fabled institutions, but the legend persisted and he had thought there would be no harm in trying. Perhaps it had worked and his luck had held. He still did not know the details or where he would be going, but when he reported to the guardhouse, he discovered that he was being summoned on "special assignment" by the Ministry of the Interior. He had become a "special-assignment prisoner" after all, just like the Gulag veteran who had made such an impression on him and warned him off general duties in Krasnaya Presnya. The future, though still obscure, suddenly seemed full of promise.

Much later, Solzhenitsyn was to look back on his nine months at Kaluga Gate with repugnance and to describe it as a low point in his life and a period of spiritual failure. This it certainly was, but it had also added significantly to his education. In Krasnaya Presnya and New Jerusalem he had glimpsed the murderous machine that kept the conveyor belts of the Gulag in motion. Here he had learned about the labour relations that made the machine necessary. And he had discovered that the land of Gulag lay not only in the distant outposts of the empire, in the far north, beyond the Arctic Circle, in the tundra and taiga of the Siberian East, in the sandy deserts and mines of the Central Asian South, but also at the very centre of the empire, in Moscow, beside Neskuchny Park and overlooking one of Moscow's famous boulevards. In short it was everywhere, like an invisible fourth dimension— "invisible," that is, to the other inhabitants of the Soviet Union.

13

SPECIAL-ASSIGNMENT
PRISONER

SOLZHENITSYN LEFT KALUGA Gate in the early afternoon of 18 July 1946 and was taken straight to Butyrki, the prison where he had spent a month the preceding summer. Passing the church cells, with their memories of Gammerov and Ingal and anxious conversations about the future, Solzhenitsyn was led into the reception wing. If the prison had seemed crowded a year ago, now it was bursting at the seams. It took eleven hours for him to complete the immutable admission procedures of search, bath, fumigation, and the endless repetition of name, date of birth, place of birth, charge, and sentence. After each short burst of activity, he was obliged to wait for hours in solitary boxes. But he no longer felt himself to be the wavering and impatient greenhorn of the preceding year, and it was almost with nonchalance that, at three o'clock in the morning, he finally entered Cell 75 and called out in a low but cheerful voice, "Who's last?" A hoarse voice replied that his place was beneath the lowest tier of bunks next to the latrine tank. Apart from this solitary reply, there wasn't a sound in the cell.

> Lit by two bright electric bulbs suspended beneath two domes, the entire cell was sprawled fast asleep, tossing in the stuffy atmosphere: the hot July air was not able to circulate through the windows, which were blocked by "muzzles." Tireless flies buzzed and flitted from sleeper to sleeper, making them twitch. Some had covered their eyes with hankerchiefs to shield them from the blinding light. There was an acrid stink from the latrine tank—its putrefaction was speeded up by the heat. About eighty men had been stuffed into a cell meant for twenty-five, and there was still room for more.[1]

The next morning, the extra boards between the bunks were dismantled and a chest pushed from the latrine tank to a position beneath the window.

As a newcomer, Solzhenitsyn had to give an account of himself and answer questions, after which he learned that he was one of many "special-assignment prisoners" in Cell 75. It turned out that the inmates consisted of two main categories: in the first were ex-prisoners of war and men repatriated from the occupied countries of Eastern Europe, all of whom had recently been investigated and sentenced for "treason" and were now waiting to learn their destinations, just as Solzhenitsyn had had to do a year earlier; the second comprised a large group of scientists like himself—physicists, chemists, mathematicians, engineers, draughtsmen—who had been gathered from all over the Soviet Union in readiness for transfer to special prison institutes where they would be able to work at their own subjects. Solzhenitsyn was relieved to have this confirmation that he was indeed destined for a prison institute.

Not many minutes had passed before he was approached by a tall, middle-aged man with a hooked nose and a grave expression on his face, who obviously possessed considerable authority in the cell. He introduced himself as Professor Timofeyev-Ressovsky, president of the "Scientific Society of Cell No. 75. Our society meets every morning under the left window after the bread ration has been served. Would you be prepared to give us a lecture on some scientific topic? And if so, on what subject?"[2]

Solzhenitsyn was both charmed and perplexed. Only the preceding morning he had been standing in the open with the carpentry brigade at Kaluga Gate, his stomach empty, his limbs heavy and aching from stooping over parquet floors, his mind dull and numbed by the monotony of the work, and now he was being asked to deliver a scientific lecture. Among these men he was something of an impostor, having had only an undergraduate training in physics and mathematics. Nevertheless, he quick-wittedly recalled the book on the American atom bomb he had read at Kaluga Gate. The chances were that the others had all been in prison too long to have learned much about it, so he offered a lecture on that. It was accepted. He was to become an expert in atomic physics somewhat sooner than he had expected when filling out the questionnaire.

It turned out that Timofeyev-Ressovsky knew almost as much about the subject as Solzhenitsyn did, understood it better, and indefatigably filled in the gaps in Solzhenitsyn's knowledge, but the lecture was judged a success. Solzhenitsyn was formally admitted to the society and got to know its dozen or so members. Nikolai Timofeyev-Ressovsky, their leader, was a distinguished geneticist. As early as 1922, as a graduate student, he had been singled out to collaborate with the eminent German biologist Vogt, who had founded Moscow's Institute for the Study of the Brain, and he later accompanied Vogt to Berlin to work with him there. In 1937 he had been ordered to return to the Soviet Union, but refused, although he retained his passport and continued to regard himself as a Soviet biologist. In fact, he had been one of the founders of the Soviet school of radiation genetics, which was why he knew so much about atomic research, and was also a biophysicist, radiobiologist, and zoologist of note. When Soviet troops entered Berlin, he had immediately placed his institute under Soviet protection, but he and another Soviet biologist, Sergei Tsarapkin, had been arrested, sent back to the Soviet Union, and sentenced to ten years for treason. Among the other members of the society were a Jewish physicist, Victor Kagan,* a composer and pianist, Vladimir Klempner, an Orthodox priest who had been captured in Europe, Evgeni Divnich, and two engineers, F. F. Karpov and Nikolai Semyonov. Semyonov had been one of the creators of the famous Dnieper Hydroelectric Power Station and Dam, one of the show-pieces of early Soviet technology, and it was he who had called to Solzhenitsyn from beneath the bunks the night Solzhenitsyn arrived. One or two of these men, like Timofeyev-Ressovsky and Semyonov, were to become lifelong friends, while others quickly disappeared from view. All, however, made a lasting impression on Solzhenitsyn in that summer of 1946. "What a cell it was!" he later wrote in *The Gulag Archipelago*. "Was it not the most brilliant in my entire prison career?"[3]

The cell was also memorable for the opportunity it gave him to rest and to recover his strength after the rigours of New Jerusalem and Kaluga Gate, even if it meant sleeping on the floor.

> In the Butyrki cells the arches supporting the bunks are very low: it had never occurred even to the prison authorities that prisoners would be sleeping under them. Therefore, the first thing you did was throw your greatcoat to your neighbour, so that he could spread it out for you. Then you lay face-down in the passageway and inched your way underneath. People were constantly walking up and down the passageways, the floors beneath the bunks were swept at best twice a month, you could wash your hands only during the evening latrine call, and even then without soap—no one could say you experienced your body as some sort of divine vessel. But I was happy! There, on the asphalt floor, in my dog's hole, where dust and crumbs were scattered from the bunks into our eyes, I was absolutely happy, without qualification. Epicurus was right: even the absence of variety can be experienced as a satisfaction when it has been preceded by a variety of dissatisfactions. After the camps, which had looked endless, after the ten-hour working day, with the cold, the rain, and my aching back, what bliss it was to lie there for whole days, to lie there sleeping and yet still get a pound and a half of bread and two hot meals a day of cattle feed or dolphin-meat. . . .
>
> They kept me in that cell for two months, and I slept enough for the year just passed and the year to come. During that time I progressed along the floor as far as the window, then went back to the latrine tank and made my way back again—on the bunks this time—as far as the arch.[4]

He found himself in a home away from home, surrounded by educated men who spoke a similar language to himself and saw their prison experiences through similar eyes. It was comforting to exchange reminiscences with veterans of many years' imprisonment and to test his impressions and devel-

* Victor Kagan later published his own reminiscences of life in this cell in *Kontinent*, no. 29 (1981). According to Kagan, the cell number was 71 (not 75), and he recalls hearing Solzhenitsyn lecture on the sound-ranging techniques he had employed at the front.

oping views against theirs. The scientific society, which met regularly every morning, gave him the sense of belonging to a friendly and exclusive small club, where there were games of chess, books (though there were always long waiting lists for the few interesting books that came their way), and, in the evenings, occasional concerts and yet more lectures and discussions. Timofeyev-Ressovsky, ever the soul of the company, would give them reminiscences of his travels in America, Italy, and Scandinavia. *Émigrés* spoke of their experiences in France, the Balkans, and other parts of Western Europe, while still others lectured on Gogol, Le Corbusier, and the habits of bees.

But not all was sweetness and harmony. Evgeny Divnich, the Orthodox priest, was passionate and convincing in his detailed denunciations of Marxism. Nobody in Western Europe, he said, believed in it any more. It was dead and buried as a political philosophy. Solzhenitsyn couldn't accept this and sprang to Marx's defence. "After all, I was a Marxist, wasn't I?"[5] It was a repeat performance of his arguments a year earlier with Yuri Y and Gammerov and Ingal, and if the flame of his conviction no longer burned quite so steadily, he nevertheless suppressed his doubts and stoutly defended the true faith.*

An unexpected meeting in the cell reminded him queasily of the ignoble way in which he had started out on his convict's career. He was already becoming accustomed to the strange twists and turns of the prisoner's voyaging about the archipelago, of the curious coincidences and criss-crossing of destinies, of the bush telegraph that brought you information about the fates of former cell-mates and the further careers of comrades whose lives you had briefly shared in a camp or transit prison. In this way he had learned of the fate of one or two cell-mates from his previous stay in Butyrki—one had been sent to Karaganda, another shot. But even so he was not prepared to bump into the elderly German civilian whom he had obliged (on the second night after his arrest) to carry his suitcase on the long march to Brodnitz. Solzhenitsyn blushed at the recollection of it, but the German seemed to have forgiven him and was truly pleased by their meeting. He had been sentenced to ten years' hard labour, and it was clear to Solzhenitsyn that he wouldn't live to see Germany again.

The days flew swiftly by. Solzhenitsyn soon found that sleep was becoming less necessary, and he joined more and more in the evening discussions and entertainments. He did some of his recitations, including poems by his favourite, Esenin (Victor Kagan remembers his reading "Letter to a Woman" and "To a Fallen Maple Leaf"). A cell-mate of about the same age, Konstantin Kioula, was writing and reciting his own verses, and for the first

---

* Kagan suggests that Divnich was not as sincere as he seemed to Solzhenitsyn and that he loved to provoke argument for its own sake. Divnich had also, it seems, had links with the Frankfurt-based NTS, or *Narodno-trudovoi soyuz* (Popular Labour Alliance), the best-organized and most militant of the anti-Soviet political groups in the emigration; many years later, after twenty years in the camps, he was persuaded to write a book about the NTS in which he denounced his former associates.

time since his arrest Solzhenitsyn felt the urge to write again. Not stories now, but poetry—poems about life in prison, rather like Kioula's, with their narrow range of subjects that meant so much to the inhabitants of the archipelago: "The First Parcel," "To My Wife," "To My Son."

In Cell 75 Solzhenitsyn learned something more about the special prison institutes for scientific research that they were all bound for. Such institutes had originated in the thirties and were the logical culmination of a number of different developments in Soviet society. On the one hand there had been the great series of purges of the technical intelligentsia, beginning with the trials of the "wrecker-engineers," and the Industrial Party, and on the other the rapid growth of Gulag and the system of forced labour resulting from the arrests made during collectivization and the purges. Initially the tendency was for all the victims to be thrown at random into the labour camps and to be used as fodder for the hard-labour brigades, regardless of whether they were engineers or peasants. But this was terribly wasteful. Moreover, it became apparent that the rooting out of the "bourgeois specialists" was not simply wasteful but was also delivering a death-blow to the nation's plans for industrialization, particularly at the ambitious tempo that Stalin had set for it. The Soviet government was hard put to it to manage without them. But it was ideologically unacceptable, and in terms of crude power politics inexpedient, to release the specialists or admit that an error had been made. And so the special prison institutes came into being, equipped with laboratories, research apparatus, workshops, and in some cases whole factories, which were then filled with prisoners capable of running them and producing results in their field of specialization.

Such prison institutes and factories were directly analogous with the labour camps thrown up to tackle the great construction projects in Siberia and Central Asia. Of course, the process of selection for them was rough and ready. Academics continued to perish digging post holes in the frozen soil of the far north, just as bricklayers continued to die in the salt mines of Siberia and fitters and turners continued to collapse in the quarries of the Urals, but the very fact of a conscious orientation towards the camps as a *normal* source of labour for every conceivable kind of project, which had begun in 1929, indicated a fundamental shift in the government's attitude towards them, and was extended to the institutes as well.

The earliest and best-known example of a prison institute was that set up for Professor Leonid Ramzin, the chief defendant in the Industrial Party trial of 1930 (whose appearance on a group photograph had led to the downfall of Solzhenitsyn's adopted "uncle," Vladimir Fedorovsky, in Rostov). Ramzin's case was unusual in that he had enthusiastically collaborated with the NKVD at his trial and been their star witness, so that he may have been promised a special reward before his conviction. In any event, he became head of an institute for the study of thermal electricity staffed almost exclusively by prisoners, and there he invented something known as the "single-pass boiler," an outstanding contribution to the thermal-energy industry that was internationally recognized as a scientific breakthrough. Ramzin was awarded a state prize for his efforts and granted a free pardon, an example that was to have a powerful influence on the attitudes of future prisoners committed to these special institutes.

It appears that a number of other Soviet technical developments in the thirties owed their genesis to work by imprisoned scientists, including a series of railway locomotives and innovations in the fields of artillery and tank construction. But the best-known and best-documented field in which prisoner research played a crucial role was the Soviet aircraft industry. In the great purge of 1937–38, large numbers of leading aero-engineers and aeroplane designers were arrested and jailed, including the outstanding designer Andrei Tupolev, who was hysterically accused of selling aircraft designs to the Germans. Once the arrests had been carried out, the Soviet air industry virtually collapsed, to which the authorities responded by putting all the factories and workshops behind barbed wire and turning them into a prison industry. Tupolev, who had been sent to a prison institute in Bolshevo, just outside Moscow, was summoned by the NKVD and asked to list all the arrested aero-engineers he knew and to head a new research and development institute in aircraft design (later known as TSAGI).* He agreed, and was joined by a number of other outstanding designers, including V. M. Petlyakov and V. M. Myasishchov—between them they were responsible for almost the entire Soviet programme of military-aircraft development in the period leading up to the Second World War. Both the Tupolev-5 bomber and the Petlyakov-2 fighter were designed and developed in Bolshevo, and a number of other aircraft were taken through the early planning stage. Later the institute was evacuated to Omsk, and in the summer of 1941 Tupolev and about two dozen of his leading engineers and designers were pardoned and released. The following year several more were released, and by the end of the war that particular prison institute was shut down.[6]

This was not the end of the prison institutes, however. A new one was set up after the war at a place called Bolshino for the development of rocket technology, and it was there that Sergei Korolyov, the "father" of Soviet space travel, invented his liquid-fuel jet engine. He, too, was rewarded with a pardon and a release. In 1946 Bolshino was split into two, one half going to Rybinsk, on the upper reaches of the Volga, about 160 miles north-east of Moscow, and the other to Taganrog, in the south. Somewhere along the line the prison institutes acquired the nickname of *sharashka*,† and in September 1946 Solzhenitsyn was dispatched to the Rybinsk *sharashka*, where jet engines

---

* An abbreviation for *Tsentral'ny aviastroitel'ny gosudarstvenny institut* (Central State Institute for Aero-construction).

† No one seems to know the origin of this term. Before the war such a prison institute was known as a *sharaga* (of which *sharashka* is the diminutive form—implying familiarity, not smallness). Professor Georgi Ozerov, an engineer, later wrote a short book about his experiences in the Tupolev institute called *Tupolevskaya sharaga* (The Tupolev Sharaga), which circulated in samizdat in the late sixties and was published (in Russian) in Frankfurt in 1973 (Possev-Verlag).

were still being made. His work, however, had nothing to do with engines and seems to have been purely mathematical. He remained there for five months before being moved to another *sharashka*, in Zagorsk. Once more he was kept away from production work, but this time was given to understand that he was here only in transit: his final destination was to be yet another *sharashka*, which was to be opened shortly.

Such a move suited Solzhenitsyn perfectly. Life in the prison institutes was easy compared to that in the labour camps. The hours were long and the prisoners were still surrounded by armed guards, but the work was not arduous and the rations were much better. At Zagorsk, Solzhenitsyn was given the post of librarian. One of the people he met there was the naval lieutenant Victor Trushliakov, the fabulous confidence trickster described in volume 2 of *The Gulag Archipelago*, who had managed to get transferred to the *sharashka* from a harsher prison by convincing the camp authorities that he was a first-class inventor. Among his many inspirations was a device for deflecting radar beams, and Solzhenitsyn was ordered to do all the mathematical calculations and formulae necessary for a realization of this project. Solzhenitsyn could make neither head nor tail of Trushliakov's fantasies, but no sooner had this project collapsed than Trushliakov invented another one, having to do with the possibility of interplanetary travel. Nothing came of that either, but one of Solzhenitsyn's engineer friends was convinced that Trushliakov was a new Newton, while another friend, Dimitri Panin, was much impressed when Trushliakov turned up at another Moscow institute and claimed to know the secret of a device for manoeuvring tanks by remote control.

Trushliakov's inventions were the fruit of that desperate urge of all the convicts to find a safe niche for themselves and somehow escape the dreadful general duties. Not only had news of the "paradise islands" of the *sharashkas* percolated through to the other camps but so had the information that a rare genius like Ramzin or Korolyov might buy his freedom with his brains, which acted as a powerful stimulus to everyone else. The authorities encouraged these aspirations, of course, for in this way the scientists and engineers revealed who they were and could be directed to more profitable work. An attempt was made to squeeze useful knowledge out of some German prisoners of war as well. In the aftermath of victory in the Second World War and its occupation of East Germany, the Soviet Union had shipped whole factories back to copy German products and belatedly learn the technology for itself. Soviet technicians learned for the first time how to make modern watches and clocks, sensitive cameras, up-to-date radios and record players, and a host of similar items. About six thousand Germans and their families were arrested and transported to the Soviet Union to work on rocket and space technology. Later, having discovered the usefulness of German expertise, the Soviet authorities thought they could find more German brains by getting their prisoners of war to fill out lengthy questionnaires on their special skills and on jobs they had held. These questionnaires were gathered up and sent to Zagorsk for evaluation, and Solzhenitsyn became the translator for a group of engineers charged with assessing their worth. But the exercise misfired. If the Germans knew enough to be useful to their captors, they either kept quiet about it or shrouded their knowledge in a fog of misleading jargon. And if they seemed to make sense and to be trying to convey something, it usually meant they knew nothing.

The most significant event of Solzhenitsyn's brief stay at Zagorsk was his discovery of the four-volume Russian dictionary of Vladimir Dahl. Dahl was the nineteenth-century lexicographer who compiled the first (and in many ways still the best) comprehensive dictionary of the Russian language. Although of Danish origin, he was dedicated to the idea of freeing literary Russian from Latin, French, and German influences, and to that end he became a great collector and student of Russian folklore and Russian folk expressions and a champion of the spoken word as a model for literary works. His is still the standard collection of Russian proverbs (a copy of which Irina had given to Solzhenitsyn in childhood), and his dictionary, like Dr Johnson's in English, became the foundation for all Russian dictionaries to follow. Solzhenitsyn found it on the library shelf soon after his arrival in Zagorsk and was delighted by his discovery. He used to be "a flat, two-dimensional creature," he wrote in one of his letters to Natalia, but then "stereometry opened up" before him.[7] What pleased him most was Dahl's habit of grouping words according to root, rather than in conventional alphabetical order, and the wide range of Dahl's vocabulary, as evidenced by the vast store of examples that Dahl had amassed with which to illustrate his meaning. Many of these were proverbs that Dahl had collected for his other work, but all his examples seemed to be filled with a lapidary folk wisdom that bordered on the proverbial, and Solzhenitsyn was amazed by their conciseness and precision. He resolved to read a page or two of Dahl every day and to memorize all the uncommon words and expressions he found there, an exercise he later dubbed his daily "literary gymnastics."[8] His purpose, he said, was not to "collect" these words but rather to immerse himself in the Russian language, to absorb its spirit and refresh himself. Later he started copying them into a series of improvised notebooks that he labelled "Selections from Dahl," which he quickly filled with his spidery handwriting. He has them still, divided into alphabetical sections, each corresponding more or less to a volume of the dictionary. They were later to form the foundation of that uniquely broad, idiosyncratically earthy lexicon that instantly identifies and sets apart Solzhenitsyn's mature literary style from that of all other Russian writers past or present.

In early July 1947 Solzhenitsyn was taken from Zagorsk to Butyrki under armed escort to await yet another move in the chess game that the authorities appeared to be playing with him. As in his previous journeys since arriving in the *sharashkas*, he and his guards travelled in the guise of private passengers, and en route he tried to slip an uncensored postcard to a fellow passenger to post for him, only to discover at the last minute that the man was a labour-camp guard homeward bound on leave.

His fourth stay in Butyrki was only fleeting. On 9 July he was shipped out again to Marfino, on the northern outskirts of Moscow, next to Ostankino Park (which housed the botanical gardens), to "Special Prison No. 16." This was the *sharashka* that became the setting for virtually the whole of *The First Circle* (Marfino becomes Mavrino in the novel), and in chapter 6 Solzhenitsyn describes the arrival of Gleb Nerzhin (based on his own experiences) there and the way in which the prison institute was established.

> A dozen and a half prisoners were summoned from the camps and brought to the ancient building of this former Moscow seminary, which was duly encircled with barbed wire. The prisoners looked back to those days as to an age of pastoral simplicity. It had been possible then to turn on the BBC at full volume in the prisoners' quarters (they hadn't yet learned how to jam it); to wander about the compound in the evenings as they pleased and to lie in the long, dewy grass, which, contrary to regulations, had not been cut (the grass was supposed to be kept short to prevent the prisoners' crawling up to the barbed wire); and to gaze at the eternal stars—or, if he was on night duty, at the mortal, sweating figure of MVD sergeant-major Zhvakun, as he raided the balks of timber and rolled them under the barbed wire to take home for firewood.[9]

The theological seminary in which the main body of the institute was housed was a neo-classical brick building that terminated in a low, hexagonal tower enclosing a vaulted church (quaintly called "Assuage My Sorrows"). It was here in the church that the library was situated and here that Solzhenitsyn worked for the first six months of his stay in the *sharashka*—once again he had been appointed librarian. Beside the church stood a grove of one-hundred-year-old lime trees and a small, vaulted house in which a bishop had formerly lived, together with a huddle of temporary buildings erected for the administrative staff.

Life here was even more comfortable than in Solzhenitsyn's previous *sharashkas*, especially during the first few months. To begin with, the *sharashka* occupied about half the main block of the seminary—the other half was still in the process of conversion by ordinary prisoners (another camp was set up next door to house them).[10] The *sharashka* inmates slept in two rooms on the second floor, on double bunks equipped with mattresses, sheets, blankets, and pillows, and each prisoner was allowed a small bedside table for his belongings. At night the blinding light of the prison and labour-camp cells was replaced by a blue-tinted bulb. Also on the second floor were a medical room and the prison commandant's office, while the floor below housed the laboratories, and the ground floor the canteen and various workshops.

It took about six months to get the institute organized, assemble the necessary equipment, prepare the laboratories for research, and fit out the workshops. Most of the equipment came from the German company of Lorentz,* whose furniture and apparatus had been shipped back to the Soviet Union in three train-loads. The work was carried out by the engineers, while

---

* Kopelev (see below) writes that the equipment came from the firm of Philips, but both Solzhenitsyn and Panin say Lorentz. Perhaps there was some from each.

Solzhenitsyn slowly sorted through the mass of technical books and journals that had been collected (in Russian and English as well as German), classified and catalogued them, and continued to do a certain amount of translation. The initial project for which the institute was being prepared was to develop a walkie-talkie radio for the police.

Undoubtedly, the most interesting thing to happen to Solzhenitsyn during those early months was his meeting, and subsequent friendship, with two men who were each in their different ways to influence his thinking and leave an indelible imprint on his imagination—Dimitri Panin and Lev Kopelev. Panin arrived in Marfino first, in October 1947, and in his memoir on this period has described his first meeting with Solzhenitsyn.

> The morning after my arrival, as I was drying my face on a government-issue towel, an impressive figure of a man in an officer's greatcoat came down the stairs. I took an immediate liking to his candid face, the bold blue eyes, the splendid light-brown hair and aquiline nose. It was Alexander Solzhenitsyn. After my transport and a month in Butyrki, I was starved for fresh air, so within moments I followed him outside. There was nobody about except for several prisoners conversing beneath some ancient lime trees in the grass-grown yard. Since I was still wearing my camp rags that gave me such a cut-throat appearance, I was quickly surrounded by the old residents—except for Solzhenitsyn, who strolled by himself some way off. But when the others had satisfied their curiosity about me, he came over and suggested we take a stroll together. I shall never forget the first thing he said to me: "As I was coming down the stairs, what should I see in the darkness of the hallway but the face of an icon of Our Saviour."[11]

Panin was indeed a strikingly handsome man. In *The First Circle* Solzhenitsyn based the character of Dimitri Sologdin on Panin, and in his description of his physical appearance likened him to Alexander Nevsky, dwelling lovingly on his high, straight forehead, regular features, piercing blue eyes, blond moustache and beard, superb physique, and erect bearing—the very figure of a medieval knight. There was something romantic and chivalrous—archaic even—about Panin's whole bearing and character, and yet his brain, especially in matters of science, was diamond sharp.

Panin was six years older than Solzhenitsyn and had witnessed scenes in the Revolution and Civil War that had filled him with revulsion for the Bolshevik regime from childhood on. Later he had become a civil engineer and had been repelled by the systematic persecution of the engineers in the early thirties, which had nourished in him an ever-fiercer hatred of the Soviet regime. At one time, it appears, he had contemplated joining a Cossack uprising in the Kuban, but nothing came of this plan. Throughout the thirties he had worked in a variety of engineering jobs, and in July 1940 had been sentenced to five years in the labour camps after being denounced by a fellow engineer. In 1943 he had been given ten more years for "defeatist propaganda," and by the time Solzhenitsyn met him, had spent seven years in a variety of labour camps in the Arctic North. During that time he had endured unbelievable privations and yet had come through them with sound health, a clear mind, and, above all, an impressive grasp of moral values and a fanatical devotion to justice.

Lev Kopelev arrived in the *sharashka* about a month later than Panin. He, too, was older than Solzhenitsyn—by five years (he became the inspiration for "Lev Rubin" in *The First Circle*) and was superficially Panin's opposite: a deeply committed Marxist, long-time Party member, and loyal supporter of the regime. He had been arrested on the same front as Solzhenitsyn and convicted on similar charges, yet he believed even more passionately than Solzhenitsyn that the whole thing was a gross error and that any day he would be pardoned. He defended the Soviet regime with even more conviction than Solzhenitsyn was now able to do, and clung to the belief that his arrest and the whole phenomenon of the camps and the purges before and after the war were temporary deviations from the norm, the result of Stalin's inadvertent misunderstandings, and would sooner or later be corrected by an all-wise Party.

Both Panin and Kopelev were men of principle, passionately committed to their separate views of the world, and they had every reason to detest one another. Yet they were the best of friends, having already met and liked one another in Butyrki before arriving at the *sharashka*. In his book on his experiences, Panin writes that he had been won over when Kopelev, a relative novice in the camps, who was still being sent parcels by his family, broke a loaf of white bread in two and handed Panin half. After seven years on starvation rations, Panin had forgotten not only how white bread tasted but how it looked. "If Lev had given me only a tiny bit of it, I would have been rapturously happy. But here was half a loaf! His grand gesture affected me. . . . A generous nature and a nobility of spirit distinguished Lev from ordinary men."[12]

Kopelev, too, was a handsome man. Of their first meeting, Panin says, "I looked up and saw, in the centre of the gangway, a striking man in the prime of life, with dark eyes and hair. He had the build of a guardsman."[13] In the *sharashka*, Kopelev grew a a beard, let his hair grow long to conceal an incipient bald patch, and looked every inch an Old Testament prophet.

It was Panin who had gone to the *sharashka* commandant to persuade him to summon Kopelev from Butyrki, although Kopelev was a philologist and literary historian and had no technical qualifications at all. Solzhenitsyn had supported Panin's recommendation on faith, disregarding the fact that his own job as librarian might be at risk if Kopelev came, since Kopelev was fluent in German and in several other languages as well. Kopelev's work in the Soviet army, where he had reached the rank of major, had been to organize anti-Nazi propaganda behind the German lines and undermine morale, and he had been arrested for opposing the hard policy taken by the Soviet army in the occupied German territories and for resisting the looting and terror carried out under the slogan "Blood for blood, death for death." He had been denounced for being "soft on the Germans" and had narrowly escaped a charge of treason. Solzhenitsyn, in *The First Circle*, sums up the complexity of Kopelev's feelings and his essential generosity of spirit when describing a small party held by some German prisoners of war at the *sharashka* to celebrate Christmas, to which Rubin (Kopelev) alone is invited from among the Russians. "For them, this enemy major who had spent the whole war spreading discord and destruction among them was the only man they felt close to and could understand." As for Rubin, he had been "reluctant to come to this celebration, but the others had been so insistent, and he was so sorry for them in their loneliness, that he could not bring himself to cast a shadow on their festivities by staying away."[14]

What Kopelev later remembered from his first meeting with Solzhenitsyn were the latter's piercing blue eyes and firm handshake. The two of them established that they had served (and been arrested) on the same Prussian front. They must have fought their way through some of the same towns and villages, and Solzhenitsyn might even have heard Kopelev's voice over the military radio. Finally, they had both been arrested by the same section of Smersh. Kopelev was genuinely delighted by this series of coincidences but noticed a slight frown on Solzhenitsyn's face as they compared their experiences. Solzhenitsyn later told him that the coincidences were so great as to make him suspicious, and he had momentarily wondered whether Kopelev was an informer. But the suspicion quickly faded. Solzhenitsyn was gratified to learn that Kopelev had shared his distaste for Soviet looting and violence in the occupied territories, and was later to incorporate a number of stories that Kopelev told him into his narrative poem *Prussian Nights*.

The two men proved to be close in other ways. Kopelev was the first prisoner in the four months that Solzhenitsyn had been librarian to ask for the newspaper files (the library had a complete run of *Pravda* and *Izvestia*). Solzhenitsyn was delighted. "It just had to be," he told Kopelev (according to Kopelev's memoirs). "We were on the same fronts and swept up by the same counter-intelligence. And we've both got the same appetite for newspapers. It's a sort of kinship."[15]

They also shared a passion for literature. Kopelev had been a young lecturer at the Moscow Institute of Philosophy, Literature, and History when Solzhenitsyn had taken his correspondence course there. Kopelev was a Germanist and a polyglot. Solzhenitsyn was chiefly interested in Russian literature, but Kopelev's passion for philology coincided with Solzhenitsyn's enthusiasm for Dahl and the history of the Russian language. Learning of Solzhenitsyn's linguistic exercises, Kopelev energetically assisted him in obtaining a complete set of Dahl for the Marfino library. Later, when Solzhenitsyn left the *sharashka* for Central Asia, taking volume 2 with him, Kopelev kept the other three; and when they were reunited in the fifties, he handed them over to Solzhenitsyn to make his set complete once more.

Last but not least, they were close politically. Kopelev approved of Solzhenitsyn's Leninist views and valued in him a political supporter, particularly in the hostile environment of the *sharashka*, where a clear majority was against Party orthodoxy. Both still identified with the establishment, both had been active members of the Komsomol, both had fought enthusiastically in the Red Army until the day of their arrest, and both felt that there had been some awful miscarriage of justice in their cases; if it could only be brought to the notice of the competent authorities, all would be put right and they would be restored to freedom. Kopelev supported his belief with a veritable bombardment of petitions (to the Central Committee, to the Supreme Court, and even to Stalin personally), which he kept up throughout his time at the *sharashka*. Solzhenitsyn, having had more experience, was beginning to cool in this respect. But he, too, on arrival in the *sharashka*, had continued to hope for an amnesty and had still dreamed of a commutation to exile, although these hopes fairly soon faded. By the end of 1947 he was ready to acknowledge them as a pipe-dream. "Whenever they start talking about an amnesty," he wrote to Natalia, "I smile crookedly and walk away."[16]

If Kopelev appealed to the loyalist and politically orthodox side of Solzhenitsyn's temperament, Panin's influence was on the side of scepticism and hostility. Kopelev appealed to his desire to believe, Panin to his urge to dissent. Panin was in some ways the engineer *par excellence*, a cool, rational, analytical thinker whose views had been tested and tempered in the fire of the labour camps. He seemed to have been everywhere in Gulag: in the far east, the far north, the Urals, European Russia. He had travelled in an infinity of prison vans and convict trains, languished in transit jails, been in punishment cells and solitary confinement, done general duties and been a trusty, fought hand to hand with the professional thieves and more than once been close to death. He was a veteran with a wealth of experience and an authority that Solzhenitsyn immediately recognized. His views were harsh and uncompromising, contradicting many of Solzhenitsyn's favourite notions, but Solzhenitsyn instinctively acknowledged their rationality and their grounding in the reality of Gulag.

On the subject of amnesties, for instance, Panin was unremittingly pessimistic. "Don't fool yourselves with day-dreams, gentlemen.* They won't let us go. If we were in the camps, maybe they'd let us out into the 'big compound' of exile. But from the *sharashka*—never. They've let us into their secrets here. . . . For all our luxuries—our mattresses, sheets, and puddings—we shall have to pay a high price. . . . No, gentlemen, there's no point in counting the days, we're in for life."[17]

Panin had enormous intellectual and physical passion and was an individualist to the marrow of his bones. He was what the Russians call a *chudak*. An "eccentric" is perhaps the nearest one can get in English, but the English

---

*Panin's persistent use of the word "gentlemen" was his way of setting himself apart from all forms of Soviet usage. In normal intercourse with one another and members of the administration, prisoners (in all the camps) were forbidden to say "comrade" and were obliged to use the term "citizen." Peretz Hertzenberg, another former inmate, says that prisoners at the *sharashka* were invariably polite to one another and always used the second-person plural *Vy* (you) instead of the more common "thou" form.

suggests rather too much crankiness and inconsequentiality, whereas *chudak* implies more of the sainted innocent and the inspired inventor. This stood out in, among other things, his invention of, and devotion to, a "language of maximum clarity." As it appears in Solzhenitsyn's novel on the *sharashka* Sologdin's (Panin's) "language of maximum clarity" looks like an inspired fictional invention (as does much else that Solzhenitsyn describes), yet he was being entirely faithful to reality. In his memoirs Panin devotes several pages to this concept, defining it as a device for refining the Russian language, purging it of all foreign words and expressions, and improving its accuracy and precision. At one point, where he talks of founding it on a vocabulary of "a few hundred basic words," he seems to toy with a concept similar to Basic English, but elsewhere comes perilously close to Hitlerian nonsense about the harm done to the purity of a language by foreign borrowings, advocating a greater Slavonicization of literary Russian that recalls the German "Aryanization" of the thirties.

It was in some ways a typical engineer's concept, and Panin thought it might even be applied to scientific language, despite the vast amount of international terminology already present in scientific Russian (as in all scientific languages). His theories evoked an answering chord in Solzhenitsyn, whose study of Dahl had led him to a preoccupation with Slavonic roots and folk language, and in Kopelev, whose philological interest was aroused. But the other two men were more professional in their linguistic pursuits and too well acquainted with the nature of the Russian language, with its vast number of foreign words and borrowings, to imagine that such a purification could work. In *The First Circle* Solzhenitsyn (not unsympathetically) parodies Panin and his theories.*

During those first few months while the *sharashka* was being organized the prisoners' schedule was extremely relaxed. Solzhenitsyn, Kopelev, and Panin lived in the larger of the two main cells, laughingly dubbed the "house of commons" (the smaller, engineers' cell was the "house of lords"). Reveille was at 7 a.m. and lights out at 10 p.m., and the working day lasted for no more than eight hours. When off duty, the prisoners could stroll in the compound, and the evenings were largely their own. The food, too, was excellent in comparison with what they had been getting: fourteen and a half ounces of white bread a day, an ounce of butter, wheat-meal porridge for breakfast, a meat course for lunch, and a dessert after lunch.

But still the prisoners were often hungry and dreamed daily of the possibility of receiving parcels, which for Solzhenitsyn, Panin, and Kopelev was temporarily excluded: the *sharashka*'s location was a state secret and couldn't be revealed to the prisoners' families, so that it took some months to set up the mechanism whereby parcels could be sent via a neutral address. Kopelev describes the modest "feast" they organized to celebrate the New Year of 1948. A luckier cell-mate had given them a quarter of a tin of concentrated

---

* In the revised, ninety-six-chapter version of *The First Circle*, Solzhenitsyn has strengthened the element of parody and shows less sympathy to Panin's views.

cocoa from his parcel. From breakfast they had saved some sugar and from supper some bread, and they obtained a couple of pots of hot water from the kitchen. This was consumed on Panin's upper bunk (similar groups of prisoners were celebrating elsewhere in the room). Panin proposed a characteristic toast: "Gentlemen . . . I am not golden-tongued [he did not want to use the word "orator"]. People usually wish one another a 'happy New Year,' but what kind of happiness is possible for us? . . . I raise this sober goblet to toast the possible. I drink to our not going hungry in the new year. . . . And to our friendship, gentlemen."[18]

Such evening gatherings of the three friends (a new and adult version of "the three musketeers") became very much the rule that winter, but on other occasions a larger group of prisoners would meet in the library to hold discussions, relate their experiences, stage impromptu concerts, or conduct poetry readings. The prime mover, according to Panin, was usually the boisterous Kopelev, who adored such gatherings. As Solzhenitsyn later noted of Rubin in *The First Circle*, he "couldn't exist without friends, he suffocated without them. He found solitude so intolerable that he couldn't even wait for his ideas to mature in his head, but hastened to share them with someone while they were still only half formed."[19] Kopelev had an encyclopaedic knowledge of Russian literature and could recite the work of dozens of poets from memory, which made him very popular and much in demand.* Solzhenitsyn also shone in these recitals. On one occasion they both read from Mayakovsky's early works (though neither cared much for the poet any more), and Solzhenitsyn read from Esenin. Kopelev also sang some popular songs by Soviet composers.

Solzhenitsyn seems to have enjoyed these performances during his first months at the *sharashka* and even revived some of his set pieces from his student days and the concerts at Kaluga Gate. In general he felt comfortable in this all-male society, enjoyed the manly comradeship, the boisterous jokes, and the feeling of oneness that derived from a sense of shared privations and shared pleasures. In a sense it reminded him of the camaraderie of the trenches—and in *The First Circle* he was to liken their cell to an ark or a ship and, by implication, its occupants to sailors afloat on the high seas. But this created problems as well, for he just as strongly felt the tug of his other interests and of his puritanical urge to work. Panin captures exactly the conflict always present in him between spontaneous gregariousness and the ascetic self-discipline that he had cultivated since childhood.

> Solzhenitsyn is a man of exceptional vitality, who is so constituted that he never seems to get tired. He often put up with our society simply out of courtesy, regretting the hours he was wasting on our idle pastimes. On the other hand, when he was in good form or allowed himself some time for a little amusement,

---

* Kopelev was evidently the originator of the satirical reworking of *The Lay of the Host of Igor* into Soviet judicial jargon, and of the fable "The Crow and the Fox" (see chapters 50 and 49 of *The First Circle*). "Buddha's Smile" (see chapter 54) was the work of Solzhenitsyn and Semyonov.

we got enormous pleasure from his jokes, witticisms, and yarns. On such occasions the flush of Sanya's cheeks deepened and his nose whitened, as if carved from alabaster. It was not often one saw this side of him—his sense of humour. He had the ability to catch the subtlest mannerisms, gestures, and intonations— things that usually escaped the rest of us—and to reproduce them with such artistry that the audience literally rocked with laughter. Unfortunately, he indulged himself in this fashion only very occasionally among his close friends—and only if it was not at the expense of his work.[20]

Kopelev also noticed Solzhenitsyn's need for solitude. They all required it from time to time, he writes, especially when walking on occasion in the yard, and then the other two would try to guard the one who had asked to be left alone and preserve his privacy. When it was Solzhenitsyn's turn, he "used to pace up and down our path, tall and thin, in his long greatcoat, with the earflaps of his army cap lowered, while Panin and I patrolled the exit from the main square in the yard"[21] to see that no one interrupted him. On such occasions, another prisoner reports, his face would be set in a mask of unapproachability.[22]

The "work" that Solzhenitsyn was engaged upon, apart from his daily linguistic exercises with Dahl, was writing, to which he had returned with an eager sense of relief as soon as he had settled at the *sharashka*. His first thought had been to continue the big novel about the Revolution that he had commenced as a student, and he had decided to go back to the beginning and start afresh. He wrote and completed some chapters under the provisional title of *Love the Revolution* but was dissatisfied with what he produced. His youthful self-confidence had vanished, to be replaced by scepticism and self-doubt. The October Revolution, which was to be the focal point of the novel, no longer shone in his mind with unclouded glory, and his title now seemed to contain a note of irony that had not been intended when he first thought of it.

Eventually, he was to abandon the project completely, but not his interest in the Revolution. Feeling inadequate to handle it, he turned to Kopelev for information. Kopelev was steeped in revolutionary history and was an ideal source for the sort of things Solzhenitsyn wanted to know. According to Kopelev, Solzhenitsyn approached him one day and said:

> What I need is the general sequence of events and the characters of the people involved. But I want you to do it without embroidery and without omissions, and as objectively and impartially as you can. I know you're biased. You're a Marxist-Leninist and must keep to the Party line. But I understand that and can make the necessary allowances. . . . Don't exaggerate, don't try to make propaganda, and don't hush anything up. Give different versions and different points of view. And don't prevent me from making up my own mind and deciding for myself. Don't pressure me.[23]

Most of Kopelev's information was imparted in whispers during their walks in the yard or *sotto voce* over cups of strong tea in a corner of the library in the evenings. On these occasions Solzhenitsyn would challenge Kopelev's interpretation of the events he was describing, and for the purposes of argument would express doubts about Lenin as well as Stalin. Was it possible to prove, he asked Kopelev, that if Lenin had remained alive there would have been no campaign against the kulaks, no collectivization, no famine? Could everything be blamed on Stalin? And they argued over Stalin, too, for although Kopelev held Stalin responsible for individual mistakes, he still regarded him as a great leader and genius. Kopelev took up a position that he himself has since described as "Red imperialism," combining Soviet patriotism with Russian nationalism. From this point of view, Stalin's main justification wasn't Marxism at all, but rather his conquest of territory "from the Elbe to the China Sea." He had made Russia great again.

Solzhenitsyn had no patience with this argument. He told Kopelev that in a book of memoirs he had read about 1917, a soldiers' meeting had been described at which an elderly veteran had interrupted an orator calling for warm-water ports with the exclamation "Screw you and your seas! What are we supposed to do, plough them?"[24] Such peasant common sense appealed to him, and he felt that Stalin had no interest in, and no time for, the common people. Lenin, Bukharin, and perhaps Trotsky had shown some concern, but not Stalin. Stalin and his supporters were interested only in more territory in which to try out their theories.

Another argument of Kopelev's that Solzhenitsyn resisted was that of historical determinism. What would have happened, he asked, if Kornilov had displaced Kerensky, if Krasnov's Cossacks had dispersed the Congress of Soviets and shot Lenin and Trotsky?* Nothing was predestined or inevitable. He had once believed in the theory of historical determinism himself, he said, but could no longer bring himself to do so, because he couldn't believe the analyses of those who had been proved wrong so many times. Even the greatest of them, Marx and Lenin, had been totally wrong in their predictions.

When it came to discussing these same things with Panin, however, Solzhenitsyn took a different tack. Panin regarded their heated debates on the truth or falsity of Marxism-Leninism with undisguised contempt. As a firm Christian, he was convinced that the Bolsheviks were the instruments of Satan, that the Revolution had been imported into Russia by foreigners and aliens, and that salvation could come only as a result of divine intervention. Russia had to purify herself of all foreign bodies, and that meant, among other things, purifying her language—hence his search for the "language of maximum clarity." Faced with this sort of argument, Solzhenitsyn switched to Kopelev's side. For all his scepticism, he could not disown the Revolution completely, and he would contradict Panin as fiercely as he had his other friend.

* In September 1917 General Kornilov led an abortive rebellion against the war minister and *de facto* leader of the Provisional Government, Alexander Kerensky. Ataman Petr Krasnov, leader of the Don Cossacks in the spring of 1918, had attempted, unsuccessfully, to enlist German support for a drive north against the new Bolshevik government in Petrograd.

At one point he sought a way out in the teaching of Eastern philosophers. Kopelev notes that one of Solzhenitsyn's favourite books, and one that he kept most thoroughly hidden from the other prisoners, was a collection of writings by sages of the ancient East. He was particularly attracted by the teachings of Lao-tse, the Chinese Taoist philosopher, and by such apophthegms as "Weapons are the instruments of unhappiness and not nobility. The noble person conquers unwillingly. He cannot enjoy killing people." And: "The more prohibitions and restrictions you have, the poorer the people. The more laws and regulations you have, the more thieves and outlaws you will have too."[25]

Kopelev shared Solzhenitsyn's admiration for this predecessor of Christ (Lao-tse also offered a version of "return good for evil"), but Panin was as implacably opposed to taking the Eastern thinkers seriously as he was to Marx and Engels. It was simply heresy, he said. True faith could not be the fruit of reason but was a gift from God, to be accepted by the heart and not the mind. Only the exact sciences were susceptible to the powers of reason. All else, including the subject matter of the social sciences and the humanities, could be understood only intuitively, and to try to study them led merely to schism and renunciation of the true church.

Among the things the three friends debated was the question of nationalism. Solzhenitsyn pointed out to Kopelev that when the war had reached a critical point for Stalin, he had rallied the nation by appealing to its patriotism and invoking not Marx and Lenin but Russian heroes of the past: Alexander Nevsky, Suvorov, Kutuzov.* Marxist internationalism was a sham. Nor was he impressed by Kopelev's assertions that internationalism was not incompatible with the fulfilment of national aspirations, that "inter" meant "between," not "above" or "without." In this, Solzhenitsyn was closer to Panin, and shared Panin's suspicions about the role of Jews and foreigners in the Communist Party. A slightly farcical illustration of Solzhenitsyn's prejudices occurred, according to Kopelev, when Kopelev came to discuss the Socialist Revolutionary party in the history of the Revolution. After Kopelev had named leaders like Gershuni, Gorovits, and Gots, Solzhenitsyn exclaimed that they were all Jews, whereas he had regarded the Socialist Revolutionaries as a party of the peasants. Solzhenitsyn also believed, according to Kopelev, that all the Trotskyites in the 1920s and 1930s had been Jews, and all Bukharin supporters Russians.

On the subject of Jewishness and its irreconcilability with the Russian national identity, Solzhenitsyn and Panin were agreed. Kopelev, they were willing to admit, knew more about Russian history and literature than they did, and spoke Russian equally well, yet also knew German and German literature very well, and if he were to live in Germany for ten to fifteen years, he would pass for a German. "But neither I nor Dimitri could do that," said Solzhenitsyn. "And it's not just us. Look at our caretaker, Spiridon. He can

---

* Alexander Nevsky had defeated and turned back the Swedes in the thirteenth century. Alexander Suvorov was a highly successful general under Catherine the Great. Field Marshal Mikhail Kutuzov was the hero of Russia's defeat of Napoleon.

barely read and write. . . . All he knows about Pushkin are some dirty jokes. But even if he were to live his whole life in Germany, or even Poland, he would remain a Russian peasant wherever he went."[26] Kopelev, said Panin, simply didn't want to own up to his true nature and admit that he was a Jew, a member of the chosen race, and not a Russian.

Solzhenitsyn greatly admired both his new friends, looked up to them as older and more experienced than he, and was grateful for their company. "It is only natural," he wrote in one of his letters to Natalia, "that men so rich in intellect, education, and experience should make such a big impression on a young man who, on the whole, was a mere provincial and had seen very little up to then."[27] He treasured their debates as marking one more stage in his education. The camps were his true universities, not the physics faculty in Rostov. And he was beginning to realize that he had fallen into a magic circle that was the freest in the whole of the Soviet Union. Where else could he have discussed so frankly and openly the true history of the Socialist Revolutionaries and the Bolsheviks, the role of Trotsky, the disasters of collectivization (Kopelev had participated in that, too, and was a mine of information), the meaning of the purges, the catastrophic start to the Second World War? In Stalin's post-war Russia every conversation they held reeked of treason and "ideological sabotage." Such opinions voiced outside the camps would have earned them a minimum of twenty-five years apiece, and even at Marfino they were obliged to speak in low voices and lard their speech with expletives to preserve the illusion of a normal labour-camp argument. If Gulag was hell, they were truly only in the first circle. Kopelev writes that he first heard this expression applied to the *sharashka* by Panin and was never sure whether Panin himself had invented it or was simply passing it on.[28] But it was left to Solzhenitsyn to seize the phrase and fill it with meaning, and that meaning had its origin in the unusual character of the *sharashka*—circumscribed yet free—and in these passionate debates between Solzhenitsyn and his two closest friends.

14

IN THE
FIRST CIRCLE

O NE OF THE many advantages of the *sharashka* was that prisoners could receive an unlimited number of letters, books, and parcels from home and could send letters out. It was true that all letters and parcels passed through the hands of the security officer, Major Shevchenko (he was later replaced by Major Shikin), for censorship purposes, but this was a tremendous advance on the usual camp regulations. There was also the comforting fact that the *sharashka* was situated on the very outskirts of Moscow. By day the prisoners could look into the unkempt grounds of the botanical gardens. By night they could see the pink glow of Moscow's lights reflected in the sky and could hear the whistle of trains leaving the capital for Riga and Yaroslavl. To Muscovites especially, it all seemed very close and accessible. And yet meetings with relatives were heavily restricted, and this created a mixture of frustration and longing in the Marfino inmates.[1]

Solzhenitsyn felt these emotions keenly, for Natalia now lived in Moscow, and it was doubly painful to have her so near and yet so inaccessible. But their infrequent meetings were a great joy to him. The first had taken place in July 1947, soon after his arrival. Owing to the secret nature of the *sharashka*, meetings were arranged at the Taganka Prison in Moscow and took place in the officers' club there, for wives and families were not supposed to know where their husbands were being held. The whole process was shrouded in an atmosphere of conspiracy and conducted according to a ritual that Solzhenitsyn has described in *The First Circle*. First the prisoners had to change out of their prison clothes and don civilian suits specially issued for the occasion. Then they were read a list of prohibitions, including strict instructions not to talk about their work or the location of the prison. At a later date, it seems, a prohibition was placed on kissing and embracing one's wife, but at this first meeting embraces were still permitted.

It was due to the top-secret nature of Mavrino that prisoners were driven to another place for their visits. Their relatives were not supposed to know the present whereabouts of these living dead, whether they were being brought in from some place a hundred miles away or from the Kremlin, from the airport or from the next world. They were only allowed to see well-fed, well-dressed men with white hands who were no longer talkative, who smiled sadly and assured them all was well and that they had all they wanted.

These meetings were rather like those scenes depicted on ancient Greek steles, showing both the deceased and the living people who had erected the monument to him. The steles always had a thin line dividing the other world from this. The living looked fondly at the dead, while the dead man looked towards Hades with eyes that were neither happy nor sad, but somehow blank— the look of one who knew too much.[2]

The location of Marfino was in fact an open secret to the Moscow wives, and Natalia subsequently went to the Ostankino Park on a number of occasions in the hope of glimpsing Solzhenitsyn through the wire. She was accompanied on these excursions by Panin's wife, Evgenia, whom she had met in the waiting-room during her first visit, and once they narrowly escaped arrest by a suspicious policeman who demanded to see their passports. They fondly imagined that the men they could see playing volleyball and lounging on the grass included their husbands, but it was impossible to get close enough to make out their faces. Solzhenitsyn did play volleyball from time to time and was reasonably good at it (though, according to Kopelev, he was a bossy player and tended to intercept passes intended for others).[3]

Natalia's and Solzhenitsyn's first meeting at the Taganka was tender in the extreme and opened a period of two years that were "the happiest of . . . our years of unhappy separation,"[4] according to Reshetovskaya, although it was to be almost a year before they were allowed to meet again. On the other hand they were able to exchange letters constantly, and the fact that they were both in Moscow, although totally cut off from one another physically, somehow consoled and reassured them, endowing their lives with a semblance of normality and driving memories of the true face of Gulag into the background.

For Natalia, these were extremely difficult times. She had succeeded in moving to Moscow and was now doing post-graduate studies in chemistry under Professor Kobozev, while living with her aunt on Malaya Bronnaya Street. It was a period of terrible shortages and overcrowding—Moscow was bursting at the seams with soldiers returning from the front and evacuees returning from the provinces, and was still reeling from the impact of the war—and accommodating Natalia had involved considerable sacrifice for the Turkins. Their "flat" consisted of a single, large room partitioned to form two smaller rooms, with a small passageway between. Aunt Veronica's mother and sister slept in one small room, and Natalia moved into the other with Veronica's daughter, the younger Veronica, who was now nineteen, while her aunt slept in the passageway. This was all that was left to them of the six room flat that Veronica had inherited from her mother, for they had been "compressed," as the saying went, into one room after the Revolution, and the other five rooms had been let to five other families, with whom they now shared the kitchen and bathroom.[5]

The Turkins had been pleased to welcome Natalia and offer her a home. They had shared her sense of shock and grief over Solzhenitsyn's arrest, although they hardly knew him, had lent a sympathetic ear to her sorrows, and had helped her find her feet in this strange, hectic, and forbidding capital city. It had been from their place that she had set out for her first meetings with Solzhenitsyn at Kaluga Gate, and it was there that she met his former sergeant Ilya Solomin, after his demobilization from the army, and heard from him the detailed story of Solzhenitsyn's arrest. Solomin told her that he had burnt the books he found stored in the howitzer case, but had managed to hide all her letters to Solzhenitsyn and was now returning them to her. He also gave her Solzhenitsyn's surviving notes on the Samsonov campaign and his front-line copy of Esenin's poetry, which Natalia immediately sent on to Solzhenitsyn at Butyrki with a new inscription inside: "Thus will everything that is lost return to you."*

Solomin, whose entire family had been slaughtered by the Germans at Minsk, now had nowhere to go and lingered at Malaya Bronnaya for a while. After much discussion and an exchange of letters with Natalia's family in Rostov, the Turkins arranged for him to move there and to occupy Natalia's old room, which he duly did. The arrangement was not a success, however. Solomin, with his barrack-room ways, old soldier's swagger (a prominent feature of Soviet soldiers returning from occupied Germany), and taste for vodka and late nights, unavoidably scandalized the old ladies and played too much havoc with their normally quiet life. The arrangement lasted less than a year, but in the meantime Solomin had succeeded in gaining admission to Rostov University to study engineering and was able to move into a university hostel.

In 1946 Natalia had also moved from the Turkins' into a university hostel. She had been reluctant to go at first. The Turkins were relatives and despite the overcrowding, she appreciated their affection and support. The hostel would be lonelier and more impersonal and would call for more self-reliance. Moreover, the atmosphere of suspicion and distrust that once again began to cloak the city as Stalin's paranoia reasserted itself meant that she dared not admit even to the existence of a husband who was a political prisoner—she would at once be expelled from the university. But the overcrowd-

---

*This is a literal translation of the Russian: *Tak i vsë uteryannoe k tebe vernëtsya.* The English translation of Reshetovskaya's book dresses this up in pseudo-biblical language, and Kopelev offers a paraphrase instead of a direct quotation. The point of the new inscription lay in its double meaning.

ing and the cramped conditions at Malaya Bronnaya were growing intolerable, and so she was obliged to make the move.[6]

The hostel was located at Stromynka and her life there, with five room-mates, was much as Nadia Nerzhin's is described in *The First Circle* (Solzhenitsyn questioned Natalia on this subject when he was working on the novel). Life was austere, as it was in most European capitals during the early post-war years. Food and clothing were rationed, the room at Stromynka was sparsely and shabbily furnished, and Natalia had only a modest graduate-student grant out of which to meet her needs. Furthermore, the oppressive secret that she was obliged to carry round with her could be shared only with Kirill, Lydia, and the two Veronicas, and this served to increase her sense of loneliness and isolation.

By the summer of 1947, when she and Solzhenitsyn had their first reunion, she was in the final stages of completing her doctoral dissertation for Professor Kobozev. The original deadline had been 1 September, but she had succeeded in getting it postponed until November. This meant that her Moscow residence permit and her place in the hostel were guaranteed for another year. After September, however, her grant came to an end, and her mother was obliged to send money from Rostov to support her. She also had no right to a ration card and was forced to buy a temporary card on the black market. Her position was most precarious. If her dissertation failed, she would be forced to look for a job and another room, or perhaps to return to Rostov. At length, at the end of November, she delivered her dissertation to Professor Kobozev, who declared himself satisfied. In December food rationing was abolished, and in January Natalia was taken on as a post-graduate assistant in Kobozev's laboratory. Her wages turned out to be less than the grant she had been getting, but she was able to manage, and she was above all relieved to be able to stay in Moscow. Throughout the spring of 1948 she prepared copies of her dissertation for the formal defence, composed an article and a lecture on the theme of her dissertation, answered some queries raised by the two chemists appointed to "challenge" the dissertation at her formal defence of it, and mentally prepared herself for the great day in June. On 23 June her formal defence took place, and her dissertation passed on a vote of twenty to two. Lydia and Kirill and some university friends from Rostov were there to hear her defence and join in the celebration banquet afterwards, and only Solzhenitsyn's enforced absence cast a shadow over her day of triumph.[7]

With her dissertation out of the way, Natalia decided to resume her musical studies and signed up for classes with a teacher called Undina Dubova at the Moscow University Club. She had never abandoned her love of piano playing and possessed her own Becker piano, a treasure that she had installed in the hostel at Stromynka, where she frequently played duets with her best friend and room-mate, Alexandra Popova. She also played fairly regularly with Kirill, and after practising hard was selected to play in concerts with some of Dubova's other pupils. Dubova was herself a pupil of the renowned pianist and teacher Heinrich Neuhaus and on one occasion took Natalia to his home to play for him. He seemed quite pleased with her playing.

Music also managed to bring her closer to her husband. Since his student days, Solzhenitsyn had not taken much interest in music, but at Marfino he became a passionate radio listener, tried to catch all the music programmes, wrote at length to Natalia about the pieces he had heard, and was enthusiastic about her return to piano lessons and her success at amateur concerts. Perhaps, he wrote, this was the "real significance" of her stay in Moscow, and he urged her to "become a great and brilliant pianist" while she was there. Later, in characteristic fashion, he began to construct ambitious plans for her. When she went to give a series of concerts in Leningrad, he hailed the news that she had developed a professional stage presence and congratulated her on having made her first visit to Leningrad not as a tourist but as "a victor among instrumentalists." He advanced the slogan "Less chemistry and more music!" and began seriously to encourage her to take up music professionally.[8]

During these years, writes Reshetovskaya, they felt extremely close to one another.

> We exchanged letters constantly, and somehow each keenly felt the life of the other. Sanya took all my affairs to heart, gave me advice, encouraged me. And I felt that everything I was doing I was doing not only for myself but also for him. It was so pleasant to cheer Sanya with my little triumphs: an examination passed with flying colours, a test lecture that went well, a complimentary remark by a professor. The letters warmed us and sustained our feelings for one another, and our meetings became celebrations in themselves.[9]

The next meeting that Reshetovskaya describes in any detail took place a year after the first, on 20 June 1948, just three days before she was due to defend her dissertation. The two of them had come to anticipate their meetings with all the ardour of young lovers again, and Solzhenitsyn wrote to her that "in the evening after work, he had walked in the yard for a long time, gazed at the moon, imagined the conversation that was about to take place between us, and thought about how I, too, was probably thinking about him 'more than the dissertation.' " He wrote that after washing his hair he had walked around "in a towel rolled up like a turban so that my hair would set properly by tomorrow,"[10] and that he would take extra care over polishing his shoes and shaving.

At their 1948 meeting Solzhenitsyn announced to Natalia an astounding coincidence: Nikolai Vitkevich had arrived in the *sharashka*.* Solzhenitsyn already knew from Natalia, via Nikolai's mother, that Nikolai had been arrested in April 1945, two months after him, and sentenced by a military tribunal to ten years' imprisonment, the standard tribunal term. And he must have known

---

*Kopelev dates Vitkevich's arrival in the *sharashka* as 1950, but Reshetovskaya confirms that it was two years earlier, in 1948.

that Nikolai had been sent to Inta, in the northern Urals, on the very edge of the Arctic Circle, to serve his sentence. But there had been no direct contact between them, and they had hardly expected to meet again while both were prisoners. Indeed, Solzhenitsyn's first response on hearing (from the Marfino security officer) that his co-defendant was on his way to the *sharashka* and that he had better "watch his step" had been one of alarm. It was a more or less fixed rule that co-defendants weren't sent to the same camp, and he suspected a deliberate provocation and the preparation of a new case against him. But his fears were quickly dissipated when he found himself face to face with Nikolai. Nikolai was given the top bunk adjoining Solzhenitsyn's, and Solzhenitsyn simultaneously moved from his lower bunk to the upper one to be beside him. After that the two friends spent many nights deep in conversation, running over the details of their arrests and investigations, comparing charges, describing their camp experiences and exchanging news of Natalia, Lydia, Kirill, and other friends. So intense were these conversations that they earned themselves the derisive nickname of "the Solzhenitsker brothers" and were the butt of many jokes by Solzhenitsyn's comrades.[11]

Their meetings outside Orel and the mock-portentous "conference of the big two" now seemed an age away, and although it appeared for a short while as if they might still be "two trains travelling side by side," in reality their formerly parallel tracks had begun to diverge. Exposure to arrest and the rigours of the Gulag had evoked different responses in them and had developed character traits that had hitherto lain dormant or been overlooked in the flush of their youthful friendship.

Perhaps the area in which this difference now counted for most was that of politics and ideas. Solzhenitsyn was still passionately engaged in the ideas that had obsessed him in youth and that were ultimately responsible for his arrest and imprisonment. He was still conducting a continual, agonizing dialogue with himself about the meaning of life, the nature of socialism, the importance of Marx, the role of Lenin, and the significance of the October Revolution (his heated debates with Panin, Kopelev, and some of the other prisoners were all part of this process). Nikolai, on the other hand, proved to be less fiery than of yore. Already as a student his opposition to the Soviet system had been tinged with quietism. He was against state interference in his personal life, detested the "big brother" mentality much more than did Solzhenitsyn, and simply wanted to be left alone. But although in some ways he had gone further in his hostility to the regime, he had always been more passive than Solzhenitsyn and had had a clearer notion of what he was against than what he would have put in its place. It had been Solzhenitsyn who had led in elaborating all sorts of programmes for improvement and in drawing up "Resolution No. 1." Now Nikolai wanted to be left alone more than ever. The camps seemed to have knocked the stuffing out of him, and he simply wanted to turn his back on it all and retreat into personal life.[12]

Another factor was partly political and partly personal. Of Solzhenitsyn's two new friends, Nikolai much preferred Kopelev (as Solzhenitsyn had predicted to Kopelev beforehand). For all his youthful rebelliousness, Nikolai had been a Party member and was the son of a Party member. He still disliked Stalin and regarded most ideology with scepticism, but he perceived that the best way to get on was to keep in with the establishment and accept its authority in return for a quiet life. But he had detested Panin from the outset (and the feeling was mutual). Panin, with his chivalry, his elevated notions of honour, his religiosity, his open contempt for the authorities, and his steadfast refusal to make a deal with them, was the type of idealist and trouble-maker whom Nikolai most distrusted—and was an uncomfortable reminder of the price of coming to terms. Nikolai's usual response when Panin entered the room, and particularly when any political discussion started, was simply to leave it. As Solzhenitsyn later said, "Nikolai's motto was that we have only one life. We were born to live, so let's live and to hell with everything else."[13]

Solzhenitsyn, however, was moving in precisely the opposite direction. Not only did he relish these political discussions and find in them rich nourishment for his own ideas but he found himself drawing steadily away from Kopelev's position and closer to that of Panin. The process is brilliantly described in *The First Circle*, where Nerzhin (Solzhenitsyn) is shown as being midway, in his political and philosophical views, between Rubin (Kopelev) and Sologdin (Panin) and arguing with both of them. The whole novel is an extended debate on the ideas and concepts that preoccupied all three of them at the *sharashka* and is, on one level, a dramatization of Solzhenitsyn's spiritual odyssey there. The struggle he shows in the novel between the two sides for possession of Nerzhin's soul resembles the struggle that took place, metaphorically speaking, between Panin and Kopelev for the allegiance of Solzhenitsyn.

Explaining later the contrast between his own position at the *sharashka* and that of Nikolai, and the course his development took, Solzhenitsyn expressed it as follows:

> For my part, I was never able to get away from politics or my convictions. It is true that I used to try to defend Marxism during the early years of my imprisonment. But it turned out that I was incapable of it. There were such strong arguments and such experienced people against me that I simply couldn't. They beat me every time. And so gradually I moved away from Marxism, and at the *sharashka* I describe an intermediate position of scepticism, when I didn't quite believe in it any more. At all events, it was a most convenient position: I don't believe in anything, I don't know anything, leave me alone. . . . Then, while still at the *sharashka*, I began gradually to abandon this scepticism. In fact, I began gradually to return to my old, original childhood concepts. Through reading Dostoyevsky, actually . . . I began to move ever so slowly towards a position that was in the first place idealist, as they call it, that is, of supporting the primacy of the spiritual over the material, and secondly patriotic and religious. In other words, I began to return slowly and gradually to all my former views.[14]

But not quite all. When Peretz Herzenberg, a fellow prisoner, said to Solzhenitsyn one day that he recognized in him a believer, Solzhenitsyn declined to confirm it. The question of religious belief, he said, was a very complex problem, and he implied that he was not ready to solve it.[15]

As for Vitkevich, the truth of the matter seems to be that he was a rather ordinary individual and that this ordinariness stood out when contrasted with the sharp originality and intellectual distinction of Solzhenitsyn's other friends. Kopelev, who got on well with Nikolai, nevertheless couldn't stand his habit of referring to famous Russian writers as "Al" Pushkin, "Mickey" Lermontov, "Nick" Nekrasov, and "Volodya" Mayakovsky.* He had developed a sentimental nostalgia for his early childhood in Daghestan, assumed an air of stoic resignation that he regarded as fitting for a man of Moslem upbringing (his dark skin and wide face enabled him to press the connection quite far, although he had not a drop of Daghestanian blood in him), and brought a Moslem narrowness to his views on women, regarding all actresses and ballet dancers as "whores" by definition, and men who married them as "unmanly." He loved listening to oriental music and was predictably flattered when Kopelev nicknamed him "Djalil."[16]

It is perhaps indicative of Solzhenitsyn's cooling relations with his old friend that no prominent place was found for him in *The First Circle*, although some aspects of the character of Ruska Doronin (notably his love affair with Clara and his occupying the neighbouring bunk to Nerzhin's) were based on Nikolai. Perhaps a factor in their estrangement was the circumstance that Nikolai worked in the vacuum laboratory and that their paths did not cross in their work. Nevertheless, their friendship survived the camps and was even revived for a brief period afterwards, but it no longer bore comparison with that intensity of feeling that had existed between them as youths and young men, before their arrest.

Among the new friends with whom Solzhenitsyn now spent much time was the camp artist, Sergei Ivashov-Musatov (who appears as Kondrashov-Ivanov in *The First Circle*, Solzhenitsyn having preserved even the double-barrelled surname). Ivashov-Musatov was a tall, skinny, exotic-looking individual who reminded Kopelev of Don Quixote, and seems to have been equally eccentric in his theories and sudden enthusiasms. On Solzhenitsyn he exercised a powerful fascination that was to last well into the period when they were both free men again. Sentenced to twenty-five years for having attended a secret reading of a novel by Daniil Andreyev,† Ivashov-Musatov had been brought straight to Marfino and ordered to paint pictures, at the rate of one a month, to decorate the offices and rooms of the prison institute. According

---

* These are the approximate English equivalents (except Volodya) of Vitkevich's nicknames.
† Daniil Andreyev was one of two sons of the well-known Russian writer of the early twentieth century Leonid Andreyev (1871–1919). In 1949 he was arrested and jailed for having written a novel that was judged "anti-Soviet," and the many friends who had visited his home to hear readings from the novel were arrested too. Kopelev mentions an engineer at the *sharashka*, Victor Kemnits, who had also been jailed as a result of hearing Andreyev read.

to Panin, Ivashov-Musatov was trained as a mathematician but had an ency-clopaedic knowledge of literature and philosophy, and subscribed to a sort of foggy theism that was not limited to any one recognized religion.[17]

Ivashov's subjects make it sound as if he somewhat resembled the pre-Raphaelites without their Christian strain: *Parsifal*, *The Holy Grail*,* *Othello and Desdemona*, portraits and landscapes dramatically painted to express strong emotions and views. It seems from Solzhenitsyn's embarrassingly lengthy descriptions of the paintings in *The First Circle* that he approved very much of Ivashov's output at the time, though he was suspicious of an excess of emotion and questioned Ivashov's romanticism in his literary pictures: did not Ivashov's doctrine of "ennobling" reality come perilously close to the cosmetic injunctions of socialist realism? On the other hand, they could also be traced back to the tradition of Russian religious art and the views of the late Tolstoy, with which Solzhenitsyn felt much more comfortable and familiar.

What seems to have fascinated Solzhenitsyn most of all was Ivashov's concept of his vocation.

> For [Ivashov] art was not an occupation or a form of knowledge. Art was the only possible way of life. For him, everything around him—landscapes, objects, human characters, or shades of colour—all had their own particular resonance, which he could unerringly identify and place in the tonic scale. . . . There was only one emotion he was a stranger to, and that was indifference. He was well known for his extreme likes and passionate dislikes, and his uncompromising opinions.[18]

Solzhenitsyn may well have been taken with one other aspect of Iva-shov's technique, brought into play when he was painting portraits. It was not sufficient for him, Ivashov asserted, simply to look at a man when paint-ing his portrait. He needed to talk to him, listen to him, observe his smile and his gestures, in order to perceive his inner nature and essential character. And that nature and that character were what he tried to capture on canvas or on paper.

The engineer Nikolai Semyonov (Potapov in the novel), whom Solzhe-nitsyn had first met in Butyrki and who reminded him so vividly of the sagacious engineers he had seen round the Fedorovskys' table as a child, became another firm friend. Semyonov had been chief engineer during the building of the Dnieper Hydroelectric Power Station, one of Stalin's prize projects, and had been captured by the Germans during the war. The Ger-mans, discovering who he was, had asked him to work for them in restoring the dam, but although Semyonov had confirmed his identity, he had refused to collaborate. He had also made no fewer than three attempts to escape from the Germans, but on his repatriation after the war he was accused of betray-ing secrets to the Germans and sentenced to ten years for sabotage. Panin detested Semyonov as an unthinking robot who was ready to do anything for

---

* Ivashov's picture *The Holy Grail* later hung in Solzhenitsyn's living-room in Ryazan.

the Soviet regime and take orders without thinking about the consequences. Solzhenitsyn in time would come to similar conclusions about the vast army of Soviet scientists who are content to take orders from above and to work to make the Soviet system strong, despite their private reservations about and even hostility to the system, but at the *sharashka* his views had still not developed that far. Theoretically, he was moving closer to Panin, but the force of habit was hard to break, and in practice he had no trouble remaining on good terms with political loyalists. Besides, what was more important to him at this stage of his life was not a man's political beliefs but his ethical stance—a view that even Panin endorsed in his friendship with Lev Kopelev.

Somewhat different from Solzhenitsyn's other friends was the Marfino caretaker, Spiridon (who appears under his own name in *The First Circle*). Like Nerzhin in the novel, Solzhenitsyn used to enjoy sawing firewood in the yard in the mornings before breakfast, usually with Panin. Panin had fixed ideas about the need to "subjugate the flesh." Invariably, winter and summer, he slept by an open window (his first words to Kopelev in Butyrki had been an admonition not to close the window), and he made a habit, even in the fiercest of Arctic frosts, of walking about the yard without a hat, with his shirt unbuttoned almost to the waist, and with a topcoat slung nonchalantly over his shoulders. In spring, the moment the snow disappeared, he would dispense not only with the coat but also with his boots and walk barefoot, seeking out the roughest ground and deliberately walking on gravel, cinders, and other material with hard edges and corners. Panin was also the first to get up in the mornings. It had been his idea to saw firewood, and he persuaded Solzhenitsyn, and sometimes Kopelev, to join him (Nerzhin rubbing himself with hoar-frost in the novel before commencing work with Sologdin is another autobiographical detail: the "walrus" still had a taste for the cold). Since the preparation of firewood was, strictly speaking, Spiridon's responsibility and since Spiridon provided the tools, the three men got to see quite a lot of him, but it was only Solzhenitsyn who cultivated him and made a point of visiting him at other times as well.[19]

Panin laughingly called it his "going to the people,"* and he was right, for Solzhenitsyn was imitating his favourite nineteenth-century writers, above all Tolstoy, in his search for wisdom at the feet of the common people. But unlike Tolstoy, he had another compelling reason: his study of Dahl's dictionary had convinced him that the path to a revitalized and healthy literary language lay through a return to peasant idioms and the popular roots of everyday speech. Spiridon was a living and accessible repository of that speech and could teach him far more than books could about the state of the living language. The fruits of this study are also to be seen in *The First Circle*, where some of the best pages (and some of Solzhenitsyn's most interesting writing) are devoted to an account of Spiridon's life in Spiridon's own speech patterns (a device Solzhenitsyn was to employ on a larger scale in *A Day in*

* Solzhenitsyn evidently took the joke in good part, for he made it one of the chapter titles of *The First Circle*.

the Life of Ivan Denisovich). But Solzhenitsyn was sufficiently aware of the paternalistic fallacies of nineteenth-century populism to distance himself from its worst excesses. By underlining, in *The First Circle*, the similarities between a Nerzhin-type intellectual and the common man in contemporary Soviet Russia, he manages to deromanticize the traditional concept of "the people" (while at the same time refurbishing it for the future use in a more fruitful and contemporary way). Only much later, in his polemical writings, did he return to a cruder concept of "the people" and betray some of the insights that had enriched *The First Circle*.

Meanwhile Solzhenitsyn was reading more than at any other time since his university days. The Marfino library contained mainly technical books but had an eclectic and eccentric collection of general books that Solzhenitsyn seems to have read in its entirety at one time or another, including Mommsen's *History of Rome*, Klyuchevsky's *History of Russia*, and works by Darwin, Turgenev, Timiryazev, and Peter Struve. In April 1948 a plan was made to organize these books into a leisure library and add to them systematically. Kopelev was put in charge of it—at Solzhenitsyn's suggestion (Solzhenitsyn had declined the task on the grounds of lack of time)—and by steadily acquiring new works, mainly in the field of literature, and taking books out on loan from the Lenin Library, was able to see that they had access to a liberal supply of good fiction and poetry. It was now that Solzhenitsyn rediscovered Dostoyevsky, finding him far more satisfying than before. According to Reshetovskaya, he also read Alexei Tolstoy, Tiutchev, Fet, Maikov, Polonsky, and Blok, and urged her to do likewise. "After all, you don't know them," he wrote, adding characteristically in parenthesis, "and neither do I, to my great shame."[20] He was apparently much impressed by that great French favourite of Russian readers Anatole France and was almost as enthusiastic about the Soviet satirists Ilf and Petrov.

Most of the writers mentioned by Reshetovskaya were poets, and it may have been no coincidence that about this time Solzhenitsyn was himself turning from prose to poetry. On his arrival in the *sharashka*, he had still been immersed in Tolstoy. "Am slowly savouring the third volume of *War and Peace*, and with it your little chocolates,"[21] he had written to Reshetovskaya; and Kopelev reports that soon after his own arrival in the *sharashka*, he had seen Solzhenitsyn poring over a volume of Tolstoy's novel that he seemed to carry everywhere with him. The margins were crammed with annotations, some of which struck Kopelev as positively blasphemous, such as "no good," "clumsy," "gallicism," and "too wordy," but when Kopelev mentioned this to Solzhenitsyn he dismissed it: "Don't try to frighten me with your authorities. That's my opinion. I wrote it for myself. Tolstoy's language is out of date now."[22] His study of Tolstoy seems to have coincided with his efforts to write *Love the Revolution* and, when that failed, with a new prose work about his life in the army. This later piece, which never acquired a title, began with a description of life in the horse-drawn transport unit, where he had first served. But when it came to describing life at the front, he keenly felt the loss of his diaries and ran into a dead end.[23]

The switch of interest from the distant past of the Revolution to the more recent events of his own life did, however, have a liberating effect on his imagination and unlocked the way for him to start writing his first long and successfully completed work, a narrative poem that finally acquired the title *The Way*. His first idea was to transpose his army chapters into verse. Since arriving at the *sharashka*, he had written a great deal of incidental verse— poems to and about his wife, a poem to Kopelev on his birthday, poems about life in the camp.[24] He was encouraged by Kopelev, who admired his talent and himself wrote verse at this time. To the list of poets they read and discussed in the *sharashka*, Kopelev adds Pushkin, Gumilyov, Pasternak, and Simonov (Kopelev points out that Solzhenitsyn was much less interested in translations: when read some Bagritsky translations by Kopelev, he responded, "What I need are Russian poems about Russia").[25] Putting his prose into verse didn't seem to work, however, and Solzhenitsyn decided to go all the way back to childhood for the start of his poem and to work forwards. The army chapters could come in as a prose epilogue to the main part of the poem, or simply remain as part 2 (this idea was also abandoned in the course of time).

Part of the reason for Solzhenitsyn's decision to return to his childhood for this poem must have been a desire to make sense of his life and to re-examine it in the light of his new feelings about Marxism, the Revolution, Soviet society in the twenties and thirties, and events, such as the purges, that he had only vaguely thought about before. In turning to verse as the medium for what was planned from the start as a longish work, he seems to have been guided as much by practical considerations as by stylistic questions. Verse was more easily memorized. In the conditions of the *sharashka*, it was possible for him and Kopelev to write their works down on scraps of paper and keep them for a while, but anything with unorthodox thoughts in it had to be carefully hidden, and when discipline was later tightened and regular searches were introduced, they often had to be burnt. Their verse could then be committed to memory and reconstituted when conditions were safer. Stylistically, the chief influences on Solzhenitsyn seem to have been the nineteenth-century poet Nikolai Nekrasov,* Alexander Tvardovsky, whose *Vasily Tyorkin* Solzhenitsyn had admired at the front,† and his beloved Esenin. All three poets were verbally inventive, racy and vigorous in their styles, and steeped in Russian folk-ways, and the first two had a strong satirical vein that matched Solzhenitsyn's present intentions. The provisional title of his poem, *Volunteers' Highway*, expressed this satirical intent; it was an ironic reference to a recent government decree bestowing this name on the old Vladimir High

---

*Nekrasov was a famous editor and poet of the 1860s and 1870s. His best-known work is the long narrative poem *Who Lives Happily in Russia?* detailing the adventures of seven peasants who set out to explore various regions of Russia on foot to find an answer to this question.
† See p. 125 and note.

Road running out of Moscow—the road along which convicts sentenced to hard labour in Siberia in tsarist times had been led from the capital in chains. The official change of name was meant to symbolize the supposed abolition by the Soviet state of hard labour and the enlistment of "volunteers" to work on the great construction projects of Siberia and the far North. In reality, 90 per cent of the "volunteers" were prisoners.

Solzhenitsyn and Kopelev were able to devote so much time to their private interests because of the small sanctuary they had constructed for themselves in the library (at a later date it was transferred to one of the laboratories). Solzhenitsyn later described some of their "home comforts" in *The First Circle:* a solid German roll-top desk with innumerable little drawers and compartments, a swivel chair, piles of books and magazines—including many unconnected with their work—and plenty of time in which to scribble notes on tiny scraps of paper "which went unnoticed amid the camouflage of official papers."[26] Solzhenitsyn had also rigged up a block of wood to which he screwed four electrical sockets—two for lamps, one for a hotplate (to boil water on), and one for a home-made cigarette-lighter of his own invention. He also had a big radio on his desk, and at night the prisoners were allowed to have earphones in their cells. (According to Kopelev, these earphones were a source of great irritation to Solzhenitsyn. He had trouble falling asleep at night, and many of the prisoners would doze off leaving their earphones still buzzing, so that it became a familiar sight to see Solzhenitsyn hopping about the cell, turning the earphones off, and cursing their careless owners.)

A favourite relaxation of the two friends was listening to music, especially on the big radio. Solzhenitsyn told Kopelev that he owed his understanding of music to Natalia, who had explained her piano pieces to him, and held that music was just as susceptible to description and rational analysis as literature. Perhaps for that reason he preferred romantic composers like Chopin, Glinka, Mussorgsky, Tchaikovsky, and Beethoven to the classicists, for then he could make up stories to accompany the music and "see" what it described. Such a utilitarian view of music was more satisfying to him than were abstract theories about melody, rhythm, and counterpoint.

Another enthusiasm was the cinema. In the first year or two at the *sharashka*, the prisoners were often allowed to watch films on Sundays. Solzhenitsyn took full advantage of this privilege and sat through two performances of the first film to be shown—*Legend of the Siberian Land*. He found he was more impressionable after his prison experiences, more easily moved, more deeply affected, and was able to relate much of what he saw directly to his own life and emotions. After seeing a film based on Pushkin's *The Mermaid*,* he wrote to Natalia that he had been very upset by the scene in which the prince behaves so harshly to the miller's daughter and had felt it as "an agonizing reproach to myself," after which he had brooded on his earlier harsh words to his wife. His "cruelty" to her had been "motivated by other reasons

---

* Pushkin's verse play of that name was written in the period 1826–32 and was never finished.

and had taken other forms," but was it any the better for that? "Must one live one's life ten times, from beginning to end, so that only for the eleventh time is one able to live it as it should be lived—without regrets and without agonizing over one's past actions?" Later he was similarly moved by a film biography of the biologist Michurin.* He felt "infinitely sorry for Michurin's wife," saying that four years previously "I would not have been able to comprehend the whole tragedy of her life so profoundly as I comprehend it now." As at Kaluga Gate, he felt that his prison experiences had softened and mellowed him. "The years go by, yes, but if the heart grows better as a result of the unhappinesses suffered, if it is cleansed by them, then the years haven't passed in vain." And on another occasion he wrote apprehensively, "If I get the chance one day to live happily, will I perhaps grow heartless again? Although it's hard to believe, still, anything can happen."[27]

His sensitivity at this time was noted by Kopelev. Kopelev's original sentence had been six years, but in March 1948 he was summoned to see the security officer and told that the Supreme Court had "amended" this to ten years; in other words, he had another seven years to go, instead of the three he had imagined. It was a heavy blow (confirming Panin's pessimism rather than Kopelev's hopes of an amnesty), and Kopelev was temporarily crushed. Panin and Solzhenitsyn responded by being especially kind to him during the weeks following this news. Panin had experienced a similar blow in 1943, and Solzhenitsyn felt intuitively what torments Kopelev was experiencing. "Solzhenitsyn tried to present himself as a grim, battle-scarred veteran, an armour-plated 'native' of the Gulag Archipelago, tested by his prison ordeals," writes Kopelev, "but he still retained an adolescent impressionability and responsiveness."[28] From that point of view, his experiences in the Marfino *sharashka* were a huge step away from the harsh lessons taught at New Jerusalem and Kaluga Gate, particularly in his first year there. He was encouraged to behave like a human being again, and allowed to relax the front of toughness and unconcern that he had acquired at his first two camps.

On 19 December 1948, shortly after his thirtieth birthday, Solzhenitsyn had another meeting with Natalia at Taganka Prison. Their relationship seemed happy and unclouded, and he prepared for it with his usual feelings of excitement. He was looking forward to hearing more news of her piano concerts and her work in the university chemistry department. But she came with an item of most unpleasant news. Security regulations were being tightened everywhere, and the entire laboratory where she worked had been declared classified, regardless of what kind of research was being done there. Solzhenitsyn has evoked this moment in *The First Circle*.

> How could she explain that even in the university almost all work had been classified as secret? All science was being classified from top to bottom. This meant a new and more detailed questionnaire about her husband, her husband's

*I. V. Michurin (1855–1935), a talented horticulturist, was taken up by Lenin after the Revolution and given lavish support for his experiments in fruit selection. The town of Michurinsk is named after him.

relatives, and his relatives' relatives. If she were to write, "My husband has been sentenced under Article 58," she . . . wouldn't be allowed to work in the university at all. . . . If she lied and wrote, "Missing without trace," she would still have to give his name, and all they needed to do was check the MVD's files and she herself could be charged for making a false statement.[29]

There was only one way to avoid dismissal, and that was to file for a divorce. Even then she couldn't write "divorced" on the questionnaire, for she would still have to give her former husband's name, and that would lead to the same results. She therefore had to do it secretly, in another city, and write "unmarried" on her questionnaire, a relatively simple expedient, since after her marriage she had chosen to retain her maiden name, which was fully provided for under Soviet law.

The news cut Solzhenitsyn to the quick. At the time he said nothing. After all, he had already offered Natalia a divorce, and in his New Year's letter to Natalia's mother in Rostov after their meeting he wrote that he was glad she had ceased to be stubborn: "This is the correct and sober thing to do. It should have been done three years ago."[30] Natalia also assured him that it was a pure formality and would make not the slightest difference to her feelings, but just as, deep down, he had been vastly relieved by Natalia's earlier refusal of a divorce, so now he was apprehensive and despondent. As he later admitted, he returned to Marfino in the "darkest despair,"[31] and some of the fears he fell prey to were later expressed in *The First Circle*.

A legal divorce? Gleb didn't feel the least regret about tearing up that piece of paper with the coat of arms on it. What did the state have to do with the union of two souls? Or the union of bodies for that matter?

But having been knocked about by life, he knew that objects and events have an implacable logic of their own. In their daily round, people never dream what contradictory consequences their actions can have. . . . Take Nadia. She was divorcing him to avoid persecution. But once having got her divorce, she would hardly notice when she married again. . . .

Nerzhin sat and sat in silence. And the rush of joy that he always experienced from such meetings and that had still filled him to bursting during the bus ride gradually receded and was displaced by gloomier and graver thoughts.[32]

Natalia, too, was depressed by this turn of events, and a New Year's dinner with Kirill and Lydia reminded her all too painfully of happier times gone by. "As I sat at the festive dinner-table, I was suddenly struck by the realization that all the members of our former fivesome were right here in Moscow. But we were not all greeting the New Year together—and the separation was due to continue for very much longer. I felt so sad that I couldn't control myself and burst into bitter tears."[33] Kirill for some reason felt uncomfortable with the subject of Solzhenitsyn's and Nikolai's imprisonment and scolded Natalia for her weakness. She had made her own bed, he said, and must now lie on it.

The application for a divorce was filed, the questionnaire safely completed (Natalia referred to Solzhenitsyn on the form as her "ex-husband"), and in due course Natalia received her security clearance. But their relationship seemed to survive unscathed. They continued to exchange affectionate letters, and were both moved when on 26 April 1949, on the eve of their ninth wedding anniversary, Natalia played in a concert in the Red Army Theatre that was broadcast over the radio and that Solzhenitsyn heard in the *sharashka*. "Somehow I just knew it. It was just as I thought it would be," he wrote to Natalia that evening. "I listened and my heart was pounding. How I wanted to catch a glimpse of you at that moment." He added that he felt inside him "as though we had seen one another on the eve of our anniversary."[34]

The concert had another happy consequence for Natalia. In 1946 she had quarrelled with her uncle, Valentin Turkin, over one of Solzhenitsyn's pleas for a pardon that she had shown him while asking for advice. Turkin had exploded and denounced Solzhenitsyn as a fool. But now, after the concert, Natalia was visited in her dressing-room by Turkin's second wife, Nina, and invited to dinner for the following week. Valentin, a noted cook and gourmet, prepared the meal, and they had a touching reconciliation. Not long afterwards, Natalia won first prize in a Moscow University musical competition and was awarded two weeks' free holiday in the university's "House of Rest" just outside Moscow for July.

Her next meeting with Solzhenitsyn was set for 29 May 1949. Antonina Vitkevich, Nikolai's mother, had been assigned a meeting on the same day and came up from Rostov in time to go to Natalia's last concert at the university. They went to their meetings together, and Natalia caught her first glimpse of Nikolai in nine years as she passed the room in which he was standing waiting for his mother. All she had time to notice was that he had grown a moustache, but they managed to exchange glances and she was pleased that he had recognized her. The meeting was in Lefortovo Prison this time. It was their first since Natalia had announced her intention to seek a divorce. Both had approached it with trepidation, but all was well between them, and Solzhenitsyn returned to Marfino holding a bunch of lilies of the valley in his hands and experiencing "an amazing sense of relief."[35]

15

THE PARTING
OF THE WAYS

The period when Natalia was going through the formalities of filing for a divorce was made doubly difficult for Solzhenitsyn by some major changes taking place simultaneously at the *sharashka*. At the beginning of 1949 Marfino was officially designated a scientific research institute and given a new chief, Colonel Anton Vasiliev (the prototype of Yakonov in *The First Circle*). The institute's first task was to be the development of a "scrambler telephone" for the use of Stalin and his top aides, and Vasiliev was to report to Beria personally on the progress that was made. At the same time, the camp was transferred from the administration of the Ministry of the Interior to the Ministry of State Security, given a top-secret classification and named "MGB Special Prison No. 1." A double barbed-wire fence was erected around the perimeter, with a "forbidden zone," consisting of a ploughed strip, between them, and watch-towers at the corners manned round the clock by armed guards with orders to shoot, just like any other labour camp. Hand-picked guards and warders were drafted in from the Lubyanka, discipline was tightened, prisoners were allowed into the compound for exercise only briefly before breakfast and lunch, and the working day was lengthened to twelve hours.[1]

Reveille was, as before, at seven, followed by breakfast. At five to nine there was a daily roll-call: the prisoners were obliged to stand by their beds while they were inspected by two officers of the guard, the one just going off duty and the one coming on. A bell rang for work at nine, which continued through to five, with an hour's break for lunch and exercise. Supper was followed by another roll-call, at five to six, and the evening shift continued from six to eleven. Very occasionally, a film was shown on Sundays, and more rarely still the prisoners were allowed out for a game of volleyball, but most of the time the working routine was strictly adhered to, and as often as not, with the exception of the evening shift, it included Sundays. At night the prisoners were locked in their sleeping quarters and the iron double-doors sealed with wax and lead. During the day the yard and corridors were patrolled by armed guards. There were also spy-holes in all the doors, and, later in the summer, the prisoners were obliged to don dark-blue boiler-suits for ease of identification. For those who stepped out of line there was a lock-up, with a punishment cell, or the threat of removal from the *sharashka* and a return to the labour camps whence they had all come.

As part of the ensuing reshuffle, Panin was assigned to the engineering design office on the second floor of the laboratory block, where he prepared drawings for telephonic control panels and later worked on a design for a mechanical voice coder. Kopelev and Solzhenitsyn were obliged to hand over the library to three women employees of the MGB and were assigned to a special research group headed by an engineer called Alexander P, to make a statistical study of the phonetic properties of the Russian language, so that it could later be broken down into its phonetic components for "scrambling" by the telephone engineers. According to Kopelev, he and Solzhenitsyn were left to work on it virtually alone and to devise their own methodology, which they both found unexpectedly absorbing. Kopelev handled the linguistic and phonetic side of the problem and Solzhenitsyn the statistics. Their task was to establish a table of the syllables used in the Russian language in ascending order of frequency. Since the science of linguistics in the Soviet Union had degenerated badly since the 1920s, they were obliged to start virtually from scratch and to apply methods culled from foreign textbooks and journals. Fortunately, the new librarian (an attractive woman lieutenant in the MGB) was able to order books freely from the Lenin Library, the Academy of Sciences, and other specialist sources, and she was also able to procure the literary texts they demanded as "material" for their studies.

At first they divided their texts into four categories: the contemporary literary language (for which they ordered books by Victor Nekrasov, Kazakevich, Panova, Babayevsky, and so on); contemporary colloquial speech (for which they ordered plays by Simonov, Virta, Sofronov); political and journalistic discourse; and the discourse of technical literature. Later they simplified this into two categories—spoken and written speech—but it still offered them a wonderful opportunity not only to read plenty of contemporary literature but also to make stylistic analyses along with their phonetic studies.

Solzhenitsyn applied probability theory to establish how many raw syllables needed to be investigated to offer statistical credibility and came up with a total of 80,000, which he amended to 100,000, to be on the safe side. He, Kopelev, and Alexander P arranged for each text to be read slowly, while a team of up to ten prisoners identified the different syllables appearing in the text and noted them down in columns of figures. Even by the technological standards of the time, it was a long-winded way of making such a count, but in three weeks they succeeded in processing all the 100,000 syllables and came up with a figure of just over 3,500 phonetically differentiated ones. Of these, about 100 accounted for 85 per cent of the usages.[2]

So pleased was Colonel Vasiliev with these results that he asked the three members of the "statistical brigade" to make reports to the institute's first scientific conference, due to be held shortly. He also transferred them into the newly formed Acoustics Laboratory one floor below, a big airy room with high ceilings that is described in some detail in *The First Circle*. Meanwhile, their old premises in the chapel (which had formerly housed the library as well) were converted into living quarters, and Solzhenitsyn, Kopelev, Panin, and the others moved back in there to sleep. This is the room Solzhenitsyn later made famous as the setting for most of the "domestic" scenes in his novel.

> The blue bulb above the wide, four-panelled doors set into the archway cast its dim light on a dozen double-decker welded cots arranged fanwise round the big, semicircular room. This room, perhaps the only one of its kind in the whole of Moscow, was a good twelve paces in diameter and was topped by a spacious dome that tapered tentlike to merge with the base of the chapel's hexagonal tower, while the apse enclosed five graceful round-headed windows which were barred, but had no "muzzles" over them, so that in daytime you could see across the highway to the park on the far side, which was wild and untended, like a forest.[3]

The rearrangement of the sleeping quarters was the result of that same expansion that took place in 1949. Another research institute was brought to Marfino and merged with the existing one, raising the total number of prisoners to about three hundred, while the security guards, MGB personnel, administrative staff, and free workers accounted for about a hundred more.

Meanwhile, the Acoustics Laboratory was put in the charge of Major Abram Trachtman (the prototype of Adam Roitman in *The First Circle*),[4] an MGB engineer and Stalin Prize winner, who set Solzhenitsyn and Kopelev to study the sound properties of the human voice, with the object of breaking them down into quantifiable and analyzable units. For this purpose they had at their disposal some apparatus, copied from an American design, that filtered and printed out the acoustical properties of the voice in the form of spectrograms—dots, dashes, thickness of line, and width of oscillation defining frequency, pitch, intensity, and amplitude. By studying and measuring the spectrograms, they were supposed to establish the degrees of clarity, fidelity, and audibility of various types of telephone line being considered for use with the scrambler phone. By the autumn of 1949 a satisfactory encoding system had been developed, but the speaker's voice still lacked clarity and audibility when decoded.

Solzhenitsyn and Kopelev quickly set up their own cosy corner once more at one end of the new laboratory. They arranged it so that they were cut off from the rest of the room by their benches and bookcases, and had a small acoustical booth beside them into which they and the other readers would go in order to read the set texts. Since they were obliged to spend much of their time wearing earphones, it was a comparatively easy matter to switch from sound patterns to classical music, or even to the BBC's Russian Service, to which they had one small radio permanently tuned.

Another luxury of their position was the presence of women, mostly employees of the MGB. Ostensibly, they were there to work as laboratory assistants and technicians, but they had another and equally important task— namely, to keep watch over the prisoners. For this purpose they were summoned to periodic confidential lectures and exhorted to keep up their guard. Major Trachtman, who in the laboratory maintained the friendliest relations with the prisoners, used to tell the women at these meetings that they were surrounded by enemies of the people, that the vast majority of the prisoners were sworn enemies of the Soviet system, and that even those who appeared to be loyal Communists (like Kopelev) were double-dealers and especially dangerous.

Most of the women heeded these warnings and restricted their relations with the prisoners to strictly business matters, but there were several exceptions. Kopelev, for instance, had a passionate affair with the neglected wife of an MGB colonel. Solzhenitsyn, too, became romantically involved with a young MGB woman whom he describes as "Simochka" in *The First Circle*, but he does not seem to have consummated the relationship. Panin also seems to have had some sort of relationship with a colonel's wife, but there were times when he resisted involvement and would relentlessly punish himself for even looking at a woman. In fits of remorse he would deprive himself of dessert by giving it to Solzhenitsyn or Kopelev, or would devise some other form of punishment whenever he transgressed.[5]

Naturally, under such artificial conditions, in which both the intellectual and the emotional pressures on the prisoners were so unremitting, there were a great many strains in personal relationships. Apart from being surrounded by watchful MGB and MVD personnel, the prisoners knew that they had informers in their midst. One "honest" informer, who had been blackmailed into co-operating with the authorities, personally warned Kopelev of his status and asked that he, Solzhenitsyn, and Panin keep their distance, because the informer did not want to betray "good people." Another informer was unmasked when a fellow prisoner found a prepared denunciation in his coat pocket.[6]

A quite spectacular exposure of the camp spying system was engineered by a dapper young mathematician from Riga called Peretz Hertzenberg. Hertzenberg was a member of Solzhenitsyn and Kopelev's articulation brigade and had taken over some of the mathematical tasks formerly performed by Solzhenitsyn. One day he was called in by the security officer, Major Shikin, and asked to spy on the other prisoners. Instead of indignantly rejecting the proposition, as Kopelev had done in a similar situation, Hertzenberg decided to play along and enthusiastically accepted the assignment. Afterwards, he went to the other prisoners and informed them of what he had done, saying that his intention was to double-cross the secret-police chief and expose his operations. The others were doubtful. They trusted Hertzenberg but feared that anyone who supped with the devil was liable to be burned. To maintain credibility, Hertzenberg was obliged to provide at least some information, and he asked the other prisoners to co-operate with him and made a point of telling them what he had said to Shikin afterwards. It did not always work out, however. He upset Solzhenitsyn considerably by informing Shikin that Solzhenitsyn kept a copy of Esenin's poetry hidden in his suitcase. Hertzenberg imagined that it would be easy for Solzhenitsyn to get it back again, since he could easily prove that it was his personal property and had not been stolen from a library or brought in by one of the free workers. But he had underestimated the book's sentimental value to Solzhenitsyn, and the difficulty the latter would experience in recovering it. It took a veritable barrage of oral and written complaints by Solzhenitsyn to get the book returned. But Hertzenberg justified his escapade by revealing to the other prisoners the date when all the camp informers were due to be paid, the method of payment, and the amount due—147 rubles. On the appointed day, a group of prisoners gathered where the mail was handed out (including money orders from fictional relatives for the stool-pigeons) and caught all the informers red-handed. There was little they could do about it in a practical way. Reprisals would have led to new charges and sentences. But it was sufficient to know who they were and to ostracize them. Hertzenberg paid dearly for his exploit, however. Not only was his double role revealed and denounced to the security officer but he was henceforth treated with reserve and a certain suspicion even by his former friends. Fortunately, he remained on good terms with Solzhenitsyn and Kopelev, met them again in the fifties and early sixties, after all three had been released, and also acted as one of Solzhenitsyn's sources for *The Gulag Archipelago*. The story of his brief career as an informer and his exploit in exposing the system was incorporated by Solzhenitsyn into *The First Circle*.[7]*

The prisoners experienced many other pressures of this kind. Panin and Kopelev, for instance, were among a group of prisoners that was invariably dispatched to Butyrki and locked up for the duration of the national holidays in May and November. Those subjected to this prophylactic measure were prisoners guilty of terrorism, attempts to escape, or more than one crime—"recidivists." Kopelev qualified because he had been sentenced three times, albeit for the same crime, and Panin because he had been sentenced a second time when already in the camps. On the occasion of the first detention, Kopelev announced his intention to go on a hunger-strike but was dissuaded by a fellow internee, Professor Vladimir Timofeyev, an elderly mathematician from Leningrad who enjoyed great authority among the prisoners. Timofeyev convinced Kopelev that protests were useless and that he should treas-

---

*Hertzenberg's trick in the book is performed by Ruska Doronin, who was based, according to Solzhenitsyn's later account, partly on Hertzenberg, partly on his old school friend Nikolai Vitkevich, and partly on a prisoner called Gusev. Hertzenberg now lives in Jerusalem.

ure his detention as a special form of freedom. In the *sharashka* they were not free, since they all had to carry out the orders of the authorities and work hard. In a prison cell, at least, they were relieved of this necessity and could think about whatever they liked. "My choice of action is strictly limited by these walls, this door, and the prison regulations. But within these *external* limits I am inwardly completely free. . . . Today the thinking Russian can be free only in jail."[8]

Timofeyev was a forceful, opinionated academic specialist who had first crossed Kopelev's and Solzhenitsyn's paths when he had made fun of their phonetic theories and contradicted their findings at the first institute conference. Sarcastic and arrogant, he easily made enemies among the other prisoners and once or twice had blazing rows with Panin over the latter's proposals for a voice coder. Solzhenitsyn was attracted to him, because Timofeyev's knowingness was backed by a truly broad erudition, encompassing not only mathematics and the sciences but also literature, the theatre, and the arts. Another source of fascination was that Timofeyev had lived in St Petersburg–Petrograd–Leningrad before, during, and after the two revolutions, had been an eyewitness to much of what took place there, and was more than happy to talk about it. Timofeyev liked Solzhenitsyn because the latter rarely argued with him. Since Timofeyev was an extreme anti-Bolshevik and anti-Communist, he naturally did not see eye to eye with Kopelev and much preferred Solzhenitsyn as a listener. Solzhenitsyn portrayed Timofeyev in *The First Circle* under the name of Professor Chelnov.[9]

The heightened security measures introduced at Marfino in the course of 1949 were not peculiar to the *sharashka*, or even to Gulag at large, but reflected the atmosphere of the country as a whole. During the years of reconstruction and consolidation after the Second World War, Stalin's suspiciousness, misanthropy, and megalomania had reached epic proportions; the impact of his obsessiveness was now to be felt in every corner of Soviet life. It was during this summer that Solzhenitsyn's former sergeant, Ilya Solomin, was arrested in Rostov on charges of anti-Soviet agitation. It appears that Solomin was even questioned about his connection with Solzhenitsyn, but this line of inquiry was not pursued, and Solzhenitsyn did not get to hear of it until many years later. At Moscow University, too the secrecy and security became stifling and soon claimed Natalia as one of its victims—though it cannot be excluded that she was the target of someone's jealousy or resentment. On the day after her June meeting with Solzhenitsyn, a fellow music student rang her and invited her to a concert by Sviatoslav Richter. She gladly accepted, terminated her experiments, and ran to the Moscow Conservatory to meet him. The following morning she was summoned by one of Professor Kobozev's deputies and reprimanded for having left the small ventilation window in her laboratory open. Natalia explained that the window was barred and that she hadn't been the last to leave that evening: there were others in Kobozev's office who had had to pass through her laboratory to get out, and normally the last person to leave would close the ventilation window. She imagined that that was the end of the matter, but on 6 June she received a notice dismissing her from the university "on the grounds of a slipshod attitude towards her work, which had expressed itself in the fact that, upon leaving her laboratory, she had neglected to close the windows and the door."[10]

Stunned by this injustice, Natalia appealed first to the university's legal officer and then to Professor Kobozev. Her former patron and protector was staying in a sanatorium just outside Moscow, recovering from a bleeding ulcer. His surgeon had been Kirill Simonyan, who had arranged an earlier visit for Natalia to consult the professor about obtaining a divorce, and now she came to him again. Kobozev knew nothing of her dismissal, but when he learned that it had been at the insistence of the security police, he told her that nothing could be done about it. The open window was simply a pretext. In view of his illness he could not intervene personally, and he advised her to leave and seek work elsewhere. He did, however, promise to arrange for her to "resign" instead of being dismissed in disgrace, for with a security charge against her, she would stand no chance of any further employment in research or education.

Natalia was obliged to seek another loan from her mother and to start looking for work. The most promising prospect seemed to be an agricultural institute that was opening in the town of Ryazan, about a hundred miles south-east of Moscow. They were looking for chemistry lecturers, and Natalia sent in her application, together with a dazzling testimonial from Professor Kobozev. At the same time she toyed with the idea of switching completely to music, a prospect that found great favour with Solzhenitsyn. But she would have to lose no time, he said, because she was already growing old for studying. She would have to find "an absolutely exceptional, but quick and sure method of becoming a professional," without going to the conservatory. "You will say there is no such way, but it must be found."[11] In July, Natalia spent her two weeks at the university's House of Rest in the company of other musicians and was encouraged by some of them to make music her profession, but still she hesitated. There would be no scholarship available to her, she would have to continue to live off her mother, and she was not sure she could face the prospect of going back to being a student again.

Soon after her holiday ended, she learned she had been rejected by Ryazan. She was obliged to start looking again and was accepted for the humbler post of laboratory assistant by the University of Gorky. She actually travelled to Gorky in August, in anticipation of starting work in September, but at the last minute received a telegram from Ryazan, offering her a lecturer's post after all. The work was more interesting and better paid, and Ryazan was much closer to Moscow—to her husband, friends, and music teacher. Furthermore, the work in Gorky was classified; she could take it only if she finalized her divorce (she had still not made her divorce from Solzhenitsyn absolute), whereas in Ryazan this would not be necessary. She hastily telegraphed her acceptance, made a preliminary visit to Ryazan in the last week of August, and on 1 September 1949 moved there to take up her new post.

Just as he had welcomed Natalia's idea of staying on in Moscow to study music, so did Solzhenitsyn congratulate her on the wisdom of moving to Ryazan. This was partly the fruit of his genuine desire to support and encourage her at this difficult period in her life. After all, he felt responsible for and guilty about most of her troubles. But he was also displaying his old talent for rationalizing and making the best of what was inevitable. As always, his optimism was able to turn everything to account. She would be better off settled in some quiet town, he wrote. "It would have taken many more years of huddling in corners and leading a semi-homeless existence" if she had stayed in Moscow to study. Now, on the other hand, she could invite her mother to come and live with her "together with your aunts and the whole menage, including the piano." In a later letter he pursued this theme: ". . . for the first time, after all these years, I have the marvellous awareness that somewhere, out there, a family home awaits me. . . . For me there can be no home without you, home can only be where you are the mistress, where you are living."[12]

These fond thoughts of home and wife were doubtless intensified by the growing discipline and harsher regimen at the *sharashka*, especially since for Solzhenitsyn in particular the autumn of 1949 brought new and unwelcome responsibilities. A telephone tap on the American and Canadian embassies had caught a Soviet diplomat trying to warn the Americans about a Soviet atom spy in their midst and the imminent handing over, in a radio shop in Manhattan, of American atomic secrets for transmission to the Soviet Union.* The diplomat's identity was unknown, and tapes of the conversation had been brought to Marfino to see whether the acoustics brigade could help. Kopelev was the first to be informed of the affair. He was summoned in secrecy to Colonel Vasiliev's office, told to listen to the tapes and to the taped voices of the three chief suspects (recorded without their knowledge), and charged with the task of identifying which one of them was guilty. A special laboratory, to be known simply as "Laboratory No. 1," would be set up parallel with the Acoustics Laboratory and would be headed by Major Trachtman. Kopelev was asked to sign a solemn declaration of secrecy and told to say, if questioned by the other prisoners, that he was working on a special coding problem.[13]

Solzhenitsyn was not directly engaged in the atom-spy project, but at the risk of incurring a heavy new sentence, Kopelev divulged the secret to him and asked for his help with some of the mathematical problems involved. It is not clear whether Solzhenitsyn had any serious reservations about it at the time, but he willingly gave Kopelev the assistance he needed. It was only later that he hit upon the idea of making the hunt for the errant diplomat the central motif of *The First Circle* and developed the ironic implications of setting a group of political prisoners to assist their jailers in sending yet one

_____

* The suggestion has been made that this telephone call was in some way linked with the Rosenberg case, but no evidence exists to confirm it.

more victim to jail. As for Kopelev, not only did he entertain no doubts at all in the matter but he was passionately keen to identify the traitor and have him caught—in this he was at one with the authorities and fully shared their contempt for this act of anti-Sovietism. Perhaps at the back of his mind he also envisaged the inviting prospect of early release if he succeeded. At all events, Kopelev—with the help of Solzhenitsyn and a team of people to dictate a variety of texts—worked flat out to establish a method for the recognition of individual human voices and got so carried away that he convinced himself, and tried to convince Trachtman and Vasiliev, that he was on the verge of inventing a new science, which he dubbed "phonoscopy" (by analogy with dactyloscopy), according to which it would be possible to identify "voiceprints" as clearly and irrefutably as fingerprints.

The claims of the new science were never recognized, but it didn't take Kopelev and his team long to establish that the guilty caller was a diplomat with the unlikely name of Ivanov.* Alas, there was no reward for this discovery, perhaps because Ivanov and the other suspects were already under arrest. Given the methods of the time, it would have cost the MGB nothing simply to execute all three if punishment had been the object, but it appears that the police needed to know which one was guilty in order to establish that there were no accomplices. It turned out, however, that Ivanov had been acting alone. He had been on the eve of departing for Canada to become second secretary in the embassy there. He had learned of the atom secrets because one of his first tasks would be to receive the stolen documents and forward them to Moscow. Kopelev firmly believed (and believes) that Ivanov was simply out for gain and was intending to defect in Canada, like Kravchenko† before him, and claim a large material reward for services rendered. There is no evidence to support or refute this hypothesis, but it would appear that few idealists were left in the Soviet diplomatic corps by the autumn of 1949, and it is quite possible that Kopelev was right.

Kopelev was not blind to the implications of his work: he was, in effect, helping the security police to track down a "criminal," something he would not have agreed to in all circumstances. In this case, however, he felt that it was his patriotic duty, regardless of his general contempt for the security organs, to help track down a traitor who was betraying his country to the imperialists and frustrating the Soviet Union's laudable efforts to achieve atomic parity. In addition, he was carried away by the intellectual challenge and, like most of the prisoners at the *sharashka*, especially the scientists, was able to divorce his larger human, social, and political preoccupations from the work at hand. The same was true, to a much higher degree, of the "robot," Semyonov, and even of Professor Timofeyev in Laboratory No. 7, who was content to restrict his thoughts and energy to the scientific problems at hand

---

* The equivalent of Smith in English.

† Victor Kravchenko was a Soviet trade representative in Washington during the war. He defected in 1944 and wrote several books, of which the most widely known is *I Chose Freedom* (New York, 1946), which became a bestseller.

and forget his generalized hostility to the regime. The majority of the prisoners accepted the carrot-and-stick philosophy of their jailers more or less unthinkingly. If they were clever—or lucky—enough to make some sort of scientific breakthrough, they might just conceivably achieve a pardon. On the other hand, if they misbehaved or stepped out of line, they would be flung back into the camps whence they had come.

An exception to the general rule was Dimitri Panin. Having experienced almost the worst that the labour camps had to offer, Panin no longer feared them. He was determined to put the respite the *sharashka* offered him to good use, but felt that if he had to return to the camps, so be it. He devised for himself an elaborate plan of private study and self-improvement with which to occupy as much of his time as possible, regardless of whether it was in official working hours or during the small amount of spare time allotted the prisoners. Apart from working on his "language of maximum clarity," he had become interested in Hegel's three laws of dialectics and was trying to relate them to the processes of thermodynamics. His intention was to try to discover whether there were universal laws of development that could be applied in fields outside the realm of physics—notably sociology, biology, and theology. Yet he, too, in his own fashion, came under the spell of the *sharashka*'s scientific programme, and especially the cryptographical research that was being carried out in Laboratory No. 7. By a combination of bluff and daring, he succeeded in winning almost a whole year for himself in which to work alone on the problem of producing a viable design for a mechanical voice coder; after concentrating intensively on this problem, he finally solved it not only to his own satisfaction but also to that of Professor Timofeyev, the *sharashka*'s leading expert in cryptology. According to Panin, Timofeyev wanted to submit the design to the authorities as a joint project, confident that it would solve the problem of creating a scrambler telephone and earn them both a free pardon. But Panin flatly refused, on the grounds that this would be helping the regime he so detested. He had set out to create the design solely to satisfy his sense of pride and to compensate for an earlier failure on a similar project. Having succeeded, he burnt all his drawings and papers and turned his back on the *sharashka*'s research. Instead of doing what he should be doing, he read only what he wanted to and by early 1950 was volunteering to do chores around the compound instead of working in the design office.[14]

It may be that Panin's gloom and resignation had something to do with the tenth anniversary of his imprisonment. Kopelev writes that at round about this time, Panin withdrew into himself and went through a species of spiritual crisis,[15] which would not be surprising, given the usual attitude of labour-camp prisoners to significant dates and anniversaries. Soon after this, Panin began refusing to work on Sundays and generally made it clear that he didn't care whether he stayed in the *sharashka* or not. In his memoir he writes that he knew that this conspicuous insubordination was bound to result in his eventual expulsion from the institute and a return to the camps, but that he now regarded such a course as preferable to working for the authorities and prayed to God to give him the strength to survive.

Panin's example appears to have had a considerable impact on Solzhenitsyn. Panin's ability to rise above his immediate surroundings and to distance himself from the system, his disregard for physical comforts and his indifference to favours, and above all his magnificent gesture in inventing the required design for a scrambler telephone and then destroying it to keep it out of the hands of the authorities, sacrificing thereby a possible pardon and his freedom, must have seemed in the circumstances almost superhuman. Here was moral grandeur on a scale rarely witnessed, an example to fire the mind as well as the imagination.

Solzhenitsyn was later to make this incident one of the focal points of *The First Circle*—some of the best scenes in the novel are devoted to Sologdin. And he placed the moral gesture of refusing to collaborate with the regime at the centre of the plot: Nerzhin's own refusal to work on identifying the unknown diplomat's voice on the telephone is both the climax of the moral debate that the novel embodies and the cause of Nerzhin's downfall and consignment to Siberia. And the serious physical consequences of his refusal enhance and underline its moral authority.*

Kopelev suggests in his book that the circumstances of Solzhenitsyn's own departure from the *sharashka* appear to have been rather different from Nerzhin's in *The First Circle* and that the moral issue, though present in a generalized form, was probably not the basic motivation for his decision to leave. According to Kopelev, there was probably no "decision" at all in the conventional sense, but rather a change in attitude and a drift in behaviour that had predictable, but not necessarily inevitable, consequences.[16] This may be true in a narrow sense: Solzhenitsyn may not have exactly planned his departure, and he appears to have been taken by surprise at the moment when it occurred, but there is ample evidence to suggest that he was mentally and emotionally prepared for it.

As Solzhenitsyn's hopes for an amnesty and justice had faded, and his faith in the Soviet regime had waned, so had his sense of alienation increased, until he came to resemble Panin in his distaste and contempt for all forms of authority. The process was a gradual one and manifested itself in various ways. Chopping wood or raking leaves, for instance, was a subtle way of showing scorn, for it demonstrated a preference for menial manual labour over the more meaningful work that the authorities demanded of them in the laboratories. So long as it was confined to the early morning and the prisoners' own time, the authorities were prepared to tolerate it, but after destroying his drawings for a coder, Panin began to insist on chopping wood every Sunday and refused to put in any overtime, and after a while Solzhenitsyn started doing the same.

Another area in which Solzhenitsyn demonstrated his growing disdain

*In the longer, ninety-six-chapter version of *The First Circle*, Solzhenitsyn has downgraded Panin's role as an example of moral rectitude (cf. Richard Hallett's detailed examination of the two versions of Sologdin in the *Modern Language Review*, April 1983), but the moral gesture of refusing to collaborate remains central to the plot.

for the administration was in the matter of complaints. Already in his earlier camps, he had discovered that oral complaints were much more effective than written ones: the written complaints were simply thrown away, whereas an oral complaint would be heard by all the other prisoners and compelled some sort of response, even if it was usually negative. At the *sharashka* Solzhenitsyn had worked this up into a fine art. Collective complaints were categorically forbidden, so he would make a complaint about something ostensibly in a personal capacity, but in reality on behalf of them all. Complaints had to be made during the morning roll-call, and Solzhenitsyn's speciality lay in keeping his complaints terse and to the point, but also in rapping them out with great speed and precision, so that they were completed during the few seconds between the time the duty officer stepped back after completing his count and the moment when he turned to leave. For example, Solzhenitsyn discovered from the regulations that each prisoner was entitled to a daily ration of five grams of flour in his soup and that nobody was receiving it. Unable to protest on behalf of them all, he simply complained that it wasn't being added to his own soup: they would have to give it to them all if they gave it to him—and they did.[17] Solzhenitsyn had also been obliged to bombard the camp authorities to get his copy of Esenin's poems back (this, too, is described in *The First Circle*). And a similar thing happened, according to Reshetovskaya, when the authorities tried to confiscate one of the volumes of the Dahl dictionary. In the course of time, these complaints came to be regarded as a kind of performance or circus turn—word would go round beforehand when a particular complaint was due—and naturally, as Solzhenitsyn grew more reckless, his complaints became more pointed and outrageous. As he wrote of Nerzhin in *The First Circle*, he "was an insolent prisoner, always demanding his rights."[18]

Solzhenitsyn's changing view of himself and the *sharashka* was reflected in other ways. He tried consciously to slow himself down, to put a curb on his impatience and impetuousness and acquire more *gravitas*. At the end of 1949 he wrote to Natalia that his mood was more equable than before and that there was nothing left "of my old hasty and convulsive attitude to life." He was living, he felt, "in harmony with time"[19] and had lost his tendency to thoughtless action, rash decisions, and disregard for others. As he wrote of Nerzhin:

Although his fair hair, parted in the middle, was still thick, skeins of wrinkles had already formed around his eyes and mouth, and his forehead was deeply furrowed. The skin of his face looked as if it were slightly sagging for lack of fresh air. But what really made him seem old was his economy of movement— that wise economy of effort by which nature husbands the prisoner's flagging strength in the labour camps. True, there was no great need for it in the lax conditions of the *sharashka*, with a meat diet and freedom from back-breaking physical toil. But knowing the length of his sentence, Nerzhin was trying, as best he could, to acquire and fix this deliberateness of movement so that it would stay with him forever.[20]

Ivashov-Musatov did a pencil sketch of Solzhenitsyn at about this time. It shows that central parting, the hair flopping to either side, and the vertical scar on the forehead. The hatching is too dark to show any wrinkles, but the most striking feature of the portrait is the eyes. The movements may have become slow and the skin on the face slack, but the eyes shine out with all their old fire and defiance.

That same winter of 1949 Solzhenitsyn wrote to Natalia urging her to complete the divorce proceedings and give up writing to him. He said that her well-being was more important than "this illusion of family relations that long ago ceased to exist"[21] and that he did not wish to cast the slightest shadow on her. His motives for this apparent volte-face after his earlier tenderness are not clear. It seems he felt a genuine desire to help his wife and set her free if that was what she really wanted. He may also have been striking a lover's attitude, confident that she would reject his magnanimous offer. But above all he seems to have been experiencing a growing mood of disillusionment, not so much despair as a stoic resignation to his fate.

Solzhenitsyn's scepticism had led him, by the end of 1949, to a point where he no longer struggled to return to the society whose leaders had rejected him, and he was no longer sure that he even wanted to. Nor was he sure that he would ever be allowed to. He had learned that paragraph 11 of Article 58 in the charges against him meant that after his sentence he would be obliged to go into "perpetual exile." Who knew what that meant, or where he would be? And under what conditions? He became aware of his full helplessness in the face of the implacable logic of Gulag, and the mood of resignation induced by this awareness implied certain consequences. If his sentence was to be, in practical terms, "endless," what was the point of maintaining this "illusion of family relations," of hanging on at the *sharashka* when the hours were getting longer and longer and the discipline tougher, and when his duties were interfering more and more with his true vocation of writing?

In March 1950 Solzhenitsyn had his first meeting with Natalia since she had moved to Ryazan. She had chosen Ryazan over Gorky in order to be nearer him, but the effect of her move had nonetheless been to estrange them. In the first place, although not engaged in classified work, Natalia still felt obliged to maintain the fiction of being unmarried, and this meant that she could no longer send parcels: in a small town like Ryazan, the news would have got out immediately. The sending of parcels was therefore taken over by Natalia's aunt Nina in Rostov. Secondly and for the same reason, Natalia was obliged to be particularly circumspect about her correspondence, and this had had a dampening effect on both of them. Thirdly, Natalia was quite simply—and naturally—caught up in her busy new life as a lecturer. She had two courses of lectures to give, as well as taking practical sessions in the laboratory, and she still kept up her piano playing and took part in a number of concerts. Her mother had been to stay for a while, and Aunt Nina had come from Rostov and spent the whole of the winter and spring with her. That very month, moreover, Natalia had been appointed head of the chemistry department.

Their meeting took place in Butyrki Prison and was subdued. Natalia repeated her assurances, already given by letter, that she had no intention of proceeding with the divorce and impressed upon Solzhenitsyn the fact that she still loved him. According to her, Solzhenitsyn was pensive. Despite his advice to her to leave him, he confessed that he had done this with his head, while his heart, as he had written in one of his letters, "had shrunk with fear—could this possibly come to pass?"[22] He also said he now regretted the fact that they had had no children, perhaps sensing that without this bond, their marriage might not survive the strains that lay ahead. Natalia, who once upon a time had felt this loss keenly, was matter-of-fact about it. It was probably too late, she said, for them to think of that now.

This meeting turned out to be their last for a very long time, for soon afterwards Solzhenitsyn set in motion the chain of events that led to his expulsion from the *sharashka* and his removal from Moscow.[23] The incident that triggered it occurred in the spring of 1950, in the Acoustics Laboratory, where Solzhenitsyn was working. The acoustics brigade was then testing a number of prototypes for a secret telephone line, based more or less closely on an American system called the "voice coder." One of the prototypes had been invented by Colonel Vasiliev, who was not only the chief of the institute but also a sound engineer of some accomplishment; when his device was tested, however, it proved to be one of the weaker models. It was Solzhenitsyn's task, as chief tester, to report on the different prototypes, and he appeared to take particular relish in criticizing Vasiliev's invention and in squashing all Vasiliev's scientific objections and arguments in its favour in front of the other prisoners. Kopelev writes that he warned Solzhenitsyn afterwards of the danger of this exploit. Only recently a young colleague of theirs, Valentin Martynov (Valentulya in *The First Circle*—the nickname was invented by Lev), had been dispatched to the punishment cells in Butyrki for arguing with Vasiliev over another prototype, and Kopelev, who knew Vasiliev much better than Solzhenitsyn did, was aware of the colonel's ire when his pride was injured.

Solzhenitsyn dismissed the warnings as unwarranted. He had built up what he regarded as an unassailable position as director of the articulation experiments. He had created, as Kopelev himself writes, "something that had never existed before—a scientifically . . . based theory and a practical methodology for the carrying out of experiments in articulation. He had become an outstanding director of the articulation readers and was truly indispensable, a fact that was recognized by everyone who had seen his work and was in a position to judge." For this reason, writes Kopelev, Solzhenitsyn was confident that Major Trachtman, if no one else, would defend his position if he was threatened—his work was essential to the smooth working of the whole laboratory. A few days later, however, Trachtman informed Solzhenitsyn that he was being removed from articulation work and would probably be transferred to the engineering design office to work with some other mathematicians on cryptology.[24]

It seems that Solzhenitsyn still had a chance to hang on at the *sharashka* so long as he would agree to do cryptology (according to Herzenberg, Trachtman was a strong supporter of Solzhenitsyn), but Solzhenitsyn was not prepared to compromise. By a strange coincidence, the civilian consultant who arrived in the *sharashka* that week to evaluate the work of the cryptologists turned out to be one of Solzhenitsyn's old mathematics professors from Rostov University. Learning that his former student was there, the professor called him in for a friendly chat and outlined the sort of work that the cryptological group would be doing from now on. Emboldened by the professor's informality, Solzhenitsyn told him in no uncertain terms that he was not interested in mathematical work and wanted to stay where he was. He was a person of some consequence in the Acoustics Laboratory and was making a real contribution to science, whereas in Laboratory No. 7 he would be just one of a crowd and easily expendable. The professor listened to him in polite silence and said nothing, and Solzhenitsyn went back to chopping wood and raking leaves (this was the way he had been filling in his time since being removed from his job in the Acoustics Laboratory). It seems that he may have imagined he was safe for a while, and that he expected to survive in the *sharashka* at least through the summer. For security reasons, it was customary for prisoners to be taken off secret work well in advance of their transfer elsewhere. But on 19 May 1950, only days after his meeting with the Rostov professor, when he and Panin were raking leaves in the yard, they were suddenly summoned to the guardhouse: "Panin and Solzhenitsyn, gather your things and get ready to move out!" Taken by surprise, Solzhenitsyn just had time to destroy some of his notes, entrust other writings and his poems to Kopelev for safe-keeping, and grab volume 3 of Dahl before hurrying to the administration block to undergo the final formalities. There he was obliged to hand in his prison clothing and put on his old garments, including his voluminous army greatcoat and a precious pair of felt boots. The prison rules forbade departing prisoners from taking a single scrap of paper with them, but he was allowed to take Dahl. Even so, he and the others were subjected to a painstaking search before being hustled into a prison van and driven off to Butyrki. Kopelev took care of the rest of his books, including the remaining three volumes of Dahl and his battered Esenin anthology, and with the help of another prisoner, who was amnestied in 1951, succeeded in smuggling everything, except the Esenin book, out to safety.* Solzhenitsyn and Panin were kept for just over a month in Butyrki (where they were soon joined by Peretz Herzenberg, who was being punished for his informer trick), and on 24 June 1950 they were shipped out to an unknown destination. All Solzhenitsyn knew was that their train would be heading east.[25]

*Kopelev names a former prisoner, later a free worker at the *sharashka*, Gumer Izmailov, as being responsible for smuggling Solzhenitsyn's books and papers out. The Esenin book was entrusted to Kopelev's girl-friend on the security staff, who later claimed to have thrown it away.

16

NOT QUITE SIBERIA

SOLZHENITSYN'S NEARLY THREE years in the *sharashka* had probably saved his life. Had he been sent straight from New Jerusalem or Kaluga Gate to continue working in the hard-labour camps it is doubtful whether he would have survived, for his body was too weak, and his mind unprepared, for the full rigours of the archipelago (he later said as much in *The Gulag Archipelago*).[1] In a sense, his earlier instinct had been right: he needed to become a trusty in order to survive. And at Marfino he had been a sort of super-trusty—as all the imprisoned scientists were in comparison with the uncertain position of the trusties in the regular camps. This privileged situation had enabled him to survive, to regain his strength, and to get his second wind. His friendships, his debates, his voracious reading, and his literary exercises had also made the *sharashka* the most rewarding stage of his "university" education in the camps; it was the richest and most varied cultural environment he was ever to find himself in. And it provided the material for his first, and in many ways best, novel: *The First Circle*.

But now Solzhenitsyn was to explore the archipelago further and learn more about that strange and sprawling empire, beginning with its lines of communication. The journey east was Solzhenitsyn's first experience of one of the key moments in the labour-camp prisoner's career—a prison transport. As he later wrote in *The First Circle*, "a transport has the same life-or-death significance for a prisoner as being wounded for a soldier. And just as a wound can be light or serious, curable or fatal, so a transport can be long or short, a momentary distraction or a shortcut to death."[2]

The "shortcuts to death" were the notorious red cattle-cars, equipped with only bare boards for sleeping on, two tiny holes under the roof for ventilation, a hole in the floor for a latrine, and occasionally a primitive iron stove, for which there was rarely any fuel. The way that prisoners were packed into these cars like sardines, locked in, and fed at irregular intervals has been vividly described by a number of writers, notably the Polish ex-prisoners who contributed to a collection of reminiscences on the subject, *The Dark Side of the Moon*, published immediately after the war.* On a long journey in the cattle-cars, you were likely either to suffocate to death, to starve to death, or, in winter, to freeze to death before arrival. Solzhenitsyn and Panin, however, travelled in the alternative to these—the only slightly less notorious "Stolypin cars," invented, apparently, by Nicholas II's minister of the interior Piotr Stolypin, in the early part of the century, but brought to perfection, like so many other instruments of tsarist repression, by the tsar's revolutionary successors. Here is one of many descriptions of this ingenious means of transport.

> [Stolypins] are the same as normal passenger coaches: a narrow corridor runs the full length of one side, with the separate cabins or compartments on the other side. The connecting doors are not solid but barred. There are no windows whatever. One side of the coach is completely blank, while the windows facing the corridor are filled with bars. None of this can be seen from outside, how-ever—they are covered with blinds—so that to look at it's a coach just like any other coach, and no one would guess that it's carrying convicts. . . .
>
> Each compartment has three shelves on either side, one above the other. Between the middle ones a board can be fixed to form a single, solid bunk. This means that generally there is sleeping room for seven—eight if you crowd up tight—but usually they cram twelve to fifteen people into each compartment or cage, and sometimes even more. And their luggage as well. And everything is stop-pered up tight, so that there is no chance of any fresh air getting in, except perhaps during a halt, when they open the door to take somebody out or shove an extra one in.
>
> The corridor is patrolled by soldiers armed with pistols. If a soldier happens to be a decent sort, he will open one of the corridor windows in passing, and for a short while a draught of fresh air will blow through the bars of the door. But some of the escorts won't give you any air no matter how much you beg them. And then the cons choke in their cages like fish thrown up on the beach.[3]

The point of shuttering the carriages was to prevent the public from seeing in and to give the impression that they were innocuous, an illusion that was fostered by their general resemblance to luggage vans and the fact that, like luggage vans, they were generally coupled immediately behind the engine (though, to judge by a comment of Solzhenitsyn's in *The First Circle*, their true function was an open secret: "You have all seen them being loaded at our railway stations, but you fearfully lowered your gaze and patriotically turned away, lest the guard commander should suspect you of something and call you over to explain").[4]

---

* *The Dark Side of the Moon* (London: Faber, 1946; New York: Scribners, 1947), with an intro-duction by T. S. Eliot.

It was possible to stuff as many as thirty-six people into a Stolypin compartment (that was the highest figure supplied by Solzhenitsyn's sources for *The Gulag Archipelago*), and Panin had travelled with as many as twenty-six (four on top, eight in the middle, and fourteen on the bottom) before his arrival at the *sharashka*.

The literature of the past fifteen years is rich in accounts of travel in these Stolypin carriages: the heat, the suffocation, the stench, the hunger, and the thirst. The usual food on such journeys is a steady diet of salt fish. The salt creates a raging thirst that is never satisfied by the meagre water ration that is handed out. And yet this water ration is sufficient to create biological urges that the guards will reluctantly satisfy only once a day—with consequences that can easily be imagined.

Solzhenitsyn and Panin were therefore relatively lucky to find themselves fifteen in a compartment—only double what it was built for—and allowed out to visit the toilet twice a day, morning and evening. The guards also agreed to open the windows on the corridor side, thus mitigating a little the stifling summer heat. The aspect of the journey that Solzhenitsyn found most heartening, however, was a spirit of freedom and defiance among the prisoners. He had already detected a change of atmosphere in Butyrki. The newly sentenced prisoners he met there had almost all received twenty-five-year terms, which was virtually a life sentence. But far from cowing them, according to Solzhenitsyn, "these twenty-five-year terms had created a new atmosphere among the prisoners. The regime had blasted us with everything it had. Now it was the prisoners' turn to say a few words—words that were free and no longer inhibited or uttered under duress, words that we had never in our lives been able to utter before, but which were essential if we were ever to understand our situation and unite."[5]

As a result of this new spirit of freedom, the political prisoners now defiantly rejected such terms as "Fascist" and "enemy of the people" to describe them. Solzhenitsyn heard prisoners vehemently answering back and even winning arguments with the guards, for which they went unpunished. And at the train's various halts not everyone averted their gaze. In the quiet station of Torbeyevo, an old peasant woman, catching sight of the prisoners through the bars of their carriage, wept silently and made the sign of the cross over them. At another halt a cheerful young woman stepped up to the Stolypin car, ignoring the threats of the guards, insisted on talking to the prisoners, and handed in a packet of cigarettes. She herself had done time in a labour camp and knew what awaited them.

A similar atmosphere prevailed in the Kuibyshev transit prison, where they were kept hanging about for over a month. The prison was housed in some converted stables, whose ancient roof was propped up with crooked tree trunks and gnarled branches. In Solzhenitsyn's cell of about 120 prisoners, there was plenty of room between the two rows of double-tiered bunks, and the mood of the prisoners was as free and easy as in the trains. One who attracted Solzhenitsyn's attention was a Ukrainian nationalist, Pavel Boroniuk, a veritable giant of a man who had earned near-universal praise by severely beating up two professional crooks who had tried to plunder the politicals in the neighbouring cell. Another was a thin and frail young Jewish student, Vladimir Gershuni, nephew of the celebrated Socialist Revolutionary terrorist Grigori Gershuni,* who despite his physical frailty insisted on challenging the guards and rejecting any form of insult. According to Panin, Gershuni had a theory that all Jews had to be brave, and he insisted on demonstrating it whenever he could. On one occasion in Kuibyshev he yelled at the KGB security officer, "Don't dare call us counter-revolutionaries! That's all in the past. We're revolutionaries again now—only this time against the Soviet regime!"—and went unpunished for it. On another he was attacked by one of the trusties after objecting to being called a "Fascist" and had to be rescued by the redoubtable Boroniuk, who was slashed with a knife for his pains.[6]

Boroniuk was one of a large number of Ukrainian nationalists, or Banderites,† as they were called, who had been sentenced in the early years after the war and were now on their way to Siberia. There were also large numbers of Estonians, Lithuanians, and Latvians from the newly annexed Baltic states, and Solzhenitsyn found himself meditating on the injustices done to these smaller nations by the Russians under Soviet leadership.

> They had harmed no one, lived a quiet, orderly life, and a more moral life than ours—and now they were to blame because we were hungry, because they lived cheek by jowl with us and stood in our path to the sea.
> "I was ashamed to be Russian!" cried Herzen when we were choking the life out of Poland. I felt doubly ashamed in the presence of these inoffensive and defenceless people.[7]

The problem of the Ukraine was both more complex and more immediate for Solzhenitsyn, because Solzhenitsyn was himself half-Ukrainian. As he was later to write in volume 3 of *The Gulag Archipelago*, "Russia and the Ukraine are united in my blood, my heart, my thoughts."[8] Nevertheless, he came to the reluctant conclusion that even the Ukrainians should be allowed to secede and found their own state if that was what they truly desired, though he still cherished the hope that in the end they would voluntarily choose to be reunited with the Russians.

Another encounter in Kuibyshev that made a lasting impression on both Solzhenitsyn and Panin (they both described it later in their books) was with a Swedish prisoner called Erik Arvid Andersen. According to his own account, Andersen was the son of a Swedish millionaire and the nephew of the English

---

*Grigori Gershuni (1870–1908) was a founder and leader of the Socialist Revolutionary party and was shot in 1908. Vladimir Gershuni had been sentenced to ten years in 1949. In the 1960s he became a leading dissident and in 1969 was committed to a psychiatric hospital.
† So called for their support of the Ukrainian nationalist leader Stepan Bandera, who during the Second World War first collaborated with and then opposed the German occupation forces with the aim of establishing an independent Ukraine.

general Robertson. During the war he had volunteered for service with the British army, had taken part in the landings at Normandy, and had fought in the Ardennes. Later he joined the Swedish army and visited Moscow as a member of a Swedish military delegation. Despite his wealthy background, he was already an admirer of the Soviet system, and this visit confirmed his opinions. On his return to Sweden he wrote a couple of articles in praise of communism and shortly afterwards was posted to West Berlin. As a member of a military mission, he had free access to East Berlin, where he started an affair with an East German singer. On one of his visits to her flat, he was picked up by MGB agents and whisked off to Moscow. His pro-Communist articles had brought him to the notice of the Soviet authorities, and they tried to cajole and blackmail him into writing another article damning the West and praising the Stalinist regime. To their surprise he refused. For a whole year he was kept under house arrest in Moscow, plied with books on Marxism-Leninism, and given a Russian tutor. Foreign Minister Andrei Gromyko, who knew his father, tried personally to persuade him to change his mind, and when Andersen persisted in his stubborness, the public prosecutor, Andrei Vyshinsky, was brought in to threaten him. Nothing worked, and in the summer of 1950 Abakumov, the minister of state security, personally read him his sentence—twenty years' hard labour.

As far as Kuibyshev, Andersen had been transported in a separate, private compartment and throughout his two years of confinement had been kept apart from the other prisoners and given special treatment. He still had a full head of hair ("a unique miracle in the world of Gulag,"[9] as Solzhenitsyn called it in *The Gulag Archipelago*), and his Swedish officer's uniform was immaculate. But now, whether by accident or design, he had been pushed into the Kuibyshev stables, and it was difficult to say who was the more shocked—he or his new cell-mates. Since his Russian was still rudimentary, whereas he was fluent in English, French, and German, he was quickly taken up by Solzhenitsyn and Panin, who were able to converse with him in one of his better languages. They were fascinated by this exotic creature from the West, whose story outstripped all but the most fantastic Gulag odysseys for romance and drama, while their bewilderment over his psychology and attitudes prefigured some of the later difficulties and disenchantments they were to encounter when they themselves came to the West.

For instance, how could the son of a millionaire become so enamoured of communism and even go so far as to extol it in newspaper articles? There was nothing in Marxism-Leninism, or in Soviet experience, to explain such a paradox. According to Marx, "being defines consciousness." Even more perplexing was the fact that a serving military officer could permit himself such a luxury. Anything remotely similar in the Soviet Union would be rewarded with a bullet in the head for treason—but in any case was unthinkable. It seemed to them that such a man might exist if he was a corrupt schemer or a credulous fool, but how then explain the fact that after he had been brought to Moscow and installed in a luxury apartment, with the offer of a fat pension for life, expensive food and drink and as many women as he liked, he nonetheless refused point-blank to collaborate and to write, from Moscow, exactly the same kind of article that he had written, in freedom and of his own free will, when still in the West? Such behaviour had baffled his captors, and it baffled Solzhenitsyn and Panin. Such firmness of purpose and principle, such steely resolve and stubborn resistance, were supposed to be the preserve of Russians, rather than of effete, compromising Westerners, especially left-leaning liberals from the upper reaches of society. Another thing that fascinated them was Andersen's unmoving contempt for his Soviet captors—a contempt that was so securely rooted in a different set of values and so unquestioning in its assumption of superiority that it differed in kind from the still-tentative and hardly won contempt that Solzhenitsyn himself was beginning to feel. There was also Andersen's continuing and implacable hostility to the Germans, expressed in a violent argument with a German *Wehrmacht* officer in Kuibyshev with whom it had never occurred to any of the Russians to quarrel. Government rhetoric was one thing, but real-life relations were something else. Government rhetoric also asserted that the Western allies had not really fought their hardest in the war against the Germans, because their hearts hadn't been in it, and Solzhenitsyn had absorbed some of that attitude. Yet here was a Westerner who far outstripped the Russians in genuine, unfeigned hostility towards the Germans. Finally, Andersen was as fiercely patriotic and as convinced of the wisdom of his wartime leaders as any Russian. Despite his fashionably leftist leanings, he passionately believed in the correctness of the policies of Roosevelt and Churchill and warmly defended them from the attacks and gibes of Solzhenitsyn and Panin, refusing to accept the Berlin blockade as a success for Stalin, or Solzhenitsyn and Panin's assertions of Soviet superiority in arms and tactics.

None of this got in the way of their friendship. Andersen was convinced that he would soon be rescued by the West from his Soviet jailers and invited his two companions, "if they ever went to the West," to visit him in Stockholm. None of them then dreamt that Panin and Solzhenitsyn would both end up in the West or that both would seek out Andersen's family in order to learn of his fate. But neither was successful, and Andersen's fate remains unknown to this day.*

In August 1950, after a month at Kuibyshev, Solzhenitsyn, Panin, Gershuni, and a number of other prisoners from the stables were transported east to Omsk, where exactly one hundred years beforehand, in January 1850, Dostoyevsky had been brought to serve his term of penal servitude. It is instructive to compare the circumstances of these two different arrivals.

Dostoyevsky and two fellow political prisoners had been met at their transit prison in Tobolsk by four of the wives of the Decembrists, still in

---

*In a later footnote to *The Gulag Archipelago*, Solzhenitsyn writes that he now believes that Andersen was probably not his real name and that he might just as well have been a Norwegian as a Swede. Many details of his story had been shown by a specialist in these matters to be false or implausible, but the essential facts of his imprisonment and special status are beyond dispute.

exile there, who had arranged a meeting with them in the prison inspector's office; the women gave Dostoyevsky and his companions a good dinner and handed over gifts of warm clothing and a copy of the gospels, the only book allowed them. It is true that the prisoners were in irons, but the wives arranged for Dostoyevsky and one of his companions to travel to Omsk by horse-sledge, instead of being marched there, and were able to persuade the accompanying gendarmes to halt the sledge en route, "as arranged in advance" (according to one witness),[10] in order to bid the prisoners a last farewell.

Solzhenitsyn and his companions were not in irons but were transported in a crowded Stolypin carriage under armed guard. They were fed on herrings and water and were forbidden, on pain of being shot, to make any contact with the civilian population. The only clothes they were allowed were those they had been arrested in or had acquired (and managed to preserve) while in jail. Solzhenitsyn still wore his officer's tunic and greatcoat and carried the suitcase that had accompanied him on his first journey under arrest from the front. Another difference was that in Dostoyevsky's transport there were just three political prisoners among hundreds of thieves, whereas in the Soviet era, the position was exactly the reverse: among the hundreds of political prisoners there was a mere handful of thieves (moreover, the political prisoners were not acknowledged as such and were not granted a special status).

Upon their arrival in Omsk, Solzhenitsyn's contingent was made to squat by the railway line to await a fresh lot of guards. It was dusk and in the background, behind the lines of stationary wagons and carriages that surrounded them, they could hear the station loudspeakers playing dance music. After a long wait, they were squashed into prison vans and taken to the Omsk jail.

Solzhenitsyn thought of Dostoyevsky and found that very little had changed since Dostoyevsky's time. The jail had been built by Catherine the Great and "wasn't like any old Gulag transit prison hastily knocked together from matchwood."

> It was a formidable jail . . . and its dungeons were particularly terrible. You could never imagine a better film set than one of its underground cells. The small, square window gave onto the well of an oblique shaft that rose to ground level. The thickness of the window's sides—three metres—gave you an idea of what the walls were like. The cell had no ceiling but was overhung with massive intersecting vaults. One wall was soaking wet where the water seeped through from the surrounding soil and formed a puddle on the floor.[11]

Ironically, it was Dostoyevsky who had been accommodated in a dilapidated matchwood shack, whereas Solzhenitsyn's home was one of the dungeons, though only for a couple of weeks. His mood was still surprisingly buoyant. He listened with great enthusiasm to a church warden (no less) singing popular revolutionary songs and to a Civil War veteran recounting popular adventure tales for the entertainment of the other prisoners; and he himself organized an evening of comic entertainment, in which Vladimir Gershuni shone by retelling humorous stories by the post-revolutionary writers Mikhail Zoshchenko and Victor Shklovsky. As had become his custom at the *sharashka*, Solzhenitsyn did not stay with the revelry until it was over but withdrew early to read.

From Omsk they were taken to Pavlodar, where they were kept in the town's permanent jail, since no transit prison existed there. But it offered a sharp contrast with Omsk. "By twentieth-century standards this was a jail to reassure, rather than horrify, to inspire laughter rather than terror. A spacious, peaceful yard, with wretched grass growing here and there, divided by reassuringly low fences into little squares for exercise. The bars on the second-floor cell windows were widely spaced and there were no muzzles, so that you could stand on the window-sill and inspect the neighborhood."[12]

It was a last rest before the ordeals that lay ahead. Pavlodar, with its squat, single-storey houses, mean streets, and beer stall opposite the prison entrance, seemed to Solzhenitsyn like an overgrown village—a relic of the pre-revolutionary past. On their arrival the prisoners had been marched through the streets, as in Dostoyevsky's time, for lack of the sickeningly familiar prison vans to take them and the whole atmosphere was easier than in Kuibyshev and Omsk. After a few days, however, they were collected by an armed escort ("I had seen many such escorts in my time," writes Panin, "but had only heard about the sort of cutthroats who made up the present one")[13] and driven out across the broad river Irtysh and into the Kazakhstanian desert to cover the last lap of their journey.

This final stage was accomplished by night in open lorries specially equipped for the purpose. The front sections of the lorries, including the cabs, were encased in metal cages. Armed guards sat behind these cages and on the roofs of the cabs with cocked rifles pointing directly at the prisoners, who were packed onto the floor at the rate of twenty-five to a lorry. They were so tightly crammed that they could barely move, and in this fashion they were jogged and jolted over the roadless wilderness for eight hours, with only a toilet stop to relieve their stiffness and discomfort.

For Solzhenitsyn this last lap of his voyage to the unknown heart of Gulag was unforgettable. He wrote later that his very senses seem to have been sharpened by the long anticipation of it, while his mind grappled with the meaning of this journey and the mystery of what lay ahead of him.

We crossed the Irtysh. We rode for a long time through water-meadows, then over dead flat steppe. The breath of the Irtysh, the freshness of the evening on the steppe, the scent of wormwood, enveloped us whenever we stopped for a few minutes and the swirling clouds of light-grey dust raised by the wheels sank to the ground. Thickly powdered with this dust, we looked at the road behind us (we were not allowed to turn our heads), kept silent (we were not allowed to talk), and thought about the camp we were heading for with its strange, difficult, un-Russian name. We had read the name on our case files hanging upside down from the top shelf in the Stolypin: EKIBASTUZ. But nobody could imagine

where it was on the map. . . . We even supposed that it might be somewhere
quite near to the Chinese border. . . .

On and on we drove. Darkness fell. It was clear from the enormous stars
hanging in the black sky that we were heading south-south-west.[14]

Just before midnight the lorries ground to a halt beside a high wooden
fence in the middle of the dark plain. The fence was floodlit and shone like a
beacon in the immense blackness of the steppe, while the dimmer lights of
an adjoining civilian settlement winked dimly a little way off. They drove
through enormous double gates into the living compound, where more lights
blazed in the serried ranks of wooden barrack huts that stretched out before
them. As in Solzhenitsyn's early jails and labour camps, the blindingly bright
lights were kept switched on all night, throwing into relief the stout bars on
the windows and the padlocks on the doors. There followed the familiar
routine of roll-call, bath, haircut, fumigation of clothing, queuing at the stores
to hand in all personal belongings, and finally assignment to their barrack
huts, where they were locked in for the night. It was the third week of August
1950.

Ekibastuz was part of a large complex of labour camps based on Dzhezkazgan, in the semi-arid steppes of Kazakhstan in Soviet Central Asia—not
quite Siberia, but almost. The entire complex, which contained sixty thousand men at its peak, consisted of so-called special camps, a new type of camp
introduced by Stalin in 1948 that took its inspiration from the tsarist system
of katorga, or hard labour. Stalin's intention was apparently to consolidate
and rationalize the entire labour-camp system as an essential component of
the economy. In the name of this rationalization, mixed camps were brought
to an end and men prisoners rigorously separated from the women. "Politicals" were also separated from ordinary criminals, and since, according to
Soviet custom, a political prisoner was regarded as far more dangerous than
a mere thief or murderer, they were placed in these special camps. A small
nucleus of professional crooks was retained in each camp to run the kitchens
and stores, to occupy all the positions of privilege and to act as informers,
but their numbers in the special camps were drastically reduced after 1948,
and for the most part they remained in the ordinary "corrective labour camps"
of the type Solzhenitsyn had been in before the sharashka.

As if to emphasize both the permanence of these new establishments
and the uniquely dangerous character of their inmates, the special camps
were reinforced with double fences of barbed wire, between which Alsatians
prowled leashed to a wire. A ploughed strip was created round the perimeter
to reveal footprints if anyone attempted to escape, sharp-pointed stakes were
set into the ground inclined towards the living compound at a forty-five-
degree angle, the guards' weapons were updated and increased, and in some
camps machine-guns were set up on the paths used by the prisoners to cover
their movements from the living compound to the work compound, or from
barrack hut to canteen. Everything was done to persuade the prisoners that

security here was absolute and that they were here for life. Release at the end of one's sentence was made to appear the exception rather than the rule (the commandant of one such camp complex boasted that in eight years he had released only one prisoner) and contacts with home and family were reduced to a minimum—two letters home a year. Incoming letters and parcels, however, were allowed at the rate of one a month, and could be acknowledged by postcards. As usual it was strictly forbidden to reveal the location of the camp or any details about the regime inside it, and all letters in and out were censored as a matter of course. To ensure security and mislead the rest of the population as to the exact nature of these establishments, the special camps were also endowed with euphemistic names. As Solzhenitsyn later noted in *The Gulag Archipelago*, it was as though some crazed poet had been called in to invent picturesque titles: "Lake Camp," "River Camp," "Meadow Camp," and so on. Who would have suspected the savage reality behind such bucolic names? Ekibastuz was part of the huge Steplag, or "Steppe Camp," to begin with, and was later renamed Lugovoi, or "Meadow Camp," and then Peshchanlag, or "Sand Camp."

In keeping with the harsh and unremitting discipline that was maintained in the special camps, Solzhenitsyn and his group were bullied by the bath-house orderlies, the store-room trusties, the warders, and the guards from the moment of their arrival. Every effort was made to inspire fear of the "special" camps, to suggest that they were more to be dreaded than anything else the prisoners had ever known and that any violations would be met with the utmost severity and brutality.

On the day after their arrival, before it had been determined exactly where any of the prisoners would work, they were temporarily employed on a variety of *ad hoc* chores, and Gershuni was ordered to dig a hole for a lamppost. Being both physically slight and weakened by the long transport, he was unable to keep up the requisite pace, as a result of which he was punched in the face and cursed by one of the trusties. Ever tense and highly strung, Gershuni threw down his crowbar and went to the commandant's office to complain. As a reward he was given eighteen days in the punishment cells, followed immediately by two months' disciplinary regime (hard labour by day, confinement to the cells by night). Thinking to escape this punishing routine by reporting sick, Gershuni tried staying in his bunk one morning and requesting a transfer to the medical post, but two burly warders seized him by the ankles and dragged him out feet first, in just his underpants, to where the other prisoners were waiting on morning parade. Gershuni resisted furiously and in the end was handcuffed and dragged back to the punishment cells, where he was kicked and beaten into unconsciousness. Later he was accused of "terrorism" for having attempted to slow his captors by clutching at anything, including some stones lying on the ground, that would halt their progress as they dragged him along. But the charge was just another form of intimidation and was dropped.

For the first day or two, the new arrivals were able to look around a bit and take their bearings. Ekibastuz had been founded exactly a year before, in August 1949, and was still not finished, although it had grown in that time from a few hundred men to nearly four thousand. The original founders had lived in tents and dug-outs on the open steppe, but now the prisoners occupied prefabricated barrack huts of a Finnish design, more of which were going up all the time. Solzhenitsyn was allocated to Hut No. 9. Each hut had a hut commander, deputy commander, and group of trusties to keep order, some of whom occupied separate cubicles of their own, while the rest of the trusties occupied a hut by themselves. As in Solzhenitsyn's early camps, all posts of responsibility in the kitchen, canteen, and stores were held by trusties, while another group of trusties monopolized the labour-assignment posts in the work compound.

After two days Solzhenitsyn's group was issued with camp numbers. First they had their fingerprints taken (this had never been done in the corrective labour camps), and then they were photographed with a little board hung round their neck displaying their number. They were also issued with four white patches that had to be sewn onto the chest, back, and left knee of their camp clothing and on the front of their peaked caps. The same numbers were then painted on these patches by the camp "artist."

The imposition of these numbers and the attempts of the camp authorities to enforce them as the sole means of identification, replacing names, seem to have burned themselves deeply into Solzhenitsyn's consciousness and to have remained forever afterwards a symbol of humiliation and dehumanization. In volume 3 of *The Gulag Archipelago*, he devotes three pages to them, describing exactly what they were made of, what they looked like, and how they were sewn on, pointing out the absurdity of tailors being appointed to cut holes in the padded jackets and trousers where the patches were to go so that they couldn't be torn off without exposure if the prisoners later escaped. In the barrack huts, a wooden board was affixed to each bunk displaying the prisoner's number, so that the warders could see it at a glance, and numbers were used on the work rolls and at roll-call in the mornings and evenings instead of names. At one point in *The Gulag Archipelago*, Solzhenitsyn denies that the impact of the numbers was chiefly psychological: "The numbers were vexatious not because of their psychological or moral effects, as the bosses intended, but for a purely practical reason—that on pain of a spell in the cooler we had to waste our leisure hours sewing up hems that had come unstitched, getting the figures touched up by the 'artist,' or searching for fresh rags to replace patches torn at work."[15] It is true that these considerations weighed heavily with a man obsessed with hoarding every minute of his free time, but Solzhenitsyn's assertion is belied not only by the space assigned to the numbers in *The Gulag Archipelago* but also by the way they form a veritable leitmotiv in *A Day in the Life of Ivan Denisovich*, including a scene where Ivan Denisovich has them renewed by the artist and meditates on the problems they cause (they also featured prominently in Solzhenitsyn's screenplay *The Tanks Know the Truth*). Finally, there is the evidence of the meticulous care with which Solzhenitsyn smuggled out his camp uniform, including the numbers, when he went into exile, and photographed himself in it; two of these photographs were subsequently included in volume 3 of *The Gulag Archipelago*.

Once the numbers had been allocated, the prisoners were assigned to brigades and sent out to work. Twenty-five members of Solzhenitsyn's group, consisting mainly of western Ukrainians, banded together to form their own brigade and were able to persuade the work supervisor to allow them to choose the fearless Boroniuk as their brigade leader. Their first task was to dig foundations for more prefabricated barrack huts to be erected, but some of the Ukrainians turned out to be skilled bricklayers, and after a fortnight the authorities turned them into a bricklaying brigade. For a while they worked on building houses for some of the free workers at the camp, but then were transferred inside the living compound to work on the camp jail. This jail, the very one in which Gershuni was already spending two months, was unfinished—only half of it had been built, and Solzhenitsyn's brigade was detailed to complete it.

It is not clear how conscious the prisoners were of the irony implicit in this task. It was the usual and universally accepted practice for prisoners to build their own camps. The men in tents who had founded Ekibastuz had been obliged to erect the fences, barbed wire, and watch-towers that would subsequently ensure that they never escaped. Barrack huts, kitchens, canteens, factories, mills, mines, railway tracks, roads—all were built by that same slave labour, which in Stalin's grand design was the key both to the construction of the Gulag system and to the development of Siberia itself.

No one perhaps gave it much thought at the time, but the paradox was apparent to Solzhenitsyn, who wrote a poem called "The Bricklayer" to express the complexity of his feelings.

> Like him of whom the poet sings, a mason, I
> Tame the wild stones to make a jail. No city jail—
> Here naught but fences, huts, and watch-towers meet the eye,
> And in the limpid sky the buzzards sail.
> None but the wind moves on the steppe—none to inquire
> For whom I raise these walls . . . why dogs, machine-guns, wire
> Are still not jail enough . . .
> . . . .
> Breaking, trimming, hammer to merry hammer calls.
> Wall after gloomy wall springs up, walls within walls;
> While we mix mortar, we smoke and await with delight—
> Extra bread, more slops in our bowls tonight.
> Back on our perch we peer into cells walled with stones—
> Black pits, whose depths will muffle tortured comrades' groans.[16]

Another irony of these months of bricklaying is that they provided Solzhenitsyn with his most vivid experience of what one might call the poetry of labour. At Kaluga Gate he had learned something of the satisfaction to be derived from physical tasks like painting and the laying of parquet floors, but there he had been a novice, and in too much emotional turmoil to savour these moments and extract much enjoyment from them. Now he felt himself to be a veteran. He knew how to husband his forces and knew exactly how much to give of himself and how much to hold back. And he had lost those wild hopes of an amnesty and imminent release. He was calmer, more at peace with himself, more dogged in his determination to endure. "Let things take their natural course," he wrote in one of his first letters home to Natalia. "I have started to believe in fate, in the regular alternation of good luck and bad, and if in the days of my youth I boldly attempted to influence the course of my life, to change it," now "this often seems like sacrilege."[17] He had begun to believe, he wrote, in the power of destiny, in the inevitable alternation between good and bad luck. He was therefore able to relax and even to enjoy his work for its own sake. No doubt he surprised himself with the pleasure he derived from this physical work.

This enjoyment later found its most vivid expression in the bricklaying scenes in *A Day in the Life of Ivan Denisovich*, where Ivan's brigade gets so carried away with its task that it ignores the whistle to stop working and go home. In the story the climax possesses its own irony, for work satisfaction is one of the "real" values that Solzhenitsyn opposes to the artificial and corrupting values upheld by the camp authorities; as such it is an essential part of the artistic scheme of the book. But the work euphoria there described is undoubtedly based on Solzhenitsyn's personal experiences at Ekibastuz, as he himself later acknowledged in volume 2 of *The Gulag Archipelago*.

> Such is the nature of man that for some unknown reason he will throw himself body and soul even into work that is abominable and hateful to him. Having worked with my hands for a couple of years myself, I, too, discovered this strange characteristic of ours to get carried away with working for its own sake, despite the fact that it may be a slave's work and promises you nothing in return.[18]

To have shown Ivan building the camp jail, however, would have introduced too much moral ambiguity into his portrait, and an electrical substation is substituted in the story, but the theme of the prisoners walling themselves in is not lost: it appears at the very beginning of the story, when the prisoners are shown hacking away fruitlessly at the frozen soil to make holes for posts to support the barbed wire that will eventually fence them in.

A Day in the Life of Ivan Denisovich is set in Ekibastuz and is based to a large extent on Solzhenitsyn's first winter there. Conditions were severe. Apart from the oppressive rule of the trusties in the barrack rooms and kitchens and the omnipresence of the warders and camp guards, the climate also bore down on them. After a dry and relatively warm autumn, disturbed only by "a thin nagging wind that made you more painfully aware than ever of the heart-breaking flatness of the steppe,"[19] the temperature suddenly plum-

meted to thirty and forty degrees below zero. As a Soviet handbook on Ekibastuz has it, the winter wind there was not "the sort of wind that rushes
through narrow city streets, bumping into tall buildings and getting entan-
gled in the trees, but a satanic blast of untamable force that had gathered
speed in the limitless expanses of the steppe where it met no obstacles."[20] It
was the sort of weather in which the mortar froze, and your bare hand, if
you let it, stuck fast to the bricks, so that the skin was torn off if you tried to
wrench it away. Fortunately, the bricklayers had mittens, but Solzhenitsyn
reported in a letter home that he had "literally burnt out"[21] both his pairs in
a short space of time and was having difficulty in keeping them sufficiently
patched to be serviceable.

On the whole he was happy to be a bricklayer and a general labourer,
instead of angling for a trusty's job, for in this he saw a means "to cleanse
my mind of the camp prejudices, intrigues, and scheming, which leave it no
time for deeper matters." It was not easy, as he and Oleg Ivanov, another
intellectual turned bricklayer, quickly found out, but its rewards outweighed
even his optimistic expectations.

> I was anxious and unsure of myself to begin with. Could I keep it up? We were
> impractical, cerebral creatures, and the same amount of work was harder for us
> than our brigade mates. But the day when I deliberately let myself sink to the
> bottom and felt it firm beneath my feet—the hard, rocky bottom that is the same
> for all—was the beginning of the most important years of my life, the years that
> put the finishing touches to my character. From thenceforth there seem to have
> been no upheavals in my life and I have been faithful to the views and habits
> acquired at that time.[22]

Peace of mind was particularly important to Solzhenitsyn at this time
because he was now immensely eager to get on with his writing. During his
long journey from the *sharashka* to Ekibastuz, he had made considerable progress with his autobiographical poem, which he had recently renamed *The
Way*,* and he was desperate not to lose momentum. "Sometimes in a sullen
work party with machine-gunners barking around me, lines and images
crowded in so urgently that I felt myself borne through the air, overleaping
the column in my hurry to reach the work compound and find a corner to
write. At such moments I was both free and happy."[23]

What is interesting here is Solzhenitsyn's use of the verb "to write."
Elsewhere he has talked of "memorizing" the poems composed in Ekibastuz,
and a legend has grown up about his method of composition there. The truth
is that both writing and memorizing were important to his method, depending upon what the external circumstances were and at which stage of the
composition he was.

In the *sharashka*, although it had been possible to write with relative ease,

---

* See note p. 44. The title is taken from one of the lines in the poem: "Where were you then, oh
way?" (The next line reads, "And how were you meant to be traversed?") Quoted in *Vestnik
RKhD*, no. 117 (1976).

he had begun memorizing his poems as a safeguard, and on leaving the *sha-rashka* for the Butyrki had been obliged to rely on his memory alone and destroy all his notes. Subsequently, in the transit prisons en route to Central Asia, he composed everything in his head and retained it with the aid of an ingenious system based on counting with broken matches. For this purpose he would lay out two rows of ten pieces of matchstick on his cigarette-case, one row representing tens and the other units. He then recited his verses silently to himself, moving one "unit" for each line and one "ten" for every ten lines. Every fiftieth and hundredth line was memorized with special care, and once a month he recited the whole poem once through. If a line was misplaced or forgotten, he would go through the whole thing again until he got it right.

This practice was not without its dangers, for to suspicious warders and the ever-vigilant stool-pigeons it might imply some secret plot to escape, and in the Kuibyshev transit prison, where he spent such a long time in the converted stables, Solzhenitsyn had hit upon another ingenious method.

> In Kuibyshev . . . I saw Catholic Lithuanians busy making rosaries for prison use. They made them by soaking bread, kneading beads from it, colouring them (black ones with burnt rubber, white ones with tooth-powder, red ones with red germicide), stringing them while still moist on twisted and soaped strands of thread and letting them dry on the window-ledge. I went over to them and said that I, too, wanted to say my prayers with a rosary but that in my particular religion I needed one hundred beads in a ring (later, when I realized that twenty would suffice, I made them myself from cork), that every tenth bead must be cube-shaped, not spherical, and that the fiftieth and hundredth beads must be distinguishable at a touch. The Lithuanians were amazed by my religious zeal (the most devout among them had no more than forty beads) but with true brotherly love helped me to put together a rosary such as I had described, making the hundredth bead in the form of a dark-red heart. I never afterwards parted with this marvellous present of theirs. I fingered and counted my beads inside my wide mittens, at roll-call, on the march to and from work, at all times of waiting. I could do it standing up, and the freezing cold was no hindrance. I carried it safely through the searches in the padding of my mittens, where it could not be felt. The warders found it on various occasions, but supposed that it was for praying and let me keep it. This necklace continued to help me write and remember right up until the end of my sentence (by which time I had accumulated 12,000 lines) and after that in my time of exile.[24]

For parallels to this astonishing feat of memory, one has to go back to the oral poets and minstrels of the Middle Ages or to the tribal bards of yore. Homer is thought to have composed and memorized *The Odyssey* in this way, and illiterate, itinerant singers memorized and recounted traditional folk-tales in the Balkans until comparatively recent times. It must be rare, however, for university graduates in the mid-twentieth century to be reduced to composing with the methods of antiquity and the Middle Ages. For Solzhenitsyn the method had serious drawbacks. So much effort went into memorizing and repeating the verses that it became increasingly difficult to compose new ones, and those that he did compose often seemed lacking in distinction. For a man with modern schooling, it was not easy to revert to the illiterate methods of the past, and so he did not rely on memory alone for long. As soon as he was able, he started writing his verses down again, at least until they could be thoroughly memorized.

Fortunately, the prisoners in Ekibastuz were allowed to have pencil and paper, but the regulations were that they had to hand in everything they had written—whether letters or simply notes for themselves—for inspection and approval by the security officer. Naturally, this was out of the question in the case of Solzhenitsyn's poem. He therefore evolved a system of secretly composing sections of verse of about twelve to twenty lines each on a tiny scrap of paper, memorizing them, and burning the paper in the stove. But on no fewer than three occasions, this system got him into trouble. On one occasion, when writing a description of the early days after his arrest and his march with seven others from Osterode to Brodnitz, he was pounced upon by a senior warder nicknamed "the tartar" and forced to hand over his piece of paper. Luckily, he was in the habit of not spelling out the more dangerous words, and "the tartar" could make no sense of it. Solzhenitsyn pretended that he had been trying to recall and write down the words of an old army song about the Soviet advance in East Prussia. On another occasion, while in the work compound, he had written about sixty lines of his verse play *Feast of the Conquerors** (which he also began while working as a bricklayer), and a fragment was found on him when he was searched on his way back to the barracks. This time he pretended it was an excerpt from a play that he was writing for the amateur theatricals that sometimes went on in camp, and the gullible warder contented himself with simply tearing the paper into pieces and handing them back to Solzhenitsyn. On the third occasion, he was found with a fragment of chapter 9 of *The Way* (eventually to become *Prussian Nights*); he explained it away as a fragment of Tvardovsky's *Vasily Tyorkin* that he had been trying to remember and write down.[25] It was the second time his path had crossed with that of Tvardovsky.

This third scrape had a sequel that is described by both Panin and Solzhenitsyn. When caught and hauled in for questioning, Solzhenitsyn had just finished writing "The Bricklayer" and had gone outside in the early morning to repeat it to himself for one last time before burning it. On his way to see the guard commander, he had managed to crumple this poem into a ball and throw it on the ground, but for the rest of that day and night was unable to go and look for it. It had to be found, for its contents made it clear that the author was in the bricklaying brigade at work on the camp jail, and since the vast majority of the brigade was Ukrainian, it would not be difficult to pinpoint Solzhenitsyn. At five the following morning, after a sleepless night, he went outside to retrace his steps and hunt for the piece of paper. A fierce

* It appears that *Feast of the Conquerors* was originally planned to be part of *The Way* but then grew into a separate work.

wind was blowing, throwing sand and even small stones in his face, and in the half-light his task seemed hopeless. After an hour of searching, he still had not found it, but just as it grew light, he stumbled across the paper wedged between two balks of timber not three paces from where he had dropped it. During that sleepless night he had prayed to God to help him. "When things are bad, we are not ashamed of our God. We are ashamed of Him only when things go well." And when he found his poem he thanked Him from the bottom of his heart: "I consider it a miracle still,"[26] he later wrote in *The Gulag Archipelago*.

Although Solzhenitsyn concealed the fact of his writing from most of the brigade, it was an open secret among his immediate friends—Dimitri Panin, Vladimir Gershuni, Yuri Karbe, Pavel Boroniuk—and in the spring of 1951, when the weather grew warm again, they would go outside in the evenings, spread their quilted jackets on the ground, and listen to him reciting passages from *Feast of the Conquerors* or *The Way*. They were proud to have this writer in their midst, made allowances for his apparent unsociability, his frequent withdrawals into his own thoughts, and did their best to see that he went unmolested and undisturbed at periods of concentration and composition.

Much of his writing was accomplished while he was actually laying bricks. "Between barrows of mortar I would put my bit of paper on the bricks and . . . write down with a stub of pencil the verses that had rushed into my head while I was finishing up the previous barrow."[27] Panin has given us a vivid picture of how he looked at such times.

> A monument should be erected to Solzhenitsyn while he is still alive, and it should represent him in a dark quilted jacket and fur hat with ear-flaps, as a bricklayer taking a rest from his work on a new wall . . . his neck wrapped in a towel, his eyes gazing into the distance, his lips whispering lines of verse, and in his hands the rosary. This is how we saw him as each week he recited for us new stanzas from his steadily growing poem.[28]

Unlike Solzhenitsyn, Panin did not think he could afford to sink to the bottom on general duties and take his chance as a labourer. Solzhenitsyn was getting regular parcels from home, whereas Panin had recently broken with his wife and family and was no longer receiving food parcels of any kind. He regarded it as a task of some urgency, therefore, to find a safe niche for himself that would protect him from the rigours of working outside and enable him to supplement the meagre camp rations. His energetic efforts in this direction soon secured a transfer from the bricklaying brigade to the wood-working factory, where he was assigned to the machine-shop and put in charge of repairs. He remained there throughout the winter and into the spring of 1951 and became friends with another engineer, named Yuri Karbe, a dour, decisive, pipe-smoking veteran of the camps who had been jailed in 1943 on charges of anti-Soviet propaganda. Karbe helped Panin obtain the post of brigade leader in one of the construction brigades, but Panin did not enjoy this work, and after a couple of months got himself transferred back to the machine-shop through his friendship with the chief engineer there, a free worker who liked Panin's technical designs. Panin took the opportunity to hand over leadership of the 104th Brigade to Solzhenitsyn, as a result of which Solzhenitsyn was able to drop his bricklaying and devote even more time to writing.[29] He had been a bricklayer for just under a year. A few weeks later, Solzhenitsyn's brigade was transferred to the machine-shop, and it continued to work there for the rest of 1951.

Solzhenitsyn has written virtually nothing about his direct experiences as a brigade leader, but in *The Gulag Archipelago* he has discussed the nature of the labour-camp brigade as a social unit and has sketched what he regards as the ideal qualities in the man chosen to lead one. The brigade was intended by the authorities as an instrument for coercing prisoners into a work tempo that was beyond their strength and for working them flat out. An unscrupulous brigade leader would curse and beat his members until they dropped from exhaustion, and could wear out several brigades in this way, while saving his own skin and surviving. But a brigade could also act as a closely knit band of brothers, helping one another, almost like a big family. "I myself knew such brigades," writes Solzhenitsyn, but points out that these were generally not the brigades assigned to general duties, but small specialized brigades of "electricians, lathe-operators, carpenters, painters," such as he had worked in at Kaluga Gate. Only a few of the bigger hard-labour brigades ever achieved such harmony.[30]

Solzhenitsyn has given us an excellent composite portrait of the ideal brigade leader in Tiurin, the ex-kulak (according to Solzhenitsyn, kulaks almost invariably made outstanding brigade leaders) in *A Day in the Life of Ivan Denisovich*. But there is no indication of whether he himself lived up to his own prescriptions. The odds are that he probably came pretty close, that in Ekibastuz he was able at last to draw with honour upon his experiences at the front and as a leader of men. No longer the novice of the clay-pits of New Jerusalem, he was now a true son of Gulag, aware of all the risks and dangers that beset him and his brigade members. We may imagine that he was a hard but fair taskmaster, adept at negotiating with the bosses and scheming to get the best-possible conditions for his brigade. It is harder, however, to see him in the role of blusterer, browbeating the work supervisors and norm setters or bawling out his men for their mistakes. Except among friends, he was still reserved, jealous of his time, a lover of solitude. And he may not have been the most energetic of brigade leaders, for Panin's whole object in handing the job over to Solzhenitsyn was to secure him more free time for his writing.* If anything, his methods would have leaned more to calculating and scheming, keeping one jump ahead of the administration and his rivals and outwitting them by brainpower rather than by brawn or bluster. It has often been

*Panin has told me that this particular brigade leader's job was uniquely easy and not to be compared to the work done by the other brigade leaders. A Chechen assistant was responsible for most of the routine connected with the job.

noted that Ivan Denisovich Shukhov contains more than a little of his creator's character, albeit transmuted into peasant terms, and there we find anticipation and cunning, stubbornness and tenacity, elevated into the cardinal
traits for survival.

17

A SON OF GULAG

EKIBASTUZ WAS AS rich in human interest as Solzhenitsyn's earlier prisons and camps, and there were writers there too. Two young students, Nikolai Borovikov and Yuri Kireyev, whose freshness and innocence greatly impressed Solzhenitsyn, turned out to be active poets, reminding him of his two young poet companions in New Jerusalem. Another poet, Anatoly Silin, a Baptist, was as adept as Solzhenitsyn in memorizing vast quantities of verse. He composed long religious poems in iambic tetrameters and could quote them for hours but, unlike Solzhenitsyn, seemed to have no system for recalling them, relying on pure memory to do the work for him. Solzhenitsyn was fascinated by Silin's steadfast meekness and humility, the firmness of his faith, and the originality of his ideas. His beliefs were idiosyncratic and had the freshness of a personal revelation. He had thought deeply about the subject of evil; some of his lines on this theme were to stick in Solzhenitsyn's mind permanently, so that he was later able to quote them in *The Gulag Archipelago*.

> Does God, who is Perfect Love, allow
> This imperfection in our lives?
> The soul must suffer first to know
> The perfect bliss of paradise. . . .
> Harsh is the law, but to obey
> Is for weak mortals the only way
> To eternal peace.[1]

Silin's very Russian emphasis on the purifying power of suffering ("By grief alone is love perfected," ran another line of his) struck an answering chord in

Solzhenitsyn and seemed to make some sort of sense—the only sense—of the purgatory they were enduring. Silin's heroic passivity attracted Solzhenitsyn as a fitting response to the despotism and brutality of the camp regime, and it is probable that Silin was the prototype for Alyoshka the Baptist in *A Day in the Life of Ivan Denisovich*.

It was here in Ekibastuz that Solzhenitsyn met the Jewish engineer Arnold Rappoport, whose story he quotes several times in *The Gulag Archipelago*, and Vasily Vlasov, once condemned to death, who was to spend twenty years in the labour camps and whose story is related at length in volume 2 of *The Gulag Archipelago*. Both Vlasov and Rappoport were to become his friends and to help him in compiling his vast epic of camp life.

Solzhenitsyn had met Vlasov as a result of his eccentric habit of squatting on his bunk after supper or shuffling along during inspections reading the only book he had brought with him to Ekibastuz—volume 3 of Dahl's dictionary. Whenever someone came over to ask him what he was reading, he invariably replied with a joke: "Dahl's dictionary. It's the safest thing there is—no danger of copping a new sentence." Vlasov, a "small man like a bantam cock, with a fierce nose and a sharp mocking look," intrigued Solzhenitsyn not only with his ebullient, pugnacious personality but also with his eloquence and the richness of his experiences. Solzhenitsyn was enraptured by Vlasov's incredible tales: "In this one man a microcosm in which half a century of my country's history was densely packed opened out before me."[2]

Another inquirer after the dictionary was a shy young Hungarian called Janos Rozsas, who had been captured by the Red Army in Hungary in 1944 and sentenced to ten years on charges that he did not understand, since they were formulated and read to him in Russian. What appealed to Solzhenitsyn was that despite his starved appearance and the pain he suffered from rheumatic fever, Rozsas resolutely refused to think about his own welfare and kept his mind on higher things. His very first remark on being told about the dictionary was "Yes, yes, a man must distract his attention to other things and not think about food all the time."[3] Rozsas had conceived a passion for Russian literature and the Russian people that outweighed all the wrongs he had suffered at Soviet hands. Solzhenitsyn discussed Pushkin, Gogol, and Nekrasov with him and introduced him to Griboyedov. He was touched by Rozsas's childlike enthusiasm for all things Russian and was to remember him with great affection. After they were both released, in the fifties, they sought one another out, and they continued to correspond long after Rozsas had returned to his native Hungary.

Despite the urge to conceal his literary interests, Solzhenitsyn was unable to keep away from the camp's cultural and educational section. Unlike Kaluga Gate, the special camp offered no concessions to those who participated in the section's activities. Consequently, there were few amateur theatricals at this time. But there was a chance to read and handle books and get to know other prisoners with similar interests. Solzhenitsyn had first gone there to have his dictionary rubber-stamped with the legend "Steplag, Cultural and Educational Section," without which it would have been confiscated; and while he was there he met a number of people who interested him.

One, whom he couldn't fail to notice, was the camp "artist," Vladimir Rudchuk, who was responsible for painting the numbers on the prisoners' clothing. A former archdeacon and reputedly once secretary to the patriarch, Rudchuk had been allowed, under some obscure camp ordinance, to keep his shock of wavy auburn hair, and was noted for his imposing figure, good looks, and the care he took over his appearance. He also sang in a vibrant bass voice, accompanying himself on the guitar, and occupied a cabin of his own. Solzhenitsyn called on him there to borrow a volume of reproductions of paintings from the Tretyakov Gallery but otherwise kept Rudchuk at a distance, suspecting him of being an informer.

More attractive to him was the even stranger figure of Piotr Kishkin, a moon-faced clown who used to dress up in a funny green waistcoat and hang around the CES, often taking an impromptu part in its activities. Kishkin was reputed to be a simpleton, and his often outrageous clowning and wise-cracks were excused on the grounds that he was not quite right in the head. Solzhenitsyn was not the only one to realize that Kishkin was no fool. On the contrary, his jokes were pointed and very daring, and frequently led to clashes with the guards. Behind the clowning there was a serious intent—to sow mutiny and bolster the prisoners' morale. He was an example of that venerable figure—the court jester or, in Russian tradition, the holy fool—and was later given a leading role by Solzhenitsyn (as Tishkin) in his screenplay *The Tanks Know the Truth*.*

The most unlikely person, for quite different reasons, whom he met in the CES was the Estonian naval officer Georgi Tenno, whose exploits he was also to describe at great length in volume 3 of *The Gulag Archipelago*.† Tenno was what Solzhenitsyn calls "a committed escaper," that is to say, from the day of his arrest in 1948 he had been committed heart and soul to the idea of escaping, dreamed of escaping, and never once gave in to apathy or despair. By the time Solzhenitsyn met him, Tenno had already planned (but failed to execute) escapes from the Lefortovo and Lubyanka prisons, had made several unsuccessful escapes from labour camps, and had recently been transferred to the Ekibastuz camp jail as a result of one such exploit. It is not difficult to see why such an indomitable and implacable foe of prison would appeal to Solzhenitsyn, although at the time of the first meeting he knew nothing of the escape attempts and could only guess at Tenno's character from his erect bearing and his habit, rare for a prisoner, of never lowering his eyes or concealing their steely glint. Tall and slim, he also stood out by virtue of the naval uniform he was still wearing, and two tattoos on his forearms. One had the word "liberty" surrounding an anchor; the other said "do or die" in English.†

*In the Paris edition of his Collected Works, Solzhenitsyn has reverted to the character's real name of Kishkin.
†Tenno was one of the many "strong men" that Solzhenitsyn came to admire in the camps (others were Panin, Boroniuk, and the Polish officer who refused food after the Ekibastuz rebellion). In this Solzhenitsyn shows a certain kinship to Dostoyevsky in *The House of the Dead*. While

Tenno was still in the camp jail when Solzhenitsyn met him, and during the day worked in the lime-kilns as part of his punishment. Unbeknownst to Solzhenitsyn, he was already plotting a new escape attempt with his friend Kolya Zhdanok—the two of them had only recently asked special permission to join the CES in order to take part in an amateur concert that was being prepared. Tenno had excellent qualifications for such a venture: in addition to being a sailor, he had worked in circuses as an acrobat and gymnast and had performed as a memory man and mind-reader. The camp authorities knew all this, and consequently, despite Tenno's notorious record, had given permission for him and Zhdanok to leave the camp jail for two hours every evening, after the other punishment prisoners had been locked up for the night, and go to the CES to take part in rehearsals.

Exploiting this opportunity to the full, the two would-be escapers had reconnoitred their new camp, noting when the guards were changed in the watch-towers and memorizing the layout. Tenno had announced that they would perform a sketch for which he needed his everyday clothes from the clothing store and a brief-case, borrowed from somewhere. And Zhdanok would require a civilian suit. When rehearsals began, they sometimes continued until late at night, so that Tenno and Zhdanok were obliged to stay over in the CES until the following morning, thus accustoming the guards to their occasional absence from the punishment block.

When all was ready, they chose a Sunday as the best day for their escape, dressed up in their concert clothes, as though going to an evening rehearsal, put their camp clothes on top, and cut their way through the fence just after dusk, when the warders were preoccupied with the evening roll-call and the perimeter guards were about to change shifts. At first their escape was wildly successful. They got clean away, succeeded in remaining at liberty for three weeks, and travelled west as far as the river Irtysh, before being recaptured, brought back to the camp, and flung into the camp jail. Eventually they were put on trial on a variety of charges, ranging from counter-revolutionary sabotage to armed robbery, and given new sentences of twenty-five years. In addition, the CES's concert party was disbanded for a year and the musical evening cancelled.

Tenno's escape attempt was not the first at Steplag, nor was it destined to be the last. A year beforehand, two men had escaped from Camp Division 1 at Dzhezkazgan and were on the run for over a month before they were caught. Then came Tenno and Zhdanok, and a few months later, in the summer of 1951, three men escaped from another camp in Dzhezkazgan, and one of them also stayed at liberty for three weeks. At about the same time, six more broke out, but they were criminals and quarrelled among themselves. A couple of them were murdered, and the rest were recaptured in a matter of days.

not (or not yet) a "strong man" himself, he sang the praises of a series of strong rebels in *The Tenderfoot and the Tart*, *The Tanks Know the Truth*, *A Day in the Life of Ivan Denisovich*, and above all in *The Gulag Archipelago*.

That same summer the inmates of one of the two disciplinary barrack huts in Solzhenitsyn's compound attempted to dig a tunnel but were betrayed by an informer in their midst. They were followed by the inmates of the other disciplinary hut, who dug an amazing seventy yards—from beneath their hut to the deep ditch that circled the camp perimeter beyond the fences and ploughed strip of no man's land. Twenty inches wide and three feet high, shored up with planks, lit by electric light bulbs and equipped with ventilation shafts, the funnel was a first-class piece of work and yet took only two months to dig—with bare hands and knives. The day of the breakout was set for 6 October 1951, and fourteen men were involved, including Tenno and Zhdanok, who had been transferred to the disciplinary hut in September. But Tenno was destined not to go with them—two days beforehand he was transferred out again. The breakout was postponed until 9 October. Zhdanok went along, and it was he who, despite his earlier experience, lost his head when a guard approached the ditch and gave himself away. Four of the others had escaped, but were quickly caught and brought back, while eight of the prisoners were obliged to scramble back to the hut and wait for the storm to burst. When it did, they were beaten to a pulp by the warders and obliged to show them where the tunnel started; even though the camp authorities had traced the tunnel back from its exit into the ditch, they were completely unable to locate its starting place inside the barrack hut.

These escapes were a relatively new phenomenon in the history of Gulag, and so were the mutinies that began breaking out in other parts of Siberia and Central Asia, news of which quickly reached Ekibastuz on the prisoners' grape-vine. Both were a more or less direct result of Stalin's introduction of special camps for political prisoners, though nobody could have foreseen it at the time. Stalin had thought that by segregating the political prisoners, inflicting harsh sentences on them, subjecting them to rigid discipline and exacting work quotas, he would cow them completely and break their spirit. But he had miscalculated on two counts. By depriving the prisoners of any realistic hope of release or improvement in their conditions, he had removed all incentive to conform or obey. Men with nothing to lose are more ready for desperate action. And by separating them out from the criminal prisoners, he had laid the basis for greater trust and loyalty between them. With fewer unreliable crooks in their midst, solidarity became possible.

Solzhenitsyn has described in great detail in volume 3 of *The Gulag Archipelago* the way in which attitudes in Ekibastuz changed and developed throughout the year 1951 (he has also dramatized them in *The Tanks Know the Truth*), and there is a parallel account in Dimitri Panin's memoirs.[5] The beginnings were modest enough. Prisoners found that they were able to trust one another sufficiently to be more or less frank in their conversations, without feeling obliged to look over their shoulders the whole time. Stealing ceased completely. Relations between brigade leaders and ordinary brigade members became friendlier and more open. With leaders like Boroniuk, Panin, Solzhenitsyn, and several others, it was possible to reason and discuss, and these friendly relations rubbed off on some of the work supervisors and norm setters from among the trusties. Even the professional thieves among the trusties felt constrained to modify their behaviour.

These changes, unfolding over a period of several months, were imperceptible at first, and affected only relations between the different groups of prisoners. Relations between the prisoners as a whole and the warders, guards, and camp administrators were if anything worse than before. The punishment cells in the camp jail and the two disciplinary huts were full to bursting. Denunciations by stool-pigeons, who still existed in the prisoners' ranks, were the one remaining weak link, and they continued unabated under the protection of the camp security officer.

But one day this situation, too, began to change. The catalyst was the arrival in Ekibastuz of a convoy of western Ukrainian "Banderites" from Dolinka, three hundred miles to the north. They had been sent to Ekibastuz after taking part in a mutiny in the Dubovka camp and setting it on fire. They were young, healthy, and rebellious, and even after being split up and distributed among the various brigades, they continued to meet and plot together.

They started off by questioning the work quotas and refusing to work until the quotas were reduced. But a more dramatic result of their arrival was the sudden suicide of a well-known stool-pigeon. At least it was passed off as suicide—the man was found hanging in the loft space of one of the disciplinary huts—but word quickly spread that he had been hanged by the Ukrainians. Two weeks later two more stool-pigeons were killed in broad daylight on two separate building sites, and shortly after that one of the trusty cooks was knifed to death by two Moslems after having insulted and beaten one of them.

From then on the informers were mercilessly tracked down and murdered one after another, usually by a group of masked Ukrainians who entered the barrack huts and knifed them in their beds. Forty-five stool-pigeons were eliminated over a period of about eight months, so that these murders became a weekly occurrence. On one occasion an informer was pursued into the office of the camp commandant, Major Maximenko, and cut down before his eyes. Another, having escaped to the hospital to have his wounds treated and bandaged, was slaughtered in his hospital bed.

As a result, the informers stopped informing, and the camp security officer and his staff no longer had any way of finding out what the prisoners were saying or thinking. The network of stool-pigeons had broken down. The rest of the prisoners then grew insubordinate. They refused to answer the security officer's questions about who was responsible, or even to go to his office at all. They became more demanding about their work conditions, and there was a sudden dearth of volunteers for the post of brigade leader. Now that the quotas had been lowered and everyone got the maximum bread rations, there was no sense in taking on extra responsibility and making trouble for oneself.

The camp authorities were at a loss as to how to respond. They couldn't call for help from their superiors at regional MVD headquarters, for that would have been to admit that they had lost control, and they would inevitably have been punished. Still less could they admit that the rebellion had political overtones. Therefore, they declared that the prisoners were guilty of gangsterism and announced that anyone caught would be put on trial and shot. When this failed, they put the whole camp on punishment regime, locking the prisoners in their huts overnight and on Sundays, forbidding them to go out to eat or to use the latrines, and revoking all privileges. But this, too, had little effect. Stool-pigeons continued to be killed, and the Dzhezkazgan Mining Trust, for whom the prisoners worked, complained that its quotas weren't being filled.

The authorities' next move was to force the prisoners to build a twelve-foot-high brick wall dividing the compound in half, but with a gate left in the middle. Simultaneously, they tried to soften the prisoners up by summoning two or three of the brigades to be photographed "for documentation purposes" and by calling a few of the men in for questioning, implying that it was all a preliminary to their release from the camp. This pretence was soon dropped in favour of individual arrests, but the "arrested" men then refused to go with the warders and were supported by their comrades. Only bodily force was capable of removing them, since it was forbidden even to warders and administrators to carry weapons inside the compound, lest they fell into the prisoners' hands.

Relations between the two sides deteriorated still further. The armed guards who escorted the prisoners to and from work became tense and openly hostile. They cursed the prisoners more than ever and baited them with taunts of "Fascists," "counter-revolutionaries," and "Banderites." In one incident, Pavel Boroniuk rushed into the guardroom to complain of the guards' behaviour, risking a beating, arrest, or worse, but was saved when the men of several brigades voluntarily and speedily lined up outside and demanded his release.

Meanwhile, the prisoners were considering ways and means of exploiting their new-found strength in other directions. They decided they would make a series of demands to have the most humiliating camp practices abolished. They would insist that the huts be left unlocked at night and the latrine tanks taken out, that their number patches be removed, that they be paid for their labour, and that they be allowed to write twelve letters home in a year instead of two. They also debated whether to insist on an eight-hour day and whether to proclaim a strike, but such a course struck them as possibly "subversive," and they gave preference to a hunger-strike.

Before they could take action, the authorities struck first. On Sunday, 6 January 1952, the prisoners in Solzhenitsyn's hut found themselves locked in after morning roll-call. When they looked through the windows, they saw the prisoners from the next hut being herded through the snow to the guardhouse, carrying their belongings. Solzhenitsyn's hut went next, and they realized that the entire camp was being regrouped and split into two, on either side of the wall they had just built. When the manoeuvre was finished, the two thousand or so Ukrainian nationalists had been put on one side and the remaining thirty-five hundred on the other. On the Ukrainian side were the camp canteen, hospital, and club, while Solzhenitsyn remained on the side with the camp jail. As a result of this gigantic reshuffle, all the brigades had to be formed afresh, and many former friends and comrades were separated. Solzhenitsyn remained a brigade leader, however, and was still in the same hut as his old friend Panin. Other members of their group to survive were Boroniuk, Gershuni, and a friend of Solzhenitsyn's called Colonel Ivanov.

For the first few days, nobody could understand the point of it all, but after about a week, ominous rumours began to circulate about sinister goings-on in the camp jail. As a result of the systematic reprisals against the stool-pigeons, a number of them, including the camp artist, Rudchuk, had earlier fled their barrack huts and sought refuge in one of the cells for their own safety. Now the authorities had hit on the scheme of picking up some of the suspected Ukrainians and throwing them one by one, not into the regular punishment cells, but into the cell occupied by the frightened and vengeful stool-pigeons. The latter had seized the opportunity to torture and maim their victims in revenge for their dead comrades, and the bulk of the Ukrainians could do nothing about it, because they were in the other compound, on the far side of the wall.

The screams of the tortured victims were heard by some of the other prisoners when they were delivering bread and gruel to the jail, and they reported what they had heard to the work brigades when the latter returned from the work compound. After two or three days of such reports, the other prisoners could stand it no longer. It was 22 January 1952, and early in the evening, just as darkness was falling, some unusual noises were heard. Both Panin and Solzhenitsyn have described what happened next. Here is Panin's version.

> As I was coming out of the canteen and tucking my spoon inside my felt boot, I caught the unmistakable sound of boards being ripped out of a fence. Klekshin, a model for a character in Solzhenitsyn's *A Day in the Life of Ivan Denisovich*, . . . was hard of hearing. Nevertheless, he, too, was startled by the noise. We exchanged glances. Near the main roadway that divided the camp in half we spotted some dark figures, running and yelling. We could not make out exactly what they were shouting. The punishment block was next to the guardhouse, just off to the right, and I ran over in that direction. . . . Some prisoners were tearing stakes out of the fence that encircled the brick jail, and using them as battering rams, were trying to knock the bars out of the windows of the stool-pigeons' cell. But the bars wouldn't give way. Then they rolled up a barrel of fuel oil [from] . . . the bakery. Three bucketsful were splashed into the cell, but before they had time to set it on fire, the machine-guns in the watch-towers went to work, and the camp guards, called from their barracks, started firing their rifles from the roadway. Most of the prisoners involved had seen service in the war, and they immediately scattered, zigzagging and keeping their heads down, just as they

must have done during an attack at the front. A minute later there was nobody in sight. Getting back to our own barrack hut would have been especially dangerous, because to reach it we would have had to cut across the road along which the rifles were laying down fire. Making short dashes, we headed for the entrance to the nearest hut, the one next to the punishment block, and stood in the doorway there.[6]

It was still necessary for Panin to get back to his own hut, since it was after lights out and all the prisoners were supposed to be locked in. Solzhenitsyn was also out in the compound and had shots fired over his head before he gained the safety of his hut. Others weren't so lucky. Some were killed by the bullets; some were caught by the warders and mercilessly beaten with iron bars. By the end of it all, about a dozen prisoners were dead.

The outburst had been spontaneous, but now, for most of the brigades, the planned hunger-strike began to come into effect. On the day after the slaughter, all stayed in their huts—with the exception of the three machine-shop brigades, two of which were led by Panin and Solzhenitsyn. It was a stupid, cowardly thing to do, as they bitterly realized when they arrived at their place of work, and both of them were later to blame themselves for their short-sightedness and lack of understanding. For all their fine words and verbal militancy, they had both been found wanting when it came to action.

On the following day the strike was total. Notes were tossed over the wall informing the Ukrainians of what was happening, and all thirty-five hundred men on the prison side remained in their huts, refusing either to eat or to work. The following day they remained inside again, lying on their bunks and ignoring the exhortations of the warders and camp officers, whose threats had now turned to pleas, to come out and work. The brigade leaders, including Solzhenitsyn and Panin, were summoned to the door and told that if the prisoners stopped their strike, nobody would be punished for what had occurred, and they could have double rations to make up for what they had missed. The brigade leaders agreed to discuss the offer with the rest of the prisoners, but it was unanimously rejected and the huts were locked again.

On the fourth morning, the officers returned, this time with some senior Gulag officials who had been flown in to deal with the mutiny. It was rumoured that the prosecutor-general of Kazakhstan himself was among them, and the tone of the officers had changed even more dramatically. As Solzhenitsyn writes in volume 3 of *The Gulag Archipelago*, it now looked like surrender: "The administration of Peshchany Camp requests the prisoners to take their food. The administration will accept complaints. It will examine them and eliminate the causes of conflict between the administration and the prisoners."[7]

This message was again passed to the brigade leaders at the door for discussion with the other prisoners. On this occasion many of them wavered, for it appeared to them that the bosses had completely given in. There seemed little point in continuing to starve themselves, especially when many were already weak from their regular meagre rations. Against this, some prisoners argued that they should hold out until their specific demands were met. Among them was Panin, who made an inspired speech urging the prisoners to hang on.

> We must think not only of tomorrow, but of the day after tomorrow as well. We all have long prison terms, but victory will at least improve the conditions of our existence, and the inevitable repressions will be much less severe than in the past. For us it will be a trifle to go hungry for a couple more days, but for the authorities it can have a decisive impact on their careers, which are more important to them than anything else.[8]

It was resolved to continue the strike, and Solzhenitsyn later told Panin, "Your voice rang out like pure silver. Your whole manner expressed conviction and faith in the rightness of our cause. This was the finest day in your life."[9]

The prisoners' resolution lasted only until early evening, however. At that point, those keeping watch at the windows shouted that Hut No. 9 had surrendered and was on its way to the canteen. Jumping up from their bunks, the other prisoners crowded to the windows in time to see a pathetic line of men, some of them holding mugs and mess-tins and some of them barely able to walk, slouching through the compound. Solzhenitsyn writes that he and his companions wept with frustration and despair. It was true that Hut 9 was a hungry hut. All its prisoners were on general duties, few of them received food parcels, and they had suffered heavily from the shooting and beating. Several of their comrades had been lying dead in their midst for the four days that the strike had lasted. There was nothing to be done. The solidarity had been broken, and one by one the other huts followed them out.

It is interesting that in their separate accounts of these events, Solzhenitsyn and Panin differ somewhat in their evaluation of their significance. Both men regard the fact that they took place at all as something of a triumph. Solzhenitsyn, in his longer and more detailed account in *The Gulag Archipelago*, sums up this aspect of the strike as follows:

> The bosses could no longer see us, no longer peer unto our souls. A gulf had opened between the overseers and the slaves!
>
> None of those who took part will ever forget those three days in our lives. We could not see our comrades in the other huts, or the corpses lying there unburied. Nonetheless, the bonds that united us, at opposite ends of the deserted camp, were of steel.
>
> This was a hunger-strike called not by well-fed people with reserves of subcutaneous fat but by gaunt, emaciated men who had felt the whip of hunger daily for years on end, who had achieved with difficulty some sort of physical equilibrium, and who suffered acute distress if they were deprived of a single

three-ounce ration. Even the goners* starved with the rest, although a three-day fast might tip them into an irreversible and fatal decline. The food that we had refused and that we had always thought so beggarly was a mirage of plenty in the feverish dreams of famished men.

This was a hunger-strike called by men schooled for decades in the law of the jungle: "You die today, me tomorrow." Now they were reborn, they struggled out of their stinking swamp, they consented to die today, all of them together, rather than go on living in the same way tomorrow.[10]

Solzhenitsyn interprets the decision to give up the strike on the fourth day, at least in the case of his own hut, as a defeat, and quotes with approval the heroic gesture of a Pole, Jerzy Wegierski, who proudly turned his face to the wall and refused to accompany the rest of them to the canteen. "If we had all been so proud and so strong, what tyrant could have held out against us?"[11] Panin, on the other hand, whose chronology differs by a day from Solzhenitsyn's,† considers that the prisoners won a victory, even though it was clear that the authorities, after making temporary concessions, would punish the ringleaders as soon as they got the chance.

In the short term, certainly, it was a victory. The prisoners were allocated double rations and on the following day, Sunday, 27 January, were given their arrears of food and allowed to wander about the camp, exchanging experiences and discussing what had happened. They were all in a holiday mood and, according to Panin, were issued with fresh bedding and allowed to watch films as well.

They were also promised that their grievances would be properly examined. Members of a commission of inquiry flew in from Karaganda, Alma-Ata, and Moscow, tables were set up in the middle of the compound, and prisoners were invited to come forward with their complaints. On the Tuesday, the brigade leaders were assembled for a more formal session in the ante-room to the bath-house, where the barbers usually operated. Solzhenitsyn was among them, and saw that the members of the commission consisted of an MVD colonel, several lieutenant-colonels, and a sprinkling of lesser officers, while the camp officers sat behind them in a second row of chairs.

The session went badly for the prisoners. The brigade leaders were mostly simple men, not much used to expressing themselves in public and overawed by the rank of their inquisitors. They were cruelly harassed and interrupted by one or two of the officers and thrown off balance by the difficulty and strangeness of it all. Solzhenitsyn writes that he could see how poorly the other brigade leaders were doing and was aware that he could do much better, but in the end he chose to be cautious. Because the commander of the

---

* This is the commonly accepted translation for the Russian camp-slang term *dokhodyaga*, meaning literally a prisoner who is on his very last legs from starvation, exhaustion, and hopelessness.
† There is also a slight discrepancy between the dates given by Solzhenitsyn in *The Gulag Archipelago* and those in a later account in *Skvoz' chad*. This account follows the dating in *The Gulag Archipelago*.

escort guards was present, Solzhenitsyn decided to concentrate his fire on him. He deplored the fact that the guards, in their conduct, had ceased to behave like "Soviet soldiers"—that they had stooped to pilfering and bullying and been responsible for prisoners' deaths. Solzhenitsyn also criticized the warders for setting a bad example to the prisoners by stealing building materials, but that was about all.[12]

It was not a particularly good or outspoken speech, as Solzhenitsyn himself later admitted. It was carefully framed in loyalist terms calculated to pander to the prejudices of his listeners, and did not say what was most important.

Panin, too, who wrote twenty years after the event, found that none of them was as heroic as he might have been. It is always easier to be wise in retrospect, of course. But the truth seems to be that they were all cowed by their years of deprivation and ill-treatment in Stalin's prisons and camps, and as a result of the twenty years of psychological preparation and indoctrination that had preceded their imprisonment. To throw off those mental and psychological shackles was in many ways harder than to discard the physical ones. Even when they had won their physical victory and forced their jailers to stay away from them, or to come as supplicants, the prisoners had been too confused, too uncertain of themselves, and above all too docile to know how to exploit their strength. It was to assist in the casting off of these psychological chains that The Gulag Archipelago was written fifteen years later, and it was not until it was written that Solzhenitsyn was free of them himself.*

For the next two weeks, the camp authorities continued to behave with circumspection and the prisoners to revel in their "victory." But one morning, when the brigades were outside the compound and on their way to work, they were ordered by their armed guards to sit down in the snow. An officer whom nobody recognized took out a sheet of paper and read out a list of names. They were all youngsters who had acted as contact men and messengers during the strike and whose names had obviously been noted by the warders. Forty of them were handcuffed and led away in one go.

After that, large numbers of prisoners were called for interrogation. Many were flung into the camp jail or posted to other camps. The trouble-makers were separated from one another. Major Cherednichenko, Maximenko's successor as camp commandant, personally threatened Panin with retribution: "Ah, Panin! I remember you—oh yes, I remember you! The wheels are turning, don't worry! We'll soon process you!" He kept his word, for on 13 February, Panin was interrogated and thrown into the camp jail (he was transported to Spassk a few weeks later). And on the nineteenth, Georgi Tenno and Pavel Boroniuk were sent away in an enormous transport of seven hundred prisoners.[13]

---

*His first attempt to give literary expression to his feelings about the rebellion was his screenplay The Tanks Know the Truth. It was not until the completion of The Gulag Archipelago, however, that he achieved full catharsis and felt free to turn to his long-planned series of historical novels.

Solzhenitsyn, however, did not accompany any of them. On 30 January, the very day after addressing the commission of enquiry, he had been admitted to the camp hospital. Some weeks before, he had noticed a small swelling in his right groin. At first he had ignored it, but it had gradually grown to about the size of a lemon, and the pain from it had increased, especially during the hunger strike. The camp hospital had remained on the Ukrainian side of the wall after the compound had been divided in two, and it was not until after the strike that Solzhenitsyn could be examined. The two doctors who saw him, after the commission had finished taking evidence, diagnosed cancer and recommended an immediate operation.

On his arrival in the hospital, Solzhenitsyn caught a glimpse of some of the prisoners who had been beaten to a bloody pulp by the warders with their iron bars, and discovered that one man had already died from his wounds. The survivors were unbowed and eagerly asked him for the latest news of the strike. The Ukrainian surgeon who was due to operate on Solzhenitsyn, a prisoner called Yanchenko, also questioned him about the strike, but was sent away on a prisoner transport before he could perform the operation. As a result, Solzhenitsyn had to wait a further ten days. It is not clear who took Yanchenko's place (a hint in *Cancer Ward* suggests it may have been a German), but the operation was performed on 12 February 1952 under a local anaesthetic, and lasted for about half an hour.

According to Reshetovskaya, Solzhenitsyn convalesced for two weeks, and if the evidence of Kostoglotov's treatment in *Cancer Ward* is to be believed, sandbags were placed on the incision to stop the bleeding and prevent further swelling. Solzhenitsyn was in considerable pain for a while and ran a high fever, but then he gathered strength quickly and made a good recovery.[14]

Coming, as it did, so soon after the turbulent events of the rebellion, which had resulted in the maiming and death of many prisoners, Solzhenitsyn's cancer and own brush with death induced him to meditate on the meaning of his own experiences. His remarks in *The Gulag Archipelago* indicate that he still felt he had done the right thing by leaving the *sharashka* and coming to Ekibastuz. The special camps were among the tougher islands in the archipelago. He had allowed himself to sink until his feet touched bottom, and had noted, with surprise and gratitude, that he did not drown. And he had risen again, not only in externals, by becoming a brigade leader, but, more importantly, in moral and spiritual terms as well.

To set oneself the aim of surviving at any price, as he had once wanted to do, was a sure path to collaboration with the authorities, corruption, and spiritual death, in exchange for material comforts. If one renounced material advantages, not only did one become morally strong but one's character improved in other unforeseen ways. In his own case he felt that the constant humbling of his pride inflicted by the camp routine was ultimately beneficial. As long ago as Kaluga Gate, he had experienced novel feelings of self-doubt and sympathy for others as a result of the shocks administered to his self-esteem by his arrest, interrogation, and sentencing to eight years' imprisonment—a sea change very much noticed at the time by Natalia. The *sharashka* had been a respite from such shocks and his life at the scientific institute a simulacrum of what it might have been outside. But now the process of buffeting had been resumed, and further changes were taking place within him.

In volume 2 of *The Gulag Archipelago* Solzhenitsyn has summarized them as follows:

> Once upon a time you were sharply intolerant, you were constantly in a rush and short of time. Now you have time with interest, you are surfeited with it, you've got months and years behind you and ahead of you, and a beneficent calming fluid begins to pour through your blood vessels—patience. . . .
>
> In the old days you never forgave anyone, you were pitiless in your condemnations and just as unbridled in your praise, but now an all-comprehending mildness underlies your uncategorical judgements. You have realized your own weakness and therefore can understand the weakness of others. And be astonished by another's strength. And wish to possess it yourself. . . .
>
> As the years go by, your heart and your hide grow armour-plated. You hasten with neither your questions nor your answers, your tongue loses its elastic capacity for easy oscillation. Your eyes do not light up with joy over good news, or darken with sorrow. . . .
>
> The rule of your life is now this: having found, do not rejoice, having lost, do not weep.[15]

It was a new variant of his old stoicism, and Solzhenitsyn here recapitulates what he had written to Natalia in his first letter from Ekibastuz, soon after his arrival. There he had recorded his willingness to bow to providence and had added, "Perhaps this belief in fate is the start of religious feelings? I don't know. It seems I am still a long way from believing in god."[16]*

Since then a year and a half had elapsed. Like most Russians, he was receptive to the idea of suffering as a purifying force. "Your soul, which was once dry, is ripened by suffering." He now felt that at last he had come to know what it meant to love one's neighbour, in Christ's sense, and to share spiritual intimacy. "It was precisely in slavery," he wrote in *The Gulag Archipelago*, "that we first learned what true friendship was."[17]

Solzhenitsyn's meditations on this theme were given added poignancy by a chance encounter in the prison hospital. As he lay in the darkened recovery room, he was visited one evening by Dr Boris Kornfeld, who sat by his bed to talk. For some reason Kornfeld told Solzhenitsyn the story of his prison conversion from Judaism to Christianity and praised Christian spirituality with a convert's ardour. He held strong views on sin and retribution and unfolded to Solzhenitsyn his theory that there was no punishment in this life that had not been preceded by a crime. "Superficially, it may seem to have nothing to do with what we are really guilty of. But if we examine our lives and think deeply about ourselves, we will always track

---

* At that time Solzhenitsyn had still been writing "god" with a small *g*. After his operation and his return to the Christian faith, he began writing it with a capital letter again.

down the crime for which we are now being punished."[18]

It is possible that Solzhenitsyn would not have remembered these words so vividly had it not been for what followed. He knew nothing of Kornfeld, except that for two months the doctor had not left the hospital or entered the camp compound, which had raised the suspicion that he was a stool-pigeon and was afraid to go there. Solzhenitsyn dismissed the idea as unlikely, but the following morning he was awakened by the sound of hurrying feet and a tramping in the corridor. Kornfeld's body was being hurried to the operating theatre—during the night his skull had been cracked by a plasterer's hammer. The operation was unsuccessful, and the dead man was placed in the morgue adjoining the room where Solzhenitsyn slept alone. It was then that Kornfeld's ominous last words returned to him with new meaning.

In *The Gulag Archipelago*, where he describes this episode at greater length, Solzhenitsyn quotes the poem that he wrote in the hospital and that marks his return to Christianity. Recalling how it had been the faith of his childhood, he describes his youthful conversion to Marxism under the influence of "bookish sophistries" and the sense of power and certainty this gave him:

> Without a rumble, faith's edifice
> Had quietly crumbled within my breast.

But then had come his journey "between being and nothingness" and his return to understanding.

> I look back with grateful trembling
> At the life I have had to lead.
>
> Neither desire nor reason
> Has illumined its twists and turns,
> But the glow of a Higher Meaning
> Only later to be explained.
>
> And now with the cup returned to me
> I scoop up the water of life.
> Almighty God! I believe in Thee!
> Thou remained when I Thee denied . . .[19]

That these were his true feelings at the time is confirmed by a letter he wrote to Natalia immediately after his release from the hospital. He had been apprehensive before the operation, he wrote, but the faith "in God's will and in God's mercy" that he had recently acquired had greatly eased his path.[20]

The closing pages of part 4, chapter 1, of *The Gulag Archipelago* ("The Ascent"), where Solzhenitsyn mentions his poem and recounts his stay in hospital, are among the most moving he has written. In them he describes not only his reconversion but also his credo, the set of beliefs to which his prison career and his sufferings had brought him and to which, with the lapses endemic to human weakness, he had tried to remain faithful ever since.

It was on rotting prison straw that I felt the first stirrings of good in myself. Gradually it became clear to me that the line separating good from evil runs not between states, not between classes, and not between parties—it runs through the heart of each and every one of us, and through all human hearts. This line is not stationary. It shifts and moves with the passing of the years. Even in hearts enveloped in evil, it maintains a small bridgehead of good. And even the most virtuous heart harbours an un-uprooted corner of evil.[21]

This was the reason, writes Solzhenitsyn, why he came to see the superiority of religion—all religions—over ideology. "They struggle with the evil *inside* man (all men)," whereas revolutions "destroy only those carriers of evil contemporary with them" and then "take to themselves as their heritage the evil itself, only magnified still more."[22]

Solzhenitsyn concludes his meditation by expressing gratitude for the years of incarceration in prisons and camps, which had enabled him to fulfil the biblical injunction "Know thyself." "Bless you, prison," he writes, "for having been in my life!" And then adds the ironic parenthesis, characteristic of his mature writing, "And from beyond the grave they answer: it's all right for you to talk—you're still alive!"[23]*

Not long after Kornfeld died, the gentle giant, Pavel Boroniuk, burst into the recovery room to bid Solzhenitsyn farewell before departing with his transport. If the evidence of *Cancer Ward* and *The Tanks Know the Truth* is to be believed, Solzhenitsyn may have been threatened with transportation himself, and there is a suggestion in *Cancer Ward* that the surgeon who carried out Solzhenitsyn's operation was also transported without warning. In the novel, the doctor shouts back to the semi-autobiographical Kostoglotov that a section of his tumour has been sent to Omsk for a histological analysis and that he should inquire there if he wants further information. Omsk is certainly the place to which doctors from Ekibastuz would have sent their samples, and it is possible that this incident is autobiographical. The removed lump was apparently a malignant lymph node, but Reshetovskaya records Solzhenitsyn as writing home to say that, according to the doctors, his tumour had not metastasized or spread to the surrounding tissues. "For that reason, the doctors assured me, there are no grounds for further concern."[24]

At the end of February, Solzhenitsyn was released from hospital and returned to the compound. Boroniuk was gone, of course. Panin was in the punishment block and soon to follow him, as were Pavel Gai, Vladimir Gershuni, and the camp jester, Kishkin. The prisoners were sullen, subdued, and full of suspicion, while the camp authorities exulted in their victory and ruthlessly rounded up all the real and suspected trouble-makers.

Solzhenitsyn did not resume his old job of brigade leader, nor did he return to bricklaying. For a while he dreamed of taking up carpentry again. "It would be good to master this trade too," he wrote in his letter home on 1 March 1952—the first for a year, because his letter of the preceding Novem-

---

* Among other things an acknowledgement that Solzhenitsyn's sentence had been light, and his experiences easy, in comparison with those of millions of his fellow victims.

ber had not arrived. He maintained his romantic prejudice in favour of manual labour, calling himself a "sissy intellectual" and complaining about his incompetence. "A thirty-year-old blockhead grows up . . . reading thousands of books, yet he can't sharpen an axe or set a handle on a hammer."[25]

But he was not allowed to be a carpenter. He was sent to work in the foundry as a smelter's mate (this was also a form of punishment, it seems), an experience he was later to draw on in writing *The Tenderfoot and the Tart*. According to the description given there, the foundry was a high-ceilinged iron building dominated by a domed, rust-red furnace that stretched from floor to ceiling, with its chimney disappearing through the roof. Beside it was a large drying-chamber built of rough brick, and there were piles of burnt earth strewn about the floor, interspersed with moulds for casting iron and a variety of shovels, crowbars, and buckets used either in fuelling the furnace or in extracting the molten iron.

The work here was probably the hardest that Solzhenitsyn had ever done. The foundry was sweltering hot, there was smoke everywhere, and he had to sweat at a variety of unskilled jobs, from chiselling slag off the furnace to stoking it and lugging the moulds about. But the foundry was also a key element in the camp's economy, making spare parts for various kinds of machinery; and it was run by a free worker, Vasili Frolov, who had a genius for fiddling the books, making articles for sale on the side, and securing excellent conditions for his workers. Solzhenitsyn based the character of Vasili Brylov, the foundry manager in *The Tenderfoot and the Tart*, on Frolov,* and Brylov's words in act 1 may be taken as indicative of the situation in which Solzhenitsyn now found himself.

Look, boys, it's not a bad life now, is it? I fix you fabulous quotas. I've worked fifteen years in the camps, I've built eleven new foundries, and I've always got on well with the prisoners. Tell me one thing you haven't got. Your bread ration's the best in the camp. You get double porridge and double soup. We make irons to sell on the side, and as for your togs, I'll sell 'em for you any time you want. And any time you want to mail a letter, just give it to me. Any time. Right now if you want. You've got your work and there's enough for me to wet my whistle.[26]

In early 1952 the special camps were made economically self-sufficient (as the ordinary camps already were). Each camp became responsible for paying its way, and a system of payments to prisoners was introduced, depending on their productivity. Some 45 per cent of the value of what the camp produced was counted as earned income, while 55 per cent went to the state. But there was a catch. Seventy per cent of the earned income was deducted to pay for the maintenance of the armed guards, dogs, fences, camp

---

* In the text of *The Republic of Labour* (which was the original name of *The Tenderfoot and the Tart*) published in the Paris edition of his Collected Works, Solzhenitsyn has changed the name back to Frolov.

jail, security officers, warders, food and clothing, and so on, leaving about 13 per cent of the total to be credited to the personal accounts of the prisoners. Anything that they earned in this way was then divided in two. Half the sum was kept back, to be handed to the prisoner at the time of his release from the camp, and the other half was converted once a month into vouchers, with which the prisoners could buy sweets, condensed milk, and similar luxuries in the camp shop, or even purchase additional meals in a specially instituted "commercial" canteen.

It was a sort of liberalization. The sums involved were quite small, but they acted as a huge incentive to prisoners; productivity (and consequently the work tempos) rose enormously. The harsh regime was eased in other minor ways. Films were shown more frequently than before, and the security officers somewhat relaxed their grip—not voluntarily, but because stoolpigeons could no longer survive among the prisoners (this was one of the few gains made by the prisoners' brief rebellion).

Apart from receiving good rations for his work in the foundry, Solzhenitsyn continued to receive monthly parcels from Natalia's aunt Nina in Rostov (paid for by Natalia). These were a "source of life" to him, as he put it in one of his letters home ("Thanks to your parcels I am alive, well, and cheerful," he had written to Nina), and had helped sustain him through the preceding icy winter and his year as a bricklayer. They contained sugar, bacon, biscuits, oatmeal, dried fruit, tobacco—and occasionally luxuries like butter and sausages (and even fresh eggs, on one occasion). Nina was also able to send him felt boots, socks, mittens, a knapsack, a kitbag, and even a pair of goggles to keep the dust out of his eyes, as well as domestic essentials like toothpaste, needles and thread, a sponge, a wooden spoon, plastic dishes, and little plastic boxes to keep things in. Just as important, in a different way, were the paper, ink, notebooks, and pencils she sent him, not to mention books by Alexei Tolstoy, Ostrovsky, Koltsov, and Blok. He read a great deal of poetry in Ekibastuz, probably to help him in composing his long epic poems at the time, and he also managed to read works by Herzen, Goncharov, Chekhov, Saltykov-Shchedrin, and Wilkie Collins.

His gratitude to Aunt Nina for her devotion and generosity was unbounded. By now she was over seventy and too old to carry the parcels to the post office herself, enlisting the services of a young relative for this purpose, but she never failed to meet Solzhenitsyn's requests and desires. "The tobacco you sent was out of this world, just as if you yourself smoked," he wrote to her on one occasion. And on another: "You are caring for me like my own mother." He owed her, he felt, "a debt too great to be repaid," and was to remember her kindness for the rest of his life.[27]

Nina's solicitude was all the more important to him now in that, for reasons he was unable to fathom, Natalia's letters were growing rarer and more distant in tone. Throughout 1950 she had written regularly at the rate of one letter a month, retailing news about her work at the Agricultural Institute, her concerts, various lectures she was giving, and her life in Ryazan.

At that time she was living in a hostel, but in February 1951 she had managed to get two rooms out of three in a communal flat in a building specially erected for teachers of the Agricultural Institute. The house was a long, low, wooden building situated on a patch of empty ground in Kasimovsky Lane, on the very outskirts of Ryazan, about a twenty-minute bus ride from the centre. Its facilities were modest—communal kitchens and toilets, no bathrooms, wood-burning stoves for heating, but at least the rooms were big enough to take a grand piano, and Natalia was able to move her piano down from Moscow. Simultaneously, her mother, Maria, had moved up from Rostov to cook and clean for her.

It was at about this time that Natalia had written suggesting that she use her summer leave to travel out to Ekibastuz to visit her husband. It was almost a year since she had seen him last, and she was feeling desperately lonely. She no longer had her Stromynka girl friends for company, and Lydia and Kirill were far away. Solzhenitsyn, however, had squashed the idea. "My dear little girl," he had written in answer to her inquiry, "coming to me here is completely useless, because a meeting is absolutely impossible. . . . We can see one another only three summers from now."[28]

Perhaps because of her disappointment over this rebuff, perhaps because of increasing loneliness, perhaps because her husband now seemed so remote and inaccessible (able to write only twice a year), Natalia found her feelings slowly changing. She started going out more on her own and became an active member of the newly formed Ryazan chapter of the Mendeleyev Society. The chapter's executive secretary was a senior lecturer in chemistry at the recently opened Pavlov Medical Institute, Vsevolod S.,* who had moved to Ryazan from Krasnodar on the death of his wife. Vsevolod, like Natalia, seemed alone in the world, and they proved to have many things in common. His training was almost identical with Natalia's, he had studied (in Voronezh) under Natalia's former professor from Rostov, and he had even applied to the Agricultural Institute at the same time as Natalia for the vacant lecturer's post that Natalia had subsequently been awarded.[29]

Natalia seems to have responded cautiously to his friendship at first, but found the fact that he was ten years older than she reassuring and comforting. Apart from escorting her to and from society meetings, he discussed her chemistry lectures with her (he was giving identical courses at the Pavlov Institute), offered her advice, and helped her with her work. Natalia's mother, Maria, appears to have liked him very much. She encouraged him to drop in for a meal or a drink even when Natalia wasn't there and did everything in her power to encourage the relationship. Despite her earlier affection for Solzhenitsyn, she regarded Natalia's continuing sacrifice of her happiness as pointless, particularly since Solzhenitsyn himself had offered Natalia her freedom and had expressed doubts as to whether he would ever be released.

In the summer of 1951, Vsevolod had followed Natalia and her mother

* Vsevolod's surname is omitted out of regard for members of his family still living in the Soviet Union.

to Rostov and had asked her to marry him. She had temporized and gone to visit her aunt and cousins in Kislovodsk, leaving him with her mother. A letter he wrote to her in Kislovodsk appears to have strongly affected her, for her own letter to Solzhenitsyn from Kislovodsk came out strained and unnaturally short. "It seemed as though you had to force yourself to begin your letter," he wrote to her at a later date. "A kind of reticence fettered your tongue, and after a few lines you broke off."[30] On her return to Ryazan, Vsevolod had met her at the station in a taxi, and from that time on there seems to have been a tacit understanding between them, although they still did not live as man and wife.

A determining factor in Natalia's decision was the arrival in Ryazan of Vsevolod's elder son, Sergei, then thirteen years old. Vsevolod had not at first told Natalia of the existence of two children by his former wife—they were staying with relatives in the south and he feared the news might alienate her. But he had told Maria, and she had broken the news to Natalia, and when Natalia saw Sergei, she was captivated by his liveliness and intelligence. The child appealed to her hitherto suppressed and dormant maternal instincts and, after a period of adjustment, he was able to accept her as a friend and mother. Oddly enough, Vsevolod, too, aroused the maternal instinct in her. Unprepossessing to look at, prematurely old for his years, he was even going deaf at the time they met and learning to use a hearing aid. But all this, plus his helplessness in dealing with the thirteen-year-old Sergei, only increased his evident need for mothering and made him more appealing.

Another contributory factor was a sudden tightening of security once more. The whole country was again under siege from Stalin's security apparatus and in the winter of 1951–52, just when the situation was growing tense in Ekibastuz (and in many other camps), Natalia was summoned by the chief of the Agricultural Institute's "special section" (responsible for security) and asked to fill out another long questionnaire like the one she had been faced with in 1948. Once more she was obliged to say that she was in the process of dissolving her marriage, and to write the necessary information about Solzhenitsyn in the column marked "former husband."

On this occasion, however, she resolved to complete the divorce proceedings. Since a divorce had to be announced in the newspaper, and since she did not dare jeopardize her position in Ryazan (where no one knew she was married), she travelled to Moscow, gave the Turkins' flat as her home address, filled in the necessary papers, and placed an announcement in the *Moscow Pravda*, which was much less read than its rival the *Moscow Evening News* (even so someone at the *sharashka* spotted it).* At the same time she handed Solzhenitsyn's notebooks, manuscripts, and other papers (including his annotated copy of *War and Peace*) to the younger Veronica Turkina for safe-keeping.

She was somewhat strengthened in her resolve by the unhappy coinci-

* The legal formalities dragged on for a while, and the divorce was not made absolute until February 1953.

dence of the loss of one of Solzhenitsyn's six-monthly letters (the one due in November 1951) and the approval of her friends. The loss meant that a whole year was to go by from one letter to the next, which stretched the thin thread of their relationship to breaking point. In the meantime Lydia Ezherets, Solzhenitsyn's as well as Natalia's friend, approved of the new marriage, and Veronica Turkina came down to Ryazan to be introduced and also gave her endorsement. In the spring of 1952, Vsevolod and Sergei moved in with Natalia and Maria on Kasimovsky Lane. He and Natalia did not go through any form of marriage ceremony but simply announced to the world that henceforth they would be man and wife.

This was the position when Solzhenitsyn left the hospital after his cancer operation and went to work in the foundry. His parcels continued to arrive (still paid for by Natalia), but her letters had now ceased, indicating that something was wrong. In March 1952 he had the chance to write again, and sent news of his operation, assuring everyone that he had recovered; and he must have written to Aunt Nina too, for he asked her to "clear up the uncertainty" for him. She dared not do it, regarding it as Natalia's duty to write and give him the news. But Natalia was too frightened: she was unwilling to upset him so soon after his cancer operation. The whole business was to drag on until September 1952, when Aunt Nina finally wrote, "Natalia has asked me to tell you that you may arrange your life independently of her."[31]

Solzhenitsyn was puzzled and irritated by this vague and roundabout means of communication—was his marriage ended or not? He wrote to Natalia again, asking her to amplify this "meaningless, enigmatic phrase" and spell out the true situation. It appears that he still hadn't given up hope of winning her back. "No matter what you've done during the past two years," he wrote, "you will not be guilty in my eyes. I shall not criticize or reproach you either in my thoughts or my words. Neither by my former behaviour nor my luckless life, which has ruined and withered your youth, have I justified that rare, that great love that you once felt for me and that I don't believe is exhausted now. The only guilty one is me. I have brought you so little joy, I shall be forever in your debt."[32] But it was too late. Reluctantly, Natalia wrote and informed him about her marriage, and that brought their correspondence to a close.

Although we have abundant evidence—in *The First Circle*—of Solzhenitsyn's feelings about his initial separation from Natalia and their first, "fictitious" divorce, we can only guess at his feelings on learning the truth of this genuine divorce, and Natalia's love for another man. What slender evidence we have suggests that he was incensed and mortally jealous. Despite his lofty declarations of Natalia's right to leave him and seek her happiness elsewhere, he seems not to have believed that she would do so; and when, at the time of their fictitious divorce in 1949, she had assured him of her continuing love and loyalty, he had confessed, with his usual candour, that that was what he had wanted all along. But now the separation was irrevocable, and it seems that Solzhenitsyn's attitude to his rival was one of deep resentment and bitterness. He later called him "a scoundrel for tempting into marriage a wife whose husband was still among the living."[33]

He was now into the last year of his sentence and beginning to look forward to his release. He knew that it was not guaranteed. There had been innumerable instances of prisoners' being charged and sentenced in the final months of their prison term, or simply not being released at all. Even if he was allowed to go, he had been told he could never return to central Russia but was destined for "perpetual" exile. Nevertheless, he had survived the purge of camp trouble-makers that had carried off Panin, Boroniuk, and the others, and with his unquenchable optimism he looked forward to making the best of whatever opportunities lay ahead. To Aunt Nina he wrote a request for textbooks on arithmetic, geometry, and other mathematical subjects. He would try to become a schoolteacher again. With his prison record, it could only be at a humble level in some out-of-the-way village or small settlement, but he still insisted that what she sent him should not be the standard textbooks. On geometry, for instance, he specified an older book, "where the text offers lots of problems for construction." As Reshetovskaya points out in her memoirs, "He was sure that a person with a mathematics degree, who had worked at mathematics in a *sharashka* as well, would certainly not have forgotten it and could easily teach it in a village school. But what Solzhenitsyn wanted was something for himself, some sort of inner satisfaction, so that even in a village school he would be almost a reformer in the method of teaching mathematics. He would conduct his courses on the highest-possible level."[34]

In April 1952, when he was studying these books in his spare time, he was surprised by a summons to see the security officer. For a moment he feared that he was not to be released after all, but it turned out that his old school friend Kirill Simonyan was being investigated by the MGB in Moscow. Kirill was now a leading surgeon in a Moscow hospital and was making a brilliant career for himself (among other things, as the author of some medical monographs). He had separated from Lydia Ezherets after a short and unsatisfactory marriage, but in all other respects seemed to be flourishing. Solzhenitsyn was asked, for reasons he could not fathom, to testify to Simonyan's "anti-Soviet attitudes" and to confirm the testimony he had given during his investigation in 1945. But he refused. Although not ashamed of the answers he had given Captain Ezepov as a green young prisoner seven years before, he was not proud of them either. As a camp veteran, he now knew how unnecessary it had been to try to answer at all. He did not confirm his former testimony, but on the contrary renounced it as extracted under duress. Kirill, he said, was a model Soviet citizen.

The exact nature of the events surrounding Kirill's arrest and interrogation is still not clear, but from a later, rather garbled account of the matter by Kirill, and from the guarded comments of one or two people who knew him in later life,[35] it is possible to reconstruct an approximate picture of what must have taken place. It appears that Kirill had been detained on some sort of homosexual charge—homosexuality was (and is) a crime in the Soviet Union (it was homosexuality, apparently, that had led to the break-up of Kirill's marriage to Lydia). Having arrested Kirill, the security organs looked at his file and presumably discovered his involvement with Solzhenitsyn. Kirill had not been implicated enough to be questioned at the time, but the "anti-Soviet" character of Solzhenitsyn's crime offered a convenient weapon with which to threaten Kirill now, and that was presumably why Solzhenitsyn was asked to "confirm" Kirill's anti-Soviet views. Solzhenitsyn's refusal must have been rather inconvenient for Kirill's investigator, but the latter chose to ignore it and showed Kirill a copy of Solzhenitsyn's 1945 testimony as if it were fresh. Kirill (like Solzhenitsyn himself and the rest of their group) was depicted there as a "harmless" malcontent, socially at odds with the tone of Soviet society and dissatisfied with many of its minor manifestations. Reading it in 1952, however, when they were all seven years older, and with the eyes of a badly frightened man, Kirill was horrified: it looked like an act of betrayal. Having achieved his purpose of scaring Kirill half to death, the investigator appears then to have offered him some sort of deal—perhaps to inform on his hospital colleagues, perhaps to perform some other kind of service. Or perhaps he was simply kept in reserve for some later occasion. Whatever it was, it had nothing to do with Solzhenitsyn at the time, but it cast a shadow over Kirill's life that was to stay with him until his death, and for which he was to hold Solzhenitsyn chiefly responsible. It also spelled (unbeknownst to Solzhenitsyn) the death of their friendship.

Solzhenitsyn spent the rest of 1952 labouring in the foundry, reading up on mathematics, and working away steadily at his poetry. His long, autobiographical poem, *The Way*, had spawned two independent works: *Prussian Nights*, a verse narrative, and *Feast of the Conquerors*, a verse play, both of them about his experiences with the advancing Red Army in East Prussia. In the course of 1952 he started a second play, *Decembrists without December*,* based on his experiences in the Smersh prison at Brodnitz, and wrote a number of shorter poems, most of which have never been published. One that was later published, with the enigmatic title of "Russia?" throws considerable light on Solzhenitsyn's developing views on Russian history.

The poem was a meditation on the poet's search for the "real" Russia, a Russia of "forthright men," "impassioned cranks," "welcoming doors," and "broad tables," as he put it, where you did not kick a man when he was down, where slavishness was not the norm, and where the wisdom of one's ancestors was not ignored. The poet's aim was not just to praise Russia's virtues and ignore her faults but also to recover a sense of the true nature of his homeland. This nature, he felt, was one that could do "without the Slavs and warm waters . . . without the sacred sword!" Wars and conquest were

---

*This play was later renamed *The Captives* and appears under that title in the Paris edition of Solzhenitsyn's Collected Works.

unnecessary to Russia, for they had brought only grief and disaster, especially to the other nations that had suffered from Russia's might.

> We have become universally hated,
> Everywhere we shall be crucified,
> They will slaughter us on the Vistula,
> And in China build us funeral pyres.
>
> The Tartar's indelible birthmark
> and the foulness of Stalinist filth
> Have marked us all! Thrice cursed
> Will be Russia's name henceforth.

Yet there was a tiny morsel of hope. However delicate and fragile she remained, the true, unique Russia was still cherished in the hearts of her hundred million people, and this Russia had still to make herself heard.

A similar theme had appeared in some passages in *The Way*, written a few months earlier, where Solzhenitsyn had addressed Russia as "my homeland, my shame," as an accursed, pitiless, ridiculous, insensate native land, unworthy of the name of mother, yet one that he could not help loving immoderately. This time he had sought the blame not only in the Tartar yoke and Stalinist excesses but also in Russian history, and particularly in the unbridled criticism and ridicule that generations of Russian writers had heaped on their homeland. "Thank you, fathers of the enlightenment! You wanted to ease our way! You sowed with great impatience—now admire what we have reaped!" Solzhenitsyn's own generation, he felt, had helped to make things worse, by living too much on the surface and not seeing through to the essence of things. Only arrest and imprisonment had opened his eyes to the truth. [36]

Exile for Solzhenitsyn was only months away. He later wrote in *The Gulag Archipelago* that in his eight years in prison and the camps, he had never heard anyone say a good word about exile, yet "the dream of exile burns like a secret light in the prisoner's mind, a flickering, iridescent mirage." It was a dream he himself had cherished from the earliest days of his imprisonment, even if he had thrust it away during the middle years of his sentence.

Now, at last, it was to be realized. Although he tried to fight down the hopes that involuntarily rose within him, to preserve a cold indifference, and to remain faithful to the stoicism he had worked so hard to acquire during his three years in Ekibastuz, he could not entirely suppress a feeling of muted exaltation. And yet, mixed with these hopes were feelings of regret. "Only on the threshold of the guardhouse," he later wrote, "do you begin to feel that what you are leaving behind you is both your prison and your homeland. This was your spiritual birthplace, and a secret part of your soul will remain here forever—while your feet trudge on into the dumb and unwelcoming expanse of 'freedom.' " [37]

Solzhenitsyn's sentence ended officially on 9 February 1953. Four days later, together with a group of other released prisoners, he was led out of the main camp gates under armed guard and marched to the railway station. Superstition decreed that you should never look back at your last prison; otherwise you were doomed to return there. According to another tradition, you should throw your spoon at it, so that it didn't pursue you (alternatively, you should not leave the spoon behind; otherwise you would be obliged to return for it). Solzhenitsyn decided to take his spoon with him. He had moulded it personally in the Ekibastuz foundry and wanted it as a keepsake.

At the railway station Solzhenitsyn's group mingled with hundreds of other prisoners brought there from other camps in the gigantic Karaganda complex. Together they were loaded into a long prison train and set off once more for an unknown destination.

18

EXILED

"IN PERPETUITY"

FOR THE FIRST few days of his journey, Solzhenitsyn retraced the route that he had followed three years earlier in coming to Ekibastuz, only this time in reverse: north to the old-fashioned prison of Pavlodar, north-east to Omsk, with its shades of Dostoyevsky, and east to Novosibirsk. Again there were the same surly armed guards, the howling dogs, the crowded Stolypins. It was hard to believe that all this presaged release. But in Omsk a good-natured warder, marvelling at their good fortune, informed five of them that they were being sent south. And in Novosibirsk they were put on a train that did indeed crawl south—through the dusty wilderness of east Kazakhstan, skirting Lake Balkhash, to Alma-Ata. From there they travelled due west to the regional administrative centre of Dzhambul, on the very border of Kirghizia, midway between Alma-Ata and Tashkent.

They arrived in Dzhambul in the dead of night and were transferred by lorry, still under armed escort, to the town jail. The next morning they were moved to the local MVD headquarters, where a lieutenant informed them that they had all been assigned to the district of Kok Terek, on the southern fringe of Kazakhstan's vast desert of Bet-Pak-Dala. A brown sheet of paper was shoved across the desk at Solzhenitsyn informing him that from this day hence he was to be exiled to the district of Kok Terek "in perpetuity" and that in the case of unauthorized departure he could be sentenced to twenty years' imprisonment with hard labour. This was the first official confirmation that he had been sentenced to exile as well as imprisonment, but it came as no surprise. All prisoners released from Ekibastuz, whether or not exile figured in their sentences, were obliged to go into exile. After signing the document, Solzhenitsyn wrote a satirical epigram that ended:

I sign with a flourish, my heart is light.
Like the Alps, basalt or the firmament,
Like the stars (no, not those on your shoulders so bright!)—
Oh, enviable fate, I am permanent!
But can every word, I wonder, be true?
Can the MGB be permanent too?[1]

Solzhenitsyn and his companions were confined to a small room for two days, before being marched back to the station. From there they set off by train back the way they had come, in the direction of Alma-Ata. But halfway there, in the small town of Chu, they were unloaded and made to continue on foot. It was stiflingly hot, and the members of the group, having cultivated the convict's habit of acquiring and retaining as many clothes as possible, were terribly overdressed. Solzhenitsyn himself was wearing long underpants and his twill trousers, two padded jackets (one filched during stock-taking at the camp), and his old, threadbare army greatcoat, which he had faithfully treasured since the day of his arrest eight years beforehand in East Prussia. In addition, they all had kitbags and suitcases to carry. They trudged for six miles along a dusty road until darkness fell, when they were locked up for the night in the jailhouse of the hamlet of Novotroitsk. The following day a lorry came to collect them and carried them bumpily over the last forty miles to Kok Terek. It was 3 March 1953, just eighteen days since Solzhenitsyn had been marched out of Ekibastuz.

They were still to all intents and purposes prisoners under armed guard, and in Kok Terek their destination was inevitably the MVD station, where they were interrogated by an officer of the MGB and asked to fill out a questionnaire and to write down a curriculum vitae. They were issued with special identity cards indicating their status as exiles (they were not allowed to have the usual internal passport) and informed that if they wished to travel beyond the district of Kok Terek for any reason, they could do so only with a special permit from the MVD. Even then they had to indicate their destination, the dates of their journey there and back, and the place where they would be staying while away. In the meantime, in Kok Terek, they were obliged to report to the MVD twice a month.

Opposite the MVD station Solzhenitsyn had spotted the village school, a low, thatched adobe building with an incongruous, neo-classical stone portico stuck on the front. When the questioning was over, he asked casually where the district education office was to be found. When the MGB officer answered his query seriously, he deduced that there would be no objection to his applying for a job there, and permission to go to the education office was granted at once. Within a few minutes Solzhenitsyn found himself walking normally down the street for the first time in eight years. He almost had to pinch himself to make sure that he was not dreaming.

I wonder whether everybody knows the meaning of this great free word. I am walking along *by myself!* With no sub-machine-guns threatening me from either flank or from the rear. I look behind me: no one there! If I like, I can take the right-hand side past the school fence, where a big pig is rooting in a puddle. And if I like, I can walk on the left, where hens are strutting and scratching immediately in front of the district education office.

I walk the two hundred yards to the office, and my spine, which seemed bent for eternity, is already just a little straighter, my manner already a little more relaxed. In the course of those two hundred yards, I have graduated to the next-higher civil estate.[2]

Putting on his usual bold front, Solzhenitsyn walked into the education office and, just as casually as when speaking to the MGB officer, announced that he would like to become a teacher. The two stout Kazakh school inspectors he found inside were surprised to see him—in these remote parts, everyone knew everyone, especially in a professional field like education. He explained that he was an exile, and after disappearing into an inner sanctum for a while, they emerged to beckon him inside. There he was greeted coolly and circumspectly by the director, "a small, lithe, attractive Kazakh woman with something feline . . . about her," who questioned him about his qualifications and his past career. What clearly interested her most were the reasons for his imprisonment, but Solzhenitsyn brazenly replied that they were a state secret and that he was not at liberty to tell her.[3]

She responded by telling him that she had no vacancies for teachers of mathematics and physics. Solzhenitsyn already knew this to be untrue. When the two inspectors had left the outer office, he had got into conversation with the typist, a plump, middle-aged Russian woman of about fifty who was herself a former prisoner, and she had told him that Kok Terek was extremely short of mathematics teachers. As for teachers of physics, there wasn't one in the entire district. But there was nothing he could say or do. The three Kazakhs were obviously frightened by his exile status and in the end compromised by asking him to fill out yet another questionnaire (in duplicate) and write out another curriculum vitae. They would let him know, they said, if a vacancy occurred.

Solzhenitsyn returned to the MVD station with its makeshift adobe lock-up. Even the MVD officers here had been affected by the easygoing southern ways of the Kazakhs, and no move was made to lock the new arrivals up for the night; they were allowed to sleep on some bundles of hay in the yard.

This first night out of prison, under the stars, was never to be forgotten by Solzhenitsyn, who wrote lyrical descriptions of how it affected him in both *Cancer Ward* and *The Gulag Archipelago*. Here is how he expressed it in the latter book.

A night under the open sky! We had forgotten what it was like. There had always been locks and bars, always walls and ceilings. I had no thought of sleep. I walked and walked and walked about the prison yard, which was bathed in soft, warm light. A cart left where it had been unhitched, a well, a drinking trough, a small hayrick, the black shadows of horses under an open shed—it was all so peaceful, so ancient, so free from the cruel imprint of the MVD. It was only the third of March, but there was not the slightest chill in the night air. It was still almost summery, as it had been in the daytime. Again and again the braying of donkeys rose over the sprawling village of Kok Terek, long-drawn-out and passionate, telling the she-asses of their love, of the ungovernable strength flooding their bodies. Some of the braying was probably the she-asses answering. I found it difficult to distinguish one voice from another, but that powerful bass bellowing was perhaps the noise of camels. I felt that if only I had a voice, I, too, would start baying at the moon: I shall be able to breathe here! I shall be able to move around![4]

As Solzhenitsyn wrote in *Cancer Ward* of Oleg Kostoglotov, "On that night he believed and hoped again, no matter how many times he had vowed never to do either."[5] Despite his desire to look on the gloomy side, the optimist in him was unquenchable.

The following day the exiles were allowed to look for private lodgings. Solzhenitsyn found a room in a tiny mud hut whose roof was so low that he couldn't stand up inside, with a single, fogged window and an earthen floor. For a bed he simply laid his padded jacket on the floor and slept on that. There were no amenities of any kind—he did not even have an oil lamp as yet (electricity was unthinkable)—but just to be alone in the dark was sheer bliss after all those years of cells and barrack huts glaringly lit by day and night.

On the very next morning, 6 March 1953, Solzhenitsyn was roused by his elderly landlady, Mrs Chadova, who seemed terribly agitated. "Go to the square and listen to what the loudspeakers are saying," she said. When he asked why, she whispered, "I'm frightened to tell you, I'm frightened to tell you."[6] In the main square Solzhenitsyn found a crowd of about two hundred people listening to a radio announcement that Stalin had died. The old men had bared their heads and were openly grief-stricken. Others looked mournful, and only a few of the younger men seemed unconcerned.

Solzhenitsyn was not merely unconcerned, he wanted to jump for joy. His arch-enemy was dead. The man who had come to personify for him all the evils and perversions of the Soviet system, author of the monstrous labour camps and monarch of the archipelago (for criticizing whom Solzhenitsyn had been flung into the abyss), had come to the end of his infamous life. Women and girls wept openly in the street, dabbing their eyes with their handkerchiefs. Concealing his real feelings and setting his face in a suitably solemn expression, Solzhenitsyn left the square and returned to Chadova's hut. The rest of the day was spent writing a commemorative poem in honour of this signal occasion, "The Fifth of March."*

Chadova's hut was not suitable for a long stay, and Solzhenitsyn found another room with a young couple called Yakov and Katerina Melnichuk, on Sadovaya Street. Their clay hut wasn't much bigger than Chadova's but was

---

*Officially the equivalent of $100, unofficially less than half of that amount in present values.

somewhat better equipped and allowed him more room. Katerina Melnichuk later described her first impression of him.

> He came . . . and put his wooden suitcase down by the front door. We shook hands. I could see that he was well-mannered and very good looking, but his clothes were in a dreadful state. Yakov, my husband, picked up his suitcase and said, "Oho! It's heavy! What have you got in there—books?" "Yes, books," he said.
>
> We made him a bunk out of boxes in the kitchen. . . . He used to burn the midnight oil a lot. We would have been asleep for ages, but he used to stay up till all hours reading by the oil lamp or writing something. He was strange.
>
> Soon after he arrived, I boiled some potatoes in their jackets and turned them out onto a plate. He picked up a potato, rolled it about in his hands and suddenly bit into it. I was alarmed. "What are you doing, Sasha? Peel it first." But he only smiled at me. He was remembering old times, I expect.[7]

Katerina recalled his getting up early—at six in the morning—and going for long walks over the steppe if it was fine. When it was not, he used to pace up and down the garden, just as he used to do in the *sharashka*. She told him to rest more and not push himself so hard, but he simply smiled and said he couldn't help it, it was what he was used to.

Solzhenitsyn now had time to look at his situation and surroundings more carefully. Exile as an institution had been common in Russia for centuries—by the beginning of the twentieth century there were about a quarter of a million Russians in internal exile at any one time. After the Revolution the new Soviet leaders promised that exile, like all the other repugnant features of the tsarist regime, would be abolished; but, like all the other repugnant features, it was not only not abolished—it was adapted and intensified a hundredfold. The numbers sent into exile had taken an exponential leap with collectivization in the years after 1929. Throughout the thirties and forties, many millions were sent into exile, including, during or after the war, whole peoples, such as the Volga Germans, the Crimean Tartars, and the Meskhetians. After 1948 it had also become the accepted practice to send almost all prisoners convicted under Article 58 ("anti-Soviet agitation and propaganda") into exile when they had served their sentences, regardless of what those sentences had stipulated.

Kazakhstan had long been familiar with the phenomenon of exile. In 1930 the Kazakhs had rebelled against the policy of collectivization, and Marshal Budenny and his famed Cossack cavalry had been sent to suppress the revolt, which they did with their usual brutal efficiency, hacking down the precious trees (in a very dry land) of rebellious peasants and putting a torch to their homesteads. Since then, Kazakhstan, with its empty spaces, had become a prime repository for exiles. In the Kok Terek district alone, there was an ethnic mixture of great variety, including Kazakhs and Russians, large contingents of Ukrainians, Volga Germans, Greeks from the Kuban, Chechens from the Caucasus, Koreans from the Far East, and representatives of just about every other nation in the Soviet empire.

Many of them had arrived in the years just before and after the war. Kok Terek, and its central village of Berlik, had consequently undergone rapid and mainly unplanned development. It was a sprawling, featureless sort of settlement, with about four thousand inhabitants, most of them exiles. When Solzhenitsyn arrived, the village had no church or mosque but possessed a cinema and a co-operative store. There was not a single asphalt road in the place. Dust was everywhere, and when it rained the roads became a quagmire and impassable. If a vehicle happened to be out in the steppe when it rained, or even on the outskirts of the village, it had to be abandoned—or the driver stayed with it—until the rain stopped and the roads dried out. For this reason, there were few vehicles in use, and the villagers preferred mules, donkeys, horses, or camels.

The main occupation in the area was agriculture, mostly cattle- and livestock-rearing, though the authorities were trying to encourage more arable agriculture, especially the growing of sugar beet. This was made difficult by the long, hot summers and frequent droughts, but a series of irrigation channels had been dug to bring water from the river Chu, and in Kok Terek itself there was an intricate network of irrigation ditches feeding the individual farms and holdings. Most water went to the state collective farm, run by Kazakhs, but private peasants were allowed to have water about once every three to four weeks, and then there was a tremendous hustle and bustle throughout the village. Competition for the water was fierce, leading to jostling and even fights, and since the water was often given at awkward times— in the middle of the night or at dawn—uproar was almost endemic.

For the first month or so after his arrival, Solzhenitsyn remained without work. He continued to badger the people in the education office, but they were visibly frightened by his political past and after a while refused to receive him at all. They even produced a document signed by the regional education office stating that all the schools in the Kok Terek district were fully staffed with mathematics teachers and had no need of more. Since the MVD had paid him the money earned and saved at Ekibastuz, he was in no immediate need and decided to bide his time. By going to the tea-room once a day for two rubles' worth of hot broth and by subsisting on potatoes, bread, and dripping, he was able to make his money go a long way. Thrift was by now second nature to him. In the meantime he occupied himself with writing out the verse he had composed and memorized in the camps.[8]

One day he was unexpectedly stopped in the street by an MVD officer and told to go with him. The officer led the way to the district consumer co-operative, a wholesale enterprise responsible for supplying all the shops in Kok Terek, and ordered him to start working there. He was signed on immediately as a "planning officer," with no questions asked, at a princely salary of 450 rubles a month,* and set to work.

---

*Officially the equivalent of $100, unofficially less than half of that amount.

He had been enlisted, it transpired, to help cope with the annual crisis brought on by the Soviet custom of holding a grandiose, nation-wide "sale" of consumer goods every 1 April. The whole exercise was little better than a propaganda trick, for no more than a few copecks were ever dropped from each item. Nevertheless, every single article for sale was affected, and this meant that every wholesale distributor and every retail shop in the country was obliged to make an inventory of its stock and set the new prices (which were centrally determined, of course). Since the task had to be accomplished almost overnight, it invariably created chaos every year.

Solzhenitsyn was quickly followed into the co-operative offices by two other unemployed exiles, V. I. Vasilenko, a former ship's captain who had arrived in the same party as Solzhenitsyn, and Grigori Samsilovich, who was still a stranger to him, although they later became friends. All three were put to work beside the fifteen permanent staff, who were already poring over enormous inventories and furiously clicking their abacuses. It was a simple and intensely boring bookkeeping operation, not at all to Solzhenitsyn's taste, but there was nothing to do but give in and get on with it.

Even so, it was not in Solzhenitsyn's temperament to obey orders blindly. Irritated by the slowness of working out all his sums on paper, he asked for a calculating machine. No one seemed to know what it was at first, and no one in Kok Terek knew how to use one, but somebody remembered that there was one in the district statistics office, and eventually this was procured for Solzhenitsyn's use.

A more spectacular piece of effrontery followed about a week later, when the going began to get tougher. The obese Kazakh chairman of the co-operative called the entire staff into his office and announced that since they were so badly behind with the repricing exercise and since the matter was urgent, everyone would henceforth be required to work from seven in the morning until two the next morning, with an hour's break for lunch and another for supper, making a seventeen-hour day. Solzhenitsyn was appalled by this news, not least because he was deep into his verse play and knew that this would deprive him of the time needed to work on it. He already resented working at the co-op at all. Seventeen hours was out of the question. And he marvelled at the sheeplike way in which everybody, including the free employees as well as the exiles, accepted this despotic injunction without a murmur.

As a political exile he could not voice his objections aloud. He would have been accused of ideological sabotage. But nobody else spoke up, so he resolved on a course of action that he had learned from experience in the camps—not to answer back, but simply to ignore the instructions and do what he wanted.

At five o'clock I rose from my desk and left. And I did not return until nine in the morning. All my colleagues were already sitting there, counting or pretending to count. They looked at me as though I were crazy. [Grigori Samsilovich], who secretly approved of my behaviour but dared not imitate me, informed me privately that the boss had stood over my empty desk screaming that he would drive me a hundred kilometres into the desert.[9]

Solzhenitsyn writes that when he heard this, his heart was in his mouth, for it was quite within the chairman's powers to get him expelled from Kok Terek. But miraculously the chairman did nothing. Kazakh lethargy, small-town dilatoriness, and the faint beginnings of a more liberal era following the uncertainty caused by the death of Stalin combined to favour him with an unexpected immunity, and he was left alone. The chairman even looked away when he passed him in the corridor.

Solzhenitsyn's stubbornness and self-confidence were soon to be rewarded in a new way. The superintendent of studies at the Berlik school, Zeinegata Syrymbetov, a young Kazakh and prominent member of the local Party organization, had been very impressed with Solzhenitsyn when he first came to ask for a job. This "tall, skinny man with the pale face and deep-sunken eyes" had struck him as rather comical at their first meeting, with his faded cavalry breeches, patched boots, and the mangy fur cap that he nervously kneaded in his lap. But Solzhenitsyn's seriousness and self-confidence had won Syrymbetov over, while his academic qualifications in physics and mathematics were well nigh irresistible.[10] The one objection to employing him had been the virtually insurmountable one of Solzhenitsyn's political past. One couldn't be too careful. But after he had been working for about a month in the co-operative, Solzhenitsyn received a call from Syrymbetov. The latter was on his way to a trade-union meeting at the Dzhambul Regional Education Office and wanted a copy of Solzhenitsyn's diploma to take with him. He was determined to employ him if he could and was prepared to take whatever political risks were necessary.

In Dzhambul, Syrymbetov pointed out to the regional director of education that it was absurd to have such a highly qualified teacher in the village and not use him. The regional director agreed and personally signed an order appointing Solzhenitsyn teacher of mathematics, physics, and astronomy in the Kirov High School in Berlik, thus bypassing the local officials who had been blocking his entry.[11]

Solzhenitsyn was overjoyed. From the very day of his arrival in Kok Terek, the tide of desire to return to his old profession had been running high. "To teach! To feel myself a man again! To sweep into the class-room and run my burning eyes over childish faces!"[12] The determined young superintendent had rescued him.

Solzhenitsyn began teaching immediately after the May holidays; he later described his emotions in *The Gulag Archipelago*.

Shall I describe the happiness it gave me to go into the class-room and pick up the chalk? This was really the day of my release, the restoration of my citizenship: I stopped noticing all the other things that made up the life of an exile.

When I was in Ekibastuz, our column was often marched past the local school. I would look at it as at some inaccessible paradise, at the children running about the yard, at the teachers in bright dresses, and the tinkle of the bell from the front steps cut me to the heart. . . . It seemed to me the supreme, heart-breaking happiness to enter a class-room carrying a register as the bell rang, and start a lesson with the mysterious air of one about to unfold wonders.[13]

Characteristically, he noted that although nostalgia and his teacher's instinct explained this craving for the class-room, it was also dictated by his hunger for esteem: "I needed the contrast after years of humiliation, after years of knowing that my talents were unwanted."

His talents were certainly wanted in Kok Terek, where he was immediately asked to take the top two classes in physics and mathematics. He found them "tragically unprepared" for their leaving examinations, due in a month's time, and threw himself joyously into the herculean task of making up for lost time. "I prescribed additional evening classes, group discussions, field-work, astronomical observations, and they turned up in greater numbers and higher spirits than if they had been going to the cinema."[14]

When the time came for the examinations, the superintendent was afflicted with an access of sudden doubt. Perhaps Solzhenitsyn was rusty and had forgotten his mathematics and physics in the camps? There had been no time to check. Syrymbetov, the only man in Kok Terek with a university degree, had been so overjoyed to find another university man that he had rushed him into the school as fast as he could manage it. He knew of the low standards of his school-leavers and was desperate to try and improve them. But what if he had blundered?

The Soviet educational system calls for leaving examinations to be taken in two parts—oral and written. The written questions are sent from the Ministry of Education in Moscow and are supposed to be opened by the teacher in the presence of his pupils and then written up on the blackboard. This is to ensure that no one knows the questions in advance. When the packet of questions arrived in Kok Terek—a day or two early, as usual—the superintendent called Solzhenitsyn and the other mathematics teachers into his office, illegally broke open the seal, and instructed Solzhenitsyn to answer the questions in the presence of the other teachers. To Syrymbetov's delight, Solzhenitsyn answered them all without difficulty.

A similar incident occurred two days later, when the examination was taking place. In the villages and hamlets around Kok Terek, the seventh-year pupils were taking a similar leaving examination at a lower level. Suddenly the telephone rang in Syrymbetov's office, and a teacher from one of the village schools came on the line: "We can't solve the questions! The answers are coming out all wrong!" Soon another teacher rang in, and then a third. The despairing superintendent summoned Solzhenitsyn and asked him whether he could answer the seventh-class questions as well. Solzhenitsyn complied, and the chastened superintendent rang back each of the schools in turn.[15]

This farcical episode reflected the abysmally low educational standards prevailing in Kazakhstan. Many of the village teachers had had only seven years of schooling, and there were other features of the local system that militated against excellence. For instance, a teacher's performance was measured by his examination results. In theory it was an excellent idea, but in practice, owing to a lack of inspection and any means of verification, it simply led to teachers' awarding high marks indiscriminately. This academic inflation was reinforced by pressure from local officials to ensure that their children got good marks, regardless of performance, and by a general unwillingness on the part of the teachers to upset their superiors. Lastly, there were the peculiar effects of positive discrimination in favour of women. In Central Asia, women had been traditionally oppressed, and the Soviet authorities were doing their best to change things and offer incentives to Kazakh women. To this end, they had introduced quotas for examination passes by women and similar quotas for places in institutes of higher education; but since not enough Kazakh women were qualified to take them, the quotas were filled with unqualified candidates. Many of these ended up as teachers, thus depressing educational standards still further.

Solzhenitsyn was irritated and affronted by this sort of petty corruption, which flourished both inside and outside the school. One source of such corruption was the precarious situation of the exiles. Of the four thousand inhabitants of Kok Terek, a majority were exiles, who were reminded at every turn of their position as second-class citizens and their dependence on the goodwill of the authorities. These reminders usually took the form of requests for "loans," accompanied by threats of dismissal if the exiles proved uncooperative.

Within the school the unofficial loans were systematized in the form of a twenty-five ruble deduction made from teachers' salaries every pay-day, and the headmaster would regularly demand fifty rubles from each teacher towards a "present" for one of his daughters' birthdays, or call individual teachers into his study to "request" a loan of up to five hundred rubles. Before graduation, the parents of Kazakh pupils were obliged to contribute a half or a whole sheep to the school—in which case a certificate was guaranteed, even if the pupil had failed—and when the local Party bosses took correspondence courses to improve their qualifications and pay (which they frequently did), it was the teachers at the school who answered the questions and completed the written tests for them.[16]

Much of this simply reflected the oriental social arrangements and tribal customs of traditional Kazakh society, but it was compounded by the corrupt centralized power of the Party hierarchy and the weakness of the law. Nor were matters helped by the passive complicity of the exiles themselves. As ex-prisoners, they expected to be ill treated and to be obliged to knuckle under, which made their oppressors' task that much easier.

Yet there was nothing inevitable about it. Georgi Mitrovich, an elderly Serb and a colleague of Solzhenitsyn's, had built a formidable reputation for himself as a scourge of all forms of corruption and backsliding, although he had served ten years for "counter-revolutionary Trotskyite activity" and was an exile. A livestock expert by profession, he had once worked in the district agricultural department, but had been sacked for exposing the local Party leaders' practice of exchanging their cows for better ones from the collective farm herd or of having their private cows fed and fattened at the collective farm's expense. After that he had been transferred to the district health department, where a similar series of events occurred, and had then moved to Solzhenitsyn's school, where he continued in the same vein, exposing illegalities at teachers' meetings, writing complaints to the regional authorities, and even dispatching telegrams to Khrushchev. He was dismissed for a while from teaching, then reinstated, then transferred to another school, and came within a hair's breadth of being rearrested, but he persisted with his fight for justice.

Solzhenitsyn did not submit meekly to the system either, refusing to award high marks for favours and rejecting, when it came, a request for a loan from the head of the Kok Terek education department. But although he admired and became friendly with Mitrovich and shared his indignation, he did not support him in his campaigns. Mitrovich was somewhat protected by the fact that he was now old and in bad health, and as a faithful Leninist (something that struck an answering chord in Solzhenitsyn emotionally, if no longer intellectually), he could attack the system "from the left," which earned him a certain degree of indulgence. Solzhenitsyn, however, had moved in the other direction and could not afford to give rein to his real opinions. Consequently he kept quiet, and to avoid voting against Mitrovich would find a pretext to slip away from meetings before a vote was taken.[17]

A more compelling reason for Solzhenitsyn's silence was his preoccupation with his writing. From the moment of his arrival in Kok Terek, he had devoted every minute of his spare time to it, despite the difficult conditions and the necessity for absolute secrecy. For the first three weeks he had had nothing else to distract him and had made splendid progress. Then had come the job at the consumer co-operative and then the teaching, so that every moment was now precious to him.

His first task had been to get down onto paper everything that he had composed and memorized in Ekibastuz. Above all, this meant *The Way* (now somewhat ambitiously called a "novel in verse"),* which he was at last able to write out in full and revise. When completed, the poem contained eleven sections or "chapters" of unequal length, preceded by a brief prologue and an equally brief introduction. It was written in a loose iambic metre modelled on the ballad form evolved by Alexander Tvardovsky for his mock-epic *Vasily Tyorkin*, the poem that Solzhenitsyn had so admired at the front. *The Way* is longer than *Tyorkin*, however, consisting of over ten thousand lines of verse

---

* It is possible that Solzhenitsyn was influenced by the subtitle of Pushkin's *Evgeny Onegin* when he called his poem a novel in verse. In fact, *The Way* has no plot in the sense that *Evgeny Onegin* has, and contains only one major character: the autobiographical hero.

("twice as long as *Eugene Onegin*," as Panin later wrote of it in his memoirs),[18] and it had been a prodigious feat to memorize it, even with the help of the rosary and the slips of paper.

The poem has not been published, except for chapter 9, which has appeared separately both in Russian and in translation under the title of *Prussian Nights*. And a part of the prologue, which was later rewritten by Solzhenitsyn, slipped out in the late sixties when quoted by a friend in an essay about his work.*

The prologue is interesting for what it tells us about Solzhenitsyn's view of his role as a writer. It begins by briefly describing his hard life in the camp. Despite his weariness, however, he feels the compulsion to write.

> . . . man is not to be prisoned in the day.
> To write! To write now, without delay,
> Not in heated wrath, but with cool and clear understanding.
> The millstones of my thoughts can hardly turn,
> Too rare the flicker of light in my aching soul.
> Yes, tight is the circle around us tautly drawn,
> But my verses *will* burst their bonds and freely roam,
> And I can guard, perhaps, beyond "their" reach,
> In rhythmic harmony, this hard-won gift of speech.

He is also explicit about his mission. He is writing not just on behalf of himself but on behalf of the millions who had died in Stalin's prisons and camps or been crippled for life by their sufferings.

> I do not write my verses for idle pleasure,
> Nor from a sense of energy to burn.
> Nor out of mischief, to evade their searches,
> Do I carry them past my captors in my brain.
> The free flow of my verse is dearly bought,
> I have paid a cruel price for my poet's rights   . . .
> . . . .
> Oh, if this were but the sum of the price paid for my verse!
> But those others paid the price with their lives,
> Immured in the silence of Solovki, drowned in the thunder of waves,
> Or shot without trial in Vorkuta's polar night.
> Love and warmth and their executed cries
> Have combined in my breast to carve
> The receptive metre of this sorrowful tale,
> These few poor thousand incapacious lines.
> Oh, hopeless labour! Can you really pay the price?
> Do you think to redeem the pledge with a single life?

*Solzhenitsyn later published some extracts in the *Vestnik RKhD*, no. 117 (1976), under the heading "On the Soviet Border." They show the hero (i.e., Solzhenitsyn) on his way from Brodnitz to Moscow under armed escort and describe his meditations on the course of Russian history (see p. 312).

> For what an age has my country been so poor
> In women's happy laughter, so very rich
> In poets' lamentations!
> Verse, verse—for all that we have lost,
> A drop of scented resin in the razed forest! [19]

Here, in outline, is the programme that was to occupy Solzhenitsyn for the next twenty years, not just in verse but in prose as well, and that was to give birth to almost all his mature works, ranging from *A Day in the Life of Ivan Denisovich* to the three volumes of *The Gulag Archipelago*.

About the rest of *The Way*, Solzhenitsyn has been extremely reticent. Four years after completing it, he told Dimitri Panin that he was rather dissatisfied with the poem, finding it long-winded and repetitive, and he spoke of rewriting it. In the early sixties, after the success of *Ivan Denisovich*, he did indeed rework some of the chapters and tone them down before offering them to *Novy Mir* under a different title (*A Cheerless Story*). *Novy Mir*'s editor, Tvardovsky, rejected them and is quoted (in *The Oak and the Calf*) as saying, "I can understand that you had to write something in the camps; otherwise your brain would have gone rusty."[20] He also told Solzhenitsyn that the poem was "the sort of thing that should be printed in 8-point type in volume 20 of your collected works."[21] In 1963, when Solzhenitsyn read the poem to Anna Akhmatova, she, too, advised him not to publish it, but to stick to prose, in which he was "unassailable."[22]

Apart from *The Way* Solzhenitsyn worked on a verse play, *Feast of the Conquerors*, also composed at Ekibastuz and committed to memory there. For many years Solzhenitsyn was even more reticent about the play than about the poem, partly because of its more controversial subject matter, but mainly because in 1965 the play, together with some of his other early works, was confiscated by the KGB and circulated among loyalist members of the Writers' Union in an attempt to discredit him. The aura of dread created around the play by subsequent bad publicity (Solzhenitsyn was obliged to renounce it when trying to get *Cancer Ward* published) led many observers to conclude that the play must contain unspeakable opinions about the Soviet political system, and it was not until many years after he had arrived in the West that Solzhenitsyn released it for publication—in volume 9 of his collected works.*

In point of fact, *Feast of the Conquerors* is not as sensational as the later controversy made it appear. It is a relatively short play of about twenty-five hundred lines, written in iambic rhyming couplets that appear to be modelled on Griboyedov's nineteenth-century comedy *Woe from Wit* (*Feast of the Conquerors* is also described as "a comedy"). There are no acts, only a succession of scenes, which all take place at an impromptu celebration banquet organized by the staff of an artillery battalion at a captured country mansion in East Prussia. Solzhenitsyn's unit had actually held such a banquet in January 1945, and many of the characters are based on fellow members of his battal-

---

* Published in 1981. An English translation appeared in 1983 under the title *Victory Celebrations*.

ion. Arseny Pashkin, the political commissar he had once wanted to describe in his novel about the war, figures as Arseny Vanin; Lieutenant Ovsyannikov becomes Lieutenant Yachmennikov; Solzhenitsyn himself is transformed into Captain Sergei Nerzhin (the first appearance of this surname in his literary works); Captain Dobrokhotov-Maikov appears under his real name (he was killed at the front shortly after the actual banquet took place); and one may readily imagine that Berbenchuk, the battalion commander, his wife, Glafira, and Captain Likharyov are also based on real-life prototypes. One further detail reproduced from the actual banquet is the use of an enormous upturned mirror as the banqueting table—an effective prop in any theatrical production.

Into this company of real-life prototypes Solzhenitsyn introduced two contending figures to propel the action along, one fictional—Lieutenant Gridnev, an officer in Smersh—and the other based on a real person who was not, however, present at the original banquet—Galina, an *émigrée* Russian girl who has come all the way from Vienna, where she lives, to be near her fiancé, who is fighting with the Vlasov forces in East Prussia. Such plot as there is deals with the discovery of Galina in a Prussian village by the artillery battalion, their assumption that she has been a prisoner of the Germans, their good-natured offer to take her along with them, and Gridnev's opposition on the assumption that she is a German spy. The only person who learns the truth about her is Nerzhin, who was a childhood friend before she departed to the West. When she informs him of her real reason for being in Prussia, he praises her for her fidelity and loyalty to her fiancé and vows to help her find him ("I have faith in our Russian future while such women as you exist").[23] He soon comes into conflict with the bumptious, self-confident Smersh lieutenant (who has designs on Galina's virtue in addition to his political suspicions), but nothing results from their clashes, and at the end of the play, Galina's fate is still unresolved.

The plot is not important, and the characters are little better than cardboard cut-outs, a pretext for Solzhenitsyn to get down to the true subject of his play, which is a debate about Russia's past and present, the pluses and minuses of the Revolution, the conflict between the revolutionary Communist values epitomized by Gridnev and the genuine human and moral values personified by almost everyone else in the play, ranging from the genial, bumbling Berbenchuk and his sagacious, far-sighted staff officers (Vanin, Nerzhin, Dobrokhotov-Maikov) down to the humble peasant lad, Yachmennikov, and including even the *émigrée* Galina. In a variety of monologues and dialogues, Solzhenitsyn examines some of the themes that were to become dominant in his mature works: the political and moral bankruptcy of Marxist ideology, the disastrous effects of collectivization, the monstrous power of the security organs, Stalin's paranoia and his abysmal performance at the start of the war as commander-in-chief, the decisive role of Russian patriotism in winning the Second World War.

It is interesting that some of these themes are expressed through the conflict between the (personally) loyal and honest Russian *émigrée*, Galina, and the (personally) disloyal—though loyal in a political sense—and dishonest Communist, Gridnev, and that the debate about Russia's historical path and destiny should be set in these particular terms. Yet Solzhenitsyn does not come out unequivocally on Galina's side. He takes a middle position, and it is significant that he hedges and qualifies many of his criticisms of Soviet society in the play precisely by placing them in the mouth of Galina, who is ostensibly (and automatically in the Soviet context) a negative character and who can be expected to criticize the Soviet Union because of her background. In the mouths of Vanin, Nerzhin, and the others, the criticism is muted or vaguely loyal, and it is only in their more positive dreams for the future that their true unorthodoxy emerges (Nerzhin's toast at the banquet is "May it be possible, in Mother Russia, to say what we think aloud!").[24]

For these reasons *The Feast of the Conquerors*, although uncommonly bold for its time, now strikes the reader as less sensational than the subsequent scandal made it seem. In an era of genuine anti-Stalinism, it might almost have passed the censorship, except for the sympathetic passages on the Vlasovites, the very mention of whom triggered an automatic and genuine loathing in Soviet readers at that time. But there is nothing truly seditious in it, nothing the Soviet security authorities could point to as totally beyond the pale, as was demonstrated after its confiscation, when no legal steps were taken to call Solzhenitsyn to account.

The same cannot be said, however, for a second play Solzhenitsyn completed at Kok Terek, *Decembrists without December* (later renamed *The Captives*).* *Decembrists* is a much longer and more ambitious work than *Conquerors*, with an enormous cast of characters, multiple changes of scene, and a text that alternates between verse and prose, though the prose predominates. Among the characters met here for the first time are Georgi Vorotyntsev, a former colonel in the tsar's army (later to reappear in *August 1914*), Lev Rubin and Valentin Pryanchikov (later to figure in *The First Circle*), and Pavel Gai, one of the heroes of *The Tenderfoot and the Tart*. Evgeni Divnich, the militantly religious anti-Communist whom Solzhenitsyn had met in Butyrki, appears under his own name, while the author's alter ego is here called Andrei Kholudenev.†

The play is set in the Smersh headquarters at Brodnitz, on the Prussian border, where Solzhenitsyn had been taken after his arrest. Again there is little plot to speak of, and no character development. The play follows the fortunes of a group of prisoners from their first arrival in the cells through investigation and questioning to their "trial" and conviction by a military tribunal. But there are several interesting formal developments. The extremely large cast of characters reflects a first attempt by Solzhenitsyn at a synthesis of all he had learned about the world of the camps. Within this synthesis he

---

*Published in volume 9 of the Collected Works in 1981. An English translation appeared in 1983.

†It may be relevant that the Russian *kholod*, which the name evokes, means "cold."

tries to encompass all aspects of the Smersh operation and to describe all the individuals involved, which means not only the prisoners (with whom the author's sympathies overwhelmingly lie) but also the Smersh personnel, ranging from the commanding general through his officers and interrogators down to the humble guards. Another feature of this synthesis is its inclusion of scenes of life among Russians who have chosen to stay behind the German lines (Galina's successors as it were) and the inclusion among the prisoners of a White Russian colonel (Vorotyntsev), a Pole, a Yugoslav, a German, a Russian who has fought with the Americans, and one who has been with the Belgian resistance.

The need to pack so much information into the confines of a stage play is one of the reasons for the play's great length, and it leads Solzhenitsyn into some interesting experiments. The diverse prisoners' voices are used contrapuntally as a kind of chorus at intervals during the play, as are the voices of the interrogators in one of the scenes. The several interrogations are shown simultaneously, side by side on the stage, with the dialogue switching consecutively from one to another, and a similar technique is used to depict the reading out of the prisoners' sentences. These devices are interesting in themselves and also go some way to vary the pace, which is otherwise rather even throughout the play's twelve scenes.

Thematically, *Decembrists* shows a logical progression from *Feast of the Conquerors*, containing many of the same ideas, but this time worked out more fully and at greater length. Perhaps the greatest development is in the treatment of the White Russians and of those who chose to remain with the Germans or fight with Vlasov's army. This time Solzhenitsyn comes off the fence and develops the thesis that Russian history was on their side, that they were more genuinely "Russian" and patriotic than the Bolshevik usurpers, and that the consequences of the Revolution had been uniformly disastrous for the Russian people. It is possible that Solzhenitsyn was "trying out" some of these ideas and not necessarily committed to them himself, but the force with which they are communicated in *Decembrists* goes far beyond anything in *Feast of the Conquerors* and makes it incomparably more inflammatory and dangerous than its more famous predecessor. It is hardly surprising that nothing was heard of it until years after Solzhenitsyn had reached the West. Had this play fallen into the hands of the KGB, his career would undoubtedly have come to a speedy and bitter end.

It must be said that neither play is particularly successful. The verse in *Feast of the Conquerors* is not as assured and inventive as that to be found in *The Way*, or as vigorous as the driving rhythms of *Prussian Nights*, although it does attain a certain Griboyedovian wit in some of the banquet exchanges. But what is interesting is the way in which both plays prefigure Solzhenitsyn's first mature work (also begun in exile), his long novel *The First Circle*. At their centre, as at the novel's, is an impassioned debate about Russia's past and future, and *Decembrists* in particular anticipates the way in which Solzhenitsyn, in the novel, was to make the microcosm of his work stand for the world outside. In *Decembrists* the character of Lev Rubin is almost fully formed and is easily recognizable as the lovable Communist we will meet again in the novel. Nerzhin-Kholudenev is less successful, perhaps because Solzhenitsyn was still unable sufficiently to distance himself from this auto-biographical character. On the opposite side of the ideological fence, the Smersh officers and investigators clearly prefigure some of the characters in *The First Circle*, but they are still too villainous, whereas in the novel they were to become more human and therefore more believable. Finally, we see Solzhenitsyn beginning to grapple with the figure of Stalin, whose statues and portraits dominate the scenery in *Decembrists* (one statue is symbolically knocked to the ground at a tense moment in the play), though it was only in the novel that Stalin was to enter the action as a living character.

The most striking scene in the play is a long debate towards the end between Vorotyntsev and a dying Smersh colonel called Prokhor Rublyov. Vorotyntsev puts forward what one might call a liberal, pre-revolutionary view of twentieth-century Russian history, in which he regards the Revolution as an avoidable disaster, while Rublyov defends the Revolution's achievements not in narrowly orthodox terms but from the viewpoint of its broadly progressive nature. It is stirringly written and sums up the arguments that appear elsewhere in the play, although as a device for the author to speak in his own voice it is too transparent to work satisfactorily as theatre. But in form and intensity, it looks forward to other notable clashes of opinion in Solzhenitsyn's later works, such as the debates between Nerzhin, Rubin, and Sologdin in *The First Circle*, between Rusanov and Kostoglotov in *Cancer Ward*, and between Lenin and Parvus in *Lenin in Zurich*.

Altogether, then, the plays must be classified as apprentice works, and the same would appear to apply to the two volumes of camp poetry that Solzhenitsyn copied out during his first year of exile, *The Heart beneath the Padded Jacket* and *When They Lose Track of the Years* (consisting of verses to and about his wife).[25] But they were essential steps on his path to becoming a real writer, and it was all as he had predicted in his preface to *The Way*:

> And one day, in distant exile dim,
> Biding my time, I will free my tortured memory from its thrall:
> On paper, birch-bark, in a blackened bottle rolled
> I will consign my tale to the forest leaves
> Or to a drift of shifting snow.[26]

Solzhenitsyn's need for peace and security in which to pursue his literary activities was finally satisfied in September 1953 when he rented a thatched and whitewashed clay hut on the outskirts of Kok Terek. His new abode consisted of a single room, with a tiny kitchen and an entrance porch, and windows facing south and west. It was unfurnished, but Solzhenitsyn had already learned how to make a bed from packing cases, and although, in Kok Terek, packing cases were like gold dust, he was able, by using his contacts at the co-operative, to buy some for two rubles each. Three went to make his bed—a mattress case stuffed with hay and wood-shavings relieved the hardness of the wood—and one served as a china cupboard. For a table, he used the old, battered suitcase that had been with him since his arrest at the front, until an exiled Ukrainian friend fashioned him a table and chair from the stunted and twisted branches of a local shrub called saxaul—no other timber was to be had in Kok Terek.

Solzhenitsyn eagerly welcomed the solitude that the possession of his own dwelling brought him. Adjoining the hut was a vegetable garden that his landlord continued to cultivate, but there was no other habitation within a hundred yards. Immediately beyond his hedge of prickly pear and the irrigation ditch that ran past his gate stretched the open steppe, with the bluish outline of the Chu-Ili Mountains rising in the distance. Solzhenitsyn continued his habit of taking daily walks and liked to wander along "a forsaken little path that wound through the fields," as he wrote to Aunt Nina, where "the silence was not of this world."[27] And in *The Gulag Archipelago* he has noted that "whenever there was a puff of wind from the steppe, my lungs drank it in greedily. In the dusk and at night, whether it was dark or moonlit, I would stroll about alone out there, inhaling and exhaling like a lunatic."[28]

Solzhenitsyn was well off by Kok Terek standards, for teachers were well paid and there was little to spend his money on. But he liked looking after himself, readily doing the shopping, cooking, and cleaning, and there was one chore that transported him back to his childhood and the pungent smells of Grandfather Semyon's adobe farm in the Caucasus. This was the need to renew the hut periodically with new layers of clay. The roof and walls needed re-doing only rarely, but every week he was obliged to replaster the floor with a mixture of mud and manure to prevent it from wearing away. On the first day after it dried, it was beautifully smooth and clean, but by the second day a layer of dust began to appear and the floor started to break up. By the end of the week, Solzhenitsyn would be raising clouds of dust every time he lifted his feet, and it would be time to renew it again.[29]

By an odd coincidence, during the very days that he was settling into his new home and preoccupied with thoughts of domesticity, he was moved by an unexpected letter from Natalia. She had obtained his address from Aunt Nina and had written in the last days of August from the Black Sea, where she was spending her summer holiday. Somewhat naïvely, she proposed a friendly correspondence in which they could indulge in a kind of platonic, spiritual communion, and she pictured their two lives as a simultaneous ascent of two "parallel staircases."

The letter touched a superstitious chord in Solzhenitsyn. It was almost as if Natalia had divined his new circumstances and the loneliness that attended his solitary state. An amateur graphologist in Ekibastuz, to whom he had shown an earlier letter of Natalia's confirming their divorce, had predicted a happy ending. It seemed to him that this was a sign, that Natalia's talk of a spiritual exchange was merely a polite cover for deeper feelings that she dared not admit openly for fear of being rebuffed. In his heart of hearts he had never believed in her love for another man. He felt sure that she had been "led astray" by Vsevolod and that she was now bored with him.

On 12 September 1953 he wrote her a tender letter of gratitude and love. Of course he was willing to take her back, he said, if she was truly prepared to turn her back on her present life and return to him. Otherwise he didn't see much point in their correspondence, since it would inevitably involve her in deception and would in any case have to cease if he should remarry. Whatever her decision, he would not feel wounded or angry, just as he had not been in the past.

> I know how weak I often was in my own life. . . . I have seen how others have behaved, and it is easy for me to understand and excuse your weakness. That Sanchik whom you once knew and loved quite undeservedly would not have forgiven you. But the present Sanya isn't even sure if there is anything to forgive. I am probably even more guilty towards you. And in any case, I haven't saved your life, whereas you have saved mine—and even more than my life.[30]

("More than my life" was a reference to Solzhenitsyn's manuscripts and notebooks, which Natalia had taken with her when she was evacuated to Central Asia during the war.)

Natalia, it seems, was taken aback by Solzhenitsyn's letter. She had no intention of leaving Vsevolod, and presumably it had not occurred to her, from the safety of her Ryazan university post and her second marriage, to wonder what impact her letter might have on her ex-husband in his lonely exile. Perhaps her letter had been but an impulsive holiday caprice, brought on by the sun and the sea? In any event, she regarded his reply as an ultimatum, and in October wrote a second letter to set him straight.

> Dear Sanechka,
> I was upset both by the contents of your letter, and by the fact that you totally misunderstood me.
> I am completely satisfied with my present life and wish for nothing more. When you have achieved the same you will perhaps understand the spirit in which I wrote to you.
> This is all I have to say to you. And so, farewell until we meet again, which will be possible only when your life becomes full in all senses of the word, not only in your work but also in the personal sphere. I trust that you will be happy. I kiss you and wish you all the very best.
> Natasha.[31]

It is not clear whether Solzhenitsyn reacted with his promised saintliness to Natalia's abrupt rejection of all his proposals, but with this letter the correspondence ended.*

---

*This exchange of letters subsequently became a point of bitter dispute between Solzhenitsyn and Reshetovskaya. Having seen only one of the three letters exchanged, I cannot say where

Solzhenitsyn soon had something much more serious to worry about. For some time now he had been plagued by a nagging stomach-ache, and in October he began to suffer from intermittent but acute pains in his groin and abdomen. As a result, he lost all desire to eat and quickly began to lose weight. The local doctors were unable to offer a satisfactory diagnosis. A gynaecologist friend, Nikolai Zubov, who was also a political exile, had attempted to treat him, but with no success, and advised him to seek permission to visit Dzhambul, where he could be seen by specialists. Solzhenitsyn was inclined to think he had gastritis or perhaps a stomach ulcer, but at the back of his mind was the memory of his operation in the camp. He had been told that it was a success, that the tumour had not invaded the surrounding tissues. Could the doctors have made a mistake?

It took him some weeks to make the necessary arrangements for a medical examination in Dzhambul. The tests for abdominal complaints turned out to be all negative, but then an X-ray revealed a tumour the size of a fist growing from the back wall of the abdominal cavity. It was almost certainly cancer. The doctors were divided over whether the tumour was a metastasis of the old one, taken out in the camp, or a new growth unconnected with it.* If it was the result of cells left behind after the removal of the lymph node, these malignant cells could have travelled through the lymphatic channels to the space behind the stomach. In any case, speedy treatment was essential, and since there was nothing to be done about it in Dzhambul, he was given a certificate for admission to the oncological clinic in Tashkent, about a thousand miles to the west.

the exact truth lies, but have endeavoured to present the picture as it emerges from Solzhenitsyn's account of the matter in his interview with me and in his published works, and from Reshetovskaya's memoirs and her unpublished letters to me in 1982.

*It is not clear whether Solzhenitsyn ever received a report of the biopsy carried out by the camp medical authorities on his first tumour. If the story of Oleg Kostoglotov in chapter 6 of *Cancer Ward* is literally autobiographical, he did not. Dr William A. Knaus, who has written the best medical analysis of Solzhenitsyn's illness (*Inside Russian Medicine* [New York, 1981], chap. 13), accepts the *Cancer Ward* version as being true for Solzhenitsyn as well.

19

CANCER WARD

FOR A POLITICAL exile to get permission to travel all the way to Tashkent was a complicated business, and Solzhenitsyn realized that he would have to return to Kok Terek for that. But before he did so he made an unscheduled—and illegal—excursion into the Chu-Ili Mountains, about a hundred miles to the east. The risks were considerable: if caught, he could have been rearrested and sentenced to a further term of imprisonment. But in Dzhambul he had heard rumours of an old man living in a village near the lake of Issyk-Kul who made infusions from a mandrake root that were supposed to be good for treating cancer.* The idea of folk-medicine appealed to him—much more, indeed, than the prospect of radio-therapy or another operation—and he resolved to find the old man and acquire some for himself. The quest proved to be not difficult, and the old man, a Russian settler by the name of Krementsov, happily sold him some of his medicine, warning him, however, that an overdose was tantamount to taking poison and that it was dangerous even to inhale it. The allowable dose was from one to ten drops, to be taken over a period of ten days, the dose to be increased by one drop each day. Then it had to be gradually decreased to one drop, and an interval of ten days allowed to elapse before starting again.[1]

Solzhenitsyn seized eagerly on this slender chance of a natural cure, bought a large quantity of the mandrake infusion, and returned with it to Kok Terek. During November and December his tumour had seemed to swell almost by the hour: "This tumour distended and distorted my stomach

---

* Dr Knaus writes that the mandrake root is a well-known folk remedy in Russia that is usually prepared in the form of tea. It contains the chemical scopolamine, which is also used in some sleeping preparations. It cannot cure cancer.

and prevented me from eating or sleeping. I was constantly aware of it. . . . But the fact that it was exerting pressure on the surrounding organs and displacing them was not the worst of it. The awful thing was that it was exuding poison and infecting my whole body."[2] The mandrake root seemed to help, however. On 11 December he wrote to an old acquaintance, Irina Arsenyeva, in Rostov that his condition had improved and his appetite had returned. Two weeks later he was still relatively cheerful, but by the end of the month he had started to go downhill again.[3] Throughout these weeks he had a sense of being at death's door and was convinced he had not long to live. Indeed, in *The Oak and the Calf* he writes that the doctors in Dzhambul had given him no more than three weeks.

It was on his experiences of these weeks that Solzhenitsyn drew for Kostoglotov's words in *Cancer Ward*:

> Although I'd been in pain for six months beforehand, the last month was agony: I couldn't stand, sit, or lie down without pain and could snatch only a few min-utes' sleep each night. So I had plenty of time to think. That autumn I learned from my own experience that a man can cross the threshold of death while occu-pying a body that is still not dead. Your blood still circulates and your stomach digests things, but psychologically you have completed all your preparations for death and lived through death itself. Everything you see around you appears to you as if from beyond the grave, evoking no emotions. Although you have never regarded yourself as a Christian—sometimes, indeed, the opposite—now you suddenly notice that you have already forgiven everyone who has insulted you and bear no more ill will towards those who have persecuted you. You find yourself indifferent to absolutely everything and everyone; there is nothing you are anxious to put right and nothing you regret. I would even say that it is a state of great equilibrium and naturalness, like that of the trees and stones.[4]

At the forefront of Solzhenitsyn's mind at this time was the problem of what to do with his manuscripts in the event of his death. He knew that if found by the authorities they would be confiscated or destroyed. He could not send them to anyone, for his mail was censored. What he needed was a reliable person who would come out and collect them and preserve them for better times, but here, too, he was in a dilemma. He and Natalia were divorced, and their sudden correspondence had ended in mutual misunderstanding. With his own family he still had no contact, and Aunt Nina was too old to make the journey. It was for this reason that he had written to Irina Arsen-yeva. He hardly knew her, but she was a former friend of Natalia's and lived in the same house as Aunt Nina. She could take the manuscripts to Nina for safe-keeping. But he could not tell her about it openly. He could only write vaguely of her coming out to Kazakhstan to "collect his belongings," which she naturally did not understand (the fact that it was a week's journey there and back by train did not make her decision any easier).[5] Realizing that it was hopeless, Solzhenitsyn resorted to desperate measures. "I hurriedly copied things out in tiny handwriting, rolled them up, several pages at a time, in tight cylinders, and squeezed them into a champagne bottle. I then buried the bottle in my garden."[6] As in the camps where he had first composed these works, literature and concealment were inextricably bound up with one another.

Meanwhile, the procedure for his visit to Tashkent had been set in motion, and Solzhenitsyn asked for permission to go during the New Year's vacation. To make the journey, he needed a permit from the MVD specifying the exact dates on which he was to travel, the place where he would stay while away, the length of time away, and the exact date of his return. He would have to register all this information with the local MVD authorities in Tashkent as well as at Kok Terek. At last the permit was issued. Donning his ancient army greatcoat and cavalry boots once more, and arming himself with a kitbag and a liberal supply of the mandrake infusion, he set off on New Year's Eve, 1953, barely able to place one foot in front of the other.

From the very start he was beset with difficulties. On New Year's Eve he was obliged to sleep in the station at Chu in order to catch the morning express to Tashkent. In obedience to the regulations, he handed in his identity card to the station officer in exchange for a room for the night. The following morning, when he went to collect his card, the duty officer was gone. He had got drunk celebrating New Year's Eve and been carried off unconscious to the nearest sobering-up station. The woman who now occupied his place could find no trace of the card and shook her head in response to Solzhenitsyn's entreaties.

The train was due at any moment, and it was out of the question for an exile to travel without an identity card. Cards would be inspected at every step of the way, and instant arrest would follow his failure to produce one. Just then he caught sight of one of the Kok Terek MVD officers strolling along the platform. The officer recognized Solzhenitsyn, who explained his predicament and showed the officer his permit. The officer was in a good mood and gave him written permission to travel.[7]

As far as Tashkent, everything went smoothly. On arrival, he made his way by tram to the MVD city headquarters and handed in his permit to stay. Then he travelled to the oncological clinic of Tashkent Hospital, but was refused admission without an identity card. In desperation he lay down on the floor of the waiting-room and refused to move until they changed their minds—an incident that he was later to use in chapter 5 of *Cancer Ward*, when describing Kostoglotov's arrival at the same clinic. Solzhenitsyn was rescued from this desperate expedient by one of the doctors who was to take over his treatment, Irina Meike, the daughter of German settlers. She quickly arranged for him to be admitted to the clinic, and the following day he entered one of the wards.

Solzhenitsyn entered the hospital on 4 January 1954, and his treatment began the very next day. Dr Lydia Dunayeva, the head of the radio-therapy department, was in charge of his case, and although she found a metastasis from the malignant lymph node, she decided that it was only a secondary tumour. The primary tumour, and the real cause of Solzhenitsyn's trouble, was a seminoma. According to medical specialists,* seminoma is a comparatively rare form of cancer that accounts for less than one-half of one per cent of the cancer cases each year, and is usually found in men between the ages of thirty-five and fifty (Solzhenitsyn had been thirty-three at the time of his first operation and was now thirty-five). Given Solzhenitsyn's weakened physical condition and the state of Soviet medicine in the early fifties, his chances of a cure were about one in three. Dr Dunayeva decided against surgery (which is now the preferred treatment in the West, followed by radiotherapy) and prescribed massive doses of radiation alone. A large purple cross was drawn on Solzhenitsyn's stomach, dividing his abdomen into four quadrants, each of which was bombarded in turn with X-rays. Three heavy rubber mats filled with lead wire were placed over the three quadrants not being treated on a given day, and a thin copper shield was sometimes used to protect Solzhenitsyn's skin from the effects of the radiation beam.[8]

According to Reshetovskaya, Solzhenitsyn's treatment lasted six weeks, during which time he had fifty-five radiation sessions of half an hour each, with a dosage of between 12,000 and 18,000 rads.[9]† This corresponds to Solzhenitsyn's description of Kostoglotov's treatment in *Cancer Ward*, where he also noted the miraculous speed with which the X-rays had begun to take effect. "This barbarous bombardment of heavy quanta, soundless and unnoticed by the assaulted tissues, had after twelve sessions given Kostoglotov back his desire and taste for life, his appetite, even his good spirits. After the second and third bombardments, he was free of the pain that had made his existence intolerable."[10] Within a couple of weeks the tumour began to shrink and Solzhenitsyn was eating well again, but then came radiation sickness, loss of appetite, and a difficult period when he felt almost as ill as when he had arrived. His spirits were also depressed by the sinestrol tablets he was obliged to take. Sinestrol contained oestrogen, the female hormone, and was administered on the principle that if seminoma was a male tumour, it might be connected with the action of the male hormones, and a female hormone would help to reduce their effect. Nowadays that theory is discredited.

Solzhenitsyn has described his condition during this period of his convalescence in one of his short stories, "The Right Hand," set in the Tashkent clinic. "My appearance was pitiful. My sallow face bore traces of everything I had gone through—the wrinkles of a camp-induced moroseness, a deathly, ashen hardness of the skin, the recent corruption of my body first by the poisons of my sickness and then by the poisons of the medicine, so that my cheeks had turned the colour of green." He tried to stroll in the hospital

---

* This account of Solzhenitsyn's illness rests mainly on Dr Knaus's analysis (see note p. 333). Knaus based himself on *Cancer Ward* and other published sources on Solzhenitsyn's illness. He does not seem to have had any co-operation from Solzhenitsyn himself.
† According to Dr Knaus, the figure of 12,000–18,000 rads refers to "air rads," meaning the amount of radiation emitted directly from the X-ray tube. Today the term "rad" refers to the dose of radiation received by the tumour, and on that definition, Solzhenitsyn probably received 2,000–3,000 rads on his abdomen and a somewhat smaller dose on his groin.

grounds, conscious of his ridiculous appearance in striped pyjamas that were too small to fit him and with his feet clad in the clumsy felt boots he had worn in the camps. After every few steps he was obliged to sit and rest, and occasionally, when attacked by radiation nausea, to lie with his head down until it passed.[11]

Judging by hints dropped in *Cancer Ward* and elsewhere, Solzhenitsyn was a difficult patient. The stubbornness, truculence, and distrustfulness of the labour-camp veteran made him reluctant to submit to orders and led to endless cross-questioning of the doctors about his treatment, while his natural restlessness made him resent his enforced inactivity and helplessness to influence events. His doctors, for their part, seem to have responded with tolerance and good humour. Irina Meike, the doctor who had rescued him from the waiting room, and Lydia Dunayeva, were both rewarded with affectionate portraits (as Gangart and Dontsova) in *Cancer Ward*.

Solzhenitsyn's independence of mind also manifested itself in his determination to cling to the mandrake root infusion that he had brought with him and with which, it appears, he surreptitiously dosed himself when no one was looking. Despite his scientific training, he seems to have nursed an elemental distrust of conventional medicine and maintained, to the very end, a superstitious faith in nature cures. At the back of his mind, at least when he arrived, was also the thought that if the pain became intolerable, and if there was no hope of a cure, the poisonous infusion offered him one last freedom—to end his life when he chose.

As life flowed back into his veins, however, the need for such a choice receded, and after a few weeks he began to recover some of his old vitality. His walks in the hospital grounds became longer and occasionally went beyond them, although this was officially forbidden to the patients. In *Cancer Ward*, he draws a cheerfully humorous portrait of himself during this period in the guise of a letter from Kostoglotov to some friends.

> The only things that can help my nausea are pickled cucumber and pickled cabbage, but of course they are unobtainable either in the hospital or the medical centre, and patients aren't allowed out of the gates. "Your relatives can bring you some," they say. . . .
>
> What can a poor convict do? I put on my boots, fasten my woman's dressing-gown round my waist with my army belt, and creep over to the place where the wall is half falling down. I clamber through the wall, cross the railway tracks, and in five minutes I'm at the bazaar. My appearance causes no surprise or laughter either on the way there or in the bazaar itself, which I take to be a sign of the spiritual health of our people, who have become accustomed to everything. I walk about the bazaar and bargain sullenly, as probably only ex-prisoners know how (pointing to some plump creamy chicken, and snapping, "How much do you want for that scrawny fowl, old woman?") What money have I got, and how did I get it? My granddad used to say, "Look after the copecks, and the rubles will look after themselves." A clever man, my grandfather.[12]

Solzhenitsyn took a keen interest in his fellow patients in the ward. For the first time since 1945, he found himself being treated as an equal, for nobody here was aware of his exile's status. On the contrary, one young Uzbek in the ward turned out to be a labour-camp guard and freely told him about his experiences, excoriating the prisoners as idlers and enemies of the people, little dreaming that he was talking to one. Solzhenitsyn's natural assertiveness meant that he was soon leading discussions in the ward and airing his opinions on this or that subject, something that he could never have permitted himself in Kok Terek. However, as he later noted of Kostoglotov, "he found that he no longer placed himself in opposition to the others, as he was used to doing, but united with them in their common calamity."[13]

In mid-March 1954 he was released from the hospital, with a warning that he would have to return again in June for a further course of treatment. This meant that although his tumour had shrunk to less than half its former size, he could not yet consider himself cured and would have to submit once again to radiation treatment. Nevertheless, he felt on top of the world. In January, when he arrived, it had been cold and pouring with rain. Now spring had arrived, and in this southern city the trees were in bud and the first early blossoms had begun to appear.

The symbolism was irresistible. As he made his way to the old city centre, Solzhenitsyn came across a church that he was surprised to find open. All the churches in Rostov had been closed in 1934, and he had expected to find the same in Tashkent. For the first time since he was a child, he entered a church again and gave thanks to God for his recovery.

In the city centre he took the opportunity to look around and make some modest purchases. Again he was reminded of his childhood; apart from his flying visit to wartime Moscow in 1943, he had not been in a city since. After the numbing world of the camps and exile, he was bewildered by the hustle and bustle, and his amazement over the consumer goods available in the shops is communicated in part 2 of *Cancer Ward*, where Oleg Kostoglotov is portrayed making a similar pilgrimage after his release from the cancer clinic. Kostoglotov's reactions are perhaps exaggerated for dramatic effect, but his route through the city is the same as that taken by Solzhenitsyn, including his ill-starred visit to the department store. In real life, however, Solzhenitsyn did buy the green-and-white striped shirt that Kostoglotov cannot afford, and returned to Kok Terek with it.

Late in the day he trekked across the city to the MVD headquarters in a distant industrial suburb, about a mile and a half from the nearest tram stop, to deregister; then he returned to the railway station, where he spent the night on the platform. It was there he encountered a rowdy gang whom he instantly recognized as former labour-camp prisoners—criminals, not politicals—and witnessed the sickening episode, described in *The Gulag Archipelago*, of the sluttish mother smashing her baby's head on the stone floor in a fit of drunken rage.

In the morning he set off for Kok Terek and on the way home paid another flying visit to Issyk-Kul to obtain a further supply of the magic mandrake root. He could not know whether his cure would last or how much of it might have been due to his secret tippling of the potent infusion.

In *Cancer Ward* there is another autobiographical scene in which Kostoglotov regards himself, for the first time in ten years, in a full-length mirror. The figure he sees there, dressed in greatcoat and boots, is most unmilitary, looking more like a convict than a soldier. "His shoulders had drooped long ago and his body was incapable of holding itself straight . . . [he] looked tormented, dishevelled, and neglected."[14] This portrait more or less describes Solzhenitsyn at the same period, and he remained painfully skinny for some time to come. A photograph of him taken in his hut in Kok Terek soon after his return reveals sunken eyes and prominent cheekbones, while the green-striped shirt bought in Tashkent hangs loosely from his gaunt frame.

These were the natural effects of his sickness and treatment, but in himself he was infinitely stronger than before, and he felt a surge of renewed hope and energy. Granted the ill fortune of having contracted cancer at all, he had been extremely lucky in having had one of the only two types of cancer (seminoma and lymphoma) that could be cured by radiation alone, and even then had survived odds of one in three to pull through. But perhaps more than just luck was involved. Cancer remains a mysterious illness whose development—and cure—is sometimes associated with mental processes. Solzhenitsyn has described his feelings before leaving for Tashkent as verging on total hopelessness, even despair. But it would appear that he never quite completely lost hope. He was by nature an inveterate optimist, a fighter to the marrow of his bones and a firm believer in the force of will-power. If mental processes can indeed influence the progress of cancer, it seems probable that Solzhenitsyn's unquenchable thirst for life and incredible powers of concentration considerably assisted him in his struggle to survive. This is not to discount the importance of the medical treatment. With only the mandrake root to help him, Solzhenitsyn would almost certainly have died. But once medical intervention had taken place, his sheer mental toughness and implacable will to live came into play and could well have influenced the speed and completeness of his recovery. He himself certainly came to believe something like that and more than once asserted, in later life, that "without a strong purpose" all living creatures are susceptible to disease and destruction. On another occasion he produced a different and somewhat contradictory explanation. The cure was "a divine miracle; I could see no other explanation. Since then, all the life given back to me has not been mine in the full sense: it is built around a purpose."[15] The contradiction may only be apparent, for a believer might argue that it was God himself who had inspired in Solzhenitsyn the will to resist and to overcome, in which case both man and divinity were working towards the same end (a view that Solzhenitsyn certainly holds now). If Solzhenitsyn's first successful skirmish with cancer had returned him to a belief in God, this second, more deadly battle seems to have convinced him that God was not merely at but also on his side.

The first beneficiary of his restored energy was the Berlik school. Solzhenitsyn genuinely loved teaching and for a while devoted himself heart and soul to the welfare of his pupils. Looking back at this period later, he declared it one of the happiest of his life.

I loved exile as if it were my second youth, although I had nothing but the school. The children, who had never had any proper instruction, were very fond of me. And what a lot of time I spent with them! . . . And it gave me enormous pleasure. . . . Real live children! They had seen nothing—they were the children of exiles—nothing. For they weren't allowed to leave that place either. . . . For them the whole world consisted of what they could see there, and what they didn't see there they would never see. My goodness, how they studied! Never in my life have I seen such eagerness anywhere.[16]

Despite the urge to spend every spare minute of his time writing, Solzhenitsyn organized a geodetic club, for which he helped the children make all their own instruments, and took them out on geodetic expeditions. He taught them astronomy, and almost every evening a group of them would come to his hut, where he would sit them down outside and study the sky with them, until they could identify every star. For this purpose he devised and built a model of the night sky in the shape of an upturned bowl. When he placed a candle beneath it, all the constellations stood out in their correct positions, each labelled with its name.

Pupils also came individually with their school problems or with pieces of homework that they couldn't do, and Solzhenitsyn was well known for his willingness to call on his pupils at home and discuss their work with them or their parents. He kept a special notebook for each class in which he recorded details of each pupil's behaviour, their likes and dislikes, preferred subjects, and spare-time interests. And nothing was too much trouble for him.[17]

One of his colleagues, the German teacher, Frieda Chernousova, was so impressed with his erudition and talents that she regarded his turning to authorship after the publication of *A Day in the Life of Ivan Denisovich* as a grave mistake. "He should never have done it. His vocation was teaching. He was a teacher of rare talent. . . . Solzhenitsyn could find the keys to unlock any child's heart." Chernousova recalled that he had an excellent knowledge of German and could read English. She also recalled a significant little scene.

One day he had gathered the pupils together to take them on an excursion. He himself was carrying his usual equipment: a knapsack over one shoulder and a camera over the other. The children were talking and shouting and making a tremendous racket. All of a sudden he rapped out a command in a voice that was unbelievably powerful and metallic: "Attention!" The class instantly fell into line and froze. It was then I realized he had once been a soldier, and no ordinary soldier either.[18]

The pupils responded to Solzhenitsyn with affection and admiration, for he had an uncanny way of bringing out the best in them. He used to burst into the class-room like a whirlwind, giving orders before he had even reached his chair: "So-and-so to the blackboard. So-and-so give me a report on the homework." It was said that he never talked down to his pupils but treated them like equals, despite his strictness. The two things he couldn't abide, according to one of the pupils, were unpunctuality and sloppiness.

"He was strict and exacting if anyone broke his word or arrived late for an appointment. He himself was never late and invariably carried out his promises, whether it was to give us an extra geometry lesson or simply to do some photography with us."[19]

One of Solzhenitsyn's most prized possessions was his camera. He had purchased it from his salary, which was one and half times the normal rate because of the extra hours he put in—thirty a week instead of twenty. Almost the first thing he did with the camera, in secret from everyone else, was to dress up in the padded jacket, trousers, and cap that had been his uniform in the special camp, complete with numbers (all of which he had smuggled out with him when he left), and use the self-timer to take a self-portrait. This was one memento he was determined to have and to keep; years later, copies of this photograph were to find their way to close friends and former camp comrades in Moscow and be kept as a talisman. He eventually published it in *The Gulag Archipelago*.

Another use to which the camera was put was filming his manuscripts. Until now Solzhenitsyn had relied not so much on holes in the ground as on a method—whose details he has never disclosed—taught him by a fellow exile of concealing papers both inside and outside his hut in such a way that they would not be found even by search parties. But with the camera he started to make microfilms, and these he inserted into the covers of two books, placed the books in envelopes and addressed them to Alexandra Tolstoy, at her farm in the United States. The name of Tolstoy, his favourite author, was a kind of symbol for him and an augury of proper treatment. "I knew nobody else in the West, not a single publisher, but I felt sure that Tolstoy's daughter would not deny me her help."[20] But he did not, it seems, ever try to send them.

Solzhenitsyn's relatively high salary meant that he could now purchase his hut instead of renting it. According to Reshetovskaya, he had a cellar built for cold storage and came to an agreement with the former owner whereby the latter would continue to cultivate the vegetable garden and they would share the produce.

At the age of thirty-five, Solzhenitsyn settled down to a life that was the nearest to normal he had ever experienced. During the day he taught at school. In the early evenings he did his chores or occupied himself with his pupils. At night and during the weekends (except for the not infrequent occasions when everyone was obliged to "volunteer" for Sunday work to help with the harvesting or other agricultural tasks), he was kept busy with his writing. As usual, he filled every minute of the day, and to the outside world presented a picture of the contented bachelor.

But as always in Solzhenitsyn's case, appearances were deceptive, and he was far from content. Perhaps his biggest problem was loneliness. Paradoxically, he had felt emotionally more secure in the camps, for there he had known where he was. The "enemy" had been easily recognizable and identifiable—camp guards, security officers, stool-pigeons, trusties—and he had known how to deal with them. He had also known exactly who his friends were. As an old convict of long experience, he had believed he could tell at a glance who was trustworthy and who not, and among camp friends there had been total trust and total confidence. They were all together at the bottom of the heap. Solzhenitsyn had had no difficulty in confiding his innermost secrets to them, and even in reading his works to them to hear criticisms. Outside the camps, however, there was no cement of common adversity to bind people together, nor the same sense of confronting a common enemy. People were anxious to get on with living their own lives. What they valued were privacy and family affairs. Even people like Mitrovich and other political exiles had a dimension to their lives that had not existed in the camps; this made it harder to get to know them properly and prevented Solzhenitsyn from completely committing himself to them. It was all very confusing, and he experienced considerable difficulty in adjusting to it.

The one exception to this general rule was an elderly couple of political exiles called Nikolai and Elena Zubov, who soon became Solzhenitsyn's closest friends. Nikolai Zubov was the gynaecologist who had advised Solzhenitsyn to seek treatment for his stomach pains, and, although in his early sixties, was still bursting with energy. Like Solzhenitsyn, he worked time and a half and was indefatigably punctilious in the execution of his duties, never hesitating to rise in the middle of the night to attend to a patient and keeping himself on call round the clock. In this impulsive energy and dedication to duty, Solzhenitsyn recognized a kindred spirit. Another reason for feeling comfortable with the Zubovs was that both had served time in labour camps before being exiled to Kok Terek, and they understood Solzhenitsyn's psychology. On the other hand, they were quite different from him in their blissful acceptance of exile as the best of all possible worlds (after the horrors of the camps) and in their readiness to forget the injustice that had been done to them.

They had come from a small town near Moscow. Elena had been married before, then, after meeting and marrying Zubov, had moved in with him and his mother, though the latter's domination of her son had stretched Elena's tolerance to the limit. It was the mother's short-sighted impulsiveness that had led to Nikolai and Elena's downfall. Some time after the war broke out, she had unthinkingly taken in a deserter from the Red Army and given him shelter for a couple of nights. Not long afterwards the deserter was caught and made a full confession about where he had stayed. Nikolai's mother was almost eighty and deemed to be beyond prosecution, but Nikolai and Elena were charged and convicted as enemies of the people. They were each sentenced to ten years' imprisonment, to be followed by perpetual exile (as in Solzhenitsyn's case, two defendants meant an organization), and were released into exile in different places: Elena in Krasnoyarsk and Nikolai in Kok Terek. After a year of writing incessant complaints and protests to Moscow, Elena had been allowed to rejoin her husband, and this was the main source of their present contentment.[21]

Not long after Solzhenitsyn got to know them, they crowned their happiness with the purchase of their own clay hut, with a garden attached. They possessed not a stick of furniture but were able to order it from the same ingenious Ukrainian who had equipped Solzhenitsyn's hut, who was an absolute wizard with the gnarled and twisted shapes of the local saxaul. Nikolai also had in him something of Tristram Shandy's Uncle Toby, for he had evolved an elaborate plan for laying out his quarter-acre garden in the form of a miniature park, complete with a central avenue, apricot trees, a vineyard, hops, tobacco plants, and a semicircular summer-house. Nothing of this existed when Nikolai proudly showed Solzhenitsyn over his bare plot, but he could see the details so clearly in his mind's eye that he referred to them as if they were already there.

Solzhenitsyn came to adore this kindly, jolly pair and spent a great deal of time in their house. "They were like a father and mother to me," he said later,[22] and they provided him with the first family environment he had known since the Fedorovskys in his childhood (they were the prototypes of the Kadmins in *Cancer Ward*). Even their two dogs, Zhuk the Alsatian and Tobik the terrier, welcomed him as part of the family, and Solzhenitsyn would take them for long walks over the dusty steppe or to the river Chu, three miles away. Tobik in time became a messenger between Solzhenitsyn's clay hut and the Zubovs'. Nikolai would tie a message to his collar and send him off to Solzhenitsyn with it, and Solzhenitsyn would send his reply in the same fashion.

Between them there grew up that trust and love that was unthinkable in Solzhenitsyn's relations with the other exiles, so much so that he confided in the Zubovs about his writing and showed them his manuscripts. Nikolai was a well-educated man with an interest in languages, architecture, history, and meteorology, as well as the medical sciences, and Elena was equally a booklover. They became his first readers (in the camps he had had only listeners) and encouraged him with their love and admiration.

In June 1954, at the start of the summer vacation, Solzhenitsyn returned to Tashkent for a further course of radiation treatment. He was given a friendly welcome by the doctors and nurses and was found to have improved enormously—he had put on weight and was looking quite well. Nevertheless, he was kept at the clinic for nearly two months. The treatment had to be interrupted at one point when his white-blood-corpuscle count dropped dangerously low, but it was thereafter continued until pronounced successful.

While killing time in the ward, Solzhenitsyn read a great deal and wrote a series of critical articles on Soviet authors with the rhetorical title *Let Us Open Our Eyes*.[23] It is possible that he was inspired by reading at the time a celebrated article in *Novy Mir* called "On Sincerity in Literature," by Vladimir Pomerantsev, an anti-Stalinist plea for more openness and honesty by Soviet writers and a veiled attack on socialist realism. In *Cancer Ward* the reading of this essay by one of the characters becomes an important part of the action (coincidentally, it was almost certainly for publishing this article that Alexander Tvardovsky was dismissed from his first period of editorship of *Novy Mir*). Solzhenitsyn never did publish his critical essays, and their contents are unknown, but they are an indication that he was once more following Soviet literary life with the interest he had shown before his imprisonment.

Upon his release from the clinic, Solzhenitsyn revisited the centre of Tashkent. This time he had his camera and paid a visit to the Tashkent zoo, another episode that was to find its way into *Cancer Ward*. The idea of the novel was conceived later the same day, as Solzhenitsyn was walking from the train stop to the MVD headquarters to deregister. Mulling over his recent experiences, he had a sudden vision of how they might fit into a novel, although it was to be another eight years before he attempted it. On this occasion he was impressed to find the MVD offices much changed and the behaviour of the chief officer much gentler and more civilized than before. It was a sign of changing times.

Once back in Kok Terek, Solzhenitsyn resumed his life with all his old vigour. He now seemed completely cured. He put on more weight and felt better than at any other time for ten years. And his thoughts turned increasingly to a subject that had never been far from his mind since his release into exile the preceding year, but that now took on a fresh sharpness and point. "I felt as if this exile of mine was like a second youth. There I was a bachelor again; I was free to marry. And life was beginning for me at the age of thirty-five. It was a very poignant feeling."[24]

The urge to know a woman again, to experience true intimacy, was very strong in Solzhenitsyn during his second year of exile. It was an elemental drive, sharpened by years of deprivation in the army, jail, and labour camps, and had by the time of his release grown into a consuming hunger for female warmth and love. It was presumably this hunger that had led him to seize on Natalia's friendly letter and to misinterpret her intentions. Interestingly, although they were written six and eight years later, both his short story "The Right Hand" and his novel *Cancer Ward*, set in this period, were infused with a sense of Solzhenitsyn's sexual longing at the time. It is possible that his feelings were intensified by the cessation of the use of the hormone tablets. But in the conditions of Kok Terek, any sort of close relationship with a woman was unthinkable outside marriage, for local society was governed by the old-fashioned, patriarchal values of the Kazakhs. Furthermore, in such a small place, everyone knew everyone else, so that any sort of secret liaison or affair was out of the question. But the indications are that it was precisely marriage that Solzhenitsyn had in mind.

Solzhenitsyn did in fact become friendly with a number of local women, particularly after Natalia's second letter, and one or two of them he seriously considered marrying. One was a Kazakh woman, another a young Russian girl, the daughter of some Russian settlers in Kazakhstan, of whom he became very fond. This was presumably the girl with whom, according to Reshetovskaya, he spent the New Year of 1955, and it appears that he did fall slightly in love with her. In the end he held back from taking the final step for fear that she might be too orthodox and too loyal to her background. She had been brought up as an enthusiastic member of the Komsomol and was forever singing or humming Komsomol songs. Solzhenitsyn feared that her attachment to the Party might prove too strong for him to break and that this would lead eventually to conflict.[25]

During the following year he tried again. At one point, apparently, he boarded a train to visit a young woman recommended by friends, but left the train in a fit of embarrassment. For a while he corresponded with a niece of the Zubovs who lived in the Urals, and also with a young Moscow student named Nara, who had been found for him by Dimitri Panin's wife, Evgenia. But nothing came of these contacts either, for he could never bring himself to carry them beyond a certain point.[26]

At the root of his fears, apart from personal misgivings, lay a concern for his work and his manuscripts. It was inconceivable that he should marry any woman without trusting her totally with his secrets, for these secrets could send him back to jail if they got into the wrong hands. For this reason he had to be immensely careful, and that was why he rejected yet another prospective financée, from Karaganda, with whom he corresponded for a while and whom he visited in the summer of 1955. Commenting on this later, he said:

> In fact I sacrificed myself. And I consider this the biggest sacrifice of my life . . . because for three years I didn't marry after spending eight years in the camps. For three years I didn't marry in order to preserve my manuscripts. And I don't know how much longer it would have gone on if I hadn't suddenly been released.[27]

Solzhenitsyn was later to repeat this refrain in volume 3 of *The Gulag Archipelago*, and it is undeniable that he came to believe it over the years, but the situation seems to have been less simple than that. For one thing, despite being in his mid-thirties, he was utterly inexperienced in the ways of women. Natalia had been his first real girl-friend, and he had been innocent when he married her, a university student with no genuine experience of life at all. She had been as naïve as he was, and they had lived out their brief year of married life in a romantic haze before the war had brutally separated them. Since then, Solzhenitsyn had spent his entire life in the company of men— three years in the army and eight years in the camps—with only one brief affair at Kaluga Gate and a platonic romance in the *sharashka* to relieve this long stretch of enforced chastity. In most respects he was a crusty bachelor, with not much more experience of women than he had had as a callow youth of twenty.

This lack of experience manifested itself in a number of ways. In the first place, Solzhenitsyn made no secret of the fact that it was precisely a wife he was looking for, an attitude scarcely calculated to encourage a relationship to the point where it could be expected to blossom. Secondly, with his bachelor habits and firm, not to say dogmatic, views on the way a wife ought to behave and fit in with his scheme of things, he was hardly the flexible and generous lover. Thirdly, he had a habit of handing prospective brides a photostat of Anton Chekhov's celebrated story "The Darling," together with an afterword by Tolstoy, and asking them whether they agreed with its conclusions. "The Darling" is about a woman who marries twice and each time adapts herself totally to her husband's character and work, and then, after being widowed a second time—and having no children—devotes herself single-mindedly to the welfare of the son of her lodger. Chekhov's intention was satirical, but Solzhenitsyn (like Tolstoy) took the portrait perfectly seriously and pointed out to his women friends that for him "the darling" represented the ideal type of wife. It appears that he solemnly asked each prospective bride whether she would swear to emulate her—which none of them apparently would.[28]

But his true bride was his writing. Having completed his tragedy *Decembrists without December*, he started another play on the camp theme, provisionally entitled *The Republic of Labour*.* This one combined elements of his experiences in New Jerusalem with episodes and characters from Kaluga Gate and Ekibastuz. Its hero was initially called Gleb Nerzhin, and the work went rapidly. "In the first flush of my happiness," he was later to write in *The Oak and the Calf*, "I wrote *The Republic of Labour*. This I did not try to memorize. For the first time I knew the joy of not having to burn a work piecemeal as I learned it by heart; the joy of writing *finis* with the beginning still undestroyed, of being able to survey the play as a whole, of making a fair copy of each successive draft, correcting it and copying it out again."[29] In its later stages the hero acquired a new name, Rodion Nemov, and the play itself was eventually to be reworked and given a new title—*The Tenderfoot and the Tart*.

The story of *The Tenderfoot and the Tart* is essentially the story of its autobiographical hero, Rodion Nemov, and follows his fortunes from the moment he arrives in the camp where it is set until he is carried off to hospital at the end as the result of an accident. As the play opens, Nemov is appointed production superintendent—just as Solzhenitsyn was at New Jerusalem. Like Solzhenitsyn, he has difficulty in persuading the other prisoners to work and meets with hostility from the other trusties in the camp. Since the camp shown in the play is based, to a large extent, on Kaluga Gate, the trusties resemble some of the people Solzhenitsyn had met there. Bershader is depicted as Solomon, and Alexander K becomes Boris Khomich in the play, while two of the characters appear under their own ames: Camille Gontoir, a stranded Belgian theatre director, imprisoned for treason; and the free worker, Vasili Frolov (in the version offered to the Sovremennik theatre, he kept his fictional name of Brylov; this is the version that was used for the translation into English). Like Solzhenitsyn in real life, Nemov is soon discharged from

* The title is ironic and comes from a popular Soviet propaganda ditty: "We are raising the banner! / Comrades, all come here! / Come and help us build / Our republic of labour!" The play opens with the playing of this song over the camp loudspeakers.

his job, and his place is taken by Khomich, after which Nemov is sent to work as an unskilled labourer in the camp foundry (the foundry reflects Solzhenitsyn's experiences in Ekibastuz—Frolov and the other foundry workers are modelled on people Solzhenitsyn met there). Finally, Nemov ends up in the hospital, just as Solzhenitsyn had done, though the cause in the play is not cancer but an industrial accident in the foundry.

The main theme of the play is the total corruption of life in the camps, the venality of all social and labour relations, and the way in which criminals and time-servers are encouraged to rise to the top of the prisoner hierarchy and the innocent are forced to the bottom. Several sub-plots reinforce this message. One concerns the difficulties of an honest brigade leader, Pavel Gai, who clashes with a group of thieves in his brigade after they refuse to work (mirroring the experience of Solzhenitsyn's colleague Akimov at New Jerusalem, who had had his kidneys smashed in revenge). In the play the forces of light prevail. Aided by a valiant young woman and ex–Red Army soldier called Granya Zybina, Gai overcomes the thieves in a violent knife fight and forces them to surrender (thus enabling Solzhenitsyn to take his revenge on reality). In the foundry, on the other hand, corruption reigns supreme. The prisoners are manipulated to produce illicit articles for sale (from which they see little profit for themselves), and when one devises a new sort of smelter to improve their work, he is tricked out of the fruits of his invention by his cynical superiors. Nemov's near-fatal accident, meanwhile, is the result of the operation of unsafe equipment and the complete neglect of any safety rules (rules that Nemov had sought, unsuccessfully, to enforce as production superintendent).

Lastly, there is the play's love interest, which gives it its title. Nemov, like Solzhenitsyn, is a regular attender at the camp's culture and education section. While acting in a camp revue, which figures as a kind of play within a play, he meets and falls in love with another trusty, called Lyuba. Lyuba returns his love, but, like the young sniper Solzhenitsyn had observed at Kaluga Gate, who was pursued and bribed into submission by the storekeeper Bershader, Lyuba is under siege from the camp doctor and finally yields to him to avoid being sent out to almost certain death on hard labour. Lyuba is the "tart," albeit a reluctant one, of the play's title, and Nemov the helpless "tenderfoot."

Interestingly enough, the sniper Solzhenitsyn had met at Kaluga Gate was obviously the model for Granya Zybina, but although in the play Granya is pursued by Boris Khomich (Nemov's aggressive usurper), Granya heroically resists his advances and is sent away on a prison transport (Solzhenitsyn thus twice revenged himself on reality). It is possible that Lyuba, at least in her positive aspects, was modelled on Anya Breslavskaya, whom Solzhenitsyn had also met at the culture and education section in Kaluga Gate, but since we have no more information about her, it is hard to be sure.

As drama the play has many faults. Nemov is not much more than an author's substitute and a passive witness of the events that take place around him. The other characters are also thinly drawn, and the drama is mainly external, in the form of fights, verbal clashes, accidents, and so on, or rests on clichés like the whore with the heart of gold, or the bravery and physical strength of ex–Red Army men and women. In practical terms, there are the problems posed by a very large cast, complicated props, and a multiplicity of sets, all of which indicate Solzhenitsyn's lack of experience with a real stage. On the other hand, the play represented Solzhenitsyn's first major attempt at a synthesis of his various camp experiences and an effort to draw wider conclusions. Writing entirely in prose was also a step forward, for it allowed him greater freedom of manoeuvre and gave him an opportunity to put his powers of mimicry into operation. Despite Solzhenitsyn's continuing tendency towards "epic" inclusiveness, his new play was undoubtedly more dramatic than any he had written hitherto. In literary terms it marked a definite advance.

The play's first readers, or rather listeners, were Nikolai and Elena Zubov, to whom Solzhenitsyn read the play in June 1955. Elena later recalled it in a letter to Natalia Reshetovskaya.

We went to see Sanya after supper one Saturday evening, just as dusk was falling, and took the dogs along.

It was nearly dark when he started reading, and after a while he lit the oil lamp. The windows were wide open. It was a bright, moonlit night, with sharp shadows. None of us felt like going to bed. On the contrary, there was a kind of swelling elation inside us.

Sanya made a note of how many minutes it took him to read each act. He was dissatisfied with the fact that they were turning out too long.

In this way we passed the night. Our impressions were incredibly vivid. By the time we left his hut, it was already dawn. We were both in a state of rapture, and I remember it as one of the high points of my life.[30]

Most of what Solzhenitsyn wrote in exile must be accounted apprentice works—even *The Republic of Labour* was reworked into *The Tenderfoot and the Tart* before seeing the light of day. But this outpouring of thoughts, ideas, and feelings on the theme of the labour camps, the release of all his pent-up frustration and bitterness onto paper, was an essential catharsis for Solzhenitsyn, enabling him to clear his mind and to work his way through to the themes that the mature artist was able to take up and transmute into works of literature.

Solzhenitsyn's writings in exile also marked an important transition from verse to prose, from the verse play, *Feast of the Conquerors*, through the mixed verse and prose play, *Decembrists without December*, to *The Republic of Labour*, entirely in prose. He was to continue writing occasional verse for a while, and his interest in the theatre and in dramatic forms was also to continue (despite his prolonged isolation from any form of theatrical life)—he was to write another play and two screenplays before he was done—but the most significant literary development in Kok Terek was his decision to go further and try narrative prose once more. It was a natural step to take. His verse had always had a strong narrative element to it, while the plays suffered from his urge to describe and explain everything, to dot all the *i*'s and cross the *t*'s. They were too wordy, too static, not dramatic enough for the stage. But by a process of trial and error, he had groped his way to the form in which he was to make all his major creations, and in the summer of 1955 he commenced work on his first big novel, *The First Circle*. It was to deal with the only period of his camp career not yet touched upon in his writings, his period in the *sharashka*, and the autobiographical hero was also to be called Gleb Nerzhin.

By 1955 the conditions of Solzhenitsyn's exile had begun to change as a result of larger changes on the Soviet political stage in the wake of Stalin's death. The event with the most widespread repercussions had been the secret arrest in June 1953 and summary execution of Lavrenty Beria, Stalin's chief of the security police and, since Stalin's death, also minister of the interior. Beria's fall had put an end to the privileged position of the security organs as a state within a state and had heralded a major shake-up both of the secret police and of the vast archipelago it controlled.

To begin with, the security service had been divided in two. Some of its functions had been handed over to the MVD, and what was left was demoted from the status of a ministry to that of a state committee. Henceforth the MGB was obliged to change its initials once again and become the KGB—the Committee of State Security—which it has remained to the present day. Meanwhile, the MVD itself was progressively stripped of its vast economic empire, and the enterprises that formed an integral part of the Gulag Archipelago were gradually handed over to the control of the economic ministries.

The repercussions in the camps, of course, had been enormous. As Solzhenitsyn later wrote in *The Gulag Archipelago*, to those in the camps "Beria's fall was like a thunderclap: he was the supreme patron, the viceroy of the archipelago! MVD officers were perplexed, embarrassed, dismayed. When the news was announced over the radio, they would have liked to stuff this horror back into the loudspeaker but had instead to lay hands on the portraits of their dear, kind protector and take them down from the walls."[31]

Beria's fall had been followed by widespread unrest in the camps; major rebellions had broken out in the special camps at Vorkuta and especially Kengir, where the prisoners had held out for forty days against their guards.* The virus of revolt that the western Ukrainians had brought from Dolinka to Ekibastuz had begun to spread everywhere, born initially of desperation, but then fertilized by the signs of demoralization visible among the camp authorities. The prisoners had begun pressing for better conditions, and after 1954, as reforms spread outwards from the centre, some of their demands had been met.

---

*Solzhenitsyn later incorporated some of the Kengir incidents into his screenplay *The Tanks Know the Truth*.

In the special camps, sewn-on number patches had been abolished, the huts had been left unlocked at night, unlimited correspondence had been allowed, and even family visits had been introduced for those who·could afford them. Not long afterwards, women had been taken off the heaviest forms of labour, money wages had been introduced for prisoners in place of vouchers, and special shops opened in which they could spend their money. In short, the camps had come more to resemble regular prisons in other countries, with the essential difference that they still held millions of innocent citizens, most of whom had never been convicted in any court of law.

This widespread liberalization of the Gulag had naturally had repercussions for the exiles as well. Exile was supposed to be a milder form of punishment. And indeed, changes had been taking place throughout Solzhenitsyn's stay in Kok Terek. The first move had come about as a result of the so-called Voroshilov amnesty, announced in March 1953 in the wake of Stalin's death. Limited to prisoners serving terms of five years or less, it had hardly affected the politicals—their sentences were usually much longer, and it was mainly the criminals who benefited. Nevertheless, a number of exiles in the Kok Terek district had been allowed to leave for home. Not long afterwards, the children of exiles had been admitted to the universities and other institutions of higher education, and the exiles themselves were no longer bullied and treated as second-class citizens (though technically they still were second class).

Changes had also taken place in the staffing and attitudes of the MVD stations. Their staff was reduced, and they became more relaxed in their supervision. The Kazakhs had in any case been more easygoing than the Russians, but now they were even milder. The necessity for exiles to report every other week was not so rigidly enforced, and travel was unrestricted within the district and became easier outside it. One after another the various national minorities were freed from the obligation to report at all, and many of them were allowed to leave. Finally there came the "Adenauer amnesty," following Adenauer's visit to Moscow in the summer of 1955, during which the German chancellor had secured an undertaking from the Soviet government to release all the German prisoners who were still being held captive ten years after the war's end. Once this had been granted, it became clear that the Soviet authorities could hardly continue to hold Soviet citizens who had collaborated with the Germans, and on 9 September 1955 the first-ever amnesty to affect political prisoners was declared. All prisoners sentenced to ten years or less were to be released immediately, and those with sentences of up to twenty years had their sentences cut in half.

Solzhenitsyn was undoubtedly stirred by this sequence of events. As always he followed the country's political and social developments with avidity and was one of the few newspaper readers to discover the announcement of the amnesty tucked away on an inside page of *Izvestia*—with no commentary of any kind. He also noticed that it was carried by no other newspaper, which meant that the government did not wish to draw attention to it. In the meantime he had bought himself a radio receiver and resumed what was to become a lifelong habit of listening to the BBC (even though it was heavily jammed), in order to know more of what was going on. Kok Terek itself was thick with rumours. It looked as if the institution of exile might be coming to an end and they would all be allowed to go home. To Solzhenitsyn's vacillations about marriage was added a new doubt: What if the bride he found suitable for life in Kok Terek should turn out differently in central Russia?

His doubts and hopes were intensified about this time by renewed contacts with his two closest camp comrades, Dimitri Panin and Lev Kopelev. Natalia had bumped into Panin's wife, Evgenia, in a Moscow department store in the spring of 1955. The two women had been friends when their husbands were in the *sharashka*, having met one another during visits, but had lost touch when Natalia moved to Ryazan and divorced Solzhenitsyn. Evgenia informed Natalia that Panin had been exiled to Kustanai, in northern Kazakhstan, and that she had visited him there, only to find him living with another woman. Nevertheless, she still wanted him back and was petitioning the authorities to get him amnestied. She asked Natalia for Solzhenitsyn's address, saying that it was one of Panin's dearest wishes to know where he was, and informed her that Panin was also in touch with Kopelev, who had recently been released and returned to Moscow. Evgenia had then passed on Solzhenitsyn's address to the two friends, and they both wrote to him in Kok Terek. They put him in touch with the Marfino artist Ivashov-Musatov, who sent Solzhenitsyn a copy of his pencil sketch done in the *sharashka*, and the three friends exchanged news with Solzhenitsyn for the first time in four years.[32]

Kopelev wrote that after returning to Moscow he had talked officials at the local police station into granting him a temporary residence permit, after which he had moved back into his old flat. Not long afterwards he had been summoned to the station and ordered to leave both flat and Moscow again, since the "Adenauer amnesty" did not apply to him. But the irrepressible Kopelev was disputing this ruling and in the meantime was determined to hang on in Moscow. Panin wrote that he, too, was confident of returning to Moscow shortly, and both he and Kopelev urged Solzhenitsyn to petition the authorities for a judicial review and to seek his own release.[33]

Solzhenitsyn has given the impression that he was somewhat reluctant at first. Having been such a naïve believer in amnesties at the outset of his prison career, he had now swung to the opposite extreme. He was cautious and suspicious. He was aware that Nikolai Vitkevich had been released a year before the end of his term and had returned to Rostov (while Solzhenitsyn was in the hospital in Tashkent), and had exchanged letters with him through Aunt Nina, but Nikolai had not been sentenced to exile, so that even if their "crime" had been identical, it did not follow that their treatment would be the same. Nevertheless, he began to write to the authorities requesting that his exile be lifted.

For a while he heard nothing. But from the BBC and popular rumour, he knew that more momentous events were taking place in the country. At the beginning of 1955 Malenkov had been ousted from power and reduced to a deputy chairman of the Council of Ministers. Bulganin was demoted from his post as minister of defence, and soon afterwards the veterans Kaganovich and Molotov also lost their influence. Cock of the walk was First Secretary Khrushchev, who consolidated his position with his devastating "secret speech" at the Twentieth Congress of the Communist Party on 26 February 1956. This celebrated speech was the first official admission of Stalin's crimes and of the immense damage inflicted on the country by Stalin's paranoia and reign of terror. It was highly selective in its revelations and denunciations, of course, concentrating on Stalin's periodic purges of the Communist Party and passing over in silence both the horrors of collectivization and the terrorization of the population at large. No apology or explanation was offered for the persecution and elimination of Trotsky and Bukharin and no mention made of the crimes with which Khrushchev himself had been associated.*

Nevertheless, the speech had an electrifying impact on all sections of the Communist world. Despite the fact that it was officially secret, news of its contents spread rapidly by word of mouth, and the text was circulated among leading Party members all over the Soviet Union. Solzhenitsyn first heard of it from the BBC and picked up further reports from some of the party members in Kok Terek. It was at once clear that this meant the virtual end of Stalin's most outstanding creation, the archipelago, and with it the institution of exile as a mass phenomenon. Solzhenitsyn was later to write in The Gulag Archipelago, "I knew that my enemy Stalin had fallen, which meant that I was on the way up."[34]

But not without a few hitches. In March 1956, after he had written his petitions, Solzhenitsyn was rather surprised to be summoned to the MVD station for "a talk." He surmised that it might have something to do with his application to be released and went along in a jaunty and relaxed frame of mind, only to discover that his interlocutor was the chief of the regional KGB. A smooth-mannered Kazakh dressed in civilian clothes, he had a rather poor command of Russian, but from his incoherent sentences it emerged that he was trying to recruit Solzhenitsyn as an informer. Solzhenitsyn wasn't sure whether he was exasperated or amused by this clumsy overture, especially at such a hopeful moment when the whole country was being liberalized. Was this provincial oaf so far behind the times that he didn't realize what was going on at the centre? Solzhenitsyn gently pointed out to the Kazakh that he was out of step with the rest of the country, that the MGB had been disbanded, and that the security service was being run down. Not a bit of it, responded the Kazakh. The KGB had been set up to take its place and had exactly the same personnel and the same tasks as the old institution. Solzhenitsyn should have been warned, but he didn't take the Kazakh's

* Notably the purging of the Ukraine in the wake of the German occupation during the Second World War.

words too seriously. It seemed obvious to him that all this secret-police stuff was coming to an end. On the other hand, the officer wouldn't give up, and Solzhenitsyn was loath to antagonize him, for he had a growing pile of seditious manuscripts in his hut, and he didn't want to attract attention or provoke the KGB's suspicion. In desperation he took the coward's way out and appealed to his illness, pointing out that as a sick man he would have difficulty enough in supporting himself and that he would have insufficient energy left over for the duties of spying. Even this didn't satisfy the KGB man at first, but in the end he grudgingly abandoned his quest. He insisted, however, that Solzhenitsyn supply him with a copy of his medical certificate. He would have to explain his failure to the higher authorities.[35]*

At last, in April 1956, Solzhenitsyn received a letter from the regional MVD headquarters informing him that his sentence had been annulled and his exile lifted. He was free to go wherever he wished. He had already given much thought to this problem and had concluded that it should be somewhere in central Russia. Theoretically he had the right to return to Rostov and to be supplied officially with a room or a flat, as was provided for in the new regulations. Nikolai Vitkevich had done this. But Solzhenitsyn had no desire to return. He longed to escape from a hot climate after his three years in Kazakhstan and he could not bear the idea of settling in a big city. The thought of all that bustle and noise and dirt repelled him. What he craved was the coolness and greenery of that central Russia that he remembered so vividly from his boyhood excursion down the Volga with Nikolai, and from his honeymoon in Tarusa. He needed peace and solitude, and a quiet corner to which to retire and lick his wounds after the battering of the past eleven years. He still wasn't sure what sort of a life awaited him back in "civilization," and he wanted an opportunity to take stock from the sidelines.[36]

With all this in mind he began writing letters to regional education departments in the provinces of Vladimir and Kostroma to see whether they had any vacancies for teachers. He also wrote a letter to Natalia in Ryazan, informing her that he was being released from exile and asking her whether she would mind inquiring about jobs in the Ryazan region, outside the city. He hastened to point out that if he should move to Ryazan, there would be "no shadow cast on your life."[37] Nevertheless it was a curious thing to do and suggests that at the back of his mind he still perhaps had hopes of some kind of reconciliation and reunion.

Before he could leave Kok Terek, Solzhenitsyn was obliged to complete the school year and mark the final examinations. Meanwhile, he sold his clay hut on the edge of the steppe, passed on his packing cases and his few sticks of furniture to the Zubovs, and on 20 June 1956 caught the train to Moscow. The journey took four days, and for the first two days the train travelled through the dusty steppes of Central Asia. On the third day they crossed the

---

*It is interesting that Solzhenitsyn was approached by the KGB in this way—for the second time in his career. He must have put up a perfect front as a loyal Soviet citizen during his stay in Kok Terek.

Volga and entered the central Russian heartland. Solzhenitsyn was overwhelmed by his feelings. He went along the corridor to a platform where the upper half of the door was open, and stood there for what seemed an eternity, gazing out at the Russian countryside. The wind rushed into his face and the tears streamed from his eyes.[38] His "perpetual" exile was over. At last he was on his way home.

20

MATRYONA'S PLACE

O N 24 JUNE 1956 Solzhenitsyn was met at the Kazan Station in Moscow
by Panin (who had been released from exile in January) and Kopelev.
He was immediately recognizable in his worn army greatcoat with flapping
skirts, but looked thinner and paler than they remembered, and his skin was
tinged with yellow from the radiation treatment. Because of his diet, he was
allowed no alcohol, and they could not drink to their reunion, but it was a
jolly occasion nonetheless. The ebullient Kopelev burst out at one point,
"Guess what? They're forming a second party." Only a few short months
ago Kopelev had been threatened with eviction from his flat and even from
Moscow and had complained to Solzhenitsyn in a letter about the difficulty
of adjusting and making friends. But now he was in the swim again and full
of the latest news. Of course, it was the wildest of wild hopes, a second
party, but Kopelev's unquenchable optimism and generous imagination made
it seem like a genuine possibility. Solzhenitsyn was impressed by what seemed
like a general mood of hopefulness and excitement in the capital and by a
relaxed freedom of speech that was quite unthinkable in Kok Terek. In
Kazakhstan you didn't even whisper about second parties, let alone talk aloud
about them on the station platform.[1]

Solzhenitsyn moved in with the Kopelevs for a while, then to the home
of one of his Georgievsk cousins, whom he had not seen since childhood, and
then to the Panins'. This gipsy life did not bother him much, since he was
still determined to go to live in the provinces. He was glad to be back in
Moscow, which he had left in prison rags six years earlier, and Kopelev tried
to persuade him to stay, but the noise and the bustle—and, above all, other
people—were too much for him. As another distinguished labour-camp pris-

oner has written, coming out of prison is like making a posthumous appearance in the world. Time has continued to pass, regardless of the prisoner's absence, and the apparent indifference of the outside world to his personal trauma creates a mood of isolation and depression. A small village in Vladimir or Kostroma Province still seemed the most desirable refuge, and Solzhenitsyn made a series of forays to investigate the possibilities. He decided to visit each district education office in turn, obtain a list of vacancies, and visit the schools. As he wrote in his short story, "Matryona's Place," "things were already loosening up a bit. When I climbed the stairs of the education offices, I was surprised to see that *Personnel* no longer lurked behind a black, leather-upholstered door, but had a glass partition in front of it as in a pharmacy. I timidly approached the window, nodded, and said, 'Tell me, don't you need any mathematics teachers well away from the railway line? I'd like to settle down there.' They carefully probed every letter in my documents, went back and forth from room to room, and made some telephone calls. It was not every day that this sort of thing happened. Everybody else asked to go to a town, and the bigger the better."[2]

In this way Solzhenitsyn got to see some wonderful villages in the heart of the Russian countryside, but they proved to be too remote for his purposes. There were no shops of any kind, not even bakeries or grocery stores, which meant that there would be no possibility of looking after himself, as he was accustomed to doing. The local people travelled enormous distances for food, fetching it home in large baskets or rucksacks, but Solzhenitsyn had no wish to expend that sort of time and effort or to be dependent on others. He decided that he had better stick close to the railway line, which would allow him ready access to Moscow.

After some weeks he came to a settlement with the unlovely name of Torfoprodukt, the headquarters of a sprawling peat-works (*torf* means "peat"), about a hundred miles east of Moscow on the main line to Kazan. Its appearance was as unprepossessing as its name: a jumble of ugly thirties-style barrack huts, some gimcrack cottages, and in the centre a grimy factory whose chimney belched black smoke day and night. A narrow-gauge railway led from the factory to some low-lying bog-lands where most of the peat was dug, and another to the main line for the transfer of the finished briquettes. Apart from having its own ramshackle station on the main railway line, Torfoprodukt was even more primitive than Kok Terek, but it was in the Russian heartland and was not too far from Moscow. Having established that it would be possible to find a room in one of the neighbouring villages, away from the smoke and the rowdiness of the workers' club, Solzhenitsyn confirmed his appointment for the autumn and returned to the capital.

Panin and Kopelev had told him of the widespread rehabilitations of former political prisoners that were then taking place, and they urged him to try to find out what his own position was. Overcoming his initial suspicion, Solzhenitsyn paid a visit to the public prosecutor's office, where he was surprised to be given the telephone number of the investigator in charge of his case and invited to ring him directly. He duly telephoned, was asked to leave the number he was ringing from, and a few days later was rung back and invited to come round to the Lubyanka "for a chat."[3]

It was now Solzhenitsyn's turn to visit that famous office on Kuznetsky Most where Natalia, like hundreds of thousands of wives before her, had first heard confirmation of her husband's arrest in 1945 and had been informed of the details of his sentence. While sitting in the waiting-room, Solzhenitsyn felt that he was being watched, and a few minutes later, when a courteous man in civilian clothes approached and introduced himself, he realized that "his" investigator had been observing him for some time.

To get to his office, the investigator led him through the unchanged, brilliantly lit corridors of the Lubyanka itself, which Solzhenitsyn had last seen as a shaven-headed prisoner on his way to and from interrogations by Captain Ezepov. According to Solzhenitsyn's account of his visit in *The Gulag Archipelago*, it was as if the new man had read his thoughts. "Ezepov?" he said, once they had reached his office. "What a brute . . . he's been demoted since then. I was in counter-espionage. . . . We didn't have people like that."

Solzhenitsyn writes that he didn't believe a word of it. He had heard Ezepov himself talk like that about other investigators, and knew that such lies were the stock-in-trade of the KGB. However, his forthcoming rehabilitation looked to be genuine enough. Taking out Solzhenitsyn's file, the new man laughed at some of Solzhenitsyn's jokes at Stalin's expense in his letters to Nikolai and praised the stories Solzhenitsyn had written at the front, which were all there as part of the incriminating evidence against him. "Here, there's nothing anti-Soviet in them. You can take them if you like and try to get them published." But Solzhenitsyn waved them away. Heavens, no, he had given up literature a long time ago and was now a humble physics teacher.[4]

His intention then was to visit Rostov and the North Caucasus, to see what few relatives and friends he still had left in the world. But before he did so, he paid a flying visit to the Urals. Elena Zubov's niece Natalia was living there. At the urging of the Zubovs, Solzhenitsyn had started writing to her during his last year in Kok Terek, and he was hoping that he had at last found a bride for himself. He stayed with Natalia and her mother for two weeks and liked the girl well enough to propose marriage (it is not known whether he had asked her to read "The Darling" beforehand), but she seems to have been frightened by his impetuosity and declined the offer.[5]

It is possible that his own heart was not entirely in it either, because a short while beforehand he had had a brief reunion with Natalia Reshetovskaya. Natalia had taken advantage of the summer vacation to travel south to collect Vsevolod's second son, Boris, then twelve years old, and bring him back to Ryazan. As a special treat, she had taken him on a steamer trip up the Don and Volga to Moscow, where she showed him the sights and bought him presents. As usual, she rang Evgenia Panin to say she had arrived, and was amazed to hear Evgenia say that Solzhenitsyn was there and wanted to see her. It so happened that she had recently made up her mind to complete her divorce from Solzhenitsyn and marry Vsevolod, so as to give his two sons a proper mother, but she did not hesitate to accept the invitation and agreed to go and see Solzhenitsyn that same evening. It was on 26 June 1956, two days after his own arrival in Moscow.[6]

Natalia was staying with Lydia Ezherets at the time and was able to walk to the Panins' flat. "I found it hard to climb the stairs," she later wrote in her memoirs. "Evgenia Panin met me and led me into the room. Sanya and Panin were sitting at a round table in the corner, drinking tea. Both stood up. Soon the Panins left us alone together, and somehow we suddenly started talking."[7]

They talked both about the past and the future, about the years spent away from one another and the years ahead. Solzhenitsyn informed her that he was proceeding with his plan of looking for work outside Moscow and would probably pick somewhere east or south-east, in Vladimir Province, not too far from the capital. Later, as he escorted her back to Lydia's flat, they took refuge in a porch from the rain, and Solzhenitsyn began to press Natalia about her reasons for divorcing him; she writes that she was too distraught to reply properly and could only blurt out something trite about fate having decreed their separation. The moment passed and they walked onwards, but before leaving her, Solzhenitsyn handed Natalia copies of the poems that he had written to and about her during his years in the camps. He evidently felt that the eloquence of his pen would better complete what could only be half said in a darkened doorway.

> Now again, again all night
> In dreams appeared
> My dear sweet wife.

Or:

> But at road's end
> There stands my home
> Where in loving vigil waits
> My own, forever mine, my wife.[8]

Soon after his visit to the Urals, Solzhenitsyn travelled to Rostov to see Natalia's two aunts, Manya and Nina, to thank them for sending him the parcels throughout his imprisonment. He also went to look at the spot where the converted stable he and his mother once lived in had been destroyed by a German bomb, and at the cul-de-sac next to the prison where they had lived before that.

Nikolai Vitkevich was now living in nearby Taganrog (he hadn't been allowed to register in Rostov itself) and was making a precarious living by giving private lessons in mathematics while studying for a higher degree in organic chemistry. Solzhenitsyn hastened to tell him about the rehabilitations and about his strange visit to the Lubyanka, but Nikolai cut him short.

It turned out that Nikolai had been summoned to the Rostov KGB head-quarters and questioned about their case. But instead of being grateful to Solzhenitsyn, he was livid. He felt that Solzhenitsyn had been poking his nose into things that were best left alone. He had no desire to be rehabili-tated. He felt safe in Taganrog. Nobody had bothered him until Solzhe-nitsyn came along, and he preferred to stay as he was.

It seemed that Nikolai had been terrified out of his wits by the summons to the prosecutor's office, for the atmosphere in Rostov was vastly different from that of Moscow—more like that of Kok Terek, in fact, than that of the capital. Whereas Moscow was in ferment, and buzzing with rumours, in the provinces little had changed. People in Rostov were as suspicious and para-noid as ever, and few knew of the contents of Khrushchev's "secret speech" or were aware of the great changes that were taking place as a result of it. Nikolai's only desire was to lie low, keep out of harm's way, and get on with rebuilding his career. He had applied to his old department at Rostov Uni-versity for permission to enroll for a doctorate and was frightened that the reopening of his case would spoil his chances.[9]

From Rostov, Solzhenitsyn travelled south to Georgievsk to visit his aunts Irina and Maria and to see his mother's grave. The two old ladies still lived in the small adobe house that Maria had purchased in 1924, Maria with her second husband in the main part of the house, and Irina in a tiny annex with a multitude of cats. Since Maria's three daughters had all made good marriages and were living in Moscow, the three old people were alone. Sol-zhenitsyn learned that Irina had returned to the religious piety of her youth and had developed some eccentric ideas. She regarded the cats as sacred animals and was always taking in new ones, so that there were never fewer than nine or ten at a time. People used to bring maimed or injured cats to her in the knowledge that she was the only one who would look after them and keep them alive.

Solzhenitsyn had no difficulty in visiting the grave in which his mother and his uncle Roman had been interred, but his father's grave had been obli-terated by the stadium. He then visited Kislovodsk to see the house in which he had been born, and the church of St Panteleimon, in which he had been baptized and which he had once seen invaded by Budenny's cavalrymen. It happened to be the feast of the ascension of St Panteleimon and the church was crammed with worshippers. A year or two later this church was also to be razed to the ground as part of Khrushchev's furious campaign to eradicate religion—Solzhenitsyn was just in time.[10]

Back in Moscow, Solzhenitsyn met Lydia Ezherets for the first time since 1944, when Lydia's father, Alexander Ezherets, had been in charge of the Barvikha sanatorium. Life had not been kind to Lydia or her father in the intervening years. Soon after the war's end, Alexander Ezherets had returned to Rostov to his post as chief medical supervisor of the Black Sea coast. At a time of bleak austerity and widespread shortages, he had used his Moscow connections to obtain medicines for people and had been liberal with his favours, and this had brought him to the notice of the Rostov security organs. In 1946 he had been charged with speculation, sentenced to twenty-five years' imprisonment, and dispatched to the labour camps, where he subsequently perished.[11]

In that same year, Lydia had married Kirill, her childhood sweetheart, and after completing her Ph.D. had started teaching German and writing occasional critical articles for some of the Moscow literary magazines. But the marriage had been a failure. Kirill was a reluctant husband, and in 1949 they had divorced, while remaining friends. Then had come Kirill's brush with the secret police, and his terrified recoil from the threat of arrest and trial, and he and Lydia had drifted apart. Meanwhile, during Stalin's last great anti-Semitic campaign at the beginning of the fifties (which had culminated in the "doctors' plot"), Lydia had been dismissed from her teaching post and barred from writing for the magazines. After Stalin's death, she had been allowed to teach again but mainly in the smaller towns in Moscow province and occasionally even farther afield. Among the towns she taught in was Ryazan, where she had often visited Natalia and had become acquainted with Natalia's second husband, Vsevolod.[12]

Naturally, Solzhenitsyn asked after Kirill, the only one of his Rostov friends he had not yet seen. Kirill was now a successful and well-known surgeon, specializing in the treatment of peritonitis. Having worked for a spell at the celebrated Sklifosovsky Institute, he had later transferred to another Moscow hospital and had written one or two medical textbooks. According to someone who met him a little after this, he was still handsome and charming in a somewhat southern way, sophisticated, elegant, and a fluent and witty talker. Women evidently flocked to him (with no chance of success, of course), and he was extremely popular with the medical students of both sexes. Lydia told Solzhenitsyn, however, that Kirill had no wish to see him, for he held Solzhenitsyn responsible for what had happened to him in 1952. It is hard to understand exactly why, since Kirill's brush with the secret police had had no connection with Solzhenitsyn whatever. But the fact that the police already had a dossier on him, and that the dossier had been compiled in connection with Solzhenitsyn's investigation in 1945, seems to have led Kirill to conclude that this new investigation was also somehow Solzhenitsyn's fault. Furthermore, he seems to have believed the KGB's assertion that Solzhenitsyn's testimony of 1945 had actually been given in 1952. Solzhenitsyn was upset by Lydia's news. He felt he had helped Kirill by refusing to testify in Ekibastuz. And he was further disturbed by Lydia's account of her marriage to Kirill and their relatively speedy divorce. Unfortunately, he passed these feelings on to their former literature teacher from Rostov, Anastasia Grunau, whom he saw a few days later in Moscow, and Grunau told Kirill, thus poisoning their relations still more.[13]

Shortly before the start of the new school year, in September 1956, Solzhenitsyn gathered up his few belongings and set out for Torfoprodukt. Spurning the smoke and racket of the main settlement, he sought a room in the neighbouring hamlet of Miltsevo, where he could immerse himself in the sights and smells of the Russian countryside. Finding a room was not easy. Most of the peasants' huts were full or had no partitions, but after making the rounds of the village in the company of a kindly woman he had met in the market, he came to the dilapidated house of a solitary widow called Matryona Zakharova.

Matryona had the reputation in the village of being a slattern, and the state of her house seemed to bear this out. The pitched wooden roof was rotting, its timbers were turning grey with mould for lack of any preservative, and the only furniture inside seemed to be a confusion of stools and benches strewn with potted plants of one kind and another. In the dim light, he could just make out the figure of a sallow-faced woman lying face down on a big, traditional Russian stove; she raised her head when he came in, without moving her body, and explained that she was recovering from one of her periodic bouts of sickness. She didn't seem particularly eager to have a lodger, nor did she refuse him outright, but insisted that he tour the village once more in a last attempt to find more comfortable surroundings.[14]

It did not seem like an obvious home for the fastidious schoolmaster, but he had taken a liking to this typically Russian *izba* with its shingled roof, fretted dormer window, and solid timbers. Although neglected, it had been built to last, with plenty of room inside for the large family that had once inhabited it. And Matryona's easygoing indifference had its attractions. She betrayed no trace of that proprietorial Russian curiosity that demands to know all your personal business before you are even across the threshold, nor was there in her manner any hint of suppressed greed at the prospect of landing such a desirable paying guest. She was offhanded to the point of rudeness. But he was pleased to note when he did return that she had climbed down from her stove and was waiting to greet him.

They quickly settled on a figure for the rent. Solzhenitsyn's wages included a free wagon-load of peat, which he placed at Matryona's disposal, and he moved in at once. They were to share the single, large living space downstairs, Matryona keeping her bed in the corner between the door and the stove and Solzhenitsyn setting up his folding cot beneath one of the four windows that lined the north wall. Beneath another one he placed a small writing-table. Since Matryona usually got up between four and five in the morning and went to bed early, whereas Solzhenitsyn stayed up late at night, and both were out during the day, they interfered little with one another, meeting mainly for the two meals that Matryona prepared for him—breakfast and supper. In keeping with her reputation, Matryona cooked badly, often burning the food or forgetting to season it, and for the most part stuck to a monotonous diet of potatoes and barley. Since the potatoes came from her kitchen garden, which was never manured, they were usually pebble-sized and tasteless. But Solzhenitsyn never complained.

More surprisingly, Matryona didn't complain either. Apart from a single goat, which she kept for milk, and the kitchen garden, she had no other means of subsistence. Because of her sickness, she had been dismissed from the local collective farm. She received no pension, not even for the husband who had disappeared while on active service—she was unable to cope with the red tape necessary to prove that he had earned one. Her fuel consisted of peat, which (in common with the other village women) she pilfered from the heaps left lying about to dry and carted home on her back. And she did a little part-time work at the collective farm, when they were short-handed, in return for payment in kind.

Solzhenitsyn was amazed by her patience and tolerance. As he got to know her better, he discovered that she had had six children, all of whom had died in infancy; that her husband had gone off to the war and never returned; that she had brought up her niece Kira as her own child; and that Kira had recently married a young railway engineer from a nearby village. He felt that perhaps this was the real reason she had welcomed him in—to take the place of her absent niece and reduce the sense of loneliness in her big cabin.

Miltsevo wasn't exactly Turgenev country. In this region of low-lying water-meadows and bog-land that sprawled on either side of the shallow river Klyazma, peat was the staple product. The surrounding forests had been cut down for fuel during Stalin's mad rush for industrialization in the thirties, and the fields themselves were scarred with peat diggings. The local agriculture was poor and mainly of the subsistence variety. But Miltsevo had its picturesque side. Matryona's house overlooked a small stream that had been dammed to form a village pond. Weeping willows, ducks, and Matryona's tumbledown cabin made up a pastoral scene straight from the pages of Esenin. Solzhenitsyn, who had known towns, the front line, labour camps, and the semi-desert of Kazakhstan, at once fell in love with it as the very essence of what he had been missing all these years: the Russian village.

As in Kok Terek, his days were filled with teaching and his evenings and weekends with writing. No longer did he feel the pressure of having to hide every scrap of paper, nor did he feel threatened by the friendly but uninquisitive Matryona. He was able to write peacefully—polishing his poems and plays and working at his novel about the *sharashka*. Publication still seemed unimaginable, but just in case, he experimented with a number of pseudonyms and finally settled on Stepan Khlynov. Stepan was a favourite Russian Christian name of his (which he was later to give to his third son), and Khlynov was the ancient name of the Russian city of Vyatka (hypocritically renamed Kirov by Stalin in honour of the Leningrad leader he had murdered).[15]*

He was at peace, but again lonely, and craved a woman's company desperately. The inability of the Zubovs' niece Natalia to make up her mind about marriage had turned his thoughts more and more to that other Natalia, his former wife, and their inconclusive meeting in Moscow. After arranging to take the job in Torfoprodukt, he had written to her informing her of his

* See note p. 176.

new address "in case you have the inclination, and the possibility, to write to me."[16] He did not know it yet, but his letter, coming after the poems he had given her, had had the desired effect. Natalia was in a turmoil. Once more she felt the lure of his imperious and romantic personality, but when she discussed the matter with Lydia Ezherets, the latter advised her not to write back. She could see in which direction the matter was heading, and she feared for the welfare of Vsevolod and the two boys, especially Boris, who at twelve was very vulnerable and had only just learned to call Natalia "mummy." Natalia, however, had already made up her mind. In some ways it seemed like the realization of her old dream of 1953. She would have the best of both worlds: marriage to Vsevolod, the satisfaction of being a mother to the boys, and a platonic correspondence with her much more interesting first husband.

She could not foresee, it seems, that Solzhenitsyn would react just as he had in 1953—not abruptly and not harshly, but with the same emotional logic. Within a very short time their correspondence assumed a more personal and affectionate character. Solzhenitsyn wrote that he was astonished by the shift in his feelings towards her and was wondering whether a new happiness was possible for them. He suggested that she try to visit him to sort out their emotions, and in late October, taking advantage of Vsevolod's absence on a trip to Odessa, Natalia arranged to go secretly to Torfoprodukt for three days, leaving the boys in the care of her mother.

On Friday, 19 October 1956, Solzhenitsyn met her at the ramshackle station of Torfoprodukt. Whatever their earlier doubts or fears, this meeting seems to have dispelled them, for on their walk along the lonely road to Miltsevo, with a bright moon shining above, they stopped in the shadow of a haystack and embraced passionately. Reshetovskaya writes that everything seemed to come back to them—their past, their youth, their early promises to one another—and it was as though the intervening years of war, camps, and separation had never been. The weekend passed in a whirl of animated conversation, questions, answers, walking and talking and taking photographs of one another. Matryona, true to her tactful and discreet disposition, said not a word and kept herself well in the background, until Natalia blurted out the whole story to her.[17]

Solzhenitsyn was aware throughout of the ultimate goal of their reunion and questioned Natalia on the seriousness of her commitment. He told her about his illness and warned her he might have only three or four years to live, but this only fired her on. If he was dying, there was all the more reason to abandon her second husband, who needed her less, and return to the first, who had suffered so much already and so desperately craved her love and affection. She was also swept along by his burning sense of mission. He showed her his plays and verse from Kok Terek and the first drafts of his novel. His confidence in himself, his utter dedication to his vocation, and his austere life-style stood in stark contrast to the soft, easygoing ways of Vsevolod, with his comfortable university career and lack of ambition. It was just like being young again. Love, ideals, soaring hopes—how could she resist it? And how could he resist that yielding, answering response to his passionate words and kisses, that womanly softness, those womanly scents, the soft rustle of a woman's clothing that he had yearned for and been so cruelly deprived of all these years?

Their letters in the weeks that followed mixed ardent affirmations of love with practical discussions of what they were to do next. Natalia went back to Torfoprodukt two or three more times, pretending to her husband that she was going to Moscow, and each new visit drew them closer and closer to one another. Solzhenitsyn made Natalia read Chekhov's "Darling" and Tolstoy's afterword to the story. He explained that he required her total submission to the restrictions that he was already imposing on himself, and would impose on her, as a result of his need for total secrecy in the pursuit of his dangerous literary interests. She would have to subordinate everything to his writing. To his enormous relief, Natalia agreed to everything. She was already devouring the tiny sheets of paper, eight inches by six, crammed with his spidery handwriting, on which he had begun his epic novel, *The First Circle*, and realized that she had a major role in it as Gleb Nerzhin's wife, Nadia. What an adventure it seemed and how exciting it all was![18]

But from Ryazan the whole thing looked more difficult. If they were to be permanently reunited—and that was what Solzhenitsyn was now demanding—she would have to undertake a proper separation from Vsevolod, and she shrank from breaking the news to him. In fact, he must already have suspected that something was afoot. She had told him of her first meeting with Solzhenitsyn in Moscow in the summer, and although she had assured him that nothing would change, he must have seen the alteration in her demeanour. Naturally accommodating, he had attempted to put a stop to the new relationship not by meeting it head on but by distracting her with trips along the river Oka in his motor boat, a holiday in the beauty spot of Solotcha in the midst of the forest, and by lavishing extra care and attention on her. All this made her decision more difficult—not to speak of the two children, whom she would be leaving motherless again.

At last she plucked up the nerve to tell him, but it seems that Vsevolod took the news very badly and was not willing to give her up without a struggle. Solzhenitsyn wrote to urge courage upon her. "I beg of you, my little girl, be firm to the end and don't stoop to a single compromise! Force me in this way to believe in your new character."[19] For Solzhenitsyn there was no problem. Still fiercely jealous of Vsevolod, he seems to have regarded him as nothing but a blackguard who had stolen another man's wife. As for the children, having never seen them or had any of his own, he possessed little concept of what it might mean to them to lose a mother for a second time, even if it was a stepmother. In years to come, he was to recognize the selfishness of his behaviour and conclude that the whole thing had probably been a mistake, but at the time he was determined. "My problem was that I thought I couldn't go on any longer, that I had to get married, that my situation was impossible. I had gone for four years without a wife. . . . And then there was no one I could tell my secret to; no one would ever understand."[20]*

On 30 October, Solzhenitsyn wrote to Natalia saying that he was firm in his decision, had "forgiven" her everything, and truly loved her once more. He was prepared, he said, to join their lives forever. Natalia and Vsevolod then came to an agreement to part after the November holiday.† There was apparently some haggling over the division of their possessions, during which Vsevolod succeeded in alienating Natalia's mother, until now on his side, but eventually he moved out to Svoboda Street, in another part of Ryazan.[21]

On 30 December 1956 Solzhenitsyn made his first visit to Ryazan‡ to spend the New Year holiday with Natalia and her mother. Maria hadn't seen Solzhenitsyn since before the war, although she had, of course, known about the various stages of his imprisonment and exile and had helped to send many of the parcels. It was an emotional reunion, and old times figured high on the list of topics for conversation. The next day, Solzhenitsyn and Natalia called at the Ryazan registry office, hoping to re-register their marriage, but Solzhenitsyn had never received an official notification of Natalia's divorce action, and it was not entered in his internal passport. A few days later, on a visit to Moscow, they hunted down a copy of the divorce order in the Moscow City Court, and the way was cleared for them to re-register (the official date of re-registration was 2 February 1957).[22]

Two months after Solzhenitsyn's return to Torfoprodukt, he received the news that his request for rehabilitation had been granted. The formal hearing had taken place on 6 February, when a military tribunal of the Supreme Court, presided over by Judicial Councillor Borisoglebsky and consisting of Colonels Dolotsev and Konev, had re-examined the circumstances of his arrest and imprisonment and heard a plea from the chief military prosecutor to annul the charges. Written evidence was received both from former military colleagues of Solzhenitsyn and from Natalia, Lydia, and even Kirill, who despite his resentment over the 1952 episode, had nevertheless written in Solzhenitsyn's defence.

The chief military prosecutor's reasons for seeking an annulment of the charges were cited as follows:

> It is clear from the evidence in this case that Solzhenitsyn, in his diary and in letters to a friend, N. D. Vitkevich, although speaking of the correctness of Marxism-Leninism, the progressiveness of the socialist revolution in our country, and the inevitability of its victory throughout the world, also spoke out against the personality of Stalin and wrote of the artistic and ideological short-

---

* Solzhenitsyn's changed view of the appropriateness of his remarriage to Reshetovskaya dates from after they had separated and he had fallen in love with another woman. He also told Kopelev at the later date that the main reason he had gone back to Reshetovskaya was that she was "the only woman he could trust," and he asked Kopelev to burn his letters to him from exile. This argument seems both to underrate the strength of his actual feelings for Natalia at the time and to show him in a worse light than he perhaps realized.

† The November holiday celebrates the anniversary of the Revolution (see note p. 31).

‡ Ryazan was coincidentally the birthplace of Solzhenitsyn's favourite poet, Esenin.

comings of the works of many Soviet authors and the air of unreality that pervades many of them. He also wrote that our works of art fail to give readers of the bourgeois world a sufficiently comprehensive and versatile explanation of the inevitability of the victory of the Soviet army and people and that our literary works are no match for the adroitly fashioned slanders of the bourgeois world against our country.[23]

The interesting thing about this plea is its revelation of how much literary criticism there was in Solzhenitsyn's early letters and how close it was to the criticisms he was to voice as a mature writer. Soviet literature's "shortcomings" and particularly its "air of unreality" were to become leitmotivs of his later criticism and the targets against which his own literary practice was directed.

The rehabilitation tribunals were as much a foregone conclusion as the Special Board sessions and military tribunals before them—nothing in the Soviet Union had changed in that respect. Verdicts were still decided before the proceedings began. It was just that attitudes had changed at the top. Nevertheless, it was sweet for Solzhenitsyn to read the tribunal's final resolution, to learn that he was still, after all, "a Soviet patriot," not guilty of any crime, and that the decree of the Special Board, passed all those years ago, in July 1945, was null and void and his case closed as unproven.

It was in fact a year of good news. First his remarriage, then his rehabilitation. But a brief cloud was cast by the sudden and tragic death of his landlady, Matryona. Matryona's niece Kira, who had moved to the village of Cherusti across the railway line after her marriage, had unexpectedly acquired a plot of ground to build on. But for some reason she was not allowed to keep it unless she could build something right away, and there was no chance of obtaining the necessary timber in time. It so happened that Matryona had willed Kira her *gornitsa*, a spacious annex to her main cabin that was more or less self-contained and no longer used. Kira's father insisted that Matryona allow the annex to be dismantled right away, without waiting for her death, and be transferred to Cherusti and re-erected on Kira's plot. Matryona agreed, and the annex was duly chopped away one evening and loaded onto two sledges pulled by a tractor. When they came to the railway line, one of the sledges got stuck. Two of the men, helped by Matryona, were trying to free it when out of the darkness, a pair of unlighted locomotives bore down on them and smashed the sledge to smithereens. All three were killed instantly, the engines were derailed, and the main-line express was stopped only just in time to avoid a major catastrophe.

Since the tractor driver had been moonlighting, his helpers had been drinking, and the locomotives should have been lighted, just about everybody was to blame and the whole affair was hushed up. Matryona's relatives, undeterred by the tragedy that had struck them (the other man killed was Matryona's nephew), quickly buried their dead and quarrelled over Matryona's inheritance.

Solzhenitsyn was caught in the middle of this episode. He had watched the annex being dismantled and towed away, had been roused from his bed and questioned by the police in the middle of the night on which the accident occurred, had attended the funeral and the wake, which was held in Matryona's house, and had subsequently moved to the house of one of Matryona's sisters-in-law, where he learnt further details of the accident and heard about the web of family envies and resentments that lay behind the disputes over Matryona's meagre possessions. It was a priceless opportunity to peep behind the scenes of Russian peasant life (not often accessible to city-bred intellectuals) and later provided the inspiration for his classic short story "Matryona's Place," in which he described the entire episode.

The rest of the school year seemed to pass in a blur of preparations for his forthcoming move to Ryazan. On visits to Moscow, Solzhenitsyn and Natalia visited his old *sharashka* friends Kopelev, Panin, and Ivashov-Musatov and their respective wives. When she was not staying with him in Torfoprodukt, he worked away at his novel, completing a full first draft by the time he was ready to move. And in June 1957 came the move itself.

Passing through Moscow, they spent a week with Natalia's uncle, Valentin Turkin, the cinema critic. Valentin had also been through difficult times since that carefree summer of 1940, when he had urged the young couple to spend their honeymoon in Tarusa. In 1948, during Stalin's campaign against "rootless cosmopolitanism" (ie., interest in foreign countries), Valentin had been publicly pilloried and his textbook on the history of the cinema banned before publication. The charge against him was that he had written too favourably on the American cinema, particularly on the pioneering role of D. W. Griffiths, and thus slighted Soviet achievements. Since he wasn't a Jew (the campaign against 'cosmopolitans" was aimed primarily at the Jews), he had escaped with a reprimand and was able to retain his post at the Institute of Cinematography. But the shock of being attacked at a time when thousands were disappearing into the camps had left its mark on him. He was still the brilliant, sophisticated man of the world who had dazzled Solzhenitsyn at their first meeting, but now had retired into himself and become even more epicurean in his private habits than when Solzhenitsyn had first met him before the war.

It was at this time that Solzhenitsyn renewed his acquaintance with Valentin's daughter, Veronica. The pretty fifteen-year-old schoolgirl with flying pigtails from before the war was now married for the second time and had a two-year-old daughter. During the day she worked in a children's library and in her spare time was studying journalism at Moscow University, where her husband, Yuri Stein, was also studying, after seven years in the air force. They still lived in the family's cramped communal flat on Malaya Bronnaya Street, together with Veronica's two aunts.

Veronica had followed Solzhenitsyn's vicissitudes with sympathetic interest ever since he and Natalia had been to stay with her and her mother during their honeymoon in 1940. In 1945, after Solzhenitsyn had been arrested, investigated, and sentenced, it was Veronica's mother to whom he first succeeded in sending news of his whereabouts; and it was with the two Veronicas that Natalia had stayed during that crowded year from 1945 to 1946, when Solzhenitsyn was successively in Butyrki Prison, New Jerusalem, and Kaluga Gate. The younger Veronica had been present when Ilya Solomin returned from the front and described to Natalia the details of Solzhenitsyn's arrest, and in 1953 she had met Solomin yet again when he, too, had returned from the labour camps. Finally, it was to Veronica that Natalia had given Solzhenitsyn's early stories and some of his books (including the profusely annotated copy of *War and Peace*) when she had left Solzhenitsyn for Vsevolod.

Veronica was thus aware of the various stages of Solzhenitsyn's odyssey through the jails, camps, and exile, and when she heard of his return from Kok Terek, she had written him a letter saying that if he was ever in Moscow, he was just as welcome at their flat in Malaya Bronnaya as in the old days. Coming at a time when he was still alone and feeling friendless and neglected, with no family to turn to, her letter had touched him, and he had responded with gratitude, saying that he appreciated her gesture all the more because he was too self-conscious, after his years in the camps, to approach old acquaintances first. But it was not until now, reunited with Natalia, that he had felt able to accept Veronica's offer.

The return to Malaya Bronnaya must have evoked vivid memories in Solzhenitsyn and Natalia and helped to cement their feeling of having completely buried the years of their separation. Veronica and Yuri welcomed them with true Russian hospitality and informed them that since they had recently acquired an additional room on the floor above their flat, Solzhenitsyn and Natalia were welcome to stay there any time they were in Moscow.

Veronica regarded the returned exile with especial interest, and it seems that a bond of sympathy and affection sprang up between her and Solzhenitsyn almost immediately. She found him much changed from the impetuous and energetic student of 1940. He was now thin and had aged far more than she had expected. His hair was dull and lifeless, his eyes somewhat sunken, lacking their old fire, his expression serious, and his movements slow and deliberate. At the same time, he seemed distant and absent-minded, although beneath the gentle exterior she sensed a hard, steely centre that had not been there before. On the whole, she liked this reserved, courteous but strong-willed figure rather more than the self-centred, bumptious student of 1941.[24]

Natalia, for her part, was in a supercharged mood of euphoria, willing to go to endless lengths to please and entertain her returned husband, full of energy and ideas, and bubbling over with happiness. It was as if she were anxious to make up for all the care and creature comforts he had missed while away and to heal the scar caused by their separation. She arranged a shopping expedition to purchase a number of items that were available only in Moscow and that they needed for their new life in Ryazan, including Solzhenitsyn's first typewriter (a Moskva-4). Between them they planned to type all the manuscripts that Solzhenitsyn had accumulated in the four years since his release from Ekibastuz—Natalia professionally, employing the touch-typing she had learned at university, and Solzhenitsyn in the classic two-finger mode. Natalia also bought tickets for a short steamer cruise down the Volga and Oka rivers, which they embarked on before settling in Ryazan.[25]

The one thing that saddened their stay in Moscow was Veronica's news of Ilya Solomin's arrest and imprisonment. It had happened in May 1946, quite soon after Ilya moved away from Natalia's aunts in Rostov and into the unversity hostel. He had been a member of a group of students who used to meet regularly for parties, discussions, and various social functions, and between flirting they had talked politics. This had aroused the suspicions of the university authorities, the group was presumably infiltrated by an informer, and the whole lot were rounded up and arrested. Ilya, as one of two who had served in the army and were therefore older than the others, had been sentenced to seven years in the labour camps for anti-Soviet agitation, and most of the rest had been given five years. Most disquieting was the news that an attempt had been made to link Ilya's case with that of Solzhenitsyn and Vitkevich (both were from Rostov), and Ilya's assertion that when shown some of the evidence in Solzhenitsyn's case, he had discovered some damaging testimony against him by Kirill. He had asked Veronica to pass this information on and to warn Natalia against her friend. It was yet one more point of potential discord between the two former school-friends, but it seems that Solzhenitsyn's inclination at the time was to dismiss it.[26]

Once in Ryazan, Solzhenitsyn and Natalia commenced their new life with a burst of activity. Her two rooms in the communal flat on the first floor had grown shabby in the five years that she had occupied them, and Solzhenitsyn, armed with the practical experience gained in the camps, set to work to rewire and redecorate them. The smaller of the two rooms was equipped with a double bed, a pair of desks, and bookcases all around the walls—for Solzhenitsyn and Natalia. Natalia's mother, Maria, continued to sleep in a corner of the larger room, which also served as their living- and dining-room combined. In this way, not only were the rooms made more convenient for their new occupant but the shade of his predecessor was exorcized in the same operation. The kitchen and toilet (there was no bathroom) continued, as before, to be shared with Natalia's neighbours.

An advantage of the wooden house on Kasimovsky Lane was that it was still on the edge of open country, and although the Ryazan suburbs were expanding year by year, encroaching ever further on the surrounding fields, it still had a quiet, tree-shaded garden. In one corner was an ancient apple tree, beneath which Solzhenitsyn constructed a bench and table for working out of doors, and in the summer they carried out a couple of loungers and spent whole days in the garden. Within a year or two the yard of the Radio Institute next door had been asphalted over and was used as an unofficial race-track by local youths on their motorcycles, and a food warehouse across the street attracted a stream of noisy lorries, but even then the garden continued to be a refuge, and in winter the "Walrus," who had always revelled in the cold, was happy to chop firewood outside.

"I don't remember ever having had such living conditions in all my life," Solzhenitsyn wrote to Dr Zubov at about this time.[27] And a few years later he was to devote one of his miniature stories, "Breathing," to the joy the garden gave him.

> Last night it rained, and the clouds are still scudding across the sky. A few drops still fall from time to time. I stand beneath the apple tree—the blossom not quite faded yet—and breathe in. . . .
>
> So what if this is only a postage stamp of a garden hemmed in by five-storey monsters. I no longer hear the roar of motorcycle exhausts, the whine of record players or the tinkling of transistors. Even if you and I are constantly made the sport of others, so long as we can breathe here under the apple tree after the rain, it will still be possible to live.[28]

21

THE SCHOOLMASTER
FROM RYAZAN

I N SEPTEMBER 1957 Solzhenitsyn started work as a teacher of physics and astronomy at High School No. 2 in Ryazan. He had first applied for the post in the spring, but owing to his prison record it had taken some time for the appointment to be confirmed. The appointments director of the Ryazan Education Department expressed amazement at the fact that Solzhenitsyn had been arrested for criticizing the "personality cult" in 1945: "Do you mean to say it existed as long ago as that?"[1] Like most uninformed Soviet citizens, she thought that Khrushchev's speech had concerned only the post-war years. Fortunately, Solzhenitsyn now had his certificate of rehabilitation to prove his innocence, and the headmaster of High School No. 2, Georgi Matveyev, whom he met at the department, turned out to have fought on the same front as Solzhenitsyn during the war.[2] After an exchange of reminiscences, no more needed to be said.

Solzhenitsyn appears to have been as outstandingly successful in his teaching in Ryazan as he had been in Kazakhstan, and for much the same reasons. His verve, his enthusiasm, his inventiveness, soon became bywords in the school, and he was found to be particularly adept at making the connection between theory and practice. In the days of his fame the headmaster told a visiting reporter, "The main thing about him . . . is his indestructible love of life and of everything in life concerned with science. Say his class is covering a particular subject. He makes a point of taking his pupils to a local factory or workshop and getting them to watch what's going on. Then he tells them to solve a problem on the basis of what they have observed at the factory. It is amazing how clear and obvious the laws of physics become when you perceive them in life around you, not even suspecting that you have been witnessing them all along." Matveyev recalled having become so absorbed in some of Solzhenitsyn's poetic descriptions of physics when visiting his class-room that he forgot what he had come for and stayed to listen until the end.[3]

Soviet clichés about an "indestructible love of life" can be discounted, of course, and it must be remembered that this account was written in the afterglow of Solzhenitsyn's success and achievement of nation-wide fame. Nevertheless, the picture of the gifted and dedicated teacher emerges with great clarity from all accounts of his work in Ryazan. He was known for keeping up with the latest developments in his subject, particularly in the field of space travel, and twice went to Moscow to lecture on the teaching of physics. He was also asked to write an article on earth satellites for the local edition of *An Agitator's Notebook* (it was never published) and spoke at a local meeting to mark the launching of the first sputnik.

Another interest put to good use was his hobby of photography. Taking over the school photography club, he introduced a passion for order and precision that was quite new to most of the pupils. Soon the dark-room was festooned with neatly typed notices—some of them in verse—containing instructions on how to develop and print, or admonishing the students against waste—and a meticulous filing system was introduced to keep track of club members' work. When a group of fellow teachers went on a brief hunting expedition, it was inevitable that Solzhenitsyn should go along with his camera.

And yet this appearance of plunging heart and soul into his teaching was only a facade, for Solzhenitsyn was careful to limit his commitments at the school and to organize his life with the utmost rigour, so as to leave the maximum amount of time for writing. He restricted his hours of teaching to fifteen a week for the first year, twelve in the second year, and eventually to only ten—the minimum to qualify as "employed" and be eligible for social security.

One of the reporters who later visited the school described his routine as follows.

> Time is so precious to him that you would take it for a mania if his creative motives weren't so crystal clear and fundamental. He arrives in his class-room just one or two minutes before the bell. He doesn't hang around after the end of classes and, without a good reason, doesn't drop into the staff room. He takes every opportunity of avoiding long meetings and conferences, not hesitating to use the help of one of his pupils to slip past the open door of the auditorium unnoticed. At the same time, he manages to get everything done. He breaks no promises, is never late, and demands the greatest exactitude from others in the fulfilment of their duties. Alexander Isayevich's punctuality is proverbial. . . . He is a person of rare self-discipline.[4]

This self-discipline naturally extended into his private life as well. Reshetovskaya has written in her memoirs of the monkish life they led during the first few years in Ryazan. "We lived by a set of strict rules on going to the cinema, concerts, and theatres. We allowed ourselves visits to the cinema only twice a month. As for concerts and theatres, these were limited to a visit every other month. All this was recorded. If we exceeded the quota in any one month, we had to abstain the following month in order to make up for it."[5]

Although she was to complain of this strict regime in years to come (and not without reason), Natalia seems to have accepted it docilely enough at the time. After all, she had read "The Darling" and been warned. Somewhat harder to accept was the isolation from her former friends. She still taught chemistry at the Agricultural Institute—for which, incidentally, she received a very good salary, thus making it possible for Solzhenitsyn to reduce his hours at the school and earn so little on his own account. But like Solzhenitsyn himself, she now spent no more time at her job than was absolutely necessary, and would rush home as soon as she could to help Solzhenitsyn on what was by now almost their joint project, the second and third drafts of *The First Circle*.

According to Reshetovskaya's memoirs, work on the second draft lasted from the summer of 1957 until mid-January 1958. An important feature of this draft was the complete reworking of the chapters devoted to Nadia Nerzhin and her life in the Moscow University hostel at Stromynka while her husband was in the *sharashka*. For this, Solzhenitsyn now had Natalia's diary to work from, and he questioned her exhaustively about her movements, thoughts, and emotions at that time, as well as about her relations with the other girls who shared her room. With a few of these he also had an opportunity to talk, especially with Alexandra Popova (Olga in the novel), with whom he and Natalia occassionally stayed when they visited Moscow.[6]

Solzhenitsyn was also able to discuss large sections of the novel with the originals of some of the principal protagonists, above all with Lev Kopelev and Dimitri Panin. Together they went over some of the scenes in which all three of them appeared, and Panin, in particular, was very active in helping Solzhenitsyn think up new themes for some of Sologdin's arguments with Rubin. Although both friends figured very prominently, Kopelev seems to have taken a more detached view of Solzhenitsyn's work and to have given him *carte blanche* in what he wrote, whereas Panin had literary and philosophical ambitions of his own and took a lively interest in all stages of the novel. In a sense this suited Solzhenitsyn quite well, for he had moved much closer to Panin's views on the perniciousness of Marxism and the evils of the Revolution, whereas Kopelev, though thoroughly disillusioned with Stalin, still preserved his faith in Lenin more or less intact. Panin also welcomed Solzhenitsyn's return to Christianity, but in 1959 he wrote him a long letter saying that faith was not enough and that before Solzhenitsyn could regard himself as a true Christian he would have to submit his will to the church. Solzhenitsyn, it appears, was not prepared to make such a submission.

A number of meetings took place in Moscow, where Solzhenitsyn also saw the painter Sergei Ivashov-Musatov and discussed his role in the novel with him. Ivashov-Musatov was not as close to him as Panin and Kopelev, but Solzhenitsyn regarded him as a creative colleague and liked to talk to him about such subjects as the role of the artist and the meaning of art in contemporary society. In the *sharashka* Solzhenitsyn had been a sincere admirer of Ivashov-Musatov's talent. He still treasured the pencil sketch Ivashov-Musatov had made of him there; and the artist's picture *The Castle of the Holy Grail* hung in his living-room in Ryazan. But now he had doubts. Ivashov-Musatov was obsessed with one project in particular—*Othello, Desdemona, and Iago*—which he had started in 1956 or 1957. Solzhenitsyn felt that it was a waste of the artist's talent and argued for more "relevance." On one occasion, in 1959, during a visit to Ivashov-Musatov's studio with Panin, Solzhenitsyn exclaimed, "I can quite understand why great artists have always drawn on the eternal subjects in Holy Scripture, and I can see why they also find inspiration in Shakespeare. But I cannot understand why an artist should be so firmly attached to the subject matter of ages so remote from ours after he has been witness to the sufferings of people close by him. Fidelity, jealousy, and treachery, as they exist in our own day, are right in front of him and all around him."[7]

Very occasionally his Moscow friends travelled down to Ryazan, and Solzhenitsyn had brief visits from old labour-camp friends living farther afield. One of these was Nikolai Semyonov, the original of the engineer called Potapov in *The First Circle*, whom Solzhenitsyn had first met in Butyrki in 1947. He was now a highly successful man who since his release had climbed back to the top of his profession. Panin still disliked Semyonov intensely, but Solzhenitsyn was very fond of him and treasured the cigarette-case that Semyonov had made him in the *sharashka* for his birthday. Semyonov's visit gave him the opportunity to show him the chapter placed into Potapov's mouth, "The Buddha's Smile,"* the original idea for which Semyonov and he had dreamt up together in Butyrki.

Contacts with these old labour camp comrades were extremely important to Solzhenitsyn for a number of reasons. The year in Torfoprodukt had acted as a kind of "decompression" period in which he had begun to recover from the tensions and psychological strains imposed by his term of imprisonment and exile, and had commenced the painful process of adjusting to "normal" life. His existence there had been of necessity solitary and reclusive. He was set apart from the rest of the villagers by his education and experiences and had been emotionally absorbed by the reawakening of his love for Natalia. But now he was obliged to fit into normal society in a far greater variety of ways, to rub shoulders with people of all kinds and in all walks of life, including those who were his educational, and in a few instances his intellectual, equals.

* The chapter is a reworking of a well-known camp anecdote that depicts Mrs Roosevelt arriving in Moscow for a goodwill visit just after the war and being shown round a model jail. The whole thing is a put-up job by the Soviet authorities, and the story describes (from the point of view of the prisoners) the way in which the elaborate deception is mounted specially for her benefit.

This was psychologically difficult for him. He still had that sense of a man who has returned from the dead and who therefore regards the normal living as somehow strange and incomprehensible. With them it was still impossible to make friends. None of the other teachers was remotely close to him, not even Matveyev, the headmaster. The only people he felt truly comfortable with were those who had shared similar experiences, former sons of Gulag who, like himself, had been innocent victims of Stalin's political terror. This sense of ease extended also to the Zubovs, with whom he carried on an intense correspondence throughout his years in Torfoprodukt and Ryazan, detailing his most intimate thoughts and plans. Their sensitive and concerned responses did much to buoy him up and soothe him during this period.

Apart from the practical utility of these meetings with his *sharashka* friends (for his work on *The First Circle*), another motive for restricting himself to their company was his need for absolute secrecy. Among his papers were three plays dealing with three of the most sensitive issues in recent Soviet history: the unbridled behaviour of Soviet troops in occupied Germany; the brutal excesses of Smersh during and after the war; and the terrorization of political prisoners by criminals in the camps, aided and abetted by the camp authorities. In addition there was his long autobiographical poem expressing sharp criticism of the Soviet regime from the very earliest days of the Revolution onwards, and numerous other "seditious" poems, including the ode on Stalin's death. Little that Khrushchev had done so far affected the light in which these works would be officially regarded. Each was, to a greater or lesser degree, "criminal," and their discovery would have led to fresh arrest and imprisonment—if not worse. It was true he had devised ingenious hiding-places for most of them, but should he attract suspicion in any way, there was a chance they would be found.

And now he was working on yet another forbidden theme—the secret prison institutes set up by Stalin for scientists to carry out research—and again needed perfect confidentiality. It was this above all that motivated Solzhenitsyn's monastic life-style. As he later wrote in *The Oak and the Calf*:

> I had to adapt my whole life to the need for tight security; make no friends or acquaintances at all in Ryazan . . . invite nobody to my home and accept no invitations—because I couldn't afford to explain to anyone that in fact I never had a single free hour. . . . I couldn't afford to let a single scrap of what I had hidden escape from the flat, or allow an observant eye inside for a moment. . . . Among my colleagues at work I took care never to reveal any broader interests and always to make a show of indifference to literature.[8]

He went to enormous lengths to cover his tracks by destroying all rough drafts and outlines as soon as they had been superseded, typing his works as tightly as possible, with no spaces or margins and using both sides of the paper, and burning his fair copies as soon as the final version had been typed—

a habit that he had started in the camps and was destined to continue until the day he was expelled from the Soviet Union, in 1974.

There is no doubt that these conditions made for immense difficulties both in writing and in everyday living. All these drafts and copies had to be burnt sheet by sheet in the Solzhenitsyns' stove, which was situated in the shared kitchen of their communal flat. This meant sitting up late until their neighbours were in bed and asleep. There were a hundred other such menial tasks to be performed with boring repetition, all of which are described (with somewhat excessive self-satisfaction) in the opening pages of *The Oak and the Calf*. On the other hand, some of these difficulties were almost certainly of Solzhenitsyn's own making, answering to what was by now an irresistible psychological imperative. There was a sense in which he needed the whiff of danger in his nostrils, partly, perhaps, to enable him to relive and recapture the emotional stresses of the past, and partly because after long years of conditioning he simply felt more comfortable in an atmosphere of embattled conspiracy.

Evidence for his attitude in these matters can be found in his response to the details of his past. For Solzhenitsyn this past was the object of profound meditation and study, its remembrance a sacred duty. Every year, on the anniversary of his arrest, he organized a "convict's day." In the morning he cut himself twenty-three ounces of bread and put two lumps of sugar in hot water for his drink. At lunch time he had a bowl of broth and a ladle of groats. And for supper he had the remainder of the bread and groats again. "And how quickly I get back to my old form," he later wrote. "By the end of the day, I am already picking up crumbs to put in my mouth and licking the bowl. The old sensations start up vividly."[9]

As he points out in that same passage in *The Gulag Archipelago*, many others did the same, and treasured their souvenirs from the camps "like holy relics." Solzhenitsyn himself treasured the padded jacket and number patches from Ekibastuz, the aluminium spoon he had made himself there, his army greatcoat, and his battered suitcase with the bayonet hole in the side.* And there were reminders of this past everywhere—for those with eyes to see. In Miltsevo he had discovered that nearly half the inhabitants had passed through the labour camps at one time or another, albeit most of them for theft. In Ryazan there was a hole in the railway fence just outside the station that for some reason was never repaired. Most passengers hardly noticed it, but Solzhenitsyn did, for it was the spot where the Stolypin cars stopped and prison vans were backed up to load or unload prisoners—even now the authorities disliked admitting their existence.

More prominent still was another kind of reminder, a massive monument to the MVD featuring a statue of a camp guard holding an Alsatian straining at the leash on the south-west side of Ryazan, where the main road came in from Mikhailov. Solzhenitsyn was even asked to lecture in a local

---

*The bayonet hole had been made by an armed guard at one of the halts when Solzhenitsyn was being transported to Ekibastuz.

labour camp soon after his arrival in Ryazan—in Corrective Labour Colony No. 2, a camp for women on the outskirts of Ryazan. The lecture was one of his usual ones on physics and space travel, but he was terribly distracted by the emaciated faces and angular bodies of the women who had come to listen to him, and he could vividly imagine the cells they had just left, their reluctance to come here, and the miserable life they would return to afterwards.

One day, finding himself in Novoslobodskaya Street on one of his visits to Moscow, he decided on impulse to enter the "Parcels Reception Office" of Butyrki Prison. It was full inside, mostly of women. This, he realized, was where his own parcels had come from. He recalled that on one occasion in Butyrki he and his cell-mates had discussed the problem of what job to take if and when they were released and what was the most useful thing they might do. All agreed that the most useful contribution would be to take a folding stool to the Butyrki parcels office, sit outside, and advise people on what went to make a perfect parcel. It should have soft sides, with nothing metal in it, and contain plastic spoons and mugs as well as food and clothing. Solzhenitsyn walked over to inspect the list of regulations hanging on the wall and wondered what chance there would ever be of putting their old plan into practice, but he had barely begun to read the notice when an MVD sergeant-major challenged him and quickly hustled him out.[10]

On another occasion he visited the block of flats he had helped build at Kaluga Gate. In those days, back in 1946, the block had been on the outskirts of Moscow and hemmed in by watch-towers and a high fence, sufficiently isolated not to draw attention to itself. Now it was lost in the anonymous suburbs that stretched for miles in all directions. A sports shop stood on the spot where the canteen and cultural and educational section had been and where, all those years ago, Solzhenitsyn had recited Chatsky's subversive monologue from *Woe from Wit*. Their old trusties' room was now part of someone's flat on the third floor, and higher up were the parquet floors he had laid and the doors he had puttied.* Placing his hands behind his back, Solzhenitsyn paced the path that he had once paced when it had been a compound, and imagined himself back in the old days. Again that feeling of having returned from the dead, of being endowed with a double vision, came back to him. The residents of these buildings had no idea that as they strolled across the central courtyard, they were stepping over the ghosts of former prisoners, one of whom had leapt to his death on this very spot. "And only those trees in Neskuchny Park . . . bore witness that they remembered everything, including me, and that it had all really happened." Unable to resist a sudden temptation, Solzhenitsyn climbed the first flight of stairs, and just below the flat where the camp commandant's office had been, scrawled in black crayon on the white windowsill, "Labour Camp Division No. 121."[11]

---

* It appears that after the publication of *Ivan Denisovich* Solzhenitsyn was invited to meet a prominent physicist then living in that very building. According to rumour, Solzhenitsyn paced the rooms and admired the fact that his floors did not squeak.

Unlike Nikolai Vitkevich and many millions of others, Solzhenitsyn was unable and unwilling to forget. In April 1958 he conceived the idea of writing an immense history of the labour camps, basing himself on his own experiences and the stories he had heard from others. He made a tentative start, before abandoning it again, on the vast enterprise that was to become *The Gulag Archipelago*. As he was later to write in the preface to volume 1, he no longer regarded his own eleven years on the archipelago "as something shameful or a nightmare to be cursed," but had come "almost to love that monstrous world." And in volume 3 he was to claim positive advantages for it. ("Life behind bars has given us a new measure for men and things. It has wiped from our eyes the gummy film of habit, which always clogs the vision of the man who has escaped shocks.")[12]

That same spring of 1958 Solzhenitsyn suffered a relapse and was obliged to enter the hospital for a course of chemotherapy. Natalia was desperately worried. Only a year ago, at her husband's urging, she had gone to the Lenin Library and read everything she could find about cancer, malignant tumours, melanoblastomas, and so on, and had come to the conclusion that Solzhenitsyn had only about four years to live. But the chemical treatment proved to be outstandingly successful, and Solzhenitsyn was discharged after only two weeks, although he continued to attend the hospital as an out-patient. He also continued to treat himself occasionally with infusions made from the mandrake root, of which he still had a supply, and with another folk-remedy made from a fungus that grows on birch trees.[13]

By the end of the treatment, Solzhenitsyn felt fitter than he had done for years and was filled with optimism. The tumour seemed to have subsided and was no longer causing him discomfort. That summer, after careful preparation, he and Natalia had their first proper holiday—six weeks in Leningrad, which Solzhenitsyn had never visited before. Characteristically, he had established a card index on the city's history and art beforehand (Natalia had done the same for its architecture), and the two of them spent much of their time wandering earnestly from monument to monument, index cards in hand, dutifully photographing and listing all the places seen, for all the world like Japanese (or Soviet) tourists.

They also went to concerts, the ballet, and the theatre. The play that impressed them most, according to Natalia, was a little-known piece by Alfred Jarry called *The Sixth Storey*, about which Solzhenitsyn later wrote to the Zubovs: "The subject is elementary. 'He' deceived 'her' and did not marry her. But here, precisely, one becomes convinced that the most important thing in art is not what is said but how it is said."[14] Later, in *A Day in the Life of Ivan Denisovich*, he was to suggest a different conclusion, when a prisoner terminates a discussion about the merits of Eisenstein's *Battleship Potemkin* with the exclamation "No! To hell with your *how* if it doesn't awaken good feelings in me!"[15] Later still, in his Nobel lecture, he was to try to find a middle way between these two extremes.

At some point in 1958 Solzhenitsyn decided to resurrect his old hobby of cycling. One motive, according to Natalia, was that he had put on weight after his chemotherapy treatment and was anxious to slim down again—an impulse that drove him to imitate Panin and start doing yoga exercises every morning. But there was more to it than that. After his long years of imprisonment and enclosure, he craved mobility; and although he was at last living in his beloved central Russia, he had seen very little of it. He needed to get out and take possession of it, physically, mentally, and spiritually. He could not afford anything more than a bicycle, but even this had its positive side, for it satisfied his romantic prejudice against the noise and smell of the internal-combustion engine,* while simultaneously reminding him of the carefree cycling tours of his youth. A bicycle brought him one step nearer that innocent past and pushed the intervening years a fraction further away.

Natalia bought a bicycle, too, and they went for excursions to the nearby Oka River and surrounding beauty spots. On one of these they visited the beautiful little village of Solotcha, nestling deep in primeval woods about thirty miles from Ryazan. Solzhenitsyn immediately fell in love with it, and it became a favourite haunt of his over the next few years. The following summer, fixing up his heavy bicycle with pannier bags and loading up with provisions, Solzhenitsyn made a longer tour alone through the lower Oka region, and the year after that he toured the upper Oka where the Moscow and Ryazan provinces meet.[16]

These were moving, bewildering, disconcerting, and infuriating journeys for the ardent pilgrim. On the purely functional level, there was the sheer difficulty of finding anything to eat or anywhere to stay for the night. There are no inns or hotels or restaurants in the small towns and villages of the Russian countryside, and no outsider is expected to travel there, particularly alone. Tourism is for groups in large cities. Solzhenitsyn could rarely find anywhere to stay and wherever he went was greeted with incredulity and suspicion. It seemed that only a thief, a spy, or a criminal on the run could be travelling at random, without an official itinerary. Good Soviet citizens could not conceive of a solitary traveller touring the countryside for pleasure, with no particular reason, and this led to all sorts of misunderstandings. There were profounder disappointments too. Visiting the ramshackle village where his adored Esenin had been born, he found only ugliness, poverty, neglect. The monastery in which the poet Polonsky was buried had been knocked to pieces and its site turned into a labour camp; the poet's abandoned grave was inaccessible inside the locked compound. In almost every village the churches had been pillaged and turned into stables, warehouses, or clubs, their bells silenced and their murals defaced. And yet Solzhenitsyn was also stirred by the sprawling undulations of the broad Russian plain, the slow meanderings of the river Oka, the smudges of wood and forest on the horizon, and the sheer defencelessness of these medieval-looking villages, each with its ruined church and bell-tower. Beneath the surface ugli-

---

* In his miniature story "Means of Transport," written not long after this, Solzhenitsyn made fun of the motor car.

ness and vulgarity of tasteless concrete boxes, loudspeakers on posts, and garishly painted windows, he could still perceive Russian history and Russian traditions shining through, and his ears were filled with the words of Russia's poets on the matchless beauty of the Russian countryside.

Much of what he saw and felt subsequently found its way into a series of miniature stories that he began to write at this time. It is not clear what led him to try this new form—prose miniatures ranging from about a hundred to three hundred words in length. They may have been suggested by Turgenev's poems in prose—the best-known example of works of this kind—or perhaps by the example of some of the Russian modernists at the beginning of the century, like Remizov or Zamyatin. Altogether he wrote about a dozen and a half in the course of the next four or five years, with titles like "Along the Oka," "Esenin's Birthplace," and "A Poet's Ashes." One of the earliest was probably "Breathing," cited earlier, and another was "The City on the Neva," recalling his visit to Leningrad.

In other respects 1958 seems to have been a quiet year for Solzhenitsyn. By the end of it he had completed a third, and for the time being final, draft of his *sharashka* novel, now called *The First Circle*, and put the manuscript to one side. He may even have tinkered with some of the material for what was to become *The Gulag Archipelago*. But he must then have turned his attention elsewhere, for when he first broke into print, it was not with any of his literary works but with an article in the local Ryazan newspaper, the *Priokskaya Pravda*, entitled "Post Office Curiosities," on the failings of the Soviet postal service, which appeared in March 1959.[17] This article, a kind of curiosity in itself, is actually rather revealing of Solzhenitsyn's psychology at the time, for it shows the way in which his barrack-room-lawyer syndrome, so noticeable in the prisons and camps, continued to operate in much the same way when he was back in civilian life.

In his later memoir, *The Oak and the Calf*, Solzhenitsyn maintained that his exasperation with the inefficiencies and bureaucratic mentality of Soviet officialdom had been held rigidly in check in Ryazan. "Though, at every step in my daily life, I collided with rude, conceited, stupid, and greedy bureaucrats of every degree and in every institution, and though I sometimes saw a chance to crash through a barrier and sweep away the rubbish with a well-aimed complaint or determined protest, I could never allow myself to do so, never take half a step out of line in the direction of rebellion, of resistance, but had always to be a model Soviet citizen, always to submit to every bully and acquiesce in any stupidity."[18] In fact, as the very tone of this passage suggests, he was not nearly as successful in suppressing his anger as he subsequently made out, and the *Priokskaya Pravda* article was a result. A year later he wrote a similar article complaining about the railway's practice of selling two tickets for the same seat, and sent it to the newspaper *Gudok* (The Train Whistle). The perfectionist temperament that was so profoundly and nobly affronted by the human waste and misery of the Gulag Archipelago was equally irritated and exasperated, it seems, by these infinitely more petty failings of the Soviet bureaucracy, but the difference was that, whereas the profounder rebellion had resulted in the writing of an excellent novel and was to produce several outstanding works of literature in the years to come, all that the lesser irritation could spawn was indignant missives to the newspapers in the spirit of "Disgusted of Tunbridge Wells." It is just as well that *Gudok* discouraged him by not printing his contribution.[19]

The interesting thing about these articles is that they show Solzhenitsyn grappling, however superficially, with themes from contemporary Soviet life as a change from his almost total immersion in the past. At about the time of his first newspaper article, in casting around for a subject to write upon, he hit upon the idea of describing his work at the school. Reshetovskaya writes, "I remember that one night my husband was seated in the corner we reserved for photography, feverishly making notes, in the weak light given out by the radio dial, for an outline of 'One Day in the Life of a School Teacher.' "[20] What became of this outline is not known, but neither the theme nor Solzhenitsyn's new-found interest in contemporary subject matter seems to have survived for long. Instead, on 18 May 1959, he transferred the idea to a story that he provisionally entitled *Shch-854*, about a labour-camp prisoner in Ekibastuz.

The story was based on an idea that had first come to him in 1952, when he was bricklaying in Ekibastuz.

> It was an ordinary camp day—hard, as usual, and I was working. I was helping to carry a hand-barrow full of mortar, and I thought that this was the way to describe the whole world of the camps. Of course, I could have described my whole ten years there, I could have done the whole history of the camps that way, but it was sufficient to gather everything into one day, all the different fragments . . . and to describe just one day in the life of an average and in no way remarkable prisoner from morning till night.[21]

For seven years this idea had lain dormant. Now it suddenly reappeared again and quickly came to occupy all Solzhenitsyn's waking thoughts. Somewhere at the back of his mind he recalled Tolstoy's dictum that a novel might take for its subject the life of all Europe for a century or the life of a muzhik for a single day. Tolstoy had tried both, and had been more successful with *War and Peace* than with *A History of Yesterday*, but Solzhenitsyn felt drawn to the narrower form. It followed naturally from his attempt to describe a day in the life of a schoolteacher, but was now centred on the subject that he felt most deeply about—the camps. At the same time, it unlocked the passions that had been thwarted by his failure to make progress with his history of the camps and opened up a new channel for them to flow into, while bringing several of his preoccupations together into a single focus: "It seemed to me that the most interesting and important thing to do was to depict the fate of Russia. Of all the drama that Russia has lived through, the deepest was the tragedy of the Ivan Denisoviches. I wanted to set the record straight concerning the false rumours about the camps."[22]

The story Solzhenitsyn wrote is deceptively simple in outline. Ivan Denisovich Shukhov is wakened on a frosty winter's morning by the sound of a hammer banging on a brass rail—the traditional camp signal for reveille. Although feeling feverish, he forces himself to leap from his bunk and start the day's ritual. As the heavily laden latrine tank is being carried out by some other prisoners, he is grabbed by a warder and sent to swab out the guardhouse. We then accompany him to breakfast in the steaming mess hall, watch him go through the monotonous and immutable procedures of the roll-call, body search, and march to the work site, and see how the prisoners reluctantly prepare to work in the sub-zero temperatures. The story then builds to a climax in which Shukhov and his fellow bricklayers become so carried away by their work that they disregard the final whistle and run the risk of being penalized for failing to stop in time and line up for the return march. Once back in the living compound, Shukhov performs a number of chores and does a personal favour for an imprisoned Moscow intellectual named Tsezar Markovich, by queuing for Markovich's parcel at the post office and saving Markovich the trouble. Markovich pays him for his favour and also lets Shukhov have his camp supper, since he will not need it that evening. Shukhov uses the money to buy some tobacco from another prisoner, performs some more little chores, chats with his barrack-room comrades, and falls asleep content. "The day was over, a day without a cloud, almost a happy day."

The story is narrated entirely through the eyes of Ivan Shukhov and from his point of view, yet in the third person, allowing the author to break into the narrative and offer his own comments and observations without interrupting the flow (rather according to Percy Lubbock's distillation of the Jamesian method). The language was colloquial, racy (to the point of obscenity in places, though Solzhenitsyn generally found euphemisms for his more colourful expressions), rich in folk idioms and allusions, yet also fresh and studded with neologisms invented by Solzhenitsyn on the solid foundation of his study of Dahl's lexical principles. Ivan Shukhov was depicted as a crafty and cunning but essentially moral picaresque hero in the Russian folk tradition (clearly a brother of Vasily Tyorkin), whose struggle for survival was sharpened by the hellish regime of the labour camps. This in itself was a considerable achievement, but Solzhenitsyn had surrounded his hero with such a rich cast of characters that he was able to endow the story with quite another dimension. There was Tsezar Markovich, a screen writer from Moscow representing the metropolitan intelligentsia; Commander Buinovsky, a naval captain from Leningrad, who had been jailed on the suspicion of espionage after having worked with the British as part of allied co-operation during the war; Tiurin, Shukhov's brigade leader, a doughty peasant who had been exiled to Siberia as a kulak during collectivization; Alyoshka, a Baptist, imprisoned for his faith; former prisoners of war; Latvian and Lithuanian nationalists, Ukrainian guerrillas, Central Asians—in short, a gallery of types representing every category of prisoner known to Solzhenitsyn. Each one occupied only a paragraph or a page or two, but the effect of their repeated appearances and combined stories was to create a panorama of Soviet life and Soviet history, a universalized portrait of suffering and oppression. Liberal hints indicated that, during these years, there had been very little to choose between life inside and life outside the camps, in other words, that the Soviet Union was one gigantic labour camp. And the character of those who survived it was perforce bitter, distrustful, long-suffering, and yet stoic and in the long run triumphant over those responsible for the oppression.

It is doubtful whether even Solzhenitsyn recognized the extent of his achievement. The story had seemed to come so easily and naturally; into it had flowed all his stored-up knowledge and experience, but set down in a kind of shorthand, concentrated and extraordinarily rich. Its elements had come from diverse corners of his past. The figure of Ivan Denisovich Shukhov, for instance, the "Shch-854"* of the title, as well as his name, had come from a soldier in Solzhenitsyn's battery. Shukhov had not been particularly close to Solzhenitsyn. It was simply that Solzhenitsyn later remembered him as a decent, honest, and likeable fellow and that somehow his face, character, and even his manner of speaking suddenly seemed to fit Solzhenitsyn's requirements. "Quite unexpectedly, without any choice on my part, . . . first the name . . . and then the face, then some of his past, where he was from and how he spoke, began to enter my tale."23

His actual biography had been quite different. He was never, so far as Solzhenitsyn knew, arrested or imprisoned, whereas the fictional Shukhov's biography was a composite of the biographies of other peasants whom Solzhenitsyn had met in the camps. And it was deliberately designed to be typical rather than idiosyncratic or sensational. There was an autobiographical element as well. "I could never have described him successfully if I hadn't myself been a simple bricklayer in the camps. One can't gain a proper understanding of the meaning of such work from mere hearsay. I describe a peasant, with a peasant's shrewdness and a convict's shrewdness, but, of course, one is bound to draw on one's own experience, just as one does when describing any character."24

For many of his leading characters, Solzhenitsyn drew on prisoners he had known in Ekibastuz. The naval commander Buinovsky was based on Captain Boris Burkovsky from Leningrad—except for one episode during the morning roll-call which was taken from an incident that had happened to Vladimir Gershuni. Tsezar Markovich, the script writer, was based on a Muscovite, Lev Grossman (who had once been a pupil of Valentin Turkin, though neither Solzhenitsyn nor Grossman had known of their connection at the time). The early life of Tiurin, Ivan Denisovich's brigade leader and the son of a family of kulaks, was based on stories told to Solzhenitsyn by someone he later referred to (in *The Gulag Archipelago*) as Nikolai K (other

* *Shch* is the twenty-sixth letter of the Russian alphabet. If each preceding letter stands for 999 prisoners in the camp, then Shukhov is the 25,829th prisoner, a vivid indication, to Soviet readers, of how big the camps were.

parts of Tiurin's character were apparently modelled on someone else). Alyoshka the Baptist and the canteen orderly, according to Captain Burkovsky in a later interview, were also based on recognizable prototypes.

Perhaps because of this adherence to real people and real events, the writing of *Shch-854* proceeded with unusual speed. By the time the school term finished, at the end of June, it was virtually complete, having taken a little less than six weeks in all. As in the case of *The First Circle*, all first drafts were burnt and the fair copy was carefully concealed.[25]

During the first part of the summer holidays, Solzhenitsyn and Natalia carried out a major reorganization of their living arrangements. The two gymnastics teachers who shared their communal flat on Kasimovsky Lane had decided to move out and go elsewhere. Solzhenitsyn suggested to Natalia that they bring her two aunts Nina and Manya from Rostov to live with them. Since Maria had moved to Ryazan to look after Natalia, they had managed alone, but Nina was now approaching eighty and Manya wasn't much younger. It was arranged for them to exchange their flat in Rostov for the extra room in Ryazan.

Solzhenitsyn was particularly grateful to Nina for all the years when she had sent him parcels, and he knew that Manya had helped as well. Their move had the additional advantage of filling the flat with one family, which made conditions much easier for the concealment of manuscripts and the burning of drafts in the kitchen stove. But it also had its drawbacks. For Nina and Manya, the move from Rostov, where they had spent their entire lives, was a painful wrench. Relations between them and Maria or between them and Natalia were not always of the smoothest. The two old ladies were not blood relatives and seem to have retained a decidedly aristocratic streak. They were reserved and somewhat haughty in their demeanour, with the curt manners of the upper class and no disposition for gossip or small talk. But they were also disastrously helpless in practical matters and therefore dependent on the practical Maria's goodwill (as well as on Natalia's salary) for their daily comforts, a dependency that they were sometimes reminded of when relations deteriorated.

For Solzhenitsyn there was the burden of living with four women, of whom three were elderly and had lived alone for most of their lives. He was used to the chattering of Maria, who loved to talk endlessly about her childhood and youth in the "good old days" and was an inveterate gossip, and he enjoyed the care and attention that these more or less unoccupied women lavished on him. But he found it difficult to endure the small talk, while the atmosphere of teacups and old lace that they created was somewhat at odds with the unvarnished manners he had acquired at the front and in the labour camps.[26]

While in Rostov to arrange the move, Solzhenitsyn and Natalia had taken the opportunity to visit a number of their old friends, including Nikolai Vitkevich, who had at last married and was completing his Ph.D. dissertation. But the two friends were further apart in their views than ever. Solzhenitsyn had been taking a keen interest in the Pasternak case. The preceding October the award of the Nobel Prize to Pasternak for *Doctor Zhivago* had created a furore in the Soviet Union, and the storm had continued well into 1959. But when Solzhenitsyn tried to discuss the subject with Nikolai, the latter was completely uninterested. He was more concerned about some sort of dispute in the chemistry department of Rostov University, where he was now working, and about the problems he was having in gaining promotion. Academic politics were more interesting to Nikolai than events in the outside world, whereas for Solzhenitsyn it was just the reverse.

From Rostov the Solzhenitsyns travelled west to the Crimea to visit Nikolai and Elena Zubov, who had been freed from exile the preceding year and had come down here to live. Their move had been complicated by the fact that one of their daughters was very ill and by their desire to visit Elena's sick and aging mother *en route*. The place where Nikolai had succeeded in finding work was not in the lush Mediterranean Crimea of Russian romantic fiction but a barren and cheerless area on the north shore. Solzhenitsyn, when he saw it, commented that it differed from Kok Terek only in that it was surrounded by sea instead of desert, but the Zubovs were their usual, equable selves and uttered no complaints.

Solzhenitsyn was delighted to see them, for the Zubovs were still his closest friends and confidants. As he had said in one of his early letters to them, "sitting down to write to you always puts me into a particularly good mood in which everything seems simple and I feel free to bare all my feelings to you. And no wonder. Only with you was I able to share three such difficult and lonely years."[27] On this occasion Solzhenitsyn brought them the completed version of *The First Circle*—they had been the earliest readers of the first drafts set down in Kok Terek, and now they would have an opportunity to compare. But he forbore to tell them about his newest work, *Shch-854*, perhaps in the interests of secrecy or perhaps because it was still not completely finished.

The two weeks that Solzhenitsyn and Natalia spent in the Crimea were unusually sedentary for them—no guidebooks, no itineraries, no timetables. In the mornings they would take a stroll to the beach and go swimming. In the afternoons it was siesta time, and in the evenings they would walk or swim once more. Even in the southern heat, however, Solzhenitsyn could not bear such inactivity for long and soon started work on a story he had been planning for some time, about the death of his Torfoprodukt landlady, Matryona Zakharova. Its provisional title was based on a Russian proverb, "Without a Righteous Person No Village Can Stand,"* but after struggling for some days with it, he seemed to run into a blind alley. According to Reshetovskaya, he felt that he had exhausted the image of Matryona and had nothing left to say about her, although his theme was still not fully devel-

_____

* "Righteous person" is an approximate translation of the Russian *pravednik*, a highly charged word meaning a virtuous person just short of a saint, but well above the average run in goodness and nobility of spirit.

oped. He therefore laid it aside unfinished.[28]

Back in Ryazan, the two of them settled down with the three old ladies in their now enlarged flat. They themselves moved into the room vacated by the gym instructors, which was twice the size of their previous one and allowed them to spread themselves a little, while the old ladies took the other two rooms. For the past year Solzhenitsyn had been teaching for only twelve hours a week, instead of his initial fifteen, and this year he asked to continue at that level, although it kept his salary very low. Throughout September and into the beginning of October, he worked at *Shch-854* once more and completed his revision of it on 11 October 1959. All in all the writing of it had taken just over three months.

Their life was now quiet in the extreme and ran more or less to a time-table set by Solzhenitsyn. In the mornings he would rise early and do his yoga exercises, after which he liked to chop and saw firewood, sometimes with Natalia. In her memoirs there is a picture of the two of them at work with a cross-cut on a hefty log of what looks like birch. To ease the task for Natalia, Solzhenitsyn introduced the idea of counting the strokes it took to cut through a single log, and devised other little games to relieve the monotony of the task.

For much of the day, Natalia was away teaching at the Agricultural Institute, and Solzhenitsyn usually had to spend a certain amount of his time at school. The headmaster had asked him to take on mathematics in addition to physics and astronomy, but Solzhenitsyn refused—the marking would take too much time. It seems that on one occasion he was even approached to take over as headmaster, but hastily declined that too. Nothing could have been further from his desires. When not at school, Solzhenitsyn read, wrote, or typed, and hated to be disturbed. He systematically discouraged visitors, with the grudging exception of his *sharashka* friends from Moscow.

Many years later, after their separation, Natalia was to accuse Solzhenitsyn of having deliberately cut her ties with her other Ryazan friends and estranged her from her colleagues at the institute. There was much truth in this. Solzhenitsyn was undoubtedly unsociable, was obsessed with his work, was utterly self-centred, and was unyielding in the demands he made on Natalia, insisting that she both assist him and observe all the conditions he set. After sixteen years of lonely, "bachelor" life at the front, in the camps, and in exile, he was also more set in his ways and more rigid in his attitudes than ever.

But there were other barriers to socializing in Ryazan that arose from Natalia's former marriage. Most of her circle of friends had been built up during her years with Vsevolod. He still lived in Ryazan, and mixing with these friends meant running the risk of meeting him too. Similarly with the scientific club and other places where her colleagues from the Agricultural Institute congregated—Vsevolod was always likely to be there. A further complication and embarrassment was that Vsevolod was now living with Natalia's and Solzhenitsyn's old childhood friend Lydia Ezherets. Lydia had never approved of Natalia's abandonment of Vsevolod and return to Solzhenitsyn, mainly because of the children, and had tried to talk Natalia out of it. After the separation Vsevolod had cried out his sorrows on Lydia's shoulder and within an amazingly short time had married her. She had kept her room in Moscow in order not to lose her registration there but was now dividing her time between Moscow and Ryazan.

Natalia largely acquiesced in her new life-style and relished the role of the writer's wife and helpmate more than she later admitted. On the domestic side she decided that it was time to turn herself into a proper housekeeper, and took lessons in cooking and sewing to help her achieve this aim. As a full-time professional woman, she had had little opportunity or taste for housework, and in any case had been looked after by her mother for all but the six years she had spent in Moscow. But now she acquired a sewing-machine (a cosy photograph of her at work on it appears in her memoirs), turned her hand to the arcane arts of pickling and bottling, produced kasha and curtains for the admiration of her husband and aunts, and tried her best to become a housewife in the traditional manner, though not always, it seems, with a high degree of success. She also typed, filed, and read things for Solzhenitsyn; and in the composition of *The First Circle* she was summoned to assist as source, collaborator, and critic. In all this, it is true, she was commanded by Solzhenitsyn, but she also seems to have found it novel and flattering and was willing to fall in with all of his schemes. In her memoirs she notes of this period that she and her husband "were living in a state of complete harmony."[29]

Solzhenitsyn was now settled for the first time in his life and was able to organize his literary affairs more systematically. In exile he had started files in which he collected information on music and literature. The literature files especially now began to bulge from the vast amount of data collected and had to be constantly rearranged and relabelled. Solzhenitsyn's method was to write out notes, in the best schoolmasterly fashion, on this or that writer and file them away in folders marked "Russian Literature," "Soviet Literature," and "Western Literature." To widen his range of knowledge, he bought an encyclopaedia of world literature, and at the same time started to build a systematic library, for which he bought, according to Natalia, books by Herzen, Dostoyevsky, Tolstoy, Hemingway, Graham Greene, Richard Aldington, and many classics from the eighteenth century. He also subscribed to Soviet collected editions of the works of Chekhov, Kuprin, Paustovsky, Prishvin, and—a childhood favourite—Anatole France, and joined three separate libraries in Ryazan.

Reading all these books was a different matter, especially since Solzhenitsyn was very strict about apportioning his time between writing and reading, and Reshetovskaya reports that he was a very slow reader. He tried, she says, to read only works that had a high reputation as models of literature, and developed a complicated and idiosyncratic system of rating them with a combination of dots, plus signs, and exclamation marks. Naturally his tastes fluctuated. He quickly went off Anatole France and Kuprin; on the other hand, he gave the very highest marks to the nineteenth-century Slavophile poet Fyodor Tiutchev, especially to his celebrated poem "Silentium,"[30] which reads as if the great poet had been able to see, across a century, into Solzhenitsyn's very soul, sending him an admonition and a warning.

A very different response was evoked by some of the Soviet authors he read. He was at first attracted by the limpid prose of Paustovsky but gradually grew disenchanted with Paustovsky's long and rambling autobiography as it appeared in its multiple episodes.* He felt that Paustovsky had become bogged down in the story of his life, "which threatens to occupy two out of the seven volumes of his collected works." Worse still, Paustovsky was deliberately avoiding the principal—and most painful—events in Soviet history, which meant that he had failed to find his true subject "in an epoch when one cannot help finding one's theme."[31]

A few months later he was similarly exercised by the first instalments of Ilya Ehrenburg's long series of memoirs, *People, Years, Life,*† which was being serialized in the liberal literary journal *Novy Mir* (New World). Solzhenitsyn felt that Ehrenburg was "arguing with the dead and trying to prove to the living that he was honest and clever," in Reshetovskaya's words. Later he somewhat modified his views and was much interested by Ehrenburg's reminiscences of the Civil War period. "There are profound thoughts there that I have never encountered elsewhere. Many of the portraits are also interesting."[32]

But it didn't alter Solzhenitsyn's general disapproval of writers who wrote their autobiographies. Reshetovskaya notes that he didn't disapprove of memoirs as such, only of memoirs by writers, feeling that they were "a product of narcissism on the part of the author" and an admission of failure, signifying the writer's "inability to elevate himself to an artistic generalization of what he has observed."[33] Spurred on by his mounting irritation, Solzhenitsyn sat down and wrote another indignant article, this time not about the post office or the railways but on a subject that was much dearer to his heart—literature (disregarding the fact that if it was published, the true nature of his interests would be revealed). Entitled "An Epidemic of Autobiographies," the article asked, "Why does a writer who is capable of *creating* need to write a simple autobiography? Those who prove worthy of it will be written about by their contemporaries or by 'literary scholars,' " and ended with a challenge: "Isn't it about time that at least magazine publishers put a stop to this epidemic of autobiographies?"[34]

Solzhenitsyn sent the article to the *Literaturnaya Gazeta* (Literary

---

*Paustovsky, a romantic novelist and story writer, was one of the Soviet Union's best-known and best-loved writers. His autobiographical cycle of five books, known collectively as *The Tale of Life*, appeared in instalments from 1946 to 1962.

† *People, Years, Life* was serialized in *Novy Mir* from 1961 to 1964 and was noteworthy for its reappraisal of the twenties and its frank treatment of proscribed writers like Babel, Mandelstam, and Tsvetaeva.

Gazette)* in November 1960 with a covering note: "I should prefer not to receive a courteous apology to the effect that 'unfortunately the editors don't have the space to publish this.' If I am right, I request that my article be published. If I am wrong, I request a rebuttal." The article was signed, "A. Solzhenitsyn. Teacher." Eleven days later the article was returned with a curt rejection and no rebuttal. Paustovsky, to whom Solzhenitsyn had boldly sent a copy of his article, did not reply at all, despite the fact that Solzhenitsyn had also praised the first part of Paustovsky's work for its form as "a chain of free-flowing novellas."[35]

It appears that Solzhenitsyn sent this article to a number of other publications in addition to the *Literaturnaya Gazeta*, but nobody was interested. As he later wrote in his own autobiography, *The Oak and the Calf*, it was probably because nobody had heard of him. In *The Oak* he further writes that although his article "looked like an attack on memoir literature generally, its real purpose was to express my exasperation with writers who had seen the great dark epoch and yet were forever trying to sidle round it, ignoring the things that mattered most, telling us nothing but trivialities, and sealing our eyes with emollients till we no longer saw the truth."[36] This was undoubtedly an important ingredient in his anger, but his distaste for literary memoirs remained very real, which is presumably whey he felt obliged to preface his own work in that genre with an apology. Solzhenitsyn was to argue later that his own memoir was "different," and certainly the circumstances of its publication were. In its goals, however, and in its "argument with time," it was not really so far removed from Ehrenburg's *apologia pro vita sua*. Age and a sense of past achievements were enough to produce a change of perspective.

---

* The *Literaturnaya Gazeta* is published three times a week and is an official organ of the Writers' Union.

22

ON THE
THRESHOLD

DESPITE ALL THESE preoccupations, Solzhenitsyn did not omit his daily "linguistic exercises" with Dahl's dictionary, which he had religiously kept up since the *sharashka*. He felt he needed this regular session in order to steep himself continually in the spirit of the Russian language and to refresh himself by repeated immersion. Years ago he had realized that the writer's task might be not just to rescue forgotten areas of Soviet experience and history from oblivion but also to liberate the Russian language from the dead weight of Soviet cant and clichés that were pulling it down. Judging the sickness of the language to be severe, he had determined on radical measures—namely, to revivify it by returning to its native and traditional roots in folklore and in folk speech. Vladimir Dahl's dictionary was the greatest repository of pure Russian language available to him. Influenced by the great German philologists of the nineteenth century, Dahl had gone to the common people to document and define the character of the Russian language. Moreover, he had responded to the genius of the Russian language by organizing his dictionary according to the roots of words, rather than the words themselves. This provided scope for illustrating and analyzing the enormous wealth of prefixes and suffixes with which Russian is endowed, constituting one of its greatest glories and offering a vast repertoire of nuances of meaning.

In the century or so since Dahl compiled his dictionary, Russian has followed the path of all Indo-European languages in becoming relatively more analytical and less synthetic, a development that Solzhenitsyn respected in his writing. But it has also suffered an unnecessary impoverishment of vocabulary and forms, partly under the weight of twentieth-century innovations in scientific and bureaucratic language, partly as a result of sheer neglect, and partly as a result of the purging of modern Russian literature of so many of its leading writers of talent. From his very first experiments in verse, Solzhenitsyn had sought to do two things: to cleanse his language of bureaucratic and industrial jargon and clichés (except where he used them for satirical purposes); and to refresh and enrich his lexicon either with old forms of words taken from Dahl or with new coinages formed according to the rules found in Dahl, but not actually pre-existing in the language. It is uncommonly difficult to illustrate this process in a language as determinedly analytical and uninflected as English, but at its lowest and most feeble it might be likened to forming the non-existent "ept" from "inept," or reintroducing an archaic word like "ruth" by analogy with "ruthless," and so on. English barely tolerates such tricks and brands them as barbarisms, but Russian is more flexible and more hospitable. Even so, Solzhenitsyn did not escape similar charges of barbarism and bathos when he was published, and his reforms were always to be controversial. Curiously enough, one of the few living Russian writers he later came to admire for his style was Vladimir Nabokov, whose linguistic virtuosity deeply impressed him. But Nabokov was altogether too Westernized in his vocabulary and syntax to serve as a model, and the two men were poles apart in their aesthetic sensibilities.

Solzhenitsyn's innovations and coinages were a highly conscious and calculated affair. Natalia noticed that in going over his writings he would make a note of all the neologisms and new expressions and mark them in the margins, taking care not to exceed a certain quota per page.[1] He realized that if he overloaded the text, his innovations would stand less chance of being accepted. He was also painstaking in his choice of names for his characters. His favourite name of "Nerzhin," for instance, had been inspired by the Belorussian village of Sverzhen, which he had come across at the front. For some reason the name of the village stuck in his mind, and he tried to adapt it. His first attempt was "Sverzhenin," but that was unsuitable because it seemed to share the same root as the Russian verb *svergat'*, "to overthrow." He then tried "Kerzhin" and only later came to his final form of "Nerzhin."[2]*

On other occasions he picked the names that appealed to him from ready-made lists. For instance, the evocative name of Shkuropatenko given to one of the prisoners in *Shch-854* belonged to one of Natalia's students at the Agricultural Institute (there is no law of libel in the Soviet Union), and the names of Gangart (in *Cancer Ward*) and Varsonofiev and Obodovsky (in *August 1914*) came from a list of pupils who had attended the Ryazan Secondary School for Boys in 1904 and whose names appeared in a book published to mark the school's centennial.[3]

In addition to Dahl's dictionary Solzhenitsyn formed a deep attachment to the same author's dictionary of Russian proverbs, a copy of which Aunt Irina had once given him in boyhood but which he had long since lost. This,

---

*Nerzhin also has overtones of the Russian *nezhny*, meaning "tender."

too, gave rise to extensive annotating, copying, and reclassifying, a task in which Natalia helped him by typing out the proverbs he had marked and filing them. His dream, she writes, was to have a big vase filled with cards on which all the best proverbs were written, so that he could pick out a card at random.[4]

In the autumn of 1960 Solzhenitsyn returned to his story about Matryona Zakharova and successfully completed it. It is not known what had prevented him from finishing it earlier, but it may have had something to do with the deeper level of meaning that Solzhenitsyn wished to achieve. The story of the old woman's penurious life and needless death in a train accident was affecting in itself, but Solzhenitsyn seems to have felt that it contained a greater significance than that, and in his final draft he was able to find a satisfactory way to dramatize and universalize Matryona's fate. At the heart of the story, in its final form, was the message that Matryona, despite her slovenly ways and low intelligence, was a genuinely good and moral person but that there was no room for her in the grasping, materialistic culture of contemporary Soviet society. Being old, infirm, and ill educated, she was at a fatal disadvantage in dealing with ambitious relatives and unfeeling local officials and was the victim of repeated injustices. When she fell ill, she was dismissed from the collective farm (the only employer in the village apart from the peat-works); since she was semi-literate, she was unable to deal with the forms thrust at her by the bureaucrats and hence received no pension; without a job, she got no allowance of peat for cooking and heating. Yet she was still expected to work for nothing at harvest time, to help friends and relations dig their cabbage patches. Her good nature was taken for granted, and her willingness to work hard exploited. The culmination was her brother-in-law's demand that she break up her house and allow him to cart away her annex for his daughter, and her death in helping him carry out this removal, which was entirely against her own interests, was her final sacrifice. "We all lived beside her," concludes the first-person narrator, "and never understood that she was that one righteous person without whom, according to the proverb, no village can stand. Nor any city. Nor our whole land."[5]

It was a story very much in the idiom of the late Tolstoy, and by implication deeply subversive. The peasants were depicted as living in poverty and squalor, totally at the mercy of despotic officials from the village soviet, the collective farm, and the peat-works, and just as alienated from them as any pre-revolutionary peasant from his landowning masters ("Just as they had formerly stolen wood from the landowners, so they now hauled off peat from the Trust").[6] By a variety of hints Solzhenitsyn even managed to suggest that they had been better off before the Revolution: at least they hadn't had to harness themselves to the plough, as Matryona and the other women did regularly every year. The whole story was also bathed in a kind of Christian light. Although there was nothing overtly religious in it and although Matryona was not represented as a believer (apart from attending church on feast-days), she and the other characters were all described and judged in terms of Christian morality, while the proverb that gave the story its name, and with which it ended, not only was traditionally Russian in character but also expressed a Christian world view. Finally there was the sweep of that last sentence. The people's travail, Solzhenitsyn seemed to be saying, was not limited to this one village he had happened to observe; it had spread through the entire land.

Having completed the story to his satisfaction, Solzhenitsyn put it aside and found himself thinking about his experiences in the hospital at Tashkent. Apparently, he was not yet ready to contemplate a major prose work on the subject, but he turned his attention to a particular incident that had shocked him at the time and remained graven in his memory. One day during his convalescence, while strolling in the hospital grounds, he had encountered a feeble old man struggling to make his way through the main gate. The man's obvious sickness and grossly distended belly made it difficult for him to walk, and he asked Solzhenitsyn to assist him as far as the admissions office to see the receptionist. Once there, the old man grew arrogant, demanding special treatment on the basis of his earlier services to the Revolution. It turned out from his documents that during the Civil War he had served in a Cheka "special detachment," where he had been responsible for hacking hundreds of people to death with a cavalry sabre. Looking at the old man's now sclerotic and enfeebled fingers, Solzhenitsyn had tried to imagine them as instruments of death and had felt repelled by the very thought of having helped him.

The figure of the revolutionary executioner was at the opposite pole to Matryona, but perhaps for that very reason spoke to Solzhenitsyn's creative impulse almost as strongly as the old woman. Employing a first-person narrative very much in the style of "No Village Can Stand," he swiftly retold the incident in the form of a short story. In a way it was a neat reversal of the Matryona theme. The narrator's Samaritan-like compassion for the old man turns out to have been lavished on a moral monster, and the reader's response is one of indignation and outrage rather than of sympathy for the oppressed. Solzhenitsyn's muse, it seemed, had two faces. *Shch-854* and "No Village Can Stand" glorified the more or less passive, martyred figures of Ivan Denisovich and Matryona, summoning compassion and humility from his readers, while "The Right Hand" smote the wicked Comrade Bobrov and appealed to the reader's sense of outrage and scorn. They were two sides of a single sensibility, often in uneasy juxtaposition with one another and wrestling for supremacy. Only with the passage of many years did the vengeful, Old Testament side of Solzhenitsyn gain ascendancy over his Christian humility.

"The Right Hand," like the Matryona story, was consigned to Solzhenitsyn's desk drawer, and he then took up a completely different kind of project—a play about contemporary life, set not in the Soviet Union but in a mythical country intended to represent a kind of composite of both East and West. "The action takes place in an unknown country at an unknown period, and the characters have international names," he later told an interviewer. "I did this not because I wanted to conceal my ideas but because I wanted to treat the moral problems of society in the developed countries, regardless of whether they were capitalist or socialist."[7] It is possible that Solzhenitsyn was also chafing over his inability to write anything that looked remotely publishable under Soviet conditions, and that by choosing a neutral terrain and a more abstract theme, he thought he might somehow produce something that would make its way into print.

The subject of the play was the return of two scientists, Alex Coriel and Philip Radagise, to a southern seaside town after a long term in labour camps on a false charge of murder, their subsequent careers, and the ensuing conflict between them. When the play opens, Philip has already been home for five years and has become head of a bio-cybernetics laboratory at the local university, whereas Alex has only just arrived after spending five years in the wilderness to gather his thoughts and readjust to freedom. They meet at the home of Alex's uncle, Maurice Craig, an elderly professor of music, a gourmet and bon vivant, who is living with his young third wife, Tillie, a journalist. Alex learns that Maurice is estranged from his daughter from his first marriage, Alda, although she lives in the same city; and in the course of his conversation with his old friend Philip, we learn of a critical difference between them: whereas Alex has come to terms with his past, is prepared to talk freely about it and even "bless" it for what it has taught him, Philip is ashamed of it, has completely banished it from his mind, and refuses to discuss it. Nevertheless, he is still perfectly friendly and invites Alex to join his laboratory, which Alex agrees to do.

In the next scene (the play is divided into scenes and has no acts), Alex has a tender reunion with his cousin Alda but is disturbed to discover how neurotic she is. He persuades her to undergo treatment at the bio-cybernetics laboratory, where techniques have been evolved to stabilize erratic personalities and cure neuroses. She agrees, and later in the play we discover that the treatment has been a success. Meanwhile, Philip is engaged in an interdepartmental battle for more funds and has decided to seek military support for his laboratory. At a party he throws to celebrate the success of his manoeuvre, he triumphantly parades the cured Alda before an admiring general and announces the establishment of a separate institute of bio-cybernetics with himself as its head. But Alex has become disillusioned with the work of the laboratory. Alda's cure has estranged her from him, and the collaboration with the military is the last straw: he announces at the party his intention to join Philip's arch-rival, Terbolm, who runs a laboratory devoted to social, not biological, cybernetics.

At the climax of the party, Tillie arrives to announce that her husband, Maurice, is dying and has expressed a last wish to see Alda. Alda bursts into tears, and it is clear that this sudden grief has undone her cure. Philip and his colleagues return to the room and accuse Alex of having deliberately let her go to Maurice out of spite. The penultimate scene shows the death of

Maurice, while an eccentric distant relative, Aunt Christina, reads the Bible over him. Alda is terribly distraught but afterwards announces her intention of returning to Philip's laboratory for more treatment, while Alex goes off to join Terbolm.

Solzhenitsyn entitled the play *The Light Which Is in Thee*, but had only a very limited success in making it relevant to both East and West. Its subject matter, the use of "biofeedback" techniques to modify the human personality, was certainly topical both in the Soviet Union and in America. Biofeedback machines were already in existence to control certain bodily malfunctions such as irregular heartbeat and hypertension, and new developments were making it possible to use them, instead of drugs, as relaxants and tranquillizers. The idea that a young woman like Alda could undergo "neurostabilization" was therefore not entirely far-fetched, and Solzhenitsyn had obviously done some homework.

But the setting of the play, the main characters, the conflicts, and even the ethical dilemma at the centre of the play inevitably reflected Solzhenitsyn's experiences and had an indubitably Soviet stamp to them. Alex was a transparent stand-in for Solzhenitsyn himself, and Philip for Nikolai Vitkevich. Maurice Craig and his young wife were modelled on Valentin Turkin and his third wife; Alda was based on Turkin's daughter, Veronica; and Aunt Christina owed her character, including a love of cats, to Solzhenitsyn's aunt Irina. The southern seaport was, of course, Rostov.

In his treatment, too, Solzhenitsyn was unable to get away from his usual preoccupations. The labour-camp theme spoke for itself (where else but in the Soviet Union would two scientists be returning to civilian life after twelve years in the labour camps?) Equally characteristic was his portrait of a fire-eating general from a "three-letter institution" (the DTF in the play—Department of Thoughts and Feelings), who had his own reasons for being interested in neurostabilization.* The scene showing Aunt Christina reading from the Gospel of St Luke over the dying Maurice was more overtly religious than anything Solzhenitsyn had done in this line before, but in other respects it followed recent developments in his thought fairly faithfully. He also underlined the significance of this scene by drawing on St Luke for his title: "Take heed, therefore, that the light which is in thee be not darkness."†

The play was quite different from those he had written before in that it was a play of ideas. Philip, Maurice, Tillie, and a number of characters associated with them represent the forces of hedonism (it is not without significance that Philip and Tillie are sexually promiscuous as well), whereas Alex and Terbolm are aware of a deeper set of values, and Alda is the "candle in the wind," buffeted by blasts from both sides. It showed Solzhenitsyn tack-

---

* Solzhenitsyn's theme turned out to be uncannily prophetic in view of the KGB's soon-to-be-initiated policy of incarcerating dissidents in mental hospitals.

† The quotation is from Luke 11:35. The play circulated under the title of *Candle in the Wind*, but in his Collected Works, Solzhenitsyn has restored the original, biblical title.

ling C. P. Snow's theme of the "two cultures"—something he was eminently equipped to do as a teacher of science and a practising writer—and indicated an extension of his range, but the characters were too bloodless, and the conflicts too obvious, for it to be very interesting as drama.

Solzhenitsyn later acknowledged his failure in *The Oak and the Calf*.

> I realized for the first time how a piece of work may stubbornly refuse to come right, even after four or five rewritings: you can throw out whole scenes and replace them with others—and it still looks hopelessly artificial. I spent a good deal of labour on it and thought I had finished—but no, it was still no good. I had based it on the true story of a particular Moscow family; I did not cheat once; I expressed only ideas I sincerely held, many of which I had long since cherished, refusing from the very first act to humour the censors—why, then, was it such a failure? Could it possibly be because I had avoided a specifically Russian setting . . . and that off Russian ground I am doomed to lose my feel for the Russian language?[8]

Nonetheless, Solzhenitsyn was pleased with his play to begin with, and owing to a rather curious incident, Veronica became its first reader. She and her second husband, Yuri Stein, had recently moved to a slightly larger flat in Chapayevsky Lane, where they also kept a room free for Solzhenitsyn, and one day Natalia rang to say that she and Solzhenitsyn would shortly be coming to Moscow and might want to spend the night there. On the evening in question, Veronica waited up for them. When they failed to arrive, she went to bed, where she had a painful dream about herself and her dead father. Later that night she woke in great distress and could not go back to sleep for a very long time. The following day Natalia rang to apologize: they had been in Moscow but had spent the night elsewhere. Noticing some sadness in Veronica's voice, Natalia asked what the matter was, and when Veronica explained about the dream, she covered the receiver and asked her to hang on for a minute. A few moments later, Solzhenitsyn came onto the phone and began to question Veronica closely about her dream and the time when she had dreamed it. Veronica asked Solzhenitsyn whether, on top of becoming a fatalist since he left the camps, he had started believing in dreams as well. Solzhenitsyn told Veronica that Natalia would explain everything the next time she was in Moscow.

After a short interval, Natalia came to Moscow and handed Veronica a brown paper parcel. In it, she said, was Solzhenitsyn's new play, two of whose leading characters were based on Veronica and her father. On the night they had been planning to come to her, just when she had dreamt her dream, they had been visiting friends in another part of Moscow. All had stayed up very late to hear Solzhenitsyn read some extracts from the play, and according to their calculations he had been reading the scene between Alda and her father at the very moment when Veronica had been having her dream. Since this was such a striking coincidence, Solzhenitsyn wanted Veronica to be the first to read the play.[9]

Oddly enough, another model for one of the characters in the play arrived in Ryazan shortly after it was finished—Aunt Irina, who paid the Solzhenitsyns a visit in January 1961. Solzhenitsyn was extremely anxious to please this favourite aunt of his childhood and went to unusual trouble, for him, to entertain her and make her feel at home. He and Natalia showed her Ryazan and took her for trips in the surrounding countryside. They even proposed that she leave her adobe hovel in Georgievsk and move closer to them. In the village of Davydovo, next door to their favourite excursion spot of Solotcha, there was a house with a garden for sale, which they were prepared to buy for her. Irina could live there, and they would visit her regularly, using the house simultaneously as a country cottage where they could rest and relax.

Irina appears to have seriously considered the idea. She liked the surroundings, and she had struck up friendly relations with Natalia's mother and aunts. But after years of solitude and a lifetime spent in the Caucasus, she was set in her ways. Above all, there was the problem of her many cats. How could she possibly get them to Ryazan, since no one in the family possessed a car and there was no question of taking them by train? Nor was there any question of leaving them behind. They were her whole life now, the object of all her thoughts and feelings, and she had developed highly idiosyncratic views about their immortal souls. She later wrote to Maria, "[Cats] are indeed the true followers of Christ. People, on the other hand, are far removed from the teachings of Christ." In the end she decided not to make the move. She was too old, she said, and "it's better not to budge the elderly from their well-worn grooves."[10]

Apart from Aunt Irina, visitors to the Solzhenitsyns were now few and far between. Natalia's aunt Zhenya came from Kislovodsk once or twice. Alexandra Popova came down from Moscow, Nikolai Potapov called on his way to a new job on the river Kama, and Panin and Kopelev appeared infrequently. One day Solzhenitsyn was astonished to receive a visit from Leonid Vlasov, the former naval lieutenant he had met on the train to Rostov in 1944, whom he had narrowly escaped involving in his downfall by describing Vlasov's views in a letter to Vitkevich. The diminutive Vlasov turned out to be the same chirpy sparrow who had captivated Solzhenitsyn during their train ride together, and the two of them got on famously. Vlasov announced that he was living in Riga but that he was obliged to visit Moscow from time to time and would call again, and before he left he invited Solzhenitsyn to visit him in Latvia.

In Ryazan, Solzhenitsyn continued to isolate himself from the mainstream of the city's life and to preserve his jealously guarded privacy. But he did make one pair of new friends, an elderly couple who in some sense came to occupy the place that the Zubovs had held for him in Kok Terek—although he continued to correspond with the Zubovs as before. The new couple, Veniamin and Suzanna Teush, were both Jews, both mathematicians, and both worked at Natalia's Agricultural Institute, where she first got to know them. Veniamin was extremely tall (well over six foot six, according to one account) and thin, with gentle, delicate features and an inner peace that was reflected in an expression of complete repose. Suzanna, his wife, was his physical and psychological opposite—not much over five feet, vivacious, smiling, emotional, and extremely sociable.

Like the Zubovs, the Teushes had also suffered at the hands of the authorities, though not to the same degree. Veniamin was a mathematician of great brilliance who had won a Stalin Prize for his mathematical research in the aircraft industry. At the beginning of the fifties, during Stalin's drive against "rootless cosmopolitans," he had been dismissed and had found it impossible to find further work in Moscow. After a long search, he had found this post in the Ryazan Agricultural Institute, and was now chairman of its mathematics department.

Despite this fall from high position and the difficulties they had experienced, neither Veniamin nor Suzanna seemed in the least bitter about it. On the contrary, they were like the Zubovs in that they seemed outstandingly equable and contented. And yet they had forgotten nothing, and it was this unusual combination of political clear-sightedness, personal composure, and reasonableness in their dealings with others that must have reminded Solzhenitsyn yet again of his old friends in Kok Terek. Both the Teushes were cultivated intellectuals in the old, pre-revolutionary tradition. Veniamin adored music and at some point had written a book about it. He was also interested in art, architecture, history, and religion, had written books on Chekhov and the history of the Jewish people, but was now devoting most of his attention to his childhood passion of anthroposophy, Rudolf Steiner's mystical religion based on the ideas of Goethe. Suzanna Teush was less interested in abstract ideas than her husband, and it is not clear whether she shared his interest in anthroposophy, but she was a woman of impeccable taste with a strong leaning towards the visual arts and a natural sense of style.[11]

The thing that seems to have impressed everybody who knew the Teushes was their absolute lack of pettiness and vulgarity. There seems not to have been a shred of vanity or falsity in their make-up. Veniamin, in particular, was frank and honest to a fault, a man of transparent integrity who could be utterly trusted. What they possessed, in short, was that elusive quality called breeding.

In the smug provincial atmosphere of Ryazan, the Teushes shone like a beacon of culture and learning, and it was not long before they and the Solzhenitsyns had become good friends. An interest in literature seems to have been the chief bond, and at some point Veniamin became Solzhenitsyn's chief reader and literary confidant—again filling the role formerly occupied by Nikolai Zubov (and carrying out a function of great importance to Solzhenitsyn). Teush read most of the works that Solzhenitsyn had written in exile and was very impressed with them, praising their originality of thought and language. But the work that he picked out as truly extraordinary was *Shch-854*. It is not clear whether the version he read was the original, longer one or a revised version that Solzhenitsyn prepared in the summer of 1961.

Perhaps it was he who advised Solzhenitsyn to remove a long polemical conversation between Burkovich and Tsezar Markovich (in which the former
explained the way the Americans had been deceived about the Soviet standard of living at Sebastopol) and who persuaded him to tone down some of
the language. At all events, Teush is said to have wept over the tale the first
time he read it. It was, he said, a work of Tolstoyan power and achievement,
with immensely far-reaching social and political implications. Soviet life and
literature, he said, could never be the same again if this book was published;
according to one source, he also told Solzhenitsyn, "There are three atom
bombs in the world: Kennedy has one, Khrushchev has another, and you
have the third."[12]

Such extravagant praise was obviously music to Solzhenitsyn's ears, but
what was he to do about it? For the time being he was concentrating on a
new revision of *The First Circle*, but at the back of his mind he was turning
over the possibility of at last revealing himself and submitting his work to a
wider audience. There were advantages and disadvantages in this. As he later
wrote in *The Oak and the Calf*, the great advantage of the underground writer
was to be able to write in complete freedom. "He needs to keep neither
censors nor editors in his mind's eye; nothing confronts him except his material."[13] And Solzhenitsyn had exploited this advantage to the full. But the
accompanying disadvantage was that he was deprived of rigorous criticism
and had no way of discovering his strengths and weaknesses or of estimating
his position in relation to the larger world of literature. Teush's praise was
all very well and had set him thinking, but he thirsted for an objective,
professional assessment of what he had written. He felt "clogged and super-
saturated" and "was beginning to suffer from lack of air in the literary underground." He also thirsted for recognition. Despite his modest facade, he had
lost none of his old ambition, none of his self-confidence and drive. If he
talked about "no hope of publication in his lifetime," he was not being insincere, but there was a strong element of insurance in such pronouncements,
an anticipation of the worst for fear that the best might never come to pass.

In many of his later statements, Solzhenitsyn has implied that all this
time he was aloof from the mainstream of Soviet literary life, took little interest in it, and regarded it as somehow trivial and irrelevant, but this is essentially a pose. As we have seen, he had tried to break into print with articles
criticizing the bureaucracy. He had submitted his article on literary memoirs
to the *Literaturnaya Gazeta*, regardless of the fact that publication would reveal
to its readers in Ryazan that he really did have literary interests. And in
truth, his thrusting, restless, activist nature was always at war with the secretive, reclusive, conspiratorial habits of the hyper-suspicious labour-camp veteran.

For many years this active and opinionated critic had, of course, followed developments in the Soviet literary world with more than ordinary
interest. Ever since reading Pomerantsev's article "On Sincerity in Literature," in the December 1953 issue of *Novy Mir*, he had kept up with that

magazine and had read in it unorthodox stories by Tendryakov and Ovech-kin and controversial articles by Abramov, Lifshitz, and Shcheglov. He also knew that Alexander Tvardovsky, whose *Tyorkin* he had so admired at the front, had been dismissed from the editorship of *Novy Mir* for daring to pub-lish them. Nor could he have missed the other contradictory signs of the Soviet Union's zigzag path towards liberalization—the dropping of the sec-ond clause from the accepted doctrine of socialist realism at the Second Con-gress of Soviet Writers in 1954;* the posthumous rehabilitation of famous but officially discredited and censored writers like Babel, Bulgakov, Koltsov, and Ivan Katayev; the rehabilitation of Olesha and Zabolotsky; the reappear-ance in print of Pasternak, Akhmatova, and Zoshchenko; and then the speeches on literature at the Twentieth Party Congress in 1956, when Sholokhov had attacked the Writers' Union in no uncertain terms and denounced its general secretary, Alexander Fadeyev ("Why has nobody told him . . . that the Writ-ers' Union is not a military unit and certainly not a penal colony and that no writer wants to stand to attention in front of Fadeyev").[14] Shortly afterwards Fadeyev had committed suicide.

All this had happened before Solzhenitsyn returned from exile (it has since been dubbed the period of "the thaw," after Ehrenburg's 1954 novel of the same name), and it would be surprising if Solzhenitsyn had not shared at least some of Kopelev's optimism. But then had come a period of confusion, encouraging Solzhenitsyn's pessimistic belief that little fundamental had changed. Khrushchev's "secret speech" had indeed spelled the end of easy certainties and ready-made solutions, but it had also opened up a yawning chasm of doubt into which nobody wished to fall. Was everything to be allowed now, or was this only a tactical retreat from the old Party line? The rehabilitations of writers from the twenties and even some *émigrés* such as Ivan Bunin seemed to open up the possibility of direct communication with the pre-Stalinist past, but did this also sanction emulation and imply toler-ance for opposing points of view? Would writers now be able to imitate the daring formal experiments of their predecessors instead of being strapped to the procrustean bed of socialist realism? The questions were endless, the answers few, and neither rulers nor ruled seemed to know exactly where they were going.

Signs of liberalism had come with the two volumes of a new miscellany called *Literary Moscow* (containing works by Pasternak, Akhmatova, and Tsvetayeva) and the serialization—again in *Novy Mir*—of a new novel by Vladimir Dudintsev under the provocative biblical title *Not by Bread Alone*. The novel was not of a very high literary quality, but what distinguished it

---

* The official definition of "socialist realism" had been set out in 1932 when the Union of Writers was founded and all Soviet writers were obliged to join. It read as follows: "Socialist realism, being the basic method of Soviet literature and literary criticism, requires from the artist a truthful, historically concrete representation of reality in its revolutionary development. More-over, truth and historical completeness of artistic representation must be combined with the task of ideological transformation and education of the working man in the spirit of Socialism."

from the usual stuff was its attack not just on insignificant incidental details but also on certain negative features fundamental to the Soviet system, such as the ruthlessness of the Party hierarchy, the untrammelled power of the bureaucracy, and the nakedness of their struggle for power. Moreover, the novel had suggested that these features were just as prominent under Khrushchev's rule as they had been under Stalin's—that nothing in the system had really changed.

There were also pointers in the other direction. Khrushchev, in a speech made in 1957 under the title "For a Close Link between Literature and Art and the Life of the People," had expressed views seemingly identical with the Stalinist line of the past: "Literature and art are an integral part of the nation-wide struggle for communism. . . . The highest social function of literature and art is to stimulate the people to struggle for ever new successes in the building of communism."[15] At the same time there rose to prominence a crude Stalinist die-hard writer called Vsevolod Kochetov, whose new novel, an "antirevisionist" tract entitled *The Brothers Ershov*, specialized in scurrilous lampoons and vicious caricatures of the liberals. It was published while Kochetov was still editor of the influential *Literaturnaya Gazeta* (although he was to lose his editorship in 1959), which gave it the weight almost of an official pronouncement. And finally there had been the disgraceful affair of *Doctor Zhivago* and the witch-hunt against Pasternak.

Here, if anywhere, was a cautionary tale for a writer like Solzhenitsyn. Pasternak had begun to work seriously on his novel not long after the end of the Second World War. He broke off in 1950, began again in 1953, after Stalin's death, published some poems from it in the magazine *Znamya* in 1954, and completed it sometime in 1955. It was clear from the note preceding the poems that Pasternak hoped for publication of the entire novel, and in 1956, in the liberal atmosphere ushered in by Khrushchev's "secret speech," he had entrusted a copy to the Italian Communist publisher Feltrinelli. By the end of that year, however, it became clear that publication would be no simple matter. Even *Novy Mir* had rejected it, explaining in a long and detailed letter of criticism (which was published two years later) that "the spirit of your novel is that of non-acceptance of the socialist revolution."[16]

Pasternak had not written an "anti-Soviet" novel, nor had he rejected the Revolution as such. His crime was much worse—he had virtually ignored it, bypassing politics altogether. His aim, he said in reply to the letter, had been "to bear witness as an artist, not as a politician. A work of art cannot be all on one plane; it has to speak on different levels"[17]—and this in a country where politics presumed to dictate everything in life, down to the very movements of a man's soul. The other sticking point was Pasternak's treatment of the intelligentsia. As his *Novy Mir* critics noted, the dying of Doctor Zhivago at the end of the twenties symbolized the virtual end of the Russian intelligentsia: "In your opinion, those members of the Russian intelligentsia whose road parted with that of Doctor Zhivago and who began to serve the people went astray from their true goal, spiritually destroyed themselves, and created nothing worthwhile."[18] To understand the flavour of this argument and the cause of Pasternak's disagreement with his critics, it is sufficient to take out the words "to serve the people" and substitute "to serve Stalin," for 1929 was the first year of the Five-Year Plan, of the collectivization of agriculture, of forced industrialization, of the terrorization of independently thinking writers, and of Stalin's undisputed ascendancy over the country.

It was probably naïve of Pasternak ever to expect his novel to be published, but he can be forgiven for thinking that after Khrushchev's "secret speech" and diatribe against Stalin, there was at least a chance. But he had not understood the reservations and limitations with which Khrushchev had hedged his denunciation. Khrushchev and his colleagues had climbed to power, with Stalin's assistance, over the backs of men like Trotsky, Bukharin, Rykov, and Kamenev. They were "Stalin's heirs" in a very real sense of the word, and they had no intention of letting his marvellous totalitarian machine run down to the point where they themselves would be threatened. The mild and pacific Pasternak, with the clear vision of an artist, was too ruthless for the blustering bullies in the Kremlin, and unfortunately premature.

Pasternak had agreed under pressure to rewrite some of his book, though not to betray its artistic message, and also to request Feltrinelli to return his copy. But it was too late. Translations were in progress in a variety of countries, and in 1957 the novel appeared, to world-wide acclaim. The following year, in October 1958, Pasternak was awarded the Nobel Prize for literature, and a veritable whirlwind raged about his head. At first he accepted it, then, under intense pressure, rejected it. The *Literaturnaya Gazeta* labelled him a "Judas," a "rabid individualist," a "malicious literary snob": "He has put a weapon in the hands of the enemy by giving the bourgeois publishing houses his book, which is saturated with the spirit of anti-Sovietism." *Pravda* called him an "internal *émigré*" and his book a "literary weed."[19] The hastily convened board of the Writers' Union took the extraordinary step of expelling him—the first such major expulsion since that of Anna Akhmatova and Mikhail Zoshchenko in 1946 (and rivalling, in its seriousness, the expulsion of Boris Pilnyak and Evgeny Zamyatin from the All-Russian Writers' Association in 1929).* And on the day that Pasternak declined the prize, V. E. Semichastny made a public speech of unparalleled violence and vulgarity, raising a theme that was to be taken up by the entire Soviet press in the days

---

* Akhmatova and Zoshchenko had been expelled after a Central Committee resolution was passed censuring the magazines *Leningrad* and *Zvezda* for their editorial policies in general and for publishing "ideologically harmful" works by Akhmatova and Zoshchenko in particular. The campaign against them was led by Andrei Zhdanov, head of the Communist Party in Leningrad and a scourge of writers. Zamyatin and Pilnyak had been expelled for publishing their nonconformist works abroad. Zamyatin's *We* had appeared in Prague, and Pilnyak's *Mahogany* in Berlin (a simultaneous Soviet edition of *Mahogany* had been banned at the last moment, thus making it appear that the Berlin publication was an intentional evasion of the censorship). During the controversy over *Doctor Zhivago*, Alexei Surkov, the secretary general of the Writers' Union, had made the links explicit: "Thus, for the second time in our history after *Mahogany* by Boris Pilnyak, a book by a Russian will be first published abroad."

to come—the idea that Pasternak should leave the Soviet Union and emigrate to the West.* Pasternak was horrified by this threat and eventually wrote a personal letter to Khrushchev begging to be allowed to remain.

Solzhenitsyn had followed the progress of the Pasternak affair with fascinated revulsion, but it is difficult to know whether he drew any direct comparisons or conclusions from it. Pasternak was a world-famous poet with a reputation dating back to before the Revolution, whereas he was a total unknown with a camp record behind him. Pasternak's novel had almost entirely evaded the issues of collectivization, the purges, and the camps by stopping short of them, whereas in *Shch-854* and *The First Circle* Solzhenitsyn had tackled them head-on by making them his very subject matter. And if *Doctor Zhivago* was anti-Soviet, what epithet could qualify *Feast of the Conquerors*, *Decembrists without December*, and some of his camp verses?

On the other hand there was encouragement to be found as well. In Stalin's day it had been unthinkable that a major writer should hand his novel to a representative of a Western publisher before it had been approved at home, let alone that it should be published abroad and not in the Soviet Union. There was also the relative mildness of the sanctions. Writers in the thirties and forties had gone to jail for far less, and others had been physically liquidated. Even expulsion from the Writers' Union was a trivial punishment in comparison with the question of survival. What the campaign showed was that there were still strict limits within which Soviet writers were compelled to operate and that those who exceeded the limits would find the full force of the Soviet media used against them. But it also showed that it was now possible to defy the government machine and remain not only alive but at liberty—at least if you had a reputation. Then there was the unexpected new force of foreign public opinion. The barbarous treatment of Pasternak had attracted indignant responses from all over the world. Telegrams and letters had flooded in, by no means exclusively from people hostile to socialism, but from writers of all shades of opinion, including Bertrand Russell, Graham Greene, Halldór Laxness, Mulk Raj Anand, and Jorge Amado. Stalin would have dismissed these protests, but Khrushchev's new policy of *détente* and increasing contacts with the West had introduced a potent new factor into the relation between Soviet writers and the Soviet government. Finally, there was the indefinable impact of the Nobel Prize itself. Had that not also conferred a considerable degree of immunity on Pasternak?

As the furore over *Doctor Zhivago* died away, the political pendulum had seemed to swing the other way again. In January 1959 the Twenty-first Congress of the Party had produced nothing to compare with Khrushchev's "secret speech" at the Twentieth Congress, even though the general line remained anti-Stalinist. But in May had come the Third Congress of Soviet Writers,

---

* Among other things, the Semichastny speech contained the following passage: "If we compare Pasternak with a pig . . . then we have to say that a pig will never do what he has done. Pasternak . . . has fouled the spot where he ate and messed on those by whose labour he lives and breathes."

where a distinctly liberal trend was visible. Konstantin Fedin, the once-respected novelist to whom Solzhenitsyn had sent his youthful stories, replaced Surkov as secretary general of the Writers' Union, and Tvardovsky's reinstatement as editor of *Novy Mir* was confirmed. Khrushchev, flushed with his success in establishing his ascendancy at the recent Party congress, even had a good word to say about Dudintsev, whom he had harshly criticized the year before.

Nevertheless, the Writers' Congress had also been notable for the number of prominent absentees. Many writers had voted with their feet and expressed their disapproval of recent trends by staying away. So obvious was it that Party spokesmen had raged about a "conspiracy of silence" on the part of the writers. The message was rammed home that the Pasternak affair had done incalculable harm to Soviet literature, and gradually a new thaw set in that was to surpass not only the original thaw of 1954 but also that of 1956–57.

This time the major role was played by young writers comparatively new to the Soviet scene. The leaders of the earlier liberalization had been members of the middle or older generations—Ehrenburg, Paustovsky, Panova, Tvardovsky, and Victor Nekrasov—whereas the new leaders were relative newcomers who had grown up since the war.

The best-known among them was a young poet called Evgeni Evtushenko, who had come to prominence in 1956 with his long poem "Zima Station" and then proceeded to turn his poetic career into a public spectacle much as Mayakovsky had done forty years earlier. Evtushenko was too young to have been moulded by Stalin's terror, and this made a great difference to his psychological make-up. He was daring, provocative, and controversial. He lacked the fear of the older generation and made a point of tackling "difficult" subjects. And having cultivated his popularity among the young and progressive, he attempted to use this as a lever for advancing the liberals' cause. Other young poets followed suit: Andrei Voznesensky, Bulat Okudzhava, Bella Akhmadulina (who was Evtushenko's wife for a while). Among prose writers Vasily Axyonov, a young doctor turned writer, played a role analogous to Evtushenko's, with his slangy tales of life among the alienated young and his exploitation of the "fathers and sons" theme, while the short story flourished as never before since the twenties. Yuri Kazakov, Daniil Granin, Yuri Nagibin, Vladimir Tendryakov, Efim Dorosh, Vladimir Soloukhin, Vladimir Maximov, and many others stretched "socialist realism" to its outer limits and helped give Soviet literature an interest and variety that it had lacked for nearly thirty years.

In all this the younger generation had been supported by certain liberal elders such as Ehrenburg, Paustovsky, Kornei Chukovsky, Samuil Marshak, and especially Tvardovsky, who gave them every encouragement and published many of them in the pages of *Novy Mir*. But there remained a strong conservative camp, with leanings towards Stalinism and a desire for strict party discipline in literature. This group included figures like Leonid Sobolev,

Alexander Dymshits, and Vladimir Ermilov, as well as the now notorious Kochetov. In truth, Kochetov had lasted only three years as editor of *Literaturnaya Gazeta*, but in 1961 he was appointed editor of the influential monthly magazine *Oktyabr* (October), which he proceeded to turn into a bastion of reaction, and was already working on a new polemical novel, *The Secretary of the Regional Committee*, which was to contain a vicious lampoon of Evtushenko.

By the time that Solzhenitsyn began to think seriously about publication, the literary world was therefore divided into two warring camps, a situation that reflected, in a sharper way, the divisions in the Party and the country. It was a novel position for the Soviet Union to be in and was undoubtedly the result of Khrushchev's anti-Stalin campaign and struggle for personal power. For the first time Solzhenitsyn could perceive prominent figures who seemed to share some of his own views on the past. Nevertheless, he still hesitated to reveal himself. "It seemed to me at the time, and not without reason, that such a revelation would be extremely hazardous: it might lead to the loss of all my manuscripts and of my own liberty."[20] What helped to change his mind was the Twenty-second Congress of the Communist Party, held in October 1961, and especially the line it took on de-Stalinization and the speech to the congress made by Tvardovsky.

The emphasis the congress placed on de-Stalinization came as a surprise to almost everyone. True, it had been maintained as official Party policy ever since Khrushchev's "secret speech" in 1956 and had been reaffirmed at the Twenty-first Congress in 1959, but after the first wave of reforms of 1956 and the consequent shock of the explosion in Hungary, the official policy had been to soft-pedal it. One reason was that Khrushchev, despite his overall ascendancy, still had powerful opponents within the Politburo. It was as though the Party leaders, after the terrors of Stalinism, had instinctively, out of self-protection, wanted to ensure that no man should henceforth be given complete hegemony. The two most powerful men after Khrushchev, Frol Kozlov and Mikhail Suslov, were hardliners who acted as an ideological brake on their impetuous leader, while the other members of the Politburo maintained a middle position between the two extremes. At the Twenty-second Congress, however, Khrushchev seems to have determined to reduce the power of his opponents once and for all; and to do this he chose to raise once more the spectre of the "anti-Party group" and the need for more reform.

It is difficult to know, in retrospect, how far Khrushchev had meant to go. As in his "secret speech" on Stalinism five years beforehand, he grew extremely emotional when speaking on the second day and appears to have been carried away by genuine feelings of outrage and regret for the past, which led him perhaps further than he had intended. At the climax of his speech, he made a dramatic promise to erect a monument in Moscow "to the memory of the comrades who fell victims to arbitrary power" and concluded, "Comrades! Our duty is to investigate carefully such abuses of power in all their aspects. Time passes and we shall die, since all of us are mortal, but as long as we have the strength to work we must clear up many things and tell the truth to the Party and our people."[21]

Superficially, it looked as though Khrushchev were carrying all before him and taking a further significant step along the road of de-Stalinization. This, at least, was how the intelligentsia chose to regard it, and they were particularly encouraged by the tone and contents of Tvardovsky's speech, which was read with close attention by the writers. Tvardovsky, a candidate member of the Central Committee in his own right, adopted a position of solid support for Khrushchev. He said that Soviet literature had benefited immeasurably from the reforms introduced after the Twentieth Congress in 1956. It had undergone a period of moral regeneration and spiritual uplift. No longer did it feel shackled by the past, and writers had flourished in the new atmosphere of freedom. But this, he felt, was still not enough. In an obvious reference to Kochetov and his friends, he pointed out that "too many writers" were finding it difficult to adjust to the new atmosphere and still yearned for the easy certainties of the past. Moreover, Soviet literature had still not taken full advantage of the opportunities opened up to it by the Twentieth Party Congress. It was still not sufficiently devoted to the Truth (with a capital T) in all its aspects and therefore was not fulfilling its responsibility to its readers. "If I am not mistaken," continued Tvardovsky,

> it was Suvorov who said that a soldier takes pride not only in his victories in battle but also in the privations he has had to undergo in the course of the campaign. We writers, when telling of the feats of labour of that wonderful soldier, the people, often keep completely silent about the privations and difficulties he has had to undergo in his great campaign. We are wounding the rightfully proud feelings of a man who has overcome all the difficulties in his path as he marches indefatigably towards his lofty chosen goal. But we should rather be reinforcing that feeling of pride and paying proper tribute to his bravery, endurance, patience, noble disinterestedness, and readiness, if necessary, to make any sacrifice. But this can be done only by showing the labours and ordeals of our people in a manner that is totally truthful and faithful to life, without varnishing and without cunningly smoothing out all contradictions. . . . The cult of personality no longer exists, but out of inertia its outworn survivals continue to echo in our literature and in our press in general.[22]

Tvardovsky's speech made a great impression on all literary circles, and not least on Solzhenitsyn in his provincial backwater. "I couldn't remember when I had read anything as interesting as the speeches at the Twenty-second Congress. In my little room in a decaying wooden house . . . I read and reread those speeches, and the walls of my secret world swayed like curtains in the theatre, wavered, expanded, and carried me queasily with them."[23] Khrushchev's emotional speech about telling the truth to the people and erecting a monument to the victims of Stalinism seemed to echo his deepest feelings. Telling the truth about these victims had occupied virtually all his waking thoughts for the past ten years, and he had a pile of manuscripts to prove it. As for Tvardovsky's speech, Solzhenitsyn couldn't help being pleased by its

military metaphors and patriotic reference to Suvorov; and its injunction to
"show the labours and ordeals of our people in a manner that is totally truthful to life" seemed to describe exactly the tale of *Shch-854* nestling in its hiding place.

Solzhenitsyn read most of these speeches in *Izvestia*, to which he subscribed (he was still as avid a newspaper reader as he had been when a student and army captain), but to be absolutely sure of getting a full version of
Tvardovsky's speech he went to the city reading-room and read it in *Pravda*.
There the thing that struck him most forcefully was Tvardovsky's words
about writers' not having taken advantage of the possibilities opened up to
them by the Twentieth Congress, and his hint that *Novy Mir* might publish
bolder and more polemical works if only it had them. Solzhenitsyn had liked
Tvardovsky ever since he had stumbled across *Vasily Tyorkin* at the front,
leading him to conclude that Tvardovsky was perhaps "our best Soviet poet."
He especially approved of Tvardovsky's peasant origins, his profound understanding of the common people, and his feel for their language. By the same
token, was it not a hundred to one that Tvardovsky himself would respond
to the peasant figure of Ivan Denisovich Shukhov and the tale of his "labours
and ordeals"?

But still Solzhenitsyn was a prey to agonizing doubts and fears. Since
the preceding spring a copy of *Shch-854* had been with Kopelev in Moscow,
and Solzhenitsyn and Kopelev had drawn up a short list of writers to whom
it might be shown. With this in mind, Solzhenitsyn had revised the text one
more time, omitting some of the biographical detail concerning the main
characters, toning down its political outspokenness, and polishing the style.
A few people had read it already. Some had praised it to the skies, others
were slightly more reserved, but all agreed on its outstanding importance as
a social and political document, and everyone wanted it to circulate. But
Solzhenitsyn was reluctant to take risks, and it was Kopelev who persuaded
him that in the aftermath of the Twenty-second Congress, the time was right
to submit the work to Tvardovsky.[24]

It would appear from Kopelev's later remarks that they had little hope
the book would be published. Kopelev's argument to Solzhenitsyn was that
since the manuscript had been shown to certain people and had made such a
deep impression, news of it was bound to travel, and there was a danger that
Solzhenitsyn might be accused of circulating the work illegally. If it was
submitted to *Novy Mir*, it would automatically be read by members of the
staff, and any further circulation could be described as accidental. It was
decided to ask Kopelev's wife, Raisa Orlova, to take the manuscript to *Novy
Mir*.* Kopelev himself preferred not to do so, because he was in the midst of

---

* It is true that Kopelev was one of those who did not have the highest opinion of *Ivan Denisovich*
when he first read it, but he was unstinting in his efforts to get it known and published. The
phrase "It is a typical production story," which Reshetovskaya attributes to Kopelev in her
memoirs, was indeed said by him, but it was offered to Tvardovsky as a possible argument to
use with Khrushchev, not as a literary appreciation. The copy that Solzhenitsyn later sent to

an acrimonious dispute with the editorial staff, including Tvardovsky, over their refusal to support a liberal anthology he was involved with called *Tarusa Pages*.[25]*

On 4 November 1961 Solzhenitsyn took a train to Moscow for one last discussion of the matter during the November holiday. To preserve his secret, he booked a room at a hotel instead of staying with Veronica or another of his friends, and saw only the Kopelevs. The hotel he had chosen was in Ostankino, near the site of the former *sharashka*, and in the intervals between reading a translation of *For Whom the Bell Tolls* (borrowed from Kopelev) he strolled along the fence still enclosing the site and recalled the crowded days he had spent there with Kopelev, Panin, Ivashov-Musatov, and his other friends.[26] It was there that he had begun to write seriously. Would the others agree with Kopelev and approve of his present enterprise, and were his old dreams of freedom and fame about to be realized, or was he thrusting his head into a noose again? Once more the optimistic activist warred with the suspicious convict within him. He was almost forty-three. Could it be that his long-awaited, eagerly thirsted-for yet involuntarily dreaded literary career was about to begin?

the Kopelevs bore the following inscription: "To my dear friends, Lev and Raya, who started the unforeseen movement of this tale."

* *Tarusa Pages* was a literary almanac edited by Paustovsky and containing positive critical appreciations of formerly taboo figures like Bunin and Meyerhold and poems by Tsvetayeva and Zabolotsky, as well as prose by some younger Soviet writers. It was widely regarded as a challenge to socialist realism and a manifesto of revisionism, and sold out its 75,000 copies in a matter of days. Tarusa is a district just outside Moscow.

23

BREAKTHROUGH

THE STORY OF how *Shch-854* made its way from an outer office of *Novy Mir* to the desk of Nikita Khrushchev and eventual publication (as *A Day in the Life of Ivan Denisovich*) has been told and retold so many times that it is now legendary, and like all legends, it has acquired such embellishments along the way that it is sometimes hard to disentangle fact from fiction. The book's physical path, however, from the Kopelevs to a copy-editor named Anna Berzer, and from her to *Novy Mir*'s editor, Alexander Tvardovsky, and thence via Khrushchev's private secretary to Khrushchev himself (and via Khrushchev onto the desks of members of the Presidium) is well attested, and there can be little doubt as to the accuracy of the general picture.[1]

Raisa Orlova delivered the manuscript to *Novy Mir* in mid-November 1961, immediately after the holiday, with strict instructions that it be passed directly to Tvardovsky. It was a week or so before Berzer got around to looking at it, but when she did, she was at once struck by its exceptional literary and political boldness and showed it to a colleague in the critical section of the magazine, Kaleria Ozerova, to check her impressions. Ozerova agreed that *Shch-854* was something quite out of the ordinary.

Both women realized, however, as the Kopelevs had done, that the story's frankness and outspokenness presented special dangers and problems. It was not that the labour-camp theme was entirely new. Solzhenitsyn has given the impression in some of his public statements (and especially in *The Oak and the Calf*) that *Ivan Denisovich* appeared in an almost total void and that there was nothing remotely comparable in existence at the time, but that is not quite true. Ever since Khrushchev's "secret speech" in 1956, the camp theme had been bubbling just below the surface, and a number of returned prisoners had written powerful and harrowing memoirs about their experiences. The memoirs of Olga Adamova-Sliozberg, for instance, were already in Berzer's possession (they were subsequently drawn upon by Solzhenitsyn for *The Gulag Archipelago*). Evgenia Ginzburg and Dimitri Vitkovsky, to name but two of the best, were hard at work on extraordinary exposures of the death camps of the Siberian Far East, and Varlam Shalamov had already completed and shown to friends his sequence of tightly crafted stories on his experiences in Kolyma.* Among the Moscow intelligentsia the closure of most of the camps and the mass rehabilitations were a prime talking point, and many manuscripts were circulating from hand to hand. Solzhenitsyn, in his isolation in Ryazan, knew little of these, for none of them had succeeded in breaking through the barriers into print. There was still a conspiracy of silence about the camps as far as literature was concerned. It was one thing for the first secretary of the Party to stand up at a congress and denounce the evils of Stalinism, but quite another for a literary magazine actually to print something on the subject (Khrushchev's "secret speech" remains to this day unpublished in the Soviet Union). And not even Tvardovsky, whose bold words at the congress had echoed Khrushchev's and who enjoyed a certain immunity as a candidate member of the Central Committee and a member of the Supreme Soviet, had been able to get a frank exposure of the camps into his journal (although *Novy Mir* was far and away the most "liberal" and outspoken of all Soviet magazines). The surface of Soviet literature, therefore, had remained virtually undisturbed by this seething commotion in the depths, and literary life was conducted as if nothing much wrong had ever happened; there were only a few dark hints to indicate the reason for the "holes" in so many people's biographies.

It was in this atmosphere that Anna Berzer contemplated what to do next. She agreed with Orlova that if the story went through the usual editorial process, it would run into insuperable difficulties. Someone on the staff was sure to try to block it out of caution or fear, and then it would be rejected like all the other manuscripts on the camps. However, she sensed that what she held in her hands was sensationally good, perhaps a masterpiece, and again she agreed with Orlova: the one man who would appreciate it and be in a position to do something was Tvardovsky. Her task, therefore, was to get it directly to him and persuade him to read it personally, but this apparently simple operation was in fact no easy matter, for reasons that have to do with the way Soviet literary magazines are organized.

Like all Soviet magazines, *Novy Mir* had (and has) an enormous staff by Western standards and a structure both bureaucratic and hierarchical. Editorially, it was divided into three sections, covering poetry, prose, and criticism respectively. Each section was staffed by rank-and-file copy-editors like Berzer and Ozerova, who represented the lower end of the hierarchy and performed the daily task of editing and correcting and preparing manuscripts

* Solzhenitsyn makes an exception for Shalamov, whose stories and verse he seems to have read as early as 1956.

for the press. It was they who dealt with the authors on a regular basis and consequently got to know them best, whether the authors were new and beginning, or old friends with established reputations. But they were not members of the editorial board, and their subordinate position was symbolized by their having their offices on the first floor, whereas the editor and his associates worked on the third.

Each of the three sections had a chief to direct it. Chief of the prose section when *Shch-854* arrived in the office was Evgeni Gerasimov, an uninspired writer and journalist who nevertheless presided over the best section in the magazine. The lively critical section was about to be taken over by the up-and-coming young critic Vladimir Lakshin, and the poetry section—to everyone's surprise the weakest, although the magazine had an outstanding poet as editor—was directed by Tvardovsky himself. The section chiefs also sat on *Novy Mir*'s editorial board, of which they were junior members, together with co-opted members like the writers Igor Sats, Alexander Maryamov, and Igor Vinogradov, while at the top of the heap sat the magazine's ruling quaternity: Tvardovsky; his first deputy editor, Alexander Dementyev; his second deputy editor, Alexander Kondratovich; and the managing secretary, Boris Sachs.

Anna Berzer knew that any one of her seniors had the right to demand to read the story and that any one of them might take fright and reject it, if only to "protect" Tvardovsky from the consequences of his possible recklessness. If the work were to get as far as the censorship board, for instance, and be rejected there, it might provoke recriminations and even sanctions against the magazine. Such fears were not without foundation. In the past questionable manuscripts had been handed straight to the security organs. Only that year there had been the notorious incident in which the manuscript of a new book by the distinguished novelist Vasily Grossman—*Life and Destiny*—had been confiscated by the KGB after the editor of *Znamya*, Vadim Kozhevnikov, had sent it to them. Grossman himself had been forced to yield up all his copies of the novel on pain of instant arrest, and even the carbon paper and ribbon used in typing it had been borne away by the police.[2]*

There was scant chance of such a response from the members of the *Novy Mir* board, but this was the general atmosphere in which even the most liberal magazine was obliged to operate, and there was a distinct possibility of a well-meaning board-member's stopping the novel in its tracks. For this reason, Berzer planned a special strategy for reaching Tvardovsky directly.

First she had the manuscript retyped. The original, according to Solzhenitsyn's usual thrifty custom, was typed on both sides of the paper, with single spacing and no margins. Merely to look at it strained the eyes and

---

* Grossman's novel resurfaced and reached the West almost twenty years later in circumstances that were even more dramatic than its disappearance. Apparently, it was secretly microfilmed by someone high up in the Party (or by the relative of a high-up) who had access to the typescript, and the microfilm was stored in a safe place. In the late seventies, a dissident Soviet writer was informed of the film's existence and arranged for it to be smuggled out. It was published in Switzerland in 1980 (an English translation is in preparation).

deterred one from reading on. Another disagreeable feature was the complete absence of an author's name. Berzer summoned Kopelev and asked him to supply one, whereupon the quick-witted Kopelev thought up "A. Ryazansky," which was duly typed in beneath the cryptic title.[3] The manuscript was ready for presentation, but the problem was how to bypass the other members of the editorial board and get it to Tvardovsky, particularly since he preferred to delegate such things and to read manuscripts only after his deputies had seen them.

Her solution was to exploit the problematical subject matter of *Shch-854* and turn it to her advantage. Approaching her immediate superior, Gerasimov, she asked him whether he would like to read "a story about the camps." Foreseeing nothing but trouble, Gerasimov waved her away. She then did exactly the same with Kondratovich and Sachs and received more or less the same response. Dementyev, the other deputy editor, was not usually on the premises, and Berzer now had the right to approach Tvardovsky. Choosing her moment and her words, she went up to his office on the third floor and laid two manuscripts on his desk: *Sophia Petrovna*, by Lydia Chukovskaya,* and *Shch-854*. They were both unusual, she said, and both controversial. *Sophia Petrovna* was about the great purge of 1937 and a mother's suffering, while *Shch-854* was about "a prison camp seen through the eyes of a peasant"[4]— it voiced, she said, the thoughts and feelings of the Russian people.

She could not have put it more cunningly or temptingly. Tvardovsky's peasant origins and predilection for peasant themes were well known in Moscow literary circles. He had made his name with his intimate portrait of Vasily Tyorkin and his poems on village and peasant life, and *Novy Mir* had a reputation as a publisher of "country prose." He would take only one manuscript home to read, he said, and without hesitation picked up *Shch-854*. Solzhenitsyn's and Kopelev's calculation that Tvardovsky would be attracted by the theme of the story had proved fully justified. The date was 7 December 1961.

It is said that Tvardovsky's custom when reading manuscripts at home was to take them to bed; that is how, one day later, he began to read *Shch-854*. After a few pages, he is said to have felt that it was inappropriate to read it in this relaxed position, so he got up, dressed, and read the story through the night, stopping only to make himself tea in the kitchen. According to Solzhenitsyn, he read it through twice and was so excited that he could not sleep afterwards and was absolutely bursting to share the good news with someone. Unfortunately, it was still early when he finished (Reshetovskaya says 5 a.m.), and Tvardovsky was obliged to contain his impatience until the relatively late hour when metropolitan intellectuals stirred from their slumbers.

There followed an avalanche of telephone calls—to Kondratovich, to

---

*Chukovskaya's novel, written in 1939–40, was a rare example of an attempt to deal with the purges in literary terms at the time they were happening. It has never appeared in the Soviet Union, but has been published in Russian in the West both under its correct name and as *The Deserted House*. Two English translations bear the latter title.

Berzer, to Kopelev—to find out who was hiding beneath that transparent pseudonym of A. Ryazansky. He was delighted to hear that the author was genuinely unknown, an obscure schoolteacher from Ryazan, and not a professional playing a trick on him. According to Reshetovskaya, he upbraided Kopelev for being so secretive about his friend and not having drawn Tvardovsky's attention to the story when Kopelev came to discuss *Tarusa Pages*. "You should be proud to have such a friend. He's got a wonderful, pure, and great talent. Not a drop of falsehood in it."[5]

What happened next is not clear. According to one writer close to *Novy Mir*, Tvardovsky insisted on reading passages aloud to his wife over breakfast. He then rushed to the *Novy Mir* offices to get some extra copies, but 9 December was a Saturday and no one was there except the cleaners. By now unstoppable, Tvardovsky broke open Berzer's desk, took out the four extra copies and dashed off to the flat of his friend Semyon Lungin, where Victor Nekrasov, another *Novy Mir* author, also happened to be staying. "A new genius is born!" he proclaimed. "Victor, go for a bottle. After all, I'm a colonel and you were only a captain."[6] Such kidding was very much in Tvardovsky's style (as was the vodka at the slightest pretext), and it may have been on this occasion that he also joked to Nekrasov: "Do you remember how one great writer went to see another great writer? I'm joking, of course, because I don't consider you a great writer. But a great writer has just been born nevertheless."[7]*

Igor Sats was summoned from home to join them, and the morning was spent in talking and growing progressively drunk. Tvardovsky was the loudest. Nekrasov later said that he had never seen Tvardovsky as excited and voluble. Usually he was restrained, even when enthusiastic about a manuscript. But on this occasion he was unquenchable, announcing that his only aim in life henceforth was to get the story into print. "I'll go to the very top, to Nikita. . . . They say that Russian literature's been killed. Damn and blast it! It's in this folder with the ribbons. But who is he? Nobody's seen him yet. We've sent a telegram. . . . We'll take him under our wing, help him, and push his book through."[8] Later, he said to the novelist Vera Panova, "Believe it or not, I've got a manuscript by a new Gogol."[9]

That same day Solzhenitsyn received a telegram from Kopelev: "Alexander Trifonovich delighted with article—very much wants to see you—come as soon as possible—congratulations and regards" ("article," of course, was the code word for *Shch-854*). Ringing up that evening, Solzhenitsyn learned of Tvardovsky's excitement and sleepless night, and the following day, on his forty-third birthday, he received a telegram from Tvardovsky himself,

---

*Tvardovsky's reference was to Dostoyevsky's first novel, *Poor Folk*, which he sent to the poet Nikolai Nekrasov in 1845, when Nekrasov was planning to launch a new literary miscellany. Nekrasov read the novel and was so impressed that he rushed to the home of the celebrated literary critic Vissarion Belinsky and exclaimed, "A new Gogol has arisen!" Belinsky is reputed to have replied, "Gogols grow in your imagination like mushrooms," but was equally impressed when he read the novel.

inviting him to come to Moscow at *Novy Mir*'s expense. As the result of a postal error, he received two copies of the telegram, as though to underline the importance of the occasion.[10]

That night, according to Reshetovskaya, it was Solzhenitsyn's turn not to sleep. His mood was one of exultation and triumph, although, throughout the day he had remained outwardly calm, merely repeating to himself over and over, "How funny . . . how funny." Tvardovsky was very much on his mind just then. A few days earlier Natalia had bought a copy of Tvardovsky's latest narrative poem, *Distant Horizons*, and Solzhenitsyn had been admiring the author's political frankness and artistic skill. Now the famous author had responded with admiration of his own. Nearly a year later, Solzhenitsyn was to write to Tvardovsky, "The greatest happiness that 'recognition' has given me I experienced in December last year, when you found *Denisovich* worth a sleepless night. None of the praise that came afterwards could ever outstrip that."[11]

On Tuesday, 12 December, Solzhenitsyn had a free day from school and caught the seven o'clock train to Moscow. Picking up Kopelev *en route*, he made his way to the *Novy Mir* offices. Tvardovsky had not yet arrived, so Kopelev took him to meet Anna Berzer and her colleagues on the first floor. Solzhenitsyn was still unaware of the role that Berzer had played in getting his manuscript to Tvardovsky, but it seems that he took an immediate liking to this diminutive and marvellously intelligent woman. Not so, however, to the second deputy editor, Alexei Kondratovich, who struck him as a pompous and self-important bore.

Tvardovsky arrived at half past one, straight from a meeting on that year's Lenin Prizes for literature. He was a big man in all senses of the word, and he greeted Solzhenitsyn gravely and politely, and with a certain solemnity too. They went upstairs to the *Novy Mir* boardroom, which also served as Tvardovsky's office, and seated themselves round the long, oval editorial table, with Tvardovsky and Solzhenitsyn at the two ends. Also present were Kondratovich, Dementyev, Sachs, Berzer, Maryamov, and, after a little while, Kopelev, who was invited to join them.

The discussion was led by Tvardovsky, who began in a more or less businesslike fashion but soon grew animated and launched into a veritable paean of praise to Solzhenitsyn's story, quoting his favourite episodes with relish and permitting a broad smile to stretch gradually from ear to ear. What made him a great editor, apart from his excellent taste, was precisely this boundless enthusiasm for works by other authors, and an ability to share in their triumphs that was rare in a poet of such achievement himself. Facing Solzhenitsyn he said:

> You have written a marvellous thing. I don't know in which schools you studied, but you have come to us as a fully formed writer. We have no need either to instruct or to nurse you. . . . The fact that you chose a small form shows you are an experienced artist. You have described only one day, and yet everything

there is to say about prison has been said. . . . Your choice of hero is excellent—
not Tsezar, for example. . . . In some ways your book is even better than [Dos-
toyevsky's] *House of the Dead:* there we see the people through the eyes of an
intellectual, whereas here the intellectuals are seen through the eyes of the people. . . . The day chosen is so ordinary that it's not even bath day. . . . You
show everyone both at the front and on the Siberian [*sic*] construction projects.
. . . One feels so sorry for the commander, and even Fetyukov evokes sympathy.
. . . And the good thing is that you don't show any horrors.[12]

In later years Solzhenitsyn was to pretend that he had remained relatively unmoved by this extravagant encomium of Tvardovsky's. Perhaps that
is why he omitted this speech (which he himself noted down) from his detailed
description of his relations with *Novy Mir* in *The Oak and the Calf* when he
came to publish the latter in 1975. It is true that he deliberately put up a
front of reserve and indifference, responding only grudgingly to the compli-
ments that were heaped upon him. But this was mainly a defence mechanism
and a sign, among other things, of his own insecurity: he could not bear to
be snubbed or disappointed after investing such great hopes in his story; he
was simply steeling himself against the worst. In fact, it is clear even from
his own account of the meeting that he was deeply flattered. This exalted
recognition was balm to his battered ego, belated recompense for all those
years of suffering and toil, and he wasn't above playing up to his hosts'
amazement over the crabbed, eccentric appearance of the original manuscript, or coquettishly flaunting his tiny salary of sixty rubles a month as a
part-time teacher in Ryazan (passing over the fact that he lived off Natalia's
salary). He thoroughly enjoyed his role of the indigent, provincial nobody
and had deliberately dressed shabbily for this solemn occasion, which only
provoked more amazement from his metropolitan companions.

The other members of the editorial board were briefer in their remarks,
and Solzhenitsyn was relieved to discover that they had very few criticisms
to make or suggestions for changes. The main problem, it seemed, was the
title, which nobody liked. After an animated discussion, in which Kopelev
also joined, they unanimously settled on *A Day in the Life of Ivan Denisovich.**

Afterwards the talk became more personal. Tvardovsky and the others
asked Solzhenitsyn about his past in the camps (Kopelev was able to join in
when they talked about the *sharashka*) and his life as a teacher in Ryazan.
They wanted to know what else he had written, but Solzhenitsyn was evasive. He told them that although he now regarded himself as primarily a
prose writer, he had begun with verse—since it was easier to memorize in
the camps—and had written quite a lot. He also told them about the occasion
in Ekibastuz when he had been caught during a search with a fragment of
verse on him and had passed it off as Tvardovsky's.

At the end of the meeting, Tvardovsky insisted on drawing up a con-

---

*The accepted title is *One Day* . . . , but the Russian "one" simply plays the role of the indefinite
article, for which Russian otherwise has no equivalent. I therefore prefer *A Day* . . . , which
lifts the stress supplied by the numeral.

tract at once. He wanted to pay Solzhenitsyn at the highest rate, but the others pointed out that the proper rate for a first publication was somewhat lower—300 rubles a signature, and this was agreed upon. The total was quite handsome compared with Solzhenitsyn's usual earnings—the advance alone exceeded two years' worth of his salary.

Tvardovsky's parting words were that he could not give a firm promise of publication, or say anything about dates, but that he promised to do his best. He also handed Solzhenitsyn the preliminary reports on the story made by his two deputies, Dementyev and Kondratovich, from which the obstacles in the way of publishing it became clear. Both editors praised the story for its literary skill and power, but both expressed doubts about its political acceptability. Dementyev was the more negative of the two: "Seen from this angle, it is horrible inside the camp and just as horrible beyond its boundaries. A difficult case: if we don't publish, it will look as though we fear the truth, and we will only drive it underground, from where it will spread all over. But publication is out of the question, because it shows life too one-sidedly, involuntarily twisting and upsetting the proportions." Kondratovich had more praise for the story but was also pessimistic about its publication chances. "It's a pity, but we probably won't be able to publish it," he began, and he ended up: "It's very talented, but how can we publish it?"[13]

Solzhenitsyn took the two reports home with him, together with a copy of the contract. When he arrived, writes Reshetovskaya, he seemed dazed. "Silently he opened his brief-case and showed us a large, thick sheet of paper on which the word CONTRACT was written in large letters. I couldn't believe my eyes. I sank down helplessly on a chair and burst into tears."[14]

In answer to Tvardovsky's pressing questions about what else he had written and might be able to offer *Novy Mir*, Solzhenitsyn had mentioned his early verse, some of his miniature prose pieces, and "a short story," having in mind "Without a Righteous Person No Village Can Stand" (he regarded his other work as too controversial to mention at that stage). He now settled down to prepare the story about Matryona for publication, toning it down a little and cutting out some of the sharper comments, and on 26 December returned to Moscow to deliver these things to Tvardovsky.

"This story can't fail to appeal to Tvardovsky," he had said to his wife while working on it, and he was right, learning of Tvardovsky's enthusiasm on his third visit, a week later, to discuss *Novy Mir*'s opinion of it. But he was disappointed by Tvardovsky's reaction to the other things he had offered. The verse was dismissed as uninteresting: "Some of it is publishable, but we want something to make a bang, and this isn't it" (to Lakshin, Tvardovsky had said that the verse wasn't worth reading). As for the miniature stories, Tvardovsky seemed perplexed by the unusual genre and failed to take them seriously, regarding them as "jottings on your scribbling pad for further use." What he yearned for as an editor was something strong and striking that could stand comparison with *Ivan Denisovich*. These little pieces were too fragile and precious, too much in a minor key to suit Tvardovsky's present requirements.[15]

The old year was almost at an end, and the school holidays had begun. It was a wonderful moment for Solzhenitsyn. Still basking in Tvardovsky's praise and the wonderment of the *Novy Mir* staff, he could relish for the first time some of the rewards of authorship, without yet suffering the responsibilities of fame and controversy. The difficulties that lay in the way of publication loomed only indistinctly in the unforeseeable future—in any case, they weren't his problem: Tvardovsky had promised to take all that on his shoulders.

Something of Solzhenitsyn's mood at this time can be deduced from a playfully affectionate letter he wrote to the Zubovs in the Crimea in response to their belated birthday greetings. The letter was begun some time before his trip to Moscow on 26 December 1961.

> My kind, dear friends,
> Don't reproach yourselves for forgetting my birthday. It doesn't feel in the least as if you had forgotten me. . . . Furthermore, my birthday this year was anyway something of a red-letter day—it was marked by a telegram from Alexander Trifonovich (not unknown for his poem *Distant Horizons*, etc.). On the twelfth I went to Pushkin Square to meet him. What will come of it all is still unclear. Maybe I will know more by the time I come to the end of this letter, in which case I will add something.

After his return from Moscow he did add something:

> You will be surprised to hear that in my spare time (being too bashful to admit it even to you) I have been amusing myself with literature, that is to say, I was foolhardy enough to attempt to write. One of the things I wrote was a yarn called *A Day in the Life of Ivan Denisovich*, and after the Twenty-second Congress I thought that the time was ripe to publish it and sent it off to *Novy Mir*. *NM*'s reaction exceeded my wildest expectations and was expressed in telegrams and expressions of delight. They decided that I was some kind of a literary rough diamond and didn't even seem to want to make any changes or corrections. All this took me by surprise, just as it will surprise you. Perhaps you will get a chance to read it one day (if they publish it). That is, the editorial board has accepted the story, has signed a contract for it, and paid me an advance of a thousand new rubles. The editors want to publish, but the chances are not very great, and it doesn't depend on them.
> So that's the news, and of course the whole thing has knocked me sideways.[16]

To celebrate the glad news, Solzhenitsyn and Natalia decided to spend the New Year in Moscow, where most of their friends seemed to be. Even Teush was there now, having retired from teaching a short while before, so that Ryazan seemed perfectly empty. The thought of Teush reminded him that this would be a good moment to review his security precautions. Ever since exile he had kept up the habit of concealing his manuscripts in case of random searches by the KGB, and of burning most of his notes and drafts. But over the years, as he had gradually returned to a normal way of life, he

had inevitably grown laxer. The sheer bulk of his archive had also grown
tremendously, until it had reached the point where he was having to conceal
well over a dozen full-length works, including an extremely long novel, together
with notes and drafts that he still needed in order to complete work in progress. Even by typing all his manuscripts in cramped single spacing, he was
unable to reduce their bulk significantly, and all this paper somehow had to
be found hiding-places that were both secure and easy to reach. There were
few friends he could trust with such a delicate task, but the Teushes were
evidently among them, and on New Year's Eve, having gone through his
manuscripts a last time and burnt what seemed no longer necessary, he and
Natalia travelled to Moscow with a suitcase containing most of the rest.

It was on this train journey that there occurred a curious incident illus-
trative of some of the tensions induced by Solzhenitsyn's secretive way of
life and the strains imposed on his naturally impetuous nature. Soon after
they left Ryazan, a drunken hooligan began to make a scene and abuse some
of the passengers not far from where Solzhenitsyn and Natalia were sitting.
None of the other men in the train raised a finger to stop him, and Solzhenitsyn felt an irresistible urge to jump up and put this insolent hooligan in
his place, but he realized that if it came to a fight, he would almost certainly
be dragged off to the police station for an explanation, and that would mean
risking his precious manuscripts. "So in order to fulfil my duty as a Russian,
I had to exercise a quite-un-Russian self-restraint. I sat there, feeling ashamed
and cowardly, staring at the floor while the women scolded us for our
unmanliness."[17]

Years later, when he came to record this incident in *The Oak and the Calf*,
the memory of it still rankled, and it also came to seem symbolic of the larger
constraints that were increasingly imposed on his natural desire to fight.

This was one of many times when my secret life as a writer robbed me—not
always in such a humiliating way, but just as aggravatingly—of my freedom of
action, my freedom to speak my mind, my freedom to stand up straight. We all
had heavy loads on our backs, but I was also dragged down, and my spiritual
energies diverted from literature, by unwieldy burdens hidden beneath the surface. My bones would ache with longing: straighten up, straighten up if you die
for it![18]

It was with a great sense of relief, therefore, that they walked out of the
Teushes' flat later that morning to stroll around Moscow, having left the case
of manuscripts in the Teushes' safe-keeping. To celebrate the occasion, Solzhenitsyn allowed himself to be persuaded to buy a new suit. It was, wrote
Reshetovskaya later, "a miracle, a real event—especially for me."[19] Certainly, Solzhenitsyn was not much given to dressing up. On the contrary, he
took a perverse pride in his shabbiness. In exile he had flaunted his fraying
army greatcoat and faded artillery breeches long after most other exiles had
rushed off to buy new clothes. And the nondescript attire donned for his first
visit to *Novy Mir* had been deliberately chosen to make an impression. The

role of downtrodden outsider matched his inner vision of his authorial persona. It was not something he could lightly abandon just because he had a
thousand rubles in his pocket.

They toasted the new year of 1962 with Alexandra Popova, and on New
Year's Day visited Ivashov-Musatov in his studio. Once again they found
him at work on yet another version of *Othello and Desdemona*, though six years
had passed since he had started it; and once again the two men fell into a
furious argument about the nature and purpose of art. A few months previously Ivashov had written to Solzhenitsyn, "Life and its manifestations
invariably provoke in me violent emotions of sorrow or joy, anger or delight,
rejection or admiration," but the drama was always seen as a personal one
played out in the life of the individual, and the figure of Othello personified
the worst tragedy that could befall the individual: faith betrayed. For Solzhenitsyn, this way of approaching life's problems seemed too private and
too abstract and somehow evaded the social evil that preoccupied his own
thoughts. His attitude, according to Reshetovskaya, was that Shakespeare's
characters had been depicted in thousands of paintings, so how could they
preoccupy an artist more than the lives of living prisoners with whom he had
shared so many hardships?[20] It was the same argument that Solzhenitsyn
had deployed on his visit to the studio with Panin in 1959, and Ivashov
offered the same reply. What interested him was not the scale of evil in
society at large but the nature of evil. What was worse, he asked Solzhenitsyn, the loss of faith in society or in one individual, when that individual
was your whole life? Which blows struck hardest, the impersonal blows of
society or a blow from your nearest and dearest?*

The next day, Natalia returned to Ryazan, and Solzhenitsyn went to
the *Novy Mir* offices to hear their verdict on "Matryona." There were only
five of them round the oval table this time—it was still the holiday period
and several members had failed to appear. Once again it was Tvardovsky
who led the discussion. As Solzhenitsyn had predicted, he liked the story
very much—for its village subject matter, for its peasant heroine, for its pure
Russian language, laced with proverbial expressions and popular diction. But
it had also placed him in something of a quandary. In the first place it was
even more critical of Soviet reality than *Ivan Denisovich*. The latter, after all,
had been set in the late forties and referred to a period and a phenomenon—
the labour camps—that were supposed to be well in the past and that had
been roundly condemned by the highest in the land. Matryona's story, however, was set in 1956, only a few years beforehand, and referred to a time
and a place that had suffered no such obloquy. As Tvardovsky saw it, the
author was "determined to show the village at its worst. You might have
given us one little glimpse of the sunny side. Everybody in sight is a degen-

*I am indebted to Martin Dewhirst for the suggestion that Ivashov-Musatov's painting may
have had a social content as well and that Solzhenitsyn misunderstood it. According to this
interpretation, the subject was allegorical. Othello stood for the Russian intelligentsia, which
had been duped by Iago-Stalin into betraying and murdering the Russian people (Desdemona).

erate or a vampire. . . . Your searching gaze has missed nothing."[21] It all added up to a devastating picture of degradation, corruption, cupidity, and moral depravity in the beloved Russian countryside.

Tvardovsky also found the treatment "a bit too Christian" for a Soviet journal, and the story "aesthetically thinner" than *Ivan Denisovich*. But worst of all was the feeling that it was too subversive to publish and that he dare not publish it, a feeling that had evidently been reinforced by Alexander Dementyev at a discussion before the meeting. Dementyev was so convinced of its unpublishability that he had declined Tvardovsky's invitation to speak to the author and had left the room before Tvardovsky launched into his monologue.

Yet despite his forebodings, Tvardovsky plainly *wanted* to publish it. He likened it to the moral tales of Tolstoy and praised its "realism without an adjective"—a reference to the Soviet distinction between the "critical realism" of the nineteenth-century classics and the "socialist realism" of Soviet authors. It was clear that Solzhenitsyn's story was much closer to "critical" than to "socialist" realism, but Tvardovsky dared not say so in front of his subordinates. He also realized by now that it would be absurd to expect any sort of orthodoxy from Solzhenitsyn. "I'm not saying you should have made Kira a member of the Komsomol," he commented at one stage, and when the discussion was over he said in his favourite jokey manner, "Please don't become ideologically reliable. Don't write anything that my staff could pass without my having to know about it."[22]

The conference had gone on for three hours, most of them taken up by Tvardovsky as he had gone round and round in circles, trying either to justify a rejection of the story or else to find reasons for publication. Anna Berzer, to whom Solzhenitsyn had taken a liking during their joint editorial work on *Ivan Denisovich*, later told him that she had never seen Tvardovsky so confused and indecisive. His literary instincts were at war with his political ones. But at the end of the day the matter was left open. Tvardovsky seemed to be saying that the story was unpublishable, but at the same time he asked Solzhenitsyn to leave it with him so that other members of the board might read it too.

Lastly, he sought to reassure Solzhenitsyn on the subject of *Ivan Denisovich*. He wasn't yet sure how to go about getting it published: "Don't try to hurry us, though. Don't ask which issue it will be in."[23] But he would do everything in his power to push it through. Solzhenitsyn believed him and was glad to leave all the arrangements to Tvardovsky. "Not everything depends on Alexander Trifonovich," he wrote to the Zubovs on his return to Ryazan, "but everything that does depend on him will be done. Neither he nor his staff can recall a work that ever had such a big impact on him. And so we will have to wait."[24]

Solzhenitsyn had decided to devote the next few months to a complete revision of *The First Circle*, making this his fourth and, he hoped, final draft of the novel. With luck, it too might be published in time. Accordingly, he returned to his routine of hurrying home from school after lessons and devoting every moment of his spare time to his writing. Once again friends and social life went by the board, and he tried to put the fate of *Ivan Denisovich* completely out of his mind. In March 1962 he wrote the Zubovs:

> My affairs in Moscow have come to a complete halt. For two months the magazine hasn't contacted me, nor I them. I think that A.T. must be having a hard time. I'll keep mum for another couple of months and then go there again. During the March holidays I shall be staying put—I shall be even busier than during term time.[25]

There were few interruptions, and Solzhenitsyn was anxious not to allow any, although he did make an exception for an unexpected visitor from Novocherkassk. It is not clear from Reshetovskaya's version of this episode how the visitor had obtained Solzhenitsyn's name or whether her arrival at their home was accidental. At all events she was a stranger, Dr Anna Dzhigurda, and she was travelling in search of a cure for her geologist son who had recently contracted cancer. Solzhenitsyn gave her a portion of the mandrake root and told her about the birch fungus that was supposed to help. In return Dr Dzhigurda, a surgeon, asked whether she might examine Solzhenitsyn, to which he agreed. "You were born lucky!" she exclaimed when she had completed her examination. His tumour, she said, had detached itself from his body and shrivelled. There was no more danger.[26] A few years later, when he came to write *Cancer Ward*, Solzhenitsyn modelled the figure of the young geologist, Vadim Zatsyrko, on Dr Dzhigurda's son.

Another interruption provoked mixed feelings in Solzhenitsyn. In February 1962 Nikolai Vitkevich moved to Ryazan to take up a post as a senior lecturer in chemistry at the Ryazan Medical Institute. Natalia looked forward eagerly to meeting Nikolai and his wife once more and renewing their old friendship, but Solzhenitsyn was not thrilled. "They'll start visiting us. We'll have to exchange presents."[27] Times had changed since the climax of their friendship during their years at the front, and Solzhenitsyn anticipated little pleasure from Nikolai's arrival now. Nevertheless, a childhood friend was a childhood friend. The Vitkeviches were welcomed on arrival, and soon the four were going on bicycle rides together and meeting at one another's homes. Despite his forebodings, Solzhenitsyn did attempt to be sociable.

By the time of the May holiday, Solzhenitsyn had finished his revision of *The First Circle* and was ready to hide several copies of it before allowing himself to relax. At least one of them went with him to Moscow, where he learned that not much had happened to *Ivan Denisovich* in the four months he had been away. Tvardovsky was perplexed as to how to approach the problem of publication. If he set the work in type and submitted it to the censorship, they were bound to reject it, and there was every chance they would report the book's existence to the Central Committee or the KGB, and that would irrevocably stop it.

The point was that Khrushchev's renewal of his de-Stalinization campaign at the Twenty-second Congress had not been quite the success the liberals had hoped for. The congress had not endorsed all of Khrushchev's proposals, the final resolutions made almost no mention of "mass repressions" under Stalin (a key phrase of Khrushchev's that had indicated an intention to go well beyond the resolutions of the Twentieth Congress), and the idea of a monument to the victims of Stalinism had been completely dropped.

Khrushchev's weakness was masked, however, by feverish activity both at home and abroad. In foreign affairs he intensified the Berlin crisis and threatened to sign a separate peace treaty with East Germany. He resumed the dialogue with Marshal Tito, a move that was intimately linked with de-Stalinization and was strongly opposed by many members of the Presidium. And, most significantly of all, he made the decision to send ballistic missiles to Cuba. At home he continued to attack Stalin in public, and in April promulgated a decree that cancelled awards, dating back to March 1944, to seven hundred former NKVD officers for the "exemplary execution of government tasks." These tasks were not specified but probably referred to the mass deportations of Ukrainians, Crimean Tartars, and other peoples from territories recaptured from the Germans towards the end of the war. The period covered by these awards, incidentally, included the time when Solzhenitsyn was arrested and affected all ranks of the security police, up to and including the former head of Smersh, Sergei Kruglov. It was another straw in the wind that Bukharin's widow was received by Khrushchev and apparently assured that her husband would be officially exonerated of the "crimes" he was alleged to have committed.*

To all appearances, then, the omens were mixed, and the main tide was not running quite so strongly for Khrushchev as appeared at the time. The main body of the Party remained suspicious of Khrushchev's domestic reforms and were made uneasy by his adventures in foreign policy. They preserved, at best, a silent neutrality between him and his opponents, waiting to see which side would win, while the conservatives made it clear that they were still a force to be reckoned with. Khrushchev therefore needed allies in his struggle for change, and he was well aware that his most reliable and eager supporters were to be found among the intellectuals.

Of all the literary intellectuals, Tvardovsky was the most prominent and most influential supporter of the Khrushchev line, and thanks to his seat in the Central Committee had a good view of the power struggle in progress there. He also had a shrewd idea of just how strong the conservatives still were, and he resolved not only that it would be necessary to circumvent them if *Ivan Denisovich* were to be published but also that its best chance lay in its being offered to Khrushchev as a weapon in his struggle for more reform. Tvardovsky therefore decided to compose a preface that would present the

---

* In the end Bukharin was not rehabilitated.

story in this light and to look for a Party connection who could get the manuscript to Khrushchev.

Meanwhile, he was basking in the reflected glory of his discovery and showing the manuscript to various luminaries in the literary establishment. One of the first to read it had been the venerable and universally loved critic and children's writer Kornei Chukovsky, to whom Tvardovsky had shown it when they were both relaxing in the government resort area of Barvikha. Chukovsky had at once recognized the story's quality and had congratulated Tvardovsky on his discovery of a major talent. Later he had the idea of writing a report on the story and sending it to Tvardovsky "in case it should come in handy for you." Headed "A Literary Miracle," the report was unstinted in its praise. Shukhov, wrote Chukovsky, was a generalized portrait of the Russian common man: resilient, stubborn, hardy, jack of all trades, cunning, and kind-hearted"—a close kin to Vasily Tyorkin. The story was written in a wonderfully pure and traditional Russian with an admixture of camp slang, which did not draw attention to itself but seemed as natural as breathing. The theme was tragic—the evil repression inflicted on innocent men over a long period of years, and their suffering at the hands of "armed scoundrels"—yet the author had not taken the path of easy indignation and fierce denunciations, and "in this lies his greatest achievement: nowhere does he express his passionate rage. He is not a polemicist but a historian."

Chukovsky noted that "this story marks the entry into our literature of a powerful, original and mature writer. . . . In every scene the author chooses the line of maximum resistance and every time is victorious." He warned Tvardovsky against trying to tinker with the text or edit it, pointing out that its apparent eccentricities showed the writer's mastery of the Russian language, not his weakness, even if a few of the near-obscenities would have to be toned down or removed. Otherwise, there was nothing in it that could not pass the censorship, for the story dealt with events that were past and was "totally dedicated to the glory of Russian man." It would be terrible to think that such a story might not see the light of day.[28]

Chukovsky's comments about the censorship and the story's innocuousness were clearly intended for Tvardovsky to show to the higher powers, and his report gave Tvardovsky the idea of collecting similar reports from other outstanding Soviet writers, since this would create a momentum for the story and help convince the political bosses that this was indeed an exceptional work of literature. He drew up a short list of authors to show it to: Paustovsky, Marshak, Fedin, and Ehrenburg. In the case of Ehrenburg, Tvardovsky was for some reason unwilling to act as the go-between himself and persuaded a reluctant Solzhenitsyn to deliver the manuscript personally. It turned out that Ehrenburg was away, but Solzhenitsyn was astonished to learn from his secretary, Natalia Stolyarova, that he had already read it. So had Stolyarova. She praised it and said she was especially pleased that Stalin wasn't even mentioned in it.* "However," she added, "I don't understand

*Stolyarova had herself served a sentence in the labour camps (after her voluntary return to the Soviet Union from Paris). She also gave Solzhenitsyn information for *The Gulag Archipelago*.

why it wasn't written from the point of view of an intellectual."[29]

In the event, Ehrenburg declined to write a report on the novel, as did Fedin. Privately, Fedin assured Tvardovsky that it was a hopeless enterprise and that he was wasting his time. Marshak, on the other hand, wrote in much the same vein as Chukovsky and made a crucial point that was to be taken up by many others when *Ivan Denisovich* was finally published: "Without exaggeration I may say that any Russian writer who reads it will make greater demands on himself, as will any reader of Russian literature. It would be unforgivable to keep this from readers."[30] Two critics, Mikhail Lifshits and E. Usiyevich, who had also been invited to comment, both insisted on the necessity of publication. Usiyevich followed Tvardovsky in comparing Solzhenitsyn to Tolstoy.

The content of these reports was concealed from Solzhenitsyn by Tvardovsky for fear of turning his head. But Solzhenitsyn was well aware that his underground reputation was growing. Anna Berzer, who had become his confidante and was the source of most of his information about events at *Novy Mir*, told him of the way the manuscript was unofficially going the rounds of Moscow. Tvardovsky was virtually ignorant of it, because the *Novy Mir* copies were strictly accounted for and lent only to selected authors for very short periods. Nevertheless, one night was enough to copy it, as Solzhenitsyn learned when he heard how four typists had recently done just that. There was a rumour that Ehrenburg had photocopied it and lent his photocopy to friends, and that someone had memorized whole pages of it and was reciting them as a party piece. Typical of the average response was that of a colleague of Anna Berzer's at *Novy Mir*, who said to Solzhenitsyn one day, "If I had to sacrifice my career to get *Ivan Denisovich* into print, I would gladly do it."[31]

Solzhenitsyn had vowed from the moment of the story's acceptance by *Novy Mir* that he wouldn't allow success to go to his head, and formal public success was still a long way off, but even this limited acclaim was powerfully flattering. "After the unbroken silence of my underground existence," he later wrote in his memoir, "two dozen such readers made me feel that the eyes of the crowd were upon me and that my fame was growing dizzily."[32]

The one remark that rankled and that he was to hear over and over again in one version or another was Stolyarova's comment that it would have been better to show the labour camp through the eyes of an intellectual. Solzhenitsyn totally disagreed, and at some point wrote the following explanation of his reasons for not doing so.

> Of course, it would have been simpler and easier to write about an intellectual (doubtless thinking of oneself all the while: "What a fine fellow I am and how I suffered"). But I decided to choose Shukhov as the line of greatest resistance. I was helped in this by the fact that, having been flung together with Shukhov in the same sort of conditions, wearing the same padded jacket and doing the same sort of work, a complete nobody as far as the others were concerned and indistinguishable from the rest of them (educational qualifications played no role at all and were if anything a point against you; your education seemed irredeemably

lost), I had a chance to feel exactly the same as they. The effect was all the more complete in that our sentences were perceived as endless. This was our "lucky" advantage over writers in the nineteenth century! Inspired by a great love for their "juniors" and feelings of self-sacrifice, those writers often did not spare themselves in their efforts to draw close to the people, but nonetheless it was impossible for them to enter into the common people's skins: the muzhik mistrusted them and sensed that they were still noblemen, while they themselves, even when ploughing the soil, could never lose sight of the fact that once they had finished work, they would return to a clean house, take a bath, and sit down to a substantial meal.[33]

Solzhenitsyn had made the same point in *The First Circle* when describing Gleb Nerzhin's experiences with "the people," and it was true. No matter how many similarities there might be between the literary philosophies of a Tolstoy and a Solzhenitsyn, the gulf between their life experiences was vast and unbridgeable, resulting in a fundamentally different approach to their subject matter. But there was another point to Solzhenitsyn's literary strategy in this tale that does not emerge from his statement. By making his hero a common peasant, Solzhenitsyn was able to seize the essence of the labour-camp experience and universalize it. An intellectual hero would have been less typical and more particular, diluting the story's power and impact. There were also temperamental reasons for preferring a peasant hero. Solzhenitsyn was not a city intellectual in the sense that his present admirers were, and he had perhaps subconsciously acknowledged this fact by his identification with Shukhov. At the same time he revealed in his choice of hero, also perhaps subconsciously, that he fully shared certain Soviet prejudices concerning the proper subject matter for serious literature.

24

A TRUE HELPER
OF THE PARTY

On his return from Moscow to Ryazan, Solzhenitsyn started planning a summer holiday visit to Siberia. It was to be his first, and he was anxious to see some of the popular landmarks—Lake Baikal, the Enisei River—that formed part of the itinerary of almost all Soviet tourists to the region.

He and Natalia set off at the end of June. Solzhenitsyn disliked the constraints of rail travel, the submission to timetables, and the fuss and bother of catching trains, but he had no choice. "Of course, it's not our style of travel," he wrote to the Zubovs from one of their stopping places. "There are too many changes of train, too many stations, and too little fresh air. You travel not on your muscles but on your nerves. But there is no other way of visiting such distant places."[1]

The journey out took almost a week, and on one of their legs Solzhenitsyn had a chance meeting that he was later to describe in *The Gulag Archipelago*. He found himself sitting beside a young MVD officer who had just completed his training at the Tavda Academy and was on his way to start work in the Irkutsk labour-camp complex. The MVD officer was friendly and talkative and told Solzhenitsyn what a mess the camps had fallen into since Khrushchev's liberalization of them, and how insolent and hostile the prisoners had become. Back in 1954 (when Solzhenitsyn was in exile), when the liberalization process began, it had been even worse, with the prisoners flatly refusing to work and buying themselves television sets with their own money. The young officer waxed indigant at the very memory of it, quite unaware of who it was beside him, drawing him on with innocent questions and sympathetic commiseration. Yet, as Solzhenitsyn realized, he was not a bad young fellow. It was simply that his training, his surroundings, and the company he kept all conspired to convince him that labour-camp prisoners were a desperate, cruel, ungrateful, and virtually subhuman race who deserved no understanding or sympathy whatsoever and who responded only to compulsion and force. Doubtless he described this angry diatribe when he called on one of his old Ekibastuz friends, Yuri Karbe, who was now living in Sverdlovsk.

In due course the Solzhenitsyns reached Lake Baikal and were impressed by its grandeur. "Baikal is astonishing," Solzhenitsyn wrote to the Zubovs, "and somehow the word 'sacred' doesn't seem out of place."* They spent several days exploring its shores and day-dreamed of building a cottage there, a project that Solzhenitsyn humorously described in that same letter to the Zubovs. "We've chosen a 'Happy Valley' where we've decided to build our cottage (300 steps above the railway line). There will be a small halt below, water from a mountain spring, solar panels on the roof to charge our batteries during the day, and paths and summer-houses among the cliffs."[2]

After they had been to Sludyanka, at the southern tip of Lake Baikal, they learned from Maria in Ryazan that a telegram had arrived from Tvardovsky, asking Solzhenitsyn to go at once to *Novy Mir*. She had informed Tvardovsky that Solzhenitsyn was in Siberia but that he could be contacted care of the post office in Krasnoyarsk, some five hundred miles west of Baikal, through which he would be passing on his return journey. Solzhenitsyn was extremely reluctant to cut short his holiday. Siberia was such an immense distance away and it had been such a huge enterprise to get there that he did not wish to waste the opportunity. But Tvardovsky's telegram awaiting him in Krasnoyarsk contained exciting news: "Cable immediately chances short visit Moscow re preparation manuscript for setting."[3]

Setting was an immense step forward. It was the stage at which the work would have to be submitted to the censorship, and Tvardovsky wouldn't have decided on it unless he had good reason to believe it would pass. Solzhenitsyn had wanted to spend some days travelling down the river Enisei, but he decided to omit that part of his journey and return to Moscow by 21 July. Tvardovsky was duly informed by telegram.

It was raining the night they arrived in Moscow. The following day, a Sunday, they hurried out to Zhukovka, a resort area on the outskirts of Moscow, where the Kopelevs had a dacha. "You're now the most popular man in Moscow," said Kopelev, "and I'm green with envy about it."[4] He told Solzhenitsyn of the praises being heaped on *Ivan Denisovich* by Chukovsky, Marshak, and the others, and about the large number of unofficial copies of the novel being passed from hand to hand. Some said there were as many as five hundred. Reports had come in of its being read as far afield as Kiev, Odessa, and Sverdlovsk. Readers were doubly anxious to grab it when they could because nobody believed that, with such a subject, it would ever get

---

* A reference to a well-known Soviet song that contains a line about "the sacred Baikal."

into print. Later, when Solzhenitsyn rang Anna Berzer, she told him that
the manuscript had been read and approved by no less a person than Khrushchev's private secretary, Vladimir Lebedev, who was proposing to show it
to Khrushchev himself. But before he did so, he wanted the author to make
certain changes, which was why Solzhenitsyn had been summoned from
Siberia.

The editorial conference to discuss these changes took place in the *Novy
Mir* boardroom at 1 p.m. on Monday, 23 July 1962. Everyone was there
again, just as at the first discussion of *Ivan Denisovich*, with the addition of a
newcomer, Vladimir Lakshin, who had just taken over the section of literary
criticism. Tvardovsky was beaming. He felt that his campaign for publication was at last beginning to bear fruit and that his unorthodox methods were
justified.

He explained to Solzhenitsyn how he and Dementyev, with some help
from Lakshin, had drafted a letter to Khrushchev in which they stated as the
unanimous opinion of the *Novy Mir* editorial board that *Ivan Denisovich* should
be published, and had requested Khrushchev to give the matter his personal
attention. (This unanimity was no fiction—Tvardovsky had insisted on taking a formal vote on it in June.) They had also quoted the favourable opinions
of several leading writers that Tvardovsky had collected through the spring
and summer. Instead of approaching Khrushchev directly, however (which
he might have done since they were personally acquainted), Tvardovsky had
judged it wiser to hand this material, together with a copy of the manuscript,
to Lebedev, who had since read the story and expressed his enthusiasm.
They had thus gained a valuable ally for the final approach to Khrushchev.

Tvardovsky then explained the changes that Lebedev wished to see made.
Most of them centred on the figure of Captain Buinovsky, the ex–naval commander and former Party member, who in the final pages is condemned to
the punishment cells for a heroic gesture of defiance. Solzhenitsyn had conceived and shown him semi-satirically, but Lebedev wanted the comedy toned
down so that Buinovsky could emerge as a "positive hero." He also wanted
Solzhenitsyn to moderate some of the language, particularly some of the camp
slang and the repeated references to the camp officers as "vermin." There
also had to be at least a token condemnation of the Ukrainian nationalists,
the Banderites (from Buinovsky if not from the narrator); the prisoners should
be shown as having some hope of freedom; and there should be a mention of
the fact that Stalin had been responsible for all these crimes.

When Tvardovsky had finished, he invited comments from the others,
and Dementyev took over; but whereas Tvardovsky's tone had been neutral
and dispassionate, Dementyev was more aggressive. He thoroughly agreed
with Lebedev's criticisms and had others of his own. The conversation about
the Eisenstein film *The Battleship Potemkin* was an insult to Soviet art and
should be cut. Shukhov's conversation with Alyoshka the Baptist about God
should also be cut, and there were many more criticisms in similar vein.
Dementyev had already irritated Solzhenitsyn by his refusal to attend the

discussion of his story about Matryona, and as early as his first visit to *Novy Mir* Solzhenitsyn had taken a dislike to Dementyev's hypocritical charm, which he regarded as a cover for political orthodoxy. Now Dementyev seemed to be standing in his way, dissipating the effects of Tvardovsky's reasonableness and infuriating Solzhenitsyn with his pedantry.

In *The Oak and the Calf* he describes himself replying as follows: "I have waited ten years and I can wait another ten. I'm in no hurry. My life doesn't depend on literature. Give me back my manuscript and I'll be on my way."⁵ Reshetovskaya repeats his description of this scene in her unpublished chapters, but also records (presumably basing herself on Solzhenitsyn's notes) that at one point his tone became more reasonable: "I will not agree to revisions that would destroy the harmony of my story or go against my conscience. . . . I cannot write for some particular category of readers, I have to reckon with my material, and I have a generalized reader in mind."⁶ Whatever the exact nature of his response, Tvardovsky was sufficiently alarmed to interject, "You don't *have* to do anything. Everything we've said today you can take or leave as you think fit. It's just that we all very much want the manuscript to get through."⁷

After this there was an awkward silence—the rest of the board-members had little to say. Only Lakshin joked that he was against removing Solzhenitsyn's veiled swear-words from the text, since he had started using some of them at home himself. Eventually, Solzhenitsyn agreed to take the manuscript away and work on it one more time, with a view to meeting Lebedev's objections. In his pocket diary he made a note next to the date, 23 July: "Difficult conference at N.M."⁸

He accomplished his task during the next three days. With Buinovsky he had no difficulties. It was no problem to reduce the comedy and stress his heroic side; and he did, after hesitation, put into the commander's mouth a criticism of the Banderites. Coming from a Party member and not the narrator, it sounded quite natural (although later, for another edition, he cut it again). It was also easy enough to tone down the language and slip in a reference to Stalin, which he did in the jokey style ("Old Whiskers") of his letters to Nikolai Vitkevich from the front. He drew the line at showing the prisoners hoping for freedom, however, and similarly refused to cut either the *Potemkin* or Alyoshka scenes.

On the whole he was well satisfied, as he wrote in a letter to the Zubovs while still engaged on this work.

> According to A.T. and Co. my story is making satisfactory progress. In literary circles there has been unprecedentedly unanimous praise: exceptionally favourable reports have come in from Chukovsky, Ehrenburg, and others. Before the last stage is tackled, I have been asked to carry out a bit more work on it, which I am doing now. Nobody is setting conditions that would cripple the book. I can hardly believe it—are we really so near?⁹

On 26 July, Solzhenitsyn handed in the revised manuscript to Anna Berzer. It is not clear how much of a hand Berzer herself had in the final editing. In Moscow literary circles she was known for her erudition and impeccable tact in handling authors and their manuscripts. She was also one of the few editors in the Soviet Union known to be totally on the author's side and adept at deceiving the censors. Certainly, she had early advised Solzhenitsyn not to make too many concessions in advance, since one could never know what would pass and what not (he later assessed the changes he made as amounting to less than one per cent of the text). Berzer was rapidly becoming the only person at *Novy Mir* whom Solzhenitsyn fully trusted.

As it turned out, he was not alone. Anna Berzer's office on the first floor of the *Novy Mir* building had become a kind of unofficial club for the liberal authors published by the magazine, where they would meet at five o'clock after a day's writing to toast "Asya," as she was affectionately called, exchange the latest gossip, and drink themselves under the table. Among the leading and more convivial members of this club were Victor Nekrasov, Vladimir Voinovich, and Naum Mendel (who published under the name of Naum Korzhavin); and on that evening of 26 July, Asya had promised them a rare treat: a meeting with the mysterious author of *A Day in the Life of Ivan Denisovich*.

The meeting was arranged at the request of Nekrasov, who had felt a sort of proprietary interest in the author ever since Tvardovsky had confided in him the morning after reading *Ivan Denisovich*. Nekrasov had also been astonished by the book and genuinely wished to express his admiration to the author, especially after hearing from Berzer what a charming and modest man he was. Solzhenitsyn, though generally avoiding Moscow literary circles, was not averse to meeting Nekrasov, for he in turn had deeply admired Nekrasov's best-known book, *In the Trenches of Stalingrad*, when he had read it in the camps in 1947 ("The book . . . wins you over with its *genuine* truth about war and is as different as heaven from earth from *everything* else that has been written about the war,"[10] he had told Natalia in one of his letters, adding that it made him nostalgic for his army days and covered the same subject matter as he had wanted to cover in his projected but unwritten war novel, *The Sixth Course*).

Solzhenitsyn's first social meeting with a group of Moscow writers turned out to be very agreeable, although as an abstemious man he was struck by the quantity of wine and vodka consumed (Nekrasov later recalled the occasion as remarkably sober by their usual standards). Nevertheless, he joined the toasts to *Ivan Denisovich*, literature, *Novy Mir*, and even Confucius—whose teaching Solzhenitsyn expounded to them and compared with Christ's. Nekrasov told Solzhenitsyn about his trips abroad and how difficult it had been, on a recent visit to Italy, to remain quiet about *Ivan Denisovich* when Soviet literature was criticized for its lack of realism.

Solzhenitsyn found Nekrasov animated, interesting, and sociable but was rather taken aback when Nekrasov suggested they pass to the "thou" form and call one another by their Christian names. The prim schoolmaster was unused to such metropolitan informality and agreed only after much hesitation. On a more serious note, Nekrasov praised Solzhenitsyn for his ability to describe a single camp in such a way that all camps were included and to write "Matryona" so that the whole countryside was described: "Tell me, how was it you were able to write 100 per cent truth? What's the secret of your art?" Solzhenitsyn replied disingenuously, "The secret is that when you've been pitched head first into hell you just write about it." Nekrasov wondered aloud what sort of impact *Ivan Denisovich* would have when it was published. Would it start a conflagration or would everything stay as before? Solzhenitsyn replied, "But it's not a sensational exposure; it's the people's point of view."[11]

The following day Solzhenitsyn went back to *Novy Mir* to hear whether the revisions he had made were acceptable. On this occasion his meeting was with Tvardovsky, Berzer, and the managing secretary, Boris Sachs. Tvardovsky and Berzer professed themselves satisfied, but Sachs wanted to cut more of the swear-words, and Solzhenitsyn agreed to remove another three. Tvardovsky then gave Solzhenitsyn a copy of his preface to read. Solzhenitsyn disliked the whole idea of a preface. Why couldn't the reader be left to make up his own mind, without being "prepared" in advance? And he particularly disliked the use of the word "happy" to describe Ivan Denisovich's day. It would seem that Tvardovsky had borrowed this idea from Chukovsky, who in his review had underlined the fact that this grim picture described a "happy day," and not one of the worst days. He had even, according to one report, suggested that this go into the title: "Ivan Denisovich's Happy Day," but this had not found favour with anyone. In response to Solzhenitsyn's objections, however, Tvardovsky agreed to remove the offending adjective.*

Tvardovsky still declined to show Solzhenitsyn the opinions written by Chukovsky, Marshak, and the others. He didn't want to spoil Solzhenitsyn, he said, to which the latter responded that the time for spoiling him was already past. And it was true, for the words "genius," "a work of genius," and similar extravagant praises were to be heard from all sides, and Solzhenitsyn had already been told by Kopelev of the gist of the famous writers' reports. Yet he remained in total command of himself and, while exulting inwardly, had steadfastly refused to betray any outward emotion. "You are taking this thing much more calmly than any of us," Anna Berzer had said to him one day. "We are all worried, but you're not." This was not quite so. Reshetovskaya notes that he was tense and wound up, finding it difficult to sleep, and had started taking bromide at night.[12]

Tvardovsky's last words as Solzhenitsyn left the *Novy Mir* office were to ask whether he had anything else to offer them. "In my view," replied Solzhenitsyn, "it's now up to *Novy Mir* to do its bit. When that happens, I won't be slow to follow it up."[13]

For the second half of the summer holidays, Solzhenitsyn planned to

---

* Tvardovsky had probably been misled by a phrase in the concluding lines of *Ivan Denisovich* indicating that it had been "almost a happy day." To call it "happy" without qualification, however, would have been a distortion of Solzhenitsyn's meaning.

take to his bicycle again. He had arranged to tour the Baltic States with his rediscovered friend Leonid Vlasov, for which purpose he took his bicycle on the train to Riga. Apart from the physical exercise and the chance to see new places, however, he had another motive for seeing Vlasov. He wanted Vlasov to repeat the story of an episode that he had been involved in at the beginning of the war and that he had first told Solzhenitsyn during their chance meeting on the train from Moscow to Rostov in 1944. Solzhenitsyn had never forgotten it and now wished to write a short story about it—he felt it was just what he needed for offering to *Novy Mir*. The title was already in his mind.

The holiday was interesting and successful. Solzhenitsyn returned bronzed and slimmer, with three rolls of film he had shot on the trip. But almost immediately he was forced to take to his bed with an attack of sciatica, a legacy of the camps. In order not to waste any time, he occupied himself in bed with revising *The Light Which Is in Thee*. Sufficient criticism had now accumulated to make him thoroughly dissatisfied with it, and he continued to work on it throughout the first half of September.

Meanwhile, the decisive moment had arrived in Tvardovsky's campaign to have *Ivan Denisovich* approved at the highest level. Khrushchev was spending the summer in the south and had left for the Crimea at about the time when Solzhenitsyn went to Riga, at the end of July. On 6 August 1962, Tvardovsky sent the revised manuscript to Lebedev, who was still in Moscow, together with his covering letter to Khrushchev and the selection of reviews. For about a month afterwards, nothing much happened, except that Dmitri Polikarpov, head of the cultural section of the Central Committee, rang Tvardovsky and asked for a copy. This was rather surprising, since the whole point of approaching Lebedev and Khrushchev had been to outflank Polikarpov, a notorious reactionary. However, news of the story's special status must have percolated to a very high level, for Polikarpov rang back later to say he would not oppose publication.

On 7 September, Khrushchev received the American poet Robert Frost, who was in the Soviet Union as part of the Soviet-American cultural exchange programme, at his villa in Pitsunda, on the Black Sea coast. Ironically, Tvardovsky was supposed to be in America carrying out the Soviet part of the exchange, but he was indisposed and could not go. Frost was accompanied by Lebedev and the Soviet poet Alexei Surkov, formerly head of the Writers' Union. According to Reshetovskaya (whose unpublished chapters contain the fullest account of these events), Lebedev and Surkov began talking about *Ivan Denisovich* in Khrushchev's presence. "What's that?" Khrushchev allegedly said. "What are you concealing from me?" [14] And when Lebedev explained, he demanded to see the manuscript.

Oddly enough (in Reshetovskaya's account), Lebedev had forgotten to bring the manuscript with him and was obliged to fly to Moscow to get it. Returning, he is said to have read extracts aloud to Khrushchev sometime between 9 and 14 September, deliberately choosing the "positive" scene of the building of the generating station for his main emphasis. Halfway through, Khrushchev summoned Mikoyan to listen, too, and is said to have been particularly touched by the way that Ivan Denisovich, when laying bricks, so carefully husbanded his mortar.

When the story was finished, Khrushchev asked Lebedev why Tvardovsky didn't simply go ahead and publish it. Lebedev pointed out that it was not so easy and reminded Khrushchev of the difficulties Tvardovsky had experienced with his own poem *Distant Horizons*. Khrushchev then said that both he and Mikoyan approved of Solzhenitsyn's story and saw no reason why it could not be published.

Khrushchev and his entourage returned to Moscow almost immediately after the reading, and on 16 September 1962, Lebedev rang Tvardovsky: "Trifonich, there is justice in this world!" That same day, Anna Berzer despatched a letter to Ryazan bearing the glad tidings: "Now we can say that *Ivan D* is on the very threshold. We are expecting news any day."[15] But there was still no official word from the Central Committee, and Tvardovsky was on tenterhooks. "If they refuse I'll resign," he is said to have threatened to his colleagues. Finally, at midday on 21 September, he received his promised call, but it was not at all what he had expected. "Deliver us twenty-three copies by tomorrow morning!"[16]

Tvardovsky was flabbergasted. He did not possess twenty-three copies. He had deliberately kept the number down so as not to let the story circulate (he was unaware of just how many *were* circulating, and it was certainly not his fault). To type up twenty-three copies was out of the question in a single night, so he grasped at the only other possibility: a limited printing of the necessary copies. *Novy Mir* didn't have its own presses, it was a dependency of *Izvestia*. Tvardovsky rang the head of *Izvestia's* printing department and arranged to have four machines set aside from printing *Izvestia* that night and reserved for printing twenty-five copies of *Ivan Denisovich*.

Berzer and Kondratovich were put in charge of the operation and allotted four proof-readers and an equivalent number of type-setters. For the latter the text presented major problems of style, spelling, and vocabulary. It was a far cry from the dull and cliché-ridden speeches of government leaders. Nor did the unorthodox nature of the contents escape them, though they were sworn to secrecy about this strange project. They worked feverishly through the night, and at dawn the next morning the copies were bound in the distinctive light-blue covers of *Novy Mir* and the plates locked away in the *Izvestia* strong-room. Later that morning twenty-three copies were delivered to the offices of the Central Committee and the remaining two to Tvardovsky (one of which he later presented to Solzhenitsyn).

Khrushchev ordered the copies to be distributed to members of the Party Presidium, and on 23 September departed for Central Asia to inspect the virgin lands and look into agriculture there. Three days later Solzhenitsyn arrived in Moscow for a short visit. Apart from Berzer's vague letter of the sixteenth, he knew nothing of the past month's events and immediately telephoned her for the latest news. "Tell me just one thing. Has he read it?"

"Yes. He liked it." Solzhenitsyn hurried round to see her, and she told him the whole story. He was naturally elated. Returning to Ryazan, he commented to Natalia, "I never thought that my entry into literature would be like this, that people would be so full of enthusiasm. . . . People have a desire to touch something that's clean."[17] Fired on by this good news, he worked away at the Vlasov story, which at that stage bore the title of "The Green Cap."

The Presidium held its meeting sometime in the middle of October. Nobody knows exactly what went on there, or indeed whether there was one meeting or two. In his own memoir Solzhenitsyn refers to only one meeting, but others, including Zhores Medvedev,* maintain that *Ivan Denisovich* was discussed at two meetings. According to them, the first time it came up on the agenda several members announced that they had not had time to read it. Other members—identified by rumour as Frol Kozlov and Mikhail Suslov—objected to the book, pointing out that the camp guards ought not to have been depicted so unfavourably. Yet another source has Khrushchev wagging his finger at the pair of them and declaring, "How can we fight against the remnants of the personality cult if Stalinists of this type are still among us?"[18] At another point he is reported to have said, "There's a Stalinist in each of you; there's even some of the Stalinist in me. We must root out this evil."[19]

If these reports are to be believed, Khrushchev did not get his way the first time, and the matter was raised at a second meeting one or two days later. Now there was mainly silence, although someone is supposed to have asked, "Whose mill would it be grist to?"[20] Goaded by this general lack of enthusiasm, Khrushchev demanded, "Why don't you say something?" And when no discussion was forthcoming, he said, "There's a Russian proverb that says silence is consent."[21] The resolution to publish was proposed by Khrushchev and seconded by Mikoyan. One last remark by Khrushchev later passed into Moscow folklore: "This isn't a campaign, it's a policy."[22]

Tvardovsky was unofficially informed of the result by Lebedev on 15 October 1962, but it was another five days before he received a copy of the official resolution. For this he was summoned to a personal meeting with Khrushchev, which lasted for more than two hours. Khrushchev, he later reported, was in a mellow, philosophical mood. He praised *Ivan Denisovich* as a life-enhancing work that was fully in the spirit of the Twenty-second Congress. It would have been harmful, however, if not so well written. Some people had wanted the camp administration to be presented in a more sympathetic light, but he had retorted, "What do you think it was, a holiday resort?" Khrushchev commented on the strange way the book had been presented for his approval and said he found the whole process abnormal. "What have we got the state machinery for?"[23] he asked irritably. However, he did not go back on his permission to publish.

Perhaps it was at this point that Tvardovsky raised the question of the

* In *Ten Years after Ivan Denisovich.*

censorship, for it is generally known that he seized the opportunity of this meeting to suggest to Khrushchev that the censorship be lifted altogether. "Babies aren't made by kisses," Tvardovsky later reported himself as saying. "Why don't you abolish the censorship of imaginative literature? Books are circulating in illegal copies—what could be worse than that?"[24]

According to Zhores Medvedev, Tvardovsky was deeply convinced of the need to abolish the censorship and had gone to the meeting with Khrushchev intending to argue for such a step. His contention was that editors were far more responsible and experienced than censors, since censors, for the most part, came from among the less successful employees of the publishing houses. "I mean, you wouldn't give them my job, would you? So why can't I, a member of the Party's Central Committee, a writer and an editor, decide whether or not to publish a particular story or a poem? After all, our entire editorial staff discusses it and comes to a decision—and then some total stranger from Glavlit, some fool who understands nothing about literature, goes and blue-pencils our decisions."[25]

According to both Solzhenitsyn and Medvedev, Khrushchev heard Tvardovsky out with some sympathy. In Medvedev's version, Khrushchev is even said to have expressed enthusiasm over the recent decision to stop censoring foreign correspondents: "We lifted the censorship on foreign correspondents and look what happened. Nothing. They told rather fewer lies."[26] Solzhenitsyn, however, feels that Tvardovsky took an over-optimistic view of Khrushchev's reactions and fell into the trap of attributing to the Soviet leader what were essentially his own opinions. But even in this more pessimistic version, Khrushchev is not seen as contradicting Tvardovsky's assertions.

In respect of the censorship their conversation remained inconclusive, but the more important practical matter was resolved. *Ivan Denisovich* could be printed. Returning to his office, Tvardovsky at once dispatched a telegram to Solzhenitsyn in Ryazan, which reached him that same Saturday evening. "Story appearing eleventh number magazine congratulations—Tvardovsky."[27] The following day Solzhenitsyn replied.

Dear Alexander Trifonovich,
      I had lately been of the opinion (and become completely resigned to the idea) that *Ivan Denisovich* wouldn't get through. So much the more unexpected and pleasant was it to receive your telegram yesterday, for which many thanks.[28]

And the day after that he wrote to the Zubovs.

Dear friends,
      As an amusing example of something that in, say, the late autumn of 1953,* I never thought I would live to see, let me inform you that *Ivan Denisovich* has been *passed for publication.* . . . I realize how radically my life is changing, what

* I.e., when Solzhenitsyn was in exile and had his second bout of cancer.

great spiritual opportunities are opening up before me, and also what spiritual dangers (fame, success, loss of conscience and feeling, hack-work). . . . At the moment I'm overwhelmed and have lots of letters to write, so please forgive my brevity.[29]

His mood continued to be one of suppressed joy. Had he allowed his natural exuberance free rein, he would have shouted his victory to the roof-tops, but years of camp training followed by more years of concealment and dissimulation had taught him to discipline his emotions and hold them in check. His natural optimism had been overlaid by a pessimism born of bitter experience, and a superstitious fear of the worst. It was for this reason that he had replied to Tvardovsky in such sober terms and kept up his bantering tone with the Zubovs, although with the latter he had allowed himself to strike a more solemn chord. But this stoicism exacted a price. According to Reshetovskaya, he began to dream more frequently. One night it was Khrushchev stopping a train and making Solzhenitsyn board it. Another night he dreamt that a big conference was in progress and that someone came out and announced that *Ivan Denisovich* had been passed for printing, after which he was surrounded by eager students of literature. On still another occasion he dreamt he was at a concert given by the well-known conductor Konstantin Ivanov and the pianist Bella Davidovich, but when the conductor bent for-wards to speak to her they turned into Tvardovsky and Anna Berzer.

Yet things seemed to be going his way. On Sunday 21 October 1962, without a word of explanation, *Pravda* published "The Heirs of Stalin," an anti-Stalinist poem by Evtushenko, in which he warned against those Stalin-ists who still held positions of power and wanted to turn back the clock. Like *Ivan Denisovich*, Evtushenko's poem was well known in Moscow literary cir-cles and had begun to circulate privately. Its sudden publication in such an authoritative organ signalled a victory for the liberals and a blow against the conservatives.

One week later, Solzhenitsyn was called to Moscow to correct the proofs. It turned out that these were the page-proofs—the final stage. As he later discovered, he was supposed to have corrected the galleys as well, but these had not been shown to him, evidently for fear that he would take back some of the changes he had agreed to. At the page-proof stage, it was impossible to make any alterations of substance.

As it happened, he had just completed his new story based on the epi-sode related to him by Leonid Vlasov, which was now called "Incident at Kochetovka Station." The episode concerned a middle-aged man who had turned up unexpectedly at a small railway station behind the front lines in the early part of the war and reported to the local commander that he had become separated from the train transporting him to the rear. He was one of several hundred soldiers who had escaped from German encirclement and were being sent to the rear to be reallocated to new units. The suspicions of the commander, a young Red Army lieutenant, were aroused by the man's evident good breeding, his "prerevolutionary" manners, and an extraordinary slip of the tongue whereby he referred to Stalingrad by its pre-revolutionary name of Tsaritsyn. The lieutenant concluded that the man was a White Russian spy who had been infiltrated through the lines at the front, and handed him over to the NKVD, knowing full well that he was condemning the man, who protested his innocence, to either death or a long prison sentence.

In Solzhenitsyn's hands the story became a parable, similar in construction to "The Right Hand" in that the reader is left to ponder the revelation that occurs just before the story's end, though the victim, Tveritinov, is an innocent sufferer like Matryona, not an agent of repression. The story is narrated by the young commander—Lieutenant Vasili Zotov, in whom Solzhenitsyn portrayed, and satirized, his own younger self: puritanical, loyal, naïve, idealistic, and fatally narrow in his blind devotion to the Soviet cause. The tragedy of the story, as told by Solzhenitsyn, is that Zotov likes Tveritinov and is drawn to him. He treats him with friendly sympathy right up until the fatal slip over Tsaritsyn, when his Soviet education and Red Army training, with their emphasis on the eternal need for vigilance, take over and cancel out this fellow-feeling at a stroke. His friendliness gives way to mortification as he suspects he has been taken in, and his subsequent hostility enables him to send Tveritinov to possible death on the slenderest thread of suspicion.

Solzhenitsyn's descriptions of the station behind the front lines and of the chaos and turmoil of the first year of the war were among the best things he had yet done, and the picture of his younger self as Zotov was richer and more three-dimensional than the autobiographical characters in the plays (in his stories up till now, the narrators had been merely observers). But "Incident" was nowhere near as tightly written as his other stories and showed a lamentable tendency to want to turn itself into a novel. There were numerous irrelevant sub-plots, and Solzhenitsyn seemed over-anxious to stuff in as much information and comment as he could (perhaps sensing that this was the nearest he would ever get to writing his novel about the war). The result was a baggy and shapeless holdall that could have done with considerable pruning before publication.

Nevertheless, Solzhenitsyn had once again displayed his talent for putting his finger on the sore spots of recent Soviet history. Among the many controversial subjects he raised in this short work were the Soviet Union's disastrous start to the war; Stalin's leading role in that disastrous start; the relative indifference of the peasants near the front as to who was winning the war; the ill treatment of soldiers who had escaped from German captivity or encirclement; and the hidden tyranny of the secret police, who continued to monitor and control the movements of Soviet soldiers and the Soviet populace even at the time of their most harrowing and tragic defeats at the beginning of the war. In his asides and comments, Solzhenitsyn was even able to bring in the thirties (as he had done in *Ivan Denisovich*), but the main emphasis was on the multiple tragedies of the war.

On the night before his departure to Moscow to check the proofs, Solzhenitsyn read his just-completed story to Natalia and to Alexandra Popova, who was staying with them for a few days, and was pleased by their praise. But as he travelled up to the capital, he was aware of a menacing storm hanging not only over him but over the entire country, a crisis that threatened just as effectively as any local or literary conflict to sweep his story away—the Cuban crisis, which had just reached its climax. Nearly a week had passed since President Kennedy had called Khrushchev's bluff over the rockets on Cuba by displaying aerial photographs of them and announcing his blockade. The question on everybody's lips was: Will Khrushchev tell his ships to run the gauntlet? Given Khrushchev's unpredictability, no one could say with any certainty whether he would or he wouldn't.

It was the eve of the November holiday, exactly a year since he had agreed to send his story to *Novy Mir*. This time, instead of staying in an obscure hotel in the suburbs, he had been booked into the luxurious Ukraine Hotel near the centre, all expenses paid by *Novy Mir*. He found the editorial offices in a festive mood. Raisa Orlova had told him how members of the editorial staff had embraced one another and done no work the preceding Monday, when they heard the news of permission to publish. "If only you knew how many people were jumping with joy, and very good people too!"[30] Now the staff gave him the latest news. Literary Moscow was agog at the prospect of seeing *Ivan Denisovich* in print. *Novy Mir* had been inundated with phone calls. The girls who did the proof-reading had gushed over Shukhov and exclaimed over the names Solzhenitsyn had given some of his characters: Volkovoi (meaning "wolfish"), Alyoshka, with its echoes of Dostoyevsky. "Now a new literature is beginning," said one of the editors.[31]

Solzhenitsyn did not see Tvardovsky on this occasion, but Boris Sachs passed on to him one last request from Lebedev. This was to remove one religious remark put into the mouth of the brigade leader Tiurin: "I crossed myself and said to God, 'Thou art there in heaven after all, Creator. Thy patience is long but thy blows are heavy.' " Playing for time, Solzhenitsyn said he would think about it and took the page-proofs back to his hotel. He sat there with the proofs on the desk before him and the radio on, listening to the latest news from Cuba. If there was to be a world conflagration, the proofs hardly seemed worth correcting. But that very weekend Khrushchev decided to back down, and the crisis began to subside. Solzhenitsyn's story would appear after all.

There remained the problem of what to do about Tiurin's invocation of the Lord. Certainly Solzhenitsyn owed Lebedev a favour. If it had not been for his energetic advocacy, the story would never have got into print at all. On the other hand, Tiurin was a key figure in the story, in some ways more important than Ivan Denisovich himself, for through him Solzhenitsyn had managed to contradict the whole official version of the history of the preceding twenty years and to smuggle in a true account of collectivization and the terror of the thirties. Lebedev had been right to spot the danger, though too late and too superficially. Solzhenitsyn pondered the request. Rereading the story, he found his camp days coming back to him, remembered his comrades and the cruel torments they had endured, and pictured their joy that at last the truth was emerging. For the first time, he writes in *The Oak and the Calf*, he wept over his tale, and realized he was bound to refuse.

During his brief stay in Moscow, Solzhenitsyn had two important meetings—with Anna Akhmatova and with Varlam Shalamov. It was Kopelev who took him to see Akhmatova on 28 October 1962.* Akhmatova was flattered to hear that Solzhenitsyn knew her *Poem without a Hero*† by heart. He told her he had found it difficult and obscure at first, but then it had become clear. She read some of her poems, and he praised her patriotism, calling her, in effect, "the soul of Russia." He also read some of his poetry to her, but she found his manner of reading strange and later told Lydia Chukovskaya that she had not been able to make much of it and that in poetry Solzhenitsyn was "vulnerable." For his prose, however, she had only the highest praise. She had read *Ivan Denisovich* in a samizdat copy and had said at the time, "I think that every one of the two hundred million citizens of the Soviet Union should read this story and learn it by heart." Now she was delighted to make his acquaintance, and the next day described him to Chukovskaya as "a bearer of light. Fresh, sharp, young, and happy. We've forgotten that such people exist. Eyes like precious stones. And stern: he listens to what he's saying." In Akhmatova's lexicon, according to Chukovskaya, this latter comment was the highest praise. Akhmatova asked Solzhenitsyn whether he realized that in a month he would be the most famous man on earth. Solzhenitsyn replied, "I've got strong nerves. I coped with Stalin's camps." But Akhmatova pointed out that Pasternak had not coped with fame. Fame was difficult to handle when it came late.[32]

The meeting with Shalamov must have been very different in tone. Shalamov had survived seventeen years in the notorious camps of Kolyma, in north-eastern Siberia, and had written a series of marvellous and carefully wrought stories about his experiences,‡ as well as some less interesting verse. Solzhenitsyn had always supposed that there must be other survivors like himself writing about the camps, but Shalamov was the only one who had come to his attention—in 1956 he had read some of his poems and had "trembled as I recognized a brother."[33] Later he acknowledged that "Shalamov's experience in the camps was longer and bitterer than my own, and I respectfully confess that to him and not to me was it given to touch those depths of

* Akhmatova was one of the candidates for the Nobel Prize that year (it was won by John Steinbeck).

† Akhmatova's long and complex poem is partly a distillation of memory, partly a meditation on history, and partly a poetical statement on Russia's destiny. It is regarded by many as the crowning achievement of her life's work, but has never been published in full in the Soviet Union.

‡ They have been translated into English in two volumes: *Kolyma Tales* (New York, 1980) and *Graphite* (New York, 1981), both translated by John Glad.

savagery and despair towards which life was dragging us all."[34] Solzhenitsyn
seems to have preferred Shalamov's verse to his prose (in *The Oak and the Calf*
he expresses the view that Shalamov's prose had suffered from the isolation
in which he had written it and that it could easily have been improved "with
no change in the range of material or the author's viewpoint"),[35] and at their
meeting he asked Shalamov to send him a selection so that Solzhenitsyn could
offer it to *Novy Mir*.

Before his departure for Ryazan, Solzhenitsyn was given the set of galley proofs that had been kept away from him by *Novy Mir* (marked "Author's
copy. Return by 25/10"), and also the twenty-fifth copy of the special edition
that had been printed for the Central Committee.

A few days after his return, he received a long letter from Tvardovsky,
in which the latter hastened to assure him that no harm had come of his
refusal to accept Lebedev's last suggestion. "Regarding that bit (where Tiurin
says that God exists), you perhaps went away feeling rather apprehensive,
but everything is all right, although I did have to 'seek advice' on that point—
one telephone call was enough to settle it."[36] Tvardovsky also gave Solzhenitsyn the annoying news that he and *Novy Mir* had been prevented from
being the first to write openly about the labour camps.

> God knows it's nothing special, but still it's happened all the same. *Izvestia* has
> just published a rubbishy story called "Rough Diamond," by one Georgi She-
> lest, where words like "nark," "grass," and "morning prayer" appear in print for
> the first time. The story's shit-awful, not worth bothering about.[37]

It turned out that Alexei Adzhubei, Khrushchev's son-in-law and editor-in-chief of *Izvestia*, having got wind of the impending publication of *Ivan
Denisovich*, had assembled his staff and harangued them for being too slow.
"Why is *Novy Mir* opening up such an important subject as the camps and
not us?" Someone had recalled that two years previously they had been sent
a story about the camps by a writer living in faraway Chita, almost on the
Chinese border, and that it had been rejected. There was no trace of it in the
office, but they had managed to trace the author, Georgi Shelest, and he had
dictated it over the telephone to them at *Izvestia*'s considerable expense. It
had then been rushed out on 6 November, in the newspaper's holiday number. In the event, the story's quality was so low that it sank without a trace,
to become merely a footnote to the saga of *Ivan Denisovich*, but Tvardovsky
was understandably upset by Adzhubei's cynical opportunism and later
snubbed him when Adzhubei tried to appear friendly.[38]

The third theme of Tvardovsky's letter was Solzhenitsyn's future and
the testing time that lay ahead of him after the publication of *Ivan Denisovich*.
Repeating Akhmatova's warning about the dangerous effects of fame ("the
brilliant rise of a big new name over the literary horizon"), Tvardovsky
expressed the hope that Solzhenitsyn would be able to preserve his dignity,
maturity, moral strength, and "the integrity of your wonderful talent." At
times, wrote Tvardovsky, he had wondered whether Solzhenitsyn's concern

for his integrity was not perhaps excessive, "amounting almost to indifference to the opportunities that the publication of *Ivan Denisovich* will open up to you," and Tvardovsky confessed that he had been a little hurt by Solzhenitsyn's guarded response to his telegram of congratulations, especially by "that feeble word 'pleasant'" to describe Solzhenitsyn's feelings, which Tvardovsky said he had found insulting. Nevertheless, it was now to Solzhenitsyn's self-restraint that he was appealing, and he hoped that Solzhenitsyn would resist the blandishments that would come his way to let other editors have "a little something" for their journals, to write screenplays, and so on. "Don't put yourself in anyone's hands, plead your prior commitment to *Novy Mir* (we have some right to hope for this), say that it takes everything that comes from your pen." In conclusion, Tvardovsky apologized for offering so much advice, "but your literary youth (despite the artistic maturity of your talent) obliges me to offer these words of caution, even if they are superfluous and perhaps even offend you."[39]

Solzhenitsyn appreciated the delicacy of Tvardovsky's letter ("Your letter was so friendly, even full of such love for me and concern over me, that I am deeply moved . . .") and wrote back at length. On seeing the fat letter from *Novy Mir*, he wrote, his first impulse had been that its editors wanted him to make more cuts. He said he was sorry if his self-restraint had caused offence, and apologized for having hurt Tvardovsky with the word "pleasant," but he added, "I should have been insincere if I had expressed myself more strongly. I felt no wild joy at the time. I may say that my whole life has trained me to expect the worst much more often than not. . . . In the camps I took to heart the Russian proverb 'Don't let good luck fool you, or bad luck frighten you.'" His greatest happiness had come, he wrote, when he learnt that Tvardovsky had found *Ivan Denisovich* worth a sleepless night. He was aware of the dangers of fame and would not let himself be devoured by it. "But I foresee that its duration will be brief, and I want to use it as sensibly as possible for the sake of the works I have already written."

Solzhenitsyn also wrote that he had long ago decided not to give a single interview or to reply to attacks on him in the newspapers, or even to reply to all the letters he received. He had been warned at the *Novy Mir* offices that plans were afoot to film his book, and had accepted the staff's advice not to get involved or to try to write the script. And he was prepared not to promise prose or verse to anyone but *Novy Mir*.[40]

The exchange showed the characters of the two men mostly at their best. Tvardovsky was warm, big-hearted, and generous, frankly delighted at the other man's success and eager to do everything he could to help. He was touchingly anxious for Solzhenitsyn's welfare, full of tactful advice and judicious comment on the pitfalls that lay ahead. At the same time he had the proprietary instincts of the editor, proud of his discovery and loyal to the new writer's talent, but also demanding loyalty in return and not hesitating to express his pique at what he took to be the younger man's ingratitude. Solzhenitsyn, for his part, responded graciously, underlined the areas where he was in agreement with Tvardovsky, and made it plain that he was fully prepared to take the older man's advice and consider himself a *"Novy Mir* author." It is true there were some reservations. Solzhenitsyn was careful to exclude "plays" from the works he would offer to *Novy Mir* (he had two more or less ready), and he stood his ground on the coolness of his response to Tvardovsky's congratulatory telegram, explaining it by his camp training. But it was all done with tact and understanding—reinforced by that extraordinary flash of insight ("I foresee that [fame's] duration will be brief") that was the hallmark of Solzhenitsyn's mature and sometimes piercing vision.

It is worth dwelling on this point because Solzhenitsyn later gave a slightly different picture in *The Oak and the Calf.* Taking the unsatisfactory nature of his subsequent relations with Tvardovsky as his starting point, he projected it back onto these early days of their friendship and implied the existence of a greater friction between them than seems to have been the case. In this sense, the unedited chapters of Reshetovskaya's memoirs are a useful corrective. Certainly, she had her own scores to settle with Solzhenitsyn by the time she came to write them, but there is nothing to suggest that she leaned to either side in her depiction of the two men's friendship. For instance, immediately after selectively quoting from his reply to Tvardovsky in *The Oak and the Calf*, Solzhenitsyn writes, "We were already on terms of such warm friendship, although we had never once met tête-à-tête, with none of his colleagues present. . . . Shortly afterwards I was at his home . . . ," and follows this with a matter-of-fact description of the delivery to Tvardovsky of an advance copy of *Novy Mir*'s November issue (containing *Ivan Denisovich*). "We embraced, and Alexander Trifonovich was as happy as a schoolboy,"[41] and so on. As usual in Solzhenitsyn's memoir, it is Tvardovsky's moods that are described and commented upon, usually slightly patronizingly, while the reader is left to conclude that Solzhenitsyn is unmoved.

The picture looks somewhat different in Reshetovskaya's version, however. First of all she quotes a further passage from Solzhenitsyn's letter to Tvardovsky.

> I've got another story ready to give to *Novy Mir*. I shall be very interested to hear your opinion of it. I was thinking of coming to see you and bringing it with me on 14 or 15 November. But now it seems you won't be there, so I'm wondering whether it's worth coming. Actually, all I want to do is deliver the story to the office as quickly as possible. . . .
> All last year I felt a desire to meet you sometime tête-à-tête, without the rest of the editorial board present, and ask your advice about all sorts of things that lie ahead. I hope we will find an opportunity in December or January? Or if it is convenient for you to come to Ryazan—be our guest.[42]

Reshetovskaya then describes how Tvardovsky responded with a telegram inviting Solzhenitsyn to come to his flat on the Kotelnicheskaya Embankment on either 15 or 16 November. Solzhenitsyn chose the fifteenth. "This was the meeting that my husband had so looked forward to," writes

Reshetovskaya, and she gives an account of the meeting as Solzhenitsyn had described it to her. Evidently the two men had talked excitedly for hours, interrupting one another, discussing their literary plans, other writers, literature in general, and agreeing on just about everything. Tvardovsky had been "tenderly solicitous" towards Solzhenitsyn and on receiving "Incident at Kochetovka station" had said tactfully, "It sometimes happens that one story is successful and the next one isn't," and had begged him not to lose heart if it was a failure. (In *The Oak and the Calf* Solzhenitsyn describes Tvardovsky as "very agitated when he took the story from me, and still more so as he read; he could not have dreaded failure more if the work had been his own.")

Reshetovskaya also describes the arrival of the proof copy of the November *Novy Mir* (omitting Solzhenitsyn's picture of the bulky Tvardovsky dancing about the room crying, "The bird is free! The bird is free!") and adds that although Tvardovsky offered it to Solzhenitsyn, the latter declined, "bringing away with him instead a rapt admiration for Tvardovsky and his childlike smile, which had somehow been miraculously preserved. . . . And when they parted, they embraced and kissed for the first time."[43]

Natalia was supposed to meet Solzhenitsyn at the station at ten o'clock that evening but bumped into him on the very threshold of their flat. He was standing there in his grey overcoat, clutching his grey brief-case, his face radiant. "My star has risen!" He told her that favourable reviews were due to appear in both *Pravda* and *Izvestia*. And according to her, he seemed "infatuated with Tvardovsky, and what he took to be the start of their true friendship."[44]

In these last days before the publication of *Ivan Denisovich*, Solzhenitsyn's life assumed an almost surreal quality. In Moscow the name of his story was on nearly everybody's lips, and its publication was awaited as a major political event. More and more people were becoming aware of the author's true name and identity, although the copies circulating still bore the original pseudonym A. Ryazansky. Sergei Ivashov-Musatov wrote that he had recently attended a gathering of a dozen old friends where the sole topic of conversation had been the keenly awaited publication of no. 11 of *Novy Mir*, which was to carry a sensational story by a previously unpublished author. "It turned out that by some sort of miracle *a half* of those present had *already* read the story and were fully aware of the author's name." They had been deeply impressed by the story's outstanding qualities and had said that all Moscow was agog and waiting for publication day. "I was astonished," wrote Sergei.

Vladimir Gershuni, his old Ekibastuz comrade, later wrote to say that he, too, had read the story "a month before publication," under the name A. Ryazansky, but had deduced who the author was after recognizing the description of Ekibastuz and particularly some of the characters, such as Buinovsky and Tsezar Markovich. "Naturally, after discovering who the real author was, I was so surprised that I blabbed about it, and rumours fly around

Moscow as fast as in camp." Other friends in the know wrote with congratulations and requests for copies—it was obvious that *Novy Mir* would sell out overnight.[45]

As a result of all this excitement, Solzhenitsyn could hardly sleep. He was still waiting anxiously to hear Tvardovsky's verdict on "Kochetovka," and was determined to exploit his impending fame by publishing as many works as he could. To this end he took out his labour-camp play *The Republic of Labour* and hastily revised it, changing the hero's name from Nerzhin to Nemov, emphasizing the romance between Nemov and Lyuba, and toning down some of the harsher expressions in the light of the experience he had gained in editing *Ivan Denisovich*. He also gave it a less political title, *The Tenderfoot and the Tart*, playing on a new vogue for camp slang that was beginning to take hold among Moscow intellectuals, and planned to take it to *Novy Mir* as soon as he and Natalia had retyped it.

Literary work was slowed, however, by his other duties. He still had to keep up his teaching and marking, and, as luck would have it, his school was being inspected during these crowded days of mid-November. On top of that, Solzhenitsyn was caught up in a curious episode concerning a fellow teacher of his, Mikhail Potapov.

Potapov was involved in a typical Soviet quarrel between neighbours over living-space and the desire of another family in the block where he lived to expand at his expense.* These neighbours, it appears, were also aching to get their revenge on Potapov's wife for having informed the authorities that some of them were drawing illegal pensions. As a result of their scheming, Potapov was framed on charges of having raped a fourteen-year-old gipsy girl who lived in the same building and of having sexually assaulted a five-year-old girl. The other teachers had first heard of these charges the preceding summer, when Potapov had been summoned to the city investigator's office and had never returned, but the trial was taking place only now, in November 1962, and it quickly became clear that the evidence was being rigged. Although excluded from the court-room, the teachers saw and heard the parents of key witnesses, all children, rehearsing them in the evidence they were to give and threatening them with dire punishment should they stumble or make a mistake.

The sentence was severe: twelve years in strict-regime labour camps. The teachers wrote a collective letter of protest to the court, as a result of which they were summoned one by one to the district Party headquarters and threatened with dismissal from their jobs for "casting aspersions on Soviet justice." Fortunately for Solzhenitsyn, impending fame made him invulnerable to the threats of the district Party, and he decided to take the matter further. No longer was he to be fettered by his anonymity and prison past. He knew that Potapov had already served nine years in the labour camps under Article 58 (the same article under which he himself had served) and

---

*This subject later found literary expression in *The Ivankiad*, by Vladimir Voinovich, translated by David Lapeza (New York, 1976; London, 1978).

that he had made things worse for himself by refusing to give false testimony
against a co-defendant. They were thus fellow veterans, and Solzhenitsyn
decided to use his position to write a protest to the Supreme Court. He was
also able to use his new Moscow connections to persuade an *Izvestia* reporter,
Olga Chaikovskaya, to investigate the case and give it publicity (it eventually
took three years to get the case reviewed).[46]

On Saturday, 17 November, Solzhenitsyn received a telegram from
Tvardovsky approving of "Kochetovka" and asking him to phone. When he
rang that evening, Tvardovsky asked him to come to Moscow the following
day to go over the story with him in preparation for its publication in the
January number of *Novy Mir*. He apologized for the short notice, but a plenary meeting of the Central Committee was to begin on Monday and Tvardovsky, as an alternate member of the committee, would be obliged to attend.
It was necessary to do the work before the meeting if the story was to meet
the deadline.

Solzhenitsyn hurried through the first snowfall of the winter to catch
the seven o'clock train on Sunday morning and meet Tvardovsky at the *Novy
Mir* offices. The preceding day had been the official publication day of the
November issue of *Novy Mir*, when the subscribers' copies were sent out and
the staff were able to buy copies for themselves and their friends. It was the
last peaceful day, the lull before the storm, and Tvardovsky told Solzhenitsyn that the atmosphere in the offices had been "just like in church." One
by one people had come in, handed over their seventy copecks in silence and
received the long-awaited copies. Triumphantly, Tvardovsky laid *Izvestia* on
the table opened at page 5, with its long review of *A Day in the Life of Ivan
Denisovich*, by the well-known Soviet writer Konstantin Simonov. To Tvardovsky's chagrin, Solzhenitsyn skimmed the first paragraph and put it aside,
saying, "Let's get down to business." Tvardovsky took this, probably correctly (though Solzhenitsyn denies it in his memoir), as an affectation and
walked out of the room, leaving Solzhenitsyn to peruse the article alone.
Solzhenitsyn later complained to Natalia that Simonov had written "nothing
about the language, about the penetration into the soul of an ordinary man,"
which suggests that he had expected rather more of this erratic establishment
writer than he admits to in *The Oak and the Calf*.[47]

They then got down to business. According to Reshetovskaya, Tvardovsky began by asking Solzhenitsyn how he wanted him to comment on
"Kochetovka"—"with or without an anaesthetic." Solzhenitsyn rejected the
anaesthetic, but when Tvardovsky produced a stream of criticisms, he vigorously rebutted them one by one, leading Tvardovsky to remark, "Why
don't you try to hold the whole line instead of fighting for every foxhole?"[48]
Nevertheless, judging from his comments in *The Oak and the Calf*, Solzhenitsyn was grateful for Tvardovsky's perspicacity in editorial matters. This
was particularly true when shortly afterwards they discussed "Matryona."
Tvardovsky had decided that he should publish the two stories together in
the January issue of *Novy Mir*. They would make quite a splash, a worthy

follow-up to *Ivan Denisovich*. Almost anything with Solzhenitsyn's name on it, he felt, was publishable now. What he was concerned about, however, was the literary quality.

His attention to detail in discussing the second story was remarkable, and Solzhenitsyn was impressed by Tvardovsky's knowledge of country life and grasp of popular custom. Examples of this superior knowledge are quoted in *The Oak and the Calf*, and it seems that Solzhenitsyn was somewhat readier to accept these corrections than in the case of "Kochetovka."* It must have been now that Solzhenitsyn's cumbersome and didactic title, "Without a Righteous Person No Village Can Stand," was replaced by the more evocative "Matryona's Place."† In addition, the action of the story was moved back from 1956 to 1953, to blunt its political sharpness and topicality. A change was also made in the other title. Solzhenitsyn had called it "Incident at *Kochetovka* Station," since Kochetovka was the real name of the station where the original incident had occurred in 1941. Tvardovsky's arch-enemy in publishing, however, and the editor of the reactionary literary magazine *Oktyabr*, was Vsevolod Kochetov, a neo-Stalinist, and it was thought to be needlessly provocative to leave such a similarity of names in a story about the effects of Stalinism. Solzhenitsyn therefore renamed it "Incident at Krechetovka Station."‡

It was probably on this visit to Moscow that Solzhenitsyn paid his second and last call on Anna Akhmatova. It appears that she read her masterpiece, *Requiem*,§ to him, but Solzhenitsyn criticized it in terms reminiscent of those he had once used in objecting to Ivashov-Musatov's Shakespeare paintings: "It's a pity your verses are always about one person's destiny." Akhmatova was evidently surprised and rejected the criticism. "Do you mean to say you can't convey the destiny of millions by describing the fate of a single person?" she asked him, and pointed out that in her epilogue she had expanded the poem's meaning to encompass "millions."‖ They apparently discussed domestic matters as well. Akhmatova asked Solzhenitsyn whether

---

* It must not be forgotten that, for all his love of the countryside and the Russian village, Solzhenitsyn, unlike Tvardovsky, was a town boy. The importance of this fact for his later idealization of the village has not, to my knowledge, been discussed.

† The customary title of "Matryona's *Home*" does not really convey the nuance of *dvor* in the Russian title *Matryonin dvor*. *Dvor* means literally the working space around a peasant's or smallholder's hut, or between wings, if the hut has them, or between the hut and outbuildings such as stables or pens. It is often translated as "yard," but Solzhenitsyn clearly means to include both the buildings and the yard. *Dvor* also has rural and folk overtones that are missing from "home."

‡ Solzhenitsyn restored the original title when he came to republish the story in his Collected Works.

§ *Requiem*, about Akhmatova's loss of a son in the purges, was written between 1935 and 1940 and memorized by Akhmatova and a few friends. It was not published until 1963.

‖ Lydia Chukovskaya, who reported this meeting, thinks that Akhmatova nonetheless took Solzhenitsyn's criticism to heart, and quotes as evidence two lines that Akhmatova later added to her epilogue: "And when, driven mad by torments, / Marched the regiments of the condemned." These two lines do not appear in the published texts of *Requiem*.

he was now thinking of moving to Moscow, but he replied, "I have several old ladies under my care," and indicated that it was unlikely. She found that he had grown more sombre since their first meeting. "There's a kind of shadow over his face," she told Chukovskaya.[49]

A week later Solzhenitsyn returned to Moscow and found Tvardovsky in an ebullient mood when he rang to confirm the time of their meeting. "Come right over on the double!" he exclaimed excitedly. When Solzhenitsyn arrived, he heard that several thousand copies of *Novy Mir* had been diverted to the bookstalls set up in the Kremlin for delegates to the plenary session of the Central Committee, which Tvardovsky had been attending all week, and that Khrushchev had announced from the platform that *A Day in the Life of Ivan Denisovich* was an extremely important work which they should all read. The delegates had trooped off to buy it and had emerged from the meeting each clutching two volumes, one red—containing materials for the plenary session—and one blue—containing Solzhenitsyn's story. Elsewhere in Moscow the magazine had sold out completely, despite the printing of several thousand extra copies, and was already a collector's item.[50]

The press was unanimous in its praise. Tvardovsky's preface had carefully prepared the ground by linking the story with the name of Khrushchev and Khrushchev's speech on de-Stalinization at the Twenty-second Party Congress.

> The subject matter of Alexander Solzhenitsyn's tale is unusual in Soviet literature. It echoes the unhealthy phenomena in our life associated with the period of the personality cult, now exposed and rejected by the Party. Although these events are so recent in time, they now seem very remote to us. But whatever the past was like, we in the present must not be indifferent to it. Only by going into its consequences fully, courageously, and truthfully can we guarantee a complete and irrevocable break with all those things that cast a shadow over the past.[51]

This was the theme taken up by the reviewers. Simonov (in the review that Solzhenitsyn had initially declined to read) wrote that the myth that Stalin had not known what was happening in the country had now been exploded forever and praised Solzhenitsyn as a "mature, unique master." Five days later, Vladimir Ermilov, a notorious secret-police informer, timeserver, and hack critic, beloved of the Soviet establishment, fulsomely praised Solzhenitsyn in the pages of *Pravda*, likening him to Tolstoy but also firmly yoking him to Party policy. "There can be no doubt that the fight against the consequences of Stalin's personality cult, taken up by the Party and the Soviet people since the Twentieth and Twenty-second congresses of the CPSU, will continue to facilitate the appearance of works of art outstanding for their ever-increasing artistic value. . . . The possibility of telling the truth has been affirmed by the Party and the people."[52]

The two leading Soviet newspapers had set their official seal on Solzhenitsyn's reputation, his respectability, and his transformation from an enemy of the people into a national hero. Catapulted to fame virtually overnight, the provincial schoolmaster from Ryazan was now acclaimed as an exemplary citizen and writer. "The Party has called writers its helpers," Simonov wrote in *Izvestia*. "I believe that Alexander Solzhenitsyn in his story has shown himself a true helper of the Party in a sacred and vital cause—the struggle against the personality cult and its consequences."[53]

25

THE CREST
OF THE WAVE

SIMONOV, ERMILOV, AND the many critics who followed them were taking
no risks when they placed Solzhenitsyn's story firmly within the bounds
of official Party policy, emphasizing its role as an instrument in the process
of de-Stalinization. This, after all, was the view of their political leader,
Khrushchev, who had authorized the story in the first place, and it is clear
that the political line to be taken had been handed down in advance. Nothing
that happens in the public domain in the Soviet Union is supposed to occur
spontaneously, least of all "spontaneous" praise or "spontaneous" criticism.
The work was thus made safe for public consumption—or so Khrushchev
thought. Even Tvardovsky's preface, with its calculated appeal to Party prejudices, served to soften and partially neutralize the story's subversive content, thereby making it more palatable to the hierarchy.

What exactly the Party line was to be can easily be gauged from the very
titles of the first reviews (the editors who wrote the headlines being closer to
Party control than the writers were): "About the Past in the Name of the
Future"; "In the Name of Truth, in the Name of Life"; "This Must Not
Happen Again"; "A Bitter But Necessary Truth"; "Let the Full Truth Be
Told"; "This Must Not Be Repeated"; "Thus It Was But Will Never Be
Again"; "In the Name of the Future." In short, ran the message, the events
and the way of life in the labour camps described in *Ivan Denisovich* undoubt-
edly existed once, and should be known about, but they belonged irrevocably to the past, to the era of the euphemistically named "personality cult."
Under the more enlightened and civilized rule of Stalin's successors, these
problems and "mistakes" had all been rectified, and it was now possible to
face the future with optimism and a sense of security.

This theme was taken up in the body of the reviews. Tvardovsky had set the tone by specifically linking the grimness of Solzhenitsyn's subject matter with Stalin's crimes and emphasizing the ability of Soviet literature to confront the problems of the past. Ermilov, true to his obsequious character, attributed the very existence of the story to the Party's wise policy of renouncing Stalinism and thanked the Party for making it possible to tell the truth. Kruzhkov, in *Ogonyok* (The Light), a mass-circulation illustrated weekly, called the story "profoundly Party-minded." Simonov approvingly quoted Khrushchev on Stalinism, and Drutse, in the literary magazine *Druzhba Narodov* (Friendship of the Peoples), took up Ermilov's theme of gratitude to the Party for having created the opportunity for such a story to be published.[1]

In a number of cases it was clear that these genuflections were little more than the ritual obeisances customarily exacted from literary critics under the Soviet Union's feudalistic rules for intellectual debate and that the work's sharper and more literary qualities had immediately been recognized. Most critics agreed with Tvardovsky (and Chukovsky in his appreciation) that the unsensational presentation of the material enhanced its impact and that the story gained in power from the author's self-restraint. They noted the "ordinariness" and typicality of Ivan Denisovich and his comrades, taking the point that they were not criminals but innocent Soviet citizens condemned to imprisonment and hard labour by an unjust regime acting illegally. Solzhenitsyn's story was a hymn to these people, to their courage, good humour, and fortitude. And its economy of means seemed miraculous. Ermilov, right for once, called it "epic," evoking the name of Tolstoy, while many others recognized the work's greater affinity with the classical Russian prose of the nineteenth century than with Soviet literature. All agreed, moreover, that despite the painful subject matter, the story's ultimate effect was to inspire hope and provide a sense of uplift.

Such a comforting conclusion was very important in the Soviet context, for one of the fundamental tenets of socialist realism was (and is) that works of art should encourage optimism and proclaim the resolution of conflicts; and what better resolution could there be than to say that the whole problem was over and done with? But the more perceptive critics were not prepared to stop there. Encouraged, perhaps, by the story's exceptional patronage, they drew rather more far-reaching conclusions.

Grigori Baklanov, a not untalented novelist and chronicler of Second World War subjects (rather in the mould of Simonov, but at that time more honest) wrote an excellent, long review in the *Literaturnaya Gazeta* in which he pointed out that *A Day in the Life of Ivan Denisovich* was one of those rare creations that change one's vision of the world, after which it is "impossible to go on writing as one did before," for it had created "a new level of dialogue with the reader, and on this level much that until recently seemed perfectly satisfactory is now hopelessly outdated and boring." Baklanov shared in the general admiration for Solzhenitsyn's main characters, shrewdly picking out the brigade leader Tiurin as equal in interest to Ivan Shukhov, but he also raised the question of the villains—the security guards, calling them "hardly Soviet," which went well beyond most official comment, for the active role of the MVD and NKVD in these repressions was usually passed over in silence. Baklanov also anticipated what was to become one of the principal objections to Solzhenitsyn's story—Why stir up the past? Why rub salt in the wounds?—saying that the only way to heal the wounds was to admit them squarely in the first place. Finally, Baklanov correctly identified two of Solzhenitsyn's most powerful underlying themes, which were nowhere stated explicitly but everywhere implied. One, that these evils had occurred because the Soviet people had blindly believed what they were told and not the evidence of their own eyes and ears; and, two, that not only would life in the Soviet Union have been better and more humane without Stalin's policies but that many of these policies had remained unchanged (contrary to what the Party line maintained).

Baklanov's analysis was echoed two weeks later in the Moscow newspaper *Moskovskaya Pravda* (Moscow Truth), by the critic I. Chicherov, who pointed out how much of Stalin's war effort—and industrial production—had been directed inwards, at controlling his own people, rather than outwards, against external enemies. And he mentioned another objection being made against the story (that it would "give comfort to the Soviet Union's enemies") only to dismiss it as a pretext for hypocrisy.

Furthest of all went Drutse in *Druzhba Narodov*. With great prescience, he declared that Solzhenitsyn's story represented a personal duel between Ivan Shukhov and Stalin (had he said between Solzhenitsyn and Stalin, he would have been even nearer the mark), in which the undoubted winner was Shukhov. It had been said, wrote Drutze, that Stalin did not love the masses. Worse than that, he had despised them and turned them into cogs, and *Ivan Denisovich* was the story of what had happened to those cogs behind barbed wire. What was needed was a restoration of their moral rights. Unfortunately, there were "certain big cogs" who found life all too comfortable "watching over the little cogs" and who were still around, making such a restoration difficult to achieve. Even more controversially, Drutse pointed to the similarities on both sides of the wire. "Are we not struck by the austere landscape of this story because we, too, as often as not, scanned the sky with morbidly strained eyes? Did we not also lay bricks, each in his own wall? . . . And didn't we also look back on each day, just like Ivan Denisovich, and with a logic inscrutable to common sense rejoice inwardly, 'Oh well, the day didn't go too badly' . . . ?" In other words, *Ivan Denisovich* wasn't just about the camps but about the whole of Soviet society under Stalin and, insofar as the "big cogs" were still in place, partly about the Soviet Union today as well.

It is no wonder that for a few, heady weeks, Soviet intellectuals thought that the censorship had been abolished. If stories like *Ivan Denisovich* could be published (which, to tell the truth, *had* evaded the censorship; had the professionals at Glavlit got hold of *Ivan Denisovich*, it would have been torn to shreds), if articles like Baklanov's and Drutse's could appear in the national press, if "The Heirs of Stalin" could be printed in *Pravda*, it began to seem that almost anything was possible. To cap it all, rumours spread that Polikarpov, the Party's top ideological watch-dog, was in trouble with Khrushchev. Apparently Khrushchev had only just got around to looking at *Doctor Zhivago*, and he felt that the novel was so highbrow that it would never have appealed to the masses anyway and was therefore not worth the international scandal that had been provoked by banning it. Since Polikarpov had been responsible, he received a reprimand, and there was talk that the Central Committee's cultural section was to be abolished and replaced by a much smaller body with more limited powers.[2]

Polikarpov's problems were compounded when he appeared at about this time at the Academy of Fine Arts to present the official Party list of candidates for the forthcoming elections. Normally, there would have been no doubt about its automatic acceptance. The academy, like the Artists' Union and most other organizations in the arts, was firmly in the hands of the conservatives, headed in this case by Victor Serov and Alexander Gerasimov, though it was true that Serov had lost his post as president of the academy the preceding year. On this occasion the unthinkable occurred: Polikarpov was hooted off the stage, and the meeting broke up in disarray. As in the Writers' Union, so in the other creative unions the liberals were in the ascendant, and everywhere the call was for less control and less censorship.[3]

In this atmosphere, in the eyes of the Moscow intellectuals, Solzhenitsyn was more of a hero than ever, and (as Tvardovsky had predicted) he was inundated with requests for "a little something" to publish or perform. To most of them he said no, if only because he had virtually nothing to offer. Tvardovsky had already seen and commented negatively on his verse. His only two publishable short stories were already with *Novy Mir*, and he regarded *The First Circle* as far too sensitive and controversial to show to anyone just yet—it was still being kept in concealment, together with the works written in Kok Terek. There remained his plays, which he had carefully excluded from his promise to Tvardovsky, and in particular *The Tenderfoot and the Tart*, which he had taken to Moscow with him when going to discuss "Matryona" and "Krechetovka."

On that trip, it seems, he had taken the play round to Oleg Efremov, the director of the Sovremennik (Contemporary), Moscow's newest and most experimental theatre, and either then or a few days later had given them a reading of it. An actor who was present described the scene as follows.

Soon after the awesome experience of *One Day*, Tvardovsky told the members of the theatre that Solzhenitsyn would shortly be coming to see us. Naturally, we held our breath: What would this mysterious new colossus be like? We waited. And recoiled in surprise when he actually appeared, because it was a very curious man who stood before us. He looked like a dental technician or a bookkeeper. His suit was made of rather good wool, but extremely old, with old-fashioned trousers as wide as the shoes—which no one in Moscow circles had worn for years. And his hat was incredibly crumpled, as if his physics pupils had played football with it in the school yard. . . .

The actor noticed nothing special about Solzhenitsyn's face, except for an impression of bad teeth,* nor did he care for his manner of reading.

He read rather badly, like a somewhat hammy provincial actor. True, he was very intense, assiduous, even zealous in his "performance," but he sometimes forgot to change voices when changing characters, so that the "tart" would come out exactly like the camp commandant—there was that kind of minor error. The reading was every bit as curious as his appearance.[4]

Nevertheless, the director and actors were deeply affected by the contents of the play. "We were professionals and accustomed to the drama, but we cried openly after the first act." This, it seems, surprised Solzhenitsyn, who commented that when he had read these scenes to former prisoners they had laughed rather than cried. But he was pleased by the excellent reception his play was accorded, as well as by Efremov's decision to put it on, though he was somewhat alarmed by the speed with which Efremov wanted to press ahead. With his experience and knowledge of the vagaries of the Soviet literary world, Efremov wanted to take advantage of the moment. And Solzhenitsyn was a hot property, whose name would automatically fill the theatre. Efremov offered to rehearse day and night and put the play on within a month, in time for the New Year holiday, and even to accept changes in the text as they went along if Solzhenitsyn wished to make further revisions. But Solzhenitsyn took fright. He did not like to be rushed—he was used to taking his time—and it seems that he also wished to consult Tvardovsky about the wisdom of such a step. He later wrote about his fears in *The Oak and the Calf*: "What if some 'top people' happened to see it before its premiere, got angry, and put the lid not only on the play but on the stories that should be appearing in *Novy Mir* any time now? The circulation of *Novy Mir* . . . was 100,000, whereas the Sovremennik auditorium seated only seven hundred people."[5]

In his memoir Solzhenitsyn attempts to throw the blame for this delay onto Tvardovsky and *Novy Mir*. Tvardovsky had not cared for the play when he read it and had told Solzhenitsyn that "it doesn't come off artistically . . . it isn't theatre," and that it was "*Ivan Denisovich* again—you're ploughing the same old field."[6] Solzhenitsyn comments that it wasn't the same old field. *Tenderfoot* dealt with an entirely different sort of camp, a regular corrective labour camp instead of the special camp of Ivan Denisovich. One can see what he means. *Tenderfoot* belonged to a different period in the development of the Gulag. For the chronicler and the historian—which Solzhenitsyn also

---

* Another Moscow intellectual who met Solzhenitsyn at about this time has commented that, although his teeth were crooked, they impressed by their strength and naturalness and relieved the general austerity of his expression. They and the eyes were invariably the first things to catch a stranger's attention.

considered himself to be—it was new subject matter. Besides, a theatrical treatment of the labour camps was bound to be different from a story (though there is no evidence that Solzhenitsyn ever used this argument). But Tvardovsky also had a point. Artistically speaking, *Tenderfoot* was the same ground as *Ivan Denisovich* and represented a regression rather than a literary advance. Consciously or unconsciously, Tvardovsky was judging Solzhenitsyn's output by the exceptional standards of his first published story, and in this he was to show a surer judgement than Solzhenitsyn himself, who had a poor appreciation of the worth of his work when it was not prose.

Of course, one cannot entirely discount the motive that Solzhenitsyn attributes to Tvardovsky—namely, his professional jealousy of other literary outlets. Soviet literary circles are no exception to the general rule in being riddled with cliques of one kind and another, not all of them based on ideological alignments; and loyalty to one's magazine, publishing house, literary institute, or theatre was often fierce and consuming, providing a sense of identity that was entirely missing from the Writers' Union, and serving as a substitute for political activities that would be normal in other societies. Alexander Dementyev, for instance, Tvardovsky's bosom friend and literary confidant, whom Solzhenitsyn disliked because of his reserved attitude to *Ivan Denisovich* and "Matryona's Place," was motivated almost entirely by his fanatical devotion to the magazine and his desire not to see its existence and role jeopardized by attempts to overreach itself. Solzhenitsyn's portrait of Dementyev in *The Oak and the Calf* is a caricature. Dementyev, according to one who knew him well, was "a cunning old fox who was totally absorbed in *Novy Mir* and devoted his life to getting it out and helping it through the censorship."[7] It is true that Dementyev would have rejected *Ivan Denisovich* if he had thought it would endanger his beloved journal, but not because he was a Party hack.

To Solzhenitsyn's irritation, Dementyev was one of those with whom Tvardovsky had discussed his play and who agreed with Tvardovsky that it wasn't suitable for *Novy Mir*. Under pressure, Tvardovsky did eventually consent to Solzhenitsyn's approaching one of the theatres. In his memoir, Solzhenitsyn records Tvardovsky's dislike of the Sovremennik ("I must warn you against those theatrical gangsters!")[8] and says that Tvardovsky suggested instead the more conservative Mossovet Theatre, run by that same Yuri Zavadsky, now aging, whose theatre studio Solzhenitsyn had once attended in Rostov. Zavadsky was an old friend of Tvardovsky's and had staged the dramatization of *Vasily Tyorkin*, but Solzhenitsyn was not attracted by this prospect, or swayed by the sentimental connection with his youth, and never made the approach, preferring instead to go to the Sovremennik.

The weeks and months following the publication of *A Day in the Life of Ivan Denisovich* were naturally difficult for Solzhenitsyn. Tvardovsky had been correct in anticipating that fame would not turn his head. He was too old and experienced for that, and all who knew him in those years agree that he withstood the pressures remarkably well. Nevertheless, the pressures were enormous and presented problems both moral and practical. He was indeed flooded with letters from all over the country, to which he and Natalia did their best to reply. The majority were friendly and admiring, but there were also hostile and even abusive epistles, many of them from members, or ex-members, of the security services and from neo-Stalinists in the Party. In due course Solzhenitsyn was to find a literary use for these letters, but in the short term they were a sharp and unpleasant reminder of a still-powerful current of opinion within the country, and distinctly upsetting in their often personal scurrility.

There were also endless invitations to attend this or that function, to become a member of this or that body, to contribute articles, lectures, stories, and to meet this or that eminent person. Most of the invitations he refused without a second thought, but membership in the Writers' Union, which was offered to him almost immediately and went through on the nod, was to prove invaluable, for it enabled him, a few months later, to give up teaching and live as a full-time writer without incurring the charge of "parasitism," a crime much publicized and persecuted during Khrushchev's rule and applied to almost anyone without a regular job.* Membership in the union also gave him pension and social-security rights and allowed him entry to the "restricted access" sections of libraries, where he could consult the books and journals that had hitherto been beyond his reach.

Fame also presented Solzhenitsyn with the dilemma of how to use it. On the one hand he was anxious to get further works into print (or onto the stage), but on the other he was frightened of committing a blunder. "I did not realize the extent of my newly won strength," he later wrote, "or, therefore, the degree of audacity with which I could now behave. The force of inertia kept me cautious and secretive. . . . I was in a hurry to stop before I was stopped, to take cover again and pretend that I had nothing further to offer and nothing further in mind." It was the old convict's mentality of suspicion and distrust ("Don't let good luck fool you . . .") that he had trained himself to live by, and years of conditioning couldn't be undone in a day—if at all. This was why he leaned so heavily on Tvardovsky for advice, while simultaneously resenting his dependence. Years later, when he came to write his memoir, this resentment rose to the surface and he was to criticize Tvardovsky for having wasted time and failing to take advantage of the favourable situation as well as for having suppressed his play. But it is clear that he was just as culpable, as he freely admits elsewhere ("my anxieties about *Novy Mir* fettered me less than my excessive caution").[9] Not surprisingly, he was pulled in two different directions, and it was to be a good three years before he resolved the doubts and misgivings that now began to beset him.

For the moment Solzhenitsyn was happy to take Tvardovsky's advice in most things, and in no area was he more faithful to Tvardovsky's recommendations than in his relations with the press, Soviet as well as foreign.

* This was the charge on which the young Leningrad poet Iosif Brodsky was to be tried a few months later, in March 1964, and sentenced to five years' compulsory labour.

Newspapermen tried to force the doors of my home and of the Moscow hotel rooms in which I stayed; there were telephone calls from embassies in Moscow to my school in Ryazan; written questionnaires were sent from press agencies. . . . I said not a single word to any of them. . . . I was afraid that if I once started answering Western correspondents, I would be asked questions by Soviet newsmen, too, questions that would predetermine my response: either an immediate act of rebellion or a life of cheerless conformity. Not wishing to lie, and not daring to rebel, I preferred silence.[10]

On the whole he was successful in his campaign to fight off any interviews. On 28 November *Sovietskaya Rossia* published a brief biographical note about him, composed jointly by himself and Tvardovsky. This called him "the son of an office worker," recorded the early death of his father from unknown causes, and after summarizing his education and army career stated that in 1945 "Captain Solzhenitsyn was arrested on unfounded political charges and sentenced to eight years' imprisonment," after which he served a period of exile. In 1957 he was "completely rehabilitated for lack of *corpus delicti*" and was now working as a teacher. This was the sum total of the information that Solzhenitsyn wanted printed about himself, and only one reporter succeeded in making a slight dent in his defences—Victor Bukhanov, of the national press agency, Novosti.

Bukhanov, like all the other journalists, was very much given the runaround. He called at the school and managed to observe Solzhenitsyn giving a lesson, but from beyond a glass partition, so that his presence "wouldn't disturb the students." He talked to Solzhenitsyn's colleagues and pupils, all of whom professed themselves amazed by his sudden success and said they had never suspected his secret life as a writer. Only the headmaster had had an inkling that he was busy with something, but had concluded he must be writing a physics textbook—"which he is fully qualified to do." His pupils reported that he was a first-rate and much respected teacher, that he was proverbially punctual, punctilious, and exacting, and that the language of *Ivan Denisovich* was not the language he used in class. All praised his highly developed sense of responsibility and capacity for hard work.

Bukhanov gleaned a number of details about Solzhenitsyn's hobbies and habits from Natalia, whom he found "cultivated and somewhat more open" than her difficult husband. "She is just as reluctant to talk about her husband as he is about himself. But being a woman she is less strict in her observation of this principle." She gave him two snapshots of Solzhenitsyn (presumably with permission), and Bukhanov heard from others that they were an ideal couple: "God grant every family the same happiness." Bukhanov also managed to visit the flat in Kasimovsky Lane, where one evening he watched Solzhenitsyn go into the yard to chop wood. "He was dressed in a padded jerkin and a fur cap with its ear-flaps and straps hanging down undone. I was astonished to be reminded of Ivan Shukhov. For all the intellectual disparity between them, the story's author and hero are united by something basic and unforgettable."

But Solzhenitsyn himself was virtually impossible to talk to.

> He continues to refuse to give interviews either to Soviet or to foreign journalists. He doesn't conceal his dislike for members of the press. . . . It is difficult for a reporter to talk to Solzhenitsyn. His invariably polite but firm "noes" reduce one to despair. I talked to him four days running in Moscow (in effect against his will) and met him in Ryazan. Solzhenitsyn conquered me with his intelligence and captivated me with his charm, but I've had enough—that was my last attempt to speak to him as my editor had instructed.[11]

For all his effort Bukhanov had got about four sentences out of Solzhenitsyn. One was to deprecate the fact that the first reviews of *Ivan Denisovich* had been written before its publication and that he had been paid for his stories before publication—a dangerous precedent. What if he could not live up to expectations? He repeated the idea that the path from writer to reader should lie only through his books, comparing his present situation unfavourably (and inaccurately) with that of nineteenth-century writers: "Nobody pestered them for sensational stories; they were simply read." And he startled Bukhanov by saying severely ("without a hint of humour in his voice"), "You'll find all that out after my funeral."

There was much that was admirable in this dogged determination of Solzhenitsyn's not to allow himself to become an empty celebrity and to preserve his modesty in the face of extreme temptation. Partly it was a matter of sheer self-preservation—it was one way, after all, of dealing with the problems posed by fame. And partly it was a demonstration of independence, a declaration that he was not like other men, that he would not be seduced down the primrose path to become a celebrity. For this reason he refused the offer of a spacious flat in Moscow. It seemed a good decision at the time—he valued his privacy and needed the isolation that Ryazan provided—although he was to regret it bitterly in later years. But there was also an element of naïvety and misunderstanding about it. Solzhenitsyn's strength as a creative writer was that he had been cut off from the normal world since early manhood and had steeped himself in the Russian classics of the past. This was the source of that amazing "purity" that everyone noticed in his work, as if he were virtually untouched by the last thirty years of Soviet literary history. Every great man, it seems, has a touch of the innocent about him. It is this that gives him that special angle of vision and single-mindedness of purpose; it is the price he pays for his singularity. Solzhenitsyn was an innocent in the ways of the world. He absolutely refused to play the game the way the press and the literary world wanted him to, or any other game—except his own, and, as it happened, that too demanded privacy, secrecy, and conspiracy ("silence, exile, and cunning").

An illustration of this mixture of naïvety and suspicion occurred when Solzhenitsyn visited the Moscow Arts Theatre to talk to some teachers and students from the theatre's drama school. He was clearly uncomfortable with the conventional format of "the writer meeting his readers" and sharply declined to talk about his personal life or working habits. The whole arrangement seemed to strike him as artificial and insincere, although once he got into his stride his unease vanished and he was perfectly charming. Even so, he couldn't resist pillorying the reporters who had pestered him in Ryazan, and as an example of journalistic superficiality, he quoted a correspondent who had visited his battery during the war to write a feature about life at the front. "I told him," said Solzhenitsyn, "that he was wasting his time. 'You won't be able to write anything useful, because tomorrow you will leave here. To understand, you have to be a part of the battery, fight with it, and not know whether you are going to live or die, or whether your comrades will live or die.' "[12]

As an indication of what sometimes sets the literary writer apart from the journalist, the example was not without merit, and Solzhenitsyn's aim in telling the story was to support his contention that the writer can write only about what he knows. But in a sense it was to underrate the role of the imagination, for writers would be severely crippled if they followed Solzhenitsyn's injunction literally. Fortunately, Solzhenitsyn himself ignored the moral of this story in his major novels.

Later that evening the subject of journalism came up again. Solzhenitsyn had begun his talk by asking whether any journalists were present and had been satisfied to hear that none was. Halfway through the evening, he suddenly broke off and exclaimed in a surprisingly angry voice, "I've been deceived! You said there were no journalists present, but I can see one in the audience." At this a young man who had been taking notes stood up and admitted to being a student journalist, but said that he had come out of curiosity and did not plan to write anything. He then launched into an unexpectedly bold attack on Solzhenitsyn's remarks. Solzhenitsyn was wrong, he said, to be so contemptuous of journalists and to think that they were automatically dishonest and would publish things against his will. As for besieging him in Ryazan, they had only been doing their job, and if Solzhenitsyn would show some understanding for their position and co-operate a little, he wouldn't have so many difficulties.[13]

Solzhenitsyn accepted the student's remarks with good humour and apologized for his harshness, but nevertheless called him over afterwards to check that he would not write anything. It was a curious episode that prefigured many later ambiguities in Solzhenitsyn's relations with the press.

There were two other attempts, besides Bukhanov's, to find out more about Solzhenitsyn's character and past. One resulted in a short and uninformative background piece by I. Kashkadamov in the *Uchitelskaya Gazeta* (Teachers' Gazette); the other, more interesting, was a longish article about Solzhenitsyn's years in exile that appeared in the Kazakhstan newspaper *Leninskaya Smena* (The Lenin Shift). Some enterprising editor discovered that Solzhenitsyn had spent his exile in Kok Terek, and a correspondent called Kungurtsev was dispatched to interview the teachers at his former school and his former landlady, Katerina Melnichuk, and to inspect the thatched adobe hut on the edge of the desert where Solzhenitsyn had lived. He was remembered with great affection. Former colleagues recalled his great erudition, former pupils his painstaking instruction and love of his subject, and all rejoiced in his present success.[14]

Although Solzhenitsyn cared little for either the privileges or the responsibilities of fame, the latter proved harder to avoid. One Saturday evening in December an official from the Provincial Party Committee came to the school to inform him that he was to report to Polikarpov at the Central Committee offices in Moscow the following Monday, 17 December, for a very important meeting. The Provincial Committee would send a car to take him (he was a VIP already, whether he wanted it or no). Solzhenitsyn decided to make a show of his independence and to resist any attempts to co-opt him. "I deliberately went along in the suit I had bought at 'Clothes for the Workingman' and wore to school; in my much-mended shoes with patches of brown leather on black; and badly in need of a haircut. This would make it easier for me to balk and feign stupidity."[15] It turned out that he had been invited to a grand gathering at the Pioneer Palace on Lenin Hills, where Party leaders were meeting four hundred writers, artists, and other members of the creative intelligentsia.

Despite his shabby dress, Solzhenitsyn was invited onto the podium to shake hands personally with Khrushchev and be introduced to the entire gathering. For the rest of the time, he sat with Tvardovsky, and during one of the intervals was introduced to a short, unassuming man in rimless glasses whose face wore a thoughtful expression. This turned out to be Vladimir Lebedev, Khrushchev's secretary and the man who had done more than anyone, with the exception of Tvardovsky, to get *Ivan Denisovich* published. Solzhenitsyn was favourably impressed by his modest manner and gladly met his request for a signed copy of his story.

The rest of the meeting was not so agreeable. Unbeknown to Solzhenitsyn, Khrushchev had been taken two weeks beforehand to an exhibition, "Thirty Years of Moscow Art," at the Manege Gallery, at which a group of modernist and abstract painters had been invited to display their art in three separate rooms. Khrushchev had been specially led into these rooms by the arch-conservatives Serov and Gerasimov, whereupon he had exploded with indignation, calling the artists parasites and pederasts, threatening them with expulsion to the West, and jeering that their canvases looked as if they had been painted by idiots.

> As long as I am chairman of the Council of Ministers we are going to support a genuine art. We aren't going to give a copeck for pictures painted by jackasses. History can be our judge. For the time being history has put us at the head of this state, and we have to answer for everything that goes on in it. Therefore we are going to maintain a strict policy in art. . . .
>
> Your prospects here are nil. What is hung here is simply anti-Soviet. It's amoral. Art should ennoble the individual and arouse him to action. . . . What's the good of a picture like this? To cover urinals with? . . . The people and government have taken a lot of trouble with you, and you pay them back with this shit.[16]

Only the sculptor Ernst Neizvestny had the courage to answer Khrushchev back, while the rest stood by in bemused silence.

The day following Khrushchev's visit to the Manege, all the leading newspapers had taken up the cry of more discipline in the arts. Editorials had appeared calling for all the unions of creative workers to be joined in one monolithic union, thus making them easier to control and less susceptible to nonconformist deviations. In the event, nothing came of this extreme demand, but Khrushchev had clearly sent out word that the arts needed careful watching, and the conservatives, who had stage-managed the campaign, were in full cry. Several Stalinists had been restored to positions of prominence. Three days after the Khrushchev outburst, Serov had been elected president of the Academy of Fine Arts, despite the earlier booing of Polikarpov, and conservatives occupied key positions in most of the creative unions, leaving only the Moscow branch of the Writers' Union as a place where liberalism still seemed in control.

Khrushchev was due to speak again that day in the Pioneer Palace, yet it seems that the writers gathered there were extraordinarily complacent—until they heard the keynote speech by Leonid Ilyichev, who was chairman of the ideological commission of the Central Committee. According to rumour, Ilyichev spoke for ten hours, which would be a record even by Soviet standards. It is more likely that the entire meeting lasted ten hours. Nevertheless, Ilyichev's speech was inordinately long. In it, he admitted that people had been asking for an end to censorship. "Exhibitions without juries, books without editors, the right of the artist to display without an intermediary anything he wishes. 'Let us create as we ourselves wish,' these people say. 'Do not restrict us.' " And he was defensive about the role of the Party and the influence of the West. But he quickly dashed any hopes that he or Khrushchev sympathized with these trends. Art, he declared (including literature), must continue to be "Party-minded." There was no such thing as peaceful coexistence between the various trends in art. Freedom of creation was a bourgeois concept alien to Marxism-Leninism. "It is the great good fortune of our art that the Party, expressing the fundamental interests of the people . . . defines the tasks and direction of artistic creation."[17]

Most of Ilyichev's speech was directed at visual artists and led on from Khrushchev's reactions to the exhibition at the Manege. "Formalism," in all its guises, was his principal target. But a number of writers were attacked, including Ehrenburg, whose memoirs were continuing to appear in Novy Mir. There was also an extraordinary clash between Khrushchev and Evtushenko. The following day, 18 December, had been set for the world premiere of Shostakovich's Thirteenth Symphony, whose first movement was a setting of Evtushenko's poem "Babi Yar" to music. Although the performance had been authorized by Khrushchev, Ilyichev now appealed to Evtushenko and Shostakovich to cancel it, while Khrushchev himself intervened to say it was inappropriate, because there was no longer any anti-Semitism in the Soviet Union. Evtushenko disagreed and refused to cancel the following day's performance. He also enthusiastically defended the modernist artists, saying he was convinced that "formalistic tendencies in their work will be straightened out in time." Khrushchev commented, "The grave straightens out the hump-backed," to which Evtushenko retorted, "Nikita Sergeyevich, we have come a long way since the time when only the grave straightened out humpbacks. Really, there are other ways."[18]

All in all, the omens were bad, but it still didn't seem possible that the great breakthrough achieved with the publication of *Ivan Denisovich* had been in vain or that the momentum of liberalization could be halted so abruptly. Indeed, *Ivan Denisovich* had been specifically exempted from criticism by Ilyichev, and the presentation of its author to the audience by Khrushchev personally was eloquent testimony to its continued high standing with the Party leaders.

The following day the Shostakovich symphony was performed, though not before Evtushenko had added some new lines to his text in the light of Khrushchev's criticisms and before the choir had attempted to resign. Apparently, they were dissuaded at the last minute by a stirring speech from Evtushenko in his best platform manner. In the evening the Moscow Conservatory was packed with liberals, though the government box was empty and the television cameras originally set up to cover this gala performance had been dismantled. The atmosphere was electric, and at the end, when Evtushenko and Shostakovich took their bows, the hall exploded in applause. It was a salute to the two men's courage, and a demonstration of liberal solidarity, as much as appreciation of the performance.

Two days later all further performances were cancelled, and a week later Ilyichev returned to the offensive at another meeting with writers, artists, and cinema workers. Again he concentrated on the artists, although this time praising Ernst Neizvestny for his "civic maturity" and singling out Evtushenko and the young novelist Vasily Axyonov for similarly "mature" behaviour. Other artists, writers, and musicians were attacked for "formalism" and refusing to toe the Party line. As if to underline that the authorities meant business, the mildly liberal editor of the influential *Literaturnaya Gazeta*, Kosolapov, was shortly afterwards replaced by the conservative Alexander Chakovsky.

It is not clear whether Solzhenitsyn attended the Shostakovich symphony concert. It is not the sort of thing he would normally have been attracted to, but all his liberal friends were there, and at least one Moscow writer (Evgenia Ginzburg) later claimed to have met Solzhenitsyn there.[19] New Year's Eve saw him celebrating in the rather unlikely company of Oleg Efremov and the actors at the Sovremennik Theatre. There were candles, fireworks, champagne, and young actresses in skimpy dresses dancing the twist— a far cry from chopping firewood in Ryazan. It is not recorded whether Solzhenitsyn danced as well.

The December issue of *Novy Mir* was very late in appearing and did not reach the news-stands until early January 1963, about a month after it should have done. It turned out that the second instalment of Victor Nekrasov's travel notes, *Both Sides of the Ocean* (the first instalment had appeared alongside *Ivan Denisovich*), had run into heavy trouble with the censors. This was the part dealing with Nekrasov's visit to America, and Nekrasov's notable fairness to the Soviet Union's ideological enemies was regarded as seditious. He had also included some remarkably sympathetic descriptions of American abstract art, which was the wrong thing to be doing at that particular time. On 20 January 1963, *Izvestia* printed a swingeing attack on Nekrasov—and by implication on *Novy Mir*—for playing a "dangerous game" in failing to attack the Soviet Union's ideological enemies and ignoring the cold war.

Not long after this, the January issue of *Novy Mir* came out, carrying Solzhenitsyn's two short stories "Matryona's Place" and "Incident at Krechetovka Station." Surprisingly, they had hardly been touched by the censors, perhaps in deference to the patronage of Khrushchev, which was perceived to be still continuing. Regular readers of *Novy Mir* and everyone with the slightest feel for literature read the stories avidly and welcomed them as proof that *Ivan Denisovich* had not been a flash in the pan and that a major new writer had arrived in their midst. The portrait of the old and humble village woman, Matryona, particularly stirred readers' breasts with its evocation of patriarchal Russia and its compassion for the "insulted and injured." The name of Dostoyevsky was now joined to that of Tolstoy in the general search for comparisons.

Solzhenitsyn's star seemed still to be riding high. Midway through January a journal specializing in the republication of fiction for a mass audience, the *Roman-gazeta* (literally, Newspaper-novel), published *A Day in the Life of Ivan Denisovich* in 750,000 copies (there may even have been a second and third impression, according to Zhores Medvedev), and a few weeks later the publishing house Sovetsky Pisatel (Soviet Writer) brought it out in book form in an edition of 100,000 copies. Both editions immediately sold out. It would probably have been possible to sell ten times as many, but Soviet publishing is not geared to the market. As in all other forms of Soviet enterprise, production runs are decided at the top, according to complex political criteria, not on the basis of demand, and the story was never reissued. Interestingly enough, Solzhenitsyn exploited the occasion of these reprints to restore some of the cuts that had been imposed on him by Lebedev and *Novy Mir* and to make a number of minor improvements. It was a bold step to take in the generally fearful atmosphere of Soviet publishing, but nobody seems to have noticed or complained.

26

FIRST DOUBTS

As the political struggle between the two main factions in the Party and the corresponding literary camps continued, there was no way in which Solzhenitsyn could keep out of it. At the political level, Khrushchev came under fierce attack by the conservatives (said to be led by Frol Kozlov) in the early months of 1963 and was severely weakened by the Cuban fiasco. He had also stirred up a hornet's nest at the November 1962 plenary session (the one at which the delegates had been seen clutching their red- and blue-covered books) by proposing sweeping administrative reforms in the Party's structure, whose ultimate effect would be to reduce the role of ideological control and make Party bosses more accountable for their decisions. This, too, was anathema to the conservatives, and it was the force and skill of their counter-attack that had driven Khrushchev (and his watch-dog over the arts, Ilyichev) onto the defensive and caused them to change their line.

But the conflict was by no means resolved, and the signs in the press were confusing. For example, as early as 11 January 1963 a critic called Lydia Fomenko made a public attack on the hitherto sacrosanct *Ivan Denisovich* in *Literaturnaya Rossia* (Literary Russia). Praising it for its "bitter truth" and literary skill, she nonetheless accused its author of failing to disclose "the full dialectic of that time." *Ivan Denisovich* expressed "a passionate 'no!' to Stalin's order," Fomenko wrote, but it "failed to rise to the philosophical level of the period, to a broader generalization capable of embracing the contradictory phenomena of that era."[1] In other words, there was no optimistic conclusion and no indication that there were "good Communists," even in the camps, who understood what was happening and would help to put everything right in the end. But the riposte to Fomenko came from, of all people, Ermilov, that same sneak and informer who had nevertheless fulfilled the "social command" and praised *Ivan Denisovich* in *Pravda* when it first appeared. Writing this time in *Izvestia*,[2] Ermilov reproached Fomenko for asking too much of the author of *Ivan Denisovich* ("Write about this as well as that!"), when the artistic unity of the story demanded that he stop precisely where he had. This did not mean he had failed to grasp the dialectic of Stalin's time; on the contrary, he had done so perfectly.

Even more confusing was the fact that the main body of the article in which these remarks appeared was devoted to a blistering attack on Ehrenburg and his memoirs in *Novy Mir*, that is to say, on a writer judged to be in the same camp as Solzhenitsyn and standing for more or less the same sort of things. Stranger still, although Ehrenburg's memoirs, dealing as they did with the period when Stalin was alive, had also been authorized by Khrushchev, it could not have been simply a case of attacking Khrushchev's favourites, otherwise Solzhenitsyn would have suffered too. Only a month or so later did it emerge that there was indeed a distinction (in the minds of the authorities) between the two men, that Khrushchev had withdrawn his support from Ehrenburg (though he was maintaining it for Solzhenitsyn), and that therefore the word had gone out to "get" him.

The occasion of this revelation was yet another meeting between the Party leaders and the writers, this time six hundred of them, which took place in the Kremlin on 7–8 March 1963. Again Solzhenitsyn was present and again *Ivan Denisovich* was singled out for praise by Khrushchev, but this time the general atmosphere was grim and threatening. "It was rigged," Solzhenitsyn later wrote, "so that the Stalinists had a preponderance of five to one . . . and the air was filled with harsh invective and destructive hostility to anything that gave off the faintest whiff of freedom."[3]

Ilyichev, the Party's ideological watch-dog, spoke on the first day and again attacked formalism and abstractionism in art. Referring to his earlier speech, he expressed satisfaction that a more orthodox line now prevailed. "What is particularly important is that, under the influence of the healthy ideas of the Party, the very atmosphere of creative discussion has changed. A number of creative workers have begun to lose their feelings of 'defencelessness,' people have been speaking out about Party-mindedness and national feeling in art, and about socialist realism, without fear of being considered reactionaries and conervatives." And he added ominously, "Everything is returning to its place" (meaning that all the conservatives were returning to their places).[4]

The real sensation came with Khrushchev's extraordinarily long speech the following day. It was clear that his main aim was to put a stop to any ideas of liberalization in the arts and to halt the trend that he himself had started. Far from showing himself sympathetic to Tvardovsky's earlier plea for the suspension of censorship in the arts, he was at pains to go the other way. "We must bring all the Party's ideological weapons, including such powerful instruments of Communist education as literature and art, into combat order," he said. "On questions of creative art the Central Committee of the Party will demand of everyone . . . that he abides unswervingly by the Party line." Like Ilyichev the day before, he attacked Ehrenburg unsparingly for his memoirs and conducted a sort of verbal tour of the arts: literature (when he abused Voznesensky and Axyonov), painting, music, the cinema, the theatre, even jazz—lambasting innovation and experiment and lauding orthodoxy, Party loyalty, and socialist realism.

At last, quite unexpectedly, he turned to the heart of the matter and addressed the central problem lying behind all the other problems—namely, the Party's attitude to Stalin and Stalinism. Ehrenburg's real crime, it turned out, had been to suggest in his memoirs that in the thirties everyone had known about Stalin's crimes but had been powerless to do anything and had therefore watched what was going on "in silence and with clenched teeth." This went much further than Khrushchev himself had gone in his speeches to the Twentieth and Twenty-second congresses, for it cast doubt on Khrushchev's claim that he and the other party leaders were ignorant of the worst excesses of Stalinism.

> Did the leading cadres of the Party know about the arrests of people at the time? Yes, they knew. But did they know that people were being arrested who were in no way guilty? No, they did not know. They believed Stalin and did not admit the thought that repression could be applied against honest people devoted to our cause.

Even more unexpectedly, Khrushchev went out of his way to speak warmly of Stalin personally and reveal that "at Stalin's funeral many people, including myself, had tears in their eyes. These were honest tears. Although we knew of Stalin's personal shortcomings, still we believed in him."

The monstrous crimes of which Khrushchev had spoken at such length in his "secret speech" were now suddenly reduced to "personal shortcomings," and Stalin was once more the beloved leader. The about-face could not have been more dramatic, and many theories have been adduced to account for Khrushchev's sudden change of tack. That his position as leader was severely weakened as a result of the Cuban crisis is without question. Undoubtedly, Kozlov and his allies were strengthened by Khrushchev's failure, and whenever there are foreign-policy problems in the Soviet Union there is always great pressure for more conformity and discipline at home. The position of Ehrenburg as a witness was also rather special, in that he, as much as Khrushchev and some of the other political leaders, had once enjoyed Stalin's favours, and although he was still telling less than he knew, there was always a chance he might go further and reveal all. The conservatives had perceived this from the beginning. At the very first meeting between the Party leaders and the intellectuals, a conservative writer, Galina Serebryakova, had electrified the gathering by revealing that Stalin's favourite secretary, Alexander Poskrebyshev, was not only (contrary to popular belief) alive and well but was also writing his memoirs, in which he accused Ehrenburg of having been an accomplice of Stalin's. This theme had been taken up by Ermilov in his attack on Ehrenburg in *Izvestia*, and now Khrushchev was returning to it again.

The point was that if, as Ehrenburg had written, "everybody knew," this implicated the Party leaders of the time far more than mere writers like himself. And this was the central dilemma of de-Stalinization, which Khrushchev, in his impulsive way, had failed to foresee—namely, Where do you stop? If de-Stalinization was taken to its logical conclusion it would indicate that most of the top leaders, including Khrushchev himself, were responsible for the crimes of Stalinism. Even more was this true of the upper levels of the bureaucracy in every sphere of Soviet life, ranging from the armed forces to the economics ministries, from the police to administrators of the arts, which is why the conservatives had such powerful support from the Party and government apparatus. Only a Nuremberg-style trial could deal with the enormity of the crimes committed against the innocent Soviet population, and since Khrushchev had no intention of going that far, he was bound to twist and turn in drawing the line. What the conservatives had apparently done was to point out to him the dangers of the path that he was following and to convince him that it would inevitably lead to disaster.

Khrushchev, therefore, had to preserve de-Stalinization in the form of a tactical manoeuvre by the Party and prevent it from becoming a major change of policy, let alone a moral crusade, which is what some of the intellectuals wanted it to be. And in the rebuke to Ehrenburg was concealed yet another axiom of Party policy, namely, its monopoly of wisdom and truth. It was one thing for Khrushchev to make speeches on Stalin's crimes, but quite another for mere writers to take up the same theme. Writers were unreliable: they could not be trusted to toe the Party line, to go just so far and no farther—not even Ehrenburg, with a lifetime of zigzagging experience behind him. When the chips were down, there could be no question of abandoning the censorship and Party control over writers, for no one could tell where this would lead.

As evidence of this danger Khrushchev revealed that Soviet publishing houses and literary magazines had been "flooded with manuscripts about the life of persons in exile, in prisons, and in the camps" since the publication of *Ivan Denisovich*. "Take my word for it, this is a very dangerous theme. It's the kind of 'stew' that will attract flies like a carcass, enormous fat flies; all sorts of bourgeois scum from abroad will come crawling all over it." It was a restatement of one of the conservatives' favourite arguments about not washing dirty linen in public, and also a reference to the enormous interest being taken abroad in *Ivan Denisovich*. The book had already been translated into all the major languages (two different English translations had appeared by January, one month after Russian publication, and two more would follow in the same year)* and was now being translated into many more, including

---

* A Soviet-sponsored translation of *Ivan Denisovich* began serialization in the *Moscow News* in December 1962 and was subsequently published by Penguin Books. The translator, Ralph Par-

those of most of the satellite countries of Eastern Europe. Speculation in the Western press about the meaning of its publication was rife, and, of course, Western commentators on the contents of the story could afford to be far more outspoken than their Soviet counterparts.

Solzhenitsyn's reputation survived this meeting unscathed, but it was clear that the whole balance of the Party's attitude had tilted strongly against him, as it had against most of the other writers associated with *Novy Mir*—Ehrenburg, Nekrasov, Evtushenko, Axyonov, Voinovich, Yashin. Indeed, a few days beforehand "Matryona's Place" had been heavily attacked by the conservative novelist and editor of *Znamya*, Vadim Kozhevnikov, in the pages of the *Literaturnaya Gazeta*. Kozhevnikov complained that there were too many "querulous" stories and tales appearing in *Novy Mir* and said that he had experienced a feeling of "deep spiritual pain" while reading "Matryona's Place."

> It seems to me that "Matryona's Place" was written by its author when he was still in a state of mind in which he could not with any depth understand the life of the people, the movement and real perspectives of that life. In the early post-war years such people as Matryona really did harness themselves to the plough in villages ravaged by the Germans. The Soviet peasantry performed a great feat in those circumstances and gave the people bread, feeding the country. This alone should evoke feelings of reverence and admiration. To draw the Soviet village as a Bunin village of our day is historically incorrect. Solzhenitsyn's story convinces one over and over again: without a vision of historical truth, of its essence, there can be no complete truth, no matter how great the talent.[5]

It was essentially the argument used by Lydia Fomenko about *Ivan Denisovich*. In that story Solzhenitsyn had "failed to rise to the correct philosophical level" and "reconcile contradictions," and in "Matryona" he lacked a vision of "historical truth." These were but euphemisms for toeing the Party line, which decreed that any shortcomings depicted in literature should be local and particular, and be contrasted unfavourably with the generally positive march of Soviet society towards a radiant Communist future. Another essential was that any shortcomings so described should be shown as being the fault of something other than the Soviet system (in this case the Germans) or as belonging to the distant past and since overcome. (The criticism would have been even harsher had the critics known that the time referred to in "Matryona" was not 1953—Stalin's time—but 1956—Khrushchev's.) In fact, the logic of this position was that no shortcomings should be described at all until after they had been corrected. The reference to the pre-Soviet and anti-Soviet Russian writer Bunin was also ominous. Bunin was held by Soviet

---

ker, who had responded to the prudishness of Soviet sensibilities by toning down some of Solzhenitsyn's saltier expressions, was falsely accused of having exercised a political censorship of the text, and a rival translation was commissioned from Max Hayward and Ronald Hingley. The latter's mid-Atlantic version was indeed racier in its vocabulary, but there was nothing to choose between the two translations in terms of accuracy, and neither was very satisfactory.

critics to have written in the nineteenth-century tradition of "critical realism," whose "task" it had been to excoriate Russian society for the evils of
capitalism and tsarism. Now that these evils had been overcome, critical realism had been superseded by "socialist realism," which could not but approve
of socialist society and be optimistic. Interestingly enough, the mention of
Bunin's name was quite perceptive on Kozhevnikov's part, for Solzhenitsyn
did admire him and had carefully annotated a volume of his stories. From
now on, however, Solzhenitsyn's avowed and perceived kinship with the
Russian writers of the nineteenth century was to be turned against him, and
he would be described more and more as a "critical realist" out of his time.

Two reviews did not constitute a campaign. Indeed, anywhere else but
the Soviet Union two negative voices among a chorus of praise would have
gone virtually unnoticed; but one of the first casualties of censorship is free
and spontaneous opinion. All public utterances instantly acquire symbolic
value and are minutely studied for "clues" to attitudes and positions. Readers
and writers alike become morbidly sensitive to nuances; virtually nothing is
ever taken at face value—nor is it meant to be. These reviews were therefore
taken as a hint, or a testing of the political weather, to see what the response
would be. And when there was no official response, the criticism grew bolder.
A critic called Lagunov lumped the Solzhenitsyn of "Matryona's Place" with
Ehrenburg, Nekrasov, Axyonov, and Evtushenko and said that what they
all had in common was a desire to "distort our reality and purposely play up
its darker, more negative aspects." Semyon Babayevsky, a best-selling peddler of Party slogans and cheap optimism, twice winner of the Stalin Prize,
wrote that it is "always much easier to describe the bad, the dark, and the
dirty than to praise the good, the radiant, and the pure. . . . What could be
simpler than to take, say, the old woman Matryona . . . and depict her in
totally black [sic] colours, and present her life in such a way that the collective
farms are to blame for everything.?"[6] In April *Oktyabr* joined its voice to the
chorus with a critical article by N. Sergovantsev.

For the time being such voices were still in a minority; and apart from
Lydia Fomenko, almost no one raised a word against *Ivan Denisovich*.
"Krechetovka," for instance, was generally praised, its setting in 1941 making it easier to accept as a description of the undesirable past. Solzhenitsyn
now thought it reasonable to press ahead with attempts to get *The Tenderfoot
and the Tart* performed. He had completed his revision of the text and was
anxious for the Sovremennik Theatre to go ahead. But in the new and changed
atmosphere, Efremov was in difficulty. It was not so simple to stage a play
about labour camps when the Party leaders had made it clear that they wanted
this subject played down. Solzhenitsyn decided to turn to his first political
patron, Vladimir Lebedev, to see whether more help would be forthcoming.
Having sent him the play at the beginning of March, he called on him in his
office on 21 March.

As it turned out, Lebedev was unhelpful. His first reaction on receiving
the play had been to ask whether Tvardovsky had read it, and when he

discovered Tvardovsky's dislike of the play, this seemed to confirm his own disinclination to get involved. The labour-camp theme was no longer desirable in literature. The Sovremennik, he said, was interested in the play only for its sensationalism and because it would fill the theatre. "I do not doubt that theatre-goers would break the doors down, as the saying goes, in their eagerness to find out . . . what sort of thing went on in the camps." But the whole thing was impossible because of those "huge fat flies" (in Khrushchev's phrase), the foreign correspondents and "home-grown philistines," who would applaud it.[7]

Three months later Solzhenitsyn went to visit Lebedev for a third and last time, and Lebedev expanded on what was wrong with *The Tenderfoot and the Tart*. What Solzhenitsyn had failed to do, he said, was to show that some people had been successfully re-educated in the camps. Somehow it always seemed to come out that the dishonest triumphed and the honest were doomed to destruction, which was a contradiction of socialist realism. Besides, the play was an "insult to the intelligentsia," since it showed so many of them fighting for privileges at the expense of their principles. Interestingly enough, word about the play had got round and had even reached Khrushchev, who thought it was a dramatization of *Ivan Denisovich*. "Let them put it on," he had said while under that impression, but Lebedev had explained to Khrushchev that the play was not about Ivan Denisovich and was not acceptable.[8]

Luckily, *Ivan Denisovich* itself retained its relative inviolability throughout 1963, although in most other respects the atmosphere steadily worsened. At the end of March the Writers' Union held a plenary session at which the "young" writers Evtushenko, Voznesensky, and Axyonov were heavily criticized on a variety of grounds; Grigori Baklanov, Yuri Bondarev, and Bulat Okudzhava among the slightly older generation, were also taken to task; and there were even rumours that Tvardovsky was to be replaced as editor of *Novy Mir*. Immediately afterwards a hysterical campaign of vilification was directed against Evtushenko for having published his *Precocious Autobiography* abroad (in the Paris magazine *L'Express*) without permission and without clearance from the Soviet censors. After that there was a lull, which may have had something to do with the fact that Frol Kozlov had a heart attack in May and disappeared from the scene, leaving the conservatives temporarily leaderless. Then, at a plenary meeting of the Central Committee in June 1963, Khrushchev back-pedalled somewhat from his earlier, hard position. He declared himself no longer in favour of a single, monolithic union for the arts. On the other hand, he had come round to thinking that a single publishing house would facilitate the Party's control, and he was still in no doubt that such control was necessary. Meanwhile, in May, Tvardovsky had given a relatively outspoken interview to Henry Shapiro, the chief Moscow correspondent of UPI, in which he had defended all *Novy Mir*'s authors and had singled out Solzhenitsyn and *Ivan Denisovich* for specially high praise.

Solzhenitsyn was aware of these fluctuations in the political arena. The publication and success of *Ivan Denisovich* had, as he later put it, drawn him into the Party's court circles, and he couldn't help knowing what was going on. Indeed, his third visit to Lebedev had been occasioned by an invitation to attend the June Party plenum, whose main theme was once again the Party's policy on the arts. Normally, such invitations were much sought after and prized, but Solzhenitsyn had absolutely no desire to spend a week in hot, sweaty Moscow listening to boring political speeches. Lebedev had been affability itself, despite his criticisms of *Tenderfoot*, confirming Solzhenitsyn's continued high standing at Khrushchev's "court." They had chatted about literature and politics. Lebedev showed Solzhenitsyn his albums of photographs of the famous, including many authors, as well as Khrushchev, Gromyko, and other bigwigs on foreign tours, and insisted on photographing Solzhenitsyn so that he could take his place in the album too. He was surprised by Solzhenitsyn's request to be excused from the plenum, but agreed to it readily enough, leaving Solzhenitsyn to hasten back to Ryazan.

It was Solzhenitsyn's last term at the school. He had given in his notice on the strength of the royalties from *Ivan Denisovich* and his two stories. There were also abundant royalties from abroad, where he had become an international celebrity overnight, and it seems that the film studio Mosfilm had contracted to produce a film of *Ivan Denisovich*. Perhaps because of this impending departure from the world of teaching, he had felt an urge to write about it, and in June completed his first story on a contemporary subject, "For the Good of the Cause." The theme was simple enough and based on a real incident that had occurred in Ryazan. A technical school, housed in makeshift, inadequate premises, is at last, after many delays and disappointments, about to move into a new, modern building. So enthusiastic are the students that they have given up their holidays and much of their spare time for nearly a year to act as unpaid labourers and hasten its completion, but at the very last moment the building is commandeered by a Moscow ministry for use as a scientific institute. Nothing that the school principal can do is sufficient to shift the corrupt district Party secretary, Knorozov, from his decision in favour of the ministry, and it emerges that the whole switch has been master-minded by the scheming director of a local factory, Khabalygin, who hopes to become head of the new institute. The principal, students, and staff of the school are deeply upset and disillusioned but are obliged to make way "for the good of the cause."

In its formal aspect the story was an uncomplicated example of socialist realism after the "thaw" of 1956. Knorozov was based on the temporarily notorious figure of A. Larionov, who had committed suicide after his shady dealings in the meat market had been exposed. Grachikov, secretary of the town's Party committee and the "positive hero" of the story, who takes the school principal's side, was based on the Party organizer in Solzhenitsyn's own school, and the character of the principal was modelled on someone else Solzhenitsyn knew. In the story they appear as little more than cardboard cut-outs (as are the students and the one other teacher who is mentioned), manipulated to illustrate the story's didactic message, and it was only the message that contained anything unusual about it, for, as in *Ivan Denisovich*, Solzhenitsyn had inverted the political moral that socialist realism was supposed to carry. Khabalygin, Knorozov, and the men from the ministry who come from Moscow to inspect the school—in other words, all members of the establishment and the upper Party hierarchy—were satirized as unscrupulous villains, while the heroes were the "little people" at the bottom of the hierarchy or outside it altogether.

A particular aspect of this was underlined in the description of the district secretary.

> It was Knorozov's boast that he never went back on his word. As it had once been in Moscow with Stalin's word, so it was still today with Knorozov's word: it was never changed or taken back. And although Stalin was long dead, Knorozov was still here. He was a leading proponent of the "strong-willed school of leadership," and he saw in this his greatest virtue. He could not imagine any other way of running things.[9]

It was the problem of Stalin's heirs in a new guise, and the message was that they were still firmly in place and still running the country as before.

It seems that Tvardovsky was pleased with the story when Solzhenitsyn delivered it to him in June, for he immediately scheduled it for the July issue of *Novy Mir*. It was at once a riposte to those who had criticized Solzhenitsyn for being unable to write about anything except the gloomier aspects of the past, especially the labour camps (even, "Krechetovka" had been about a man destined for the camps) and a blow in the struggle against the neo-Stalinists—just what *Novy Mir* needed, especially now after the Party plenum, when Khrushchev had slightly opened the gates for the liberals again. Solzhenitsyn, too, was satisfied by Tvardovsky's prompt response and in general felt hopeful about the way his career was developing.

Among other omens that encouraged Solzhenitsyn's optimism at this time were some unexpected encounters with the establishment. In February 1963 he had been invited to address seventy members of the Soviet Union's supreme Military Tribunal, that same tribunal under whose auspices the Special Board had sentenced him in 1945 to eight years' imprisonment and perpetual exile. He was even able to joke about it and was met with a sympathetic response. They told him endless horror stories about the camps and the work of the tribunal in the past, answered his questions willingly, seemed genuinely indignant, and discussed *Ivan Denisovich* with sincere admiration. "I looked about me," Solzhenitsyn later wrote, "and was amazed: they were human beings! Completely human! Now they were smiling, and frankly explaining how they had only wanted to do good."[10] Solzhenitsyn realized that there was an element of show in it all, but the very fact of their meeting him spoke volumes about the change. The deputy chief military prosecutor, Colonel D. T. Terekhov, had also received him in his office and described to him the arrest and investigation of Stalin's former minister of state security

Victor Abakumov and of the secret-police official who had master-minded the "doctors' plot,"* Mikhail Ryumin, both of whom Terekhov had interrogated before they were shot. Solzhenitsyn recognized in him a man of exceptional forcefulness, honesty, and talent, of the kind who might cleanse the land of injustice, and felt that there might really be on the way a new order that was ready to reform Soviet society.[11]

But not everything looked rosy that summer, for the honeymoon period of his friendship with Tvardovsky appeared to be fading a little, and a certain amount of friction was creeping into their relations. On Solzhenitsyn's side it was occasioned by an uncomfortable sense of being patronized. Of the many works he had offered Tvardovsky for publication, Tvardovsky had taken only three short stories: "Matryona," "Krechetovka," and now "For the Good of the Cause." Solzhenitsyn's lyric poems, some extracts from *The Way*, his miniature stories, his labour-camp play, and perhaps also *The Light Which Is in Thee* (though it is not clear whether Solzhenitsyn had yet shown him this play) had all been rejected. Moreover, Solzhenitsyn had a suspicion that Tvardovsky had somehow played a role in the Sovremennik's decision not to proceed with *Tenderfoot*, and he resented the fact that Tvardovsky had failed to put in a good word for it with Lebedev. He felt that it had been one thing to defer to Tvardovsky's judgement when he was unknown, but now he was world famous and, in many people's judgement, a better writer than Tvardovsky.

Tvardovsky, for his part, seems to have felt that he was in a position of tutelage *vis-à-vis* Solzhenitsyn and that he had a proprietary right to Solzhenitsyn's work, in view of the unprecedented and successful campaign he had waged to publish *A Day in the Life of Ivan Denisovich*. He had recognized in Solzhenitsyn a natural ally, and he certainly hoped, with Solzhenitsyn's help, to advance the cause of his magazine, but he also thought, not without justification, that Solzhenitsyn owed him something too. It must also be acknowledged that in matters of literary judgement he had right on his side, for everything he had rejected of Solzhenitsyn's so far had been second-rate, and everything he had accepted, apart from "For the Good of the Cause," had been excellent. Indeed, one can only admire his restraint in not jumping on the bandwagon of Solzhenitsyn's popularity at the slightest opportunity.

The differences of taste and interest between the two men also emerged in Tvardovsky's response to Solzhenitsyn's suggestion that *Novy Mir* published Shalamov's poetry. To his astonishment, Tvardovsky was uninterested in their labour-camp themes and rejected them on grounds of form—they were "too much like Pasternak." As Tvardovsky later wrote to Shala-

---

* In November 1952 nine Kremlin doctors were arrested and charged with conspiring with the British and American intelligence services to murder Soviet leaders, and were said to have been responsible for the death of Andrei Zhdanov in 1948. Since the doctors were Jewish, the accusations had anti-Semitic overtones, but the doctors were saved by the death of Stalin in March 1953 and were released a month later. The whole episode is usually referred to as the doctors' plot.

mov, they were not the sort of thing at all, in his opinion, that would appeal to *Novy Mir*'s readers.[12]

Solzhenitsyn conceded Tvardovsky's right to regard himself as a better judge of poetry—Tvardovsky was a famous poet. But as it happens, Solzhenitsyn had stumbled across a peculiar prejudice of Tvardovsky's. Andrei Sinyavsky, who had recently contributed a long article on Pasternak to *Novy Mir*, reports that although Tvardovsky had supported the article on political grounds, he had said to him, "I've only one request to make of you—please don't make Pasternak out to be a classic." Tvardovsky was convinced that Pasternak was a minor poet, destined to sink without a trace. He also exclaimed one day with distaste, "He's no better than that Mandelstam,"[13] meaning that he didn't care for either of them. He was, it seems, extremely hostile to modernism in all its forms, holding that a writer should be popular and read by the masses. This was what had so endeared Solzhenitsyn to him, for they were cast in the same mould and shared the same literary values. Shalamov, on the other hand, was a modernist. Even his short stories, despite the rawness of their material, were highly wrought and polished, with an emotional restraint that went well beyond Solzhenitsyn's in *Ivan Denisovich*. Solzhenitsyn was willing to tolerate the modernism for the sake of the subject matter,* but Tvardovsky was not. It was this intolerance, coupled with Tvardovsky's jealousy, that explained why *Novy Mir*'s poetry section was so weak.

A certain disharmony between the two men also sprang from their different perceptions of the world. Tvardovsky was the most remarkable Russian editor of his time, but he was a Party member and a high Soviet functionary, and this was very important to him. A writer who worked with him over many years has characterized him as follows:

> Tvardovsky was not a political radical by nature, he was a Party loyalist and very influenced in his behaviour by this, but he was also a superb editor and had an unerring instinct for literary quality. He was constitutionally incapable of publishing inferior work, he sought excellence in everything, and it was this that led him into politically dangerous waters, particularly when he decided to publish *Ivan Denisovich*. He didn't look for trouble, he didn't want trouble, he didn't like trouble when it came, and he did his level best to get out of it, but he was drawn into it by his own high editorial standards, and on that front he wouldn't compromise. He was therefore constantly finding himself put into ambiguous situations in which he felt deeply unhappy and very uncomfortable, but there was nothing he could do about it.[14]

Despite this inner conflict—or perhaps because of it—Tvardovsky was a past master at Soviet literary politics and at manoeuvring to get the maximum possible past the censors and their political mentors. He found the

---

*Despite feeling that Shalamov's prose style had suffered from his isolation, Solzhenitsyn was still able to admire his achievement. He once told Kopelev, "You can't get a razor-blade between his words."

tactics of it absorbing, even exhilarating, but it was precisely here that Solzhenitsyn parted company from him. Solzhenitsyn's loyalty was to a system
of literary (and increasingly political) values older and more disinterested
than those of the Soviet establishment, values that he had imbibed from his
immersion in the classical Russian literature of the nineteenth century. As
he later wrote of Tvardovsky, "he was too ready to believe that this system
was all-embracing and durable. He could not imagine anyone rejecting the
system from the outset. He could not imagine my discerning or knowing
things about literature or politics that he himself could not see or did not
know."[15] This judgement, characteristically harsh, puts the blame all on one
side and perhaps exaggerates Solzhenitsyn's own feelings at this time, but it
does point to a fundamental difference between the two men.

Solzhenitsyn was able to take this stance because he was an outsider.
His prison experiences had set him apart for all time from the Soviet establishment and the world of political and social orthodoxy. As he later noted
in *The Oak and the Calf*, "I could never be so candid with [Tvardovsky], so at
ease with him, as I could with dozens of people on whom the groves of Gulag
had cast their indelible shadow."[16] The dividing-line between them was still
the barbed-wire fence and the ploughed strip, a ghostly barrier that continued to separate the oppressed "us" from the privileged "them." It was membership in this grim club that still guided Solzhenitsyn in many of his judgments
of others, and from which he derived an essential element of his own identity.

Nor can one discount Solzhenitsyn's egotism, ambition, and iron resolution. Even if he understood Tvardovsky intuitively and intellectually, he
was not prepared to make any allowances or to budge an inch from his plans.
One of his enduring strengths, as a writer and as a man, was this absolute
refusal to compromise; but it made for some difficult relationships and some
turbulent scenes, especially in his dealings with his editor.

One such scene occurred in July 1963. Solzhenitsyn and Natalia were
in Moscow on their way back from Leningrad. Solzhenitsyn was in a dud-
geon about some changes that Boris Sachs had allowed the censors to make
in "For the Good of the Cause" without asking his permission (among other
things, they had removed the word '"strike" from his description of the protest the students proposed to stage), having only just discovered them when
the July issue of *Novy Mir* appeared. Here was a perfect example of his differences with the magazine. Such practices, he told Tvardovsky, had become
so normal that no one noticed them any more. Tvardovsky sided with Sachs
and accused Solzhenitsyn of "flaunting his principles." But Solzhenitsyn felt
betrayed. For him, every word counted. Even if other authors acquiesced in
such treatment of their works, he was not going to join them.[17]

This little contretemps then escalated into a more serious confrontation.
Tvardovsky had just returned from a meeting with Ilyichev to discuss the
composition of the Soviet delegation to a conference of a hundred writers
that was to be held in Leningrad the following month. The conference was

to be a symposium on the novel jointly sponsored by UNESCO and the Communist-inspired Community of European Writers (COMES). It was one of a series of events (the just-completed Moscow International Film Festival was another) designed to demonstrate the Soviet Union's policy of cultural coexistence with the West. After some pleading, Tvardovsky had managed to secure the inclusion of Solzhenitsyn in the Soviet delegation, which, in terms of Soviet literary politics, meant a signal boost for *Novy Mir* and the entire liberal camp.

As it happens, Tvardovsky had just come round from one of his periodic drinking bouts—his answer to the insoluble problems that beset him. It had been a particularly difficult summer, and he had been taking to the bottle somewhat more than usual. His eyes were still bloodshot, his skin sagged, and he was chain-smoking with nervous concentration; but he was also elated by his success with Ilyichev, and he confidently expected Solzhenitsyn to agree to go. But Solzhenitsyn refused point-blank. He was still furious with the censors, he detested Tvardovsky's drinking habits, and he was determined not to waste his time at conferences. As he later wrote, "It would be quite impossible to say what I thought, and . . . to go there like a pet monkey would be shameful." But Tvardovsky was appalled: "I made it my business to see justice done. You can refuse if you like, but it's your duty to be there in the interests of Soviet literature."[18]

Victor Nekrasov, who was present during this conversation, sided with Tvardovsky. He himself could not go, because he was still under heavy attack from the authorities for his travel notes. An official "investigation" into his behaviour abroad had been going on in Kiev for months, and he was on the brink of expulsion from the Party. He felt that Solzhenitsyn ought to go, not so much for the sake of Soviet literature as for Tvardovsky's sake. According to Nekrasov's account of the scene, Tvardovsky openly pleaded with Solzhenitsyn and virtually went down on his knees to him, but Solzhenitsyn was adamant. He gave no explanation and no reasons, and Nekrasov felt that for the first time he was seeing a completely new side of Solzhenitsyn. In his view Tvardovsky deserved support, if only in the form of gratitude and a human response to his misery.[19]

The COMES meeting went ahead without Solzhenitsyn, who writes that he was obliged to decamp from Ryazan on his bicycle to avoid giving a negative answer to all the telegrams and official invitations that came for him. It was not a success, for it revealed a wide chasm between Western and Soviet writers in their attitudes to literature. In desperation Ehrenburg was freed from disgrace and dispatched to Leningrad by Khrushchev personally to pour oil on troubled waters, and in a speech of brilliant diplomacy he did do something to draw the two sides together, but there was no real meeting of minds. There was, however, a curious postscript. In an apparent attempt to underline the Soviet Union's sincerity in seeking closer ties with the West, Khrushchev invited a group of twenty-eight writers to his villa at Pitsunda, on the Black Sea. There he treated them to one of his long, rambling speeches that took in Cuba, Hungary, China, tsarism, Stalinism, disarmament—anything but culture, in fact—and was incongruously threatening in tone. Then he suddenly broke off and invited Tvardovsky to read aloud his long satirical poem "Tyorkin in the Next World." "Tyorkin," with its earthy peasant idioms and untranslatable expressions, was just as baffling to the Western writers present as Khrushchev's speech, but the extraordinary thing about it was its daring political content, as daring in its way as *Ivan Denisovich*, which had condemned the poem to circulate underground for much of the nine years since it was written.* It seemed that Khrushchev was anxious once again to use literature to demonstrate his broadmindedness and to dissipate, by this gesture, the gloom induced by his uncompromising speech. Three days later, "Tyorkin" was published in *Izvestia*.[20]

An interesting aspect of Solzhenitsyn's description of his argument with Tvardovsky in *The Oak and the Calf* is the insularity it reveals on the part of both men with regard to contemporary literature. Tvardovsky is quoted as saying that the symposium would in any case be pointless, since there were no novels worth arguing about: "It is doubtful whether a novel can be written in our time." To this, Solzhenitsyn boastfully ripostes, "*Cancer Ward* was already begun, *The First Circle* had been finished a year before, but I didn't know in what form I dared offer it to Tvardovsky. And I was supposed to sit in a symposium, bound and gagged, listening to forty mouths chorusing, 'The novel is dead!' 'The novel is obsolete!' 'There can be no more novels!'"[21] Yet this was a conference attended by William Golding and Angus Wilson, Alain Robbe-Grillet and Nathalie Sarraute, Hans Magnus Enzensberger and Jean-Paul Sartre, where novels by Günter Grass, Heinrich Böll, Samuel Beckett, Graham Greene, and Saul Bellow were also discussed. It was hardly likely that the death of the novel would be the main point on the agenda—it was little more than a rhetorical slogan to draw attention to the main subject matter. Solzhenitsyn, by reason of his long years of imprisonment, and Tvardovsky, as a result of his ideological blinkers and ignorance of foreign languages, had barely heard of the names of the leading European and American novelists of the time, let alone read and understood them. Yet they were quite ready to dismiss them out of hand. Meanwhile, at the symposium itself, the senior Soviet delegates (though not Tvardovsky and not Ehrenburg) devoted their efforts to a violent attack on Joyce, Kafka, and Proust and a justification of their non-publication in the Soviet Union. Despite Khrushchev's half-hearted liberalization, the Soviet Union as a whole was still in the literary Dark Ages.

In August, Solzhenitsyn did escape on his bicycle. He and Natalia went

---

*"Tyorkin in the Next World" was begun, and largely completed, in 1954 and was said to have been circulating in samizdat since about 1957. A continuation of *Vasily Tyorkin*, it purported to show Tyorkin's adventures in the "next world" after his death, but the next world bore a surprising similarity to Stalin's Russia, which was mercilessly criticized and satirized by Tvardovsky. The poem appeared in *Izvestia* on 18 August 1963, and a few days later in *Novy Mir*, no. 8 (1963).

on a carefully planned tour of "Russian antiquities," setting out from Me-shchera, in Ryazan Province, and cycling through the provinces of Ivanovo and Yaroslavl to Moscow—through the heartland of ancient Russia. They visited the picturesque, unspoiled cities of Suzdal, Vladimir, and Rostov the Great, inspecting the monasteries, churches, and fortifications of the Middle Ages, taking photographs, making notes, and camping out overnight. Soon after arriving back in Ryazan, they set out on another ride, this time to Tula Province and Yasnaya Polyana, Tolstoy's estate. For Solzhenitsyn, with his deep love of Tolstoy, it must have been in the nature of a pilgrimage; but he had started collecting material once more for his big novel on the Revolution, now tentatively called *The Red Wheel*, and it may be that he was already planning the scene that was eventually to appear in *August 1914* in which the young Sanya Lazhenitsyn (based on Solzhenitsyn's father) confronts an aging Tolstoy at Yasnaya Polyana to ask him for his thoughts on the purpose of life and the writing of poetry.

On this Tula trip, they also paid a visit to Kulikovo Field, site of the famous fourteenth-century battle between the Russians and the Tartars, a turning point in Russian history. There they inspected the ruined medieval church of St Sergius of Radonezh, whose iconostasis had been chopped up for firewood, whose flagstones had been carried off by the nearby villagers to pave their yards, and whose cupolas had been plundered for their tin. They clambered up the unusual cast-iron tower erected in 1848 to mark the site of the battle and made the acquaintance of the dogged and faithful care-taker, Zakhar Dmitrievich. Zakhar fascinated them by his prickly gruffness, by his dedication to the church and monument, and above all by the devotion with which he had sewn a special pouch inside his tattered jacket in which to carry and cherish the Kulikovo visitors' book. Disgusted by the disrepair into which the site had been allowed to fall and yet captivated by its air of desolation, Solzhenitsyn spent a whole day wandering about the field, recon-structing the epic battle that had been fought there, and he and Natalia spent the night in the caretaker's hut at the latter's invitation. Two years later Solzhenitsyn described the caretaker, the monument, and the day he had spent there in one of his finest short stories, "Zakhar the Pouch."

By the time the Solzhenitsyns returned to Ryazan, a new controversy was breaking over "For the Good of the Cause." On the very last day of August, a deputy editor of the *Literaturnaya Gazeta*, Yuri Barabash, pub-lished an article—"What Is Justice?"—in which he called the story "a fail-ure." He was right, but for the wrong reasons, since he maintained that the defects of "Cause" "had much in common with those that critics had already noted . . . in 'Matryona's Place.' " Solzhenitsyn's main mistake, he wrote, had been to "operate with abstract categories that were empty of concrete social content," and his view of life, as reflected here, was just as "archaic" as in the earlier story.[22]

The *Literaturnaya Gazeta* followed this up by printing three readers' let-ters supporting Barabash's criticism. Then, quite unexpectedly, it published another article in favour of the story, this time by the mildly liberal novelist Daniil Granin, who praised it as a contribution to the necessary democratization of Soviet life and a plea for greater justice. Almost immediately after that the paper changed tack yet again with another attack both on the story itself and on Granin's defence of it, adding an editorial note to the effect that Solzhenitsyn had violated the canons of socialist realism by "mechanically transplanting . . . the tradition of critical realism to socialist soil." By then it was October, and, appropriately enough, the ultra-conservative magazine (and *Novy Mir's* chief ideological adversary) *Oktyabr*, edited by Kochetov, published a harsh attack on both "Matryona's Place" and "For the Good of the Cause." In the same issue *Oktyabr* printed a glowing review of a new work about the labour camps called *Endurance* by a former prisoner, Boris Dyakov. Dyakov was a loyal Communist who had remained faithful to the Party and who had survived his ordeal by becoming a trusty. He rejected Solzhenitsyn's criticism of the trusties as parasites and stool-pigeons and praised them as loyal helpers of the regime.[23]

At this juncture *Novy Mir* returned to the fray with three readers' letters praising "For the Good of the Cause," only to find itself attacked by the *Literaturnaya Gazeta* for selecting only favourable letters and suppressing the unfavourable ones. This drove *Novy Mir* to investigate its readers' letters in detail and to discover that it had received a total of fifty-eight letters about the story, of which fifty-five were completely in favour, two had stylistic criticisms, and only one was hostile—and couched in such abusive language that it was unpublishable. These facts were conveyed to the *Literaturnaya Gazeta* in a "letter to the editor," at the end of which *Novy Mir* revealed a little secret. Twelve of their favourable letters had been sent simultaneously to the *Literaturnaya Gazeta*, which had published not one. It was the *Gazeta* that had been guilty of suppression, not *Novy Mir*.[24]

The debate then died down, but what was interesting about it was not just the light it threw on the tug of war between the conservatives and liberals or on the fluctuations of Solzhenitsyn's reputation but also the fact that it took place at all over such a mediocre story. From the point of view of the passion displayed and the space devoted to them, virtually no distinction was made between "Matryona" and "Cause," yet one was a masterpiece and the other a pot-boiler. And "Cause" attracted far more attention than Solzhenitsyn's much better story "Incident at Krechetovka Station." At the same time, nobody bothered to say how badly written "Cause" was—the conservatives because they had other, more damning accusations to make against it, and the liberals because they didn't want to damage their case. It was a typical instance of politics completely overriding literary values.

27

LENIN PRIZE
CANDIDATE

Having given up his teaching post, Solzhenitsyn now had immeasurably more time in which to pursue his literary career. His first preoccupation was to get something else into print. His two plays and his verse had proved frustratingly unpopular with Tvardovsky and other knowledgeable readers, and much else that he had "in his desk drawer" was politically unacceptable, including his major work *The First Circle*. He felt, however, that if he picked out some chapters from the novel, they might just get by, and so he chose those dealing with the relationship between Gleb and Nadia Nerzhin and offered them to Tvardovsky as "a fragment," without revealing that it was part of a completed novel. In *The Oak and the Calf* Solzhenitsyn writes that Tvardovsky rejected them as being about "that prison theme again,"[1] but Reshetovskaya throws a slightly different light on the matter. According to her, Tvardovsky liked the chapters but thought that to start publication of the novel before he saw the rest of it and in this fragmentary fashion "would be unwise and might ruin the whole project."[2]

Solzhenitsyn had meanwhile turned his mind to a new topic, which he hoped would be more suitable—his experiences in the cancer hospital in Tashkent. The idea of writing a novel on this subject had first occurred to him when he was walking back to the MVD office from the tram-stop in Tashkent in 1955. It had lain dormant until a few months earlier, when he had made a tentative start on it before putting it aside to work for a while on *The Red Wheel*. Now he was ready to return to it again, particularly since he felt that the subject would be more acceptable to *Novy Mir* than that of *The First Circle*. Tvardovsky seemed delighted with the idea and was all for including it in the announcement of works to be published in *Novy Mir* in the coming year. But he didn't like Solzhenitsyn's projected title, *Cancer Ward*. It was too direct and outspoken for the Victorian sensibilities of Soviet readers and might be interpreted as political and allegorical. He suggested something blander, like "Patients and Doctors," but Solzhenitsyn was indignant over this naked political calculation and the subordination of literary to nonliterary criteria. Tvardovsky's proposed title was like "a smear of porridge on a plate,"[3] and he flatly refused to accept it. When the *Novy Mir* announcement appeared, there was no mention of any new work by Solzhenitsyn.

Although they had failed to agree on Solzhenitsyn's next literary venture, it did not prevent Tvardovsky from continuing to build on his first one, and later that year he nominated *A Day in the Life of Ivan Denisovich* for the 1964 Lenin Prize, with *Novy Mir* as the nominating institution.

Lenin Prizes are awarded in the Soviet Union for what are adjudged to be the best examples of literature, art, science, and technology each year, and nominations may be made by the relevant unions and professional bodies. In literature, the list of nominations was announced in the *Literaturnaya Gazeta* on 28 December 1963. Apart from Solzhenitsyn the leading candidates were Oles Gonchar, head of the Ukrainian Writers' Union, for his novel *The Sheep Bell*, an uncomplicated tale about life in the Ukrainian steppes; Daniil Granin, for his novel about scientists, *Into the Storm*; Egor Isayev, for his poem *Court of Memory*; Galina Serebryakova, for a trilogy of novels on the life of Karl Marx, *Prometheus*; Alexander Chakovsky, editor of the *Literaturnaya Gazeta*, for his novel *Light of a Distant Star*; and Leonid Pervomaisky, for his novel *Wild Honey*. As is clear from some of the titles and subjects above, if literary merit had been the criterion, there would have been no contest. *A Day in the Life of Ivan Denisovich* stood head and shoulders above the rest and was the only entrant that was indisputably a work of art. Everyone knew it. But literary prizes are rarely a question of pure merit, least of all Soviet literary prizes, and the Lenin Prize is the most eagerly sought after, and thus the most politicized, of all. It is also conspicuously bestowed as a mark of the establishment's favour.

From the start, therefore, the question that dominated the debate over the prize, both privately and publicly, was, Would Solzhenitsyn be allowed to get it? The composition of the judging committee was not reassuring. Apart from Tvardovsky, the only member with any independence of mind was Mikhail Sholokhov, and he was crusty and unpredictable, with a marked preference for Party loyalists. The rest were timid mediocrities and, astonishingly by Western standards, included two of the candidates: Chakovsky and Isayev. A third candidate, Gonchar, was an ex-officio vice-chairman of the prize committee.

To a certain extent, committee members were tied by the nominations made by the organizations they represented. *The Sheep Bell* and *Into the Storm*, for instance, had been proposed by the board of the USSR Writers' Union, while *Prometheus* was the nominee of the Writers' Union of the Russian Republic. Because of the conspicuous safety of its subject matter, *Prometheus* had the most nominations of all—including one, according to Zhores Medvedev, from the Directorate of Weather Bureaux of the Central Provinces, which gives one some idea of the processes at work behind the prize awards. It was reasonably clear that, given their own preferences, committee members would plump for something safe and uninspiring, but clearer still that they would do what they were told: if an order came from on high to vote for *Ivan Denisovich*, they would do so without blinking. And here lay the chief hope of Solzhenitsyn's supporters.

At first there seemed to be something of a bandwagon rolling in Solzhenitsyn's favour. In mid-January 1964 *Izvestia* published an interview with the prototype of one of the most memorable characters in *Ivan Denisovich*, Captain Buinovsky, the loyal Communist naval captain who is dispatched to the punishment cells for arguing with the guard commander in one of the closing scenes of the book. His original, Commander Boris Burkovsky, was now curator of the naval museum of the cruiser *Aurora* in Leningrad, and he enthusiastically confirmed the truthfulness of Solzhenitsyn's portrayal of Ekibastuz and its prisoners (thus refuting conservative accusations of exaggeration). By the greatest irony, Burkovsky asserted that the men in the camps, like the prisoners in the novel, had in their hearts "never broken with the Party, and had never identified the evil done to them with the Party or our system. I and thousands like me were physically torn from the Party and people, but our hearts and thoughts were still with both."[4] This was undoubtedly true of Burkovsky, but it hardly coincided with Solzhenitsyn's portraits in his story. On the other hand it made perfect propaganda for the Lenin Prize.

At the end of January the official mouthpiece of the Party, *Pravda*, published a strong article in favour of *Ivan Denisovich* by Samuil Marshak,[5] winner of the Lenin Prize the preceding year, and at a Writers' Union meeting in early February to discuss the nominations, letters urging support for Solzhenitsyn were read out from Kornei Chukovsky and Ilya Ehrenburg, while Lev Kopelev took the floor to endorse his old friend. *Novy Mir* also published in its January number an extraordinarily long and detailed article by Vladimir Lakshin called "Ivan Denisovich, His Friends and Foes." Lakshin analyzed all the articles that had appeared on *Ivan Denisovich* throughout the year, carefully dissecting the hostile critics' arguments and rebutting them one by one.[6]

But the conservatives were not inactive, either, and in February developed their counter-attack. At a combined meeting of the Moscow and the Russian Republic branches of the Writers' Union, *Ivan Denisovich* was heavily criticized by Dmitri Eremin (once a scourge of Dudintsev's *Not by Bread Alone*), a secretary of the Moscow Union, and by two "experts": Boris Dyakov, author of *Endurance*, and, for some reason, General A. Todorsky. Much time was devoted to a vicious attack on Lakshin and his article, for it was still felt safer to assault Solzhenitsyn's supporters than the author himself, who had, after all, once been endorsed by Khrushchev. All this was then reproduced, together with an approving editorial note, in the *Literaturnaya Gazeta* (without any indication that the *Gazeta*'s editor—Chakovsky—was a rival candidate).[7]

Lakshin's article had stirred a storm of controversy. The young Yugoslav critic Mihajlo Mihajlov (later to become a dissident in Yugoslavia), who was visiting Moscow, was told by Lakshin that since the publication of his article he had been receiving up to 150 letters a day, almost all of them favourable. He told Mihajlov of a saying then current in Moscow: "Tell me what you think of *One Day* and I will tell you who you are."[8] The idea of *Ivan Denisovich* as a kind of litmus paper had been voiced by one of the first critics to write about it the preceding year, I. Chicherov, and even as this debate was in progress Veniamin Teush was writing an article, "A. Solzhenitsyn and the Writer's Spiritual Mission," in which he commented (somewhat extravagantly) on this phenomenon.

> The atmosphere around Solzhenitsyn has been filled with spinning and ever-expanding spiritual hurricanes: a hurricane of love and a hurricane of hatred. *Ivan Denisovich* has become a sort of touchstone, or, as one reader put it, an X-ray apparatus that virtually automatically sorts people into the living and the dead, with dead, withered souls.[9]

Teush had been given access to the hundreds—perhaps even thousands—of letters that Solzhenitsyn had received as a result of the publication of *Ivan Denisovich* and "Matryona," and he built his article around a classification of this material and an analysis of the responses. He found, naturally enough, that an overwhelming majority of readers favourable to the stories had themselves suffered in the labour camps, or had relations or close friends who had served and often died in them. They were supported by others who were appalled and shamed by the revelations made by Khrushchev, Solzhenitsyn, and others about Stalin's terror and the horrors of Gulag, and by those members of the intelligentsia, the Party, and the bureaucracy who sincerely desired a change for the better and a more humane society. Together they composed a majority of those who wrote. On the other side were former prisoners, like Boris Dyakov, who had survived more or less comfortably in the camps by co-operating with the authorities; former camp guards and officers of the camp administration; and members of the Party or the bureaucracy who were either implicated in Stalin's crimes and still shared his ideas or who simply believed in strong-arm methods and feared that change of any kind would bring anarchy and the loss of at least some of their privileges.

These divisions reflected more or less accurately the divisions in society at large, and for this reason it was easy for the two main camps to fall in behind their leaders and take up positions for the political battle over the Lenin Prize. In this sense the struggle over *Ivan Denisovich* was very much part of a larger struggle then in progress. But the reasons for the ferocity with which this particular battle was fought also have to do with the peculiar qualities of the story itself, which completely transcended the social and political dimensions of its success.

These were, in the first instance, its literary qualities. It is hard for Westerners to grasp just how bleak and barren the Soviet literary scene is and was (especially in the early sixties), how parched and starving Soviet readers are for contemporary literature of any quality. If one casts one's mind back over the nearly forty years since the Second World War, one finds barely half a dozen writers whose names stand out as possibly having world-class literary talent: Akhmatova, Pasternak, Solzhenitsyn, Brodsky, Sinyavsky, Nadezhda Mandelstam, Nekrasov—and three of these were of an older, pre-war generation. Dozens of Soviet writers have been translated into English and other foreign languages, but most stand out only because of the emptiness of their surroundings, so that, ironically, it is easier for a third-rate Russian writer to be translated into English—provided he provokes a political scandal—than for a second-rate French writer or a first-rate Italian one.

As one critic has aptly noted, most Soviet so-called literature consists of editorials in verse or in rhythmic prose. They are read and listened to because they fulfil the function of a free press—not that literature is free in the proper sense of the word, but it is freer than the actual press itself, and its writers are sufficiently skilful to smuggle in ideas and issues that get smothered in the newspapers. (This is not, by the way, to be taken as a slander on the writers. Many of them perform miracles by way of allegory or indirection, and in another setting would certainly do as well as anyone else.) In *belles-lettres* they can be more daring—within limits—and are therefore listened to and read with more respect.

In such a setting *A Day in the Life of Ivan Denisovich* was also perceived as an editorial—an editorial of uncommon daring, force, and impact. But much more than that, it was a genuine work of art. Paradoxically, as the English critic Max Hayward has noted, although *Ivan Denisovich* was published in Moscow for avowedly political reasons and was received both there and abroad mainly as a political sensation, it was one of the few Soviet prose works since the war that could stand completely as a work of art and be discussed exclusively in terms of its aesthetic achievement, quite apart from its political qualities. It was a universal statement about the human condition, and it was for this reason that comparisons were made with Tolstoy and Dostoyevsky and that hungry readers cherished the book.

Thus far, one supposes, the Western reader is able to follow and sympathize, but there was another dimension of the book that is difficult to describe and summarize, but without which no account of the impact of *Ivan Denisovich* would be complete. This dimension one can only call spiritual, not out of any sentimental regard for the attributes of the alleged "Russian soul" but simply because it relates to that sphere of human existence where morality and faith converge and whose workings are beyond our conscious understanding. It is a sphere that in the Soviet Union has been so scorched by Marxist theory and Soviet practice that it had seemed, during Stalin's rule at least, to have succumbed to total atrophy.

Perhaps the simplest way to illustrate the impact of *Ivan Denisovich* and what it meant to Soviet readers is to reproduce some of the comments quoted by Teush. "My face was smothered in tears," wrote one woman. "I didn't wipe them away or feel ashamed, because all this, packed into a small number of pages of the magazine, was mine, intimately mine, mine for every day of the fifteen years I spent in the camps." Another woman: "I wept and laughed. . . . I can weep now, but at the time there were no tears." And a man: "Although I wept as I read it, at last I felt myself to be an equal citizen with all the rest, whereas up to now I felt only hostile looks reminding me of Pechora and Norilsk."* And another: "For me and others like me your story was the last hope that justice still exists somewhere, that it has not vanished or died out." And another: "At last the chill of estrangement is beginning to melt. We too, all of us, are being given some human sympathy."

Even more striking were readers' responses to the author himself: "I kiss your golden hands"; "Thank you for your truthfulness"; "Let me bow to the ground before you, dear friend"; "Thank goodness that you exist . . . look after yourself. Your existence is our happiness"; "We love you, we believe you, we wish you health and strength, thank you"; "Please accept our love and gratitude, beloved writer, great writer"; "Thank you for your love and courage". And, at greater length:

Thank you, dear friend, comrade and brother! Thank you for your tremendous achievement, thank you from the bottom of my heart. I would give you anything, anything. Reading your story I remembered Sivaya Maska and Vorkuta† . . . the frosts and blizzards, the insults and humiliations. . . . I wept as I read— they were all familiar characters, as if from my own brigade. . . . Thank you once more! Please carry on in the same spirit—write, write. . . . Keep well, dear friend. You have already left your name in the history of Soviet literature, and nothing can wipe it away.[10]

Perhaps all this does reflect the "Russian soul"—in its emotional fulsomeness and hyperbolic expression. But it also reflects the spiritual wasteland that was Soviet literature before the appearance of *Ivan Denisovich*, and the enormous sense of spiritual and psychological relief induced by reading Solzhenitsyn's story (and reinforced by "Matryona's Place"). In these circumstances the debate about *Ivan Denisovich* took on a significance that had never attended the discussion of any work of Russian literature before, either before or since the Revolution. It was indeed a literary struggle and a political struggle, but it was also a struggle for the hearts and souls of the Russian people.

Solzhenitsyn was inundated with such letters, which had kept coming throughout 1963 and which now increased again as a result of the debate over the Lenin Prize. One consequence of his conscientious reading of them was the unpleasant discovery that although the Gulag Archipelago no longer

* Two of the biggest and most notorious labour-camp complexes in Stalin's time.
† Notoriously harsh labour camps in Siberia.

harboured millions of political prisoners, it had not, as Khrushchev proclaimed, been entirely dismantled, and still numbered its victims in hundreds
of thousands. Among the letters that reached him in Ryazan were scraps of
torn and crumpled paper uncannily reminiscent of the creased triangle he
had once smuggled out of Krasnaya Presnya to Natalia, bearing evidence of
present injustices and innocent victims still behind barbed wire. There was
little he could do publicly, other than go on writing in the same way, but he
resolved to do what he could behind the scenes, and in January 1964 exploited
the publicity surrounding his nomination for the Lenin Prize to arrange some
meetings with a number of government representatives.

His first meeting was with the legislative proposals commission of the
Supreme Soviet of the USSR, which was just then engaged in producing a
revised corrective-labour code to replace Stalin's code (although, as Solzhenitsyn remarks in *The Gulag Archipelago*, Stalin's code had existed only on
paper and was ignored in practice). The eight commissioners expressed an
interest in hearing Solzhenitsyn's views on how the code might be reformed,
and he spoke passionately in favour of liberalization. Surely, he said, removing prisoners from their families, depriving them of their freedom, segregating them in labour camps, and obliging them to do work that was different
from their trade was sufficient, without piling on extra punishments and
humiliations. Could they possibly imagine how painful this was? They should
try to reform the prisoners, not just punish them, in order to return them to
society. Solzhenitsyn also pointed out the injustice of the Khrushchev "reform"
of 1961, which had introduced three different regimes for labour-camp prisoners: normal, strict, and special. The latter two disciplinary regimes, he
explained, were designed systematically to humiliate and exhaust the prisoners, partly by means of starvation. Could they not at least increase the
number of food parcels a prisoner was allowed to receive? Could prisoners
not be allowed more letters and family visits and be guaranteed Sundays off?

In short, Solzhenitsyn urged a general humanization of the labour-camp
regime, but he was hampered by the parameters of their discussion. In the
first place, he was speaking on behalf of those he took to be innocent, and his
plea for greater mercy and liberalism in the treatment of the prisoners reflected
this belief; but he could not voice it aloud, for this would have cast a slur on
the workings of Soviet justice generally. The commissioners, by contrast,
were convinced that they were dealing exclusively with hardened and dangerous criminals and that only coercion and severity had any chance of working. Secondly, Solzhenitsyn was obliged to accept the good faith not only of
the commissioners but also of the Supreme Soviet and the Party in their
proclaimed desire to introduce reforms, whereas he grew convinced in the
course of the meeting that the exercise was wholly cosmetic and that the
authorities were essentially uninterested in change.

He found himself rebuffed and even lost for arguments. The commissioners' reasoning was smooth and deft: he was behind the times and out of
touch. "I leave feeling tired and jaded," he later wrote. "I even feel a little

less sure of myself, whereas they are not the least bit shaken. They will do just as they please, and the Supreme Soviet will confirm it unanimously."[11]

Solzhenitsyn paid visits to the minister for protection of public order, Vadim Tikunov, and to the Institute for the Study of the Origins of Criminality. The minister was more friendly and agreed with some of Solzhenitsyn's criticisms of the harshness of labour-camp conditions but was equally immovable when it came to judging the prisoners' characters or proposing changes. He was more or less satisfied with the camps the way they were and offered to take Solzhenitsyn to see one, but Solzhenitsyn declined, because he was convinced he would be taken to a camp specially designed for showing to visitors and because, if he went as a ministry guest, he would be incapable of looking the prisoners in the eye. "I left with the weary conviction that there was no end to it. That I had not advanced my cause by a hair's breadth and that they would always take a sledge-hammer to crack a nut. I left depressed by the realization that two human minds could think so differently. Prisoner will understand minister when he ensconces himself in a ministerial sanctum, and minister will understand prisoner when he, too, goes behind the wire . . . and in return for his freedom is offered the chance to master a machine."[12]

Solzhenitsyn's third meeting, with members of the research staff of the Institute for the Study of the Origins of Criminality, was the friendliest of the lot, and he was impressed by the way the researchers frankly disagreed with one another and held a range of opinions. On his way out, however, he had a brief meeting with the director, Igor Karpets, who turned out to be as dogmatic, reactionary, and opinionated as anyone he had met. Karpets was vehemently against any suggestion of "babying the prisoners," justified the harsh measures applied in the camps, and was in no doubt at all that their purpose was not re-education but "retribution." The most piquant fact about Karpets, as Solzhenitsyn discovered afterwards, was that he was the Soviet representative in the International Association of Democratic Lawyers, of which he was nothing less than vice-president.[13]

The reason that Solzhenitsyn was received at all by these bureaucrats was that he was now an establishment figure in his own right. Indeed, his position in society and his way of life had changed out of all recognition in the year or so since *Ivan Denisovich* had been published. Free of the school at last, he was able to travel more often to Moscow and Leningrad to use the libraries there. His favourites in Moscow, according to Reshetovskaya, were the Basic Library of Social Sciences and the Central Archive of Military History. In the latter he searched for material on the Samsonov campaign for *The Red Wheel*. While digging there, he turned up some information on his father and even found the name of the church in Belorussia where his parents had married.[14] In Leningrad he preferred the main public library for conducting research.

An essential adjunct of this new-found freedom and mobility was the small, green Moskvich he had bought at the end of 1963 with some of the royalties from *Ivan Denisovich*, overcoming a squeamish distaste for the internal-combustion engine that had inspired his satirical prose poem "Means of Transport" ("this most absurd of all earth's creations. . . . All it can do is clatter and screech . . . and belch out gob after gob of stinking black smoke").[15] Hitherto he had preferred the bicycle. He had also once gone on record as stating that he would never buy a car, since a man's psychology changes when he climbs behind the wheel. Be that as it may, "Denis," as he nicknamed his car, would take him more and more often away from Ryazan, if not to Moscow or Leningrad, then to his favourite village of Solotcha, where he stayed in the picturesque cottage of an elderly peasant woman, Agafya, who reminded him in more than one respect of Matryona Zakharova.

Away from Ryazan also meant away from Natalia, who was beginning to feel uneasy about his frequent absences from home and to wonder whether she could keep up with her celebrated husband. Solzhenitsyn's sudden fame had been a trial for her as well. It was very pleasant to be invited to fashionable Moscow restaurants, spend New Year's Eve at the Sovremennik, and be on first-name terms with the famous. Natalia had been more impressed by it all than her husband had. But she was always aware that she was present on sufferance, as the great man's consort, and that without her marriage no one would have cast a second glance at her. It is possible that this would not have bothered her overmuch—it was a common enough situation for the wives of the famous—but there was Solzhenitsyn's puritanism, parsimony, and mania for secrecy to contend with at the same time. There was nothing she would have liked better than to take some of their sudden wealth and go out and buy herself a new wardrobe, fit out their flat with new gadgets, or sit back and relax a bit, calling on friends and taking life easy. But with Solzhenitsyn such frivolity was out of the question, and life for her went on much as before. They did discuss the question of whether Natalia should leave the Agricultural Institute. She had ceased doing any original research, she was socially estranged from most of her colleagues by her husband's unsociability, and the work was no longer very interesting. But Solzhenitsyn pointed out that an author's income was quite uncertain and irregular and that it might be premature to leave just yet.

Her one consolation was her music. She continued to play the piano regularly and still dreamt from time to time of being able to make it her career, though the chances were by now remote. Solzhenitsyn had nurtured her illusions earlier by promising that when he was published, their circle would widen and she would meet others who shared her interest and ambitions. But, in the event, it had been essentially his circle that had widened, and she had remained at home with her mother and aunts in Ryazan.

To compensate for this, Natalia had occupied herself with minor secretarial work, opening and in some cases answering letters, sorting them and putting them away in numbered folders. Solzhenitsyn's filing system was as meticulous as ever. There were separate folders for the different categories of mail, and for a variety of newspaper and magazine articles, such as folder no. 28 for "Reactions from Abroad." Then there were the manuscripts and various drafts, as well as all the research material Solzhenitsyn was amassing from the libraries. In this way Natalia felt she was able to be useful and was comforted by the knowledge that she was participating in her husband's career.[16]

As for Solzhenitsyn it was natural that he should want to get away from time to time from the claustrophobic flat in Kasimovsky Lane, with its three old ladies, however obliging and helpful they might be. Formerly, there had been the school to offer a break, but now there would be none unless he had other reasons to leave. And he had plenty. The world was his oyster, and after losing the best part of his youth in the camps and exile, he was keenly aware of a sense of having to make up for lost time. So it was nothing exceptional when, towards the end of January 1964, Solzhenitsyn telephoned Natalia from Moscow to say that he was moving on to Leningrad to do some work in the public library there. Leningrad had become a favourite resort of Solzhenitsyn's ever since his first trip there, in 1958; and the preceding year he had met and become good friends with the distinguished literary critic Efim Etkind and his wife, Ekaterina Zvorykina.

This latter meeting had been the direct result of a "fan letter" from Zvorykina to Solzhenitsyn after she had read "Matryona's Place." He had been impressed by the quality of her letter and on his next visit to Leningrad had simply rung and asked for permission to call. Their meeting was a success. The Etkinds were people of vast erudition and learning, with a very Russian passion for the arts and a highly developed taste. They were also possessed of a high seriousness that greatly appealed to the earnest Solzhenitsyn. For their part, they were amazed to find him so cheerful, talkative, and young-looking. This wasn't at all the gloomy ex-convict of the *Novy Mir* photograph. Solzhenitsyn's ebullience, indeed, had had a comical sequel. Etkind's translation of *The Resistible Rise of Arturo Ui*, by Bertolt Brecht, was then running at the Leningrad Bolshoi Theatre, and the Etkinds and the Solzhenitsyns went along to see it. Since only three tickets were available (and those only because Etkind had told the box-office whom they were for), Etkind watched from the director's box. Soon after the curtain went up, he saw Solzhenitsyn slip from his seat in the second row into an empty seat in the front row. Solzhenitsyn did not know it, but the man sitting next to him was Vasily Tolstikov, the chief of the Leningrad Communist Party, and he proceeded to guffaw all the way through the play, applauding the politically sharp passages and turning round to the two wives behind him to draw their attention to the numerous Soviet parallels. What Solzhenitsyn's reaction was when he discovered who his neighbour had been is not known, nor whether Tolstikov ever discovered who *his* noisy neighbour was.[17]

It would seem that Solzhenitsyn felt particularly at ease in Leningrad, perhaps because he was away from a lot of the people who knew him in Moscow and removed from the literary establishment. He disliked having to pay the penalty of fame. Reshetovskaya relates that one day in the summer of 1963, Solzhenitsyn was accosted at the trolleybus-stop by a young author, Tatyana Kazanskaya, who begged him to read the manuscript of a short story she had written. He did so reluctantly and sent her a detailed critique, but when she sent him another story, he declined to reply.

As a successful author, he was beginning to receive more and more of these requests, especially through the mail, and he decided to resort to a means of defence not uncommon among the famous—a form letter, which he meticulously labelled "Form No. 1." Reshetovskaya quotes it in her memoirs:

Dear ——
You have sent me your manuscript and asked me to comment on it (revision, advice, can it be published).

I regret that you did not ask my consent beforehand. It may appear natural to you that any writer can, and should, give you his opinion about the level and quality of your work, and that this does not present any difficulty for him.

However, this is very laborious work: to give a superficial evaluation, after barely leafing through the pages, would be irresponsible; you could either be groundlessly discouraged or just as groundlessly encouraged. To give a professional critique, however, requires a serious self-immersion in your manuscript and an evaluation not only of the writing but also of the goals you have set for yourself as a writer. (After all, your aims and those of your reviewer may not necessarily coincide.)

The condition of my health and my late arrival on the literary scene compel me to place an extreme value on my time and make it impossible for me to comply with your request.

Believe me that a nameless (to you) reviewer who is constantly occupied with work of this sort for a magazine, say *Novy Mir*, would be able to satisfy you better than I.

With best wishes,
[Signature][18]

On one of Solzhenitsyn's visits to Leningrad another encounter with an admirer had led to a happier outcome. Among the many hundreds of letters he had received was one from a lady in her late fifties called Elizaveta Voronyanskaya, who had written in embarrassingly fulsome terms to offer him secretarial help: "There are thousands of us, but you are one! And not one of us dare claim your attention. One cannot be angry with the person to whom one prays. I await your telephone call with impatience."[19] Solzhenitsyn had requested her to meet him at the public library, and Voronyanskaya later told Reshetovskaya how she had sat and observed him for forty minutes before going up to him. The thing that had fascinated her most was the way he repeatedly tossed his pencil in the air and caught it again in mid-flight, without lifting his eyes from the book he was reading. She had been too bashful at first to make the approach, but eventually did so and was not disappointed by her idol. She told him she was due to retire shortly and would be happy to type manuscripts and help him in any way she could, an offer that Solzhenitsyn gratefully accepted.

In February 1964 Solzhenitsyn was back in Leningrad again and working at the public library, while Natalia, in Ryazan, was rehearsing in her spare time for a piano recital she was scheduled to give at the beginning of March. Solzhenitsyn was expected back well before then, since they had made it a rule, since their reunion in 1957, always to celebrate their birthdays together, and Natalia's birthday was on 26 February. In the middle of the month, however, Natalia received a telegram from Voronyanskaya asking permission for Solzhenitsyn to stay on in Leningrad for an extra week. According to the account in her memoirs, she was not particularly disturbed by the fact that the telegram came from Voronyanskaya. It probably meant that Solzhenitsyn had gone into seclusion to work faster. Apart from researching in the library, he was working on a major revision of *The First Circle* in order to be able to show it to Tvardovsky, reducing it from ninety-six to eighty-seven chapters and toning it down politically. Voronyanskaya was retyping the novel for him.

They eventually met in Moscow on 25 February, on the eve of her birthday, and the meeting was not a success. The birthday present he had bought Natalia gave her no joy, and she criticized the smart new sweater he was wearing. He said that Voronyanskaya had picked it out for him and persuaded him to buy it, but Natalia was not convinced. From Moscow they returned separately to Ryazan within a few days of one another, but the atmosphere between them was still awkward. According to Natalia, Solzhenitsyn seemed particularly irritable; when asked what the matter was, he replied stiffly, "An act of betrayal has been committed in our home." Natalia asked by whom, and he explained that it was Maria, Natalia's mother, but refused to go into detail.[20]

They were just then preparing a trip to Tashkent to visit the hospital where Solzhenitsyn had been a patient in 1955. He was planning to collect material for *Cancer Ward*, and he promised Natalia he would explain everything then. They set off for Tashkent on 17 March. The weather was bitterly cold in Ryazan, but when they registered at the Hotel Tashkent it was like summer. For the first day or two the research went badly. Solzhenitsyn was welcomed at the hospital like a celebrity and was genuinely pleased to see his former doctors again, including the chief of the radiology department, Dr Dunayeva, and the chief surgeon, Dr A. M. Statnikov. But the beaming smiles and carefully arranged inspections of the hospital's work set up for him were artificial and distracting, and not even his participation in the doctors' rounds, dressed in a white coat, brought him anywhere near the naturalness he sought. For the first time in his life, he found himself "collecting material" like a typical Soviet writer, publicly and with the help of the authorities; but the falsity of it all made it seem like a waste of effort. Collecting material had to be done anonymously, without letting the people observed know that you were a writer, whereas here his very presence was putting everyone on edge. Nevertheless, having come for two weeks, he decided to persist. He was at least able to gather a mass of technical data and check his memories of the physical appearance of the cancer clinic, as well as study the work of the doctors in a way that had been quite impossible as a patient.

Finally, on 23 March 1964, Solzhenitsyn and Natalia had their "explanation." Maria's "act of betrayal," it appeared, had been to speak too freely to one of Solzhenitsyn's female visitors about some details of his cancer. Her description of the illness's consequences had touched on certain matters of an intimate nature that Solzhenitsyn regarded as improper for communication to another woman. Natalia later wrote in her memoirs that she refused to believe it at first but that when Solzhenitsyn named as his source the university teacher he had recently visited in Leningrad, she was obliged to concede that her mother had been indiscreet. It did not take her very long to realize, however, that if the Leningrad woman was able to discuss subjects of this degree of intimacy with Solzhenitsyn, his relationship with the woman must be considerably closer than she had imagined, and this must have been the reason why he had returned so late from Leningrad. There ensued a painful scene, during which Natalia wept and Solzhenitsyn begged her understanding. According to Natalia, he said he could not help himself. He was torn between the two of them and loved them both. His feelings for Natalia were quite different, he said, from those he felt for the other woman. They were "two planes that could never intersect." He would, he said, love Natalia even more deeply if she would allow him to keep his new partner and not leave him, since gratitude and admiration would be added to his original feelings for her. "You have helped me to create one novel. Permit me to allow her to help me create another!" To collect material for his next novel (not *Cancer Ward*, apparently, but *The Red Wheel*), he needed to go on a walking-tour through the villages of Belorussia and East Prussia and required a companion. Natalia was physically too weak for such an expedition and too old, whereas the other woman was younger and stronger and had more stamina.[21]

Behind many of his arguments lay the unspoken view that a writer was different from other men and needed to know a variety of women for the purposes of research. Up till now he had relied mainly on Natalia for information about how women thought and felt, but he wanted to broaden his range and experience. As if to underline his point, he openly studied Natalia's reactions as she struggled to come to terms with his news, at one moment admiring her pallid visage and finding that suffering enhanced her beauty, at another asking her to jot down her thoughts and feelings in her diary, so that he could read them later (which he did, taking down extracts, according to Reshetovskaya). At some point he exclaimed complacently over the change that had taken place in his personal life since the time when he had last been in Tashkent, nine years beforehand: "At that time I didn't have a single woman in my life, and now I have two."[22]

On their return to Ryazan, relations continued to be strained between

Solzhenitsyn and Maria, and Natalia left to spend a week in Moscow. From there she wrote saying that she found it impossible to share him with another woman and that he should choose between them. If he couldn't make up his mind, he should leave anyway, since it would be unbearable to live side by side when they were estranged. Solzhenitsyn replied that he couldn't understand why he should be "chased out of the house for telling the truth" and that he needed a peaceful home for the sake of his work. Eventually, they compromised on a suggestion of Natalia's that they partition the flat to form a separate study for Solzhenitsyn, so that the two of them could sleep in separate rooms "until he could make a decision." Builders were called in, a new partition was quickly built, and in no time they had settled down under the new arrangement. Solzhenitsyn, however, continued to agonize over what to do and after some weeks resolved to drop the woman from Leningrad. His decision was communicated to Natalia by telling her that she could remove the woman's letters from "File No. 21, The World of Scholars" and destroy them.[23]

A couple of months later, before departing on a trip in his car, he left Natalia a letter that he told her to open if she was feeling lonely. In it he wrote about their recent crisis, saying it had convinced him more than ever that no one could be as devoted to him as she was and that there was no one with whom he felt more at ease.

> If you think about it deeply and examine your feelings, you will find that our ties have grown stronger and more durable over the years. Everything recedes and will pass away as transitory and subject to decay—upset feelings, the clash of egos, fits of temper, and unjust accusations. Remember, they never lasted very long; they were always ousted by love and our boundless compassion for one another. If you are hurt, I at once feel the hurt as well. . . . I am not being rhetorical, because that's the way it is—nothing but death can come between us. But let it be a long time before it does.[24]

While Solzhenitsyn and Natalia were experiencing this painful rift, the Lenin Prize committee was reaching the final stage of its deliberations. According to Zhores Medvedev, Tvardovsky had been more or less confident of victory for *Ivan Denisovich* until the end of February. In March, however, there had been an abrupt change of mood at the top. A long article by Tvardovsky in praise of the story was denied publication in the press, and when Tvardovsky asked Lebedev to find out what had happened, the latter was told by Khrushchev, "Let's not bother ourselves with that, it's the business of the prize committee to decide." It seemed that some sort of deal must have been struck between Khrushchev and his opponents.[25]

When the time came for the committee's final series of deliberations, on 10 April, the entire first day was taken up with a discussion of *Ivan Denisovich*. Instructions must have been given to have the story removed from the list of works early, before the secret ballot was taken, since it was clear that under conditions of secrecy it would win without difficulty. Resolutions of this kind are usually taken by a show of hands, and it must have seemed to the authorities like a convenient way of disposing of the matter before the real voting began. Members of the Party were under orders to vote according to instructions, and all the Russian writers present, with the exception of Tvardovsky, voted to have *Ivan Denisovich* dropped. Ironically, it was representatives of the other arts who were against removing *Ivan Denisovich*, and the first day's voting ended in a stalemate.

The next day, Solzhenitsyn was in Moscow and called on Tvardovsky at his office to hear how the first round of voting had gone. Tvardovsky was sitting stunned in front of an open copy of *Pravda*. "*Das ist alles*,"[26] he said heavily to Solzhenitsyn, addressing him for the first and last time in a foreign language. *Pravda* had announced in an editorial note that *Ivan Denisovich* was obviously unsuitable for the Lenin Prize, since it failed to meet the high standards set by previous winners, was lacking in the necessary Party spirit, and did not observe "the best traditions of the Russian literary language." It was a clear signal of the authorities' intentions.[27]

Pravda had arrived on the news-stands just two hours before the final ballot was due to be held, and when the session opened, the committee chairman, N. S. Tikhonov, tabled a formal resolution to eliminate *Ivan Denisovich* from the list. Tvardovsky objected that this was against the rules and was supported by the veteran film director Mikhail Romm and several others; Tikhonov, although supported by the minister of culture, Ekaterina Furtseva, was unable to persuade the committee to agree with him. At that point Sergei Pavlov, chief of the central committee of the Komsomol, got to his feet and declared that it was impossible to award the prize to Solzhenitsyn "for political and legal reasons." He had heard, he said, that Solzhenitsyn had surrendered to the Germans during the war and afterwards had been convicted on a criminal charge, of which he had never been cleared. According to Medvedev, Tvardovsky had leaped to his feet and shouted, "It's a lie," to which Pavlov responded, "You will have to prove it's a lie."[28]

Tvardovsky was helpless to do it on the spot. Pavlov, a well-known hardliner who had been one of the first to criticize *Ivan Denisovich* many months before, was an influential figure in Party circles and a close associate of Vladimir Semichastny, chairman of the KGB. It could be that he had information unknown to the others. Tvardovsky, Romm, and many cinema and theatre people present continued to oppose the resolution, but this time it was passed on a show of hands.

During the break that day Romm said to Tvardovsky, "If Solzhenitsyn doesn't get the prize no one else will," and he was right. In secret ballot after secret ballot, each of the other works was rejected in turn, including the Party's official favourite, *The Sheep Bell*, by Gonchar. Once more the committee was obliged to adjourn without a decision. The next day the Central Committee's propaganda chief, Leonid Ilyichev, came and stood in the room while Tikhonov put *The Sheep Bell* to the vote one more time. The message was clear, and reluctantly the committee voted in favour. Gonchar, who had already won the prize before, was once again made the winner.

Tvardovsky had already sought out Solzhenitsyn in order to get a copy of his certificate of rehabilitation, but the certificate was too brief to refute Pavlov's calumnies, and Solzhenitsyn had been obliged to use his connection with Colonel Terekhov to obtain a fuller version, which had taken a whole extra day. When he obtained it, Tvardovsky took it to the next committee session and asked for permission to speak. "The last time we met," he said, "Comrade Pavlov asserted that Solzhenitsyn's military record was not irreproachable and that I must prove that this was untrue. I have here a document issued by the Supreme Court of the USSR. I shall hand it to the secretary of our committee and ask him to read the full text of the Supreme Court's ruling."

The secretary took the document and read out the full contents, including a summary of Solzhenitsyn's military record, details of the charges against him, and the Military Tribunal's judgement that there had been no case to answer and therefore no crime. Pavlov rose to his feet: "I am defeated. I offer my apologies." But the damage had been done—the prize had gone elsewhere. The slander had also proved extraordinarily effective, a fact that was noted in the appropriate places and stored away for future reference.

28

NOT ANOTHER
PASTERNAK

SOLZHENITSYN ACCEPTED THE Lenin Prize committee's decision philo-
sophically, although he was aware of the prize's symbolic importance
and the boost his victory would have given not only to himself but also to
the liberal cause as a whole. In his memoir he suggests he was in two minds
about it. "Winning the prize would have had its advantages: it would have
consolidated my position. But there were more disadvantages. . . . An
'established position' carried obligations—to be loyal and grateful."[1] Yet his
presence in Moscow during the judging and his meeting with Tvardovsky
indicate that he was keener on winning than he would later care to admit.
Certainly, the defeat of his book, and with it of Tvardovsky and *Novy Mir*,
did nothing to improve his chances of further publication.

To get something published was now Solzhenitsyn's chief preoccupation, and throughout the spring and early summer of 1964 he carried out a
thorough revision of *The First Circle* to make it more palatable to the authorities. In its original form the novel had stuck with extraordinary fidelity to
the facts of Solzhenitsyn's imprisonment in the *sharashka* and the work he had
been engaged on there, although it had telescoped events from his three years
at Marfino into just over three days. The central narrative thread of the novel
was the Soviet diplomat's telephone call to the American embassy to warn it
of the espionage rendezvous in New York. Solzhenitsyn had begun the novel
with this and then had switched to the *sharashka* (called Mavrino in the book),
to the team of prisoner scientists working on voice prints and their remorse-
less search for the identity of the erring diplomat (called Innokenti Volodin).
The leading members of the team were Lev Rubin (modelled on Kopelev),
Gleb Nerzhin (based on Solzhenitsyn himself), and, slightly to one side,

Dimitri Sologdin, for whom the prototype had been Panin. Volodin was in due course arrested, and in the closing chapters of the novel was shown entering the Lubyanka and enduring all its humiliating reception procedures as a prelude to interrogation. The novel ended with the refusal of Nerzhin to continue working at the *sharashka* and his departure for an unknown destination in the general camps.

Around this bare framework Solzhenitsyn had constructed a noble and comprehensive narrative encompassing almost the whole of Soviet society. At its centre, and described in the greatest detail, were the imprisoned scientists, a company of volatile, highly intelligent, and articulate intellectuals who, in their working hours, carried out the scientific tasks assigned to them (creating a walkie-talkie radio, a scrambler telephone, and a voice decoder) but who, in their free time, passionately debated major issues of philosophy, politics, and morality, and above all the rights and wrongs of Soviet history. Their debate was given added poignance by the fact that they were all the innocent victims of that history, and it was broadened by the illustrations Solzhenitsyn offered of the way that history was working itself out in other areas of Soviet society. At the lower extreme of this *univers concentrationnaire* were the regular hard-labour camps (of the type that Ivan Denisovich inhabited, and worse). These were largely off-stage in *The First Circle*, though it was made clear that all the privileged scientists in the *sharashka* had come from that nether world and constantly risked being sent back there if they should slip or step out of line. It was the upper layers that concerned Solzhenitsyn now, the first circle of hell (where the scientists were) and above. In addition to the lives of the prisoners, he was able to depict those of their guards and bosses, the MVD and MGB personnel and the military scientists in charge of the prison institute—notably Adam Roitman (based on Major Trachtman) and Anton Yakonov (based on Colonel Vasiliev). Through them, Solzhenitsyn was able to make connections with the higher reaches of the Soviet security services, the Party, and the government, up to and including the minister of state security, Victor Abakumov, and even Stalin himself. Through some of the free workers at the *sharashka*, Solzhenitsyn was also able to trace paths to the Soviet intelligentsia and ultimately to the erring diplomat, Volodin, and his family, so that almost the whole of Soviet society was connected by the silken threads of Solzhenitsyn's narrative and portrayed as a single web, in which it was sufficient for one strand to be jerked for the whole net to be set swaying.

In this way Solzhenitsyn achieved in *The First Circle* a perfection of artistic form akin to that of *A Day in the Life of Ivan Denisovich*, endowing the reader with a sense that the whole of Soviet society, including the inmates of the camps, was bound together in an indissoluble symbiosis, in which the society of the camps was but a microcosm of life outside. But in *The First Circle* he had achieved it with infinitely more richness and diversity, and made explicit what was only implicit in *Ivan Denisovich*—namely, that in the oppressive anthill of the contemporary Soviet Union, those in the labour

camps were freer than those allegedly and formally "at liberty." Paradoxically, the land of Gulag was the only place where a Soviet citizen had nothing
further to fear.

The principal illustration and expression of this freedom in the novel
were the debates between the prisoners, notably between Nerzhin, Rubin,
and Sologdin, though many more prisoners were drawn into the discussions
in the course of the narrative. The two sides of the central issue were personified by Rubin and Sologdin—Rubin, the Leninist, rejecting Stalin but still
clinging to the socialist ideals of the Revolution; and Sologdin, the Christian
and militant anti-Communist, asserting the prior claims of morality and personal faith. Nerzhin was shown as oscillating between the two (rather as
Solzhenitsyn had done between Kopelev and Panin in real life), but gradually
moving closer to Sologdin as his faith in Marxism and the justice of the Soviet
system was eroded. At the centre of Solzhenitsyn's fictional universe were
morality and the claims of conscience; and the "message" of this crucial debate,
insofar as it could be reduced to a formula, was that man should "believe his
eyes and not his ears," should listen to his moral instinct and his conscience
and behave accordingly. It was in line with this precept that Nerzhin was
shown, at the end of the novel, voluntarily abandoning the *sharashka*, where
he was involved in helping an immoral government and embracing the dangers of banishment to Siberia.

There were numerous sub-plots in the novel. One concerned Nerzhin's
relationship with his wife Nadia (modelled on Natalia), who was studying at
Moscow University and dared not reveal that she was married or where her
husband was living. Another told the story of Nerzhin's innocent romance
with an MGB lieutenant at the *sharashka* called Simochka, while still others
described relationships between the prisoners and their wives, or between
prisoners and some of the women who worked in the institute. Innokenti
Volodin's family relationships occupied a significant place in the narrative,
and in one part of the novel, Solzhenitsyn entered into Stalin's mind and
attempted to offer a psychological portrait of the tyrant from inside. The
novel was also filled with stories and anecdotes, including a spoof reworking
of the medieval Russian epic *The Lay of the Host of Igor*,* in the form of a
Soviet-type trial of Prince Igor for treason, and a satirical account of a mythical visit to Butyrki Prison by Mrs Roosevelt, for which some show cells are
prepared and the prisoners issued with special clothing and luxuries for the
duration of her visit.

The problem that Solzhenitsyn faced in his revision was how to make
the novel less controversial politically and more acceptable to the censorship.
One way was to cut certain chapters altogether—for instance, one on Lenin,
a satirical analysis of dialectical materialism, one about the need for resistance
(called "The Word Will Smash Concrete")† and two showing Innokenti's

---

*Probably written in the twelfth century, the *Lay* is the only Russian work of medieval times to
have become a classic and is known to every Russian schoolchild.
†This chapter was renamed "On the Back Stairs" when the novel was restored to its full length
of ninety-six chapters.

gradual conversion from Soviet orthodoxy to a position of scepticism and distrust. Elsewhere he cut scenes and lines and dropped some of his sharper statements.

This still left many things requiring change, and of these the most fundamental concerned the nature of Innokenti Volodin's telephone call at the beginning of the book. In his original version, Solzhenitsyn had stuck to the true story of the atomic secrets, but it was obvious that this version could never be printed in the Soviet Union. With its morbid sensitivity towards all things military and connected with security, the Soviet censorship would never have permitted it. Indeed, he would have courted arrest by submitting it for publication in the first place. Solzhenitsyn therefore changed the subject of the conversation to a warning to a well-known Soviet doctor not to hand over some medicine to a Western colleague on his next trip abroad, since the gift would be used against him and he could be arrested.*

From the point of view of the plot, the substitution was very neat and allowed the novel to preserve its original shape, but its consequences in other respects were rather far-reaching. In terms of the moral debate about whether or not the prisoners should agree to help the government, it had a trivializing effect: the handing over of medicine to a foreign doctor and the betrayal of the dangers involved to the Soviet doctor concerned could hardly be compared with trading in atomic secrets and with the betrayal of a Soviet agent to a foreign embassy. The truth was infinitely more dramatic than the fictional substitute, and Solzhenitsyn has several times lamented the necessity of making the change. Yet in some respects the change was for the better. In the question of espionage and the acquisition of military secrets, the behaviour of the Soviet government was not essentially at variance with the practice of other governments. It is far less easy to condemn such behaviour as morally reprehensible than it is to despise the actions of a government that hounds and persecutes its citizens simply for contacts with foreigners—even for humanitarian purposes, such as the sharing of medicine. Both types of activity were going on, and both involved the active participation of the security services, but the medical theme shows clearer evidence of moral baseness than espionage does. Furthermore, although Solzhenitsyn and many dissidents were eventually to reach a point where they would whole-heartedly oppose and condemn the acquisition by the Soviet state of any more powerful weapons whatever, there were few Soviet citizens—if any—not already behind bars, who could have reached that conclusion by 1949, when the action of the novel takes place. Even in 1964, most people would still have been equivocal about it. In purely fictional terms, therefore, the new (fictional) motivation worked better than the old (true) one.

The relationship between real life and fantasy in the novel was important in another respect. The novel was, after all, based on real people in a real place at a real time. Many of the characters' prototypes knew of Solzhenitsyn's fictionalization of them, and some, like Kopelev, Panin, and Semyonov,

---

* Solzhenitsyn had the background of the "doctors' plot" in mind when he altered the character of the telephone call.

had helped Solzhenitsyn with some of the scenes. Most approved of what he had done or simply shrugged their shoulders and gave him *carte blanche*, but what would Kopelev make of his fictional double's new motivation? It was perfectly plausible, and in the circumstances of the labour camps the prisoners would have had very little choice anyway. The fictional Lev Rubin (whatever Kopelev in real life might have done) would have had little difficulty in rationalizing away any ethical objections that sprang to mind. The Party, after all, could never be *that* wrong. And in any case, fiction was fiction. It was understood that novels had to obey their own laws and couldn't be tied too tightly to the real-life events that inspired them.

Nevertheless, Solzhenitsyn felt constrained to show a copy of the new version to Kopelev, who with his wife, Raisa Orlova, spent two days reading it and a further day discussing it with Solzhenitsyn. They both had a number of objections, which Kopelev later summarized in a long letter to Solzhenitsyn, setting out his views on the novel as a whole. "Muster your patience," he wrote, "read it, and then may heaven guide you." The most interesting point in the letter seems to have been Kopelev's division of the novel into two layers: what Solzhenitsyn had seen and depicted from nature and what he had imagined (i.e., life in the *sharashka* and life outside). According to Kopelev, the scenes in which Solzhenitsyn had written out of his own experience were immeasurably stronger than the rest, and this led to an "inner duality" in the novel, weakening its total impact, for he found it difficult to believe in "those homunculi who perforce are conceived in newspaper and archival test-tubes."[2]

The scenes Kopelev had in mind appear to have been those describing Soviet "high society" and the intelligentsia. Kopelev had a right to criticize because he knew them far better than Solzhenitsyn (indeed was a member of them) and understood how they worked. While he may have taken umbrage at the fact that Solzhenitsyn had made fun of the Moscow intellectuals and caricatured them, it was also true that some of Solzhenitsyn's simplifications sprang from ignorance of his subject matter. Another irritating feature of Solzhenitsyn's novel, from Kopelev's point of view, was the self-confidence with which he pronounced his verdict on these circles, leading Kopelev to protest in his letter that Solzhenitsyn appeared to be imbued with a dangerous certainty that he held "all the truths in the hollow of his hand." Kopelev felt that Solzhenitsyn had strayed out of his depth and that certain parts of the book had suffered as a result.

Kopelev's criticism holds additional interest in that it offers a kind of commentary on the book's central motif of believing one's eyes and not one's ears. On one level Solzhenitsyn persuades the reader that he should believe the misery, poverty, and corruption he sees all around him and not fine words and promises about the radiant future that lies just around the corner. In the book it was Rubin, Kopelev's fictional double, who was most subject to this roseate delusion, and Rubin's character more or less faithfully reflected Kopelev's at that period. Yet now Kopelev was in a way turning Solzhenitsyn's own maxim against him. In attempting to describe people and aspects of society that he did not know and had not seen, said Kopelev, Solzhenitsyn was being false to the truth, and in these passages his narrative lacked verisimilitude.

Kopelev's reproach was to become a commonplace of criticism of Solzhenitsyn's fiction in later years and is the first recorded instance of its being made (though there had been murmurs about his portrayal of the Moscow intellectual Tsezar Markovich in *A Day in the Life of Ivan Denisovich* somewhat earlier). Much debate has taken place over the perceived disparity in Solzhenitsyn's works between the autobiographically grounded passages and those that were entirely imagined. Solzhenitsyn acknowledged the gravity of the charge in his letter of reply and rejected it as too sweeping. "It is not for me to judge," he wrote, "but I would be a dead duck if I were to believe that I cannot write out of my imagination, for one cannot see everything for oneself." He was also able to point out that Kopelev had underestimated *Ivan Denisovich* and "Matryona's Place": "Wouldn't I have been an oaf if I had listened to your advice on both occasions? Therefore you cannot ask me to accept your tastes without convincing proof."[3] It was a good point but did not necessarily invalidate Kopelev's criticism on this occasion.

The success of *Ivan Denisovich* and the short stories (with the exception of "For the Good of the Cause") was undoubtedly due to their having been firmly rooted in autobiographical reality, just as many of the best scenes in *The First Circle* derived their power from the same source. But there were many striking scenes, characters, and episodes with no autobiographical basis, and not even the scenes depicting Stalin, later to be much criticized, were as weak as some have alleged.* It is true, however, that Solzhenitsyn did seem to need a firm autobiographical substratum from which his imagination could take off and that his own particular brand of realism flourished so long as it remained in close touch with that substratum—or could draw on it when the author projected himself into other characters—but tended to wither and become artificial when too far removed from personal experience.

It would appear from Reshetovskaya's account of this exchange that Kopelev also commented unfavourably on the interrogation chapters, but how exactly is unclear. Admitting that others had made a similar criticism, Solzhenitsyn promised to give the matter some thought and also said he would do everything in his power, within the limits posed by the form of the novel, to mitigate the negative effects on the character of Rubin of the change of plot.

Three years later, when the novel was circulating in samizdat, Solzhe-

---

* According to one source, Victor Ilyin, then secretary of the Moscow branch of the Writers' Union (and reputed to be a lieutenant-general in the KGB), once asked Solzhenitsyn, after reading *The First Circle*, whether Solzhenitsyn had ever met the former minister for state security Victor Abakumov, for the portrait of him in the novel was "very, very accurate." It appears that Solzhenitsyn had gathered a lot of information from the prosecutor D. Terekhov, who was responsible for interrogating Abakumov after Stalin's death (Abakumov had been arrested in connection with the "doctors' plot"). Incidentally, Chekhov, among others, had criticized Tolstoy in terms similar to those used by the critics of Solzhenitsyn, saying that it had been a major error to introduce the figure of Napoleon into *War and Peace*.

nitsyn sent Kopelev a letter in which he referred to these earlier discussions about the plot. "As you know," he wrote, "there were weighty reasons why I couldn't give an accurate description of what actually happened. At the same time I was determined to preserve the central theme: that an excellent man with ideal convictions needs no practical criteria of good and evil, since he is sufficiently guided by his convictions." He had been in a hurry at the time, he wrote, and that was why he had picked up the typical theme (for the period described) of "giving away medical secrets." But he had not foreseen what unpleasant consequences there would be for Kopelev, when readers took the novel too literally. "I must say I had never expected such a primitive approach from literary men. To think that the literary public, which has more experience than most of the relationship between a prototype and invention, should insist so obstinately on confusing a prototype with a fictional character, and a plot with the true course of events. I hope, nevertheless, that this refers only to a tiny minority and that it won't be generally read that way." Solzhenitsyn wrote that he had had similar discussions with other prototypes in the novel but that it was less of a problem for them, since they were not known in the literary world. Kopelev should regard this as a "letter of rehabilitation" and show it to anyone who, after reading the novel, might refuse to shake his hand.[4]

Not everything, in fact, had been plain sailing with the other prototypes. Sologdin in the novel allowed his decoding device to be burnt, just as Panin had done in real life, but whereas Panin had also refused to co-operate with the authorities, had gone off to Ekibastuz rather than co-operate (and had played no small role in persuading Solzhenitsyn to do the same), the fictional Sologdin destroyed the design only as a tactical measure and kept the details in his head in order to bargain with Colonel Yakonov for a reward. Moreover, Sologdin stayed in the *sharashka*, leaving Nerzhin to go off alone, whereas Panin had done the opposite.

There is no evidence that Panin was unduly upset by this alteration in his biography at the time. On the contrary, he took an active part in helping Solzhenitsyn modify his fictional double in order to make him more acceptable to the censors, for the real-life Panin had been more outspoken and more openly anti-Communist in 1949 than it was possible to admit even fifteen years later. Panin willingly helped Solzhenitsyn invent new dialogue and new arguments to put into Sologdin's mouth, and he seems to have been flattered to be asked to do so. But he was also guided, it appears, by a certain vanity, which manifested itself in a desire to see himself portrayed in a flattering light. And in later years, when he came to write his own memoirs, he expressed the hope that in revising *The First Circle* yet again, which he knew Solzhenitsyn to be doing, Solzhenitsyn would bring his fictional counterpart closer to reality. "I hope that when it is published, Sologdin will be rehabilitated by the author and transformed from a lady's man and a careerist into something more worthy of, and nearer to, his living prototype."[5]

At last the revision was finished. The novel was reduced from ninety-six to eighty-seven chapters (this was the version that was to travel round the world and be translated into foreign languages), and its politically sensitive material was softened. What remained was still controversial by Soviet standards, with its detailed description of one of the hitherto-secret prison institutes, its vivid account of the hostile relations between prisoners and guards, its bleak picture of Soviet society at large, and its daringly hostile depiction of Stalin. Yet there was a small chance that it would jump the hurdles standing in front of it.

With his usual thoroughness and his flair for planning, Solzhenitsyn set about preparing the ground. For some time now he had been convinced that the first person to see it "officially" must be Tvardovsky. Just as Tvardovsky had at once perceived the literary worth of *Ivan Denisovich* and been prepared to take all sorts of risks to publish it, so, felt Solzhenitsyn, would he warm to the new novel and stake his reputation as before. The problem was how to get it to him, and he decided that the simplest and surest way was to invite Tvardovsky to Ryazan to read it there. Tvardovsky accepted at once and travelled down on 2 May 1964, the Russian Easter Saturday. Solzhenitsyn and Natalia met him at the station. Tvardovsky was wearing a light-blue raincoat and blue beret that accentuated the brilliant blueness of his eyes, and Natalia, who was meeting him for the first time, was struck by his grave courtesy and the melancholy expression on his youthful face.

The four days that Tvardovsky spent with the Solzhenitsyns and his behaviour while reading *The First Circle* have since been described by Solzhenitsyn in a celebrated (and, in the Soviet Union, controversial) chapter of *The Oak and the Calf*.[6] Over dinner the first evening, Tvardovsky tactfully warned Solzhenitsyn not to expect too much, saying that every writer had his disappointments. The next day, after reading several chapters, he commented, "Great stuff!"—but again cautioned that it was too early for him to pronounce judgement. In the evening, however, after liberal helpings of vodka and cognac had loosened his tongue, he became quite garrulous, and during a leisurely walk to the post office to telephone his wife he treated Solzhenitsyn to a torrent of informed gossip about the upper echelons of the Party (revealing that Brezhnev had once been punished by Stalin) and to his views on literature, praising Bulgakov and disparaging Leonov and Mayakovsky. Solzhenitsyn tried to persuade him that his deputy editors were not worthy of *Novy Mir*, Kondratovich being a fool and Dementyev a sinister fifth-columnist of the Party. Tvardovsky dismissed the criticisms as exaggerated but did confess somewhat wistfully that his dream was to have a deputy capable of making decisions and managing the magazine in his absence, thereby conceding that neither Kondratovich nor Dementyev quite fit the bill.

The next morning, Tvardovsky insisted on having some cognac on his desk to replace the Thermos flask of tea with honey that had sufficed on the first day. Solzhenitsyn strongly disapproved but was unable to dissuade Tvardovsky. Since Tvardovsky was occupying his study and since he found it impossible to write when visitors were present, Solzhenitsyn puttered about in the yard outside or with his car, listened to the BBC news on his short-wave radio, and popped in from time to time to check how far Tvardovsky had got and to monitor his reactions. He need not have worried. Tvardovsky was touchingly eager to like the book, and his enthusiasm was visibly growing. Half-way through he commented, "No, no, I don't believe you'd go and spoil it in the second half!" And after chapter 64: "You'd have a job to spoil it now, right at the very end."

Perhaps the greatest compliment he paid the novel was the way he entered so deeply into its atmosphere and spirit. On the third evening, he questioned Solzhenitsyn eagerly about life in prison and the camps and listened attentively to Solzhenitsyn's description of the circumstances of his arrest. The world that Solzhenitsyn unfolded struck him as simply incredible. When he had first read about the *sharashka*, he had said to Solzhenitsyn, "My goodness, what an imagination you've got to dream up something like that. It's absolutely amazing, you begin to believe it all." He absolutely refused to accept that it had really existed. At another point he had remarked, "You are a terrible man. If ever I came to power, I'd put you away," and later he developed the joke, saying that Solzhenitsyn was not to worry, since he (Tvardovsky) would bring him some food parcels and even smuggle in some brandy. Then, as the liquor took hold of him, he imagined himself going to prison—perhaps for publishing *The First Circle*—and by the end of the evening was asking Solzhenitsyn to play the role of an MGB lieutenant and shout commands at him, which he would then, as a prisoner, obey.

In the end, despite his distaste for these excesses, Solzhenitsyn was obliged to undress Tvardovsky and put him to bed. But before long, he and Natalia were awakened by a loud noise. When he went into the room, all the lights were on. Tvardovsky was sitting at the desk in his underpants talking loudly to himself, shouting prison commands, and leaping to his feet to stand at attention; then he slumped over the desk and mumbled self-pityingly about the sacrifice he was going to make. Solzhenitsyn watched for a while and then intervened. He and Tvardovsky talked for an hour or so, had a smoke, and Tvardovsky went back to bed as meek as a lamb.

On the fourth day, Tvardovsky finished the novel, shedding a tear over the jilting of Simochka by Nerzhin, laughing at the antics of "Valentulya" Pryanchikov, and identifying with some of the other characters. During and after an excursion to see the Ryazan kremlin he gave his verdict. Artistically, the novel was beyond praise. Solzhenitsyn's narrative energy, he said, was derived from Dostoyevsky. It was a firmly constructed novel, with not a superfluous page, inspired by the Russian classics but not imitative of them. It created a whole world into which the reader could be absorbed and in which he could lose himself. At the same time, Tvardovsky felt that its overall message was consonant with Party policy ("it contains no condemnation of the October Revolution"), although he couldn't help remarking wryly on Solzhenitsyn's encyclopaedic settlement of old scores: "You are Tolstoy, but you can forgive Soviet power nothing."[7]

The only criticisms he offered concerned the Stalin chapters. He asked for the complete removal of one chapter, "Study of a Great Life," devoted to proving that Stalin had collaborated with the secret police, and suggested (echoing one of Kopelev's criticisms) that Solzhenitsyn should be less confident about the details of Stalin's private affairs, since no one really knew what they were. He also had a few reservations about the character of the peasant Spiridon, saying that Solzhenitsyn had made him out to be too crafty and cunning. Later he came to feel that the spoof of *The Lay of the Host of Igor* was over-literary and also a candidate for omission. Nevertheless, he was convinced it was a "great novel" and said that his ambition was now to publish it.

Solzhenitsyn's little stratagem had worked. Tvardovsky was as enthusiastic and committed as he had been with *Ivan Denisovich* and at once made arrangements for his colleagues to read it. They, however, had considerable reservations, as the meeting of *Novy Mir*'s editorial board on 11 June showed. Tvardovsky introduced the discussion by stressing not only the novel's exceptionally high quality but also its difficult political character: "By the normal standards of Soviet criticism, not only should this novel be scuttled but the author should be prosecuted. But what sort of people are we? Can we evade this responsibility? Who would like to give us a lead? Who is willing to take the plunge for once?" Predictably, few were anxious to take the plunge. Kondratovich found the novel artistically powerful but excessively polemical and decided to play safe: "It's impossible to publish. And morally impossible not to." Sachs was against immediate publication and called for a second reading. Like Kopelev, he found the chapters set outside the *sharashka* much weaker than the rest and suggested that they be dropped. He echoed Tvardovsky's comment in Ryazan that Solzhenitsyn seemed unable to omit anything in his criticisms of Soviet society, to which Solzhenitsyn replied that it was true: "It's second nature with me. I can't bypass any important question." Dementyev was also highly doubtful. He conceded the power of the writing but feared that the novel's critique went far beyond the personality cult and called even the Revolution into question. "On the philosophical side the author has no answers to the question 'What is to be done?' Behave decently—is that all he can tell me?" And later in the discussion he added plaintively, "Can't the author think a bit more kindly of people and of life?"[8]

Nevertheless, Dementyev did not come out openly against publication, and Lakshin and Maryamov were strongly in favour, so that Tvardovsky felt justified, in his summing up, in concluding that the board's overall opinion was favourable and that the decision was to publish. But he knew that the others were unhappy with the decision, and he also knew that a decision to publish was only the first step. The big problem would come in getting the novel through the censorship. He decided to repeat his original ploy of showing the book to Lebedev. Unfortunately, Tvardovsky's relations with Lebedev were no longer as warm as before. The two of them had recently clashed over Lebedev's request to Tvardovsky to reject the last instalment of Ehrenburg's memoirs, which Tvardovsky had refused. Tvardovsky therefore approached the matter even more cautiously than before, giving Lebedev only a quarter of the novel to read and pretending that it was from a work still in progress.

But times had changed. Lebedev returned the chapters to Tvardovsky with a comment that the novel was a libel on Soviet society and advised him, "Keep this novel well hidden. Don't let anybody see it." When Tvardovsky demurred and pointed out that it was not like the Lebedev of old to say such a thing, Khrushchev's secretary retorted, "If only you knew *who* has now taken a dislike to *Ivan Denisovich* and regrets that it was ever published." Publication of Solzhenitsyn's first story, it seems, was one of the many things now being thrown in Khrushchev's face as evidence of his mistakes, and this was indirectly confirmed by another source who described Khrushchev's wife as having complained to a retired general, "Oh, if only you knew what we've had to put up with because of that Solzhenitsyn. We shan't be meddling any more, that's for sure."[9]

That avenue was definitely closed. Nothing daunted, Tvardovsky (egged on by Lakshin) concluded a contract with Solzhenitsyn, paid him an advance, and when later drawing up his publication plan for 1965, boldly announced that Solzhenitsyn "was working on a big novel" for *Novy Mir*. The announcement was published in the July and August numbers of the magazine, when readers were invited to take out their subscriptions for the following year.

In the aftermath of the Lenin Prize decision, Solzhenitsyn's public position was undoubtedly weaker than before. In May 1964 both the leading literary newspapers had published attacks on *Ivan Denisovich*. Yuri Barabash, in a long article in the *Literaturnaya Gazeta*, concentrated on Lakshin's "friends and foes" article in *Novy Mir*, while Vsevolod Surganov, in *Literaturnaya Rossia*, accused Solzhenitsyn of choosing the wrong sort of hero for his stories, saying that it was "not the Matryonas and the Shukhovs" that the Party looked to in its struggle to improve the countryside. In June the *Literaturnaya Gazeta* gave Lakshin an opportunity to reply but accompanied his letter with an even longer editorial note rejecting the critic's views, and in the July number of the journal *Moskva*, G. Brovman denounced *A Day in the Life of Ivan Denisovich* as falling short of the Party's requirements.[10]

Generally, it was a time for keeping quiet and out of the public eye. And since progress was now stalled on *The First Circle*, Solzhenitsyn tried to interest some theatres in *Candle in the Wind*. Again they all rejected it, partly because of recent political developments, but also, it seems, because they were not much impressed with it dramatically. Solzhenitsyn found this difficult to understand. He was aware, by now, that his play was no masterpiece, but he felt that its apoliticism and its non-Soviet setting (at least superficially) gave it a much better chance than his other works, and he still could not accept that it was as bad as all that. Discussing his efforts to get it staged with a friend some time later, he explained defensively, "When a man has a couple of daughters to marry off, it is only natural that he should try to fix the elder one up first."[11] What he meant, perhaps, was "uglier" rather than elder, for *Candle* was written last. Curiously enough, he was rather fond of this marriage metaphor, for when inviting Tvardovsky to Ryazan he had adapted it to fit *The First Circle:* "Alexander Trifonovich, the novel is ready. But do you know what it's like, surrendering a novel to a publisher when you intend to write only two in a lifetime? It's like marrying off a son. Pretend it's a wedding and come and stay with us in Ryazan."[12]

There were no takers for the play or, it seemed, for the miniature stories that Tvardovsky had so brusquely rejected. But these, at least, had met with a better reception from others who had read them, and Solzhenitsyn decided that nothing would be lost if he allowed them to circulate unofficially among friends and sympathizers in samizdat.* It was a calculated risk. Samizdat was not a new phenomenon. It had come into existence in the late fifties as a result of the clash between the intellectuals' post-Stalinist hunger for more freedom of expression and the continuing repressiveness of the censorship. Demand for copies of the banned *Doctor Zhivago* had given it a considerable boost, and now the swing of the pendulum towards stricter controls was leading to a new upsurge, one that was all the stronger, for the appetites aroused by Khrushchev's liberalization had been frustrated by his retreat.

Solzhenitsyn had kept his distance from samizdat till now. All his literary dealings had hitherto been strictly legal, and despite the growing criticism of his work, he was still a respectable member of the establishment. Putting works into samizdat was a small step into the unknown. There was something risky, something almost bohemian about it, which was not at all to Solzhenitsyn's taste, and he knew that Tvardovsky and the rest of the *Novy Mir* board would not like it at all. The unofficial, pre-publication circulation of *Ivan Denisovich*, for which Tvardovsky himself had been unwittingly responsible, had already led to recriminations. Solzhenitsyn dared not admit that this time it was he who had done it. On the other hand, he resented the fact that he could not publish the stories openly, and he was anxious to see what would happen if they circulated. At the very least it was an insurance against oblivion.

He did not have long to wait for an echo. He had first let the stories go in the spring of 1964. Within months they were circulating in hundreds of copies and soon reached the provinces. What particularly heartened him was the general approval of his defence of religion in them, one of their features that had made them unacceptable to Tvardovsky and *Novy Mir*. So quickly did they circulate that by the autumn they had reached the West and appeared in Russian in the *émigré* literary magazine *Grani*, published in Frankfurt (which was, in due course, to create new problems).[13]

By the time news of this event reached Moscow, there was something much bigger to worry about: Khrushchev's overthrow. The "palace revolu-

---

*Literally, "self-publishing house," by analogy with *Goslitizdat*, the state publishing house in the Soviet Union. Samizdat is the collective name for works of literature or documents that circulate from hand to hand, usually in typewritten form.

tion" occurred in mid-October. It was not directly connected with Khrushchev's policy of de-Stalinization, controversial as this had been, but rather with his repeated zigzags in policy, his penchant for experimentation, and his disruptions of the Party hierarchy. At home he had caused massive discontent in the Party apparatus with his attempted division of the administration into industrial and agricultural sectors. This had introduced an element of competition and direct responsibility that was most unwelcome to the bureaucracy. He had also offended the KGB—that state within a state—by reforming its structure and reducing its numbers and status, and he had blundered with his agricultural reforms. Abroad, his initial policy of peaceful coexistence with the West had made many of his fellow leaders uneasy, and then the Cuban adventure had badly undermined his prestige. Finally, he had developed and encouraged his own miniature "personality cult," which had antagonized his colleagues in the leadership and made them hostile to him.

His fall was thus the result of many factors, but overall it was a victory for the conservatives, and naturally those opposed to de-Stalinization and the exposure of Stalinist crimes took advantage of the occasion to intensify their campaign further. The censorship, they felt, should be strengthened, attacks on Stalin's personality cult halted, and Stalin himself partially rehabilitated.

For Solzhenitsyn the fall of Khrushchev was most alarming. In a direct sense he owed his spectacular rise to him, and given the feudal nature of Soviet politics, it was possible that when the king fell, everyone connected with him would fall too. He panicked and rushed to see Tvardovsky at his new dacha in Pakhra. It seemed to him that in this new atmosphere *The First Circle* was too dangerous for publication and stood no chance of acceptance by the censors. It might even provoke reprisals against him. The old convict's fear and suspicion welled up all the more strongly for having been suppressed during the years of his success, and he suggested to Tvardovsky that he take back *The First Circle* from *Novy Mir* and substitute, as the "big novel in progress," *Cancer Ward*, a large part of which had been completed.

Tvardovsky was taken aback. Although once an admirer of Khrushchev, he was perfectly prepared to accept the Party's decision, and since he had decided that Solzhenitsyn's novel was not "against the Revolution," he saw no reason to conceal its existence or indulge in dubious stunts of substitution and deception. By his anxiety, Solzhenitsyn was in effect giving the game away and revealing that *The First Circle* was more subversive than Tvardovsky realized, but fortunately Tvardovsky did not react to this. What did worry him was the possibility that the novel was being passed around and circulating in samizdat. News of the publication of Solzhenitsyn's miniature stories in the West had hit Tvardovsky hard. Apart from experiencing a twinge of jealousy, he had made inquiries and discovered that *Grani* was considered highly anti-Soviet. He did not suspect Solzhenitsyn himself of having sent the stories to *Grani*. He knew enough to understand that their free circulation in samizdat had led to that. But he did suspect Solzhenitsyn of either carelessness or duplicity, and he sought assurances that the same thing was not happening with *The First Circle*.

Solzhenitsyn promised him that this was not the case, but he was not being entirely honest with Tvardovsky. Although *The First Circle* was not circulating, it was certainly being read. At least one copy was kept at Veronica Stein's flat in Moscow, where it had been perused by many in her circle, and Zhores Medvedev, who got to know Solzhenitsyn at about this time, had been told of another flat where a copy of the typescript was kept, and a couple of months later was allowed to go there and read it.[14] More importantly, Solzhenitsyn was about to take the momentous decision to send a copy secretly to the West.

Just how he came to this decision is not clear. Perhaps the publication of his miniature stories in the West had suggested the idea; perhaps it was Khrushchev's downfall and the alarm he had felt that precipitated the need for some sort of insurance policy; or perhaps it was simply that an opportunity had presented itself. It appears that sometime during the preceding year he had been introduced to a writer called Vadim Andreyev. Andreyev would have attracted his attention on a number of counts. He was the son of the celebrated writer Leonid Andreyev; he was the brother of another writer, Daniil Andreyev, who had served ten years in Vladimir Prison for having written a politically unacceptable (and never published) novel—it had been for listening to Andreyev read from that novel that Solzhenitsyn's *sharashka* friend Ivashov-Musatov had been arrested and imprisoned; and he was a writer himself. But perhaps the most important and interesting fact about Vadim Andreyev, from Solzhenitsyn's point of view, was his ability to travel freely between Moscow and the West. Having found himself in the West with his father after the Revolution, he had retained a patriotic love of Russia and had repeatedly applied for Soviet citizenship, which he was granted while continuing to live in the West. In the 1950s he had moved from his post as chief corrector with the Soviet delegation to the United Nations in New York to work with the Soviet mission in Geneva, and after 1957 had begun to visit the Soviet Union regularly. He had also had several books published there.* He was exceedingly dismayed by the apparent re-Stalinization of Soviet life, however, and being an admirer of Solzhenitsyn, he was more than willing to help him.[15]

Solzhenitsyn transferred the shortened version of *The First Circle* to three rolls of microfilm and passed them to Andreyev to carry out. With his penchant for conspiracy, Solzhenitsyn proposed that Andreyev wear a money-belt under his shirt and conceal the microfilms there, but Andreyev pointed out that nothing was designed to attract more attention, if discovered, then a belt under his shirt, and he simply slipped the three canisters of film into the pocket of his raincoat.[16] As a trusted visitor, he was not searched at the

---

*It was after reading Vadim Andreyev's memoir of his father in 1963 that Solzhenitsyn had asked to meet him. His interest at that time had been purely literary

airport and passed through customs with no trouble.* Solzhenitsyn received the news of their safe arrival with deep satisfaction, particularly since another friend, living in the Soviet provinces, to whom Solzhenitsyn had entrusted a complete set of his writings, had burned them in panic on hearing of Khrushchev's overthrow. There was one more complete set in the provinces and an incomplete set with the Teushes, but the burning of the manuscripts underlined the need for care. Of *The Feast of the Conquerors*, for instance, there remained but two copies, one of them with the Teushes. If more alarms occurred, he might be in danger of losing it completely. The discovery of the West as a safe alternative was a comfort and a relief, and enabled him to secure his rear.

In his panic over Khrushchev's downfall, Solzhenitsyn had moved to the Teushes and spent the rest of October and most of November 1964 either there, at Veronica Stein's, or at Chukovsky's dacha in Peredelkino. He no longer felt safe in Ryazan and needed peace and quiet in which to write. He also thought it wise to lie low until the political atmosphere had cleared, and he had accumulated many projects he wanted to work on. Accordingly, at the end of November, he retired to Agafya's cottage in Solotcha and settled down to a spell of solid writing that was to last throughout the winter.

Project number one was a history of the labour camps for which he had begun to make notes in 1958. At that time the project had seemed too ambitious and incapable of fulfilment. There had been no hope of access to official sources on the subject or even to the "reserved" sections of the public libraries, where all the published materials were kept. The circle of his labour-camp acquaintances, though wide, had also been insufficient to supply the necessary variety of information. He had discharged a part of his indignation in the writing of the plays, *The First Circle*, and *Ivan Denisovich*. But the very publication and success of *Ivan Denisovich* had created a new situation by bringing him an enormous flood of readers' letters.

Many of these letters had been a revelation to Solzhenitsyn. They disclosed information about camps, regions, and regimes that he had never heard of before, and through them he was introduced to hundreds of tragic and heart-rending biographies. Almost as enlightening, in their different way, were the letters from ex-guards and MVD personnel, oozing with spite and hatred for the author of *Ivan Denisovich* and reaffirming the heartless philosophy on which the labour-camp system was based. But the greatest surprise was the letters from prisoners still in the camps, as Solzhenitsyn later admitted.

> When Khrushchev . . . . gave permission for the publication of *Ivan Denisovich*, he was quite sure that it was about Stalin's camps and that he had none of his own.

* Solzhenitsyn does not mention Andreyev's name in his account of these matters in *The Oak and the Calf*. Since then, however, Vadim Andreyev has died, and it is therefore possible to reveal his identity.

Tvardovsky, too, when he was worrying the highest in the land to give their imprimatur, sincerely believed that it was all in the past, that it was over and done with. . . .

Tvardovsky can be forgiven. Around him, everybody in public life in Moscow was sustained by this one thought: "There's a thaw, they've stopped snatching people, we've had two cathartic congresses, people are returning from nowhere, and in large numbers!" The archipelago was lost in a beautiful pink mist of rehabilitations and became altogether invisible.

But I—even I—succumbed. . . . I, too, genuinely believed that the story I had brought [Tvardovsky] was about the past. Could *my* tongue have forgotten the taste of gruel? I had sworn never to forget. . . .

"As the paunch grows, the memory goes." I did get fatter. I fell for it and— believed. I let myself be persuaded by the complacent mainland. Believed what my own new-found prosperity would have me believe.[17]

For the past several months Solzhenitsyn had been collecting material on the camps. Much of it came in unsolicited, but to fill the gaps and make his inquiry comprehensive, he sought out many of his correspondents and asked them to answer questions or to write down detailed accounts of their experiences. He also gathered material from friends and former fellow inmates—Panin, Kopelev, Karbe, Gershuni, Rappoport, Susi, Tenno. As news of his enterprise spread secretly among sympathizers and ex-prisoners, the number of people helping him gradually increased. Some of these assistants managed to find rare early publications on the history of the camps or obtain copies of little-known documents, and as a member of the Writers' Union, Solzhenitsyn could now use the "reserved" sections of the libraries. Thanks to his fame, he also had contacts in high places. He could not confide in many of them, but even at high levels, especially in the universities and scientific institutes, there were men and women who had served sentences in the camps and who were willing to take risks for the sake of his undertaking.

Solzhenitsyn spent most of the winter of 1964–65 in Solotcha working on what was to become *The Gulag Archipelago*. He drew up the overall plan of dividing the work into seven parts and commenced work on parts 1 and 5. These were the easiest: part 1 was mainly historical, dealing with the origins of the labour camps and the development of the legislation making them possible, while part 5 was largely autobiographical and described Solzhenitsyn's experiences in Ekibastuz and the prisoners' rebellion of 1952. At some point in the early part of 1965, he took time off from his writing to make the first of three visits to Tambov, about two hundred miles south-east of Ryazan, to investigate the peasant revolt that had occurred there in 1920–21. Not surprisingly, he found the local survivors extremely relucant to talk about it and information difficult to come by, but he learned enough to regard the trip as worth repeating at a later date.

Solzhenitsyn broke off his work on the camp history only for the New Year holiday, for which he returned to Ryazan. New Year's Eve was spent with the Vitkeviches in Kasimovsky Lane but was not a success. Nikolai

declared that there no longer seemed to be any frankness between them, to
which Solzhenitsyn replied that when frankness between people ceased, they
should stop seeing one another. Later they discussed *The First Circle*, which
Solzhenitsyn had given Nikolai to read—it contained one or two episodes
based on Nikolai's experiences. Nikolai said that he had had time to read
only a few chapters but that he disliked the novel's tone of omniscience and
the author's love of categorical judgements. He poured scorn, as he had been
wont to do in the *sharashka*, on Tolstoy, Dostoyevsky, and "the classics" and
was even more contemptuous of "those who regard themselves as their dis-
ciples." When Solzhenitsyn asked him whom he had in mind, Nikolai retorted,
"You, for instance." The evening ended in a quarrel, and the following day
Solzhenitsyn went around to the Vitkeviches' flat and took the novel back.
Some time later that year, according to Reshetovskaya, the Vitkeviches had
a baby boy. She urged Solzhenitsyn to forget his differences with Nikolai
and offer his congratulations. Solzhenitsyn replied, "I don't see how the birth
of a child is a greater event than the birth of a novel. After all, they rejected
my *Sharashka*."[18]

By the following spring, Solzhenitsyn was back in Ryazan, but he no
longer felt comfortable there. The flat on Kasimovsky Lane was shabby,
cramped, and uncomfortable. After the mud hut of Kok Terek and Matryona's ramshackle cabin, it had once seemed positively luxurious, but now,
with his experience of Moscow living, it had lost its lustre. The wood-burning stove was cumbersome and inconvenient, and the shared kitchen and
toilet were both psychologically and practically a burden. With Natalia's
mother and two elderly aunts constantly present (and getting older and more
infirm), it was a strain to spend the whole day at home writing. His study
bedroom was no longer large enough to hold all his reference books and
materials, and the last straw was the siting of a warehouse across the street,
where heavy lorries revved their engines from morning till night. Solzhenitsyn, ever sensitive to noise, could not bear it.

Some months previously he had persuaded Natalia to ask for a different
flat—their accommodation was provided by the Agricultural Institute, and
the only possibility of moving was to get the institute to find them another
one. But he had come to the conclusion that it would be wiser to leave Ryazan
altogether. It was too far from Moscow, too cut off from his friends, from
the literary world, and from contacts with abroad. Since Khrushchev's overthrow he had gone in constant fear of some sort of reprisals against him.
Nothing, in fact, had occurred to confirm his fears, but he still felt isolated
and vulnerable.

The pity of it was that he had refused the flat in Moscow offered him
by the Writers' Union after the publication of *Ivan Denisovich*. He had turned
it down on the grounds that Moscow was too noisy and dirty, and he had
enjoyed demonstrating his independence of the establishment by showing
that he didn't need its favours. But now, when he had changed his mind, it
was too late. The political establishment did not want to know of him any
more, and Natalia's requests to the Agricultural Institute went unheeded.

In the spring of 1965 Solzhenitsyn took up the idea of moving to the small town of Obninsk. The idea had been suggested by the biochemist Zhores Medvedev, whom Solzhenitsyn had met for the first time the preceding November. Medvedev was well known in liberal Moscow circles for his opposition to the biological theories of Stalin's former protégé T. D. Lysenko. He had attacked Lysenko openly in the journal *Neva* (The Neva) in 1963 and had written an outspoken book, *Biological Science and the Personality Cult* (later published in the West as *The Rise and Fall of T. D. Lysenko*), that no one dared print but that circulated widely in samizdat. The preceding summer, Medvedev had been attacked in the Soviet press by the president of the All-Union Academy of Agricultural Sciences, M. A. Olshansky, and this had provoked Solzhenitsyn into writing him a rare fan letter.

> Respected Zhores Alexandrovich,
>
> This summer I read your "Essays." I cannot recall for literally years being so haunted by any book as I was by this one of yours. Its sincerity, cogency, simplicity, scrupulous construction, and accuracy of tone are beyond all praise. Its relevance to the present day goes without saying.
>
> I know that many readers have found it very exciting even though biology is remote from them. No one can remain indifferent to its future.[19]

Solzhenitsyn had gone on to say that he had been planning to call on Medvedev in Obninsk—where Medvedev worked at the Institute of Medical Radiology—"the day before Olshansky's despicable article appeared," but his journey had taken him another way. However, "at a moment so crucial for you, I would like to shake your hand warmly and say how proud I am for you, for your love of the truth and of science in our country."

Eventually, in mid-November 1964, the two men had met in Moscow and made a favourable impression on one another. It turned out that they had a common friend: Professor Nikolai Timofeyev-Ressovsky, with whom Solzhenitsyn had shared a cell in Butyrki Prison in 1946. Medvedev informed Solzhenitsyn that Timofeyev-Ressovsky had been in the Urals but was now in Obninsk, although at a different institute from Medvedev's.

There were other coincidences as well. Medvedev had first taken his magazine article on Lysenko and genetics to *Novy Mir* in the summer of 1962, but its editors, though sympathetic, had turned him down, because, as they put it, they were already planning to publish one strongly anti-Stalinist contribution, and two would have been excessive. The one they possessed—a story by an "unknown schoolteacher from Ryazan"—was being shown to Khrushchev for his personal approval, and *Novy Mir* was anxious not to upset him (Khrushchev was known to be a supporter of Lysenko's eccentric theories and had even threatened to close the Timiryazev Agricultural Academy, one of the oldest centres of learning in Russia, because of its opposition to Lysenko). Medvedev had formerly worked for the academy and had then been obliged to take his present job in Obninsk, and his article had been published in *Neva*.[20]

Solzhenitsyn was very interested by this story. He undertook to approach the *Novy Mir* editorial board about Medvedev's book and argued his case at one of its meetings. Tvardovsky somewhat impatiently cut him short, saying that they were "all agreed" on the book's excellence and on the desirability of publishing it, but simply needed to ask the author to make some "small cuts." These cuts later escalated to "large cuts," and a decision on whether to publish was repeatedly postponed, until in the end nothing was done. The "moment" for Medvedev's views had by then irrevocably passed.[21]

When Solzhenitsyn decided, in the spring of 1965, that it would be wise to move away from Ryazan and closer to Moscow, he made plans to spend part of the month of May driving through the provinces of Tula, Yaroslavl, Vladimir, and Kaluga, as well as through Moscow Province, to look for somewhere suitable. His itinerary would take him through Obninsk, and he wrote to Medvedev to express the hope that the two of them could meet and that Timofeyev-Ressovsky would be there as well. Medvedev replied that it would be a pleasure and that perhaps Obninsk would be a suitable place for him to live. One of the criteria for choosing a spot was the availability of work for Natalia, and since Obninsk was the site of several scientific institutes, it seemed to offer solution to the problem.

The Solzhenitsyns arrived in Obninsk on 30 May 1965. Solzhenitsyn was delighted to meet his old cell-mate again, and the two of them recalled that hot, sweaty July of 1946 when they had met in the crowded cells of Butyrki Prison and Timofeyev-Ressovsky had solemnly invited Solzhenitsyn to address the "Scientific Society of Cell No. 75" on the subject of nuclear physics. It is not clear whether Solzhenitsyn confided in the professor about his history of the camps, but he must certainly have questioned him, for the details of Timofeyev-Ressovsky's career both before and after the Butyrki meeting were later incorporated into volume 1 of *The Gulag Archipelago*.

The following day the four of them strolled round the town and down through the park to the river. A blaring loudspeaker destroyed the tranquillity of the scene, but Solzhenitsyn and Natalia were impressed, and decided that Natalia should apply for a vacant position as a chemist at Medvedev's institute. Within a month they heard that the institute's academic board had elected her almost unanimously (by eighteen votes to two), and the Solzhenitsyns began to plan their move. But their optimism was premature. It seemed that the Kaluga Provincial Party Committee had been alerted to the possibility of Solzhenitsyn's moving to the area and for some reason was against it. Pressure was put on the director of the Radiology Institute to delay an announcement, and the appointment remained unratified.[22]

Meanwhile, certain changes had occurred in Moscow as a result of the shake-up following Khrushchev's downfall. Leonid Ilyichev, Khrushchev's ideological chief, had been replaced by Piotr Demichev. In July, Demichev had a meeting with Tvardovsky and among other things expressed an interest in meeting "that Solzhenitsyn." Tvardovsky was immensely pleased by this mark of favour from the new ruling group and took it as a sign that *Novy Mir* must be on its way up again.

It so happened that Solzhenitsyn called to see Tvardovsky that very day. He had good reasons of his own for wanting to meet Demichev and agreed to go at once, whereupon Tvardovsky picked up the phone and arranged a meeting for 15 July 1965. Tvardovsky was delighted to find Solzhenitsyn in such an accommodating mood; backed up by his staff, he attempted to persuade Solzhenitsyn to write him a "viable little story." Solzhenitsyn had not had anything published for two years, and it was essential for him to appear in print again. But he had nothing "viable" to offer and, with his head full of *Gulag* and his thoughts on the camps, felt remote and estranged from these city intellectuals and their political calculations. He was also irritated by their attempts to "smarten him up" for his interview with Demichev. This summer, for the first time, he had grown a beard, which struck Tvardovsky and the others as an absurd affectation. They begged him to shave it off and also to don a suit and tie and not turn up at the Central Committee headquarters in his favourite summer attire of an open-neck shirt worn outside his trousers.[23]

Whether he heeded their advice about the suit is not known but Solzhenitsyn's meeting with Demichev was amicable. The latter was cool and admonitory at first, voicing all the familiar Party reservations about *A Day in the Life of Ivan Denisovich* and "Matryona's Place." Solzhenitsyn replied in detail, refuting the various allegations of the critics one by one, and then in turn attacked the orthodox camp stories by Dyakov and Shelest. He complained about some of the slanders that had begun to be whispered about him behind closed doors: that he had been a prisoner of war or had collaborated with the Germans—the kind of thing started by Pavlov during the Lenin Prize deliberations.

Gradually, according to Solzhenitsyn's account of the meeting, Demichev thawed and Solzhenitsyn thawed too—to such an extent that he confided in Demichev about the next novel he was writing: *Cancer Ward*. Demichev was at once put on his guard. Wasn't the title too morbid and the subject too pessimistic? "Generally speaking, which are you—a pessimist or an optimist?" "An unshakable optimist," replied Solzhenitsyn. "Can't you tell from *Ivan Denisovich?*"[24]

Solzhenitsyn writes that his aim, throughout these exchanges, was to calm any fears that Demichev might have had about his causing difficulties and to portray himself as a quiet, retiring, slow-working introvert whose only desire was to eschew publicity and get on with his writing. He almost sabotaged this aim by his very vehemence in defending himself, but in the end seems to have more or less succeeded. "I can see you really are an honest, straightforward Russian," said Demichev towards the end of their conversation. "You really are a very modest man. You have nothing in common with Remarque." Having earlier noted apprehensively, "You are a strong personality" and "the attention of the whole world is fixed upon you," he ended with an almost audible sigh of relief: "*They* have not been given a second Pasternak."[25]

29

ENTER THE KGB

THE INTERVIEW WITH Demichev seemed an excellent sign, and Solzhenitsyn was reasonably confident that he had made a good impression. Demichev had also been of practical help. When told of the obstacles being put in the way of Natalia's appointment in Obninsk and their plans to move to that town, Demichev at once put a call through to the Kaluga Provincial Party Committee and ordered them to let the appointment proceed. Two days later, the first secretary of the Kaluga committee went to the institute to discuss the matter with the director, and the day after that the director summoned the Solzhenitsyns to his office and informed Natalia that she was to start on 1 September.

At last the matter seemed settled, and to mark this satisfactory outcome, Solzhenitsyn purchased a modest plot of land with a small summer-house on it in the picturesque hamlet of Rozhdestvo, district of Naro-Fominsk, not far from Obninsk. It was evidently part of a local dacha co-operative that had been established after the death of Stalin, when city workers were encouraged to buy plots of land for allotments and even smallholdings, and allowed to build small cottages on them. At that time the regulations were reasonably generous by Soviet standards, and people could buy plots of up to about a quarter of an acre, so that Rozhdestvo presented a pleasant checker-board of copses, gardens, fields, and large allotments. With his penchant for nicknames, Solzhenitsyn quickly dubbed his cottage "Borzovka," in honour of its previous owner, Borzov, and moved in at once in order to spend the rest of the summer there.

In truth the "cottage" was nothing more than a primitive wooden shack, consisting of a single, large room downstairs and an attic above, with a small, rustic balcony and a corrugated iron roof. There was no running water, no gas or electricity, and no toilet, and in winter it was uninhabitable because of the cold. In summer, however, it was idyllic. Its very simplicity appealed to Solzhenitsyn. He immediately rigged up a makeshift study in the attic, safe from the floods of the small river Istya bounding his garden. The following year he built a lean-to garage. And from now on he spent as much time here as he could, sometimes sharing it with Natalia, when she came for weekends or during a vacation, but mostly living alone, caring and cooking for himself and concentrating on his writing. Not since acquiring his mud hut in Kok Terek had he felt so independent and carefree.

This was the first patch of ground I had ever been able to call my own. I had a hundred yards of stream to myself, and an extraordinary feeling of intimacy with the natural world about me. Almost every year the little house was partly under water for a while, but I always hurried there as soon as the floods began to recede, although the floor-boards would still be wet and a tongue of water from the gully crept up to my porch in the evenings. On cold nights all the water is drawn back into the river, leaving a covering of glassy white ice over the sloping water-meadows and in the gully. It hangs, a brittle film, over a vacuum, and in the morning falls away in big pieces as though someone were walking over it. On warm nights, though, the river does not sink, the flood-water does not withdraw, but laps and babbles all night long. Even in daytime the roar of lorries from the high road cannot drown the sounds of the river in spate, and I can sit for hours listening to its mysterious gurglings, feeling my health return hour by hour. One minute I hear a heavy gulping, the next a sharp crack (a loose branch, lodged in a willow tree when the water was higher, has fallen), and then the even murmur of many voices begins again. The sun, blanched by the clouds, is reflected in the racing water. Then the higher ground begins to dry out, and you can caress the warm earth with your rake, clearing it of withered grass to let the new green blades through. Day by day the water falls, and now you can take your fork and clear the banks of the rubbish and drift-wood cast up by the river. Or simply sit thoughtlessly sunning yourself on the old work-bench or the oak seat. There are alders growing on my patch, and nearby there is a birch wood, and every spring the weather signs are there to be read: if the alders come into leaf before the birches it will be a wet summer; if the birches are earlier than the alders, a dry one.[1]

During that first summer in Rozhdestvo, Solzhenitsyn continued to work on his camp history, which about now probably acquired its title of *The Gulag Archipelago* (a phrase first coined by Solzhenitsyn in *The First Circle*). In addition, he made a start at last on the work that had been his life's dream, his epic on the October Revolution, which was no longer called *The Red Wheel* but code-named *R-17*. By what seemed like a miracle, the notes he had taken and the chapters he had written as a student in Ryazan had all survived, saved by Natalia, handed over to Veronica during Natalia's marriage to Vsevolod, and handed back by Veronica to Solzhenitsyn again after his return from exile.

In outline, the plan of the work had not changed much at all. Solzhenitsyn still regarded the 1914 Battle of Tannenberg and Samsonov's defeat as the key to the events that followed, including Russia's collapse and the Revolution. He found, when he came to them, that he was able to incorporate some of the scenes written in Rostov nearly thirty years beforehand virtually without altering them. He was also able to adapt material from other early attempts at this subject—*The Sixth Course* and *Love the Revolution*. In other respects, however, there were big changes. Lenartovich, the Communist hero of the original version, now became the anti-hero and underwent a considerable transformation, mirroring the change in the epic's basic philosophy from pro-Communist and pro-Marxist, with an optimistic view of the Revolution, to a darkly pessimistic evaluation of the "disaster" of October 1917.

With this fundamental shift of emphasis went an equally profound reappraisal of Russian society before the Revolution. From his days in the Komsomol until almost the end of his imprisonment, Solzhenitsyn had held a more or less negative view of tsarist Russia and, like most young men, had dismissed the experiences of his forebears and the life they had led as uninteresting and irrelevant. Such feelings had been strengthened by Soviet propaganda and his personal need to lie about his family and conceal his true origins.

Since his disillusionment with Marxism, however, and his return to some sort of Christian faith, he had begun to view the past in a new light. Things that had seemed automatically and unquestionably bad when regarded through Marxist spectacles now took on a new aspect, and as Solzhenitsyn began to re-examine pre-revolutionary Russia, he discovered quite another side to it. A crucial role in this re-examination was played by members of his own family. In youth and early manhood, aided by the fact that he was a virtual orphan, he had grown away from them, and had come to regard himself as virtually alone in the world, apart from his wife. In Ekibastuz and in Kok Terek he had been literally alone, but this had provoked in him, on his "return from the dead," a curiosity about his remaining family and a desire to pick up the broken threads and learn more.

That was one reason he had gone south in 1956—to Rostov, to revisit the scenes of his childhood, to Georgievsk, to find Aunts Maria and Irina and see his mother's grave, and to Kislovodsk to visit the house where he was born. He had also been reunited with his stepcousins, Maria's daughters, both of whom had married soldiers (both their husbands had been purged and exiled in 1937 and rehabilitated in 1956, the same year as Solzhenitsyn). They had much in common and much to talk about when they all met in Moscow. In 1960 Solzhenitsyn had gone south again, and it may have been then that he established contact with the one surviving aunt on his father's side, Evdokia, and the husband of his deceased aunt Anastasia. It may also have been then that he learned that his step-uncle, Ilya, had been exiled to Siberia during the collectivization of the early thirties. Two years later, in 1962, he had visited Ilya during his Siberian journey, and Ilya had since been to stay with him in Ryazan.[2]

Through talking to his uncle and aunts, Solzhenitsyn had been able to put together a clearer picture of his family's past and to reclaim for himself the ancestry he had once disregarded. Four people, in particular, stood out in his mind as holding the key to his own character and development: his mother and father; his aunt Irina; and his grandfather Zakhar Shcherbak, the "only man in the family" throughout his early childhood. Like most children and adolescents, he had taken his mother more or less for granted and not paid a great deal of attention to her. By his own admission, she had not been able to influence him and had usually not dared speak her mind, yielding to him in almost everything.[3] Having rejected Russia's past and therefore his mother's past, he had simply ignored whatever life she might have had before and separate from his own existence. This had led him to reproach himself after his mother's death, and there is a scene in *The First Circle* where the diplomat Innokenti Volodin (who is endowed with certain elements from the author's life) searches for a book and stumbles across his mother's old letters and diaries.

He did, incidentally, find the book and was later to read it, but the important thing he discovered was not in the book but in the letters and the life of the mother he had never before understood, and had been fond of only as a child. . . .

. . . Towards his mother—always concerned for him, but always vaguely worried, nostalgic, always surrounded by books and hot-water bottles—he had felt superior, as sons usually do, never suspecting that she had any life of her own, apart from himself, his childhood, his needs, never thinking about her being ill and in pain, or her dying at the age of forty-seven.

His parents had lived very little together. Innokenti had never had any reason to ask himself what their short married life had been like, and it would not have entered his head to question his mother.

But now, there it all was in her letters and diaries. Their marriage had been a whirlwind, like everything else in those years. Circumstances flung them together, and circumstances had kept them apart, and in the end parted them for good. And his mother had not been just an adjunct to his father, as she had always appeared to him—she was a world in herself.[4]

This appears to be directly autobiographical, though it is not clear when Solzhenitsyn was first shown his mother's letters and diaries. It must have been on one of his early visits to Georgievsk, for the above passage appears in the version of *The First Circle* that was shown to Tvardovsky.

Solzhenitsyn goes on to describe batches of letters tied up with coloured ribbon, bundles of theatre programmes, old newspapers, photographs, notebooks, magazines, all of them breathing an atmosphere that was totally unfamiliar to Innokenti and that he had formerly disdained. In his mother's handwriting he finds reminiscences of her life as a student. "One description went straight to his heart, of a white June night in Petersburg when his mother, as an enthusiastic teen-age girl, went with a crowd, all equally carried away, all crying for joy, as they met the Moscow Art Theatre troupe at Petersburg Station." And Solzhenitsyn comments, "A breath of that joy touched Innokenti. He knew of no such theatre company today, and if there was one, he could think of no one staying up all night to meet it—except for representatives of the Cultural Department with bouquets ordered on expenses. Certainly no one would weep for joy on such an occasion."[5]

The key element in this passage is Innokenti's discovery of his mother's jottings on "ethical considerations," in which she praises such old-fashioned concepts as compassion and tolerance, and he is particularly struck by one formulation: "What is the most precious thing in the world? It seems to be the consciousness of not participating in injustice. Injustice is stronger than you are, it always was and it always will be, but let it not be committed through you." There are similar passages on "Truth, Goodness, and Beauty" (all with capital letters), and Innokenti realizes that "six years ago, he would not have noticed" these passages.

At the end of it all, he comes to another realization (omitted from the version shown to Tvardovsky).

> These yellowing pages confronted him with the abounding variety of conflicting currents and ideas, the imaginative freedom and anxious foreboding that was the Russia of the 1910s—the last pre-revolutionary decade, which Innokenti had been taught in school and college to regard as the most rotten and shameful in the entire history of Russia, so pitiful that had the Bolsheviks not extended a helping hand, Russia would simply have crumbled from within and collapsed in ruins.
>
> Yes, it had been a much too garrulous decade, in part too self-confident, in part too helpless. But what a crop of new shoots, what a sprouting of ideas!
>
> Innokenti realized that up till now he had been robbed.[6]

The fresh idea that he now had of his mother was inseparable from his idea of pre-revolutionary Russia. And Solzhenitsyn links this with another idea that makes perfect sense in terms of the novel and of Innokenti's marriage, but that also contains more than a grain of autobiography: "His mother had prevailed: risen from the grave, she took her son away from her daughter-in-law."[7]

From this part of the past, it was but a short step farther back to Grandfather Zakhar and his family. In 1964, during a trip to the south, Solzhenitsyn paid a visit to his grandfather's old estate near Armavir. Zakhar's mansion, dilapidated and neglected but still sturdy, was now occupied by a collective farm. Solzhenitsyn had no difficulty in entering and walking around and was quickly able to identify the former dining- and drawing-rooms, the various bedrooms, and other parts that he had heard described or seen in photographs. Afterwards he prowled the gardens and was impressed to see that Zakhar's original layout had remained more or less unchanged, with its orchard, avenues of poplar and plane trees, kitchen garden, rose garden, and so on. Everything was overgrown and terribly neglected now, but the principal features had proved surprisingly durable.

Solzhenitsyn hung around for the best part of a day, taking notes and writing down his impressions. He would dearly have liked to question some of the old men he saw working on the farm. Many of them would have known Zakhar and could doubtless have given him vivid descriptions and much valuable information. But he dared not, for fear of revealing his identity. The shade of his grandfather did, however, materialize at one point during his wanderings. While contemplating the empty reservoir, which had once supplied the house and gardens with piped water and which he remembered having seen brim full in some photographs, he caught sight of a pair of small boys playing nearby. "Why is the reservoir dry?" he asked. They told him that "old Shcherbak had put a spell on it." Solzhenitsyn asked them who Shcherbak was, and the boys explained that he had once owned the place but that when it was expropriated during the Revolution, he had put a curse on it, so that the water wouldn't flow any more.[8]

For more information about Shcherbak and his life, Solzhenitsyn had to turn to Aunt Irina in Georgievsk, whose earlier tales he remembered from his childhood. He asked her to write her memoirs for him, since she was virtually the only one alive who could remember it all. Aunt Maria, his mother's sister, might also have been able to provide some information, but she lacked Irina's education and intelligence. Nor did she hold the same fascination for Solzhenitsyn that Irina did, for he was as anxious to hear about her life as he was about Shcherbak's.

Solzhenitsyn's reunion with his aunt and the relationship he established with her also appear to have been fictionalized in the full, ninety-six-chapter version of The First Circle, where Innokenti, after scrutinizing his mother's papers, suddenly feels an impulse to call on an elderly uncle and learn still more about the past. He finds his uncle living in a crooked little wooden hovel, one storey high, in a cobbled street that runs directly between the walls of houses, so that no trees or gardens are to be seen. The door, with fretted panels, leans at a crazy angle and Innokenti is unable to obtain any answer to his knocks or to gain entrance through a tiny gate leading into the yard. The street seems empty, until he catches sight of an old man approaching slowly, carrying two full buckets of water. The old man is skinny, has one shoulder higher than the other, and is concentrating so hard on his task that he pays no attention to Innokenti. The latter, however, recognizes the old man as his uncle and they embrace.

The uncle ushers Innokenti into the entrance passage of his tiny house and firmly bolts the door. Innokenti finds himself in an interior like none he has ever seen before.

> The short passage had a low ceiling, a microscopic window looking out onto the gate, two cupboards, and two regular doors. . . . And in all the rooms, and between the rooms, all the doors were askew, some lined with felt, others folding, with old-fashioned patterned carving. To go through any of them, you were obliged to bend your head and also to keep it clear of the lamps hanging from the ceiling. There were three tiny rooms, all with windows facing the street, and the air inside was heavy and stale, for the double windows had been stuffed with cotton wool, tiny glasses, and coloured paper, so that only the ventilation panes

could be opened, but even these had strips of shredded newspaper hanging in them: their constant trembling in the draught frightened the flies away.[9]

Innokenti's sense of the grinding poverty of his uncle is reinforced by the uncle's clothing: his shirt is unmentionable, his jacket in rags, his trousers held together only by patches, his boots a cobbler's nightmare. Innokenti is depressed and repelled. He had come with the idea of staying the night, but his impulse now is to leave as quickly as possible. Gradually, however, as his uncle lovingly shows him round the house and small court-yard garden, Innokenti warms to his uncle's dignified acceptance of his lot, to his sharp intelligence, and to his sly humour. For his uncle is not oblivious to his poverty; he comments wittily on it and can see himself from the outside. More importantly, he proves to be a perceptive critic of the life he observes around him, and as their intimacy grows, Innokenti learns of his uncle's active hostility towards Lenin and Stalin and his conviction that Soviet power is both alien and illegitimate. He has remained faithful, in other words, to the beliefs and values he held before the Revolution.

Throughout this chapter the fictional demands of the narrative have to be met, and it would be excessive to identify the characters of Innokenti and his uncle with those of Solzhenitsyn and his aunt in every detail. That the physical appearances and living conditions of the fictional uncle and real aunt do more or less coincide, however, was later confirmed by a photograph of Irina at her gate that appeared in *Stern* magazine in 1974, and there are reasonable grounds for believing that the psychological understanding between uncle and nephew reproduces fairly accurately that which grew up between the real-life nephew and his aunt.

There remained the figure of Solzhenitsyn's father, about whom least of all was known. Again we find echoes in the life of Innokenti. "Innokenti didn't remember his father . . . but those around him never tired of telling the son about him. . . . Innokenti was used to feeling very proud of him."[10] There was little Solzhenitsyn could do to fill the void, however. He remembered his mother's stories, but there was hardly anyone alive who had known his father. Solzhenitsyn would have to re-create him, and *R-17* would be in part the realization of this aim.

The peace and quiet of Rozhdestvo was a godsend. He could write all day and every day if he wanted, and yet he was within an hour and a half of Moscow if he needed to go there. And in the summer of 1965 he went there quite often, sleeping at the Steins if the need arose to stay on. In August he and Natalia went to central Russia on a camping holiday, on which they were joined by Dr Zubov, who had come up from the Crimea specially for the occasion. They gathered in the Steins' flat to make the final preparations, and on the evening before their departure the Teushes dropped in for a drink and a chat, accompanied by two young friends of theirs: Ilya Zilberberg, an engineer and anthroposophist disciple of Teush's, and his wife, Ellya. The appearance of comparative strangers in the flat on social occasions was com-

mon enough in those days. Solzhenitsyn was such a mysterious and enigmatic figure that people were eager just to take a look at him, and those lucky
enough to know someone in his circle often availed themselves of the chance.
Solzhenitsyn seems to have taken their presence in good part, and conversation revolved around the question of whether there could be a return to the
past (meaning a return to Stalinism) in Soviet society. The general opinion
was that there couldn't. Despite some ominous signs since Khrushchev's
departure, it was felt that liberalization had gone too far, and authorities like
Nadezhda Mandelstam were quoted as believing in the impossibility of a
reversal. On another topic, Solzhenitsyn quoted the case of Chaadayev,* the
nineteenth-century thinker who had encoded his manuscripts and hidden
them sheet by sheet in different books in his library. Only in Soviet times,
one hundred years later, had they been discovered and decoded, and they
had been prepared for publication, but publication had then been banned
because of the manuscripts' "reactionary content." This curious incident had
obviously made an impression on Solzhenitsyn and he later cited it in the
opening pages of *The Oak and the Calf*.[11]

The evening broke up relatively early because the Solzhenitsyns wanted
to prepare for their departure the following day. It was then that Solzhenitsyn seems to have shown some curiosity about the two strangers in their
midst. Ilya Zilberberg later remembered seeing Solzhenitsyn and Teush conferring in a corner and looking in his direction, from which he deduced that
he was the subject of their discussion. Whatever was said by Teush seems to
have been satisfactory, however, for a few minutes later Solzhenitsyn invited
Zilberberg to help him fit the roof-rack onto his little Moskvich, and they
chatted about motoring matters before amicably parting.[12]

It is not known where the Solzhenitsyns spent their camping holiday—
it may have been in the Tambov region, which Solzhenitsyn was studying
for the purposes of *The Gulag Archipelago* and his proposed novel about the
Revolution. But while they were away, there were some ominous developments in the political world. An important ideological conference took place
to discuss Party policy. According to Solzhenitsyn, it was dominated by
Alexander ("Iron Shurik") Shelepin, a former chairman of the KGB, who in
1963 had been appointed chief of a new Party-state control committee to
enforce ideological orthodoxy. Shelepin is thought to have played a major
role in the overthrow of Khrushchev (although the latter had appointed him)
and to have retained close links with the KGB through the appointment of
his friend Vladimir Semichastny as his successor. At all events, his promotion to full membership in the Presidium in 1964 had been widely regarded
as a reward for his and the KGB's services during the coup.

At the August conference Shelepin is said to have been a leading advo-

---

*Piotr Chaadayev was a friend of Pushkin's who underwent a conversion to mystical Christian-
ity and whose *Philosophical Letters* were harshly critical of Russian history and Russian society.
When the first letter was published, in 1836, Chaadayev was declared insane and placed under
medical supervision. Most of his writings were not published in his lifetime.

cate of closer ideological control. Coexistence with the West should not take on pacifist overtones or imply the "ideological disarmament" of the Soviet people, but should be accompanied by a sharpening of the struggle in the field of ideas. De-Stalinization was sapping the people's will and should be halted, and it was time to resurrect Stalin's "useful'" concept of "enemies of the people." Particular attention, it seems, was paid to cultural matters. Zhdanov's 1946 decrees on literature had been sound and should be revived.* *Novy Mir* should be investigated and prevented from giving so much comfort to the bourgeois enemy. There were even rumours that the KGB had called for the arrest of "a thousand intellectuals" as a precautionary measure, but this was probably a later reaction to the events that followed.

Solzhenitsyn heard about these things upon his return from holiday. They reinforced the fears that had never been far from his mind since the fall of Khrushchev, and his first thought was for his novel with *Novy Mir*. Its chances of being published now seemed more remote than ever. Tvardovsky's enthusiasm remained high, but the position of the magazine was too precarious for him to take any major risks at the moment, and he lacked the connections in high places that he had possessed under Khrushchev. Solzhenitsyn had heard on the grape-vine that he, Solzhenitsyn, had also been criticized at the ideological conference for "distorting the true picture of the labour camps." He felt exposed and vulnerable, especially because the pages of *The Gulag Archipelago* were lying on his desk, and he decided that the safest course would be to forget all ideas of publication for the moment and get *The First Circle* back from *Novy Mir*.

On 6 September 1965 he went to see Tvardovsky at his dacha in Pakhra to ask whether he could take the novel away. Tvardovsky had been drinking and was in an irritable, obstinate frame of mind, so that when Solzhenitsyn made his request, it seemed to catch Tvardovsky on the raw and trigger off other resentments. He reproached Solzhenitsyn, not for the first time, for having let his miniature stories circulate in samizdat and thus reach the West. This was a particularly sore point with Tvardovsky, for that spring he had been summoned to see Polikarpov at the ideological section of the Central Committee, confronted with a copy of *Grani*, and asked to explain the stories' appearance there. In the eyes of the authorities, the interest of an openly anti-Soviet journal in the work of any Soviet author was proof that that author was at best politically unreliable, and at worst actively collaborating with the Soviet Union's enemies. Tvardovsky had told Polikarpov that it was inconceivable that Solzhenitsyn had had anything to do with their publication, and that in any case "most of the stories" were not his work. But since then he had learned that the Soviet women's magazine *Semya i shkola* (Family and School) had actually set them up in type and was planning to publish them, with Solzhenitsyn's active help and connivance. Such a step was out of the question for works that had already appeared in the West—presumably *Semya i shkola* didn't know this and Solzhenitsyn was deceiving them on this point. But worse still was the prospect that Tvardovsky himself would be exposed as having lied to Polikarpov, and all this for stories that he genuinely believed to be second-rate. Solzhenitsyn could at least have told him about the negotiations with *Semya i shkola*. "I put my head on the block for you, and what do you do?"[13]

Tvardovsky also had harsh words to say about Solzhenitsyn's beard. There were rumours, he said, that Solzhenitsyn had grown it so that if he wanted to slip across the frontier, he could shave it off again and cross unrecognized. He revealed that at a meeting he had attended in Novosibirsk a written question had been handed in asking whether it was true that Solzhenitsyn had once worked for the Gestapo, and that Polikarpov had virtually accused Solzhenitsyn of handing *Grani* his stories himself.

Given Tvardovsky's aggrieved and petulant tone and the strained atmosphere of the meeting, these snippets of information emerged as accusations rather than as the warnings they were presumably meant to be, and it was Solzhenitsyn's turn to take umbrage. He was not the sort of man to forgive a slight, and although the camps had succeeded in mellowing him for a while, his attitude to those who were not close personal friends had not really changed very much. Tvardovsky's words hurt, and he carefully noted them down for the book of memoirs he was planning to write (he had been taking notes since the day of his first editorial conference at *Novy Mir*, but it was only recently that the idea had begun to form in his mind of putting them into a book). Apart from feeling resentful, he remembered the notorious recent confiscation by the KGB of Vasily Grossman's novel *Life and Fate** and was genuinely apprehensive that the same might happen to him.

In explaining the matter to Tvardovsky, he bungled it, however, and instead of being honest told a schoolboy fib about wishing to "correct the grammar." Tvardovsky was incredulous, and even more so when Solzhenitsyn at last explained his true motive. There was nothing wrong with the *Novy Mir* safe, he said, and refused to let the novel go. Then he asked that just one of the four fair copies be left at *Novy Mir*, which had, after all, signed a contract to publish it and paid Solzhenitsyn an advance. The book was rightfully theirs. But Solzhenitsyn was adamant, and his iron will easily prevailed over Tvardovsky's. The following day he went to the *Novy Mir* offices and removed all four copies in a suitcase brought specially for the purpose. He took the suitcase to the Teushes, who had just returned from their summer holiday, and left it there with three copies inside. A fourth was delivered to the literary critic Yuri Kariakin, at *Pravda*. For some reason, although he no longer trusted Tvardovsky or *Novy Mir* to keep his manuscript safe, Solzhenitsyn still had faith in the ultra-orthodox *Pravda* and was still hopeful that the newspaper's mildly liberal editor, Alexei Rumyantsev, would publish one or two chapters as he had promised.[14]

* See note p. 412.

With these deliveries safely accomplished, Solzhenitsyn returned to Rozhdestvo in a much more relaxed state of mind. The date was 8 September. Four days later, on 12 September, Veronica Stein arrived in a state of great agitation, bearing two items of bad news. The preceding evening the KGB had raided the Teushes' flat and carried off all three copies of *The First Circle*. Three days prior to that, on the very day Solzhenitsyn had returned to Rozhdestvo, the KGB had arrested the literary critic Andrei Sinyavsky, for smuggling stories to the West.

Solzhenitsyn was petrified by this news. According to Veronica, all the colour drained from his face, leaving it an ashen grey, and he was momentarily speechless.[15] He thought at first that he must have walked into a trap, and he bitterly regretted having removed the novel from *Novy Mir*. Surely it gave as much cause for his arrest as the works Sinyavsky had sent to the West. What was the meaning of it all? As at the time of Khrushchev's overthrow, his feelings were akin to panic. He wondered whether the police were looking for him, and whether perhaps they had already been to his flat in Ryazan and searched it. Perhaps they were on his track at that very moment? It was late afternoon. Throwing all his manuscripts and some clothing into the car, he decided to set off for Tvardovsky's. Despite the fact that they had only just quarrelled and that he had ignored Tvardovsky's advice in removing the novel, he felt that Tvardovsky was the only person who could advise him. But before leaving he had the presence of mind to have his photograph taken, so that his misery might be registered for posterity.[16]*

Solzhenitsyn drove to Tvardovsky's by a circuitous route, so as to avoid entering Moscow. He ran out of petrol about a mile short of his destination and had to walk the last bit of the way, carrying a jerrycan in his hand. Tvardovsky reacted to the news of the novel's confiscation with admirable calm. Gone was the petulance and chagrin of the preceding week; in its place were sincere distress and a grave determination to sort the matter out. After prolonged thought he decided that the best course would be for him to approach Demichev the next morning. Then he changed his mind and suggested that Solzhenitsyn write Demichev a letter. They sat down to draft it together, but disagreed over the wording. Solzhenitsyn was for a strong protest and wanted to refer to the novel's "illegal" removal, but Tvardovsky was more cautious. Who knew what was legal and illegal when the security service was involved? He insisted that the tone of the letter be kept mild and respectful.[17]

After very little sleep that night, Solzhenitsyn drove into Moscow, where he was greeted by news of fresh calamities. Only the day before, a second writer, the little-known Yuli Daniel, had been arrested by the KGB. More to the point, it turned out that at the time when *The First Circle* was confiscated, the KGB had also found and taken the archive that Solzhenitsyn had deposited with Teush two and half years ago. This archive contained not only early versions of *Ivan Denisovich*, "Matryona's Place," *The Republic of*

---

*The photograph appears in *Solzhenitsyn: A Pictorial Record*, p. 60.

Labour, and so on, none of which was very important, but also copies of his early camp verses and his verse play, *Feast of the Conquerors,* one of his most "anti-Soviet" works. Only a very few intimates had ever seen the play, and he had never attempted to "lighten" it for publication. It was too inflammatory, too damning. And now it was in the hands of the KGB.[18]

It looked to him as if his brief but glorious literary career was already over.

30

THE
TURNING-POINT

THE KGB RAID and the confiscation of his novel and archive constituted the most serious blow to strike Solzhenitsyn since his cancer of twelve years beforehand. According to his later assessment, he felt it worse even than his arrest eight years before that.

The catastrophe of September 1965 was the greatest misfortune in all my forty-seven years. For some months I felt as though it were a real, unhealing physical wound—a javelin wound right through the breast, with the tip so firmly lodged that it could not be pulled out. The slightest stirring within me (perhaps the memory of some line or other from my impounded archive) caused a stab of pain. . . .

Throughout this period I felt a constriction in my chest. There was a sickening tug somewhere near my solar plexus, and I could not decide whether it was a spiritual sickness or a foreboding of some new grief. There was an unbearable burning sensation within me. I was on fire, and nothing helped. My throat was always dry. I felt a tension that nothing would relax. You seek salvation in sleep (as you once did in prison): let me sleep and sleep and never get up again! Switch off and dream untroubled dreams! But within a few hours the shutter of the soul falls away and a red-hot drill whirls you back to reality. Every day you must find in yourself the will to put one foot in front of the other, to study, to work, to pretend that the soul can and must do these things, although in reality your mind wanders every five minutes: Why bother, what does it matter now? . . . In your daily life you seem to be acting a part. You know that in reality it's all gone pfft. It is as though the world's clock had stopped. Thoughts of suicide— for the first time and, I hope, the last.[1]

How serious these thoughts of suicide were is not certain. Solzhenitsyn referred to them again in volume 2 of *The Gulag Archipelago*, but from there

Solzhenitsyn's grandmother Evdokia Shcherbak, and his aunt Maria (standing) circa 1900. (Private collection)

The Shcherbak family, circa 1921. Standing at the back are Roman, Irina, Maria, and Maria's second husband, Fyodor Garin; sitting are Zakhar, Taissia, and Evdokia. The child on the left is Solzhenitsyn; the other may be one of Maria's stepchildren. (Private collection)

The house in Kislovodsk where Solzhenitsyn was born. (Private collection)

Roman Shcherbak's Rolls-Royce, circa 1910. Roman's wife, Irina, is sitting in the back with Taissia. (Private collection)

Solzhenitsyn in Rostov, aged six and a half, 1925. (Seuil)

School photograph taken in 1935. Second from the left at back is Nikolai Vitkevich, with Solzhenitsyn beside him; immediately in front of them is Kirill Simonyan; to Kirill's left (with braids) is Lydia Ezherets; to his right is Anastasia Grünau, their literature teacher. (Bobbs-Merrill)

Solzhenitsyn as a student at Rostov University.
(Seuil)

Solzhenitsyn and Natalia Reshetovskaya
immediately after their marriage, in 1940.
(Bobbs-Merrill)

Taissia in the late 1930s. (Bobbs-Merr

Solzhenitsyn wearing his Patriotic War medal after participating in the Soviet recapture of Orel in August 1943. (Seuil)

Solzhenitsyn reading Gorky's *Matvei Kozhemyakin* to Natalia during her visit to the front in spring 1944. (Seuil)

Solzhenitsyn and Vitkevich at the front in 1944, just after signing "Resolution No. 1." (Seuil)

Solzhenitsyn at the Marfino *sharashka* on his thirtieth birthday. Permission to be photographed was granted as a reward for good work. The suit was provided by the prison authorities. (Private collection)

The main building of the *sharashka* (formerly a seminary) and the setting of *The First Circle*. (Ardis)

Solzhenitsyn as he looked at Ekibastuz. Having smuggled his number patches into exile, he took this photograph immediately after his release. (Seuil)

Solzhenitsyn outside his mud hut in Kok Terek in 1955. (Private collection)

Solzhenitsyn in Kok Terek after his successful treatment for cancer in Tashkent. (Private collection)

Solzhenitsyn with two of his pupils in the village of Miltsevo in 1956. (Private collection)

Natalia Reshetovskaya at Miltsevo after being reunited with Solzhenitsyn in 1956. (Private collection)

The house on Kasimovsky Lane in Ryazan where Solzhenitsyn and Reshetovskaya lived (ground floor left, with three windows) from 1957 to 1969. (Private collection)

Solzhenitsyn on Ryazan Station on the day of his arrival in spring 1957. The hole in his suitcase had been made by a convoy guard's bayonet when he was still a prisoner. (Private collection)

Sawing wood at Kasimovsky Lane. (Private collection)

The tennis player, 1959. (Private collection)

In the garden at Kasimovsky Lane, 1958. *Left to right:* Maria Reshetovskaya (Natalia's mother), Solzhenitsyn, Elena Zubov, Nikolai Zubov, Natalia. (Private collection)

Solzhenitsyn at his rustic writing table in the woods at Solotcha (1963), where he worked on *Cancer Ward* and wrote "For the Good of the Cause." (Private collection)

Solzhenitsyn's summer cabin at Rozhdestvo, which he purchased in 1965. (Private collection)

Solzhenitsyn at Rozhdestvo on the day he learned
that his manuscripts had been confiscated by the
KGB, 12 September 1965. (Seuil)

Solzhenitsyn with his two closest friends from his *sharashka* days, Lev Kopelev (Rubin in
The First Circle) and Dimitri Panin (Sologdin) at Rozhdestvo in 1967. (Seuil)

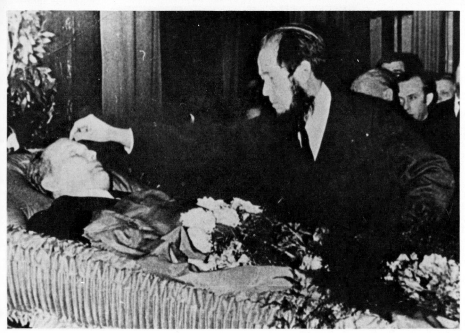

Solzhenitsyn making the sign of the cross over Tvardovsky in his coffin (December 1971). (Seuil)

Solzhenitsyn's room at Chukovsky's dacha in Peredelkino after he had left it for the last time. The pitchfork was intended for self-defence in case of need. (Private collection)

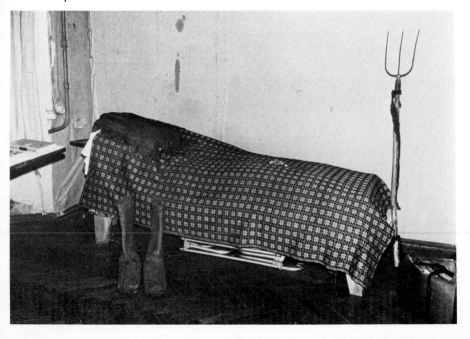

Solzhenitsyn with Heinrich Böll in Langenbroich on the day of his expulsion from the Soviet Union, 14 January 1974. (UPI)

Solzhenitsyn with press photographers outside his house in Stapferstrasse, Zurich, spring 1974. (Rex Features)

Solzhenitsyn receiving the Nobel Prize in Stockholm four years late, December 1974. (Rex Features)

Solzhenitsyn at Harvard, June 1976. (Wide World Photos)

Solzhenitsyn and his second wife, Natalia Svetlova, at the AFL-CIO luncheon in New York in July 1975. (Rex Features)

it is equally clear that the idea of suicide was really quite alien to Solzhenitsyn's basically sanguine and optimistic temperament. Apart from that period in 1965, he writes, "I was convinced throughout my life that never in any circumstances would I contemplate suicide," and he goes on to state his opinion that "a suicide is always a bankrupt, always a man in a cul-de-sac, a man who has lost the game of life and doesn't have the will to continue the struggle." In such circumstances it takes "more will-power to stay alive than to die."[2]

Will-power Solzhenitsyn certainly had, but according to his memoir, intermittent feelings of hopelessness persisted for about three months, during which he daily expected to be arrested. He psychologically prepared himself for arrest and a long imprisonment. He decided that he would refuse to cooperate with any investigation and composed a ringing declaration in advance: "Conscious of my responsibility to my predecessors in the great literature of Russia, I cannot recognize or accept the right of gendarmes to supervise it. I will answer no questions under interrogation or in court. This is my first and last statement."[3]

One may easily believe that these were the worst months of Solzhenitsyn's life, but it was not in his nature to remain inactive in the face of danger, and with his characteristic resilience he took steps to avert further disasters. The most immediate risk was presented by his notes and unfinished drafts for *The Gulag Archipelago*, which he had taken to Moscow with him when hastily leaving Rozhdestvo. With the aid of some ex-prisoners who were helping him gather information for the book, he transferred everything to a remote spot in the provinces. He also completed and delivered his letter to Demichev and arranged for the fourth copy of *The First Circle* to be retrieved from *Pravda* and delivered to *Novy Mir*. Quite apart from the confiscation of the other three copies, there was now no hope that extracts would be published in the Soviet Union's leading daily. Rumyantsev, the mildly liberal editor on whom Solzhenitsyn had pinned his hopes, was dismissed as part of the general upheaval, and his successor, Mikhail Zimyanin, chairman of the Journalists' Union, was known to be a hardliner and a crony of Brezhnev's.

A sign of the tension that Solzhenitsyn was under at this time—and of the generally strained atmosphere in Moscow literary circles—was the row that Solzhenitsyn had with Tvardovsky over the return of his novel. The ground for it had already been prepared by their disagreement over Solzhenitsyn's letter to Demichev. Tvardovsky had been further upset to learn of the confiscation of the archive, including a play that Solzhenitsyn himself acknowledged was—by Soviet standards—virtually treasonable. When the novel was returned to *Novy Mir* by Karyakin, Solzhenitsyn seems to have expected Tvardovsky to welcome it back and lock it up in his safe again, but Tvardovsky refused. He was badly frightened by the news of Solzhenitsyn's "anti-Soviet" play and took the view that Solzhenitsyn himself was to blame for the confiscation by having removed the novel in the first place.

In *The Oak and the Calf* Solzhenitsyn builds a big scene out of this incident and compares Tvardovsky unfavourably with Pushkin when the latter was editing the journal *Sovremennik*. It is inconceivable, he writes, that Push-kin would have turned away a novel being similarly hunted by Bencken-dorff,* and he describes himself as leaving Tvardovsky's office with his "orphaned and unwanted novel" under his arm.⁴ It is possible that Tvardov-sky's fear at this juncture was excessive, but it is hard not to regard Solzhen-itsyn's later account of it as exaggerated. Tvardovsky had every reason to feel vulnerable. Sinyavsky, the better-known of the two arrested writers, was one of *Novy Mir's* star critics and a highly controversial one, celebrated for his spirited advocacy of Pasternak's poetry and his satirical attacks on Party stal-warts. The arrest of Sinyavsky was as much a black mark against *Novy Mir* as was the confiscation of Solzhenitsyn's archive, and Tvardovsky felt doubly threatened. In a more cohesive and less hagridden society, Tvardovsky, Sol-zhenitsyn, and the families and friends of Sinyavsky and Daniel might have got together and made common cause against the common enemy, but the legacy of Stalinism was still strong. Not only was there not the remotest chance of such solidarity being manifested but even within the separate cir-cles there were splits and backbiting, and individuals were often left to fight their battles alone.†

A week or so later, this painful rift was widened by Tvardovsky's refusal to publish a letter that Solzhenitsyn had written defending himself against Party-inspired rumours that he had collaborated with the Germans. Solzhenitsyn implies that Tvardovsky's chief reason was injured pride, because the top copy of the letter had been sent to *Pravda* (before Solzhenitsyn knew of Rumyantsev's dismissal) and only a carbon to *Novy Mir*, but a careful reading of his memoir reveals that Tvardovsky's rejection was part of a deeper disagreement with Solzhenitsyn's entire strategy over this period. In addition to writing to Demichev, as Tvardovsky had suggested, Solzhenitsyn had also fired off letters of protest to Brezhnev, Mikhail Suslov, and Yuri Andropov (asking Zhores Medvedev to post them in Moscow). In his account of the affair, Solzhenitsyn says he was afraid that Demichev might suppress his letter, but it seems equally likely that he was simply following his old camp practice of firing off as many protests as he could. To Tvardovsky, who had a direct connection with Demichev, it looked as though Solzhenitsyn were simply trying to go over Demichev's head and thus over Tvardovsky's as well, and this appears to be the real reason why Tvardovsky refused to help.⁵

In essence it was a conflict of perceptions. Tvardovsky was very much a man of the Soviet establishment. He knew better than most how the Party and government hierarchies worked, who was responsible to whom, who owed whom a favour, and how one worked the levers of power that were available. But he was fully prepared to abide by its rules and in the end

---

*Count Alexander Benckendorff was chief of the secret police under Nicholas I and became Pushkin's particular tormentor after the Decembrist rebellion of 1825.
†In a postscript to *The Oak and the Calf*, Solzhenitsyn later conceded that his comparison of Tvardovsky with Pushkin·had been unfair and that Tvardovsky had behaved reasonably in not wishing to take back *The First Circle* after the KGB raid.

submit to whatever he was told. Solzhenitsyn, on the other hand, had spent too many years outside the system ever to fit in comfortably again, and after the confiscation of his archive, he felt that he might be battling for his very life. In these circumstances, anything was allowed, just so long as he survived. What did it matter to whom he wrote and in what order? But to Tvardovsky it looked like wilful self-indulgence.

They parted on very bad terms, and Solzhenitsyn drove back to Rozhdestvo to rejoin Natalia. So far as he could tell, very few people yet knew of his precious summer-house, and he took great care to see that any letters he sent were posted in either Ryazan or Moscow. But it was isolated and exposed, and he felt vulnerable there. If the KGB did find out about it, he could be picked up and jailed before anyone knew. Moreover, there no longer seemed to be much point in Natalia's staying on—her job in Obninsk had still not materialized, and she would have to return to Ryazan for the start of the school year.

The farcical story of how Natalia was finally excluded from the Obninsk institute was further depressing evidence, if evidence was needed, of the amazing lengths to which the Soviet authorities were apparently prepared to go now to thwart Solzhenitsyn's most innocuous plans. Quite apart from the confiscation of the archive (and there seems to have been no connection between the two sets of events), nothing could have been more calculated to reinforce Solzhenitsyn's growing sense of fear and apprehension. Despite Demichev's phone call of July and the categorical assurance of the director of the institute that Natalia's appointment was guaranteed, the necessary confirmation by the Academy of Medical Sciences in Moscow had not been forthcoming. Instead, the academy had ordered that all the dossiers of the successful applicants for some sixty senior and junior vacancies that were being filled that summer be submitted for scrutiny, and finding nothing irregular in Reshetovskaya's application, it had arbitrarily cancelled all appointments. Since many of the junior staff had already been engaged and had resigned from their previous jobs, this meant throwing them out of work, but the academy was adamant and decreed that "all staff engaged as a result of the examination are to be dismissed from the posts they are holding."

A new examination commission was appointed to replace the old one, and the whole examination was held again. Again, Reshetovskaya was selected for appointment, whereupon the academy adopted a special resolution to change the composition of the institute's academic council. Seven Obninsk scientists were dismissed and replaced by five appointees from Moscow, who attended only one meeting—that at which the second round of voting was due to take place. Even now the voting was supposed to be by secret ballot, which still gave Reshetovskaya a chance, so the vote was postponed indefinitely on the grounds that no ballot papers had been prepared. Finally a special meeting of the presidium of the Academy of Medical Sciences was called in Moscow with only one item on the agenda: Should Reshetovskaya be allowed to take part in the competitive re-examination for the post of senior scientific assistant at the Medical Institute in Obninsk? A galaxy of top brass attended the meeting, as well as Zhores Medvedev, who had been active, with Timofeyev-Ressovsky, in lobbying Demichev and others on Reshetovskaya's behalf. From the papers in from of him, Medvedev saw that Reshetovskaya's application and supporting documentation had been subjected to the most rigorous scrutiny; it was equally clear that not the slightest weakness had been found in her qualifications. Nevertheless, the presidium recommended that Reshetovskaya be excluded from the competition on the grounds that an employee of an agricultural institute could not possibly fit into a medical institute, even as a chemist. The institute's director, Professor Zedgenidze, refused to implement the recommendation, saying that it was illegal to exclude her, whereupon the academy cancelled the "chemical" vacancy altogether and had it rescheduled as a "medical" vacancy under the jurisdiction of the Ministry of Health. Strictly speaking, such a transfer required the approval of the Council of Ministers of the USSR (the approximate equivalent of the British cabinet—at least in theory), and it may be that the appointment was even discussed at that level, but nothing was ever made public about it.[6]

Medvedev and Timofeyev-Ressovsky both suffered as a result of their exertions on Reshetovskaya's behalf. Medvedev was denied an already agreed exchange visit to the United States to work in a genetics laboratory there, and Timofeyev-Ressovsky was almost denied an American prize for his research. An attempt was made to persuade him to reject the prize on the grounds that its award was a provocation, but Timofeyev-Ressovsky refused, and the insignia were informally delivered to him by a visiting vice-president of the American Academy of Arts and Sciences before the Soviet authorities were able to intervene.

By the time this little drama had played itself out, Natalia was back in Ryazan and Solzhenitsyn had found a new refuge: the dacha of Kornei Chukovsky at Peredelkino, the writers' colony just outside Moscow. Chukovsky had pronounced A Day in the Life of Ivan Denisovich "a literary miracle" when given it by Tvardovsky to read. Like Ehrenburg and Marshak, he was an elderly survivor of the years immediately before and after the October Revolution, but as a literary critic and children's writer he had survived the years of Stalinism physically intact and morally uncompromised, and was universally loved and respected. He had first met Solzhenitsyn in 1963, when Solzhenitsyn called on him at his villa in Peredelkino. Chukovsky was meticulously neat in his habits and, according to an eyewitness, had called for his tie beforehand, saying, "The greatest living writer of our country is coming to see me, and I must be properly dressed."[7] Solzhenitsyn, wearing a light-blue knitted shirt, grey sailcloth trousers, and an anorak, had surprised everyone present by his cheerful informality and by the athletic way he had bounded up the stairs. Earlier reports of his cancer had persuaded them that Solzhenitsyn was a seriously sick man, but he had laughed and told them that although the tumour in his stomach had been "this big" (showing them two clenched fists), it no longer bothered him and was completely cured. Over lunch the two men had discussed Dostoyevsky, Gorky, Zoshchenko, and other writers, and afterwards they had visited Pasternak's grave together.

Thereafter the two men became friends, though not meeting very often, because of Solzhenitsyn's distance from Moscow. Even when he did come he generally avoided Peredelkino. It was too fashionable, and he had no desire to go where other writers congregated. But Chukovsky had remained solic-itous of Solzhenitsyn's well-being. On one occasion he had asked Solzheni-tsyn whether he had enough money to live on. Solzhenitsyn replied that he was all right. "The main thing is not to spend too much money on yourself." Pointing to his shoes with inch-thick soles, he had added, "These will last me eight years at least."[8] In early 1965 the two men had discussed for the first time the possibility of Solzhenitsyn's coming to work at Chukovsky's dacha (Chukovsky was now away a great deal receiving medical treatment at the government sanatorium in Barvikha—where Second Lieutenant Solzhe-nitsyn had once spent his weekend on leave from the front). Nothing had been decided then, but in the aftermath of his archive's seizure Solzhenitsyn went to see Chukovsky again, and Chukovsky repeated his offer.

Apart from the comfort and convenience, Peredelkino was a much safer place than Ryazan. Solzhenitsyn was too isolated in Ryazan, without friends or influence. He had made enemies there with his story "For the Good of the Cause," based on a true incident in Ryazan, and Medvedev has suggested that one of the reasons for the authorities' reluctance to let him move to Obninsk was that they had established an efficient system of surveillance in Ryazan and didn't want to have to start again in another town.[9] If Solzheni-tsyn happened to be arrested in Ryazan and a scandal ensued, it could always be shrugged off as an excess of zeal on the part of local officials, whereas in Obninsk or Moscow the authorities would have to do it openly and face a public outcry.

Solzhenitsyn moved into Peredelkino sometime before the end of Sep-tember. Apparently the original plan had been for him to use a couple of rooms above the garage, but in the end he occupied a ground-floor room opening off the dining-room, which had formerly been used by Chukovsky's daughter Lydia, also a writer. Chukovsky's rooms were upstairs. Solzheni-tsyn insisted, however, on looking after himself, doing his own shopping, cooking, and cleaning, and would not hear of anyone else's doing it for him.

All the houses in Peredelkino are set well back from the road and are surrounded by trees and large gardens. It is a perfect place to find peace and solitude, and here Solzhenitsyn settled down to await developments and brood on the meaning of the KGB raid. It was here that Kopelev telephoned to inform him that "his case" had been passed to the public prosecutor* and here, too, that the Etkinds found him when they called on their way back to

---

*This is what Solzhenitsyn writes in *The Oak and the Calf* (p. 398), but it is not quite accurate. Everyone else involved agrees that it was never "the Solzhenitsyn case," but always "the Teush case."

Leningrad from a holiday in the south. Solzhenitsyn was sitting alone in his room. Although it was evening, he had not bothered to switch on the light and was unoccupied—a phenomenal rarity for a man so proverbially busy. His face was grim and drawn when he told them about the loss of his archive, but he perked up sufficiently to chat during the evening and later accompanied them to the station.[10]

At other times he paced the garden.

> I strolled for hours through the dark cloisters of the pine trees in Chukovsky's grounds with a heart empty of hope, vainly trying to comprehend my situation, and, more importantly, to discover some higher sense in the disaster that had befallen me. . . . I had come to grief and I did not understand. I seethed. I rebelled. . . . I had long ago come to understand the meaning of my arrest, my deathly illness, and many personal misfortunes, but this disaster I could make no sense of. It rendered meaningless everything that had gone before.[11]

What made his situation hardest to bear was his complete ignorance of the motives for the KGB raid. He had first supposed that he was followed from *Novy Mir* after picking up the copies of *The First Circle* and that the KGB had swooped on Teush's flat just as soon as they knew where the novel was, fearing that Solzhenitsyn was about to put it into samizdat. Discovery of the the archive containing his early works must have been a lucky and unexpected bonus. But that theory was demolished when he learned that the archive had been confiscated not from Teush but from Ilya Zilberberg, the young engineer and anthroposophist he had met on the eve of his holiday. There had been two raids simultaneously, one to pick up the novel and the other to confiscate his archive.

This evidence of prior planning based on the KGB's evident foreknowledge of what they were seeking showed the raid in a much more sinister light, and it must have been the shock of this discovery that had turned Solzhenitsyn's mind to thoughts of suicide. It also appears to have induced a feeling of blind panic, which led him into the fateful error of isolating himself from the other people involved in the affair and the case that grew out of it. It was an understandable reaction during those early days when he literally awaited arrest, but in the weeks that followed he was cut off from first-hand information about how the case was progressing and prevented from learning important facts that might have changed his perception of the KGB's motives and intentions.

Instead, he brooded on the event in the solitude of his room, making only occasional sorties to contact the Steins and learn from them how the investigation was going. He could not understand why the KGB agents had chosen to raid Zilberberg as well as Teush. How had they learned of the archive's whereabouts, and when and why had Teush given it to his young friend in the first place? From Veronica and Yuri Stein he learned that Zilberberg was an ardent admirer of Teush's, a frequent visitor to his home and an occasional visitor of the Steins as well. He was therefore well acquainted with those of Solzhenitsyn's unpublished works that had been passed around among friends to read—*The First Circle*, *Candle in the Wind*, the *Miniature Stories*—as well as with certain items restricted to a much narrower circle, such as *The Way*, *The Republic of Labour*, and early camp verses. All of these had become part of a much larger flow of unofficial reading that was so popular and hungrily devoured in Moscow literary circles at the time, and although Solzhenitsyn had always been careful to distinguish between works that could go into samizdat and be copied and those that could only be read, in the relaxed atmosphere of the early sixties these restrictions were interpreted fairly liberally. Furthermore, the Steins' flat was well known as a literary "salon" where a great deal of samizdat was discussed and passed around. What the Steins were unable to tell Solzhenitsyn was what else, if anything, Teush might have shown Zilberberg, and for some inexplicable reason neither they nor Solzhenitsyn seem ever to have asked. Solzhenitsyn did have a single meeting with the Teushes to clarify certain details, but this question appears not to have been raised. Solzhenitsyn jumped to the conclusion that Teush and Zilberberg had been unforgivably lax with his papers, had read them in their entirety, and had discussed their contents over a tapped telephone.[12]

At that stage Solzhenitsyn seems to have regarded Zilberberg as the chief culprit in the affair, a theory that was influenced, perhaps, by the hypothesis that Zilberberg was an informer. Later he came to blame Teush more, describing him, in his own account of these events, as "a thoroughly decent fellow but, alas, careless, a muddler, a happy-go-lucky conspirator." According to Solzhenitsyn, he had visited Teush to remove the main portion of his papers shortly before the raid took place, but Teush had "broken the rules," extracted things to read, and out of carelessness failed to replace them again. Consequently, instead of leaving only safe works in Teush's possession, Solzhenitsyn had left some of his most sensitive material, and it was this that Teush had transferred to Zilberberg and that had fallen into the hands of the KGB. As for Zilberberg, Solzhenitsyn writes that he "did not know and had not checked up on" him as a possible recipient of his papers and was unaware of Teush's intention.[13]

Seen from Solzhenitsyn's vantage-point and in the light of his conviction that the KGB raid was directed exclusively at him, this scenario contains a great deal of logic, but Zilberberg has since written a book on the subject that puts Solzhenitsyn's version into doubt.[14]

The first thing Zilberberg makes clear is that Teush passed the archive to him only in the summer of 1965 and not earlier in the year, as Solzhenitsyn apparently first thought. Teush did so because he was planning to go away for two months and was afraid to leave sensitive material lying about in an empty flat, particularly since he had reason to believe that he was under some sort of surveillance himself. The preceding year he had written his long article on *Ivan Denisovich* and its importance for Soviet society. Although he had strictly limited the number of copies to five and had forbidden its distribution in samizdat, one copy had "got away" and there had been a rumour of its circulation. There had also been one or two suspicious incidents involving a snoopy neighbour and a strange telephone call. Teush had therefore decided to entrust all the remaining copies of the article, together with Solzhenitsyn's archive, to his young friend while he was away.

As it happened, Zilberberg was also planning to go away for a month in mid-August, but since his mother was staying in Moscow and since their communal flat was shared with two other families, he felt there was little likelihood of anyone's breaking in while he was away. In fact, there was no break-in, but on the day of his return, on 11 September, he was visited by agents of the KGB and the archive was removed, together with a large quantity of his own papers. By this time, Teush was also back in Moscow, and his flat was raided on the same day.

Zilberberg demonstrates that the archive was handed to him by Teush in a sealed parcel and that the seal was found to be intact by the KGB agents at the moment of confiscation. He reproduces the exact wording on the search record drawn up by the agents, which includes item no. 10, "a white paper packet measuring 38 cm x 24.5 cm. The packet bears a rubber stamp marked 'mechanical engineering.' On being opened, the packet was found to contain a brown envelope, in which were found a number of typed and handwritten manuscripts."[15] The record goes on to list about two dozen items, some of them anonymous, a few signed with Solzhenitsyn's real name and several with his pseudonym "Stepan Khlynov." Zilberberg states categorically that he had read neither *Feast of the Conquerors* nor any other work in the archive that had not been passed round to everyone in their circle, so that he could not have "talked on the telephone" about them or shown them to anyone else.

Zilberberg gives a detailed description of his interrogations at the Lubyanka by the investigator in charge of the case and of his consultations with Teush on how to respond. The name of the case throughout was given as the "Teush case," and the subject of the investigation was said to be Teush's article on Solzhenitsyn. According to the investigator, this "libellous" and anti-Soviet article had been discovered in the luggage of a foreign tourist as he was leaving the country. Although the article was unsigned, investigations had led the KGB to Teush, and they were now trying to determine how many copies existed and whether the article had been distributed by Teush. Under Soviet law at the time, the composition and possession of "libellous" manuscripts was not a crime, whereas deliberate circulation was. The investigator made it clear that the KGB had been tapping a number of telephones for quite a while, including those of Zilberberg and Teush, but he needed more substantial evidence if charges were to be brought.

Some of this was communicated to Solzhenitsyn by the Steins at the time, but it seems he found this explanation of the case difficult to believe. Why would the KGB have gone to the trouble of a double raid simply to confiscate an article about him, especially when the flats they visited contained his original works? Surely it could not have been a colossal coincidence? In time he was to conclude that the confiscation of *The First Circle* had indeed been a coincidence. The detectives had been on their way out of Teush's flat when they spotted Solzhenitsyn's suitcase on top of a cupboard (not under the bed, as some reports have maintained). Suzanna Teush had tried to put them off the scent by claiming it was hers, but the KGB men had insisted on opening it and had carried it off with all the other papers they confiscated.[16] But the archive seemed to be another matter. Solzhenitsyn's suspiciousness and almost superstitious dread pointed his mind away from chance and in the direction of a premeditated act as the only explanation for the raids. Years later he would attribute the confiscation to an even grander design—the work of divine providence.

The problem with the premeditation theory was that it required a certain bending of the facts to make it fit. In *The Oak and the Calf*, where Solzhenitsyn offers a condensed description of these events, he deliberately minimizes the degree of his friendship with Teush, calling him merely "a friend of my wife" when he takes the archive to him and "a retired professor of mathematics and an anthroposophist" when the archive is stolen, while exaggerating Teush's impracticality in contrast with his own "excessive foresight" and "cool calculation." In one paragraph he claims that he had removed most of his archive before the raid, leaving behind "only semi-overt things of secondary importance," but in the next reveals that this was not so, explaining the discrepancy by saying that Teush had taken out things to read and had failed to put them back where they belonged.[17]

Solzhenitsyn's account is in fact self-contradictory. We are asked to believe that in 1962, while not yet famous, Solzhenitsyn had deposited his cherished archive, including a play that could place his life in danger, with someone who was no more to him than a friend of his wife's, a "careless muddler" and "happy-go-lucky conspirator." And that when he came to remove it, Solzhenitsyn did not bother to check its contents, despite the fact that the manuscript of the dangerous play, *Feast of the Conquerors*, was supposed to be his sole surviving copy.* The provisional conclusion to be drawn from these statements is that far from being the far-sighted master plotter of his own self-portrait, Solzhenitsyn, too, was guilty of monumental carelessness, in which case it was not fair for him to blame Teush. The search record also shows that Teush couldn't have been as careless as all that, for he took the trouble to pack up the archive neatly and seal it before passing it to Zilberberg for the period while he was away. This seems hardly to square with the image of a man who leaves his friend's papers strewn around his flat and

---

*There is a mystery about Solzhenitsyn's assertion that he had left with Teush his "sole surviving copy" (*poslednii ekzemplyar*, in Russian) of *Feast of the Conquerors*. This copy was confiscated by the KGB and never returned to Solzhenitsyn, yet Solzhenitsyn published the text of the play in volume 8 of his Collected Works. In an accompanying note Solzhenitsyn writes, "The lost text was later restored (*vosstanovlen*) by the author." *Vosstanovlen* can also mean "recollected," so the suggestion may be that Solzhenitsyn was able to rewrite it from memory.

discusses them over the telephone with another friend. It is also inconceivable that Teush wrote his long article, containing quotations from Solzhenitsyn's early verse and abundant extracts from readers' letters on *Ivan Denisovich*, without Solzhenitsyn's permission and approval, so that there could be no question of his "breaking the rules" by reading them. It is true, according to Zilberberg, that Solzhenitsyn did remove some sensitive material not long before the raid took place, but this was related to *The Gulag Archipelago*, on which Solzhenitsyn was working at the time. Finally, when Solzhenitsyn writes that he did not know Zilberberg, he is contradicted not only by Zilberberg's testimony but also by that of the Steins, who introduced him to Zilberberg.[18]

The question arises as to why Solzhenitsyn should have persisted with this tendentious version of events. Part of the answer must be sought in the didactic character of *The Oak and the Calf*, which is by no means a simple memoir, but a cautionary tale with a moral, intended to show how David almost slew Goliath (or how the calf did much more than merely butt the oak). In this allegory David had to be shown as more consistent and farsighted than he actually was, and his opponents (and even bystanders) as stupider and more incompetent. Secondly, the crisis seems to have accentuated certain elements in Solzhenitsyn's character that were, to say the least, ambiguous. That inner self-confidence and driving ambition that fuelled his will to succeed (and that were largely responsible for his huge success) could and did transform themselves, under pressure, into intolerance and ruthlessness. At the same time his faith in his own instincts and intuition was intensified to the point where he no longer wished to listen to the voices of others. As driving forces in his career, such traits had their positive side, but when they entered personal relations they could become negative and destructive, a tendency already noted by his friends Vitkevich and Kopelev. Rightly or wrongly, Solzhenitsyn preferred to stand alone, and that meant relying on his own strength and cunning for survival and disregarding others.

It would appear that by going into hiding, Solzhenitsyn also cut himself off for a time from sources of information about what was happening elsewhere in Moscow, and this, too, hindered him from making a just appreciation of his situation. The Steins have indicated that investigations in the Teush case went considerably wider than their immediate circle and encompassed, among others, the *Novy Mir* critic Vladimir Lakshin. Lakshin was well known as Solzhenitsyn's most eloquent public champion, but the immediate reason for his being questioned was a letter he had written to Teush commenting favourably on Teush's article.[19] This was a serious matter, for it seemed to point to distribution. Fortunately, Lakshin had returned his copy of the article after reading it, so no case for circulation could be made apart from the copy that turned up at the customs.

Lakshin's involvement in the investigation served to link the case with *Novy Mir*, and through *Novy Mir* with the Sinyavsky-Daniel case. Lakshin, as head of the critical section, had commissioned Sinyavsky's latest articles for the magazine and could therefore be said to suffer guilt by association. Yuri Stein was asked by the investigator whether he was acquainted with either Daniel or Sinyavsky, but he avoided answering by saying that he was being questioned as a witness in the Teush case and couldn't see the relevance of the question.

All this strengthened the belief that the KGB was engaged in a concerted attack on the literary intelligentsia generally, a belief that was widely shared in Moscow at the time and led to the panic over samizdat. In his memoir Solzhenitsyn appears to give credence to that view, linking the attack with the ideological conference that had taken place in August, but he consistently underplays the furore that surrounded the Sinyavsky-Daniel case. One gets the impression that he was frustrated by this sudden switch of the spotlight and jealous of the publicity they attracted. He complains in his memoir that nobody in the West paid attention to the confiscation of his novel until two months later, implying that the KGB agents—and the foreign press—should have been concentrating on him rather than on them: "[The KGB] had not merely an adequate but an embarrassingly abundant collection of material on which to base charges against me, ten times more than they had against Sinyavsky and Daniel—and yet for some reason they didn't take me."[20]

From this distance in time it seems that the raid on Teush and Zilberberg was in reality a fishing expedition by the KGB men. They were aware that the Teushes' and the Steins' flats were both frequented by Solzhenitsyn, and the discovery of Teush's article offered an excellent pretext for snooping around. It may be that some zealous KGB officer was also seeking to distinguish himself and earn promotion. But the raid was carefully calculated. To search either of Solzhenitsyn's own residences would have been too openly provocative, and there were no legal grounds for doing so. Even to search the Steins' flat would have caused a stir—they were Solzhenitsyn's relatives and he had a room there. But a friend was a different matter, especially a friend who had written a "criminal" article. And so, it seems, the KGB agents made a speculative raid, little suspecting the haul that their fishing would yield, and stumbled across riches so unexpected that it took them several months to understand what they had acquired and to decide what to do.

To say that Solzhenitsyn's reaction to this raid was probably based on a misconception is not in any way to minimize the agonies of mind that he endured or to suggest that, in the long run, his relations with the Soviet authorities would have ended any differently. It was his name, after all, that had attracted the KGB's attention to Teush, just as it was the KGB agents' move that led to the discovery and confiscation of the archive. And once it was in their possession, they were bound sooner or later to put it to use. But the indications are that they were not looking for it and had stumbled across it by accident. Furthermore, the most dangerous item in it, *Feast of the Conquerors*, did not bear Solzhenitsyn's name, and he could have won a lot of time for himself by denying authorship. His assumption that the KGB had known in advance of his archive and its contents naturally altered his perspective and behaviour and had incalculable consequences for the future, complicating, and in some instances poisoning, his relations with family and friends and leading him into a confrontation with the Soviet authorities some years earlier than might otherwise have been the case.

It is easy to be wise after the event. The KGB is free to strike when, where, and how it likes, unfettered by any but the flimsiest provisions of the law. It can choose its moment, take its victims by surprise, and sow panic with contemptuous ease—no one has described this better than Solzhenitsyn himself. And its victims are frightened and confused. In the secretive and paranoid atmosphere of the Soviet Union, fear quickly gives way to a frantic search for reasons and motives, and a feeling of guilt is present from the start. What Soviet citizen can place his hand on his heart and declare that he is guilty of nothing? In the Soviet security service there is a saying: "Give us the man and we'll find the crime." And so the victim, aware of these attitudes, begins to do the prosecutor's work for him, involuntarily absorbing the values of the guilt-ridden society around him.

What is interesting is that even a labour-camp veteran like Solzhenitsyn should have been so vulnerable to this kind of pressure. A careful reading of *The Oak and the Calf* reveals that he was tormented for months after the raid, that he felt truly helpless and afraid. But he tries to obscure this fact by projecting the thoughts, attitudes, and ideas of his later years back to a period when they existed only in embryo and when the public persona that later became famous was just beginning to take shape. In this account, the man Solzhenitsyn is displaced by the myth of Solzhenitsyn. According to the myth, the author was bold, brave, and far-sighted from the very outset of his career and was let down only by the mistakes and cravenness of others (or by misplacing his faith in others). He claims to have seen through the shams and deceptions of the literary establishment from the start, planning his campaigns against it with the vision of a prophet and the strategic cunning of a general. There is a kernel of truth in this picture. Solzhenitsyn did hold aloof from official literary circles and had always conducted himself as something of an outsider, but he was prepared to participate and make compromises. He joined the Writers' Union, attended meetings at the Kremlin and in Ryazan, made friends with "liberals" in the literary establishment and competed keenly for the Lenin Prize. The one area in which he fiercely resisted compromise (and it was the most important) was in the actual content of his writing, but in other matters he was more flexible. At the very moment of the confiscation, he was expecting—and hoping—that extracts from *The First Circle* would be published in *Pravda*. And he would continue to make accommodations in the immediate years ahead, although they were destined to grow fewer and fewer.

September 1965 was a turning-point not because a fearless hero suddenly realized what his destiny was but because a brilliant writer anxious to make his mark on the world and still trying to come to terms with his society's leaders was suddenly kicked in the stomach. He reacted as anyone would—with fear and panic. Perhaps the next blow would be a knife in the ribs. Twisting and turning like a hunted animal at bay, he searched for a way out and in his initial turmoil sought to put the blame on anyone but himself. Later, bit by bit, he subdued his fear and fought back, and it was then that he became a hero. A man without fear is no hero; the man who overcomes his fear is. The importance of the events of September 1965 was not that they turned Solzhenitsyn into a hero but that they gave him a chance to become one. But only a chance. True greatness lay in taking it.

31

A PERIOD
OF ADJUSTMENT

SOLZHENITSYN'S FUTURE ACTIONS depended to a large extent on what sense he could make of the disaster that had befallen him, and in his search for answers he turned to Dahl's collection of Russian proverbs, which he took to reading daily, "like a prayer-book."[1] There he soon found some comfort. "Grief won't kill you, but it will knock you off your feet," he read. "Whatever your troubles, don't put your head in a noose." More significantly: "One man dies of fear, another is brought to life by it." And: "If trouble comes, make use of *it* too." These and many more he noted down for their aptness and possible future use (many were incorporated into what was to become *August 1914*). Meditating on these enigmatic messages and how to interpret them, he thought of his career to date and what meaning it held for him. Outwardly it appeared to have ground to a halt. His principal theme—the labour camps and their moral implications for Soviet society—was totally at odds with what the authorities wanted from their writers. Since the fall of Khrushchev, they were doing their best to forget that the camps had ever existed and to suppress any further mention of them. That was why he had become so unpopular with official circles and why the prospects for his still-unpublished work looked so bleak: they almost all dealt, in one way or another, with the theme of the camps.

On the other hand, he still benefited from the tremendous popularity he had reaped with *Ivan Denisovich* and his short stories, and readers' letters continued to reach him. Some of them had put him in touch with sources for *The Gulag Archipelago*, and some he planned to use in the book itself, following the example of Teush in his ill-fated article. Perhaps, in recalling the contents of those letters—the love, gratitude, the hero-worship, the joy—he also remembered the solemn adjuration of one prescient reader.

Russia is predominantly a writers' country. No matter how things are going, we have always felt better when we have a Turgenev, a Tolstoy, a Chekhov. It wasn't enough for us for a writer to be a good writer, even a great writer. He had to be someone whom we could love. You are someone we loved from the start, and we are grateful to you, for man does not thrive without love. . . . We are very proud of you, Comrade Solzhenitsyn—your glory is our glory. If you were to betray the big truth, it would be a tragedy for all of us. Once Russia had Yasnaya Polyana, once we had Melikhovo, and now there is Solzhenitsyn in Ryazan. I am not saying this just to flatter you, I am telling myself. . . . Take care of yourself, Alexander Isayevich, because now that you've written *Ivan Denisovich*, your life no longer belongs to you alone. I don't suppose you even realize who you are and what you have become for the rest of us.[2]

"Your life no longer belongs to yourself alone"—it was this above all other readers' messages that was to stick in his mind and become his guiding star. In a sense it echoed what he had long thought about himself, but it was important to have it confirmed and to be reminded of an additional reason why he had to overcome his setback.

In the short term he simply had to hold on, and he decided that his best course was to make himself visible, both physically and by appearing in print, so as to avert the possibility of a secret arrest. Within a few days of the raid, he attended a Shostakovich concert and told some fellow writers about the confiscation of *The First Circle;* and soon afterwards he put in an uncharacteristic appearance at the Central Writers' Club for a party to celebrate the birthday of Sergei Smirnov, a minor writer of books about the Second World War. The following day, he went for another audience with Demichev, who had still not answered his letter complaining about the confiscation of his novel and archive and demanding that they be returned to him. Tvardovsky had spoken to Demichev twice by telephone, only to be given evasive answers, and Solzhenitsyn himself was snubbed. Instead of Demichev an assistant received him, and their conversation got nowhere. One or two days later, the Ryazan Provincial Party Committee informed him that his letter to Demichev had been referred to the prosecutor general of the USSR.

In the hope of getting at least something into print, Solzhenitsyn sent Tvardovsky his play *Candle in the Wind* and in the third week of November went to *Novy Mir* to discuss it. Tvardovsky pronounced it "very stageable" but found the allegorical foreign country in which it was set too transparent a substitute for the Soviet Union. He disagreed, he said, with the equation made between the vices of East and West: "I can't accept that point of view without drawing a line between capitalism and socialism." If it were up to him, he would publish it with a disclaimer saying that the magazine could not share the author's point of view. Solzhenitsyn said that that would be fine, but Tvardovsky still demurred—in the last analysis the decision would not be his, and he was sure the censorship would reject the play.

Before leaving, Solzhenitsyn handed Tvardovsky his short story "The Right Hand," about the old man in Tashkent who had once wielded a sabre in a punitive detachment. It was one of Solzhenitsyn's shortest and most economical stories, and one of his best. Tvardovsky liked it very much: "The descriptive passages are very good; all in all, this is the most terrifying thing you have ever written." But again he was doubtful whether he could publish it.[3]

Solzhenitsyn's next move was to submit an article on language to the *Literaturnaya Gazeta*, which, to his surprise, published it (though not, it seems, before clearing it with Demichev). Taking part of a Russian proverb for its title, "It Is Not the Custom to Whiten Soup with Tar . . ." (". . . We've Got Sour Cream for That" is how the proverb continues), the article was a sharp polemic with an earlier article on the Russian literary language by the academician Victor Vinogradov. Vinogradov's article attracted rather a lot of comment in the *Literaturnaya Gazeta*, and Solzhenitsyn's reply was one of several, but in tone it was the sharpest, resembling what we know of his earlier broadsides against the post office, the railways, and the writers of autobiographies. In *The Oak and the Calf* Solzhenitsyn later dismissed the article as hastily and superficially written, but it is interesting as the only programmatic statement he has ever made about language,* and it describes some of the thinking behind his own stylistic and lexical innovations.

Reproaching Vinogradov for his poor use of language and for neglecting such authorities on Russian style as Dahl, Herzen, and Andrei Platonov, Solzhenitsyn diagnoses the problem of modern literary Russian as follows:

> Ever since Peter the Great's time, either as a result of the sheer violence done to it, or from the pens of the educated classes who always thought in French, or because of the playfulness of translators or the haste of writers who knew the value of time and thought but not of the word, our written language has suffered in its vocabulary, in its grammatical structure and, most importantly of all, in its syntax.

Solzhenitsyn then analyzes each of these three last-named categories. The Russian vocabulary has shrunk, he writes, and suffers from the importation of too many foreign words. Solzhenitsyn is not against foreign words completely (he doesn't adopt the position of Sologdin in *The First Circle* on the "language of maximum clarity") and sees the utility of many of them, but he feels that Russian borrowing has been indiscriminate and excessive. As for modern Russian grammatical structure, it emphasizes what is European and what links Russian with other Western languages, but leans away from those features that are specific to Russian and define its true character. This is particularly noticeable in word formation, which has been unduly influenced by German practice (in the formation of compounds and verbal nouns) at the expense of shorter and more expressive native formations. Thirdly and most importantly, Solzhenitsyn points to a progressive movement away from a truly Russian syntax. As examples of what a proper syntax should be, he

---

* A recent announcement about the forthcoming volume 10 of Solzhenitsyn's Collected Works indicates that it contains an article by Solzhenitsyn on Russian grammar.

quotes a number of the proverbs he had recently been reading and praises their pithiness, vividness, and economy of expression. He also advises writers to pay more attention to the structures of the spoken language and recommends a policy of verbal innovation—"the carefully calculated use (in the author's narrative) of words which, although they do not live in contemporary speech, are so closely situated [to it] and are used so aptly by the author that they may catch the fancy of people when they are speaking and thus be returned to the language."

As a description of Solzhenitsyn's own views and procedures, the article is very revealing, and he concludes by once more invoking the shade of the great lexicographer Vladimir Dahl and stating a sort of credo.

> As I understand it, the decisive decades are perhaps already upon us, when it is still within our power to put things right—by jointly consulting, explaining to one another and ourselves, and being strict with ourselves. For the chief abuse of the Russian literary language comes from us, from our pens, when they are too hasty and slide too easily over the paper.
>
> Let us slow and control their race! It is still not too late to correct the shape of our literary (author's) language, so as to restore the conversational lightness and freedom of popular speech.
>
> Again it was Dahl who said that we can all gradually (none of us alone and not at once) replace all that is bad by the good, all that is long by the short, all that is obfuscated by the plain, all that is shadowy by the clear, the commonplace by the vivid, and the flabby by the strong.[4]

In another attempt to break into print and secure a hearing for himself, Solzhenitsyn decided on the radical step of submitting some of his works to magazines other than *Novy Mir*. Tvardovsky had read and rejected, for a variety of reasons, almost everything he had shown him recently, and Solzhenitsyn was resentful. He felt Tvardovsky was treating him simply as a piece of literary property, confident that Solzhenitsyn had nowhere else to go. *Novy Mir* was far and away the most liberal and outspoken magazine in Soviet Russia, and Solzhenitsyn was more outspoken still, so it seemed hardly likely that anyone else would publish him.

But Solzhenitsyn had other ideas. Partly out of wounded pride and partly, it seems, out of sheer desperation at remaining unpublished for so long, he decided to try elsewhere—and not just anywhere, but the arch-conservative publications *Moskva*, *Ogonyok*, and *Literaturnaya Rossia*. To each of these he sent four stories: "The Right Hand"; "Zakhar the Pouch," based on his cycling trip to Kulikovo; "What a Pity," based on a true incident involving the daughter of a former fellow prisoner;[5] and a fourth story that Solzhenitsyn does not specify and has never published. All except "The Right Hand" had been completed in the autumn of 1965.

Kopelev termed this move "Hadji Murad's defection," having in mind Tolstoy's story about the Caucasian military commander who defected to the Russians after quarrelling with his leader, and in the context of Soviet literary politics it really did seem like an act of betrayal, which is why Solzhenitsyn went to some pains to keep his approaches secret from Tvardovsky and *Novy Mir*. In *The Oak and the Calf*, he later defended this move; not only was he impatient with *Novy Mir* but he writes that at bottom he could see no significant ideological difference between *Novy Mir* and its conservative opponents. All were equally loyal to the Party, and none dared question the basic tenets of communism.* But he then went on to qualify this statement by writing that *Novy Mir* "was the only judge in Soviet literature whose artistic and moral verdict on a work commanded assent and indelibly marked its author," and he conceded that *Novy Mir* set the standards for all others to follow.[6]

More to the point was Solzhenitsyn's feeling that he had to be a free agent. Despite all that *Novy Mir* had done for him, he was constitutionally incapable of belonging wholly to any one camp or faction. It was too cramping. He could not submit to anyone else's "rules" or expectations, and the most honest explanation of this comes at the end of his list of reasons in *The Oak and the Calf* (where he partly contradicts his earlier rationalization).

> All I wanted was to eliminate an untried possibility—who could tell, it might produce something—by offering my stories, and especially "The Right Hand," to the notorious "conservative wing" (as though that wounded bird the Soviet press had any other!) and seeing whether it would swallow them. What if their differences with *Novy Mir* had become so irksome to them that they would set ideological loyalty at naught and carefully steer my stories between the horns of their own beloved censorship—simply in order to "kidnap" me for their side? There wasn't much of a chance, but even this "degree of freedom" should, I thought, be utilized—if only so that I would not blame myself later. If I saw "The Right Hand" published even by the gendarmes' press, I would not feel ashamed.[7]

At first the move looked successful. Two of the periodicals that Solzhenitsyn approached—*Ogonyok* and *Literaturnaya Rossia*—were weeklies, and it helped that all four stories were short. Anatoli Sofronov, the editor of *Ogonyok*, came up to town and assembled his entire editorial board to greet Solzhenitsyn, not omitting to mention that he, too, was a native of Rostov. Having read the stories, he said he would publish all of them except the one that Solzhenitsyn regarded as the most important, "The Right Hand." *Literaturnaya Rossia* also treated him as an honoured guest but was more circumspect, offering to publish only "Zakhar the Pouch." After that, *Ogonyok* turned down "What a Pity" as well, leaving only two stories out of the four that he wished them to publish. *Moskva*, a monthly literary magazine like *Novy Mir*, did not reply at all, and so Solzhenitsyn decided to take all the stories back

---

*With the benefit of hindsight it is possible to see that another reason for Solzhenitsyn's attraction to these journals was their increasingly nationalist orientation, as opposed to *Novy Mir*'s internationalism. This division was obscured at the time by the more obvious split along "liberal versus conservative" lines.

and offer the one undoubtedly publishable story, "Zakhar the Pouch," to *Novy Mir*.

He must have had some difficulty in explaining his "defection" to *Novy Mir* when he called there on 2 December, but he decided to put on a bold front and explain it by Tvardovsky's repeated rejection of his works. Fortunately, Tvardovsky was not there that day, and Lakshin and Dementyev accepted both the explanation and the story. Later they suggested that, in view of its patriotic theme, it might be possible to place the story in *Pravda* or *Izvestia*, and approaches were made to both papers. *Izvestia* got as far as setting it in type, but in the end never published, and the story eventually appeared in the January 1966 issue of *Novy Mir* (the three remaining stories never appeared at all). As it turned out, it was to be Solzhenitsyn's last work to appear officially in the Soviet Union, but no one suspected it at the time.

Tvardovsky got to hear of "Hadji Murad's defection" a few days later than the others and reproached Solzhenitsyn for disloyalty, as a result of which they had a quarrel. Tvardovsky felt that Solzhenitsyn was being high-handed, selfish, and wilful, intent on putting his own interests first and his own idiosyncratic interpretation onto every event. "If you piss in his eye, he'll say it's dew from heaven!"[8] he exclaimed exasperatedly at one point, whereas Solzhenitsyn felt that Tvardovsky's "insensitive assumption of the right to patronize me" could be justified only by the latter's superior understanding, which he felt Tvardovsky lacked. They argued over the confiscation of the archive, Solzhenitsyn's removal of *The First Circle* from the *Novy Mir* office, Solzhenitsyn's spate of letters to four Central Committee members instead of to Demichev alone, and Tvardovsky's recent visit to Paris, where, according to Solzhenitsyn's information, he had said not a word about Solzhenitsyn's difficulties with the authorities and had implied that all was well with him. All this took place in front of the entire editorial board and practically ended in an open rupture; when it was over, the two men shook hands coldly before Solzhenitsyn departed.[9]

The double life that Solzhenitsyn had become used to after leaving the labour camp and that had dwindled during his brief official career now reasserted itself in a novel way. The material he had collected for *The Gulag Archipelago* was obviously growing too sensitive, especially since the seizure of his archive, and he could not afford to be caught working on it either at his hide-out in Rozhdestvo or in Peredelkino. He therefore decided to travel into the countryside to where his notes and early drafts had been hidden and work on them there, and set off immediately after leaving Tvardovsky. But first he had to shave off his beard. This was particularly ironic, because one of the issues that had most irritated him in his recent arguments with Tvardovsky had been Tvardovsky's sarcastic comments about his beard and the laughing suggestion that Solzhenitsyn was growing it in order to be able to shave it off and cross the border incognito. In his memoir Solzhenitsyn returns to this theme again and again, perhaps because Tvardovsky, in jest, had put his finger on one of Solzhenitsyn's most enduring foibles—his love of mystification and conspiracy. His past experiences at the hands of the security service had been no joke, but one cannot escape the feeling that Solzhenitsyn took a certain boyish delight in playing at disappearing and reappearing, having his letters posted from places other than where he was living at the time, dressing up (or, more often, down), and keeping his movements secret. Now, in shaving off his beard, he was doing precisely what Tvardovsky had predicted, albeit with a different destination in mind.*

Solzhenitsyn's response to persecution by the authorities was characteristic of his generation. The conspiratorial style of the secret police (and indeed government) had been met with conspiracy on the part of the people, deception with deception, cunning with cunning. In Stalin's time, when Stalinist psychology ruled, these had been the only methods that worked—even if not very effectively. This was why Tvardovsky, a man of a slightly older generation, was able to understand Solzhenitsyn so well. In the early sixties, however, this psychology began to be challenged. Khrushchev, as in so many other things, had played his part by lifting the lid off the bubbling cauldron of Soviet society and letting some of the steam escape. And now, when his successors were trying to jam the lid on again, they were discovering that it wasn't going to be easy.

One of the signs of escaping steam had been the phenomenon of samizdat. Ever since the mid-fifties it had been gathering momentum, until it had become a sizeable cottage industry, and there were few self-respecting intellectuals in Moscow, whether supporters of the Soviet regime or not, who had not read at least several works in this form and did not possess forbidden typescripts themselves. The works in question were for the most part by earlier Russian authors who had fallen into disfavour and been banned—Bulgakov, Mandelstam, Gumilyov, and so on. Their works had in time been augmented by Pasternak's *Doctor Zhivago* and some of his poetry; Tvardovsky's "Tyorkin in the Next World" (before it was published); Solzhenitsyn's *Miniature Stories;* essays and non-fiction by the Medvedev brothers and other controversial authors; works on the labour camps by Shalamov, Vitkovsky, Evgenia Ginzburg, and others; and by translations of Western works that were unable to find a publisher in the Soviet Union (the copy of Hemingway's *For Whom the Bell Tolls* that Solzhenitsyn had read in November 1961 fell into this category). It was partly the growing popularity of samizdat that had caused the KGB to strike at Teush the preceding September, in the forlorn hope of being able to suppress it.

Meanwhile, a parallel development had taken place at roughly the same time, although at a slower pace and in a slightly different way. This was the publication abroad of works by Soviet authors that had never appeared in the Soviet Union and had not been approved by Soviet censors. The example had been set, in a way, by Pasternak, with the publication in Italy of *Doctor*

---

* It is possible that Tvardovsky's hostility to Solzhenitsyn's beard was derived from a sense that it also symbolized Solzhenitsyn's traditionalist and conservative sympathies, which Tvardovsky was reluctant to accept.

Zhivago. It was said at the time to be the result of a misunderstanding between Pasternak and his Italian publisher, Feltrinelli, but there can be little doubt that foreign publication was what Pasternak wanted or that publication had a devastating impact on Soviet public opinion. It was the first such evasion of the Soviet censorship since Stalin's clamp-down on literature at the beginning of the thirties, and the lesson was not lost on Pasternak's successors.

The first writer to follow in Pasternak's footsteps had been his young friend and admirer Andrei Sinyavsky. As early as 1956 Sinyavsky had written his controversial story "The Trial Begins" and the brilliant critical essay "On Socialist Realism." Despairing of publication at home, he had sent them to the West, and in 1960 they had been published under the pseudonym of Abram Tertz. In the same year Mikhail Naritsa's *Unsung Song* had appeared in Frankfurt (pseudonym—Mikhail Narymov), and a year later, Yuli Daniel's story "Hands" was published in Paris under the pseudonym of Nikolai Arzhak. At around this time two other writers sent works abroad. Alexander Esenin-Volpin, son of the poet Esenin, published a modest volume of verse, *A Leaf of Spring*, under his own name in 1961, and in 1962 Valeri Tarsis published two stories, "The Bluebottle" and "Red and Black," in England, under the pseudonym of Ivan Valeri. During the next three years, a spate of stories appeared in the West by Sinyavsky, Daniel, and Tarsis, thus establishing the idea as a regular practice and putting the Soviet authorities on the defensive.

The authorities had not remained inactive, however, and their reaction to these developments had led to a sequence of events between 1962 and 1966 that marked a psychological change in the relation between the government and its critics and the emergence of the phenomenon that was later to become known as the Democratic or the Human Rights Movement. The authorities' first move, as soon as they had discovered his identity, had been to commit Naritsa to three years in a mental hospital. That was in 1963, the year in which they had tried to do the same to Tarsis. Tarsis, however, was made of sterner stuff. He had already exposed his pseudonym, saying that it had been the publisher's idea, not his, and this fact had saved him, because when news of his committal reached the West there was a wave of protest that forced his release, whereupon he wrote another story, "Ward 7," based on his experiences, and again sent it to the West under his own name. At this point he was interviewed by the KGB and threatened with a "road accident," to which he is said to have replied, "What of it? A crown of thorns will suit me very well. Remember, no one will believe you even if I am run over by accident or a brick falls on my head. Abroad they will still think that the blood-stained secret police killed Tarsis. Therefore, not only will you not kill me but you'll even look after me and move heaven and earth to see that I don't die."[10]

Few people had ever talked to the KGB like this, let alone boasted about it afterwards and held press conferences to which Western correspondents were invited, as Tarsis did. Exploiting his notoriety to the full, he defied the authorities for nearly a year, giving interviews and hearing his words beamed back that same evening by the BBC and other foreign radio stations. Although a translator and minor writer of long standing, he was not popular or well known in established literary circles and had little influence there, but he made a big impression on young nonconformists like Vladimir Bukovsky and his friends, who were just beginning to get interested in social issues, and his example encouraged a group of young poets to hold readings in Mayakovsky Square and also to send their poetry abroad. Calling themselves SMOG, which was said to stand for the Russian words meaning "boldness, thought, image, and profundity" (also satirically interpreted as "the youngest society of geniuses"),* they held several meetings and vigorously circulated their works in samizdat, for which they were attacked in *Komsomolskaya Pravda* (the organ of the Komsomol, or Young Communist League) in June 1965. Five days later Sergei Pavlov, first secretary of the Komsomol and scourge of all liberal tendencies (it was he who had scotched Solzhenitsyn's chances for the Lenin Prize by alleging that he was a collaborator) denounced them in *Pravda* itself. "A bunch of layabouts," he said, "have met somewhere and declared themselves the Youngest Society of Geniuses, and the Western press immediately begins to talk of the upheaval of a whole generation."[11]

Another and bigger influence on the young nonconformists was Esenin-Volpin. Esenin-Volpin had been incarcerated in mental hospitals three times. He was indeed a true eccentric of the sort utterly to baffle a Party functionary—absent-minded, shabbily dressed, whimsically humorous, and wholly other-worldly in his personal behaviour. He was not primarily a poet, but a mathematician and a logician, and in the early sixties had begun to train his formidable mind on the problem of Soviet legality. He concluded that the concept of "Soviet man" lay at the root of the government's habitual disregard for legality, for it was simply a device for blackmailing people into unquestioning submission to the dictates of the Party. By manipulating the terms "Soviet" and "anti-Soviet," the Party was able to superimpose a political value judgement on what should have been a simple question of law and to exact obedience to government actions that were literally illegal. There was no law, for instance, compelling Soviet citizens to be "Soviet people" or to support the building of communism in their country and obey ideological directives. All that a citizen of the USSR was legally obliged to do was obey the written laws, and these happened to be, on paper, remarkably liberal, guaranteeing freedom of speech, assembly, worship, and all sorts of other rights. Of course, the whole system was structured on the assumption that no one would actually claim these rights and that the sole arbiter of who should enjoy them, and when, was the Party, which backed its claims with coercion. But there was nothing to prevent the citizen from simply withdrawing his support from this system and observing only the written laws. If enough people did so, the system would collapse from within.

---

*I.e., *Smelost', Mysl', Obraz, Glubina;* or *Samoye Molodoye Obshchestvo Geniyev.*

Esenin-Volpin's ideas had their first practical effect in December 1965, three months after the confiscation of Solzhenitsyn's papers. While Solzhenitsyn was away in his country hide-out working on *Gulag* and while the authorities were still making preparations for the trial of Daniel and Sinyavsky, a small number of public-spirited individuals, including Bukovsky, Yuri Galanskov, Esenin-Volpin himself, and several others, organized a public demonstration in Pushkin Square to demand that the trial of the two writers be an open one. On 5 December, "Constitution Day" in the Soviet Union, about two hundred people gathered in the square and unfurled placards reading, "Respect the constitution" and "We demand an open trial for Daniel and Sinyavsky." Bukovsky wasn't there, having been arrested three days earlier and confined to a mental hospital, and Esenin-Volpin was obliged to arrive in a friend's invalid carriage to escape detection, but the demonstration was a notable success by Soviet standards and has since been regarded as marking the formal arrival on the Soviet scene of the "dissidents."[12]*

The trial of Daniel and Sinyavsky, which took place from 10 to 14 February 1966, marked a further step forward in the consciousness of Soviet liberals and nonconformists. In secretly sending their works abroad and publishing under pseudonyms, Sinyavsky and Daniel had been conforming to the standard Soviet ethos of conspiracy and cunning that had reigned since the twenties. It had been done according to the same reasoning that had guided Solzhenitsyn in his plans to send his works to Alexandra Tolstoy, and to send a microfilm of *The First Circle* to the West. Naritsa had behaved similarly. But Esenin-Volpin and Tarsis had broken out of that mould by using their own names, and in the course of their trial, Sinyavsky and Daniel broke out of it further. Unusually in a Soviet show trial, the two defendants refused to admit their guilt or express repentance. On the contrary, they defended themselves vigorously against all the charges, and their defiant and eloquent final pleas subsequently circulated in samizdat and became popular reading.[13]

Solzhenitsyn, in his hide-out, listened avidly to BBC reports on the progress of the trial and was pleased by the defendants' final speeches, though he seems still to have grudged the enormous publicity accorded the trial in the West, feeling that it had obscured for a time his own difficulties with the regime and the damage done to him by the confiscation of his novel. On his transistor radio he also listened to reports of the award of the Nobel Prize for literature to Mikhail Sholokhov, an extraordinary obeisance to the Soviet establishment at a time when Sholokhov's real services to literature lay nearly

---

*For some reason the English word "dissident" was taken over to indicate the political nonconformists grouped together in the Democratic (or Human Rights, as some preferred to call it) Movement, although there is a perfectly good Russian word, *inakomysliashchii*, meaning more or less the same thing. It could be that the Russian word is too cumbersome or that the people involved liked the Western ring of "dissident" (or that the Western term was used derisively by the dissidents' opponents and simply stuck). I am not aware of when the word first made its appearance in Russian, but it must have been at around this time.

thirty years in the past. When news of the award had broken, in the autumn of 1965, attempts had been made to persuade Sholokhov to intercede on behalf of Daniel and Sinyavsky, and their English publisher had flown to Stockholm to urge him to intervene, but to no avail.[14] What the award did do was muddy the waters of international protest, a process that was aided by the Soviet authorities' sudden decision to allow Tarsis to emigrate to the West. This, too, was a first—the first time a prominent opponent of the regime had been allowed to leave unhindered for the West since the twenties—and understandably it confused people. It implied that if a Soviet writer published his works secretly in the West he would go, if discovered, to a lunatic asylum or a labour camp like Naritsa, Sinyavsky, and Daniel, whereas if he published openly under his own name he might go scot-free. It is not clear whether that was the message the authorities wished to convey, but it must have impressed itself as such on many people's minds, including Solzhenitsyn's. Solzhenitsyn may also have meditated in his retreat about the symbolic importance of the Nobel Prize and have seen a relevance to the predicament of Sinyavsky and Daniel in the publicity it generated. He had already absorbed the lessons of the Pasternak affair. Here was new evidence of the prize's power.

The Moscow to which Solzhenitsyn returned in March 1966 was a vastly different place from the city he had left four months previously. The Sinyavsky-Daniel trial and the vociferous propaganda campaign that accompanied it in the press had succeeded in temporarily cowing most of the literary intelligentsia. The Writers' Union, having illegally expelled Sinyavsky as early as the preceding November (i.e., before the trial) had recently issued an abject statement supporting the court's verdict of "guilty" and the sentences of seven years' imprisonment for Sinyavsky and five for Daniel. Established writers had hurriedly dropped their interest in samizdat, and liberal magazines like *Novy Mir* were clearly on the defensive. On the other hand, in circles distant from the establishment, Moscow's tiny band of dissidents were emboldened by the results of their protest in Pushkin Square. Three of the younger ones, it is true, including Bukovsky, had been committed to mental hospitals as a punishment, but there was no wave of trials and the protesters' morale was high.

Solzhenitsyn's position had also improved slightly in his absence. The investigation of the "Teush case" had been completed in February 1966—aided by Teush's admission of authorship of the offending article—and it had been decided not to prosecute. Solzhenitsyn and his friends came to the conclusion that the probable reason was that a second literary trial would not have brought extra dividends. On the contrary, it might have been judged excessive and have provoked even greater controversy than the first. Besides, the authorities now had the archive in their possession, and that seemed to offer more interesting possibilities, though with their usual ponderousness they had still not decided what to do with it. They did not hand it back to Zilberberg when they returned some of his other papers, nor did they comply with Solzhenitsyn's requests that the archive be returned to him.

In practical terms, Solzhenitsyn's position was improved by the offer of a new flat in Ryazan, possibly as a result of representations recently made on his behalf by a group of prominent Soviet intellectuals headed by the physicist Pyotr Kapitsa. Solzhenitsyn had been introduced to Kapitsa the preceding autumn by Zhores Medvedev, and the two men had got on very well. Kapitsa, who had worked with Rutherford in England before the war and was the Soviet Union's most distinguished nuclear physicist, had told Solzhenitsyn about his clashes with Stalin and Beria, particularly after his refusal to work on the Soviet atom bomb in 1945, after which he had been placed under house arrest for nine years. He showed Solzhenitsyn an article he had recently written and submitted to *Pravda* in answer to an attack by Rumyantsev on the intelligentsia (the article was never published), and it was clear that his liberal views and his hostility to Stalinism in all its forms coincided very closely with Solzhenitsyn's. There was no mention then of Solzhenitsyn's difficult living conditions in Kasimovsky Lane, but Medvedev had told Kapitsa about them at some length during an earlier visit, as well as about the abortive attempt to move to Obninsk, and at the beginning of 1966 Kapitsa, Chukovsky, Shostakovich, Paustovsky, and Smirnov had written a letter to the Central Committee drawing attention to the author's poor accommodation and requesting that he be given a flat in Moscow. The Moscow request was ignored, but the Central Committee did instruct the Ryazan City Council to offer Solzhenitsyn a new flat, and out of the four offered, he chose a spacious, three-roomed flat in an older building in Yablochkov Passage, overlooking one of the inner-city squares (he and Natalia had often skied there when he was still a schoolmaster).[15]

In earlier times Solzhenitsyn had often thought how nice it would be to live in one of these solid nineteenth-century houses with high ceilings, but for a variety of reasons the opportunity had come too late. The three principal rooms still had to accommodate Natalia's mother and aunts, as well as him and Natalia, so they were still overcrowded. In the meantime, Solzhenitsyn had grown if anything even more sensitive to noise and extraneous intrusions than before, so that the roar and bustle of the busy square below his windows now seemed to him unbearable, particularly after the hush of the countryside where he had worked on *Gulag,* and the peace and quiet of his beloved Rozhdestvo. Then again, it was still Ryazan, and although the inner tumult provoked by the confiscation of his archive had now abated, he continued to fear further sallies by the KGB and the possibility that some "accident" would happen to him on the quiet.

But the most important reason for his unease in Yablochkov Passage was the cooling of his relations with Natalia. Not since their quarrel in Tashkent over Solzhenitsyn's female friend in Leningrad had their relations been normal, and in the interim, it seems, there had been other women as well. To many women in Moscow, Solzhenitsyn had proved very attractive. Tall, self-confident, and not at all bad-looking, he would have caught the eye by his looks and vitality alone, but added to that was his legendary fame, his charm (when he needed it), his articulateness, and an endearing naïvety in the ways of the opposite sex. In no way was he a Don Juan; he was too inexperienced for that. But he was sensitive to women and seems to have felt that having missed so much in his earlier life, he could be permitted a modest fling in middle age.

It would be a wonder if Natalia, herself middle-aged, had not resented these little adventures, and it may be that the separate-rooms policy she had inaugurated after Tashkent had rebounded on her. But it appears that it was not just a question of sexual jealousy but of jealousy of a wider and more diffuse nature, brought on by their physical separation. In his search for peace in which to concentrate on his writing, Solzhenitsyn had taken to spending more and more time alone, first at the cottage in Solotcha and then in the summer-house at Rozhdestvo. Solotcha was relatively near, and Natalia had been able to go there for days and weekends, but Rozhdestvo was much farther away and increased the degree of their separation, both physically and psychologically. Then had come the dramatic events of September 1965, Solzhenitsyn's disappearance into hiding at Chukovsky's dacha, and the following spring his literal disappearance to work on *The Gulag Archipelago*. Throughout this time Natalia had been tied to her lectureship in Ryazan, and she resented Solzhenitsyn's long absences. She did not understand why it was so important for him to go away all the time, and she felt that his shock and fear after the confiscation of the archive were exaggerated. While he was at Chukovsky's, Natalia had not been able bear the thought of his absence any longer and had demanded that he leave Peredelkino and return to Ryazan at all costs, giving as her reason the rather foolish excuse that her friends in Ryazan thought she had been abandoned.

There was also the problem she had in coping with his fanatical dedication to his writing, his career, his fame, and increasingly his role as a symbol of opposition and as a man with a mission. At the time of *Ivan Denisovich* she had fully shared in his success. She had gone almost everywhere with him, met famous people, helped answer the floods of letters, and been his confidante. In the writing of *The First Circle* she had taken an active part, describing to him her most intimate feelings while he was in the camps and evoking her life at the hostel in Moscow. She had watched the genesis of *Cancer Ward* and been with him in Tashkent, and she had helped with the first drafts of *The Gulag Archipelago* in its original form, before *Ivan Denisovich* was published. But since then *The Gulag Archipelago* had become a wedge between them. Many of the 227 informants who helped him wanted their identities concealed. There were secret meetings, confidential letters, hushed conversations that had to be kept from everyone, including Natalia. Psychologically, and of necessity, a part of Solzhenitsyn was plunging back deeper into the world of the convicts that he had never completely left. Camp veterans were his main helpers, they surrounded him, they represented a part of Solzhenitsyn's experience that Natalia could not share with him, and they had risen from the past, as it were, to reclaim him.

Meanwhile, another but lesser part of him had been claimed by the Moscow establishment. The visits to *Novy Mir* and meetings with Moscow writers and editors had continued. His friendship with Chukovsky had brought him into contact with Chukovsky's daughter, Lydia Chukovskaya, author of *Sophia Petrovna*, the novel about Stalin's purges that Anna Berzer had offered Tvardovsky to read simultaneously with *Ivan Denisovich*.* Lydia had a wide circle of prominent literary friends, including Anna Akhmatova, and Lydia and her daughter Elena soon became devoted to Solzhenitsyn and began to help him with his literary chores. The Chukovskys also offered him the use of their flat in Moscow.

At the same time, ties with some of his old friends had been loosened. With Nikolai Vitkevich he had quarrelled. With Panin and Ivashov-Musatov, both of whom Natalia knew well, his relations had cooled. With the Teushes he had grown distant since the loss of his archive, and only with Kopelev, of their old circle, had he remained as close as before. But Kopelev was also a member of the literary establishment, a friend of Tvardovsky, Chukovskaya, and dozens of other writers, and so there was no conflict.

As a result of all this, Natalia had begun to feel cut off and excluded from more and more of his life, and her vanity was injured. After all, being the wife of Russia's most famous living writer was not a bad position to have, and she had relished the perquisites of his fame. She enjoyed receptions, conferences, concerts, and dinner parties—the social round of Moscow literary life—and could have done with more. It was bad enough that her husband did not care for these things, was eccentrically and exaggeratedly indifferent to the trappings of success and the privileges it brought, but at least he should not be perceived to have abandoned her or, still worse, be seen in Moscow in the company of other women.

Solzhenitsyn, for his part, could not see things from her point of view. For him, work always took precedence over everything else. He still believed, as he had in his youth, that family life and emotional relationships were of only secondary importance, and he had always assumed that Natalia, too, would put his work before her own interests. It was his work that had driven him to Solotcha and Rozhdestvo, and he had moved to Peredelkino not to be near other women but to evade arrest and to continue writing. He was shocked by Natalia's outbursts and her ultimatum to him to return. The word "divorce" had rung in the air again, for the first time since Tashkent, but the idea had made Natalia hysterical. It would drive her mad, she had said, or else she would commit suicide—anything rather than leave him. And he had recoiled and promised that as soon as the crisis was over, he would return to Ryazan.[16]

When he did return in the spring of 1966, their immediate task had been to move their belongings to the new flat and settle in, and this he and Natalia

---

* *Sophia Petrovna* never did appear in the Soviet Union.

had accomplished during her spring vacation. Perhaps this went some way towards restoring Natalia's spirits, but Solzhenitsyn was soon restless again and unable to work. As soon as he could, over Natalia's protests, he moved to Rozhdestvo in order to work on *Cancer Ward*. Part 1 was nearly finished. He felt that it would be more acceptable to the authorities than *The First Circle* and hoped that it would enable him to be published again.

While Solzhenitsyn was sorting out these domestic arrangements, the Twenty-third Congress of the Communist Party was held in Moscow—the first since Krushchev's dismissal. Its dominant tone was one of political retrenchment and ideological discipline, marking a decisive end to the period of the Khrushchev "thaw." Literature was represented not by Tvardovsky, who on this occasion was not even a delegate (thus ensuring that he could not be re-elected a candidate member of the Central Committee), but by the new Nobel laureate, Sholokhov, well known for his reactionary views and unwavering support of the Party line. A number of speakers, including Khrushchev's successor, Leonid Brezhnev, castigated rebellious intellectuals for "defaming and slandering our system," saying that they did not express the true feelings of the Soviet intelligentsia, while others criticized films, plays, books, publishing houses, and magazines (including *Novy Mir*) that were "ideologically harmful" and gave, in the words of the first secretary of the Belorussian Communist Party, "a distorted picture of our Soviet life, revelling in individual deficiencies and difficulties, encouraging scepticism and lack of political consciousness, and intentionally depicting our leaders as opponents of the collective." It was left to Sholokhov to mention the case that was uppermost in everybody's minds—that of Daniel and Sinyavsky. The two writers were traitors and misfits who would have been shot during the Revolution, declared Sholokhov. They were "immoral," and he was "ashamed" of those who defended them, for they were defaming the Soviet state.[17]

Sholokhov had in mind the wave of internal protest set off by the verdicts on Daniel and Sinyavsky, and especially a letter to the congress signed by sixty-three Moscow writers representing the flower of Soviet literature (the signatories included Chukovsky, Ehrenburg, Shklovsky, Kaverin, and Dorosh, of the older generation, Voinovich, Akhmadulina, Okudzhava, Dombrovsky, Samoilov, and Morits among the younger ones). The signatories recognized that the case was uniquely important for Soviet literature because it marked the first time in Soviet history that writers had been sentenced in a court of law explicitly for the content of their fictional writings—all earlier repression had been by administrative decree or on charges ostensibly unconnected with writing. "Although we do not approve of the means by which these writers published their work abroad," they wrote, "we cannot accept the view that their intention was anti-Soviet . . . the condemnation of writers for the writing of satirical works creates an extremely dangerous precedent and could impede the progress of Soviet culture." They begged the authorities to release the two writers and allow the letter's signatories to stand surety for them.[18]

A number of prominent liberal names were missing from this letter, among others those of Tvardovsky, Nekrasov, Evtushenko, and Voznesensky. Indeed, no one from *Novy Mir*'s board signed the letter at all, a glaring omission apparently due to the fact that the magazine was already in considerable difficulty and didn't want to exacerbate its position. The same seems to have been true of Nekrasov and certain other liberal writers. Solzhenitsyn's non-appearance on the list apparently had a different cause. Maria Rozanova, Sinyavsky's wife, approached Solzhenitsyn through Timofeyev-Ressovsky in Obninsk. Solzhenitsyn sent a message back that he would not sign, because he "disapproved of writers who sought fame abroad," a reason that struck Rozanova as excessively "Soviet" and shocking in a writer famous for his liberal sympathies.[19] She did not know, of course, that Solzhenitsyn had himself sent various works to the West, albeit as a precaution, and had in fact contemplated such a course as early as 1954 (as Solzhenitsyn later revealed in *The Oak and the Calf*). But she thought it strange and somehow out of character with what was known of the public Solzhenitsyn, and the news, when it got around, caused the first, slight dent in his reputation with the Moscow liberals.

Indeed, it was an extraordinary reason for a man in Solzhenitsyn's position to give. In *The Oak and the Calf* he takes Tvardovsky to task for having held similar views: "This idea, that work published abroad was irretrievably lost, and its author disgraced, stayed with Tvardovsky through all the years I knew him." Yet there can be no doubt that this was the view he took of Daniel and Sinyavsky's action, for in a part of that same memoir, written a year later, he refers to their "literary schizophrenia" and makes it quite clear that he disapproved of their behaviour in publishing in the West.[20]

Behind this puritanical attitude there seems to have stood a more purely emotional and less rational impulse than Solzhenitsyn was prepared to acknowledge at the time, namely, his drive to act completely alone and his instinctive recoil from groups or factions of any description. It was this instinct that had kept him from ever identifying himself fully with *Novy Mir* or allowing himself to be regarded as automatically a member of any particular camp. He was a born outsider, and the instincts that were driving him away from his wife, his former friends, and his old way of life were also causing him to distance himself from literary and intellectual allies. Henceforth he would act and fight alone, caring only for his own role and his own particular battle. At the same time, this battle was saved from sterile egotism because it was not simply for his own personal satisfaction but also on behalf of all those who had suffered unjustly and, as he saw it, of the entire Russian people. Here lay his mission, and by definition its fulfilment was a solitary undertaking. Signing letters on behalf of others and maintaining friendships or cumbersome personal relationships that demanded time and energy were nothing less than distractions from the main goal, and paled into insignificance in comparison with the overriding purpose of his life.

It may have been that this new sense of mission, of "representing" something and someone, played a role in Solzhenitsyn's refusal to meet Jean-Paul

Sartre in the spring of 1966. Sartre and Simone de Beauvoir were in Moscow to visit old friends among the Soviet literary establishment, among them Ehrenburg. Having published three of Solzhenitsyn's stories in *Les Temps Modernes** (including "Matryona's Place"), they expressed a wish to meet him. Solzhenitsyn had a meeting with their Russian interpreter but, according to Simone de Beauvoir, explained that he could not meet them, because Sartre was a writer whose work had all been published. "Every time he writes a book he knows he will be read. So I really do not feel I can talk to him: I should suffer too much." Simone de Beauvoir interpreted this to mean that Solzhenitsyn was both too proud and too shy to meet Sartre, because he felt he couldn't speak to him on equal terms (though Sartre, as she points out, had almost certainly read more of Solzhenitsyn's than Solzhenitsyn of Sartre's).

In his own account of this episode, Solzhenitsyn writes that his real reason for refusing was Sartre's role in canvassing Sholokhov for the Nobel Prize the preceding year, thus inflicting "the most hurtful insult imaginable on Russian literature." He had told Sartre's interpreter, he says, that it was no use for the two writers to meet when one of them was gagged and had his hands tied behind his back. He feared that Sartre might use their meeting to bolster his own reputation for broadmindedness while doing nothing to help Solzhenitsyn in return. "Let him help us to get published first" was his comment to the interpreter. It was a very Soviet response and perhaps reflected a certain paranoia on Solzhenitsyn's part. It may also have contained an element of rationalization. Solzhenitsyn's knowledge of the West, of Westerners and Western literature, was almost zero, and he may have shrunk in any case from meeting one of the most famous figures in Europe, especially when that figure was not someone he admired. On the other hand, it could be said that he was once again showing his disdain for "appearances" and empty gestures.[21]

It appears that Solzhenitsyn's changing view of himself did not pass without notice and was reflected in certain aspects of his outward appearance as well as in his bearing. Vladimir Lakshin, who was so upset by Solzhenitsyn's portrayal of Tvardovsky in his memoir that he wrote an essay of rebuttal (and therefore may be suspected of being a little partial in his comments) has described the impression that Solzhenitsyn's transformation made on him in the sixties.

> I remember him as a modest Ryazan schoolteacher in a plain Russian shirt with rolled-up sleeves and open collar; I remember his energetic efficiency, his firm handshake, the unexpectedly cheerful, open smile that would light up his otherwise rather glum features. He seemed to be untouched by the seduction of the sudden world-wide fame that had burst upon him: he was firm in his convictions,

*According to Victor Nekrasov, it was he who had delivered a copy of *A Day in the Life of Ivan Denisovich* to Sartre in December 1962. He had been about to depart for Paris when Tvardovsky had given him a copy of *Novy Mir* fresh from the presses and asked him to deliver it personally to Sartre immediately on his arrival. Sartre had thus been one of the very first foreign publishers to receive a copy.

but tolerant and patient, straightforward, cordial in his relations with slight acquaintances. . . .

But towards the end of the 1960s he did begin to change somewhat. He acquired a more dignified bearing, and a tone of peremptory self-assurance crept into his voice with increasing frequency. The miserly attitude towards time, which even previously had been one of his ingrained characteristics . . . grew into a fussy preoccupation with haste, which expressed itself in a lack of attention to whoever happened to be talking to him. At the time, one overlooked these trifles. Now, with hindsight, I see in them more clearly the logic of changes that were taking place within Solzhenitsyn himself.[22]

The critic Grigori Svirski has written that when he first got to know Solzhenitsyn, during the early sixties, the latter had a rather touching appearance. Invariably dressed in cheap, baggy clothes that looked as though they had been bought in some country store, he had the slight stoop of the typical schoolmaster. His expression was straightforward, open, and trusting (Svirski quotes Akhmatova as having said that Solzhenitsyn had "a soft face"). But after 1967 Solzhenitsyn's face grew hard and inflexible, and his manner imperious. By the end of the sixties he was dressed more expensively, and Svirski speculates that one of Solzhenitsyn's motives for growing a beard may have been to disguise his native frankness and lend himself more gravity.[23]

A number of people have remarked that from now on Solzhenitsyn began to regard himself as even more apart from the main body of the intelligentsia than before. A friendly observer puts the blame for this more on the other intellectuals than on Solzhenitsyn. They had become over-confident in their ability to bring about liberal changes in the Soviet Union, she has said, and consequently were more shocked than Solzhenitsyn was by their failure to do so. When things began to go wrong during and after the Sinyavsky-Daniel trial, they expected Solzhenitsyn to act as one of them and join them in their protests, whereas he felt less immediately involved than they, less responsible for the failures, and therefore less inclined to make public gestures. Others have put a less charitable interpretation on Solzhenitsyn's behaviour. From then on, in their view, his actions were dictated by one simple rule: Would a given action help or hinder him in his personal battle with the authorities? Every step, every decision whether to help someone or not, whether to intercede or keep quiet, had to be undertaken in terms not of what it would do for the other person but of how far it advanced the main cause. Every move had to be planned according to a larger strategy, and it was this that determined his behaviour.

There is some justice in both these observations. It must not be forgotten, however, that Solzhenitsyn's sense of mission was deep-rooted, dating back to his early youth, or that he was already engaged in a clandestine operation that was to have immense significance both for Soviet dissidents and for the Soviet rulers—the writing of The Gulag Archipelago. For this he was obliged to co-operate with hundreds of assistants and informants—not just the 227 principals referred to in his introduction but also dozens of correspondents up and down the country, who had got to hear of his project on the grape-vine and were eager to help. And yet, at the same time, absolute secrecy had to be preserved while this ghostly army of former convicts and their sympathizers laboured behind the scenes to produce the eyewitness accounts and provide the often rare documents and books that Solzhenitsyn needed for his work.

The gathering and sorting of the necessary materials and the composition of *The Gulag Archipelago* indeed constituted an extraordinary, epic, and very Russian enterprise, collective in its general character, yet inspired, led, and brought to fruition by a man of immense energy, will, and creative power. In intellectual terms it resembled nothing so much as one of those vast and vaunted construction projects of the early Soviet years, like the Bratsk Hydroelectric Dam or the White Sea Canal or, rather, one of their literary equivalents, like the commemorative book on the White Sea Canal compiled by 36 eminent Soviet writers under the guidance and editorship of Maxim Gorky (after no fewer than 120 writers had travelled on an inaugural inspection voyage along the canal). The difference was that whereas the character of these projects was faked—the voluntary component non-existent, the enthusiasm phoney, the labour compulsory, and the leadership backed by force—Solzhenitsyn's project was the real thing, the fruit of genuine passion and conviction and a labour of selfless love. It was, if you like, a literary riposte to *The White Sea–Baltic Stalin Canal* (though very much more than that), just as *A Day in the Life of Ivan Denisovich* had been, in its way, a riposte to the thousands of fake "construction novels" that had preceded it.

But the difficulties in the way of bringing this project to fruition were enormous. In June 1966, for instance, Solzhenitsyn broke off from his work on *Cancer Ward* and travelled north to have a look at the White Sea–Baltic Canal for himself. He would have liked to sail along its entire length, but this proved impossible, for there were no passenger steamers on it at all. To travel on a freighter would have required him to identify himself and state a purpose, and he felt that he was now too notorious to take the risk. Instead, he drove to the southern end of the canal where it leaves Lake Onega and walked along it for several miles. To his amazement, it was virtually deserted, and during the eight hours he spent there only one cargo ship passed in either direction, each loaded with cheap timber. A guard commander (the canal was guarded by sentries) informed him that there was little traffic because the canal was too shallow for most cargo ships and that it couldn't be opened to tourism "because the Americans would rush over to see it." Its original function had been military, to enable the fleet to be transferred from one sea to another, and although the canal was virtually useless for that purpose, the security argument remained in force. The whole thing was a gigantic white elephant, built at the cost of a quarter of a million lives and untold millions of rubles.[24]

Later that summer Solzhenitsyn drove south as far as Odessa and the

Crimea, calling on correspondents, picking up material, and whenever possible visiting places that figured in his narrative. But again there were problems. The average provincial Russian is highly suspicious of strangers—any strangers—especially when they start to ask awkward questions. As Solzhenitsyn pointed out when already in the West, it was extremely difficult to gather firsthand information. "I went to Tambov Province, for instance, to where the peasant rebellion had broken out—there are still eyewitnesses living there, but they are all afraid to talk to a stranger about it, and I myself was frightened to question them for fear of putting a speedy end to my expedition."[25]

One other chore that Solzhenitsyn accomplished that summer was to write a further letter to Leonid Brezhnev, protesting once more against the confiscation of his archive and the statements being made against him at secret Party meetings. "Slanderers employing even official propaganda channels . . . have declared in various provinces that I, an officer who fought the entire war in the same unit and was awarded two active-service medals, was either a traitor, a collaborator, or in effect a member of the Gestapo." Apart from reports of this kind, Solzhenitsyn had received information about mysterious dealings with his confiscated play and novel, information that came from sources within or close to the upper reaches of the Party. *The First Circle* was being passed around among senior members of the Central Committee and the Writers' Union, and *Feast of the Conquerors* was being shown both to these and to leaders of the Artists' and Musicians' unions, the calculation being that their content was so blatantly anti-Soviet that all right-thinking Communists were bound to be revolted by them. Such an assumption was somewhat unfair to the novel. It is true that *The First Circle* was ultimately anti-Communist in content, but the political message was well buried and Solzhenitsyn had toned it down from his original, sharper version. It was more overtly anti-Stalinist than anti-Communist, and until the confiscation there had been grounds to hope that it still might see publication one day. But taken in conjunction with *Feast of the Conquerors*, it did not stand a chance—and that was the point of the KGB's strategy. This "anti-Soviet" play composed in the labour camps would be used to discredit Solzhenitsyn's entire output.[26]

It is not clear how much Solzhenitsyn's letter said about the circulation of these works. In his memoir he writes that his first inclination had been to be sharp in tone but that the journalist Ernst Henri* persuaded him to be more diplomatic. In the end, he aimed his reproaches at the Writers' Union rather than at the Party itself and also offered a sort of apologia for his vision of the role of the writer.

> I know that my works strike some people as too sharp, exposing unpleasantnesses in our past and contemporary life that for some reason they would prefer literature to keep quiet about. But if the writer is not permitted to express the people's

---

*Ernst Henri is the pen name of Semyon Rostovsky.

common pain and anxiety, if the writer cannot be a kind of cybernetic "feedback" for his society, then the writer is unnecessary and literature will be replaced by cosmetics. Sickness can be cured only if it is diagnosed and named in time—driven inwards, it festers. There were writers in the twenties who warned about Stalin's character and the personality cult, but they were liquidated instead of being heeded. As the proverb goes: Friend and your flatterer I cannot be.[27]

The letter was posted at the end of July 1966 and was never answered or acknowledged. Solzhenitsyn came to feel, however, that it had helped his cause with the authorities, and it may also have contributed to his obtaining permission for part 1 of *Cancer Ward* to be discussed at a Writers' Union meeting in the Central Writers' Club later that year.

32

THE BEST FORM
OF DEFENCE

SOLZHENITSYN HAD COMPLETED part 1 of *Cancer Ward* in Rozhdestvo in the early summer. Like *A Day in the Life of Ivan Denisovich* and *The First Circle*, it described a group of people cut off from the mainstream of society and isolated in a smaller, artificial world whose boundaries were arbitrary. In this case it was not a labour camp but a cancer clinic—the Tashkent clinic that Solzhenitsyn had attended in 1954. The novel's action was set a little later, in 1955.

As in all novels* set in such "closed" institutions, the characters had been chosen to represent a cross-section of society. The two principal patients were Oleg Kostoglotov, a former labour-camp prisoner now in administrative exile (as Solzhenitsyn himself had been when undergoing treatment), who was suffering from cancer of the abdomen, and Pavel Rusanov, a high-ranking official in the Communist Party, with cancer of the neck. These two were the protagonists in the ideological and ethical conflict that lay at the

---

*Solzhenitsyn did not in fact accept the epithet of "novel" to describe *Cancer Ward*; he preferred the traditional Russian term of *povest'*, which can be approximately translated as "tale." He explained his reasoning in *The Oak and the Calf*: "The dividing lines between genres are becoming more and more blurred in our country, and the result is a devaluation of forms. *Ivan Denisovich* is of course a short story, though it is a large and dense one. Less substantial than the story is the novella—it is light in construction and clear-cut in subject and ideas. A tale *[povest']* is what too many of us readily call a 'novel.' There are several story lines, and the action almost inevitably extends over a fairly long time. A novel *[roman]* (odious word! surely we could find a better one?) differs from a tale not so much in size, nor in the duration of the action (compression and a rapid tempo can also be virtues in a novel), but in the number of destinies it embraces, the breadth of its horizon, and the depth of its ideas" (pp. 24–25 n.). Nevertheless, I personally prefer the term "novel" to describe *Cancer Ward* and have used it throughout.

heart of the novel, a conflict between materialism, political expediency, and selfishness on the one hand, and altruism, spirituality, and compassion on the other. Kostoglotov, the champion of altruism, was autobiographical in conception and undoubtedly served as the mouthpiece for many of Solzhenitsyn's own views, although the details of his arrest and imprisonment were partly based on the experience of his former sergeant Ilya Solomin. Through Kostoglotov, Solzhenitsyn was also able to introduce the charming, old-world figures of a pair of elderly exiles named the Kadmins (based on Nikolai and Elena Zubov), and between them, these three characters represented the forces of decency and affection. But whereas the Kadmins had overcome the malignity of the society in which they found themselves with submission and love, Kostoglotov's defence of personal liberty and search for justice and compassion were truculent and aggressive, and there was little doubt as to where Solzhenitsyn's true sympathies lay. Kostoglotov was the champion of freedom against the forces of political paternalism and authority.

Rusanov, his opponent, personified authority, and through Rusanov and members of his family, Solzhenitsyn offered a picture of the corrupt way in which the Party establishment operated to control society and of its authoritarian attitudes to the people it governed. Despite a heroic attempt on Solzhenitsyn's part to be objective in his portrayal, the character of Rusanov came out close to caricature, while that of Rusanov's daughter Aviette, a young establishment poet moving in fashionable literary circles, overstepped the bounds of realism altogether. In the last chapter, where she was shown visiting her father and cheering him up with all the latest gossip from literary Moscow, Solzhenitsyn mercilessly satirized the capital's intellectuals, going well beyond the sarcastic picture of the intelligentsia that he had painted in *The First Circle* (and hinted at in *Ivan Denisovich*).

Arrayed around these two protagonists were the other patients, two of whom could be said to stand for Rusanov's view of the world, and one for Kostoglotov's. Rusanov's allies were Efrem Podduyev, a former construction worker (and congenital liar) who was suffering from cancer of the mouth; and Vadim Zatsyrko, a young geologist and Party loyalist (inspired by the story of the lady doctor who had visited Solzhenitsyn in Ryazan to obtain some of the mandrake-root infusion for her son) who had cancer of the leg. Each represented a different facet of the materialist attitude to life: Podduyev a negative one of opportunism and deception, and Zatsyrko, who was portrayed as being in the heroic mould of the positive heroes of Soviet fiction, a more attractive one of self-abnegation in the name of the cause. Kostoglotov's ally, Dyoma, a sixteen-year-old schoolboy also suffering from cancer of the leg, simply represented childlike honesty and human perplexity in the face of the enormous, and seemingly unjust, challenge of his illness.

The confrontation of all these characters with the terrifying threat of death from cancer lent the novel an existential resonance that was more overt than that in either *Ivan Denisovich* or *The First Circle* (although death had been an unseen presence in both of them), and Solzhenitsyn explicitly drew attention to this element by the rather crude device of having Podduyev read Tolstoy's *The Death of Ivan Ilyich* and undergo a sort of conversion. This later led many critics to praise *Cancer Ward* for being more profound than Solzhenitsyn's other novels. Yet it is clear that unlike, say, *The Magic Mountain* or *The Rack* (with which Solzhenitsyn's novel has been compared), *Cancer Ward* was not about the existential dilemmas posed by death or the meaning of death, or even about the meaning of illness in a fundamental way, but rather about the light that illness and death throw on the ethical dilemmas with which life confronts us, particularly in their social and political application. The hidden theme of *Cancer Ward* was in fact de-Stalinization and its implications for the health of Soviet society. This was why the action of the novel was set in 1955, when de-Stalinization had begun in earnest but was still being fiercely debated and opposed; and a close examination of the ebb and flow of Kostoglotov's and Rusanov's illnesses reveals that there is an intimate and reciprocal relation between them. When Kostoglotov's recovery is at its height (coinciding with successes in the policy of de-Stalinization), Rusanov's sickness intensifies; when Kostoglotov experiences a relapse (usually associated with some parallel political setback), Rusanov is shown to be on the up and up.

It was in this context that the relationship between Kostoglotov and his doctors acquired its true meaning. Solzhenitsyn's portrayal of the doctors in *Cancer Ward*—particularly of Lyudmila Dontsova, the head of the radiology department (based on the real-life Lydia Dunayeva), and her assistant Vera Gangart (based on Irina Meike), and their daily cares—was later widely praised as a triumph of old-fashioned realism (it was, if anything, "real" socialist realism, or socialist realism as it might have been without the ideological trimmings, rather in the manner of the celebrated building scene in *Ivan Denisovich*). But Kostoglotov was shown coming into conflict with them over the question not simply of what his treatment ought to be but of who should decide it and on what grounds. In so doing, Kostoglotov raised the issue of whether a man had the right to dispose of his own life, and of the ethical and also political dilemmas posed by the paternalism, however benevolent and even idealistic, that the doctors exercised in wielding their power. Dontsova argued that the doctors had the right to determine the treatment and to use it on the patient, whatever the consequences, because they were the experts and their aim was to save the patient's life (even if they inadvertently ruined or destroyed it as a result of the malignancy of the illness or the inadequacy of the treatment). It was not difficult to see that these arguments contained a metaphor for socialism or that Solzhenitsyn was opposing personal liberty to the well-intentioned despotism of the doctors. In part 1 of *Cancer Ward* the dilemma was not resolved. The doctors did, after all, save Kostoglotov's life, when his preferred method of dosing himself with the mandrake-root infusion and relying on faith and will-power had failed. On the other hand, there remained the larger question, Saved his life for what? For what sort of life, what sort of society, and what sort of country?

The question was raised but not answered in part 1. At the end of the part, Kostoglotov seemed to be in the ascendant. He was much recovered from his sickness and able to enjoy life again, so much so that he was engaged in a double flirtation in the hospital—by day with Dr Gangart and by night with a pretty young nurse called Zoya. Rusanov, by contrast, was going through a difficult period, leaving the reader with a sense of optimism. However, the first part's last words were spoken by Rusanov's daughter Aviette and had either an ominous or an ironic ring to them, depending on one's point of view. "Don't worry," she told her father, "everything is going to be all right. *Everything.*"

Solzhenitsyn had submitted the novel, like all his other works, to *Novy Mir* as soon as it was ready, and on 18 June there was a meeting of the journal's staff to discuss it. Generally, according to Solzhenitsyn's version of the meeting, the more junior people present (Lakshin, Maryamov, Berzer) were in favour of publication, while the older members of the editorial board (Dementyev, Kondratovich, Sachs) were against. The latter's objections were of two kinds. They found the composition of the novel lumpy and shapeless, and they disliked its tendentiousness, particularly in individual scenes, such as a conversation in the hospital ward about Stalin's culpability for the Leningrad blockade and the chapter on Aviette's visit to her father. Igor Vinogradov, who had recently joined the board, announced, "If we don't print this, I see no reason for our existence," and Tvardovsky, summing up, spoke powerfully in the novel's favour.

> Art does not exist in this world to be a weapon in the class struggle. Once it knows it is a weapon, it loses its fire-power. We are quite free in our judgements of this piece of yours: we are no more concerned with whether it will get by or not than if we were discussing it in the next world. . . . The work is topical in that it presents a moral reckoning on behalf of a newly awakened people. . . . Unfinished? Great works always bear the mark of incompleteness. *Resurrection*, *The Possessed*—try to think of a single exception. . . . This is something we want to publish. If the author will work on it a little more, we will launch it and fight for it to the limit of our powers—and beyond![1]

It sounded almost like a repeat of the decision to launch *Ivan Denisovich*, but Tvardovsky was not without his criticisms. He still disliked the title, he agreed that the Leningrad blockade discussion was one-sided and wanted Hitler mentioned as well as Stalin, and he, too, felt that the Aviette chapter was a lampoon on the intelligentsia and should be omitted. Solzhenitsyn, as was by now his custom, had made a virtually stenographic record of everything that was said and answered the points one by one. He absolutely refused to tone down the character of Rusanov, as some of those present had suggested, or to soften his references to the system of administrative exile. But he did agree to make most of the changes proposed by Tvardovsky, and a week later he returned the manuscript, revised and shorn of the Aviette chapter, with an alternative title suggested in brackets: *The Ward at the End of the Avenue*.

Unfortunately, by the time they came to discuss it a week after that, Tvardovsky had changed his mind. He demanded further cuts and alterations along the lines earlier suggested by Dementyev and Sachs, and began to drag his feet over publication. The circumstances were not favourable. The magazine was already having great trouble with Alexander Bek's novel *The New Appointment* and Simonov's *War Diaries*, both of which had been announced but were being held up by the censors.* He wasn't sure whether they could take on yet another controversial major work. Besides, "we have to have the sort of manuscript in which we can defend any passage whatsoever because we share the ideas expressed in it. . . . But Solzhenitsyn, alas, is the same as he has always been. . . ." Perhaps they would try for publication the following year. On that basis he was prepared to sign a contract for the novel at once and offer an advance of 25 per cent. In the meantime Solzhenitsyn could be getting on with, and perhaps finishing, part 2.[2]

Solzhenitsyn was intensely irritated by this unexpected turn of events. He had been genuinely happy to be reconciled with Tvardovsky and had basked in the latter's sincere praise of the novel's artistry, but now all his old doubts and resentments returned. He felt that Dementyev and Sachs, whom he distrusted and had always regarded as his enemies, had been working on Tvardovsky to change his opinion and had engineered matters so that they were present at this second meeting, whereas Lakshin and Solzhenitsyn's other supporters were absent. Concealing his feelings, however, he simply said that he would not sign a contract and would take the manuscript with him.

The *Novy Mir* debacle had important consequences for Solzhenitsyn. In the first place it hastened a decision that he had already been moving towards but that he might have postponed if publication had seemed a real possibility—namely, to let his novel circulate in samizdat. In this way he would get the readers he so desperately craved and would reach at least a limited public, whereas with *The First Circle* he had reached virtually nobody. Secondly, he could restore the cuts that he had reluctantly made in response to *Novy Mir*'s demands. And thirdly, he felt morally free of *Novy Mir*. Up till now, a sense of obligation had bound him to Tvardovsky and his magazine, however erratically of late, and it was a relief to shed it. His resolve to try samizdat was fortified by a conviction that he had nothing to lose. His panicky fears about what the authorities might do to him when they had read and digested *Feast*

---

* *The New Appointment* was a novel about the death of Sergo Ordzhonikidze, Stalin's fellow Georgian and people's commissar for heavy industry during the thirties. Ordzhonikidze was the only government leader to protest against Stalin's terror and to be killed as a result. The novel was never published and subsequently circulated in samizdat. Simonov's *War Diaries* were said to be a relatively unexpurgated account of his experiences as a war correspondent during the Second World War, and to contain severe criticism of Stalin. They have not been published or, to my knowledge, appeared in samizdat.

of the Conquerors had proved groundless. All they had done was distribute it among themselves and somewhat step up their campaign of slander, but this could hardly hurt him, since the people who were reading it were hostile to him anyway. If anything, it helped, for it added to his reputation, and each negative rumour spread about him provoked a score of rebuttals from well-wishers. It also demonstrated the authorities' helplessness. If that was all they could manage, he had little to fear. Nothing he released now could be as damaging as his play.

News of the novel's circulation (though still in a highly restricted fashion) among certain Moscow intellectuals soon reached Tvardovsky, who was livid at what he took to be a breach of *Novy Mir*'s security. He tried to get in touch with Solzhenitsyn to check the matter, but the latter, though aware of Tvardovsky's efforts, had no desire to talk to him and wrote a letter instead.

> If I thought you were upset because the tale* has become known to others besides the editors of *Novy Mir* . . . I should be bound to express surprise. . . . Every author has this right, and it would be strange if you ever intended to deprive me of it. What is more, I cannot allow *Cancer Ward* to repeat the dismal career of my novel *[The First Circle]*: first there was an indefinite period of waiting, during which the author was repeatedly asked by the editors not to show it to anyone else; and then the novel was lost both to me and to those who should have read it, but it is being distributed to a few select persons on a secret list.[3]

Solzhenitsyn later heard that Tvardovsky had wept when he read this letter, but he remained unmoved. The break with *Novy Mir*—and with Tvardovsky—was almost complete. He was on his own now, which was exactly what he wanted.

His latest idea was to try to achieve something through the Writers' Union, which he knew included a number of liberals among its rank and file, particularly among the younger members. It had looked as if an opportunity might present itself at the Writers' Congress planned for June, to which he would have had access as a bona fide member of the union, but the congress was postponed until the end of the year, and Solzhenitsyn was impatient to move quicker than that. He therefore managed to arrange for a discussion of *Cancer Ward* to be held at the Central Writers' Club in Moscow. After three months of delays and three postponements, the meeting was held on 17 November 1966.

It was billed as an "expanded session" of the Bureau of the Creative Prose Association of the Moscow Writers' Organization within the Russian Republic's branch of the Writers' Union. In other words, it was at a relatively low level and was one of a series of occasional meetings to discuss individual books. But as the chairman, G. Berezko, noted, the attendance on this occasion was extraordinarily high (fifty-two writers were present), and it appears that tickets for the event were extremely hard to come by. Berezko

---

*I.e., *Cancer Ward*. See note p. 563.

also indicated that the meeting had been called at Solzhenitsyn's request and that the usual reason for such sessions was "a difference of opinion between the author and the publisher," suggesting that Solzhenitsyn's purpose was to outflank *Novy Mir*. This was presumably why Tvardovsky had instructed his staff not to attend.[4]

By and large, the writers who gathered in the club that afternoon were Solzhenitsyn's sympathizers and supporters. Of his known opponents in the literary hierarchy, only Zoya Kedrina addressed the meeting. Notorious for her recent role as a "social accuser" in the trial of Sinyavsky and Daniel, where she had appeared on behalf of the Writers' Union, she was noisily heckled when she rose to speak, and Victor Nekrasov led a mass walk-out long before she had finished. For this reason, criticism of the novel was fairly muted and more or less followed the lines of the arguments made earlier at *Novy Mir*. Many people were made uncomfortable by the portrait of Rusanov, which they felt revealed too much hatred on the part of the author and therefore constituted an artistic failure. Others felt that the labour-camp theme intruded overmuch, or were disturbed by the novel's "naturalism."[*] There was widespread criticism of the Aviette chapter, which was described as farcical and exaggerated, and a few people expressed unease over the way in which discussions of Tolstoy's story *The Death of Ivan Ilyich* and of Vladimir Pomerantsev's article "On Sincerity in Literature" seemed to have been "dragged into" the novel artificially.

Against this was set a chorus of praise in favour of *Cancer Ward* and in favour of its publication. Solzhenitsyn was compared, in his literary methods and preoccupations, with the classics of the nineteenth century, and parallels were drawn between the novel and Tolstoy's story, mostly to the novel's advantage. With reference to more recent literature, Solzhenitsyn's fate was compared with that of Babel, Bulgakov, Platonov, Zamyatin, Zabolotsky, Zoshchenko, Akhmatova, and Pasternak—all of them classics of the Soviet era who had suffered heavily at the hands of the authorities for the courage and honesty of their writing. Alexander Bek's blocked novel was recalled, and many speakers expressed indignation that two such outstanding works were being denied publication.

The best contributions came from the veteran novelist Veniamin Kaverin and from Arkadi Belinkov, a brilliant and fiery critic who had himself spent thirteen years in the camps for his "anti-Soviet" writings. Kaverin pointed out that in addition to talent, Solzhenitsyn had two indispensable qualities for a great writer: "inner freedom and a powerful striving for truth." He was the most impressive of a whole group of promising new writers who were revitalizing Soviet literature. "The new writing has arrived, and the old, reptilian, crawling literature that understood service to society as a straight line between two points . . . is finished. Who now remembers the books that were published in . . . millions of copies and that were full of lies, distor-

---

[*] A reference to some of the medical detail in *Cancer Ward*, and perhaps to Solzhenitsyn's frank, by Soviet standards, treatment of Kostoglotov's sexual yearnings.

tions, and praise of Stalin, open or camouflaged, and remote from the truth?" *Cancer Ward* should be published immediately, for "all efforts to silence Solzhenitsyn are doomed to failure. He cannot write differently from the way he writes."[5]

Belinkov put his finger still more accurately on what made Solzhenitsyn so special. "The outstanding merit of the works of Alexander Isayevich is that they were actually written. A man got to the point of writing the books he wanted to write." There were many other writers, said Belinkov, with great experience of life and perhaps the talent to write excellent books about it, but for some reason they never had. Solzhenitsyn had done it, and he had restored Russian literature to its former greatness. But he was not just a traditionalist, as some people seemed to think. "Solzhenitsyn creates a new system of Russian prose, because he introduces into the composition of his art new, unknown, or forgotten ideas of good and evil, life and death, and the relationship between man and society. The apparently traditional nature of his style is similar to the art of the Renaissance, which was close to the art of the ancient world, but only at a distance and on casual inspection. Solzhenitsyn's writing is not only similar to the Renaissance; it is in fact the renaissance of Russian spiritual life."[6]

At the conclusion of the discussion, Solzhenitsyn was invited to comment. He thanked the participants for their many kind words and above all for their professional criticism. His years of solitude as a writer had had both advantages and disadvantages. The fact that he had been writing virtually for himself meant that he had never had to wonder whether this or that work would "pass." On the other hand, in isolation one inevitably became less demanding of oneself, and it was essential to receive informed criticism of one's work. That was why he had requested this discussion, particularly since he was being deprived of publication and the natural responses of his readers.

He went on to discuss some of the points raised by the other speakers, "not in the spirit of petty polemics" but simply in the interests of clarification. First there was the title, *Cancer Ward*: Was it meant to be a symbol?

Some speakers have said that there was a cancerous growth in our society. Yes, there was. But that wasn't what I had in mind. When I called the book *Cancer Ward*, it was the sickness I had in mind, and the struggle against this sickness. I boldly gave it this title because I reckoned that I would not depress the reader or reduce him to despair. . . . I used it because I reckoned to overcome it in resolving the question of the struggle between life and death. That was why I quite calmly employed this title, that and no more.

Another question concerned the confinement of the action within the walls of the hospital ward, thus curtailing the view offered of Soviet society as a whole. Wasn't this unnecessarily restrictive? Solzhenitsyn thought not.

Recently I have come to the conclusion that literature can never describe the whole of our world, can never encompass everything . . . But it has one interesting quality. Let me make a comparison with mathematics. It seems to me that any work of literature can become a cluster of planes. In mathematics, a cluster of planes is defined as an aggregate of planes all passing through a given point . . . . Each author chooses a point corresponding to his experience and inclinations. But each point can have a myriad planes passing through it, tilting in all possible directions. . . . And you can take any subject you like. This subject was suggested to me by my illness, which gave me a chance to obtain a virtually professional knowledge of it so as to verify my treatment. I might not have chosen the cancer ward, but something else entirely. But if you want to go beyond the confines of the cancer ward, you will find those same planes everywhere.[7]

Solzhenitsyn then touched on a number of other questions. Since 90 per cent of the speakers had been critical of Rusanov, he felt there must be something to this criticism, but, unfortunately, no one had been able to indicate a way of putting the character right, and he was still puzzled about how to proceed. As for the Aviette chapter, he agreed that it was farcical but said that he had put into her mouth only statements and opinions actually uttered by real people and reported in the Soviet press. It was his little joke against certain kinds of critics. The collection of Tolstoy stories, including *The Death of Ivan Ilyich*, had actually been on the shelves of his ward when he was in Tashkent, as had the copy of *Novy Mir* containing Pomerantsev's article "On Sincerity in Literature," and both had led to discussions in the ward. He could truthfully place his hand on his heart and say, "I have invented nothing."[8]

Just before he sat down, Solzhenitsyn tossed in a small surprise. Since his negotiations with *Novy Mir* over the novel had proved inconclusive, he had sent it off to two other reviews, *Zvezda* (The Star) and *Prostor* (Expanse), the former based in Leningrad and the latter, less well known, in Alma-Ata (by going to the provinces, Solzhenitsyn was trying to circumvent Moscow's veto). His announcement had the desired effect. Before the chairman was able to close the meeting, a number of speakers demanded to know what decision was being taken. Lev Kopelev proposed that a transcript of the discussion be sent to *Zvezda* and *Prostor*. Another speaker suggested that *Moskva*, the magazine of the Moscow branch of the Writers' Union, and its publishing house be approached to publish the novel and that any decision reached should be by the entire meeting, and not just the secretariat. In the end, two resolutions were passed, one to send off the transcripts, the other to urge publication as soon as possible.

Pressing home his advantage, Solzhenitsyn immediately asked, "May I conclude from our discussion that when I finish the second part, I can bring it to the Moscow Writers' Organization?" "Of course," replied the chairman, to general applause. "And I would ask you, Alexander Isayevich, in my own name and in the name of those present today, to visit us more often and take part in our life and our discussions."[9]

The meeting was a minor triumph for Solzhenitsyn—and had the additional virtue of putting dozens more copies of *Cancer Ward* into circulation in samizdat. As news spread of the discussion, more and more people wanted to read the novel, and those who had participated in the discussion were pressed to lend copies, if they had them, to friends and to friends of friends, where further copies were made and passed on.* In this way, pressure was built up on the authorities to do something about it. It was a relatively new tactic for Solzhenitsyn (though he had tried it, in a limited and modest way, with his *Miniature Stories*), and he was impressed with its efficacy. He was beginning to realize the value of the Soviet Union's still tiny, but growing, body of independent opinion and to appreciate the importance of publicity, particularly when it was amplified by foreign radio stations broadcasting back into the Soviet Union. Furthermore, beyond that body of Soviet listeners to foreign broadcasts there was the foreign public itself, and its opinions, too, were important to the Soviet authorities. The possibilities for exercising influence, it seemed, were far greater than he had once imagined.

During that crowded month of November 1966, he proceeded to put these new discoveries to the test. A Japanese newspaper correspondent, Komoto Sedze, had recently sent him a request for an interview or for written replies to five questions. Solzhenitsyn had routinely refused such requests up till now, but this time he decided to accept and arranged to meet Sedze at the Writers' Club the day after the discussion of *Cancer Ward*. It was a brilliant and bold tactical move. The club was such a public place that when Solzhenitsyn met the correspondent, with his official interpreter and a photographer from the Novosti press agency, who set up floodlights to take pictures, the club employees and bystanders assumed it must be official, whereas Solzhenitsyn had deliberately not sought the necessary permission and was acting quite outside the normal Soviet regulations. The interview lasted only about twenty minutes (Solzhenitsyn discovered that Sedze himself had been a Soviet prisoner of war and had spent three years in the labour camps), but the written answers to Sedze's questions had already been prepared, and Solzhenitsyn simply had to hand them over.[10]

In view of the novelty of this direct communication with the outside world, Solzhenitsyn's statement was fairly circumspect. He did not refer to the confiscation of his novel and archive or to the ugly rumours that were being circulated about him at secret meetings, but he did mention the existence of *The First Circle* and the fact that it had not been published, as well as his two unpublished plays, *The Tenderfoot and the Tart* and *Candle in the Wind*. He also described the subject of *Cancer Ward* and indicated that he hoped to finish the second part quite soon. Asked to offer his views on a standard cliché, "the writer's duties in defence of peace," he gave a characteristically individual answer: "I shall broaden the scope of this question. The fight for peace is only part of the writer's duties to society. Not one little

*This may be an exaggeration on my part. Arkady Belinkov writes, in *Novy Zhurnal*, no. 93 (1968), that Victor Ilyin handed copies to union members personally, one at a time. Each member was obliged to sign for his copy and to read it in a room specially set aside for that purpose. In this way, further circulation of the typescript was restricted. It is probable, however, that some copies got away.

bit less important is the fight for social justice and for the strengthening of spiritual values in his contemporaries. This, and nowhere else, is where the effective defence of peace must begin—with the defence of spiritual values in the soul of every human being. I was brought up in the traditions of Russian literature, and I cannot imagine myself working as a writer without such aims."[11]

Another personal rule that Solzhenitsyn now broke was his refusal to make public appearances. The first time was almost by accident. A friend casually asked him while they were walking in the street whether he would agree to speak at the Kurchatov Institute of Physics. Sensing that this would give him another opportunity to make his presence felt in the capital, Solzhenitsyn assented, and the meeting was fixed very quickly, so that there could be no official interference. While preparing this lecture, Solzhenitsyn stayed at the Steins' flat, and Veronica Stein was the involuntary witness of how much it meant to him. Returning from her office in the late afternoon, she thought she heard his voice and imagined he must be saying something to her. When she popped her head inside the door of his room, however, she found him rehearsing a scene from *The First Circle*—where the engineer Gerasimovich has a brief prison visit from his wife—and as he looked up, she saw tears in his eyes.[12]

When Solzhenitsyn arrived at the institute that evening, he found six hundred people present and was given an enthusiastic reception for his readings from *Cancer Ward*, *Candle in the Wind*, and the ostensibly "forbidden" *The First Circle*. News of his appearance quickly spread, and soon he was inundated with invitations from all over Moscow. He accepted as many as he could, and everything seemed to be arranged: permissions were granted by the directors of various institutions, dates established, notices put up, and invitations sent out, but at the last minute each lecture was cancelled. At the Karpov Institute, Solzhenitsyn arrived in the car that had been sent for him only to find a notice pinned to the door: "Cancelled owing to the author's indisposition."[13]

It turned out that the Moscow City Party Committee had been ringing round to warn everybody off, threatening the institute directors with reprisals if they went ahead with their meetings. Semichastny, the head of the KGB, denounced Solzhenitsyn's effrontery at Party ideological conferences and briefing sessions for Party propagandists, but, paradoxically, his fulminations only increased Solzhenitsyn's self-confidence. If that was all the head of the dreaded KGB intended to do to him, there was no danger. It was difficult, however, to find other platforms to speak from, until, quite unexpectedly, he was invited to the Lazarev Institute of Oriental Studies (a previous meeting there had been cancelled) for November 30. With a premonition that this might be his last opportunity, Solzhenitsyn went along prepared to speak as well as to read; after treating his listeners to two chapters from *Cancer Ward*, he seized on a question from the audience in order to get a few things off his chest.

I must explain why, although I used to refuse to talk to reporters or make public appearances, I have now started giving interviews and am standing here before you. I believe, as before, that the writer's business is to write, not to haunt public platforms, not to keep explaining himself to newspapers. But I have been taught a lesson: the writer exists not to write but to defend himself. . . . There is a certain *organization* that has no obvious claim to tutelage over the arts, that you may think has no business at all supervising literature—but that does these things. This organization took away my novel and my archive, which was never intended for publication. Even so, I said nothing, but went on working quietly. However, they then made use of excerpts from my papers, taken out of context, to launch a campaign of defamation against me, defamation in a new form—from the platform at closed briefing sessions. What can I do about it? Only defend myself! So here I am! Look, I'm still alive. Look, this head is still on my shoulders. Yet, without my knowledge and contrary to my wishes, my novel has been published in a restricted edition and is being circulated among the chosen—people like Vsevolod Kochetov, the chief editor of *Oktyabr*. Tell me, then, why should I deny myself similar privileges? Why shouldn't I, the author, read you chapters from the same novel here today?[14]

It was an extraordinary performance, and these were extraordinary words to be heard from a public platform in the Soviet Union. Solzhenitsyn was carried away by the strength of his feelings—recklessly, exaltedly. He imagined he could see before him the face of Semichastny, and his resentment knew no bounds. "In a loud voice, and with a feeling of triumph and simple joy, I explained myself to the public and *paid him back*. An insignificant convict in the past, and perhaps in the future too, . . . I had been granted an audience of half a thousand and the freedom to speak!" The son of Gulag was truly unbending his knees and straightening his back. As he later wrote when describing this scene:

You would have to live through a long life of slavery, bowing and scraping to authority from childhood on, springing to your feet to join with the rest in hypocritical applause, nodding assent to patent lies, never entitled to answer back—all this as slave and citizen, later as slave and convict: Hands behind your back! Don't look round! Don't break ranks!—to appreciate that hour of free speech from a platform with an audience of five hundred people, also intoxicated with freedom.[15]

But even more important was another sensation that accompanied this explosion of anger and truth: "This was perhaps the first time, the very first time, that I felt myself, saw myself, making history."

The legend of Solzhenitsyn was being born. He read some chapters from *The First Circle*, but this time the most provocative ones, the most political ones, instead of the domestic chapters he had read at the Kurchatov Institute. Within days the news of his outburst and of his daring defiance of the KGB had travelled round Moscow, but Solzhenitsyn was no longer there to hear it. Also contributing to the legend were those sudden disappearances of his, and at the beginning of December he shaved off his beard once more and slipped away to his hide-out to work on *The Gulag Archipelago*, not so much a musketeer as a pimpernel. He was beginning to live a life now that far surpassed, in excitement and danger, the lives of his fictional heroes.*

Between December 1966 and February 1967, Solzhenitsyn produced his second draft of the first six parts of *The Gulag Archipelago*, revising and retyping over fifteen hundred pages in two and a half months. Always a strenuous worker, he surpassed himself on this occasion, working sixteen hours a day in two shifts. He had read somewhere the theories of the German doctor Beckmann that sleep was more refreshing—and that you needed less of it—if you went to bed at sundown and rose with the sun the next morning. Going one better than the theory, he established a routine whereby he went to bed at eight o'clock each evening and rose again at two. From two to ten in the morning, he worked his first shift, took a break for an hour, then worked again from eleven in the morning to seven in the evening, and then had a further free hour before going to bed again. He also washed, cleaned, and cooked for himself, and as a result of this killing timetable, he had one or two bouts of illness.[16]

He did not omit to take his faithful transistor radio with him—the idea of being without news was unbearable, even in his rural solitude—and somehow found time to listen to the BBC, Radio Liberty, and other Western stations. Apart from his usual curiosity, he was listening for news of his interview with Komoto Sedze, which the latter had agreed to publish during the first week of the new year (not only had Solzhenitsyn gone over to the offensive with his new tactics of communicating directly with abroad, but from the very outset he also tried to control both what was published and when and where). He was puzzled and disappointed to hear nothing, and concluded that either Sedze had grown afraid or the interview had been suppressed by his editor. Solzhenitsyn's little "bomb" had failed to go off. (Only much later did he discover that he was wrong. The interview had been published in Japan, but no echo of it had reached the West. He had overestimated the closeness of the cultural ties between Japan and the Western world.)

Irked by this failure, but in other respects encouraged by the general success of his new policy of openness, Solzhenitsyn pondered his next move. As early as the preceding July he had hit upon the scheme of writing an open letter to about a hundred of his fellow writers. The idea had been suggested to him by a similar open letter written in the spring of 1966 by two priests attacking the behaviour of the officially approved Orthodox church.[17] To write and send such a letter would be a gamble, for the challenge would be

---

*While Solzhenitsyn was away, the authorities carried the campaign against him into his home town of Ryazan. The district ideological secretary, Alexander Kozhevnikov, denounced Solzhenitsyn at a local Party meeting for his "harmful influence on Soviet youth" and quoted passages from *The Feast of the Conquerors* under the mistaken impression that he was citing *The Tenderfoot and the Tart*. Natalia got to hear of it and personally delivered a letter of protest to an astonished Kozhevnikov.

far weightier and more overt than anything he had done before. On the other hand, lesser-known personalities were now writing such letters all the time. The Sinyavsky-Daniel trial had provoked a whole spate of them, not only of the mild variety that he had refused to sign but also more outspoken ones, such as the eloquent letter that the young intellectual Alexander Ginzburg had addressed to Premier Kosygin or the fiery denunciation of Mikhail Sholokhov by Lydia Chukovskaya after Sholokhov's disgraceful remarks at the Party Congress. If he were to do something similar, with his fame and reputation behind him, the impact would be enormous. None of these other authors of open letters had been arrested or charged with an offence, so the chances of getting away with it seemed good. However, he needed a pretext, and he decided that the forthcoming Congress of Soviet Writers would be the ideal moment. The congress had just been postponed until the spring of 1967, which would give him time to make the necessary preparations.

When he returned to Ryazan at the beginning of March, the government seemed to be becoming even more restrictive than before. In December it had ratified a new decree establishing two new paragraphs of the criminal code directed against "anti-Soviet" statements and unauthorized demonstrations. But the opposition was also stronger. A group of distinguished academicians and intellectuals, including Shostakovich, Kaverin, Mikhail Romm, Igor Tamm, and—a relatively new name on such appeals—Andrei Sakharov, had signed a letter of protest when the decree was first promulgated, and in January a group of young people had demonstrated in Pushkin Square against the new law, although several of them were arrested as a result. Also arrested were Yuri Galanskov, for publishing a new samizdat journal, *Phoenix 66;* Alexander Ginzburg, for compiling a "white book" on the Sinyavsky-Daniel trial and sending it to the West; and two of their friends, for helping them. In February, shortly before Solzhenitsyn's return, two of the young demonstrators had been tried and one of them, Victor Khaustov, sentenced to three years in a labour camp. Like Sinyavsky and Daniel before him, Khaustov had held firm under cross-examination and did not renounce his opinions or admit any guilt.[18]

Solzhenitsyn must have been aware of these developments, but the demonstrators and young poets were remote from those members of the literary establishment that he knew, and his own immediate concern was to secure a final decision on *Cancer Ward.* Part 2 had been almost completed before he went away, and with his usual love of mystification he had arranged for his not quite final draft to be forwarded to Tvardovsky a month before his return, thus leading Tvardovsky to think he was in Ryazan rather than somewhere quite different. Relishing this opportunity to exercise his old labour-camp skills of "throwing up a smoke-screen," and his role of the cunning outsider, he had accompanied it with an elaborately misleading letter informing Tvardovsky that the latter could be "the first reader of part 2" if he wished and assuring him that their inability to agree over part 1 had in no way affected his attitude to *Novy Mir.* "I continued to follow the activities and the policy of your magazine with complete approval." This was untrue, but Solzhenitsyn felt he needed to flatter Tvardovsky to lull his suspicions and make things easier for himself. In his account of the matter, he suggests that he was already anticipating rejection by Tvardovsky and was simply trying to keep things polite, but subsequent events indicate that he had not really given up hope. Part 1 had been rejected by both *Zvezda* and *Prostor*, and three other magazines had declined to publish extracts. *Novy Mir* was his last hope.[19]

Solzhenitsyn had ended part 1 of *Cancer Ward* on a relatively optimistic note. Kostoglotov's illness was under control, and he was full of hope, whereas the Party official Rusanov was still sick and viewed the future with misgiving. In part 2, however, the pendulum gradually swung the other way. Kostoglotov's cure was more or less completed, but at the cost of severe radiation sickness and unknown damage to his libido from the hormone treatment. His romances with Zoya and Dr Gangart both ended inconclusively. He had neither the appetite for physical sex with the one nor the psychological strength to sustain a marital relationship with the other. The novel ended enigmatically, with Kostoglotov paying a visit to the Tashkent zoo, where the animals reminded him of people he knew (a fierce, yellow-eyed tiger recalled Stalin, though Stalin's name was not mentioned explicitly). One animal was missing from its cage. A macaque monkey had been blinded when someone threw tobacco in its eyes, and the monkey's fate was compared, metaphorically, to Kostoglotov's. The "tobacco," in his case, had been his labour-camp sentence and his illness; and "no one" was responsible, just as the monkey's assailant had remained anonymous. He had survived, but the cure had almost killed him, and he remained a sort of cripple.

Rusanov, by contrast, was completely cured and had been discharged even before Kostoglotov—the car taking him away had narrowly missed running down Kostoglotov in the driveway, a suitably symbolic expression of their mutual antagonism.

In part 2, more attention was paid to the personalities and work of the doctors than had been possible in part 1, and some new figures were introduced. Dr Oreshchenkov, a retired general practitioner who obviously enjoyed the author's approval, was made to embody a surprising plea for the virtues of private medicine; and the humane surgeon, Lev Leonidovich, with a more than usual sympathy for the sufferings of his patients, turned out to have learned his compassion in the labour camps, like Kostoglotov. Together with Dontsova and Gangart, these "good" doctors were placed in opposition to their venal chief, Nizamutdin Bakhramovich, and his hangers-on, who were lazy, technically unqualified, and interested only in personal advancement. The ultimate fate of the good doctors was perhaps symbolized by Dontsova's discovery that, as a result of too much exposure to the X-rays (in the selfless pursuit of her duty), she herself had contracted cancer.

Two new patients in part 2 were also of interest for Solzhenitsyn's grand design. Maxim Chaly, an unscrupulous Communist "businessman" who had learned how to manipulate the system, was a naturally ally of Rusanov's, and a lugubrious librarian called Shulubin gravitated to Kostoglotov. Shulubin, an Old Bolshevik and a loyalist, was suffering from a severe and terminal form of rectal cancer, which endowed his conversations with Kostoglotov with a particular pathos and urgency. Once a true believer, he had become thoroughly disillusioned with the cruelty and corruption of Soviet society, but not with socialism. Into his mouth was placed an eloquent plea for "ethical socialism," based as much on the ideals of the Russian socialists of the late nineteenth century as on the theories of Lenin and the Bolsheviks. What Shulubin advocated was perhaps an early variant of "socialism with a human face," and so persuasive was his reasoning that for several years he was taken to represent Solzhenitsyn's own views on socialism. Only much later did Solzhenitsyn reveal that this was not so. He had passed that point long ago in his own development, but had found it interesting to make the best possible case for socialism through the medium of a sympathetic character. His own views, as embodied by Kostoglotov, Oreshchenkov, and the Kadmins, entailed a rejection of socialism, but they had of necessity to be camouflaged if he was to stand any hope of Soviet publication.

When he arrived at the *Novy Mir* offices on 16 March 1967 to discuss the novel once more, Solzhenitsyn found that although the entire editorial board had read part 2, the meeting with Tvardovsky was to be tête-à-tête. Tvardovsky was in a deep depression. In the course of the winter, the Central Committee had sacked his two most faithful deputies, Dementyev and Sachs, without even asking him. *Novy Mir* had been attacked in *Pravda* and was finding it harder and harder to get things past the censorship. And Tvardovsky himself was under a cloud. After failing to be re-elected to the Central Committee, he had been rejected by the Supreme Soviet and had been ostentatiously passed over for a medal that was awarded to colleagues who had toed the Party line—Sholokhov, Fedin, Leonov, and Tychina. As a result, he was more preoccupied than ever with the fate of his magazine. He had managed to maintain the quality of his editorial board by signing up the liberal writers Efim Dorosh and Chingiz Aitmatov, but his freedom of manoeuvre was greatly limited and he feared that there was little hope of publishing *Cancer Ward* during the coming year. He was desperately sorry about this, because he had found part 2 "three times better" than part 1 and had only the highest praise for it.[20]

One may assume that Solzhenitsyn was disappointed by this news. There was no one else in the Soviet Union likely to print it, and publication was still his goal. But his chances seemed even slimmer after the two men had become embroiled in a silly quarrel of the sort that had spoiled their two previous meetings. Tvardovsky was irritated by some news that had been passed to him the day before by Georgi Markov, a member of the Writers' Union secretariat, to the effect that *Cancer Ward* had been published in the West. If this was true, it made his task of securing Soviet publication impossibly difficult, and he was angry with Solzhenitsyn for manoeuvring behind his back. Solzhenitsyn tried to soothe him by explaining that it was only one chapter and that it had appeared in Czechoslovakia, which was hardly the

West. He explained that in response to a request, he had sent them a chapter that had also been offered to several Soviet magazines. He added that since then he had also given an interview to a Slovak journalist (simultaneously slipping in the information that a few months previously he had been interviewed by a Japanese correspondent as well).

It turned out that Tvardovsky knew about the Japanese article. He was due to leave for Italy the next day for a meeting of COMES and had been briefed on the latest developments before his departure—that was probably why he had been told about the *Cancer Ward* chapter as well. And this, too, was a bone of contention between them. Almost their first quarrel had been over Solzhenitsyn's refusal to go to Leningrad for the COMES symposium in 1963. In the winter of 1965, Tvardovsky had been in Paris for a meeting of COMES and had refused to comment on the confiscation of Solzhenitsyn's novel and archive, assuring Westerners that Solzhenitsyn was well and working normally, while Vigorelli, the secretary general of COMES, had been reported as saying that he had had "a friendly chat" with Solzhenitsyn and been told that the novel and archive had been returned to him. Solzhenitsyn now reminded Tvardovsky how much he hated Vigorelli for this statement and hinted that he expected better behaviour of Tvardovsky on his forthcoming visit to Rome.

As tempers rose, Tvardovsky exclaimed over *Cancer Ward*, "Even if publication depended entirely on me, I wouldn't publish it!" When Solzhenitsyn asked why, he replied, "Because of your non-acceptance of the Soviet regime. You refuse to forgive the Soviet regime anything. . . . You refuse to forget anything. You have much too good a memory!" Solzhenitsyn tried to explain that he was fully in favour of the Soviet regime in its original form—freely elected deputies to independent workers' soviets—but that a writer could not be false to his memory and describe things otherwise than as they were. Tvardovsky invoked the collective farms as a "sacred" aspect of Soviet society that Solzhenitsyn refused to respect, but Solzhenitsyn pointed out that collective farms were not mentioned in his novel and that the true objections to the book lay elsewhere. "What really casts its shadow over the whole book is the prison-camp system. No country can be healthy while it carries such a tumour inside it" (he was, incidentally, contradicting his statement at the Writers' Club the preceding November that there was no symbolism in it). He also reminded Tvardovsky of something that he himself had not known until he started receiving letters in response to *Ivan Denisovich*—that Khrushchev, who had presided over the run-down of Stalin's labour-camp empire, had also been responsible for establishing a new network of camps almost as oppressive as Stalin's, and that these camps were still in operation.*

Nevertheless, Tvardovsky insisted that Solzhenitsyn had gone too far.

---

*In one respect—that of the food provided in the camps—Khrushchev's were said to be worse than Stalin's (according to one story, Khrushchev, when presented with the budget for the camps, halved the amount for food because he was appalled by the cost). It was under Khrushchev's rule that three kinds of camp regiment were introduced, according to the rations provided and the restrictions imposed on the prisoners: normal, intensified, and severe.

"Say what you like, you must make some concessions to the Soviet regime. In the long run, you can't afford *not* to—you can't fight a howitzer with a pea-shooter." Until six months earlier, Solzhenitsyn would probably have agreed with him, but now he was not so sure. He felt that writers at last had a howitzer of their own—public opinion—and he was determined to exploit it to the hilt. *Cancer Ward*, he told Tvardovsky, was already circulating, and nothing could stop it now. If nobody would publish it in the Soviet Union, it no longer mattered to him. "My books can wait, Alexander Trifonovich. I shall die, and every word will be accepted, just as it is. Nobody will want to correct them!" Tvardovsky was irritated by these high-flown words and pooh-poohed them as self-infatuation. Solzhenitsyn, he felt, was striking attitudes. "There's nothing easier than telling yourself that you're the only brave one, and all the rest are poltroons, always ready to compromise."[21]

Tvardovsky did not know of Solzhenitsyn's resolve to write an open letter to the Writers' Congress, nor did he know that in addition to sending a chapter of *Cancer Ward* to Slovakia, Solzhenitsyn had that very week (perhaps even that day) handed a complete copy of Part 1 to the Slovak journalist who had interviewed him. This journalist, Pavel Ličko, who was also a translator from Russian, had written to Solzhenitsyn some months previously to inquire about his latest work. In response, Solzhenitsyn had sent him ten pages from *Cancer Ward*, and Ličko had arranged for their publication in the Bratislava *Pravda*. It was a world scoop, and Ličko was subsequently asked to visit the Soviet Union and try to get an interview with Solzhenitsyn. He was well equipped for the task, having served as an officer in the Soviet army during the war and speaking fluent Russian, but when he approached the Writers' Union in Moscow, he was repeatedly told that Solzhenitsyn was busy or ill, or even almost dying, and could not receive visitors. Ličko was also denied a permit to visit Ryazan. Having sent a telegram to Solzhenitsyn and received an invitation to visit him, however, he had managed to pull sufficient strings through his military contacts to obtain the permit and had travelled to Ryazan in the week preceding Solzhenitsyn's talk with Tvardovsky; there he had spent six hours in Solzhenitsyn's company at his new flat in Yablochkov Passage.[22]

Unfortunately, Ličko proved to be an erratic witness, who later embroidered his story of this unique visit to Solzhenitsyn's home, so that his subsequent accounts of what he saw there are not to be fully trusted. He did, however, take down a relatively ungarbled account of Solzhenitsyn's life and views (Solzhenitsyn later wrote to him listing some of the worst mistakes), and the interview, when it appeared in the Bratislava literary magazine *Kulturni Život* (Cultural Life) on 31 March 1967, attracted a great deal of attention, becoming a prime source of information about the reclusive author for some years to come. In it, Solzhenitsyn gave the fullest and frankest account of his life yet to appear anywhere, underlining his military record, pointing out that he had been sentenced not in a court of law but by the "extra-judicial decision" of a special tribunal, and listing his labour camps and his place of exile. Among his literary works he drew special attention to *Cancer Ward*, of which he said he had just completed part 2; *The First Circle*, which he said had taken him nine years, off and on, to complete; and his plays *The Tenderfoot and the Tart* and *Candle in the Wind*. Of the latter he commented, "I do not think I was successful with it. Nevertheless, both the Vakhtangov and Lenin Komsomol theatres wanted to stage it at one time." He also mentioned his miniature stories and said he was aware that they had appeared in translation in the English magazine *Encounter*, although he had had nothing to do with it.

As interesting as the details of his biography were the views he expressed on literature. He admitted that he was not well read in world literature. Owing to the circumstances of his life, he had had time only for Russian literature. Nevertheless, he had decided opinions on what to expect in the near future. "I have a subjective impression that literature in Western Europe, perhaps because it has not experienced any upheavals for the past several decades, may be rather shallow. The foundation of literature lies in the deep experiencing of social processes. Eastern Europe, in which I include Russia, has endured profound upheavals. For this reason I am very hopeful for its literary future." Russian literature in particular, he said, had always been characterized by its sensitivity to suffering, but now it was exposed to dangers of a different kind. "In our country you sometimes hear that writers should paint a pretty picture of what is going to happen tomorrow. This is false and justifies lies. Such literature is cosmetics." The duty of the writer was not exclusively towards society but also toward each individual within society, and their interests did not always coincide. The individual had many problems that the collective did not know how to solve.

Solzhenitsyn also elaborated on an idea that had caught his attention at the Writers' Club discussion of *Cancer Ward*. Yuri Karyakin had been one of those who expressed reservations about the portrayal of Rusanov, and had quoted Camus's words that art of the higher kind should not play the part of prosecutor. Solzhenitsyn had replied at the time that this raised the issue of "the correlation between the present time and eternity" in a work of art, and now he took up the idea once more.

> The writer needs to maintain a balance between the two categories of the present and eternity. If his work is so topical that he loses his view of things *sub specie aeternitatis*, then his work will quickly die. And conversely, should he devote too much of his attention to eternity and neglect actuality, his work loses its colour, force, and "air." The writer stands at all times between this Scylla and Charybdis and should forget neither the one nor the other.

Two further points of note emerged from the Ličko interview. One was that Solzhenitsyn did not regard it as unusual or even necessarily undesirable for society to persecute its writers. "There have been many cases in which society treated a writer unjustly and he fulfilled his vocation nevertheless.

The writer must be prepared for adversity. This is an occupational hazard. The writer's lot will never be easy."

Secondly, Solzhenitsyn voiced his thoughts on his preferred method of composition in his novels. The genre he regarded as most interesting, he said, was the "polyphonic novel" (a term first coined to describe the novels of Dostoyevsky). Solzhenitsyn's definition of the polyphonic novel seemed to differ a little from the accepted one. In his view, the touchstone of the polyphonic novel was that it had no one hero. "The way I interpret polyphony, each character, as soon as the plot touches him, becomes the main hero. That way, the author is responsible for, say, thirty-five heroes and doesn't give preference to any one of them." He had written two books in this way, he said, and was planning to write a third.[23]

It was a few days after this interview that Solzhenitsyn had given Ličko a copy of part 1 of *Cancer Ward*. His idea seems to have been to get the novel published in a "friendly" East European country if publication was impossible in the Soviet Union, and Czechoslovakia was particularly suitable just then, in view of the liberalization that was taking place in the months preceding the "Prague spring." Bratislava was also a good choice. It was less in the limelight than Prague, so that plans for publication there would be less likely to attract attention.* At a later date Ličko was to claim that Solzhenitsyn had asked him to seek publication in England or Japan as well, "since he believed that England and Japan had the most deep-rooted cultures in the world."[24] In view of certain conflicts in Ličko's evidence, this story was disbelieved by most of those who heard it; but in the light of Solzhenitsyn's known ideas and plans at this time, it is not entirely implausible. Later, under pressure at home, Solzhenitsyn denied that he had "authorized" anyone to publish *Cancer Ward*, but it is quite possible that he had a contingency plan whereby Ličko was to act if anything untoward should happen. He was still apprehensive about the possible results of his forthcoming open letter, and he anticipated all kinds of unpleasantnesses, up to and including arrest. It is equally plausible that Ličko confused what Solzhenitsyn was saying to him, but unlikely that he imagined the whole idea of publication in the West.

The theory that Solzhenitsyn may have envisaged Western publication of *Cancer Ward* is given credence by a similar move that he made a month later, when he gave explicit instructions for *The First Circle* to be published in the West. The person he entrusted with this mission was Olga Carlisle, an American journalist of Russian descent and the daughter of the man who had carried out the microfilms of *The First Circle*, Vadim Andreyev. Carlisle was in Moscow to collect material for an anthology of Soviet poetry that she was preparing. Although he had never met her before, Solzhenitsyn was influenced in her favour by the kind of subjective "signs" that appealed to his intuition: her kinship with Vadim Andreyev (and through him with her grandfather, Leonid Andreyev), and the fact that her maternal grandfather had been the Socialist Revolutionary politician Victor Chernov. Her pedi-

---

* The Slovak edition of *Cancer Ward* was actually printed and bound and lying in the warehouse when the Warsaw Pact forces invaded Czechoslovakia, but it never went on sale to the public.

gree on both sides, from Solzhenitsyn's point of view, was impeccable. Furthermore, she was a good friend of Kornei Chukovsky (who had put Solzhenitsyn in touch with her) and, to cap it all, her photograph had stood on the desk where he worked in Chukovsky's dacha. He had studied it many times, without ever thinking that he would one day meet this attractive woman and call on her for help. Chukovsky's information that she was in Moscow must have struck him as a wonderful coincidence or even an "act of God," which is how he described to her Ličko's recent visit to Ryazan. They were walking back to her hotel from the flat where they had met (for the second time, that evening), and Solzhenitsyn described to her the details of his difficult situation and his plans for dealing with it. The KGB was trying to throttle him into silence, he said, but he had outflanked it by giving part 1 of *Cancer Ward* to Ličko, and now he wanted her to see that *The First Circle* appeared in the West, first in America and then in other countries.

"It is a big book—my life," he told her, adding that it was his most important work, the one that mattered and would hit the Soviet leadership the hardest. He also told her he wanted it to "stun public opinion throughout the world. Let the true nature of these scoundrels be known." At the same time, absolute secrecy would have to be preserved and no mention made of his participation in this decision. "You can imagine what would happen to me if you were found out." He also told her of his plan to send an open letter to the forthcoming Writers' Congress in May and asked her to do what she could, as a journalist, to get it publicized in the West. Carlisle seems to have accepted the assignment eagerly. Flying to Western Europe, she contacted her father in Paris and took the microfilms from him. By the end of April 1967 they were in America.[25]

Solzhenitsyn's most important novel was now launched on the road to publication in the West. Part 1 of his second novel was half-way there, while *The Gulag Archipelago*, his ultimate exposure, was almost complete and in the safe-keeping of trusted friends. The decks were therefore cleared for Solzhenitsyn's letter to the congress. The first draft had been finished the preceding summer, when Solzhenitsyn first thought of the idea, but since then had lain untouched. On his visit to Moscow, however, Solzhenitsyn took the opportunity to show this draft to Chukovsky, Kaverin, Kopelev, and one or two others, and to ask their advice. On 24 March he returned to Ryazan and in three days wrote out a completely revised text. The principal change he introduced was to make the letter less personal and more general. Originally, it had resembled some of his earlier (private) letters to the authorities, concentrating on the confiscation of his novel and archive and listing his personal grievances. Now it began with a resounding denunciation of the Soviet system of censorship, went on to rehearse the injustices perpetrated against Soviet writers over the preceding forty years, and only then referred to the persecution and harassment inflicted on himself. From a personal, if eloquent, plea for justice for one man, it had turned into a thunderous denunciation of the entire conduct of the literary establishment, and was no longer a petition but a demand for justice for all. According to Reshetovskaya, Solzhenitsyn's favourite listening during the days when he was composing the letter was Beethoven, and much of it was written with Beethoven's Ninth Symphony playing in the background.[26]

When the letter was finished, Solzhenitsyn found himself at something of a loose end and tried to catch up on correspondence, writing a letter to Shalamov and thanking Vladimir Soloukhin for his *Letters from a Russian Museum* ("How Russian it is, how characteristic, the collection of names and objects, and how very timely!").* He put together a critical article on Griboyedov from notes written earlier, and even found time to read some stories mailed him by beginning writers and to send them his comments. But somehow he could not settle, until the thought crossed his mind that he might not survive the release of his open letter unscathed and that it would be a good idea to write a sort of valedictory literary testament (for which he also had notes ready). In a month of sustained elation, from 7 April to 7 May, he wrote over 150 pages of an *apologia pro vita sua*, describing and analyzing his thoughts and actions from the moment he had decided to offer *Ivan Denisovich* for publication up to and including his most recent quarrel with Tvardovsky.[27] His account was selective, polemical, and hugely entertaining, a step-by-step justification of his past behaviour and a rollicking denunciation of his enemies. In these pages he could let his hair down and give vent to his deepest feelings, but he also had a didactic intent: to explain to himself and others how it was that he had reached the end of his tether and why he had decided to launch his open letter. It was a means of coming to terms with himself in the lull before the impending storm and was eventually to form the basis of the first four chapters of his "literary memoir," *The Oak and the Calf*.

There remained only the task of sending his open letter to the intended recipients. With the help of Natalia and several assistants in Moscow, he prepared 250 typed copies of the letter, each signed with his own hand, and in the last five days before the congress had them posted from different districts in Moscow (never more than two in the same box) to outwit the postal censorship. The recipients were chosen with meticulous care and included all the people whom Solzhenitsyn regarded as honest and genuine writers, leading members of the Writers' Union and other public figures, a sprinkling of *apparatchiks* to confuse the KGB, and writers representing each of the non-Russian republics. Curiously enough, Solzhenitsyn placed great hopes in the non-Russians (but was disenchanted by their reactions when the congress took place).[28]

This careful planning was the hallmark of Solzhenitsyn's style of operations, and it duly bore fruit. The vast majority of the letters reached their destination, and well before the opening day of the congress, on 18 May 1967, the text was being circulated in samizdat, so that there was hardly a congress delegate who didn't know about it.

---

*Soloukhin's book, published in 1966, was about icons and icon collecting, and contained, among other things, an impassioned plea for the preservation of Russian churches and their contents.

33

LETTER TO THE
WRITERS' CONGRESS

T HE FOURTH ALL-UNION Congress of Soviet Writers was intended to be
a solemn affair to celebrate the fiftieth anniversary of Soviet power,
which was one of the reasons why it had been held over from the preceding
year. According to Zhores Medvedev, preparations for the congress were
exceptionally thorough. Both the Writers' Union and the ideological department of the Central Committee were determined to ensure a facade of complete unanimity, to which end the lists of writers who wished to speak were
carefully scrutinized and the texts of all the speeches approved in advance.
A special commission was set up to accomplish this task, and speakers were
warned that they must on no account depart from their prepared statements.
It was feared that some delegates might try to raise the subject of Sinyavsky
and Daniel, whose imprisonment was still a rallying point for opposition to
the Party line. And to make doubly sure that there would be no untoward
incidents, no guests were invited from the other creative unions (artists, composers, musicians, and so on). As a result, the enormous Main Hall of the
Kremlin Palace of Congresses was four-fifths empty when the congress
opened.[1]

It was clear that the organizers had done their job well. Observers found
it the dullest congress in the entire history of the Writers' Union. Once
Demichev had demanded absolute loyalty to the doctrine of socialist realism
in his opening address, there was nothing further to discuss, and the general
tone was summed up towards the end of the congress by a complacently
ironical Sholokhov: "Judging by the past few days, everything is going as it
should with good people: quietly, peacefully, calmly, with no sharp speeches
and no unnecessary outbursts—in other words, everything in the garden is

lovely, so that everyone breathes freely and smiles benevolently, and the atmosphere in the auditorium is so tranquil that some in the audience have been dozing off."[2]

Whether Sholokhov's irony was meant to be pointed is not clear. He certainly was no friend of Solzhenitsyn, but he could hardly have been unaware that behind the scenes the atmosphere was anything but tranquil. Just about every delegate present was aware of Solzhenitsyn's letter, and by the second or third day all of them had read it. It was the main topic of conversation in the intervals between the sessions, at mealtimes and in the corridors of the congress hall, completely dominating all other concerns. Never had the contrast been greater between the unruffled, dead surface of Soviet literary life and the seething passions underneath. For the first time since the early thirties, a writer was trying to make a connection between the real problems facing Soviet literature and the empty formalities of its ceremonial.

Solzhenitsyn had divided his letter into three parts. In the first he confronted head-on a subject that had not been tackled since the late twenties: the censorship. Nowhere in the Soviet constitution, he wrote, was there any provision for a censorship board. Its very existence was illegal, which was presumably why it was never publicly mentioned. Yet it gave arbitrary power over writers to individuals who hadn't the faintest idea of literary merit. "A survival of the Middle Ages, censorship has managed, Methuselah-like, to drag out its existence almost to the twenty-first century. Perishable, it attempts to arrogate to itself the prerogative of imperishable time, of separating good books from bad." Soviet writers, continued Solzhenitsyn, were not supposed to express their own judgements on man and society, and when they did, their works were mutilated beyond recognition. He then listed some of the specific absurdities of the censorship and the writers who had suffered from it, ranging from Dostoyevsky to Pasternak. Curiously enough, he also struck a nationalistic note, pointing out that "from the national point of view" the censorship was short-sighted and foolish.

> Our literature has lost the leading position it occupied at the end of the last century and the beginning of this one. . . . To the entire world the literary life of our country now appears immeasurably more dull, trivial, and inferior than it really is. . . . Not only does our country lose by this—in world opinion—but world literature is poorer for it too. If the world had unrestricted access to all the fruits of our literature, if it were enriched by our spiritual experience, the whole artistic evolution of the world would move in a different way, acquiring a new stability and rising, indeed, to new heights.[3]

Solzhenitsyn formally proposed "the abolition of all censorship" of imaginative literature and the granting of independence to publishers.

In the second part of his letter, he dealt with the role of the Writers' Union. The union not only had failed to defend a long list of persecuted Soviet writers but had itself often led the persecution. There was no need for this tradition to be maintained, he wrote, and he proposed that union guarantees to defend its members should henceforth be clearly formulated "so that past illegalities will not be repeated."

Thirdly and lastly, Solzhenitsyn called on the union to consider his own case and defend him against the persecutions to which he had been subjected. He repeated the complaints (and more) he had voiced in his lecture at the Lazarev Institute: about the confiscation of his works, their restricted circulation among Party loyalists, the campaign of slander against him conducted at Party meetings, the blocking of *Cancer Ward*, the refusal to perform or publish his plays and screenplay, the refusal to reprint any of his published works in a collected edition,* and the cancelling of his public lectures. "Faced with these flagrant infringements of my copyright and 'other' rights, will the Fourth Congress defend me or will it not? It seems to me that the choice is not without importance for the literary future of some of the delegates themselves." Solzhenitsyn concluded with a ringing declaration that he would fulfil his duty as a writer "in all circumstances—from the grave even more successfully and incontrovertibly than in my lifetime."

In this, his first polemical public statement written for a large audience, Solzhenitsyn had typically gone to the heart of the matter in naming censorship as the chief enemy of Russian literature and in divining that it was the one subject the congress organizers would want to avoid. His letter went well beyond his earlier statements and set a pattern for many public utterances to come, mixing concern for national pride and the national interest with a more specialized care for the fate of the national literature and alarm over the treatment of his own works, linking them firmly as different facets of the same, central problem. In other words, the central problem of Russian literature and the problem of Solzhenitsyn were one and the same thing.

After seeing to the delivery of the copies of his letter, Solzhenitsyn had stayed on in Moscow to find out what the response would be, half hoping that he would be invited to the congress to defend and discuss it. On 19 May, he had lunch with Kapitsa, who thoroughly approved the contents of Solzhenitsyn's letter and later commented, "The technological revolution will do far more for general prosperity than any socialist revolution."[4] For the next two days Solzhenitsyn stayed in Peredelkino, discussing possible strategy with Chukovsky and others, and on the day of the congress opening gave a reading at a research institute in the Moscow suburb of Bogorodskoye. The hall was half empty, and the reading (of the Spiridon chapters from *The First Circle*) did not go well. Solzhenitsyn then read some of his miniature stories and his letter to the Congress. It was the only public reading of the letter in Moscow (Solzhenitsyn stood up to read it after having sat to read from his works) and had an immediate impact on his otherwise lukewarm audience, who greeted it with genuine applause.

---

* Solzhenitsyn was all the more disturbed by the absence of such a collected edition in the Soviet Union because he had just learned of the publication of one by Possev in West Germany (indeed a friend had recently brought him a copy from there).

But it was not the congress platform, and that evening, after dinner with the academician Tamm and a group of his colleagues, Solzhenitsyn heard from his friend Boris Mozhayev that there had been no mention of the letter in the public sessions of the congress, although most of the delegates had talked of nothing else in the corridors outside. The next day, the Solzhenitsyns lunched with Shostakovich and his young wife, Irina Supinskaya, who fetched them in her car and took them to Shostakovich's luxurious dacha in Zhukovka. Shostakovich, too, seemed to approve of Solzhenitsyn's letter, called him a "truth-seeker," and presented him with a signed record.[5]*

Meanwhile, the congress continued as the authorities had planned, and only one person present found the boldness to challenge the leadership. A writer named Vera Ketlinskaya got up and complained that although it was admissible to criticize or dislike this or that author, it was intolerable simply to ignore someone and pretend that he did not exist, "as our speakers have done with regard to the talented author Solzhenitsyn." She was evidently greeted with loud applause (the stenographic record has a suspicious blank space where applause would normally be recorded),† but that was all, and there was no mention of Solzhenitsyn's letter.[6] Medvedev tells the story of a popular poet who, after downing several drinks at a party, announced his intention of going up to the platform the following day and reading the letter aloud to the delegates. He even extracted a solemn promise from another writer present, who was due to chair one of the following day's sessions, to call on him at the appropriate moment. But when the next day's sessions began, the prospective chairman was absent, and his replacement read out an apology, saying that the other writer had been unexpectedly taken ill. The poet was unable to take the initiative himself, and thus the contents of the letter remained excluded from the debate.

The ease with which this was accomplished may be ascribed to the careful way in which the delegates to the congress had been picked beforehand. Hardly anyone of independent views attended, a circumstance that was all the easier to arrange because of the natural distaste of most writers of consequence for being marshalled and manipulated like puppets. But there was plenty of support in the form of unofficial letters and telegrams to the congress. The most significant, urging an open discussion of Solzhenitsyn's letter, had eighty-three signatures on it, including those of just about every writer, critic, and editor of consequence in literary Moscow (though with the exception of Tvardovsky, Lakshin, and the upper echelons of *Novy Mir*).[7] A number of writers wrote individual letters, of which the most outspoken came from the young prose writer Georgi Vladimov, who went even further

---

* According to Shostakovich's memoirs *(Testimony)*, as edited by Solomon Volkov, Shostakovich and Solzhenitsyn fell out two years later, after Solzhenitsyn had criticized Shostakovich's Fourteenth Symphony (1969) for its undue pessimism.

† In the unpublished chapters of her memoirs, Natalia Reshetovskaya confirms that there was applause. She reports Solzhenitsyn as having been told that Tvardovsky was among those who applauded.

than Solzhenitsyn in his denunciation of the iniquities of the censorship and the pusillanimity of the union leaders.

Solzhenitsyn was gratified and genuinely surprised by the success of his letter. In his memoir he confesses, "I had written and disseminated my letter like a man voluntarily mounting the scaffold," fully expecting dire consequences from his effrontery.[8] That was why he had gone to so much trouble to put his affairs in order and send his manuscripts safely to the West before acting. His words about accepting death and speaking from beyond the grave, while rhetorical, undoubtedly reflected a dread of the reprisals that he anticipated from the government side. Yet nothing happened and nothing was said, not even after the letter had appeared in the West and was broadcast back again. Solzhenitsyn does not say so in his account of the matter, but this, too, he had arranged by handing a copy to Efim Etkind on the eve of the latter's departure for a literary conference in Vienna. Etkind passed it to a Swedish editor of his acquaintance and asked him to see that it appeared in all the major Western newspapers, and this duly happened on 31 May, shortly after the congress ended.[9] A photographer who visited Solzhenitsyn at Chukovsky's dacha that week found him pacing the garden with his transistor radio in his hand,* waiting impatiently to discover whether the BBC had obtained the text of his letter and would broadcast it back.[10]

He did not realize how successful he had been, however, until he attended a public meeting organized by the Writers' Union on 31 May 1967 to celebrate Paustovsky's seventy-fifth birthday. Paustovsky had long been an idol of the liberals, and even Solzhenitsyn shared the general respect for him, despite having criticized his autobiography in the past. The meeting had been organized as a kind of liberal counterblast to the Writers' Congress, which few of them had attended, and was full to overflowing (over 900 writers were estimated to be present). Kaverin, as chairman, made a long speech in praise of Paustovsky's career, in the course of which he defined three main strands in Russian literature: the romantic (of which Paustovsky was the best living exemplar); the "dramatical grotesque," typified by the late Bulgakov; and philosophical realism, whose leading exponent at that time was Solzhenitsyn.[11]

At some point during the meeting, Kaverin went up to Solzhenitsyn and complimented him on his tactics. "What a brilliant move that letter of yours was!" And Solzhenitsyn was even more surprised to learn that Tvardovsky approved of his letter, although Tvardovsky had not signed the collective letter of support.[12] His information about Tvardovsky's attitude came at second hand, and he did not know that Tvardovsky had done more than approve or write in support, that he had been active behind the scenes. The secretariat of the Writers' Union had called a confidential meeting immediately after the congress to discuss how to respond to Solzhenitsyn's letter. They had regarded the letter as a "blow below the belt" and wanted to reply

* According to Natalia Reshetovskaya, the radio was a gift from the Japanese correspondent Komoto Sedze.

in kind, but the degree of support for Solzhenitsyn within the Writers' Union and the hullabaloo created abroad by the publication of the letter had caused them to have second thoughts, and Tvardovsky (supported, it seems, by Simonov and Polevoi) had vigorously persuaded them to take a different line. They should publish a statement, he said, confirming that there was no blemish on Solzhenitsyn's war record, admitting that his letter contained things that deserved attention, but sternly admonishing him for the "sensational" manner in which he had behaved. Having grudgingly accepted this suggestion, the secretariat asked Tvardovsky to invite Solzhenitsyn to their offices to confirm that this would satisfy him before they submitted their proposed statement to the Central Committee for final approval (one of the reasons they always moved so slowly and ponderously was that everything had to be approved by the Central Committee's ideological section before any action could be taken). Tvardovsky experienced his usual difficulty in tracking the elusive author down but finally reached him on 8 June 1968, just before Solzhenitsyn was to leave for Rozhdestvo. Over the telephone, he implored him to drop everything and come at once to *Novy Mir*, but Solzhenitsyn was suspicious. He thought that Tvardovsky wanted to persuade him to make a retraction. If not, and if Tvardovsky was ready to publish something, he would let him wait until after the weekend. The BBC had announced three readings of his letter during the next few days, and he preferred to wait for these to make his position stronger.[13]*

He therefore arranged to see Tvardovsky on 12 June, and only then did he learn about the union's climb-down and the reasons for Tvardovsky's sense of urgency. Tvardovsky rushed him off at once to the union's offices (situated in the house that Tolstoy used as his model for the Rostovs' residence in *War and Peace*) to meet Voronkov and three other members of the secretariat, including the loyalist Georgi Markov. The meeting lasted for a couple of hours and was friendly. Markov explained hypocritically that Solzhenitsyn's letter couldn't be discussed at the Writers' Congress, because "the agenda was too tight," but that now they were ready to consider it and hoped that Solzhenitsyn would help them "find a way out" of the difficult situation they were in (meaning the clamour from abroad for an explanation of their attitude). Solzhenitsyn, as usual, had come well equipped, bringing copies of his earlier letters to Brezhnev and Demichev, as well as of his letter to the congress, and he informed them of its prehistory, starting with the confiscation of his archive and ending with his dismay at receiving no answer to his complaints. That was why, as a last resort, he had resolved to address the congress (though he fibbed that his reason for not sending the letter when it was first composed was his desire for moderation).

Markov and company feigned sympathy ("Of course Comrade Brezhnev

---

*It appears that, between listening to the BBC broadcasts, Solzhenitsyn spent much of that weekend learning how to use a scythe. Natalia Reshetovskaya reports that when she arrived in Rozhdestvo on 14 June, Solzhenitsyn had scythed the entire plot—the first time she had known him to do such a thing.

never got to see your letter") but were clearly disturbed by the fact that Solzhenitsyn had produced his congress letter in so many copies and that it had got abroad so quickly. Had it been his intention to appeal to the Soviet Union's "enemies" over the head of the union? Not at all, replied Solzhenitsyn innocently. He had prepared sufficient copies to reach all the delegates to the congress, because in the past his letters in single copies had been pigeon-holed and never answered. As for the circulation of the letter abroad, he had had nothing to do with it. It had come about because of the union's delay in answering him. They should have called him to the platform, allowed him to read it into the record, and then discussed it.

Solzhenitsyn's logic was unassailable. The secretariat members were almost certain that Solzhenitsyn had deliberately moved to outflank and put pressure on them, but they were too dim-witted, and too hampered by their inability to call a spade a spade, to be able to counter his arguments.

The conversation then moved to *Cancer Ward*. Solzhenitsyn was wrong, said Markov, to say that *Novy Mir* had refused to publish his novel, and he appealed to Tvardovsky to confirm this fact. Tvardovsky agreed, dismissing the argument he had had with Solzhenitsyn over part 2 as "just talk." The secretariat members were worried about the circulation of *Cancer Ward* (and, to a lesser extent, *The First Circle*) in samizdat and about rumours that they might even be abroad. Solzhenitsyn simply replied that he was not to blame, but Tvardovsky seized on their anxieties to secure an advantage. "That's just why I say that *Cancer Ward* must be published immediately. That will put a stop to all the hullabaloo in the West and prevent its publication there. We must put excerpts in the *Literaturnaya Gazeta* two days from now, with a note that the story will be published in full."

Solzhenitsyn was astonished to hear them agree, and then to be actually thanked for coming and explaining. In Tvardovsky's limousine on the way back to *Novy Mir*, Tvardovsky planned which chapter to offer to the *Literaturnaya Gazeta*, while Solzhenitsyn savoured the fruits of victory. "That day I experienced for the first time in my life . . . what it feels like to make a successful show of strength. And how well they understand that language . . . . that and no other, from the day they are born."[14]

Unfortunately, the triumph was short-lived. No statement from the Writers' Union appeared in the *Literaturnaya Gazeta*, nor did an extract from *Cancer Ward*. Solzhenitsyn heard that it had been vetoed by the cultural department of the Central Committee at the suggestion of Demichev.* Demichev was feeling particularly hostile towards Solzhenitsyn since some-

---

* Natalia Reshetovskaya, on the other hand, has suggested that Solzhenitsyn himself may have been partly to blame by delaying his meeting with the secretariat for four days. An earlier meeting would have given the *Literaturnaya Gazeta* five or six days in which to set a chapter from *Cancer Ward* and include it in the relevant issue, whereas the two days that were left were too short a time and produced the delay that gave Demichev his chance. She adds the interesting observation that Solzhenitsyn's original account of the meeting was much more positive than the one he eventually published, and that the satirical tone and sceptical comments were added only in November, when the prospects for publishing *Cancer Ward* were already much worse.

one in the KGB had sent him a tape of Solzhenitsyn describing their meeting to friends and mimicking Demichev in the process (on such minutiae does Soviet literature depend). As a delaying tactic, Demichev suggested that all forty-two secretaries of the Writers' Union should read not only both volumes of *Cancer Ward* but also *The First Circle* and *Feast of the Conquerors* before coming to a decision, which would take some time. Before sending off the manuscript of *Cancer Ward*, Tvardovsky asked Solzhenitsyn to make one or two cuts to render it less provocative, to which Solzhenitsyn agreed.[15]

By now Solzhenitsyn was well advanced in his preparations for writing the first in his series of planned novels on the period of the First World War and the Revolution. Volume 1, now to be called *August 1914*, would deal primarily with General Samsonov's campaign against the Germans on the eastern front, and especially the Battle of Tannenberg, marking Russia's first big defeat in the war. He still had the material he had collected when a student in Rostov, but he needed some local colour and extra background information. Accordingly, he and Natalia decided to take a trip that summer to East Prussia and Lithuania, accompanied by Efim and Ekaterina Etkind, to inspect some of the places in which the novel's action occurred.

Just before they left, Solzhenitsyn was involved in a collision in his Moskvich and was obliged to get the body repaired (it had been rammed and stove in from behind after he braked to avoid a pedestrian). Getting a repair done quickly through the official repair shops in the Soviet Union is almost impossible, but Solzhenitsyn found an enterprising mechanic who was a specialist in working on the side, and became quite fascinated by this man's cheerful ingenuity in cheating his bosses. Solzhenitsyn had recently accepted a commission from Mosfilm to write a screenplay that he had intended to set in a school, but he now resolved to make the mechanic his hero and, during the first week of July, jotted down preliminary notes for what was to become his screenplay of *The Parasite*.[16]

Almost the first use Solzhenitsyn made of the car after its repair was to take down an unorthodox interview. He was visited by a former labour-camp prisoner called Leonid Samutin, who before his arrest had fought with Vlasov's forces on the German side. Solzhenitsyn at once interviewed him for *The Gulag Archipelago*, but not trusting the walls indoors, he took Samutin into the garden and sat him in the Moskvich to ask him some questions.[17]

The Solzhenitsyns and the Etkinds finally set off in the second week of July. Their first goal was a village near Smolensk, where Solzhenitsyn sought out Tvardovsky's brother, Konstantin Tvardovsky, who, unlike the famous editor, had stayed on the land and worked for the village's collective farm. From there they drove north-east into what had once been East Prussia. Apart from inspecting the terrain over which Samsonov's army had fought, Solzhenitsyn wanted to revisit the places where he himself had fought with his artillery battery, and he was filled with nostalgia when they arrived. As usual they camped along the way, spending cheerful evenings around the campfire, during which Solzhenitsyn recited the whole of *Prussian Nights* to the Etkinds from memory.

He was not able to follow his routes all the way—some of the places where Samsonov had fought and where he himself had been now belonged to Poland. But he was able to soak up the physical appearance and atmosphere of these forests and marshes, to visit the solid and once-prosperous Prussian villages that had formerly so impressed him, and to tour old Königsberg (now Kaliningrad), with its memorial to Kant and its air of bourgeois stability. Driving into Lithuania, the Solzhenitsyns parted from the Etkinds and continued on to Latvia to stay for a while with Olga Zvedra, the widow of the noted revolutionary leader Ivan Karpunich. Solzhenitsyn planned to write about Karpunich and Olga in his historical novel and had come to question Olga and study her papers.[18]

It would appear that during the course of the summer of 1967 Solzhenitsyn came close to being reconciled with his old school friend Kirill Simonyan. As long as nine years ago, he and Natalia had sent greetings to Kirill on the occasion of the latter's fortieth birthday, but Kirill had not replied (he later claimed not to have received anything, owing to his change of flats). Now it was Kirill who initiated the first move. According to the sketchy account he has given of it in his pamphlet about Solzhenitsyn, Kirill and his sister Nadezhda had been provoked by the controversy surrounding Solzhenitsyn's letter to the Writers' Congress to write to him and suggest a reunion. The first response apparently came from Natalia, who asked Kirill to write Solzhenitsyn a more personal letter, and Kirill wrote again. It seems that either then or in a later letter Kirill must have mentioned his suspicions about Solzhenitsyn's role in his interrogation of 1952 and referred to the fact that he had been shown the record of Solzhenitsyn's own interrogation, for in a reply dated 26 June 1967 Solzhenitsyn reproached Kirill for having been duped by the KGB into believing that Solzhenitsyn's statements of 1945 had been made in 1952. He also regretted that Kirill was opening old wounds at such a time.

According to a former friend of Kirill's, Kirill was alarmed by the very outspokenness with which Solzhenitsyn referred to such sensitive matters and by the fact that he had sent his letter through the open post—Kirill was convinced that his own letters were subject to being opened by the KGB and felt that the same might also be true of Solzhenitsyn's. He therefore wrote a carefully worded letter in which he accused Solzhenitsyn of taking a one-sided view of life. "Objectively speaking, you have become the standard-bearer of Fascist reactionaries in the West. . . . Lenin, whom I'm convinced you love and honour just as much as you used to, yes, and old Marx and Engels too, would have condemned you in the severest fashion. Think about it!" These sentiments did more or less reflect Kirill's sentiments at the time, but apparently he stressed them in case his letter should fall into the hands of the KGB.

It appears that Solzhenitsyn did not take offence, for further correspondence led the two men to arrange a meeting, but when Solzhenitsyn turned up at Kirill's flat, there was no reply to the bell. After waiting in the lobby for about an hour, Solzhenitsyn scribbled a note and returned to slip it through the door. When he opened the flap of the letterbox, he caught sight of Kirill's slippered feet standing stock still in the hallway: Kirill was evidently too frightened to open the door. Solzhenitsyn lowered the flap and left, and the two friends never met, either then or later.[19]

Towards the end of the summer, Solzhenitsyn retired to Rozhdestvo and plunged into work on the first volume of his historical epic. Before disappearing, however, he sent word to Olga Carlisle to proceed at full speed with the preparation of the American translation of *The First Circle* and to aim for publication in the winter of 1968, in approximately eighteen months' time. A few weeks later, Carlisle came to Moscow to secure Solzhenitsyn's approval for the rather cumbersome arrangements she had made. In addition to retaining a translator (Thomas Whitney, a friend), she and her husband, Henry Carlisle, proposed to act as editors: her husband would also be the book's literary agent for foreign sales, another friend would act as a lawyer to draw up the necessary agreements with Harper & Row—who would prepare to publish in strictest secrecy—and another friend, Harrison Salisbury (the Soviet-affairs specialist of the *New York Times*), would guarantee to the publisher the book's quality. Whether it was made clear that all this would cost large sums of money in editorial, agency, and legal fees and in incidental expenses is not known (the translator, having inherited a small legacy, had agreed to work for nothing). In her book on the subject, Olga Carlisle reports Solzhenitsyn as saying that money was no object. "Money must be spent freely, nothing must be spared. There must be no thought to money."[20] In view of the later controversy that erupted between them, it may be doubted that Solzhenitsyn, with his seven-year-old boots and habit of feeding himself out of tins, had the slightest idea what fabulous sums could be spent in America on these subsidiary literary services.

Meanwhile, there was no movement on *Cancer Ward*. Towards the end of August, Solzhenitsyn had suggested to Tvardovsky that they sign a contract for the novel. That would formalize the situation and might provide some momentum towards publication. But Tvardovsky refused, saying he could not do so without permission. Not long afterwards Solzhenitsyn heard a rumour that *Cancer Ward* was to be published in Italy. The rumour proved false, but it provoked Solzhenitsyn into writing a letter to the Writers' Union secretariat pressing them to come to a decision on *Cancer Ward*. It was four months, he wrote, since over a hundred writers had supported his letter to the Writers' Congress, and three months since four members of the secretariat had agreed to publish a statement refuting the slanders about him and to "look into" the question of publishing his novel. In that time new slanders had been spread by Party activists (to the effect that he had defected to Egypt or England) and he had heard that *A Day in the Life of Ivan Denisovich* was being secretly removed from Soviet libraries. *Novy Mir* was ready to publish *Cancer Ward* but was awaiting permission to do so.

Does the secretariat believe that my story will silently disappear as a result of these endless delays, that it will cease to exist, so that the secretariat will not have to vote on whether to include it in, or exclude it from, the literature of this country? . . . At the 12 June meeting I warned the secretariat that we must make haste to publish the story if we wished to see it appear first in Russian, that under the circumstances we could not prevent its unauthorized appearance in the West.

And he increased the pressure by blaming the union in advance.

After the senseless delay of many months, the time has come to state that if it does happen, it will clearly be the fault (or perhaps the secret wish?) of the secretariat. . . . I insist that my story be published without delay![21]

Instead of treating this as an open letter, Solzhenitsyn made forty-two copies and sent them to the forty-two secretaries who were supposed to be reading his novel, plus one to the secretariat office, and he did not show it to anyone. The response came quicker than he had anticipated. On 18 September 1967 Tvardovsky summoned him to *Novy Mir* and told him that three days previously the secretariat had held a meeting to consider a reply and that it would meet on 22 September, with Solzhenitsyn present, to discuss the whole question again. At the secretariat meeting, Tvardovsky had held out for publication of *Cancer Ward* and had been supported by two of the members, while several others had appeared to waver. "Things aren't altogether hopeless," he told Solzhenitsyn. Nevertheless, the meeting on the twenty-second would be a difficult one. All the secretaries had been given *Feast of the Conquerors* to read and were highly indignant about it. Their strategy would be to concentrate on *Feast* at the expense of *Cancer Ward*, and it would be Solzhenitsyn's and Tvardovsky's task to reverse these priorities. (Tvardovsky was practically the only member of the secretariat not to have read the play: he refused to accept it from the KGB, and Solzhenitsyn said he had no other copy available to give him. Simonov was another who had honourably refused to read it.)

Solzhenitsyn agreed to write out a preliminary statement in which he would try to deflect attention from *Feast*. He also wrote down some answers to possible questions and meticulously prepared some clean sheets of paper, numbering them and ruling in the margins, on which to note down a record of the discussion. He had taken to doing this not only at *Novy Mir* but whenever he was involved in literary discussions, calculating that the sight of him taking down their words would inhibit even his most rabid enemies and induce an element of caution. Coincidentally it enabled him to keep his head down and have time to think before answering some of the hotter questions.[22]

The gathering took place in the former "Rostov mansion," started at 1 p.m. and ended at 6 p.m. Konstantin Fedin, chairman of the Writers' Union, had been called in to preside, although he was seventy-five and in poor health. As a reasonably talented novelist of the twenties and thirties, Fedin had once possessed a certain authority among the writing fraternity but had squandered most of it as a result of his cowardly behaviour during the Pasternak affair. It was the authority of his office, not the man, that was now needed, and the certainty that he would remain loyal to his political masters. Interestingly enough, some of the more prominent writers on the secretariat, including Sholokhov, were absent from the meeting, but there were still over thirty members present, as well as an ideological watch-dog from the cultural department of the Central Committee, Comrade Melentyev, who took notes throughout. It was, in general, a far more hostile assembly than that which had gathered at the Writers' Club some ten months earlier.

The secretariat had taken the precaution of convening two hours before Solzhenitsyn's arrival to agree on the line to be followed (presumably laid down by Melentyev). In this sense it was to be a typical Soviet business meeting, with the main decisions taken in advance and the roles of the participants well rehearsed. The only problem this time was that the sacrificial victim had prepared a different script and was determined to thwart the leaders' intentions.

In his opening speech, Fedin expressed distaste for Solzhenitsyn's latest letter. He found it threatening and offensive, a slap in the face of his colleagues ("We are made to appear as scoundrels rather than representatives of the creative intelligentsia"), and an attempt to force their hand. In this he was supported by several others, including Voronkov, who broadened the attack to include Solzhenitsyn's relations with the West. How did his letter to the congress reach the "filthy bourgeois press" so soon, why was it being broadcast so eagerly by foreign radio stations, and why didn't Solzhenitsyn answer this "loathsome bourgeois propaganda" and dissociate himself from it?

The temperature rose rather quickly. At one point Solzhenitsyn snapped that he was "not a schoolboy" obliged to jump to his feet and answer each question as it was asked. He would take several and answer them together (in this way he was able to answer only those he chose to and ignore others). Alexander Korneichuk, a third-rate Ukrainian playwright, alleged that Solzhenitsyn's letter had been broadcast before the congress opened. Not so, said Solzhenitsyn. But instead of replying to the question of how it got abroad, he counter-attacked with one of his prepared answers.

> Very suggestive and effective use is made here of the word "abroad," as if it referred to some high authority whose opinion is greatly respected. Perhaps this is understandable to those who flood our literature with lightweight sketches about life abroad. But this is alien to me. I have never been abroad. . . . Throughout my life I have had the soil of my homeland under my feet. Its is the only pain I feel; it the only subject I write about.

He recited once again the various slanders and sanctions he was being subjected to through secret Party channels and offered chapter and verse. News of a secret directive banning the library circulation of *A Day in the Life of Ivan Denisovich* and ordering its withdrawal from the shelves had come to him in several letters, one of which, from the Crimea, he quoted verbatim.

The statement that he had defected to Egypt had been made by a Party propaganda official in the Moscow suburb of Bolshevo. The allegation that he had gone to England had been made by a Major Shestakov in Solikamsk. Party activists in various parts of the country had accused him of collaboration during the war and said that he had been released from the camps either by mistake or before his time was up. Vladimir Semichastny, a former head of the KGB, had accused him of "materially supporting the capitalist world by not collecting his royalties," and so on.

After this fighting response (which, among other things, testified to the excellence of Solzhenitsyn's sources), the balance of opinion shifted a little in Solzhenitsyn's favour. Afanasy Salynsky and Konstantin Simonov, supported by Tvardovsky, suggested that *Cancer Ward* be published and a communiqué issued defending Solzhenitsyn's record. Fedin held back, saying that Solzhenitsyn should first make a statement denouncing the use made of his name by "our enemies in the West." Korneichuk, noting Solzhenitsyn's evasions ("You were asked questions but you failed to answer"), weighed in with that orthodox view of world affairs that Solzhenitsyn refused to take into account: "Do you not realize that a colossal, world-wide battle is being fought under very difficult conditions? We cannot stand aloof. With our works we defend our government, our Party, our people. . . . We travel abroad to carry on the struggle." Korneichuk added how upset he had been by Solzhenitsyn's "nasty, insulting . . . foul" play, *Feast of the Conquerors*. Vadim Kozhevnikov concurred. But it was left to the senior secretary present, Alexei Surkov (a prominent baiter of Pasternak), to spell out the real objections to Solzhenitsyn and his novel. The publication of *Cancer Ward*, he said, "would be more dangerous than Svetlana's memoirs"* and would be used against the Soviet Union. "The works of Solzhenitsyn are more dangerous to us than those of Pasternak: Pasternak was a man divorced from life, while Solzhenitsyn has a bold, militant, ideological temperament and is a man possessed by an idea."

When discussion turned more specifically to *Cancer Ward*, a new argument was introduced—namely, that Solzhenitsyn was not a talented writer anyway. Sergei Baruzdin, a writer of children's books, said he had never been impressed by Solzhenitsyn's works. Toktobolot Abdumomunov, from Kirghizia, said that *Cancer Ward* was too gloomy ("There are many tedious passages, repetitions, and naturalistic scenes"). The Georgian Irakly Abashidze confessed that he had been unable to read more than 150 pages, and Berdy Kerbabayev, from Turkmenia, had found it "nauseating."

Solzhenitsyn attempted to stem the tide first of all by renouncing *Feast of the Conquerors*. At the very start of the meeting, he had read out a prepared statement saying that he had "long since disowned" this play, which was the work not of the mature writer Solzhenitsyn but of the nameless prisoner Shch-232, written at a time of hopelessness when millions were being repressed.

* The reference is to Stalin's daughter, Svetlana Alliluyeva, who published her memoirs, *Twenty Letters to a Friend*, in 1967 shortly after she had defected to the West.

"I now bear as little responsibility for this play as many other authors would wish to bear for speeches and books that *they* wrote in 1949," he had said threateningly. And now he added a new thrust: "If *Feast of the Conquerors* is ever widely circulated or printed, I solemnly declare that the full responsibility will fall on the organization that has the only remaining copy. . . . It is this organization that is disseminating the play."

Solzhenitsyn also attempted to answer some of the criticisms of *Cancer Ward*. He denied (not altogether truthfully) that the title and subject matter were symbolic. The book was rooted in autobiography, and its texture was too dense to be a symbol. Nor was the story "anti-humanitarian." In it, life conquered death. "But I do not believe that it is the task of literature . . . to conceal the truth . . . or to tone it down." Moving to more comfortable ground, he was able to demonstrate the misconceptions on which a number of the more detailed criticisms had been based, and he concluded by urging them to publish *Cancer Ward* quickly, before copies reached abroad.

There were signs that not all the speakers were against this idea. Even some of those who had attacked *Feast of the Conquerors* expressed satisfaction that Solzhenitsyn was willing to renounce it publicly. It was suggested that if *Cancer Ward* were sufficiently revised in consultation with *Novy Mir*, a way might still be found to publish it, despite the criticisms that had been heaped upon it. But in the end the whole issue got bogged down in the question of who was to make a statement first. Solzhenitsyn insisted that it was up to the Writers' Union to publish his letter and refute the slanders about him. "Konstantin Alexandrovich [Fedin] says it is I who must resolve the situation. I am bound hand and foot and gagged—how am I to resolve it? It seems to me that this would be an easier matter for the mighty Union of Writers. My every line is suppressed, while the entire press is in the hands of the Union." Fedin was adamant that it should be the other way round, and again it was Surkov who put the matter in a nutshell. "You should state whether you dissociate yourself from the role ascribed to you in the West," he said, "that of leader of the political opposition in the USSR."

Portraying this meeting later in *The Oak and the Calf*, Solzhenitsyn employed his favourite metaphor of a battlefield (he called it his Borodino)* and described himself as a triumphant general putting his enemies to flight. "Deploying my forces ever more boldly, steadily broadening the front, setting the bounds of battle to suit myself, no longer merely answering their questions but following my own plan, I drive them headlong over the field of Borodino to their remotest defence works." There was talk of artillery salvoes, wheeling cavalry, and marching dragoons—good, stirring stuff—but at

---

*The Battle of Borodino took place in 1812 between the Russians and Napoleon's invading army. At the time it seemed to have ended in stalemate, but it in fact marked a turning-point in the war and the virtual end of Napoleon's advance. Tolstoy celebrated the battle in nationalistic terms in a famous section of *War and Peace*. Solzhenitsyn first made the comparison in a letter to Tvardovsky (quoted by Reshetovskaya in her unpublished chapters), explaining it by saying, "For a long time neither side could understand the meaning of what had happened or who had won. But the French were mistaken in celebrating the fact that they had held on to their territory."

best it was a draw, as Solzhenitsyn was obliged to admit at the end of his account: "The field of battle is in their hands. Nowhere, not an inch of ground have they yielded."[23] He was a writer, after all, not a general.

What was new and truly encouraging about this encounter was that it had taken place at a meeting of the Writers' Union secretariat and not in a court of law. The first writers to defend their views in public and to defy the Soviet establishment (and incidentally to defend the publication of their works in the West)—Sinyavsky and Daniel—had been obliged to do so from the dock. Since then many other young dissidents (neither writers nor well known) had pronounced a similar defiance of the authorities from the dock, but only Solzhenitsyn had been able to carry his argument within the portals of power and there stand his ground. Tvardovsky, for one, was filled with admiration. "I was delighted—for your sake and ours," he wrote afterwards to Solzhenitsyn, praising "the manifest superiority of truth to any and every dirty trick and to 'politics.' "[24] In his somewhat optimistic view, there had been a shift in his and Solzhenitsyn's favour, and he wrote that he was now ready to sign a contract for *Cancer Ward*.

Three days later the BBC broadcast to the Soviet Union a detailed account of the meeting. According to Reshetovskaya, Solzhenitsyn was not responsible this time, for he was in Rozhdestvo typing up his own notes on the gathering. But he was very pleased. He was no longer "a needle in a haystack" and would no longer be forgotten by the European media.[25]

But already there were new clouds on the horizon. In the course of the meeting, two Writers' Union secretaries from Central Asia had come up with a fresh idea: Solzhenitsyn should be expelled from the union. A few days later, this was followed by a letter to the secretariat from none other than Sholokhov, which was read aloud at a union meeting. According to Solzhenitsyn, the whole thing ended rather farcically. Sholokhov had written that he could no longer "remain in the same union with an anti-Soviet type" like Solzhenitsyn, whereupon some of the Russian writers proposed a vote on it. Leonid Sobolev, the chairman, took fright. The voting might go the wrong way and backfire: What if Sholokhov were expelled instead? There was some hilarity over this, but the issue was serious, especially when Sholokhov could openly demand that Solzhenitsyn "should be prevented from writing." Sholokhov was the union's single most influential member.[26]

It seems that the inner circle of top Party officials had already made up its mind that Solzhenitsyn was a lost cause, and was determined to try to neutralize him. On 5 October 1967 the editor of *Pravda*, Mikhail Zimyanin, addressed a private gathering at the Press House in Leningrad and compared Solzhenitsyn to Valery Tarsis. Tarsis was mad, said Zimyanin, and the Western campaign on his behalf had ceased only with Tarsis's expulsion to the West.

Now Solzhenitsyn occupies an important place in the propaganda of capitalist governments. He, too, is a psychologically unbalanced person, a schizophrenic. Formerly he was a prisoner and, justly or unjustly, was subjected to repression.

Now he takes his revenge on the government through his literary work. The only topic he is able to write about is life in a camp. This topic has become an obsession with him. Solzhenitsyn's works are aimed at the Soviet regime, in which he finds only sores and cancerous tumours. He doesn't see anything positive in our society.[27]

Zimyanin revealed that he, too, had been given *Feast of the Conquerors* to read and said it was obvious that Solzhenitsyn's works "could not be published." Only if he wrote "stories which correspond to the interests of our society" would the authorities change their mind. Otherwise, Solzhenitsyn should go back to teaching physics.

In the meantime three more of the young participants in the demonstration in Pushkin Square had been tried and sentenced for their activities. Vladimir Bukovsky, one of the main organizers, was sentenced to three years in a normal-regime labour camp, while Vadim Delaunay and Evgeny Kushev, both of whom turned state's evidence and pleaded guilty, were given suspended sentences of one year. Bukovsky had made a fighting speech protesting his innocence of any criminal activities and demanding that the provisions of the Soviet constitution be observed, including those that prescribed the standard freedoms of speech, press, assembly, and belief. "We know that freedom of speech and of the press is above all the freedom to criticize. No one has ever been forbidden to praise the government. . . . You accuse us of trying to discredit the KGB by our slogans, but the KGB has discredited itself so effectively there is nothing we can add. . . . We have not committed any crime. I absolutely don't repent of having organized the demonstration. I believe it has done its job, and when I am free again I shall organize other demonstrations."[28]

Again a book of documents was compiled containing a full description of the trial, together with the trial of Khaustov and Gabai. The compiler and editor was a young physicist named Pavel Litvinov, grandson of the former Soviet foreign minister Maxim Litvinov and his English wife, Ivy. Litvinov was summoned to the KGB headquarters at the Lubyanka and warned that if the documents appeared, either in the Soviet Union or the West, Litvinov would be held responsible and charged under Article 190/1 of the criminal code. "You understand . . . that such a record could be used against us by our ideological enemies, especially on the eve of the fiftieth anniversary of Soviet power. . . . We are only warning you, but the court will prove you guilty. . . . Imagine if all the world were to hear that the grandson of the great diplomat Litvinov was involved in such a thing—it would be a blot on his memory."

Litvinov acknowledged no such thing and on returning home neatly turned the tables on his persecutors by writing down their entire conversation from memory and sending a record of it to *Izvestia*, the *Literaturnaya gazeta*, and some Western Communist newspapers with a request for publication. "Such actions by the security services are tantamount to open blackmail and I protest. I ask you to publish my letter so that, in the event of my arrest, the circumstances leading up to it will be public knowledge." Shortly after-wards, the documents that Litvinov had compiled began to circulate in sam-izdat, and in due course appeared abroad as a book, *The Demonstration in Pushkin Square*. Contrary to expectations, Litvinov was not arrested and con-tinued to circulate samizdat materials and make protests.[29]

It was the eve of the fiftieth anniversary of the October Revolution, which the government was anxious to celebrate with great pomp and a show of strength and unity. The military parade in Red Square on 7 November 1967 was bigger and more impressive than ever, and Moscow was full of delegations from every corner of the globe. Party functionaries were too busy with their guests to pay much attention to dissident intellectuals.

Solzhenitsyn had made a quick trip to Rostov and Georgievsk in Octo-ber to collect more material for *August 1914*, had been in Moscow when Zimyanin made his scurrilous remarks in Leningrad, and now returned to Ryazan to get down to his novel. Before he could begin, however, he felt compelled to write up the latest episodes in his conflict with the authorities and composed the first supplement to his growing memoir, which he opti-mistically called "The Noose Snaps" (describing events since his letter to the congress).[30]

He also had a considerable amount of correspondence to get through. His mail had increased steadily since the publication of *Ivan Denisovich* and had recently taken a quantum leap in the aftermath of his letter to the con-gress. There were also many readers' responses to the samizdat copies of *The First Circle* and *Cancer Ward* now circulating in Moscow and other big cities. Of these, one of the most interesting was a long letter from Shalamov on his reading of *The First Circle*. Shalamov wrote that it was a novel "of which any writer in the world could be proud" and praised Solzhenitsyn's idea of "giv-ing a geological cross-section of Soviet society from top to bottom—from Stalin to the caretaker Spiridon." He also liked the fact that Solzhenitsyn had mainly described events that he had witnessed or lived through. "The reader who has experienced Hiroshima and the concentration camps, the gas chambers of Auschwitz, revolutions, and wars will be insulted by invented subjects and invented fates."

It was an interesting variant on Kopelev's earlier remarks about the superiority of the autobiographical passages in *The First Circle*, although more positive. But Solzhenitsyn was still unable to agree. He could not endorse Shalamov's implicit conclusion that documentary prose would drive out fic-tion. He had a high regard for prose founded on documents ("so long as the author doesn't drown in his documents but fuses them together so that they live"), but why should one exclude the other? In his view, documentary prose could never replace the fictional novel, "whose main attraction and enchantment lies not merely in its narrative truth to life but in the spiritual flight of a great artist's personality, and even in its play. This adds a unique lustre to the narrative, and it is this that makes us shudder." Solzhenitsyn also made a distinction between invention and creation. Readers might well

be insulted by *invented* subjects and fates, but not if they had been truly
created by the author.[31]

Another interesting letter he wrote at about this time was to three students who had recently visited him and had sought his guidance on various
ethical matters. The subject of the letter was justice and conscience. Solzhenitsyn clearly thought it important, because he later released the letter into
samizdat.

> Obviously [justice] is a concept inherent in man, since it cannot be traced to any
> other source. Justice exists, even if there are only a few individuals who recog-
> nize it as such. Love of justice seems to me to be a different sentiment from love
> of the people (or at least the two coincide only partially). . . . There is nothing
> relative about justice, as there is nothing relative about conscience. Indeed, jus-
> tice *is* conscience, not a personal conscience but the conscience of all mankind.
> Those who clearly recognize the voice of their own conscience usually also rec-
> ognize the voice of justice. I consider that in all social or historical matters (if we
> are . . . touched by them spiritually) justice will always suggest a way to act (or
> judge) which will not conflict with our conscience.[32]

It was, in a minor way, a credo, a statement of the belief that underlay
the creation of all Solzhenitsyn's works up to this time, but especially *The
First Circle* and the three vast volumes of *The Gulag Archipelago*. What was
particularly interesting was the separation of "love of justice" from "love of
the people." Solzhenitsyn undoubtedly aspired to the latter, as the Spiridon
chapters in *The First Circle* and the story of Matryona had shown. But there
is little doubt that "love of justice" was the prime motivating force in his
writing (and his behaviour generally), a burning passion that consumed him
day and night, whereas "love of the people" was somewhat harder to achieve.
Like Tolstoy before him, he willed his love, and like Tolstoy he came quite
close to experiencing it through the very strength of his desire, but it was
secondary, and in his heart he recognized this. Justice was what he really
thirsted for, the defeat of falsehood and lies. "Please don't tell me that 'everybody understands justice in his own way,' " he wrote in that same letter to
the students. "No! They can shout, they can take you by the throat, they
can tear your breast, but convictions based on conscience are as infallible as
the internal rhythm of the heart."

That last sentence, which might have been written with Solzhenitsyn's
enemies in the Writers' Union in mind, certainly described his own determination, though his growing self-confidence was still tempered by doubts:
"Call no day happy until it is done; call no man happy until he is dead," he
wrote in mid-November, concluding the latest instalment of his memoir.[33]

Immediately after its completion, Solzhenitsyn went to Moscow to see
Tvardovsky about *Cancer Ward*. Tvardovsky was not there. He was out at
his dacha in Pakhra and apparently not well. Solzhenitsyn tried the Writers'
Union, but the secretary of the Moscow section, Victor Ilyin, informed him
that there would be no discussion of part 2—"the secretariat hasn't approved

it." While in Moscow, Solzhenitsyn paid another visit to Kapitsa, who expressed unease over Solzhenitsyn's growing intransigence: "Why are you so uncompromising?" He called for the first time on Evtushenko and was amazed by the luxuriousness of Evtushenko's flat. The oval table they sat at had supposedly come from Versailles. Even more exotic was Rostropovich's flat, where he went next, with its Greek-tiled kitchen, antique furniture, and souvenirs brought from all over the world. They ate off English plates with pictures of English tourist attractions on them and drank from Hungarian glasses stamped with crowns.[34]

Solzhenitsyn had met Rostropovich for the first time only two weeks before, in Ryazan. Rostropovich had given a concert there with the Moscow Symphony Orchestra (Solzhenitsyn and Natalia had attended) and the following day turned up unannounced on Solzhenitsyn's doorstep. When Maria opened the door he had said, "I'm Rostropovich. I've come to embrace Solzhenitsyn," and had virtually walked straight in, quickly conquering the reserved Solzhenitsyn with his impulsive friendliness and charm. The two men had talked for a couple of hours and Solzhenitsyn was surprised by the breadth of Rostropovich's interests—"unusual in a musician." Rostropovich had explained that most musicians were limited by the long hours they had to spend practising, but he had been blessed with an excellent memory and therefore didn't need to practise very much. When they parted, Rostropovich had absolutely insisted that Solzhenitsyn visit him in Moscow, and now Solzhenitsyn was complying.

As before, Rostropovich was brimming over with good humour ("he literally bellowed with joy, hearing my voice on the telephone," Solzhenitsyn later wrote to Natalia) and on this occasion insisted on drinking *Brüderschaft* and going on to Christian-name terms. He was ebullient, witty, spontaneous, mercurial, completely irresistible, and the two men quickly became friends. A little later, according to Reshetovskaya, after reading Solzhenitsyn's two novels, Rostropovich wrote that he would long remain under the deep impression of Solzhenitsyn's genius. Solzhenitsyn replied that he was equally under the spell of Rostropovich's musical genius, sunny disposition, and scintillating ideas but later added a sombre note of interrogation about Rostropovich's future reputation: "We have a habit in this country of demanding of our geniuses sympathy for the national sorrow."[35]

Solzhenitsyn finally went to see Tvardovsky in Pakhra on 24 November 1967, to try to persuade him to do something more about *Cancer Ward*. He drove out with Lakshin in *Novy Mir*'s equivalent of a company car, a black Volga from *Izvestia*'s car pool. Both men were aware that Tvardovsky had been indulging in one of his periodic drinking bouts. Lakshin told Solzhenitsyn on the way how Tvardovsky had been deprived of the editorship of *Novy Mir* in 1954 because of his drinking. He had got drunk on the very day of a meeting with Khrushchev to discuss the magazine's future and had failed to turn up, as a result of which he was sacked. Only in 1958 had he been able to take over again.

Tvardovsky was suffering from a hangover and was very subdued when he came out to greet them, quoting, with mournful humour, the words that Tolstoy puts into the mouth of the defeated Austrian General Mack in *War and Peace:* "You see before you the unfortunate Mack." Solzhenitsyn tried to persuade him that the recent Writers' Union discussion had gone better than Tvardovsky realized and that now was the time to send several chapters of *Cancer Ward* to the printers and have them set up in type. He would even make the changes suggested by *Novy Mir*. But Tvardovsky was sceptical. It wouldn't be possible without some sort of go-ahead from the Central Committee's cultural department, and Tvardovsky had just had a row with them on the very subject of Solzhenitsyn. They had pressed him, for the umpteenth time, to read *The Feast of the Conquerors*, and Tvardovsky had lost his temper and given them too frank a piece of his mind. Lakshin came up with an alternative plan. He had heard that the cultural department's main objection to permitting any movement hinged on Solzhenitsyn's refusal to denounce the use of his name being made in the West. If Solzhenitsyn would agree to write a letter for the correspondence columns of *Novy Mir*, surely they would be able to carry some chapters of *Cancer Ward* in the same issue? Tvardovsky rejected that as well. He saw no point in such a letter or in trying to push *Cancer Ward*. The situation looked too black to him, and he had no will to try to change it.

Solzhenitsyn was very depressed by the sight of Tvardovsky in this state. He detested heavy drinking and had repeatedly lectured Tvardovsky on its evils, not least after Tvardovsky's performance in Ryazan while reading *The First Circle*. For Solzhenitsyn, alcohol was the writer's greatest enemy. Victor Nekrasov recalls being rung up by Anna Berzer on one occasion and informed that Solzhenitsyn was coming to Moscow the next day and wished to see him "between 4.15 and 4.54 p.m." about "a very important matter." Nekrasov had arrived for their meeting with a quart of vodka in his overcoat pocket and proposed that they take a drink while they talked, but Solzhenitsyn was horrified. After a terrific struggle, he agreed to accept a thimbleful. Then he drew himself erect, looked at Nekrasov solemnly, and said, "Victor, you must drink six times less than you do." The affable Nekrasov was nonplussed and said jokingly, "But why not five times or seven times less? Why six? I'll settle for five, but not six." Solzhenitsyn was not amused and launched into a passionate speech about the evils of alcohol and how vodka was ruining the national literature. Writers had to be disciplined and hard-working, and not let their will be sapped by drink.

Solzhenitsyn was right about the effects of vodka on Russian writers—it is an occupational disease—but there was a painful absence of humour and tolerance about his attitude to it, as about his whole manner. At another point in their conversation, Solzhenitsyn asked Nekrasov whether he ever travelled by train. Nekrasov said no, he preferred to go by plane. Solzhenitsyn retorted that this was a mistake. "In a plane you meet nobody. But if you go by train you can meet other people, find out how they live, and talk to them." Nekrasov said it reminded him of a story told about Tolstoy and his aristocratic disciple Chertkov. Tolstoy had told Chertkov that he should no longer travel first class by train but should go second class to show his humility. Chertkov had obeyed—and hired an entire second-class coach for himself the next time he went on a journey.[36]

Solzhenitsyn's gloom after his unsuccessful meeting with Tvardovsky was soon dissipated by a letter from Voronkov, the secretary to the board of the Writers' Union. Voronkov wrote to ask whether Solzhenitsyn had had any further thoughts about writing a letter to dissociate himself from Western propaganda. Taking this as a sign of weakness on the union's part, Solzhenitsyn wrote a strong reply in which he didn't mention Voronkov's question but asked a series of his own: Would the secretariat refute the slanders being spread about him by Party officials (including Zimyanin, whose remarks had been reported to Solzhenitsyn by this time)? What measures were being taken to get his works unbanned in universities and public libraries? When would *Cancer Ward* be published? When were the confiscated copy of *The First Circle* and his archive going to be returned to him? What about an edition of his collected stories, as Simonov had suggested? And for good measure he threw in a question about the Universal Copyright Convention and another as to why he hadn't received an official transcript of the recent meeting in the Writers' Union.

It was an excellent expression of his growing belief that the best form of defence was attack, and it seemed to have worked, for two weeks later he received word from Tvardovsky that Voronkov wanted to see the two of them in his office. They went there on 18 December 1967 (again in an *Izvestia* Volga) and found Voronkov, accompanied by another Writers' Union official, Sergei Sartakov, in an affable and accommodating mood. He had already indicated to Tvardovsky by telephone that he hoped *Novy Mir* had concluded a contract with Solzhenitsyn for *Cancer Ward* and paid him an advance, and his generally friendly comments had raised Tvardovsky's expectations sky-high. Tvardovsky was sure that someone "up top," perhaps Brezhnev himself, had given the word to go ahead, which meant that they might at last be able to print an extract in the *Literaturnaya Gazeta* to consolidate their position. On greeting Solzhenitsyn in the *Novy Mir* offices in Moscow, Tvardovsky had presented him with a copy of his latest volume of poetry, inscribed, "To dear Alexander Isayevich on this day of hope, 18-12-67." But Voronkov turned out to be as evasive as he was affable, and was impossible to pin down. Tvardovsky spoke of Bulgakov and the scandal that his best novel had not seen the light for nearly thirty years.* Did they want to have the same thing happen to Solzhenitsyn's novels? Solzhenitsyn referred to the processes of history and pointed out the odd circumstance that no one had actually banned *Cancer Ward*, so why wouldn't they let it be published? Voronkov indicated that Tvardovsky could proceed at his own risk, but Tvardovsky

---

* *The Master and Margarita* had been published (in a censored form) a year earlier in the journal *Moskva*, no. 11 (1966) and no. 1 (1967).

said that that was unprecedented: as a journal of the Writers' Union, *Novy Mir* needed the explicit permission of the union to publish controversial works. At one stage Voronkov agreed to discuss Tvardovsky's proposal of publishing a chapter from *Cancer Ward* in the *Literaturnaya Gazeta*, and seemed ready to endorse a one-volume edition of Solzhenitsyn's already published stories with a preface by Tvardovsky (the preface also to be printed in the *Literaturnaya Gazeta*). But again, when it came to making a final decision, he took refuge in bureaucratic formalities: there would have to be a meeting of the secretariat, he would have to have some sort of letter from Solzhenitsyn first.[37]

It seemed like yet another stalemate, but on this occasion Tvardovsky was not to be deflected. His fighting spirit had been roused. The letter and the meeting seemed like unimportant details in comparison with the importance for Russian literature of getting *Cancer Ward* into print. Since Voronkov had not uttered an outright "no," he would take it as a "yes." Returning to the *Novy Mir* offices, he at once gave instructions for the first eight chapters to be set up in type for inclusion in the January 1968 issue, and went personally to the *Izvestia* printing works to see that it was done promptly. The following day an editorial conference was held to draw up a list of corrections and changes that Solzhenitsyn would be asked to make, and then Solzhenitsyn himself was invited to discuss the list. Lakshin, Dorosh, and Kondratovich regarded the list as very short. Solzhenitsyn pretended to find it "long," but there was nothing in it he disagreed with, except a request to cut the scene with the Japanese, which he refused to do, on grounds of plot. The only real disagreement came over the chapter headings, which Tvardovsky wanted to remove but which Solzhenitsyn insisted should stay as they were: "You can take eight chapters or twenty-one chapters, but without the headings I refuse to let it go ahead." At length, agreement was reached to leave the headings, and Tvardovsky insisted on concluding a contract with Solzhenitsyn and paying him the full amount of the advance. This generous gesture assured Solzhenitsyn of a sufficient income for at least the next two years.

Solzhenitsyn returned to Ryazan to correct the galley proofs. According to Reshetovskaya, he was more elated than he subsequently divulged in *The Oak and the Calf* but was still sceptical about the outcome. "There is a strange, phantasmal air of unreality about everything that has happened so far," he told her. "Generally there's the same sort of commotion as there was when they printed *Ivan Denisovich*. If everything turns out the way they've planned, it will be fantastic. But it's possible that nothing will happen at all. It will become clear only gradually—for us in Ryazan on Wednesday, depending on what's in the *Literaturnaya Gazeta*."[38]

His entire future hung in the balance, and he did not know what to think when, on 24 December, a telegram arrived from Tvardovsky begging him to return to Moscow on Tuesday the twenty-sixth. He decided that yet another duel with the secretariat was in prospect and, after skiing for a couple of hours in Solotcha to clear his head, sat down to prepare arguments and answers as he had done in September. He was due to leave Ryazan on the

11 a.m. train to Moscow, but something caused him to change his mind at the last moment and to return home. He told Natalia that when he got to the station, there was a long queue of people waiting, and no tickets were being issued, because the train was delayed for an hour and a half. This meant that he couldn't possibly get to Moscow before 5 p.m., which would be too late. Natalia tried to persuade him that he would still be in time for a meeting on Wednesday, or could go on Wednesday morning, but Solzhenitsyn refused. The trains and stations were packed with people flocking to Moscow to do their New Year shopping, and he did not wish to face the discomfort and inconvenience of it all. Instead, he sent a telegram to *Novy Mir* asking whether he could come on 2 or 3 January.

Reshetovskaya reports that she was perplexed by this sudden apathy on the part of her husband and was at a loss to explain it—and still could not do so when she came to write about it ten years later.[39] Interestingly enough, Solzhenitsyn slides over it in his own account of those days, saying nothing of his prior preparations to put up a fight in Moscow and simply referring to the "excruciating discomfort" the journey would have caused him. Nor does he mention the events of the next few days.[40]

On Tuesday the twenty-sixth, the day he returned from the station, Solzhenitsyn phoned an editorial assistant in the prose section of *Novy Mir* (at her home, not at the office) and learned that the purpose for which he was being summoned to Moscow was to make some sort of statement for the secretariat. This confirmed his worst suspicions, and strengthened his resolve not to go, but to depart for Solotcha as he had originally planned. Before leaving Ryazan, he wrote a note for Natalia with strict orders not to disturb him at Solotcha and with precise instructions on how to deal with any further messages: "Answer any telegrams with a letter or telegram either in your name or in mine, saying that all the tickets had been sold for the train in Ryazan and that it was impossible to get on the next one. And end by wishing the entire editorial staff a Happy New Year." To Voronkov she could also write either in her own name or his, saying (in her own name) that she would not see her husband until the school holidays at the end of January. If in his name, she was to write, "I consider that my presence is not necessary for ending the sanctions to which I have been subjected: everything was discussed on 12 June and 22 September, and almost everything lies within the power of the secretariat. But in accordance with your invitation, I will not refuse to attend a meeting of the secretariat at the close of my winter working period at the beginning of March." If the demands for Solzhenitsyn to go to Moscow were exceptionally urgent, Natalia could book him a ticket for 3 January *"but not the second."*

The next day, another telegram arrived in Ryazan from Tvardovsky. Two days after that Natalia spoke to his secretary by telephone, and booked a ticket for 2 January despite Solzhenitsyn's warning. When she joined Solzhenitsyn for New Year's Eve, he was in the midst of writing part 6 (entitled "Exile") of *The Gulag Archipelago* and was in high good humour, but he still refused to go to Moscow and insisted that she go instead. He dictated to her seven detailed answers to the seven arguments he thought Tvardovsky most likely to use, including one to the probable request to make a statement. He would not do anything of newspaper-article length, he said, but only a broad overview, which "would not differ much from his letter to the congress and would give little comfort to anybody." A writer's statements were his books, and it was these that were being banned. "Until I am published I am nobody, and I have nothing to say about *anything*."

When Natalia saw Tvardovsky in Moscow on 3 January 1968, she passed on Solzhenitsyn's views together with a covering letter to Tvardovsky. In it Solzhenitsyn urged Tvardovsky to ignore any conditions being set by the secretariat and to send his eight chapters directly to the censorship office. "As distinct from obtaining my 'repentance' or 'regret,' such a step doesn't require you to do a deal with your conscience, and therefore it's open to you, as open as your next breath. Just send it off, and don't bother to lobby or persuade anyone! Just sent it off as a normal editorial procedure." Solzhenitsyn wrote that he feared Tvardovsky was being pressured into wheedling some sort of recantation out of him, however mild and however confidential, so long as it was in written form. But his "inner, spiritual well-being," he wrote, was "dearer to him than the fate of his books," and he wouldn't give the secretariat "a single line of a promissory note" until they came out into the open and publicly admitted that they would not publish *Cancer Ward* and his collected stories without such a written statement from him.

It was Solzhenitsyn at his most uncompromising, but Tvardovsky informed Natalia that it was too late anyway. "To tell you the truth," he said, "all they wanted from him was a brief internal note addressed to the secretariat. I wanted to dictate it to him. It would have gone approximately as follows: 'I do not regret and do not withdraw a single word of my letter, but I am sorry that it has provoked a reaction among those to whom it was not addressed. . . .'"

Reshetovskaya records that Tvardovsky did not seem angry with Solzhenitsyn, only immensely sad and bewildered. Tvardovsky said that he understood why Solzhenitsyn had not wanted to write such a letter and that it did not matter any longer. Later Solzhenitsyn learned that Tvardovsky had tried his old ploy of going straight to the Central Committee's cultural department in an attempt to bypass the Writers' Union, but the department had referred him to the union secretariat again. Tvardovsky told Natalia that a lot hinged on *Cancer Ward*. If he could get it published, the way would be open for many other works. But the literary world was polarized. "Some writers sincerely wish *Cancer Ward* to be published, but there are others who detest it—what will happen to their own novels if it gets through?" He also said, "Alexander Isayevich judges everything from the point of view of the stars . . . but if I leave, what will happen to the magazine?" And growing irritable for a moment: "Why does he have to hide himself all the time? I'd even send a helicopter for him!"

Reshetovskaya writes that in her opinion, this episode was a third turning-point in Solzhenitsyn's relations with the Soviet authorities (after the publication of *Ivan Denisovich* and the confiscation of his archive) and blames his stubbornness and intransigence (as much as the obtuseness of the Writers' Union) for this failure to be reconciled and be accepted back into the Soviet fold. There is something to be said for this point of view, and certainly his turning back at the Ryazan station strikes one as arbitrary and almost irrational in its capriciousness. He had prepared carefully for the meeting in Moscow, and one can only speculate on what would have happened had the train arrived and departed on time. But in his position there was also an underlying logic. It may be that had he written a confidential note for internal consumption only, *Cancer Ward* would have been published, with incalculable consequences for himself and Russian literature. But the question was, Would the Writers' Union keep its word? And if it did with regard to *Cancer Ward*, would it keep the letter secret too? The odds were that it wouldn't, or that it would hold possible publication over Solzhenitsyn's head as a threat. Such a brief and (on the face of it) uncompromising letter seemed to Reshetovskaya and Tvardovsky a small price to pay for the prize of publication. On the other hand, Solzhenitsyn's moral purity, his absolute refusal to compromise on fundamental issues, was his greatest asset, which gave meaning to his life and work. It may be that this was not the best place to draw the line. He was capable of compromise, as he had shown in his reworkings of *The First Circle*, *The Tenderfoot and the Tart*, and, to a lesser extent, *Cancer Ward*. Perhaps he should have gone to Moscow after all, negotiated with the devil, and pushed *Cancer Ward* through regardless (this would certainly have been better for Soviet literature as a whole and for the liberals around *Novy Mir*, if not for him personally), but he was surely right in perceiving a deep and ultimately unbridgeable chasm between what he believed and stood for, and what the Soviet regime would tolerate. If it was not clear before, the writing of *The Gulag Archipelago* would have taught him this truth (it was symbolic, perhaps, that he chose to work on *Gulag* at precisely the time he was supposed to be in Moscow).

The accident of the delayed train may simply have triggered or crystallized in Solzhenitsyn's mind a decision that was bound to be taken sooner or later. And that it was sooner may have had something to do with Solzhenitsyn's innate irascibility and stubbornness. But it is hard to believe that it was ultimately of fundamental importance. What is significant, however, is Solzhenitsyn's decision to keep more or less silent about this incident in his memoir. No hint of hesitation was given there. Everything was portrayed as neatly cut and dried, and Tvardovsky, with all his torments, was patronized as a pathetic loyalist at the mercy of his Party superiors. It makes for a more heroic, but less interesting, portrait of the artist as an infallible crusader.

On 5 January 1968, at the request of the Central Committee, the secretariat of the Writers' Union met specifically to discuss the possible publication of *Cancer Ward*. Tvardovsky and Simonov were in favour of publication, but the hardliners—Fedin, Sholokhov, Leonov, Surkov, Tikhonov, and Mikhalkov—were against, and again a letter from Solzhenitsyn was mentioned as an essential condition of progress. Squeezed between the secretariat's intransigence and Solzhenitsyn's stubborn refusal to co-operate, Tvardovsky made a last, desperate attempt to salvage the novel by writing a long, confidential letter to Fedin, a key figure in the affair, in which he eloquently expounded the case for publication. His principal argument was the novel's literary excellence. While not regarding Solzhenitsyn as "a perfect and faultless artist who is above criticism," he had not the slightest doubt that *Cancer Ward* was a major work of art "written by a master." There was also Solzhenitsyn's symbolic importance as the most outstanding living writer of Russian prose (though Tvardovsky did not stress this point—Fedin himself was a novelist of once-considerable stature) and the initiator of a renaissance in Soviet fiction. Quoting the words of the novelist Grigori Baklanov about *Ivan Denisovich*, "After the appearance of Solzhenitsyn's novel, we clearly cannot go on writing as we have been writing up till now," Tvardovsky pointed out that not only had several authors been directly influenced by Solzhenitsyn but absolutely no one had remained unaffected by him. Like it or not, Solzhenitsyn had become the focal point of Soviet literature, around which everyone else turned.

How absurd then, continued Tvardovsky, that the question of whether or not to publish *Cancer Ward* had got bogged down in what had come to be known as the "Solzhenitsyn affair"—a reference to Solzhenitsyn's open letter to the Writers' Congress and the supposed unacceptability of its unorthodox form. It was this letter that now stuck in the gullets of the Writers' Union officials and caused them to demand some sign of "repentance" and submission on Solzhenitsyn's part before passing his novel. Even worse, wrote Tvardovsky, was the union's attempt not to address itself to the substance of Solzhenitsyn's letter but simply to "charm it out of existence in the privacy of the literary establishment," to hush it up and cancel it by a new letter. In keeping with this policy of secrecy, the union was now suggesting that Solzhenitsyn's new letter could be secret too: it would just be placed on the file to satisfy his hostile critics. "To think," commented Tvardovsky bitterly, "that the solution of this whole complex problem should depend on this one never-to-be-published 'document', that . . . a 'document' of a couple of pages is more important to us writers than a completed 600-page novel which . . . would be the pride and ornament of our literature."

Among other things, Tvardovsky tried to warn Fedin that it was almost too late. He hinted at Solzhenitsyn's growing indifference to the publication of his books in the Soviet Union, the appearance of copies of *Cancer Ward* abroad and its almost certain publication there, although Solzhenitsyn could "not possibly be accused of trying in any way to earn the good opinion of the West." There was also the growing circulation of Solzhenitsyn's works in samizdat, as a result of which his popularity was growing "at an astonishing rate." As an editor, Tvardovsky pointed to another aspect of the affair that was causing him great concern—Solzhenitsyn's novel was "at the head of a queue of other important and valuable works that are being held up (. . . Simonov's *One Hundred Days*, Bek's *A New Appointment*," and so on). "The publication of *Cancer Ward* would not only be a literary event in itself; it would also remove this bottle-neck, as when a car at the head of a traffic jam moves on. It would certainly benefit Soviet literature in its present—frankly speaking—depressing and critical state, and it would dispel the atmosphere of silence, bewilderment, uncertainty, and passive waiting."[41]

Almost immediately, Kaverin sent a separate letter to Fedin along similar lines, but without practical results. All that came back was a telephone call from Fedin ordering Tvardovsky to break up the type—an order he was bound to obey, inasmuch as *Novy Mir* was an organ of the Writers' Union. Later, it is true, Fedin thanked Tvardovsky for his frank and outspoken letter and hinted that he had at one point spoken to Brezhnev about Solzhenitsyn. But he declined to say whether he had pleaded on Solzhenitsyn's behalf or tried to get the novel published. He simply shrugged his shoulders and implied to Tvardovsky that there was nothing to be done.[42]

The whole enterprise had ground to a halt, and Solzhenitsyn's attempt to dynamite his way through the barrier of official suspicion and hostility with his letter to the Writers' Congress had, in a local and immediate sense, been a failure. But on the larger scale ("from the point of view of the stars") it was a very different story. Contrary to his initial forebodings, Solzhenitsyn had survived the storm unscathed, and his reputation had grown phenomenally, both at home and abroad. Far from hurting him, the conspiracy of official silence surrounding his name had had the opposite effect. He was now more famous and revered than if his novels had been published, and was acquiring an aura of infallibility and invincibility that grew with every failed attempt to silence him. Of course, the novels were there in samizdat to be read by a few, and they rightly enhanced his reputation as Russia's greatest living writer, but for the thousands—perhaps millions—of his admirers who hadn't been able to read these works it hardly mattered: his very life, his behaviour, his courage, and his defiance were becoming symbols of resistance to oppression and beacons of liberty for others.

34

PLAYING THE
WESTERN CARD

WHEN SOLZHENITSYN RETIRED to Solotcha, his original intention had been to make a start on the historical epic that he regarded as his chief life's work and for which he had made such careful preparations. Settling down in Agafya's cottage, he had taken out his student notebooks, surrounded himself with pictures of Samsonov's generals, and attempted to write, but the words would not come, and he was overawed by his subject. So keen had been his longing for this moment, so powerful his dreams and so delayed their fulfilment, that when the moment of consummation came he had found himself impotent. In *The Oak and the Calf* he claims that "God has spared me creative crises, fits of despair, and impotence," but elsewhere in that contradictory and boastful memoir he freely admits that when he came at last to the Samsonov book, "the lines flagged and petered out, my hand slipped feebly from the page."[1] It was a simple case of writer's block, and it was to get over it that Solzhenitsyn had turned once more to *The Gulag Archipelago*.

Throughout December, January, February, and March he worked unremittingly. After dealing with the subject of exile, he still had to write up the history of the show trials, and it was during this last intensive stint on the book that he studied the printed materials collected for him by friends and ex-prisoners, and incorporated them into the main narrative. Once again he drove himself hard. Although no longer attempting the two-shift system he had adopted in his secret hide-out, he regularly worked for twelve to fourteen hours a day, and his health began to crack under the strain. He started suffering from painful headaches and high blood pressure. From long hours of sitting he developed lumbago and sciatica and found it increasingly hard to sleep at night. At one point, it seems, he contemplated attending some sort of specialized clinic for treatment but was told that he would have to go to a resort on the Black Sea for an extended period of time, which was out of the question given his current commitments. Somewhat later, at the request of Reshetovskaya, Zhores Medvedev wrote to friends in America in the hope of obtaining some pills for this condition, but without success. There was nothing suitable on the market, and the intended go-between was prevented from visiting the Soviet Union at the appropriate time.[2]

That same winter an emissary from Olga Carlisle arrived in Moscow. Rumours had reached America that a rival edition of *The First Circle* was being prepared in Italy, allegedly with Solzhenitsyn's approval. Did he know anything of this and had he given it his authorization? Solzhenitsyn replied that he hadn't and that the Carlisles should proceed with their plans for U.S. publication as agreed. More than that, they should advance the publication date to the coming June. He evidently felt that the time was ripe for an all-out attack on the Soviet establishment, and the sooner it took place the better. But he must also have had in mind the large number of samizdat copies of the novel that were now circulating in Moscow. One Western specialist who visited the Soviet capital not long afterwards has described the response when he asked to read the novel.

> I received a photographed copy, two extremely bulky volumes, with pages half as big as [a newspaper]. Onto every page were glued four photographs of type-written pages, just big enough to be readable. The typing was bad. So were the glueing and the photography. Some pages were hardly legible. Quotations from foreign languages had simply been left out by the typist.[3]

Not long after this, according to the same visitor, samizdat editions of *Cancer Ward* were fetching up to seventy-five rubles on the black market.

Solzhenitsyn assured his visitor that if a pirate edition of *The First Circle* should appear before the American one, he would publicly denounce it and acknowledge only the American edition as full and correct. But he was reluctant to sign a letter of authorization—such a document would compromise him if it fell into the wrong hands. He needed to preserve his freedom of action for a long as possible. What he did do, however, to reassure his visitor that the Carlisles had his backing, was to send word of a larger and even more important book that he was just finishing and that he intended to entrust to them for eventual publication in the West. Its very existence had to be a closely guarded secret for the time being, but it would be sent to them by the following June. The book he had in mind, although he did not name it, was his almost-finished camp history, *The Gulag Archipelago*.

It is curious, looking back on it, that Solzhenitsyn should have taken the risk of mentioning the book at all at this time. Inside the Soviet Union its existence was known only to his ex-prisoner informants and a narrow circle of friends. Of these, almost none had read the whole work, and all were forbidden to mention it. Solzhenitsyn may have calculated, as Olga Carlisle thought, that by passing on such news he was strengthening her authority with his American publisher, Harper & Row, and this it certainly did, particularly in the absence of a letter of authorization, but it is hard to conceal an impression that Solzhenitsyn was acting impulsively, that he thought of this boost for the Carlisles virtually on the spur of the moment. It wouldn't have been the first time that he behaved in this fashion—one has only to recall the impulsive way he took the copies of *The First Circle* to Teush for safe-keeping, even though, according to his own account, he no longer trusted Teush and had recently removed some of his manuscripts from Teush's flat as a precaution. Nor would it be the last—in a matter of months he would be in danger of losing the entire manuscript as a result of carelessly supposing that the KGB knew nothing of his cottage in Rozhdestvo. It was as if the rigid discipline he imposed on 95 per cent of his life could not operate without a safety valve, as if these sudden impulses and lapses were the price he paid for the strain of keeping everything else under control.

He may also have been made reckless by a sense of euphoria. Ever since his letter to the Writers' Congress the preceding spring, he had been riding a wave of success. Despite the official silence surrounding his letter, he had received dozens of messages of support from other writers, and he was aware that he was not alone in challenging the Soviet establishment.

In January 1968 the trial had opened of the four young people involved in the compilation and circulation of documents about the Daniel and Sinyavsky trial: Alexander Ginzburg, Yuri Galanskov, Alexei Dobrovolsky, and Vera Lashkova. Two of them had been in trouble with the authorities before, Ginzburg for compiling the first (and best-known) literary journal in samizdat, *Syntax*, in 1960, and Galanskov for writing unofficial poetry and for compiling another well-known samizdat almanac, *Phoenix*, in 1961. In 1966, disgusted with the verdicts on Daniel and Sinyavsky, Galanskov had compiled a second issue of his almanac, *Phoenix 66*, in which he published only works that had been refused by publishing houses or the censorship. This, too, was one of the charges against him.

The trial lasted four days, and the sentences handed down on the two principal defendants were the same as for Daniel and Sinyavsky: Galanskov was sentenced to seven years' imprisonment in strict-regime labour camps and Ginzburg to five years'. Dobrovolsky, who co-operated with the prosecution, got two years, and Vera Lashkova, the typist, was sentenced to one year.[4] In some ways the trial was a repeat performance of the earlier trial: the court-room was packed with KGB men in civilian clothes (representing "the public"); only a handful of the defendants' closest relatives were allowed to attend, mostly for very short periods; the prosecution was given full rein in presenting its case, while the defence was prevented from calling most of the witnesses it named; and the verdict and sentences had the air of having been decided well in advance.

Taken in conjunction with the trials of the Pushkin Square demonstrators the preceding September and February, it looked as though the authorities were determined to crush dissent once and for all. But yet again, despite the heavy sentences, moral victory went to the dissenters. To begin with, the trial had attracted a great deal of publicity even before it began. This was a result partly of its clear connection with the Sinyavsky-Daniel trial and partly of the demonstration organized by Bukovsky and his friends to draw attention to it (which had led to its own trials and protests). Another factor was the interest shown by some of the foreign correspondents in Moscow, who learned of Ginzburg's arrest the day after it had occurred and were quick to publish the news abroad. Because the pre-trial investigation had taken so long (nearly a year, thus probably breaking Soviet law, which, with one proviso, allowed only nine months), there had been time to mobilize opinion among the intelligentsia, and at least three open letters had been addressed to the authorities appealing for the trial to be truly open and for the public to be admitted. Among the more than a hundred signatories of these letters were established writers like Kosterin, Axyonov, Iskander, and Akhmadulina, a few academicians, and a host of university professors, teachers, editors, journalists, artists, and so on. Particularly noteworthy was the large number of prominent scientists who signed the third of these appeals, including a distinguished mathematician by the name of Igor Shafarevich. Someone else who had intervened privately on behalf of the defendants was the brilliant nuclear physicist Andrei Sakharov ("father" of the Soviet H-bomb), who in February 1967 had appealed to the Central Committee not to proceed with the trial. His letter was not made public at the time, and he revealed its existence only some months later.

Even more striking than the pre-trial publicity, however, was the amount of controversy aroused during and after the trial. Among the many friends of the defendants locked out of the court-room were Pavel Litvinov and Larisa Bogoraz (who at that time was married to Yuli Daniel). Frustrated by their impotence and alarmed by what they heard from the defendants' relatives about the cynical way in which the prosecution was violating legal norms, they wrote an impassioned plea to "world public opinion." In it they denounced the trial as a witch-hunt and a mockery, and after describing numerous instances of the rigging of evidence by the court authorities, they appealed to people around the world to demand the prisoners' release and a retrial: "Citizens of our country! This trial is a stain on the honour of our state and on the conscience of every one of us. . . . Today it is not only the fate of the three accused that is at stake—their trial is no better than the celebrated trials of the 1930s, which involved us all in so much shame and so much bloodshed that we have still not recovered from them."[5]

The evocation of Stalin's show trials was deliberate, as was the authors' demonstrative rejection of Stalin's legacy by employing a form of appeal that had not been resorted to since the twenties, before Stalinism had tightened its grip. To emphasize this message, Litvinov and Bogoraz handed their statement directly to Western correspondents outside the court-room (they, too, having been locked out), without going through the pretence, as Litvinov had done the preceding October, of sending it to the Soviet press as well. "We are handing this appeal to the Western progressive press and ask that it be published and broadcast by radio as soon as possible. We are not sending this request to Soviet newspapers, because that is hopeless."[6] That one little word "progressive" remained as the only sop to official opinion. In all other respects the challenge was drastic and unmistakable.

Such activities by the dissidents could not fail to interest Solzhenitsyn. Until now he had been almost as remote from them as had Tvardovsky and his other friends in the Soviet literary establishment, but events were conspiring to drive him closer. It seemed that only a miracle had preserved him in 1965 from joining Sinyavsky and Daniel behind bars. At the time he had recoiled and mentally censured the other two writers for their duplicity in sending their works abroad. But the intervening two and a half years had seen a sea change in his attitude, and it was now he who was sending his books abroad and leading a distinctly double life. It was true that he planned to publish under his own name, but that was a measure of the way the times had changed and a sign of his increasing self-confidence. Others were clearly going further. Both Litvinov's recent statements had contained a direct challenge to the Soviet authorities (and above all to the KGB); and by handing the latest one to foreign correspondents, Litvinov had exorcized the old bogy of "contacts with Westerners" and "abroad." More than that, he was deliberately calling upon the foreign press and foreign radio stations to convey his message to the Soviet people, and thereby put pressure on the Soviet government.

It was at about this time that Litvinov released his book of documents on the trials of Bukovsky, Khaustov, Delaunay, and Kushev—*The Demonstration in Pushkin Square*—after having carefully ensured that one copy had reached the West and would be translated there. He was also busy collecting materials on the Ginzburg-Galanskov trial and made no secret of his intention to compile another book, although he was the object of more or less permanent surveillance by the KGB. This time the material was plentiful, for the sentencing of the two young student writers had aroused an even greater storm than that of Daniel and Sinyavsky. It was as though, the first time around, the intellectuals had been caught napping, and now were determined to make up for it and demonstrate their opposition to government bullying. In the course of January, February, and March about thirty open letters protesting against the conduct of the trial were sent to members of the government and circulated in samizdat. One signed by prominent writers, journalists, and artists included the names of Axyonov, Antokolsky, Iskander, Kaverin, Kornilov, Paustovsky, and Voinovich, while others attracted up to 220 signatures at a time. They came from many different parts of the country, and almost all quoted the original appeal by Litvinov and Bogoraz, which they had heard over foreign radio stations or seen in samizdat.

Litvinov, to whom copies of these letters had been sent, realized that he and Bogoraz had broken through an important barrier by addressing the West directly. Not only had they succeeded in arousing public opinion abroad

(Bertrand Russell, Graham Greene, and François Mauriac were among the many Western writers who protested). More importantly, they had aroused their fellow citizens as well and had created a platform, albeit limited and insecure, for further appeals and protests. For the first time since the twenties, an incipient public opinion was coming into being in the Soviet Union and henceforth would have to be reckoned with.

They were not the only ones to realize it. The authorities reacted by publishing two long articles about the case, one in *Izvestia* (*Izvestia* had already published two other articles, one before and one during the trial) and the other, aimed at young people, in *Komsomolskaya Pravda*. The purpose of both articles was to blacken the defendants by portraying them as agents of the Frankfurt-based NTS, the *émigré* opposition group that was proving most successful in getting news and manuscripts out of the Soviet Union and publicizing them in its political weekly, *Possev*, and its quarterly literary journal, *Grani*. The NTS had long been a thorn in the Soviet government's side, if only because it was the sole effective opposition left among the Russian *émigrés* and because its programme of Christian Socialism could hardly be portrayed as "capitalist." A strenuous attempt was therefore made to build it up as a sinister centre of subversion, training "spies and saboteurs" to infiltrate the Soviet Union and undermine it from within. "The parasites of yesterday," wrote *Komsomolskaya Pravda*, "stand accused today of having criminal ties with the White émigré organization NTS, whose task is the overthrow of the existing order in the USSR and the restoration of a bourgeois regime; of obtaining from the NTS anti-Soviet literature and disseminating it in our country; of sending materials to the West that contain slanders on our people and our homeland; and of engaging in manipulations involving the receipt of currency from abroad." Elsewhere the NTS was described as "a White *émigré* organization that formerly served Hitler and is now supported by the U.S. Central Intelligence Agency," and Galanskov, Ginzburg, and Dobrovolsky were accused of "espionage" and "treason," although their actual conviction had been on the less serious charge of "anti-Soviet propaganda."[7]

These articles backfired, however, in that they provoked a new hail of protests and open letters, and in March 1968 the editor of the *Literaturnaya Gazeta*, Alexander Chakovsky, intervened with an article called "Reply to a Reader." The article was noteworthy for its defensive tone and went to great lengths to try to neutralize the mass of protests that had come from abroad. Equally interesting was a comment slipped in near the beginning. "I would also like to add that people who find the Soviet system odious and are tempted by the fate of Tarsis, who vanished into the Lethe of the West, ought to be given the opportunity to share his fate. And instead of giving such people food and drink at the nation's expense in prisons or corrective labour colonies, the responsibility for their keep should be shifted to the American, English, or West German taxpayers."[8] Chakovsky's article in turn brought forth a barrage of protests, but then the official press fell silent until the summer.

Behind the scenes an attempt was made to stem the flow of publicity about the trial and punish those who had protested on behalf of the defendants. At the beginning of February the KGB summoned members of Ginzburg's and Galanskov's families and warned them against "spreading false information" about the trial. Soon afterwards Litvinov, Bogoraz, General Grigorenko,* and Pyotr Yakir† were called in for a similar purpose. More ominously, Alexander Esenin-Volpin and a young poet called Natalia Gorbanevskaya were forcibly confined to mental hospitals in mid-February. After about a week Gorbanevskaya was discharged, but it was not until May that Esenin-Volpin was released, and then only after two letters in his defence had been signed by over a hundred distinguished academicians, mathematicians, and scientists and sent to the minister of health (one made its way abroad and was broadcast back by foreign radio stations, thus adding to the publicity). At the same time, many of the Communists who had signed protest letters were expelled from the Party, and a number of them lost their jobs, while others were deprived of privileges or moved to inferior positions.

At the Writers' Union moves were afoot to deal similarly with members who had signed the protests, but the secretariat ran into considerable resistance. Hints in the literary press that certain writers might be expelled brought a delegation (said to include Axyonov, Tendryakov, and Evtushenko) to headquarters to say that if this happened, 100 writers (some said 150) would resign on the spot, and Kaverin informed the secretariat that he, Chukovsky, Paustovksy, and Pavel Antokolsky‡ were also prepared to resign. By the time a formal meeting was called on 17 April, the secretariat was prepared to content itself with handing out warnings and reprimands. Among those rebuked were Kopelev (who had also blotted his copybook by supporting Solzhenitsyn's letter to the Writers' Congress), and about thirty other writers. In a parallel action, the literary critic Grigori Svirski was expelled from the Communist Party for a fiery speech he had made to the Writers' Union in January in support of Solzhenitsyn's letter.§

Litvinov and his friends were now awash with material on the trial and its aftermath and worked furiously at putting it all together in a new "white book." At the same time, they conceived the idea of starting a regular publi-

*General Piotr (or Petro, as he now prefers to be called) Grigorenko was a distinguished war hero during the Second World War and was promoted to major general in 1959. In the early sixties he became disgusted with Khrushchev's policies and as a result of his energetic protests was confined to a mental hospital in 1964. Thereafter he became an active dissident and was best known for his defence of the rights of the Crimean Tartars (deported from their homeland by Stalin after the Second World War). He emigrated to the West in 1977.

†Pyotr Yakir is the son of the former army commander Iona Yakir, who was executed, on Stalin's orders, in 1937. Pyotr Yakir spent his entire childhood and youth in prisons and labour camps and was released only in 1954, after Stalin's death. In the mid-sixties he became a leading dissident in Moscow.

‡Pavel Antokolsky was a minor but honest poet of the older generation. He also wrote a personal letter to Solzhenitsyn in support of Solzhenitsyn's letter to the Writers' Congress.

§Solzhenitsyn later bumped into Svirski outside the block of flats where both Svirski and Kopelev lived, questioned him closely about the circumstances of his expulsion, and urged him to stand firm.

cation, a samizdat journal, in which to publish some of the vast amount of information they were receiving from various parts of the country. Unlike earlier samizdat journals, it would be factual and descriptive, a kind of news magazine for the dissidents and their supporters, whose numbers seemed to multiply by the day, and would concentrate on chronicling the excesses of the authorities and the attempts of various individuals to protest and fight back. Thus was born the unofficial *Chronicle of Current Events*, whose first number appeared in April 1968. Taking advantage of the fact that the United Nations had proclaimed 1968 "International Human Rights Year," the *Chronicle* placed Article 19 of the UN's Universal Declaration of Human Rights (proclaiming the right to freedom of expression) on its masthead and made violations of this article—such as the Ginzburg-Galanskov trial—the main object of its investigations. Its first editor and guiding spirit was Natalia Gorbanevskaya. Simultaneously, a young historian who had earlier been exiled for his unconventional views, Andrei Amalrik, suggested that the loose coalition of dissidents that had emerged as a result of the Ginzburg-Galanskov trial call itself the Democratic Movement, and this was widely accepted, although Human Rights Movement came to be used in parallel with it and was positively preferred by some.

Solzhenitsyn appears to have been deeply interested in these developments. Many of the people protesting on behalf of Ginzburg and Galanskov had earlier supported his letter to the Writers' Congress. There was clearly a community of interest, and like the authorities, Solzhenitsyn realized that some sort of a breakthrough had occurred. In March 1968, on one of his visits to the capital, he sought a meeting with Litvinov and Bogoraz to discuss the dissidents' methods and goals. He had already been in touch with them through intermediaries, sending congratulations on their appeal to world opinion and signalling his approval of the way Litvinov had turned the tables on his KGB interrogators, but now he evidently wished for a closer acquaintance. They arranged to meet early one morning at the flat of Litvinov's parents. Solzhenitsyn arrived punctually, bursting with energy and *bonhomie*, and at once began to question them about their long-term plans. Litvinov and Bogoraz indicated the Czech reform movement as their model (the "Prague spring" was well under way by this time) and said they hoped for similar developments in the Soviet Union. Solzhenitsyn was unimpressed. The Czech movement was being led by Communists, he said, but they had no counterparts in the Soviet Union. Nor were the Soviet intelligentsia or the Soviet workers as much to be relied upon as their Czech equivalents.

Litvinov quoted the case of Anatoli Marchenko, the worker who had just completed an amazing exposure of the labour-camp system under Khrushchev and Brezhnev.* There was talk of offering the book to *Novy Mir*, not so much because *Novy Mir* was expected to publish it (it was too sensational for that), but simply in order to legalize its existence and afford the

---

* *My Testimony*, published in the West in 1969.

author some protection—much as Kopelev had intended when encouraging Solzhenitsyn to offer *Ivan Denisovich* to *Novy Mir* in 1961—and Litvinov asked Solzhenitsyn his opinion. Solzhenitsyn had apparently read Marchenko's book in samizdat and had a very high opinion of it, but he advised against sending it to *Novy Mir*. It would only embarrass Tvardovsky and his colleagues and make their position even more difficult than it was already (it was in fact offered to *Novy Mir*, and also to *Znamya*, but without result, and Marchenko was eventually arrested and jailed).

The conversation lasted about an hour and a half, and Litvinov had the distinct impression that they were being "inspected" by Solzhenitsyn to see whether he should throw them his support. He was obviously deeply interested in what the Democratic Movement was doing, and gave them the impression that he generally shared their views, without, however, being over-eager to link forces in any formal way. A short time later he sent them a page of text in which their role in standing up to the Soviet authorities was described in glowing terms. They were asked to burn the page after having read it; they subsequently learned that it was a page from the last chapter of *The Gulag Archipelago*.[9]*

Solzhenitsyn did not see Litvinov again, though it appears he had similar meetings with Bukovsky, Ginzburg, and several others. He was fundamentally a lone wolf and not disposed to run with the pack. He may also have been discouraged by the aura of bohemianism that surrounded the dissidents, who were mostly far younger and more informal than he. Having mustered the courage to throw off the bonds of political conformity, many dispensed with the social conventions as well, while a common danger bound them together into a close-knit, conspiratorial circle. Jobs and other social obligations were often ignored (many of the dissidents had in any case been dismissed for their political activities), and thus they felt themselves to be outsiders in more than one respect. To the somewhat puritanical Solzhenitsyn, much of their behaviour was uncongenial. Similarly, the dissidents advocated, and practised, democracy in their personal relations as well as in political theory, and neither was particularly attractive to Solzhenitsyn. What drew him to the dissidents was their civic courage and the audacity with which they challenged the authorities, an audacity that so far had exceeded his own. But he was disturbed by their disregard for discipline, their liberal social values, their egalitarianism, and, as it seemed to him, their uncritical admiration of the West.

It was at about this time that he met a man who was to prove profoundly congenial to him, both in personality and in his political and religious convictions—Igor Shafarevich. Shafarevich was a brilliant mathematician (he had become a full professor at Moscow University at the age of twenty-one),

---

* Interestingly enough, when Litvinov questioned Solzhenitsyn about rumours that he had written a book called *The Gulag Archipelago*, Solzhenitsyn denied that he had, and asked Litvinov to tell his friends that these rumours were not true. Even more interesting is the fact that when *The Gulag Archipelago* finally appeared, the page about Litvinov and Bogoraz was missing.

a corresponding member of the Academy of Sciences and, outwardly at least, a pillar of the Soviet intellectual establishment. Solzhenitsyn, with his scientific background and through his friendships with Zhores Medvedev, Timofeyev-Ressovsky, Kapitsa, and Tamm had had easy access to these circles but had not been impressed with what he saw. Most top scientists, he felt, were too wrapped up in their field of study or too obsessed by their material privileges to bother themselves with social and ethical questions. In this he was overly pessimistic, for among scientists, too, certain attitudes were changing. There had been several scientists and mathematicians among the signatories of the letters in defence of Ginzburg and Galanskov. Scientific institutes like those at Obninsk, and science-oriented cities like Novosibirsk, were decidedly freer in their intellectual atmosphere than the rest of the country—as Solzhenitsyn had discovered a year or two beforehand when giving his readings. And Shafarevich was one of those concerned academicians who had spoken up for Ginzburg and Galanskov without fear for his reputation.

Their first meeting was not auspicious. Shafarevich had just been to Yugoslavia and insisted on showing Solzhenitsyn his snapshots of the Adriatic, a tiresome ritual that convinced the latter that Shafarevich was not different from most of his colleagues. But at subsequent meetings Solzhenitsyn discovered in this tall, rugged individual, still only in his mid-forties, "the strong and vigorous grip of an independent mind uncluttered with stereotyped preconceptions, capable of sifting the wheat from the chaff." Shafarevich had interests far beyond his narrow field of mathematics. He was passionately fond of music, (he had written a study of the "flawed genius" Shostakovich). He was interested in the phenomenon of socialism (in its Soviet variant) and was inclined to take a metaphysical view of it as a spiritual disease or a sickness of the soul that afflicts nations at various times and in various regions of the globe, independently of their national history. But the quality that most endeared him to Solzhenitsyn and drew the two of them together was his passionate patriotism. As Solzhenitsyn later wrote:

> Shafarevich was from birth inseparably tied to Russia, the land and its history: they are one flesh, with a common bloodstream, a single heartbeat. His love of Russia is a jealous love—to make up for the past carelessness of our generation? He looks insistently for ways to use his head and his hands so as to requite his country for the love it inspires in him.[10]

By the time of these meetings, Solzhenitsyn had almost finished *The Gulag Archipelago*—all that remained was to type out the final manuscript in several copies and distribute them in various hiding-places. One chapter, based on readers' letters to him and to *Novy Mir* with their reactions to *Ivan Denisovich*, seemed not to fit, but rather than waste it, Solzhenitsyn gave it to his friends to read and encouraged them to let it circulate in samizdat.[11] It was a summary of readers' responses, both positive and negative, accompanied by a commentary by Solzhenitsyn, and covered some of the same ground that Teush had gone over in his early article on *Ivan Denisovich*. In Solzhenitsyn's survey, however, the more fulsome responses were eliminated, and more space was given to the negative and sometimes highly critical letters that he had received, mostly from members or ex-members of the security services. At the time when Teush wrote, such people had seemed to be in eclipse, but time had shown that, on the contrary, it was they who were in the ascendant in Brezhnev's Russia, and Solzhenitsyn was anxious to expose them.

In early April 1968 Solzhenitsyn moved to his summer-house in Rozhdestvo, anticipating two months of peaceful labour typing up and collating *The Gulag Archipelago* amidst the warmth of spring. But it was not to be. Spring was late that year, and Saturday, 13 April, produced a heavy snowstorm. Sunday the fourteenth produced a different kind of surprise. Tuning in to the BBC's evening programmes, Solzhenitsyn heard with trepidation that some extracts from *Cancer Ward* had just appeared in the *Times Literary Supplement* in London. It was both expected and unexpected. He had a fairly shrewd idea that one or another copy of the novel must have reached the West by now, but he had deliberately not inquired too closely in order not to incriminate himself. Let it find its own way there once the initial push had been given—in that way he could preserve his innocence and honestly swear that he wasn't responsible.

Such a position was important—it was sufficient to have only *The First Circle* to worry about. The next day, Natalia arrived post-haste from Ryazan to inform him that Tvardovsky was in a panic and searching for him everywhere. Neither she nor Solzhenitsyn knew exactly what the reason was—Tvardovsky's alarm dated from before the BBC broadcast. But Solzhenitsyn felt sure that it must be connected in some way with *Cancer Ward* and hastened to cover his rear. Keeping fast to his theory of attack, he decided that now was the moment to make public his record of the September meeting of the Writers' Union secretariat, where a half promise had been made to publish part 1 of *Cancer Ward*. In the course of the winter, he had had friends prepare fifty copies for just such an occasion. He had also prepared fifty copies of Voronkov's November letter to him and his reply (which he had had the satisfaction of hearing broadcast by the BBC in February—the leak came from Voronkov's end). To these he added a fresh letter of his own in which he summarized the state of the stalled negotiations over *Cancer Ward* and drew attention to its appearance abroad. "A year has passed and the inevitable has happened: recently, chapters from *Cancer Ward* were published in the *Times Literary Supplement*. Nor are further printings precluded—perhaps of inaccurate and incompletely edited versions. What has happened compels me to acquaint our literary community with the contents of the attached letters and statements, so that the position and responsibility of the secretariat of the Writers' Union will be clear."[12]

It was a brilliant piece of work. It laid the blame squarely on the Writers' Union, diverting attention from any possible role that he himself might have played in the affair; and it enabled him to throw up a smoke-screen over the issue of the accuracy and completeness of the manuscript that was in the West, and eventually of the quality of the translation. In this way he avoided committing himself on the main issue—did he or did he not approve of the publication of his manuscripts in the West?—while expressing indignation over a decidedly minor aspect of the problem.

Having prepared his fifty copies, Solzhenitsyn planned to dispatch them to fifty selected members of the Writers' Union. It was a rather cumbersome way of writing an open letter without declaring it open—someone was sure to leak its contents to the West, and he would not be held responsible. Litvinov and the dissidents were already handing their letters to Western correspondents, but Solzhenitsyn was still too cautious to do that. He was still, however precariously, a member of the Soviet establishment (and a member of the Writers' Union) and felt that he was obliged to preserve appearances. He couldn't afford to have it known that publication in the West was precisely what he wanted and had been working for.

When everything was ready, he took the copies to Moscow to meet whatever challenge lay ahead. As he had guessed, it was connected with *Cancer Ward*. Tvardovsky had received a telegram from the editors of *Grani*, the literary magazine associated with the dreaded NTS: "We hereby inform you that the Committee for State Security through the medium of Victor Louis has sent a further copy of *Cancer Ward* to the West so as to block its publication in *Novy Mir*. We have therefore decided to publish this work immediately."[13]

Tvardovsky was in a thunderous mood. If *Grani* published *Cancer Ward* in Russian, it would put an end to all his hopes of publishing the novel in *Novy Mir*, and simultaneously to his efforts to "save" Solzhenitsyn for Soviet literature. Almost as bad were the implications of guilt by association. Barely two months had passed since the Soviet press had painted the NTS in the most lurid colours. The mere presumption of a connection between this *émigré* organization and Ginzburg and Galanskov had been regarded as sufficient to damn them. Solzhenitsyn was no dissident, but the consequences of his novel's being published by the NTS were incalculable. And the publication would inevitably cast a shadow on *Novy Mir* as well. The only way out was for Solzhenitsyn to write a strong letter of denunciation (which might serve, who knew, as that anti-Western letter so long and ardently sought by Fedin and the Writers' Union: Tvardovsky was at one with them now).

Tvardovsky did not doubt that Solzhenitsyn would write such a letter—he had already promised Demichev as much, eagerly supported by Lakshin and Kondratovich. But Solzhenitsyn was evasive. Taken aback by the *Grani* telegram (though not as upset as the others), he tried to brush it aside by showing Tvardovsky his letter to members of the Writers' Union. But that only poured more fat on the fire: Tvardovsky was appalled. At that very moment the government was planning to strengthen the criminal code and intensify sanctions against dissenters. The thing for Solzhenitsyn to do was to demonstrate his loyalty by sending *Grani* a telegram. He had to show everyone where he stood—for *Novy Mir's* sake as well as his own. Solzhenitsyn reluctantly agreed and was given Lakshin's office for the purpose, but the words would not come. He needed a pause to think. With difficulty he persuaded Tvardovsky to give him a little more time and went off to the Chukovskys' dacha to discuss the whole affair with Lydia. The idea of writing a purely loyalist letter or telegram was repugnant, but the matter was clearly serious. How could he wriggle out of it this time?

A careful perusal of the telegram provided an answer. First there was the unusual circumstance of its delivery—how many telegrams from anti-Soviet organizations abroad were delivered by the ever-vigilant Moscow post office to their rightful addressees? Perhaps it was a forgery or a provocation? If not, what were *Grani's* motives in sending it? There was little Solzhenitsyn could do in a practical way to stop publication of his novel or to interfere with other copies going abroad. Was *Grani* trying to "protect" him or to damage him further? Above all, who was Victor Louis and where had *he* obtained the manuscript? By sheer chance he discovered that Victor Louis was a Moscow newspaperman with an unusual background. His real name was Vitaly Levin, and he had spent a number of years in the labour camps, where his "good" behaviour and co-operation with the authorities had earned him a Moscow residence permit and complete freedom to travel abroad. He was now married to the daughter of a wealthy Englishman, possessed a luxurious flat in Moscow and a country house in the exclusive village of Bakovka, and worked as a foreign correspondent for the London *Evening News*. It had been Victor Louis who, the preceding year, had taken an extra copy of Svetlana Alliluyeva's memoirs to the West and blunted their impact by arranging for a pirate translation to appear before her own edition. His supplier was said to be the KGB.

The intervention—or, rather, alleged intervention—of such a dramatic and shadowy figure was a godsend to the beleaguered Solzhenitsyn ("If Victor Louis hadn't existed, I should have done well to invent him"). In drafting the required letter to the Writers' Union, he did indeed protest against the publication of his novel in *Grani*, but the focus of the letter became the identity and activities of Louis, his possible connection with the KGB, and the dilatoriness of the Writers' Union in not permitting publication of *Cancer Ward* in the Soviet Union (thereby ensuring its prior appearance abroad). "This episode," concluded Solzhenitsyn, "compels us to reflect on the strange, dark ways by which the manuscripts of Soviet writers can reach the West. It constitutes a drastic reminder to us that literature must not be put in such a position that literary works become a profitable commodity for any scoundrel who happens to have a visa. The works of our authors must be given the possibility of publication in their own country and must not become the plunder of foreign publishing houses."[14]

It was hardly the searing denunciation of the pernicious "neo-*émigré*" journal (as Tvardovsky had called it) that Tvardovsky had demanded, much less the anti-Western diatribe that the Writers' Union was seeking, but it seemed to contain sufficient disparaging references to the Western greed for "profitable commodities" and "plunder" to hold the line for a while, and Solzhenitsyn returned to Rozhdestvo with a feeling that he had done well to keep his head. But his troubles over *Cancer Ward* were only beginning. An unidentified friend (called "A.E." in *The Oak and the Calf*) came quickly with more bad news. Two Western publishers—the Bodley Head, in London, and Mondadori, in Italy—were engaged in litigation over which of them had the rights to *Cancer Ward*, and the Bodley Head was claiming Solzhenitsyn's authorization. This was more dangerous than the *Grani* affair, for the Bodley Head had acquired its copy from Pavel Ličko in Bratislava, and it was well known that Ličko had visited Solzhenitsyn in Ryazan—indeed, he was the only foreign journalist to have penetrated there. Solzhenitsyn hastily composed yet another letter for dispatch to *Le Monde* and *L'Unità* in the West (both considered "respectable," from a Soviet point of view, because of their left-wing sympathies), with a copy for the *Literaturnaya Gazeta*. The initial draft was so anti-Western that some friends persuaded him to tone it down, but even then it proved to be the harshest and most anti-Western document he had yet produced, and came close enough to the denunciation that the Writers' Union had been demanding of him for it to be accepted and published by the *Literaturnaya Gazeta*, albeit with a delay of two months (by which time it was too late to be of help in that cause). In it, Solzhenitsyn denounced the Mondadori–Bodley Head quarrel and made his categorical disclaimer.

> I declare that *no* foreign publisher has received a manuscript of this novel from me, or any authorization to publish it. Therefore, I do not recognize as legal *any* publication of this novel, present or future, carried out without my authorization, and I do not accept that anyone has the right to publish it. All distortions of the text, which are inevitable considering the number of copies involved and their uncontrolled distribution, are harmful to me. I categorically condemn and prohibit all unauthorized adaptations for the screen or stage.
>
> I already know from experience that *A Day in the Life of Ivan Denisovich* was spoiled by haste in all the translations. The same fate evidently awaits *Cancer Ward*. But money is one thing, literature is another.[15]

Like all Solzhenitsyn's public statements in this vein, the letter was another masterpiece of ambiguity. While refusing to acknowledge that any Western publication of *Cancer Ward* was authorized (and denying any personal involvement), he reserved his "categorical" condemnation and prohibition only for stage and screen adaptations, which weren't in question at the time. Similarly, he again sought to divert attention from the main issue by denouncing the "uncontrolled distribution" of his work, "distortions" in the text, and the vexed problem of bad translations, subjects that genuinely concerned him but were hardly the chief worry of the Soviet authorities. He was treading a fine line, however, and the very vehemence of his statement led to much confusion among his supporters and sympathizers in the West.

The accepted view of the majority was that he truly did not want publication in the West. This not only accorded with the general picture of Solzhenitsyn as a left-of-centre "socialist" writer in close harmony with the pregressive socialist views espoused by Tvardovsky and *Novy Mir*, and loyal to the Soviet government line, but also fitted with his apparent repudiation of the *Grani* publication and his strenuous efforts to be published in the Soviet Union itself. People who held this view feared that if a link could be established between Solzhenitsyn and Western publishers, he would be arraigned on the same charges as Daniel and Sinyavsky three years earlier and liable to heavy punishment. A leading American specialist on Soviet literature, Kathryn Feuer, summed up these fears when she told a *Time* magazine reporter, "How tragic if, accustomed to operating in a free society, [Western publishers] have misjudged the situation and are playing into the hands of Solzhenitsyn's enemies, while thinking to serve freedom and literature."[16]

The resulting pressure led two American publishers, Frederick Praeger and E. P. Dutton, to drop plans to publish *Cancer Ward* and issue a public statement about it. Olga Carlisle, who was making final preparations with Harper & Row to reveal the forthcoming publication of *The First Circle*, was also feeling queasy. What if Solzhenitsyn should feel compelled to denounce her as well? *Time* magazine's Soviet affairs specialist, Patricia Blake, had somehow got wind of the Harper & Row project and was doing everything she could behind the scenes to put a stop to it. A close student of Solzhenitsyn's career and devoted to his cause, she feared that Solzhenitsyn's very life would be placed in danger if publication went ahead, and this was virtually the consensus among Western specialists on Soviet literature.

Olga Carlisle at least had Solzhenitsyn's personal assurance that he wanted her to proceed and would not denounce the publication of *The First Circle*, and indeed he never did. But the situation with *Cancer Ward* was more complicated. The Bodley Head had obtained its copy from an astute English journalist named Nicholas Bethell, who had made contact with Pavel Ličko in Bratislava and smuggled the manuscript out in his lap while being driven in a friend's car (these were the months of the "Prague spring," when controls on the Czech frontier were very lax and Westerners could come and go with relative ease). The Bodley Head, however, under pressure from critics of its plans, had wanted assurances that Ličko was empowered to authorize publication and had brought him to London in March, where he swore a confidential affidavit confirming that Solzhenitsyn wished to have the novel published. Solzhenitsyn had asked him, said Ličko, to publish *Cancer Ward* in Czechoslovakia and to find "a responsible publisher in the West" and had indicated that the two countries where he would prefer publication first were England and Japan, which had "the two most deep-rooted cultures in the world."[17] To protect Solzhenitsyn, Ličko's testimony was kept secret, but the Bodley Head's claim of authorization was public knowledge, and the British publisher at once brought out a Russian-language edition to establish copyright.

Meanwhile, the Italian publishing house of Mondadori had acquired a manuscript from a different source and was preparing to publish it, in Russian, almost simultaneously.

A mystery remains as to the real nature of Solzhenitsyn's dealings with Pavel Ličko. In *The Oak and the Calf* Solzhenitsyn makes only a glancing reference to "some Slovak reporters" who had visited him in Ryazan (Ličko had always implied he was alone, but he may not have been, of course), not mentioning Ličko by name or indicating that he had given him a copy of *Cancer Ward*. On the contrary, when referring to its impending publication, Solzhenitsyn writes that "*Cancer Ward* was precisely the book I had never tried to pass to the West. I had had offers, there were ways, but somehow I had always refused without knowing why. But if it had found its own way there, that was how it should be. God's appointed time had come."[18] Solzhenitsyn was not above lending God a helping hand if there was a risk of His being late for His appointed time, but how are we to explain this confident denial? Forgetfulness? Disingenuousness? Deliberate mystification? It could be that Ličko had simply exceeded his brief. There is no doubt that Solzhenitsyn had approved the novel's publication in Slovakia. A month or two later he was to write to the Tatran publishing house in Bratislava expressing his pleasure over the news that they planned to publish it (they never quite did—the stocks were still in the warehouse when the Warsaw Pact invasion took place in August). At the same time, he expressed regret that they had evidently translated it from one of the "itinerant" versions that lacked his final corrections of the preceding December, which may have indicated a forgetting of Ličko's role in taking it there, but was more likely to be another smoke-screen to protect his position. The letter, after all, was sent through the regular mail to an official publishing house in a Communist country.[19]

It is not clear why Solzhenitsyn should be so anxious to deny complicity in the foreign publication of *Cancer Ward* when he has freely admitted to having sent *The First Circle* abroad shortly beforehand. At the time his concern was understandable. Ličko's signing of an affidavit, even in confidence, really did appear to place Solzhenitsyn in jeopardy, and one can understand the vehemence of his denial. But now it seems only mysterious, unless Solzhenitsyn's resentment of Ličko is so strong that he wishes to deny him any part in the story.*

Having composed his letter to *Le Monde* and *L'Unità*, Solzhenitsyn lost no time in taking copies to the offices of the *Literaturnaya Gazeta* and *Literaturnaya Rossia* in Moscow. Their first response was to promise immediate publication, in return for which Solzhenitsyn agreed to postpone sending the letters abroad for a couple of days. Publication in the Soviet Union would

---

* Such was the atmosphere of suspicion and distrust surrounding this episode that because of his wartime connection with the Soviet armed forces, Ličko was suspected by some of having links with the KGB. This suspicion appears to have been unfounded. In 1970, after the Warsaw Pact invasion of Czechoslovakia, Ličko was sentenced to eighteen months' imprisonment on charges of having damaged Czechoslovakia's interests abroad and corrupted Czechoslovak youth.

provide a better shield and obviate the need actually to send them, since the letter's appearance in Moscow would obviously be reported abroad. But when nothing happened, Solzhenitsyn acted. The *Le Monde* letter went off as planned. In the case of *L'Unità*, however, he decided to make use of the presence in Moscow of the Italian Communist literary critic Vittorio Strada, once a leading light in COMES and still a frequent visitor to Moscow, and asked him to take the letter back to Italy.

It wasn't quite the direct appeal to foreign correspondents that the dissidents were now specializing in, but it was a further step in that direction, and it almost brought Solzhenitsyn to grief. Despite his relatively privileged status, Strada was searched by the customs on his way out and Solzhenitsyn's letter was confiscated, together with a quantity of samizdat. Solzhenitsyn was told of this at the time but paid no particular attention to it until a few weeks later, when a letter arrived out of the blue summoning him to the customs office at Sheremetyevo Airport "in connection with . . . a matter concerning you personally." Not wanting to appear submissive, he wrote back suggesting a meeting at Veronica Stein's flat in the city centre, and in due course met one of the customs officers, accompanied by someone who was evidently from the KGB, to discuss the matter. The visitors were models of politeness, but momentarily startled Solzhenitsyn by producing not only his letter but also a copy of his transcript of the Writers' Union meeting to discuss *Cancer Ward*. One look told him that it had been typed on a strange typewriter, so it was easy to disclaim it. He even feigned indignation at Strada: "It was intended for home consumption." When it came to the letter, which he could not disclaim, he decided on an elaborate bluff and went over to the attack. How dare they intercept his letter? It was very important for it to appear in the Italian press for the honour of Soviet literature. "A letter attacking a pirate publisher was on its way to an Italian Communist newspaper. It would have been useful to the Italian Communist party! Why did you hold it up?"

Solzhenitsyn even tried to persuade the customs officer to post the letter on for him and offered to provide a stamp, but the officer balked, and the interview petered out with neither side the winner.[20] It showed yet again, however, that boldness paid, that merely to stand up to the Soviet bureaucratic machine (so difficult for the average, brainwashed Soviet citizen to do) was to wreak a fundamental change in one's relations with it, and that the bureaucrats themselves were helpless when faced by a challenge in place of the usual weak submission. At the same time, there was fresh cause for anxiety. The customs' letter had been delivered to his shack in Rozhdestvo, a place whose whereabouts he had kept secret from all but his closest friends. If the post office knew where to find him, it meant that the KGB knew as well, and the tiny cabin was awash with hundreds of pages of the half-typed *Gulag Archipelago*.

It was time to hurry. For the rest of May, Solzhenitsyn and Natalia rushed to finish typing final copies and to make microfilms of the whole book.

The work was finished on 2 June 1968. Almost immediately he heard of an opportunity to send the film out to the West—Vadim Andreyev was in Moscow and would shortly be leaving for Western Europe. There was some risk involved—a search by the customs could not quite be ruled out—but Andreyev was not likely to run into trouble. After a delay of about a week, he left on 9 June.

The circumstances were such that Solzhenitsyn would not know for about another week whether the mission had been safely accomplished. He attempted to settle down to some work. On the very day the typing of *The Gulag Archipelago* was completed, he had received news of Harper & Row's Russian edition of *The First Circle*, together with their announcement of its forthcoming appearance in English. He had also just received a copy of the Mondadori Russian-language edition of *Cancer Ward*.[21] That meant that he had not one but two big novels out in the West simultaneously and that his bridges to the Soviet literary establishment were now burned. There was no chance whatever that either work could be published at home. It had all happened so fast, and while so much else was going on at the same time, that he had hardly had a chance to assimilate the idea. Only recently Sinyavsky and Daniel had been jailed for publishing their stories in the West, and he had lain sleepless and quaking, waiting for the police to come for him after the confiscation of his archive. Yet here he was, three years later, alive and well and flourishing, while his books, banned at home, had begun to travel the world.

But the shadow of *Gulag* was still hanging over him. Had it reached the West safely, or had it been intercepted by the customs? He tried to do some work on *The First Circle*. Now that there was definitely no chance of its appearing in the Soviet Union, he regretted that he had let the shorter version go. It was time to restore the missing nine chapters, chapters that had been controversial to begin with, but in which he could afford to be even bolder now that the die was cast. But he found it impossible to work. The agony of suspense over his microfilms was too great. If they should go astray, if they fell into the hands of the KGB the way his letter to *L'Unità* had done, his days of freedom were numbered. True, it would take the KGB some weeks to establish the author, which would give him time to arrange his affairs and prepare for the worst, but there was too much autobiography in the book for him to remain undetected, and the style was easily identifiable by experts. In a fever of anxiety he packed his bags and fled once again—to a safe flat without a telephone. But still the days flicked by without news.

> My work was going to pieces. I was short of air, short of room to move. I couldn't even go near the windows, in case someone spotted a stranger. I had put myself in jail, except that the windows had no "muzzles" and I was not on short rations. But oh, how reluctant I was to go to the Lubyanka![22]

For a few days he was the hunted convict again, reliving the agonies of his imprisonment (already relived so intensely once, in the writing of *The*

Gulag Archipelago) and fearing for his life. But then came the news that the microfilms were in the West and that he was safe. "Big fish" had reached Paris and within a matter of days had been picked up by the Carlisles and taken to America. The process of publication was to be the same as for *The First Circle*. Thomas Whitney would translate, the Carlisles would edit the translation, and Harper & Row would be the publishers. The difference was that this time there were fifteen hundred pages of tightly packed manuscript to deal with—more than three times as many as in *The First Circle*. On the other hand, no date had been set for publication. The translator and editors seemed to have all the time in the world to prepare Solzhenitsyn's *magnum opus* and get it right.

As for Solzhenitsyn, he could not say when he would be ready to publish. Apparently, he was thinking of publication in about two years' time, but the main thing was that the manuscript was safe. He had done the first part of his duty to the victims of the Gulag, both living and dead. The testimony was complete. But to publish it would be to let off a bomb, in whose explosion he himself might perish. For this sacrifice he was not yet prepared, particularly since he hoped to make a start at long last on his historical epic. Let the translation into English be made ready while he started work on a task even more gargantuan than *The Gulag Archipelago*, and one he had long regarded as the most important of his life.

35

PORTRAIT OF THE
ARTIST AT FIFTY

T HE *LITERATURNAYA GAZETA* printed Solzhenitsyn's letter to Western
publishers on 26 June 1968, two months after he had written it. The
delay was evidently due to two factors. First, the decision on whether to
publish or not had been referred upwards, probably to the Central Committee. Secondly, the decision, when it came, must have been accompanied by
an instruction to publish a separate article setting out the official view of
Solzhenitsyn's letter and of Solzhenitsyn generally, and this had taken some
time to compose and clear.

The article was called "The Ideological Struggle and the Writer's
Responsibility" and was anonymous, though it was rumoured that the authors
were two literary critics and loyal Party members, Vitaly Ozerov and Boris
Ryurikov (both of whom had been present at the secretariat's discussion of
Cancer Ward). The article's anonymity implied that it was the official view of
the *Literaturnaya Gazeta* and therefore of the Writers' Union. Part 1 of the
article was devoted to a review of the world-wide ideological struggle between
the Soviet Union and the West, and the use that Western propagandists were
making of the actions of those dissenters who were also writers. These writers, said the newspaper, were untalented impostors, ranging from the
"graphomaniac and schizophrenic" Tarsis through the "homunculus" Svetlana Alliluyeva to the "underground lampooners . . . Ginzburg, Galanskov,
and their ilk." It was true that certain respectable writers had been deceived
into expressing support for these "slanderers and adventurers," but the overwhelming majority of Soviet writers "who cherish their good name and the
honour of their homeland . . . convinced that their work cannot be divorced
from the interests of the people and the Party and from the ideas of socialist

society" were determined to rebuff Western attempts to co-opt them, and the article approvingly cited Anatoli Kuznetsov, Vladimir Tendryakov, Valentin Katayev, and Galina Serebryakova as writers (and "liberals") who had refused to be manipulated.

Having thus lined Solzhenitsyn up with the schizophrenics and adventurers, the *Literaturnaya Gazeta* went on to describe his career in terms that would support such a view. *A Day in the Life of Ivan Denisovich*, the published short stories, and Solzhenitsyn's nearly successful candidacy for the Lenin Prize were passed over in silence. Instead, the article concentrated on Solzhenitsyn's dealings with the Writers' Union, including his letter to the Fourth Writers' Congress and his subsequent correspondence with the secretariat. Solzhenitsyn, it said, had refused to take any part in the public life of the union and had insisted on going his own way. In his letter, which "had violated the generally accepted norms of behaviour," he had made impossible demands. At the Secretariat's discussion of *Cancer Ward*, he had behaved demagogically, and in his later letters he had issued a series of ultimatums designed to blackmail the Writers' Union into complying with his wishes.[1]

In all this there was more than a grain of truth. It was clear that Solzhenitsyn's aggressive tactics in dealing with the union had not gone unremarked in the proper quarters. And the anonymous authors of the article were able to score a number of points. The reproduction of Solzhenitsyn's original letter to the congress in multiple copies, they pointed out, had virtually guaranteed widespread publicity, since copies were bound to reach the West. Similar tactics with subsequent letters to the secretariat indicated a definite desire on Solzhenitsyn's part to exploit Western public opinion. Solzhenitsyn's letter denouncing the foreign publication of *Cancer Ward* had come too late to prevent its appearance, and Solzhenitsyn had directed his concern more against possible distortions of his novel than against the actual fact of publication. But in other respects the article was a travesty. Having accused Solzhenitsyn of hypocrisy, the *Literaturnaya Gazeta* went on to describe as "nonsense" the charge that Solzhenitsyn's "files and manuscripts . . . had been taken from him," since they were not "manuscripts" but typed copies and had been removed not from Solzhenitsyn's flat but from "a certain citizen Teush," a peddler of anti-Soviet propaganda. This provided the excuse for yet one more tirade against *Feast of the Conquerors* and a denunciation of Solzhenitsyn's disclaimer of responsibility as insincere. "How can we pretend that such a play does not exist if A. Solzhenitsyn, having entrusted the safekeeping of his works to a supplier of anti-Sovietism to the foreign world, thereby lost all control over them and over the play in particular?"

It was clear that the principal point at issue, as it had been all along, was still Solzhenitsyn's refusal to dissociate himself from the West and to write a public denunciation of "Western propagandists."

One had hoped that A. Solzhenitsyn would finally recognize the need to speak out in sharp protest against the actions of foreign publishers, would disavow his unbidden 'guardians,' and would declare, for all to hear, his unwillingness to have anything to do with the enemy provocateurs of our country. But Solzhenitsyn did not do so. . . .

The writer A. Solzhenitsyn could devote his literary abilities completely to his homeland and not to its ill-wishers. He could, but he does not want to. Such is the bitter truth.[2]

The *Literaturnaya Gazeta* had got the best of both worlds. It had published Solzhenitsyn's letter, which though not nearly militant enough by Party standards, was still the most anti-Western statement he had ever made, and it had used the occasion to launch a wide-ranging attack on all aspects of Solzhenitsyn's behaviour. It was the first official response that Solzhenitsyn had ever received to his letter to the congress and was to set the official line for some months to come. And yet, while totally negative in tone and content, it could have been worse. No actual sanctions were threatened. And it did leave loopholes. While *The First Circle* was denounced as "containing malicious slander on our social system," *Cancer Ward* was merely described as "in need of substantial ideological revision," and after criticizing Solzhenitsyn's refusal to attack the West, the anonymous authors had added, "Whether A. Solzhenitsyn wishes to find a way out of this cul-de-sac depends primarily on himself." In other words, it was still possible for him to make amends by producing a statement. Then, it was implied, there might be a chance for his "ideologically revised" books to be published.

It was, as Solzhenitsyn rightly divined, a reply from weakness, and he had not the slightest intention of complying. But others were outraged by the cynical, sneering tone of the piece, its anonymity, and the fact that this was the first frontal attack on Solzhenitsyn after two years of silence. Lydia Chukovskaya, who had grown friendly with Solzhenitsyn during his long stays at her father's dacha and who had grown steadily more radical in her political views over the same period, wrote a thundering defence of Solzhenitsyn that rivalled his own statements in its eloquence and excoriating irony. "You see, they have to invent a way of dealing with a writer who still carries on exposing Stalinism *after* the command has been given to forget about it," she wrote. And about his letter to the congress:

When I read this extraordinary letter for the first time, it seemed to me that Russian literature itself had looked back over the path it had trodden, pondered and weighed everything it had had to suffer, counted up its losses and its casualties, prayed to the memory of the persecuted—those who went to their destruction outside the prisons—weighed up the loss to the spiritual wealth of our country through the persecution of writers, and, with the voice of Solzhenitsyn, uttered the words: "Enough! This must not go on! We shall live differently!"[3]

Valentin Turchin, a young physicist, wrote another eloquent letter in Solzhenitsyn's defence and circulated it in samizdat. At the end of it, he announced that he was cancelling his subscription to the *Literaturnaya Gazeta* and suggested that others who felt likewise should do the same. It is not known how many complied, but Zhores Medvedev states in his book on Solzhenitsyn that in Obninsk, at least ten research scientists responded to Turchin's call and mailed their July copies back to the newspaper's editor, Alexander Chakovsky, as a mark of disgust.[4] There were many letters in this vein. As so often happens with officially inspired attacks in the Soviet press, the rebuttals they evoked were more effective than the original accusations, and this particular article raised a small storm of protest. But there were other letters, too, almost certainly officially inspired, sent not to the *Literaturnaya Gazeta* but to Solzhenitsyn personally. One such purported to be from a teacher of mathematics in Solzhenitsyn's native North Caucasus. "You are a schizophrenic with a vile, black soul, and all you can do is corrupt the souls of others by filling them with your bile and your fanatical hatred of all things Soviet. And so, of course, the anti-Soviet radio stations and rotten publishers in the West are delighted to arm themselves with your filth. And you gladly offer them your evil-smelling trash, for which there isn't and cannot be any demand among us."

It was the same message as the newspaper's, phrased in more direct language, and it ended with a frankness that went beyond the newspaper's officialese, reflecting more accurately the true feelings of the KGB: "There's no room for you in our country. Get out! Stop bothering us. Get out of this life altogether. . . . Can't you understand that neither you nor your filth is needed by *any* of us Soviet people? Scram! I think it was a mistake to let you out of jail. You should have been shot. And only the genuine humaneness of our government permits you to exist. Get out!" The letter was signed by Lydia Kizieva, mathematics instructor at a teachers' training college in Stavropol, in the Caucasus. Had the sponsors of the letter planned that it should come from Solzhenitsyn's native province?[5]

The authorities were clearly casting about for the best way to deal with the problem that Solzhenitsyn posed for them and had not made up their mind. The *Literaturnaya Gazeta* article was a holding operation, leaving a small loophole through which Solzhenitsyn could return to the fold should he so desire, and it seems that there was no agreement on what to do next. At this point someone must have suggested that the best way to discredit the author was to send *Feast of the Conquerors* to the West and let it be published there. Its anti-Soviet sentiments and especially its open sympathy with the Nazis' Vlasovite allies were calculated to arouse a wave of indignation against Solzhenitsyn, particularly among his supporters on the left. Discussion of this idea must have reached a fairly advanced stage, because in late summer, on a routine visit to the Central Committee's cultural department from *Novy Mir*, Lakshin and Kondratovich were confidentially informed that a copy was already in the West and was due to be published by Mondadori. Solzhenitsyn was finished, they were told, and would certainly go to jail.[6]

Alarmed by this intelligence, the two men informed Tvardovsky, who at once started looking for Solzhenitsyn. Solzhenitsyn, as usual, was hard to find, but when he heard of Tvardovsky's reason, he rushed to see Tvardovsky at his dacha. Tvardovsky repeated the story in greater detail and anxiously asked Solzhenitsyn whether he still possessed any copies of the play. He was eager to read it, but he still could not bring himself to accept a copy from the secretariat (which effectively meant from the KGB). Solzhenitsyn assured him that he possessed no copies, and that, if the work should ever reach the West, it could only do so via the KGB.

Their meeting was the most cordial for many months. Tvardovsky was reading a samizdat work by Zhores Medvedev on the difficulty for Soviet scientists of maintaining links with abroad, and praised the book highly.* Solzhenitsyn, who had grown friendly with Medvedev as a result of the latter's efforts to get Natalia a post in Obninsk, was both pleased and surprised. In former years Tvardovsky had been suspicious of samizdat (and had refused to publish Medvedev's book on Lysenko) but now seemed to have changed his mind and was reading a great deal of it. Furthermore, Tvardovsky (albeit involuntarily) had a new work in samizdat himself—his January letter to Fedin in defence of Solzhenitsyn. This circumstance, and the fact that the subject of the letter was Solzhenitsyn, drew the two men together. They discussed other works in samizdat, and Tvardovsky confessed that he now listened to the BBC (insisting that the two men listen together when it was time for the news), and confided in Solzhenitsyn that he had sacrificed an article on Marshak and was holding up the publication of a volume of his collected works because of a refusal to remove some remarks on Solzhenitsyn from the text.

Solzhenitsyn felt so warmed by this meeting that he confided to Tvardovsky the existence of *The Gulag Archipelago*, and offered to let him read it. Judging from some of Solzhenitsyn's remarks in *The Oak and the Calf*, he expected such a reading to open Tvardovsky's eyes still further to the iniquities of the Soviet past and to strengthen the spirit of rebellion that he sensed was growing in him. Soon afterwards, he took steps to extract a copy of the manuscript from a distant hiding-place and brought it to Moscow to show Tvardovsky, but other events intervened and Tvardovsky could not find the time to read it.[7]

The meeting at Tvardovsky's dacha took place on 16 August 1968. Four days later there occurred an event that was to mark the end of an era throughout the whole of Eastern Europe and the USSR—the Warsaw Pact invasion of Czechoslovakia. The liberalization of the Party and government in the latter country, and the attempt to introduce "socialism with a human face," had in their way been a logical culmination of the policy of de-Stalinization inaugurated by Khrushchev in 1956. If the Hungarians had been premature in attempting to draw conclusions from de-Stalinization overnight, the Czechs and Slovaks seemed to have followed a safer and more evolutionary path,

* The book was eventually published in the West as *The Medvedev Papers*, with the subtitles *Fruitful Meetings between Scientists of the World* and *Secrecy of Correspondence Is Guaranteed by Law* (London, 1972).

and had waited for the reforms to be initiated by the Party itself. Nothing, it seemed, could stop them from taking their own destiny in their hands and producing the first genuine and stable liberalization of a Communist regime that the world had yet seen. But on the black night of 20 August the attempt was brought to an abrupt and brutal end by Soviet tanks, and the Soviet government demonstrated once again that it would tolerate no challenge to its centralized and absolute power.

The impact of this invasion on the Soviet population as a whole is not known, since no instruments exist for ascertaining or measuring such data. But the impact on the Soviet intelligentsia was crushing. The liberalization in their own country, initiated by Khrushchev, had been braked and then reversed under Leonid Brezhnev, but so long as liberalization persisted in neighbouring Czechoslovakia, there was a sense that the original impulse still had some momentum, that all was not lost, and that liberal reforms might even return to the Russians from their more fortunate neighbours to the West. With the crushing of the Czechs, however, it became clear that, on the contrary, everything was over and that things from now on would become even bleaker at home.

The majority of Soviet intellectuals felt bewildered and oppressed by this cruel blow—and perhaps ashamed of their country's despotic action—but were too cowed and frightened to take positive steps. Only one group thought differently: the tiny band of activists responsible for starting the *Chronicle of Current Events* and the Democratic Movement. At the time of the invasion, they were attending the trial of Anatoli Marchenko, the author of *My Testimony*. Copies of the book were already circulating in samizdat and had reached abroad, but Marchenko's trial, which opened on the very day of the invasion, was officially for the minor offence of breaking the internal-passport regulations.[8]

At an impromptu meeting, seven friends of Marchenko who had been attending the trial as unofficial observers decided that they would organize a demonstration the following Sunday to protest against the invasion of Czechoslovakia. There was no chance of attracting public support. Spontaneous demonstrations are anathema to the Soviet authorities and are heartily feared by the average Soviet citizen. What awaited them was certain violence from the police, arrest, and probable imprisonment. And so it was. At noon on Sunday, 25 August 1968, the seven young people walked into a corner of Red Square (the old Execution Ground, a favourite tourist spot in front of St Basil's Cathedral) and sat down, holding makeshift banners with slogans on them: "Hands off the CSSR" and "For Your Freedom and Ours." Among them were two women. One, Natalia Gorbanevskaya, had her small child with her in a pram. The other was Larisa Bogoraz, and among the men was Pavel Litvinov. Predictably, the demonstrators were pounced upon, their banners ripped to pieces, and they themselves punched and thrown into police cars—but not before they had been seen by sufficient people for the news to carry round Moscow and then abroad, whence it was broadcast back into the Soviet Union that same evening.[9]

As Anatoli Yakobson wrote soon afterwards, these seven individuals saved the honour of an entire nation. But apart from this one heroic gesture, there were few other signs of protest. In all the scientific institutes, higher-educational establishments, creative unions, literary magazines, and so forth, special meetings were called by the Party to obtain endorsements of public statements applauding the invasion of Czechoslovakia, which were then printed in the Soviet press. Only a few brave spirits refused to sign, thereby risking their jobs and their reputations. At *Novy Mir*, only Igor Vinogradov objected. Even Tvardovsky felt obliged to go along with the general line, if only for the sake of shielding his already beleaguered journal. But in his individual capacity Tvardovsky resolutely refused to sign a collective letter by Soviet writers in support of the invasion, despite the huge pressure that was put upon him and the further damage to his reputation in official quarters.

Solzhenitsyn found himself in a quandary. For some time past he had regarded Czechoslovakia with a special sympathy. In July of the preceding year the playwright Pavel Kohout had caused a sensation by reading Solzhenitsyn's letter to the Fourth Writers' Congress aloud to a congress of Czech writers, after which the letter had acted as a rallying cry for part of the Czech reform movement. Solzhenitsyn had also received many invitations to go to Czechoslovakia (none of which he had been allowed to accept) and was aware of the impending publication of *Cancer Ward* in Bratislava. He was therefore particularly shocked by the news of the invasion—and shocked, too, that he had seen it coming and not realized it. He was staying in Rozhdestvo at the time, completing his revision of the ninety-six-chapter version of *The First Circle*, and had ignored the obvious signs: "For days and nights on end, tanks, trucks, and service vehicles had been pouring southwards along the high road a hundred yards from my cabin, but still I supposed our leaders were doing it only to frighten the Czechs, that these were just manoeuvres."[10]

Solzhenitsyn writes that his first thought was to compose a public statement in the vein of Herzen's celebrated essay "Lament," written a century earlier.* He would take it to a number of prominent liberals in the Soviet intelligentsia (he mentions Shostakovich, Rostropovich, Kapitsa, and Tvardovsky as candidates), get them to sign it jointly with him, and make it public. With this in mind he did, it seems, compose a brief statement along the lines of "I am ashamed to be a Soviet" but at the last moment shrank from showing it to anyone. He considered issuing the statement on his own but decided against that, too, fearing that he would call down further official wrath on his head.†

* Published in Herzen's journal *Kolokol* (The Bell), 3 March 1863, in response to Russia's brutal suppression of the Polish rising of that year. It included the words "When I walk down the street, I am afraid to be recognized as a Russian."
† On the very day when Litvinov and his friends demonstrated in Red Square (25 August), Solzhenitsyn was visited in Rozhdestvo by Panin and Kopelev and their wives, and spoke then of imitating Herzen and of somehow making a protest. Raisa Orlova, Kopelev's wife, objected that Kopelev couldn't stand another prison sentence, to which Solzhenitsyn replied, "This is no time to think of the consequences. But I can't for the life of me think what to do. One thing is clear—letters won't be of any help."

This at first sight surprising decision was not in fact uncharacteristic. At the time of the protests over the Daniel and Sinyavsky trial, Solzhenitsyn had shown his distaste for signing collective letters. And his instinct in making public statements was to stick to the familiar ground of literature—or to the even more familiar ground of his own problems and his duel with the authorities. He was not ready to act with the selfless and uncalculating bravado of the young dissidents of the Human Rights Movement, nor yet to become a tribune of the people.

Justifying his decision later in *The Oak and the Calf*, Solzhenitsyn wrote that neither the time nor the cause was right for him.

> This is the question to ask: Am I crying out against the greatest evil? Cry out just once and perish for it—yes, if you have never seen anything so horrible in all your life. But I have seen and known many worse things. . . . To cry out now would be to deny the whole history of our country, to help in prettifying it. I must preserve my vocal chords for the *great* outcry. . . . Wait until they begin translating *Gulag* into English.[11]

But this explanation is unconvincing. There was no chance of Solzhenitsyn's "perishing" for a protest over Czechoslovakia. On the contrary, being already a pariah, he had less to lose than most other people and would simply have been acting true to the authorities' opinion of him. Nor would a cry over Czechoslovakia have "denied" Soviet history: to denounce one injustice is not to approve of other, unmentioned injustices. Solzhenitsyn was simply being prudent. As he writes about that same period in another context: he who fights and runs away, lives to fight another day.

Solzhenitsyn tried to preserve his position by writing that "from then on I bore an additional weight on my back. At the time of Hungary, I was a nobody, and it didn't matter whether I cried out or not. Now it was Czechoslovakia, and I held my tongue." But then he went on to criticize Tvardovsky and the *Novy Mir* staff for behaving in basically the same way, for toeing the line in order to save the magazine for future battles. It is hard to see that there was any essential difference between them, and one cannot escape the impression that in his description of these melancholy events, Solzhenitsyn tried to have it both ways. On the one hand, he seemed to say, he took the sensible path and saved himself for bigger things, but on the other he really was a hero, because he felt indignant, drafted a statement, and almost got others to sign it. This, he felt, gave him the right to be contemptuous of Tvardovsky for also doing nothing about Czechoslovakia.

The pity is that his self-centered account tended to obscure who the real heroes were—the tiny band demonstrating on Red Square—and the remarkable fact that members of the opposition were all heroes in their different ways: the dissidents, Solzhenitsyn, Tvardovsky. In a spectrum of opposition and dissent from their government's oppressive action, the dissidents were at the left extreme, with Solzhenitsyn and Tvardovsky in the middle and the conformists on the far right. Solzhenitsyn may have been farther to the left than Tvardovsky, but both were hampered by their ties to the establishment and their different plans for future battles. It was the classic dilemma of all members of Soviet society opposed to their rulers but unable (or unwilling) to cut themselves loose by going into total opposition, with all its fearsome consequences. Solzhenitsyn's movement towards this latter position was steady and inexorable and had been continual during the three years since the confiscation of his archive, but he had not yet travelled the whole distance. He still had a toe-hold in the establishment and could not follow the dissidents into open rebellion.

Another outstanding individual who was beginning to feel this dilemma keenly was the nuclear physicist Andrei Sakharov. Sakharov, a pillar of the Soviet scientific establishment, thrice a Hero of Socialist Labour and "father" of the Soviet H-bomb, had begun to take an interest in public-policy questions as early as 1958, when he tried to get the Soviet moratorium on nuclear testing extended. Unsuccessful then, he had returned to this question in 1961 and 1962 and had been instrumental in persuading the Soviet leaders to sign a nuclear test ban agreement with the United States in 1963. At the same time, Sakharov had broadened his scientific and political interests. He had intervened in the education debate then raging in the Soviet Union, helped to destroy the influence of Lysenko's pseudo-scientific theories in the fields of biology and genetics, and in 1966 was one of the twenty-five co-signatories of a letter to the Twenty-third Congress of the Communist Party calling on its leaders not to rehabilitate Stalin. These activities had made Sakharov decidedly unpopular with the Soviet establishment, and he was steadily demoted in his scientific work, though remaining an academician. But what signalled a major rupture with his former colleagues and the Party leaders was his celebrated memorandum "Progress, Coexistence, and Intellectual Freedom," released in May 1968, a few months before the invasion of Czechoslovakia. The memorandum called for a genuine coexistence and cooperation between the Soviet Union and the United States and canvassed the idea of a convergence of their two social systems. This would mean changes for both sides, and in the Soviet Union would require complete de-Stalinization, the ending of censorship, the release of political prisoners, and a reform of the economic system.

The memorandum at once began to circulate in samizdat and in August 1968 was widely published in the West, as a result of which Sakharov was removed from secret work and given to understand that his status would be irrevocably altered. Almost simultaneous was the invasion of Czechoslovakia, signalling the effective end of that period of liberalization timidly inaugurated by Khrushchev and inexorably throttled by Brezhnev.

Solzhenitsyn was among those who read the memorandum in samizdat in 1968, just as he had evidently noted Sakharov's name on some of the petitions interceding for Galanskov and Ginzburg, and he was intrigued by the eminent physicist's attempt to grapple with some of the larger questions that were also troubling him. There was, one feels, a hint of rivalry in Solzhenitsyn's feelings towards Sakharov—Sakharov had got his memorandum in first—but Sakharov was also one of the people he had had in mind to sign the statement on Czechoslovakia, and he decided to seek a meeting with him anyway. The two men met a few days after the invasion of Czechoslovakia, in the house of a mutual acquaintance (although recently dismissed from secret work, Sakharov was still circumscribed in his movements and could go only to places that he was in the habit of visiting and that had previously been checked by security agents).

Solzhenitsyn found himself charmed by Sakharov's "tall figure, his look of absolute candour, his warm, gentle smile, his bright glance, his pleasantly throaty voice, the thick blurring of his *r*'s" and by his carefully knotted tie and buttoned jacket, betokening an old-fashioned gentility that was some-what at variance with Solzhenitsyn's own preference for generally more informal attire. The contrast in dress, to judge from Solzhenitsyn's account of the conversation, was reflected in their talk, which with interruptions lasted for four hours. Solzhenitsyn's manner seems to have been importunate, excitable, even hectoring. He was anxious to dispute Sakharov's ideas and criticized him unceremoniously, not hesitating to put forward his own views on the problem of Russia's future, without stopping to think whether he might be hurting Sakharov's feelings. Sakharov, for his part, was calm and reserved, polite and affable, and listened carefully. "He was not in the least offended," writes Solzhenitsyn, "although I gave him reason enough. He answered mildly, tried to explain himself with an embarrassed little smile, but refused to be the least bit offended—the mark of a large and generous nature."[12]

Solzhenitsyn did not omit to mention Czechoslovakia, but Sakharov seemed as perplexed and helpless as he. No other prominent figure had made a move, and the two of them evidently did not feel strong enough to make a gesture on their own. The seven demonstrators on Red Square thus remained virtually isolated. Apart from occasional refusals to sign official letters of support for the invasion (or diplomatic "illnesses" coinciding with the meet-ings where decisions to send such letters were taken), the only other overt protests consisted of the circulation of a few anonymous leaflets, the appear-ance of some political graffiti, and the writing of one or two letters. Mindful of the mistake they had made with the trial of Ginzburg, Galanskov, and company, whose year-long investigation had allowed a considerable head of steam to be built up behind the protest movement, the authorities moved rapidly to deal with the demonstrators. Gorbanevskaya, as the mother of a three-month-old child, was remanded for a psychiatric examination, pro-nounced mentally disturbed, and released into the care of her mother. Victor Fainberg, a tourist guide, had been so badly beaten that he couldn't be shown in court and was similarly recommended for psychiatric examination—he was later diagnosed to be suffering from "residual symptoms of schizophre-nia" and confined to a special psychiatric hospital (meaning a prison hospital) in Leningrad. As for the remaining five, their investigation was concluded with unprecedented speed on 12 September, their trial opened on 9 October, and by 12 October 1968 it was all over. Two of the demonstrators, Vladimir Dremlyuga and Vadim Delaunay, were sentenced to three and two and a half years imprisonment respectively in normal-regime labour camps. Pavel Litvinov, Larisa Bogoraz, and Konstantin Babitsky were sentenced to five, four, and three years of internal exile in Siberia. On the very eve of the demonstration, Litvinov had put the finishing touches to his massive documentation of the Ginzburg-Galanskov case, *The Trial of the Four*, and launched it into samizdat, and Natalia Gorbanevskaya was performing the same service for Litvinov and her fellow demonstrators. *Red Square at Noon* was to appear ten months later and describe these events, and the trial that followed, in minute detail.

At the time when these events were unfolding, Solzhenitsyn was preoccupied with a long-term dream of his that at last seemed to be approaching reality, namely, to finance the construction of a church. The outward signs of his religious belief had been few since his return from exile. In Ryazan, he had never gone near the local church, but after the publication of *A Day in the Life of Ivan Denisovich*, and especially "Matryona's Place," with its overt religious message, he had made the acquaintance of a number of Moscow priests, including such prominent and outspoken preachers as Father Alexander Men, Father Dimitri Dudko, and Father Vsevolod Shpiller. He was also known to have written a number of prayers, of which only one had circulated in samizdat and then appeared abroad. Known simply as "Prayer," it resembled some of his miniature stories in tone and structure: "At the height of earthly fame I gaze with wonder at the path that has led me through hopelessness to here—to where I have been able to convey to mankind some reflection of Thy radiance," it began, and continued in the same vein.

There was nothing mystical or intimate about his prayer. It expressed his faith in the Lord, his confidence that the Lord would assist him to continue with good works, and reflected his eminently practical attitude to religion—God was there to help him accomplish things. Solzhenitsyn also seemed to have little interest in the clerical aspects of the church or in its pastoral work. Panin, who was eventually to convert to Roman Catholicism, had frequently admonished him for his reluctance to submit to the authority of the church and had accused him of the sin of pride. And Natalia Reshetovskaya has stated that Solzhenitsyn never kissed the hands of Orthodox priests, as true members of the church were supposed to do; nor did he seem attracted to the mysteries of the church ritual.

It is rather surprising, therefore, that he should have come to the idea of building a church, but this was now what he had in mind, and he intended to finance it from his foreign royalties. The church was to be called the Church of the Holy Trinity, and its architect was to be a dissident artist named Yuri Titov. According to Reshetovskaya, it was intended to be quite a big complex, with a reading-room and library, and an adjoining lecture hall. Only the best priests would be invited to serve, and the church would be sumptuously decorated. In August and September, Solzhenitsyn, Titov, and some of their friends among the priests set out to look for a suitable site, and their preference rested on the district of Zvenigorod (where the appropriately named camp of New Jerusalem had once been situated). Titov produced a number of designs for the church, some of them apparently quite spectacular, but in the end it was never built (at least one of the priests felt that Solzhenitsyn would do better to spend his money on restoring ruined churches rather than on building a new one). Rumours that Solzhenitsyn was to build a church flew round Moscow for many months, and it was alleged that he had made some sort of deal with the government in order to have access to his royalties from abroad, but this latter rumour was patently not true, and speculation died after a while.[13]

Meanwhile, Solzhenitsyn soon returned to Rozhdestvo, where he learned of the publication in the West, in quick succession, of *Cancer Ward* and *The First Circle*. Part 1 of *Cancer Ward* was the first to appear, having been published in England by the Bodley Head in the last days of August. The reviews were respectful but somewhat inconclusive. Most reviewers noted the author's tendency to discursiveness and his old-fashioned ideas about causality and narrative structure, but they saluted the seriousness of the theme and Solzhenitsyn's courage in daring to write openly and honestly about forbidden topics. In the end, however, apart from describing the novel's plot and subject matter, they preferred to suspend judgement until part 2 was available.

Less than two months later came the publication of *The First Circle* (which, in the United States, preceded the appearance of *Cancer Ward*), an altogether bigger and more newsworthy event. Harrison Salisbury, in the Sunday *New York Times*, called it "the greatest Russian novel of the last half of the century" and made the obligatory comparisons to Tolstoy, Dostoyevsky, and Chekhov (invoking the shades of Hugo, Balzac, Zola, Thackeray, and Dickens elsewhere in his review). Franklin Reeve, in the *Chicago Tribune*, wrote that Solzhenitsyn was one of the finest novelists now living anywhere, whether in Eastern Europe, Western Europe, or North America, and many commentators repeated Evtushenko's widely quoted remark that Solzhenitsyn was "Russia's only living classic." The sense of occasion was heightened by an avalanche of news stories describing Solzhenitsyn's embattled situation in the Soviet Union and speculating on how his novel had reached the West (and whether its publication would now harm him); and selection by the Book-of-the-Month Club helped to ensure that within a week or two *The First Circle* had entered the best-seller lists and was climbing rapidly. But there were also demurring voices. The novel's nineteenth-century aura, structural looseness, and strong documentary element disappointed many. "The world of Joyce, Mann or Proust doesn't exist for [Solzhenitsyn]," wrote one. He seemed to be unacquainted with Freud or Kafka, had no knowledge of modern depth psychology or with other contemporary writings on prison camps, and had written a novel that was "less modern" than *Doctor Zhivago* or *The Master and Margarita*.

The British responses had fewer reservations, perhaps reflecting a greater admiration of traditional realism than was prevalent in the United States. Julian Symons, in the *Sunday Times*, called it a "majestic work of genius," whose exploration of people's behaviour in extreme situations made "the mass of contemporary fiction dealing with this theme look trivial by comparison." Ronald Hingley (in *The Spectator*), trumping Harrison Salisbury, described Solzhenitsyn's novel as "arguably the greatest Russian novel of the twentieth century," while those who acknowledged its untidy construction and old-fashioned technique nonetheless praised its daring conception and its surprising buoyancy of tone (the British were much more receptive to Solzhenitsyn's sardonic humour than the Americans seem to have been). Raymond Williams, in *The Guardian*, introduced the interesting idea that *The First Circle* was more important and convincing than *Cancer Ward* because it was less like literature, and he met the challenge of its unusual subject matter by refusing to recognize "the frontiers between the imaginative and the real." Solzhenitsyn had refurbished traditional realism and transformed it in order to be able to describe a new reality.*

An unfortunate by-product of the mysterious manner in which the two novels had arrived in the West was the still-simmering controversy over whether the author had desired publication or not, while new disputes broke out over copyright and the quality of the translations. In the case of *Cancer Ward*, the Bodley Head, with the help of Pavel Ličko, had more or less secured its copyright to the title in England and had quickly published a Russian text to support its claim, but rival Russian texts were published on the Continent, notably by Mondadori in Italy (in addition to the Possev text that had started the rush), and in America no fewer than four publishers had announced their intention of publishing it there. After the appearance of Solzhenitsyn's statement in *Le Monde*, two of them, Dutton and Praeger, had withdrawn, leaving two others to fight it out. Farrar, Straus and Giroux claimed copyright on the basis of the Bodley Head edition, and accused the rival Dial Press of piracy. Dial countered that Farrar, Straus and Giroux and the Bodley Head were endangering Solzhenitsyn's safety, and perhaps even his life, with their claim to authorization, and issued their own translation of the entire novel in early 1969. By this time, the Bodley Head had also prepared a translation of volume 2, so that Farrar, Straus and Giroux were able to issue the novel in one volume almost simultaneously with Dial.

In the matter of translations, there was not much to choose between them. The Bodley Head version had been done by Nicholas Bethell and a Soviet *émigré* journalist called David Burg.† It was not a distinguished piece of work, bearing many signs of the haste and extensive editing to which it had been subjected, but the Dial translation was no better: its flatter and

---

*It is not clear whether Williams was aware of the fact, but a similar claim had been made for Tolstoy in his lifetime, who was praised for his ability to "erase the boundaries" between literature and life.

†His real name is Alexander Dolberg.

more literal rendering of the original Russian simply reflected American taste in this matter, rather than having any greater accuracy.

A more serious difference of taste had manifested itself in the translation of *The First Circle*. There had been no problems over copyright, but Thomas Whitney's original translation also bore signs of extensive editing (in this case mainly by the Carlisles) and was rejected outright by Collins, the English publishers. Collins commissioned three of England's best translators—Max Hayward, Ronald Hingley, and Michael Glenny—to produce a new version (it was published under the pseudonym of "Michael Guybon"), but their translation, though somewhat smoother and more literary than Whitney's, also contained a large quota of errors and was, if anything, even further from the texture and spirit of the original.

It looked uncomfortably like a repetition of the squabbles and multiple competing translations that had been such a feature of the foreign publication of *Ivan Denisovich* six years earlier, and gave Solzhenitsyn considerable cause for concern. Then, as now, it helped to divert attention from literary matters to the purely political sensation that seemed inseparable from Solzhenitsyn's name and all his work. Under normal circumstances, it might never have happened. Solzhenitsyn is the sort of meticulous author who would have taken a personal interest in the selection of his translators (as he has done since his arrival in the West), and would have demanded a voice in the arrangements that were made, had he been given the opportunity. But then, nothing was normal in his literary career, and this haste, this jostling competition between over-eager publishers and their harried translators, was but a by-product of the secrecy, the web of conspiracy, and the atmosphere of political intrigue that enveloped his every move. His books had become contraband, and the Soviet authorities had succeeded, through their persecution of the author, in surrounding them with the aura of forbidden fruit. Solzhenitsyn (given his outlaw status) was not entirely dissatisfied with this process, for the persecution, like most attempts at censorship, was doomed to produce the opposite of what was intended. It simply spotlighted his work, inflated his reputation, and, by drawing world-wide attention to him, reinforced his immunity. In a sense the authorities played into Solzhenitsyn's hands, and the poor translations and competing editions might have seemed a small price to pay for the protective publicity they afforded (the competition and the ensuing recriminations merely magnified Solzhenitsyn's attraction for the sensation-hungry Western press). Only later did these inadequate translations begin to loom as a problem, and by that time Solzhenitsyn had forgotten their temporary practical utility in his struggle with the Soviet government.

The Soviet authorities were not averse to trying to exploit the situation they had brought about. Some of Solzhenitsyn's friends feared that Solzhenitsyn would be put on trial for having sent his manuscripts abroad, but Solzhenitsyn himself seems to have been confident that that wouldn't happen. "No," he said one day in response to a question from Zhores Medvedev, "I think that's unlikely. They've already exhausted themselves in that direction with the trials of Sinyavsky, Daniel, and the rest. Now they've got to think up something new."[14]

Meanwhile, nobody seemed to know what had become of Victor Louis's copy of *Cancer Ward*. Perhaps it was the one that ended up at the Dial Press or that reached Dutton or Praeger before they abandoned their intention of publishing the novel themselves. Certainly it contributed to the general confusion, and not long after his trip to Europe, in September 1968, Victor Louis himself turned up in, of all places, Rozhdestvo. Solzhenitsyn knew from the customs officers that his summer cabin was known to the authorities and therefore probably under surveillance, but he was nonetheless surprised to find Victor Louis openly on his doorstep.

Ostensibly, Louis had come to explain that he had not taken a copy of *Cancer Ward* to the West, but his real purpose was to try to interview Solzhenitsyn. Solzhenitsyn was repairing his Moskvich and crawled out from beneath it, covered in oil, when his unexpected visitor arrived. The moment Solzhenitsyn discovered who it was, he refused to answer any questions and ordered Louis off the premises. Louis returned on 24 September, however, and was able to take a number of pictures of Solzhenitsyn's cabin with a telephoto lens, which he later sold to the West German illustrated weekly *Stern*. Some time afterwards, Louis hawked around the West a purported "interview" with Solzhenitsyn, but a careful reading reveals that all the direct quotations in it came from other sources and that Solzhenitsyn had said not a word to Louis himself.

The "interview" eventually appeared, after many refusals, in the *International Herald Tribune*, with a prefatory note explaining Louis's role as a privileged Soviet journalist and a purveyor of material that the Soviet authorities wished to send to the West. Louis's piece said nothing new; it was interesting chiefly as an example of "soft" propaganda. Solzhenitsyn was disparagingly compared with Dostoyevsky and Tolstoy, his cabin at Rozhdestvo mockingly likened to Tolstoy's estate at Yasnaya Polyana (and his beard to Tolstoy's, which was nearer the mark). Louis also summarized the accusations recently made against Solzhenitsyn in the *Literaturnaya Gazeta*, adding that Solzhenitsyn owed his cunning and his ability to manufacture alibis to his experiences in the labour camps. But these experiences had also been his undoing: "The time Solzhenitsyn spent in camp and in exile shocked him so deeply that he became one-track-minded and can hardly keep off this subject in his work."

This had become a leitmotiv of official criticisms of Solzhenitsyn, as had the accusation that he was working for the enemies of the Soviet Union, especially the NTS, abroad. But Louis added a new and up-to-date twist of his own. The NTS, he wrote, accompanied its publication of Solzhenitsyn's works in the West with advertisements stating that "the construction of a Communist society does not worry Solzhenitsyn. . . . Soviet power and the Party are not named in his story, but they are present there as evil foes of life and mankind." Yet Solzhenitsyn, "who is a member of the Writers' Union," did not protest against these statements. What seemed like a *non sequitur* about the union was then followed up and expanded: "He disagrees with the Writers' Union on many counts, but he doesn't want to return his membership card because it gives him considerable advantages. . . . Nor would the Writers' Union like to expel him, because he is a popular author." In other words, the Writers' Union *would* like to expel him. It was the first time the subject had appeared in print, even in this negative form, and the cautiousness of its formulation was an indication of indecision on the part of the authorities. At the same time, it was a useful trial balloon and offered an excellent opportunity to test foreign reactions and to prepare foreign public opinion for what might now logically follow. Perhaps this was the "something new" that Solzhenitsyn had predicted to Medvedev.[15]

At the end of November 1968, Solzhenitsyn paid another visit to Tvardovsky and *Novy Mir*. He had with him a copy of *The Gulag Archipelago* for Tvardovsky to read, just as he had promised some weeks before. But Tvardovsky was busy again and hard to pin down. He was having a room added to his dacha to hold all the complimentary books he had been sent over a lifetime in the literary world, and was too busy supervising the workmen to come to the office. At last he appeared in Moscow, on 24 November, for a meeting of *Novy Mir's* Party committee, and afterwards the two men talked in Tvardovsky's office. Tvardovsky was preoccupied and pensive. He had recently been a candidate for membership in the Academy of Sciences, but had been turned down on orders from above. He was also apprehensive about his letter to Fedin, which had just been broadcast by the BBC. He felt it might compromise him further. But about the BBC's current readings from *Cancer Ward* he was enthusiastic and generously complimentary, telling Solzhenitsyn, "You're more famous in Europe than I am now." He asked Solzhenitsyn how he was surviving and offered him money from his own pocket, but Solzhenitsyn declined. What he would like, he said, was a further advance from *Novy Mir* on *Cancer Ward*—60 per cent, instead of the 25 per cent he had already received. This was more difficult for Tvardovsky, since he had to get permission for such a payment from the *Izvestia* accountants, but he promised to do his best (and in due course was successful—getting the whole of the advance for Solzhenitsyn, instead of just 60 per cent).[16]

There was no question of showing *The Gulag Archipelago* to Tvardovsky on this occasion. There was too little time, and Solzhenitsyn needed to stay with Tvardovsky for the several days required to read it. He could not afford to let the manuscript out of his sight, or run the risk of accidents. They arranged the reading for May Day the following spring: Tvardovsky would go to Rozhdestvo—to Solzhenitsyn's "hunting lodge," as he playfully called it, which he now knew about—and read *The Gulag Archipelago* there, just as he had read *The First Circle* in Ryazan.

What Solzhenitsyn did have to show Tvardovsky was his freshly completed screenplay of *The Parasite*. The screenplay had been commissioned by friends at the Moscow Film Studios (Mosfilm) the preceding year in order to provide him with some money, although there was little hope that the film would ever be made. Solzhenitsyn, it seems, still nursed a fascination with the cinema, although he was not hopeful either. *The Parasite* was a comedy (unique in Solzhenitsyn's *oeuvre*), but he had not been able to resist taking a politically controversial subject—elections—and making satirical fun of them. Even when he had removed some of the more subversive passages, it was still rather too sharp for the prevailing atmosphere.

The screenplay describes the adventures of a privileged young Moscow girl, Elvira, when she tries to get her damaged car repaired quickly in a strange provincial town. She is referred to the mechanic Pashka, notorious for his skill in cheating the garage where he works and carrying out repairs on the side (he is the "parasite" of the screenplays's title), and he agrees to help. But first he must satisfy two important, queue-jumping clients who are clamouring for his assistance as well, an army major and the chairman of the local electoral commission—the chairman's repair job is particularly important because the following day is election day. Pashka completes the work and then stays up all night to repair Elvira's car (falling slightly in love with her in the process). The next morning he learns that the Party bosses are searching for him. He flees with Elvira in her half-repaired car. After a comical chase, his pursuers catch up with him and inform him that it is election day (he has forgotten) and that he is guilty of the crime of not voting—the only man in the town not to have done so. He willingly allows himself to be dragged to the polling station, so that the election chairman can have his 100 per cent turnout and close the polls, as usual, ten hours ahead of schedule.

The Parasite was the lightest work Solzhenitsyn had yet written and had some amusing scenes, such as the initial collision between Elvira and an army vehicle and the chase through town and countryside. Solzhenitsyn also got in some thrusts at the petty bribery of small-town life and the ridiculous hypocrisy of the Soviet electoral process, but the characters were caricatures—even the amusing Pashka, who was modelled on the Ryazan mechanic who had repaired Solzhenitsyn's car for him. One scene in particular, in which a stranger was shown breaking all the unwritten rules by insisting on voting secretly, stuck out as a naked polemic, even though it was based on a true incident that had happened to Georgi Tenno.[17]

Solzhenitsyn delivered three copies of the script to Mosfilm on 26 November 1968, where it was presumably read and shelved.[18] Tvardovsky and the editorial staff of *Novy Mir* also read it but found it too sharp for publication, even with one section (presumably that based on Tenno) removed. Tvardovsky's joking comment after reading it was that Solzhenitsyn's place was "inside" and "the sooner the better."[19] After that the screenplay languished among Solzhenitsyn's papers and did not appear until 1981, when it was published in volume 8 of his collected works in Russian.

That November, Henry Carlisle went to Moscow to seek further instructions on the preparation of *The Gulag Archipelago* for publication. The launching of *The First Circle*, apart from the question of the unsatisfactory translation, had been a great organizational and commercial success for the Carlisles and Harper & Row, and the publishers had sold the rights for other translations all over the world. They were disturbed, however, by the disputes and sometimes rancorous litigation that had broken out between the various publishers of *Cancer Ward*, and by rumours that Solzhenitsyn had written a revised and longer version of *The First Circle* that he was contemplating releasing as well. This second prospect would spoil the impact of the Harper & Row edition and throw doubt on the ownership of the copyright. Journalists and rival publishers were already questioning Harper & Row's credentials, yet the publisher was sworn to secrecy: nobody knew of Olga Carlisle's role as Solzhenitsyn's representative and of the authorization he had given her.

Solzhenitsyn's situation was apparently too delicate for Henry Carlisle to meet him face to face. A message was passed through an intermediary, and Solzhenitsyn replied similarly. He was satisfied with the publication of *The First Circle*, would not release the additional chapters he had written, and wanted Olga Carlisle to handle *The Gulag Archipelago* in the same fashion as the first book—with one proviso. She was not to enter into a contract with Harper & Row until the translation was ready (which he hoped would be in 1970). She should then send a coded message and wait until he gave her instructions to proceed. Only in the event of his arrest or death should she go ahead on her own.[20]

Together with these instructions Carlisle brought two requests to the West. One, from Solzhenitsyn, was for a small tape recorder. The other, from Kornei Chukovsky, was for telegrams and letters of congratulation to be sent to Solzhenitsyn on his fiftieth birthday. Quaint as the custom may seem to Westerners, fiftieth birthdays are an occasion of great importance to Soviet writers. For the vast majority who enjoy official approval, it is marked by adulatory articles and statements in the literary press (and in the national press, as well, if the author is important enough) and shoals of telegrams and letters to his home, not only from official bodies like the various levels of the Writers' Union (all-union, republic, province, and town) but also from "workers' collectives" and committees all over the country. Such outbursts of acclaim are carefully orchestrated, but they do sometimes coincide with true popularity, as had been the case with writers like Tvardovsky and Nekrasov. There seemed little chance of Solzhenitsyn's birthday being so marked, and Chukovsky was anxious that the impetus should come from elsewhere. Telegrams and letters from abroad would demonstrate world-wide support for Solzhenitsyn and strengthen his position in his duel with the Soviet authorities.

Solzhenitsyn spent his birthday, 11 December 1968, at home in Ryazan. Telegrams, letters, and messages of support did indeed pour in from abroad, and there were many laudatory articles in the Western press to celebrate the occasion. But what truly surprised and moved Solzhenitsyn was the enormous volume of congratulations he received from within the Soviet Union.

No one had been officially informed. There was not a word in the *Literaturnaya Gazeta*, either before or after his birthday. But letters and telegrams began arriving a full week beforehand and were being brought to the flat at the rate of up to seventy at a time. On the day itself, postmen were calling at thirty-minute intervals, so that Solzhenitsyn, Natalia, her mother, and aunts were unable to open the letters quickly enough before the next batch came. By the end of the week, there were more than five hundred telegrams and about two hundred letters, and a further hundred messages arrived at *Novy Mir*. According to Zhores Medvedev, *Novy Mir* also sent an official telegram, as did the Ryazan and Voronezh branches of the Writers' Union, the Czech Writers' Union, and a number of Moscow theatres.[21]

The tone of most of the letters revived memories of those he had received after the publication of *Ivan Denisovich*. "Please do not lay down your pen." "I rejoice that our generation's sufferings have at least produced such sons." "You are my conscience." "We read your books on cigarette papers, which makes them all the more precious to us. If Russia is paying dearly for her great sins, it is surely for her great sufferings, and so that shame may not utterly demoralize us that you have been sent to her." Tvardovsky wrote, "May you live another fifty years and may your talent lose none of its splendid strength. All else passes, only the truth will remain." And Lydia Chukovskaya: "In you the dumb have found their voice. I can think of no writer so long awaited and so sorely needed as you. Where the word has not perished, the future is safe. . . . You have restored to Russian literature its thunderous power."[22]

Solzhenitsyn was deeply stirred by these messages, although he tried not to show it outwardly, even to his family. Veronica Stein, his sole guest on that memorable day, reports that after helping the women to open and sort the letters in the morning, Solzhenitsyn disappeared into his study to work. He came out briefly for lunch and to drink tea with some local women who had called to congratulate him—neighbours who helped him with typing, copying, sending out duplicated letters, and so on—and then went back to work again, while Natalia showed the visitors some holiday slides. All in all, it was typical of Solzhenitsyn to treat it as a normal working day, even if he was glowing inside. He hated making concessions to convention, feeling that it bred hypocrisy and obliged him to behave in ways that were false. He also disapproved of gift-giving. He had a theory that it was an intrusion on another's privacy. To give someone a present is inevitably to impose your own taste on that person and therefore to limit and constrain him. He tried to avoid receiving gifts himself and rarely gave them, except in the form of money or purely utilitarian objects.[23]

This unbending attitude to the harmless courtesies of everyday life showed Solzhenitsyn's penchant for taking theories to extremes. As a result, even his best impulses and most attractive qualities could express themselves with such uninhibited force that they became oppressive, cancelling out the initial pleasure they evoked. Solzhenitsyn was not incapable of generosity—quite the contrary. Zhores Medvedev describes in great detail Solzhenitsyn's attempts that year to obtain an expensive drug from America for the ten-year-old daughter of a friend in Ryazan who had developed an acute form of leukemia. He was prepared to spend up to five thousand dollars of his American royalties to pay for the drug. In the event, the drug was obtained for nothing but did not prove as effective as had been thought, and the little girl died two years later.[24] Solzhenitsyn's offer to use foreign royalties from *Ivan Denisovich* referred to funds that were blocked to him personally, but later, when money from the Nobel Prize became available to him, he was generous to friends in need and had no hesitation in sending them sums of money. Like many proud and self-centered people, he was a better giver than receiver.

His fiftieth birthday was therefore treated much like any other day. Solzhenitsyn not only liked to ignore the conventions, he took a secret and perverse delight in flouting them (thus demonstrating that he was not indifferent). But it was not entirely a normal working day. Buoyed up by this tidal wave of love and admiration from his loyal readers ("Let me scorn mock modesty and admit that I held my head high that week"), he spent part of the time in his study composing a suitably solemn acknowledgement: "I thank the readers and writers whose greetings and good wishes on my fiftieth birthday have so moved me. I promise them never to betray the truth. My sole dream is to justify the hopes of the Russian reading public." There was nowhere in particular he could send it—no Soviet newspaper would publish his words without instructions from above. But for form's sake he addressed it to the *Literaturnaya Gazeta* before releasing it into samizdat.[25]

Solzhenitsyn was now at the height of his powers and had every reason to feel pleased with himself. He had entered into a single-handed duel with the strongest and most ruthless government in the world and had more than held his own. His losses had been the confiscation of his archive, the public attacks on him, the refusal to publish *Cancer Ward* and *The First Circle* in the Soviet Union, and poor translations in the West. His victories had been his letter to the Fourth Writers' Congress, his completion and the safe dispatch abroad of *The Gulag Archipelago*, and the publication of his two major novels abroad. He was physically safe and had embarked at last on his series of historical novels.

To his admirers, especially inside the Soviet Union, he symbolized freedom, independence, purity, justice—and in a narrower sense embodied the hope that the reforms of the Khrushchev era and the move towards the de-Stalinization of Soviet life were not entirely lost. He was not alone in this—the dissidents were fighting the same battle, often with a greater disregard for their personal safety. But what Solzhenitsyn uniquely possessed was his literary talent and his charisma. He had a natural instinct for battle tactics—for knowing when to advance and when to retreat, when to attack and when to defend, when to kick up a fuss and when to keep quiet. It was here that his convict experiences stood him in such good stead. In *The Gulag Archipelago* he had seen the camps as a metaphor for the whole of Soviet society (the metaphor had appeared in *Ivan Denisovich* and *The First Circle* as well, but *The Gulag Archipelago* made it explicit and developed the metaphor with greater complexity)—the Soviet Union was one big labour camp. In dealing with its leaders, Solzhenitsyn instinctively drew on his past experience with the camp bosses. It was one of the keys to his success (and also the key to some of his failures). As he himself was to put it to Tvardovsky a year later:

> This is a different age—not that in which you had the misfortune to live the greater part of your literary life—and *different* skills are needed. Mine are those of the world of forced labour and the camps. I can say without affectation that I belong to the Russian convict world no less, and owe no less to it, than I do to Russian literature. I got my education there, and it will last forever. When I am considering any step of importance to my future, I listen above all to the voices of my comrades in the camps, some of them already dead, of disease or a bullet, and I hear clearly how they would behave in my place.[26]

The camps had bred their own antidote: the one place where truth had been preserved in Stalin's Russia—the gulag—had sent its messenger to haunt the greater gulag of Soviet Russia itself. And combined with this implacable will to reveal the truth and this incomparable battle instinct was the artist's flair for self-dramatization and the power to communicate in vivid, unforgettable language the nature and progress of his struggle.

Of course he could hold his head high, and of course he was the object of passionate admiration, of idolization even, and deservedly so. At the same time there was the mystery of his personality, the secrecy surrounding his daily life—dictated partly by the exigencies of his struggle, but also consciously manipulated by Solzhenitsyn. The artist was not content with mere art: he would make a dramatic parable of his life as well, and art from that parable, and a parable from that art (his memoir, *The Oak and the Calf*, would put the finishing touches to both). There was a holy innocence—as well as calculation—about the gusto with which he fashioned his role, playing hide-and-seek with Tvardovsky and other friends, acting the Scarlet Pimpernel in matters great and small.

It added to the mystery and fascination of his image, lending him an aura that was of the greatest assistance in his battle with the authorities. And if this was true inside the Soviet Union, it was even more so abroad, where the mystery of his personality was compounded by distance and ignorance. An example of the effect this produced in bystanders was an article, in the form of a pen portrait, by an anonymous Soviet intellectual, which reached the West shortly after Solzhenitsyn's fiftieth birthday and was published first in the *émigré* journal *Vozrozhdeniye* ("Rebirth") and then in some Western newspapers. It is interesting both for its more or less reliable description of Solzhenitsyn's physical appearance and for the idealized and lyrical haze through which the writer views Solzhenitsyn's personality. Physically, Solzhenitsyn is described as follows:

He has an original and fascinating appearance. His eyes are blue, not light blue but an intense blue, with a youthful sparkle—you might even say scintillating—and when he looks at you they grow warm and confiding. His features are big, and he's a big man generally, with broad shoulders and big hands, but well shaped. He's blond, and despite having something Nordic and Scandinavian in his appearance, very Russian. His hair and beard are both fair, his face (the upper part) icon-like, his eyes lively and kind. He speaks rather fast and very to the point; he's purposeful, self-disciplined, businesslike and precise, but at the same time a bit of a dreamer, with a touch of pleasant naïvety about him. He's modest, but conscious of his role and worth. He speaks figuratively, without using a single cliché, and his language is simple, unaffected, without a trace of mannerism—it is a pleasure to listen to, it is good, pure, genuine Russian.

Meeting Solzhenitsyn, continues the unknown author, "was an enormous event in our grey life," especially when he was compared with the people one met every day.

You experience Solzhenitsyn as a real Man (with a capital letter): there is not the slightest trace of timidity or embitterment in him, there is nothing petty or dishonourable in his make-up, everything about him is in a major key, organically major, there is no posing or affectation. Optimism, faith in the future, extraordinary simplicity, directness, and an enormous, almost childlike interest in everything around him—in the people he meets, in their work and opinions, and all this benevolently and without bias.[27]

In other words, a secular saint. To a people starved of spiritual nourishment and desperate for beauty, justice, and truth, Solzhenitsyn was as if heaven-sent, God's messenger on earth, a reassurance that the Russian people and Russian literature had not lost their spirituality. In a country with a centuries-old tradition of deifying its great men, it was inevitable that Solzhenitsyn would sooner or later reach the moment of his apotheosis.

36

EXPULSION FROM
THE WRITERS' UNION

I<small>T IS IN</small> the nature of things that no man be successful in all that he under-
takes or experience complete happiness in every department of his life,
and at precisely this moment of his greatest fame and popularity, Solzhenitsyn was experiencing, in his private life, the exact opposite of his public
success. His marriage was about to collapse.

A sign of what was afoot was a seemingly trivial incident witnessed by
Veronica Stein on the very day of his fiftieth birthday. For some years past,
Solzhenitsyn had been allowing Natalia to handle almost all his correspondence. This gave her an opportunity to keep up with what he was doing and
to feel wanted and useful. On the evening of his birthday, Solzhenitsyn
emerged from his study and handed Natalia a letter to post to Elena Chukovskaya (Lydia Chukovskaya's daughter), in which he informed Elena that he
would be coming to Moscow in three days' time and would like to stay at the
Chukovskys' dacha. On reading it, Natalia created a noisy scene, accusing
Solzhenitsyn of being selfish and never thinking of her. Why couldn't he go
to Moscow on a weekend so that she could accompany him? A row broke
out that lasted until bedtime, completely ruining the latter part of the birthday. After Solzhenitsyn had gone to bed, Natalia continued sobbing well
into the night in the small room where she and Veronica were sleeping.[1]

At the root of this outburst lay Natalia's jealousy of his Moscow friends
and probably Elena in particular. For most of the past two years since Solzhenitsyn had fled to the Chukovskys after the confiscation of his archive,
Elena (known universally as "Lyusha" in Moscow literary circles) had been
helping him with his work, gradually increasing her involvement to the point
where in all but name she had become Solzhenitsyn's private secretary. By

profession she was a chemist like Natalia herself, but slightly higher up the ladder, a senior researcher at the Moscow Institute of Organic Chemistry. She was also Kornei Chukovsky's favourite granddaughter (her father, Tsezar Volpe, had died in the war, leaving her an orphan) and from him, and from her mother, had absorbed a lifelong passion for literature.

Elena was in her mid-thirties when she met Solzhenitsyn and was unmarried—as she is to this day. Perhaps the very strength of her personality has something to do with it. When asked to describe her, friends come up with an assortment of flattering adjectives: noble, disinterested, dedicated, generous, intelligent, broad-minded. But they also indicate a quizzical, sceptical mind, absolute independence of spirit, a good sense of humour, and a sharp tongue adept at puncturing affectation and pomposity. The picture is of a clever, subtle, discriminating person with a mind of her own. And yet, with all these qualities, she is also one of those strong, saintly Russian women who seem to find their deepest satisfaction in life in devoting themselves to others. While her grandfather was alive, it was he who lay at the center of her affections and to whom she dedicated the bulk of her attention. During his declining years and especially after his death, although she continued to worship his memory and work on his literary archive, she seems to have transferred the focus of her attention to Solzhenitsyn. In him and his work her noble, generous nature found a cause fully worthy of her character and talents.

Because Elena is still living in the Soviet Union and has not written about it herself, it is impossible to describe the full extent of her work for Solzhenitsyn. Ever since publishing *Ivan Denisovich*, Solzhenitsyn had been accustomed to receiving secretarial help from admirers and friends. Much of the day-to-day work had been done by Natalia, insofar as she had been able to combine it with a full-time job, but with the flood of correspondence that followed the publication of *Ivan Denisovich* and with the lengthy revisions of *The First Circle* and *Cancer Ward* (the few photocopiers that existed in the Soviet Union were kept under lock and key—and still are), the labour was clearly too much for her, so that others in both Ryazan and Moscow were brought in to help. Elizaveta Voronyanskaya, in Leningrad, accompanied Solzhenitsyn on one or two research trips as an amanuensis and typed up final versions of *The First Circle* and *The Gulag Archipelago*. Reshetovskaya writes, "My husband could approach her with literally any request any time, and she would do everything she could for him." She had even learned to type for Solzhenitsyn's sake, and there were many like her.[2]

Natalia was thus willy-nilly distanced from her husband's work, which from being the product of one man at his desk had turned into a cottage industry, especially when, in 1964, he launched in earnest into *The Gulag Archipelago*. There was the very size of the task. Interviewing or reading letters from 227 ex-prisoners, registering and copying the interviews, obtaining and absorbing a mass of factual printed material, typing and retyping sections of the enormous manuscript, correcting and copying a final draft of well over two thousand pages—all this required an army of helpers, not to speak of intermediaries for arranging confidential interviews or scouring provincial libraries for obscure and hard-to-find books. When he came at last to begin *August 1914*, he used the same system, and again there was no lack of volunteers. Finally, there was the work required by his public campaign against the authorities. Two hundred and fifty copies of his letter to the Writers' Congress had had to be typed, addressed, and mailed from a variety of postboxes in Moscow, as did forty-four copies of his letter to members of the Writers' Union secretariat, with his transcript of the *Cancer Ward* discussion. Others were typed for samizdat or for carrying abroad, and many of the sympathizers who helped in this way reported back to Solzhenitsyn on the proceedings of meetings they had attended or the remarks made by ideological spokesmen at closed meetings of the Party faithful. Only in this way was Solzhenitsyn able to learn what Zimyanin had said to a meeting of journalists, or of the instructions issued to provincial librarians to remove his books from the shelves. These snippets of information Solzhenitsyn would then hoard until, with his inimitable flair for tactics and timing, he judged the moment right to make them public, sowing confusion among his enemies and rejoicing his friends. For this not insignificant group of people, Solzhenitsyn's struggle was their struggle, he was their leader and standard bearer, and it was this idea that Pavel Ličko had clumsily tried to convey in his BBC interview in London in 1967, but which a poor translation had converted into the image of Solzhenitsyn at the head of a "private army."[3] There was an "army," an army without arms, a largely silent mass of supporters content to assist him behind the scenes or to back him passively, and for the most part unwilling to come out into the open and risk their security.

In such circumstances it was inevitable that Natalia should get pushed somewhat to one side and that others should emerge to take on the extra work. Elena gave up some hours at her institute and worked part-time in order to devote herself more fully to it, and thanks to the weight of her personality, her drive, and her energy quickly came to occupy a special position in Solzhenitsyn's esteem, enjoying his complete confidence and trust. She was also one of the few people whose criticisms he heeded. With her outspokenness she did not hesitate to comment on his writing, particularly his political writing, and he frequently took her advice.

For Natalia the whole thing was bewildering. From being an obscure lecturer at an agricultural institute, she had gone on to become the consort of Russia's most famous and acclaimed writer. The doors of *Novy Mir*, of the Taganka and Sovremennik theatres, of the Writers' Club, and almost of the Kremlin itself had been thrown open to her. She had hob-nobbed with the mighty and was simple and straightforward enough to have enjoyed this sudden prominence. But her husband, from the start, had reacted strangely to his fame. He had often avoided the great, declined their invitations, and insisted on skulking in his own backyard. In a way this guaranteed a continuation of their domestic cosiness. In her book on their life together, there are two photographs of them taken in Ryazan that seem to sum up her vision of their married life. In one of them she is shown sitting at an electric sewing-machine, while Solzhenitsyn leans over her with a bemused smile on his face. In the other she is playing the piano and gazing into the distance, while he, in homage to a thousand Hollywood movies, leans on the back of the piano in an attitude of contemplation.

This was Natalia's image of how their marriage ought to be: a bourgeois paradise, an island of calm and domestic bliss amidst a sea of troubles. When this calm was ruptured by sudden fame, she was still willing to become the gracious consort of a celebrity, to play the part of the famous man's wife, entertain and be entertained, enjoy the privileges and fulfil the duties of a person in the public eye. But none of this was for Solzhenitsyn. The picture that Victor Louis and the Soviet media had begun to present of him as a greedy philistine eager for creature comforts, luxuriating in his foreign royalties and social success, was totally wide of the mark. He could not have cared less for worldly goods and social acceptability (the portrait owed more to how Writers' Union officials themselves behave and feel than to any accurate assessment of Solzhenitsyn). Quite the contrary, he felt positively uncomfortable without a hair shirt of some kind. The thing that absorbed 90 per cent of his energy and time was "the cause": collecting material, writing, distributing, devising strategy. It was this that had progressively swallowed up more and more of his life, leaving almost no time for domestic concerns. And what it now brought in its wake was odium and insults, brickbats instead of plaudits, and continual harassment by the political and literary establishment.

Even this, Natalia could probably have borne—side by side with the man she loved. She was loyal to her husband and would have followed him anywhere. But his fame had coincided with other developments in their relationship that conspired to drive them apart. First, there had been the incident with the woman in Leningrad. Such an occurrence was almost inevitable in the light of Solzhenitsyn's celebrity. He was deeply fascinating to many women, with his romantic past, his air of mystery, and his vibrant personality. Many of his most devoted helpers were women, and it is more than probable that their motives were mixed: the cause was noble, but its champion was masculine and not at all bad-looking. Voronyanskaya, though no longer young and though apparently disinterested, had been a party to the Leningrad romance and had helped to deceive Natalia over Solzhenitsyn's real reasons for being there. And Voronyanskaya was one of Solzhenitsyn's principal literary assistants as well.

The Leningrad incident had been patched up, although it had led to separate rooms. But equally serious had been the domestic repercussions of the confiscation of Solzhenitsyn's archive and his hasty departure from Rozhdestvo (and therefore from Ryazan). Solzhenitsyn truly thought that his life was in mortal danger. Yet within days of his arrival in Peredelkino, Natalia had been on the telephone demanding his immediate return to Ryazan. She felt lonely and abandoned, she said, and was also threatened by the myste-rious raid on Teush (the Teushes were her friends too; Teush had been *her* colleague). She could not understand why Solzhenitsyn should want to spend such a solemn and decisive moment away from her.[4]

Perhaps this fatal misunderstanding was bound up with a more pro-found psychological trauma. It was the KGB raid that had reminded Solzhe-nitsyn so forcefully of his convict past and that hastened a reversion to his old way of thinking—to a period and a frame of mind that was outside his relationship with Natalia. The true son of Gulag had been abandoned by her and indeed was not known to her. The man she received back into her mar-riage and into her bed had been rehabilitated, born again, to all intents and purposes a respectable Soviet citizen. But now he was diving down to the depths again, depths to which she could not follow.

The fact that Solzhenitsyn's destination after his dive had been the Chu-kovskys was partly accidental. Kornei, Lydia, and Elena could have been only dimly aware of Solzhenitsyn's state of mind when he went to them, of the complex reorientation taking place in his mood and his thinking. But they could certainly follow him mentally and spiritually, and there was a certain appropriateness, if not inevitability, in his finding refuge with them.

Natalia's jealousy of Elena, therefore, was many-layered and not just conventional. It might have been conventional once, for Natalia was sensitive to sexual rivalry, and Elena's devotion to Solzhenitsyn certainly seems to have had emotional overtones. A friend of both women who wandered into Elena's room one day was amazed to find the walls, shelves, and bookcases plastered with photographs and mementoes of Solzhenitsyn. When he made some platitudinous comment, she shook her head and said, "That's all over now."[5] This is not to say that the relationship was any other than platonic or that Natalia's personal feelings for Elena were necessarily unfriendly. It was perhaps that Solzhenitsyn's post-birthday departure to Elena's somehow symbolized everything that had gone wrong with their marriage in the pre-ceding three to four years.

Natalia may also have been aware of the unflattering comparisons that could be made between Elena and herself. Elena was a sophisticated Mus-covite, steeped in culture and a member of a famous literary family. She had read all the books, and more, that Solzhenitsyn had read and had a far broader cultural background than he. Natalia, by comparison, was a provincial school-marm. She was a gifted amateur pianist and out of a sense of duty tried to read one or two of the "thick" magazines, but her real interests barely went beyond the meetings of the Ryazan chapter of the Mendeleyev Society and amateur dramatics at the institute. Of all the friends that she and Solzheni-tsyn had in common at the time and who have commented on the subject, only Dimitri Panin recalls being impressed by her intellect. He found her brilliant in everything she touched—chemistry, music, photography—a vivacious, if moody, companion and a thoughtful, hospitable host.[6] Others, including some who were later to take her side in the split with Solzhenitsyn, found her affected, gossipy and vain, bourgeois in her tastes, and limited in her opinions.

Such judgements may reflect the time and circumstances of people's first meetings with Natalia. Panin recalls her chiefly from a period when she and Solzhenitsyn were falling in love again and during their early years in Ryazan. Others met her only in the aftermath of *Ivan Denisovich*, when Solzhenitsyn's fame was throwing the first strains on their marriage. Veronica Stein, her cousin, affirms that Natalia is at heart a spontaneous, emotional woman who reacts equally strongly to good and bad news. "If she's in a bad mood, she's plunged into despair."[7] But what seems to have tipped the scales of opinion against her was her pretentiousness and her sometimes comical attempts to live up to the role of "the great writer's wife." Zhores Medvedev recalls that whenever she accompanied Solzhenitsyn, she would refuse to let him out of her sight, and insisted on sitting in on all of his conversations, no matter what the subject. Medvedev came to the conclusion that she was trying to hear and memorize everything so that she could write it down once she got home, and he was not surprised to learn soon afterwards that Natalia was keeping a diary. Another friend remembers her as a terrible name-dropper, while a third describes her as mimicking her husband: "I'm sorry," she would say, looking at her watch, "I can spare you only ten minutes"—when time was not really a problem.[8]

It seems that all this represented her idea of how a writer's wife should act, and she reinforced this image of herself by reading heaps of literary memoirs. Her particular favourite, according to Veronica Stein, was the diary of Tolstoy's wife, which she read several times. At one stage she bought a notebook, divided it into columns, and wrote out the psychological characteristics of Tolstoy and his wife as she perceived them (again, it seems, in imitation of her husband's method of analysis—he was doing the same with Lenin). She then went through the notebook putting ticks against the qualities she felt she and her husband shared with the Tolstoys, and crosses where she felt they were different. Perhaps it was at this moment that she conceived the idea of someday writing a memoir of her own.*

Insecurity clearly had a lot to do with her behaviour and her loneliness. It should not be forgotten that in his years in Ryazan, Solzhenitsyn had virtually cut her off from her former friends and colleagues. He and Natalia had had no social life to speak of, and it was all for the sake of his work, his need for secrecy. Then, for the sake of his work, he had had to spend long periods away from Ryazan and consequently away from her, and for the sake of secrecy (over *Gulag*) to exclude her from many of his arrangements. To him it seemed both inevitable and logical (forced on him by circumstances, by a cruel government), and her resistance seemed blind selfishness. In their increasingly frequent quarrels, he accused her of "tearing his guts out" with her nagging and of completely disregarding his literary work and professional

---

* In the unpublished chapters of her memoirs, Reshetovskaya states that it was the reading of a volume of Van Gogh's letters that provided the main impulse for her to undertake them.

problems. He told her that he could not endure such a life. She was sucking more energy out of him than his writing and public activities put together.[9]

To her, his fanatical devotion to his work and his longer and longer absences in Moscow seemed equally selfish. After the incident with the Leningrad woman, she had been pathologically jealous, endlessly questioning him on where he was going, turning out his pockets, trying to catch him out. This behaviour had prompted him to start giving her his unsealed letters. Then she had gone through a period of estrangement. She had complained that since their marriage he had overshadowed her and cramped her development, quoting Nikolai Vitkevich and her mother and aunts in support. She tried to move away from him, to take less interest in his work, to develop her own interests in amateur photography and especially in music.[10] Solzhenitsyn encouraged her in these plans and helped her to get lessons for a while from the celebrated and eccentric Soviet pianist Maria Yudina. Yudina was politically bold (she had read Pasternak's poems at some of her concerts when Pasternak was in disgrace) and was noted for her religious piety. She deeply admired Solzhenitsyn, having sought him out after the publication of *Ivan Denisovich*, and readily agreed to teach Natalia (although it was true, as Solzhenitsyn had written to her, that Natalia "wasn't developed enough for a teacher of her calibre"); and it appears that the two women became quite good friends.[11] Natalia's efforts to break away from her husband's spell, however, ultimately failed. She was too dependent on him, too lonely on her own, and he was still the only source of glamour in her life, even if he wouldn't behave conventionally. She was still Mrs Solzhenitsyn, it was her one consolation, and she wanted the world to see and acknowledge it, to witness her by his side.

Unfortunately, not even this seemingly small concession was easy for Solzhenitsyn to make. He simply could not see why it was important to her. He himself set little store by appearances and seemed unaware of the nuances that lay behind them. And his unawareness was compounded by his indifference to personal relations. As he later confessed, "I had a theory that one's personal life should be regarded as secondary . . . and the key to my behaviour was that I really treated it that way and I was constantly making mistakes." According to his ideas, personal life should account for only about 5 per cent of one's time and emotions, while the other 95 per cent should be devoted to professional duties. It was no wonder that he neglected personal life and failed to understand his wife's needs. Instead of offering her a partnership, he was passive, simply buying time and a quiet life.

> She used to keep demanding that I spend more time with her, pay her more attention, and be more affectionate, and this happened every time she came to me . . . but the moment she arrived everything would be gloom and endless conversations, and all my work would just slip from my hands . . . until she left again. And I was always soothing her and saving things up the whole time. That's a perpetual mistake of mine and the cause of many errors I've made, not only in this sphere but elsewhere as well. If only I could carry on with my work

uninterrupted, if only we could arrange it so that private matters didn't get in the way of work, if only I could get another chapter written, finish this book, and then something else. . . . And so I let things slide year after year, and things got worse and worse, but all I wanted was not to be interrupted and to get on with my work.[12]

The conflict was probably insoluble. They were locked into a marriage that brought less and less satisfaction to either of them and in which the needs of one contradicted the needs of the other. And yet, until 1968, no immediate threat had seemed to be in view. But earlier that year Solzhenitsyn had acquired another woman helper who combined Elena Chukovskaya's interest in literature, strong will, and talent for organization, with qualities that were infinitely more appealing and dangerous. Natalia Svetlova was not only adept in the ways of underground typing and the preparation of samizdat but also young, beautiful, and alluring.

Like Solzhenitsyn, Natalia Svetlova was a mathematician. At the time of their meeting, she was working for her doctorate and was a teaching assistant to Professor Kolmogorov at Moscow University, who regarded her as one of his star pupils. In 1960, while still only twenty, she had married an even more brilliant young mathematician named Andrei Tiurin, by whom she had had a son, Dmitri, in 1962. In 1964 they had decided to part, and were divorced a year later, though remaining on the friendliest of terms. Natalia's mathematical training obviously offered one affinity with Solzhenitsyn, but more important was her interest in literature. As early as the fifties she had been reading the still-forbidden poetry of Akhmatova and Pasternak. Later she had been one of a group of young people who attached themselves to Nadezhda Mandelstam and helped her with secretarial work. Among other things she had typed out Osip Mandelstam's *Voronezh Notebooks*, much of his poetry, and some stories by Bulgakov.[13]

Through her involvement with samizdat, Svetlova had recently got to know a number of dissidents. This had started with her introduction to Gorbanevskaya in 1967. Soon afterwards she had met Ginzburg, Litvinov, Larisa Bogoraz, and many of those associated with the foundation of the *Chronicle of Current Events*. After Ginzburg's sentencing, in January 1968, she had also become friendly with Ginzburg's fiancée, Irina Zholkovskaya. She did not count herself as a militant, however. Apart from signing one collective letter to *Komsomolskaya Pravda* to protest an article slandering Ginzburg and his co-defendants,[14] and briefly attending one or two trials, she had preferred to stick to the literary side of dissent, and she regarded some of the more outspoken dissidents as reckless and extreme.

Her first meeting with Solzhenitsyn had occurred in the small flat on Vasilievsky Lane near the Central Post Office, where she lived with her mother, Ekaterina (an aeronautical engineer and herself a formidably intelligent and efficient woman), her stepfather, David Svetlov, her grandmother, and her small son Dmitri. A mutual friend (possibly Shafarevich) had brought Solzhenitsyn there for the express purpose of introducing them, and it seems that the attraction between them was immediate and mutual. What Solzhenitsyn particularly liked about her was her pugnacious character, her quickness of mind, and her versatility. She had an answer for everything, and a practical flair that seemed capable of overcoming every difficulty. With her knowledge of the ways of samizdat and the world of the dissidents, she was also able to be very useful to him. He later said of his attraction to her:

> She thinks with electronic rapidity. . . . In an instant she's able to come up with the strongest argument and give it to you. . . . She has such fighting spirit, she was born to do battle, and that's what brought us together. . . . She simply joined me in my struggle and we went side by side. . . . She has a firm and excellent grasp of any situation, is very intelligent, and always has lots of ideas on how to act, what to do, and what response to make.[15]

Of the physical and emotional attraction between them, Solzhenitsyn has never spoken. One friend who occasionally stayed at the Chukovsky dacha when Solzhenitsyn was there recalls being discreetly asked to keep out of the way "between three and four" one summer afternoon in 1968, since Solzhenitsyn was expecting a visitor. Later he was seen to leave with his arm round the waist of a then-unknown woman. As for Svetlova, it seems to have been almost love at first sight. Soon after their first meeting she told a woman friend, "That's the man for me," and she later said (in another context) that, much as she had admired and respected her first husband, Tiurin, she had not known what love was until she met Solzhenitsyn.[16]

For the first year or so of their relationship, virtually no one outside her family circle knew of it. Natalia Svetlova was renowned for her discretion and told none of her friends. On the contrary, she began to edge away from her dissident contacts (except Irina Zholkovskaya), partly to secure her secret, but also as a natural result of her increasing involvement in Solzhenitsyn's affairs. With his penchant for impetuously following his instinct, he quickly handed over to her all the conspiratorial side of his activities—preparing and copying texts, distributing them among trusted friends or concealing them in prepared hiding-places, keeping track of where everything was, following up news of leaks, and generally acting as adjutant to Solzhenitsyn's general. By the end of 1968 and the time of his fiftieth birthday, Solzhenitsyn thus had two strong, capable, dedicated women assisting him with his affairs. Elena Chukovskaya looked after his above-ground activities, as it were, directing research and helping him interview sources and collect material for his historical novels, while Natalia Svetlova dealt with the submerged and secret part of his work. Of course, the division was not watertight, but it was broadly thus, and it perfectly suited Solzhenitsyn's mentality and his preference for keeping his life compartmentalized. It meant that no one person could know everything that he was doing, and below the level of his two principal secretaries, friends and acquaintances were even less aware of the full ramifications of his growing "establishment."

Also excluded from many important aspects of this arrangement was Natalia Reshetovskaya. Her exclusion had been gradual, dating from the move to Chukovsky's dacha in 1965, but it was inexorable, which partly accounted for the painfulness of the squabble on Solzhenitsyn's birthday. Perhaps it was her sense of this growing estrangement that led her to make a desperate attempt to close the gap between them. Two months after Solzhenitsyn's it was her own fiftieth birthday (Kopelev was the only guest), and she chose this moment to announce that she was making her fiftieth birthday the occasion of her early retirement from the Agricultural Institute. At fifty, she could look forward to a reasonable pension from her employers, but more important, she said, was her realization that she had for too long ignored her husband's literary affairs and was now anxious to assist him again. Accordingly, she would help him gather material for *August 1914* and resume some of her secretarial duties.[17]

Solzhenitsyn appears to have been both irritated and baffled by this move. The last thing he wanted was to have Natalia meddling in his work, particularly if it led her to discover the exact position and role of the other Natalia. On the other hand, too vehement a rejection would have aroused his wife's suspicions. He therefore devised a number of harmless tasks for her to perform, such as interviewing old ladies for their memories of pre-revolutionary Russia and the First World War and reading some peripheral documents and secondary literature. At the same time, he seems to have tacitly encouraged her growing interest in memoir writing and to have directed her attention principally to the early years of their marriage and to files of his letters from the time of their life in Ryazan.

To a certain extent this acted as a sop to Natalia's vanity, but it did nothing to remove her simmering resentment over his long absences from home and the humiliation of his neglect of her. She consoled herself by reading his earlier letters to her and dwelling on memories of their cosy life in Ryazan. But this only served to underline the reality of her present loneliness, a loneliness that was compounded a little later, when she was obliged to enter the hospital to have a lump removed from her breast. Cancer was suspected, but proved not to be the culprit. Just as depressing, from her point of view, was Solzhenitsyn's absence throughout her stay in the hospital. He was away on a research trip (probably with Svetlova) and was either unaware of Natalia's operation or else judged it impossible to return. For Natalia it was a crushing blow. No operation, apart, perhaps, from a hysterectomy, is more calculated to undermine a woman's confidence in herself (and in her continuing attraction for her husband) than an operation for suspected breast cancer. Yet Solzhenitsyn was—or seemed—completely indifferent to it, and no visits by friends and family could compensate for his absence. On being collected from the hospital by Veronica Stein, Natalia launched into a bitter tirade against her husband's heartlessness. Veronica defended him on the grounds of his literary mission and his dedication to his vocation, and the two cousins had a terrific row from which their relationship never fully recovered. Cordiality was restored, and they continued to meet regularly, but from now on a certain coolness crept in where before there had been warmth and trust.[18]

Apart from these domestic upheavals (and there were more in the course of the year), 1969 turned out to be relatively calm on the public front. In the early months of the year, Solzhenitsyn learned that both *The First Circle* and *Cancer Ward* were on the best-seller lists in almost all Western countries (*The First Circle* lasted for seven months on the American list), although many of the translations left much to be desired. Some, in the case of *The First Circle*, had been made from English instead of the original Russian.[19] He heard also that in France he had been awarded a prize for "the best foreign book of the year" and that in the United States he had been elected a member of the American Academy of Arts and Sciences (Boston).

At some point near the beginning of the year, Solzhenitsyn invited General Grigorenko, who was now one of the most prominent dissidents in the Democratic Movement, to visit him in Solotcha. After an exhausting struggle to rid himself of the agents who followed him everywhere, Grigorenko boarded the train for Ryazan only in the evening, and arrived at Solotcha in the small hours of the following morning. Solzhenitsyn was waiting up for him and impressed Grigorenko with the simplicity of his ways. The hut was every bit as primitive as the one Solzhenitsyn had lived in with Matryona. His present landlady had one room and Solzhenitsyn the other. At night he slept on the traditional peasant stove and, as usual, prepared all his own food. While they were chatting, Grigorenko noticed a sheaf of blank paper cut up into small pieces lying on the table, and asked Solzhenitsyn why it was so small. Solzhenitsyn took out a similar sheaf of paper that was covered with tiny, spidery handwriting, and explained to Grigorenko that it all had to do with his methods of concealment.

> This here is an entire day's work. Before going to sleep, I have to remove it from the house and will never see it again. I never keep what I have accumulated during the day in the place where I am working. If I need to go out for any reason, I put everything I have written, together with the clean sheets, into my pocket. Wherever I live, I always have several hiding-places scattered about. If a stranger comes, particularly a suspicious-looking stranger, I put everything I've written, and the clean paper, into one of these hiding-places. Let me emphasize that that includes both the clean paper and my pencil. Everything around me has to be clear, without the slightest hint that I am working. When you knocked, I put everything in my pocket. If I hadn't recognized you, everything would have been transferred to one of my hiding-places.

The two men stayed up all night talking. Again it looked like one of Solzhenitsyn's inspections, but it turned out that he was especially interested in hearing about Grigorenko's wartime experiences; when Grigorenko had finished, Solzhenitsyn repeatedly urged him to devote his time to writing an unvarnished history of the war. "I don't see anyone else who could do it," he told Grigorenko. "It's criminal for a man like you to spend his time running from trial to trial and writing appeals for the victims that the authorities always ignore." Grigorenko could not agree and felt that his comrades in the Democratic Movement would regard it as a betrayal if he abandoned them for writing. He was no intellectual, he said, and was not sure he had the ability anyway.[20]

The rest of that winter and spring was a quiet time for Solzhenitsyn. The *Literaturnaya Gazeta* predictably ignored Solzhenitsyn's letter thanking his readers for their fiftieth-birthday greetings, and it did not appear anywhere until the Russian-language newspaper in Paris, *Russkaya Mysl* (Russian Thought), published it in May. That same month, Solzhenitsyn was tipped off that the Writers' Union was seriously considering expelling him. In the context of the time, this was a serious step. The only precedents for it in post-war years had been the expulsions of Anna Akhmatova and Mikhail Zoschenko, in 1946, and of Pasternak, in 1958, after the publication abroad of *Doctor Zhivago* (Sinyavsky, too, had been expelled, while in jail). Similar treatment of Solzhenitsyn would place him on a par with his predecessors as a renegade and turncoat, but for him it would also have grave practical consequences. Zoshchenko and Akhmatova were established writers, and Pasternak already had his dacha in Peredelkino, a steady income, and an assured position in Soviet letters when he was attacked: he could absorb the blow without too much physical discomfort. Solzhenitsyn, however, would lose the threadbare but still effective covering of legitimacy which was all that stood between him and complete official isolation. Without a union card he would have no official place in society: like Brodsky before him, he would be technically unemployed and therefore a "parasite," in the legal definition of the term, which was a criminal offence. He would lose other benefits, too, like his pension rights, his right to social security and medical insurance, his right to employ a secretary, and his access to libraries. In short, his vulnerability would be immeasurably increased, and hence the opportunities to punish him.

For the moment the proposal remained at the discussion stage, and the authorities seemed at a loss as to how to proceed. Solzhenitsyn continued to be denounced at secret meetings, and at some of these a new slander (in the eyes of those making it) was introduced: Solzhenitsyn's name was pronounced as "Solzhenitser." At one meeting in Moscow, according to Zhores Medvedev, a member of the audience was so puzzled that he sent up a note explaining to the lecturer that he was mispronouncing the writer's surname. "Not at all," replied the lecturer, "it's not a mistake. The person known to you as Solzhenitsyn is really Solzhenitser, and he's a Jew."[21]

Even more farcical was a clumsy attempt, also reported by Medvedev, to blacken Solzhenitsyn's character by impersonation. One day rumours began to circulate in Moscow that Solzhenitsyn had "taken to drink." Alleged eyewitnesses reported that Solzhenitsyn had been seen at a well-known restaurant, the Slavyansky Bazaar, ordering sumptuous dinners, drinking extravagantly, pestering any women who happened to be present, and lavishly tipping the band to play "old Russian songs" for him. Soon afterwards the orgies shifted to other restaurants, and then an actress from one of the Moscow theatres came to see Lev Kopelev with a strange story. Apparently Solzhenitsyn had telephoned the theatre's manager and told him he was writing a new play. For professional reasons, he had said, he wanted to get to know a certain type of actress, and the manager had agreed to send along two candidates the following day. The two young women had had a jolly meal, and the writer chose one of them to meet in the Vega restaurant a day later. This was the actress who had now come to see Kopelev, who was well known as Solzhenitsyn's friend. Kopelev immediately made arrangements to accompany her and invited several other friends as well. When "Solzhenitsyn" saw them, he took fright but was escorted, unharmed, to the nearest police station. His papers identified him as Alexander Shalagin, former deputy director of some sort of theatre school, and some tattoos on his arm as a former criminal inmate of the labor camps. He did not say who had commissioned him, nor was he detained or ever charged. Nor did he seem to realize that the real Solzhenitsyn was well known for his dislike of alcohol.[22]*

The real Solzhenitsyn was barely aware of these manoeuvres. After a winter of hesitation, he had plunged into writing *August 1914*. The first parts of the novel to be completed were the chapters on the Battle of Tannenberg and Samsonov's defeat and suicide. Somewhat to his surprise, Solzhenitsyn had received a permit to work in the Historical Museum and was given access to all the military records on the early part of the First World War. It is true that some security men called round to discover what he was up to, but when they learned the subject of his investigations they left him in peace. While handling these documents, Solzhenitsyn took the opportunity to investigate whether his father was mentioned in any of them, and was enormously pleased to come across several references to Isaaki's service at the front. With the help of Elena Chukovskaya and other friends, he had also amassed quite a collection of books of his own, and Zhores Medvedev reports that when he called on Solzhenitsyn in Rozhdestvo that summer, he found him "surrounded by piles of photograph albums of the First World War. They were mainly German albums. With characteristic thoroughness the Germans had recorded battle scenes and the most important political events of the period."[23]

Work on this book naturally turned Solzhenitsyn's thoughts back not only to Russia's history but also to his family's past. In 1956, when he had travelled south to see his aunts after returning from exile, he had been impelled by a kind of elemental yearning to make contact with his roots and restore the bonds broken by imprisonment and exile. Since then he had been back

---

* This incident had a farcical sequel. Kopelev instituted a private network of vigilantes after this to monitor the KGB's activities and keep watch for Solzhenitsyn. One day he reported to Solzhenitsyn that another impostor had been regularly visiting a certain address where he evidently saw a woman friend. Solzhenitsyn asked for details of the address and exploded. It was he whom Kopelev's men had been watching, and the address was Svetlova's.

several times to gather information about his family, knowing that he would one day write about it in his novels. And now, when he examined this material more closely and pondered it, he must have realized how much his perspective had changed since his confident youth. He was closer to his childhood, and to his parents and their generation, than at any other time since the early thirties. Tales of the horrors of the Civil War, of the lootings and murders, of the siege of Kislovodsk, must have come back to him vividly, together with his mother's and Irina's stories of Grandfather Zakhar, their estate, and the halcyon years before the First World War and the Revolution, when patriarchal Russia seemed to be rousing itself from the sleep of centuries and modernizing its economy and industry, while retaining its archaic social fabric and its reverence for the mysteries of revealed religion.

His view of the Revolution had changed too—dramatically. For many years now, he had rejected Stalin and Lenin and their teaching and had concluded that the Revolution was a disaster. But the notion that the Revolution was somehow predestined and inevitable was hard to shake off until one examined what had preceded it, and the context in which it had taken place. The more he thought of it, the more he concluded that the Revolution had been avoidable and that it had been the stupidity, short-sightedness, and mistakes of the tsar, of the tsarist high command, and of Russia's statesmen that had led her to catastrophe. As for the intelligentsia, it, he felt, bore the heaviest responsibility of all, an opinion in which he was strongly reinforced by his discovery of a famous pre-revolutionary collection of essays entitled *Landmarks*.

Landmarks had been published in 1909 by a group of eminent thinkers, scholars, and writers of the time. Foremost among them were the religious philosophers Nikolai Berdyayev and Sergei Bulgakov, the economist and liberal politician Peter Struve, and the literary historian Mikhail Gershenzon. All of them had grown up in an intellectual atmosphere dominated by populist socialism and Marxism. Struve, for instance, had been a leader of the "legal Marxists," then of "revolutionary liberalism," until he finally arrived at a form of liberalism that was patriotic, religious, and almost nationalist, while rejecting the excesses of imperialism. The main thrust of *Landmarks* was to denounce the current Russian intelligentsia as anti-religious, unpatriotic, and materialist, in thrall to so-called scientific socialism and contemptuous of the spiritual values that were a necessary condition of the nation's intellectual, cultural, and moral health. As Gershenzon wrote in his preface to the volume, its authors were united by their "recognition of the primacy both in theory and in practice of spiritual life over the outward forms of society, in the sense that the inner life of the individual . . . and not the self-sufficient elements of some political order is the only solid basis for every social structure."[24]

Landmarks had caused a tremendous stir when it first appeared, and later became the foundation of a new national liberalism that proved highly popular in Russia just before and during the First World War. Prince Mirsky, in his famous *History of Russian Literature*, describes the book as instrumental in kindling a patriotic spirit in 1914 and inspiring the White Army during the Civil War. Struve, meanwhile, went on to become "the principal brain of anti-Bolshevism" and the best and most influential political writer among the post-revolutionary *émigrés*.

Struve and company managed to produce a kind of sequel to *Landmarks* in 1918, after the October Revolution. Called *De Profundis*, it lamented the Revolution as a fulfillment of the authors' earlier forebodings and was immediately suppressed, as was *Landmarks*. Only in 1967 did *Landmarks* surface again, in a reprinting in Paris by the Russian-*émigré* publishing house YMCA Press, an edition that may have fallen into Solzhenitsyn's hands too. It is possible that echoes of the philosophy of *Landmarks* had reached Solzhenitsyn already in his childhood through the opinions of his aunt Irina or his mother, both of whom had spent time in White Army territory and could be reckoned to be sympathetic to a form of religious liberalism. Perhaps some such ideas had cropped up in those intellectual conversations around the dinner table at the Fedorovskys' in Rostov. At all events, Solzhenitsyn seems to have been highly receptive to the views of Berdyayev, Struve, and their circle, and to have experienced the reading of *Landmarks* as a revelation. Here was something that rejected Marxism and Bolshevism four-square and embraced the Christian faith, without lapsing into the extremes of monarchism and reaction. It also explained the Russia he dimly remembered from the stories of his childhood far more convincingly and vividly than did the Bolshevik myths he had imbibed at school and university. And it allowed him to place his own family and forebears in a context that made intellectual and emotional sense and that fitted with everything he had learned about pre- and post-revolutionary Russia in the "university" of the camps.

At the same time, *Landmarks* offered Solzhenitsyn a patriotic alternative to the liberal, Western-influenced ideas of the dissidents in the Human Rights Movement, and to the science-based (and equally Western-influenced, in Solzhenitsyn's view) theories put forward by Sakharov in his memorandum. Indeed, it may have been his reading of *Landmarks* and *DeProfundis*, in the spring of 1969, that impelled him to put onto paper his criticisms of Sakharov's memorandum in a more systematic form. This essay, "As Breathing and Consciousness Return," was the first of what was to become a long series of critical and polemical articles by Solzhenitsyn in the ensuing ten years, and is noteworthy (in contrast to his later essays) for the gentleness and thoughtfulness of its tone, as if Solzhenitsyn had been infected with the tone of Sakharov himself.

Solzhenitsyn's purpose in making his critique was not simply to welcome Sakharov's unprecedented essay but also to clarify and challenge some of the ideas in it and move the debate forward. "The way back, which our country will soon face—the return of breathing and consciousness, the transition from silence to free speech—will also prove difficult and slow, and just as painful, because of the gulf of utter incomprehension that will suddenly yawn between fellow-countrymen, even those of the same generation and place of origin, even members of the same close circle." Solzhenitsyn went on to illustrate the gulf by criticizing Sakharov's memorandum on a number of points. Too much attention was paid by Sakharov, he wrote, to other countries' problems, and not enough to his own. Sakharov was also too timid to attack one of the main roots of evil in the Soviet system—Marxist ideology—and mistakenly reserved all his criticism for Stalinism. "A close study of our modern history shows that there never was any such thing as Stalinism, either as a doctrine, or as a path of national life, or as a state system. . . . Stalin was a very consistent and faithful—if also very untalented—heir to the *spirit* of Lenin's teaching."

Solzhenitsyn criticized Sakharov's belief in convergence, technological progress, and socialism and his disdain for nationalism. But perhaps the most interesting passages in his article were those in which he took issue with Sakharov's views on intellectual freedom and democracy. Intellectual freedom was all very well, he wrote, but what had it done for the West. "We see [the West] today, crawling on hands and knees, its will paralysed, uneasy about the future, spiritually racked and dejected." In itself, freedom was no answer. Nor were democracy and the multi-party system, which the dissidents seemed to idolize. "Party" meant just a part of something. "Every party known to history has always defended the interests of this one part against— whom? Against the rest of the people. . . . And every party . . . levels and crunches its members." It was time for the Russian people to rise above Western conceptions to a loftier viewpoint and look for "extra-party or non-party paths of national development."

Despite these reservations about Sakharov's memorandum, Solzhenitsyn nonetheless professed to find in him an ally. Sakharov's call for a new world leadership and a world government surely implied a rejection of both "socialism" (of the Soviet variety) and Western democracy. "We have quite a different principle—that of authoritarian rule. Whether such a government proved very bad or excellent, the means of creating it, the principles of its formation and operation, can have nothing in common with modern democracy."[25]

It is doubtful whether Sakharov would have agreed; but what is striking here is the date when these views were expressed—1969, a full five years before the publication of Solzhenitsyn's *Letter to the Leaders*, which was to cause such a stir when it appeared in 1974, with its apologia for an authoritarian form of government. For the moment, however, Solzhenitsyn was not prepared to release to the larger public this statement of his political views, and he contented himself with sending a copy privately to Sakharov with a request that he not show it to anyone.

To the outside world, Solzhenitsyn remained a liberal—a "progressive" even—firmly associated with *Novy Mir* and its policy of more or less loyal opposition and its programme of a "return to Leninism," rather as Sakharov was arguing. But beneath the facade of comradeship the cracks between Solzhenitsyn and *Novy Mir* were also steadily widening. Suspicious from the first of Dementyev, Sachs, and Kondratovich, Solzhenitsyn now turned away from his former ally Vladimir Lakshin. Formerly he had held Lakshin in the highest regard, describing him as "a very gifted literary critic . . . who can stand comparison with our best nineteenth-century critics," and in 1964 and 1966 had written expressing his gratitude to Lakshin for his excellent and courageous articles on *Ivan Denisovich* and "Matryona."[26] But since March 1967, when Dementyev and Sachs were dismissed and Lakshin became Tvardovsky's confidant and *de facto* deputy editor (the official deputy editor's job went to Kondratovich), Solzhenitsyn had gradually become dissatisfied with Lakshin's caution and respectability. He seems to have felt that Lakshin was acting as a drag on Tvardovsky's progress towards a more radical attitude to the political establishment.

The differences between the two men were a result as much of Solzhenitsyn's evolving views as of a change on Lakshin's part, and this emerged with particular clarity in September 1969, when Solzhenitsyn paid a routine visit to the office after an absence of several weeks. The chief subject of discussion when he arrived was a polemic that *Novy Mir* had been conducting with the monthly magazine *Molodaya Gvardia* (Young Guard) and then with *Ogonyok* and a "managers'" newspaper called *Sotsialisticheskaya Industria*. The dispute was over two articles published the preceding year in *Molodaya Gvardia* by a literary critic named Victor Chalmayev.[27] Chalmayev's views added up to a reactionary mishmash of Brezhnev-style communism and old-fashioned Russian chauvinism with Slavophile overtones—a mixture that was sometimes dubbed "National Bolshevism" (by analogy with National Socialism) by its opponents, although it was then just beginning to be formulated. The West was denounced as hopelessly corrupt and degenerate, "choking on a surfeit of hate" and the fount of all evil. Attempting to build bridges with it, to import its technology or, even worse, its consumer goods or its culture, was a complete waste of time and even dangerous—the West's infection might spread to the East. The Russian tradition, on the other hand, was pure and lofty, fed by a "sacred spring." It had degenerated somewhat under the trivializing impact of television, the cinema, the mass media (all imports from the West), but it could reform itself by turning back to its roots, drawing inspiration from the Russian village, the moral and spiritual values of the Russian people, the pure idioms of popular speech. There were mystic references to the sacramental power of the native soil, even an invocation of Holy Russia, her "saints and just men born of a yearning for miracles and loving kindness": Sergius of Radonezh, the Patriarch Hermogen, Serafim of Sarov. All this, according to Chalmayev, had culminated and found its finest expression in the Russian Revolution, that "sacramental act" that had crowned a thousand years of glorious history.

To most Soviet intellectuals, sentiments like these had an ominous ring to them. They evoked memories of the "Black Hundreds" of tsarist times—Ku Klux Klan–type societies glorifying the Russian past and specializing in anti-Semitism and pogroms. Above all it was seen as a blast not only at the Westernizing liberals, but at the intelligentsia as a whole, with its European manners, its internationalism and remoteness from the "true" Russian people. Amid the outcry that followed, *Novy Mir* had commissioned Dementyev to write a reply, which it ran in its June number. Dementyev had attacked Chalmayev for his obscurantism and poured scorn on his patriotism, his extraordinary (and "un-Leninist") genuflections to church history, his reactionary Slavophilism, his praise of an unrealistic, bucolic utopia, and his hostility to modernization. This was not Marxism-Leninism, he wrote, but a "dogmatic perversion." Marxism-Leninism was internationalist, progressive, and in favour of modernization. Dementyev was in turn fiercely attacked (in the crudest terms) by *Ogonyok* and by "a worker" in *Sotsialisticheskaya Industria*, to which Tvardovsky had replied in the August number of *Novy Mir*.

When Solzhenitsyn turned up in September, he was naturally expected to show sympathy for *Novy Mir* and the liberals against the reactionaries at *Molodaya Gvardia*, but he produced a sheet of paper from his pocket setting out all the points on which he agreed with Chalmayev and all those where he thought Dementyev was wrong. For while he shared some of *Novy Mir*'s disgust with Chalmayev's bombastic tone, cheap rhetoric, and extreme xenophobia, he had nonetheless been surprised and pleased to find in it certain themes and ideas that were appearing, to the best of his knowledge, for the very first time in an official Soviet publication, and he felt it was important to distinguish these from the dross that made up the rest of the article. The themes that interested him in particular were Chalmayev's appeal to Russian, as opposed to purely Soviet, patriotism, his praise of the early Russian church and Russian saints, nostalgia for Russian village life and popular culture, and reverence for the uniqueness of the Russian national tradition. Solzhenitsyn was disposed to agree with Dementyev that it was absurd to regard these aspects of Russian life as culminating in the Russian Revolution, for the Revolution was a product of Westernization and Western influences. But whereas Dementyev, and *Novy Mir*, tended to reject the Russian national tradition in the name of the Revolution, Solzhenitsyn had reached an opposite view— that it was necessary to reject the Revolution in the name of the Russian national tradition. He could not say this to the *Novy Mir* people in so many words, nor did he care to point out the degree to which he shared Chalmayev's repugnance for the West (as indicated in his private letter to Sakharov), for that would have antagonized his friends even more, but he did make it clear how strongly he disagreed with Dementyev's reply.

Solzhenitsyn had been particularly irritated, it seems, by Dementyev's insulting references to *Landmarks* (just as he had been favourably impressed by Chalmayev's indirect quotation, at one point in his article, of *De Profundis*), which Dementyev (quoting Lenin) had termed "the renegade's Encyclopaedia" and had himself called "that symposium of shame." Had Tvardovsky ever read *Landmarks*, Solzhenitsyn wanted to know? Or Dementyev either, for that matter? And if not, why were they insulting it in their magazine?

Tvardovsky was confused. He had barely heard of *Landmarks* (and was unaware that Solzhenitsyn himself had discovered it only a few months beforehand). Solzhenitsyn had insisted on dragging him into Lakshin's office to repeat the question and to ask Lakshin to obtain a copy. Lakshin had responded coldly (he was evidently better informed than Tvardovsky), thus confirming Solzhenitsyn's increasingly poor opinion of him.

It was probably now, under the influence of his debate with Sakharov and his growing disillusionment with *Novy Mir*, that Solzhenitsyn began to think seriously of creating his own journal. In *The Oak and the Calf* he writes that the idea had first occurred to him as early as 1965. But it was only in the summer of 1969, while taking a trip with Svetlova to the river Pinega, in the north of Russia, that he appears to have planned the project in more detail. He envisaged it as a samizdat journal, and with his usual thoroughness and love of plotting, Solzhenitsyn elaborated a plan that seemed conspiratorially foolproof: "there would be a distribution department, a more deeply hidden operative editorial staff, and a still more deeply hidden shadow staff to take over if the original team came to grief, and to set up a second shadow staff."[28] In any event, nothing came of this plan, but it may have started the chain of thought that led Solzhenitsyn, a few years later, to sponsor a collection of essays by himself, Shafarevich, and a group of friends. Shafarevich may well have been a party to the journal idea too. He was close to both Svetlova and Solzhenitsyn, and it seems that he exercised a considerable influence on Solzhenitsyn's thinking at this time, particularly in strengthening his feelings of patriotism. It may have been Shafarevich who introduced Solzhenitsyn to *Landmarks* and *De Profundis*.

It cannot have been a coincidence that the whole question of love and loyalty to one's country and the ethics of leaving it was prominent in Solzhenitsyn's mind that summer. Over the years, consciously or unconsciously, he had grown more or less accustomed to the idea that he might some day escape—or be pushed—abroad. And he had welcomed the prospect. "Through the years I had never changed in one thing—the conviction forged in me by the camps, the thought I shared with my comrades there: that our zombies must be struck down by our knowledge of the camps, but from outside. There I should have all my weapons ready to hand; not a single word need ever again be suppressed or distorted or blunted." It was only the preceding year, when he confided this thought to Svetlova, that he had come up against stiff resistance to it. She was shocked, and adamant that he was wrong; and Shafarevich, with his fanatical love of the motherland, had supported her. "I have hardly met anyone like him," Solzhenitsyn later wrote, "in his readiness to die in and for his homeland, rather than seek safety in the West."[29]

As if to point up their debate, the novelist Anatoli Kuznetsov defected to England while they were still on holiday by the Pinega, creating a minor sensation in both East and West. Kuznetsov blamed his decision to defect on the stifling Soviet censorship and on the KGB's habit of manipulating writers by enlisting them to inform on one another and rewarding them with foreign trips in exchange for carrying out commissions for the KGB. Initially, dissidents and liberals in the Soviet Union greeted the news of Kuznetsov's defection with approval, but in making his public denunciations of the KGB, Kuznetsov revealed that he had also agreed to co-operate with the secret police in order to be allowed abroad, and conceded that in his dealings with the censorship (especially over his celebrated novel, *Babi Yar*) he had been less than bold. His frank admissions touched off a larger dispute among Soviet writers that eventually resolved itself into a condemnation of his behaviour, even by most liberals. Andrei Amalrik, who had recently completed his own brilliant contribution to the debate about Russia's future—*Will the Soviet Union Survive until 1984?*—summed up the general feeling in an open letter to Kuznetsov, in which he drew a distinction between external and "inner" freedom. Kuznetsov, he wrote, had been so blinded by his desire for external freedom that he had paid too heavy a price for it. What was more precious was inner freedom, such as the dissidents had attained for themselves; Sinyavsky and Solzhenitsyn were two writers who had rightly chosen inner freedom as their primary goal. (Interestingly, he quoted Solzhenitsyn's position as being "for the Soviet regime and . . . opposed only to its particular or general shortcomings," which is indicative of the position Solzhenitsyn occupied in the public eye at that time.) True, they had paid a high price— Sinyavsky in the form of a jail sentence—but not in moral and spiritual terms, and that was what was important.[30]

Solzhenitsyn himself was not prepared to go as far as Amalrik. He must have had a sneaking admiration for Kuznetsov's feat—not least for the deep conspiracy in which Kuznetsov had laid and carried out his plans, even to the extent of burying his manuscripts in the ground (a tactic familiar to Solzhenitsyn) and concealing his intentions from his wife (was Solzhenitsyn not engaged in similar deceptions?). Surely it took nerve, guts and skill to do that, especially in view of the strength of the forces he was up against. But, as he comments in his memoir, "We are an irrational people. We wallow and flounder in liquid dung for decades and grumble that things are bad. Yet we make no effort to struggle out of it. And if someone does scramble clear and runs away, we yell, 'Traitor! Renegade!' "[31]

Solzhenitsyn had an additional reason for feeling uneasy about this new hullabaloo over connections with the West, for he was just then making preparations for a new and unprecedented step of his own—the engagement of a Western lawyer to protect his literary estate and look after his interests in the West. He wanted to take this step because he feared for his physical safety and consequently for the safety of his manuscripts. Engraved on his heart was the memory of how the KGB had already descended once and confiscated his novel and archive, all of which had disappeared into limbo. For some time he had been concerned about what steps to take. He no longer trusted Natalia. For a while he had thought of entrusting his estate to Elena Chukovskaya and had already discussed it with her. But soon after the appearance of Natalia Svetlova on the scene, he had resolved to transfer everything to her. She had the necessary skill and drive to conceal it safely and preserve it for posterity, and she was now his closest confidante. But it was necessary to have a fall-back position. So long as Svetlova was in the Soviet Union, and associated with him, her life, too, was in potential danger, and in the long run the only truly safe repository was the West.[32]

In October 1969 Solzhenitsyn was able to show Tvardovsky twelve sample chapters from *August 1914*—dealing with the Samsonov campaign. Tvardovsky was enthusiastic, and delighted that Solzhenitsyn's writing revealed no sign of flagging. "Solzhenitsyn is a man of extraordinary talent," he told Zhores Medvedev, "perhaps even more so than Gorky. I'm in the middle of reading some chapters from his new novel about the First World War, Prussia, the defeat of Samsonov's army. Fascinating prose, an entirely new key."[33]

That same October, Kornei Chukovsky died after a long illness. He was eighty-seven and was given a pompous funeral befitting his former status as the grand old man of Soviet literature. For some reason, Solzhenitsyn didn't attend—he must have arranged to take his farewell of his benefactor privately, before the main event. And Chukovsky continued his generosity to Solzhenitsyn even from beyond the grave. A wealthy man from his royalties, a ruble millionaire, he made a bequest to Solzhenitsyn that was to keep the latter in funds for another three years.

Soon after the funeral Solzhenitsyn returned to Ryazan for the first time in many months. He planned to work on a chapter on Lenin for *August 1914* and was amused to find that a portrait of his subject had been hung on a building across the street from his study window in time for the November holiday. But on the morning of 3 November his work was interrupted by a ring at the door. A secretary from the Ryazan branch of the Writers' Union thrust a piece of paper into his hand requesting him to attend a meeting at three that afternoon on the "ideological education of writers." The invitation struck him as rather unusual. He was rarely in Ryazan, and even more rarely attended meetings of the local Writers' Union. Including himself, its membership barely came to half a dozen. How did they know he was in town, and why were they meeting today? He sensed that it must be something to do with himself. Interrupting his work, he gathered up some clippings and drafts that he had put aside for just such an eventuality (neatly stacked in a folder labelled "The Writers' Union and Myself") and wrote out some notes for a speech.

Arriving five minutes early in order to secure a good seat, Solzhenitsyn was surprised to find only one person there—Vasily Matushkin, the branch secretary. Solzhenitsyn settled himself at a round table, spread out his pencils, papers, and notebook, and prepared to keep a record of the meeting. Experience in Moscow had shown him that the official records of such meetings, if kept, were never made available, even to the participants, yet they could be a useful weapon when used in the right way. Four more writers came in together, accompanied by a grey, bureaucratic-looking figure who introduced himself as Franz Taurin from the secretariat of the Russian Writers' Union in Moscow. Five other dark-suited individuals also entered the room, one of whom came over to Solzhenitsyn and shook his hand. Solzhenitsyn did not know who he was, and only later did he discover that it was Alexander Kozhevnikov, ideological secretary of the Regional Party Committee.

The ostensible purpose of the meeting was to hear a report from Taurin on a recent meeting of the union secretariat and a resolution passed there on "Measures to Intensify Ideological Educational Work among Writers." It seemed one of those routine gatherings organized on the Party's usual conveyor-belt principle of relaying to the provinces details of ideological decisions taken in Moscow: Party emissaries fan out all over the country to bring the word to the provinces and ensure that the Party line is carried down to the lowest level. Taurin spoke about the disgraceful behaviour of Kuznetsov in deserting his country; members of the Russian Writers' Union were extremely indignant, he said, and were insisting that indoctrination procedures be stiffened and controls tightened on writers travelling abroad.

For a moment Solzhenitsyn relaxed. Taurin had almost reached the end of his report without mentioning his name once, though he did indicate that the Moscow branch was investigating charges of ideological laxity against Lev Kopelev, Lydia Chukovskaya (both friends of Solzhenitsyn), and Bulat Okudzhava. But in his very last sentence, Taurin added that something had also been said about a Ryazan member, "Comrade Solzhenitsyn."

This proved to be the cue for the attack proper to begin. Matushkin spoke first. He accused Solzhenitsyn of not taking part in the work of the Ryazan branch of the Writers' Union, of failing to help young writers and to join in discussions of their work. But this, it turned out, was only a beginning. Solzhenitsyn's true crime was that "all of his recent writing (true, we have no knowledge of it, we haven't read it . . .) is at cross purposes with what the rest of us are writing. . . . When our motherland was besmirched with the help of his writings and Alexander Isayevich was told how to reply . . . he failed to react, he felt he knew better." Therefore, said Matushkin, there was no room for Solzhenitsyn in the Writers' Union, and it was time they parted company.[34]

Matushkin was followed by Nikolai Rodin, Sergei Baranov, Evgeni Markin, and Nikolai Levchenko, local writers of no note, who repeated Matushkin's charges and added little of their own. Only Markin seemed to vacillate: "I find myself depressed by the extraordinary swing of the pendulum from one extreme to the other. I was working on the staff of *Literatura i Zhizn* (Literature and Life) when unprecedented tributes were being paid to Solzhenitsyn. Since then there has been a swing in the opposite direction: never have I heard such harsh views expressed about anyone as about Solzhenitsyn." Markin had other criticisms to make of the Union, and it seemed for a moment that he might go against his fellow members, but in conclusion he announced tamely, "I fully agree with the majority of the writers' organization."*

---

*Markin subsequently repented of his role in the expulsion and wrote two poems that were thinly disguised allegories of Solzhenitsyn's fate: "Weightlessness" and "The White Buoy." The poems appeared in *Novy Mir*, no. 10 (1971), and caused a considerable stir.

When the other writers had had their say, Solzhenitsyn was allowed to speak. He declared that it was not true he had refused to participate in the work of the local branch: he had done what he could whenever he stayed in Ryazan. He had also asked for *Cancer Ward* to be discussed by the branch, but Moscow had refused to send the necessary copies. As for the letter he was supposed to write, he pointed out that he had twice written letters to the union secretariat, responding to all the points they had raised, but the secretariat had never once replied to him. He then rehearsed the saga of the non-publication of *Cancer Ward*, his letters to *Le Monde* and *L'Unità*, the *Literaturnaya Gazeta*'s refusal to publish his letter until it was too late, the interference with his correspondence, especially at the time of his fiftieth birthday, the harassment of his friends and of anyone who had anything to do with him. Finally, quoting Nekrasov (the nineteenth-century poet) and Tolstoy, he emphatically denied that he was painting reality too black—or doing anything other than what his great predecessors had done. As for the pendulum Markin had mentioned, yes, there was a pendulum, the pendulum of de-Stalinization, which was now swinging back the other way, but it was impossible to forget the crimes of Stalin. Russian writers owed it to their people, and especially to the younger generation, to tell the truth. Only then could further injustices be prevented. Solzhenitsyn repeated the last words from his letter to the Writers' Union: "I am, of course, confident that I shall fulfil my duty as a writer in all circumstances. . . . I am prepared to accept even death—yes, death and not merely expulsion from the union." And he concluded, "Well, then, take the vote—you've got a majority. But remember: the history of literature will some day show an interest in this meeting of ours."

At this point Kozhevnikov, the watch-dog of ideological purity, intervened to restate the Party line: "The congress rejected your letter as uncalled for and ideologically incorrect. In that letter you repudiate the guiding role of the Party—but that is what we take our stand on, the guiding role of the Party." Nikolai Levchenko then got to his feet and read the previously prepared resolution:

> In view of his anti-social behaviour, which contradicts the aims and objectives of the Union of Writers of the USSR, and of his gross violation of the basic provisions of the statutes of the Union of Writers of the USSR, we resolve that the writer Solzhenitsyn be expelled from the Union of Writers of the USSR. We request the secretariat to endorse this decision.

The resolution was carried unanimously.

On his way out of the meeting, Solzhenitsyn was stopped by a solicitous Taurin: "I strongly advise you to go up and see the secretariat right away. Tomorrow they are holding their plenary meeting, and it would be in your own best interest." Solzhenitsyn was sceptical. It seemed out of the question that they would confirm such a decision and expel someone within twenty-four hours of the original resolution, especially *in absentia*. If they did, it would be unconstitutional and would demonstrate that they had regarded the Ryazan decision as a foregone conclusion (it was also the start of the November holiday, when by tradition no official business was ever transacted). It did not seem possible that they would go to such lengths at such a time. And so he hurried instead to the post office to find the only coin-operated inter-city phone in Ryazan, and phoned the news through to *Novy Mir*. Then he returned home to write up his record of the meeting.

The following day he had the satisfaction of hearing news of his expulsion broadcast by both the Voice of America and the BBC, and of posting a copy of his "Record" to Moscow for distribution in samizdat. In the Ryazan Party offices there was consternation. What spy had the BBC posted in Ryazan to report such news so quickly? But in Moscow the Union outsmarted Solzhenitsyn. On 5 November 1969 the secretariat held a confidential meeting to ratify the expulsion. According to Zhores Medvedev, only one writer voted against—Daniel Granin, from Leningrad, who felt that such a decision should be taken only in the presence of the accused writer.[35] When he later returned to Leningrad, Granin was reprimanded by the first secretary of the Leningrad Party Committee, Tolstikov, and dismissed from leadership of the Leningrad branch of the Writers' Union. Meanwhile the secretariat decided to keep its decision secret for a while to make sure that when the news got out it would be irreversible. Nikolai Levchenko was ordered to man the telephone in Ryazan and tell all callers from Moscow that there had been no expulsion and that he knew nothing about it. This led certain Western correspondents to report that the expulsion was a false rumour, and it was nearly a week before the original report was confirmed.[36]

Solzhenitsyn had miscalculated, and was absolutely livid when the news reached him two days later. He sat down and penned his bitterest and most eloquent broadside yet against the dinosaurs in the secretariat.

Shamelessly trampling underfoot your own statutes, you have expelled me in my absence. . . .

Dust off the clock face. You are behind the times. Throw open the sumptuous heavy curtains—you do not even suspect that day is already dawning outside. . . . The time is near when each of you will seek to scratch your signature from today's resolution.

Blind leading the blind! You do not even notice that you are wandering in the opposite direction from the one you yourselves announced. At this time of crisis, you are incapable of offering our grievously sick society anything constructive and good, anything but your malevolent vigilance, your "hold tight and don't let go!"

Openness, honest and complete *openness*—that is the first condition of health in all societies, including our own. . . . He who does not wish this openness for his fatherland does not want to purify it of its diseases, but only to drive them inwards, there to fester.[37]

Solzhenitsyn did not release the letter at once. Having got these feelings off his chest, he attempted to settle down again to work on *August 1914*, but inspiration would not come. He was too upset, smarting from his defeat and seething with pent-up rage. At the back of his mind was that old fear again: Was Ryazan safe? Just as after the confiscation of his archive, he was prey to a mounting sense of panic. It would be all too easy to do away with him before anyone could find out about it. In a motor accident, perhaps. A familiar pick-up truck had appeared outside his front door, keeping him under surveillance. He decided it was necessary to leave and seek greater safety once more. Packing his manuscripts, books, and a few personal belongings into a case, he said goodbye to Natalia, Maria, and the two aunts and took the train to Moscow. It was 11 November 1969. He perhaps did not know it, but it was the virtual end of the Ryazan period in his life, begun twelve years before in a haze of domestic bliss. On that occasion he had arrived arm in arm with Natalia Reshetovskaya, unknown, unsung, an obscure provincial teacher. Now he was leaving in a blaze of publicity, world-famous, controversial, at the eye of the storm, and, for the time being at least, alone.

37

THE TAMING
OF *NOVY MIR*

SOLZHENITSYN'S DESTINATION IN Moscow on this occasion was not the
Chukovskys' flat or their dacha in Peredelkino but Rostropovich's dacha
in the outer Moscow suburb of Zhukovka, a quiet, leafy district of spacious
houses and large gardens reserved for Soviet notables and top Party leaders,
to which access was virtually barred for the general public. In fact there were
two Zhukovkas: "Zhukovka 1," also known as "Sovmin," where the Party
leaders lived behind a brick-and-iron palisade and to which entry could be
gained only by a special pass; and "Zhukovka 2," or "Academic Zhukovka,"
a more informal settlement inhabited by top Soviet scientists (Sakharov had
a dacha here), musicians and composers like Rostropovich and Shostakovich,
and many leading academicians. The police were much in evidence here—
not to harass the residents but to guard them against unwelcome intrusions
from outside—and there was a certain irony in Solzhenitsyn's finding refuge
inside this privileged zone.

Had he wished, he might have gone to Zhukovka much earlier, for Rostropovich had been urging him to move in for almost a year. He had fairly
recently built a new wing consisting of a garage for three cars with a small
flat above (two rooms, kitchen, and a bathroom). The flat had been built and
furnished for a young Leningrad cellist whom Rostropovich had intended to
befriend and teach but who for some reason had failed to come, and was
therefore perfect for Solzhenitsyn's purposes. Nevertheless, Solzhenitsyn had
declined at first. He felt he didn't know Rostropovich well enough. But in
the course of 1969 they had become good friends and now he had decided to
accept. In fact, his formal use of the flat had commenced the preceding September, but he had continued to spend more time in Ryazan than in Mos-

cow, and it was only after his expulsion that the move to Zhukovka was made more permanent.

The move naturally came as a great relief. Solzhenitsyn quickly christened Rostropovich's miniature estate "Seslavino,"* and Rostropovich he called "Steve." The grounds were particularly lovely, with paths winding between oak, birch, and pine trees and benches scattered here and there. Rostropovich, a great collector, planned to line the paths with some old street lamps that he had brought back from Paris—"so that not only Pushkin and Dostoyevsky but also Solzhenitsyn shall walk under them," as he ebulliently explained one day.† But Solzhenitsyn hated the idea. He disliked ostentation of any kind, and in any case preferred to be able to see the stars.[1]

The one problem with the move was that it further complicated his relations with Natalia. There seemed to her to be something more permanent about the Zhukovka arrangement than there had been in Peredelkino. Here his quarters were self-contained and very comfortable by Soviet standards. There was not the same sense of obligation to his hosts, and his independence was more complete. Furthermore, this new separation ran counter to her plans to be a literary wife and help her husband with his work, as well as to consult him over the writing of her memoirs. She had given up her teaching post in order to devote herself to his affairs once more, and now he was leaving again. It is not clear what arrangement they finally came to. According to Veronica Stein, there were some angry scenes before she allowed herself to be persuaded to remain behind in Ryazan and to visit Solzhenitsyn only occasionally.[2] According to her own account, however, it was more or less the other way around: she moved into Zhukovka and visited Ryazan only from time to time.[3] In any case, one of the rooms at Zhukovka was assigned to her use, and she seems to have come and gone fairly frequently.

Solzhenitsyn's other immediate destination in Moscow on 11 November was the offices of *Novy Mir*. He was not looking forward to this call, for he had an uneasy feeling that Tvardovsky would be upset by his expulsion and would be alarmed by its implications for the future of *Novy Mir*. He was not altogether wrong. Tvardovsky had been receiving threatening telephone calls from the Central Committee about the composition of his editorial board. Further changes were about to be demanded, and Tvardovsky was seriously contemplating resignation. Glad of a chance to take a positive role, Solzhenitsyn urged Tvardovsky to stand firm. The magazine was still well worth saving, still the best they had, and Tvardovsky shouldn't make it easy for his detractors by going voluntarily. Let them be forced to dismiss him and show their hands.

Solzhenitsyn toyed with the idea of showing Tvardovsky the reply to the Writers' Union secretariat that he had prepared in Ryazan, but decided against it. It was too strong and outspoken. Tvardovsky would try to per-

* From the Russian *sei* ("this") and *Slavin*, meaning "belonging to Slava." Slava is the short form of Rostropovich's first name, Mstislav.
† The quote is from Natalia Reshetovskaya. Pushkin was never in Paris.

suade him not to send it, and that would lead to an argument or possibly worse. His instinct was confirmed when he showed it to another *Novy Mir* writer, his friend Boris Mozhayev. Mozhayev, no coward himself, was appalled by the bitter outspokenness of Solzhenitsyn's statement. "You can't possibly send a letter like that," he said. Better to make a formal appeal to the union and follow the regular channels. But Solzhenitsyn would not be budged. As he later wrote in *The Oak and the Calf*:

> In my opinion it's the most Russian thing imaginable to take a swing and— wham! For one brief moment you feel yourself to be a worthy son of your country. Brave? I'm not brave. There's no one more timid. I have written *Gulag*, but I keep it quiet. I know something about the camps as they now are, but I don't say anything. I kept quiet about Czechoslovakia, and for that alone I must drag myself into action now. What Lydia Chukovskaya once said about political protests was right: "If I don't do it, I can't write about the things that matter. Until I pull this arrow out of my breast, I can think of nothing else."[4]

On 12 November the *Literaturnaya Gazeta* made its formal announcement of Solzhenitsyn's expulsion ("the behaviour of A. Solzhenitsyn is of an anti-social nature and fundamentally conflicts with the principles and aims formulated in the constitution of the Union of Writers of the USSR"),[5] and Solzhenitsyn released his reply into samizdat. As in previous instances, his open letter created a minor sensation, but for the first time he did not receive the unanimous approval of his usual allies. Many of the writers grouped around *Novy Mir*—who regarded themselves, however outspoken they might be, as a "loyal opposition" (some were still Party members)—took exception to his description of Soviet society as "grievously sick" and especially to a passage in which he jeered at the sacred dogma of the class struggle: "Should the Antarctic ice melt tomorrow, we would all become a sea of drowning humanity, and into whose heads would you then be drilling your concepts of 'class struggle'?"[6] In this and similar statements Solzhenitsyn had come considerably closer than before to showing his true political face in public, and the morbidly sensitive Soviet intellectuals, keenly aware of the slightest political nuance, were quick to detect the heresy implicit in his angry words.

According to Medvedev, many took the "Mozhayev line," feeling that Solzhenitsyn had overstepped the mark and should have exhausted all legal measures to gain reinstatement in the Writers' Union before speaking out.[7] They were influenced in this by the general air of caution that had prevailed in the country since the invasion of Czechoslovakia the preceding year. Before that, Soviet liberals had felt emboldened by the example of Dubček and his allies (who were all members of the Czechoslovak Communist party, and therefore also "loyal" in their opposition to Soviet orthodoxy), but afterwards they withdrew into their shells and took cover.

Solzhenitsyn also lost ground, it seems, among some more conservative supporters who regarded themselves as "patriots." So long as he was seen as an "innocent victim" of the authorities, condemned to silence by the non-publication of his novels, these people felt a definite solidarity with him. But the moment he moved into overt political opposition, their support fell away. Let him write as many stories and novels as he liked, and let them be published. But he should stay away from politics.

For these reasons support for Solzhenitsyn's letter was much more muted than he had expected. "With my usual over-optimism, my usual premature assumption of success, I had expected another mass movement among the writers, a battle, perhaps another mass exodus from the Writers' Union. But none of this was to be. There was no real persecution, there were no arrests, no thunderbolts . . . people were tired and had lost all urge to resist."[8] There was an outspoken telegram from Lydia Chukovskaya, and a couple of open letters appeared in Solzhenitsyn's support, one signed by fourteen people and another by thirty-nine (though there were hardly any writers among the latter), but according to Solzhenitsyn only seventeen members of the union registered some sort of protest. The most noteworthy was a visit by seven Moscow writers to Voronkov to point out that it was disgraceful for a writer as eminent as Solzhenitsyn to be expelled by the votes of a handful of obscure and unknown writers from the provinces, and to demand that the expulsion be discussed by a plenary session of the Writers' Union with full publicity. This, they asserted, was not only their own opinion but expressed the view of a large number of writers in the union. Voronkov promised to pass their request to the higher authorities, but the only result was that the Party members among the seven were summoned by their district Party committees and given a reprimand for violating Party discipline. It was reported that at a meeting of the prose section of the Moscow branch of the Writers' Union, twenty-two writers voted against a resolution approving the expulsion, but the names of the dissenters are not known.[9]

Perhaps more painful than any of this for Solzhenitsyn was Tvardovsky's response. Already a nervous wreck because of the pressures being heaped on *Novy Mir* by the Central Committee, and still reeling from the blow of Solzhenitsyn's expulsion, Tvardovsky is said to have exploded on being shown a copy of Solzhenitsyn's letter. "He's finished us!" was his first reaction, meaning that the letter would be used against *Novy Mir*. And he tried to track Solzhenitsyn down so that he could summon him for a discussion (he knew nothing of the Rostropovich arrangement). But Solzhenitsyn was determined to lie low in Zhukovka until the initial storm had died down. A few days later, judging that Tvardovsky's rage would have subsided, he sent him a conciliatory letter, in which, among other things, he explained his reasons for phrasing the open letter as he had.

> By writing this letter . . . I have shown that I shall resist to the last; that when I say, "I will lay down my life," I am not joking; that I shall continue returning blow for blow, and perhaps hit still harder. So that if they are wise, they will think twice before touching me again. . . . I feel that my whole life is a process of rising gradually from my knees, a gradual transition from enforced dumbness to free speech, so that my letter to the congress and this present letter have been moments of high delight, of spiritual emancipation.[10]

Typically, despite the friendly tone, Solzhenitsyn still felt constrained to deceive Tvardovsky as to his present whereabouts by arranging for his letter to be carried all the way to Ryazan and posted from there. Tvardovsky should think that he was still out of town.

The letter seems to have had its desired effect. "Well," Tvardovsky is reported to have said after reading it, "he was entitled to write as he did: after all, he was in a camp while we were sitting around editing magazines."[11] In conversation with Zhores Medvedev later that month, he was even more complimentary. He compared Solzhenitsyn to a bird that fiercely defended its young when attacked by a bird of prey, as opposed to those birds (writers) who ran away under pressure. "One should judge a man not by his hot-tempered letters but by his work." Tvardovsky compared Solzhenitsyn to Gorky, and his letters to the authorities with Gorky's letters to Lenin (and Lenin's to Gorky), in which no punches had been pulled. But those letters, he added, had all since been locked away so that nobody knew of them any longer.[12]

It was ironic that Tvardovsky should invoke Lenin in defence of Solzhenitsyn at a time when Solzhenitsyn himself had gone far beyond "a return to Leninism" in his own thinking about the future. The chapter he was even then writing for *August 1914* was a debunking of Lenin, and it was a measure of the psychological and political distance between the two men that Tvardovsky did not realize the true position. The "thirty-nine" had also quoted Lenin as a defender of pluralism, and Zhores Medvedev, the only individual to write a personal open letter in support of Solzhenitsyn, had linked his remarks to a general attack on Stalinism and the re-Stalinization of the Party. Only Solzhenitsyn's confidants—Natalia Svetlova, Igor Shafarevich, and that tiny circle of trusted friends who had been allowed to read the full version of *The Gulag Archipelago*—realized how much further down the opposition road Solzhenitsyn had already travelled.

Another interesting difference between Solzhenitsyn's latest letter to the union and his letter to the Writers' Congress was in the huge volume of support the latest letter received from the West. Perhaps it was because the issue of expulsion from the Writers' Union was clearer-cut cut than the somewhat more technical questions of the workings of the Soviet censorship, the difficulties of publishing, and the campaign of official slander against him enumerated in his first letter. Expulsion was a punitive sanction, whereas the letter to the congress had led only to official silence and slanders under the counter.

The first response came in mid-November in a telegram from the International PEN Club to Konstantin Fedin, expressing shock and imploring him to intervene personally to reverse the ruling. Fedin's reply was a masterpiece of Soviet stonewalling: "I regard your telegram as an unprecedented interference in the internal affairs of the Writers' Union of the USSR, the observance of whose rules lies exclusively within its competence." On the same day, a long statement was put out by the French "National Writers'

Committee," rehearsing all the sanctions carried out against Soviet writers in the past and concluding unctuously, "Yet despite all this, we still wish to believe that . . . there will be found in the high councils of the nation, to whom we owe the Dawn of October and the defeat of Hitlerian fascism, men capable of realizing the wrong that has been done and of putting it right. This—for the common cause for which we live, fight, and die." Among the signatories were Jean-Paul Sartre, Elsa Triolet, Louis Aragon, and Michel Butor. Another protest to Fedin came in early December from an international group of writers bristling with famous names: Arthur Miller, John Updike, Truman Capote, Kurt Vonnegut, Carlos Fuentes, Yukio Mishima, Günter Grass, Heinrich Böll, Friedrich Dürrenmatt, Jean-Paul Sartre (again), and Igor Stravinsky, many of whom joined the British writers W. H. Auden, A. J. Ayer, Graham Greene, Rosamond Lehmann, Muriel Spark, Philip Toynbee and some more French, German, and American writers in signing one of the strongest letters of protest ever to appear in the London *Times:* "The silencing of a writer of Solzhenitsyn's stature is in itself a crime against civilization. . . . Should this appeal fail we shall see no other way but to call upon the writers and artists of the world to conduct an international cultural boycott of a country which chooses to put itself beyond the pale of civilization until such time as it abandons the barbaric treatment of its writers and artists."[13]

There was little chance that the Soviet authorities would respond to such threats (nor was there ever any sign that the threat would be translated into action when the Soviets refused to budge). Indeed, an editorial in the *Literaturnaya Gazeta* three weeks before the *Times* letter had made the authorities' determination quite clear. Solzhenitsyn, said the editorial, had virtually made common cause with the enemies of the Soviet system. His letters, statements, and manuscripts were travelling abroad through illegal channels "organized and steered by a practised hand. . . . The enemies of our country have elevated him to the rank of 'leader' of 'the political opposition in the USSR,' which has been fabricated by them."[14] The only really serious charge in the article was the allegation that part of Solzhenitsyn's royalties from *Ivan Denisovich* had been paid by the American publisher Praeger to an organization called the International Rescue Committee,* which, the newspaper said, had organized "hostile acts" against the Soviet Union and its allies. But Ekaterina Furtseva, the Soviet minister of culture, who was in Paris during the last days of December, repeated Fedin's line that "the Solzhenitsyn affair is a domestic affair," adding, for the benefit of foreign public opinion, that "if he writes good books we will publish them."[15]

Meanwhile, evidence was emerging of the ludicrous lengths to which the Writers' Union had been forced to go to effect the expulsion in the first

---

* Praeger's intentions in paying the money to the committee were evidently honourable, in that they did not want to take Solzhenitsyn's royalties for themselves, but it was naïve and shortsighted to assign them to such a cause. Evidently, only the first year's royalties were paid over in this way.

place. Issue no. 12 of the by now indispensable *Chronicle of Current Events* contained a description of the Gogolian events that preceded the meeting in Ryazan. It appeared that the expulsion had been planned at the beginning of November. The secretary of the Ryazan branch of the union, Ernst Safonov, had been so appalled at the prospect that he had volunteered for an appendicitis operation and gone straight to hospital. Of the five remaining branch members, four had been summoned for individual interviews and informed of what was expected of them (the young poet Evgeni Markin was promised a flat if he co-operated, and was duly awarded one). A fifth writer, Rodin, was ill in the town of Kasimov, 120 miles away, but on the day of the expulsion was dragged from his bed and obliged to drive to Ryazan. One hour before the meeting, the five writers were grilled by the ideological secretary of the Ryazan party and given their final instructions; after the meeting, another secretary visited Safonov in hospital to obtain his vote, for it had to be unanimous. Safonov refused at first, but was obliged to comply a month later.[16]

Perhaps one reason for the generally muted response of Soviet liberals to Solzhenitsyn's expulsion was a perception that the government had definitely made up its mind that winter to reassert close control over all areas of cultural and intellectual life, and that it was dangerous to draw attention to oneself. Certainly the pressure was considerable, and it quickly became clear that after "dealing with" Solzhenitsyn, the authorities were anxious to get to grips with those whom they saw as his backers and supporters at *Novy Mir* (little suspecting the fissure that had opened up between Solzhenitsyn and *Novy Mir*).

The primary target was Tvardovsky himself. A sort of index of Tvardovsky's standing in official eyes had been provided during the year by the fortunes of his latest long poem, "By Right of Memory," which he had started in about 1966 and completed, in a revised version, in the middle of 1969. A copy of the early version had been submitted by Tvardovsky to the magazine *Yunost* ("Youth") as early as 1967, but the magazine had rejected it. After reworking the poem, Tvardovsky had decided to publish it himself in *Novy Mir* and in the spring of 1969 had set it in type, intending to publish it in the April issue. It was rejected by the censors, however. Tvardovsky had resubmitted it for the May issue, and again in June, but on both occasions it was rejected. Tvardovsky had then had twenty proof copies of the poem bound separately (rather along the lines of *Ivan Denisovich* seven years earlier), one of which he presented to Solzhenitsyn and another to Roy Medvedev. His intention was to supply the remaining copies to members of the Writers' Union secretariat and perhaps to the ideological section of the Central Committee, so that publication of the poem could be "discussed" at a higher level, but all his overtures were rebuffed and the copies declined.

A factor in this rejection may have been the poem's contents. For the first time Tvardovsky had turned to his childhood for inspiration and could not help dwelling on the fate of his father, who had been proclaimed a kulak and deported to Stalin's labour camps. Solzhenitsyn had found the poem too mild and apologetic, yet the very mention of the labour camps and Stalin's repressions had become taboo, and there were many lines that could cause offence. Tvardovsky was evidently aware of this, for he explicitly refused, in the poem, to hide behind the skirts of the censorship and to express the things that burned his soul. It was the poet's duty "to utter all the unuttered omissions of the past."[17]

Unfortunately, Tvardovsky had arrived at such sentiments too late for them to be published openly in the Soviet Union any more. But there was more to the official ban than just a distaste for the contents of Tvardovsky's poem. The time had evidently come for him and his magazine to be silenced, and this was the simplest way for the authorities to show their displeasure. Then, in the late autumn of 1969, the authorities benefited from what seemed like an amazing stroke of luck. Tvardovsky's poem appeared in the hated NTS journal *Possev*. Tvardovsky was immediately summoned to the Central Committee and asked to explain. Of course he could not, but it was demanded that he write a stinging statement denouncing the publication and pouring scorn over the NTS. Tvardovsky did so willingly, the more so since the poem had been given a different and provocative title ("On Stalin's Ashes") and had been printed in its earlier and less finished version of 1967. What he seems to have overlooked in his ready indignation, however, was that the poem couldn't have reached *Possev* through samizdat, since it had never been circulated in its earlier version. It could only have been supplied by someone at *Yunost*, which suggests that it might have been deliberately planted.

Tvardovsky wrote his statement, and the Writers' Union did what it had done with Solzhenitsyn's disclaimer over *Cancer Ward* two years previously—it suppressed it for three to four months, so that Tvardovsky appeared not to be reacting. In the meantime, Voronkov started putting pressure on Tvardovsky to resign. Similar suggestions had been coming from the Writers' Union secretariat for over a year now, but only at the end of 1969 did the pressure become irresistible. At first there was an attempt to accomplish the matter politely. Tvardovsky was invited to hand in his resignation for "health reasons" (that old Soviet stand-by), and the pill was sugared by the simultaneous offer of a permanent secretaryship in the Writers' Union—a highly paid sinecure that was the equivalent of being kicked upstairs. When Tvardovsky still refused, it was decided to get at him by changing his staff. Officially, the Writers' Union had no authority to dismiss an editor, but it could dismiss and appoint members of his editorial board. The usual thing was to do this in consultation with the editor, but *in extremis* the editor's wishes could be ignored. This had happened in the case of Dementyev and Sachs in 1967, and now the union used its powers again to fire Kondratovich, Lakshin, Sats, and Vinogradov—all the section heads and all Tvardovsky's trusted lieutenants. In their place came five mediocrities, third-rate hacks who were guaranteed to take union orders and toe the Party line.[18]

This was accomplished at a special meeting of the secretariat that was held—typically—in Tvardovsky's absence in the first week of February 1970. Tvardovsky appealed, but his appeal was rejected, and an announcement of the changes appeared in the *Literaturnaya Gazeta* for 11 February. In the same issue, the newspaper published Tvardovsky's long-delayed disclaimer over "By Right of Memory," so that the well-schooled Soviet reader would get the message: Tvardovsky was being punished for allowing his work to be published abroad (which was only part of the truth).

To rub salt in the wounds, the Writers' Union summoned Tvardovsky that same day to a meeting to discuss relations with COMES, the European Writers Association, of which Tvardovsky was the Soviet vice-chairman. Vigorelli, the association's secretary-general, had sent a vigorous protest on behalf of the association over the union's expulsion of Solzhenitsyn, and the meeting was being held to determine the Soviet reply. In fact, there was nothing left to decide, since the decision had been taken at a higher level. Tvardovsky was instructed to write a stiff letter to Vigorelli, announcing his resignation from the post of vice-chairman and Soviet withdrawal from the association as a whole. Just as a liberal literary journal, or its liberal editor, was no longer needed, so the pretence of co-operation with the rest of Europe could now be dropped, and with it the Soviet figure-head.

Tvardovsky needed no more urging. The replacement of his editorial board behind his back and his abrupt removal from COMES added up to a comprehensive humiliation both at home and abroad. He sat down at once and wrote a letter of resignation from *Novy Mir*.

It was the end of an era, and by the time it occurred, the end was no longer unexpected. For weeks before the actual announcement, Moscow had been full of rumours, and in the last days, in early February, writers and friends of *Novy Mir* had flocked to the elegant offices in Maly Putinkovsky Lane, partly as a show of solidarity, partly out of curiosity, and partly, it seems, out of a subconscious desire to pay their last respects to the dying journal. And yet the whole thing was strangely muted. Solzhenitsyn describes a group of writers, led by Mozhayev, hastily composing a last-minute collective letter to Brezhnev.[19] But the text was kept secret, even after Tvardovsky's resignation. On the very last day, the offices and corridors were packed with sympathetic visitors, standing about in groups, smoking and wondering what was going to appear in the *Literaturnaya Gazeta* on the morrow. When the final announcement came, they accepted it calmly, fatalistically, almost as a relief. In the next few weeks, Efim Dorosh, a talented prose writer, A. Maryamov, and M. Khitrov announced their resignations from *Novy Mir*, giving the Writers' Union a clean sweep of the liberals, but apart from that, there was remarkably little public reaction to the change. Only two written protests circulated in samizdat, and both were anonymous—a bad sign when dozens of human-rights activists were willingly going to jail for signing their protests with their right names.

Solzhenitsyn's attitude to these events seems to have been contradictory. On the one hand, he couldn't but be depressed and angered by the virtual suppression of the one decent journal that remained in the Soviet Union and by this brutal humiliation of Tvardovsky. On the other, he himself had gone far beyond *Novy Mir*, had outgrown it years ago, politically and artistically, and had therefore come to regard it, somewhat patronizingly, as excessively timid and conformist. In his view, *Novy Mir*'s position in the vanguard of Soviet literature had been outflanked and overtaken by samizdat, and the editors had become far too complacent and smug in their easy assumption of moral and literary superiority over their rivals. But then again, despite this difference in attitudes, he felt himself inextricably linked with *Novy Mir*, both in the public's eyes and, to a lesser degree, in his own. The ups and downs in his own fortunes invitably reflected on the journal, and he was uneasily aware that Tvardovsky and his staff had often suffered from their association with him. Similarly, the rise and fall of *Novy Mir*'s reputation affected him too—there was little chance that he would prosper at a time when the journal was down. And this he resented, just as he resented Tvardovsky's tutelage and attempted patronage of him, and was jealous of the older man's symbolic position as the conscience of Soviet literature (a position to which he himself aspired, consoling himself with the not incorrect assumption that if Tvardovsky was the conscience of *Soviet* literature, he, Solzhenitsyn, was the conscience of *Russian* literature and hence in a far older tradition).

These contradictions emerged in those February days of waiting. Like the other writers in the *Novy Mir* stable, Solzhenitsyn felt impelled to show himself and express his solidarity. His apartness from the multitude was demonstrated by his being locked up with Tvardovsky in his office while the others thronged the corridors. It was their first meeting since the November storm over Solzhenitsyn's expulsion, and the two embattled writers seem to have felt close once again. Solzhenitsyn took the part of loyal friend and urged Tvardovsky not to resign from *Novy Mir* until the last possible moment when things got worse. He also advised Tvardovsky to be careful with his letter on the *Possev* affair and to disown not his poem but only the incomplete version of it published in the West (much as Solzhenitsyn had earlier disowned incomplete versions of *Cancer Ward*, but not the novel itself). Tvardovsky was not up to such subtleties, however, and had already delivered his letter, just as he had made up his mind to resign, and Solzhenitsyn's urgings were in vain.[20]

The two men met again on 12 February 1970, the day after the announcement in *Literaturnaya Gazeta*. This time Solzhenitsyn irritated Tvardovsky with his criticisms of Tvardovsky's letter and with an attempt to stand up for the junior members of *Novy Mir*'s staff, such as Anna Berzer and the other copy editors.[21] In the weeks that followed, Solzhenitsyn seems to have elevated Tvardovsky's alleged disregard for his staff, and his attachment to hierarchical structures within the office, to a cardinal sin of Tvardovsky's regime, and in conversations with other *Novy Mir* authors—and in letters to Lakshin and various members of the board—he developed a comprehensive critique of *Novy Mir* that was later set out in *The Oak and the Calf*. According to this, "*Novy Mir*'s whole existence had consisted of constant compromises with the censorship and with Party policy." The magazine was crippled by its commitment to democratic socialism and its choice of roles as the articulator of a "loyal opposition" within the Soviet system. If *Novy Mir* was a window, it was "a warped window crudely hacked in a rotten wall, and blocked . . . by an ideological screen of its own choosing." Because of this, wrote Solzhenitsyn, the magazine was doomed from the start, and when the end came, it was bound to be ignominious. "There are many different ways to die. In my view, *Novy Mir* died an unlovely death without even uncurling its spine." Solzhenitsyn maintained that from the point of view of a reader and writer of samizdat, there was not all that much to choose between *Novy Mir* and all the other conforming journals. "The desperate fight between *Novy Mir* on the one hand and *Oktyabr* and the whole 'conservative wing' on the other strikes me as nothing more than the contending forces that jointly constitute surface tension, creating between them a solid film, as it were, which prevents even the most active molecules from bursting out from the depths below." Nor was there likely to be much difference between the old *Novy Mir* and the new one. To make his point brutally clear, Solzhenitsyn offered his support to Tvardovsky's replacement, Valery Kosolapov (who had briefly been editor in chief of the *Literaturnaya Gazeta* and then director of a publishing house), and encouraged other writers to do the same.[22]

It was a cruel verdict on the journal, but not entirely unjust. *Novy Mir*'s window was certainly imperfect, though not too imperfect to let through the brilliant beams of light from *Ivan Denisovich* and "Matryona," or the bright rays of Victor Nekrasov, Aitmatov, Shukshin, Tendryakov, Dombrovsky, Trifonov, Vladimov, Voinovich, and many others. And although Tvardovsky's *Novy Mir* had formed part of that ideological membrane that extends over the whole of Soviet public life, no journal had done more to bend, stretch, or pierce that membrane than *Novy Mir*, and Solzhenitsyn knew it. Furthermore, if his strictures were true of *Novy Mir* under Tvardovsky, what would the magazine be like under Kosolapov?

One is left with the impression that for Solzhenitsyn it was more a question of cold calculation. There was nothing to be done to save Tvardovsky, and it was better to look to himself and the future. If the authorities felt satiated by their dispersal of the *Novy Mir* board, they might let something daring slip through again, just to show that the magazine hadn't been killed. And that something might even be by Solzhenitsyn. *August 1914*, except for one chapter, was in many respects orthodox from a Soviet point of view, and certainly in comparison with Solzhenitsyn's previous novels. This, or something like it, seems to have been the fantastic notion in Solzhenitsyn's head and the motivation for his complete public silence on the demise of Tvardovsky's *Novy Mir* (Solzhenitsyn criticized the lateness and feebleness of the writers' attempts to protest against the changes at *Novy Mir* but nowhere indicated that he was willing to write or sign anything himself). It was a repeat of

Hadji Murat's defection, of his earlier approaches to *Moskva* and *Ogonyok* with his short stories when things were getting difficult at *Novy Mir*, and Solzhenitsyn saw no difference. He was beholden to no magazine, loyal to no editor. But he still felt obliged to rationalize and justify his behaviour with a critique of his old friends.*

Actually, the dichotomy that Solzhenitsyn perceived between samizdat and works published in *Novy Mir* was not as clear-cut as he suggested. Many works intended for *Novy Mir* eventually found their way into samizdat, and some that were so outspoken they seemed destined for samizdat actually appeared in the pages of *Novy Mir*. But in any case the distinction paled before the fact that the authorities' move against *Novy Mir* was paralleled by similar moves against samizdat, against the dissidents, and above all against the *Chronicle*. In December 1969 Natalia Gorbanevskaya, chief inspirer and editor in chief of the *Chronicle*, had been arrested again and taken to the Serbsky Psychiatric Institute. A mental examination the month before had pronounced her sane, but this time the notorious Dr Lunts† got to work on her and had no difficulty in arriving at a diagnosis of "sluggish schizophrenia," a disease known only to graduates of the Serbsky Institute and to Soviet psychiatrists specializing in political cases.[23]

Meanwhile, General Grigorenko (who had spent an unnecessary year in a psychiatric hospital as early as 1964–65) had been lured to Tashkent by a fake telephone call, arrested, examined, found sane, transferred to Moscow (to that same Serbsky Institute), and pronounced insane; he was brought to trial on 26 February 1970, after which he was dispatched to a psychiatric prison hospital in Chernyakhovsk, near the Polish border. Shortly afterwards, his friend and fellow campaigner Ivan Yakhimovich was similarly pronounced insane by the Serbsky Institute and, at his ensuing trial, sent for compulsory treatment to a psychiatric hospital of a normal (not prison) variety.[24]

The practice of committing sane individuals to mental hospitals for political reasons is said to date back to Stalin's time and to have been instituted by Vyshinsky in the thirties. After a brief lull during the early years of de-Stalinization, it seems to have come into vogue again in the early sixties. Esenin-Volpin had been incarcerated in a mental hospital for a year in 1960 for having sent a collection of his verse and a philosophical essay to the West with the help of an American tourist. Two years later Tarsis had described his forcible internment in the Kashchenko Mental Hospital in his short story "Ward 7," and from 1963 to 1965 the young dissident Vladimir Bukovsky

---

* In his "sixth supplement to *The Oak and the Calf*," written in 1978, in which he commented on Lakshin's criticisms of his book, Solzhenitsyn conceded that he had been too harsh on Tvardovsky and *Novy Mir* and that Tvardovsky had had no choice but to resign when he did.

† Dr Daniel Lunts was head of department no. 4 of the Serbsky Institute and as such had a special responsibility for political detainees who were referred to the institute. He had played a prominent part in diagnosing leading members of the dissident movement as suffering from mental illness.

had been confined to a mental hospital in Leningrad (where he met General Grigorenko during the latter's first spell inside). Later came the attempts to commit Gorbanevskaya and Fainberg to mental hospitals after the Czecho-slovakia demonstration in Red Square, and the policy was evidently increas-ing in popularity with the KGB, for in May 1970 occurred the biggest and juiciest scandal so far.

On the twenty-ninth of that month, a group of policemen led by a major and accompanied by the head doctor of the Kaluga Psychiatric Hospital and the Obninsk town psychiatrist crowded into the flat of Zhores Medvedev, twisted his arms behind his back, and led him away before the astonished eyes of his family and friends. When asked why they had produced no doc-uments, the major replied, "We are organs of force, and you can complain to whomever you like."[25] The next two days were a public holiday, so it was three days before Zhores's twin brother, Roy, was able to see him. It was then necessary to wait for a special commission to examine Zhores, and when the commission found nothing wrong with him, another was summoned from Moscow, which consisted of "experts" from the Serbsky Institute (so suspi-cious was Roy Medvedev of the reputation of Dr Lunts that he was able to have him excluded). This commission did not announce its findings but reported directly to the Ministry of Health in Moscow.

The incarceration of Zhores Medvedev raised a hurricane of protest. On 31 May the Kaluga Hospital was deluged with telegrams from prominent Soviet scholars and writers, including the academicians Kapitsa, Sakharov, Tamm, Engelgardt, and Astaurov, and the writers Tvardovsky and Tendrya-kov. Another batch of letters and telegrams went to the Ministry of Health, the Central Committee, and the chief prosecutor's office. On 4 June a larger group of leading academicians called on the world's writers, scientists, and scholars to institute a total cultural boycott of the Soviet Union until such time as Medvedev was freed and given an apology, and more telegrams were sent to government ministries. On 9 June a group of eminent Soviet figures, including Tvardovsky, accompanied Roy Medvedev on a personal visit to the Kaluga Hospital. When he saw Tvardovsky in the visitors' room, Zhores later wrote, and when they embraced, "I found it difficult to restrain my tears."[26] But it was to be another week before he was released, and then only after a high-ranking delegation, led by Mikhail Keldysh, president of the Academy of Sciences, had called on the minister of health personally to express concern.[27]

Solzhenitsyn also took up the cudgels on Medvedev's behalf. As early as 2 June he drafted a protest that was so outspoken his friends persuaded him to tone it down. He decided not to release it until the fifteenth so as not to harm Medvedev with his pugnacity. It was a new departure for Solzheni-tsyn to speak out on behalf of another individual. There had been signs of a change of policy in his strong letter on his expulsion, where he had taken the opportunity to mention Lydia Chukovskaya and Lev Kopelev, but the Med-vedev statement was harsher than anything he had ever published before, and it is significant that he should refer to his prison experiences when writing about it in his memoir: "During my time in the camps I had got to know the enemies of the human race quite well: they respect the big fist and nothing else. The harder you slug them, the safer you will be."[28] Therefore, after starting with a personal tribute to Medvedev (whom he described as "a man of subtle, precise, and brilliant intellect and of warm heart"), he quickly moved to a general denunciation of this whole phenomenon in Soviet society (a point that was underlined by the statement's title: "The Way We Live Now").

> If only this were the first case! But this devious suppression of people without searching for any guilt, when the real reason is too shameful to state, is becoming a fashion. Some of the victims are widely known, many more are unknown. Servile psychiatrists, breakers of their Hippocratic oath, see social concern, excessive ardour, excessive sang-froid, brilliant or abundant gifts, as so many symptoms of mental illness.
>
> . . . It is time to think clearly. The incarceration of free-thinking people in madhouses is *spiritual murder*, it is a variation on the *gas chamber*, but is even more cruel: the torments of those done to death in this way are more evil and protracted.[29]

Imperceptibly, Solzhenitsyn was shifting the ground of his protests from purely literary to more general social concerns, and in so doing he was taking up a position much closer to outright political opposition than most people realized at the time. The reference to "gas chambers" was an indication of the direction in which his mind was moving, but this was put down to moral outrage rather than a calculated change of approach.

On 17 June 1970 Medvedev was released without explanation, but the chief psychiatrist at Kaluga Hospital partly gave the game away when he admitted that he had been shown some of Medvedev's samizdat writings as evidence of the latter's "psychic sickness." One of these was the Lysenko book, and the other was his recently completed book *International Scientific Co-operation and National Frontiers*. The intention (which was not without a certain ingenuity) must have been to discredit this highly idiosyncratic work, with its surrealistic examples of Soviet deviousness, by throwing doubt on the author's sanity. Another possible reason was Medvedev's recent application for a new job. In the summer of 1969 he had been illegally dismissed from the Obninsk Institute of Radiology on the insistence of the local Communist Party, and it had taken him nine months—and three court cases—to get the necessary references from his former institute to enable him to apply elsewhere. Eventually, he had been able to apply for a vacant post at the Moscow Institute of Medical Genetics, and the applications were due to be judged the very week that Medvedev was thrown into the hospital.[30]

Clearly, the KGB had overstepped the mark. It made the whole of educated Moscow aware that, as Solzhenitsyn put it, "tomorrow this can happen to any one of us" and that it was only Medvedev's international reputation as a geneticist (the case was widely publicized in the Western press) and his prominence in scientific circles in Moscow that had saved him. Bukovsky, Esenin-Volpin, and Grigorenko had suffered worse, and for each of them there were dozens of unknown innocent victims being laced into strait-jackets and injected daily with stupefying quantities of powerful drugs. So far, news of these horrors had reached only the dissidents, and for respectable, if liberal, members of the Soviet establishment, the Medvedev incident was the first hint that something more serious was wrong. A corner of the veil had been lifted for just a moment, and it was enough to send a shudder through all who peeped underneath.

When Medvedev went to thank Solzhenitsyn for his intervention, he found him in his cabin at Rozhdestvo hard at work on the final chapters of *August 1914*. He looked more cheerful than when Medvedev had seen him in the spring, which can probably be attributed to the happiness he always found when able to retreat into his writing. The winter and spring of 1970 had also been a time of considerable anxiety for Solzhenitsyn personally. The preceding December, at the height of the uproar over his expulsion from the union, an extract from *Prussian Nights* had suddenly appeared in the West German newspaper *Die Zeit*, with an editorial promise that the rest would follow shortly. Feverish telephone calls and visits to a variety of flats had uncovered an unauthorized copy of the poem made by the friend of a friend four years before, when the atmosphere had been more relaxed and samizdat had been circulating more freely. Now, after keeping it secret for four years, the friend's friend had lent it out, and a copy had leaked to the West. Further telephone calls succeeded in halting its publication in *Die Zeit* and getting the manuscript back again.

A similar scare ballooned over the circulation of an early chapter from Solzhenitsyn's memoir, *The Oak and the Calf*. The existence of the memoir was a much deeper secret than that of *Prussian Nights*, and its "escape" therefore all the more alarming. Again there were phone calls, secret visits, and frantic huddles until the leak was found—one of Solzhenitsyn's closest and most trusted friends had made an unauthorized copy and lent it out. In such cases Solzhenitsyn was implacable: "We called up the culprit. We arranged to meet her. Sobbing, she confessed. She was struck off our list for the future. I confiscated the booty."[31]

Worse still were two new developments in the West. One was the news that KGB agents were peddling Solzhenitsyn's early play *The Feast of the Conquerors* to Western publishers and theatres. Fortunately, the French National Writers' Committee came to the rescue again with a statement in *Le Monde* warning that "the work in question is one whose publication the author has forbidden and which, circulated against his will, has served as grounds for bringing political charges against the author."[32] The statement pointed out that publication in the West would not only conflict with his author's title to copyright but might also serve as the pretext for a political trial. The publicity seems to have worked, for nothing more was heard of the play for a while.

The other development was the appearance of articles in the Western press reporting the existence of *The Gulag Archipelago*. Nicholas Bethell had visited Moscow in February 1970 and picked up word that Solzhenitsyn had recently completed "a new novel" of that name that he was "keeping under lock and key."[33] A similar story appeared in the London *Times*, and there were one or two further mentions of the book in America, including one in *Time* magazine. So persistent were these rumours that Solzhenitsyn himself turned up on one occasion to meet a Western correspondent and warn him off the book.[34]

Solzhenitsyn had particular reason not to want *Gulag* to escape his control that spring, for he was in the process of rethinking the entire timetable for its publication. His original plan had been to publish it that year, but that was before he fell in love with Natalia Svetlova and before he was properly launched on the writing of *August 1914*. His new love gave him powerful reasons for not wanting to incur the jail term or deportation that the publication of *Gulag* risked bringing him, while absorption in his epic about the early years of the century had shown him how much material he still needed to collect. He was anxious to postpone the moment of decision for as long as possible—and to be in command of the decision himself when the moment came.

Another factor was that he was still undecided on how best to proceed with Western publication. After the initial appearance of *Cancer Ward* in England, he had secretly granted the Russian rights to the YMCA Press in Paris, the republishers of *Landmarks* and *De Profundis* and the publishers of many religious works that he greatly admired.* It was his intention to grant the copyright of *August 1914* to the YMCA Press as well, and also perhaps of *The Gulag Archipelago*. The problem with the latter was that when he had informed Olga Carlisle of this intention the preceding year, she had been very upset. Her understanding was that she and her husband would control world copyright through Harper & Row, just as they had done with *The First Circle*. Solzhenitsyn, however, was dissatisfied with their handling of *The First Circle*. He had heard of the British publisher's poor opinion of the Whitney translation, the decision to commission a new one, and of the disastrous French translation from English. Therefore, when the Carlisles had sent a messenger to Moscow that spring, he had informed them that they were to concentrate on the English-language translation only and that the basic copyright of the work would go to YMCA.

The whole situation was exceedingly delicate, and he was alarmed to hear of an article in the London *Times* reporting that "*The Gulag Archipelago*

---

*The YMCA (IMKA in Russian) Press is part of the *Russkoye studencheskoye khristianskoye dvizheniye* (Russian Student Christian Movement), founded in Paris ifn 1924 to unite Russian yough dispersed by the First Emigration (after the Revolution) and to promote an Orthodox Christian outlook among them. The press was founded a year later and specializes in works of Orthodox Christianity.

. . . was being offered for sale in Europe and America." Solzhenitsyn sent frantic coded messages to the Carlisles in the mistaken belief that they were responsible for the leak. One began:

> Dear Friend,
> We are well, but the springtime is unusually warm. Everyone suffers from the heat.
> We are deeply disturbed to learn that the doctor's advice has not been followed and that travel has been permitted to various countries.
> Complete rest is essential now. How can this be misunderstood? Sergei's life depends upon it.[35]

"Suffering from the heat" meant that Solzhenitsyn and his friends were being closely watched. "Travel to various countries" referred to the *Gulag* manuscript, and "the doctor" and "Sergei" were, of course, both Solzhenitsyn. The Carlisles answered firmly that they were not to blame and that the manuscript entrusted to them had not left their hands. But it took time for such messages to travel back and forth, and in the paranoid atmosphere of Moscow the long delays only increased Solzhenitsyn's distrust. In replying to this affirmation, Solzhenitsyn emphasized the need to wait once more and moved a step farther away from his commitment to Harper & Row. He had been premature, he acknowledged, in asking the Carlisles to inform the publisher about the book. However, so long as the manuscript was still in their possession, it did not matter.

These anxieties and the strenuous efforts needed to deal with them naturally took their toll of Solzhenitsyn's physical strength, his nerves, and his time. As he later wrote in his memoir, "If I recalled and described them all in detail, you would see that throughout those years most of our effort and anxiety was expended . . . on alarms, excursions, reconnaissance raids, anticipatory moves, and precautions . . . in short, on saving the situation by whatever means we could."[36]

Insofar as Moscow was concerned, they were just about able to contain the situation, but to control the situation abroad was much more complicated, and it was to this end that Solzhenitsyn had decided on the novel step of retaining a Western lawyer. Expense was no problem, since he now had considerable sums of money lying in Western banks in the form of uncollectable royalties on *The First Circle* and *Cancer Ward*. A properly authorized lawyer would be able to take charge of these royalties and would quickly pay for himself many times over. He would also enable Solzhenitsyn to overcome most of the difficulties created for Soviet authors by the Soviet government's refusal to sign the Universal Copyright Convention. This refusal, a hangover from the enthusiastic rejection of all forms of bourgeois property that was fashionable immediately after the Revolution, meant that no Soviet books were protected by copyright outside the Soviet Union, and no foreign books inside it. Culturally and commercially, this was immeasurably to the Soviet advantage: they needed Western publications, especially scientific publications, far more urgently than the West needed theirs, and saved millions of dollars in the process. But for the Soviet authors of *belles-lettres*, it created great problems—and for the authors of unofficial works not even published at home, like Solzhenitsyn, still greater ones, since it opened the way to (and actively encouraged) piracy. This was why there had been so much trouble with pirated editions of *The First Circle* and *Cancer Ward* and why it was so easy for people like Victor Louis and other recipients of KGB-supplied manuscripts to fish in these troubled waters. When *Possev* published *Cancer Ward* and *Die Zeit* announced the publication of *Prussian Nights*, Solzhenitsyn hadn't a legal leg to stand on, and there was nothing he could do about threats to publish *Feast of the Conquerors*. But with a Western lawyer in place, he could exercise his rights under Western law and exert some sort of author's control.

The lawyer chosen for this role was Dr Fritz Heeb of Zürich. He had no particular experience of literary matters (which was to lead to recriminations in the future) but was at one end of a chain of acquaintances that led from him, through some European social democrats with connections in both Switzerland and the Soviet Union, to Lev Kopelev and Solzhenitsyn. One circumstance in his favour was that he could in no way be described as a "capitalist profiteer." His father had been a prominent Swiss Social Democrat who had known Lenin, Trotsky, Rosa Luxemburg, Paul Axelrod, and many other Communist notables of the time. Heeb himself had been a member of the left-wing Swiss Social Democratic party nearly all his life and had represented the party in the Zurich cantonal parliament for eight years. At the time of his assignment he was in his late fifties, a taciturn, reticent, somewhat dour Swiss burgher with a puritanical notion of honour and a highly developed sense of duty—the ideal person to defend Solzhenitsyn's rights disinterestedly and with tenacity.

The arrangement had been in place since the turn of the year (it was Heeb who managed to keep the rest of *Prussian Nights* out of *Die Zeit*), but it was not until March 1970 that Heeb had issued a five-point public statement. Solzhenitsyn had retained him, said Heeb, because his books could no longer be published in his own country but only abroad, and he needed someone to represent him. Secondly, since neither the Union of Writers nor the Soviet literary agency Mezhdunarodnaya Kniga would protect his author's rights abroad, he was obliged to take steps of his own. Thirdly, now that Solzhenitsyn had been expelled from the Union, there was no hope of an improvement in his situation. Heeb's instructions were to prevent the unauthorized publication of Solzhenitsyn's work abroad, to check and if possible improve the quality of translations of his work, and to forbid adaptations for film, radio, or television. "All publishers are hereby informed that any publication of my client's work can in the future take place legally only with contractual authorization by the author or his legal representative." There was also a special point covering "maliciously circulated false statements" to the effect that royalties from Solzhenitsyn's books had been given to "subversive anti-Soviet organizations"—a reference to the earlier *Times* article on this subject and the political capital made out of it by the *Literaturnaya Gazeta*. "I am empowered to state," wrote Heeb, "that royalties due to Alexander Solzhenitsyn are being kept intact. After his death, they will be disposed of according to his wishes."[37]

It was a bold stroke, totally unexpected, it seems, by the Soviet authorities and yet apparently legal. By expelling Solzhenitsyn from the union they had in a certain sense fallen into a trap. The arrangement with Dr Heeb had been planned well before the expulsion, but by announcing it now, Solzhenitsyn made it seem that it was simply the result of his expulsion. It was an excellent example of Solzhenitsyn's brilliant ability to counter-punch on the run and to turn tactical defeat into strategic victory. That orthodox-sounding paragraph distancing him from "maliciously circulated statements" and "subversive anti-Soviet organizations" was also a masterpiece of camouflage, adding a veneer of Soviet respectability to what was in essence a profoundly un-Soviet action.

38

THE NOBEL PRIZE

Solzhenitsyn was not the only Soviet writer to be exploring openings in the West in 1970. As early as the preceding December, Andrei Amalrik had written to some Western newspapers about his attempts to obtain foreign royalties from his two samizdat books, *Involuntary Journey to Siberia* and *Will the Soviet Union Survive until 1984?* which had enjoyed considerable success in the West. "I wanted to prove that a Soviet citizen, like the citizen of any other country, has the right to publish books not issued in his own country, to do this under his own name, to fix personally with the publishers the terms of publication, and to enjoy all the author's rights flowing from this." Typically for a member of the Democratic Movement, Amalrik had approached the matter frontally, without guile, and had been rebuffed. His publications in the West were termed illegal, and he was informed that at best he could receive money from the West as "a gift," which would be taxed at a much higher rate than royalties, but not through the regular channels. Amalrik was now drawing attention to this trickery, he wrote, so that he could publicly shame the Soviet government. "While Stalin would have shot me for publishing my books abroad, his pitiful heirs are only up to trying to appropriate a part of my money. This confirms my view about the degeneration and growing decrepitude of this regime, which I have expounded in my book. . . ."[1]

The book in question, *Will the Soviet Union Survive until 1984?* was almost certainly the reason why Amalrik was arrested in May 1970, at the time when Medvedev was put away and Gorbanevskaya was being examined in the Serbsky Institute. Interestingly, his long essay had also been prompted by Sakharov's memorandum and was part of the same debate that Solzhenitsyn had joined, albeit covertly, with his confidential letter to Sakharov. But Sakharov was himself evolving. In March 1970 he had composed a new document addressed to Brezhnev and the Central Committee in which he modified some of the ideas put forward in his memorandum and proposed a much more concrete programme of reform. Called *Manifesto Two*,* this document was signed jointly with Valentin Turchin and Roy Medvedev, and undoubtedly bore their impress.

The chief plank in their programme was "democratization" of the existing system, a gradual, evolutionary democratization that was to be carried out under the direction of the Communist Party and with the aim of "strengthening the Soviet socialist system, the socialist economic structure and . . . socialist ideology." The document called for economic decentralization, an effort to join the "second industrial revolution" ("we are falling further and further behind America"), a relaxation of the censorship, a reform of education, and the observation of certain basic human rights, such as the release of political prisoners and the elimination of internal-passport restrictions. In essence, it didn't go far beyond what Sakharov had said before (and in certain respects was more cautious), but its approach was more systematic and in its style and language it paid more respect to Soviet political convention.[2]

At the same time, Sakharov was growing more outspoken in his other statements. In May 1970, together with Turchin, the academician Leontovich, and a physicist named Valery Chalidze, he protested against violations of the law in the recent trial of General Grigorenko in Tashkent, and a couple of weeks later was a member of the delegation that visited the minister of health on behalf of Zhores Medvedev. He also wrote an open letter to Brezhnev warning that the policy of committing sane men to mental hospitals was a threat to the freedom of science and was endangering international co-operation as well as Medvedev personally.

It would appear that there was a general drive that spring and summer to crush dissidents of all kinds and introduce a stricter discipline, especially among the intellectuals. A sign on the literary front was the elevation of the children's poet Sergei Mikhalkov to the post of first secretary of the Writers' Union of the Russian Republic, and the award to him of that year's Lenin Prize for literature. Mikhalkov had first distinguished himself as the scourge of dissidence in April 1968, when, in an article in the *Literaturnaya Gazeta* (with the typically Soviet title "Whose Side Are You On?"), he had denounced those few members of the Writers' Union who had protested against the trial of Ginzburg and Galanskov and called for tighter discipline. Further articles of this sort (one in *Pravda*) had appeared in May and June of that year, and in 1969 Mikhalkov had become one of the principal assailants of Solzhenitsyn. It seemed likely that his elevation was not unconnected with these efforts. Almost simultaneously, Franz Taurin, who had orchestrated the Ryazan

---

*This is the title given the document in the collected essays of Sakharov. It is not clear whether this was Sakharov's own name for it.

meeting to expel Solzhenitsyn, was appointed to head the prose section of *Novy Mir* in place of Dorosh.[3]

According to Solzhenitsyn, a decision in principle to expel him from the country had been taken as early as the summer of 1969. The idea was not new. Heavy hints had been dropped in a number of articles and public statements by Party officials, and Nicholas Bethell had been told in the spring that if, as Solzhenitsyn's translator, he were to invite Solzhenitsyn to the West, there would be no problem in getting the latter a passport and visa.[5] But now the Presidium itself was said to have drafted the necessary order depriving him of Soviet citizenship, and a patriotic "request" for his deportation had come formally from twelve members of the Writers' Union. A decision was then made, according to this story, to delay the expulsion until after the dust of the Medvedev affair had settled, so that it wouldn't look like a crude reprisal. And then, as a *deus ex machina*, came the news that François Mauriac, supported by about fifty other French writers, had nominated Solzhenitsyn for the Nobel Prize for literature. This was in July 1970, and again it complicated matters. Solzhenitsyn was convinced that he had been a candidate for the Nobel Prize the year before, in 1969, and that the decision to expel him from the Writers' Union had been a direct result of his failure to get it. The timing certainly appeared to support such a theory. The original decision to expel him had been postponed from the summer of 1969 until October, but immediately after the award of the prize to Samuel Beckett, in the last week of October, the wheels had been set in motion again. It may have been coincidence, but Solzhenitsyn didn't believe it was.

All in all, he had a curious and uniquely Soviet attitude to the Nobel Prize as an instrument in a larger struggle. It may, indeed, have been the first occasion in the history of the prize when a writer deliberately set out to capture it and himself helped to prompt the campaign for his nomination. In *The Oak and the Calf* Solzhenitsyn writes that he had dreamed of winning the prize ever since first hearing of it in the camps, before he had a published word to his name. A powerful new impetus came with the award of the prize to Pasternak, in 1958, though he was disappointed by Pasternak's meek acceptance of the abuse hurled at him and his rejection of the prize. He, Solzhenitsyn, would behave differently. He would accept the prize, go to Stockholm, and make a fighting speech, even if it meant never returning to the Soviet Union, for he could then publish everything he wanted. "For all this, the lot of an outcast was not too high a price to pay (and in any case, I could picture myself returning before many years were out)."[6]

The clarity of this picture owes a certain amount to hindsight, but it undoubtedly reflected his thinking in 1969–70.* Therefore, when a representative of the Swedish Academy canvassed the idea with Kopelev (at Evtushenko's flat) in the summer of 1970, Kopelev had little hesitation in saying that if awarded the prize, Solzhenitsyn would not humiliate the academy by

---

*Natalia Reshetovskaya reports that Solzhenitsyn kept a list of Nobel Prize winners in his desk and updated it each year after the announcement of that year's winner.

refusing it. Throughout the rest of that summer and autumn, Kopelev, Etkind, and others with contacts among foreign writers energetically lobbied for the prize to go to Solzhenitsyn, and Moscow was abuzz with rumours months before the recipient of the prize was due to be announced.

The Swedes were aware of the political implications of awarding the prize to Solzhenitsyn. The Pasternak award had almost led to an international incident between the Soviet Union and Sweden (though the Swedish Academy is, strictly speaking, an independent body that in no way represents official Swedish policy). The award to Sholokhov seven years later was widely seen as a sop to the Soviet government to make up for the earlier scandal and had delighted the Soviet establishment, which hastened to make as much political capital as it could out of what was supposed to be a strictly literary award. But if the prize now went to Solzhenitsyn, it was obvious there would be an even bigger scandal than before, for Solzhenitsyn, as Surkov had rightly noted three years earlier, had "an animated, militant, ideological temperament" that was at the opposite pole to Pasternak's. The debate in Sweden, both within and without the academy's walls, is said to have been earnest and fierce. The appearance of both *The First Circle* and *Cancer Ward* in Swedish translations that year had strengthened Solzhenitsyn's case, as did the support expressed for him by the International PEN Club, which had always had a strong base in Stockholm. Earlier in the year the Bulgarian PEN Centre had been moved to cancel a round-table conference it was sponsoring because of letters signed by Pierre Emmanuel, the international president of PEN, and other prominent PEN members denouncing Solzhenitsyn's expulsion from the Writers' Union, and now PEN was to consider, at its Edinburgh conference in the autumn, a proposal to make Solzhenitsyn an honorary member of every PEN centre (there were upwards of sixty) in the world.[7] On the other side, preparations were set afoot in the Soviet Union to form a special delegation of writers to go to Sweden, under the leadership of Konstantin Simonov, to try to block the award by mobilizing left-wing political opinion there.

Solzhenitsyn had gone back to his Rozhdestvo hide-out and was working hard to finish *August 1914*. With typical meticulousness he planned to complete the work in the third week of October, immediately before the Nobel Prize announcement, which for literature was traditionally made on the fourth Thursday of the month. There were few interruptions. In July, Tvardovsky celebrated his sixtieth birthday, and Solzhenitsyn sent him a telegram: "Dear A.T., I wish you spacious days, precious discoveries, a happy creative life in your ripe years! Through all our constant quarrels and disagreements I remain immutably your deeply affectionate and ever grateful Solzhenitsyn." Tvardovsky acknowledged it with a message of his own, in which he said, among other things, "Though I often differ from you in my views, I never falter in my esteem and love for you as an artist."[8]

At a distance the two men could be warm and affectionate with one another—only when shut up in the same room did their egos collide and explode. But for Tvardovsky these were difficult days. Still one of the Soviet Union's leading literary figures, he was bound to have his birthday marked by encomiums in the official press, and indeed all the main newspapers carried articles about his career, some of them accompanied by photographs. But an instruction had been issued forbidding all mention of Tvardovsky's anti-Stalinist poem "Tyorkin in the Next World" or of his editorship of *Novy Mir*—although he had spent sixteen years of his life at the head of the magazine and had made it world famous. Most readers were perfectly well aware of this fact, just as they recognized the message of disapproval behind the silence. Not only had Tvardovsky to be expelled from his magazine but his nose had to be rubbed in the dirt as a lesson to others. And to cap this lesson in squalid revenge, editors were forbidden to approach Tvardovsky for interviews or samples of his work, as was customary at such moments. Kicking a man while he is down is an essential part of Soviet governmental therapy.

Apart from these public indignities, Tvardovsky's health was giving cause for alarm. Towards the end of the summer, he suffered a stroke that left him partially paralysed. At the Kremlin Hospital for Soviet notables, pleurisy was diagnosed and treatment with cupping glasses and poultices prescribed. Only after two weeks did the doctors discover their blunder and realize that it was cancer and too late to operate. But even unto the doors of death Tvardovsky was pursued by government mendacity and double-dealing. The doctors were strictly forbidden to mention his stroke in their public bulletin. As a leading official writer later explained, "The word 'thrombosis' was not to be mentioned at all . . . people might connect a thrombosis with the *Novy Mir* business, whereas cancer is from God."[9] Tvardovsky was given about a month to live by the doctors.

At the beginning of October, Solzhenitsyn was back in Rostropovich's dacha in Zhukovka and putting the final touches to *August 1914*. On 8 October 1970, with two weeks to go to the Nobel announcement and the deadline for completion of his novel, he was unexpectedly called to the telephone by Rostropovich's cleaning lady. An excited friend informed him that he had just been awarded the Nobel Prize. Solzhenitsyn refused to believe it—the announcement was two weeks early, it had to be a mistake. But the friend had heard it from an impeccable source—the Norwegian journalist Per Egil Hegge, who represented both Norwegian and Swedish newspapers in Moscow and was in constant touch with Stockholm. The caller wanted to know whether he could give Hegge Rostropovich's telephone number (the cellist was not in the directory), since the foreign press in Moscow was besieging Solzhenitsyn's friends with requests for interviews, and it was feared that sooner or later they would get the number anyway, and perhaps even descend on Solzhenitsyn in person. To this Solzhenitsyn seems to have given his grudging assent.

Hegge himself telephoned Solzhenitsyn about half an hour later. In the meantime one or two other friends had rung Solzhenitsyn to say they had heard the news on foreign radio stations, but Solzhenitsyn was still incredulous. When Hegge got through, Solzhenitsyn sounded both irritated and agitated. He virtually stammered his replies, and his first words were full of suspicion: "Where did you get this information from?" After Hegge told him of the Swedish Academy's official statement, he fell silent and refused to comment. "I am not prepared to give interviews. But I should like you to convey my thanks to the Swedish Academy privately. I repeat—privately." Hegge gently explained to him that this was hardly good enough on such an occasion and that the whole world was interested in Solzhenitsyn's reaction. Solzhenitsyn asked him to wait while he fetched pencil and paper and drafted a statement.[10] According to his memoir, his original intention (assuming he got the prize) had been to keep silent for a week and see how the Soviet authorities reacted, but the early announcement and Hegge's persistence took him by surprise.[11] A refusal to make a statement might be interpreted as evasion and cowardice. Thinking fast, he rattled off a brief and pointed reply: "I am grateful for the award. I accept the prize. I intend to come and receive it on the traditional day insofar as this depends on me. I am well. The state of my health is no obstacle to my making the trip."[12]

Solzhenitsyn's true feelings on hearing the news can only be guessed at. His self-control was absolute, and his prompt and firm acceptance was designed to underline the fact that there would be no repeat of the Pasternak fiasco, while the emphasis on his good health and fitness was intended to deprive the Soviet authorities of that time-honoured pretext for keeping people at home: "He's too sick to travel." In Solzhenitsyn's case, such an excuse would have enjoyed widespread credibility because of his well-known experience of cancer. Rumours of poor health had surrounded him continually since the early days of his fame and had served as a convenient smoke-screen when it suited his purposes. But it would have been an unfortunate reversal if this had now been turned against him.

A formal telegram from the academy reached Solzhenitsyn on 10 October, informing him that the prize was being awarded to him "for the ethical force with which he has pursued the indispensable traditions of Russian literature." Solzhenitsyn thanked the academy in a return cable, repeated his intention to go to Stockholm, and commented, "I regard the decision on the Nobel Prize as a tribute to Russian literature and to our troubled history"— thereby deliberately adding a political dimension to what some in Sweden were presenting as a purely literary affair.[13]

Not that it mattered much, for the political dimension did not escape the Soviet authorities. They might have been wiser to keep silent and ignore the matter, but tempers in the Writers' Union were apparently too frayed, and this was too good an opportunity to be missed by Solzhenitsyn's enemies. Reacting with uncustomary speed, *Izvestia* and *Pravda* printed a statement by the Writers' Union on the very day of the official telegram, denouncing Solzhenitsyn as the darling of "reactionary circles in the West," accusing him of illegally sending his works abroad, and criticizing the Swedish Academy: "One can only regret that the Nobel committee has allowed itself to be drawn into an unseemly game, undertaken by no means in the interests of the development of spiritual values and literary traditions, but dictated by speculative political considerations."[14]

The same theme was repeated, with variations, in *Sovetskaya Rossia*, *Literaturnaya Gazeta*, *Komsomolskaya Pravda*, and other organs of the Soviet government. The English-language *Soviet Weekly* added a literary appreciation of the Nobel laureate.

> Solzhenitsyn is a run-of-the-mill writer with an exaggerated idea of his own importance. His tragedy is that he has given in too easily to the flattery of people who have no scruples about the means they use to struggle against the Soviet system.
>
> But he must surely realize himself that his literary gifts are not only below those of the giants of the past but also inferior to many of his Soviet contemporaries—writers the West chooses to ignore because it finds the impact of truth in their writing most unpalatable.[15]

Soviet Weekly brought up the comparison with Tarsis once more, while *Komsomolskaya Pravda* suggested the parallel of "that other Nobel laureate" André Gide, allegedly condemned by his fellow countrymen for his "collaboration with Hitler's monsters." That same week, the *Literaturnaya Gazeta* claimed that Solzhenitsyn's Nobel Prize nomination had been originated by a right-wing *émigré* newspaper in Belgium called *Chasovoi* (The Sentinel), and a week later published extensive extracts from two articles critical of Solzhenitsyn, one from the American Communist newspaper the *Daily World* ("A Provocation in the Spirit of the Cold War"), and the other from an obscure Swedish newspaper called *Norrskensflamman* ("A Stockholm Newspaper Condemns the Decision of the Swedish Academy"), which it passed off as the informed opinion of influential circles in the West. Both articles were cited in *Pravda* the same day (and probably in a host of regional Soviet newspapers as well). On 28 October the *Literaturnaya Gazeta* returned to the fray with derogatory quotations from the Bulgarian and East German press, and on 4 November printed a critical statement by the presidium of the East German Writers' Union condemning the award yet again.[16]

In the rest of the world, however, the prize was hailed as a just reward for an outstanding body of work, even by Communist newspapers in France and Italy. The French literary reviews devoted substantial supplements to an analysis of Solzhenitsyn's books and philosophy, and the Anglo-Saxon papers lauded him in editorials. The political overtones of the award were not overlooked, causing a few on the left to express certain reservations about the motives of the Swedish Academy, but generally it was felt that in the modern world, politics and literature are inextricably intertwined and that the academy had shown realism and bravery in recognizing this fact.* As the

---

*One member of the jury, Arthur Lundquist, openly dissented from this view. In December he issued a statement to the press saying that the academy had played into the hands of the Soviet Union's enemies. "I have never said how I voted when Solzhenitsyn was awarded the prize, but I regard its award to him as a mistake." Lundquist's statement was quoted in *Pravda* on 12 December 1970.

London *Times* pointed out, one of the original criteria for awarding the prize had been that the work in question should show "idealistic tendencies," and no one could dispute this quality in Solzhenitsyn's books.

At home there were disappointingly few letters and telegrams of congratulations—no more than about fifty, according to Zhores Medvedev[17]—perhaps because of the official pressure that had been exerted on individuals who congratulated Solzhenitsyn on his fiftieth birthday (interviews with the KGB, Party reprimands, and so on), perhaps because of a general atmosphere of timidity and depression, and perhaps because others were intercepted by the post office. There could be no doubt, however, that the remaining liberals among the intelligentsia were heartened, while those in open opposition to the regime did not hesitate to express support. A number of messages got through, including one signed by thirty-four human-rights dissidents and another smuggled out of the camps: "Barbed wire and automatic weapons prevent us from expressing to you personally the depth of our admiration for your courageous creative work, upholding the sense of human dignity and exposing the trampling of the human soul and the destruction of human values."[18] It was signed by Yuri Galanskov and over two dozen others. Most encouraging of all was a note from some old comrades of his own labour-camp days: "We hotly dispute the Swedish Academy's claim to have been the first to appreciate your valour as a writer and as a citizen at its true worth. We jealously cherish our friend, our cell-mate, our comrade of the prison trains. . . ."[19]

Solzhenitsyn's base of support within the Soviet Union was narrowing, but outside the country it was broader and stronger than ever, and on 14 October he decided to capitalize on his new status by trying to negotiate once more with the authorities. Spurning the Writers' Union, he turned directly to the political establishment in the form of Mikhail Suslov, responsible for ideology in the Politburo and the man who had among other things, been instrumental in ousting Khrushchev. In a way it was an odd choice—Solzhenitsyn had been Khrushchev's protégé and certainly favoured his policies over his successor's. But Suslov was now all-powerful in ideological matters. Furthermore, Solzhenitsyn had once been introduced to him by Tvardovsky, had quite liked the man, and had formed the impression that Suslov liked him too. Faithful, as ever, to his instinctive hunches, he decided to write Suslov a personal letter setting out his "terms" for an agreement.

Solzhenitsyn suggested diplomatically that the ban on his works had been placed there by "unscrupulous officials of the Writers' Union," who had given the Party false information, and he made the following proposals: one, that *Cancer Ward* be published immediately ("the banning of this story . . . is a pure *misunderstanding*"); two, that his existing works be replaced in the libraries and that persons reading or asking for them no longer be punished; three, that a collection of his short stories be prepared for the press. If these steps were taken, wrote Solzhenitsyn, it would normalize his situation in Soviet literature and allow him to receive the Nobel Prize in "much more favourable circumstances." In return, he would submit his new novel, *August 1914*, for official publication, since there was nothing in it that could cause offence or create "difficulties" with the censorship.[20]

This was Solzhenitsyn's second attempt to negotiate with the government, as opposed to simply defending himself against attacks or counter-attacking in his turn, and his tactic was clearly to go over the heads of the Writers' Union leaders and to try to split them from their political bosses in the Central Committee. Judging from his later comments in *The Oak and the Calf*, he was optimistic about the outcome. "If I could have set in train just the things suggested there . . . it would have meant a change not only for me but in the whole literary situation, and in time not merely the literary situation." Particularly fascinating were his remarks on gradualism. "Although my heart yearned for something more, something decisive, still, those who change the course of history are the gradualists, in whose hands the fabric of events does not tear. If there were any possibility of changing the situation in our country smoothly, we ought to reconcile ourselves to it and do just that."[21] It was a far cry from "taking a swing" and showed that in some circumstances Solzhenitsyn was prepared to compromise, an interesting position for one who had recently torn *Novy Mir* to shreds, quarrelled with Tvardovsky, and broken with Lakshin over their "pusillanimous" attempts to work with the system and liberalize it from within. It is true, as he also writes, that he was offering this deal from a position of strength and that, technically, he "wasn't giving an inch." But he was consciously abandoning Russian editions of *The First Circle* (even the eighty-seven-chapter version, not to speak of the full ninety-six), if only for a time, for the sake of coming to an arrangement, and he was postponing *Gulag* into the indefinite future.

What he really wanted to do, it seems, was to buy time—time to think, time to absorb the import of the award, and time to make the necessary arrangements should matters for some reason come to a head and he decide, or be obliged, to leave the country. But the letter disappeared into the void, and the only answer he received was in the form of abusive articles in the official press.

Quite apart from literary and political considerations, there was one other compelling reason why Solzhenitsyn needed to play for time at this juncture, and that concerned his increasingly tangled family life. The early announcement of the Nobel Prize had introduced chaos into what was already a tense and difficult situation between himself and Natalia Reshetovskaya and had caught Solzhenitsyn unprepared. At this remove it is difficult to be precise about what happened during that turbulent autumn, but both Solzhenitsyn (through the intermediary of Veronica Stein) and Reshetovskaya have provided accounts that coincide in all but the smallest details, and it is clear that their quarrel exercised a direct influence on Solzhenitsyn's behaviour throughout the controversy over the Nobel Prize. Indeed, his actions cannot be explained without some reference to what was going on behind the scenes, nor understood without some indication of the intolerable strain he was under while having to make the most difficult and complicated decisions.

It appears that throughout the first half of 1970, he and Natalia had subsisted in some form of uneasy coexistence. According to one source, she had become tired of being able to make only short visits to him, and one day in spring had simply turned up at Zhukovka with all her luggage and announced her decision to stay indefinitely.[22] Solzhenitsyn had been upset, not least because it cramped his relations with his new circle of friends, and especially with Svetlova. There were recriminations and squabbles, and it seems that Natalia already suspected she had a rival of some kind. But the situation had been eased when they both moved out to Rozhdestvo for the summer. Solzhenitsyn always felt more comfortable there, and he was eager to finish *August 1914*. There were also things he wished to discuss that were too confidential for Moscow—even Zhukovka might have microphones.

The most immediate issue had been what to do if he won the Nobel Prize. He was determined to go and collect it, but it was quite possible he would be forbidden to return. According to Reshetovskaya, he had said he would take her with him—if she agreed to live abroad—but the problem was what to do about her mother and aunts. Fortunately, they had been able to discuss the situation with Maria when she came to Rozhdestvo for their traditional celebration of her name day, on 4 August. Maria had said she did not want to be a burden to them, but Solzhenitsyn insisted she wouldn't be. However, neither he nor Natalia could think of what to do about her aunts, and this aspect of the problem was left unresolved.[23]

Shortly after Maria's return to Ryazan, Solzhenitsyn had asked Natalia whether she would leave him to work alone at Rozhdestvo and would go back to Zhukovka for a while. Natalia had agreed reluctantly and spent the rest of August sorting through Solzhenitsyn's correspondence and making notes for her projected memoirs. Rostropovich and his wife, Galina Vishnevskaya, were away at the time, but Natalia had seen quite a lot of their daughters and sometimes accompanied the eldest, Olga (a cellist, like her father), on the piano in the main house. Natalia had felt abandoned and frequently wept when alone.

On 26 August, Solzhenitsyn had been to see her and was apparently distressed to find her so unhappy. There was another scene between them, in the course of which Solzhenitsyn told her about his infidelity and tried to justify it in terms of literary research. According to Reshetovskaya, he had said, "Please understand me, I have to describe lots of women in my novel. You don't expect me to find my heroines round the dinner table, do you?" He was a writer, and writers should be judged differently from other men. He asked Natalia whether she had sought advice from friends like Suzanna Teush (Suzanna had been Natalia's sole confidante in 1964 after the Leningrad incident) and suggested she do so. He also told her he would return to Zhukovka on 5 September. Natalia was horrified to have her suspicions confirmed—she would have preferred to live with the uncertainty—and did take advice, not from Suzanna Teush, but from Father Vsevolod Shpiller, an

Orthodox priest who had been friendly with Solzhenitsyn. Shpiller advised her to leave her husband for a while and found her a room in Moscow. She decided to move there on the day when Solzhenitsyn returned to Zhu-kovka.[24]

Solzhenitsyn, meanwhile, had just received an astonishing piece of news: Svetlova was expecting his baby. This was doubly surprising. In the light of his cancer and the radiation treatment in Tashkent, it seems he had regarded himself as probably sterile and had in any case sternly set his face against all thought of having children. As he had forcefully informed Natalia many years earlier, children would get in the way of his work, and that was not to be countenanced under any circumstances. But now, faced with the actual fact of Svetlova's conception, he felt deeply stirred. He was almost fifty-two, old enough to be a grandfather and at a time of life when he imagined that things like fatherhood were unthinkable, yet God had presented him with this sudden mystery, a late gift of providence. To a man of his religious disposition, with his belief in signs and mystic occurrences, it must have seemed like a divine signal, an omen to which he was bound to submit.

The practical implications, however, presented formidable difficulties. Svetlova was all for keeping it a secret. She declared that she was resigned to a life of secrecy, and told Solzhenitsyn she was prepared to bring up the child alone if necessary, if that was what Solzhenitsyn wanted. Solzhenitsyn, however, felt it was essential to give the child a name and could not tolerate the thought of concealing his fatherhood. On the other hand, he accepted Svetlova's suggestion that they need not marry and that he should stay for-mally married to Natalia. She was too old to make a new life for herself and should not be abandoned. Accordingly, after a great deal of agonizing, he wrote Natalia a confessional letter of eleven pages, informing her of the impending birth of the baby and saying that he intended to admit paternity. He did not name the mother and asked Natalia not to try and guess, saying that the other woman was not just a passing fancy in his life, but was not trying to tear him away from Natalia either; although pleased to be having a child by him, she would not insist on marrying him.[25]

Solzhenitsyn wrote in tender terms of his past life with Natalia. She was always telling him not to negate the past, and he was not negating it. She could be proud of their long years together, and she had every right to write her memoirs, whatever happened to the two of them in the future. She was in his blood and in his heart, forever dear to him, and that was why this letter was so hard to write. But he had been obliged to write it because of the critical position he was in with regard to the Nobel Prize. He faced the dan-ger of being forced to go abroad and never seeing his child, and leaving the mother behind for good, and he was not sure he could do that. On the other hand, he could not make up Natalia's mind for her or live with the conscious-ness that he had thrown her aside and spiritually murdered her. If his life had remained normal, he would never have wanted to leave her and never have forced her to choose. But now it was up to her to decide; she should weigh and judge everything that had happened. It was not a question of making external changes but of Natalia's undergoing a change of heart. Could she rise to such heights of magnanimity and benevolence that would make him her worshipper for ever more and create beautiful, lofty relations that would last beyond the grave? He begged her forgiveness for posing such an agonizing question; the fault was all his. He regarded himself as responsible for her well-being for the rest of her life. May God bless her in coming to the right decision.[26]

Not expecting to find Natalia at Zhukovka any more, and not knowing where she would be, Solzhenitsyn summoned Veronica Stein to Rozhdestvo and asked her to pass the letter on. Veronica did so on the night of 5 September, the night that Natalia moved from Zhukovka. Natalia arrived at the Steins' flat just before midnight, when Yuri Stein was in bed and Veronica in her night-clothes. Natalia, dishevelled and distraught, launched into a diatribe against her husband. It was the worst possible moment to give her the letter, but after several cups of tea and more talk, Veronica felt that Natalia was calm enough. She also nurtured the naïve hope that Solzhenitsyn's invitation to his wife to return and live with him would somehow outweigh the news of the baby and perhaps mollify her.

It was a vain hope. After swiftly skimming the letter, Natalia tore it to pieces and rushed from the room. Veronica, in dressing-gown and slippers, followed her down to the street and persuaded her to return while she got dressed and went with her. They would walk to Natalia's home together, and Veronica would try to talk her round. Natalia returned, but then dashed away again, slamming the front door behind her. Veronica had to wait for Yuri to return (he had dashed after Natalia but failed to catch her) before they could go out. They searched the street, a nearby park, and the nearest metro and bus stops, but could find no trace of her. The following morning, after a sleepless night, they telephoned Natalia's friends to see whether she was with them, and rang the police. But no one had seen her. Finally, with a feeling of dread, they rang Solzhenitsyn at Zhukovka to tell him what had happened. "I know," he said sepulchrally. "It's all right. She's here."[27]

The cause of their alarm was that for years now, since her first serious altercation with Solzhenitsyn, in the spring of 1964, Natalia had been in the habit of making threats of suicide. Only once, in Tashkent, had she said anything about divorce, and at that time Solzhenitsyn had pooh-poohed the idea. Since then she had never mentioned it but had reacted with hysteria to all talk of separation. According to Solzhenitsyn, she had invariably threatened that she would either kill herself or go mad, and every time he had retreated and thought the crisis would pass of its own accord. It had been with such threats that she had demanded his return from the Chukovskys to Ryazan after the confiscation of his archive in 1965, when he thought he faced arrest. In February 1966 she had again summoned him by telegram from a distant hiding-place where he was working in deep secrecy on *The Gulag Archipelago*, and he had expected some serious news, only to be told that she was bored and lonely and "couldn't wait a day longer." Such scenes had flared up intermittently over the years and were common knowledge to the rest of their family and friends, and Solzhenitsyn had taken her threats seriously, so much so that he had at one point hidden the infusion of the mandrake root that he still kept in Ryazan, lest Natalia should be tempted to use it.[28]

Veronica and her husband were highly relieved, therefore, to hear that Natalia had not done anything drastic, though they soon learned that their fears had not been totally unjustified. It turned out that after leaving them, Natalia had just managed to catch the last electric train in the direction of Zhukovka. The train had terminated several miles short, and she had had to walk the last part along the tracks. After gaining admittance (Solzhenitsyn was not at home), she had slashed her thumb and written in blood on a sheet of paper the single word "I" followed by a question mark. Then she had crossed it through, also in blood, and stuck it over the bed in Solzhenitsyn's room before retiring to bed herself. Solzhenitsyn had returned to find it there the following morning.[29]

Natalia had indeed intended, it appears, to attempt suicide and to do it at Zhukovka, but her nerve had cooled during her long walk, and by the time she arrived she had begun to hope that when he saw her, Solzhenitsyn would somehow change his mind. But their conversation the following morning was cool and strained. Solzhenitsyn wanted to know whether she had read his letter, and when she said she had torn it up before getting to the end, he gave her another copy to read (it had taken him a week to write it, he said, and expressed exactly what he wanted to say). He insisted she go through it before saying any more. When she had finished, she told him she was willing to take the baby, but couldn't accept his continuing to see the mother. Solzhenitsyn said that that was impossible, and they argued ineffectually for a while. Natalia wanted to know the mother's name, but Solzhenitsyn said (evidently to avoid a scene) that he would tell Suzanna Teush and that Natalia could find out from her.[30]

Eventually, Solzhenitsyn was successful in calming Natalia, and she returned to the room Father Shpiller had found for her for the next few weeks. They did, it appears, have several more tense and unfruitful discussions, without coming to any conclusions.

It was while these talks were going on that Per Hegge and the others had telephoned with their news about the Nobel Prize, and this had at once transformed the atmosphere. Natalia was enormously excited and proud. She was the wife of a Nobel laureate. "Aren't you going to congratulate me?" she said to Veronica the next time they met. "Half the prize is due to me." She decided that she should move into Zhukovka to help her husband "receive foreign correspondents" and take care of the mail—just as she had done in the old days in Ryazan. Solzhenitsyn was reluctant, but thinking that it might be a prelude to a real agreement between them and knowing how genuinely delighted she was by his success, he allowed her to come back. Not that he intended to receive correspondents—quite the contrary. He was even incongruously glum when the Rostropoviches and the Titovs turned up at supper time to congratulate him. But there were indeed letters to be written, and it was Natalia who went to the post office to send Solzhenitsyn's telegram of reply to the Swedish Academy confirming his acceptance of the prize. She later said to Veronica, "I could easily have put 'I can come with my wife,' but I didn't."[31]*

Despite this brief interlude of seeming normality, relations between them remained tense and strained. It quickly became clear that although Natalia was eager to have a share of the glory, she had no intention of accepting any of Solzhenitsyn's conditions concerning the other Natalia and the baby. On the contrary, she seems to have felt that the public spotlight of the Nobel Prize would force Solzhenitsyn to stay married to her to avoid any suspicion of scandal (and she later came to believe that his long letter to her had been written also to avert a scandal). She was determined to keep him at any price, and this again led to stormy scenes, violent arguments, recriminations, and tears.

It must have been in the midst of this struggle that Solzhenitsyn was startled, on 11 October, to hear a knock on the front door and, when he opened it, to find four Western correspondents standing on the doorstep. Alarmed by this unexpected intrusion, he spoke to them through the half-opened door and refused any interviews, making the excuse that he was a guest at Rostropovich's dacha and could not invite them in. When reporting this incident to the outside world, the AP correspondent noted that "Solzhenitsyn's rust-coloured beard and his flashing eyes made a somewhat terrifying impression as he peered through the half-open door," and described how, after excusing himself hastily, Solzhenitsyn had "banged the door shut and locked it, leaving the correspondents standing in the mud outside."[32] It sounded rude and unfriendly and added to the mystique of Solzhenitsyn as a crusty recluse, but on this occasion the correspondents could have had no idea of the real human drama unfolding inside.

It seems that Natalia then moved out for a few days, but on 14 October returned again. Over dinner, Solzhenitsyn told her that he was becoming more and more attached to the other woman, and asked Natalia whether she couldn't make a sacrifice for the sake of the three of them. The following morning, the fifteenth, Solzhenitsyn was surprised to hear no sound from Natalia's room long after her usual rising hour. After some time, he grew restless and at about nine in the morning dropped a heavy book on the floor to see whether there would be any reaction. There was none. Opening the door, he found Natalia lying in bed with saliva dribbling from her mouth. She had taken an overdose of sleeping tablets. He remembered that in one of the neighboring dachas, a medical orderly was in permanent attendance on

---

*A reference to the text of the telegram from the Swedish Academy, which read in part, "We hope that you and your wife will be able to come to Stockholm on 10 December to receive the prize." In confirming his intention to go, Solzhenitsyn made no mention of Natalia.

the academician Tamm, who was slowly dying. He quickly fetched the orderly, and the orderly gave Natalia an injection. Solzhenitsyn then rang Veronica Stein for help, and she suggested he ring the Kopelevs, who were able to summon two doctors from a nearby writers' clinic, a man and a woman, who could be trusted to keep the matter secret. Natalia was in a coma, and the doctors insisted, over Solzhenitsyn's objections, that she be taken to a hospital, but the problem arose of where. Under Soviet law, attempted suicides should be taken to a psychiatric hospital, but this was obviously out of the question—the scandal would be too great and would make a formidable weapon in the hands of the Soviet government. Fortunately, one of the doctors was able to get her admitted to the surgical ward of a nearby hospital, where she was taken by ambulance and put in a private room.[33]

It appears that the first tablets had paralysed her oesophagus, making it impossible for her to swallow the rest, and this had saved her life, but it was twenty-four hours before she recovered consciousness. When she did so, she immediately recognized Veronica, who was sitting with her, and burst into tears. She asked why they had saved her and said she had genuinely wished to die—a fact she later confirmed in a letter to Kopelev (in which she reproached him for his part in rescuing her). Later that day she was visited by a woman police doctor (the police were automatically notified of all suicide attempts, and not even in this case could the formality be avoided), but when the doctor heard the cause of the attempt, she took a robust view and dismissed the affair as the result of a normal family quarrel. Since a relative (Veronica) was with the patient and since the doctor did not suspect their true identity from their names (Reshetovskaya, Stein), she agreed not to pursue the matter and to submit a purely formal report.

That evening Natalia was transferred to the psychiatric ward of another hospital, where a friend worked and was able to make the necessary arrangements. Veronica and another cousin took turns at sitting with Natalia, and later Suzanna Teush and Alexandra Popova sat for a while. All this time Solzhenitsyn stayed away. His mood was one of cold fury. "How could she do this to me?" had been his first words to Kopelev. "How *dare* she do this to me?" And to Veronica he said it was the last straw. He had offered Natalia "reasonable terms," and she had responded with this act of extremism. He said he felt no further obligations to her.[34]

Natalia, however, was anxious to see him. Earlier she had raved to Veronica about Solzhenitsyn returning to her and the three of them settling in Rozhdestvo, where they would found a museum. Solzhenitsyn would write his novels, and she would work at her memoirs, while Veronica helped the two of them. About the baby and Svetlova there was no word. When Solzhenitsyn failed to appear, she suggested she might agree to a divorce after all and begged Veronica to persuade him to come to the hospital. Solzhenitsyn was extremely reluctant, but agreed when Veronica told him that Natalia was now filled with friendly feelings towards him and was considering a divorce. It was eleven days since Natalia's suicide attempt, and the meeting was fairly amicable. Natalia, having put on a fresh night-gown and dressing-gown and made herself up, was extremely animated. She asked Solzhenitsyn to accompany her into the ward where the other women patients were. She wanted them all to know that she was married, and overcoming Solzhenitsyn's objections, she hustled him inside. Once there, she suddenly announced in front of everyone that he was taking her home. The doctor was called and protested that it was too early, but Natalia was possessed of a manic energy and succeeded in overcoming everyone's objections. The doctor reluctantly discharged her, and Veronica and Solzhenitsyn escorted her home. On the way, Natalia babbled incessantly about the need to get a divorce and proposed that they go to Ryazan the next day and make an official application. Solzhenitsyn agreed, but declined to take her back to Zhukovka. Natalia's mother, Maria, had been summoned from Ryazan to Veronica's flat, so Natalia consented to go there and meet Solzhenitsyn at the station the following day.[35]

The next morning, 27 October, they met and travelled down to Ryazan. On the way to the station, Natalia unexpectedly announced that she would not agree to a divorce after all and would refuse all summonses to appear in court. At the station, she cheered up again, joked about how nice it was to be travelling with her husband once more and how it was like a second honeymoon (characteristically, Solzhenitsyn had brought some pages of *August 1914* to correct on the train). When they arrived in Ryazan, they went straight to the registry office to apply for a divorce, but the officials there were clearly dismayed. Solzhenitsyn's notoriety overwhelmed them, and none dared take responsibility for setting the wheels in motion without explicit orders from above. Solzhenitsyn and Natalia then went to the Regional Executive Committee headquarters, which was in charge of all registrations in Ryazan, but news of their mission had preceded them, and no one was prepared to take action. Frustrated, they returned to Moscow with nothing accomplished, and Solzhenitsyn took up residence in Zhukovka once more, while Natalia went to stay with some friends, promising to return for a divorce application after the November holidays.[36]

This was the emotional and family background against which Solzhenitsyn had to deal with the storm raised by his winning of the Nobel Prize, to handle negotiations with the Swedish Academy, and to make his decision about whether to go to Stockholm to accept the prize. Originally, it seems, his intention had genuinely been to go, even if it meant being prevented from returning to the Soviet Union. Only when abroad could he publish *all* the works he had written and write the whole truth fearlessly and without restraint. This was one reason he had started smuggling his works abroad—so as to be prepared when the time came. And it was not until 1968, when he met Svetlova, that he had encountered any serious opposition to this idea. Even then, his conviction of its correctness was not shaken.

So thoroughly had I digested this lesson that in 1968, when [Svetlova], shocked by my attitude, fervently tried to persuade me that it was just the opposite—

that if I were *outside*, my words would bounce off the iron integument around our country, whereas while I was inside, the porously receptive mass would absorb them, fill in the gaps, supply what was left unsaid or merely hinted at—I was shocked in my turn. I decided that she thought this way only because she had never been in a camp.[37]

In 1969 the subject had come up again, when Solzhenitsyn had discussed the provisions of his will with Svetlova and decided to make her his chief executor. He was still convinced that sooner or later he would have to go abroad (this was another reason to retain a Western lawyer), and when they had discussed their proposed magazine, Solzhenitsyn had made contingency plans for him to participate from abroad. There had been at least two occasions when he had already been psychologically prepared to go. The first had been in November 1969, after his expulsion from the Writers' Union, when the Voice of America had mistakenly broadcast the news that "the writer Solzhenitsyn is to be expelled from the Soviet Union." For a moment Solzhenitsyn had believed it and had steeled himself for departure. Another moment had come shortly afterwards, when the Norwegians announced that Solzhenitsyn would be welcome in their country and offered him an official residence for writers. Solzhenitsyn had a soft spot for Norway—the only country in Europe that "never for a minute forgot or forgave the invasion of Czechoslovakia"—and cherished sentimental notions of its similarity to his homeland: ". . . a northern country, with a winter like ours in Russia. With peasant utensils, wooden cups and dishes, just like those in Russia." Solzhenitsyn had found himself thinking of nothing else for days and had again been ready to go. Had the Soviet government pushed at that moment, it would have found little real resistance.[38]

But now, a year later, the situation was rather different. He had survived his expulsion from the Union, and the furore had died down (until the Nobel Prize award, at least). He had left the camp theme behind him and launched into a series of novels that required research in Russia and a close knowledge of Russia. Since they were historical novels, the authorities might even agree to publish one or two, or at least turn a blind eye, as he had suggested to Suslov. Meanwhile, Natalia Svetlova, Shafarevich, and others of their circle had talked to him of patriotism (his very theme in *August 1914* was that of patriotism, of love of the homeland—and of patriotism betrayed). And now, finally, he had a deeply personal stake in staying, because of the revelation that Svetlova was expecting their child. In theory this was not supposed to count. He and Svetlova had evidently agreed at one point that if he got the prize he should go. There must also have seemed a chance that she and their child might follow—whether or not he got a divorce from Natalia. But there appeared to be little prospect of a divorce in the immediate future. Natalia had failed to turn up after the November holiday—perhaps hoping that Solzhenitsyn would go abroad and take her with him—and it seemed inevitable that the authorities, alerted by Solzhenitsyn's appearance in the registry office in Ryazan, would exploit the situation to their advantage. So theory was one thing, but practice, even in Solzhenitsyn's case, quite another. As he ruefully noted in his memoir, "By way of mocking reproof, to teach me not to judge my predecessors too hastily, I was left teetering paralytically on the knife-edge of decision."[39]

None of this behind-the-scenes drama was known to the outside world. The opacity and secretiveness of Soviet society played into Solzhenitsyn's hands (he was becoming a past master at exploiting it to his own advantage), and not even the persistent foreign press corps in Moscow suspected what was going on. When Per Hegge, the most astute and best informed of them, tentatively inquired about Mrs Solzhenitsyn and whether she might be travelling to Stockholm if Solzhenitsyn decided to go, he was informed variously that she was "ill" (that good old Soviet alibi) or, in more convincing detail by Zhores Medvedev, that she had recently had a hysterectomy and was suffering from a hormonal imbalance, since the proper hormone treatment was not available in the Soviet Union. The medical detail was impressive, and from the embarrassment that Hegge detected in the faces of the people he questioned, he deduced that it was unwise to probe any further.[40]

Perhaps fortunately for Solzhenitsyn, the reaction of the Swedish government, and of certain circles close to the academy, to his winning of the award also turned out to be ambiguous. Already in the first days after he had sent his telegram of acceptance, he had begun to hear of mutterings, relayed from Stockholm, about his remark that the prize was a tribute to "Russian literature and our troubled history," which was regarded as provocative. In the weeks leading up to the Nobel ceremony on 10 December, the Swedes proved embarrassingly eager to disclaim any political dimension to the award and to damp down any controversy that might be raised by Solzhenitsyn's going to Stockholm. Solzhenitsyn therefore had a genuine political pretext for his eventual decision not to go and was able to conceal and resolve his personal dilemma in the smoke and thunder of public controversy.

The difficulties began when Solzhenitsyn, seeking to obtain the advantages of a Nobel ceremony without the risk of being shut out of the Soviet Union, decided to explore the possibility of holding some sort of alternative ceremony in the Swedish embassy in Moscow. He seems to have hit on this idea within about two weeks of winning the prize, for in the last week of October Per Hegge was approached by Zhores Medvedev with just such an inquiry. Hegge had known Medvedev from the time of Medvedev's release from the mental hospital—a mutual friend had introduced them at the time—and it had been through Medvedev that Hegge had sought an interview with Solzhenitsyn if he won the Nobel Prize. Medvedev met Hegge again on 28 October and passed him a whole string of questions from Solzhenitsyn on the details of the Nobel ceremony, what the travel arrangements would be, where Solzhenitsyn would stay in Stockholm if he went, and so on. At the same time he asked Hegge to find out what the chances were that the prize could be handed to Solzhenitsyn at the Swedish embassy in Moscow, and whether Solzhenitsyn could visit the embassy himself at noon on 27 November—either to apply for his entry visa to Sweden or to make arrangements for a ceremony in Moscow. For his personal visit, however, Solzhenitsyn wanted a letter of invitation from the Swedish embassy in case he was stopped by a police guard outside.

Hegge promised to find out everything he could both from the Swedish Academy in Stockholm and from the embassy in Moscow, and arranged to meet Medvedev on 20 November. Medvedev said that Solzhenitsyn would come too. Hegge approached the Swedish embassy and was told that the embassy could not write a letter of invitation to Solzhenitsyn but that Solzhenitsyn was welcome to come to the embassy at the stated time. The embassy spokesman added that it was out of the question for a ceremony to be held at the embassy, since the embassy's task was "to maintain good relations with the local authorities." This order had come from Stockholm. Hegge was taken aback by this double refusal and pointed out that five years beforehand, Ambassador Jarring had invited Sholokhov to an official dinner at the embassy and personally congratulated him. Was he not afraid of the comparison between then and now, and how it would look to the outside world? It was also possible, Hegge felt, that Solzhenitsyn would decline to go without an invitation.[41]

Hegge met Medvedev and Solzhenitsyn on 20 November. In the meantime, Solzhenitsyn had been receiving information direct from Stockholm about the ceremony. He was told by the academy and the Nobel Foundation that they feared demonstrations against him by Maoist students and that for the sake of his own peace and safety, they would accommodate him not in the Grand Hotel, where all the other laureates stayed, but in a "quieter and more secluded spot," where he could have a "secure apartment" in which to live. He had also received the programme, with pictures of previous laureates in dinner-jackets and black tie and tails, and realized that he, too, would have to dress up and attend banquets. He would also have to deliver a brief, three-minute speech at the main banquet, and a longer Nobel lecture later in the week. One problem was that with all the family turmoil at home and the official attacks on him in the Soviet press, he was too troubled to sit down and write a proper speech, and the journey to Stockholm and his participation in the formal ceremonies there had begun to seem more and more unreal. By the time he went to see Hegge, he had already made up his mind not to go, and instead of a Nobel lecture had written a letter setting out his reasons for staying away and for broaching the idea of a ceremony in Moscow. This he would ask Dr Karl Ragnar Gierow, secretary of the Swedish Academy, to read out on his behalf at the banquet.

At the meeting with Hegge, Solzhenitsyn was no longer interested in the Stockholm arrangements, but rather in confirming his visit to the embassy, finding out whether the embassy would convey his letter to Gierow through the diplomatic pouch and whether they would agree to a ceremony. The three men (including Medvedev) met outside the Lenin Library in the early evening and strolled along the Kalinin Prospekt to talk. Hegge was impressed with Solzhenitsyn's nonchalance and self-control. His news was all bad, but Solzhenitsyn took it all impassively and did not lose the cordiality with which he had first greeted the Norwegian journalist. He did, however, as Hegge had predicted, announce that he wouldn't go to the embassy without an invitation, even though Hegge pointed out to him that there were never policemen on duty outside the Swedish embassy and that gaining admittance would be no problem.

Before parting, Hegge and Solzhenitsyn arranged to meet the following week, on 26 November. Solzhenitsyn's letter to the academy was to be an open one, and he wanted Hegge to have a copy for the press. They met at the library again and went for another walk. There was an amusing moment when Solzhenitsyn stopped in a dark doorway to hand him the letter and Hegge noticed the name of the institution on the door: "Institute of Marxism-Leninism." Solzhenitsyn literally jumped when Hegge pointed this out to him and insisted on moving to somewhere else. He then surprised Hegge by saying that he would go to the Swedish embassy the next day after all, but at 10 a.m. instead of at noon. When Hegge protested that he had told them Solzhenitsyn wasn't coming, Solzhenitsyn merely asked him to go there early the next morning and say that he had changed his mind. When Hegge queried the change of time, Solzhenitsyn said it was because he didn't trust the embassy employees and wanted to catch them off-guard. Hegge protested that this was preposterous. No matter how badly—in his eyes as well as Solzhenitsyn's—the embassy was handling the matter, there was no reason to distrust the staff. Solzhenitsyn agreed to modify the time to 10:45 and Hegge went to advise the Swedish embassy the next morning.[42]

Solzhenitsyn's meeting with Ambassador Gunnar Jarring was brief and businesslike. Jarring was at that time the United Nations mediator in the Arab-Israeli conflict, in addition to being the Swedish ambassador to Moscow, and was said to have an interest in U Thant's job as UN secretary-general when the latter vacated it. He seemed hardly likely to do anything to offend a superpower with the right of veto over U Thant's successor, and his behaviour confirmed it. He was polite but reserved. Solzhenitsyn informed him that he had decided not to go to Stockholm and wished to send a letter informing the academy of this fact. Could it go by diplomatic bag? Jarring assented. But when it came to the question of a ceremony in the embassy in Moscow, he vigorously discounted the idea. He was prepared to present the medal and diploma privately to Solzhenitsyn in his study, "without an audience," but a reception was out of the question: "It's never been done that way." Solzhenitsyn asked him to think the idea over and discuss it with the Swedish Academy, since there had never been a case quite like his before.[43]

The letter that Solzhenitsyn sent to the academy gave three reasons why he had changed his mind about going to Stockholm, each of them only partly true. First, there were the onerous Soviet procedures for obtaining a passport to travel abroad, including the need to obtain character references from the Party (an unlikely requirement in Solzhenitsyn's case); then the danger that, in view of the hostility of the Soviet government to the award, he would be deprived of the chance to return to his native land; and thirdly, his distaste for the formal (and tiring) ceremonies and dislike of the fuss that his visit would cause. He also expanded on the controversial phrase in his earlier telegram about "Russia's troubled history": "Inwardly I share [the prize] with those of my predecessors in Russian literature who, because of the difficult conditions of the past decades, did not live to receive such a prize or who were little known in their lifetime to the reading world or even to their countrymen in the original." He added a request that the academy consider the possibility of presenting the prize to him in Moscow. There was no word about the personal drama that was the real reason for his refusal to go.[44]

The academy had apparently intended to keep this letter secret until 10 December, the day of the ceremony, but Solzhenitsyn wanted the news of his decision made public sooner than that and had taken the precaution of giving a copy to Hegge (with a three-day embargo). In his account of the matter, Solzhenitsyn suggests that the letter leaked at the Stockholm end, but his version is sufficiently vague to leave open the possibility that he himself was responsible. At all events, the academy sent a telegram of apology and asked for a fresh statement for the banquet. Taking and adapting a paragraph from his unfinished Nobel lecture, and bearing in mind the date of the ceremony, Solzhenitsyn wrote as follows:

> I hope that my involuntary absence will not cast a shadow over today's ceremonies. Among the greetings delivered on this occasion, you will expect one from me. I desire even less that my words should cloud this solemn occasion. Yet I cannot close my eyes to the remarkable fact that the day of the Nobel Prize presentation coincides with Human Rights Day. Nobel Prize winners are bound to feel that this coincidence places a responsibility upon them. Everybody present in the Stockholm City Hall must see a symbolic meaning in this. So let none at this festive table forget that political prisoners are on hunger-strike this very day in defence of rights that have been curtailed or trampled underfoot.[45]

It was a powerful statement, and once again Solzhenitsyn had gone to the root of the question that bothered him most, with his brilliant appeal to the symbolism of Human Rights Day. It was also acutely embarrassing to his symbolic hosts in Sweden. Solzhenitsyn had not named the country in which political prisoners were planning a hunger-strike, but it was clear which one he meant. Solzhenitsyn took the statement to the Swedish embassy for transmission, but Jarring was away and his deputy wriggled and squirmed in his desire to avoid sending it. Solzhenitsyn was relentless, however, and defeated all the man's arguments against it. Only later did he learn that the deputy had spent his own money to fly to Finland over the weekend and post the letter from there, rather than risk abusing the diplomatic pouch.

Even then the statement failed at the last hurdle. At the Nobel banquet on 10 December, Dr Gierow pronounced a brief encomium on Solzhenitsyn's work and career, praising him as a great humanist and democrat. He took care, however, to distance himself from "Western" interpretations of Solzhenitsyn's books, and dwelt at greatest length on his first work, *Ivan Denisovich*, quoting, of all newspapers, *Pravda*, to demonstrate how loyal Solzhenitsyn was. At the end, when he came to read Solzhenitsyn's statement, he omitted the last sentence about the hunger-strike. It was, it seems, too provocative for the academy to swallow.

The Swedish diplomat's journey to Finland had been in vain, as Solzhenitsyn realized when he listened to radio reports of the Nobel ceremony that same evening. He sat with a handful of friends, who had gathered in Rostropovich's attic bar to celebrate the occasion. Never mind, he would release the statement into samizdat the following day.

39

THE START OF
A VAST ENTERPRISE

In the weeks following the Nobel ceremony, news began to trickle through to Moscow of the way it had gone. From reports it became clear that Solzhenitsyn's absence had both cast a shadow over the proceedings and in a peculiar way also dominated them. At the end of his prepared speech, Dr Gierow had added the impromptu remark that "the Swedish Academy regrets the reason why Alexander Solzhenitsyn has deemed it impossible to be with us today" and said that the prize would be awarded to him "at a place and time still to be agreed." There was a long pause that seemed to some observers to contain a compound of embarrassment, shame, and silent respect for the missing writer, while those who looked for the empty chair that was supposed to be there were surprised to find it had been forgotten. The silence was ended when the king of Sweden rose to his feet and led the assembly in a round of applause. Professor Arne Tiselius, a former winner of the Nobel Prize for chemistry, said in his keynote speech afterwards, "we appreciated . . . the motives that have prompted [Solzhenitsyn] not to attend. The homage just rendered is, if anything, reinforced by his absence."[1]

There were one or two side-shows as well. The academy had put on a display of Solzhenitsyn's works that was moved from the reception to the banquet and then back to the academy again. A Swedish human-rights organization had put together an even bigger exhibition that was displayed in the premises of the Workers' Educational Centre in Stockholm. The Educational Centre abutted the Grand Cinema, where a world première of the Anglo-Norwegian film of *A Day in the Life of Ivan Denisovich* (starring Tom Courtenay) was given for the benefit of the royal family and the remaining prize winners, but the exhibition was ostentatiously boycotted by the Nobel Foundation on the grounds that it contained, among hundreds of other books, copies of Solzhenitsyn's works published in Russian by the NTS. The Soviet embassy, which had been active throughout in bringing pressure to bear on the Swedish Academy and the Swedish authorities, managed on the fourth or fifth day to have the exhibition closed on the grounds that it was a threat to Soviet-Swedish relations. The Nobel ceremony itself and all associated events were boycotted by representatives of the Soviet Union and the countries in the Soviet bloc.[2]

These squalid manoeuvres were standard Soviet practice and barely raised an eyebrow in the bustle and clamour of Nobel Prize week (one of the successes of Soviet propaganda has been to persuade the rest of the world that such behaviour is more or less normal, at least on the part of Communist countries). But it had its effect on the Swedish Academy, which refused to accept *any* books from the closed exhibition for its own collection and grew decidedly timid in its dealings with Solzhenitsyn. It soon emerged that among the materials he had forwarded at the academy's request was a brief autobiography of about three pages, which he urged the academy to make public at once, since he was "deprived of a platform in the Soviet Union."[3] For some inexplicable reason the academy declined and said it would publish the autobiography in its year-book nine months later, until which time the document would remain secret. Feeling bound by his obligations to the academy, Solzhenitsyn did not release it into samizdat, so that many facts of his biography remained unknown for another year, adding to the mystery of his past.

Meanwhile, the larger controversy around his name continued to rage world-wide. In November, shortly before the Nobel ceremony was due to take place, Rostropovich had created headlines by releasing a long open letter about Solzhenitsyn to the world's press. Announcing that it was "no longer a secret" that he was sheltering Solzhenitsyn in his house, Rostropovich declared that he had been impelled to write his letter by the Soviet campaign against Solzhenitsyn's Nobel Prize. It was the third time, he said, that a Soviet writer had been given the Nobel Prize. In two cases the award had been regarded as a "dirty political game," but in one (Sholokhov's) as a "just recognition of the outstanding world significance of our literature." If Sholokhov had declined to accept the prize, Rostropovich would have understood that the Soviet authorities no longer trusted the objectivity and honesty of the Swedish academicians, but now it appeared that the Soviet authorities accepted the Nobel Prize sometimes with gratitude and sometimes with curses. Rostropovich referred to earlier campaigns against Shostakovich, Prokofiev, and other composers and cited a long list of senseless censorings and bannings with which he was personally acquainted. He was not concerned with political and economic questions, he wrote, but wished that somebody would explain to him "why in our literature and art people completely incompetent in this field so often have the final word? Why are they given the right to discredit our art in the eyes of our people?" It was always, it seemed, because "there was an opinion" handed down from on high. Rostropovich concluded that after his letter "there will undoubtedly be an 'opinion' about me, but I am not afraid of it. I openly say what I think. Talent, of which we are proud, must not be submitted to the assaults of the past. . . . Solzhenitsyn seeks the right through his suffering to write the truth as he sees it, and I see no reason to hide my attitude towards him at a time when a campaign is being launched against him."⁴

Rostropovich had apparently drafted his letter while on a visit to London at the end of October to receive the gold medal of the Royal Philharmonic Society, but it was only when back in Moscow in November that he decided to make it public (it was formally addressed to the editors of *Pravda*, *Izvestia*, *Literaturnaya Gazeta*, and *Sovetskaya Kultura*, none of which published it), and he posted it on the eve of his departure for a concert tour in West Germany. Some observers concluded from this that he would not be punished for it, but he was immediately banned from going abroad again (already-arranged tours to France and Finland were cancelled) after his return from Germany, and in time began to find that his Soviet tours were being cancelled as well.

From a different source came another open declaration in support of Solzhenitsyn. On 10 December, the day of the Nobel ceremony, Arthur Miller announced in the *New York Times* that he, too, after a long run as a popular author in the Soviet Union, had been banned from Soviet stages and that a television production of one of his plays had been suddenly cancelled, either as the result of a preface he had written to a book of photographs, *In Russia*, by his wife Inge Morath, or for having signed an outspoken letter in defence of Solzhenitsyn at the time of his expulsion from the Writers' Union. Whatever the reason, Miller declared his solidarity with Solzhenitsyn and Rostropovich and his disgust with this new evidence of Soviet intolerance.⁵

Until now some foreign observers had professed to see a certain leniency in the Soviet government's attitude to Solzhenitsyn over the Nobel Prize affair. Most of the official attacks, they felt, had been directed as much against the Swedish Academy as against Solzhenitsyn himself, and there had been nothing like the scurrilous insults hurled at Pasternak. This was true, but probably reflected the authorities' uncertainty and the problems caused them by Solzhenitsyn's greater pugnacity, rather than any sudden feelings of remorse or indulgence. This was borne out on 17 December when *Pravda* published a wide-ranging attack on the whole phenomenon of dissidence, with Solzhenitsyn featured as public enemy number one. There was little new in it. Solzhenitsyn was labelled a "spiritual *émigré*, hostile and alien to the entire life of the Soviet people," who had tried to "blackmail" the Writers' Union by threatening that his works would find their way to the West and then conniving at their appearance there. *Feast of the Conquerors* was mentioned again. But perhaps the most menacing note was sounded in the comparison between Solzhenitsyn, Tarsis, and Anatoli Kuznetsov on the one hand, and Solzhenitsyn, Bukovsky, and Amalrik on the other. This was the first time that Solzhenitsyn had been lumped with the dissidents in the official press. Tarsis and Kuznetsov had gone abroad, while Amalrik had just been sentenced to three years in a labour camp and Bukovsky would shortly be in the dock again. The inference was plain: one or the other awaited Solzhenitsyn in the not too distant future. Another theme was that all these individuals were the tools of Western intelligence services. It was an argument that would resurface again and again in the years ahead, in ever new variations.

The article was signed with the *nom de plume* "I. Alexandrov," which is customarily reserved for authoritative statements by the Soviet leadership, and therefore had the force for loyal Soviet citizens that a papal decree has for Catholics. It was followed by harsher outbursts in *Krasnaya Zvezda* (Red Star), the organ of the Soviet armed forces, and *Kommunist vooruzhennykh sil* (Armed Forces Communist), a newspaper devoted to questions of ideology and propaganda. According to Zhores Medvedev, surveillance of Solzhenitsyn's friends and family circle was intensified, and pressure was applied on the Norwegian government to have the journalist Per Hegge withdrawn.[6]

For most of December and January, Solzhenitsyn was too preoccupied with family affairs to pay much attention to what the Soviet press was saying about him. While his quarrel with Natalia simmered on, playing havoc with his nerves and keeping him jumpily on the defensive, Natalia Svetlova, her mother, stepfather, and son were able to exchange their small flat in Vasilievsky Lane, plus a smaller, two-room flat that Svetlova still owned in a university co-operative, for a big, old-fashioned, four-room flat in Kozitsky Lane, also just off Gorky Street. The extra space came just in time, because on 30 December 1970 (slightly prematurely) Svetlova gave birth to a son. Solzhenitsyn chose for him the quaint and archaic name of Ermolai, based, he said, on the Greek Hermes—"herald of the people."

An immediate result of the child's birth was that Svetlova was dismissed from her job. For the past six months she had been carrying out research and lecturing in applied mathematics at the Labour Institute in Moscow. A friend had obtained the post for her, despite knowing of her pregnancy and who the father was. In a typically Soviet compromise, he had told her that this might create difficulties for him but that she should stay until the baby was born and see what happened. If the institute bosses kicked up a fuss, she would have to go quietly; if they didn't, she could stay. In the event, the bosses didn't wait for explanations but simply dismissed her the moment they learned the news, taking it as self-evident that she would accept it. Not long afterwards her mother, Ekaterina, was dismissed from her engineering job for becoming the grandmother of Solzhenitsyn's child.[7]

In February 1971 Tvardovsky was discharged from the Kremlin Hospital, having made an astounding recovery. His thrombosis had been resolved, his paralysis was partly gone, and he was able to speak again, albeit with difficulty. Soon after his return home, Solzhenitsyn and Rostropovich went to see him. Solzhenitsyn knew how delightedly Tvardovsky had received the news of his Nobel Prize in hospital. "Bravo! Bravo! Victory!" he was said to have cried to the nurses. To Roy Medvedev, who had visited him at the end of October, he had said, "It is our prize too," meaning *Novy Mir*'s.[8] Solzhenitsyn found him still partly paralysed and gave him the freshly completed typescript of *August 1914* to read (Tvardovsky had seen an earlier version the preceding spring, but not the complete text). He also read him his letter to Suslov—reminding Tvardovsky that it was he who had introduced them—and told him of all the difficulties surrounding the Nobel Prize and his manoeuvres to get it presented in Moscow. Tvardovsky could still hardly speak, but intermittently beamed his interest and approval. Before leaving, Solzhenitsyn devised a system of different-coloured markers so that Tvardovsky could indicate which parts of *August 1914* he liked and which parts he didn't—he was still anxious to have Tvardovsky's opinion, despite their many squabbles. The markers were for use in case Tvardovsky's speech failed to improve or deteriorated.

It must have been just before or just after this visit that Solzhenitsyn finished the third part of *The Oak and the Calf*, in which he described his expulsion from the Writers' Union and the breaking up of *Novy Mir*. There we find strident criticism of Tvardovsky's behaviour and the harsh and unfeeling reflection on Tvardovsky's cancer that was to shock so many readers when the memoir was published: "Cancer is the fate of all who give themselves up to moods of bilious, corrosive resentment and depression. People can live through hardship, but from hard feelings they perish."[9] Yet in the next part of the memoir, describing Solzhenitsyn's February visit, there was an immensely tender description of Tvardovsky's disablement and of the understanding between the two men.

> AT's powers of active response were paralysed, but kindly feeling streamed from his eyes unstemmed, and his face, exhausted as it was by illness, still retained its old, childlike expression.
> When AT was particularly anxious to finish saying something and could not manage it, I helped him out by taking his left hand—which was warm, and free and alive. He squeezed my hand in reply, and in this way we understood each other well enough. . . . Understood that all was forgiven between us. That all the bad things, the hurts, the troubles, might never have been.[10]

Which mood represented the true Solzhenitsyn? Both, of course, which is what made him so baffling to deal with.

Negotiations with the Swedish embassy had come to a temporary halt. The Soviet authorities had in the end expelled Per Hegge, and Solzhenitsyn was having trouble with the Nobel lecture that he had promised to write. He felt drained by the emotional stresses he was undergoing and found himself listless and apathetic. "I had thought of my Nobel lecture beforehand as a scouring peal of bells. This, more than anything else, made the prize worthwhile. I sat down to it, I even wrote it, but it came out in a form difficult to digest." He was anxious to write about social and political problems, whereas he had deduced from the speeches of his predecessors that the main theme should be art and literature. He tried to combine the two, but friends to whom he showed the lecture pronounced it a failure. Solzhenitsyn then wrote to the Nobel Foundation asking whether he might forgo the lecture, since he was having difficulty sticking to the theme, and the foundation readily agreed. However, in an effort to "shield" the author, as it thought, from the adverse publicity attendant upon an admission that he preferred to write on social and political themes, the foundation invented a reason of its own. Solzhenitsyn would not be writing a lecture, it announced, because he did not know how to deliver it. If he sent it openly through the mail, it would be intercepted by the censorship; if he sent it secretly, he would be accused of committing a crime.[11]

The intention was perfectly laudable, but it backfired. The foundation could not see that this seeming admission of his impotence—and acceptance of the Soviet rules—was for Solzhenitsyn more damaging than the real reason. When he heard the Nobel announcement on the BBC's Russian Service, he was furious and the next day fired off a telegram to Nils Ståhle, the foundation's director. It is not clear whether Ståhle received it, but a few days later Solzhenitsyn released it to reporters in Moscow. "I am extremely surprised by your explanation of the motivation for my refusal to deliver a Nobel lecture. I never expressed any such thing to you. If some explanation is necessary at all, you ought to cite the truth: the very genre of the lecture on literature is alien to me—to talk of the nature of art, creation, and beauty and to avoid broad judgments on present social life and its ulcers. . . . I sincerely ask you to correct your mistake and make it public."[12] Characteristically, he now resolved to write the lecture after all.

There were other niggles and anxieties that spring. The Nobel Prize brought with it the sum of about $78,000 at the then current rates of exchange, and Solzhenitsyn wanted to have at least a part of it to take care of his new family. The Soviet authorities, however, could not miss this opportunity to make life difficult for him. When he asked for $3,000 to be transferred to his account in dollar certificates for use in Moscow's hard-currency shops, the government insisted on levying a 30 per cent tax. Solzhenitsyn protested that this was prize money and not subject to tax, but the government refused to listen.

That spring an attempt was made to evict Solzhenitsyn from Rostropovich's dacha in Zhukovka. It was understandable that Solzhenitsyn's presence there rankled. Zhukovka and the adjacent district of Barvikha were élite enclaves, completely closed to ordinary Soviet citizens, let alone to social outcasts like Solzhenitsyn. And Solzhenitsyn was living there quite unofficially, without being registered. One day in March, he returned from a short jaunt on skis to find a small police delegation awaiting him, led by the head of the Moscow regional passport office, Anosov. This was not the first visit by the police. A captain had called to see him the preceding autumn but appeared to have been satisfied when Solzhenitsyn informed him that he was a guest of Rostropovich. Now the police had returned in greater force and at a higher level—there was a major in addition to the head of the passport office, and another captain as well.

Solzhenitsyn was aware that his situation was delicate. According to Soviet law, every Soviet citizen was supposed to be registered in his place of main residence, and Solzhenitsyn's registration was in Ryazan. This move against him was therefore not unexpected. But he hadn't the slightest intention of complying and with his usual thoroughness had already composed a letter of protest to the police, ready to send off (and release into samizdat) the moment that anything happened: "Serfdom was abolished in our country in 1861. The October Revolution is said to have swept away the last remnants of it. I am, therefore, a free citizen of this country, not a serf or a slave. . . ." When Anosov and the police officers informed him of the purpose of their visit, he was not surprised and greeted them calmly, even affably, trying to bluff them into dropping the whole matter and implying that they would get into some kind of undefined "trouble" if they persisted with their mission. When they insisted that he do something about obtaining a residence permit or return to Ryazan, and informed him of their decision to report him, he lost his temper and exclaimed defiantly, "I won't do it! Make my own way to Ryazan? I'll neither go nor let myself be carried there. And if the court issues an order? I won't obey it! If I go, it will be in chains!"[13] As usual with bureaucrats, the histrionics worked. The police delegation withdrew abashed, and Solzhenitsyn was not obliged to release his fiery letter on "serfdom" after all.

But Solzhenitsyn's private life was still in turmoil. Natalia had failed to return to Moscow after the November holidays, and he had no idea where she had gone or what her plans were. In fact she had gone to the countryside to stay with some friends from the Agricultural Institute in Ryazan, and had taken Solzhenitsyn's early letters with her, especially those written from the *sharashka* and later in 1956, when they were coming together again. She immersed herself in their tender and eloquent rhetoric, so replete with affirmations of eternal love, vividly recalling the years of their greatest happiness and lulling her into a belief that her marriage could still be saved. Her Ryazan friends, in whom she had once confided when deciding to leave Vsevolod and return to Solzhenitsyn, seem to have encouraged her in the belief that a divorce was avoidable, and she decided to travel north to Riga to consult a lawyer there. On the way, she classified and copied out extracts from Solzhenitsyn's letters to support the point that he truly loved her and had sworn eternal fidelity, but the lawyer was obliged to disabuse her: a divorce in their circumstances, where there was another woman and a baby, was virtually guaranteed under Soviet law. The letters touched only the moral aspect of their relations and had no bearing on legal matters. She advised Natalia to look for a job and to adopt a child if, as she claimed, she felt so strongly about her childlessness.[14]

Natalia was not satisfied with this and returned to Ryazan. On the way to Riga, under the influence of Solzhenitsyn's old letters, she had decided to make a start on her memoirs at last and found that the writing acted as a form of therapy. For several weeks she worked away at the opening chapters, and the more she wrote, the more she convinced herself that a divorce was unthinkable. Eventually, she returned to Moscow, but the very thought of Solzhenitsyn with Svetlova and the child made her insanely jealous, just as a visit to her mother in Ryazan and the sight of their flat brought on uncontrollable fits of weeping. Her isolation in Moscow was compounded by a quarrel with the Steins. She felt that Veronica had betrayed her by going to meet Svetlova and see the baby and by accompanying Solzhenitsyn to the Sovremennik Theatre after Natalia's "disappearance," as if to set the seal of public approval on Solzhenitsyn's new family. Natalia found such behaviour on the part of her cousin disloyal and "demonic" and refused to have any more to do with her. Another painful spot was her relationship with her former piano teacher Maria Yudina. Yudina was shocked by the rift between Natalia and Solzhenitsyn, but Natalia could not bring herself to tell Yudina who the other woman was, because Svetlova (who had been baptized only recently) was Yudina's god-daughter. Yudina subsequently learned the truth from Nadezhda Mandelstam and planned to write Solzhenitsyn a letter, but soon afterwards caught pneumonia and died without doing so.[15]

Natalia and Solzhenitsyn finally met again on 26 February 1971—Natalia's birthday. Solzhenitsyn, according to Natalia, was filled with remorse, wept, and said how relieved he was that Natalia had taken sleeping tablets instead of the mandrake infusion and had survived. When she asked whether she could move back to Zhukovka with him, he said that he would rather not just yet and that she should "wait a year," meaning a year from the time of her attempted suicide. He feared that otherwise Zhukovka would only remind her of what had happened there and have a depressing effect on her. In return, he agreed that he would do nothing about a divorce until then, so that she would have time to recover her strength and build a new life.[16]

The knowledge that Natalia was set against a divorce was extremely painful for Solzhenitsyn, and life was made even more difficult when Natalia began visiting their old friends (the Kopelevs, Chukovskys, Etkinds, Panin, Suzanna Teush, Father Shpiller) to seek their support and to show them extracts from the letters she had been reading (she also sent some of the extracts to Solzhenitsyn himself to remind him of his former love for her). Although discreet and tactful by nature, she now flaunted these intimacies as weapons in her private struggle, and Solzhenitsyn did not know how to react. Seemingly all-powerful in his confrontation with the Soviet government, bestriding the world's stage with his books, his public statements, and his actions, he was yet helpless when faced with the wrath of a discarded woman. One is reminded of Cyril Connolly's dictum that "in the sex war, thoughtlessness is the weapon of the male, vindictiveness of the female," and no remark could better summarize the relations between the Solzhenitsyns. Not the least of the many surprising features of Solzhenitsyn's memoir, *The Oak and the Calf*, is the veil of silence he draws over this dramatic struggle, which paralleled and at times completely overshadowed the public battle he was engaged in. Only occasionally does he drop his guard and slip in a hint about the true state of affairs—as in the following explanation of his exhaustion in the spring of 1971.

> I felt this way largely because that side of my life which tension and ceaseless motion had caused me to disregard, to let slip, to leave out of account, came to the fore, painfully forced itself upon me, left me more exhausted than another man would have been in my place, drained more of my strength perhaps than all the pot-holes on the highway of my life. For the preceding five years I had put up with a deep, an abysmal marital rift, and had continually postponed any decisive action: I was invariably short of time to finish some work, or some part of a work, and every time I backed down, coaxed, wheedled, just to gain another three months, one month, two weeks of precious working time, so as not to be torn away from what mattered most to me.[17]

Now that his mind was made up, however, he still found himself uncharacteristically helpless. At the same time, he was depressed and debilitated by the knowledge that he could do practically nothing for the moment to aid and protect Svetlova and their child. Without a divorce, he was powerless to marry her and give the child his name. This meant that if the worst came to the worst, and he was imprisoned or exiled abroad, she would have no standing in his affairs. She would have the right neither to visit him, nor to follow him abroad, nor to receive his income, nor to manage his literary estate. He could not obtain for her any of the money that was rightfully his without going through a humiliating procedure specially devised for this purpose. After Solzhenitsyn had protested against the levying of the tax, the Ministry of Foreign Trade had decreed that each of his applications to receive a portion of the money should be examined by a special committee and that each time it should take a separate decision on whether to pay the money over, in what form, and at what exchange rate. In this way the Nobel Prize winner was effectively prevented from enjoying his prize.

To overcome some of these difficulties, Solzhenitsyn made a redoubled effort to see that his last will and testament was properly legal and watertight, and sent a copy to Dr Heeb in Switzerland. As an earnest of Solzhenitsyn's newly awakened concern for political and religious opponents of the regime, the will decreed that in the event of Solzhenitsyn's death, disappearance, or imprisonment, a fund for social purposes would be set up to help political prisoners and their families in the Soviet Union. The money for it would come from his royalties, particularly the royalties from *The Gulag Archipelago*, and he hoped that others would make contributions once the fund was established. Elaborate arrangements were made for the publication of his still-unpublished works, and Natalia Svetlova was designated his main beneficiary and main executor. In the event of his death or disappearance, the will was to be published world-wide within two weeks, and in such circumstances, "no protest from me, in writing or by word of mouth, from prison or in any other place where my freedom is restricted, can cancel or modify a single point or a single word in this will."[18]

In addition to his will, Solzhenitsyn succeeded in sending to Dr Heeb the balance of his literary archive, including an additional copy of *The Gulag Archipelago*. He was not prepared to publish it yet. On the contrary, he had decided to put off publication for several more years. Had he gone to the West, as he had half expected, to collect the Nobel Prize, he would have published it right away, according to his original plan. But now he was "trying to think up an excuse for deferring it, for delaying the cup that I could not in the end put from me." He decided that he was justified on two grounds. First, publication might hurt some of the 227 ex-prisoners who had given him their testimony. Secondly, he needed more time to write his series of novels on the Revolution. "The Gulag was only the offspring of the Revolution and heir to it: if I had had to write about Gulag in secrecy, writing about the Revolution required even greater secrecy, deeper burrowing, stranger contortions. To make haste with the Revolution was even more important, certainly no less urgent. And as things had happened, it was I who must do it." It was, of course, a rationalization of other needs, as Solzhenitsyn secretly acknowledged to himself (". . . it was not just an excuse, though if I am to be strict with myself I shall do better to acknowledge it as such"), and in the end he hit on a compromise: he would postpone a decision until Lenin came to play a decisive role in his series of novels. This would come in about book 4. At the rate he was going, that might give him from three to six years more. In the meantime, he would suppress the chapters in which Lenin appeared in the first three volumes, much as he had done with the controversial chapters in the original version of *The First Circle*. Having made this decision, he felt, as he reports, much happier. "This final deadline brought light and ease into my life. For the time being, postpone everything else, and work, work, work. But after that, a head-on clash was inevitable. There were no more loopholes."[19]

But he still needed to have an additional copy of *Gulag* in the West, for relations with the Carlisles were beginning to deteriorate, and he felt he no longer completely trusted them. Olga had been to see Dr Heeb the preceding summer and had arranged to hand over a sum of money representing the world-wide royalties of *The First Circle*. The sum would have been greater, apparently, had she not insisted that she should keep some back as a reserve against expenses on *Gulag*, but it would still not amount to as much as Solzhenitsyn had anticipated. Secondly, Olga was decidedly reluctant to let any part of the manuscript of *The Gulag Archipelago* out of her hands and, according to Solzhenitsyn, was refusing to let Dr Heeb have a copy. She still felt that she should control world-wide publication, and Solzhenitsyn did not wish to provoke an open break, partly because he feared his secret might come out and partly because he was genuinely grateful to Olga Carlisle for what she had done for him. What is more, she had recently informed him—or so he understood—that the English translation of *Gulag* was ready, which meant that when the time came the all-important American edition could be published in a matter of weeks.[20]

With his literary affairs more or less in order, Solzhenitsyn was ready to deliver his next blow to the Soviet government—the open publication in the West of *August 1914*. It meant a great step forward from his previous position with regard to *The First Circle* and *Cancer Ward*. Then he had been obliged to dissemble, pretending that he had had nothing to do with Western publication and disapproved of it and that he would prefer publication in his homeland. Now he knew that Soviet publication was out of the question, even though there was little in the novel to which the Soviet censorship could take exception. He was irrevocably *persona non grata*, beyond the pale, and not even a eulogy of Brezhnev could appear over his name. He could therefore afford to come out into the open.

Even so he felt the need for some sort of smoke-screen, however thin and transparent, and he decided to offer the novel to a number of Soviet publishing houses first. The chances that they would accept the offer were infinitesimal, but it would blunt any future accusation that he was turning his back on his homeland or deliberately going abroad first. He could always say that he had offered them the novel in good faith and that they had rejected it, and that only then had he sought publication abroad. The problem was that he did not wish to send the manuscript, because he was afraid of its being copied and finding its way into samizdat before he could publish it himself. At Rostropovich's suggestion, he sent letters to seven publishers informing them of the novel's completion and asking them whether they were interested in publishing it. There were obvious risks involved—one of the publishers might ask to see it—but in the event, none of them did, and the way ahead was clear.

This strategy of camouflage worked beautifully, as is clear from a Moscow dispatch that appeared in the *New York Times* that spring.

> Solzhenitsyn was reported today to have offered his latest novel *August 1914* to several Soviet publishing houses in the hope that the authorities would end the ban on the printing of his works in this country.
>
> Friends . . . said that early last month Mr. Solzhenitsyn sent letters . . . inquiring if they were interested in seeing the manuscript.
>
> As of a few days ago, Mr. Solzhenitsyn had not received a reply.

The friends in question were reported to have described Solzhenitsyn's actions as "stubborn," since they had advised him to take the manuscript personally to the publishing houses and not wait for them to reply. The article continued:

> But the 52-year-old novelist has refused to show the manuscript in advance for two reasons, they said. The first relates to his feeling that as the winner of the Nobel Prize, he should be approached by the publishers. The other is a fear that the manuscript might be smuggled overseas if he allowed it to circulate freely.[21]

The deception was complete. Not even the friends he used to pass information to the press knew the full story, so that one of his major fears appeared to be foreign publication. This cover would be blown as soon as the Paris edition appeared, but for the time being no one could suspect what was in store—once again, the Soviet authorities seemed to have been put in the wrong.

On 11 June 1971 the charge was detonated. The YMCA presented to the press gleamingly fresh copies, still smelling of printer's ink, of *August 1914*, complete and unabridged, in the original Russian. The accompanying statement was brief and noncommittal, merely noting that the subject of the novel was the early days of the First World War on the eastern front and that it was the first of a planned multi-volume work. The author's copyright was emphasized, and Dr Heeb was said to be ready to prosecute any unauthorized publication or translation.

Curiosity about the novel was intense. The first rumours of its existence had leaked as early as the preceding November, at the height of the fuss over the Nobel Prize, but despite the novel's title, nobody had quite expected the severely historical novel that it turned out to be. Solzhenitsyn's chief subject was indeed the start of the First World War, and in particular the disastrous advance of General Samsonov into East Prussia and his resounding defeat at the Battle of Tannenberg. This was the subject that Solzhenitsyn had studied with such ardour all those years ago in the libraries of Rostov, as a callow youth of nineteen, and he was immensely satisfied to have brought it to fruition. It seemed an affirmation of the rightness of his choice of subject, and of a continuity and consistency in his career that he had feared broken by his imprisonment and exile.

The Samsonov campaign was what he called a "nodal point" (a term borrowed from mathematics) in history, a moment in the sweep of time that exemplified the development—and conflict—of forces critical for man's destiny. Each of his planned series of novels would be devoted to one nodal point (which is why he was calling them "nodes" or "knots" rather than novels), consisting of ten to twenty days described in great detail and density, and the aim was to plot the graph of this period of Russian history by fixing these points along a curve. In discussing this first volume later, Solzhenitsyn had this to say about his intentions.

> My idea in the first node was as follows. I couldn't portray the whole of the First World War, even though its history has never been told in our country, so I decided to choose a single event—a battle—and through it show the whole war. I had made this choice as early as 1937, when I was only nineteen. . . . And it's characteristic that when I returned to this subject many years later, in 1969, I was able to keep a number of the earlier chapters in the same compositional function, though of course the texture, the actual writing, and the images had to be reworked in that I was an adult now.[22]

Solzhenitsyn had been able to draw on his military experiences for the battle scenes. The technology was different, of course, but military strategy had not changed all that much, and his memories of artillery service were put to particularly good use in *August 1914*. Solzhenitsyn had not yet fictionalized his army experiences, which seemed such a natural subject for a man with a military cast of mind and a fondness for military metaphors. As he noted in *The Gulag Archipelago*, his army novel had "gone up in smoke" in the Lubyanka furnaces when his notebooks were burned. But here it was at last, in extended and loving detail, the experiences that Solzhenitsyn had garnered in fighting over this terrain in 1944–45, but transposed backwards in time. In a very real sense (and this was noted by readers), a part of his heart had remained in East Prussia, whose neat villages and apple-pie farms were to stay forever with him as an image of European civilization.

It was no accident that Solzhenitsyn's father had also fought in this campaign or that he turned up in the novel under the barely disguised name of Isaaki (nicknamed "Sanya") Lazhenitsyn. Indeed, most of the members of Solzhenitsyn's family appeared in the pages devoted to scenes behind the lines in provincial Russia, including Grandfather Zakhar, Uncle Roman, Aunt Irina (all under their own Christian names, though with Shcherbak metamorphosed into Tomchak), and above all his mother Taissia (here renamed Xenia). Also here were Taissia's stern schoolmistress and patron, Alexandra Andreyeva (Kharitonova in the novel), with her husband, daughter, and son, and mixed up with them, the Fedorovskys (Arkhangorodskys) from Solzhenitsyn's own childhood. So his youth—that other untouched period—was partly here too, especially in the descriptions of his paternal grandfather's farm in Sablia and his reminiscences of Rostov. Rostov in the New Economic Policy period was hardly different from what it had been before the First World War, and it was that atmosphere, those colours, and those sights and smells that Solzhenitsyn associated with what he now took to be the golden age of pre-revolutionary Russia. What he had not known and seen personally in his childhood he had made up for with conversations with his relatives during visits to Kislovodsk, Pyatigorsk, Georgievsk, and Armavir in 1956 and 1964.

These pastoral scenes of the North Caucasus and southern Russia were obviously the "peace" parts of what was Solzhenitsyn's bid to write a twentieth-century *War and Peace*. Spiritually and intellectually, he had in many ways abandoned Tolstoy for Dostoyevsky, but the old sage's influence on him was still strong, as was shown by Solzhenitsyn's argument in the pages of *August 1914* with Tolstoy's theory of history (Isaaki is portrayed as literally meeting and arguing with Tolstoy about something else—Tolstoy's theory of love) and above all by the force of Tolstoy's example. He was, for Solzhenitsyn, the very model of what a major Russian author ought to be.

When *August 1914* appeared, Solzhenitsyn was more than usually nervous about readers' reactions. For the first time he had stepped out of his immediate experience and tried to deal with a period not his own. He had done his research with typical thoroughness, right down to the study of social minutiae. Andrei Sinyavsky's wife, Maria Rozanova, who was friendly with Natalia Svetlova and had once trained as a jeweller, tells of being introduced to Solzhenitsyn at about this time and of being asked to advise him on what jewels ladies wore before the Revolution, and on what occasions. She told him what she knew, and he jotted her answers down on an elaborate chart he had compiled, covering dress, jewellery, and various other aspects of social behaviour.[23] This was for his next novel, *March 1916*, but the same technique had evidently been applied to *August 1914*. The winter before releasing *August 1914*, he had also distributed thirty copies of the novel to friends with a questionnaire that they were to fill out, detailing their criticisms—"because the historical novel was new to me."[24] He had evidently anticipated more criticism than usual, and this made him extra sensitive to it.

One touching detail is that he was particularly anxious to have Tvardovsky's opinion of the novel, and one reason for his dismay at finding Tvardovsky paralysed and unable to talk in February had been his disappointment at not being able to hear Tvardovsky's verdict. On a return visit in May, he had found Tvardovsky considerably improved—he was able to move one whole side of his body and to talk a little—and Solzhenitsyn had been gratified to hear his novel pronounced "marvellous." Despite his patronizing attitude to Tvardovsky's social and political views, he still respected the older man's literary taste, and nothing was more important to him than the latter's approval.

The initial impact of the book's publication on the West was inevitably political and commercial. The boldness and originality of Solzhenitsyn's gesture (not to speak of its apparently impeccable legality) immediately caught the world's headlines: once again the intrepid and embattled author had outwitted his clumsy persecutors, while the book's appearance in Russian set off a wild scramble for translation rights among Western publishers that far exceeded the early competition for *Cancer Ward* and *The First Circle*.

Solzhenitsyn was under the impression that with a Western lawyer in place and with himself releasing a single copy of *August 1914* for initial publication in Russian, he could control its translation, distribution, and publication in the West as successfully as any "normal" author from a "normal" country, and in a manner that would make up for the deficiencies in the publication of his earlier works. But the battery of obstacles—extra-legal, legal, social, and psychological—placed in the way of such an operation by the Soviet authorities proved to be too much for him. Without the possibility of direct and open communication, he was obliged to delegate everything to intermediaries, and above all to Dr Heeb, who, with all his industry, integrity, and dedication to Solzhenitsyn's cause, was unable to cope with the enormity of the task.

Faced with an avalanche of telegrams, letters, and phone calls from interested publishers, but inexperienced in literary matters, Heeb took the apparently sensible step of placing world rights to the novel in the hands of Dr Otto Walter of the small, independent German publishing firm of Luchterhand. Heeb was familiar with Luchterhand as the publishers of the German edition of *Cancer Ward*. The preceding year he had confirmed their edition as the "official" one in his eyes and had granted them the exclusive right to bring out a new translation of Solzhenitsyn's short stories and prose poems in a single volume. Luchterhand had acquired their original title to *Cancer Ward* from the Bodley Head in England, and Heeb had simultaneously recognized Bodley Head's world rights to *Cancer Ward*, as well as to Solzhenitsyn's play *The Tenderfoot and the Tart* (which the Bodley Head had recently published in a limp translation under the even limper title of *The Love-girl and the Innocent*). In doing so, Heeb seems implicitly to have recognized Pavel Ličko's original claim to represent Solzhenitsyn in this matter— a claim with some justice, though Solzhenitsyn later denied it, and it is not clear whether that was part of Heeb's plan. It was a side-effect of his pragmatic idea of finding someone capable of handling the matter, and Heeb had apparently been more pleased by his dealings with the *Cancer Ward* team (Bodley Head, Luchterhand, Farrar, Straus and Giroux, in America, and Mondadori, in Italy) than by those with *The First Circle* team, consisting of the Carlisles and Harper & Row. Not surprisingly, the relevant rights to *August 1914* went to none other than Luchterhand, the Bodley Head, Farrar, Straus and Giroux, and Mondadori.

The decision was controversial at the time. It was well known in America that Farrar, Straus and Giroux were far from being the highest bidders: Little, Brown, of Boston, had offered $600,000 for the U.S. rights, almost twice what Farrar ultimately paid. In Germany, Fischer (the German publishers of *The First Circle*) offered $80,000, Suhrkamp $165,000, and Langen-Müller an undisclosed amount that they claimed was "in any case more than anyone else had offered," but Luchterhand paid only $104,000 for the entire world rights.[25] The arrangement was presented as a triumph for literary values and the integrity of the small companies over the cheque-wielding affiliates of conglomerates, and it is true that the personal qualities of the men heading these firms (Otto Walter, Max Reinhardt, of Bodley Head, and Roger Straus, of Farrar, Straus and Giroux) weighed heavily with a man of such obvious sincerity as Dr Heeb. But it cannot be said that the cause of better translations, which Solzhenitsyn had announced as one of his twin aims in retaining Dr Heeb, had been noticeably served by the deal. The Bodley-Farrar translation of *Cancer Ward* (Solzhenitsyn's easiest book) had been less than distinguished, their translation of *Tenderfoot* pathetic, and their "new" version of *Ivan Denisovich* (prepared as a basis for the film script) was an uninspired rehash of the two main existing translations. In Germany, Luchterhand had produced a lacklustre *Cancer Ward* (distributing the work among three translators for speed), and the translator of a new *Ivan Denisovich* version had removed her name from the translation as a result of "editorial improvements" made by the publisher. In short, there was no existing reason, other than the "niceness" of the proprietors, to expect any better translations from these houses than from others, or any improvement on the past. It was a cosy arrangement that, as the translation arrangements—and the result—were ultimately to show, moved Solzhenitsyn not a whit forward in his quest for accurate versions of his works. Only in France was a sort of progress made. Luchterhand sold the rights for *August 1914* to Editions du Seuil, a committed Catholic publishing house with a strong interest in social and political issues. Apart from having recently issued a collection of documents on the "Solzhenitsyn affair," Le Seuil had had no contact with Solzhenitsyn's works until now, but it was to assume an increasingly important role in the future.

Solzhenitsyn's other aim in publishing directly in the West was to put an end to pirated editions of his works, but in this, too, he was only partially successful. Within two months the indefatigable Alexander Flegon* had brought out an unauthorized photocopy of the YMCA original, with illustrations supplied by Flegon himself. He then had the effrontery to offer translation and serial rights to the very companies that had signed an agreement for them with the Bodley Head. At the same time, as a result of Heeb's refusal of the highest bids for the novel and the deals he concluded at more modest terms, rumours began to circulate, especially in Germany, that Heeb was not Solzhenitsyn's true representative at all or that he was deliberately flouting Solzhenitsyn's interest for the sake of some other, more mysterious goals. So persistent were these rumours that Solzhenitsyn was obliged to issue two statements on the subject, one of which he sent to Heeb and the other to Per Hegge in Norway, asking the latter to publicize it in the Western press. Among other things he denounced Flegon by name, and the Bodley Head was able to stop this illegal edition by means of a writ in the British courts.[26]

Not long afterwards, on 21 October 1971, the Langen-Müller publishing house of Munich announced to a startled world its publication that day of a complete German translation of *August 1914* in a print run planned to reach one hundred thousand copies. The translator, Alexander Kaempfe, had apparently translated nearly six hundred pages of dense and difficult Russian into eight hundred pages of German in about fifteen weeks—if not a record, then at least a major feat of translation. Kaempfe, although he had worked in haste, was no hack. He was recognized as one of Germany's top translators from Russian, and the embarrassing part of it was that Luchterhand had also tried to commission him, but he had declined on the grounds that he was "too busy." His defection was a double blow, particularly since the German record of translating Solzhenitsyn was no better than the English.

*Flegon specialized in publishing Russian-language editions of works that had appeared in the Soviet Union in samizdat and had no copyright protection. He had earlier published Russian editions of both *Cancer Ward* and *The First Circle* (neither of them authorized) and had produced photographic reprints of *A Day in the Life of Ivan Denisovich* and "Matryona's Place" from the texts in *Novy Mir*. In the case of *August 1914*, Flegon argued that the work had circulated in samizdat prior to its publication by the YMCA Press and therefore did not fall under the copyright laws. He also claimed, when challenged in court by the Bodley Head, that in publishing his novel abroad, Solzhenitsyn had broken Soviet law and that he therefore could not claim copyright in it. Thirdly, he maintained that Solzhenitsyn's agreement with Dr Heeb was also illegal under Soviet law and thus null and void. He lost on all three counts.

Of the two main *Ivan Denisovich* translations, one had been translated not from Russian but from English, while the other was the work of four different hands. The Luchterhand experience with their *Ivan Denisovich* and *Cancer Ward* has already been mentioned, and even *The First Circle*, the work of only two translators, had been spoiled by haste.[27]

Luchterhand's embarrassment over the Kaempfe translation was compounded by the fact that their own plan was to bring out the translation the following August, a whole year hence, for someone had conceived the curious notion that it would be a nice publicity gimmick if all fifteen planned translations of the novel were issued in the same month—"August" in August. This, too, was to end up causing problems, but for the time being, Luchterhand tried to plug the dam by securing an injunction against Langen-Müller. Herbert Fleissner, a swashbuckling Sudeten German who had made a fortune out of his popular newspapers and who was the managing director of Langen-Müller,* also tried to claim that Solzhenitsyn's novel had circulated in samizdat and therefore was in the public domain. When it was pointed out that samizdat did not constitute publication under the terms of the Universal Copyright Convention (Solzhenitsyn had been careful not to give it to samizdat anyway), he changed his tune and argued that Solzhenitsyn had had foreknowledge of his translation and approved it. This was easily demonstrated to be false, and Fleissner lost his case.[28]

A subsidiary reason of Solzhenitsyn's for wanting to publish his book openly in the West was his desire to reach readers in the Russian emigration and to ask for their help. He was aware that the older ones would not only remember many of the events he was describing but also see them from a perspective that was different from the accepted Soviet one. In the freer atmosphere of the West, they would have been able to preserve documents, letters, and family archives that were too dangerous for Soviet citizens to possess. In a special postscript to the novel, after explaining how he saw his historical task, Solzhenitsyn described his difficulties and concluded with the following appeal.

> I am now publishing the first node of my work for Russian readers abroad with a simultaneous plea for criticism, corrections, and supplements, especially with regard to historical personages on whom I have little material. . .
>
> I would be grateful for any unpublished materials relating to subsequent years, but strictly with respect to the following places. . . .

* It appears that Fleissner had both personal and professional reasons for wanting to pull off his coup. As a German who had been expelled from the Sudetenland after the war, he was in any case bitterly anti-Communist. One company in his publishing group had published one of the original German translations of *Ivan Denisovich*, and Fleissner seems to have felt that he had a personal interest in Solzhenitsyn. But perhaps the main motive was Fleissner's wish for a major literary scoop to affirm his importance as a publisher. Sometime beforehand, he had been manoeuvred out of the exclusive German publishers' club known as Books of the Nineteen, supposedly on account of the flamboyancy and sensationalism of his popular newspapers, and his place had been taken by none other than Luchterhand. He therefore had a double motive for wishing to upstage Luchterhand on this occasion.

I am hopeful that the publishers will take on themselves the work of collecting for me any material that is sent in.[29]

There was an extra stroke of boldness in this appeal. The Russian *émigrés* had traditionally been regarded by the Soviet government as unmentionable. Every effort was made to portray them as renegades and traitors, the person-ification of counter-revolutionary decadence and black reaction. To maintain contact with or show an interest in them was in itself potentially seditious, and Soviet citizens were encouraged to ignore the *émigrés'* existence com-pletely and regard them and their children as consigned to "the rubbish bin of history." Publishing a book that not only might be read sympathetically by *émigrés* but was specifically intended "for Russian readers abroad" was doubly provocative, and it announced yet another of Solzhenitsyn's ambi-tious intentions, namely, to bring the departed Russian millions back—met-aphorically, at least—into the national fold, to heal the split caused by the Revolution and Civil War, and to show that it was by no means irrevocable or irreversible. It was part of that same impulse that had informed his sym-pathetic portrayal of former Vlasovites and *émigrés* in his early (unpublished) plays. The Russians were all one people and should be together. His passion-ate desire was for national unity and harmony, matching his deeply felt reli-gious impulse towards the old Russian ideal of *sobornost** in national life. Like all his other intellectual enterprises, it was vastly ambitious and, also like them, seemed to fly in the face of history. But that was not sufficient to deter him now. If one of his aims in publishing his big series of novels was to reverse the consequences of the October Revolution, the other was to restore unity to his divided and suffering people.

Sobornost is difficult to define. Briefly, it suggests that a familial, spiritual consensus should replace formal legalism as the guiding principle of national life and that unity should be the nation's goal. The idea goes back to medieval times and was later taken up by the Slavophiles and by the Russian religious philosopher Nikolai Berdyayev.

40

DEATH OF
A POET

I T WAS SOLZHENITSYN's fate to launch all his major books after *Ivan Denisov-ich* into a critical vacuum. *The First Circle* and *Cancer Ward* had leaked out in fits and starts to Russian readers through samizdat and then through foreign editions. There never was a "publication date" with readers' and crit-ics' responses flowing in as a natural consequence and in an even tempo. Instead, the responses arrived piecemeal, usually distorted by political pres-sures of one kind or another, and the mass of Russian readers remained igno-rant of his works. In the case of *August 1914*, there had at least been a publication date in Paris, but apart from the responses of a small number *émigré* readers (and critics in *émigré* journals) who were able to absorb it at once, there was again an unnatural silence. Western reactions to the book would have to wait until the translations appeared, and Soviet Russian responses until sufficient copies had trickled back to the homeland to find an informed readership there.

In the official Soviet press throughout 1971 there were not only no reviews but no responses of any kind. Such silences in the past had usually been short-lived, indicating a period of indecision until the Central Committee's ideological department had determined what the official line should be, but on this occasion the silence stretched right through the summer and autumn and into winter. It began to seem that the authorities had grown wiser and were going to try the more intelligent tactic of simply ignoring Solzhenitsyn's manoeuvre and waiting for the memory of it to fade. But a disquieting inci-dent in the summer indicated that this was probably not the case, and that something threatening was being prepared.

As so often happens, the revelation of what was afoot was the result of a series of accidents. Deprived of the opportunity of living at Rozhdestvo that summer (he had agreed to let Natalia have the use of their cottage and because of the extreme tension between them was unwilling to risk a meeting with her), Soltzhenitsyn felt restless and disoriented. At the same time, he felt an urge to travel south and revisit the scenes of his childhood and youth and gather more material. The writing of *August 1914* had returned his thoughts to this period with particular force, and even more to the years preceding his birth. As he mulled over his plans for the following novels in his series, dealing with the years of the Revolution and Civil War, he must have recalled the stories told him by his mother and aunts and have tried to reconstruct their lives in Rostov, Armavir, and Kislovodsk, both before and after the Revolution. The stories that had awed and terrified him as a child, that had subsequently been dismissed as exaggerated old wives' tales and counter-revolutionary propaganda during the years of his confident orthodoxy, and that had returned to haunt and fuel his rage in the writing of *The Gulag Archipelago*, now awaited the direct efforts of his pen in his chronicle of the times. He felt a need for greater detail about the early experiences of his family, and had accordingly written to Aunt Irina in Georgievsk—now eighty-two and more eccentric than ever, but still vigorous and lucid—to ask her to write down her memories for him. In August 1971 he set off for the south to visit her. He was travelling with a friend in the friend's car, and they had got as far as Tikhoretsk—within spitting distance of his grandfather's old estate and half a day's drive from Georgievsk—when the car heater came on and jammed. The two men tried to carry on with the windows open, but the heat in the North Caucasus in August is intense, and it was impossible to continue. They got out of the car and attempted to disconnect the hoses. It was midday. Solzhenitsyn was wearing a pair of shorts and nothing else. As the sun blazed down out of a clear blue sky, the temperature went up into the nineties, and Solzhenitsyn was smitten with sunstroke.* Well before evening his arms, legs, chest, and back had swelled up and become covered with huge blisters, and he was vomiting. Every movement caused him intense pain. For the "walrus," heat was the deadliest enemy.[1]

Frightened by the idea of booking Solzhenitsyn into a local hospital, the friend managed to get him to the nearest railway station and put him in a sleeper for Moscow. He then telegraphed Ekaterina Svetlova to meet the train, warning her that she would have to take someone along to help carry or support the stricken Solzhenitsyn. Ekaterina asked a young engineer colleague, Alexander Gorlov, to go with her to the Kursk station, where they found the swollen Solzhenitsyn prostrate in his bunk, barely able to move or walk. With difficulty they got him back to Rostropovich's. A doctor diagnosed an extreme form of heat allergy and commenced a course of treatment that had to be continued for four months before Solzhenitsyn was able to walk and move without pain.[2]

It was now that the accident led to unforeseen consequences. Once the

---

* It appears that Solzhenitsyn's sensitivity to heat and the sun was a consequence of the malaria he had contracted while on his honeymoon in 1940.

swelling was down, Solzhenitsyn was able to turn his mind to everyday domestic matters and asked Gorlov to go to Rozhdestvo to pick up a spare part for his car—he was planning to repair the clutch and there was a nearly new clutch plate at the cottage. Armed with instructions on how to find the key and a note of explanation for Natalia in case she should be there, Gorlov set off on the afternoon of 12 August, planning to be back by early evening. When he reached the cottage, he was surprised to find the outer door open and the inner one latched from inside, and to hear voices within. Suspecting nothing, he knocked loudly once or twice, opened the inner door, and walked in.

Almost at once two men ran down the stairs from the attic room and asked him roughly what he was doing there. Gorlov asked them the same question but was suddenly seized from behind and hustled out of the door. His arms were twisted behind his back, he was struck a heavy blow on the head that knocked him out for a few seconds, and when he recovered consciousness, he was being dragged face down in the direction of the surrounding woods. Convinced that he had stumbled across a gang of burglars and was about to be killed as the only eyewitness, Gorlov shouted the only thing that might give them pause for thought: "You'll answer for this! I'm a foreigner!"[3]

The ruse worked. The two men dragging him relaxed their grip, and Gorlov broke away. He did not get far, however, before another group of men pounced on him. There was a fierce struggle, during which the corners of Gorlov's mouth were torn; he was repeatedly punched in the face and was kicked and pummelled about the body. All this time he was yelling at the top of his voice for help (his mouth had been torn when the men tried to shut him up), and soon a crowd formed as people came running from the neighbouring cottages. The men were told to release Gorlov when their leader was threatened by one of the locals with a big stick. The leader attempted to pass the whole thing off by pretending that Gorlov was drunk; when this failed, he produced a red pass from his pocket and waved it under the nose of the man with the stick. He was a captain in the KGB; the "gang" were his men. In no time the crowd melted away and Gorlov was taken to the Naro-Fominsk police station, where the captain gave his name as "Ivanov."

Gorlov was ordered by the police to write an explanation of his presence at the cottage, and Captain "Ivanov" demanded that he sign a statement swearing himself to secrecy. Gorlov refused. On their way back to Moscow in Gorlov's car, "Ivanov" questioned Gorlov thoroughly on his family and career, learning that he was a doctoral candidate in engineering and had a wife and a twelve-year-old son. "I must tell you this," said the captain. "If the owner of the cottage or indeed anyone else gets to know about what happened today, you will lose everything you have. Not only will you be putting your entire career at risk, and never get to defend your doctoral dissertation, but your son and wife will suffer too. And if we consider it necessary, we'll send you to jail."

Gorlov got back to his home, shaken and weak, between nine and ten that night and told his worried wife he had been attacked by some drunks. The following morning, he informed Ekaterina Svetlova of exactly what had happened, and she left the office where they both worked to tell Solzhenitsyn. Later that day, Gorlov was summoned to the personnel department, where he found Captain "Ivanov," in uniform this time, and a man in civilian clothes, who proceeded to "explain" to him the reasons for the incident at Rozhdestvo. The Naro-Fominsk police, they said, had been tipped off that a local burglar was planning to raid Solzhenitsyn's cottage, and had set an ambush for him. It was unfortunate that they had not secured the owner's permission first, but since he was away, they had let themselves in and lain in wait. When Gorlov arrived, they had mistaken him for the burglar and tried to arrest him, and it was only his violent resistance that had forced them to beat him. Having now investigated the matter and learned that Gorlov was an exemplary Soviet citizen, they wished him to know that no charges would be pressed.

It was transparently dishonest, but Gorlov was satisfied to have his honour vindicated and relieved to hear that the police had no intention of taking any further action. Solzhenitsyn, however, was far from relieved. The raid on the cottage showed that the official silence over *August 1914* was only a tactical measure and that behind the scenes the authorities were looking for evidence to discredit him. Gorlov had told of seeing several men make off from the cottage with folders and boxes. It was possible that the boxes contained electronic equipment intended for eavesdropping, and the folders could have contained letters or manuscripts. He thought he had been careful to remove everything that could be incriminating before Natalia moved in for the summer, but it was always possible that he had overlooked something (the following year he discovered a full set of carbons of *The Oak and the Calf* in the cottage, and a similar set from *The Tanks Know the Truth;* they must have been there at the time of the raid—he had meant to burn them and had forgotten; fortunately, the KGB had overlooked them too). A Rozhdestvo neighbour later informed him that a group of policemen had returned at four the next morning—either to finish the job or simply to tidy up the mess.

Solzhenitsyn was still in bed and swathed in bandages when the news came, but he at once recognized the raid as a dangerous escalation of hostilities. The 1965 raid, resulting in the capture of his archive, had been accidental, as it were, and directed to other purposes, but this was a deliberate trawl for incriminating material, and the physical violence inflicted on Gorlov contained a menace that had largely been absent till now. Following his old precept that attack was the best form of defence, Solzhenitsyn drafted and released into samizdat a furious open letter to Yuri Andropov, chairman of the Committee for State Security and head of the KGB. "For many years," the letter began, "I have borne in silence the lawlessness of your employees: the inspection of all my correspondence, the confiscation of half of it, the tracking down of my correspondents, their persecution at work and by state agencies, the spying around my house, the shadowing of visitors, the tapping of telephone conversations, the drilling of holes in ceilings. . . . But after the raid yesterday I will no longer be silent." Solzhenitsyn went on to give a summary of the Gorlov incident and concluded, "I demand from you, citizen minister,* the public exposure of all the intruders, their punishment as criminals, and a public explanation of this incident. Otherwise I can only conclude that they were sent by *you*."[4]

An open attack on the KGB was something that Solzhenitsyn had not contemplated before, but on this occasion he was so enraged and upset that it came naturally to him. He capped it by sending a copy of the letter to the chairman of the Council of Ministers, A. N. Kosygin, demanding that the government investigate Andropov if the latter refused to respond. He had contemplated demanding Andropov's dismissal, but friends talked him out of it, saying that he could only harm himself and make himself look ridiculous if he overplayed his hand.

Of great interest for his psychology at this time is the letter he sent to Gorlov to explain his motives in making the incident public. Gorlov was in the country when the open letter was released, and returned to find himself a household name to readers of the world press and among Soviet listeners to foreign radio stations. It was a great shock, particularly because he had hoped, after his last meeting with "Ivanov," that he would be left in peace and the whole episode forgotten. Solzhenitsyn's open letter, however, ensured that this was not to be. Gorlov was caught in the cross-fire, and it was with mixed feelings that he read the copy of the open letter, which Solzhenitsyn forwarded to him via Ekaterina Svetlova, and the accompanying letter of explanation.

Dear Sasha,

I am overwhelmed by your boldness, bravery, and firmness of purpose—I see in them a sign of the new times and a new generation. I embrace you sincerely! I suffer for your scratches and bruises, but I hope that they will pass—unlike your action.

I want you to understand and believe and trust me: only *maximum* publicity and noise can offer you any reliable defence—you will stand in the world's spotlight and no one will dare touch you! That is why I took it upon myself to decide the matter for you—today I am writing an open letter to Andropov and will give it to samizdat.

Try to believe me and convince your family that any attempt to hush the matter up and conceal it will simply help *them* to smother you silently. I would even like to give your address and telephone number in the samizdat copies, so that people will know who you are and can telephone and write to you.

It is rarely given to a man in a single day (after a sleepless night—itself the result of a good deed) to test and prove both his physical and moral courage, and not to be found wanting in either one.

Once more I embrace you! Get better and be strong![5]

*Solzhenitsyn's use of the term "citizen" to address a minister was a calculated snub. The usual Soviet term is "*comrade* minister."

Solzhenitsyn's judgement on the benefits of publicity was undoubtedly correct insofar as it concerned himself. Publicity was virtually his only weapon, and he had become a virtuoso in its deployment. But it is questionable whether it was of similar utility to an otherwise loyal and conforming Soviet citizen like Gorlov, whose ambition in life was not to oppose the political system or become a dissident but to defend his dissertation and flourish as an engineer. In the course of the next few weeks, his life was turned upside down. The foreign radio broadcasts (which nobody was supposed to listen to, but which everyone in Moscow knew about) had made him a celebrity. He was an intimate and confidant of Solzhenitsyn. Friend and family rallied round, but an increasing number of colleagues at work refused to speak to him or even acknowledge his presence. Anonymous letters began arriving at the office and at the institute, some supporting and some attacking him. He was summoned to the Lubyanka to give an explanation and told that Solzhenitsyn was wrong: the whole affair was the work of the Naro-Fominsk police and had nothing to do with the KGB. When Gorlov decided to write an official complaint to the police and demand an apology and compensation, he was summoned to Naro-Fominsk and offered the same explanation as at the Lubyanka (and by "Ivanov" at his office before that): the police had been waiting for burglars and had mistaken him for a criminal.

Despite these persistent explanations that it was only the police, Gorlov invariably found someone present at these meetings who was dressed in civilian clothes and refused to give his name or rank—and it was usually the same person. Nevertheless, he was finally offered an apology by the Naro-Fominsk police and decided to accept it. Somewhat surprisingly, Solzhenitsyn, too, received an apology of sorts. A few days after his open letter to Andropov, someone from the KGB rang Rostropovich's dacha and left a message that Solzhenitsyn should address his protests not to the KGB but to the police. Solzhenitsyn then wrote to the Ministry of the Interior and about six weeks later received an official reply, which ended as follows:

> The events you refer to were the result of a misunderstanding and of the personnel in question exceeding their responsibilities. The guilty parties will be severely punished for their misdemeanours. This incident is all the more unpleasant in that, as you know, great efforts are being made by the police to strengthen socialist legality, reduce the incidence of violations of citizens' lawful rights, and raise the cultural level of our employees.
>
> We regret what has occurred.[6]

It was the usual bureaucratic waffle, but at least the principle of police culpability had been accepted, and it seemed that the incident might well be regarded as closed. Gorlov was anxious to consider it so and informed the police of this. Only in the months and years ahead was he to discover that it was not so easy after all and that, whereas the police were willing to settle, the gentlemen in civilian clothes had other opinions. Captain "Ivanov" had not been joking when he warned Gorlov to hold his tongue. Gorlov was the innocent victim in a larger struggle.*

Solzhenitsyn's dealings with the police in the summer and autumn of 1971 were not confined to the Gorlov affair. In September he received another visit from Anosov of the passport office and another man in plain clothes. Anosov wanted to know whether Solzhenitsyn had done anything about registering his residence. Six months had passed since his last visit, and the situation could not continue indefinitely. Solzhenitsyn was itching to cause a scene and on this occasion had even laid his statement about not being a serf on the desk between them, but Anosov's tone was so mild and apologetic that it did not seem the right occasion. All he wanted was an assurance that Solzhenitsyn would at least go through the motions. Seeing what seemed like an opportunity to exploit Anosov's concern, Solzhenitsyn brought up the subject of his new family and his desire to join them in Moscow. "Even when I'm legally married, they still won't give me a Moscow permit, will they?" "What do you mean?" replied Anosov. "They're obliged to by law." The two policemen prepared to depart amicably, and Solzhenitsyn was not forced to make his public declaration, but he did decide to remind them of his intransigence just in case. He would, he said, see to it that any attempt to remove him from Rostropovich's received the maximum publicity: "I shall refuse to leave if the police order me to, and I shall refuse to attend the court, so you'll have to sentence me to internal exile."[7]

After this little incident Solzhenitsyn's excitement subsided, and he was able to turn his mind to another question that had suddenly become topical again—the award of his Nobel Prize. For nine months nothing had happened, and no move had been made to arrange for the presentation of the prize, but in the first week of September 1971, Per Hegge published a book in Oslo, called *Middleman in Moscow*, in which he gave a detailed account of his activities as a go-between in the preceding year between Solzhenitsyn and the Swedish embassy and of the abortive negotiations for the delivery of the prize. Hegge strongly criticized the Swedish diplomatic staff in Moscow, and by implication the Swedish government, for refusing to accede to Solzhenitsyn's request for a presentation ceremony at the embassy. The Swedes had told him, he said, that they were aware that the refusal to present the prize "didn't look very heroic" but that the embassy's duty was to "maintain good relations with the Soviet authorities, and a ceremony for the sharply criticized author Solzhenitsyn might prove embarrassing." The Swedes had asked Hegge not to write anything about the negotiations, but Hegge had refused, saying that the embassy's servile attitude to the Soviet Union deserved to be exposed.[8]

Publication of the book provoked a stormy debate in the Swedish parliament. Olof Palme, the Swedish prime minister, declared that Solzhenitsyn would have been welcome to receive the prize at the Swedish embassy if he

---

*Gorlov was subsequently dismissed from his institute and prevented from defending his doctoral dissertation. He emigrated to the United States in August 1975.

had consented to do it without a ceremony. But a ceremony "might have been interpreted as a political manifestation against the Soviet Union." Subsequently, Palme was obliged to expand his remarks in a letter to the *New York Times* (after the *Times* had published an editorial critical of his position), and he repeated his view that presentation of the prize in the embassy, with any sort of audience present, was bound to have political repercussions.[9]

The timing of Hegge's book and the ensuing controversy struck Solzhenitsyn as particularly apposite. The United Nations was about to begin a new session and elect a new secretary-general: Gunnar Jarring, whom Hegge criticized, was known to covet the job, and his chances would be greatly reduced. Another advantage was that the announcement of the 1971 prize winners was only three weeks away, so that again the Nobel Foundation would be in the public eye. And despite the extra work that this circumstance must have been causing him, the secretary of the Nobel Foundation, Karl Ragnar Gierow, chose this moment to announce that he was writing to Solzhenitsyn once more to see whether arrangements might still be made for him to present the prize in the Swedish embassy in Moscow.

Solzhenitsyn replied to Gierow instantly on hearing news of the announcement on the radio (Gierow's letter did not arrive until three weeks later). In order to conceal this embarrassing discrepancy, Solzhenitsyn left the date open and dispatched his letter to a friend in the West for forwarding at the appropriate time. In it he informed Gierow that he was still willing to accept the prize at the embassy, but not without a small ceremony. Ambassador Jarring had insisted on a purely private transaction, but Solzhenitsyn could not see the point: "To agree to such a proposal seemed to me an insult to the Nobel Prize itself. It would be as though it were something to be ashamed of, something to be concealed from people. As I understand it, Nobel Prizes are conferred publicly because the ceremony has a public significance."[10] To ram home his point, Solzhenitsyn wrote separately to Per Hegge in similar, but blunter, terms, asking Hegge to make his letter public. "Palme's answer in parliament," wrote Solzhenitsyn, "is very surprising. Is the Nobel Prize actually stolen property that must be handed over behind closed doors and without witnesses?"[11]

Solzhenitsyn was anxious not only to have a ceremony but also to find an opportunity to read his newly completed Nobel lecture. Having abandoned the original version at the beginning of the year, he had recently returned to it and rewritten it. "This time I somehow succeeded in ridding the lecture of any otiose propaganda or political content, drawing it more tightly together round the theme of art." He still expected it to make a splash and wanted to ensure the best conditions for it. That was why, he wrote to Hegge, "the delivery of the insignia must be done in public and on condition that I am allowed to give my Nobel lecture."[12]

Gierow wrote to Solzhenitsyn again in November explaining that he had had a meeting with Gunnar Jarring, and that Jarring had told him that the embassy in Moscow had no room suitable for a public lecture. There could thus be no ceremony. "But," he added, almost as an afterthought, "I am naturally always ready to come to Moscow to hand over the Nobel diploma and medal, if some fitting form can be found, either in the embassy or, as far as possible, in any other place convenient to you."

This gave Solzhenitsyn the idea of holding the ceremony not in some official institution but in a private flat—in Natalia Svetlova's flat in Kozitsky Lane—and on 4 December he wrote a long letter to Gierow, expressing his gratitude for the latter's generosity of spirit, "which shines through this obstacle-strewn situation like a shaft of light," and outlining his plan. After making sarcastic fun of Ambassador Jarring—"The whole vexing situation has apparently arisen only because the Swedish embassy in Moscow simply does not have the *accommodation* for any other procedure (does this unfortunate circumstance mean that it never holds receptions?)"—and suggesting that the whole thing may have been the result of a "semantic misunderstanding" ("Do Mr Jarring and his superiors perhaps think that a 'public' or 'open' procedure necessarily implies a mass audience?"), Solzhenitsyn put his finger on the real objection to his original proposal.

Alas, I fear that it is not superficial semantics that separates us from the tenants of those premises but an unexpected discrepancy in our views as to where the frontiers of *culture* run. The Swedish embassy has a cultural attaché on its staff, and no doubt has within its purview all sorts of cultural questions, transactions, and events—but, we may ask, does it regard the presentation of a Nobel Prize (regrettably, on this occasion, to myself) as an event in cultural life that helps to draw our peoples together? If not, if it is seen, rather, as an incriminating shadow that threatens to blight the whole activity of the embassy, then, however spacious the accommodation, no place can ever be found for the procedure that you and I, Mr Gierow, have in mind.

Solzhenitsyn proposed his alternative of a ceremony in Svetlova's flat. "This flat, it is true, is certainly no more spacious than the Swedish embassy, but forty or fifty people can be fitted in quite comfortably by Russian standards." What the ceremony lost in formality it would gain in warmth and cosiness. Besides, "can you imagine, Mr Gierow, what a load we shall be taking off the mind of the Swedish ambassador and indeed of the Swedish Ministry of Foreign Affairs?" If this plan failed, the insignia could remain in Stockholm. "They will lose none of their value for that. And perhaps some day, even if it is only after my death, your successors will, with a proper sense of the occasion, present the insignia to my son."

The letter was again deliberately made public by Solzhenitsyn (thus circulating around the globe) and Dr Gierow replied that he accepted the idea. It remained only to fix a date, and after further correspondence in private, they agreed to set the ceremony for 9 April 1972—the first day of the Orthodox Easter.[13]

In the midst of these negotiations came the not unexpected news that Tvardovsky had died. In November 1971 his condition had deteriorated so seriously that he had been readmitted to the Kremlin Hospital, and his death came on the night of 18 December. Tvardovsky's status as one of the outstanding literary figures of his time was unassailable. News of his death was prominently featured in all the main Soviet newspapers, and the official obituary listed nearly all his achievements as a poet, public figure, and editor. In the many separate articles written in his memory, however, virtually no mention was made of his triumphant editorship of Novy Mir or of his more controversial poems, "Tyorkin in the Next World" and "By Right of Memory."[14] Nor would Soviet readers have learned from these obituaries of Tvardovsky's discovery of the greatest Russian writer of modern times, or of his many battles on Solzhenitsyn's behalf—with the Central Committee, the Writers' Union, and the censors. In death, as in life, he was pursued by the hostility and vindictiveness of the Writers' Union and its satraps.

It was thus a bitter and disgraceful irony that in death, according to immutable Soviet custom, his body, too, was given over to his enemies. In the USSR, where absolutely nothing that impinges on official life can be private or spontaneous, important people are invariably given state funerals. A "funeral committee" is formed by colleagues and functionaries, and this committee organizes the entire ceremony and pays the expenses. In Tvardovsky's case, it was a group of bigwigs from the Writers' Union, and the funeral ceremony was arranged for 21 December. The leave-taking was to be held at the Central House of Writers, on Herzen Street, starting at noon, and the interment would be at the Novodevichy Convent, on the banks of the Moscow River, where many prominent Soviet figures were buried.

Zhores Medvedev has provided us with a graphic description of the day of the funeral itself.[15] Only members of the Writers' Union were supposed to be admitted to the ceremony, and the six hundred seats available were filled up well before midday. But in addition to official visitors, thousands of unofficial ones had come to pay their last respects, and the hall where the funeral was to take place was jammed with people filing past the flower-strewn coffin in a never-ending line. This continued all morning, with funeral music playing in the background, until the doors were closed for the ceremony itself. The speeches were lacklustre and perfunctory, delivered by third-rate writers who owed their presence in the hall to their role as functionaries of the Writers' Union rather than to any literary merit. Not one of them was a close friend of Tvardovsky,* and again no mention was made of the last ten years of Tvardovsky's life or his achievements at Novy Mir. The ceremony was very short, and the union secretary in charge of the proceedings, Sergei Narovchatov, asked everyone except the writer's family and close friends to leave the hall. A young woman rose to her feet:

> Why are you closing the meeting so soon? Is it possible that no one is going to say that we are burying our civic conscience here? That Tvardovsky was forcibly

---

*On the contrary, the Tvardovsky family had specially asked the Writers' Union not to include in their delegation Mikhail Suslov, one of Tvardovsky's bitterest enemies while the latter was alive. The union ignored their plea and included Suslov just the same.

removed from his work, that he was compelled to leave *Novy Mir*, that his last poem was not published? That they shut his mouth before he shut it of his own accord?

At this point the official ushers on duty began to converge on her and shout her down, but she quickly gathered up her things, pushed her way towards the exit, and was lost in the general crowd.

At the interment it was a similar story. Medvedev boarded a trolleybus to make his way to the Novodevichy Convent, but although most passengers rose from their seats as they approached the cemetery, the bus drove straight past and did not stop for another mile or so. The authorities had thought of everything. Bus drivers had been told that the cemetery stop was "out of use" that day and ordered not to halt there. When Medvedev arrived back at the cemetery (it was a bitterly cold day, with a heavy frost), he found all the approaches cordoned off by phalanxes of policemen, while the main entrance, opposite the underground station, was barred by a row of soldiers. When he tried to walk through, he was grabbed and frog-marched back again, and told that only people with cards from the Writers' and Journalists' unions were to be admitted. He eventually got in by tagging on to a group of school-children and pretending to be one of the teachers (a school class is an obliga-tory part of the window-dressing provided for such occasions); he estimated that about 250 people had got in to attend the interment. One of them, an ordinary-looking man carrying a plastic bag, tried to push his way through to the front when earth was sprinkled over the coffin. He said he had brought some of "Tvardovsky's native soil, earth from Smolensk, from the mound over the communal grave of the men who fell in the liberation of Smolensk. They call it the 'hill of heroes.' "

Solzhenitsyn also attended the funeral, arriving very early. Although no longer a member of the Writers' Union, he did not bother to show a pass and the ushers dared not keep him out. Throughout the ceremony he sat in the front row with Tvardovsky's widow and children, and only at the end did he go over to Tvardovsky's open coffin and make the sign of the cross over him. He accompanied the family to the cemetery (on the insistence of Mrs Tvardovsky—the ushers wanted to stop him), where he stood bareheaded in the freezing wind, publicly kissed Tvardovsky before the coffin was nailed up, and joined in tossing some soil into the grave when the ceremony was concluded.

His presence created a sensation in its own right—so rarely did he appear in public these days—and was clearly recognized as symbolic. It attracted, among other things, the entire Moscow corps of foreign correspondents, and innumerable photographers, who captured Solzhenitsyn's expression and movements at every significant stage of the ceremony. Solzhenitsyn was nat-urally aware of the stir he would cause and was later accused by Vladimir Lakshin of having exploited the funeral for his own ends:

It is now obvious that to Solzhenitsyn the death of Tvardovsky was primarily a means of making a public appearance and of showing off under the arc-lights.

Stricken by our loss, we failed to realize this at the time. The only thing that struck us as odd was Solzhenitsyn's reply to Tvardovsky's younger daughter, who invited him to make his last farewell to her late father in the small mortuary at Kuntsevo, where only close friends were to assemble on the eve of the funeral and where there would be no pomp and no crowds. "No," replied Solzhenitsyn, "my whole day is already planned out. I'll come to the lying-in-state at the Central House of Writers tomorrow, as I have already noted in my diary." And he arrived, having skilfully stage-managed his entrance and attracted a horde of photographers—insolent, sweating with zeal, behaving offensively by standing with their backs to the casket and firing off flashbulbs point-blank at Solzhenitsyn as he sat in the front row beside the widow, hastily scribbling his impressions of the ceremony in a notebook and preparing to make his theatrical farewell gesture—with a kiss and the sign of the cross—to the man who could no longer answer him back.[16]*

Despite the excessive bitterness, there is undoubtedly an element of truth in this accusation. Solzhenitsyn needed the publicity at this juncture and almost certainly calculated his effects. But there was more to it than cold egocentricity. Solzhenitsyn was well aware of the authorities' efforts to turn Tvardovsky's funeral into a non-event—what they feared above all was a public demonstration, such as had taken place at Pasternak's funeral. Solzhenitsyn was determined to thwart them and do just that—turn it into a demonstration. He owed it to Tvardovsky's memory, and to Russian literature, and he succeeded. *Novy Mir* had been cut down almost without a whisper. Its staff had gone quietly; Tvardovsky had been shunted into retirement without the slightest hitch. His death was the last opportunity to mark the occasion, to bring home to those Russians who cared, and to people in the rest of the world, the meaning of what had happened. Solzhenitsyn had a unique flair, it is true, for attracting and exploiting publicity, but on this occasion it served not only his own cause but also a larger one, as he made clear in his farewell elegy to Tvardovsky, which he released nine days after the death (the traditional day of the memorial service in Russian custom).

There are many ways of killing a poet. The method chosen for Tvardovsky was to take away his offspring, his passion, his journal. The sixteen years of insults meekly endured by this hero were as nothing so long as his journal survived, so long as literature was not stopped, so long as people could be published in it, so long as people could go on reading it. . . .

. . . In the guard of honour we see the same seedy dead-beats who hunted him down with unholy shrieks and cries. Yes, it's an old, old custom of ours, dating back to Pushkin's time: dead poets must fall into the hands of their enemies. The body is speedily disposed of, and the situation saved with glib speeches.

They plant themselves round the coffin like a circle of stones and think they have isolated it. They break up our only journal and think they have won. . . . Madmen! When the harsh voices of the young ring out, how you will yearn for

---

* According to one source, Solzhenitsyn is supposed to have said after the funeral, "I really let them have it. I even made the sign of the cross over him."

this patient critic, whose gentle, admonitory voice was heeded by all! Then you will be fit to tear at the earth with your hands to bring Trifonich back again. But by then it will be far too late.[17]

A stirring elegy like this and the dramatic appearance at the funeral were things that only Solzhenitsyn could bring off. They were theatrical, yes, but they made the historical point with unmatchable emphasis. Within hours press photographs of the funeral had been flashed round the globe, and Solzhenitsyn's words, when released a few days later, travelled abroad with equal speed. Lakshin and Tvardovsky's other loyal friends were obliged to mourn in private, at informal gatherings such as that described by Zhores Medvedev after a visit to his grave on the fortieth day after Tvardovsky's death. Most of those present were writers, and amid the eloquent tributes to Tvardovsky one writer reminisced about Tvardovsky's foresight: "Do you remember that meeting of the editorial board when it was clear already that the storm-clouds were gathering and he said, 'They want to put out our fire. But it's too bright to be blown out or quenched with water. If they are going to put it out, they'll have to scatter all the smouldering, red-hot pieces to the four winds. Then it will be extinguished.' "[18] Those present may well have entertained feelings for Tvardovsky stronger than Solzhenitsyn's, and certainly their sadness was keenly sensed (and shared) by Medvedev. But the truth was that they had indeed been scattered and their fire extinguished, whereas Solzhenitsyn's fire burned brighter than ever—and was intense enough to light up that melancholy landscape sufficiently clearly for everyone else to see it.

41

WHOSE LIFE
IS IT ANYWAY?

SOLZHENITSYN HAD GOOD reason to prize the publicity that Tvardovsky's funeral brought him that winter, for he was beset with personal and political problems more serious and more numerous than ever. They were converging in a most alarming manner and threatened to become totally unmanageable unless he could do something to resolve them.

In his personal life, he continued to experience difficulties with Natalia. They had not seen each other throughout the summer. After spending some time in Rozhdestvo, Natalia had travelled south to the Crimea for her summer holiday. There she had struck up a friendship with a middle-aged widower, who subsequently met her at the station in Moscow with flowers and escorted her about town for a while,* but although his attentions soothed her battered pride, she did not take him as a serious alternative to Solzhenitsyn and was still opposed to a divorce. When they met in Kuntsevo in October as formerly agreed—on the first anniversary of her suicide attempt—Solzhenitsyn offered her an ultimatum: either divorce amicably and remain friends, or he would take her to court. She countered with a reminder that he had said she could return to Zhukovka after a year, but Solzhenitsyn informed her it was too late: Natalia Svetlova had moved in with their baby, and he had no intention of turning her out.[1]

About a week later, on 25 October 1971, Solzhenitsyn submitted a formal divorce claim to the district court in Ryazan on the grounds that his

---

* Solzhenitsyn seems to have suspected that Natalia's new friend was connected with the KGB and had been assigned by them to court her, but Reshetovskaya says that this was not so and that her friend never asked her any questions about Solzhenitsyn. On the contrary, he left when the divorce proceedings started up again because he feared the publicity.

marriage to Natalia had irretrievably broken down, and that it could not be restored again. He had recently had a child (his first) by another woman—Natalia Svetlova—and since his first marriage was childless, there was no reason why he should not be granted a divorce in order to marry the mother of his child. He had tried, he said, to secure a divorce by mutual consent over the past year, but Natalia had consistently refused. He also listed their joint property: his ancient Moskvich, bought with the royalties from *Ivan Denisovich;* a new Moskvich that he had just bought for Natalia's use; a share in a co-operative garage in Ryazan; a grand piano; and various items of domestic furniture. Apart from the ancient Moskvich, he was prepared to grant Natalia possession of all these goods and of all the money in their savings account and to renounce his share of their flat in Ryazan.*

The hearing took place on 29 November 1971. Natalia did not oppose Solzhenitsyn's application outright, but asked for a postponement on the grounds that there were problems over the division of property—namely, their cottage at Rozhdestvo, which could not be decided by the court in Ryazan but had to be resolved elsewhere. She delivered a long speech in which she described the history of their first marriage, separation, second marriage, life in Ryazan, and joint work on his literary projects. Quoting liberally from his letters to her, she tried to show that their love for one another was extraordinary and eternal, that their childlessness was his fault rather than hers, and that he had never wanted children anyway. As a climax she quoted the letter in which he had confessed to her his love for Svetlova and offered her the choice of what to do about it. This choice had apparently been removed from her now because of her suicide attempt. "I have reconciled myself to many things that are unavoidable, but I will never be reconciled to the fact that the man who had been closest to me—and will always be closest—in my life is now abandoning me. Abandoning me when I am past fifty and on the brink of old age. Leaving me alone with three old ladies, ranging from eighty-one to ninety-three years old. When my health has been completely undermined by our tragedy. Throwing me into a void." She expressed her conviction that this was out of character for him, the result of a "temporary delusion" that could not last long, and that he would soon come to his senses.

Natalia concluded by asking for a six-month adjournment, which the court granted. Solzhenitsyn suspected that the authorities might have seized on his divorce case as an opportunity to harass him, and might be behind this delay, but it seems likely that the judge was influenced by the distraught and weeping Natalia, who was literally on the verge of hysteria. Solzhenitsyn was furious and informed Natalia that she had won "six dead months." During that time he would neither see her nor answer her letters, except on strictly business matters.[2]

---

* According to Reshetovskaya, Solzhenitsyn had had the help of the advocate Sophia Kallistratova in drawing up his petition. Kallistratova was well known in Moscow for her spirited defence in court of a number of leading dissidents.

He attempted to fulfil his vows, but Natalia seemed to feel that she could use this six-month reprieve to get her husband back again. She resumed visiting their joint friends, to whom she quoted the passages from Solzhenitsyn's letters that she had copied out for the court. She complained of his cruelty and despotism, of the fact that he had always overshadowed her, exploited her, and sacrificed her to his work. She was indeed a pitiful figure, and there was sufficient truth in her accusations for the friends to be discomfitted. An older woman abandoned for a younger, prettier one (whatever the other reasons for the change) will always be an object of compassion, and a number of friends took her side, including Panin and the Etkinds. Natalia insisted on trying to arrange meetings with Solzhenitsyn against his will, and put pressure on their friends to force him to see her.[3]

In January 1972 Solzhenitsyn tried to gain a respite by writing to Natalia's mother, Maria, in response to her reproach that he was showing "unbelievable cruelty" by refusing to open Natalia's letters. All he wanted, he wrote, was "six months of peace," before the next court hearing, in order to get on with his work. Meeting Natalia literally made him ill for days afterwards and simply gave her an excuse to indulge in the pipe-dream that he would return to her. But that would never happen. Before the divorce hearing he had told her that after the divorce the way would be open for them to have human relations, but Natalia had preferred "a dead piece of paper," so let her enjoy it.[4]

Just as Natalia delved ever deeper into the past to find signs of his love for her (and had burnt his letters of more recent years, according to one report), so did Solzhenitsyn drag out their past quarrels and differences to prove the opposite. Perhaps he should never have married her at all, he suggested. And how coolly Natalia had taken his departure for the front. And later divorced him and married another man when he was in the camps. And then spurned his frantic cry for help when he had believed himself to be dying in exile and had wanted her to come and visit him. In short, he had reached the point where all he could think of was how to wound her. And yet, even now, Natalia clung to her marriage with a desperate tenacity that would have been pitiful, had not her abjection alternated with bouts of fierce hatred.

Perhaps the nadir was reached when Natalia passed on to Solzhenitsyn, through the medium of Panin, what she called her ultimatum: "If he doesn't save me from the humiliation of a divorce, I shall take my revenge on him." Solzhenitsyn was furious and answered her in a postscript to his letter to Maria. Natalia, he wrote, was possessed of an insatiable vanity, which distorted her view of the world. She knew that he no longer loved her, but she insisted on clinging to the empty shell of their marriage long after its essence had disappeared. All she wanted was her "position" as his wife, and if she couldn't have that, she was obviously determined to revenge herself on him in any way she could. That was why she insisted on telling all their former friends that he was a despot and had mistreated her. Unfortunately, many

of them had believed her, and he simply did not have the time to go around
giving his side of the story. Besides, it was demeaning for a man to waste
time complaining to others about his suffering. The point was that his marriage to Natalia was dead, and the reason she could not see it was that she
simply did not understand him. In fact, she had never understood him; she
had been too preoccupied with herself and her own affairs. He now loved
another woman; he had no doubts whatever about this new relationship and
would not enter into negotiations of any kind on the subject of his divorce
from Natalia.[5]

To the Soviet authorities, the divorce wrangle must have seemed a godsend, particularly as Solzhenitsyn had appeared to hold the initiative in his
struggle against them with the surprise publication of *August 1914*. It was
now over six months since the novel's appearance in Paris, and there had
been not a word on the subject in the Soviet press. Nor had there been any
other overt moves against him since the KGB agents' ill-fated encounter with
Gorlov in Rozhdestvo the preceding August. It seemed almost as if they were
preparing to leave him in peace. But the calm was, as usual, illusory. In
reality, the struggle was about to shift and embrace another aspect of his
private life—his biography. It was here that the public and private counts
against him fused, and in January they burst into the open.

On 12 January 1972 the *Literaturnaya Gazeta* appeared with a banner
headline on one of its inside pages: "*Stern* Magazine on Solzhenitsyn's Family." It turned out that in November the Hamburg illustrated weekly had
run a big story on Solzhenitsyn's ancestry, announcing that he had come
from a wealthy family, whose dispossession by the Revolution was the reason for Solzhenitsyn's hostility to the Soviet regime. The magazine's Moscow correspondent, Dieter Steiner, described how he had travelled south to
Georgievsk to locate and interview Solzhenitsyn's aunt Irina. Accompanying
the article was a picture of her, wrinkled and bent, standing in the doorway
of the ramshackle clay hovel that she had occupied for thirty years. Other
photographs, some of them provided by Irina, showed the big house in Kislovodsk where Solzhenitsyn had been born, Uncle Roman's Rolls-Royce,
Irina in boarding-school uniform, and Solzhenitsyn as a student and on his
first visit to Irina in 1956, after his return from exile.

The gist of the *Stern* article was that Steiner, having recognized the autobiographical element in *August 1914*, had set out, like any good investigative
Western journalist, to follow up an interesting story. He had discovered that
the Irina Tomchak of the novel was in fact Irina Ivanovna Shcherbak, a
resident of Georgievsk, and had interviewed her there. Here is how Steiner
describes their meeting.

The old lady—bowed and almost blind, but vigorous and still completely lucid—
lives in the annexe of an old farmhouse. Her room is six feet by nine, has an
earthen floor, a sloping ceiling, and whitewashed walls. She sits on an iron bed,
with a framed icon and a wooden crucifix overhead. Her dog Druzhok ("Friend"),

a decrepit, shaggy mongrel is asleep under the bed. A quarter of the room is taken up by a brick oven, on top of which are a saucepan, two tin plates, and a bag of flour. As I sat down on a rickety bench, Irina said, "You can see for yourself what sort of a life I have now, after fifty-three years under the commissars. From the state I get ten rubles a month, and Sanya sends me another fifteen. I am his only living relative."⁶*

According to Steiner, Irina told him some of the history of the Shcherbak family and gave or lent him the account of her memories that she had written down at Solzhenitsyn's request. She seemed irritated that Solzhenitsyn had never come to pick them up, and was apparently unaware of Solzhenitsyn's mishap on his way to see her.

The bulk of the article consisted of Steiner's summary of her remarks, accompanied by juicy and damaging titbits from the "memoirs." Irina appears to have spoken with some asperity of her in-laws, referring to them as "a family of boors" and describing the south Russian landowners of the time in general as "living like swine," with thought only for wine, women, and cards. She was sharply critical of Solzhenitsyn's mother, Taissia, and contemptuous of Natalia, whom she called "the daughter of a Jewish businessman" and denounced as a loose woman for having left Solzhenitsyn temporarily for another man. Such opinions are compatible with what one knows of this cranky, short-tempered, and indomitable little old lady, but at the age of eighty-two, despite Steiner's praise of her lucidity, her mind was clearly wandering, and her rambling narrative was a mishmash of truth and imagination. Steiner was content to take most of what she said at face value, and by judiciously quoting from *August 1914* to fill the gaps, he managed to paint a picture of Solzhenitsyn and his family that was simultaneously patronizing and damaging. In this version of events the Shcherbaks had been reactionary barbarians, vulgarly squandering their ill-gotten wealth until it was removed from them by the Revolution. Solzhenitsyn's mother had been a haughty provincial who put on airs, his father a tsarist officer who died because he could not face the victory of the Reds. "A hunting accident was the official explanation—probably it was suicide," commented Steiner maliciously. Solzhenitsyn himself, in Steiner's portrait, was heartless, ungrateful, grasping, bourgeois in his tastes and habits, and a secret counter-revolutionary, while his wife was frivolous and unfaithful—and a Jew.

This was the article that the *Literaturnaya Gazeta* now splashed in its inside pages—with certain modifications. Irina's comment about "a family of boors" was used to introduce the article, and most of her—and Steiner's—derogatory remarks were faithfully reproduced. But there was no reference to Irina's scathing comment on the fifty-three-year rule of the "commissars," to their economic achievements visible in her pension of ten rubles a month and miserable living conditions, or to the quotation from *August 1914* with which Steiner opened his article: "Russia must now be governed by idiots;

---

*This was not correct. Solzhenitsyn had cousins living in Moscow and an uncle in Siberia.

Russia can never be any different." On the other hand, not satisfied with Steiner's limitation to only one side of the family, the *Literaturnaya Gazeta* had despatched a correspondent to the village of Sablia to gather incriminating material on Solzhenitsyn's father's side of the family as well. "We are, of course, far from any idea of making a direct, vulgarly sociological connection between a man's origins, upbringing, and the circumstances of his youth, on the one hand, and his activities as a mature adult on the other," began the second article sanctimoniously and went on to assert that Solzhenitsyn's grandfather Semyon Solzhenitsyn had once owned five thousand acres and twenty thousand sheep, employed over fifty labourers, possessed, besides a couple of farmsteads, two big "manor houses" in the village of Sablia, and been a leading member of the board of a Rostov bank. Solzhenitsyn was alleged to have been wealthy on both sides of the family, and therefore— vulgar sociological considerations apart—doubly damned.

The writer of the second article had also come up with a potential "find"— another relative of Solzhenitsyn's by the name of Xenia Zagorika, the daughter of his long-dead uncle Vasily and hence his cousin. Perhaps disappointingly for the *Literaturnaya Gazeta*, Xenia had been only six months old when Vasily died, in 1919, and had been brought up by foster parents. She knew nothing of her celebrated cousin or his family. But because she was a simple country girl, she did enable the *Literaturnaya Gazeta* to introduce a touching digression on the subject of the flourishing collective farm where she worked, which now occupied the former land of the Solzhenitsyns, and to underline the high standards of living of contemporary villagers ("every house has piped water, 640 out of 800 houses have television sets, 600 have gas, 1,112 newspapers and journals are delivered per 1,000 of population"), while upbraiding Steiner for ignoring this modern miracle in his story.[7]

It might have seemed from this rebuke that the *Literaturnaya Gazeta* was reprinting the *Stern* story in all innocence, as it were, and simply taking issue with the *Stern* reporter over his alleged ideological bias. But it was more complicated than that. Dieter Steiner, a competent foreign correspondent of wide experience, had little Russian and scant knowledge of Soviet society and literature. It is most improbable that he had spotted the autobiographical element in *August 1914* himself; and he certainly did not go to Georgievsk on his own initiative, if only because Georgievsk belongs to that three-quarters of the Soviet Union that is totally closed to foreigners. In fact, as Solzhenitsyn later discovered, three men had visited Aunt Irina in her hovel and had made a total of five calls. The notes she had given them to read were supposed to be given back, but they had been taken away, together with the photographs, and were never returned. From the fact that all three men were said to have spoken excellent Russian, Solzhenitsyn concluded that Steiner had not been there at all, but that was wrong. Steiner was there and had his photograph taken with Irina, although the photo was not published. Steiner was also briefly in Sablia, but despite the *Literaturnaya Gazeta*'s mock indignation, he was not allowed to leave his car, and the only photographs he obtained were taken through the car's windscreen.[8]

It was another example of the Soviet technique of sponsoring, or even writing, an article for publication in a foreign newspaper and translating it back for Russian readers as an example of what "The West" thinks about a certain topic. The *Literaturnaya Gazeta*'s main feature was full of inaccuracies and distortions, but these could be conveniently blamed on Steiner, and he in turn could blame them on the faulty memory of an eighty-two-year-old woman. What the *Literaturnaya Gazeta* added on its own initiative was equally egregious. In its early editions, the photograph of Irina's ornate villa in Kislovodsk was described as Semyon's village house in the Stavropol steppes, and Solzhenitsyn's father's name was rendered as "Isai" (a mistaken deduction from Solzhenitsyn's patronymic "Isayevich"), undermining the *Gazeta*'s claim that its information had been gathered from eyewitnesses in Sablia itself.

According to Zhores Medvedev, the articles in the *Literaturnaya Gazeta* provoked much mirth in Moscow literary circles. Two of Solzhenitsyn's chief adversaries in the literary establishment, Alexander Chakovsky, the editor of *Literaturnaya Gazeta*, and Sergei Mikhalkov, the first secretary of the Russian Writers' Union, were descended from much grander families than Solzhenitsyn, and Mikhalkov's grandfather still had a whole village named after him—Mikhalkovo. Clearly, the "vulgar sociological line" had to be handled with care.[9]

Solzhenitsyn, however, was not amused. Only a few months earlier he had issued the "official" version of his biography in the form of an autobiographical sketch for the Nobel Foundation, to be printed in its year-book. He had mentioned the fact that his father had served as a volunteer officer in the First World War and had died in the summer of 1918, before his son was born, but had said nothing of the circumstances of his father's death or his origins. Similarly, he had written nothing more of his mother than that she had been a shorthand typist in Rostov-on-Don, had remained alone and in poor health, and had brought him up in modest circumstances—somewhat fewer facts than he had conveyed to Pavel Ličko in 1967.

He was exceedingly alarmed and annoyed by the *Stern* article and its sequel in the *Literaturnaya Gazeta*, which took him completely by surprise. Having disguised the surnames and changed the first names of many of the relatives described in the novel (was it significant that he could not bring himself to change just two: Isaaki, his father's name, and that of Aunt Irina?), he had felt sure that they would not be recognized and that no attempt would be made to track down the one important survivor.[10] Up till now he had been able to exercise some sort of control over information about his former (and private) life, but things were beginning to get out of hand. First his divorce and now his origins were being turned against him, and he knew that the Soviet authorities would use any weapon they could to discredit him. Soon afterwards he learned that a Major Blagovidov of the KGB had been dispatched to check the files of Moscow University for 1914 and investigate all the Isaaki's there, in the hope of proving that Solzhenitsyn was a Jew after all. Once again his father's strange Christian name had misled the investigators (and they evidently forgot to inform the *Literaturnaya Gazeta* of their inquiries, where the name appeared as Isai); and, of course, they drew a blank.[11]

Solzhenitsyn was equally worried by another problem. Over the past year or two, he had become aware of projects by Western authors to write biographies of him.* On the whole he did not disapprove. Though he was unwilling to participate directly in their preparation, one of the projects—by an American journalist, George Feifer, and an *émigré* journalist, David Burg (co-translator of *Cancer Ward*)—had received his tacit approval in the summer of the preceding year.[12] Since then, Feifer had had many conversations with Veronica Stein and other friends of Solzhenitsyn, but in July 1971 he had been detained at Sheremetyevo Airport, questioned, searched, and relieved of his detailed notes. A draft text that he then sent to Veronica for checking contained too much speculation—mixed with accurate information—for Solzhenitsyn's comfort, yet to refute the speculative parts required more disclosure than he was ready for. Solzhenitsyn seems to have concluded that a biography would cause more trouble than it was worth, especially in the light of the KGB's fishing expeditions. Having already warned Feifer in July to stick to literary matters and leave his private life alone, he now felt impelled to go further and issue a generalized warning, through Dr Heeb, to all potential biographers.

> I understand that certain "biographies" of me are due to appear shortly in the West, including some that will contain information of a mainly non-literary character. This information is being collected by the authors without my knowledge or my agreement, often in dark and roundabout ways by interviewing people who knew me at one time or another, but who are often not informed at all. The material collected in this manner is supplemented with imaginary facts and motivations which must be invented, since the true circumstances and motives of my work cannot be known to anyone, owing to the isolation in which I live. The collection of "information" in this way is no different from police spying. I regard the publication of such biographies during an author's lifetime as ill-mannered and immoral, especially since they are bound to involve living people who are exposed and have much to lose from such publicity. I can defend myself against such publications in no other way than by asking authors, editors, and publishers to respect my right to privacy.[13]

At the same time Solzhenitsyn sought a convenient means to refute publicly the half-truths and distortions in the *Stern* and *Literaturnaya Gazeta* articles. His first reply was given to the Moscow correspondent of the West German newspaper *Die Welt*, but for some reason it got lost in transmission.

---

*I, too, had visited Moscow in June 1970 and had talked to Kopelev about the possibility of writing a biography of Solzhenitsyn. Kopelev and others convinced me, however, that it was not the best moment and that Solzhenitsyn was unlikely to co-operate on such a venture.

Solzhenitsyn then asked Zhores Medvedev to arrange an interview with the correspondents of the *New York Times* and the *Washington Post* in Moscow (then Hedrick Smith and Robert Kaiser). The interview was shrouded in secrecy. Medvedev put Smith and Kaiser through an elaborate series of preparatory manoeuvres and communicated with them and Solzhenitsyn in mysterious codes. The interview was originally set for 4 April 1972, but was then moved forward by Solzhenitsyn to 30 March, and took place in Svetlova's flat in Kozitsky Lane. A few days beforehand, under the cover of darkness, Medvedev showed the correspondents the way and gave them their final instructions. They were to bring tape recorders and cameras so that they could record and photograph Solzhenitsyn, but at the same time should try to look as inconspicuous as possible. This they did by putting on old clothes and, in Kaiser's case, by wrapping his modern equipment in old copies of *Pravda* and carrying them in a typically Muscovite string bag.[14]

What followed was a memorable confrontation between Western and Eastern notions of news gathering, interview techniques, and the management of publicity. Smith and Kaiser had prepared their questions in advance while ice-skating at an outdoor rink in Moscow (to avoid the possibility of being eavesdropped on by KGB microphones). They were fairly fresh to the Soviet Union, having been there but seven months, and had only a sketchy knowledge of the Russian language and of the darker reaches of Soviet society. On the other hand, they were experienced newspapermen, well trained in the hard-nosed tradition of American investigative reporting, observant, adaptable, and well able, as they thought, to tackle any assignment with confidence. They had not then encountered Solzhenitsyn's imperious will and steely resolve, or imagined to themselves the full danger of the knife-edge upon which he was living.

They arrived at the flat shortly after noon—Solzhenitsyn himself unbolted the door and let them in—and the encounter began affably enough. Solzhenitsyn shook hands, introduced them to Svetlova and their son, Ermolai, now fifteen months old and babbling in baby language, and ushered them into his study, in which all the curtains were drawn. Smith later wrote that the easy informality of those first few minutes disarmed him, for he had expected to be "over-awed by this living classic of Russian literature." Solzhenitsyn, in fact, was "warm and engaging. He was also physically more dynamic than I had expected, bounding out of chairs, moving with athletic ease across the room. His enormous energy was palpable. For a man who had suffered so much, he looked well." Smith noted that Solzhenitsyn's steel molars flashed when he smiled and that a dark tobacco stain on his index finger marked him as a heavy smoker.

This accord quickly vanished once they got down to business. The original intention had been for the two reporters to send their questions in advance, but they had been prevented from doing this when Solzhenitsyn brought the interview forward. After apologizing for the sudden haste (but without explaining it), Solzhenitsyn took from his desk two copies of a thickish manuscript and placed them before the two correspondents. This was his "interview," complete with questions as well as extensive answers. Solzhenitsyn wanted it published in full. Smith, who had been determined in advance not to let himself be "used" by Solzhenitsyn, was thrown completely off balance.

I was stunned. What an irony, I thought. This is the way it is done at *Pravda* and here is Solzhenitsyn, whose entire being reverberates with his furious battle against censorship, a man who in the great tradition of Pushkin and Dostoyevsky had dared to assert the writer's indepence, producing a pre-packaged interview. How could he be so blind or vain? I thought of walking out.

"This is outrageous," I muttered to Kaiser.[15]

It did not occur to Smith or Kaiser that a man with his back to the wall, being watched by all-powerful enemies for the slightest slip, might have had a more than common interest in an accurate portrayal of his thoughts and views. Solzhenitsyn did not help, of course. It was beneath his dignity to persuade or explain. His situation, he felt, was self-evident. And despite his extensive exploitation of the Western press in his struggles against the authorities, he hadn't the remotest idea how that press really worked. His only previous interview had been with the obedient Japanese correspondent Komoto Sedze, and before that with Soviet correspondents in Ryazan. But for Western reporters this was a breach of journalistic ethics, a plant, a fake interview. They demanded the right to put their own questions (they had come with ten) and to select and edit the answers.

There followed several hours of intensive bargaining. First, the two Americans read the "interview" through—painfully slowly, with assistance from Svetlova. Both were impressed with parts of it, but the long explanations of Solzhenitsyn's ancestry in answer to the *Stern* allegations struck them as long-winded and irrelevant. Both declared that no more than half could be used by their respective newspapers ("Not even the American President gets more"—which was perfectly true). Since the document was over seven thousand words long, this was eminently fair, particularly for a daily paper (even of the gargantuan proportions of American newspapers), but Solzhenitsyn would not budge: all or nothing.

Later he offered a compromise. The two reporters could use what they liked if they promised to get the rest of the interview printed in other publications. The reporters said they had no power to do that, and Solzhenitsyn left the room. A moment later he returned and asked whether a Swedish correspondent could take the rest of the interview and print the parts the Americans omitted. The two Americans objected that there was no such Swede, at which Solzhenitsyn disappeared and returned with a blond young man in his wake. This was Stig Frederikson, the correspondent of the Scandinavian News Agency in Moscow, and he was willing to print the whole of Solzhenitsyn's interview a day after it appeared in America.

The two Americans were dumbfounded. They had had no idea there was another correspondent concealed in the flat, though they concluded that he had not come for an interview but was somehow involved in the negotiations that were then in full swing to hold a Nobel Prize ceremony. Solzhenitsyn had simply seized on his presence as offering a way out of the impasse. And it did. The Americans quickly agreed to this new suggestion, and the young Swede was hustled out again. The two correspondents still insisted on putting some questions of their own, however. A few meshed more or less easily with Solzhenitsyn's text and were substituted for the novelist's simplistic and sometimes naïve original proposals. Others were ruled out by Solzhenitsyn as being too broad or too political. "In general," he explained, "a writer decides what he will talk about." Eventually, he agreed to let them tape one of his negative answers, in which he explained why he could not answer a certain question, and after this he allowed them to repeat the process question by question. "He discussed every answer with Natalia before giving it," writes Kaiser in his account of the meeting. "She offered extensive advice, some of which he accepted. The sport of it seemed to please him, though he was obviously nervous about a situation he could not fully control. (We learned later that when he played back his tape, he was disappointed that his language wasn't more polished.)"[16]

Kaiser offers one or two other interesting details about the photographic session—pictures were taken of Solzhenitsyn, Natalia, and Ermolai separately and then together as a group. In posing with the family, Solzhenitsyn was all smiles, but when his own picture came to be taken he absolutely refused to smile: "It's time to be serious," he said, composing his face into a solemn mask for posterity. At one point he searched for a red pencil to underline something he thought important and would not accept Kaiser's offer of his blue pen for the purpose: it had to be red. At another he expressed concern that his interview not be published on 1 April lest people think it was a hoax. Kaiser also noted the now bulging belly, pushing at his loose pullover, and the stubby, powerful, worker's hands with their scarred right thumb, but was overwhelmed by Solzhenitsyn's "radiant smile" and the intense concentration of his bright blue eyes. Indeed, both correspondents were deeply affected by Solzhenitsyn's dominating personality and steely will (and correspondingly grateful for Natalia's diplomatic tact and sense of humour in the negotiations) and left with a sense that the afternoon had lasted far longer than four hours.

The interview appeared in two separate versions on 3 April. As the first full interview that Solzhenitsyn had ever given to Western correspondents, it received front-page billing in both the *Washington Post* and the *New York Times*, and in the many other newspapers around the world that reprinted one or the other version. Kaiser's article as it appeared in the *Post* was fairly short (the *Guardian* in England ran it at considerably greater length) and was presented as a straight story, without the question-and-answer format (except in the *Guardian* again), whereas the *New York Times* story was much longer. In addition to an introductory article by Hedrick Smith, there was almost a full page of questions and answers. Both papers carried photographs of Solzhenitsyn and his family.

The printed stories concentrated on Solzhenitsyn's current difficulties with the authorities and on the campaign then being waged in the Soviet press against *August 1914*. Solzhenitsyn, as usual, had been scathingly eloquent about the situation he found himself in. "A kind of forbidden, contaminated zone has been created round me and my family," he was quoted as saying. "To this very day there are people in Ryazan who have been dismissed from work for visiting my home a few years ago."[17] He went on to describe the cowardly and illegal way in which Svetlova had been dismissed from her job when it was learned that she had borne Solzhenitsyn's son, the punishment meted out to Moscow housing officials for having allowed Svetlova and her parents to exchange their two former flats for the more spacious one in Kozitsky Lane, and the everlasting problem of surveillance. If he met anyone to work on his book, he said, that person would come under suspicion. "As soon as he leaves my house, he will be as closely followed as if he were a state criminal, and they will investigate his background. And they then go on to find out who this man meets and then, in turn, who that man is meeting."

Solzhenitsyn told them in detail about the campaign of harassment and threats he had been subjected to, starting with the confiscation of his archive in 1965, and the official whispering campaign conducted against him at Party meetings. "They say, 'Solzhenitsyn voluntarily gave himself up to the Germans—no, he surrendered a whole battery. And he served as a policeman in occupied territory—that is, for the Germans. Or even better, he fought with Vlasov. Even better, he worked right in the Gestapo. On the surface, everything is quiet, no defamation, but under the crust is the cancer of slander.'"

Solzhenitsyn also talked about the difficulties he had experienced over the award of the Nobel Prize, the publication of *August 1914*, and in carrying out his work for the sequel to it—*October 1916*. The fuss over the Nobel Prize, he said, was an insult to all former winners, including the Communist poet Pablo Neruda. In the case of *August 1914*, he had been accused of smuggling the manuscript abroad without informing the Soviet authorities of its existence, whereas the truth was that he had offered it to seven Soviet publishers without receiving a single response. As for researching and writing *October 1916*, his status as a pariah and a "non-person" put unusual difficulties in his way. "I live in my own country, I write a novel about Russia, but it is as hard for me to gather material as it would be if I were writing about Polynesia."

And what was it all for? "The plan," said Solzhenitsyn, revealing the real reason for giving the interview, "is either to drive me out of my life or out of the country, throw me into a ditch or send me to Siberia, or to have me dissolved 'in an alien fog' as they write."

The interview was a huge success and attracted world-wide attention to Solzhenitsyn, as he had privately predicted. Readers in the West recognized this as an unprecedented step, indicating a new threshold of desperation in Solzhenitsyn's situation and a need for even greater public support than before. But still Solzhenitsyn was not satisfied. The *Washington Post* editors had shrunk Kaiser's article to a fraction of its original length, and Solzhenitsyn resented Hedrick Smith's presentation of their meeting as too novelettish.[18] True to his desire for journalistic autonomy, Smith had begun his story with the questions and answers that he had insisted on recording from Solzhenitsyn at the end of their meeting, thus leaving less space for Solzhenitsyn's own questions and answers and framing them in (from Solzhenitsyn's point of view) "extraneous" material. Worst of all, there had been almost no room for Solzhenitsyn's detailed exposition of his ancestry. The *Post* had ignored this part of the interview, while the *Times* had confined itself to some comments about his parents and childhood. Solzhenitsyn's feelings on this matter were conveyed to Smith in a tart little note some days later,[19] and the whole text was released into samizdat to rectify the omissions. Shortly thereafter, the text appeared in Russian in the West and was later translated in its entirety.

One of the many things that had puzzled Smith and Kaiser about the interview was its timing. It was common knowledge in Moscow that Solzhenitsyn's privately arranged ceremony for the delivery of the Nobel Prize had been set for Sunday, 9 April, just ten days after his meeting with the two correspondents. Solzhenitsyn had insisted on talking about it in his interview. Dr Gierow, he said, had agreed to come on the ninth. In addition to close friends, Solzhenitsyn was inviting those whom he called "the most eminent representatives of our artistic and scientific intelligentsia—some writers, the chief producers at our leading theatres, important musicians, actors, and certain academicians."[20] Solzhenitsyn declined to name them for fear of causing them unnecessary difficulties if the ceremony failed to take place, but we know from his memoir that there were to be about sixty altogether and that the selection criteria were as follows: "We had to draw up the guest list so as to invite no one whose civic behaviour was in any way questionable, to omit no one whose standing in the artistic or scientific world entitled him to an invitation, and at the same time to invite guests who really would come and not funk it." The list had been drawn up and the invitations prepared with Solzhenitsyn's usual attention to detail and regard for secrecy. Each invitation was handwritten by Solzhenitsyn and included a detailed plan showing exactly how to get to Svetlova's flat (the block had about twenty entrances), where the ceremony was to be held. The ceremony was set for a Sunday so that it could take place in daylight (it was due to start at noon), when the KGB would be prevented from harassing the guests under the cover of darkness, and even then some "fearless door-keepers" were appointed to keep overzealous KGB agents at bay (and to take care of stone throwing, the cutting off of the electricity, or anything else that might be dreamed up and attributed to "hooligans" or technical "accidents"). Delivery of the invitations had commenced on 1 April, and Solzhenitsyn was gratified by the response. "The number of writers, producers, and actors who accepted surprised me:

to think that such courage, such a longing to stand upright, such a feeling of shame to be slaves forever, still survived in so many people." But "there were, of course, refusals too, sickeningly in character, from people of international reputation who had nothing to fear"[21] (but Zhores Medvedev writes that "the one or two people who declined had entirely valid reasons for doing so").[22] On the day when Solzhenitsyn met the two American correspondents, the arrangements were all complete and only the invitations remained to be delivered, so why did he choose this moment to speak out? Was it not a deliberate provocation to the authorities, a challenge to them just when Solzhenitsyn needed to keep quiet for a while—at least until the ceremony was over? And why did he advance the interview at the last moment, as if to ensure that whatever they wrote was printed before the ceremony was due to take place?

In his own version of these events, Solzhenitsyn offers no immediate answer to this conundrum. He brushes over the fact that it was he who invited the correspondents in the first place (as if they themselves had asked to come) and makes no mention of the last-minute advancement of the interview. The answer is probably to be found, however, in certain other aspects of the Soviet press campaign that was unleashed against him in the first three months of 1972.

One of the most disturbing features of the original *Stern* article, apart from its biographical "revelations," had been a passage suggesting that *August 1914* was not really a historical novel, but a thinly disguised allegory describing the Soviet army as Solzhenitsyn had known it in the Second World War. "Cunningly exploiting a well-tried method that has shielded him in the past from going to jail for treason, he has placed the action in pre-revolutionary times. Whoever reads *August 1914*, however, is at once aware that in depicting events from the past, the author is dealing with the problems of the present."[23] The vulgar cynicism and stupidity of this remark suggest that it may have been KGB inspired. Whatever the case, the *Literaturnaya Gazeta* inevitably reproduced it, commenting that "many Western newspapers and magazines emphasize the anti-Soviet tendency of this novel" and quoting a review by Anatole Shub in the *Washington Post* to bolster this conclusion.[24]

On 23 February, the *Literaturnaya Gazeta* had followed up with two more articles allegedly republished from foreign newspapers. One, by Marina Stütz, said to have appeared in the West German *Deutsche Volkszeitung* (the organ of the West German Communist Party), simply dismissed the novel as a "banal apologia for the theory of convergence," but the other, by a Finnish journalist called Martti Larni, was a far more poisonous affair. Picking up where *Stern* and *Literaturnaya Gazeta* had left off, Larni underlined the "anti-Soviet" message of the novel, repeated *Stern*'s allegation of allegorical intent, and carried the argument a stage further. Solzhenitsyn's sympathetic contrasting of the efficiency and discipline of the German army in the First World War, with the inefficiency, corruption, and disorganization of the Russians was intended as a barely disguised parallel with the Second World

War. In the Second World War the Germans were pursuing the same imperialist aims as in the first, only this time they were led by Hitler and the Nazis. *Ergo* (though Larni refrained from spelling this out) Solzhenitsyn sympathized with the Nazis. In conclusion Larni reverted to the comparison of Solzhenitsyn with another "denatured intellectual" who had abandoned his homeland and "dissolved in a London fog"—Anatoli Kuznetsov (though the name was superstitiously omitted).

The interesting thing about the Larni article was that, although billed as the translation of an article that had appeared in a Swedish newspaper called *Norrskensflamman* (published by a faction of the Swedish Communist party in the provincial town of Luleå), it was nothing of the sort. In an interview given to the Finnish newspaper *Uusi Suomi* three days after his article in the *Literaturnaya Gazeta*, Larni revealed that he had never heard of *Norrskensflamman* and that his article had been commissioned directly by the *Literaturnaya Gazeta*. Moreover, he had not read *August 1914* himself but was simply replying to the Anatole Shub review that the Russians sent to him.

This information reached Solzhenitsyn too late for inclusion in his interview (though he was able to get off a gibe at the "alien fog"), but it made no difference to the gravity of the inference. Solzhenitsyn also had what he regarded as reliable evidence that a definite decision had been taken at the highest level to arrest and expel him. Chakovsky, the editor of the *Literaturnaya Gazeta*, was reported to have said as much at an editorial meeting;[25] the operation was apparently intended to take place sometime in mid-April. This, it seems, had been the real reason for Solzhenitsyn's sudden decision to advance his newspaper interview and make a pre-emptive strike, even if it did threaten the Nobel ceremony. Other factors may have been the impending visit to the Soviet Union of President Nixon (hence the choice of American newspapers), when the Soviet authorities would not want an international incident, and Solzhenitsyn's developing theory of verbal guerrilla warfare. One of the best tactics, he had discovered, was to string a series of statements and moves together into a "cascade" in rapid succession to one another: "Events crowd in thick and fast at moments of crisis . . . but you can also increase their density deliberately by exploiting the unique characteristics of our Soviet bigwigs: their obtuseness, their slow-wittedness, their inability to keep two concerns in mind at once."[26]

The interview and the forthcoming Nobel ceremony constituted two elements in the cascade; a third was Solzhenitsyn's "Lenten Letter to the Patriarch," which just then was also creating a stir. Solzhenitsyn had conceived the idea of writing to the patriarch the preceding Christmas Eve, after listening to the Christmas service on a Western radio station and hearing a pastoral letter addressed to Russian Orthodox Christians in the West by Patriarch Pimen of Moscow. Among other things, the patriarch had appealed to parents to foster a love of the church in their children and to set them a personal example. Solzhenitsyn, perhaps with the cares of fatherhood now at the forefront of his mind, was moved by this appeal, but also stung by the hypocrisy of a church that could address such words to *émigrés*, while remaining completely silent in its own country. Again there was that stab of indignant rage. "At once I was fired to write to him! I had no choice but to write!"[27]

The task proved a difficult one. Solzhenitsyn had to inform himself on the policies and possibilities of the Orthodox hierarchy in Russia before he could write convincingly, and then adopt the correct forms and tone in which a loyal subject of the church should address so august a personage. The latter was particularly hard for a man used to speaking out in Solzhenitsyn's peremptory manner, but he had finally managed it and had sent his letter to the patriarch on 17 March. At the same time, he gave it to one or two friends in the church to read, thinking that it would not become public before Easter and before his newspaper interview, but he had miscalculated. A copy quickly made its way abroad and was published there, whence it was broadcast back into the Soviet Union by Western radio stations. To Solzhenitsyn's evident surprise, it created something of a furore.[28]

The gist of the "Letter" was that it was hypocritical for the Russian Orthodox church to preach a course of behaviour abroad that it was unwilling to embrace at home. "Why is your honest appeal directed only to Russian *émigrés?* Why do you call only for those children to be brought up in the Christian faith? Why do you admonish only the distant flock to 'discern slander and falsehood' and be strong in truth and justice? And we—what should we discern? Should we or should we not foster in our own children a love of the church? . . . The Russian church has its indignant opinion on every evil in distant Asia or Africa, yet on internal ills it has none—ever." Solzhenitsyn's principal criticism was that the church had sold out to the state, that it existed in a condition of abject subjugation to the secular authorities and had needlessly forfeited the right to propagate the faith. Solzhenitsyn compared the past half century of religious neglect with Russia's glorious religious past—and also with the very different state of affairs in Poland. He drew attention to the wholesale destruction and despoliation of Russia's churches, the material and spiritual poverty of the Russian people deprived of all beauty, all faith, and all transcendence in their lives, and the catastrophic consequences for their future. And he pointed out that his was not the first warning. Two courageous priests, Father Nikolai Eshliman and Gleb Yakunin, had written a similar warning seven years earlier to Patriarch Pimen's predecessor, and Archbishop Ermogen of Kaluga was still sequestered in a monastery for having dared to forbid the closing of churches and the burning of icons and church books. Yet no action had been taken, and the Orthodox church was still secretly managed by a quasi-governmental council for religious affairs. "A church dictatorially ruled by atheists is a sight not seen in two thousand years," commented Solzhenitsyn acidly. The consequences were that the church's money was given away for non-religious purposes, while there were no funds for the repair of churches; priests were powerless in their own parishes and had to seek special permission just to visit the sick or attend a ceremony.

What sort of reasoning can convince one that the consistent destruction of the spirit and body of the church by atheists is the best means for its preservation? Preservation for whom? Certainly not for Christ. Preservation by what means? Falsehood? But after falsehood, what sort of hands should perform the Eucharist?

Your Eminence! Do not disdain completely my unworthy cry. You will probably not hear one like it every seven years. Do not allow us to suppose, do not force us to think that for the bishops of the Russian church, earthly authority is higher than heavenly authority, earthly responsibility more terrifying than responsibility to God.[29]

The "Lenten Letter" was Solzhenitsyn's most eloquent and moving public statement since his letter to the Fourth Writers' Congress. In tone and form it was of a piece with his elegy for Tvardovsky, written shortly beforehand, and his recently completed Nobel lecture, which he planned to deliver on 9 April. And yet the responses to the "Lenten Letter," not only by government officials but also by some fellow Christians and dissidents, were more hostile than Solzhenitsyn could have imagined.

On the government side, the hostility was clearly due to the fact that Solzhenitsyn had touched a sensitive nerve. Atheism is a corner-stone of the Soviet state (it is the "state religion") so that his attack on it was tantamount to heresy. By appealing to the Orthodox church to repeal or renegotiate its lopsided concordat with the state, Solzhenitsyn appeared to be attacking one of the sacred foundations of the Soviet system and attempting to turn the clock back to pre-revolutionary (and possibly even pre-Petrine) times. It was, in conventional parlance, a counter-revolutionary proposal, though it could not be assailed as such, because it was cloaked in ecclesiastical terminology.

The hostility of fellow Christians and fellow dissidents was somewhat more surprising. The attitude of the dissidents, most of whom were liberals, seems to have been that the whole appeal was irrelevant. What was the point of the Orthodox church anyway, emasculated and muzzled as it had been for decades? And many seem to have been misled by the tone and language of the "Letter" into dismissing its concerns as a storm in an ecclesiastical teacup, completely overlooking the letter's far-reaching, political implications. As for fellow Christians (and Christian dissidents), they were split. Some approved of the "Letter" as a timely reminder of the church's present subjugation and its duty to release itself in the future, but others saw in it only a gratuitous and self-serving attack on a patriarch and clergy who were doing their best under impossible conditions and were in no position to answer back. The weightiest exponent of this second view was Father Sergei Zheludkov, of Pskov, a leading Christian dissident who had lent his support in the past to "liberals" like Pavel Litvinov and Anatoli Marchenko but who had not hesitated to criticize Sakharov's ideas when he disagreed with them. Zheludkov had recently written a book on church reform* that may have aroused Sol-

---

* *The Church of People of Goodwill*, in which Zheludkov argued that there were many Christians who did not belong to the church but who should be counted as members anyway. Zheludkov

zhenitsyn's interest in the subject in the first place, but he certainly did not share Solzhenitsyn's views. Solzhenitsyn had told the truth, said Zheludkov in an open letter to Solzhenitsyn, but not the whole truth, for the whole truth was that it was impossible for the Orthodox church in the Soviet Union to become an island of freedom in a sea of unfreedom. It was a miracle that the church existed at all, but it did so only because it accepted the state's terms. "What would you have us do? Insist on all or nothing? Try to go underground, which is unthinkable given the present system? Or try to fit into the system and exploit those possibilities that are allowed? The Russian hierarchy took the second decision."

According to Zheludkov, the patriarch was powerless either to answer Solzhenitsyn or to act on his proposals, other than by abdicating. Solzhenitsyn was further damaging the church by attacking it and would only make its work more difficult and give comfort to its enemies. Solzhenitsyn had no right to try to compel people to accept suffering and martyrdom. And he included two accusations that must have been particularly upsetting to Solzhenitsyn: that the "Lenten Letter" consisted of "talented half-truths that could prove to be more harmful to many than outright lies"; and that Solzhenitsyn was out of touch with the people: "The problem of providing children with a Christian education arises today only in those few families who are part of the rebirth of the Christian intelligentsia."[30]

In short, it was an argument for "realism," humility, and modesty in the face of Solzhenitsyn's maximalist demands for, as it seemed, heroism, self-sacrifice, and martyrdom. As such, it was a kind of recapitulation, on different territory, of Solzhenitsyn's former polemics with Tvardovsky and *Novy Mir*. Solzhenitsyn, however, had come a long way since his *Novy Mir* days, aided immeasurably by his work on *The Gulag Archipelago* and *August 1914* (not to speak of his self-discovery in the writing of his memoir, *The Oak and the Calf*), as well as by the experience gained in his struggle with the authorities, and he referred to this in his brief answer to Father Zheludkov. Zheludkov had pointed out that, in times gone by, he and others had defended Solzhenitsyn when he was under attack and that Solzhenitsyn should not therefore attack the defenceless patriarch, particularly when the author was now protected by his fame. "Are you saying that 'no one can act alone'?" wrote Solzhenitsyn. "Everyone can, and one person can—so it's not true. Had you even heard of me nine years ago? And are you now going to the other extreme—that everything is 'safe' for me now? How did this come about? Doesn't that mean there is a way?"[31]

For Solzhenitsyn there certainly had been a way—this was his unique achievement. Recapitulating his early life's history in the course of writing *The Gulag Archipelago*, and then the history of his rise to fame in *The Oak and the Calf*, he had perceived a pattern and a plot. The stories of Gleb Nerzhin, Oleg Kostoglotov, and even Ivan Denisovich had been fragments of a larger

also published a religious journal in samizdat, *V puti* (On the Path), and was a prolific writer on church and religious matters.

whole, but he had been unable at the time to discern the grand design that lay behind those fragments—or at best had glimpsed it only momentarily. In each of those fictional works the hero had struggled for moral selfhood, inner freedom, and spiritual understanding. They had been voyages of self-discovery, and at the same time searches for the holy grail. Now, in his mature years, he had himself become the searcher for the holy grail. His life was the story, the work of art, and he was simultaneously its hero and its maker. But this wasn't sufficient for Solzhenitsyn. Every story had to have a moral and a lesson, and his life, too, bore a lesson if you looked closely enough at its details. It was the story of a voyage from innocence to experience, from ignorance to knowledge, from sinfulness to moral improvement—if not to moral perfection. And this was a lesson that should and could be brought to the notice of others and that others could learn from.

The dawning of such a realization must naturally have been a slow process lasting over many years, but it seems that Solzhenitsyn's open letter to Father Zheludkov, written on 28 April 1972, was the first occasion on which he openly alluded to it in print. The "Lenten Letter" was imbued with the spirit of this discovery from beginning to end, which was presumably why Father Zheludkov had found it "pretentious" and why many other intellectuals took a dislike to its tone without quite knowing why. The faint whiff of an odour of sanctity had begun to rise from Solzhenitsyn's pages.

Interestingly enough, this new note of exaltation was recognized by another of Solzhenitsyn's ecclesiastical admirers, Father Alexander Schmemann, dean of St Vladimir's Orthodox Theological Seminary in New York State and a regular broadcaster of religious programmes to the Soviet Union over Radio Liberty. It may even have been a broadcast of Schmemann's that inspired Solzhenitsyn to compose his "Lenten Letter." Solzhenitsyn had long admired Schmemann at a distance, and the admiration was mutual. Well over a year before, Schmemann had published a long article on Solzhenitsyn in the YMCA *Vestnik* in Paris, in which he had tried to demonstrate that Solzhenitsyn was the first major *national* writer to appear in the Soviet period, that he was overwhelmingly a Christian writer who could not be understood without reference to the philosophical and theological beliefs of the Russian Orthodox church, and that Solzhenitsyn was in the great line of Russian classics stemming from Pushkin.[32] Solzhenitsyn had read the article and liked it. "It gave me a lot," he later wrote to a friend in Western Europe, "and told me a lot about myself and Pushkin that I didn't know, explaining why I always felt such an affinity for his sense of the world and the key in which he writes. The article also formulated some important aspects of Christianity that I was unable to put into words."[33]

Father Schmemann had read Solzhenitsyn's "Lenten Letter" as soon as it reached the West and been deeply impressed with it. Above all he noted its elevated style and biblical rhythms, as if the author had been addressing his words not just to mere mortals but to all eternity, and he immediately identified the tone: "In the Old Testament, in the history of the ancient chosen people, there was the astonishing phenomenon of the *prophets*. Strange and extraordinary men who could not experience peace and self-satisfaction, who swam, as they say, against the tide, told the truth, proclaimed the heavenly judgement over all untruth, weakness, and hypocrisy." These were the opening words of Schmemann's Easter sermon over the radio, and he went on to draw the logical comparison: "And now this forgotten spirit of prophecy has suddenly awakened in the heart of Christianity. We hear the ringing voice of a lone man who has said in the hearing of all that everything that is going on—concessions, submission, the eternal world of the church compromising with the world and political power—all this is evil. And this man is Solzhenitsyn."[34]

Solzhenitsyn the prophet—it was not he who had said it first, but he was listening to Schmemann on the radio and was "profoundly moved to hear that my favourite preacher had given me his approval. This in itself was my spiritual reward for the letter, and for me, conclusive confirmation that I was right."[35] A hitherto unspoken conviction of his rightness (and righteousness) would begin to inform his public actions and statements more boldly from now on—and some of his private ones too. In the years ahead he would spy "the finger of God" in events that befell him, discern "miracles" in the behaviour of others, and come to regard himself as "a sword" in the "Hand of the Highest" when going forth to do battle against his enemies.[36] The tenor of his writing in *The Oak and the Calf* would take on a more biblical note, and his vision of his role in the passion play of his life would become still more elevated and sublime. He was not just a writer, or a moralist, or a leader of public opinion, but the instrument of a higher power, and his life was no longer his own.

42

DIVORCE

A FOURTH ELEMENT IN Solzhenitsyn's "cascade of blows" to be aimed at the Soviet authorities in the spring of 1972 was his Nobel lecture. Having resolved to complete it after all, he had struggled with it throughout the preceding autumn and finally succeeded in finishing it in good time. He was rather pleased with it, in fact, since he felt that he had not compromised and had still managed to convey his political message by indirection ("I had said a *very* great deal, said all that really mattered"). He contemplated the reading of it at his improvised ceremony with considerable trepidation, feeling that it was "the most dangerous of all the actions" he was to undertake that year.[1] It is not difficult to see why. Although the outward form of the lecture was a meditation on art and the role of the artist, Solzhenitsyn had managed to include in it as comprehensive a denunciation of Soviet society as he had yet written anywhere.

In describing his path to the Nobel Prize, he recalled his days in the "Gulag Archipelago" (this was his first public use of the term outside the pages of *The First Circle*—the existence of a book of that name was barely suspected in 1972), "in a column of prisoners in the gloom of bitterly cold evenings, with strings of camp lights glimmering through the darkness," and the bleak prison-camp world in which so many had perished: "An entire national literature remains there, buried without a coffin, even without underwear—naked, with only an identifying tag on one toe." Those few who survived had expected to find a world eager to hear their message about the hell they had gone through (and to do something about it), but were stunned by the world's indifference. "It was a world which upon seeing a slimy bog exclaimed, 'What a charming meadow,' and of concrete stocks said, 'What an exquisite necklace.' Where some were shedding unstanchable tears, others danced to carefree music."

How was this possible? Solzhenitsyn explained it by the existence in the world of different scales of values, and by the different perceptions we bring to events according to their distance from us. Without naming which parts of the world he had in mind, he drew a contrast between attitudes to freedom, violence, and crime:

> There are different scales for punishment and wrongdoing. According to one, a month-long detention, banishment to the countryside, and "solitary" with white rolls and milk all stagger the imagination and fill columns of newsprint with wrath. But according to another scale it is both commonplace and forgivable to have sentences of twenty-five years, punishment cells with ice on the walls where prisoners are stripped to their underwear, lunatic asylums for normal people, and shootings at the border of unreasonable individuals who for some reason insist on trying to flee.

To make clear just whom he was addressing he added, "Our hearts are especially at ease over that exotic land about which we know nothing, from which no tidings ever reach our ears except the belated and banal conjectures of a few foreign correspondents."

The task of art, and of literature and the writer, was to overcome these differences of perception. Literature was condensed experience, the living memory of nations. ("But woe to that nation whose literature is cut short by the intrusion of force. This is not merely interference with 'freedom of the press' but the sealing up of a nation's heart, the excision of its memory.") It could speak not only to its own people but other peoples as well, and thus serve the cause of world unity.

> I believe that world literature is fully capable of helping a troubled mankind to recognize its true self in spite of what is advocated by biased individuals and parties. World literature is capable of transmitting the concentrated experience of a particular region to other lands so that we can overcome double vision and kaleidoscopic variety, so that one people can discover, accurately and concisely, the true history of another people, with all the force of recognition and the pain that comes from actual experience—and thus be safeguarded from belated errors.

Solzhenitsyn's vision of art and literature was thus strictly utilitarian, and he made this clear in a long digression on the horrors of the twentieth century and the spectacle, as he saw it, of a world collapsing in anarchy. According to this view, the East (including—especially—China) was lost to a barbarism that now threatened to engulf the whole world. The West, though still free, was being shaken to it foundations by terrorism, crime, and a rising tide of random violence, in the face of which its will was being paralyzed by affluence, apathy, and cowardice. "The spirit of Munich dominates the twentieth century. A timorous civilized world, faced with the onslaught of a suddenly revived and snarling barbarism, has found nothing to oppose it with except concessions and smiles." The United Nations had been set up to rectify some of these problems, but had been a complete failure, had become an organization of "united governments" rather than of nations, and was powerless to intervene. Matters were made worse by a complete "blockage of information flow" between the two parts of the planet, leading to entropy and ultimately to destruction. But it was precisely here that writers could help, could step in to overcome the blockage, take over the role of the United Nations, and bring peoples together. "In a fortunate instance, this could save an entire nation from a redundant, erroneous, or even destructive course, thereby shortening the tortuous paths of human history."

Solzhenitsyn was aware, perhaps, that few writers would perceive their role in this light, and theoretically he conceded "the right of the artist to express nothing but his personal experiences and his observations of himself, disregarding all that occurs in the rest of the world," but the very formulation of it indicated his disapproval. Just as, in his answer to Father Zheludkov, he had denied wanting to "force" people to make sacrifices, but had defended his right to summon them for this purpose, so, in his lecture, he summoned writers to the idea of a larger commitment.

He had begun his lecture by invoking Dostoyevsky's words "Beauty will save the world," interpreting them as a cryptic reference to the "tri-unity of Truth, Goodness, and Beauty," all of which were necessary to a work of art, but it is clear that Solzhenitsyn's position was still closer to that of his other literary hero, Tolstoy, especially in Tolstoy's later period. Like the elderly Tolstoy, Solzhenitsyn's emphasis (in this triad) was on "truth," as emerged with particular clarity from the closing pages of his lecture.

> We shall be told, What can literature do in the face of a remorseless assault by open violence? But let us not forget that violence does not and cannot exist by itself: it is invariably intertwined with *the lie*. They are linked in the most intimate, organic, and profound fashion: violence cannot conceal itself behind anything except lies, and lies have nothing to maintain them except violence. Anyone who has once proclaimed violence as his *method* must inexorably choose the lie as his *principle*. . . . [Once established,] violence no longer and not necessarily lunges straight for your throat—more often than not it demands of its subjects only that they pledge allegiance to lies, that they participate in falsehood.
>
> The simple act of an ordinary brave man is not to participate in lies, not to support false actions. . . . But it is within the power of writers and artists to do much more: *to defeat the lie*. For in the struggle with lies art has always triumphed and always will. . . .
>
> Russia's favourite proverbs are about *truth*, forcefully expressing a long and difficult national experience, sometimes in striking fashion: *One word of truth shall outweigh the whole world*.
>
> It is on such a seemingly fantastic violation of the law of conservation of mass and energy that my own activity is based, and my appeal to the writers of the world.[2]

Unfortunately, this stirring appeal was not to be made in Moscow before a select audience of liberal artists, writers, and academicians as Solzhenitsyn had planned. On 4 April, 1972, on the evening of the day when his interview with Kaiser and Smith appeared in the Western press, the Soviet authorities announced that they were refusing a visa to Dr Gierow to travel to Moscow to present the prize. The blow was supposedly softened by a suggestion that Dr Gierow might be permitted to travel at "some other, more convenient time," and the Swedish foreign minister announced the following day that there was still a possibility the prize would be presented at the Swedish embassy in Moscow—provided the ceremony did not become a "political demonstration." But the Soviet statement was a bluff and the Swedish one a pious and empty gesture: there was no chance that Solzhenitsyn would accept it.[3]

Solzhenitsyn writes in his memoir that the Soviet action in refusing the visa (and thus effectively cancelling the ceremony) was committed in pure pique over his interview and with unseemly haste, but this seems unlikely. By his own account, the Soviet government moves with painful slowness and rarely acts without carefully considering the issues beforehand. What he omits to say is that a gathering of prominent liberal intellectuals of the kind he had invited would in itself have been a political demonstration. The Swedish embassy was quite right to regard it as such (whether it was right to refuse to act as host is another matter). Even if the Soviet authorities had not known what was in the Nobel lecture, they realized Solzhenitsyn was not the person to let the occasion pass without a statement to mark it and that since foreign correspondents had been invited as well, it was equally certain that Solzhenitsyn's words would instantly travel abroad. The correspondents' presence, in fact, would ensure that the ceremony was not private, as Solzhenitsyn insisted, but public, and the idea of a public event not under the control of the authorities was simply unthinkable. Solzhenitsyn's interview may have served as a convenient pretext, but the decision itself was inevitable.

Solzhenitsyn responded with his usual tactic of writing an angry letter to Gierow and releasing it to the press. Insisting still on the private nature of his planned ceremony and predictably rejecting the Swedish foreign ministry's "belated concession," he pointed out that the Swedish conditions were insulting. The guests he had invited were all busy people who could not be expected to alter and reschedule their plans a second time, while he would regard it as "humiliating," to both Dr Gierow and himself, if he were to receive the Nobel insignia from the hands of anyone other than the permanent secretary of the Swedish Academy. "Under the rules of the . . . academy, as they have been explained to me, it can keep the Nobel insignia for an indefinite period. If I do not live long enough myself, I bequeath the task of receiving them to my son."[4]

Not entirely by way of a joke, Solzhenitsyn had invited to his Nobel ceremony Ekaterina Furtseva, the minister of culture (some speculated that it was this "insult" to a member of the government that had provoked the government to retaliate), and two Soviet correspondents, one from *Selskaya Zhizn* (Agricultural Life) and another from the trade-union newspaper *Trud* (Labour), these being, as Solzhenitsyn ironically explained, the only two major Soviet newspapers that had not attacked him. A "correspondent" from *Selskaya Zhizn* actually appeared at the appointed time (the only one to do so) but backed away when Natalia Svetlova invited him to step in for a private conversation with Solzhenitsyn. Later inquiries revealed that no one had heard of him at *Selskaya Zhizn:* his KGB superior had evidently forgotten to tell him the ceremony was cancelled.[5]

Trud sent no one, not even a police agent, for two days before the projected ceremony it had broken its self-imposed restraint and published an enormously long attack on *August 1914* by a Polish journalist named Jerzy Romanowski. The same article appeared simultaneously in *Literaturnaya Rossia*, covering three full pages, and was alleged (by *Trud*) to have been translated from a Polish article published in a paper called the *Wroclawski Tygodnik Katolikow* (Wroclaw Catholic Weekly) the preceding month.[6] Just why this charade of republication had to be adhered to is unclear, unless it was to indicate that no Soviet writer or critic had sullied his mind by actually reading Solzhenitsyn's novel, but it did not take the ingenious Zhores Medvedev long to prove that the article was not a translation from Polish, but, on the contrary, had been translated into Polish from an original Russian version. This was shown by the spelling of certain proper names—Barbara Tuchman, quoted in the article, appeared in the Polish version as "Takman," a phonetic transliteration of how it would appear in the Cyrillic alphabet. And all the quotations from Tuchman's book *The Guns of August* had been translated into Polish from Russian, not from the original English.[7]

The Romanowski broadside was followed five days later by a much shorter article in the *Literaturnaya Gazeta* entitled "Which Russia Is Solzhenitsyn Crying For?" by an obscure Belorussian writer named Leonid Proksha, accompanied by a selection of "indignant" letters from a sprinkling of outlying republics—Azerbaijan, Armenia, Kirghizia, Moldavia—and from provincial Russian cities, designed to show that the Soviet condemnation of Solzhenitsyn's novel was universal and unanimous. Proksha's article and the letters were described as a spontaneous response to the earlier articles by Larni and Stütz, and thus produced the ludicrous spectacle of commentaries on a novel that none of the writers had read, based on an article by Larni, who had also not read the novel and was responding to a review by the American journalist Anatole Shub.[8]

One week later the *Literaturnaya Gazeta* appeared with two more attacks on Solzhenitsyn. The shorter one, entitled "In Harness with the Enemy," was signed by five Belorussian writers, led by Maxim Tank. A much longer article, "Who Calls the Tune?" by an Italian writer named Eusebio Ferrari, was said to have been translated from a Milan-based magazine, *Calendario del Popolo*. Oddly, the Italian writer devoted a good half of his space to Solzhenitsyn's reviled play *Feast of the Conquerors*, which was not known to have circulated in Milan but which he claimed to have heard about from "people who have read it.'"⁹ Once more the indefatigable Medvedev did some digging and came up with the information that Ferrari was completely unknown in Milan, lived in Moscow, and had sent his article from there. Judging by the respective publication dates, the "translation" must have been prepared before the "original" had had time to arrive in Italy.¹⁰

This ponderous and clumsy campaign would have been farcical had it not carried such menacing overtones. But despite its scope and vituperativeness, it fizzled out in the end. In his Nobel lecture (still unpublished in view of the cancellation of the ceremony), Solzhenitsyn had written of the "protective wall" erected round him by the support of foreign writers: "Throughout these last years, when my work and my freedom did not collapse, when they seemed to hang in mid-air in violation of the laws of gravity, seemingly supported by nothing at all—except the invisible and mute tension of the cohesive film of public sympathy—throughout those years I gratefully and quite unexpectedly came to know the support of the world-wide brotherhood of writers." And now, too, the "cohesive film" worked. Ferrari's article even ended with a plaintive résumé of Solzhenitsyn's repeated refusals to disavow his supporters in the West and with a defensive "reply" to those foreigners who asked why Solzhenitsyn's works could not be published in his homeland. "In the Soviet Union it is a principle that no works calling for the replacement of the existing socialist order can be published," wrote Ferrari, "so why should an exception be made for Solzhenitsyn? And if there are to be no exceptions, what is the alternative?" To publish masses of "anti-Soviet" works just to prove that they were anti-Soviet was clearly absurd. And so, he concluded, "it is impossible to come to any other conclusion than that the attitude that has been formed in the Soviet Union towards Solzhenitsyn answers to the logic of the struggle of the proletariat for the victory of communism". It was an extraordinarily feeble end to what was to be the last public attack on Solzhenitsyn in the Soviet press for nearly a year and a half.

Mercifully, there were no further attempts to drag Solzhenitsyn's private life through the mud in this series of articles, but the issue did surface again in a rather different quarter—in a new samizdat journal called *Veche* (a name for the medieval "assembly" of certain self-governing Russian cities). As its name indicated, *Veche* was patriotic and traditionalist in orientation. It had been founded the preceding year by a moderately well known dissident named Vladimir Osipov, a veteran of the Mayakovsky Square poetry readings (along with people like Ginzburg, Galanskov, Bukovsky, and Edward Kuznetsov) as long ago as 1960, who had later served eight years in the camps for his unorthodox views. But whereas Bukovsky, Galanskov (until his death), and Ginzburg had joined the mainstream of the Democratic Movement, and Kuznetsov the campaign for the emigration of the Jews, Osipov had embraced a romantic variety of Slavophilism and belief in a Russian national revival. "We have no desire to belittle the qualities of other nations," he had written in 1971 in response to Western press accusations that his new journal was chauvinistic. "We want only one thing—a strengthening of Russia's national culture and patriotic traditions in the spirit of the Slavophiles and Dosto-yevsky, and a reaffirmation of Russia's originality and greatness."[11]

It would not be surprising if Solzhenitsyn was interested by such a pro-gramme, since it echoed views that had formed in his own mind, and Osi-pov's stirring editorial statement of Russia's moral degradation and need for reform, in the first issue of his magazine,[12] must have evoked a powerful response in him.* He seems therefore to have been fairly receptive to the idea of a meeting with Osipov. Just as he had earlier met and held discussions with members of the Human Rights and Democratic movements, so he appears to have wished to know more about this patriotic and religious trend, which on the surface, at least, seemed so much more congenial to his way of think-ing. It is not clear when they met, but Osipov was enormously impressed by Solzhenitsyn. "For the first time in my life, I physically experienced a man's distinction," he later told a friend. "He is totally possessed by that inner process taking place inside him. You can literally feel the thoughts of a great man in constant motion—and you are distracting him with your conversa-tion."[13]

Solzhenitsyn must have struck Osipov as the ideal romantic figure-head for a movement of Slavophiles, and he asked Solzhenitsyn to become a con-tributor to *Veche*. Solzhenitsyn declined on the ground that the magazine's shape and level were not yet clear enough.[14] It would appear that, despite Osipov's disclaimers, *Veche* was too chauvinistic for Solzhenitsyn's taste. An inhibiting feature of the magazine, from Solzhenitsyn's point of view, must have been that it appealed for support not only to dissidents and nonconformists but also to government and Party circles. In its first issue the magazine had approvingly quoted Lenin as asking, "Is the feeling of Great Russian nation-alism alien to us?"—and answering his own question, "No." So anxious, in fact, were the editors not to appear to be threatening the status quo that some dissidents suspected the magazine of having links with the KGB, and it was many months before the rumours died down. For Solzhenitsyn, the very invocation of Lenin's name was probably too much, let alone the idea that one might look to sections of the Party for a defence of Russian patriotism. In a year or so he would pick up the idea himelf—perhaps under the influ-ence of *Veche*—but in 1971 and 1972 the thought was untenable.

Whatever the level of Solzhenitsyn's interest in *Veche*, the magazine's interest in Solzhenitsyn continued to be very great, and it soon involved itself in the question of his relations with Natalia Reshetovskaya and the history

---

*Among other things Osipov wrote, "Our moral state leaves a great deal to be desired. Drunk-enness of epidemic proportions. The collapse of the family. The astounding growth of uncouth-ness and vulgarity. The loss of even an elementary perception of beauty. Foul language run riot; a symbol of the brotherhood and equality of the pigsty. Envy and spying. A don't-give-a-damn attitude to work. Thievery. A cult of bribery. Double-dealing as the norm of social behaviour. Is this all we amount to? Can this be the great nation that gave to the world such a plethora of saints, ascetics, and heroes? Have we even the right to call ourselves *Russians?*"

of their marriage. The occasion for this involvement was Irina Shcherbak's harsh criticism of Natalia Reshetovskaya in *Stern* and the *Literaturnaya Gazeta*. *Veche* apparently decided to take its own steps to refute the slanders of the *Literaturnaya Gazeta*. In its fourth issue it published an editorial note: "We are deeply shocked by the *Literaturnaya Gazeta*'s unprecedented outburst against Solzhenitsyn and his family. Solzhenitsyn's enemies have tried and are trying to blacken the glorious name of this heroic writer, who for the last decade has been Russia's conscience. We are offering our pages to a group of readers who are much concerned for the good name of Solzhenitsyn and also the good name of his wife."[15]

There followed a long article—in the form of a letter and an interview with Natalia's mother, Maria Reshetovskaya—in which the false facts in the *Stern* and the *Literaturnaya Gazeta* features were refuted and a more or less true version of Solzhenitsyn's marriage given, with the exception that the idyllic state of his relationship with Natalia was pictured as lasting until April 1970, when "they celebrated twenty-five years of marriage in their Ryazan flat" (two years after he had met Svetlova). The authors of the article also quoted and reproduced a letter Aunt Irina had written to Maria thanking her for the wonderful time she had spent in Ryazan during her visit in 1961 and refuting the *Stern* allegation that Solzhenitsyn and Natalia had been ashamed of Irina's poverty-stricken appearance and had hidden from her at the Ryazan station.

It might seem from these efforts that the letter's authors, and the editors of *Veche*, were unaware of the rift between Solzhenitsyn and Natalia and of the birth of a baby to the second Natalia—but not at all. Their purpose, as revealed in a coda to the letter, was none other than to try to heal that rift and somehow restore Solzhenitsyn's marriage to its original harmony. The *Literaturnaya Gazeta* attack was construed as being directed not only against Solzhenitsyn but in particular against his marriage, while its destruction was seen as one of the newspaper's primary aims. "To whose benefit would it be," asked the letter's authors, and "what do they want of Solzhenitsyn?"

According to the authors, unnamed enemies had struck at Solzhenitsyn's "Achilles' heel" the preceding year—presumably a reference to his falling in love with Natalia Svetlova or perhaps to the birth of her child—and all that remained now was to "wrench him from his native land." Their vision of what would follow from this was apocalyptic:

> If they are successful in this, *no matter in what form*, Solzhenitsyn's mission will be at an inglorious end. Russia's enemies, Solzhenitsyn's enemies, will at last have achieved their cherished goal. A game for large stakes is being unsuccessfully played around the figure of Solzhenitsyn, and it is evidently on an international scale. The publications in *Stern* and *Literaturnaya Gazeta* are the best proof of that. It is unclear what role in this game has been assigned to Alexander Isayevich's credulity and sometimes childish naïvety.
>
> That the leader of the opposition, or he who pretends to this role, must be irreproachable is a truth not in need of any proof, good at all times and for all

peoples. Solzhenitsyn's exceptional position in our society places his marriage on the level of a state marriage.

Disregard of these demands will irrevocably lead to Solzhenitsyn's reverse transformation into a "private individual."[16]

It was an interesting Russian variant of the Western press dictum that the lives and wives of public men must be open to public scrutiny. According to the dissident writer Mikhail Heifetz (now in Israel),* who later met Osipov in a labour camp and discussed these matters with him, there were some people on *Veche*, including Osipov himself, who genuinely sympathized with Reshetovskaya as a wronged wife and felt that Solzhenitsyn's treatment of her was the work of "dark forces." If only those forces could be exposed, their hero would perceive the folly of his ways and return to the path of rectitude. Another faction within *Veche*, however, led by the magazine's chief ideologist, Ivanov (who wrote under the pseudonym of "A. Skuratov"), had taken strong exception to what they regarded as the anti-patriotic character of *August 1914* ("Skuratov" published a sharply critical review of the novel in *Veche* no. 4) and felt that Solzhenitsyn's moral turpitude in personal matters was but a reflection of a larger and more significant failure.[17]

The question arose as to the nature of the "dark forces" supposed to be influencing Solzhenitsyn. One scapegoat was distressingly obvious: the Jews. Solzhenitsyn's new consort was Jewish on her mother's side (the fact that she was Russian on her father's side and a member of the Orthodox church was either unknown to these critics or did not count); *ergo* Solzhenitsyn was being manipulated by the Jews. Osipov, it seems, was not disposed to follow that line of argument, but he did consider that some other dark force might be influencing Solzhenitsyn for the worse—namely, the Freemasons.

The idea sounds fantastic, a typical notion of the lunatic fringe (which in a way it was). But suspicion of the Freemasons has a long pedigree in right-wing Russian circles: they have been blamed for causing both the First World War and the Russian Revolution, as well as many other related disasters. According to Heifetz, Osipov was not 100 per cent convinced by this theory, but he saw sufficient logic in it to seek a second meeting with Solzhenitsyn and warn him of the danger. Solzhenitsyn appears to have listened politely to Osipov's warning and to have assured him that his fears were greatly exaggerated.

Heifetz thinks that Osipov was to a certain extent being manipulated by "Skuratov" and some of the more extreme nationalists standing behind him. It appears that they had come to the conclusion that Solzhenitsyn was no longer their man and that the time had come to put some distance between

---

*Heifetz was sentenced to four years in the labour camps and two years' internal exile in 1974 for having written a laudatory introduction to a samizdat collection of the poetry of Iosif Brodsky (Brodsky had been expelled from the Soviet Union two years beforehand). He served his sentence in full and was allowed to emigrate to Israel immediately after completing it, in March 1980.

him and themselves. Throughout the sixties they, like almost everyone opposed to the Soviet regime in one way or another, had been able to adopt Solzhenitsyn as their common standard and feel comfortable supporting him: he had seemed an innocent victim of the system, and his own views on a whole range of subjects were sufficiently foggy for him to be given the benefit of the doubt. Indeed, all had wanted him on their side then. With his open letter to the Writers' Congress, however, and a succession of increasingly pugnacious statements since, Solzhenitsyn had transformed himself into an active opponent of the regime who could no longer be perceived as merely a victim. In this he was going further than the nationalists wished to do: they were happy to retain an authoritarian political order but wanted it based on Christianity and the Orthodox church in place of Marxism and the Party. From this point of view, Solzhenitsyn's attack on the church in his "Lenten Letter" had struck them not only as a dangerous apostasy but as the last straw. In a strange sort of way, their criticisms, in the end, turned out to be amazingly similar to those levelled against him in the official press—that he was "unpatriotic," "immoral," and "a traitor."

It is most unlikely that Natalia Reshetovskaya shared any of the ideological preoccupations of her *Veche* supporters or was indeed even aware of them. She was being exploited by them. But she was grateful to *Veche* for its defence of her, for the rosy glow thrown over her relations with Solzhenitsyn and the note of martyrdom injected into her depiction as a wronged and abandoned wife; and to show her gratitude, she offered *Veche* for its next number some extracts from her memoirs. "Dear Mr Osipov," she wrote in an accompanying letter, "allow me to express my sincere thanks to you personally and to your journal for speaking out in defence of my name. As a mark of my profound gratitude, allow me to offer your journal two chapters from my memoirs with the right of first publication."[18]

The two chapters, "Recognition" and "On the Threshold," appeared in *Veche* no. 5, in May 1972, and as a sign of the confusion then reigning in samizdat publications, carried Reshetovskaya's original dedication to "the radiant memory of Alexander Trifonovich Tvardovsky." The former leader of the liberal Marxist "loyal opposition" to the regime must have been anathema, in ideological terms, to most members of the editorial board, but they swallowed it nonetheless.

The two chapters dealt with the period 1961 to 1962, when Solzhenitsyn offered *A Day in the Life of Ivan Denisovich* to *Novy Mir*, was "recognized" by Tvardovsky, and became friends with him, so there was a clear logic to the dedication. Presumably, Osipov welcomed the chapters because he still had the highest regard for Solzhenitsyn and wanted him on the journal's side. But they must have been distasteful to "Skuratov" and his friends, who wanted to move away from Solzhenitsyn. On the other hand, the very fact that the chapters were by Solzhenitsyn's estranged and embittered wife could also have struck them as a good thing, since this seemed automatically to place *Veche* in opposition to Solzhenitsyn.

It may be that because of this circumstance some members of the editorial board took it for granted the memoirs would be hostile. But Reshetovskaya's text proved to be remarkably favourable to Solzhenitsyn. Drawing heavily on his letters to the Zubovs and on his correspondence with Tvardovsky, Reshetovskaya had produced a faithful and, on the whole, well-written account of their life in Ryazan before and after Solzhenitsyn's submission of the novel, and of the drama and excitement of its acceptance. What Solzhenitsyn thought of them is not clear. Presumably, he was relieved by their lack of distortion and vituperation—and by the fact that, given the relative obscurity of *Veche* and the suspicion with which it was regarded by the mainstream of the dissident movement, the chapters passed virtually without notice, both in the Soviet Union and abroad.

But Solzhenitsyn was far from calm about the continuing dispute over the facts of his private life, whether past or present. In his interview with Smith and Kaiser, he had again emphasized his irritation with Westerners who were preparing to write biographies of him; having heard from Veronica Stein that Burg and Feifer, the most advanced, were reluctant to restrict themselves to literary matters, he attacked them by name in the hope of persuading them to alter their plan. "Fame is deep trouble," he told Smith and Kaiser, "it consumes a lot of time to little purpose. At least the authorities don't drag me along to meetings as they do others—I'm thankful they expelled me. It was good to work when nobody knew me, nobody exercised his pen making up fairy tales about me or went around collecting lavatory-wall gossip, like those rascals Burg and Feifer."[19]

In February 1972 Solzhenitsyn's old friend and camp comrade Dimitri Panin had taken advantage of the Soviet government's modest emigration concessions to travel to the West. He had recently left his first wife and remarried. His second wife, Issa, though Catholic in faith, was Jewish by birth and thus able to fit into the Jewish quota, and take her husband with her. The two friends had become estranged in the last two or three years, especially after Solzhenitsyn's split with Natalia and Panin's remarriage, but they met for a cordial farewell, and when Panin spoke of writing his memoirs, Solzhenitsyn extracted a promise that discussion of his own life would be limited to the distant past and not touch on recent events. He for his part agreed to remove Panin's testimony from *The Gulag Archipelago* so that Panin could use the material for a book of his own.[20]

Not much more than a week later it was the Steins' turn to travel West. Yuri Stein was Jewish, and because of his involvement in the dissident and Jewish movements (not to speak of his connection with Solzhenitsyn), he had not been able to find a regular job for four years. Their departure was preceded by a meeting with Solzhenitsyn that turned into a flaming row. In packing up her flat, Veronica had found a copy of Burg and Feifer's manuscript, which she had been asked to comment on. She had already told Solzhenitsyn of her misgivings about the book, but just to make sure, she had given the manuscript to Zhores Medvedev to read, since his English was

much better than hers. Medvedev had his own interest in reading Burg and
Feifer's manuscript, since he was preparing a biographical study of his own
to be called *Ten Years after "Ivan Denisovich,"* which was scheduled for release
into samizdat (or publication in the West) at the end of the year. Medvedev
had been raised in the Soviet Union and was writing with Solzhenitsyn's
guarded approval, so he was well aware of the political minefield he was
treading and of his subject's acute sensibilities. When he saw what the two
Westerners had produced, he spotted not only numerous errors but also those
speculations and reconstructions that might either damage Solzhenitsyn
politically or touch on a sensitive nerve. He was also dismayed by what he
felt to be the distorted representation of his own role in Solzhenitsyn's affairs.
He wrote the authors a long letter putting them straight on his own actions,
and informed Solzhenitsyn of his misgivings. The latter, already rattled by
the way in which his private life had become a battleground, angrily accused
the Steins of compromising him and told them, "You got me into this, now
you can get me out of it." He asked them to do everything they could to stop
the book when they got to the West.[21]

The Steins travelled to Vienna at the beginning of March 1972, from
there to Rome, and eventually to the United States. They were visited and
lobbied not only by Burg and Feifer and their friends but also by Western
opponents of the biography, who had succeeded in getting one publisher to
drop it and were putting pressure on others to do the same. In June, Veronica Stein put out a statement under the somewhat melodramatic heading
"Alien Hands." Repeating Solzhenitsyn's accusations in his recent interview,
she described the history of her co-operation with Feifer in the preparation
of the book, her warning to him that it contained too much gossip and too
much fictional material from Solzhenitsyn's works passed off as fact, Solzhenitsyn's warning to Feifer, and her unsuccessful efforts to persuade the latter
to revise the book. She claimed that the biography was misleading, superficial, and tactless, but her main objection was that it threatened Solzhenitsyn's safety. "Its principal harm . . . lies in the fact that some of these
conjectures, rumours, and riddles . . . can provide a pretext for a new wave
of persecution against the writer. . . . It is . . . well known how in the Soviet
Union facts are juggled and falsified for the purpose of casting even the slightest
aspersion on Solzhenitsyn's past and how shamelessly 'reviews' by allegedly
objective foreign critics are instigated and then reproduced in the Soviet press
to confuse Soviet readers and turn them against the . . . writer."[22]

It was the same argument that had raged over whether to publish *Cancer
Ward*—and the biography's case was not helped by the fact that one of its
authors ("David Burg") had been a co-translator of that novel. Publication
then had not hurt Solzhenitsyn (he had secretly welcomed it), but this was
different. His whole situation had become tenser and more precarious.
Bystanders were justifiably puzzled as the argument spread through the
Western mass media and spilled over into the literary weeklies. Had that
"cohesive film of public sympathy" and that "protective wall" of world public

opinion praised so gratefully by Solzhenitsyn in his Nobel lecture not been created, in part, by articles and books about him? Surely a biography—a sympathetic biography—could only add to and strengthen that wall? And if it was a flawed and unsuccessful book, wasn't that simply the risk one took with Western attitudes to openness and publicity? Solzhenitsyn had freely turned to the Western press and Western opinion to support him in his struggle but was then irritated and disappointed with the results in the *Washington Post* and the *New York Times*. He simply did not understand the methods and values of a free press. Did he want the advantages without the disadvantages?

These and similar arguments were later to be used by Burg and Feifer in their polemics with critics of the biography, offering a curious parallel, in some ways, to the arguments of the *Veche* authors that Solzhenitsyn's private life was of public interest. The answer to the question, however, had to be yes: Solzhenitsyn did want the advantages without the disadvantages. His overriding justification was that he was engaged in a daring and unprecedented struggle that placed his very life in danger, and that only he could be the judge of what might and might not bring him crashing down. As in all other spheres of his existence, he felt that everything had to be sacrificed to the success of his mission.

In this sense, Veronica Stein had a right to attack the biography, and Solzhenitsyn had every right to instruct her to do so, but Burg and Feifer were the unfortunate victims of two sets of circumstances. One was that the times had changed between the moment they began their researches and the time when they were ready to publish. In 1969 and 1970 Solzhenitsyn's biography had not been the political issue it later became, and his overall political position had been nowhere near as tense as it had become by the end of 1972. Solzhenitsyn was therefore justified in wishing to cut back on or alter the tenor of the personal material that appeared in the book. But instead of simply informing the authors of this fact with a clear explanation of the reasons (which would have involved a tacit admission of his complicity), he was led by his preference for devious and conspiratorial methods of communication and by his usual peremptoriness to issue a simple edict not to publish at all or to cut so much material from the book as to make it meaningless. It may be that he panicked when he realized just how much of his life he had given away directly or indirectly through Veronica, or that he recognized only belatedly the potential harm the book might do to his political situation, but his volte-face came extremely late and in a manner most upsetting for the two authors and for the friends of Solzhenitsyn who had supplied them with information. These friends, having perceived the depth and violence of Solzhenitsyn's anger, and having in some cases experienced its consequences themselves, hastened to line up behind him and support his denunciation of the biography.

Veronica Stein's public statement was too late to stop the book—by the time she made it, the galley proofs were in her hand—and it duly appeared in September 1972: The reviewers had mixed reactions. Some felt that a reasonably professional job had been done, others that it was sensationalizing and superficial, and particularly dissatisfying in its concealment of its sources (in this respect the authors had played into the hands of their critics), but few seriously suggested that it would harm Solzhenitsyn in any significant way. It all looked like a storm in a teacup. The authors appeared to have cut or toned down some of the more dubious passages under the impact of the bad publicity. The controversy simmered on for several more months, Dimitri Panin and later Zhores Medvedev adding their condemnation to that of the Steins, but by the end of 1972 the book had faded from view and had no detectable consequences.

It was just about then that another aspect of Solzhenitsyn's private life became the object of international concern. In his interview with Smith and Kaiser, Solzhenitsyn had referred to his financial difficulties: "You see, since the royalties from *Ivan Denisovich* I have had no real earnings, nothing except the money left me by the late K. I. Chukovsky, and now that is running out. I lived for six years on the royalties and three years on the legacy."[23] This wasn't strictly true. Tvardovsky had personally signed a contract for *The First Circle* in 1964, after which Solzhenitsyn had been paid part of the advance, and in 1968 Tvardovsky had paid him 60 per cent of the advance on *Cancer Ward* (later giving him the full balance). Solzhenitsyn had also been paid by Mosfilm for his film script and had been receiving certain sums from the Nobel Foundation as instalments of his prize (the two Natalias and he himself had all been seen in the Moscow shops that sold goods only for foreign currency or currency certificates). Evidently, Solzhenitsyn had been exaggerating for rhetorical effect. He wanted to underline his point that he was unable to afford a secretary or to gain access to the by now astronomical Western royalties deposited with Dr Heeb. And unspoken, but probably very real, were the fears that he would have difficulty in continuing to support both Natalia Reshetovskaya and his new family.

But this little-noticed section of the interview was to have unexpected consequences. In December 1972 an American novelist and screen writer named Albert Maltz, who had been blacklisted and jailed in the 1950s as a result of the McCarthy hearings, publicly stated that he was willing to make available to Solzhenitsyn the considerable ruble royalties that had accrued to him from the publication of his novels and stories in the Soviet Union (over two million copies).[24] The story made headlines and provoked the Soviet minister of culture, Furtseva, to say that Maltz did not have any royalties in the Soviet Union, because "my country does not subscribe to the Universal Copyright Convention." She added that Solzhenitsyn was "well-off" and not in need of assistance.[25]

Solzhenitsyn himself then returned to the fray. He was deeply touched by Maltz's offer, he said, and would accept it. "Because of the desperate nature of my situation, I would accept the money as a loan, even if it is very embarrassing, but with obligatory repayment." He went on to describe a situation that was almost pathetic: "For seven years they have denied me money and housing. I have no roof of my own, and I have nothing with which to buy even the most modest small house. My only car, which I had been using for nine years, was sold to prolong my existence, and I have not got any other kind of a car."[26] This provoked two more offers of Soviet royalties from Robert Penn Warren and Bernard Malamud, both of whom had been published very successfully by the Russians.[27]

Solzhenitsyn's picture of his conditions was again vastly exaggerated, and the Soviet authorities hastened to counter it with their own set of half-truths in an article by a Novosti correspondent, Semyon Vladimirov, that appeared in the *New York Times* in early January 1973. Vladimirov offered a glowing portrait of Solzhenitsyn's Rozhdestvo cabin ("a sturdy, two-storied building with a garage and garden . . . standing on the bank of a picturesque river") and of the two "comfortable" flats allegedly available to him—one in Ryazan with Natalia Reshetovskaya, and the other in Moscow with Svetlova. He also described the "three cars" that Solzhenitsyn allegedly owned, one registered in Ryazan in the name of Reshetovskaya, and two in Moscow, registered to Solzhenitsyn and Ekaterina Svetlova, respectively.[28]

Six weeks later, Vladimirov's article was answered (also in the *New York Times*) by Zhores Medvedev, who had just arrived in the West after being unexpectedly granted a visa to do medical research in England. Medvedev ridiculed Vladimirov's idealized picture of Solzhenitsyn's wealth and comfort. The "sturdy, two-storied building" was an unheated cabin, the "river" a small stream that any schoolboy could jump over, two of the three cars belonged not to Solzhenitsyn but to the people in whose names they were registered, and Solzhenitsyn, having left Reshetovskaya, was not allowed to live with Svetlova, because he had been refused a Moscow residence permit. "If the writer came to live with his 'real' wife . . . for a period of more than two to three days, he would be fined for the first offence and sent to jail for repeated violation of this police rule." Medvedev pointed out that in the case of the cars, it was a legal offence for an individual to possess more than one. If Vladimirov was correct, "why have officials not started an action against the writer for this violation of a state law?"[29]

At this point the dispute was entered by Natalia Reshetovskaya. In a statement supplied by Novosti, she poured ridicule on Medvedev's version of the situation, underlined Solzhenitsyn's wealth in terms of Western royalties, but above all recalled the history of her marriage to Solzhenitsyn and accused Medvedev and other friends of Solzhenitsyn's of trying to conceal or distort the nature and duration of that marriage. It was a painful document, rambling and almost incoherent in places, written by a distraught and unhappy woman. Referring to the earlier discussion of money matters, she commented, "No millions can compensate for loss of faith in a man. It has fallen to my bitter lot to learn through Solzhenitsyn himself what lies and violence are. And yet he proclaims lies and violence 'the greatest evil in the world' in his Nobel lecture." Natalia revealed the hitherto closely kept secret that she had "laid hands on herself" in 1970 and that, a month ago, her mother had died prematurely "partly as a result of this incident," leaving her to care for

her two aunts, now eighty-four and ninety-five. She also informed readers
that she had recently completed her memoirs "in response to fabrications in
the Western press and by 'good friends' " and was planning to publish some
chapters of them in the near future.[30]

Two and a half weeks later, Natalia partly reversed herself. In another
letter to Novosti, made available to Western correspondents by her friends,
she accused the agency of taking advantage of her unhappiness and distorting
her words. Two reporters had recorded her original statement on tape and
returned with a transcript for her to approve. "I was offered a . . . text that
was significantly different from the original and even contained phrases and
expressions I would not use. . . . Being in an extremely depressed condition
in connection with my spiritual trauma . . . I . . . mistakenly agreed with
the text I was offered and inserted in it just a few corrections."[31]

The reason for Natalia's "spiritual trauma" and sudden reversal of position was that in the interval between the two letters her divorce from Solzhenitsyn had been completed. The adjournment of six months granted her by
the Ryazan court had expired in July 1972, and when Natalia sought and
obtained yet another adjournment, Solzhenitsyn had appealed the decision
to the Supreme Court in Moscow. The hearing had been set for November
1972, but in September, Svetlova had borne Solzhenitsyn a second son, Ignat,
and this seems to have influenced Natalia to agree to a settlement. On 18
October the two women had met, on Natalia's initiative, for the first and
only time. The meeting was subdued. The two women shook hands, and
Natalia asked Svetlova whether she had ever thought about her. Svetlova
replied that she herself was divorced and was on good terms with her former
husband and that she had expected the same to be the case with the Solzhenitsyns. She was sorry, she said, for the grief she had caused Natalia. The
following day, Natalia had written to the Supreme Court saying that, in view
of the birth of a second child to Svetlova, she withdrew her objections to the
divorce. She had sent a copy of her letter with a covering note to Svetlova,
but the tone of the note appears to have upset the younger woman, and she
had sent a cool reply that in turn offended Natalia.[32]

It is quite likely that Natalia would have withdrawn her consent at that
point, particularly since the court failed to acknowledge her declaration, but
it was just then that Maria, now eighty-two, had been struck down by a
heart attack, and on her deathbed extracted a promise from Natalia to go
through with the divorce as planned. Natalia had filed the necessary papers
shortly before Maria died, in December 1972. On 27 January 1973 Natalia
and Solzhenitsyn had met at a memorial service for Maria, and on 15 March
they had been divorced by consent at the register office in Ryazan. In addition to the money and property already promised Natalia in his original divorce
petition, Solzhenitsyn had also settled a quarter of the Nobel Prize money
on her. The only outstanding item they owned in common was the cottage
at Rozhdestvo, and this they agreed for the time being to share.[33]

Natalia's statements in her first newspaper article that she had initially
refused Solzhenitsyn a divorce because she wanted him to take the "moral

responsibility" for their divorce and that she "could not imagine life apart from . . . Solzhenitsyn" and feared being "flung into the emptiness of a lone old age" were thus perfectly true. But what had provoked her to write her letter to the *New York Times* in the first place had been resentment over the "slanders" that had been directed at her by Medvedev, which seemed to her to be but a repeat of some of the things that had appeared in the *Literaturnaya Gazeta* and that till now had gone unanswered (except by the little-known *Veche*). It is not clear how much of this she said to the Novosti reporters who came to see her, but it appears that she did show them the *Veche* chapters, and they in turn showed them to Vladimir Semyonov, the Novosti correspondent who had written in the *New York Times* about Solzhenitsyn's "great wealth."

Someone at the agency then got hold of the original *Stern* article for her, which contained more of Aunt Irina's innuendoes than the *Literaturnaya Gazeta* version, and this put her into a rage. She insisted on a meeting with Solzhenitsyn and demanded that he publicly vindicate her, since he had said nothing in her defence in his long interview with Smith and Kaiser. Solzhenitsyn declined, promising her a "posthumous rehabilitation" instead, but this was not acceptable to Natalia. She informed him that in that case she would be obliged to publish her memoirs to defend her reputation, and would do so through Novosti. It may be that she also spoke about the possibility of publishing his letters at this time (presumably to vindicate her assertions of his former love for her) or simply spoke of including extracts in her book. Whatever the case, in May 1973 Solzhenitsyn issued through Dr Heeb a general warning that copyright in the letters belonged to him, and that he would sue anyone who sought to publish them. The next month, Natalia was introduced to Semyonov, who charmed her with his erudition and good manners and completely won her over by informing her that he had once been a student of her uncle, Valentin Turkin, the film historian, and had visited his home. Semyonov told Natalia that she would have "complete freedom" to write whatever she wanted, and on 18 June 1973 she signed a contract with Novosti for a book of memoirs, with delivery set for six months later.[34]

With the divorce at last out of the way, Solzhenitsyn was free to marry Natalia Svetlova, and a quiet service took place about a month later at an Orthodox church in the Moscow suburbs. He was not able to move in with her and the children, however, for he still did not have a residence permit. One of the absurd aspects of his divorce action had been that the court had refused his first appeal on the grounds that Solzhenitsyn was not living with his new family and therefore was not a part of it. But earlier the authorities had rejected his application for a permit to live with Svetlova on the grounds that he was not married to her. The argument was thus circular and utterly contrived. For the time being, though, he would have to live with the absurd situation that it created.

43

COMING INTO
THE OPEN

SOLZHENITSYN'S FAMILY DRAMA and its reflection in the Soviet and foreign press had led to the appearance of the first cracks in the hitherto monolithic support shown him by opposition-minded members of the Soviet intelligentsia. The high-water mark of that support had coincided with the award of the Nobel Prize for literature in 1970, but since then a certain wavering had become discernible. Many admirers not affected by the family dispute were disturbed by the tenor of his interview with the two Western correspondents, by the conservative and, as it seemed, anti-Western tenor of his Nobel lecture, and by the pieties of his "Lenten Letter." This split was shown to have widened still further in the responses to *August 1914*.

By the end of 1972 the novel had been in print for eighteen months, but the response of Soviet readers had been retarded by the scarcity of available copies. Their predicament and its partial solution were described by the editor of a collection of unofficial reviews of the novel that appeared in the last months of 1972.

> We must bear in mind how difficult it is to *obtain* Solzhenitsyn's new book at all. And not only difficult, but dangerous. It is smuggled in from abroad and retyped or reproduced by other means. Nevertheless, the articles here show clearly that absolutely all our contributors . . . are well acquainted not only with this novel but with Solzhenitsyn's entire output. The degree of danger entailed is itself a measure, so to speak, of the dynamic force of readers' interest in the subject.[1]

Interest had been fanned by the official campaign against the novel the preceding January and February, which resulted not only in *Veche*'s response to certain of the Soviet press's allegations but also in the compilation of these independent reviews. Entitled *Reading "August 1914" in the Homeland*, the collection contained a wide spectrum of opinion.

The comparison and contrast with Tolstoy's *War and Peace*, which Solzhenitsyn was inviting by the juxtaposition of his battle scenes with scenes of life at the rear and by his polemic with Tolstoy's theory of history, was the framework within which most of the writers examined the novel, and opinions were divided as to which parts they preferred. On the whole, they seemed to find the war sections the more exciting. Solzhenitsyn, it was felt, excelled in the description of men in action, and his account of Samsonov's retreat and suicide was almost unanimously hailed as the high point of the novel. But reservations were expressed about the plethora of detail in the exhaustive descriptions of advances and retreats and the minutiae of military strategy and tactics; the narrative line, many felt, tended to be obscured by an excess of information. As for the scenes of "peace," these were generally felt to be leisurely and charming, but too fragmentary and slight to make a judgement on, while the characters still lacked the vividness and vitality of Tolstoy's creations.

The most controversial aspect of the novel, and the occasion of the deepest split among reviewers, was its underlying political philosophy. The corrosive portrait of a corrupt, cowardly, and criminally inept ruling class (including the tsar and his entourage) that Solzhenitsyn had drawn was generally too much for those patriots and nationalists who approved of his positive picture of a buoyant and flourishing pre-revolutionary Russia, and his apparently pro-German sentiments offended them even more. "Skuratov," whose article from *Veche* was included in the collection,[2] accused Solzhenitsyn of being anti-Russian and the dupe of German propaganda, while another *Veche* author added "anti-monarchism" to the list of Solzhenitsyn's sins. "Skuratov" contrived to find in Solzhenitsyn's praise of engineers and industrialization echoes of Sakharov's theory of "convergence" and therefore Westernism—further evidence, in his view, of Solzhenitsyn's hostility to Russia. "Westernizers," on the other hand, were offended by Solzhenitsyn's negative attitude towards the intelligentsia, and particularly towards the liberals and social democrats. In this respect, the character of Lenartovich attracted much attention. A social democrat (that is, in Russian terms of the period, a Communist), Lenartovich was shown as having adopted a defeatist attitude from the very beginning of the war and as behaving like a coward during the fighting, in contrast to the heroism displayed by the upper-class staff colonel, Vorotyntsev, and Lenartovich's "pair" and opposite, Yaroslav Kharitonov. Critics felt that this characterization was not only anachronistic ("defeatism," except among the Bolshevik leaders in exile, had become fashionable in Russia only in the last year of the First World War) but also heavily biased and not terribly convincing. One wonders whether they unconsciously detected the difficulty that Solzhenitsyn had experienced in turning the Communist hero of his original plan for the novel into one of its principal villains.

Also controversial were Solzhenitsyn's language and literary devices. In language he had moved a long way from *Cancer Ward* and even from *The Gulag Archipelago* (unfamiliar to readers as yet) and was developing his style in two specific directions. On the lexical level, he was still attempting to bring his language closer to what he regarded as its true Church Slavonic and Old Russian roots. This involved the liberal use of archaisms and the introduction of many neologisms—words freshly coined by Solzhenitsyn according to the regular rules for word formation in Russian, but not used before. On the syntactical level, he sought the maximum possible degree of terseness and compression, along the lines advocated by his latest literary hero, Evgeny Zamyatin (author of *We* and other works in the twenties).* In addition, he made a strenuous effort to capture folk rhythms and idioms in his language, studding his narrative with proverbs, popular sayings, unexpected inversions, and provincialisms, many of them archaic and obscure.

The effect of this on Russians is hard for a foreigner to grasp or reproduce. Zhores Medvedev, in discussing the novel, quotes a reader who complained that after a hundred pages he became bogged down in "unnecessary neologisms and anachronisms" that he could not stomach.[3] Among the samizdat critics, there were some who also found the language artificial and stylized, especially in the "peace" scenes, though it was generally acknowledged to work better in the passages of military action. Another reader wrote, by contrast, that "the best thing about the novel is the language—extraordinarily vivid, condensed, full of surprises, new word formations that enrich our literature and go to make up Solzhenitsyn's unique style. . . . Whatever else you may say about the novel, Solzhenitsyn takes the Russian language further forward than any other writer has managed to do this century."[4]

Another surprise was Solzhenitsyn's literary devices. Interspersed with passages of traditional realism were cinematic sequences, montages of pre-revolutionary newspaper headlines, advertisements and street posters, proverbs printed in bold capital letters, and brief chapters of historical summary and exegesis. The cinematic passages and montage technique had been borrowed from Dos Passos, whose novel *1919* Solzhenitsyn had come across and read in the Lubyanka immediately after the war.[5] Solzhenitsyn's approach differed from Dos Passos's "seeing eye" technique, however, in that his attempts to reproduce the cinematic effect were more exhaustive and literal, reflecting the devices he had used in his screenplay *The Tanks Know the Truth* to convey the actual sensation of viewing a film, rather than rendering it impressionistically, while his newspaper montages reflected that fascination with the sheer vitality and even vulgarity of a free press that he had experienced when reading through his mother's papers and clippings for the first time. Such vivid variety had been a revelation to a Soviet citizen raised on the grey sludge of the Soviet press, and he presumably hoped that its reproduction would evoke

---

*Evgeny Zamyatin (1884–1937), one of the finest Russian writers of the twentieth century, has been sadly neglected. His brilliant dystopian novel *We*, written in 1920, prefigured (and influenced) both Huxley's *Brave New World* and Orwell's *1984*. His expressionist prose was noted for its extraordinary concision.

similar wonder in his readers. It did not meet with much enthusiasm, however, and although these experimental flourishes did not provoke the same
controversy as his language, they did not find many defenders either.

Despite these misgivings, *August 1914* was correctly perceived as a radically new departure for Solzhenitsyn, and even the controversy around it
differed from earlier controversies over his works. In those the controversy
had resided principally in Solzhenitsyn's differences with the Soviet government and his attempts to overcome or circumvent them, and this had defined
the nature of his support, even among some political "loyalists." Now the
true controversy was located among his natural supporters.

Part of the reason for this development may be found in Zhores Medvedev's explanation of why he reacted to *August 1914* with less enthusiasm
than to the earlier works. Solzhenitsyn's first books, writes Medvedev, had
been "emotionally exhilarating" to read because they dealt with events that
"revived smouldering memories, stimulated a complex mixture of feelings
. . . resurrecting for some the events of their own life and forcing others to
remember the fate of their fathers, brothers, sisters, husbands, wives, and
friends. Such is the history of our country that I don't know anyone who
would not identify the fate of Solzhenitsyn's heroes with the fate of his nearest and dearest."[6] In his new book, however, Solzhenitsyn had turned to a
period remembered only by the very elderly, so that its direct emotional
impact was weakened. Content receded in urgency and importance to take
its place beside style and form as only one among many relevant elements in
the novel.

In this way, *August 1914* became the first of Solzhenitsyn's works to
float partially free of the rigid critical framework imposed by Soviet ideological categories of "for or against." His best books had always transcended
that category, but they had also fitted into it fairly snugly and had lent themselves to that characterization: who was "for" the authorities was against him,
who was "against" the authorities was for him. But by turning back to history and by publishing his work uncensored and abroad, he was able to
escape the constraints of the Soviet either/or and to achieve a position that
would have been absolutely normal for a writer in most other parts of the
world—to have his novel read and criticized on its merits—but that was fresh
and somewhat unsettling for Soviet readers (and for Solzhenitsyn himself).
This in turn disrupted the unanimity of opinion that had enveloped his earlier works. His supporters hitherto had formed an ill-defined but palpable
"party" opposed to the party in power, and each new work, quite apart from
its literary qualities, had been greeted as another plank in the "party" platform—a process from which even the weaker works had benefited. But *August
1914* refused to fit into the old categories. It "split" the opposition in different
ways, leaving many of them puzzled and bewildered. And because of the
book's artistic unevenness and weaker aesthetic impact, it was harder to defend
on purely literary grounds.

Solzhenitsyn was painfully aware of these conflicting reactions and conscious that his novel had failed to trigger off the usual unanimous chorus of praise, but he chose to take a narrowly political view of the reasons for it.

It is . . . from the appearance of *August 1914* that we must date the schism among my readers, the steady loss of supporters, with more leaving me than remained behind. I was received with "hurrahs" as long as I appeared to be against Stalinist abuses only; thus far the entire Soviet public was with me. In my first works I was concealing my features from the police censorship—but by the same token, from the public at large. With each subsequent step, I inevitably revealed more of myself: the time had come to speak more precisely, to go even deeper. And in doing so, I should inevitably lose the reading public, lose my contemporaries in the hope of winning posterity. It was painful, though, to lose support even among those closest to me.[7]

There is a degree of truth in this interpretation, but it is not the whole story. It was by no means only the "anti-Stalinists" (for which read "Leninists") who were disenchanted with Solzhenitsyn's novel. It was the "liberal democrats" too (who formed a majority among his supporters), as well as the extreme wing of the nationalists. And there were other, more disinterested critics who were simply disappointed with it on literary grounds.

This last response came out with particular clarity in the foreign reviews, which overlapped in time with the samizdat articles. The main Western editions of the novel had been synchronized to appear more or less simultaneously in August 1972—a feat of sentimental timing that was entirely to the taste of the author (though not requested by him) but that extracted an additional price of its own, particularly in the case of the English-language edition, whose translator was later to list financial blackmail and physical breakdown as among the pressures he was subjected to in trying to meet his deadline.[8] Inevitably, it was a publishing event of the first magnitude. The vast sums of money expended on the rights were quickly recouped as the novel went straight onto the best-seller lists. By November it had climbed to number two in the important American market (it was never quite to make it to number one), and when the list for the whole of 1972 was published, it again appeared in second place, outselling books by Irving Wallace and Taylor Caldwell and even Frederick Forsyth's *The Odessa File*—though the latter had been held back to catch the Christmas trade.

The reviews of the novel were decidedly mixed. Like Russian readers, the reviewers noted Solzhenitsyn's abandonment of personal testament for historical inquiry and generally regretted the loss of intensity that this entailed. Like the Russians, too, they generally preferred the battle scenes to the rest, though some found even these too encumbered with their documentary sources. Reading them, wrote one critic, was "like being inside the bound volumes of military memoirs" or contemplating "a war seen from staff maps."[9]

Shapelessness was a worry of most commentators on the novel. It was well known that this was the first in a series and that broken-off narrative lines were to be continued in later volumes. But there are many precedents for novels in series, and it was felt that each volume should have an aesthetic cohesiveness of its own. As for the formal devices—the cinematic passages, the newspaper clippings, and the proverbs—they struck Western readers as no less old-fashioned than Solzhenitsyn's brand of realism, distractions from the main narrative rather than additions to it.

All this created difficulties for the generally well disposed reviewers. As the American novelist Herbert Gold wrote, it was a question of tact: How to reconcile this "clumsy fictional apparatus" ("clumsy in technique, outdated in form, episodic to distraction,"[10] as the *New York Times* reviewer called it) with its lofty aims ard Solzhenitsyn's patent sincerity and courage?[11] One way out of the dilemma was to examine the novel's historical and political ideas, concentrate on the content and forget the form, though here, too, the critics ran into difficulties. Mary McCarthy, in a determinedly sympathetic review, pointed out that Solzhenitsyn's novel seemed almost deliberately designed to offend the sensibilities of Western liberals—in other words, the sort of people most likely to be reviewing it. Its political line was reactionary, it lauded patriotism and nationalism over revolutionary discontent and internationalism, and it was unreservedly hostile to the pre-revolutionary Russian intelligentsia. Nor was its approach to its historical material "escapist" or objective: it was committed and partisan. Every character, every episode, was planned to ram home the same message. It was not just a novel but an impassioned homily, a "moralized myth" for the times.[12]

The overall response, in short, was one of respectful bewilderment: Why had Solzhenitsyn turned his back on what were plainly his strengths as a novelist—his ability to transform and universalize deeply felt personal experience—and buried himself in the "remote" past? And why had he abandoned his favourite variety of solid realism for an excess of historical documentation tricked out with the dubious experimentalism of the twenties? Comparisons to Tolstoy or Dostoyevsky now struck the reviewers as grotesquely inflated. Margaret Mitchell, Pearl Buck, James Michener, and Maxim Gorky were the names now invoked, and one reviewer committed the sacrilege of comparing Solzhenitsyn to his arch-enemy and *bête noire*, the first secretary of the Writers' Union, Konstantin Fedin.

One aspect of Solzhenitsyn's enterprise, perhaps, did not receive its proper due in the Western reviews, and that was the manner in which *August 1914* fulfilled the programme that Solzhenitsyn had prescribed for writers in his Nobel lecture: "Literature transmits . . . condensed experience from generation to generation. In this way, literature becomes the living memory of a nation. It . . . safeguards a nation's bygone history and . . . preserves the nation's soul." Soviet citizens have been cut off from so much of their history for so long that they have become totally disoriented and ahistorical in their thinking. Solzhenitsyn saw his task, in his historical novels, as being to oppose that disorientation and reawaken his countrymen's historical awareness, thus forcing them to re-examine old assumptions. At the same time, he was reopening crucial questions to which the Soviet regime felt that it had long ago provided definitive answers, showing, among other things, that pre-revolutionary Russia had had not just two choices—for the tsar or for revolution—but a third as well: to build something completely different. Behind this was the further, unspoken thought that if the choice had existed then, perhaps—in however attenuated a form—it still existed now.

For Westerners, the inner logic of Solzhenitsyn's development was obscured by a radical difference of context. For them, pre-revolutionary history was no secret or mystery. The orthodox Soviet version of history was but one of several versions available to them, and Solzhenitsyn's version would become another. But for Soviet readers it was a revelation to hear one of their own writers (however unorthodox and anathematized) broach issues that were strictly taboo. Solzhenitsyn had remained true to his vocation of saying the unsayable, of pointing to the august emperor's shameful lack of clothing, and it was entirely logical that he should take his investigation of the phenomenon of Soviet power back to its roots and origins. The question of the artistic merits of his enterprise was another matter, as was the system of values that informed his treatment of the subject, but the very service he performed in turning his readers' attention to this period was inestimable, and was wholly consonant with the ambitious aims he had set himself. He did indeed provoke a debate about Russia's past (and future) that continues to this day.

By the time this discussion took place he was well into the writing of the second volume in the series, *October 1916*, and already tracing out the main lines of the third, *March 1917*. These two were evidently to be more closely linked with one another than with volume 1; and since they brought the action up to the difficult events surrounding the February Revolution, they would obviously be of crucial importance to the success or failure of the whole enterprise. Perhaps for that reason, he found them harder to write than volume 1.

At the same time, he began preparations for the publication of a collection of essays on social, political, and religious themes relevant to contemporary Russia. It is not clear whether the idea for such a collection grew out of his earlier plan to publish a journal or was meant from the beginning as an independent project. At all events, it seems that at some point since 1969 he had dropped the journal idea as impractical and over-ambitious. Or perhaps he simply yielded to an alternative plan for a journal first proposed by Vladimir Bukovsky in the winter of 1971–72 and taken up by the novelist and short-story writer Vladimir Maximov after Bukovsky's imprisonment in January 1972.[13] A leading participant in the latter project was an acquaintance of Solzhenitsyn's called Mikhail Agursky. Agursky, an unconventional Zionist who had links with *Veche*,* was ambitious to make his mark in dissident

* *Veche* no. 5 had printed a long letter from Agursky pointing out that Zionists and the Russian nationalists were not, as was commonly supposed, in conflict with one another, since both favored the affirmation of their peoples in their separate homelands—a theory that was highly congenial to Solzhenitsyn. In a sense, the plan for a journal came to fruition when Maximov founded *Kontinent* in the West.

circles as a kind of honest broker between Jews, liberals, and nationalists, and he saw the journal as a possible means of achieving this. Solzhenitsyn apparently knew and approved of the project, though he had no wish to participate personally.

The collection of essays was a different matter entirely. The stimulus for the collection seems to have been a series of five articles that had appeared in no. 97 of the *Vestnik RSKhD* (Herald of the Russian Student Christian Movement), published in Paris by the same company that had published *August 1914.** The articles, anonymous and pseudonymous, had been sent from the Soviet Union by a group of liberal Christian intellectuals concerned about the future of the Soviet Union, and they had painted a bleak picture of Soviet society and the state of Russian culture. What must have particularly caught Solzhenitsyn's eye was that two of the writers had been directly inspired by the example of *Landmarks* and had quoted it in their essays, while their themes were very much in the *Landmarks* tradition and spoke to his own interests: the role of the intelligentsia, Russian nationalism, the renaissance of religious feeling in the Soviet Union, the character of the Russian people. One of the writers even called for a programme of mass repentance by the Russian people, an idea that must have struck a responsive chord in Solzhenitsyn's thinking.

But the impulse to join in this debate arose not from a desire to endorse and support the writers in *Vestnik* (though there was much that Solzhenitsyn agreed with in their essays) but from an urge to contradict and refute them. For a central plank in their arguments was that the chief danger to a healthy development of society was "Russian messianism," the idea that the Russians had somehow been chosen by God to play a special role in history and to lead other peoples to a truer understanding of the world. Solzhenitsyn felt that the writers showed an arrogant contempt for Russian tradition, had an inflated estimate of the importance of the intelligentsia, and displayed cowardice in not revealing their real names.

He therefore decided to produce a counterblast, taking as his model the admired *Landmarks* and its less well known successor, *De Profundis.* To make the identification more explicit, he dreamed up an eccentric Russian title, *Iz pod glyb* (From under the Rubble),† that deliberately echoed the Russian for *De Profundis: Iz glubiny.* He himself decided to write two essays for the collection—on national repentance and the role and nature of the intelligentsia, and to include his unpublished letter to Sakharov on Sakharov's memorandum, with a postscript relating it to the arguments of the *Vestnik* authors. Other contributors to the volume were to be Igor Shafarevich (Solzhenitsyn's co-editor), Mikhail Agursky, and two obscure young historians of art and

---

* The *Vestnik PSKbD* was founded in 1925 as the organ of the Russian Student Christian Association. See note to p. 693.

‡ The English title of the book was provided by myself, when I prepared the English translation after discussing it with Solzhenitsyn, but it is not really satisfactory. *Glyb* suggests something heavy and immovable, as well as what has settled in one place for a long span of time.

religion, Evgeny Barabanov and Vadim Borisov.

The anthology was to be Solzhenitsyn's first attempt at some sort of group action and was the first indication of a desire to define for himself his own platform and his own "party" within the growing debate in dissident circles about Russia's future. For most of the years of his fame, he had preserved a jealous distance between himself and the other dissidents, meeting a few of them individually and privately from time to time, but hardly ever making common cause with them and never identifying himself with them in public. Only once had this principle been breached. In the chaos and hullabaloo surrounding the award of the Nobel Prize in the winter of 1970, distracted by the crisis with Natalia, he had allowed himelf to be co-opted as a corresponding member of the Committee for Human Rights, recently founded by Valery Chalidze, Andrei Sakharov, and another young physicist, named Andrei Tverdokhlebov. The committee's aims, inspired mainly by Chalidze, were to make a systematic and comparative study of Soviet and international law in the field of human rights, to try to persuade the Soviet authorities to observe the laws they already had, and to bring those laws, if possible, closer to international norms. In many respects it was a continuation of the ideas of Esenin-Volpin about instilling a "consciousness of legality" into Soviet society, and Esenin-Volpin was appointed one of two expert consultants to the committee (the other was Boris Tsukerman, also a physicist).

It seems probable that Solzhenitsyn had agreed to join only because Sakharov asked him and that he regretted it almost immediately, for he had taken no active part in the committee's deliberations, except to persuade the other members in May 1971 to accept his new friend Igor Shafarevich as a member (after which Shafarevich seems to have operated more or less as Solzhenitsyn's agent). Solzhenitsyn was in fact out of sympathy with the committee's rather pedantic legal approach and took particular exception to two reports by Chalidze. One, entitled "The Rights of Persons Declared Mentally Ill," recommended that patients in mental hospitals be given certain sexual rights, which offended Solzhenitsyn's sense of moral propriety, while another, "Notes on the Meaning of the Concept of 'Political Prisoner,' " struck him as absurd and superfluous.[14]

Another aspect of the committee's activities that must have disturbed Solzhenitsyn, though he was silent about it at the time, was its enthusiastic involvement in the swelling campaign for the right of Soviet Jews to emigrate. The idea of a Jewish emigration had been born in the aftermath of the Six-Day War, in June 1967, and had received new impetus after the invasion of Czechoslovakia in 1968. The first had aroused feelings of pride and national identity among Soviet Jewry, and the second had deprived them of the hope of a real improvement in Soviet conditions, especially as both events had provoked outbursts of anti-Semitism in the Soviet press. The issue was masked for a while by the fact that many Jews were active in the Human Rights Movement and in producing and distributing samizdat. Their "cause" seemed naturally bound up with the larger cause of more human and civil rights for all. But in 1970 the Jews had decided to launch their own samizdat journal—modelled on the *Chronicle of Current Events*—with the pregnant title of *Exodus*. That same year, the government had organized a press conference of prominent and successful Jews to demonstrate that accusations of discrimination were false, but this had led in turn to a celebrated "Letter of the Thirty-nine" demanding the right to emigrate to Israel with renewed vigour and, in June, to the even more celebrated attempt by twelve Soviet citizens, mainly Jews, to hijack a plane in Leningrad and fly it to Israel. The death sentence imposed on two of the "conspirators," Mark Dymshits and Edward Kuznetsov, in December (it was subsequently commuted to life imprisonment)* only served to heighten the clamour—especially abroad—and by 1971 the authorities had weakened on this one point and begun to allow significant numbers of Jews to emigrate.[15]

Among the non-Jews most active in supporting the Jewish activists were Chalidze and Sakharov. For Chalidze it was a question of legality and civil rights: at the request of Soviet Jews he drew up numerous appeals and petitions and represented them in their negotiations with the authorities. For Sakharov it was a question of morality and human rights, and he, too, had begun to appeal on behalf of individual dissidents and to appear at their trials.

For Sakharov it had also become a personal issue. In 1970 he had met the half-Armenian and half-Jewish dissident Elena Bonner at one of the trials he attended. Like Solzhenitsyn, Sakharov fell in love just short of his fiftieth birthday (though unlike Solzhenitsyn he was a widower), and he married Elena Bonner in 1971. Like Solzhenitsyn, too, he came under considerable influence from his new wife—more so, according to those who have known both men. Elena Bonner was closely connected with the movement for Jewish emigration and was even pretending to be the aunt of one of the two leaders of the "hijacking plot" (Kuznetsov), so that she could visit him in the camps. Inevitably, Sakharov became closely involved, and it was Sakharov, as one of the few non-governmental observers admitted to the appeal by Kuznetsov and Dymshits against the death penalty, who had emerged from the court-house afterwards to inform the waiting crowd that "we have won" and that the death sentences had been commuted to fifteen years in the labour camps. "If you need any help," he had added, "call me or Chalidze."[16] In October 1971 he had written a special appeal to the Soviet government entitled "Let Soviet Citizens Emigrate," calling for the law to be changed and an amnesty to be granted to all who had been jailed or victimized (including many non-Jews) for expressing a wish to emigrate.

---

* Although the charge was hijacking, it seems that the members of the group involved were hardly equipped to carry out a proper hijacking, but rather wished, out of despair, to draw attention to the plight of the Soviet Jews and their desire to emigrate—in which they were ultimately successful. Kuznetsov's *Prison Diaries* (London and New York, 1975) give an excellent account of the motives and aims of the "hijackers."

Solzhenitsyn was not opposed to the desire of many Soviet Jews to emigrate or their having the right to do so. Indeed, he felt more at home with Zionists of the type of Agursky than he did with those who demanded additional rights for the Jewish population at home. There was no conflict between the brand of Russian nationalism that attracted Solzhenitsyn and the Jews' wish to build their own nation in Israel. But Solzhenitsyn felt that the right to leave the country was secondary, that the enormous publicity the Soviet Jews were drawing in the West was distracting attention from the more important struggle of the whole population for more rights inside the Soviet Union. Furthermore, the emigration campaign was having far more success than the larger struggle. In 1971 more than fourteen thousand Jews had been allowed to leave for abroad, and in 1972 there were to be more than thirty thousand. The need seemed greater elsewhere.

Solzhenitsyn did not resign from the Human Rights Committee, and in the minds of both the dissidents and the government, he therefore remained associated with the human-rights movement in a way that he had not been earlier. This had become clear at Vladimir Bukovsky's trial in January 1972, where Bukovsky was accused of compiling information about the committal of political prisoners to mental hospitals (which had brought him into close touch with the Human Rights Committee). The prosecutor deliberately linked Bukovsky's activities with Solzhenitsyn's "lampoons on the Soviet people, which blacken the achievements of our homeland and the dignity of the Soviet peoples," and declared Solzhenitsyn to be the "inspirer" of anti-Soviet activities like Bukovsky's.[17] This was at the time of the *Stern* article and the assault on *August 1914* in the Soviet press, and it was fairly obvious that the campaign had been sanctioned by the same security forces that set out that winter to suppress the *Chronicle of Current Events*, the *Ukrainian Herald* (a dissident journal modelled on the *Chronicle*), and *Veche*. Word seems to have gone out from the government that all forms of uncensored writing were to be cut short once and for all. Hundreds, if not thousands, of searches were carried out in Moscow, Leningrad, Kiev, Vilnius, and the scientific research and industrial centre of Novosibirsk (Solzhenitsyn's works were among those automatically confiscated if found). In the Ukraine alone, over a hundred arrests were made and tons of documents confiscated. Another wave of preventive arrests occurred on the occasion of President Nixon's visit to Moscow in May 1972 to inaugurate the new superpower policy of *détente* ("Telephones were disconnected, activists faced sudden calls for military retraining or two-week jail terms for 'hooliganism,' members of the [Jewish] Information Committee were kept in prisons far from Moscow until the president departed"),[18] and the Novosti press agency issued a special 106-page booket called "The Press on Solzhenitsyn." Consisting exclusively of Soviet press attacks on the author, the booklet had a print run of two thousand copies in English, two hundred in French, and but one hundred in Russian, while a shorter version appeared in two thousand copies in English.[19] The culmination of the campaign came in June 1972 with the arrest of two leading dissidents, Piotr

Yakir and Victor Krasin, and their subsequent interrogation by the KGB. Both men cracked under questioning and gave their investigators sufficient information about the workings of the *Chronicle of Current Events* and the people behind it to close the *Chronicle* for a while and get dozens more dissidents arrested.[20] By the spring of 1973 it seemed that the authorities had succeeded in their aim. Samizdat was quieter than before, the *Chronicle* and *Veche* had suspended publication, Andrei Amalrik was sentenced to camp for the second time (for "anti-Soviet propaganda"), the investigation of Yakir and Krasin ("Case No. 24," as it was called) was proceeding with a great deal of fanfare, and the number of individuals able and willing to stand up to the authorities was smaller than at any other time since the beginning of the Democratic Movement in the mid-sixties.*

It was in these circumstances that Solzhenitsyn grew close for a time to the only other figure in the Soviet opposition with a stature approaching his own—Andrei Sakharov. Sakharov had long since lost his official status as one of the Soviet Union's top scientists, but he retained his membership in the Academy of Sciences, continued to do work at the Lebedev Institute, and still had the use of a flat in Moscow and an official dacha in Zhukovka. It turned out that the latter was but a hundred yards from Rostropovich's dacha, and between 1970 and 1972 the two men had a number of meetings. It was Solzhenitsyn who initiated them, by sending Sakharov his critique of the latter's "Memorandum" and later discussing it with him. It seems he felt sufficiently close to Sakharov to invite him to contribute to *From under the Rubble*, especially after Sakharov had modified some of the ideas in his "Memorandum" in a "Postscript" sent to Leonid Brezhnev in June 1972. Here Sakharov had introduced some new thoughts about the decay and corruption of Soviet society and for the first time stressed that a moral and spiritual regeneration would have to accompany social and political reforms. He also proposed the setting up of an "International Council of Experts" to advise national governments, an idea of which Solzhenitsyn thoroughly approved, although in other respects Solzhenitsyn was less enthusiastic about Sakharov's tactics. He recognized in Sakharov's defence "not of 'mankind' or 'the people' at large but of each individual victim of oppression a devotion to truth and a love of humanity with a miraculous power to heal our ills," but he felt that by his innumerable appearances at trials and his numerous open letters, Sakharov was needlessly expending his energies and exhausting himself. Sakharov's important statements, such as his "Postscript," tended to get overlooked in the welter of less important declarations and thereby lost their impact. Such behavior was diametrically opposed to Solzhenitsyn's own. Whereas Solzhenitsyn meticulously planned each public statement and carefully abstained from getting mixed up in the affairs of other dissidents, Sakharov continually fired off declarations and letters in all directions and kept

---

*The *Chronicle* later restarted, after an eighteen-month hiatus, and continues to this day. Yakir and Krasin decimated the Democratic Movement by naming dozens of names. They were eventually tried in August 1973 and given token sentences.

open house for anyone who cared to visit him. As a result of this "incorrigible urge to champion the persecuted," as Solzhenitsyn wrote of him, and of his extraordinary generosity and humility, Sakharov had become the people's tribune.[21] Solzhenitsyn, on the other hand, was proud, suspicious, secretive, and aloof. He, too, was the people's tribune, but only of the collective people and on his own terms.

There was, in the event, no meeting of minds or of personalities. Sakharov found the idea of *From under the Rubble* "uninspiring" and declined to participate. Solzhenitsyn was suspicious of the dissidents who clustered round Sakharov in ever-greater numbers and feared that any secrets confided to Sakharov would find their way to his visitors and eventually to the KGB. "We were no longer left alone for the space of a single conversation," wrote Solzhenitsyn later. "So we condemned ourselves to separate action, and when we met we merely exchanged news and opinions on events already in the past." Gradually, these meetings became less frequent, and in the spring of 1973 the Sakharovs visited Rostropovich's dacha for the last time. "They were in a gloomy frame of mind. . . . Even [Sakharov's] posture had changed. Instead of sitting straight and tall on his chair as he used to when we first met . . . he slumped against the back of the chair so that his baldish head was pulled tightly downward and his shoulders were up around his ears." Sakharov was coming under increasing pressure from the authorities, who had been victimizing his children and stepchildren at school and work, and he was contemplating the possibility that the children might go abroad and that he, too, might emigrate.[22] Here was a notable point of difference between the two men, and it may be presumed that Solzhenitsyn attempted to argue against it before they parted. It was to be nearly nine months before they met for one last time, and then it would be not in Zhukovka but in Moscow, when both men were under intense pressure.

As it happened, Solzhenitsyn was feeling increasingly restive in Zhukovka. Later he was to write nostalgically of "my life at Rostropovich's dacha, in blissful conditions such as I had never known in my life (peace, country air, and urban comfort),"[23] but the price of his comfort was growing too high. Rostropovich, after his open letter and refusal to expel Solzhenitsyn from his dacha, had been subjected to a string of humiliating insults and increasingly severe sanctions. First he had been forbidden to travel abroad to fulfill his concert engagements there (formerly he had spent up to six months of every year on foreign tours).* Then he was banned from all radio and television concerts in the Soviet Union. He was also banned for two months from playing with the Moscow Philharmonic Orchestra, but vigorous protests by Moscow's leading musicians caused the ban to be lifted again. Worst of all, he was deprived of his work at the Bolshoi Theatre—his favourite post. At the same time, his name was cut from all newspaper descriptions of con-

---

*One consequence of this decision was that the first performance of the Polish composer Lutoslawski's First Cello Concerto, which was dedicated to Rostropovich, had to be postponed indefinitely, as did the performance of a similar concerto by Benjamin Britten.

certs where he had performed, his photograph was removed from a wall display marking the fiftieth anniversary of the Bolshoi orchestra, and his wife, the well-known opera singer Galina Vishnevskaya, was simultaneously humiliated and squeezed out of Soviet musical life.

Solzhenitsyn felt that it was not right for "one artist to wither so that another might flourish" and decided to leave Rostropovich's home in the spring of 1973. Now that his marriage to Svetlova was legal, he applied again for a Moscow residence permit,* only to be told by the chief of the Moscow Passport Office (who turned out to be that same Anosov who had called on him in Zhukovka) that residence permits were not the province of the police department, but were decided upon by a "council of honoured pensioners;" there was therefore nothing he could do to help (this message was said to have come "from the minister [of internal affairs] personally").[24]

Solzhenitsyn held his peace but deduced that word had gone out to increase the pressure on him. He was not mistaken. In June he received an anonymous letter: "We are not gangsters, if you will give us $100,000 we guarantee in return the safety and tranquillity of your family." This was followed by another: "There will be no third warning, we are not Chinese. Once we've lost confidence in you we shall be unable to guarantee anything." The messages were crudely pasted up from printed sources; and to reinforce the point about not being Chinese, a lock of kinky hair was included in one of the letters. Later came a third: "Well, bitch, you never came! Now you've only got yourself to blame. We'll straighten you out. Just you wait!"[25]

Solzhenitsyn was not unduly worried by these threats. He was convinced they were inspired by the KGB, as undoubtedly they were. The Sakharovs, too, were unexpectedly visited by two Arabs claiming to be members of the Black September terrorist group and threatening to kill Sakharov if he continued to make public statements in favour of Israel. "We never warn people twice," said one of the men, echoing the letters of Solzhenitsyn. Sakharov also received threatening letters posted in Lebanon and other countries—at a time when his mail was closely controlled by the authorities and 90 per cent of it failed to arrive.[26]

In his own case Solzhenitsyn decided to make a pre-emptive strike by writing directly to the KGB.

> I am sending you copies of two inept anonymous letters, although you already have other copies in your file.
>
>   I have no spare time to play detective with you. If this story has any sequel, I shall publicize it, together with other methods by which your department has persistently interfered with my private life.[27]

It was not the first time he had employed such a tactic. In 1972, when his correspondence with Dr Heeb and with Sweden was being intercepted,

* Olga Ivinskaya, Pasternak's former secretary and companion, describes meeting Rostropovich in a train at about this time and Rostropovich's boast that he would use his influence to get Solzhenitsyn a residence permit. Rostropovich failed, of course, and that was another reason why Solzhenitsyn felt he had to move.

he had included a little note with two of his letters which read more or less as follows: "You may read this letter, copy it, subject it to chemical analysis, and do whatever else you wish, but it is your duty to see that it is delivered to the addressee. If you do not, I shall publish a public protest against you that will not bring honour to the post office." Both letters evidently reached their destinations minus the note, and after that, Solzhenitsyn began to receive more mail.[28] On this occasion, too, his letter was acknowledged, first by a receipt slip and then by a telephone call saying that his message had been passed to the police.

Nevertheless, to be on the safe side, Solzhenitsyn decided to move Natalia Svetlova and the children to a dacha in Firsanovka, just outside Moscow, for the summer. Svetlova was now expecting their third child, and he didn't want her to be upset by the letters, threatening telephone calls, and other disturbances they were getting in Moscow. Personally, he found Firsanovka too noisy for really serious work—it was near the airport and aeroplanes were constantly flying overhead—so he spent part of the summer at the cottage in Rozhdestvo.* He did, however, work on his essays for *From under the Rubble* at Firsanovka and began two major political and social statements—"Peace and Violence," a response to the international debate then in progress on the subject of *détente*, and *Letter to the Leaders*, on Soviet internal policies.

His aim was apparently to lie low that summer, keep writing, and stay out of harm's way, and this may have contributed to his continuing reluctance to become involved with other dissidents. But some of the tensions engendered by this policy surfaced briefly in July, when Vladimir Maximov was expelled from the Writer's Union. Maximov had been periodically in difficulties with the authorities for two years, mainly as a result of the publication in the West of his powerful novel of disenchantment with the Soviet system, *The Seven Days of Creation* (itself not uninfluenced by Solzhenitsyn), after it had been repeatedly rejected by the Soviet censorship. In January 1972 Maximov had been reprimanded, urged to publish a disclaimer in the Soviet press (like *Cancer Ward*, the novel had been published by the NTS), and when he refused, obliged to submit to a psychiatric examination—which, however, had no serious consequences. In the meantime, Maximov had moved close to dissident circles, becoming a frequent signer of open letters and protests on human rights, and a friend and confidant of Sakharov, Chalidze, Shafarevich, Galich, and many others. At one time, while still a member of the Writers' Union, he had employed Bukovsky as his secretary to protect the latter from charges of parasitism, and it had been then that he and Bukovsky had discussed their plan for a new samizdat journal.

After his expulsion in July, Maximov wrote an angry letter to Solzhe-

---

* Solzhenitsyn was unable to spend more than a part of his time there, because he still shared the cottage with Reshetovskaya and did not like to be there when she was. He was hoping to resolve this difficulty by having an extra cabin built in the grounds, after which he proposed to transfer ownership of the cottage itself to Reshetovskaya. Late that summer, however, they quarrelled over a letter Reshetovskaya had written him, and Solzhenitsyn changed his mind.

nitsyn quoting Solzhenitsyn's words in his Nobel lecture about the "world-wide solidarity of writers" and asking why it always seemed to flow in only one direction—from other writers to Solzhenitsyn, but never from Solzhenitsyn to other writers. If Solzhenitsyn's voice had been joined to the voices of others protesting his expulsion, and if Solzhenitsyn had manifested the solidarity he demanded from others, the impact would have been immeasurably greater and the authorities would have felt more hampered in applying sanctions against him.[29] In its way it was a repeat of some of the charges made against Solzhenitsyn for refusing to join the protest over Daniel and Sinyavsky, but this time it carried more weight, for Solzhenitsyn was much more famous now and his immunity all the greater. It may have been that he also sensed an implicit (negative) comparison with Sakharov, because on this occasion he answered the charge, although his resulting letter was evasive. He had, he wrote, interceded for Maximov in private, though not in public (in his interview with the two American correspondents, he had used Maximov's difficulties over *The Seven Days of Creation* to make a general point about literature's being above criminal sanctions, but not about Maximov himself), because he felt that public interventions would devalue the impact of his protests. Later, in *the Oak and the Calf*, he offered a further gloss on his position. "I did not defend him," he wrote, "for the same reason that I had not defended any of the others: licensing myself to work on the history of the Revolution, I had absolved myself of all other duties. . . . An artist has no other recourse if he does not want to overheat himself with ephemeral concerns and boil dry."[30] Nevertheless, at his next interview with Western correspondents (for which, as before, he wrote both the questions and the answers), Solzhenitsyn made a point of mentioning Maximov by name: "He is an honest, courageous writer with a disinterested and self-sacrificing devotion to truth, and he has had great successes in his quest for it. So his expulsion from the lying Writers' Union is perfectly normal."[31]

Another writer who briefly made Solzhenitsyn's acquaintance that summer was Andrei Sinyavsky. Sinyavsky had been quietly released from the labour camps two years earlier and was inevitably without a job. He was given to understand, however, that although neither he nor his wife was a Jew, if they applied for exit visas to go to the West, they would not be refused. Accordingly, they were preparing to move to Paris. Sinyavsky's wife, Maria Rozanova, had been introduced to Natalia Svetlova by their mutual friend Irina Zholkovskaya while Sinyavsky was in the camps,* but their husbands had not met until Solzhenitsyn invited the Sinyavskys to Firsanovka in the summer of 1973. Their meeting was cordial. The two men

---

* Solzhenitsyn and Svetlova's first son, Ermolai, had been born slightly prematurely, and when he began to ail at about six months, Maria Rozanova introduced Svetlova to a paediatrician who did not fear for his reputation with the authorities in the light of Solzhenitsyn's notoriety. The Sinyavskys and the Solzhenitsyns subsequently sent their children to the same nursery school in Moscow, and Natalia Svetlova helped organize a summer camp in Koktebel, to which many of the dissidents, including the Sinyavskys, sent their children in the holidays.

strolled in the woods (to evade any microphones), where they discussed literature and related matters. Solzhenitsyn voiced his well-known sentiments about the importance of history to Soviet writers and asked Sinyavsky whether he contemplated writing on historical subjects when he got to the West. Soviet distortions of history, he said, had created a heavy burden for Russian writers, and he implied that all writers ought to share it.[32] Sinyavsky, according to his own account, replied evasively, but it must have been clear to both men that their attitudes to literature and to the tasks of the writer diverged so fundamentally that there was little to discuss. It is hardly surprising that when a couple of months later Solzhenitsyn came to list the contemporary Russian writers he admired and to name those who constituted, in his view, the mainstream of Russian literature, Sinyavsky was not among them.[33]

Solzhenitsyn also had mixed feelings about Sinyavsky's decision to go to the West. In *The Oak and the Calf* he writes that he was "chilled and saddened" to think that ever-fewer people were willing to "endure Russia's destiny, wherever it might lead," and that he himself would have cut a poor figure if he had joined those who emigrated after receiving the Nobel Prize. These were the kinds of sentiments he had come to regard as correct of late, partially, it seems, under the influence of his second wife and Shafarevich. But the very mention of the subject in those terms indicates a doubt, or an element of posturing. Elsewhere he reveals that about a month later, in a moment of sudden candour when walking with Shafarevich, he had commented on the beauty of the Russian countryside and added, "How vividly we shall remember all this if . . . ever we are somewhere else, away from Russia!"[34] Shafarevich had reacted with predictable horror and reproached Solzhenitsyn for such sacrilege, but the thought was clearly in Solzhenitsyn's mind and could not so easily be dismissed.

Solzhenitsyn would have continued to keep a low profile that summer had events not conspired to alter his plans and to sweep him away on their current. The initial impetus came from Sakharov. At some point in June 1973 he gave a wide-ranging interview to Olle Stenholm, a correspondent of the Swedish radio and television network, which was broadcast on 2 July. In it, Sakharov revealed himself to be far more pessimistic about Soviet society than ever before. "I'm sceptical about socialism in general. I don't find that socialism offers us anything new on the theoretical level, or a better way of organizing society." And: "There's nothing new . . . about this socialism. It's simply capitalism developed to its extremes. . . . We . . . have the same kind of problems as the capitalist world, the same criminality, the same alienation of the individual. The difference is that our society is an extreme case, with maximum lack of freedom, maximum ideological rigidity, and, most typical of all, maximum pretensions about being the best society, though it is far from that." Sakharov admitted that there was not much anyone like himself could accomplish, but "one always needs to create ideals for oneself, even when one can see no direct way of realizing them," and he described himself in political terms as "a liberal, a gradualist if you like."[35]

Within two weeks Sakharov was violently attacked by Tass and accused of "slandering the Soviet Union"—a criminal charge. To underline its gravity, he was summoned on 16 August to the office of the deputy prosecutor general, M. P. Malyarov, and warned that he was giving comfort to the enemies of the Soviet state and being used by foreign intelligence services. "Any state has the right to defend itself," said Malyarov repeatedly. "There are appropriate articles in the criminal code, and no one will be permitted to violate them."[36]

Sakharov denied having broken the law and, when he returned home, wrote out a transcript of the interview from memory and had it typed in multiple copies. Following Pavel Litvinov's earlier example, he released this document to foreign correspondents but went a step further than Litvinov by holding an impromptu press conference to denounce the government's tactics of harassment and intimidation. In his answers to journalists' questions, Sakharov touched on the intimidation of other dissidents, the harassment of his and Elena Bonner's children from their former marriages, his own professional and financial problems, and the larger political situation, but the most controversial statement he made was in connection with *détente*.

> *Détente* without democratization, *détente* in which the West in effect accepts the Soviet rules of the game would be dangerous, it would not really solve any of the world's problems. . . . It would mean trading with the Soviet Union, buying its gas and oil, while ignoring other aspects of the problem. I think such a development would be dangerous because it would contaminate the whole world with the anti-democratic peculiarities of Soviet society; it would enable the Soviet Union to bypass problems it can't solve on its own and to concentrate on accumulating still further strength. . . . It would mean cultivating a closed country where anything that happens may be shielded from outside eyes, a country wearing a mask that hides its true face.[37]

For his press conference Sakharov had deliberately chosen the fifth anniversary of the Soviet invasion of Czechoslovakia, 21 August, and it was on this symbolic date that Solzhenitsyn also entered the arena. Having recently completed a fresh version of his letter to the Soviet passport authorities, he addressed it to the minister of the interior, N. A. Shchelokov. It was a protest against the April refusal to grant him a permit to reside in Moscow and a declaration that Solzhenitsyn would ignore the ruling. In it he got off, at last, his bitter words on serfdom: "The demeaning, compulsory 'passport' system, in which his place of residence may not be chosen by the individual but is chosen for him by the authorities . . . probably does not exist even in colonial countries today. . . . However, I take this opportunity to remind you that serfdom in our country was abolished 112 years ago, and we are told that the October Revolution wiped out its last remnants. Presumably, I . . . am neither a serf nor a slave and should be free to live wherever I find it necessary."[38]

It is typical of Solzhenitsyn's caution that, having composed this fiery statement and dated it 21 August, he nonetheless held it back for two days until he had given another interview to Western correspondents. He did not care for these interviews very much, finding them "a poor genre for writers: you lose control of your pen, the shape of your sentences, your diction; you fall into the hands of reporters with no feel for the things that move you." He considered that the two American correspondents Smith and Kaiser had "made a hash" of his earlier interview, and this time he chose a different American and a Frenchman. The results were no better: "*Le Monde* shredded and garbled this interview, too, and even secreted the full text in the French Foreign Ministry," he later wrote.[39] But he was again able to release his own version into samizdat, and that was sufficient to make the effort worthwhile.

The interview marked an extension of and an advance on the previous one of eighteen months ago. Listing the various threats and harassments he had recently endured, including anonymous letters and phone calls and threats to have him killed in a car accident, Solzhenitsyn commented sardonically that in view of the round-the-clock surveillance he was subjected to, if any harm came to him or he were killed, "you can infallibly conclude, with one hundred per cent certainty, that I have been killed by or with the approval of the KGB." He alluded briefly to his difficulties in getting a residence permit, to his progress on the sequels to *August 1914*, to the recent Soviet signing of the Universal Copyright Convention, and to other literary matters, but the bulk of the interview, perhaps in response to Maximov's reproaches (and the example of Sakharov), was devoted to social and political problems, the current state of the human-rights movement, and a spirited defence, name by name, of the individual victims of Soviet persecution. Maximov himself was mentioned again, together with Zhores Medvedev (who had just been deprived of his Soviet passport in London), Igor Shafarevich, Andrei Amalrik, General Grigorenko, Vladimir Bukovsky, Anatoli Marchenko, and well over a dozen others, including the most prominent members of the Ukrainian dissident movement. Solzhenitsyn showed himself to be a close reader of the *Chronicle* and took the opportunity to defend that publication, too, and to deny persistent rumours that the authorities had succeeded in closing it down.

Among other things Solzhenitsyn expressed his conviction that the situation of Soviet human-rights campaigners and political prisoners was far worse than that of similar victims in right-wing countries then in the human-rights spotlight—Greece, Turkey, Portugal, and Spain—and that many in the West were guilty of hypocrisy in equating the two sides. There had never been an amnesty for political prisoners in the Soviet Union in all its fifty years of existence, and access for the press and outside observers was non-existent, whereas all these things existed under right-wing regimes. In the light of the debate then in progress on the subject of jamming, he pointed out that "the jamming of Western radio broadcasts in the East . . . robs international agreements and guarantees of all meaning, because they cease to exist in the minds of half of mankind." And on Western attitudes to human-rights abuses in the Soviet Union, he stated, "It is important to understand that the East is not at all indifferent to protests from public opinion in the West. On the contrary, it goes in deadly fear of them—and them alone—but only when it is a matter of the united, mighty voice of hundreds of prominent personalities, the opinion of a whole continent. . . . Our prisons retreat and hide from the light of world publicity."[40]

Some of these ideas were an elaboration of what Solzhenitsyn had written, in more Delphic form, in his Nobel lecture, but at the end of his statement he offered a newly matured thought on the relative psychologies of those who lived in the West and those human-rights activists who lived in the Soviet Union.

> There is one psychological peculiarity in human beings that always surprises me. In times of prosperity and ease, a man will shy away from the least little worry at the periphery of his existence, try not to know about the sufferings of others (and his own in the future), make many concessions even in matters of central, of intimate importance to him, just to prolong his present well-being. Yet a man who is approaching the last frontier, who is already a naked beggar deprived of everything that may be thought to beautify life, can suddenly find in himself the strength to dig in his heels and refuse to take the final step, can surrender his life but not his principles!
>
> Because of the first quality, man has never been able to hold on to one single plateau he has attained. Thanks to the second quality, mankind has pulled itself out of all kinds of bottomless pits. . . .
>
> We must not accept that the disastrous course of history cannot be corrected, that the Spirit, if it has confidence in itself, cannot influence the mightiest Power in the world.[41]

A sign of Solzhenitsyn's continuing caution was his request to the correspondents of Le Monde and the Associated Press (the other news organization involved) to hold up publication of his interview for one week. He could not have known, of course, that before the week had elapsed the authorities would stage the long-delayed trial of Krasin and Yakir. Piotr Yakir, the son of the renowned Soviet army commander Iona Yakir, who had been purged and shot by Stalin in 1937, and his friend Victor Krasin had now been under interrogation for fourteen months in a case specifically intended to break the Chronicle of Current Events. Both men had spent many years in prisons and camps and both confessed to underground activities both real and false, including links they had had with Western émigré organizations. During the course of the investigation, over two hundred dissidents were questioned and in many cases obliged to undergo wrenching personal confrontations with Yakir and Krasin under the eyes of the KGB interrogators; some of them capitulated and gave evidence against the Chronicle. At the instigation of the KGB, Yakir wrote a letter to Sakharov urging him not to allow his name to be used "for purposes of propaganda against our homeland." Sakharov had not referred to this letter in his press conference but had foreseen that the coming trial would undoubtedly be used to link the dissident movement with "anti-Soviet organizations abroad," and he had publicized the KGB warning that for each new issue of the *Chronicle* that appeared, a given number of dissidents would be arrested, and everyone involved given punitive sentences.[42] Solzhenitsyn, too, had indicated his concern over the trial and had attempted to defuse its impact by ridiculing it in advance. It was "just a dismal repetition of the clumsy Stalin-Vyshinsky farces," he told the *Le Monde* correspondent. "In the thirties . . . these farces, despite the primitive stagecraft, the smeared grease-paint, the loudness of the prompter, were still a great success with 'thinking people' among Western intellectuals. . . . But if no correspondents are to be admitted to the trial, it means that it has been pitched two grades lower still."[43]

The trial opened on 27 August, less than a week after Sakharov's and Solzhenitsyn's interviews, and was given maximum publicity in the Soviet press. No Western correspondents were admitted. They were, however, invited to an extraordinary press conference staged for Yakir and Krasin by the KGB and shown in part over Soviet television. Yakir and Krasin repeated the charges they had made against the *Chronicle* in their confessions, including the allegation that Solzhenitsyn had been a regular reader of the *Chronicle* and that "copies had been systematically passed to him for evaluation."[44]

A big campaign was simultaneously opened in the Soviet press against Sakharov and Solzhenitsyn. The initial stroke was a letter in *Pravda* on 29 August signed by forty members of the Soviet Academy of Sciences, denouncing Sakharov for his "anti-patriotic" utterances and accusing him of jeopardizing *détente*. Two days later another letter appeared, which linked Solzhenitsyn's name with Sakharov's and accused the two of them of "slandering our social and state order" and summoning the West to return to the cold war. This letter was signed by thirty-one members of the Writers' Union, including such comparative moderates as Chingiz Aitmatov, Vasyl Bykov, Sergei Zalygin, and Konstantin Simonov, in addition to predictable hardliners like Fedin, Surkov, Chakovsky, and Sholokhov. During the next week or so, the campaign mushroomed and spread from *Pravda* to *Izvestia* and the *Literaturnaya Gazeta*. On 1 September, Sakharov was attacked by members of the Agricultural Academy, on the second by members of the Medical Academy, on the third by composers and musicians (including Shostakovich, Khachaturian, and Oistrakh), on the sixth by artists, economists, and technologists.

Every effort was made to suggest that the entire intelligentsia—indeed the entire nation—loathed and detested Sakharov (Solzhenitsyn was mentioned less often) as a renegade and traitor, sabotaging *détente* and the Helsinki accords. As a staff writer on the *Literaturnaya Gazeta* later told Hedrick Smith, "we had lists of people to call—some of them very important writers—and we would simply tell them what the Party expected them to say."[45] Letters in support of Sakharov and Solzhenitsyn, on the other hand, were simply ignored and handed over to the KGB (its officials made monthly inspection visits). But on this occasion the picture was more complicated than usual. Perhaps because the public's hopes for *détente* had been raised unusually

high or because the authorities were more than customarily adept in manipulating Sakharov's words, there really did emerge a ground swell of popular
opinion against him. Smith quotes a young and by no means blinkered Soviet
economist who explained to him during the campaign that it was "quite natural for people to consider men like Sakharov and Solzhenitsyn as traitors. It
is very simple: Sakharov and Solzhenitsyn are turning to foreigners for help.
The imperialists are using these two, and . . . imperialism is our main enemy.
So if our enemy is using these people, then naturally it must mean that they
are traitors. Sakharov called for the West to punish our country, to keep us
from getting most-favoured-nation tariffs from the United States. So of course
he is considered a traitor and it is a normal duty for people to join a campaign
to denounce him."[46]

Curiously enough, Sakharov received painful proof of this attitude in a
most roundabout way. Immediately after giving his press conference, he had
left for a holiday on the Black Sea. While lying on the beach near Sochi, he
heard transistor radios pouring out a stream of invective against him and had
the uncomfortable experience of listening to people around him discuss the
broadcasts and denounce the "traitor" for his oppositions to *détente*. At one
point Sakharov asked his neighbours whether anyone had actually read what
this Sakharov had said, and suggested that it might be worth finding out—
"perhaps he has good intentions after all"—but nobody seemed interested,
and his wife hustled him away. If the sunbathers discovered his true identity,
they might be tempted to assault him.[47]

The campaign was also successful in driving a wedge into the intellectual community to separate the sheep from the goats. Inevitably there turned
out to be very few goats, either in the writers' community or among scientists. The vast majority of those approached were dragooned into signing
critical statements of one kind or another, making them accomplices in the
repression. In this way they were compromised, and guilty consciences drove
them to be even more critical of the outspoken few, whom they blamed for
having forced them into making such painful choices. "The honest man makes
the silent ones feel guilty for not having spoken out," said Valentin Turchin
to Hedrick Smith when the campaign was over. "They cannot understand
how he had the courage to do what they could not bring themselves to do.
So they feel impelled to speak out against him to protect their own consciences."[48] Turchin spoke with some authority in the matter, having been
one of the few to defend Sakharov publicly. As a result, he had been the
object of unanimous condemnation at a mass meeting called by his computer
institute, but open supporters could be counted on the fingers of two hands.

Fortunately for Sakharov and Solzhenitsyn, the world-wide interest in
détente at that moment and the focusing of Western attention on the Soviet
Union were to prove their salvation. In Britain, France, Germany, and the
United States a growing body of public opinion began to question whether
détente was worth the price, or indeed possible with "a dictatorial regime"
and a "tyranny." The non-persecution of Sakharov and Solzhenitsyn was

made a touchstone of further co-operation, and it was emphasized at all levels in the West that any sanctions against them would put an end to *détente*. Perhaps the most influential intervention was that of the president of the American Academy of Sciences, who deplored the attack on Sakharov by forty Soviet academicians and sent his opposite number at the Soviet Academy a succinct telegram: "Harassment or detention of Sakharov will have severe effects upon relationships between the scientific communities of the USA and USSR and could vitiate our recent efforts toward increasing interchange and cooperation."[49] This was on 9 September 1973. A day later, Senator Wilbur Mills, chairman of the House Ways and Means Committee in Washington, remarked that he was against increased trade with the Soviet Union until the persecution of people like Sakharov and Solzhenitsyn ceased.

Almost at once the Soviet press campaign against Sakharov and Solzhenitsyn was halted—the Western threats seemed to be taking effect. The U.S. Congress was just then debating the Mills and Jackson amendments,* and the Soviet government was reluctant to worsen its image still further. But Sakharov and Solzhenitsyn did not fall silent. Sakharov, as before, was the more outspoken and pugnacious of the two. Having returned from his holiday, he gave a press conference on 8 September on the Soviet abuse of psychiatry for political purposes. On the ninth he followed this up with an interview with a Dutch radio station on the same subject. On the twelfth he issued a statement refuting the main accusations made against him in the Soviet press, asserting that he was not a warmonger and not against *détente*, but simply for a genuine *détente* in which human rights would be respected and internal tensions relaxed. Finally, on the fourteenth he sent an open letter to the U.S. Congress appealing to it to support the Jackson amendment and to insist on the Soviet Union's acknowledging the right of emigration as a condition of receiving most-favoured-nation status. The letter was set in capital letters in the *Washington Post* and appears to have had a decisive impact on American congressmen, for the amendment was passed in the teeth of opposition from President Nixon and Secretary of State Henry Kissinger.[50]

Solzhenitsyn, meanwhile, was concentrating his attention on the two important, programmatic essays that he had begun that summer: "Peace and Violence" and *Letter to the Leaders*. "Peace and Violence" was an amplification of some of the ideas he had advanced in his Nobel lecture—ideas, he now felt, that had been missed or misunderstood because of the indirect way in which they were expressed. He thought the time had come to make them more explicit and to link them to the theme of peace and *détente*, much as Sakharov was doing in his public statements. He appears to have been much preoccupied with Sakharov and Sakharov's views that summer and autumn.

---

*These were amendments to a bill proposed by President Nixon to ease trade with the Soviet Union by granting the latter "most favoured nation" status, a device to give the Soviet Union access to credits and to reduce tariffs on its exports to the United States. The amendments were intended to make this status dependent on the Soviet Union granting freer emigration to the Soviet Jews.

In his interview with *Le Monde* and the Associated Press, he had discussed and defended Sakharov at some length, offering his own idiosyncratic interpretation of Sakharov's importance: "There is in his behaviour a profound significance, a lofty symbol, a logical working-out of his own destiny: the inventor of the most destructive weapon of our age has submitted to the overpowering pull of the World's Conscience, and the eternally afflicted conscience of Russia. Weighed down by our common sins, and the sins of each and every one of us, he has abandoned the abundantly good life of which he was assured and which destroys so many people in the world today, and has stepped out in front of the jaws of all-powerful violence." The Soviet government's charges against Sakharov he called "absurd" and "shameless" and pointed out that in his suggestions for reform Sakharov invariably showed himself to be well informed and constructive. Nevertheless, said Solzhenitsyn, there were many things he could not support in Sakharov's concrete proposals, and it appears that his two essays were an attempt to formulate these differences and offer alternatives.[51]

"Peace and Violence" was completed in August 1973 and was first offered to *Le Monde*, but the French newspaper rejected it, and Solzhenitsyn was obliged to seek another publisher (a new experience for him). On 31 August he heard that the Nobel Prize committee in Oslo had short-listed forty-seven candidates, including Presidents Nixon and Tito, for the Peace Prize, which struck him as ridiculous (he had not then heard of the even more surrealistic nomination of the eventual winners, Kissinger and Le Duc Tho). He decided to adapt his essay into a proposal of Sakharov for the prize and sent it off to Per Hegge at *Aftenposten* in Oslo (showing Sakharov a copy to warn him). The essay appeared on 11 September. Sakharov immediately signified his acceptance of the nomination, but there were procedural difficulties. The nomination had come too late for 1973 and was rejected. The idea appealed to some British and Danish parliamentarians, however, and to some people in other countries, who pressed for Sakharov's candidacy to be switched to 1974 if 1973 was out of the question, and this was eventually done.

Almost simultaneously, Solzhenitsyn completed and sent off his *Letter to the Leaders*. The idea for it had come to him while he was finishing the first draft of "Peace and Violence," but whereas the latter was concerned with "foreign policy," *Letter to the Leaders* contained a set of proposals for the alteration of Soviet policy in domestic matters as well. Solzhenitsyn had written it in a mood of high excitement. The *Letter* "had suddenly begun to exercise such a pull on me, I was so overwhelmed by the crush of ideas and phrases, that for two days at the beginning of August I had to abandon my main work, let the spate expend itself, write it all down, and order it in sections." Solzhenitsyn continued to work on the *Letter* throughout August and completed it on the last day of the month. His initial plan was to release it to the press at the same time as "Peace and Violence" and double their impact, but Natalia Svetlova dissuaded him: let the Soviet leaders receive the *Letter* first and have time to think about it, before it became public knowledge. Otherwise, they would be tempted to dismiss it as propaganda.[52]

Since most attention was paid to the *fact* of Solzhenitsyn's nomination of Sakharov for the Peace Prize, the ideas propounded in his essay were generally overlooked, though one or two correspondents in Moscow, to whom Solzhenitsyn had given the Russian text, did note that it was Solzhenitsyn's most outspoken attack to date on Western liberals and what he called their policy of "appeasement" towards the Soviet aggressor. The correspondents also noted his criticisms of the U.S. Senate and the British Labour party (especially Prime Minister Harold Wilson) for "hypocrisy," and his bewilderment over the burgeoning of the Watergate affair, which, in common with the vast majority of the Soviet population, he regarded as an incomprehensible self-inflicted wound. The essay was not widely translated or discussed, however, and it disappeared from the international press before its contents could become widely known.

Throughout the rest of September, Western publicity in favour of Solzhenitsyn and Sakharov continued to mount. Thousands of prominent scientists, writers, artists, and other intellectuals signed petitions and telegrams of support. The U.S. House of Representatives heard a motion proposing that the two men be made honorary citizens of the United States. A leading newspaper commented that "the Solzhenitsyn-Sakharov affair . . . is fast escalating into a major international incident. . . . [It] is swiftly reaching into American political life."[53] And it seemed that the campaign was for once having results. On 13 September 1973 the Soviet Union ceased jamming certain foreign radio broadcasts for the first time since the Second World War. In the same week General Grigorenko was transferred from a mental hospital to a normal hospital, and Evgeni Barabanov, one of the participants in *From under the Rubble*, emerged unscathed from a press conference at Svetlova's Moscow flat, where he had announced his refusal to respond to a KGB summons.

On 21 September the Soviet Union took another step towards co-operation with the West by signing the Universal Copyright Convention and establishing its own special agency for handling copyright matters (VAAP).* Since the exact wording of the relevant legislation was kept secret, there were persistent rumours that the new Soviet agency would use its powers to cut off samizdat or blackmail Western publishers into renouncing unofficial Soviet manuscripts. But Solzhenitsyn found an ingenious way of challenging this notion. For some time he had been trying to think of a way to publish some extra chapters from *The First Circle* that he had cut when preparing the novel for publication in *Novy Mir*. Accordingly, he announced that he was now releasing two chapters (chapters 44 and 88) into samizdat. If the Soviet Union was serious about preserving the rights of Soviet authors, it would protect these chapters from "arbitrary publication in the West."[54] No action was in fact taken by VAAP or by the Soviet government, either to defend or to

* *Vsesoyuznoye agentstvo avtorskih prav* (All-union Agency for Authors' Rights).

encroach upon Solzhenitsyn's copyright, and subsequent events showed that the fears of a censorship role for the new copyright agency had been somewhat exaggerated. The chapters were published in the West without hindrance.

By mid-September 1973 the storm of publicity raging in both East and West around the figures of Solzhenitsyn and Sakharov was beginning to die down. Their positions looked stronger than ever. Two lone individuals had severely shaken the monolithic Soviet government's policy on *détente*, had exerted a direct influence on the policies of its powerful adversary, the United States, and yet seemed immune from reprisals by virtue of their world-wide fame and reputations. In *The First Circle* Solzhenitsyn had written, "For a country to have a great writer—don't be shocked, I'll lower my voice—is like having a second government."[55]* Could it be that the prophecy was coming true?

* An interesting extension of the nineteenth-century critic Vissarion Belinsky's dictum that "writers are Russia's parliament."

44

THE GULAG
ARCHIPELAGO

SOLZHENITSYN'S MOOD WAS buoyant in the summer of 1973, yet at the back of his mind one unresolved problem continued to nag him: what to do about *The Gulag Archipelago*. The original plan had been to publish in 1969, shortly after he completed it. The chance of receiving the Nobel Prize had caused him to put the matter off, and after the award was made known, he had more than half expected to go to the West, where he could publish the book at his leisure. He had changed his mind about that too. The year 1970 had gone by, and 1971, and at the end of 1972, after much agonizing, he had decided to postpone the moment once again. His conscience was not entirely easy with that decision—he felt he had a duty to the millions of dead Gulag victims to publish at once. On the other hand, he could rationalize the postponement by envisaging the reprisals to which he (above all, he) and others of his two hundred witnesses would be subjected once the book appeared. But the determining factor was his desire to continue work on the sequels to *August 1914*. For these he needed more time—and access to sources in the Soviet Union—and he resolved to delay *The Gulag Archipelago* at least until Lenin began to play a major role in the series. Lenin had already appeared in one chapter of *August 1914*, but Solzhenitsyn had suppressed that from the published version and could easily do the same with the next two volumes. Only in volume 4 would Lenin play such a prominent role that it would be impossible to conceal the author's attitude to him, and that would come out, according to Solzhenitsyn's calculations, sometime in 1975.[1]

It is possible that this decision was influenced by certain difficulties Solzhenitsyn was experiencing in arranging for foreign translations of *The Gulag Archipelago*. In October 1972 Solzhenitsyn had written to Olga Carlisle that

Harper & Row were to have the rights only to the English-language edition
and that he was very concerned about the quality of the translation.

> I am especially sensitive about the English translations . . . and to speak hon-
> estly, I am not pleased with any of the big translations. Some of them reduce me
> to despair. Meanwhile, a lot more will depend on how the translations of *August*,
> *October*, *March*, and . . . [*Gulag*] are understood and received. This is not simply
> my author's sensitivity, on this the whole solidity of my legs depends, and I
> cannot yield to *anyone* out of goodwill.[2]

He did, he wrote, still wish Olga Carlisle to be responsible for the English
translation. He felt that she wanted this and that he owed her a debt of
gratitude for her work on *The First Circle* and her help with *Gulag*. But Carlisle was still dissatisfied and in January 1973 had sent him an ultimatum:
either she should have full control over the world rights or she would withdraw altogether. It had taken two months for her letter to arrive, and he had
answered her immediately: "Your letter has greatly saddened me, especially
for its lack of keeping with the *spirit* of the book we are now talking about."
He dealt with her objections to the new arrangement one by one and begged
her to reconsider. "I will be sincerely happy if you keep the right of translation [into English] for yourself, to be ready at the agreed date and without
going beyond the limitations of my conditions for all translators and publishers."

These "conditions" appear to have been arrived at by Solzhenitsyn only
slowly, in the course of thinking about Western publication, and he knew
that Western publishers would probably "cringe" when they learned about
them. "Under these conditions, the publishing house will have *extremely small*
profits. This must be so, so that this book does not become a commercial
commodity and will not be sold at demented Western prices ($10! This is 60
rubles. This cannot even be conceived of by our compatriots!)"[3]

At the same time, Solzhenitsyn concluded that it would be helpful if the
foreign translations appeared more or less simultaneously with the publication in Russian: the publicity would be much greater, and his own position
thereby strengthened. But he was beginning to have serious misgivings about
the American translation. According to his memoir, Carlisle had informed
him in 1970 that the translation was "ready."[4] Yet in her 1973 letter she had
written that only a "first draft" was complete, while "a substantial part" existed
in "a more finished style." For Solzhenitsyn (after four and a half years) this
was not enough.

> If . . . your decision [to withdraw] should be irreversible, I see one way of ter-
> minating the affair, just for all and offensive to no one: FIRE. Your greatly
> unfinished work (because I cannot consider a literal translation to be even the
> beginning of a translation, it being a stage which is usually completely unneces-
> sary for translators) cannot be considered the "property of [Thomas Whitney]"
> (as you write) since and insofar as the work is paid for. . . . Thus, upon comple-

tion of the payment . . . all the materials of the translation must be, by you personally or by your representative, BURNED, let us say inside the fireplace of Dr H[eeb] and in his presence.

Whether the Russian manuscript should be burned as well, Solzhenitsyn left to Olga Carlisle and Dr Heeb to decide and suggested that a new English translation be started "from zero." But he could not help feeling bitter, he wrote, "that for some completely secondary, unnamed reasons you have determined to stain the movement of this book, which is not a literary commodity but a link in Russian history."[5] It was as well he had decided to postpone publication for two more years, and perhaps it was a relief when he heard that the Carlisles had decided to withdraw from the project altogether and to leave it in the hands of the man who had done the donkey work so far, the translator Thomas Whitney.

This was the rather unsatisfactory position in September 1973 when Solzhenitsyn received electrifying news from Leningrad: the KGB had tracked down and confiscated a copy of *The Gulag Archipelago*. The first message reached him on 1 September and was confirmed on the third. His devoted typist, Elizaveta Voronyanskaya, had been interrogated by the KGB and had divulged the whereabouts of one of the copies. Voronyanskaya herself was dead, probably a suicide. There was little he could do on the spur of the moment. He was in the midst of completing and dispatching final copies of "Peace and Violence" and *Letter to the Leaders*, but a few days' thought convinced him that the game was up: with his *magnum opus* in the hands of the KGB, the only thing left to do was to order its speedy publication in the West. The Russian text was ready, and there was hope that the translations, if rushed, would not be too far behind. He sent word secretly to Dr Heeb at once and on 5 September announced the existence of the book, and his decision to publish it, to Western correspondents in Moscow. He described the book as a history of the labour camps that contained "only real facts, places, and the names of more than two hundred persons who are still alive," but was careful to specify that it covered the years "1918 to 1956" (that is, stopping short of the Brezhnev period).[6] Ironically, although it was Solzhenitsyn's most important news of the month, it was almost completely overlooked in the flood of indignant publicity about the press campaign against him and the merits and demerits of *détente*.

Solzhenitsyn did not dare go personally to Leningrad to investigate Voronyanskaya's death for fear of stepping into a trap, and it took him several weeks to piece together a hazy picture of what must have happened. The sixty-seven-year-old typist, lame and in poor health, had been arrested in the first half of August. Her modest room in a communal flat had been ransacked, and she was taken to the "Big House" (the KGB headquarters in Leningrad), where she was unremittingly interrogated for five days and nights. Eventually, she cracked and revealed that a copy of the book was buried in the garden of a dacha at Luga, not far from Leningrad. The dacha belonged to Leonid Samutin, the former labour-camp prisoner and Vlasovite who had visited Solzhenitsyn in Ryazan (it was he whom Solzhenitsyn had questioned in his car) and been one of his 227 informants for the book. The KGB had released Voronyanskaya but had kept her under some sort of house arrest to prevent her informing Solzhenitsyn, or anyone else, of what had happened. But its agents had not gone to collect the book. They were apparently waiting for Samutin to leave his dacha, so that they could go while he was away and keep their possession of the book a secret.

Their plans had been upset by the unexpected death of Voronyanskaya some two weeks after the interrogation. It is still not clear on which day she died. The body was taken to the Leningrad morgue in strictest secrecy and was not shown even to the family before being sealed into a coffin for burial. The cause of death was given as "death by asphyxiation"—Voronyanskaya was said to have hanged herself. The funeral took place on 28 August 1973 and was attended by Samutin. The following day, Samutin telephoned Efim Etkind in Leningrad to inform him of Voronyanskaya's death, and the two of them arranged to meet at the cemetery, where Samutin informed Etkind of the search of Voronyanskaya's flat, the interrogation, and the confiscation of her "private archive." Etkind deduced from this that Samutin meant *The Gulag Archipelago* and telephoned Solzhenitsyn in Moscow to give him the news. According to Solzhenitsyn's later reconstruction of events, however, Etkind had made a mistake. The manuscript had not yet been taken, and it was Etkind's telephone call that triggered the search (both Solzhenitsyn's and Etkind's telephones were being tapped at this time). Only three days later was the loss of the manuscript finally confirmed.[7]*

The most galling aspect of this tragic affair was that Solzhenitsyn had thrice asked Voronyanskaya to burn her copy of the manuscript, and at the third time of asking she had assured him it was done. But, fearing that other copies might be lost, she had secreted her copy in Samutin's garden "just in case" (burial, burning, or confiscation seem to have been the fate of most of Solzhenitsyn's manuscripts at one time or another). The only source of information about Voronyanskaya's last days and hours was another woman living in the same communal flat, who told lurid and contradictory stories of a hanging body with bloodstains and even knife wounds on it. It later emerged that this woman was the niece of one of Leningrad's senior prosecutors and that a family of workers had only recently moved out of the flat to make way for her. She, too, moved out again very soon after Voronyanskaya's death, and Voronyanskaya's room was sealed.[8]

Solzhenitsyn had no doubt that the KGB's capture of the book was a

---

*I have tried to reconstruct the chronology of events surrounding Voronyanskaya's death from Solzhenitsyn's literary memoir *(The Oak and the Calf)*, from his "sixth supplement" to the memoir, published in *Vestnik RKhD*, no. 137 (1982), and from the few fragments about it that appear in Efim Etkind's *Notes of a Non-conspirator* (Oxford and New York, 1978), but many aspects of this episode remain to be clarified. That the KGB found a copy of *The Gulag Archipelago* at Samutin's dacha after interrogating Voronyanskaya for several days is beyond dispute, however.

decisive moment in his life. His most outspoken work on the camps ever—
easily outdoing the notorious *Feast of the Conquerors* in its excoriation of Soviet
excesses—it was bound to bring retribution on his head. At first sight it
seemed a greater disaster than the seizure of his archive in 1965. And yet his
mood was quite different. "Not for a single hour, not for a minute, was I
down-hearted on this occasion," he later wrote.⁹ The difference was that in
1965 he had been taken completely by surprise and had by no means hardened in his opposition to the Soviet regime. On the contrary, it was the KGB
strike against him that had reawakened his worst fears and provoked a reversion to the convict's paranoia that he had been slowly casting off. Since then
he had consciously embraced the role that the KGB had, as it were, thrust
upon him, and had come successfully through a hundred crises, emerging
stronger and more battle-hardened from each one. By now his fears, though
ineradicable, were considerably less than before, and he had acquired a faith
in divine guidance: "I had enough experience . . . to know from the prickling
of my scalp that God's hand was in it! It is Thy will!" Even so, he might
never have mustered the strength, he felt, to publish *Gulag* voluntarily, not
while he was unharmed and still had work to do in the Soviet Union. But
just as before, the KGB had taken the matter out of his hands. They were
all at the mercy of a mightier force. "I had glimpsed the finger of God: Sleep-
est thou, idle servant? The time has long since come and gone. Reveal it to
the world!"¹⁰

When the unthinkable happened, Solzhenitsyn was still under the influence of the euphoria engendered by his and Sakharov's successes in their
unequal struggle with the Soviet authorities. For a moment it seemed that the
two Davids might succeed in thwarting Goliath. The entire Western world
appeared to be on their side. In his Rozhdestvo hide-out, Solzhenitsyn kept
his ear glued to his short-wave radio for news of the battle. One more heave,
it seemed to him, and some real changes might be on the way. Not so long
ago he had written of a key character in *August 1914:* "Ever since his youth,
Vorotyntsev had been obsessed by a profound desire to be a good influence
on the history of his country, by either pushing it or pulling it—by the roots
of the hair, if necessary—in the right direction." That passage had ended
with a rueful admission: "But in Russia that kind of power and influence
wasn't granted to anyone who wasn't fortunate enough to be close to the
throne; at whatever point Vorotyntsev attempted to exert pressure and however much he exhausted himself trying, the effort was always in vain."¹¹
Now, at last, Vorotyntsev-Solzhenitsyn must have felt that his hour had
come. Towards the end of October, he drew up a list of possible courses of
action the authorities might take. *Gulag*, he felt sure, was being passed "directly
from the experts to the top bosses, right up to Andropov himself," and its
effect would be devastating: "The blood must have turned to ice in their
veins; its publication might be fatal to the system."¹²

So what would they do? Solzhenitsyn foresaw half a dozen options. The
first was to kidnap his children as hostages, but he was ready for that. "We

had . . . made a superhuman decision: our children were no dearer to us than the memory of the millions done to death, and nothing could make us stop that book." They might try to intercept the manuscripts in the West by breaking in and stealing them, or bring legal pressures to bear, perhaps under the new copyright law. Or simply intensify their efforts to blacken and intimidate him. For all these he was equally prepared. But there was one last option that he secretly hoped they would choose—to negotiate. "Against this last I put a large question mark," he writes in *The Oak and the Calf*, quoting a remark of Demichev's that had once been passed along to him: "Negotiate? With Solzhenitsyn? He won't live to see the day!" After which Solzhenitsyn adds defensively, "I didn't really believe in them [negotiations], didn't want them for myself, couldn't visualize them." But he had done everything he could to prepare for them and make them possible. His foreign and home policies had been set out in "Peace and Violence" and *Letter to the Leaders*. The latter had deepened and expanded upon the anti-Western sentiments in the former, and *The Gulag Archipelago* had been equipped with a deceptive chronological indicator, "From 1918 to 1956." It appears likely that part 7, dealing with the camps after 1956, would have been held back by Solzhenitsyn if Brezhnev had really entered into negotiations (which was why Solzhenitsyn had announced the same chronology to the press). On the day he posted his *Letter*, Solzhenitsyn had felt that it "couldn't be more timely: they had realized at last that we were a force to be reckoned with." And he had acceded to his wife's request that the existence of the *Letter* be kept a secret "in the infinitesimal hope that they would read it."[13]

As if in answer to his prayers, the day after he had drawn up his table of options, Solzhenitsyn did get a kind of offer to negotiate—not from the government or the Central Committee but from Natalia Reshetovskaya. He had seen her two days beforehand at Rozhdestvo. They had had a furious row, and he was not anxious to see her again so soon. But Natalia was insistent, and he deduced from the meaningful tone of her voice that it was not just a personal matter but had some sort of political dimension as well.

They met at the Kazan Station (the terminus for Ryazan) later that same day, 24 September 1973. According to Solzhenitsyn, Natalia said that she had been speaking to "certain people" and had come to discuss the possible publication of some of Solzhenitsyn's suppressed works. The prime candidate was *Cancer Ward*. Was Solzhenitsyn, she wanted to know, prepared to negotiate for the publication of *Cancer Ward*? Would he sign a publisher's contract and keep quiet about the fact that she had come here to offer him this concession? After all, it had been his refusal in 1967 to go to *Novy Mir* and sign a "mild" letter on Western publication that had led to the ban in the first place.

She told him he was wrong to keep attacking the security organs. It was the Central Committee that was persecuting him, not the KGB. "It was they who published *Feast of the Conquerors*, and what a mistake that was!" She said she had recently made many new and influential friends in high places, and they were far cleverer than Solzhenitsyn gave them credit for being. If they had been searching for his manuscripts, it was Solzhenitsyn's fault: "You tell the world that your most important works are still to come, that the flow will continue even if you die, and that way you force them to come looking." Evidently with *The Gulag Archipelago* in mind, she asked him, "Why don't you just make a declaration that all your works are in your exclusive possession and that you won't publish anything for twenty years?"[14]

Solzhenitsyn writes that the bargain did not strike him as a very good one, though he played along with the conversation for the sake of appearances and genuinely wavered over *Cancer Ward*. Politically, it was no longer important to him, but the prospect of publication in the Soviet Union was alluring. He said he would agree to publication—in full and with nothing cut. He also said he would agree to keep quiet about their conversation and her offer (though it appears he didn't intend to for one moment). The irritating thing from his point of view was that he was being obliged to conduct these negotiations on such a low level—with his ex-wife. On the other hand, he was exultant that "they" had chosen to negotiate with him at all and was sure that she had been dispatched by someone in an official position. This seemed to be confirmed when she cautiously asked him whether he would agree to talk to somebody "a bit higher up," and explained that her aim was to help him: "I believe that in the discussions I have had, and in particular chapters of my memoirs which I have sent to certain people, I have succeeded in explaining your character, defending you, and making your lot easier." Solzhenitsyn, she said, was surrounded by fools: "Somebody is deceiving you, inflaming your suspicions, practicing some terrible emotional blackmail on you, inventing imaginary threats." She said it was time for him to come to his senses and talk, but Solzhenitsyn was not prepared to negotiate in this indirect and unsatisfactory way, and told her that he would speak "only to the Politburo" and only "about the nation's destiny, not my own." The conversation then degenerated into another personal wrangle, and they parted with nothing resolved.[15]

In his dramatic account of this meeting in *The Oak and the Calf*, Solzhenitsyn expresses his conviction that Natalia was acting under orders from the KGB (with whom she must have been put in touch by Novosti) and that the two of them were being watched, photographed, and recorded by secret policemen in plain clothes on parallel platforms. Indeed, this scene forms one of the high points of his book and was the reason, he writes, why he broke off relations with her afterwards. Reshetovskaya, however, in a separate account of this meeting, has thrown considerable doubt on Solzhenitsyn's interpretation. The meeting, and the suggestion for negotiations, she writes, were entirely her own idea, conceived in desperation after their row at Rozhdestvo as a last feverish attempt to avert a permanent rupture.*

---

* See note to p. 801. After their quarrel over the Rozhdestvo cottage in the late summer, Solzhenitsyn had informed Natalia Reshetovskaya that he did not wish to see her or communicate with her again.

She had begun by using her contacts at Novosti to approach someone. in the Party, probably in the ideological department of the Central Committee, since that was where most of Solzhenitsyn's problems had arisen. This person, whom Natalia promised not to name (and has still not named), was extremely cautious, and felt that Solzhenitsyn would not agree to negotiate or make concessions, but said that he would certainly agree to talk to Solzhenitsyn if the latter came to the Central Committee and that there might be a chance of doing a deal over *Cancer Ward*. As for the KGB, Natalia writes that her sole contact with that organization had been shortly beforehand, when its agents had come to question her about *The Gulag Archipelago* and to try to discover whether she knew of any further copies. As Solzhenitsyn's former wife, she was an obvious target for questioning, especially since she was mentioned in Voronyanskaya's diary as one of the typists. The diary had contained one or two other names as well, about which the KGB had also questioned her, and that was why she in turn was to mention these names during her meeting with Solzhenitsyn (leading him to accuse her of having given them away herself).

This, then, was the background to Natalia's meeting with Solzhenitsyn, and she had fixed it up in the fantastic and forlorn hope that if she could somehow be the instrument of his reconciliation with the government, she would earn his undying gratitude and thereby salvage their relationship. It was a pathetic enterprise, and she was hopelessly out of her depth, arousing his suspicions all the more and ruining their relations forever. But her assertion that she was not the cat's-paw of the KGB rings true, and her belief that Solzhenitsyn later exaggerated his suspicions is supported by two further pieces of evidence. She had set their rendezvous, she writes, inside the station building, and it was Solzhenitsyn who had insisted that they walk to the far end of one of the platforms, from where he could see everyone for yards around and make sure that there were no microphones or eavesdroppers. If they were spied upon, it was not pre-arranged with her.

In her view, Solzhenitsyn arrived at the opinion that she was being manipulated by the KGB only much later, probably as a way of rationalizing his total rupture of relations. The point was that she had written him a "nervous letter" about their differences over the Rozhdestvo cottage, in which she had taunted him with being a puppet of Svetlova. This letter she handed to him at the station. Three weeks later she received a bitter reply, breaking off relations and informing her that he had withdrawn his request to have the cottage transferred to her. But there was no mention at that time of their Kazan Station meeting or of any suspicions that Natalia had been acting for the KGB.[16] This accusation did not arise until later.

Solzhenitsyn could not go back to Rozhdestvo in these circumstances, for fear of running into Natalia (it was in any case the end of the season), nor could he stay in Moscow without a residence permit, and he had promised to leave Zhukovka for good. Fortunately, the Chukovskys came to the rescue again. Lydia Chukovskaya had followed the Sakharov-Solzhenitsyn battle against the Soviet press with the greatest interest and had herself entered it in early September with one of her clarion calls in their defence.* Now she invited Solzhenitsyn back to Peredelkino again, and at the beginning of November he moved in.

In some ways it was just like old times. In her book *Process of Exclusion*, describing her own path to expulsion from the Writers' Union, Chukovskaya describes the comfortable relationship that Solzhenitsyn had established with her family after his first invitation to Peredelkino in 1965. He had soon had the keys both to Peredelkino and to their flat in Moscow, she writes, and had come and gone as he pleased. Sometimes he would come for a day, sometimes a week, and sometimes a month, and would then disappear for ages. "Whatever the circumstances, whether he was being praised to the skies or persecuted, it made no difference. . . . we both continued to go our own way, keeping to our own style of life, timetable, and the work that life had set for us."[17]

Chukovskaya draws a marvellously sympathetic portrait of Solzhenitsyn's routine during the winter of 1973–74. Solzhenitsyn always remained "sovereign master of his life" wherever he was. "Everywhere and at all times he had this rigid and unbreakable daily timetable, calculated not in hours but in minutes." He went to bed and got up very early, and always insisted on preparing his own food, eating it in the kitchen so that he could simultaneously listen to foreign radio broadcasts (on which he made notes) without disturbing her. If they ever met, it was always on the "neutral" ground of the kitchen, dining-room, or the corridors, and they never exchanged more than a few words.

> A conversation (if it wasn't about work or something that had given rise to that work) was relaxation, leisure, and Solzhenitsyn and leisure were incompatible. It was as if at some point in time—I don't know when and why—he had sentenced himself to imprisonment in some corrective labour camp with the strictest possible regime, which he then rigorously imposed on himself. He was both convict and overseer. The degree of vigilance he exercised over his own behaviour was probably even more unremitting than that exercised by agents of the KGB. The lesson was intended for heroic shoulders, for a lifetime's labour with no days off, and the principal instrument of this labour was total and well protected solitude. . . . He allowed himself no indulgences and sat down to work at the crack of dawn. Occasionally, I would find a brief note on the refrigerator: "If you are free at nine, we can listen to the radio together." This meant that on that day he would finish the lesson earlier than usual and was giving himself an unexpected breather of twenty minutes—to listen, to talk, to ask questions, to answer them.[18]

Chukovskaya found him equally punctilious in respecting her own habits and way of life. One day, after hearing her whisper to guests when she

---

* Chukovskaya called her open letter "The People's Wrath," an ironic reference to the officially inspired letters in the press from ordinary workers who usually began by expressing their "wrath and indignation" over the sins of Solzhenitsyn, Sakharov, and their ilk.

was seeing them off late at night, he threatened to move out if she inconvenienced herself for his sake. Occasionally, he would accompany her to the Peredelkino cemetery to visit her father's grave, and she was amazed and touched by the assiduity with which he assisted her over rough patches in the path or warned her of obstacles (she is extremely near-sighted). And although he came and went with mysterious and unexplained suddenness, he never left the dacha without sticking a note to the refrigerator informing her of the date and time of his departure.

Solzhenitsyn's custom was to work six days a week and spend the seventh in Moscow—usually a Monday. He always carried a rucksack on his back, in which he brought provisions from Moscow for the week ahead. He generally preferred foods that took up little space, were easy to prepare or consume, and contained a high number of calories—chocolate, condensed milk, canned food that could be quickly heated on the stove—he was indifferent to their culinary qualities. His room was one of two small rooms that opened off the dining-room on the ground floor, spartanly furnished with a large desk, a simple wooden wardrobe, and a hard, narrow divan on which he slept. There was no rug on the floor. Behind the wardrobe Solzhenitsyn kept a peasant pitchfork that he said was to ward off burglars or attackers if they came for him: in the Soviet criminal code a pitchfork, unlike a knife or a club, is not considered a weapon.[19] Solzhenitsyn may also have had visions, if he stayed long enough, of forking hay in the Chukovskys' garden. He liked to undertake these simple peasant tasks—in moderation—like some of his nineteenth-century predecessors.

So regular was Solzhenitsyn's routine that it seemed to make him an easy target for surveillance, and there was no shortage of spies. A writer who happened to be staying in the Writers' Residence at Peredelkino that winter reports that after Solzhenitsyn's arrival the residence suddenly filled up with third-rate hacks known to be informers for the KGB. But Solzhenitsyn had his own methods of evading them. Whenever he wished to visit Moscow secretly, he would telephone his wife at bedtime to wish her good-night, put a night-light where it could be seen through the window, then slip through the garden and over the back fence onto a quiet street at the back of the house and walk through the lanes to the next station down the line, Michurinets. Once in Moscow he would sometimes pretend to leave the city and return by a different route, often walking many miles to accomplish his aim. He enjoyed the exercise and found the whole cat-and-mouse game exhilarating, taking a boyish delight in outwitting his clumsy opponents.[20]

On one such visit to Moscow, he had his last meeting with Sakharov. They had not seen each other since September and not been in contact since the end of October, when Sakharov's flat had been invaded by the "Arab terrorists" and Solzhenitsyn had sent the scientist a letter of commiseration and support ("Would they have dared to act without receiving permission? . . . This is only the latest method. What can answer the free words of a free man? . . . Only hired killers remain")[21] and had rhetorically vowed to avenge him if Sakharov should come to harm. On 1 December, Sakharov and his wife came to Svetlova's flat. In the course of November, Elena Bonner had been repeatedly called in for interrogation by the KGB—ostensibly because of the publication in the West of Edward Kuznetsov's *Prison Diaries*, which Bonner admitted to having sent out of the country. Both she and Sakharov were exhausted by their struggle and by anxiety for themselves and their families. "I shall be put inside in two weeks' time," said Bonner dejectedly; "my son is a candidate for the camps, my son-in-law will be banished as a parasite within the month, my daughter is out of a job."

A major topic of the conversation was an invitation to Sakharov to teach at Princeton. News of the invitation had emerged during Sakharov's press conference at the beginning of September. He had indicated that he would like to go—especially as his wife's children had been invited to another American university—but only on condition that he could return, which seemed unlikely. Both Chalidze (who seems to have arranged the Princeton invitation) and Zhores Medvedev had been told they could go abroad for a limited period and return, yet both had been tricked out of their passports and deprived of citizenship once they were there. But throughout the autumn and winter of 1973 the idea of Solzhenitsyn's and Sakharov's going to the West, either voluntarily or under compulsion, had continued to occur like a leitmotiv in speeches and the press and was reinforced by the departure of so many others. Sakharov revealed that he had taken the first step of asking for a character reference from his institute. His intention was to take his family abroad and then return. When Solzhenitsyn suggested that Sakharov might not be readmitted, the latter said he would present himself at the frontier and oblige them to let him in. It was bravado, of course; Solzhenitsyn sensed that Sakharov did not really want to go and probably wouldn't apply. And he himself argued strongly against it.[22]

At Peredelkino, Solzhenitsyn seems to have occupied himself with mainly secondary tasks in preference to the next volume in his historical series, probably as a result of the strain he was experiencing as the days ticked by to the appearance of *The Gulag Archipelago*. He had asked for it to be published in Paris on 7 January, the Orthodox Christmas Day. Meanwhile he worked on his third supplement to *The Oak and the Calf*, bringing the story up to his last meeting with Sakharov, finished "Repentance and Self-limitation in the Life of Nations," and worked on his third contribution to *From under the Rubble*— "The Smatterers"*—which was completed towards the end of January. In doing this, he continued to observe a rule he had set for himself twenty years beforehand during his exile in Kok Terek. Every evening at dusk, he would

---

*This English title was also supplied by me. Solzhenitsyn's neologism *Obrazovanshchina* appears to have been formed by analogy with the derisive term *intelligentshchina* used by Berdyayev in *Signposts* to describe the intelligentsia. Solzhenitsyn's word is derived from the Russian for "schooling" and implies that anyone who has been to school in the Soviet Union, and has a smattering of knowledge, tends to think of himself as an *intelligent*, or intellectual. The article contains a harsh critique of the intelligentsia in Soviet times.

stroll into the garden with a black satchel over his shoulder, take out the drafts he had finished with that day, and set fire to them, even if there was snow on the ground. He also tried to take some exercise, sometimes on skis, sometimes pacing the path that ran from fence to fence. One day Chukovskaya asked whether he didn't get bored walking up and down. "No," said Solzhenitsyn. "I got used to it in the *sharashka*."[23]

At lunch-time on 28 December 1973 as he was eating his usual, quick meal in the Chukovskys' kitchen and listening to the radio (one of the BBC's daily news programmes in Russian was at 1.45 p.m.), Solzhenitsyn heard that volume 1 of *The Gulag Archipelago* had just been published in Paris—nine days earlier than planned. According to his memoir, he took the news calmly and continued eating. A little later in the day, however, he scalded his hand on the gas boiler and was obliged to go to Moscow for treatment. That evening he held a private celebration with his wife and a few friends at her flat. It seemed unbelievable. "What a burden I had shed. Secretly, surreptitiously I had carried it and had brought it safely to its destination! And now it was no longer on my back, but set where all could see it—that unwieldy stone, that great petrified tear."[24] Solzhenitsyn had shed tears, real tears, in the living and the writing of it, and was to do so again when he listened to extracts over the radio. But for the moment his overwhelming feeling was one of relief and immense joy.

On New Year's Day he again took stock of his situation and drew up another list of possible actions the government might take. This time it included murder, imprisonment, internal exile, and deportation as worst-case possibilities, but the first two seemed to him unlikely and the next two barely conceivable. For some reason, he had grown confident they would do nothing. "My wife and I did not seriously expect swift reprisals. Time and again we had got away with it. You begin to delude yourself that your impunity will continue indefinitely." Much more probable were a new press campaign against the book, attempts to discredit his character, and legal action in the West to halt publication. The head of the new copyright agency, Boris Pankin, had threatened to intervene in December, a week before the book appeared, but the American publishers of the book, Harper & Row, announced they would welcome a suit and would fight it all the way, at which the Soviet authorities fell silent. The last two possibilities that Solzhenitsyn foresaw were negotiations and retreat (by the latter he meant a decision by the government to swallow the book and accept that the evils it described had ended in 1956). In the hope that something of the sort might still happen, he sent instructions to the West to postpone publication of his *Letter to the Leaders*. His original plan had been to publish it twenty-five days after *Gulag*, but since *Gulag* had appeared early, he wanted to give the Kremlin more time to digest the letter. "I believed that they might feel drawn in different directions. It was unimaginable that not one of those at the top would find something to think about in the *Letter*. (At the very least, *new men* on their way to the top might see in it a possible path for themselves, a way out of the impasse.)"[25]

The question arises, To what extent was Solzhenitsyn deceived by his own ambition? He had always been prone to romanticize his life, to turn it into yet another novel, not least in *The Oak and the Calf*, where most of these ruminations occur. Was there ever a chance that the Soviet leaders would listen to him (even as a young man, on his way to the Lubyanka, he had wondered whether they were taking him to Stalin)? Did he really think that Natalia Reshetovskaya had been sent to him by the KGB—or by someone higher? And that his children might be kidnapped and he himself murdered? To what extent had he become the captive of his self-created myth and of his own literary imagination (or was he creating it after the fact)? Along with his searingly effective and deadly accurate denunciations of Soviet sins went a strain of rhetorical exaggeration that sometimes seemed to take flight from reality. Ever since his letter to the Fourth Writers' Congress, he had talked of fulfilling his duty to Soviet literature "from beyond the grave" and of being "prepared to accept even death" in the service of that cause, affirmations that had the ring of metaphorical truth but hardly reflected a real and present danger. This sense of unreality—or of exaggeration—had occurred again in parts of his interviews with Western correspondents and in his recent letter to Sakharov: "If they should ever succeed in . . . an attack on you while I remain alive, you may be certain that I shall dedicate what remains of my literary powers and my life to ensuring that the murderers do not win, but lose."[26] It was a noble sentiment, but what did it mean? One has only to try to imagine Sakharov saying something of the kind to realize the high-flown key in which it was pitched and the slight aura of artificiality that it carried. Certainly, Reshetovskaya had been of the opinion at their meeting on the Kazan Station that he had lost touch with reality, that he was inventing imaginary threats, and she had accused him of being a "fanatic." She had her own anxieties and fears to contend with, of course, and her own conspiracy theory: "Somebody is deceiving you, inflaming your suspicions, practising some terrible emotional blackmail on you." But the very fact that Solzhenitsyn treated her as an emissary and was convinced (or convinced himself) that they were being photographed and taped on the open platform testified to a highly coloured vision of reality, if not symptoms of genuine paranoia.

We will presumably never know whether any Soviet leader bothered to read the *Letter*, but the authorities were clearly undecided on how to respond to *The Gulag Archipelago*. Once the book had appeared, the publicity in the West was as usual enormous. Again, it seemed, the author had challenged the Soviet leaders head-on and had again taken them by surprise. In a statement accompanying the Russian edition, Solzhenitsyn explained that he had delayed publication to protect the ex-prisoners who had provided him with testimony (which was not the whole truth) and that he had been forced to publish now by the KGB's discovery of the manuscript (which was). What caught the Western press's attention, however, was his comparison of Soviet crimes with Nazi crimes, his claim that Germany (West Germany, at least) had healed itself by bringing its war criminals to trial, whereas the Soviet Union's body politic was festering and rotting from the corruption that still consumed it, and could be cured only by similar radical surgery. It was noted that his book was, as he called it, both a "monument of solidarity with all the martyrs and the dead of 1918 to 1956" and an appeal "to the two hundred million inhabitants of my country and the whole of mankind."[27] There was no doubt that *The Gulag Archipelago* went far beyond any of Solzhenitsyn's previous works in its comprehensive documentation of the labour-camp system, its catalogue of cruelty and injustice, going right back to the beginnings of Soviet society, and its trumpet call for a bringing of the perpetrators to justice and for a new era in Russian life. As a German (Communist) newspaper noted, the book constituted "a burning question mark over fifty years of Soviet power, over the whole Soviet experiment from 1918 on," while another expressed Solzhenitsyn's own secret hope: "The time may come when we date the beginning of the collapse of the Soviet system from the appearance of *Gulag*."[28]

It was a full five days before the Soviet government responded with a commentary distributed by Tass. Calling the book "a novel," Tass asserted that Solzhenitsyn had already "confessed his hatred for the Soviet social order" and for the October Revolution in his "autobiography"—presumably a reference to the autobiographical note that Solzhenitsyn had sent to the Nobel Foundation. Now Solzhenitsyn was praising the tsarist regime as "liberal," and the Nazis as "merciful" to Russian prisoners of war, and singing his "old song" about the injustices of the labour camps. His whole purpose was simply "to poison the atmosphere of *détente*, to sow mistrust between peoples, to blacken the Soviet Union, its people, its policies," and that was why his book was being excerpted and praised in the Western bourgeois press, especially those right-wing organs that praised the "Fascist junta in Chile . . . bloody reaction in Greece . . . the crimes of the South African racists," and so on. This was followed a day later by a stronger commentary repeating the accusations that Solzhenitsyn was anti-*détente* and pro-German and adding that he was a "renegade" attempting to "cover up for those who became traitors to our motherland in the Second World War." His book was "a malicious slander against our socialist state" and had become the "foundation and pivot of the anti-Soviet campaign that is being spread throughout the pages of foreign newspapers."[29]

It was fairly clear from this initial response that the commentators had still not had time to read the book properly and were reacting to certain snippets and extracts that had appeared in the West. Indeed, their accusations barely went beyond what had been said in the press months before, and it seemed that Svetlova's prediction of nothing worse than "vituperative articles" was being borne out. Solzhenitsyn retired to Peredelkino to complete his last essay for *From under the Rubble* and to listen to the excerpts from *The Gulag Archipelago* that were already being broadcast by Radio Liberty. Although that station was still jammed, the readings could be heard with complete clarity, and for once he sacrificed part of his rigid schedule to listen to his own creation.

According to those who saw him during this period, he was completely calm, even relaxed, and had time to interest himself in the affairs of others. Throughout the preceding year, pressures had been increasd on writers to toe the line, and two of the most rebellious, Lydia Chukovskaya and Vladimir Voinovich, were due to be summoned to special sessions of the Writers' Union board, at which, it was rumoured, they were to be expelled—Chukovskaya for her open letter, "The People's Wrath," and Voinovich for publishing his works abroad. On 6 January 1974 Solzhenitsyn wrote a letter to Sara Babyonisheva at the union asking her, as a friend of Lydia Chukovskaya's, whether she couldn't organize some kind of collective opposition to the board's pre-arranged decisions. "For how much longer are our writers going to behave like chickens—each waiting submissively until its turn comes to be slaughtered and not interfering with the slaughter of others?" People who behaved like that did not deserve the name of writers and had no business writing. If they took no action, "the company of respectable writers deserves no less contempt than its official leadership." Babyonisheva had permission to quote him on this and show the others his letter if necessary.

The first board meeting took place on 9 January, without a hitch. Chukovskaya was summoned, excoriated, and duly expelled with no opposition, and no members of the union were admitted besides the board—not even Babyonisheva, who asked to be allowed to accompany Chukovskaya because the latter was half blind. Chukovskaya knew nothing of Solzhenitsyn's intervention at the time and was surprised, on her return that evening, to find him waiting for her, eager to hear her story. He questioned her closely on the details of who had said what, and she was taken aback by his intensity. What, she wondered, was the secret of Solzhenitsyn's immense inner force?

> It was in his ability to concentrate himself, the whole of himself . . . to gather up and concentrate . . . his individual "I" on the "I" of another. Now he was concentrated on me and my pain. Totally. Absolutely. It was as if he had pulled some lever inside himself—a switch—switching on his full attention, which he could then switch off again whenever he wanted. If he hadn't acquired this faculty—with all his being, with all his substance to experience the pain of others—how could he have created Matryona, not to speak of the entire population of the archipelago?[30]

She related the events of the meeting to him. Solzhenitsyn became agitated. "Do you mean to say that no one stood up for you? . . . No one at all?" She said of course not. He said, "I feel I'm going to weep," and she felt he meant it. But afterwards the absurdity of the whole procedure became apparent to them, and their tears turned to laughter at the pathetic effrontery of the hacks who had solemnly lectured her on decency and morality. Relaxed, Solzhenitsyn's face struck Chukovskaya as that of a simple worker not long out of the village—a fitter, say, or a mechanic. But soon Solzhenitsyn switched off again. "The lever worked without a hitch. It was time for the convict to return to his barrack hut for the evening roll-call. More than time, in fact, otherwise he'd lose the next morning's work." Solzhenitsyn handed her her notes on the meeting. "He was a different man—no longer listening, but hurrying past."[31]

As it turned out, Voinovich was not summoned until six weeks later; unlike Lydia Chukovskaya, he refused to go, terming such secret meetings illegal and adding sarcastically, "I do not wish to participate in illegal activities of any kind."[32]

By the following weekend Solzhenitsyn seems to have concluded that the immediate threat to himself had receded. There was a trickle of articles against him in the press, mainly reprints from Communist publications in Eastern and Western Europe, and the well-known *Pravda* columnist Yuri Zhukov devoted his weekly television programme to a rebuttal of *The Gulag Archipelago*. Zhukov commented that although Solzhenitsyn seemed to want to become a martyr, "we do not want to help him," while Western analysts felt that the Soviet Union would not want to jeopardize the next stage of the European Security Conference talks, due to open in Geneva the following week, by persecuting Solzhenitsyn and demonstrating their disregard for the "free circulation of ideas."[33] All of them, as it turned out, were wrong.

45

DEPORTED

On 14 January 1974 *Pravda* published an 1,800-word commentary headed "The Path of a Traitor," setting out the government's case against Solzhenitsyn in greater detail than hitherto. Many of the charges were the same as before—that he was a counter-revolutionary, an internal *émigré*, a "defector to the camp of the enemies of peace, democracy and socialism," that he was trying to disrupt *détente*, and so on. But this time the pseudonymous author "I. Solovyov" linked these themes to Solzhenitsyn's entire career and asserted that Solzhenitsyn had been a renegade from the beginning. As the "scion of a rich landowner," wrote Solovyov, Solzhenitsyn was naturally advocating a return to a capitalist and landowning form of society, and as a disciple of the pre-revolutionary Kadet party, he was prepared to betray his country to bring about a reversal of the October Revolution. Solzhenitsyn was anti-patriotic, anti-Russian, and pro-German (equals "pro-Nazi"). By quoting from *Gulag* out of context, "Solovyov" sought to demonstrate that Solzhenitsyn was "literally choking with pathological hatred for the country in which he was born and grew up, for the socialist system and the Soviet people." He was a traitor, a sympathizer with the White *émigrés*, and, on top of all else, a rich speculator in his own right, with three cars, a dacha, and "a Swiss lawyer to look after his bank accounts." He had earned a small fortune from placing his "anti-Soviet lampoons" on the Western market.

Pravda having laid down the Party line, the rest of the Soviet press followed suit with either the identical article or what amounted to a paraphrase. Only the *Literaturnaya Gazeta* distinguished itself by adding some original ideas and rhetoric of its own. Solzhenitsyn, it wrote, was under the direct control of his imperialist masters and had gathered his material for *Gulag* not in the Soviet Union but from working "in close contact and accord with the most rabid reactionaries and cold warriors." He was suffering from an "overtly bestial hatred for everything Soviet" and was no better than a reptile: "In daylight, all reptiles look disgusting."[1]

That same day there came an official hint that Solzhenitsyn should leave the country. In a radio broadcast, his old adversary Sergei Mikhalkov stated, "There is no need to fear that anybody might wish to hold him fast and not let him go should he wish to find a place for himself in a society in which he and his works will serve the struggle against socialism and communism, and he need have no doubt that he will be able to find such a place."[2] Mikhalkov doubted, however, that Solzhenitsyn would go voluntarily.

As if on cue, Natalia Svetlova's flat was subjected to a barrage of anonymous telephone calls and letters. Among the calls were such choice efforts as "Some of us have done time without betraying our country—get it? We won't leave that son of a bitch above ground much longer." "Isn't that Vlasovite dead yet?" "My [former] idol is the scum of the earth." Threats were made to murder Solzhenitsyn, to poison his food, and to harm his children, and at times the phone was so busy that it was impossible to call in or out. Svetlova bore the brunt of this campaign with great fortitude, occasionally answering the callers back and informing them that their words were being taped (which they were).[3] A few of these threatening calls were made to Peredelkino, and Lydia Chukovskaya was threatened as well.

Perceiving the danger of this new campaign, Solzhenitsyn reacted sharply. On 15 January he informed Western correspondents of the scurrilous letters and telephone calls and denounced the Writers' Union for having expelled Chukovskaya. Her real crime, he alleged, was that of harbouring him at Peredelkino, and that was why she had been singled out for punishment. Three days later he issued a more detailed rebuttal of the charges levelled against him in the press, pointing out that none of them was supported by the contents of *The Gulag Archipelago* and that most of the "quotations" in the articles were phoney. The *Literaturnaya Gazeta* had quoted from part 4 of the book, not yet published, indicating that the author of the article had been briefed by the KGB. The lies that Solzhenitsyn was "pro-Fascist" and a traitor were being disseminated to whip up popular hatred against him.

A day later he gave an interview to *Time* magazine. He denied that his book was intended to damage *détente* or that it would do so, provided *détente* was between peoples and not their oppressors. He also denied that he and Sakharov were appealing to Western governments or "reactionary circles" in the West to intervene in Soviet affairs and return to the cold war, as was alleged by his critics; but he simultaneously attacked the suggestion of "the Medvedev brothers" that reforms in the Soviet Union could come about only from within. Speaking more positively about *The Gulag Archipelago*, he indicated that it was a summons to "personal, public, and national repentance," a call "to purify the atmosphere," and he pleaded with Soviet young people to "refuse to participate in the lie," an idea he had been nursing for some time now and about which he had written a separate appeal ("Live Not by Lies"). Unable to make up his mind on when and how to publish the appeal, he contented himself with summarizing its main argument: "Everyone must stop co-operating with the lie. . . . In our country, the lie has become not just a moral category but a pillar of the state. In recoiling from the lie, we are performing a moral, not a political, act."[4]

In the last weeks of January and the first weeks of February 1974, the campaign against Solzhenitsyn took some bizarre forms. On Gorky Street, not far from Svetlova's flat, a poster was put up in a show-case depicting Solzhenitsyn's collected works in the form of a banner being carried at the head of an anti-Soviet orchestra. The banner was decorated with a yellow skull and cross-bones on a black background. One musician banged a drum labelled "anti-Soviet campaign," another was playing a battered trumpet marked "anti-Communist slander," while a four-line piece of doggerel underneath described "the traitor Solzhenitsyn" as having fallen into a slanderous fever and become "the standard of anti-Soviet forces abroad."[5] Headlines in the Soviet press now referred to him routinely as a renegade, Vlasovite, traitor, Judas, blasphemer, counter-revolutionary. He was described as an ally both of the Maoists and of the hawks in the Pentagon. Mildly liberal writers like Konstantin Simonov and the Ukrainian Oles Honchar, both of whom had themselves been attacked in the past, were pressed into making public denunciations of *The Gulag Archipelago*, and the usual array of "honest workers" assailed Solzhenitsyn in letters to the press about a book that none of them had read.

The pressure from the other side was also considerable. On 22 January, a large group of American intellectuals demonstrated in Solzhenitsyn's favour outside the National Press Club in Washington. The following day the BBC External Services and their German equivalent, the Deutsche Welle, began broadcasting excerpts from *The Gulag Archipelago* in Russian. That same week, the book appeared in a German translation, and two weeks later in Swedish, thus adding to the ground swell of Western opinion in Solzhenitsyn's favour. Smuggled copies of the Russian edition had already begun to appear in Moscow. They were passed from hand to hand, each reader being allowed a maximum of twenty-four hours to read the entire volume. The only weak spot in this foreign response—a significant one from Solzhenitsyn's point of view—was the absence of the American translation, which he regarded as the most necessary to his continuing safety, for the Americans had only news reports to guide them in their responses. In September, when Dr Heeb had written to the Carlisles for a copy of their translation of volume 1, he had been sent an unedited first draft of Thomas Whitney's translation (five years after work had supposedly begun on it). When checked for accuracy, the draft turned out to require a great deal of further work before it could begin to approximate to Solzhenitsyn's energetic and fiery original. By the time this had been established, three months had elapsed, and a serious editing of the translation had only just been started when the German and Swedish editions appeared.

On 2 February, Solzhenitsyn made another public statement in reply to his critics, on the fourth Lydia Chukovskaya released an open letter in his defence, and on the seventh Roy Medvedev defended Solzhenitsyn in an interview (Sakharov had twice spoken up for Solzhenitsyn in interviews in January). All of them praised *The Gulag Archipelago* as a truthful and necessary book. Sakharov described it as "a stone that will finally shatter the wall dividing mankind. It is a wall of mistrust and lack of understanding created by lies, wickedness, cowardice, and stupidity. . . . This stone has been cast by a sure and powerful hand." Medvedev, while expressing reservations about some of Solzhenitsyn's conclusions, declared the book to be "completely authentic" in its basic facts and a unique contribution to Russian and world literature. Chukovskaya, true to her pugnacious nature, concentrated on refuting the government's slander campaign against Solzhenitsyn and on underlining *The Gulag Archipelago*'s true meaning: "Solzhenitsyn, a living tradition, a living legend, has once more run the blockade of silence. He has reinvested the deeds of the past with reality, restored names to a multitude of victims and sufferers, and, most importantly, he has re-endowed events with their true weight and instructive meaning."[6]

These isolated protests were but voices crying in the wilderness, however, and were reported only abroad, doing little to breach that "wall of mistrust and lies" referred to by Sakharov within the Soviet Union. Indeed, this wall was being built higher by the day. Of particular distress to Solzhenitsyn was the discovery that the KGB had begun to blackmail some of his childhood friends into making statements against him. One of the first to be approached was his old school friend Kirill Simonyan, whom Solzhenitsyn had named in a footnote to chapter 4 of *The Gulag Archipelago* and reproached for some hostile comments during their exchange of letters in 1967. Guessing that Simonyan would be still further insulted by Solzhenitsyn's footnote—in which he expressed regret that Simonyan had *not* been arrested in 1945, for then he would have understood Soviet society (and Solzhenitsyn) better—the security organs showed the footnote to Simonyan and put pressure on him to make a public denunciation. A colleague at his Moscow hospital remembers entering Simonyan's office at this time and finding him holding his head in his hands and weeping.[7] Judging by his later behaviour, he must have promised to write something but was able to avoid making a statement right away.

Nikolai Vitkevich (whom Solzhenitsyn had referred to as "Nikolai V" in *The Gulag Archipelago*) was tracked down to Bryansk, where he was now a full professor in charge of the chemistry department of a large research institute. It was suggested to him that he too make a statement critical of Solzhenitsyn. When he refused, he was visited by the second secretary of the Regional Party Committee and persuaded to go to Moscow, where he would be acquainted with "some documents" pertaining to his and Solzhenitsyn's wartime arrest. Being a member of the Party and a senior professor, he could hardly refuse a second time, and in Moscow was shown that same record of Solzhenitsyn's original, 1945 investigation that had been shown to Simonyan in 1952. The passage of nearly thirty years since the events described in the record appears to have erased from Vitkevich's mind all memory of the atmosphere of terror reigning at that time, of the prisoners' dread of the security organs and the investigators' skill in rewriting and distorting testimony. Vitkevich had consciously suppressed his memories and had "edited" them to suit the prevailing orthodoxy. According to Natalia Reshetovskaya (who later discussed it with him), Vitkevich had behaved differently from Solzhenitsyn at his investigation. Whereas Solzhenitsyn had tried to outwit the investigator by weaving a fantasy (the typical vice of the story-teller) from his correspondence and diary, substituting innocuous "crimes" for the more serious charges the investigator was threatening him with, Vitkevich had simply admitted his guilt and refused to embellish on it. When he now came to read Solzhenitsyn's investigation record, therefore, he was apparently genuinely shocked by the difference in their behaviour and by Solzhenitsyn's inventions.[8]

This does not excuse Vitkevich's action in now denouncing his former friend, but it does make comprehensible his statement that the day on which he read Solzhenitsyn's investigation record was the "most terrible day of my life." He had defended Solzhenitsyn in his testimony, he said, but the latter had defamed not only him but also Simonyan, Lydia Ezherets, and even his own wife, Natalia, by inventing a plot to form a secret anti-Soviet organization. It was this attempt at co-operation that had resulted in Solzhenitsyn's being sentenced to only eight years' imprisonment, whereas he had been sentenced to ten. Vitkevich stated that after his release from the camps, he had been in the same position as Solzhenitsyn,* and "no little bitterness had accumulated in me too." However, he had experienced "a benevolent attitude" towards him on the part of the people he came into contact with, including government officials, had been enabled to complete his post-graduate studies, and now held a chair in a large institute. "No matter where I have worked, no one has ever been embarrassed or worried about my past, and my work, family, and the years of new impressions have today completely expunged from my mind any sense of hurt over those now distant times."[9]

In an interview that Vitkevich gave to Leo Gruliow of the *Christian Science Monitor*, Vitkevich went considerably further. He asserted that he had decided to protest to Novosti after hearing references to himself in Voice of America broadcasts. This was not true, if only because he was nowhere identified in them, but he tried to cover up by saying that he had "identified

---

* Vitkevich had not been in the same position as Solzhenitsyn after serving his camp sentence, because he had not been additionally sentenced to "perpetual exile." In fact, Vitkevich had been back in Rostov almost a year by the time Solzhenitsyn's exile was commuted and he was allowed to return home.

himself from the context." He also claimed to have seen copies of Solzhenitsyn's interrogation record at the time of his rehabilitation in 1957, as well as more recently, and to have been deeply shocked even then; and he minimized the seriousness of his and Solzhenitsyn's interrogation and sentences and implied that Solzhenitsyn's reaction to them was "abnormal." Perhaps worst of all, he denied that there had been "many millions" in the labour camps, attributing Solzhenitsyn's allegations to a desire to "stress his tragic biography," and produced the utterly specious accusation that Solzhenitsyn had "violated his human rights" by writing about him without authorization— despite the fact that only his first name and initial had been given in *The Gulag Archipelago* and that in *The First Circle* he had been disguised under a different name altogether.[10]

It is not clear how much of this Vitkevich believed and how much of it was a cynical invention placed into his mouth. Leo Gruliow described him as "speaking slowly in a low voice," indicating reluctance or depression. Natalia Reshetovskaya suggests that it was a mixture of genuine indignation, naïvety, and bad faith, brought on by fear of the security organs. When Natalia asked him whether he thought Solzhenitsyn was to blame for his—Vitkevich's— arrest, as some people later concluded from his remarks, he said he did not.[11] Solzhenitsyn reacted with predictable pain and fury in his statement of 2 February, pointing out sarcastically the holes in Vitkevich's statement as well as the fact that he was being accused, in essence, of co-operating with the security organs—a course constantly urged on loyal Soviet citizens as their sacred duty.

This latest invasion of his private life and past served notice on Solzhenitsyn of how his persecutors were now likely to proceed: *The Gulag Archipelago*'s autobiographical sections would be scrutinized for information about relatives and friends and pressure put on them to refute individual episodes and discredit both author and book. There were, unfortunately, rich possibilities in this approach, as Solzhenitsyn warned (in the hope of forestalling some of them) in his statement: "In this book I have told the reader intimate truths about myself that are much worse than all the bad things their timeservers can fabricate. That is the point of my book: it is a call to repentance, not a pamphlet."[12]

It seemed from this context that when Natalia Reshetovskaya virtually simultaneously gave an interview to a correspondent from *Le Figaro*, she, too, was acting under KGB pressure. The correspondent, Robert Lacontre, certainly could not have visited her in Ryazan without the assistance of the security authorities, for Ryazan was out of bounds to foreigners; and the Novosti agency, which arranged the interview, must have taken it for granted that the interview would be hostile to Solzhenitsyn. But Natalia was still an independent spirit and, as in the Kazan Station episode, appears to have been acting out of a sincere, if confused, desire to "help" Solzhenitsyn.

On the subject of *The Gulag Archipelago* she offered an original and not uninteresting interpretation. Underlining the author's qualification of it as "an experiment in artistic investigation," she maintained that this disqualified it as a work of scholarship or history. It was not a history of the Soviet Union or even a history of the camps, but a history of "camp folklore." During his years in prison, she said, Solzhenitsyn had met a vast number of prisoners, and being a man of intense curiosity, he had found it natural to question them on their experiences. "He has a fantastic memory, which is why he was able to preserve all those stories, and if he recounted some of them in *Ivan Denisovich*, *The First Circle*, and even *Cancer Ward*, all the rest of this folklore not yet used was condensed and combined in *The Gulag Archipelago*."[13]

At a later point in her life, Natalia came to regret her denigration of *The Gulag Archipelago*,[14] though her comments throw more light on its method of composition and its structure (and on some of its faults) than she is probably aware. Its contents were not, of course, "folklore" in the sense of being untrue, but they had, in large part, been filtered through the minds and imaginations of the 227 witnesses who had helped Solzhenitsyn, as well as through his own, and this endowed them with a form and colouration that were not too dissimilar from certain attributes of folk literature. It would appear, however, that this was not what Reshetovskaya meant either. Her intention, quixotic as it may seem, was to help Solzhenitsyn—by suggesting that the West was exaggerating the book's political importance and by implying that Solzhenitsyn himself may have been the victim of disinformation, albeit involuntary, at the hands of his collaborators.

That her intentions were benevolent is borne out by the rest of the interview, in which she underlined the fact that she had known Solzhenitsyn since 1936 and that he had always been "unswervingly loyal (in the political sense)" in his earlier years, accepting Soviet policy unquestioningly. And he had not changed at the front. If, during his imprisonment, he had written "that unfortunate book" *(Feast of the Conquerors)*, he had written it at a time when his resentment was justified. He had in any case later repudiated it, which demonstrated that it no longer represented his point of view.

Natalia repeated to Lacontre her theory that Solzhenitsyn's tragedy was a result of the Writers' Union's refusal to publish his works. "He no longer knew whom he was talking to; he went round in circles. He didn't want his books published in the West. He wanted them published here, but the thing acquired such momentum that it was difficult to stop it." And once his books had appeared in the West, she said, he found himself in an extraordinarily complex and difficult situation that could not fail to affect his psychology. "His state of mind came close to that which he had once experienced in the camps and which he ought to have got over but which returned in the end in much the same form as before."

The appearance of Natalia's interview within a few days of Vitkevich's served only to confuse foreign observers still more. Neither statement appeared in the Soviet Union. Not for the first time, one had the ridiculous spectacle of interviews given in the Soviet Union being completely suppressed there and published only abroad, while the Soviet press chose to dig up and reprint—

or print for the first time—strident articles by Western journalists who were unknown and unread in their own countries. On the face of it, there seemed a certain symmetry in this selective approach to what to print and what not to print, but the symmetry was fraudulent: the stature and newsworthiness of a Solzhenitsyn or Sakharov—as well as Chukovskaya, Medvedev, and even Natalia Reshetovskaya—were not to be compared with those of the obscure hacks paraded by the Soviet newspapers. *Le Figaro*, puzzled by the interview's friendly tone, wondered in a headline whether this signalled a particularly clever manoeuvre by the Soviet authorities or a genuine change of heart. After all, Solzhenitsyn himself in his recent statement had indicated that Reshetovskaya, Vitkevich, and others were being manipulated by Novosti. The situation did not seem as bad as it had a week or two before, and the consensus was that although the public attacks on Solzhenitsyn had been vicious, they were dying down again, and the danger of arrest was receding.

Solzhenitsyn seemed to share this view, for on 7 February he noted in his diary, "Forecast for February: apart from attempts to discredit me, they aren't likely to do anything, and there will probably be a breathing space."[15] He was proved wrong the very next day. Svetlova rang in the evening to say that a messenger had tried to deliver a summons from the public prosecutor's office requiring Solzhenitsyn to report to his office at 5 p.m. that day. She had refused to accept the summons on the grounds that it was improperly drawn up, but the matter was obviously serious. Since it was a Friday, Solzhenitsyn decided to stay in Peredelkino for the weekend and continue his work. He would go to Moscow on Monday morning as usual. Though undoubtedly worried by this latest move (enough, at least, not to be able to work properly), he seems not to have regarded it as exceptional or final. Sakharov had also been summoned to the public prosecutor's office a few months previously, had been warned about his behaviour, and had then given a press conference to denounce the warning. Nothing had happened to him. Could it be a similar manoeuvre?

On Monday, 11 February, making no special arrangements, telling no one where he was going, and leaving his Peredelkino room in its usual state of neat preparedness, Solzhenitsyn set off for Moscow. Soon after his arrival at Svetlova's flat a second summons arrived. By now Solzhenitsyn had had time to think about what his response would be. Instead of signing to acknowledge receipt, he typed out and affixed to the summons another bold challenge.

In the circumstances created by the universal and unrelieved illegality enthroned for many years past in our country . . . I refuse to acknowledge the legality of your summons and shall not report for questioning to any agency of the state.

Before requiring citizens to observe the law, you must learn to carry it out yourselves. Free the innocent people now in prison. Punish those responsible for mass extermination, and the false informers. Punish the administrators and the special squads who carried out the policy of genocide (the deportation *of whole peoples*). Deprive the local and departmental satraps of their unlimited power over citizens, their arbitrary use of courts and psychiatrists *today*. Satisfy the *millions* of lawful but suppressed complaints.[16]

In *The Oak and the Calf* Solzhenitsyn writes that he was optimistic about his ability to survive the prosecutor's challenge, but the provocativeness of this reply suggests otherwise. So does Solzhenitsyn's action in promptly telephoning a number of Western correspondents to inform them of his action and inviting them to take a public statement from him. The statement consisted almost entirely of an extract from the still unpublished part 7 of *The Gulag Archipelago*—the part dealing with the period from 1956 to the present, about which Solzhenitsyn had been keeping quiet till then. By making it public, he was openly challenging the Brezhnev regime.

The theme of the passage was that although the political prisoners in Soviet labour camps were now numbered in thousands, rather than the millions of Stalin's time, Soviet law had not changed in any fundamental way. It was still at the mercy of the political leaders and the bureaucracy, could still be flouted or manipulated with impunity, and therefore could, at any time, be adapted to accommodate a return to Stalinist terror if the leaders showed sufficient determination. "We have called this chapter 'The Law Today,' " the statement ended, "but really it should be called 'There *Is* No Law.' The same perfidious secrecy, the same fog of unrighteousness, hangs in the air around us, hangs over our cities more densely than the city smoke itself. A powerful state towers over its second half-century, embraced in hoops of steel. The hoops are there indeed, but *not* the law."[17]

There was no response to Solzhenitsyn's challenge that day. Solzhenitsyn and Svetlova felt themselves to be in a kind of limbo. One fear was undoubtedly that Solzhenitsyn would be arrested, for they discussed in some detail what his behaviour should be during his investigation, trial, and subsequent imprisonment. Solzhenitsyn was determined not to co-operate with the authorities in any way, or to do prison work. He might even try to write in prison, he thought—say, a history of Russia for children, which he had begun to think about since the birth of his own sons. But he didn't think he could hold out for more than two years in jail—long enough for his remaining works to be published in the West, but no more.

He and Svetlova also cleared the literary backlog as best they could. All Solzhenitsyn's unpublished works had by now been microfilmed and securely hidden or spirited to the West, and there remained only some mopping up to do. They made a microfilm of Solzhenitsyn's preface to *A Current of "The Quiet Don,"* a samizdat book analyzing Sholokhov's famous novel and seeking to demonstrate that Sholokhov was not the sole author, but had plagiarized it. Solzhenitsyn had apparently agreed to help the anonymous writer get his study published in the West. Overnight, unable to sleep, Solzhenitsyn did some further work on his *Letter to the Leaders*. Having delayed Western publication of the letter, owing to the fierceness of the Soviet press attack on *Gulag*, he now wanted to alter the letter's conciliatory tone. It might look like weakness, he felt, to be making such overtures to the Soviet leaders after the publication of *Gulag* and the harsh Soviet response. And after his latest aggressive statement, there was less reason than ever to appear compromising. Another factor, not touched upon by Solzhenitsyn, seems to have been his desire to appear less contemptuous of the West. Whether this was the result of criticism from friends or perhaps of a premonition that he himself might soon end up in the West, the fact remains that he removed a number of passages disparaging Western democracy and Western institutions, and considerably modified some of his harsher strictures.* The resulting text was still critical of the West, but it no longer painted quite so black a picture of the West's decadence.[18]

The following day seemed to start quite normally. Solzhenitsyn and Svetlova spent the morning at their separate desks, dealing with correspondence and minor literary chores. In the afternoon, while Solzhenitsyn was walking the five-month old Stepan in his push-chair in the yard, he was visited by Igor Shafarevich, who had come to bring him the manuscript of his just-completed book *The Socialist Phenomenon* and to discuss their plans for *From under the Rubble*. Shortly after they had gone upstairs to the flat again, there came a ring at the front door. Leaving the door on the chain, Svetlova reported that two men had come from the prosecutor's office "to clear something up." Solzhenitsyn went to the door and opened it, whereupon the two men burst inside, followed quickly by six others who had been waiting round a corner of the landing. Their leader took an official document from a folder, thrust it at Solzhenitsyn to inspect and sign, and informed him that he must accompany the assembled policemen to the prosecutor's office immediately.

Solzhenitsyn was thunderstruck. He had described this very procedure in the opening pages of *Gulag*: "[Arrest] is a sharp night-time ring of the bell or a brusque knock at the door. It's the brazen entry of the unwiped boots of unsleeping agents. . . ." He had made endless plans with Svetlova about how they would behave if the police came for him—how they would use delaying tactics, how they would rush to the telephone and inform their friends, how they would refuse to admit more men than there were adults in the flat at the time, so as not to be outnumbered. Yet when the actual moment came, he had been caught napping. "I was in a state of witless shock, as though flames had suddenly enwrapped and paralysed me. . . . Dolt! Is this all the good your training has done you? What's become of your much-vaunted wolfish prison ways?"[19] He was no better—and no wiser—than those helpless "rabbits" whose tragic impotence he had chronicled in *Gulag*.

The one gesture he was able to make before being led away was to go into his study and fetch his prison sack, which was supposed to be ready with his prison necessities inside. Since the readiness of this sack has entered

---

*A copy of the original text is in my possession, since I asked by Dr Heeb to arrange for the translation of the *Letter* into English and for its publication in England and America. The original text was sent to London in late September. Then came the order to delay publication, and afterwards an amended text to be substituted for the original one.

Soviet folklore, it is worth recording that (by Solzhenitsyn's own admission) it wasn't there—he must have left it in Peredelkino. He was obliged to take a child's school satchel and empty it of confidential papers under the very noses of his police escort, having foolishly allowed them to follow him into his study. In short, he behaved just as distractedly, and made as many mistakes, as any other person would do on being arrested. He did manage, however, to don the threadbare cap and shabby sheepskin overcoat that he had preserved from exile and that he had been keeping for just such an eventuality.

The arrest had begun disastrously for Solzhenitsyn. Always able hitherto to keep one step ahead of the authorities, he had surrendered the initiative, and he was to remain at a disadvantage throughout the short duration of this, his second imprisonment.

He had planned to adopt a policy of complete non–co-operation with the prison authorities. "I was quite sure . . . that in jail I would not accept the humiliations to which Soviet political prisoners are subjected. I myself had written so much in *Gulag* about the way in which even in the twenties our young people had upheld the proud traditions of earlier Russian political prisoners: not standing up when prison officers came into the room, etc., etc." Yet when he was taken to Lefortovo Prison, he forgot these resolutions, too, and did just the opposite (some of the finest pages in *The Oak and the Calf* are devoted to an unsparing description of how Solzhenitsyn had wanted to behave and how he did behave—a happy instance of the novelist taking over from the polemicist). On arrival in Lefortovo he meekly submitted to being stripped and searched ("like a cow standing stock still to be milked"), to handing over his watch and other belongings and signing the receipt, to undergoing a medical examination. He even rose obediently to his feet when reminded to do so by the newly arrived Colonel Komarov, the prison commandant. The only thing he argued for was to be given back his cross, but the guards refused on the grounds that it was made of metal and therefore not allowed. Solzhenitsyn was obliged to concur.

The other miscalculation he made was that he would be given special treatment befitting a prominent person. In his account of his arrival, he describes how he imagined a high Party official being posted somewhere out of sight to observe this "not altogether ordinary moment in the history of Lefortovo." But there were no special arrangements, and no concessions to Solzhenitsyn's fame. After enduring the immutable reception procedures, he was taken to a cell—not a solitary cell, as he had imagined, but one with two other men in it: petty currency speculators, newly arrested like himself.

About an hour or so after his arrival, he was summoned from his cell by Colonel Komarov and led into the office of a small, bald-headed official who turned out to be Mikhail P. Malyarov, the deputy prosecutor general of the USSR—that same Malyarov who had interviewed Sakharov. With a minimum of formality, Malyarov informed Solzhenitsyn that he was being charged under Article 64 of the penal code with treason—a charge, although Malyarov did not say so, that carried a penalty ranging from ten years in prison to the death sentence. At this point Solzhenitsyn at last recovered his composure and refused to sign the document that Malyarov pushed across the desk to him. He also made his long-planned declaration: "I shall take no part in either your investigation or your trial. You must carry on without me." Malyarov, according to Solzhenitsyn, showed no surprise and asked Solzhenitsyn simply to sign to confirm that he had been informed. This was too old a trick to catch an ex-convict, and Solzhenitsyn refused, whereupon the "interview" was brought to an end.

Back in his cell, Solzhenitsyn had a difficult night. His pillow was too low for a man with high blood pressure, but there was nothing he could do about it. The following morning he was taken out for another medical examination, this time more thorough than the first: the prison authorities did not want to be accused of mistreating their prisoner. Discovering that his blood pressure was high, they gave him some medicine to bring it down before returning him to his cell. After breakfast he was taken out again and given a fresh white shirt and tie to put on. He had already been provided with a suit and new shoes the preceding day, and now he was supplied with shoelaces and an overcoat and cap. He protested that he wanted his own clothes returned but was told by Colonel Komarov that this was impossible: "Later, later. . . . Right now you're going on a journey." No more details were given, and Solzhenitsyn leaped to the conclusion that at last his old dream was about to be fulfilled.

> Where was I going? I had no doubt about it. To see the government, that very Politburo of theirs, of which Mayakovsky had once dreamed. At long last we would have our first—and last—discussion. I had at times found myself looking forward to the moment when light would break in on them, when they would suddenly be interested in talking to me—and surely it would be in their interest?
>
> The conversation would be a serious one, perhaps the most important of my life. There was no need to plan it: I had carried a plan in my heart and in my head for a long time. Arguments would suggest themselves. I would be utterly unconstrained and talk to them as their subordinates never did. . . .

The prison officers appeared to be in some confusion. At first they were in a hurry, but Solzhenitsyn was then returned to his cell to wait. After some delay, he was led out again and taken to the same office where he had been charged with treason the day before. On his way into the room, he still anticipated a meeting with some member or members of the Politburo and was staggered to find only Malyarov again. Once Solzhenitsyn was seated, Malyarov informed him that he was to be deported.

> By decree of the Presidium of the Supreme Soviet of the USSR: for the systematic execution of actions incompatible with Soviet citizenship and harmful to the USSR, Solzhenitsyn A. I. is to be deprived of Soviet citizenship and evicted beyond the borders of the Soviet Union, today 13 February 1974.[20]

Solzhenitsyn does not record that he was given any choice or that he objected. He had more than half expected it. The idea had been in the air for a couple of years now and, in the weeks since the publication of *The Gulag Archipelago*, had been revived in a number of influential quarters both East and West. It must also have come as something of a relief. His defiant thoughts of refusing to co-operate and holding out for two years in jail had quickly evaporated on contact with the realities of prison life. It was clearly beyond his strength. "I had promised my wife that whatever happened, I would stick it out in jail or in a camp for two years. Just till I knew that all my work had been published and I could die content, knowing I had hit them where it hurt. But now I saw that I had promised more than I could deliver. I could have held out for years, adapting myself to any angle from the vertical, so long as I had air and silence and a chance to write. But here I would surely be done for in two months."

Malyarov's statement undoubtedly lifted a burden from Solzhenitsyn, but he did not want to give the deputy prosecutor the satisfaction of seeing it. He demanded that his family be allowed to go with him. Malyarov said that it was impossible but that the family could follow afterwards. Solzhenitsyn demanded guarantees and asked to be allowed to write a statement to Podgorny, the Soviet president. After a moment's hesitation Malyarov agreed, but all Solzhenitsyn could think of was to list the names and ages of his family, including his mother-in-law and stepson. It was only a gesture, but it enabled him to save face. To be awkward, he tried informing Malyarov that he was unfit to travel by air, but Malyarov's response was noncommittal.

Solzhenitsyn was returned to his cell for lunch and then led out to a waiting limousine. On the way, his cross and his watch were returned to him (but not his clothes), and he broke off a hunk of Lefortovo bread and stuffed it into a pocket. The limousine drove to Sheremetyevo International Airport, where Solzhenitsyn was ushered into the forward cabin of a waiting jet-liner, accompanied by seven secret-service men (and one doctor) in civilian clothes. The cabin was empty except for Solzhenitsyn and his escort. It was a regular Aeroflot flight to Frankfurt that had been held back for three hours. Passengers and inquirers had been told that the delay was due to "fog."

The flight lasted about two and a half hours. As the plane took off, Solzhenitsyn bowed to his native soil and crossed himself, causing some bewilderment to his police escort. There were some farcical moments later when two detectives insisted on accompanying him to the toilet and keeping the door open while he was inside, but otherwise the flight seems to have been normal. The plane landed shortly after 4 p.m. local time (6 p.m. in Moscow). When Solzhenitsyn tried to leave his seat, he was ordered to wait for a while. Then he was allowed to don his new (Czechoslovak) overcoat and cap and make for the exit. Just as he reached the door, one of the escorts stepped up and handed him five hundred German marks—a gift from the KGB. He descended the steps, half expecting to see a KGB man on either side of him, but there was none, only a ring of German officials at the bottom. A ground hostess came forward and presented him with a rose, and a German official, Peter Dingens, greeted him on behalf of the German Foreign Ministry. He stepped into a waiting car (his second limousine that day) and was whisked off at top speed, with a police escort back and front, to the country home of his old friend Heinrich Böll, in the hamlet of Langenbroich, west of Bonn.

Throughout this time Natalia Svetlova was in complete ignorance of what was happening to her husband. For the first hour after his arrest, her telephone had been cut off, but she had been able to make three calls before the line was cut again and to communicate the news of Solzhenitsyn's arrest to friends. Her mother had managed to reach some Western correspondents from a nearby call-box before also being cut off. In no time at all the flat had been swamped with visitors: friends, sympathizers, dissidents, and correspondents. Sakharov and four friends went off to picket the public prosecutor's office, partly to express a protest and partly to see whether Solzhenitsyn would emerge again. When told that he wasn't there, they had returned to Kozitsky Lane, where there were more people than ever. The visitors now included Sakharov, Shafarevich, Yuli Daniel, Natalia Gorbanevskaya, Vladimir Voinovich, Vladimir Kornilov, and about two dozen others. Everybody present sensed that this was a public event of the first magnitude; they somehow wanted to be there to show solidarity as well as to help if possible. At some point the telephone was restored again and from then on never stopped ringing: Stockholm, Paris, New York, Amsterdam—the whole world wanted to know what was happening. At 9.15 p.m. the prosecutor's office rang through to say that Solzhenitsyn was being detained for the night.

The question arose of what to do with the bewildered children in all this throng and whether to take them elsewhere, but it was decided to put them to bed as usual. Natalia Svetlova and her mother, Ekaterina, had no time to worry about them. They were frantically at work in Solzhenitsyn's study, sorting through piles of manuscripts, documents, letters, and microfilms to see which could be burnt and which had to be hidden. A search was expected at any moment, and they worked through the night, burning unwanted papers on a large tray and then in a basin on the kitchen floor. By morning they were more or less ready, but fortunately the search never came.*

Overnight, Svetlova had also found and released to Western correspondents (through Robert Lacontre, summoned from his bed in the small hours) Solzhenitsyn's statement—prepared, as usual, well beforehand—on the occasion of his arrest: "I declare in advance that any criminal proceedings against Russian literature, against any single book in Russian literature, or against any Russian author are improper and invalid."[21] The statement reiterated Solzhenitsyn's determination not to co-operate in any trial or to work while in jail. "In this way I leave [the authorities] the simple recourse open to all

---

* At least one search was carried out in Ryazan, at the home of friends of Solzhenitsyn's called the Radugins. Solzhenitsyn felt, when he later learned of it, that the KGB had been looking for a copy of *The Oak and the Calf*.

arrant bullies: to kill me quickly for writing the truth about Russia's history." The next morning, Svetlova released his programmatic declaration "Live Not by Lies," setting out at greater length the advice he had given to young Russians in his last newspaper interview, and sent a copy to Dr Heeb in Zurich with instructions to publish. When Heeb telephoned her that day, she also instructed him to set in motion the provisions in Solzhenitsyn's will for the publication of his remaining works. She wasn't quite sure whether the time for that had yet come, but intended it as a warning to the KGB's wire-tappers. There was still time to rescind it if necessary.

On the morning of 14 February, Svetlova was kept in constant suspense. It was impossible to get through to the public prosecutor's office by telephone, and nobody knew where her husband was. In the rest of the world, the press and broadcasting media had erupted with reports on how the arrest had been carried out—mostly based on interviews with her—but they knew nothing more than she did, and the Soviet media were as usual silent. Then came rumours and reports that Solzhenitsyn was on his way to or had arrived in Germany. Svetlova described the news as "a great misfortune" and expressed her dismay, refusing to believe it until she had heard from Solzhenitsyn himself. It was only after he had rung her from Heinrich Böll's house that she accepted the fact and confirmed that she and the children would eventually join him.

The timetable and manner of Solzhenitsyn's expulsion are thus not in doubt, but a certain mystery still surrounds the choice of West Germany as his destination and the arrangement to go to Heinrich Böll's. The idea that Solzhenitsyn might be expelled to Germany seems to have arisen in connection with a speech that Chancellor Willy Brandt delivered in Munich on 2 February. In an unscripted aside, Brandt had referred to Solzhenitsyn's difficulties and to the tradition of free speech in Germany and had said, "Mr Solzhenitsyn would be able to live in freedom and work unhindered in the Federal Republic."[22] At the time it was thought to be an impromptu remark, but German government sources later indicated that the remark had been deliberately added at the last minute. Whatever the case, a representative of Tass requested an official transcript and transmitted it to Moscow (though Tass itself never reported the speech). It would obviously suit the Soviet government to send Solzhenitsyn to Germany, since one of the things he was accused of was pro-German sympathies, and the symbolism would not be lost on the Soviet public, but German officials have steadfastly denied that there was a deal. However, about a week after Brandt's speech a Soviet visitor to Bonn is said to have predicted that Solzhenitsyn would be expelled precisely to West Germany, though no one took much notice of the remark at the time, for it seemed no better and no worse than other speculations then in the air.

If official sources are to be believed, it was only on the evening of Tuesday, 13 February, that the German government had any inkling of what was planned. The Soviet ambassador to Bonn, Valentin Falin, phoned Paul Frank, an undersecretary at the Foreign Ministry, and asked for an interview early the next morning to discuss "an important matter." At 8.30 a.m. on Wednesday, Falin informed Frank that the Soviet Union wanted to expel Solzhenitsyn to Germany, and asked whether the Germans would accept him. Willy Brandt was at that moment chairing an urgent meeting of the cabinet and was reportedly surprised when the news was given to him, but he at once gave his approval and left his personal secretary to deal with the arrangements.[23]

It is at this point that mystery supervenes. The Soviet ambassador is said to have informed Frank that Germany was Solzhenitsyn's own choice when informed of the decision to deport him and that Solzhenitsyn had asked to be taken to stay with Heinrich Böll on arrival. This made perfect sense, since German was Solzhenitsyn's best (if not only) foreign language and since Böll was the only Western writer he counted as a personal friend. On the other hand, if the supposition that the Soviet government was influenced by Brandt's speech is correct, Germany could have been the government's choice, and it was simply camouflage to pretend that Solzhenitsyn had requested it.

This would mesh with Solzhenitsyn's assertion (in his memoir) that he did not know his destination until he landed in Frankfurt and saw the name on the airport buildings. But there are problems with his account too. It is clear, for instance, that Solzhenitsyn and his escorts travelled alone in separate cabin at the front of the plane, and he has described the twenty-seat cabin behind as also being empty.* He even suggests at one point in his story that "a special plane" had been provided for him, and elsewhere that he was the "only passenger." Yet earlier he writes that before take-off "the passengers, some of them with little children, were exhausted by the delay," and a *Washington Post* reporter talked to one of those passengers (a Yugoslav) after the plane had landed.[24] If this was the case, it is straining credulity to suggest that the crew of a scheduled flight, with a complement of disgruntled passengers aboard, would omit the usual announcements on take-off and landing.† Similarly, Solzhenitsyn refers to the presence aboard this Soviet plane of copies of the *Frankfurter Allgemeine Zeitung*, yet writes that he drew no conclusions from it, other than that some members of his escort might be diplomats. Finally, Solzhenitsyn told reporters at Langenbroich, when asked whether he regarded exile as the only way out for him, "I learned about this only at 1 p.m."[25] "This" presumably referred to the fact of his exile, and also to the journey, for he had objected to flying. But did it not also include his destination?

---

*Here, too, is a mystery. Solzhenitsyn was said to have flown in a TU-154, which Jane's *All the World's Aircraft* describes as having only two cabins—one smaller at the front, and one larger behind it. Did Solzhenitsyn's memory deceive him (perhaps as a result of the extraordinary circumstances) as to the layout of the cabins, or was a different aircraft substituted for the usual one on this route?

†On the other hand it is possible that the loudspeakers were switched off in the cabin in which Solzhenitsyn was travelling.

The question of who first suggested Böll is also problematic. It is not unlikely that the Soviet authorities thought it up for themselves. Solzhenitsyn's friendship with Böll must have been known to them from their wiretapping and surveillance, and the idea sounded plausible enough. On the other hand, Böll himself thought at one time that it was Solzhenitsyn's idea, "because I am the only living author in the Federal Republic whom he really personally knows."[26] On another occasion, Böll indicated that he thought the suggestion had come from Willy Brandt, "because a hotel would have been unsuitable."[27] The point is that if Solzhenitsyn made the suggestion, he must have known that he was headed for Germany.

The issue was not regarded as important at the time but has since acquired a certain significance in the light of Solzhenitsyn's polemics with other dissidents on the whole question of emigration. For Solzhenitsyn, "voluntary" emigration from the Soviet Union has come to be regarded as an act of betrayal, and he has harshly criticized those dissidents who left the Soviet Union of their own accord, as opposed to being forcibly put on a plane—usually straight from jail, as in the cases of Bukovsky, Ginzburg, Edward Kuznetsov, and a small number of others. In this category, Solzhenitsyn places himself. His critics, however, maintain that the choice presented to other prominent *émigrés* (Iosif Brodsky, Pavel Litvinov, Andrei Sinyavsky, and a host of others) was not much different from Solzhenitsyn's: emigrate or go to jail. This is why it matters (though not very much in the long run) whether Solzhenitsyn was truly a blind and ignorant victim until the moment he stepped off the plane in Frankfurt, or had learned his fate a few hours earlier in Moscow and had accepted it. Like many other mysteries in his life, this one has still to be resolved.*

Whatever the true facts of the case, Solzhenitsyn's departure from the Soviet Union was a major event. Just as Solzhenitsyn had managed to conduct his whole struggle with the Soviet authorities in the glare of world publicity, so his expulsion was headline news. Reporters were present both in

---

* Solzhenitsyn writes in *The Oak and the Calf* that after he had been informed of the decision to deport him "my steps seemed lighter all the time, my feet touched the floor more lightly. I was soaring, floating up from this tomb." But by the time he reached Germany, he was anxious to emphasize to everyone that he had been given no choice. In the *Oak* he mentions that in Moscow, on the day of his departure, "there was a rumour, launched in haste, before they could tidy up the loose ends, that [I] had voluntarily chosen expatriation rather than imprisonment." Solzhenitsyn does not say who was responsible for the rumour, or who, for that matter, was responsible for "tidying up the loose ends." It may be that Solzhenitsyn was not asked to choose, but there is no evidence that he was anything other than delighted by the decision to send him abroad or that he seriously attempted to force the issue and seek a different outcome. Indeed, he ends his account of the matter with the comment that "for one moment of mental aberration they [his family and supporters] thought, 'Better a Soviet camp than live out your days abroad,' " making it clear that for Solzhenitsyn such a thought *was* an aberration. There is also a cryptic reference in the *Oak* to what looks like a difference of opinion between himself and Natalia Svetlova: "Life has so many jolts and jars, and when the closest of friends are jolted apart even for a day, they cease to think alike." This would explain Svetlova's dismay when first told by correspondents that Solzhenitsyn had flown to West Germany.

his Moscow flat and at Frankfurt and in Langenbroich throughout the final hours of the drama—and virtually standing at both ends of the telephone when Solzhenitsyn rang Natalia Svetlova with the details of his departure. The Soviet Union's repressive attitude to dissent and contempt for its own citizens, even its most famous citizen, was dramatized yet again and unforgettably.

But it was much more than just a media event, for the expulsion was real and irreversible, an arbitrary, brutal reprisal against the Soviet government's most daring and dangerous opponent. It was a crushing blow to Solzhenitsyn's hopes of staying on and continuing his fight within the Soviet Union, and a no less serious blow to the now dwindling band of Soviet dissidents. On the same day that Solzhenitsyn was expelled from Soviet soil, Vladimir Maximov was informed that he, too, could go to the West. Sinyavsky had already gone, and within the next few years many more prominent dissidents would follow. In one sense these were acts of desperation on the part of the government and admissions of defeat: whereas Stalin would simply have had them killed or silenced, the present Soviet leadership was unable to contain and control its dissenting citizens and was obliged to expel many of them, including this most awkward one of all. But from another point of view, it was a victory for the regime. The chess players in the Kremlin had found just the right strategy. To put Solzhenitsyn on trial and jail him (there are no innocent defendants in Soviet political trials) would have created a world-wide furore, disrupted relations with the West, and put an end to *détente*—at least for some time. To let him remain free was too great a risk, especially after his latest challenge to the public prosecutor. But expulsion allowed the Soviet government to rid itself of its bitterest opponent, while avoiding charges of excessive cruelty and repression. The storm of bad publicity and Western indignation could be ridden out, and after that it would be business as usual again.

FIRST MONTHS
IN THE WEST

THE HAMLET OF Langenbroich, in the Eifel hills west of Bonn, normally has a population of about one hundred inhabitants. On the evening of Solzhenitsyn's arrival, it had been swollen to more than twice that number by reporters and television crews from all over the world (not to speak of a contingent of German police to control them). First reports that Solzhenitsyn was bound for Böll's house had emerged at about lunch-time, when the interior minister of the state of North Rhine–Westphalia, Willi Weyer, told reporters in Düsseldorf that Solzhenitsyn was already in Germany and staying with Böll. The minister was premature, but an agency report of his remarks sent hordes of newsmen rushing there, and others to Frankfurt airport, after German government sources had confirmed that Solzhenitsyn was truly on his way. When they discovered that the airport had been sealed off, they, too, rushed to Langenbroich, so that by the time Solzhenitsyn arrived, the approaches to Böll's modest converted farmhouse and its front yard were jammed with cars and people and bathed in the bright light of arc lamps. The whole ceremony of the arrival was carried live on German television.

Solzhenitsyn, clutching a bunch of daffodils presented to him by the interior minister (perhaps to make up for his earlier lapse) was hugged and kissed on both cheeks by Heinrich Böll before being ushered into the farmhouse. Inside he was told that he would have to say something to the waiting press, and a few moments later he emerged to confront the microphones. "You must understand that I am very tired and worried about my family," he said in heavily accented German. "I must telephone Moscow—this morning I was in jail." Switching to Russian, he thanked the reporters for their patience but insisted that he could make no statements and would give no interviews. "I have given too many interviews in the recent past. Now I must simply collect myself and understand my situation. . . . I ask you not to come here tomorrow and surprise me or Mr Böll." At the end of this little speech, he raised his hands above his head in an athlete's gesture of victory.[1]

The entreaty to the pressmen not to return the next day was superfluous—they never left. A goodly number remained in the cobbled yard the whole night (despite the February cold) or prowled round the house and tried to peer in at the back windows, while others dozed in their cars. The next morning, new contingents appeared, swelling the crowd to even greater proportions.

On the night of his arrival, Solzhenitsyn had been nervous and exhausted. He detested not being in control of events, not knowing what was going to happen next, and being obliged to appear before the world in (brand new) clothes not of his own choosing. It was also one of the few occasions, he told Böll, on which he had been without his notebook and pencil.[2] He felt naked and at the mercy of others. But the following morning he was his old self again—relaxed, friendly, calm, and controlled. Strolling outside with Böll in the latter's orchard to get some fresh air, he willingly signed copies of his books and posed for photographs. But he firmly declined to answer questions or give interviews, even when he recognized old friends among reporters in the crowd and invited them in for a chat. Per Hegge, one of those invited in, reports that he found Solzhenitsyn in unexpectedly good form, full of sardonic jokes and supremely practical in his approach to the problems that lay ahead of him. "He looks far less sad than I think he is," Hegge told another reporter.[3] Janis Sapiets of the BBC's Russian Service, who had never met Solzhenitsyn, found himself being hugged and thanked for his religious programmes on the BBC, to which Solzhenitsyn had been an avid listener.[4] Robert Kaiser, of the *Washington Post*, was called over and told that just a few days earlier, Solzhenitsyn had been trying to reach him in Moscow, not knowing that Kaiser was in Europe on a skiing holiday.[5] Others who went in included Hans Björkegren, Solzhenitsyn's Swedish translator, and Dimitri Panin, who was now living in Paris. It was like a miniature court, and all who went into the house found Solzhenitsyn calm and smiling. As for the good-natured and self-effacing Böll, he was "like a stranger in his own house," according to Hegge, but not at all put out or resentful of this upheaval. On the contrary, he did everything he could to cushion the shock for Solzhenitsyn, carried messages back and forth, and acted as intermediary with the outside world.

There was something touchingly incongruous in the conjunction of these two Nobel Prize winners. Böll was then under heavy attack in Germany for his left-wing views and alleged sympathy with left-wing terrorists. On his coffee-table lay a book on the terrorists, *Free Passage for Ulrike Meinhof*, and on the wall hung a treasured portrait of Rosa Luxemburg. He was detested in Germany by the very people who most admired Solzhenitsyn. And yet there was a certain logic in it too. Solzhenitsyn's camouflage as a man of left-wing convictions, aided by a clever choice of helpers in the West, had not yet slipped sufficiently for his conservative political views to have become well known, especially to those who had not read *August 1914*. *The Gulag Archipelago* had only just appeared, and the *Letter to the Leaders* had not yet been released. But the two men were both rebels. Solzhenitsyn, moreover, was extremely grateful to Böll on a personal level for all the favours the latter had done him, while Böll's admiration of Solzhenitsyn was genuine. He had praised Solzhenitsyn's novels as well as his *Gulag Archipelago* in reviews (the latter as recently as 9 February) and was not one of those naïve souls who confuse the Soviet dictatorship with socialism. What he would think of Solzhenitsyn's views of the West was still in the future, but on the Soviet present the two men were more or less in agreement.*

Solzhenitsyn's decision not to make a fuller statement on his first day in the West was partly tactical. He still did not know enough about his wife's situation in Moscow to take any risks, and she and the children were in a sense hostages to his good behaviour. But there were deeper reasons too. "I had been transplanted so quickly that I hadn't even had time to decide how I felt about it, let alone make a speech about it," he wrote later. The idea of speaking impromptu, without preparing in advance, was completely alien to him, as he had shown in his dealings with Western reporters in Moscow. Another factor weighed heavily with him but was misunderstood at the time: How would his words and actions be received in the Soviet Union—not only by his enemies but by his friends? "I suddenly felt that I would demean myself if I indulged in abuse from afar, if I spoke out where everyone speaks out, where speaking out is permitted." As it happened, his silence was also misinterpreted in Moscow, but that was a risk he had to take.[6]

A good part of that first day was spent conferring with Dr Heeb, who had travelled from Zurich as soon as he heard the news of Solzhenitsyn's expulsion. The modest doctor had never met his famous client before and was taken aback by how tall and brawny he seemed ("like a lumberjack"). Their meeting commenced with a jovial bear-hug that warmed the cockles of the cautious lawyer's heart before they got down to business. The first problem was where Solzhenitsyn should live. Germany seemed out of the question, for political reasons. Indeed, Solzhenitsyn had already been issued with a German travel document enabling him to go abroad. But he was torn between Norway, to which he had been invited and had a sentimental attachment, and Switzerland, where Dr Heeb lived and kept Solzhenitsyn's papers. In the end, they agreed on Switzerland.

The journey to Zurich the following day was another media circus. Heeb wanted Solzhenitsyn to fly, but Solzhenitsyn flatly refused: he hated aeroplanes and insisted on going by train. This meant travelling to Cologne by

---

*A year later, in Paris, Solzhenitsyn explained the basis of his friendship with Böll: "Certain West German journalists try to present us as enemies: in reality, we are personal friends. There is a similarity in our general concepts of the world, even if we differ in our interpretation of certain events."

car and running the gauntlet of the correspondents posted outside the house. Someone suggested a helicopter as far as Cologne, but again Solzhenitsyn was adamant. And so, on 16 February 1974 a vast motorcade wound its way out of Langenbroich and down the mountain, and then sped along the autobahn to Cologne. At its head were Solzhenitsyn and his friends, with a police escort, followed by an ever-lengthening convoy of reporters. Once in the city, the motorcade created chaos, refusing to stop for red lights, blocking intersections, and snarling up the traffic for miles around. By the time they reached the station, Heeb, at least, was a bundle of nerves.

In Cologne, Solzhenitsyn expressed an innocent desire to visit the famous cathedral, but the podium linking cathedral and station was a sea of photographers and tourism was out of the question. The nearest Solzhenitsyn could get was the roof of the station post office, to which he was led via a back entrance and from which he had an uninterrupted view of the east front. On the train all was chaos again. In addition to the couple of hundred journalists who had boarded it in Cologne, more seemed to get on at every station along the way, so that when the train arrived in Zurich, it seemed to have none but journalists on board. They arrived in the middle of the rush hour. The crowd of reporters and cameramen there to greet them was swelled by curious commuters, and they had the utmost difficulty in struggling from their compartment to a waiting car.

Solzhenitsyn, according to Heeb, was infuriated by all this attention and absolutely refused to make the slightest concession to the journalists. As a result, the siege continued at Heeb's flat. Reporters ringed the building and stood on guard all night, questioning the milkman about the Heebs' consumption of dairy products and keeping a lookout for other callers. Several cameramen sneaked into the garden beneath the Heebs' flat and concealed themselves in the shrubbery. When Solzhenitsyn stepped onto the balcony that evening for a breath of fresh air—having first taken the precaution of dowsing the lights inside—a battery of arc lights flashed on and the photographers started taking pictures.[7]

It is easy to sympathize with Solzhenitsyn in such conditions. Anyone who has been confronted by a crowd of baying journalists in pursuit of a story or by photographers jostling for pictures will know what an unnerving experience it can be, even for a Westerner. For a Russian newly arrived from the Soviet Union, where the press is under total control, it is terrifying. But there was another side to the matter as well. As Solzhenitsyn's encounters with Smith and Kaiser (and other reporters) in Moscow had shown, he regarded the press as something to be turned to in an emergency, but otherwise ignored. Like most Russians, he could not conceive of journalists' having their own set of professional rules or requirements or as having a duty to something called "the public"—a duty that sometimes ran counter to their own desires. Nor was he comfortable with the notion that the price of freedom was the freedom to write trash as well as articles of high quality, to be trivial, sensational, irresponsible, as well as serious and objective. For Solzhenitsyn, freedom of the press meant the freedom to be serious and write the truth (as he saw it). Anything else was anarchy. Unfortunately, he was not helped in arriving at a true appraisal of the press's strengths and weaknesses by the people among whom he landed. Heinrich Böll, for all his admirable qualities as man and writer, has a particularly jaundiced view of the Western press (having suffered from its vices). He despises its shrillness, its sensationalism, its commercialism, and is blind to many of its virtues. Dr Heeb, as a lifelong socialist and idealist, is no admirer of the press, and these two earnest friends could only have strengthened the prejudices that Solzhenitsyn brought with him from Moscow. As a result, when other friends with more experience of the media suggested that a quick, ten-minute press conference would satisfy the journalists and get rid of them, at least for a day or so, and pointed out that nothing was more calculated to provoke them than this wilful evasiveness and silence, Solzhenitsyn refused to co-operate.

Not surprisingly, a game of cat and mouse ensued between Solzhenitsyn and the reporters. The first day saw them following him into and out of shops, on and off a Zurich tramcar and to a special showing of Alexander Ford's film of *The First Circle*, which Solzhenitsyn did not like (he later called it "poor" and "irresponsible").[8] In order to avoid the reporters, Solzhenitsyn and his party dodged out early, but back at Heeb's flat it was the same siege atmosphere as before, and both Heeb and Solzhenitsyn were seething with resentment. The breaking-point came the next day when the mayor of Zurich, Sigmund Widmer, took Solzhenitsyn on a tour of the hilly district of Sternenberg, about an hour's drive east of Zurich. Solzhenitsyn liked the area very much, saying it reminded him of the North Caucasus where he was born, but he was driven to distraction by the antics of two French *paparazzi* who refused to leave him in peace. "You're worse than the KGB," he roared at them. "Go away. I want to be alone."[9] By breakfast time the next morning, his words had travelled round the world and only made the situation worse.

Finally, in a half-hearted attempt to improve matters, Solzhenitsyn arranged to give an interview, but characteristically gave it exclusively to one reporter—Frank Crepeau of the Associated Press—and then only because he had recognized Crepeau on the street as a former Moscow correspondent. Once again he insisted on making written answers to each of the questions and later distributed the "authorized" Russian text to counter any distortions that might creep into the Western version. Solzhenitsyn repeated to Crepeau his feelings about certain photographers but said that in general he was overwhelmed by the warmth and friendliness with which he had been greeted by ordinary people and that he much appreciated their support. His principal worry was the fate of his family and of the extensive archives he had gathered for writing his historical novels. If the Soviet authorities were to confiscate his archives, it would be "spiritual murder," but he was reasonably confident his wife would be able to preserve them and bring them out of the country, although it was an enormous burden for her. Exile was like being uprooted from the soil that fed you; it was painful and disorienting. But it was possible to put down new roots: "Even old trees can be transplanted and thrive in new surroundings." He was an optimist by nature, and he didn't exclude the possibility of returning.[10]

However, even this attempt at mollifying the press backfired on Solzhenitsyn. His recognition of Crepeau from Moscow led to a rumour, perhaps started by a jealous colleague, that the reason for Solzhenitsyn's friendliness was that Crepeau had brought him a letter from his wife. When such reports appeared in the press, Solzhenitsyn typed out an angry denial and read it to the reporters outside the house. He did not need any letters to be brought, he said, since he talked to his wife every day by telephone. Calling the Western press "childish" and "irresponsible," he concluded, "I insist that the name of the correspondent who gave this evil announcement should be made known and that his newspaper or agency widely publicize in my name that he is a liar not worthy of the name correspondent." When he had finished reading this modest demand, he handed copies to the reporters present.[11]

The following day he again burst out against a group of newsmen who were dogging his footsteps: "This is the fifth day. You have a thousand pictures. Leave me alone." But it is typical of a certain ambivalence on his part that after arriving outside the house in the Spiegelgasse, where Lenin had once lived, he looked round for the television cameras and was disappointed not to find them there. He had wanted to record this historic moment for posterity and to publicize his controversial opinions of Lenin's historical role.[12]

One of the subjects raised by Crepeau and still being speculated on by the press was the question of Solzhenitsyn's future domicile. Persistent rumours had mentioned Scandinavia as a possible alternative to Switzerland, and on 21 February, one week after his arrival in the West, Solzhenitsyn gave them new currency when he set off by train—alone and in semi-secret—to Norway via Copenhagen.

The idea of his settling in Norway had been raised as long ago as 1970, soon after his expulsion from the Writers' Union and well before he won the Nobel Prize. It had come from a group of Norwegian intellectuals led by an artist specializing in religious subjects named Victor Sparre. In an article written by Sparre and signed by himself and several others, it was suggested that Solzhenitsyn be invited to live in Norway and be offered the "House of Honour" in Oslo—the former house of the Norwegian author Henrik Wergeland, which was periodically put at the disposal of eminent writers.[13] Nothing came of the idea, but Solzhenitsyn heard of it and mentioned it in his Nobel lecture. In 1972 he asked Per Hegge for the names of the people who had signed the article, and subsequently made contact with Sparre after Sparre had visited Moscow but failed to meet him. Solzhenitsyn was grateful for the Norwegians' efforts, he wrote, and had particularly warm sentiments for Norway.

> I believe that Norway and Russia have much in common in our northern rural life (as it used to be, of course, not as it is today). They say that you, too, use wooden dishes, just as we do.

    Until now I have also considered the Norwegian spirit to be one of the finest and staunchest in Europe.

    I warmly shake your hand. Give my heartfelt thanks to your colleagues, who in such a moving way were ready to receive me four years ago.[14]

This letter had been sent in December 1973, mere weeks before Solzhenitsyn's expulsion. On the day after the expulsion, a huge demonstration had been held in Oslo, and a torchlight procession had made its way to the Soviet embassy carrying a big banner: "Welcome to Norway, Solzhenitsyn." Another house had been found for him (to purchase, this time), the former home of the Norwegian Nobel Prize–winning novelist of the twenties, Sigrid Undset, near Lillehammer, in central Norway, and Solzhenitsyn had been informed of this by Per Hegge in Langenbroich. Solzhenitsyn was again touched and took the offer seriously. Despite Hegge's insistence that the whole idea was sheer romanticism, he was now on his way to see for himself.

    In Copenhagen the crowds of newsmen and well-wishers were as big as in Zurich, and he was applauded as he boarded the overnight ferry for Oslo. The following morning, as the ferry pulled in, he could be seen standing on the bridge with a big brass telescope slung from his waist, as if in command of the ship. Again there were crowds, including hordes of newsmen, and again Solzhenitsyn refused to talk to them, despite a plea by Hegge (himself a correspondent) that if only he gave the press ten minutes, they would go away satisfied and leave the author in peace. But Solzhenitsyn was adamant, and so his four days in Norway were a repetition of the circus in Switzerland, with reporters and cameramen clambering onto trains, driving behind his car, and lying in wait for him at every opportunity, while he and his party played hide-and-seek and tried their best to disappear.

    Their first journey was to Lillehammer to see the Undset house, where they were entertained by Sigrid Undset's son Hans. Hans was a jovial host, lavish in his hospitality, but it was clear at once that the house was too remote and the interior too like a museum to the memory of its former owner. They looked at some other properties, including the luxurious home of a wealthy art collector and the home of a well-known Norwegian painter, but neither the elegant furnishings of the former nor the abstract paintings in the latter appealed to Solzhenitsyn's taste, and soon they abandoned the search in favour of tourism.[15]

    Solzhenitsyn liked the Norwegian countryside, the mountains, the solitude, and the snow. One night was spent at a remote farmhouse. Contemplating the animals in the barn that evening, Solzhenitsyn spat violently onto the ground and exclaimed angrily, "To think of the misery that damned collective-farm system has brought to my country! We should have an agriculture like yours—every man with his own small farm."[16] He took great interest in the history and customs of old Norway as described to him by Sparre and Hegge, and filled pages of his ever-present notebook with their stories; but not for a moment did he forget what he had left behind. His watch was still set on Moscow time (and would remain so until Svetlova arrived). Everywhere he went, he took a big transistor radio with him, and at the appropriate times tuned in to the BBC programmes in Russian. And every morning he had long conversations by telephone with Svetlova in Moscow.

On his last night he went to see the film of—*A Day in the Life of Ivan Denisovich*, starring the English actor Tom Courtenay and made in Norway by the Finnish director Caspar Wrede. It was more faithful to the original book, and less pretentious, than *The First Circle*, and apparently to Solzhenitsyn's liking ("It is a good, honest film; it just lacks Russian local colour," he said of it some months later).[17]

Solzhenitsyn eventually decided against living in Norway because it was too much on the periphery of Europe and because the language was so strange to him. "At my age it would be difficult to learn a new language," he told Sparre. He felt that he and his wife would not be near enough to the Russian *émigré* communities of Western Europe and that the language barrier might create difficulties for the education of his children.[18] Per Hegge had been right. Despite the wooden platters and handmade furniture, it was not the place for a celebrated author with world-wide contacts and political ambitions.

Having decided to stay in Zurich, Solzhenitsyn began to cast about for a place in which to live and in which to welcome his family. The latest reports from his wife said that it would take about a month to pack up all his books and papers, complete the necessary formalities, and get everything shipped out. Such was the Soviet reverence for the printed word that every book and document had to be inspected and registered before it could be taken out of the country. This meant that a large part of the archive would have to go by "unofficial" channels, since there was much that Solzhenitsyn did not wish to have inspected. By far the most difficult and dangerous part of Svetlova's task would be to ensure that these materials were transferred without a hitch. She was not helped by the fact that baby Stepan had just gone down with a bout of pneumonia, but on the telephone and in conversation with friends, she remained her usual calm and determined self and was confident she could cope with everything.

Solzhenitsyn was assisted in settling in Zurich by his new friend and patron Mayor Widmer. A bluff, energetic, and capable local political leader, Widmer had taken an instant liking to Solzhenitsyn (who reciprocated the feeling) and was determined that this world-famous writer should be made welcome and comfortable in the city in his charge. Widmer found a city-owned house for Solzhenitsyn to rent in the quiet suburban Stapferstrasse, not far from the town centre. It was a square, detached three-storey villa with green shutters and a small garden, set well back off the road and guarded by a gate that opened only when a buzzer was pressed from inside. Perhaps from neglect—or from design—the gate had no bell, so that unannounced callers, including curious reporters, had little chance of being admitted. It might have seemed ideal for Solzhenitsyn, but he was not much happier there than at Heeb's. He still did not like living in the city, even in one of the quieter parts, and seems to have felt strangely vulnerable there. Widmer was able to come to the rescue again by offering Solzhenitsyn the use of his farmhouse in Sternenberg (shown him during their earlier visit). The farmhouse was situated in a remote area of the Zurich uplands, at the highest point above sea level in the canton of Zurich. The farms round about were modest in size and the land poor, the farmers being little better off than peasants in the context of Switzerland. Solzhenitsyn was attracted by this austerity, not to speak of the peace and solitude, and at once moved his books to the farm, returning to Zurich only on weekends. At the farm he was able to look after himself, purchase milk, eggs, and provisions from the local farmers or in the nearby village, and live more or less as he had in Russia. Above all, he was able to write, for which he had a burning need just now. He was eager to complete the story of his literary career in the Soviet Union, *The Oak and the Calf*, and fix the events of his last days in the Soviet Union while the memories were still fresh. Sternenberg became a lifeline for him, that provider of space and air without which he could not write or breathe.

Meanwhile, the indefatigable Widmer had been in touch with the Swiss Ministry of Justice about political asylum for Solzhenitsyn and his family, and early in March Solzhenitsyn accompanied him to Bern to meet the minister, Kurt Furgler. A personal visit was not necessary, but Solzhenitsyn was curious to see how the Swiss judicial machinery worked. One thing that surprised him was to see the square in front of the Bundeshaus in Bern crowded with peasants and farmers and their market-stalls. It was a marked contrast to the Soviet Union, he said, where government buildings usually had huge empty spaces around them and the people were kept out. It was hard to imagine Red Square or the Kremlin crowded with market-stalls, instead of being the empty and impersonal wasteland they were.[19]

Asylum was granted very quickly, and visas were issued to Natalia Svetlova, her mother, and the children in Moscow. There was some anxiety that the Soviet authorities might make difficulties for Svetlova's son by her first marriage, Dmitri. It is a favourite trick in such cases to put pressure on the former spouses of emigrants to refuse permission for their children to leave, but no move seems to have been made on this occasion, and Andrei Tiurin readily assented to Dmitri's departure.

The family left Moscow on 29 March, just over six weeks after Solzhenitsyn's expulsion. They were preceded by 1,400 pounds of luggage, comprising the innocuous part of Solzhenitsyn's archive and library, and Solzhenitsyn's favourite, old-fashioned desk (presented to him by a grateful reader of *Ivan Denisovich*). Svetlova had made the announcement two days earlier, six weeks to the day since Solzhenitsyn's expulsion, and that night there had been a kind of wake at the flat in Kozitsky Lane. Crowds of dissidents and well-wishers came to say their last farewells. The atmosphere was tense and tearful. Svetlova circulated among the guests, who included Kopelev, Yuli Daniel, Alexander Ginzburg, and many other well-known figures, as well as her first husband and some Western correspondents, and embraced each one in turn.

She also made a fiery farewell statement fully in the spirit of her husband's work. "It is painful to part from Russia," she said, "painful that our children are condemned to a life without a homeland, painful and difficult to leave friends who are not protected." The only thing that made it bearable was a conviction that she and her family would return. As for her husband's expulsion, "they can separate a Russian writer from his native land, but no one has the power and strength to sever his spiritual link with it, to tear Solzhenitsyn away from it. And even if his books are now set ablaze on bonfires, their existence in his homeland is indestructible, just as Solzhenitsyn's love for Russia is indestructible." It was an eloquent declaration, and in her final words Svetlova evoked the memory of the wives of the Decembrists a century and a half earlier, when following their husbands to Siberia. "My place is beside him, but leaving Russia is excruciatingly painful."[20]

Two days later the members of family rose at dawn to make their journey. A convoy of six cars carried them and their twenty-eight pieces of luggage to the airport, arriving at 5.40 a.m. The Soviet customs officers were scrupulously polite, but unremitting in their procedures. Each carefully labelled and numbered suitcase was opened, scrutinized, and closed again. The cabin bags were searched minutely. Every scrap of paper was carefully examined, a tape was taken out and played over, and all members of the family were made to empty out their pockets. After an hour the inspection was finished. Then came more tearful farewells—with Kopelev, with Shafarevich, with Gorbanevskaya, with Evgeni Pasternak, son of Boris Pasternak, with Alexander Gorlov. About thirty people had gathered to see them off. "Kiss Alexander Isayevich for us," shouted a girl in the crowd. "Tell him we shall not forget him."[21] A young man made the sign of the cross. Four hours later the scene in Zurich was somewhat different, but also tense. An armoured personnel carrier with a heavy machine-gun was parked in front of the plane immediately it landed, and Swiss police with automatic rifles stood on guard. Solzhenitsyn and Dr Heeb, in Heeb's car, had been allowed onto the tarmac, and a crowd of reporters and photographers jostled behind a red-and-white chain-link fence. Solzhenitsyn grimaced at the sight of the press, but having gone on board to greet his wife in private, he emerged to offer a perfect pose, with Ignat and Ermolai on either arm, his wife beside him, and Stepan in a carry-cot. There were no statements or interviews, just one word, uttered in response to a reporter's question in Russian: "All's well that ends well?" "Yes."[22]

In the world of public affairs, from which Solzhenitsyn seemed temporarily to have withdrawn but which he continued to follow with unremitting interest, the storm over his expulsion was at last beginning to die down. The Western response had concerned itself with two main aspects of the expulsion: Solzhenitsyn's personal tragedy and the impact of his expulsion on *détente*.

To cope with Solzhenitsyn's statelessness, no fewer than four countries had publicly offered him asylum: Germany, France, Britain, and Norway. His personal odyssey from Moscow to Germany, Switzerland, and Norway and back to Switzerland again was sympathetically followed by millions through the mass media. Generally, there was relief that his physical safety had been assured and that he was not to be put on trial or jailed, while it was felt that the Soviet authorities had made the best of a bad job. Provided Solzhenitsyn's family was allowed to join him, it was the most humane solution possible, short of allowing him to stay in the Soviet Union and continue working.

With regard to larger political questions, it was pointed out that the last Soviet citizen to be forcibly expelled against his will had been Lev Trotsky, in 1929—the inevitable deduction being that the Soviet Union had changed little in the interim (a point Solzhenitsyn had made forcefully in *The Gulag Archipelago*). It was also noted that the expulsion was illegal. There was no provision for it in the Soviet penal code; it was simply an act of political expediency, yet another echo of the inglorious past. But the subject that concerned most commentators was the likely impact of the expulsion on *détente*. Henry Kissinger, then secretary of state to President Nixon, had attempted to pre-empt discussion by announcing that *détente* would not be affected. "The necessity for *détente*," said Kissinger on the day that Solzhenitsyn was expelled, "does not reflect approbation of the Soviet domestic structure. . . . The necessity of *détente* is produced by the inadmissibility of general nuclear war under present conditions." Solzhenitsyn's personal plight was irrelevant: "Our human, moral and critical concern for Mr. Solzhenitsyn and people of similar convictions should [not] affect the day-to-day conduct of our foreign policy."[23] But others thought differently. Nuclear disarmament was only one aspect of *détente*. Other parts included provisions for the freer movement of people and ideas. If the Soviet Union was not willing to introduce some relaxation into its home affairs and its dealings with its East European empire, and to behave even marginally like a civilized country, perhaps *détente* was not worth the trouble—certainly not if it seemed to sanctify the Soviet suppression of all forms of dissent at home. Solzhenitsyn's desperate action in challenging the government over the absence of a rule of law in the USSR was a signal that the Soviet political system had not changed and had no intention of changing and that *détente* on its side was a sham.

Such a perception was widespread in the United States and Western Europe and for several weeks seemed to have the upper hand. The long Soviet campaign against Solzhenitsyn, Sakharov, and the other dissidents had made its mark on Western public opinion, and there was a feeling that the base of support for a policy of *détente* was steadily narrowing—rightly, in the view of many; wrongly, in the view of those who supported Kissinger.

This was the calculated risk the Soviet authorities had taken when they decided on the expulsion. For a moment it had seemed that their policy would be to play the matter down. The first news had reached Soviet citizens in a laconic dispatch from Tass quoting the text of the Supreme Soviet decree and adding that Solzhenitsyn's family would be allowed to join him. The following day the same announcement was tucked away on the back pages of the leading newspapers, but this was only the usual lull while the ponderous Soviet propaganda machine got up a head of steam. On 15 February 1974 *Pravda*, *Izvestia*, and a number of other newspapers had splashed prearranged letters over several pages. Headlines such as "The People's Will," "The People Reject the Turncoat," "A Traitor Gets His Desserts," and "The End of a Literary Vlasovite" indicated the direction the campaign was to take, while editorials compared Solzhenitsyn to Tarsis and Anatoli Kuznetsov and asserted that, like them, he would disappear without a trace. As one well-known propagandist elegantly put it, "Foreign reactionaries to whose tune Solzhenitsyn danced, not free of charge, have plenty of grounds to grieve and rage. . . . Solzhenitsyn was interesting to them when he was here. The 'melodies' of his ideological subversive activity caressed their ears when they sounded from our country. But now he is a covered trump card to them. When Solzhenitsyn's bosses realize that the game is lost, they will dump him."[24]

The centre-piece of the campaign was a 10,000-word article by Professor Nikolai N. Yakovlev, an Americanist and doctor of historical sciences, in *Voice of the Motherland*, a Soviet newspaper published for sympathetically inclined *émigrés* by the Soviet Committee for Cultural Links with Compatriots. This article, which later appeared in an abridged form in the *Literaturnaya Gazeta*, set out the Soviet government's case against Solzhenitsyn in the greatest detail. The context for Solzhenitsyn's traitorous activities, wrote Yakovlev, was the peaceful competition between the two superpowers and the growing movement in favour of *détente*. Solzhenitsyn (like Sakharov and the other dissidents) was against *détente* and was giving succour to American supporters of the cold war. Yakovlev analyzed those works of Solzhenitsyn's that gave most offence: *August 1914* and *The Gulag Archipelago*. The first of these was "an indictment of the [Russian] autocracy from the point of view of the bourgeoisie," a position that coincided with that of A. I. Guchkov and the Octobrists (a conservative group to the right of the Constitutional Democrats). The other distinguishing feature of *August 1914*, wrote Yakovlev, was that it had coincided with the German propaganda of the time (and since) in exaggerating the importance of Samsonov's defeat, while undervaluing Russian victories on the south-eastern front, and repeated a theme that had been picked up by Hitler and the Nazis during their own initial advance. That explained why Solzhenitsyn, at the very moment of the Soviet advance into East Prussia (against those Prussian militarists before whom Solzhenitsyn "mentally bent the knee"), had occupied himself with "spreading vile rumours designed to undermine the morale of the troops," for which he was rightly removed from the front and sent back to Moscow (there was no mention that this was an entirely new charge, or of Solzhenitsyn's rehabilitation, in Professor Yakovlev's summary of these events).

It was out of resentment and spite, wrote Yakovlev, that Solzhenitsyn later produced his "lampoons," above all *The Gulag Archipelago*. *Gulag* was filled with the class hatred of a "scion of the wealthy bourgeoisie" for the class that had supplanted his own, and with hatred of the October revolution. It was a travesty of the historical truth, completely ignoring the terror of the Whites and the reasons why the Red terror was a justifiable response. Yet even the Americans, after their own revolution, had violated the human and civil rights of half a million of their citizens who remained royalists and supported George III, and many of the latter had been killed. Equally reprehensible had been Solzhenitsyn's defence of General Vlasov and his supporters, his assertion that Soviet victory in the war had been a "disaster" for the Soviet population, and his bitter philippics against Churchill and Roosevelt for not having opposed, or even fought against, the Soviet Union at the end of the war. Yakovlev devoted a couple of thousand words to a painstaking analysis of post-war relations between the allies, showing that many of the Western leaders had wanted to make war on the Soviet Union but had been held back by the latter's strength and military might.

The most interesting aspect of Yakovlev's essay was not its content, only parts of which were new, but the academic garb in which it was clothed and the (barely sustained) attempt to maintain a civilized tone of voice. Yakovlev cited a wealth of sources: George Kennan, Harry Truman, Eisenhower, Milyukov, General Golovin, and numerous historians, American, English, and Russian. Parts of his argument—for instance, on the exact significance of the Battle of Tannenberg to the allies in the First World War, or the reasons why the British and the Americans agreed to Soviet occupation zones after the second—might have come from independent textbooks on these subjects, and it was only when dealing with emotional subjects like *détente* or the history of the Revolution that Yakovlev lapsed into the cruder forms of Soviet rhetoric. His article must have been months in preparation—he showed great familiarity with the text of parts 1 and 2 of *The Gulag Archipelago* (he avoided repeating the gaffe of a *Literaturnaya Gazeta* commentator, who had quoted from later, unpublished parts)—and henceforth was to serve as a mine for other Soviet journalists. It also seems to have had the stamp of the highest official approval.[25]

Since this essay was intended for readers outside the Soviet Union, a certain elevation of tone was perhaps to be expected anyway. Items for domestic consumption did not have to be composed under such restrictions. The Soviet Union, which prides itself on not having a gutter press, was nevertheless able to find room for the following tasteless doggerel in its "satirical" magazine *Krokodil:*

> An advertisement for a brothel screams,
> Where, on the farthest reaches
> Of lewdness, spite, and degeneracy
> Madame Solzhe is fornicating mightily.
>
> Hating Russia fiercely,
> Abusing her people,

Madame sells her homeland
For foreign currency.
....
Madame always tells her guests:
"I am not a prostitute, gentlemen.
I, gentlemen, am a dissident."[26]

The aim of this press campaign was, as usual, to demonstrate that "the people" were unanimous in their condemnation of the renegade, but among the intelligentsia, the authorities did not find much support. The only noteworthy writer to make a statement was the aging Valentin Katayev, who six years previously had endorsed Solzhenitsyn's letter to the Writers' Congress but who now, for some reason, had been obliged to turn against him. The authorities were also able to publish letters from Metropolitan Serafim of Krutitsky and Kolomna, and from the Academician Kolmogorov, but except for them, they had to fall back on old faithfuls like Sergei Mikhalkov, Boris Dyakov, and Boris Polevoi. Nevertheless, they seem to have been successful in persuading the common people, who were utterly dependent on the Soviet media for news, of the justice of their case. An American correspondent who approached people in the street found that the majority supported the expulsion.* One woman said she couldn't understand why the authorities had waited so long. Others said that Solzhenitsyn should have been tried for treason and executed. A teacher commented that it would have been all right if Solzhenitsyn had stuck to writing novels, but he should never have "given up literature for politics." That same evening, Moscow television carried interviews with five workers on the subject, one of whom got so carried away by his description of what he would have done to Solzhenitsyn that the sound had to be turned off. The successive waves of propaganda against the writer were clearly having their effect.[27]

But unofficial voices had been raised on the other side too. Sakharov and a group of prominent dissidents (including Maximov, Litvinov, and Marchenko) took issue with the Soviet press campaign and launched an appeal for the Soviet Union to publish *The Gulag Archipelago*, to open the archives of the Cheka, GPU, NKVD, and so on, to assist in the creation of an international tribunal to investigate the crimes of the security organs, and to allow Solzhenitsyn to return to his homeland and work in peace. Other writers who protested were Lydia Chukovskaya, Roy Medvedev, Kopelev, Shafarevich, Agursky, and Voinovich. Voinovich had again been summoned to appear before the board of the Writers' Union for a disciplinary hearing, but he refused to go, repeating that since the meeting was to be held behind closed doors, it was illegal. "We have nothing to discuss," he wrote, "because

---

*Street interviews in the Soviet Union are not usually reliable, since the average Soviet citizen cannot be expected to tell a correspondent the truth (the risks are too great). Hedrick Smith, however, was well aware of this problem when he did his interviews and knew how to read between the lines of the responses he got and to distinguish between a genuine and a fake answer.

I express my own opinion and you say what you are told to say." He was duly expelled on 21 February, which led to protests by two more writers, Vladimir Kornilov and Konstantin Bogatyrev.[28]

Perhaps the most interesting protest—the only recorded protest by an establishment writer—was that of Evgeni Evtushenko. On 17 February, Evtushenko released a long and eloquent letter in which he revealed that a concert based on his poetry scheduled for the preceding Saturday had been abruptly cancelled. The reason for the cancellation was that on hearing of Solzhenitsyn's arrest, Evtushenko had phoned the KGB for confirmation and then sent a telegram to Brezhnev. "I voiced my anxiety about the fate of the writer and how this might affect the prestige of our motherland, but in a polite way, avoiding sharp expressions," he wrote, "but in response to my sincere, confidential appeal there followed immediate, crude, and humiliating punishment." Evtushenko had a genuine interest in defending Solzhenitsyn, for in a sense his own rise to fame with "The Heirs of Stalin" was inextricably linked to *A Day in the Life of Ivan Denisovich*, as both were to Khrushchev's de-Stalinization campaign. This emerged from the rest of his statement, in which he referred to the evils of Stalinism and the "shocking ignorance" of the younger generation about Stalin's purges, because books and newspapers now hushed up all mention of the truth about that period. Evtushenko admitted that he had read *The Gulag Archipelago* and said that while he remained a socialist and disagreed with many of Solzhenitsyn's ideas, the book nonetheless contained "terrible documented pages about the bloody crimes of the Stalinist past."[29]

Naturally, none of this got into print in the Soviet Union, but there was one muffled squawk of alarm in the literary magazine *Yunost*. A poem by Boris Slutsky, "Not Quite," appeared to deal with the situation of Solzhenitsyn.

> Destroyed by humiliation
> and not simply by destruction,
> a man still sometimes rises
> and threatens them all—
> all who humiliated him,
> believing they were destroying him
> completely.[30]

The poem went on to describe this man as "trampled, slandered, the object of whispering campaigns," yet never losing hope and retaining the "God-given ability to return blow for blow." The magazine had been passed by the censors in January, so the poem was not a response to the expulsion but referred, rather, to Solzhenitsyn's position generally. The publication date of 18 February could not have been more appropriate, however, and led to excited whispers in the corridors of the Writers' Union.

But it was still only "a fist in the pocket"—an indirect gesture of defiance that carried no risks, whereas Solzhenitsyn was demanding, by example and in his last appeal, "Live Not by Lies," that Soviet citizens go one step further and adopt a policy of non–co-operation with the authorities—in effect, practise passive disobedience. "Live Not by Lies" was now circulating widely in dissident circles and shortly gave its name to a samizdat collection of documents on the subject of Solzhenitsyn's expulsion. The documents covered the period from August 1973, when Solzhenitsyn decided to publish *The Gulag Archipelago*, to the weeks immediately following the expulsion and included, besides statements by Solzhenitsyn and his supporters, letters and statements hostile to him, in an attempt to give both sides of the argument. There were also letters of support from unknown citizens who had written to *Pravda* or *Izvestia* and had their letters rejected, together with an account of a confidential Party lecture by an anonymous colonel in which it was said that President Pompidou had been warned by the Soviet government that his forthcoming official visit would be cancelled "if he doesn't stop all the newspaper fuss about that book" in France. The lecturer had revealed that "many demand the exile or arrest of Solzhenitsyn, but we are under so much pressure on his account that that would only add fuel to the anti-Soviet propaganda."[31]

The chief topic of conversation in the samizdat collection was the document that had given the book its name, Solzhenitsyn's "moral testament": "Live Not by Lies." The declaration had been written some four years beforehand and was an attempt by Solzhenitsyn to summarize his views on what steps might be taken by private citizens to bring about a moral improvement in Soviet society. The Soviet situation was very bad, wrote Solzhenitsyn in his preamble. "Things have almost reached rock-bottom. A universal spiritual death has already enveloped us all, and physical death will soon flare up and incinerate us and our children. But just as before, we continue to smile in cowardly fashion and mumble with tied tongues—what can we do to stop it? We haven't the strength." But the Russian people did have the strength and had already achieved a certain freedom of opinion in samizdat and in private conversations. All that was needed was a determined effort to translate these private achievements into the public sphere.

> Let us admit it: we have not matured enough to march into the squares and shout the truth out loud, or to express aloud what we think. It is not necessary. It is dangerous. But let us refuse to say what we do not think. This is our path, the easiest and most accessible one, which allows for our inherent, deep-rooted cowardice. . . . Once we realize where the perimeters of falsehood are (everyone sees them in his own way), our path is to walk away from this gangrenous boundary. If we did not paste together the dead bones and scales of ideology, if we did not sew together rotting rags, we would be astonished how quickly the lies would be rendered helpless and would subside. That which should be naked would then really appear naked before the whole world.*

*Compare this with Thoreau on slavery: "If *one* honest man . . . ceasing to hold slaves, were actually to withdraw from this copartnership, and be locked up in the county jail thereby, it would be the abolition of slavery in America."

Solzhenitsyn's advice to Soviet citizens was not to sign, print, or make untruthful statements, even under pressure, not to allow falsehood into their art or scientific work, not to attend meetings or demonstrations under duress, and not to subscribe to newspapers and magazines that deliberately twisted the truth. The choice, he wrote, was relatively simple: "Either truth or falsehood: towards spiritual independence or towards spiritual servitude."[32]

47

TAKING
POSITIONS

T HE QUESTION THAT hovered in many people's minds after the expulsion
was what the effect would be on Solzhenitsyn's reputation in the Soviet
Union. The Soviet authorities thought they had answered it in their press
campaign, but as Roy Medvedev pointed out in an unpublished letter to
Izvestia, Solzhenitsyn was bound to continue writing about his homeland,
"and his books will continue to be important and necessary to us, though it
will become even more difficult to obtain them, and reading them will entail
danger and risks." Sakharov, in a telephone interview with a Milan newspaper, asserted that Solzhenitsyn's role as the most important Russian writer
"does not depend on where he lives and writes" and that he was sure that
Solzhenitsyn would exploit to the full the possibilities that living in the West
offered him to continue his great work.[1]

"Live Not by Lies" was in a way an assurance that Medvedev and Sakharov were right, though this clarion call to moral betterment and civic
courage did not have quite the resonance that Solzhenitsyn had hoped for.
But he was not one to let matters rest there. In Norway, Victor Sparre had
complimented Solzhenitsyn over dinner one evening on always seeming to
be on the attack. Solzhenitsyn had accepted the compliment "by tightening
his fists around his knife and fork and shadow-boxing." He had told Sparre,
"I don't sit and wait for the enemy to hit me. I strike first. I guess at the
enemy's next trick. I avoid fighting on his ground. I attack when he least
expects it and where I am strongest. The KGB mustn't think they've got the
initiative by deporting me. I've got something ready for them any day now."[2]

That "something" was his *Letter to the Leaders*. The revised version had
been set in type for some time, and because of the delay he had ordered in

January, the translations were ready too. Now he was in the West, there was no reason for hanging back, and he authorized the Russian publication for 2 March 1974. The translations followed a day or so later. *Letter to the Leaders* was in many ways the most important statement Solzhenitsyn had made since the publication of *Ivan Denisovich*. For the first time he stepped forth before his readers naked and unadorned, uttering his own opinions in his own voice, and the result was a severe shock to a majority of his admirers both East and West. He in turn was shocked by their expressions of incredulity, and the ripples from that first major political statement have not yet subsided.

The *Letter* was in the form of a manifesto, a programme of radical reform and renewal that Solzhenitsyn proposed as the best way "to avoid the catastrophe with which we as a nation are threatened." It was divided into seven parts. The title of part 1 spoke for itself: "The West on its Knees." In it, Solzhenitsyn developed some of the ideas he had tentatively put forward in his Nobel lecture and "Peace and Violence." The West was in a state of collapse "as the result of a historical, psychological, and moral crisis affecting the entire culture and world outlook which were conceived at the time of the Renaissance and attained the peak of their expression with the eighteenth-century Enlightenment." The Soviet Union, on the other hand, was "at the peak of . . . staggering successes" and in a period of unprecedented expansion, but it, too, was threatened by the rise of Red China as a world power. Part 2, "War with China," dealt with the possibilities of such a war and forecast certain defeat for the Soviet Union if it should ever take place. The prudent course was to avoid a collision with China, and the surest way of doing that was to jettison the main source of conflict between them—Marxism, "that murky whirlwind of *Progressive Ideology* that swept in on us from the West at the end of the last century and that has tormented and ravaged our soul quite enough."

It was in parts 3 and 6, however, that Solzhenitsyn expounded the more radical elements of his programme for survival. Civilization had reached an impasse, he wrote, and faced economic and ecological disaster. The doctrine of material progress was false. The West would probably realize it in time, and with its superior adaptability would change course. The Third World would choose not to follow the Western path at all. But what about Russia— "with our unwieldiness and our inertia, with our flinching and inability to change even a single letter, a single syllable, of what Marx said in 1848?" The only answer was to abandon material progress and turn backwards and inwards. In Russia's case, this meant ceasing to meddle in the affairs of Asia, Africa, and Latin America, withdrawing from its empire in Eastern Europe, and turning to its national heartland: Siberia and the North-east. There "we can build anew: not the senseless, voracious civilization of 'progress'—no; we can set up a stable economy without pain or delay." On the details of this economy, Solzhenitsyn was somewhat vague but generally adhered to the "small is beautiful" line of argument. Starting afresh in the North-east would enable Russia "to avoid repeating the disastrous errors of the twentieth century—industry, roads, and cities, for example." Urban life was utterly unnatural, as was proved by the universal popularity of out-of-town dachas. Solzhenitsyn's pastoral vision of what life should really be like was quite different.

> You are all old enough to remember our old towns—towns made for people, horses, dogs—and streetcars too. Towns which were humane, friendly, cosy places, where the air was always clean, which were snow-clad in winter and in spring redolent with garden smells streaming through the fences into the streets. There was a garden to almost every house and hardly a house more than two stories high—the pleasantest height for human habitation. The inhabitants of those towns were not nomads; they didn't have to decamp twice a year to save their children from a blazing inferno. An economy of non-gigantism with small-scale though highly developed technology will not only allow for but necessitate the building of *new* towns of the *old* type. And we can perfectly well set up road barriers at all the entrances and admit horses and battery-powered electric motors, but not poisonous internal-combustion engines, and if anybody has to dive underground at crossroads, let it be the vehicles and not the old, the young, and the sick.

Among the more practical reforms Solzhenitsyn advocated were the abolition of collective farms, the eradication of corruption and bribes, the removal of the state tax on vodka (to reduce its importance to the economy), and an end to compulsory military service. Such service was morally harmful to the nation's youth, while a reduction in the armed forces, especially the air force, would "deliver our skies from the sickening roar of aerial armadas . . . breaking the sound barrier, roaring and booming, shattering the daily life, rest, sleep, and nerves of hundreds of thousands of people, effectively addling their brains by screeching overhead" (was this heartfelt plea written during his summer in Firsanovka?).

In part 6 Solzhenitsyn dealt more fully with the question of ideology, "a primitive, superficial economic theory" that was now "decrepit and hopelessly antiquated." Marxism was not accurate or scientific; moreover, it had failed to predict a single event and was thoroughly crude and mechanistic. Nor was it necessary to the country any longer, as it might have been in the twenties and thirties, but was "a sham, cardboard, theatrical prop—take it away and nothing will collapse, nothing will even wobble." Yet it was the source of so much misery and corruption, the reason why a "universal, obligatory force-feeding with lies" was now "the most agonizing aspect of existence in our country"—worse than all the material miseries, worse than any lack of civil liberties. "Cast off this cracked Ideology!" wrote Solzhenitsyn. "Relinquish it to your rivals, let it go wherever it wants, let it pass from our country like a storm-cloud, like an epidemic. Let others concern themselves with it and study it, just so long as we don't!"

It was in part 7, "But How Can All This Be Managed?" that Solzhenitsyn came to the most controversial part of his proposals. In some sense they echoed ideas that Sakharov and Roy Medvedev had put forward in the past—the introduction of freedom of expression, the observation of the constitution, the abolition of the absolute monopoly of the Party over society while leaving it in control of the commanding heights—the army, the police, industry, transport, communications, and foreign trade. But Solzhenitsyn's political vision was of quite a different order. On the basis of his study of Russian history, he wrote, he was an opponent of all revolutions. For that reason, and because "the sudden upheaval of any hastily carried-out change of the present leadership . . . might provoke only a new and destructive struggle, leading to only a dubious gain in the quality of the leadership," he was against sudden change now. Nor was he in favour of "that turbulent 'democracy run riot' in which once every four years the politicians, and indeed the entire country, nearly kill themselves over an electoral campaign" and in which "a judge, flouting his obligatory independence in order to pander to the passions of society, acquits a man who, during an exhausting war, steals and publishes Defense Department documents."* Not even the "established democracies" of Western Europe appealed to him as examples, for their systems would not work in Russia. "Here . . . for sheer lack of practice, democracy survived for only eight months. . . . *Émigré* groups . . . still pride themselves on it to this day and say that outside forces brought about its collapse. But [it] . . . was *their* disgrace . . . because . . . they turned out to be ill prepared for it themselves, and Russia was worse prepared still." In the last half-century, that preparedness had diminished still further. Russia had her own way, a thousand-year-old authoritarian order that had preserved the "physical and spiritual health of her people intact." "*Order* is not immoral if it means a calm and stable system. But order, too, has its limits, beyond which it degenerates into arbitrariness and tyranny." The difference between the present authoritarian order and the past was that in the past it possessed "a strong moral foundation" rooted in the Orthodox religion. Solzhenitsyn himself saw "Christianity today as the only living spiritual force capable of undertaking the spiritual healing of Russia"—but he was not asking for any special privileges for the Christian religion, simply that it be permitted to coexist with other faiths and ideologies. Finally he came up with a totally surprising suggestion—to bring back the soviets of the twenties.† "The soviets . . . were in no way dependent upon ideology . . . they always envisaged the widest possible consultation with all working people. Would it still be within the bounds of realism or a lapse into day-dreams if we were to propose that at least some of the real power of the soviets be restored?"³

Once more, Solzhenitsyn made headline news. The London *Sunday Times* ran the 15,000-word *Letter* in full, the *New York Times* devoted a whole page to it, and similar prominence was given in other countries. But the response

---

* A reference to Daniel Ellsberg and the Pentagon Papers.
† Solzhenitsyn had in mind the democratically elected workers' councils in the form in which they had existed before being taken over by the Communist Party.

was not at all what Solzhenitsyn had expected. His fierce opposition to Marxist ideology was noted, of course, as were his scathing criticisms of Soviet corruption and Soviet inefficiency, but the two aspects of the *Letter* that attracted most attention were his dismissal of Western democracy and his prescription for Russia of an authoritarian political system, tempered, if possible, by a renewed faith in Orthodox Christianity. Up till now it had been more or less taken for granted that all Soviet dissidents were pro-Western and in favour of a Western-style democracy, and few in the West were sufficiently conversant with Solzhenitsyn's political writings of the last year and a half to have detected any significant difference between his views and those of the rest. It came as something of a shock, therefore, to discover that Solzhenitsyn was neither pro-Western nor a democrat and that his principal allegiances were to "God and Mother Russia," as one magazine headlined it.

Western readers were also surprised by Solzhenitsyn's warnings, in not quite so many words, against the "yellow peril" of China's millions (though he expressed warm sympathy for the individual Chinese) and by the unbridled nationalism that peeped through in some of his digressions: "For half a century, since 1920, we have proudly (and rightly) refused to entrust the exploitation of our natural resources to foreigners. . . . But . . . now, when it has been revealed that the world's energy resources are drying up, we, a great industrial superpower, like the meanest of backward countries, invite foreigners to exploit our mineral wealth and by way of payment suggest that they carry off our priceless treasure, Siberian natural gas—for which our children will curse us in half a generation's time as irresponsible prodigals." Solzhenitsyn's calls to the Soviet leaders to turn their backs on industrial progress and revert to a patriarchal form of society were dismissed as the utopian day-dreams of a crank. But perhaps the most damaging aspect of the whole affair was the unearthing by the *New York Times* of Solzhenitsyn's original version of the letter, before he had softened it for publication. By comparing the two, the *Times* was able to establish that the first version, sent to Brezhnev and his colleagues, was more anti-Western than the second, naming the United States and Great Britain specifically for their failures in democracy, describing the first as "ungovernable" and the second as incapable of dealing with a "handful of terrorists" (in Northern Ireland). It also contained the following intriguing passage (deleted from the later version):

> It was those baited and despised "Slavophiles" who long ago pointed to the chief defect of Western democracy—that it has no *ethical foundation*. This means that its highest recourse is only the constitution and that under its rules, without any additional moral constraints or conditions, parties and classes enter into a conflict between interests, simply of interests and nothing higher.[4]

The *New York Times* demonstrated that the *Letter* released to the public was not, as it purported to be, the *Letter* that Solzhenitsyn had sent to the Soviet leaders. It was virtually identical in tone, but subtly different in content, and

Solzhenitsyn had neglected to point this out in publishing it.*

For a moment it seemed that the Kremlin's gleeful predictions of a speedy rift between Solzhenitsyn and his Western admirers might be coming true. In less than a month after his expulsion, he had succeeded in splitting opinion about him as never before. Yet it was an inevitable part of the risk he ran in making his position clear for the first time, and as much the fruit of his literary honesty as of his personal impetuosity and his inclination to make hasty judgements. For in questioning the prospects of democracy in Russia, he was again going to the very heart of a painful and much avoided problem. As he had written (with some exaggeration) in his preface, "Our intelligentsia is at one in its concept of a desirable future for our country (the broadest possible freedoms) but is equally at one in its total lack of action to realize that future." The question was: What if those freedoms are not possible? What should Russia do then? And Solzhenitsyn was among the first to spell out the unpopular notion that some (or perhaps most) of those freedoms were not attainable in the immediate future. Once more he was moving the debate forward onto fresh ground, and he was deeply disappointed by the negative reactions shown to it in the West.

One problem was that his preface had got lost in the English translation, so that the above explanation did not appear in England or America.† Nor did his note that, while some of his practical proposals "might occasion surprise," he was prepared to "withdraw them at once if someone offers not a witty critique but a constructive course of action, a better and, most importantly, fully realistic way out, with clear paths ahead."⁵ As he wrote in his conclusion, he realized that he was taking upon himself "a heavy responsibility to Russian history." But "not to take upon oneself the task of seeking a way out . . . is an even heavier responsibility."

On 31 March 1974, two days after Svetlova's arrival, Solzhenitsyn gave an interview to the AP correspondent in Switzerland, Roger Leddington, in an attempt to clear up what he called American misconceptions. A mutual understanding between the Soviet and American peoples, he said, was essential but was "difficult to establish from afar, using the superficial and often insufficiently thought-out judgements of the daily press." His *Letter* had been subjected to "primitive and even mistaken interpretations" in the American press, even before publication, and especially in the *New York Times*. His

---

* The *New York Times*'s analysis of Solzhenitsyn's *Letter* was correct in all essentials. What the *Times* did not reveal was that it had obtained a copy of the original text of the *Letter* by deception. After I had offered the *Times* a translation (at Dr Heeb's request), the *Times* sent a correspondent to the YMCA Press in Paris and requested a copy of the Russian text in my name, which it then proceeded to have translated in secret (by a London team that included three of my friends). Thus, when Solzhenitsyn distributed his amended text, the *Times* found itself in possession of the original and made this the basis of its news story. The *Times*'s trick did nothing to dispel Solzhenitsyn's low opinion of the Western press.

† Unfortunately, the preface somehow got detached from the main text in the confusion surrounding its secret dispatch from Paris to London. As a result, only the second and later editions of the *Letter* in English include Solzhenitsyn's preface.

suggestions had been for the peaceful withdrawal of the Soviet Union from foreign conquests "on a scale far exceeding that which they dream of achieving by nuclear *détente*," yet he had been accused of nationalism. Similarly, when he had proposed following the recommendations of the Club of Rome, he had been accused of utopianism. "In this way, the press is capable of introducing incomprehension between distant parts of the planet rather than international understanding." In other words, the press was acting in a manner diametrically opposed to the role of literature as described by Solzhenitsyn in his Nobel lecture.[6]

Solzhenitsyn's strictures on the American press would have been more convincing if his *Letter* had been more enthusiastically received by his comrades in the Soviet Union, but the sad fact was that there, too, it was widely criticized—often on the same grounds as those advanced in the West. Andrei Sakharov, while paying tribute to Solzhenitsyn as a writer and especially to his "great book," *The Gulag Archipelago*, took issue with his nationalistic concern for the sufferings of the Russian people alone, pointing out that other peoples in the Soviet Union had suffered just as much. Nor did he agree that all Russia's troubles had come from the West or that ideas could be divided into "Western" and "Russian" ones. Ideas, from the scientist's point of view, could only be true or false. There was much, he wrote, with which he could agree in Solzhenitsyn's *Letter*, but he was disturbed by its "isolationism" and anti-Western tone. He also felt that Solzhenitsyn was falsely idealizing the Russian past and that Russia need not resign itself to an authoritarian regime. Democracy was possible in Russia, and for that it needed the help of the West, even the "convergence" he himself had advocated in his 1968 memorandum. Sakharov pointed to some uncomfortable parallels between Solzhenitsyn's latent xenophobia, strident patriotism, presumption in favour of the Orthodox church on the one hand, and the policies of Stalin and his followers during and after the Second World War on the other. They were only parallels, he wrote, but they made him uncomfortable, for even if Solzhenitsyn was advocating a "mild" version of these arrangements, it was known from history that "mild ideologists" were always followed by far harder practical men.[7]

Sakharov's criticism was of particular significance, because, as Sakharov himself noted, the *Letter* had specifically taken up some of Sakharov's earlier arguments and attempted to refute them. Solzhenitsyn clearly saw Sakharov as his principal ideological adversary (among the dissidents), and Sakharov's essay further clarified the differences between the pro-Western "rationalists" like Sakharov and the anti-Western traditional nationalists of Solzhenitsyn's type. Henceforth these two groups would be dubbed "Westernizers" and "Slavophiles," after their nineteenth-century ideological forebears, and although there was much to differentiate them from their predecessors, there remained sufficient similarities to make the comparison useful.

The Sakharov essay was written at the beginning of April 1974. Together with Solzhenitsyn's *Letter*, it soon gave rise to a whole unofficial literature on the subject of Russia's future and the prospects for reform. These essays were collected by Mikhail Agursky and released into samizdat in June 1974 under the collective title *What Awaits the Soviet Union?* and the subtitle *A Collection of Articles on "Letter to the Leaders."* Among the contributors were Roy Medvedev, who confessed to being "disillusioned" with Solzhenitsyn's proposals, which he deemed unrealistic and hardly worth arguing with; Agursky himself, who found Solzhenitsyn's programme "pragmatic" and "constructive"; Vladimir Osipov, who took issue with Sakharov's criticisms of Solzhenitsyn; and ten other authors of varying degrees of intelligence and competence.

The usefulness of Solzhenitsyn's *Letter* from the point of view of concerned Russians was that it drew attention once more to the problem of Russia's future and brought into greater prominence the debate that had been going on, in rather subterranean fashion, between various groups of dissidents for some time. Thanks to Solzhenitsyn's incomparable vividness of expression, it also set the agenda for future discussions of this burning issue. Needless to say, nowhere among the responses to his *Letter* did he admit to finding that "constructive course of action," that "fully realistic way out," that would persuade him to withdraw his proposals. On the contrary, he would broaden and elaborate on them, but hardly change them, in the years that lay ahead.

A question that had arisen during Solzhenitsyn's interview with Leddington was whether he intended to visit America. President Nixon, presumably advised by Kissinger, had been one of the few Western leaders not to express official sympathy with Solzhenitsyn or to offer him asylum, for fear that it might jeopardize his plans for a meeting with Leonid Brezhnev that spring or interfere with the European Security Conference then in progress in Geneva. On 16 February, however, a Republican congressman had suggested inviting Solzhenitsyn to address a joint session of Congress, and on the eighteenth, Senator Jesse Helms proposed a resolution to make Solzhenitsyn an honorary citizen of the United States: if passed, he would become only the second honorary U.S. citizen (the other was Winston Churchill). Helms also wrote to Solzhenitsyn to invite him to the United States,[8] and soon afterwards George Meany, president of America's main trade-union organization, the AFL-CIO, wrote to invite Solzhenitsyn to be the organization's guest and "to travel widely in our diverse country [and] communicate freely, to the extent of your wishes, with the American people."[9]

Solzhenitsyn declined both invitations on the grounds that, after the upheaval of his expulsion, it was essential he get down to literary work again ("at my old level and tempo") in order to regain his equilibrium. He wrote that he was extremely grateful to Helms for his generous offer and support, and in a further exchange of letters he attempted to clarify his political views as set out in *Letter to the Leaders.* To George Meany he was even warmer. Expressing his "great respect" for Meany as "one of the most farsighted, reasonable, and steadfast public figures in the United States," he wrote that he had been particularly pleased to find Meany's name on the invitation and that he would always be grateful to the AFL-CIO for having published a map of the Gulag camps long before most people were aware of the problem. While declining to come immediately, he left open the possibility of a later visit.[10]

These were genuine reasons for not visiting America immediately after his arrival, but it is possible that Solzhenitsyn was influenced by his feeling that he was still misunderstood there. In his second letter to Helms, he had repeated at greater length his criticisms of the American press treatment of *Letter to the Leaders*, and he was clearly stung by some of the bad publicity. Another irksome bone of contention was the continuing non-appearance of the American edition of *The Gulag Archipelago*. The editing of the text had finally got under way only in January 1974, and at the time of Solzhenitsyn's expulsion very little progress had been made in getting it ready. While the publishers, Harper & Row, were prepared to go to extreme lengths to have the book printed and bound at record speed, they were prevented from doing so by the unsatisfactory state of the text.

Towards the end of March 1974, Olga Carlisle paid a visit to Solzhenitsyn to try to explain her role in the affair and account for the delay. According to her, it was Dr Heeb's fault. A complete translation of volume 1 of *The Gulag Archipelago*, polished and edited by her, had been ready and available for publication since the preceding June, but Heeb had omitted to ask her for it, and she had not offered it, because of her break with Solzhenitsyn shortly before that. Heeb had therefore received Whitney's unedited first draft, and the further delay was due to the slowness of the "expert" whom Heeb had nominated to work on the translation.* Solzhenitsyn was polite but distant as he listened to her explanations. Then he mentioned the point that weighed on his mind most of all about the non-appearance of the American translation. "Olga Vadimovna, had *The Gulag Archipelago* come out in time, they would never have dared expel me! I had a fabulous strategy worked out, all ready to be set in motion. A whole campaign."[11]

Was Solzhenitsyn correct, and would he have survived in the Soviet Union if the American translation had appeared? He certainly thought so, for he had said the same thing in a telephone conversation with the publishers the day after his expulsion, and he was to repeat it in *The Oak and the Calf*. His reasoning was that his entire position in the Soviet Union rested on world-wide publicity, and above all on the words and actions of the United

*I was that "expert," and it was I who determined that Whitney's first draft needed extensive revision before it could be published. Unfortunately, I had no idea (and I don't think Dr Heeb did) that a revised text already existed—nor did I have the slightest idea of Olga Carlisle's involvement in the project. The reasons for the delay were many. I was obliged to wait three months after pronouncing the text inadequate before being called in to revise it, which was to give Thomas Whitney time to work on it too. I was then asked to revise nearly 700 pages in three weeks to fit in with the publisher's schedule—an impossible task, hence the delay. As it was, the entire operation was hopelessly rushed, and the resulting text has to be added to the long list of inadequate translations of Solzhenitsyn's works.

States. In his calculation, the contents of *The Gulag Archipelago* were so sensational, and so damaging to the Soviet Union, that the storm of protest they would have provoked in the United States would have forced the latter to take some drastic action, such as breaking off all talks with the Soviet Union and declaring *détente* stone-dead. Alternatively, the United States might have made the safety of Solzhenitsyn a condition of further good relations, while the intensive publicity would have made it harder for the Soviet authorities to act against him. It was even possible, in Solzhenitsyn's view, that the pressure might have produced a crack in the monolith and a chance to press the arguments in *Letter to the Leaders* even more seriously. Whether this was a realistic possibility is hard to tell. Solzhenitsyn had already stretched the power of the word in the Soviet Union beyond all previous limits and had demonstrated his enormous faith in its possibilities. His theory on the American translation of *Gulag* was a further demonstration of that faith, and its validity will never be known.

For these many reasons, Solzhenitsyn did not feel ready to visit the United States, and settled down in Zurich to sort out his papers and start writing again. His main literary objective was still to continue with the sequels to *August 1914*, but before that he was determined to complete the book that he had kept a total secret from all except his wife: his memoir, soon to be called *The Oak and the Calf*. In Sternenberg he had made considerable progress with it, and by June the whole thing was finished. He was also determined to set the record straight concerning his earlier "censored" works. Suppressed chapters of *The First Circle* were beginning to appear in Russian in the YMCA *Vestnik* in Paris, and he was preparing full and authorized texts of his other novels and stories. In addition, he made arrangements for the YMCA Press to publish *Prussian Nights* in Russian and to bring out a disc of himself reading it, which he had recorded earlier in the Soviet Union. Simultaneously, he began to look around for a film producer to work on his screenplay *The Tanks Know the Truth*.[12]

Meanwhile, the nature of the impact of Solzhenitsyn's expulsion on East-West relations and on the dissident movement in the Soviet Union was becoming clearer. On international relations the impact was very limited. President Nixon and Secretary of State Kissinger were desperately eager to make their visit to Moscow, and nothing could be allowed to hinder that. At the preparatory talks in Geneva for the forthcoming European Security Conference, where human rights and the freer movement of people and ideas were supposed to be central topics, the expulsion was not even mentioned. Ironically, it was the Communist parties of Italy, Sweden, and Yugoslavia (but not France) that seemed to be most upset by the move, and there was anxious talk about a Soviet return to Stalinism. Naturally, such a speedy loss of interest in the West had its effect on the Soviet dissidents. Their desire for the Russian edition of *The Gulag Archipelago* was intense, and copies were changing hands for as much as eighty rubles at a time. But there was also an increased fear of being caught, and a feeling that to support Solzhenitsyn had become much riskier than before. With his protective presence removed, many intellectuals felt demoralized and exposed, and there was a general sense that the Soviet government's bold move in expelling the writer had been (for the government) a striking success.

Solzhenitsyn himself was not disposed to accept this situation meekly; in the course of the spring and summer, he released a number of statements designed to make his presence felt and put pressure on the Soviet authorities. In April he protested against the expulsion from Moscow of Victor Nekrasov and Alexander Ginzburg, amplifying his earlier definition of Soviet society as one where a fully fledged policy of serfdom was in place. "This is the source of Soviet serfdom: permanent registration in one's place of residence and the impossibility of going anywhere beyond the jurisdiction of the local authorities without their permission."[13] Later the same month, he drafted and signed, jointly with Shafarevich (who was still in Moscow), a petition for the release of General Grigorenko from the mental hospital in which he had been incarcerated, and in May he protested on behalf of Gabriel Superfin, a young literary scholar who had helped him in his research, and Efim Etkind, who had just been drummed out of the Herzen Institute in Leningrad for his friendship with Solzhenitsyn.* In his statement on Ginzburg, Solzhenitsyn referred to Ginzburg as an "official of the Political Red Cross," a description that puzzled observers until Ginzburg himself clarified the matter with a separate statement saying that he had taken charge of a fund to help the families of political prisoners and that the main source of money for the fund was Solzhenitsyn.[14]

In fact, the status of political prisoner no longer existed in the Soviet Union. It had been abolished by Stalin in 1937, and with it the Committee to Aid Political Prisoners (headed in those days by Gorky's former wife, Ekaterina Peshkova), popularly known then as the "Political Red Cross." Aid to the victims of political persecution had always been a Russian tradition, however, and it was revived again in the mid-sixties by members of the Democratic Movement. In 1970 an attempt had been made to organize this aid on a more regular basis, and it was at around this time that Solzhenitsyn had begun donating a part of his royalties. He had always intended the royalties from *The Gulag Archipelago* to go to such a cause as well, and in Zurich he lost no time in setting up the Russian Social Fund to Aid Political Prisoners and Their Families, which was properly constituted as a charitable foundation under Swiss law. Theoretically, other people were invited to contribute to the fund too, but in practice the overwhelming bulk of the money consisted of the proceeds from *The Gulag Archipelago*. The fund was officially launched in April 1974, and Ginzburg was put in charge of collecting names and distributing aid within the Soviet Union. It was for this reason (not formally, but in fact) that he had been expelled from Moscow and obliged to leave his family and reside in Tarusa, a small town about eighty miles to the south,

*There were several counts against Etkind, including his earlier defence of Iosif Brodsky, but the Solzhenitsyn connection seems to have been the deciding factor.

and placed under administrative surveillance, but it did not stop him from announcing the existence of the fund and inviting applications. The president of the fund, he said, would be not Solzhenitsyn but his wife, Natalia Svetlova. Solzhenitsyn, meanwhile, made a similar announcement in Zurich.

Just as, since the beginning of the year, Solzhenitsyn had reversed his former policy and begun to speak out on behalf of individual dissidents, so he now began to speak openly and actively on the subject of *détente*. In a letter to the U.S. congressmen Donald Fraser and Benjamin Rosenthal, who had solicited his views on *détente*, Solzhenitsyn wrote that while true *détente* was "not only necessary but mankind's only salvation," the "pseudo-*détente*" being negotiated by Nixon and Brezhnev was a fraud, since only the United States was making concessions. The Soviet Union was bound to cheat, just as North Vietnam was cheating on the truce arranged by Kissinger, since there were no guarantees built into it. Solzhenitsyn criticized not only Kissinger but also Willy Brandt and his recent statement that he would have attempted *détente* even with Stalin. Did that mean, asked Solzhenitsyn, that Brandt would have advocated *détente* with Hitler as well?[15]

Towards the end of June, Solzhenitsyn repeated these views directly to the American people in a lengthy television interview with Walter Cronkite. He had been bombarded with requests to appear on television ever since his arrival in the West and had steadfastly refused. But the painful work of revising the American translation of *The Gulag Archipelago* was now finished, the book was timed for publication in the last week of June, and Solzhenitsyn apparently wanted to erase from American minds the bad impression left by his earlier criticisms of the American media. The choice of Cronkite to do the interview was presumably dictated by Cronkite's audience ratings in the United States, but in other respects it was unfortunate. Cronkite did not appear to be well briefed on life in the Soviet Union and had little grasp of Solzhenitsyn's career and writings, so that the interview was rambling and unfocused and the questions vague, with no attempt made to follow up the answers or press for clarifications.

Apart from *détente*, he again talked about his attitude to the press and explained why he had been shocked by the journalists' behaviour. But this time he was more conciliatory. He was fully aware, he said, that the Western press had helped him to survive, for which he was "very grateful." And he explained his position more precisely. "Not only am I not critical of the system of freedom of the press but, on the contrary, I consider it a great blessing that the West has a free press. But I feel that not only the press but every profession and every individual must know how to use freedom, and know where to call a halt and set a moral limit." He also pointed out, like Amalrik before him, that the aggressive, investigative instincts of Western journalists somehow seemed to evaporate when they reached Moscow, or at least underwent a rapid cooling: the press was quite capable of applying double standards in its work.

Another topic he returned to was *Letter to the Leaders*, again insisting that he had been misunderstood. He had not said that he *preferred* an authoritarian system of rule, or that it was better than democracy, but simply that under present Soviet conditions, he did not see a way of bringing democracy to Russia without a new revolution, and he was against revolutions in principle. It was true he had criticized Western democratic methods, and to a large extent he stuck by that, but that had been written in the Soviet Union; having now seen the Swiss system at work, he felt he had to make an exception at least for Switzerland. It did not mean, however, that the Swiss system could be exported to England, France, or America, still less to the Soviet Union. Every country was different and had its own traditions and possibilities.

Similarly, he did not want his criticism of America to be taken too literally. He liked to make a distinction between peoples and governments, and whereas he was very hostile to the American government's foreign policy, he did not extend this hostility to the American people.

> Please believe me, and I want to say this to you here today, that independently of your government's policies, there exists among the Russian people a steadfast sympathy for the American people, which has come into being despite the lies in the press (our newspapers have written first one thing and then another), and that there is a kind of inner compatibility between the Russian and American peoples. Your generosity, for instance, and your magnanimity are very well understood by our people, probably because we are alike in this—Russians are also generous and magnanimous.[16]

The interview was a great success in America—and was shown in many other countries as well. Television, the medium of the masses, the eye of the man in the street, had been allowed into the mysterious Russian's home, shown into his living-room, and seen him revealed as a human being like the rest of us. Passionate, yes; vehement, yes, but also likeable and manageable, and very charming in close up.

This was not the impression created by volume 1 of *The Gulag Archipelago*, which had appeared in French a few weeks earlier and now came out in England and America. A dawning sense that this was possibly one of the great books of the twentieth century, fed in the first instance by reports of the Russian and German editions, now received massive confirmation as hundreds of thousands of copies of the book (soon to be followed by millions of paperbacks—in America alone over two million) rolled out into the bookshops and thence into the hands of incredulous readers. Starting with its slitheringly evocative title (*Arkhipelag Gulag* sounds even more reptilian in the original Russian) and puzzling subtitle, *An Experiment in Literary Investigation*, it was perceived as strange and unique, a conducted tour of a chamber of horrors almost without parallel in modern literature.

It was, of course, the contents that attracted most attention and comment. In principle, the story that Solzhenitsyn had to tell was not new to well-informed Western intellectuals. What *was* undoubtedly new, however, was the comprehensiveness of Solzhenitsyn's compilation, the intensity and passion of his formulation, and the devastating judgement he pronounced on fifty years of Soviet history. These things were uttered with the unique authority of someone who had lived through and survived the system (and even been a part of it for a while), who had seen it from the inside—not by one of the dozens of Westerners, or even émigrés or refugees, who had chronicled these monstrosities from a greater distance.

The immediate comparison that sprang to reviewers' minds was the Holocaust.[17] Regardless of the degree of similarity, the Holocaust had made a deeper impact on Western minds than the Gulag because it was closer and had destroyed millions of Westerners and people with connections to the West, and also because Westerners were conscious of a certain complicity. Solzhenitsyn's achievement was to impress on Western minds the horror of the Gulag with almost the intensity that earlier discoveries had done for the Holocaust. A large part of his success was due to sheer literary power. Critics agreed that it was one of Solzhenitsyn's very best books, citing the extraordinary richness and complexity of his central metaphor: an archipelago that stretched for thousands of miles, made up of islands, bays, peninsulas, capes, promontories, and an ocean into which flowed hundreds of rivers, streams, and rivulets. To an English commentator, the sensation of reading Solzhenitsyn's prose was that of being "disconcerted by the shriek and roar of the high wind, the sustained passion of the irony, the violence of apostrophe and invocation." But the hyperbole was justified because Solzhenitsyn was "re-creating horror, and the result is a phantasmagoria of good and evil, the intensity of experience refuelled periodically by injections of the author's personal emotions." There were scenes worthy of Goya, shades of Hieronymus Bosch, echoes of Swift; it was an elegy, an indictment, but also a merciless factual catalogue of evil upon evil.[18]

The evocation of the Holocaust was not accidental, for Solzhenitsyn's book was also, as he had said in the Soviet Union, an act of contrition on behalf of a whole nation, a call to repentance, much as the Germans had been called upon, as a nation, to repent the sins of nazism. Indeed, Solzhenitsyn invoked the example of the Germans for emulation and called upon his countrymen to rise to similar heights of self-abnegation and penitence (offering yet one more reason for his official Soviet critics to excoriate him as a traitor).

There was no way to measure the "success" of such a gargantuan undertaking, but *The Gulag Archipelago* was no doubt enormously successful in imprinting the Soviet tragedy on the world's consciousness.* Since the time of the book's appearance, the very word "Gulag" has come to have the same threatening ring to it, to bear a similar charge of metaphysical horror, as the word "holocaust"; yet, unlike "holocaust," it had not existed as a word before

---

* The impact of *The Gulag Archipelago* was particularly great in France, where the Soviet Union continued to enjoy greater sympathy from the intellectuals than in any other Western country. Georges Suffert, the editor of *Le Point*, was hardly exaggerating, in the French context, when he remarked that *The Gulag Archipelago* had "forever eclipsed the beacon of communism."

Solzhenitsyn used it, but was merely an ugly bureaucratic abbreviation.* Solzhenitsyn had enriched the world's vocabulary. At the same time, the book was a political event of prime importance for the image of the Soviet Union in world affairs. George Kennan, by no means a cold warrior, called it "the greatest and most powerful single indictment of a political regime ever to be levelled in modern times" and asserted that the book was bound to have a "major effect" on the Soviet regime: "This merciless indictment . . . is too devastating to be ignored. The Soviet leaders cannot, just by ignoring it themselves or attempting to smother it with falsehood, consign it to oblivion or cause it to remain without consequences. It is too large for the craw of the Soviet propaganda machine. It will stick there, with increasing discomfort, until it has done its work."[19]

The success and impact of *The Gulag Archipelago* carried a lesson for Solzhenitsyn that he was most unwilling to learn—namely, that the power of the written word issuing from the pen of Solzhenitsyn the creative artist was out of all proportion to the power he wielded as a publicist and journalist. There are indications that he was at least aware of this dichotomy. To Cronkite he had expressed regret that he felt unable to concentrate on his creative work and was obliged to make public statements all the time. He would not do it, he said, if his country did not have its system of constant repression, did not destroy people for dissidence, and did not seem to want to expand over the entire globe. Unfortunately, it did, and therefore he felt the statements were necessary. He did not seem to realize that direct political statements like his *Letter to the Leaders* and his somewhat strident views on *détente* were doing him more harm than good, and undoing his reputation as a writer. Or if he did, he still felt unable to stop.

Throughout it all, Solzhenitsyn's personality remained to most people an enigma. The mystery with which he had deliberately surrounded his personal life and character in the Soviet Union, although dispelled a little by the public nature of his arrival in the West, still clung to him after his decision to settle in Zurich and was enhanced by his aversion to giving interviews. He needed the seclusion to sustain his single-mindedness and dedication, yet at the same time it served to spark people's curiosity and provoke them to even greater efforts to learn more about him.

The portrait that gradually emerged from the descriptions of people who had got to know him was complex and in some ways contradictory. Janis Sapiets, the BBC commentator, who like millions of others had idolized Solzhenitsyn from afar, was surprised to find him "not a tall man" and quite ordinary looking. "After all, you have been listening to his words, reading his books, you have seen his stern face in the photographs everywhere. To you he is a symbol of a kind of giant fighting the power of the state. Then you suddenly meet him and it's an ordinary person sitting there."[20] Like so many others who met him during his first days in the West, Sapiets was

*Gulag (*GULag* in Russian) is an acronym for *Glavnoye Upravleniye Lagerei* (Chief Administration of the Labour Camps).

impressed by Solzhenitsyn's calmness and self-control. Nikita Struve, his publisher at the YMCA Press in Paris, spent several days in Zurich with him and was amazed by Solzhenitsyn's ebullience and *joie de vivre*. It was as if a great weight had been lifted from his shoulders, and he was enjoying it to the full.[21] In Norway he had surprised his travelling companions by his robust humour and his capacity for clowning. When the press had become particularly importunate at the farm where he was staying the first night, he had dressed up in borrowed clothes, donned a red pixie hat, and posed nonchalantly for pictures with Sparre in similar garb.[22]

Heinrich Böll understood Solzhenitsyn's lighter side, for he had seen it in intimate conversation in Moscow. As he told a *Spiegel* reporter, there was a "dimension of humour" to Solzhenitsyn. The Russian writer was not exactly an optimist, but somehow "sanguine by nature, full of hope and strength," and therefore basically cheerful.[23] This was the secret of his relaxed manner when among friends. But Böll understood something else as well. "It's true he is a very polite man," he told a journalist friend, "extremely polite when you talk to him, when he listens to you, thanks you and smiles, and looks at you with his bright blue eyes. But he is also inflexible, polite but inflexible."[24] It was the inflexibility that came out in his public persona and made him so difficult to deal with. It was real enough, for inflexibility and stubbornness were part of the secret of his success in standing up to the Soviet government; and Solzhenitsyn was not above exaggerating it to frighten casual bystanders away. It suited him to seem stern and unapproachable, for in that way he protected his peace.

Within a short time after Natalia Svetlova's arrival, Solzhenitsyn was able to settle down to a regular way of life. During the week he generally went alone to Widmer's farm in Sternenberg to write, leaving Natalia and her mother to cope with the household and children, sort out his archive, and deal with callers and the mail. On the weekends he would return again and try to cram all his business into two or three days. But the task was almost hopeless.

To begin with there was the mail, mountains of which soon filled the attic to overflowing. So many sacks of it had accumulated by early April that Solzhenitsyn felt obliged to issue a public statement thanking his numerous correspondents *en bloc* and apologizing for his inability to answer them. He had been inundated, he wrote, by an avalanche of letters, telegrams, parcels, presents, invitations, and congratulations from every corner of the world. Even if he ceased all literary activity, it would take him over six months to answer them all. Therefore, he was resorting to the only possible response, a statement to the press. "I heartily thank everyone who has written to me and beg you to excuse my physical inability to answer each one of you." He was touched and moved by the warmth and support he had experienced from all sides and hoped to repay it with his literary work.[25]

It was a little reminiscent of the form letter he had once sent out to young writers soliciting his advice, but whereas, then, he had had little choice, having no means to employ secretarial help, now there was less excuse for it. He had arrived in Zurich a rich man. The full extent of his wealth was not known—guesses ranged from a quarter of a million to two million dollars—but it was well within his means to hire a secretary and additional help, even if only on a temporary basis. But Solzhenitsyn did not—partly for good reasons and partly for bad. On the positive side, Solzhenitsyn had a strong liking for simplicity. He was a genuinely modest man in his domestic arrangements. The house on Stapferstrasse was plainly and simply furnished—even impersonally: the whole time Solzhenitsyn was there, it had an air of impermanence about it, as if the inhabitants were just passing through. Solzhenitsyn could not tolerate fuss of any kind. His meals were also plain and simple, even with guests present, and there was no formality, apart from prayers said by the children. The idea of having a secretary was extremely unattractive to him. It smacked of ostentation, hierarchy, bureaucracy (on however small a scale), and repelled him as pretentious.[26]

On the other hand, there was something unrealistic and selfish about this arrangement, as if Solzhenitsyn were reluctant to come to terms with the consequences of his fame. He accepted the power and influence it gave him but did not welcome the responsibilities and the loss of time (and of freedom of action) that fame brought with it. He wanted to remain untrammelled and independent, as free to act and respond as he had been when he was unknown, but yet to have others listen to him and come running when he wanted them to. This attitude placed an enormous strain on his immediate family, and especially on Natalia Svetlova. She ended up working an even longer day than he, struggling to remain a mother and wife as well as a secretary. But she willingly accepted the burden. When asked that summer whether she didn't feel she should be able to share the work-load, she replied that no one else could possibly interpret her husband's wishes and requirements. These were so complex and idiosyncratic that it would take months to train someone, and both she and Solzhenitsyn were too busy to break off and do it. Besides, she added, giving away what was probably the overriding reason, Solzhenitsyn could not trust anyone but her with his personal and political affairs.[27]

This amateurish disregard for organization led to chaos in many areas. As the unanswered letters piled up in the attic on Stapferstrasse (leading to all sorts of suspicions, misunderstandings, and frustrations on the part of Solzhenitsyn's unsuspecting colleagues and well-wishers), he and Natalia rushed frantically from task to task, trying to keep up and inevitably falling further and further behind. Between whiles they would have lengthy sessions with Dr Heeb, whose own small office was almost as overwhelmed as they were.

It seemed a strange way for a world-famous Nobel laureate to arrange his affairs, but then Solzhenitsyn was no respecter of custom or precedent. Having been flung out to the West, he regarded it as more important than ever to maintain the momentum that had brought him thus far. The best way to do that, it seemed to him, was to behave as far as possible as if nothing had changed. And so he established his small household almost exactly along the lines that it had run in Moscow, got back to his old writing routine, and tried to ignore the inconveniences that this change in his circumstances had forced upon him.

48

CLARIFICATIONS

I T HAS BEEN suggested that Solzhenitsyn was uncomfortable in Zurich and found the Swiss rather bourgeois and boring and that this was why he turned his back on them and immersed himself in his own world. But that is to misread his urge for privacy and his sense of his vocation. It is true that his literary work occupied the bulk of his time and thoughts and was directed towards his fellow Russians and his homeland. But Solzhenitsyn took a definite interest in his new surroundings, formed several friendships, and was not unhappy with his experiences there.

One of his best friends, Mayor Widmer, was able to open many doors for him. It was Widmer who had first showed Solzhenitsyn around Zurich and its environs and indicated where to find the places that Lenin had visited and stayed in. Very soon after Solzhenitsyn's arrival, Widmer had taken him to evensong at the Benedictine monastery of Einsiedeln, outside Zurich. Solzhenitsyn liked the service but found it "cold" and impersonal in comparison with Russian rites. Widmer also arranged dinner parties for the Solzhenitsyns to meet local people of interest to them and had no difficulty in persuading Solzhenitsyn to come. On the contrary, the writer expressly asked to meet as many Zurich people as possible and greatly enjoyed these evenings.

Widmer was pleasantly surprised by the interest that Solzhenitsyn took in Swiss life and manners, for he, too, had expected the latter to be more aloof. When Zurich's famous spring festival took place, at the end of April, Solzhenitsyn made a point of standing on a corner for some hours to watch the parade go by. Another time he asked to attend the ceremony, held once a year, at which the Zurich City Council awards a silver candlestick to an

outstanding contemporary artist. As it happened, Rostropovich had offered
to give a free concert in honour of the occasion, and Marc Chagall had agreed
to attend, so that the celebration dinner afterwards was a very Russian affair.
Widmer also took Solzhenitsyn on a car tour of Switzerland. On the St Gott-
hard Pass, Solzhenitsyn paid homage to the Suvorov Memorial and explained
to Widmer the importance of General Suvorov to Russian history.[1]

Another friend was Dr Fred Luchsinger, editor-in-chief of the *Neue Zürcher
Zeitung*. Solzhenitsyn had felt grateful to the Zurich newspaper ever since it
had published the story of the confiscation of his archive in September 1965—
the first and almost the only newspaper to do so—and was particularly pleased
to meet its editor. With Luchsinger he liked to talk politics, especially international politics, but Luchsinger was able to show him something of Swiss
politics as well.

Solzhenitsyn was already well disposed towards the Swiss political system before he came. What he liked, he told Luchsinger at their first meeting,
was the fact that Swiss democracy was organized in small units, such as the
village and the canton, and that the emphasis was on local self-determination
and the participation of the entire population. It reminded him, he said, of
the democratic system that had existed in medieval Novgorod. On another
occasion he told his Swiss publisher, Otto Walter, that he was much impressed
by the treatment Alexander Herzen had received when he sought political
asylum in Geneva in the nineteenth century. Geneva had asked the federal
government in Bern whether there would be any difficulties if Herzen was
granted permission to reside there, and the government had replied that it
was up to the city to decide. "This," said Solzhenitsyn, "really is democracy
from the base, when a city can decide questions of national policy for itself."[2]

By the time of his interview with Cronkite, Solzhenitsyn had become
even more convinced of the virtues of Swiss democracy and was unequivocal
in his praise.

> Swiss democracy has some amazing qualities. First, it is completely silent and
> works inaudibly. Secondly, there is its stability. No party and no trade union,
> by going on strike, taking a sharp turn or a sudden vote, can shake the system
> here, provoke a coup or the downfall of the government—no, it's a stable system.
> Thirdly, it's an upturned pyramid. That is, there's more power at the local level
> . . . than in the cantons, and more power in the cantons than with the govern-
> ment. . . . Furthermore, democracy is everyone's responsibility. Each individual
> would rather moderate his demands than damage the whole structure. The Swiss
> have such a high sense of responsibility that there are no attempts by groups to
> seize something for themselves and elbow out the rest. . . . And look how the
> national problem has been solved: three nations, four even, and the same number
> of languages. There is no state language, no domination of one nation by another,
> and that's the way it's been for centuries, and everything is in its place. Naturally
> one can only admire such a democracy.[3]

This statement is interesting as the most explicit description Solzhenitsyn has so far offered of what he understands by the term "democracy" and

as the firmest indication of his approval. He hastened to qualify his remarks, however, by repeating his conviction that no one could expect to transplant the Swiss system to other countries, least of all to the Soviet Union, and indicated that his main objection to other forms of democracy was the latitude they gave to the "unbridled play of the passions."

Some months later, knowing of his interest in such matters, Luchsinger offered to take Solzhenitsyn to see the annual election in Appenzell, a village near the Austrian border. Solzhenitsyn agreed, provided no one was told in advance, for he did not want it turned into a media event. The election was held on a Sunday, and Solzhenitsyn chose to attend the service in the local church. Inevitably, he was recognized, and by the time he emerged, virtually the whole village was standing outside to greet him and demanding autographs. Solzhenitsyn explained that he signed only books, whereupon the village bookshop was opened and every book by Solzhenitsyn was sold on the spot. It turned out that the election speeches were all in dialect, which Luchsinger translated into High German for Solzhenitsyn's benefit, and Luchsinger found himself apologizing for the reactionary, almost xenophobic tone of some of the speakers, who were vigorously opposed to the admission of a dozen residents of Italian origin to full voting rights. But Solzhenitsyn thought this quite all right and said he understood them perfectly. "If these people want to stay on their own and don't accept foreigners, that's all right with me, and you don't have to excuse it."[4]

Solzhenitsyn later wrote about the election himself. What he had particularly admired were its traditional forms ("all the men carried swords or daggers as a sign of their right to vote—women and children didn't have them") and ancient rituals. Voting was done by a show of hands, in full view of everyone, and the decisions were ultra-conservative: no foreigners, no new taxes, and no increase in the unemployment benefit. "It was the voice of the people. The question was irrevocably decided—without newspaper articles, without television commentaries, without senate commissions, in ten minutes and unchangeably for a whole year." He was also impressed by the speech made by the Appenzell "mayor," Raymond Brogher, who pointed out that in the fifteen hundred years of its existence, the canton of Appenzell had made no fundamental changes in its electoral procedures, had never succumbed to the "madness of total freedom," and had always believed that neither the individual nor the state could be guaranteed freedom without discipline and the preservation of honour. "The state cannot function rationally without an admixture of aristocratic and even monarchist elements." The democratic system required a firm hand, and the stability of the state depended not on beautiful articles in its constitution but on the quality of the holders of power.

A separate section of the speech dealt with world politics, the weakness of America in Vietnam, the dangers of Soviet aggression—included, one suspects, precisely in Solzhenitsyn's honour, though there is no trace in his account of any awareness that his presence at this remote ceremony might have introduced its own pressures and distortions. At all events, he solemnly asked for copies of all the speeches made both during the election and at the banquet afterwards—at which he was undoubtedly the guest of honour ("they were honouring not the writer but the warrior against evil, as the mayor made clear in his speech")—and declared himself a fervent admirer of Swiss grass-roots democracy, which had grown "not out of the ideas of the Enlightenment but directly out of the ancient forms of the commune."[5]

Natalia usually accompanied her husband on these outings, but life was harder for her than for Solzhenitsyn in Zurich. For one thing, there was the problem of language. Solzhenitsyn's German, though rudimentary on his arrival, quickly improved with practice, and he was not shy about making mistakes. Natalia did not know a word. To remedy the situation, it was arranged for her and her mother Ekaterina to take lessons, but they found themselves so busy with family and literary affairs that there was little time to study and progress was slow. The Widmers were very conscious of this problem. Mrs Widmer took Russian lessons and she and her husband arranged excursions to the mountains for just the four of them. Natalia loved climbing and felt very much at home there. She and Solzhenitsyn taught the Widmers some Russian songs, and the four of them would sing lustily as they walked the mountain paths. The only stipulation Solzhenitsyn made was that it should not be too hot.[6] As before, he could not bear too much sunshine, whereas it could never be too cold for him.

There was one other group with which Solzhenitsyn mixed during his first several months in Zurich, and that was the rather large Czech *émigré* community. The way it had come about was rather strange—and it was to have even stranger consequences. Shortly after his arrival in Zurich, Solzhenitsyn became very friendly with a middle-aged Czech couple, Dr František Holub and his wife. The Holubs had emigrated from Czechoslovakia in 1969, after the Soviet invasion, along with many others in the Zurich Czech community, but no one knew very much about them. Holub was rumoured to have been a diplomat in Rumania, but he told another Czech that he was a linguist and had been working in Rumania on the compilation of a Czech-Rumanian dictionary. He also claimed to have helped smuggle some of Solzhenitsyn's manuscripts to the West through Rumania.[7] As for Mrs Holub, her Czech was so fluent that most people did not realize she was of Russian origin and had moved to Czechoslovakia only after her marriage. In Prague she had worked for Pragokonzert, the state-run body that was responsible for all foreign tours by Czech musicians and for exchanges with other countries. At such an institution, she may be presumed to have come into contact with the Czech security organs, for all tours and exchanges are closely controlled by the secret police in countries of the Communist bloc.

Owing to the secrecy with which he surrounded his domestic life in Zurich—and to the outcome of this friendship—Solzhenitsyn has never revealed how he met the Holubs. Widmer, one of the people closest to Solzhenitsyn, thinks that Mrs Holub simply came to Solzhenitsyn's house with bread and salt—the traditional Russian symbols of hospitality. Given that Solzhenitsyn's gate was kept locked and that there was no outside bell, this is hard to believe, though she could have waited until someone came out. On the other hand, on his very first day in Zurich, Solzhenitsyn had overruled the protests and fears of his friends to receive a Russian woman who claimed to be from Ryazan and who had brought him a bunch of roses and lilac. The woman gave him a note bearing a proverb specific to Ryazan and said she chose lilac for her bouquet because Ryazan is filled with lilac in the spring. Solzhenitsyn had been touched, had kissed her hand, and had asked her about her feelings in exile, to which she had replied that she hoped to see Russia again one day.[8]

It is not inconceivable that this woman was Mrs Holub (though the report describes her as "young," whereas Mrs Holub was middle-aged), for she refused to give her name. But even if she was not, Solzhenitsyn's impulsive response was characteristic, and he would probably have responded in a similar manner to someone bringing him the traditional bread and salt. Whatever the case, within weeks—and possibly within days—the Holubs had become Solzhenitsyn's unofficial advisers in Zurich, Mrs Holub taking over unspecified duties of a secretarial and public-relations nature.

A factor in Solzhenitsyn's willingness to welcome this Czech couple was his general fondness for Czechoslovakia, and his gratitude for Czech and Slovak efforts to get *Cancer Ward* published. He also felt a certain obligation to Czech intellectuals as a result of the impact his letter to the Writers' Union had had on Czech writers when it was read out to the Czech Writers' Union in 1967. He therefore asked the Holubs to introduce him to the Czech community settled in and around Zurich, and this led to the organization of two formal events—a visit to a Czech art gallery and a meeting between Solzhenitsyn and a group of some locally prominent Czech *émigrés*. Both events took place in the spring of 1974.

The art gallery was located in Pfäffikon, a village about three-quarters of an hour's drive from Zurich, where some thirty Czechs had gathered to meet the great Russian writer. The semi-abstract paintings and bas-reliefs of the Czech *émigré* artist Jan Kristofori, which were on view, could not have been much to his conservative taste, but he made polite noises and gracefully accepted the gift of a bas-relief from the gallery's owner, Oskar Krause. When Krause mentioned that he, too, had been a political prisoner and had served time in Czech jails, Solzhenitsyn embraced him and wept, and later invited him to the meeting in Zurich, which was due to take place the following week.[9]

The Zurich meeting was held in the Holubs' flat in the centre of town. Again there were about thirty Czechs present, many of them different from the ones who had been at the gallery. There the majority had been, like Krause himself, refugees from communism of many years' standing, whereas at the Holubs' flat the majority had left only after 1968. This meant, among other things, that the political complexion of the group was also different.

Many of these *émigrés* had been supporters of "socialism with a human face," had even been members of the Party, and therefore were less in accord with Solzhenitsyn's political views than were Krause and his friends. Indeed, after Solzhenitsyn had left, his views on Soviet expansionism, the irredeemable evils of socialism, and the illusions of *détente* were widely criticized, and a certain air of disenchantment was evident among those present.[10]

The meeting passed off quite amicably, however. The Czechs were honoured and impressed to be meeting this famous man in such friendly surroundings, and the Holubs, though faintly obsequious in the Viennese manner, were able to keep the conversation flowing in the desired direction. They had asked their guests to bring gifts for Solzhenitsyn (a request that would certainly have infuriated him had he known of it) and at one point ostentatiously introduced him to "our Czech Solzhenitsyn," a young writer by the name of Tomáš Řezáč, who presented Solzhenitsyn with his latest book. Řezáč was a slightly controversial figure in the Czech emigration. The son of two prominent establishment writers in Czechoslovakia (Václav Řezáč and Emma Řezáčova), he had been known in Prague as a rather untalented orthodox journalist who traded on his parents' fame. His emigration, with his wife, Lida, had come as a surprise to everyone, but by emigrating later than most others, he had antagonized both the reformist socialist *émigrés* of 1968–69, and the anti-Communist *émigrés* of an older generation. He was thus something of an outsider. In 1973 he had surprised everyone by writing a rather good spy novel, *Dwarf on a Swing*, which was published by an *émigré* Czech publisher in West Germany.[11] The novel's author was not known at first, for Řezáč had published it under a pseudonym, and the revelation of his authorship had produced a minor sensation among the Czechs. This was the flimsy basis for Mrs Holub's flattering description of him as "a Czech Solzhenitsyn." Since the fact of his authorship had been revealed only the preceding December, he was still something of a local celebrity.[12]

A Czech publisher who attended the meeting had objected to Řezáč's presence on the grounds of his pro-Communist sympathies but was told by Holub that it was at Solzhenitsyn's request, because Řezáč spoke fluent Russian.[13] It seems most unlikely that Solzhenitsyn had a hand in the invitation, but Řezáč did indeed speak good Russian and was seen to have several exchanges with Solzhenitsyn. Later, it was arranged with Solzhenitsyn for Holub to edit the translation of *The Gulag Archipelago* into Czech and for Řezáč to translate *Prussian Nights*. Neither proved to be very efficient at his work. Holub, although he gave up his lowly job at the international-press-cutting agency where he worked, knew hardly a word of Russian and succeeded only in slowing up the work of the seven translators of *The Gulag Archipelago;* and Řezáč never finished. Řezáč seemed unable to find regular work of any kind, and all of a sudden, in 1975, disappeared back to Prague, leaving his wife (and debts) behind and taking the manuscript of *Prussian Nights* with him. Meanwhile, Solzhenitsyn was apparently tipped off by the Swiss police that the Holubs were not quite what they had seemed to him, and he ceased to employ them in any capacity at all. Shortly afterwards, Dr Holub was killed in a road accident.

It is curious that Solzhenitsyn seems never to have suspected his new-found friends of any sinister intentions. Perhaps it was because they were Czech and he expected trouble to come directly from the Soviet Union itself. He must have known that Mrs Holub was Russian-born, but could have had any suspicions lulled by the fact that she had lived in Czechoslovakia so long. Similarly, he seems never to have discovered that Řezáč's Russian was so good because he had spent five years studying at a counter-espionage college in Moscow. There were other Czechs in Zurich who could have told Solzhenitsyn some of this, but they were defeated by the barrier thrown up by the Holubs. Solzhenitsyn was sufficiently suspicious and reclusive to cut himself off from the Czechs at large by employing the Holub couple to guard him, but he never dreamt, it seems, of suspecting the guards themselves.[14]

It was perhaps another sign of his impulsiveness, a spontaneous quality that was permanently at war with his acquired suspiciousness and near paranoia. And yet he was still the secretive plotter of yore. It showed in small things: the telephone number on his dial was a false one; favoured friends were instructed to put a small green cross on their letters to distinguish them from the ones that went straight into the attic; visitors to the house were strictly enjoined not to tell anyone they had been there. And it informed Solzhenitsyn's larger activities as well. Contacts with the Soviet Union were naturally shrouded in secrecy, but Solzhenitsyn insisted on enveloping his negotiations with agents, publishers, translators, journalists, politicians, and even friends in a similar veil of conspiracy. The arrangement for which he strove, just as in the Soviet Union, was to place himself at the centre of a gigantic spider's web, with lines of communication leading directly from him to each individual or organization he was dealing with. At the same time, it was essential to his purposes that each line be kept distinct from the others and that no one at the other end know who was on the other lines. In a sense this was a personal quirk, acquired from his years in the labour camps. In another, it was a profoundly Soviet instinct, inherited from the days when Lenin led a small, conspiratorial party surrounded by enemies. But it also lent itself wonderfully to manipulation and control by the person at the centre of the web. In the Soviet Union it had been a perfect device to oppose the larger and stickier web of Party control. Those involved in it, even in the West, had willingly agreed to play their obedient parts for the sake of the greater cause. But now that Solzhenitsyn was in the West himself, it began to break down. The individuals he was dealing with, though geographically spread, were less numerous and often knew one another, so that, despite the vows of secrecy, they would compare notes and discover a larger part of the picture. On the other hand, they often didn't, and would find themselves involuntarily competing against one another or getting in each other's way. This had been part of the problem with the publication of *Letter to the Leaders*, had also complicated the revision of *The Gulag Archipelago*, and was to cause further problems with the translation of *The Oak and the Calf*.*

There was something absurd in this web of conspiracy, and yet Solzhenitsyn had some cause to be suspicious and afraid, for the Soviet authorities were still determined to discredit and harm him by all possible means. Their actions ranged from petty vindictiveness to elaborate forgeries and physical threats. Upon arriving in Zurich, for instance, and opening up her luggage, Natalia had discovered that all the tape recordings in one suitcase had been erased by the Soviet customs. A few of the tapes had been of Solzhenitsyn reading extracts from his works, but the majority had borne family stories and recordings of the children as babies while learning to talk, all of which had been wiped clean in Moscow.[15]

Shortly after this, Solzhenitsyn learned of an elaborate KGB plot to compromise him by sending forged letters in his name. The effort had been made in 1972, when letters had been sent to Vasili Orekhov, the director of a Brussels organization called the Russian National Association, interested in tsarist military history. The letters, in Solzhenitsyn's handwriting and purportedly signed by him, were posted in Prague and gave a variety of return addresses, one of which turned out to be the office of the Czech airline and national tourist organization. The telephone number on that letter indicated another district of Prague, where both the Soviet embassy and the headquarters of the Czech secret police were located. Evidently the plan had been to lure some Russian *émigrés* from the West to Prague, arrest them, and accuse Solzhenitsyn of having "links with anti-Soviet organizations," but for some reason the plan had misfired.[16]

Solzhenitsyn also learned in Zurich about the sanctions taken against his friends in the Soviet Union and the frantic efforts to erase his name from Soviet history. On the day after his expulsion, an order had been issued by Glavlit† for all Solzhenitsyn's works to be removed from public libraries.‡

---

*Again I speak from experience. My draft translation of the first quarter of *The Oak and the Calf* was secretly shown to a colleague (who was unaware of the identity of the translator) in the guise of a finished product and condemned as "unfit for publication." This story has a happy ending. The project was handed over to Harry Willetts, who has turned out to be Solzhenitsyn's ideal translator. His versions are head and shoulders above those by any other translator into English.

† An acronym for *Glavnoye upravleniye literatury* (Chief Administration of Literature), a shadowy body responsible for, among other things, the censorship in the Soviet Union.

‡ Glavlit was presumably acting at the behest of the KGB, which had produced its own "inspection reports" on Solzhenitsyn's works. Two of these were later reproduced in the *Chronicle of Current Events*, no. 36 (May 1975). On *A Day in the Life of Ivan Denisovich* the KGB had this to say: "The contents of this short novel are ideologically harmful. The author describes events connected with the period of Stalin's cult of personality and tendentiously concentrates on the events in one day in the life of prisoners, and on the severity of their living conditions. There is an exaggerated emphasis on the allegedly unbearable cruelty of the camp regime." And on *Cancer Ward:* "Like his other works, it is written on a labour-camp theme in a rough kind of slang. The author describes the period from 1937 to 1954 . . . exaggerating and blowing out of proportion the mistakes and shortcomings that took place then. He defames our social and political system and libels Soviet reality."

Since only *Ivan Denisovich* had appeared in book form, this meant the simultaneous removal of all copies of *Novy Mir* in which his stories had appeared. At the same time, a series of raids had been carried out on the homes of friends in Ryazan, Moscow, Leningrad, and other cities. In one case the police staged a faked robbery but gave the game away by leaving a note in the typewriter: "We love Solzhenitsyn so much that we took along his work."[17] Vadim Borisov, one of Solzhenitsyn's collaborators on *From under the Rubble*, was officially warned not to correspond with Solzhenitsyn on pain of arrest. Then there was the more elaborate case of Etkind in Leningrad. Etkind had been dismissed from the Herzen Institute and expelled from the Writers' Union mainly because of his friendship with Solzhenitsyn. But Etkind had also been a friend of the poet Iosif Brodsky and had been involved in the compilation of a five-volume samizdat collection of Brodsky's poetry by two young Leningrad writers, Mikhail Heifetz and Vladimir Maramzin. Not long after Etkind's expulsion, Heifetz and Maramzin had been arrested on charges of anti-Soviet propaganda—based on a controversial preface by Heifetz that Etkind and Maramzin had approved—and were later sentenced to five and four years' jail, respectively.[18] Thanks to his confession of guilt, Maramzin received a suspended sentence and was allowed to emigrate, while Heifetz served his term before also emigrating to Israel. Heifetz later concluded that the whole "Case No. 15," as it was called, was part of a wider effort to intimidate writers and intellectuals in the wake of Solzhenitsyn's expulsion and to warn them that henceforth dissent would be kept under tighter control.[19]

Meanwhile, in Zurich anonymous callers continued to telephone threats to his home, especially concerning his children, or offered "sympathetic warnings" against the intentions of Western gangsters. But as Solzhenitsyn said in an interview with *Time* magazine, "My experience has proved to me that all the gangsters in my life come from one and the same organization"— the KGB.

Nor was the propaganda onslaught halted. In the spring of 1974 the Novosti press agency published a short book in several languages called *The Last Circle*, a collection of articles and statements denouncing Solzhenitsyn and supporting the decision to expel him. Included in its contents were many old items, such as the *Stern* and *Literaturnaya Gazeta* articles on his family background, Reshetovskaya's letter to the *New York Times* and her interview with *Le Figaro*, and Vitkevich's statement, but there were also some new titbits, such as an attack by Father Shpiller and an interview with Malyarov, the deputy public prosecutor, in which the latter accused Solzhenitsyn of having deliberately dressed up in old, shabby clothes to answer his summons, so as to give the impression of having only rags and tatters: "Even a fisherman returning from a fishing trip on a rainy day looks more refined." Malyarov alleged that Solzhenitsyn had taken the news of his expulsion quite calmly, had asked to go by train via Helsinki rather than by plane, and had requested some different clothes for his journey to the West.[20] The latter

detail sounds rather suspicious in view of Malyarov's naïve boast that Western reporters who saw Solzhenitsyn in Frankfurt had "unanimously mentioned in their dispatches the splendid brown fur hat of the unexpected guest
and other particulars of his wardrobe." Perhaps it had been Malyarov's idea
to dress Solzhenitsyn up in new clothes and this was his way of claiming the
credit.

In August 1974 the Italian publisher Teti (by arrangement with Novosti)
published a more significant book—*In Dispute with Time*—by Natalia Reshetovskaya.* This was supposedly the volume of her memoirs that she had
been working on since 1969, but it soon became clear that Novosti had cut
them down significantly from the original version, and had done a great deal
of "positive" editing and rewriting. Of the two original chapters that had
appeared in *Veche*, only isolated sentences and phrases had survived. The
overall tone had been changed from friendly and objective to hostile and
sneering, and Reshetovskaya's apparatus of footnotes and references to sources
had been omitted entirely. The story that Reshetovskaya now had to tell was
that of a vain, ambitious, egocentric young man who had been unpopular at
school, had neglected his mother, and had exploited all his friends for his
own ends.

A particularly egregious passage was devoted to the subject of the scar
on Solzhenitsyn's forehead. In twenty years of marriage, wrote Reshetovskaya, it had never occurred to her to mention it or ask her husband how he
had acquired it. "It was only in 1973, a good third of a century after we met,
that I learned the origin of this scar from the distinguished surgeon and doctor of medicine Kirill Simonyan, who had been a classmate of my husband."

The distinguished doctor told her that Solzhenitsyn had sustained the
scar as a result of his "nervous disposition": "You surely must know that
Sanya was very sensitive as a child. He couldn't bear it when anyone in the
class received a higher mark than he did." Such was the strength of this
jealousy, it seemed, that the blood would drain from Solzhenitsyn's face and
he would look as if about to faint. "On one occasion the history teacher,
Bershadsky, began giving Sanya a dressing down, and Sanya really did faint,
striking his head against a desk and inflicting a deep gash in his forehead."

According to Reshetovskaya (or Novosti), Solzhenitsyn's arrest at the
front was his own fault, for he had harboured pro-German and counter-
revolutionary ideas and was by implication a traitor to his country. His
investigation and sentence were just and humane; the KGB interrogators had
bent over backwards to be fair to Solzhenitsyn, who fawned on them and
denounced his friends to save his own skin. "It is paradoxical but a fact,"
wrote Reshetovskaya (or Novosti) at one point, "that the investigation had to
defend people against my husband's calumnies."[21] The latter part of the book
was notably episodic and scrappy, and seemed to proceed on the principle of
describing and discussing only incidents that Solzhenitsyn had used in his

---

* The Italian title was *Mio Marito Solgenitsyn*. Extracts appeared in *Il Tiempo* in June 1974.

works or mentioned in various interviews. In this way it turned into a kind of polemic with him on the nature of the reality he was describing, while revealing few facts that were not previously known.

At the same time, there was surprisingly little about the emotional aspects of Solzhenitsyn's marriage to Reshetovskaya. He was alleged to have been cold and indifferent in later life, and selfish in his domestic arrangements. His affair with the Leningrad woman was briefly described late in the book. But the narrative came to a discreet end in 1964, with no mention of the appearance of her rival, the second Natalia, of the stormy years from 1968 to 1973, of her suicide attempt, and of their negotiations for a divorce, even though the memoirs were dated as having been written between 1969 and 1974.

There were other glaring omissions as well. Stalin was barely mentioned. Solzhenitsyn's Stalin scholarship at Rostov University was referred to euphemistically without indicating the dictator's name. Khrushchev was not mentioned anywhere, not even in connection with *Ivan Denisovich*, nor was Solzhenitsyn's candidature for the Lenin Prize or the confiscation of his archive and his later campaign against the Writers' Union. In short, it was a most peculiar concoction and raised the question of whether Reshetovskaya had anything to do with the final edition at all. If she did, it was only after her own words had been sifted and manipulated by a hidden hand. And the purpose behind it all was inadvertently revealed on page 84 of the English edition. After persistently denigrating *The Gulag Archipelago* and supporting Vitkevich's allegations of betrayal during their investigation, Reshetovskaya purportedly wrote, "And probably neither I nor Vitkevich would ever have addressed ourselves to events long gone by had Solzhenitsyn not discussed these matters in *The Gulag Archipelago*, that same *Archipelago* that has so many pretensions to being 'the voice of truth' and 'the veritable truth.' "22* In other words, the task set by Novosti was still at all costs to undercut *The Gulag Archipelago* and discredit its author, and that was why both Reshetovskaya's life and her husband's had to be twisted to serve the cause. Solzhenitsyn, ran the message, was a petulant egomaniac, disloyal to family and friends, unscrupulous in his overweening ambition, obsessed with the imaginary wrongs done to him and his eight years in the camps, and furiously intent on wreaking revenge on the benevolent country and government that had cherished and reared him.

Not surprisingly, even with such a negative portrait as this, the book was not for sale in the Soviet Union. Nor were the usual decencies observed for the sake of camouflage: no censor's number, no date of printing, no indication of the number of copies. The aim was to influence foreign opinion, and, to this end, translation rights were auctioned in a number of languages and went for fairly large sums.

Solzhenitsyn's initial intention was to denounce the book and attack

* The phrasing was less explicit in the Russian edition. Reshetovskaya made a number of changes to the text while the English version was being translated, and this was one of them.

Reshetovskaya, but on reading it he found it so unconvincing and so feeble that he thought better of it. "What fools they are," he said after reading it. "If they had left it to her, she would have done me far more damage. They've made the book weaker, not stronger."[23] To attack it would only be to draw more attention than the book deserved, and he was proved right, for the translations, when they were published the following year, attracted little notice. He did, however, threaten to prosecute the Italian publisher Teti, who announced a forthcoming volume of Solzhenitsyn's letters to Reshetovskaya, for copyright violation. When the case came to court, a few months later, Solzhenitsyn lost, but for some reason Teti never proceeded with this plan.

As he had shown in his dealings with the Czechs, one of Solzhenitsyn's many concerns during his first year in Zurich was to make common cause with intellectuals from the other countries of Eastern Europe (nearly all under Soviet domination, of course) and bring their joint influence to bear on Western Europe. He had mentioned it in his interview with Cronkite. For the first time in centuries, he said, Russians, Czechs, Poles, Hungarians, Rumanians, Lithuanians, and Germans shared common experiences and had a common point of view, especially on the activities of the West. He had noticed it himself. What was needed now was a dialogue between Eastern and Western Europe. "It seems to me that it is exceptionally important for the West to listen to the united voice of Eastern Europe, for the whole of Eastern Europe together could tell much that is useful and important."[24] His meetings with the Czechs had confirmed him in this idea, as had a brief meeting with Jerzy Giedroyc and Jozef Czapski of the Paris-based Polish magazine *Kultura*. When Vladimir Maximov, who had left the Soviet Union a couple of months after Solzhenitsyn, came to seek his support for a new Russian-language literary magazine to be published in Western Europe, Solzhenitsyn was enthusiastic—on condition that the magazine was not exclusively Russian, but adopted a platform of co-operation with the other peoples of Eastern Europe ("except Marxists"). He also proposed a name for it—*Kontinent*—to symbolize the interdependence of the two halves of Europe, and agreed to contribute occasional articles and extracts from his literary works (he drew the line, however, at joining the editorial board or letting his name appear on the mast-head).[25] When the first issue appeared, in September 1974, it contained a letter of welcome from Solzhenitsyn in which he again emphasized the virtues of unity—first, among the Russian intelligentsia, now scattered in a diaspora; secondly, between Russians and Eastern Europeans; and, thirdly, between Eastern and Western Europe: "The intelligentsia of Eastern Europe speaks with the united voice of suffering and knowledge. All honour to *Kontinent* if it is able to make this voice heard. Woe (which will be not long in coming) to Western Europe if its ears fail to hear." He also contributed an unpublished satirical chapter from the full version of *The First Circle:* "Dialectical Materialism—the Progressive World View."[26]

Unity of all kinds was very much on Solzhenitsyn's mind that summer.

His sudden appearance in the West had brought him into direct contact for the first time with all sections of the numerous and widely dispersed Russian emigration and with its three main "waves": the first, consisting of survivors of the White Russian emigration from the time of the Revolution and the early twenties; the second, consisting of those who had managed to escape during the Second World War; and the third, consisting of Soviet *émigrés* of the past few years, of which he himself was a member (though he rejected the epithet *émigré*). Solzhenitsyn was uniquely popular with all three waves and was well placed to see both the mistrust with which they regarded each other and the warring factions within each wave. *Kontinent*, he hoped, would be a vehicle for bringing them closer together. Another possible vehicle was the Russian Orthodox church outside Russia. In September 1974 the Russian Orthodox Church Abroad was due to hold its assembly in Jordanville, New York, and invited Solzhenitsyn to attend. He declined to go in person but wrote a letter setting out his views on the church and its relations with other branches of the church within and without the Soviet Union. It was a mistake, he wrote, for the Russian Orthodox Church Abroad to continue to quarrel with its rival body, the Russian Orthodox Church of America, and to accuse it of "submission to atheist forces" because of its recognition of the Moscow patriarchate. He himself was one of the Moscow patriarch's strongest critics, but that did not mean that the church in the Soviet Union was dead or completely under the thumb of the government. On the contrary, it was very much alive, and growing in strength all the time. It was wrong to regard it as "fallen" or to think that a genuine leadership of the church could be exercised from abroad. Such internal dissension in the church was a tragedy. It was because of similar dissension in 1917 that the Revolution and Civil War had come about, and indeed the Orthodox church had not been whole or healthy since the great schism of the seventeenth century, when the Old Believers had been persecuted for refusing to accept the reforms of Patriarch Nikon. Since then, the history of the Orthodox church had been one of ever-increasing disunity, and it was now clear that 1917 was the fruit of the reforming efforts of Nikon and of Peter the Great. The only way back, or rather forwards, was to come together with the other churches and promote unification. If this were achieved, a reborn church might even serve as an example to others.

> We as the church must attain forms that are not merely a restoration or a replica of pre-revolutionary forms. They must be of such elevation and so suffused with an unfading sense of search that perhaps even the Western world, seized by an unquenchable spiritual longing, will be drawn to follow us. The incomparable bitterness of the Russian experience indeed holds out such a hope.[27]

There is no reason to doubt the sincerity, indeed the passion, with which Solzhenitsyn held these views. They not only reflected his thinking during his last months in the Soviet Union but were also to run like a leitmotiv through his statements and interviews during his next few years in the West.

But they sat most uneasily with other views that Solzhenitsyn began to express at this time, and above all with his practice, in his private and professional life, of imperiously settling scores with both former friends and opponents. Rather than promoting unity, many of his statements and actions sowed dissension and discord and involved him in those classic *émigré* squabbles that he claimed to scorn.

The first of these had occurred on his very first day in the West, at Heinrich Böll's house, when Dimitri Panin came to see him. Panin had been living in Paris since his departure from the Soviet Union in 1971, and in 1973 had published his reminiscences. Solzhenitsyn had known of his plan in Moscow and had given it his blessing, and Panin had agreed with Solzhenitsyn on the limits within which he would describe their friendship in the *sharashka* and Ekibastuz, and had promised not to deal with events after the date of their release. Panin had kept his word but, perhaps foolishly, had allowed his memoirs to be marketed under the title of *The Memoirs of Sologdin* (the fictional name under which he had been described in *The First Circle*). In Langenbroich, Solzhenitsyn had accused Panin of "exploiting his name in the West" and had asked him to leave, saying that he no longer wished to have anything to do with him.[28] Some eight months later, after hearing from a mutual friend that Panin was ill and in straitened circumstances after an expensive heart operation in Geneva, Solzhenitsyn sent him a cheque, but Panin returned the cheque uncashed. The two men never met or corresponded again.

By the time of the cheque incident, Solzhenitsyn had also quarrelled irrevocably with Zhores Medvedev. In 1973 Medvedev had published his book on Solzhenitsyn, *Ten Years after Ivan Denisovich*, prepared with Solzhenitsyn's knowledge and approval, and also limited to the public aspects of Solzhenitsyn's life and career. Among the illustrations, he had included a photograph of Solzhenitsyn's personal invitation to his planned Nobel ceremony at Svetlova's flat and—at least in the first printing*—a photograph of the reverse side, showing Solzhenitsyn's plan of how to get to the flat. Solzhenitsyn had been informed of this, and he had sent Medvedev a sharp letter on the subject. He had also written criticizing some of Medvedev's statements while in the West and accusing him of capitalizing on his and Sakharov's reputations, but at the time of his arrival in Zurich he still seems to have regarded him as a friend. In the summer of 1974 Medvedev planned a journey to Germany and wrote to Solzhenitsyn to ask whether he might call. Solzhenitsyn replied that he was too busy, and there the matter was left. A couple of months later, Medvedev was invited to Oslo by the Norwegian PEN Club to give a lecture; during a question-and-answer session afterwards, he was asked about Sakharov's candidacy for the Peace Prize (Solzhe-

---

* The initial Russian edition of Medvedev's book appears to have run into a number of difficulties at an early stage, owing to copyright and other problems, and there seem to have been at least two versions, and possibly three. The revised edition that circulated most widely contained among its illustrations neither the text of the invitation nor the plan.

nitsyn's nomination of Sakharov had been carried over from the preceding year, and the interest in Oslo was particularly great: the Peace Prize is awarded in Norway and not Sweden). Medvedev, according to his own account, declared his support for Sakharov but expressed strong reservations about the quality of the prize, suggesting that it had to do more with political than with moral questions.[29] This reply caused umbrage among some of his Norwegian listeners, who drew the conclusion that Medvedev was against awarding the prize to Sakharov, and a letter was sent to Solzhenitsyn (and to *Russkaya Mysl*, the Russian-language newspaper in Paris), accusing Medvedev of attacking Sakharov. *Russkaya Mysl* ignored the letter, but on 11 September Solzhenitsyn wrote a thunderous denunciation of Medvedev, accusing him of having made a whole series of pro-Soviet statements since the preceding summer. "In an astonishing way, Z. Medvedev always knows what the Soviet government would like to hear and says it more cleverly and appositely than the whole paid apparatus of the Central Committee's propaganda section."[30] Solzhenitsyn's letter was sent to the London *Times* (which refused to print it because of its inflammatory language) and to *Aftenposten* in Norway, where it appeared on 20 September 1974. Medvedev was horrified and rang Solzhenitsyn in Zurich. Natalia answered the telephone, refused to let Medvedev speak with her husband, and the conversation apparently foundered in a welter of mutual recrimination.[31]

Medvedev may have been made to suffer partly on account of his brother, Roy, still in Moscow, who had just published two long articles sharply critical of Solzhenitsyn. One, an essay on *Letter to the Leaders*, had made fun of some of Solzhenitsyn's ideas and been given great prominence in the German weekly *Der Spiegel*, while the other was a critical review of volume 2 of *The Gulag Archipelago*, which had appeared in Russian in June. Roy Medvedev, like other dissident readers of volume 2, had had high praise for its literary qualities but disputed some of its facts and took issue with its bitter anti-Marxism and wholesale denunciation of all Soviet political leaders. "Regrettable bitterness," wrote Medvedev, leads Solzhenitsyn "to that very 'impatience and infallibility of thought' that he blames Marxism for."[32]

Indeed, Solzhenitsyn's popularity among his fellow dissidents, both inside and outside the Soviet Union, was somewhat on the wane. Neither *Letter to the Leaders* nor "Live Not by Lies" had been met with much enthusiasm, and further dismay was spread by two press conferences given in November 1974 to launch the YMCA publication, in Russian, of *From under the Rubble*, in which Solzhenitsyn had played a leading role. The first press conference was given in Moscow on 14 November by four authors represented in the collection: Igor Shafarevich, Mikhail Agursky, Evgeni Barabanov, and Vadim Borisov. Their aim in holding the conference in Moscow was to emphasize a point that Solzhenitsyn made later, namely, that "all the articles in this collection . . . were written in our native land and offer solutions not from outside our country but from within." The message was driven home by Shafarevich, who ended his remarks with a diatribe against the very idea of emigration—and, by implication, against all those who had gone into emigration over the past few years. The freedom to emigrate, Shafarevich allowed, should exist in every country, but in the Soviet Union it had acquired an exaggerated importance and had led to a disastrous "emigration of culture," to the departure of the "best representatives of our literature, criticism, and music." In a sense it included Solzhenitsyn, but Solzhenitsyn was an exception because he was the only one who had been forcibly expelled. All the others had left "voluntarily," even if they now claimed that they, too, had been expelled or had been driven out by threats. "Those representatives of Russian culture who left voluntarily simply couldn't withstand the pressure that, for example, millions of believers have withstood for decades. In other words, they lacked the necessary spiritual qualities. . . . And if that is the case, what possible contribution to culture could they make?" As an example, Shafarevich mentioned the case of Andrei Sinyavsky and held up for particular ridicule a phrase from Sinyavsky's article in the first issue of *Kontinent:* "Russia, you bitch, you'll pay for this too!"[33]* Sinyavsky, said Shafarevich, was absolutely right to leave. "It would be pointless for him to put up with discomfort for the sake of this country, and he has nothing at all to offer it."[34]

Shafarevich's remarks received considerable publicity, and two days later, when he held his own press conference in Zurich, Solzhenitsyn attempted to play down Shafarevich's more controversial statements. He, too, however, had already gone on record, in his Cronkite interview, as holding essentially the same views on emigration: "The people who emigrate are generally those who run away to save themselves from our horrible conditions. Much braver people, steadfast and devoted to their country, stay behind to improve the situation." He also criticized Sinyavsky at his press conference, holding his remark to be a blasphemous and impermissible slur on "Mother Russia."

In the rest of his press conference (which lasted close to four hours in his home in Zurich), Solzhenitsyn concentrated on introducing the contributors and their articles. He claimed that "in the last fifty-five years, the Soviet Union has not known a collective work of such scope, with such a serious approach to the problems it poses," and referred to himself and the others as "our movement." Their programme was "in no way political" but existed on another and higher plane. "To create a good and just society we must first become good people. . . . This is why I call the programme that I propose for my country a 'moral revolution.' " The ideas set out in *From under the Rubble*, he said, were an extension and an elaboration of the ideas in *Letter to the Leaders* and "Live Not by Lies," and he could not understand why these

---

*Shafarevich's paraphrase of Sinyavsky was abbreviated—Sinyavsky had written that Russia would have to pay for abandoning and discarding its despised Jews—but the word he took exception to was "bitch," failing to grasp its rhetorical function in Sinyavsky's argument. Shafarevich may also have been settling a score on Solzhenitsyn's behalf, for in that same article Sinyavsky had disparaged literary realism (and therefore by implication Solzhenitsyn's works) as old-fashioned and of limited appeal (according to Sinyavsky, "the flowering of prose" has not yet occurred in Russia in the twentieth century).

had been received so coldly both in the Soviet Union and in the West. Even Sakharov, he was sorry to say, had misunderstood him.* Solzhenitsyn then dealt with Sakharov's objections in greater detail, took a side-swipe at "those antediluvian Marxists" the Medvedev brothers, ridiculed "two Labour prime ministers," Harold Wilson and Gough Whitlam, for their appeasement of communism, and answered Günter Grass's criticism of *Kontinent* for taking money from Axel Springer: "I consider Günter Grass a fine and honest man," he said, "who, unfortunately, lacks a profound insight into the East—like almost everyone in the West, alas!" The Russian *émigrés* would have been glad to accept money for their magazine from the Left, but the Left never offered any. Springer, in any case, was hardly to be compared with a regime that had starved and murdered its own population and that had crushed the Berlin rising in 1953, Hungary in 1956, and Czechoslovakia in 1968. Why did Grass and his colleagues allow their books to be published in the Soviet Union and accept Soviet money for them?[35]

The press conference was a powerful performance by Solzhenitsyn. As Western reporters were beginning to learn, he possessed great self-confidence and total self-control. He could win points as much by charm as by forceful argument. And yet *From under the Rubble* made no more of an impression than his *Letter to the Leaders* and "Live Not by Lies." When asked whether he regarded the book as being on a level with its model, *Landmarks*, he had replied evasively and modestly, though it was clear from his introductory remarks that he did. Yet apart from two of his own three contributions, the articles were lightweight and fugitive, variations on themes that he himself had adumbrated elsewhere, but written by literary amateurs, with none of his passion, sparkle, and mordant wit. Nor were his own contributions the best of their kind. "Repentance and Self-limitation in the Life of Nations," it is true, glowed with a kind of fiery humility (the sort of humility that Tolstoy was very good at, more self-righteous than pride itself), but "The Smatterers" was so brimming with invective against the writings of other dissidents, so bitter and shrill in its contempt for others' opinions and others' ideas, that it hardly rose above the level of monthly journalism. Moreover, it was ridiculously at odds with the humility and penitence that Solzhenitsyn preached elsewhere in the volume. "Self-limitation" for Solzhenitsyn, it seemed, was to be directed towards more abstract entities like "history," "the people," or "other peoples" but not towards individual fellow writers and dissidents either inside or outside the Soviet-Union. In no way could this collection be compared to the classic essays of Bulgakov, Berdyaev, Gershenzon, and Piotr Struve at the beginning of the century, and it only detracted further from Solzhenitsyn's reputation for him to assert that it did. One good thing that eventually came out of it, however, was that it spurred others to reply and to produce answering volumes of their own, and this had been part of Solzhenitsyn's intention.

---

* Solzhenitsyn published a "reply" to Sakharov in *Kontinent*, no. 2 (1975).

Before the year was out, Solzhenitsyn made two more statements to the press. The first, an interview with Janis Sapiets of the BBC's Russian Service, was intended primarily for a Soviet audience and took place one day after his conference with Western journalists. In it Solzhenitsyn repeated many of the ideas he had discussed the day before, but raised two new subjects that were to recur in his statements with increasing frequency in the years ahead. The first addressed the question of how repentance was possible for nations rather than individuals and whether Solzhenitsyn believed in the collective guilt of a whole people. Solzhenitsyn instanced the Germans who after the Second World War had recognized and expiated such guilt. Another example was the guilt of colonizing nations, and he added, "Or take the well-known story about how the British in Austria, after the war, handed over some one and a half million people to the Soviet Union, knowing they would be ruthlessly punished there."* The reference was to large numbers of Russian and Ukrainian *émigrés* from the first and second emigrations who had lived peacefully in Yugoslavia, Austria, and Germany between the wars and during the war but who Stalin had demanded be repatriated as "war criminals" at the end of the Second World War. Solzhenitsyn had heard about them in the labour camps and had heard how "the British betrayed us." Was this not, he asked, an example of collective national guilt? In volume 1 of *The Gulag Archipelago* he had touched on this subject, calling it "the last secret" of the Second World War,[36] and it still festered. "In Britain democracy is well established, there is the right to demand explanations, to ask questions, yet thirty years have passed and it is only now that, with great difficulty, this secret is being unearthed."[37]

The other theme, in a way not unconnected, was the special role that the Russian people was destined to play in history. The Soviet Union, he said, was more than ready for a moral revolution. In fact, that revolution had already begun because the Russian people had retained "spiritual reserves" that were absent elsewhere. "Religion in our country has spread much more widely, and its roots are much deeper than in the West, where nobody has tried to obstruct religion."[38] Through suffering, the Russian people had acquired spiritual depth, and he quoted Shafarevich in *From under the Rubble*: "If . . . to acquire supernatural strength one must go through death, then we can say that Russia has passed through death and can now hear the voice of God."[39]

Solzhenitsyn's last public appearance of the year was his visit to Stockholm in December to collect, four years late, his Nobel Prize for literature. In a short but pugnacious speech at the award banquet, he apologized for having caused the Swedish Academy "so much trouble" but added that he

---

* Several books have been published on this subject since Solzhenitsyn drew attention to it in *The Gulag Archipelago*. Among them are *The Last Secret*, by Nicholas Bethell; *Victims of Yalta*, (published as *The Secret Betrayal* in the United States), by Nikolai Tolstoy; and *Pawns of Yalta: Soviet Refugees and America's Role in their Repatriation*, by Mark R. Elliott. Latest estimates put the number of people repatriated at close to two million.

had had plenty of trouble of his own. However, the Nobel Prize had given him enormous support and prevented him from being crushed by persecution. He wanted to thank the academy for that and to offer thanks also on behalf of "that vast unofficial Russia which is prohibited from expressing itself aloud, which is persecuted both for writing books and even for reading them." Referring to accusations that his award had been a political decision, he commented that these were the words of "raucous loudmouths" who knew no better. "We all know that an artist's work cannot be contained within the wretched dimension of politics." Not surprisingly, the ceremony was boycotted by the ambassadors of the Soviet Union and the six countries of Eastern Europe and Cuba (for whom these words were evidently intended).[40]

Two days later, Solzhenitsyn gave another of his marathon press conferences. He was in an ebullient mood and easily fielded the questions put to him, conscientiously writing them down (apart from those that came to him already in writing) and answering them in groups. In response to a question about Raoul Wallenberg,* Solzhenitsyn revealed that he had been to see Wallenberg's mother but had nothing new to say about the case, except that "a whole epoch" had elapsed since Wallenberg's arrest, in which time imprisoned nationalists in Africa and elsewhere in the Third World had emerged from jail and become presidents and prime ministers, which illustrated the singular cruelty and vengefulness of the Soviet regime. This led on to a question about Amnesty International, which Solzhenitsyn was reported to have criticized. Solzhenitsyn replied that Amnesty International was "a noble idea . . . apparently so much at one with the truth." But because there was so much inequality in the numbers of the arrested and the conditions of their imprisonment between Eastern, Western, and Third World countries, the famous even-handedness of Amnesty, although well-intentioned, was a sham. So much was known about countries in the West and in the Third World that there was no difficulty in obtaining information about prisoners there and applying pressure, whereas in the Soviet case, it was impossible to obtain exact or detailed information, and pressure was limited by the harshness of the Soviet censorship.

Turning to questions arising from his earlier interviews, Solzhenitsyn once more defended his *Letter to the Leaders* and appeared to modify his attitude to democracy. "I am not against democracy as such," he said, "and not against democracy in Russia, but I am in favour of a sound democracy, and I want us in Russia to move toward it smoothly, cautiously, and slowly." This was more positive than anything Solzhenitsyn had said on the subject before, but he remained sceptical about the Western varieties of democracy,

---

*Raoul Wallenberg was a Swedish diplomat who single-handedly helped thousands of Jews escape from Hungary during the Second World War. He was arrested by the Soviet occupation forces after the war and disappeared into the camps, where he was reportedly seen by other prisoners as late as the 1970s. The Soviet authorities maintain that he died in the forties. His fate has become something of a *cause célèbre* in the last few years. There have been international petitions for an inquiry and for Wallenberg's release, all without result so far.

though conceding that the West's problems were "psychological and moral" rather than political. This seemed to leave open the possibility that its political institutions were not so bad, but Solzhenitsyn did not say that. He did say, however, that although his views on the West had not basically changed since his arrival in Switzerland (because "I could see it already over there"), nonetheless, "you can tell from my answers . . . that over here I am beginning to look at things in a different way perhaps."

In other answers, Solzhenitsyn dealt at some length with the views of Roy Medvedev and Medvedev's recent book on Stalinism, *Let History Judge*. There was a new theory coming into existence, he said, that was also gaining popularity in the West. "First they surrendered Stalin, while Lenin was defended. But now it is difficult to defend Lenin, so they surrender him, too, and they retreat to the next trench-line and defend Marx. But anyone who reads Marx carefully will find some perfectly Leninist formulations and Leninist tactics, continuous appeals for terror, violence, and power seized by force." The Soviet system *was* Marxist, and Marxism led inexorably to a Soviet type of society. As for Medvedev's reviews of the first two volumes of *The Gulag Archipelago*, he felt it was somewhat unfair to refer to this as a dialogue. As he put it more pungently on another occasion, "I write a book, he writes a review; I write a book, he writes a review—and they call that a dialogue between equals."[41]

Solzhenitsyn also answered questions about his attitude to an earlier Soviet Nobel Prize winner, Mikhail Sholokhov. In August, Solzhenitsyn had sponsored the publication in Paris of *The Stream of "The Quiet Don"* by a deceased Soviet literary critic whom he called simply "D." The thesis of the book was that it was not Sholokhov who wrote most of his celebrated novel, *The Quiet Don*, but a Cossack writer (who died in the Civil War) named Fyodor Kryukov, from whom Sholokhov had stolen the manuscript. In his introduction to the book, Solzhenitsyn supported the theory that Sholokhov was not the author, instancing Sholokhov's extreme youth at the time of the events described in the novel (he was fifteen) and of the completion of the first volume of the book (when Sholokhov was twenty); Sholokhov's unproductiveness ever since; the mediocrity of what he had produced; and the internal evidence in the book that its author was a Cossack, whereas Sholokhov was an *inogorodni*, or Russian outsider.

Solzhenitsyn had a certain insight into these problems, since he, too, was from an *inogorodni* family and had been brought up in Rostov, on the very edge of the Don Cossack lands described in *The Quiet Don*. And he repeated that he was sure Sholokhov hadn't written the novel. It was common knowledge in the Soviet Union, he said, and had been since before 1929, when five Soviet writers published a letter in which they wrote, "Rumours are being spread that Sholokhov is not the author of *The Quiet Don*. Please let us know the names, and we will take measures via the GPU." This "official reply," said Solzhenitsyn, spoke for itself. On the other hand, Solzhenitsyn said he was not convinced that it was necessarily Kryukov who wrote the bulk of the novel, since the evidence was all circumstantial, and Sholokhov's papers had "unfortunately" been destroyed at the outbreak of the Second World War. But Kryukov was the strongest candidate, and someone other than Sholokhov must have written the bulk of the book. A recent article by Konstantin Simonov in *Der Spiegel* denying the charge was simply ridiculous, and he was surprised at Simonov's stooping to such a task.

Lastly, Solzhenitsyn had some sharp things to say about Western publishing practices. The subject arose in connection with a question about whether Solzhenitsyn had found freedom "in capitalist society." "For a writer who thinks only of his material and of realizing his plans satisfactorily, there is no absence of freedom anywhere in the world," he replied. "He is always free, even in prison." There were, however, external constraints on a writer's freedom, even in the West, and these arose usually as a result of commercial considerations. The main force in publishing were the booksellers, who had so many rights over the way a book was presented and sold that one might be forgiven for thinking that it was they who had written it, rather than the author. Another problem was translations. He had suffered unduly, he said, from hastily prepared and bad translations in a number of countries, mainly because publishers sought translators who would accept very small fees, or else paid so little that good translators were obliged to rush and skimp in order to make a living. This was one aspect of the literary trade that was infinitely better managed in the Soviet Union, where fees were substantial and the translator's standing was high and where, because of the censorship, many of the best creative writers had turned to translation as a means of remaining honest. He was so worried about this problem, he said, that he was now trying to introduce a system in the West of higher rewards for translators—at least where his own books were concerned.[42]

As in Zurich, the conference had lasted about four hours, and again Solzhenitsyn displayed his energy and stamina by ending as fresh and vital as he had begun, earning a round of applause from the assembled correspondents. The postponed visit to Stockholm had been a great personal success, his presence there overshadowing the 1974 winners of the literature prize (Harry Martinson and Eyvind Johnson from Sweden) and most of the other current prize-winners, including the former Irish foreign minister (and former chairman of Amnesty International) Sean MacBride and the former Japanese prime minister Eisaku Sato, joint winners of the peace prize. After nearly a year in the West, he remained a feature of the political landscape, someone whose views were eagerly sought after and widely disseminated, and, despite his skirmishes with the press, a natural celebrity, whose every pronouncement continued to make news. In that sense, the Soviet government's calculations had come to naught. Solzhenitsyn's views were as influential as ever. The slight erosion of his authority as a writer and thinker was entirely his own doing and had no connection with Soviet propaganda. It stemmed from readers' disappointment with works like *Letter to the Leaders* and *From under the Rubble* that had been completed before he left the Soviet

Union and would have been published anyway. Perhaps the only change was that he was now more accessible and had more opportunity to air his opinions, which did indeed contribute to the damage. But he was still the most celebrated writer of the moment, well able to command a world-wide and sympathetic audience.

ON THE MOVE

SOLZHENITSYN'S VISIT TO Stockholm signalled an end to his period of retreat in Zurich and the start of a spate of intensive travelling that was to take him to six countries on two continents within the next eighteen months.

His immediate literary tasks were all completed. *The Oak and the Calf* was with the printers, volume 2 of *The Gulag Archipelago* and *From under the Rubble* were being translated into Western languages, volume 3 of *The Gulag Archipelago* was scheduled for publication in Russian the following year, and in his work on the sequels to *August 1914* he had come to a temporary halt. Thanks to his unexpected arrival in the West, he had suddenly acquired access to masses of new material about the Revolution and Civil War, as well as the opportunity to meet survivors and eyewitnesses of that period. As a result, he was obliged to rethink his plan for the series, and he was content to leave the whole thing in abeyance for a while, until he had had time to examine some of this material and clarify his ideas.

There was one respect, however, in which this new material had had an immediate impact on his writing, and that was on his treatment of Lenin in volumes 2 and 3 of the series. Finding himself in Zurich, where Lenin had spent some of the most eventful years of his exile, Solzhenitsyn had been able to enrich his pages not only with local colour but also with material drawn from the Zurich archives and from people who had known Lenin at first or second hand—he was able to interview, among others, the son of Fritz Platten, the Swiss Social Democrat who had conducted Lenin in the railway carriage through Germany. His two original chapters, written in the Soviet Union and regarded as finished, had grown to eleven. "I believed I already understood what made Lenin tick before I left the Soviet Union," Solzhenitsyn later told an interviewer. "But I learned lots of new facts in Zurich, so that when I reread the things Lenin had written there in the light of what I now knew, they took on a fresh meaning. . . . Basing myself on his books, I hadn't been able to understand him the way I later did in the light of the Zurich material."[1]

During his year in Zurich, Solzhenitsyn had also made some major changes in the conduct of his literary affairs. The fiasco over the American translation of *The Gulag Archipelago* had caused him to take a close look at the publication arrangements for all his books in the West, and he was very dissatisfied with what he found. In the case of *Gulag*, he had stipulated that he would take only a 5 per cent author's royalty (which he intended to put into the special fund anyway) and that all the publishers should take no more than a 5 per cent profit either (this had extended also to the Italian-based Erich Linder literary agency, which had handled the non-English rights on Dr Heeb's behalf).* It had all been done as he directed, but with his ingrained suspicions of Western cupidity, Solzhenitsyn seems to have concluded that there was a virtual conspiracy to defraud him and insisted on undertaking a thorough investigation of his own. In an abrasive meeting with Linder's Zurich representative, Paul Fritz (Linder had also handled the non-English rights for *The First Circle*), Solzhenitsyn demanded a complete accounting for every foreign edition and interrogated him on the seemingly high cost of the book in German—owing, it appears, to a sudden rise in the cost of paper and the German publisher's need to obtain enormous amounts of it at short notice. Solzhenitsyn, according to Fritz, "kept producing little scraps of paper from his pocket" with different questions on them and wrote down the answers in one of his little notebooks. He brooked no argument or discussion. Every time Fritz contradicted him or produced a philosophical reply, "he would give a little smile and change the subject."[2]

The initial exchange had taken place in October 1974 without the presence or participation of Dr Heeb, after which there had been a silence until December, when Solzhenitsyn summoned Fritz and announced that since he was placing all his literary affairs in the hands of the Paris publisher Le Seuil, the Linder agency should renounce and hand over its *Gulag* contract forthwith. Dr Heeb had instructions to terminate their agreement starting on 1 January 1975. Fritz refused, there was a stand-up row, and the subsequent negotiations between Solzhenitsyn, Le Seuil, and Erich Linder in Italy were acrimonious in the extreme, resulting in a compensation payment to Linder for the loss of his contracts and in the assignment of everything to Le Seuil.[3]

An unfortunate casualty of this explosion was Heeb himself. Solzhenitsyn had never shown him any particular warmth after the cordiality of their first meeting at Böll's house, and their relations since then had been on a strictly business footing. The reasons for this may have been partly political.

* It appears that at some point Solzhenitsyn wrote to all the publishers of *The Gulag Archipelago* asking them to donate their 5 per cent profits to the Russian Social Fund as well. It is not known what response he received.

Heeb was a social democrat with left-wing leanings, whereas Solzhenitsyn no longer made a secret of his conservative views or of his conviction that any form of socialism was a Trojan Horse for communism. Personally, the two men were perhaps too dissimilar to have much common ground. Solzhenitsyn seems to have been put off by Heeb's reserve, his very Swiss sense of decorum, his slight stiffness of manner, feeling more at home with Fred Luchsinger's gregariousness and Mayor Widmer's heartiness. Not even when studying Lenin had Solzhenitsyn gone to Heeb for information, although Heeb's father had known Lenin personally and had often met him when the latter lived in Zurich.[4] Solzhenitsyn's dismissal of Heeb, however, was on the grounds of the latter's inability to handle literary matters, an accusation that, even if true, hardly justified the lack of ceremony with which the final severance was made. Heeb and his friends refuse to speak of the matter, but it is clear that the lawyer now regards his former client with considerable bitterness.

With these various chores out of the way, Solzhenitsyn evidently felt free to travel. He began modestly, with some car journeys to different parts of Switzerland, on one of which he intended to meet his celebrated compatriot and now Swiss neighbour Vladimir Nabokov, who lived in Montreux. Solzhenitsyn had long had ambiguous feelings about Nabokov and his work. On the one hand he admired his talent and recognized his mastery of Russian prose, but on the other he deplored the fact that Nabokov had turned his back on Russia and gone his own way. He later expressed his feelings in one of his interviews.

> Nabokov is a writer of genius. However, once he had left Russia, I am sorry to say, he abandoned Russian subjects. He was a member of that generation that could have written marvellously about our Revolution. But he didn't do it. And now it is necessary for people of a younger generation—mine, for example—to carry out this task. In other words, the circumstances of his life (or perhaps it was his own decision) prevented him from placing his colossal, I repeat colossal, talent at the service of his homeland.[5]

According to Natalia Svetlova, as long ago as 1971, Solzhenitsyn had exercised his prerogative as a Nobel Prize winner to nominate Nabokov for the literature prize and had sent Nabokov a copy of the letter.* There had been no reply, but soon after his expulsion Solzhenitsyn had received a note of welcome from Nabokov, saying that the latter would be happy to see him if a meeting was ever convenient. Solzhenitsyn had acknowledged the note, but it was only when he and Natalia planned a tour that would take them through Montreux (Nabokov lived at the Palace Hotel) that he thought of taking up the offer, and he wrote to Nabokov to say that they would be

*Mrs Vera Nabokov has confirmed that Solzhenitsyn wrote to Nabokov after receiving the Nobel Prize, but she is unable to say whether a copy of his letter nominating Nabokov was attached.

passing through Montreux on such and such a date, and would it be convenient to call? If so, would Nabokov mind confirming the arrangement? By the time of the Solzhenitsyns' departure from Zurich, there had been no reply to their letter, and although they telephoned the house each day, no answer had come by the time they reached Montreux. Uncertain of what this silence meant, they reached the hotel, crawled past the end of the driveway debating whether to go in, and eventually decided to drive off, fearing that Nabokov might be ill or have some other compelling reason for not seeing them that day.

Some weeks later, Maximov came tó see the Solzhenitsyns after visiting Nabokov. He told them that the Nabokovs were most perplexed and distressed by their non-appearance. Unaware that Solzhenitsyn was awaiting confirmation, the Nabokovs had ordered lunch for four in a private dining room of the hotel and had sat there for over an hour, waiting for their guests to arrive. When no one came, they had not known what conclusion to draw. Maximov took it upon himself to telephone Nabokov and explain the nature of the misunderstanding, but the two principals did not speak to one another, and in the end did not meet.[6]

In early April 1975 Solzhenitsyn went abroad again, this time to Paris, to mark the forthcoming publication of *The Oak and the Calf* in Russian. At the offices of his regular Russian publishers, the YMCA Press, he was met like a conquering hero—it was as much as some of his humbler Russian admirers could do not to kiss his hand. He was also able to confirm Le Seuil as his French publisher and literary agent, at a crowded press conference for which a hundred journalists had waited over two hours and which was terminated after the sixth question for "lack of seriousness."[7] But Solzhenitsyn was not indifferent to the requirements of publicity. On the contrary, he was now well aware of where the true power of the Western media lay, as he showed by agreeing to appear on a three-and-a-quarter-hour television marathon to answer questions from three French journalists.

A good deal of the discussion centred on Solzhenitsyn's still-controversial *Letter to the Leaders* and his provocative statements to Walter Cronkite. Once more he expounded his message that he was not hostile to the West but simply alarmed by its hedonism and materialism. "It's not your liberty we are criticizing, but the use you make of it." He repeated that he preferred an authoritarian political order because he was against the totalitarian societies that grew out of democracy's failures. He also expressed his admiration for Israel as a state with a guiding idea—"It is the only religious state in the West, a model that is difficult to attain for Western countries"—and he praised the Israelis for "their courage and their firmness in the face of the dangers that surround them."[8]

A theme that was much publicized in the press during Solzhenitsyn's visit was that of emigration. Shafarevich's sharp condemnation of the *émigrés* at the Moscow press conference to launch *From under the Rubble*, and Solzhenitsyn's more guarded remarks in Zurich, had aroused widespread resentment both inside and outside the Soviet Union. Perhaps the weightiest rebuttal came from Yuli Daniel, who had chosen to stay in the Soviet Union despite severe harassment by the authorities after his release from the labour camps and who fully met Shafarevich's criteria of self-sacrifice and patriotism (living in far more straitened circumstances than anything Shafarevich had had to endure). Daniel defended the right of artists to emigrate, saying that while such a course might offer the supreme spiritual test, a true artist was always linked to his homeland by an unbreakable umbilical cord.[9] Another authoritative opponent was Rostropovich, who had emigrated in 1974 in response to the official freeze imposed on himself and his wife, Galina Vishnevskaya, after they had sheltered Solzhenitsyn.* In a long letter published in full in the Russian émigré press, Rostropovich detailed the many sanctions imposed on his work. To remain, he wrote, would have meant spiritual and artistic death. It had been a question of emigration or extinction, and in no sense could such a move be called "voluntary."[10]

Like Yuli Daniel, Rostropovich had diplomatically addressed his remarks to Shafarevich, and he was followed by four other prominent writers who had recently emigrated: Vladimir Maximov, Victor Nekrasov, Andrei Sinyavsky, and Alexander Galich, who upbraided Shafarevich for the "impermissibly insulting tone" of his remarks. But it was clear that beside (or behind) Shafarevich stood the more redoubtable figure of Solzhenitsyn, and it was to him that another distinguished recent émigré, Pavel Litvinov, addressed an open letter that was published in Paris shortly before Solzhenitsyn's arrival, together with Solzhenitsyn's reply.[11] Litvinov took issue not only with the two press conferences but also with some of Solzhenitsyn's other public utterances; he condemned their harshness of tone, intemperate language, and intolerance of the opinions and actions of others, of which the decision to emigrate was only one. He also suggested that a distinction existed between Solzhenitsyn's literary and polemical works: "In your books you destroy the myth that there are quick and obvious solutions to the various problems that people face, yet in your public statements you create the impression that a single solution exists and that you know what it is. And then you start to believe it yourself."

Solzhenitsyn did not address this charge in his reply, on the grounds that Litvinov gave no examples, and in many respects his response was ambiguous. He was not, he said, against emigration as such. "I consider, of course, that everyone who desires to emigrate must have the right to do so freely and that all obstacles placed in the way of emigration are barbarous and a monstrosity." But emigration was "at all times and in all places a weakness, an abandonment of one's native land to the oppressors," and it was wrong to describe a weakness as heroism. He also made a distinction between

---

* Rostropovich and Vishnevskaya were granted permission to leave the Soviet Union after Senator Edward Kennedy personally interceded with Brezhnev during a visit to Moscow. They left with Soviet passports, but their passports were revoked not long after they had arrived in the West.

the first two Russian emigrations, which had been "grand popular movements" of millions of people, and the third emigration, which was nothing
but a "thin slice" off the Jewish emigration to Israel. While it was acceptable
for *émigrés* to "labour incessantly" to restore political liberty and spiritual
health to their native land, and to seek to return to it as soon as possible
(which was more or less the position, according to Solzhenitsyn, of the first
and second emigrations), it was not acceptable to "squander the years thus
saved in making malevolent attacks" on the homeland. Solzhenitsyn had
nothing against those who were "tired," had extenuating personal circumstances, or wished to protect their health, but he simply could not praise
"those persons who claim that their heart calls them to Russia but who march
in the opposite direction. . . . They quit a passionately loved but dangerous
Russia (taking advantage of a possibility that is far from available to everyone)
in order to set themselves up here in the West, to give unilateral explanations
and to act as the authorized ambassadors of an immense country that has no
voice of its own."

Solzhenitsyn did not spell out exactly who was labouring to return spiritual health to the homeland and who was making the malevolent attacks on
it, nor did he commit himself to any direct opinion on the departure and
subsequent actions of Litvinov, Rostropovich, Maximov, Nekrasov, Galich,
and Sinyavsky, but the clear implication was that the members of the first
and second emigrations fitted the first category, while the majority of the
third emigration fitted the second. A small minority—which obviously included
Solzhenitsyn himself—could presumably be exempted from this charge altogether, either because they had kept silent or because they laboured incessantly to re-create political liberty and spiritual health inside mother Russia.
Solzhenitsyn did not answer Litvinov's main charge—that he was guilty of
"laying down a closed system of normative ethics" (in other words, of proposing a set of values of the "either/or" variety, to replace the "either/or" of
the Soviet Communist Party)—and he still seemed to be proposing some sort
of norm for *émigré* behaviour, without spelling out or defining just what it
was that determined whether he was for or against a given individual's actions
and words.

Much of the heat of this battle stayed within the confines of the *émigré*
press and did not impinge on his French audience. They, on the contrary,
were overwhelmed by the force of his personality as seen on television (five
million Frenchmen tuned in—more than double the usual number), convinced by his burning sincerity, and captivated by his charm. *L'Express* called
him "a giant . . . a new prophet, the herald of a great religious movement,"
and attributed his greatness to the enormous suffering he had endured. For
Paris Match he was "a genius . . . the equal of Dostoyevsky," and even for
Jean Daniel, the editor of the independent socialist *Nouvel Observateur* and a
participant in the television programme, who had attracted Solzhenitsyn's
ire as the spokesman for the Left, Solzhenitsyn was "grace personified." But
it was Raymond Aron who best defined the nature of Solzhenitsyn's impact

on the thinking French. Solzhenitsyn's views on Vietnam, Chile, and Portugal could be discounted, wrote Aron, as those of an uninformed exile, but he sowed confusion and consternation because he belaboured the soft underbelly of Western intellectuals and the very point where they were dishonest. Solzhenitsyn was saying, If you turn a blind eye to the big Gulag (in the Soviet Union) why are you so self-righteously indignant about the little ones (in the right-wing dictatorships)? Camps are camps, no matter what colour they are, whether red or brown. The entire Western intelligentsia was guilty to a greater or lesser degree of this error, wrote Aron, and the leftists most of all. But Solzhenitsyn, with "his grandeur, his faith, his love, and his eloquence," had been more than a match for such views.[12]

Within two weeks of these debates, after his flying visit to view the Appenzell election, Solzhenitsyn was in Canada. Unlike the Paris visit, this journey was carried out in great secrecy, and its purpose was for Solzhenitsyn to seek a new place to live. He had been badly shaken by the Holub episode in Zurich and was convinced that the KGB had mounted a large-scale operation there to keep him under surveillance and perhaps plan his assassination. Despite the friends he had made and his easy access to the mountains, he began to find the atmosphere of Zurich claustrophobic. He longed for the wide-open spaces and northern continental climate of his beloved Russia, while wishing to put a much greater distance between himself and its present rulers than Switzerland allowed. Someone must have suggested that Canada was the place to try, and he spent the first two weeks of May touring Quebec and Ontario and inspecting properties.

For the duration of the Orthodox Easter, Solzhenitsyn abandoned his search to stay with an Orthodox priest near Montreal (at whose home he met for the first time his old admirer Father Alexander Schmemann), leading to a flurry of rumours that he had decided to become a monk and was seeking a religious community in which to live, and a house nearby for his wife and family. These rumours were perhaps fuelled by the fact that Solzhenitsyn was travelling without his wife and for some of the time in the company of the Reverend Kirill Bulashevich, an Orthodox priest, and was making a point of visiting the many religious communities dotted about Canada, but they were also the fruit of the great secrecy in which his visit was shrouded. Natalia in fact joined him half-way through his tour, and together they travelled to Canada's western provinces.

Because of his desire for secrecy, Solzhenitsyn refused all requests for interviews but did agree to a short meeting with the Canadian prime minister, Pierre Elliott Trudeau, and taped a three-and-a-half-minute broadcast for the Ukrainian service of Radio Canada International. It was a typically austere and provocative message. Recalling that his grandfather had been Ukrainian, that he himself was one-quarter Ukrainian, and that the fate of the Ukrainian people was therefore dear to him (he addressed them as "dear brothers"), Solzhenitsyn used the occasion to tear into the West once more. During the Soviet famine of 1933, he declared, six million people had died, but "insensitive Europe ignored the tragedy of the Ukrainian people. Even photographs of the dying villagers taken by the American photographer Tom Walker were not printed by Western editors." The difficult situation of the West at present, said Solzhenitsyn, had its roots in the West's incomprehension of the fate of the Soviet peoples.[13]

From western Canada, Solzhenitsyn took a coastal ferry to Juneau, in Alaska, for his first step onto American soil. His destination was Sitka, the former capital of Alaska, seat of Russian Orthodoxy there from the time when Alaska was a Russian possession, and still the site of an Orthodox cathedral and the home of the spiritual head of the Alaskan Orthodox church, Bishop Gregory. Solzhenitsyn spent three days with Bishop Gregory, listening to stories of the Orthodox community in Alaska, inspecting the church's archives, and absorbing the atmosphere. The severity of the climate and austerity of his surroundings appealed to his spartan instincts, and he particularly enjoyed a visit to Old Sitka, about six miles away, with its ruined Fort of the Archangel Gabriel. Founded by the first Russian governor of Alaska, Alexander Baranov, in 1799, and destroyed almost immediately by the Tlingit Indians, it was an eloquent relic of Russia's imperial past.[14]

In early June 1975, Solzhenitsyn moved south to California to visit the Hoover Institution on War, Revolution, and Peace at Stanford University. Like his Canadian visit, this one was unheralded by advance publicity; it was only after he had been there a week that he reluctantly revealed his presence and agreed to make a statement to the press (Hoover's director disclosed that Solzhenitsyn's original intention had been to leave as secretly as he had arrived). He had come to Stanford, he said, to inspect the Hoover Institution's archives on the history of twentieth-century Russia, the richest collection in the West, and had accepted an appointment as an honorary fellow in order to return and do research for his series of novels on the Revolution. The documentation was in many respects unique: "It is the kind of original source material that the Soviets, in order to rewrite history, either destroyed or refuse to make available to scholars." He looked forward to using the Hoover library for the rest of his life.[15]

At some point Solzhenitsyn must have informed George Meany, president of the AFL-CIO, that he was now prepared to take up his invitation to deliver a speech to American union members. Meany announced in mid-May that Solzhenitsyn would speak in Washington at a special banquet to be held in his honour at the Washington Hilton Hotel on 30 June and that Solzhenitsyn would arrive a few days beforehand. Solzhenitsyn then dropped out of sight for a month and did some sightseeing across the country. Among other things, he made a pilgrimage to the California home of Jack London. A part of the attraction of Alaska seems to have derived from his reading of London. According to Bishop Gregory, Solzhenitsyn told him that as a child he had read "everything Jack London ever wrote" and that ever since then he had wanted to visit the "mysterious, unapproachable land" of Alaska.[16] Another visit, lasting for several days, was to a community of Old Believers settled near Woodburn, in Oregon. Solzhenitsyn had long been sympathetic to this sect and wanted to see for himself how successful they had been in transplanting their archaic version of Orthodoxy and conserving its ancient rituals. According to one newspaper, their success had been outstanding: as a non-member of the sect, Solzhenitsyn was not permitted to enter the church (a regulation of which he thoroughly approved).[17]

By the time Solzhenitsyn arrived in Washington, the sense of anticipation there was enormous. As a curtain-raiser, Solzhenitsyn had contributed an article to the *New York Times* called "The Big Losers in the Third World War," which appeared on 22 June. The Third World War, according to him, was already over—it had begun at Yalta (where "the cowardly pens of Roosevelt and Churchill" had signed away the whole of Eastern Europe) in 1945, and just ended with the American defeat in Vietnam. In essence the article was a restatement of the ideas contained in the opening pages of his *Letter to the Leaders*, but more extreme and more despairing. In the thirty years since the Second World War, wrote Solzhenitsyn, the West had "plummeted downwards" in a spiral of enfeeblement and decadence. More countries and people had been surrendered than were ever surrendered following any military capitulation, and that was why it was no empty figure of speech to say that the Third World War was already over and the West defeated. "I have described the situation as it appears clearly to the average man . . . from Poznan to Canton, but Western spirits will need great firmness, and Western eyes great clarity of vision, to discern and accept the evidence of a constant, methodical, triumphant instigation of violence throughout the world emanating from one source for almost sixty years." There was no longer any point in worrying about the Third World War; the task now was to stop the fourth.

Almost simultaneously came the American publication of *From under the Rubble*. Not surprisingly, reviewers concentrated on Solzhenitsyn's own contributions, and in particular on his attacks on the dissidents associated with the Democratic Movement and his arguments for some form of authoritarian rule to follow Communist totalitarianism. These were not much appreciated, and it was borne in on some critics that Solzhenitsyn was much more effective in attacking other people's ideas than he was in proposing positive schemes of his own. A Russian critic in the *New York Review of Books* repeated Litvinov's earlier criticism of the difference between Solzhenitsyn's literary work and his polemics: "Deprived of narrative flesh and stripped of their multidimensional fictional expression, the writer's moral judgments lose their power to convince. They are the same yet different, so that it is always possible to refute Solzhenitsyn's one-sided public pronouncements by examples from his fictional works."[18]

Solzhenitsyn was now in Washington. It had been agreed that he would give two speeches under AFL-CIO auspices, one in Washington on 30 June 1975 and one in New York ten days later. The Washington speech was delivered at the Hilton Hotel to an audience of 2,500 people, and Solzhenitsyn spoke in Russian from notes (his words being simultaneously translated into English). It was a new venture for him, his first full-dress speech in the West, as opposed to interviews and press conferences, and Solzhenitsyn delivered a virtuoso performance, full of oratorical skills, that had a powerful impact on his mainly trade-union audience. His words were frequently interrupted by applause, and at the end he received a standing ovation.

On the face of it, it was another triumph, but to anyone who admired Solzhenitsyn's skills as a novelist and his ability, as an artist, to confront the complexities of society and history without fear or undue prejudice, it was a dismal effort, worse than anything he had done before. Alternating shallow ingratiation ("Brother workers . . . as a former bricklayer, foundry man, and manual labourer . . .") with gross flattery ("the USA has long shown itself to be the most magnanimous, the most generous country in the world"), Solzhenitsyn pandered outrageously to his audience's prejudices with cheap gibes about Western capitalists being allegedly responsible for "the Soviet Union's powerful military and police forces . . . that are used to crush our freedom movement in the Soviet Union" and their "burning greed for profit that goes beyond all self-control and all conscience." Tendentious half-truths ("world democracy could have defeated one totalitarian regime after another. . . . Instead, it strengthened Soviet totalitarianism, helped it bring into existence a third totalitarianism, that of China, and all this finally precipitated the present world situation") gave way to brazen demagoguery ("if all these countries together [England, France, the United States, Canada, Australia, and other countries] couldn't defeat Hitler's little Germany, what are they going to do today, when more than half the globe is flooded with totalitarianism?"),[19] and the resulting diatribe was more appropriate to a tub-thumping machine politician (or a crusading union leader) than to the painfully honest and truth-seeking creator of *Ivan Denisovich*, "Matryona's Place," and *The First Circle* or to the unflinching but scrupulous annalist of *The Gulag Archipelago*.

One can only speculate about the reasons for this extraordinary outburst. Although his press conferences had provided a sort of introduction, Solzhenitsyn was unaccustomed to speaking publicly and virtually off the cuff to a large audience. Moreover, he was in Washington, capital of the world's "other" superpower, and completely unfettered, with the freedom to say whatever he wanted. The experience must have been quite disconcerting, and to hear his words being greeted with spontaneous applause, in place of the sullen silences or curses he was used to experiencing in the Soviet Union, utterly intoxicating. How many times, in the prisons and camps, had he and his comrades vowed to trumpet the truth about their situation to the world if they survived! He had kept his compact, but from within the Soviet Union it had still been difficult to speak clearly and in terms that compelled the world's attention. Then it had seemed that if only he went abroad—or *when* he went abroad—he would be able to make up for all those difficulties, to shout his message to the skies, and then the world would understand. With his profound (and profoundly Russian) belief in the power of the word—

confirmed, it seemed, by the Kremlin's fear of the word—he could not help imagining that "the truth" would shake sceptical Westerners to the core and totally transform their attitude to the Soviet Union. A year in the West had undermined that belief, and it would appear that in sheer desperation, he had allowed the embittered convict to take over and speak in the enraged tones of a disillusioned son of the Gulag. This must have accounted for the shrillness and extremism of his harangue. And yet the pity of it was that in allowing himself to be carried away and in devoting so much of his time to the sins and omissions of "the West" (in his eyes apparently a monolithic structure for the past seventy years), which he poorly understood, he allowed his genuinely valuable insights into the nature of communism to be overshadowed, and in the end was left with only a few minutes into which to squeeze some salutary warnings about the danger of a spurious and one-sided *détente*. Even here the very emotionalism of his speech led to a misunderstanding of his words. Like Sakharov and many others, Solzhenitsyn sought to distinguish between a sincere and durable *détente* (accomplished by genuine disarmament) and the simulacrum that the Soviet Union was currently trying to pass off on the West as the real thing. But because of the extravagant tenor of the speech as a whole, he was widely reported as being totally against *détente* and in favour of a new "cold war."

In New York on 9 July, in another one-and-a-half-hour speech delivered to an audience of about a thousand people, Solzhenitsyn refuted this charge. The speech was punctuated by homely Russian proverbs, Khrushchev-style, and there were some more extravagances, notably an obsession with Portugal and Solzhenitsyn's conviction not only that Portugal and India had been lost to communism but that Italy and France were destined to follow shortly. There were some more tendentious readings of recent history, some selective quotations from Marx, Engels, Lenin, and the American press, but in sum the speech was infinitely more restrained and thoughtful than its Washington counterpart. On this occasion Solzhenitsyn concentrated on what he knew— the psychology, social and political assumptions, and world view of the Soviet leadership, and the social conditions of the Soviet people—instead of airing his prejudices about life in the West. The picture he painted of an implacable, omnipotent, and cunning communism toying with the West was grossly exaggerated, but he did ram home the essential truth that the goal of communism remained what it had always been—in Khrushchev's immortal words, "to bury capitalism"—and that the Soviet press, despite the Soviet leaders' pious words about *détente*, continued to present its readers with a chorus of hate about all things Western and the West. He repeated his wish for a true *détente*, calling for a policy of "the open hand" (to show no weapons were concealed) to replace the distorted *détente* of the moment, but said that until that was forthcoming, it was necessary to maintain trade sanctions and to withhold loans or technology from the Soviet state. The Communists boasted of their strength and superiority. In that case, said Solzhenitsyn witheringly, **"all I ask of you is that as long as this Soviet economy is so proud, so flour-**

ishing, and yours is so rotten and so moribund, stop helping it. Where has a cripple ever helped an athlete along?"[20]

Only in one place did Solzhenitsyn apply his literary skills to the matter in hand.

> There is a word, very commonly used these days, called "anti-communism." It is a very stupid word, badly put together. It makes it appear as though communism were something original, basic, and fundamental. Therefore it is taken as a point of departure, and anti-communism is defined in relation to communism. Here is why I say the word was poorly selected. . . . The primary, the eternal concept is humanity. And communism is anti-humanity. Whoever says "anti-communism" is saying, in effect, "anti-anti-humanity." A poor construction.

Solzhenitsyn proceeded from this to produce a fallacy of his own—"That which is against communism is for humanity"—but it did not detract from the value of the original insight.*

Solzhenitsyn's private movements, as usual, were shrouded in deep secrecy to avoid the attentions of the press. In Washington he had had confidential meetings with George Meany and a few union leaders and also with Jesse Helms, the Republican senator who had proposed him for honorary citizenship the preceding month (but who was too conservative for even the AFL-CIO to invite to the banquet at the Hilton). He had also had a reunion with Rostropovich (who had recently moved to the United States and apparently bore Solzhenitsyn no ill will over the emigration controversy) and did some private sightseeing in a hired car. In New York, Solzhenitsyn met the Russian community after attending a service in one of the Russian Orthodox churches ("the atmosphere was electric and there was complete silence until Solzhenitsyn entered and executed a deep bow before the iconostasis," according to one eyewitness),[21] and visited the library of Columbia University to inspect its Archive of Russian and East European History and Culture. While there, he announced his intention of sponsoring a series of books on Russian history since 1900 that would "correct the false impressions of the Russian Revolution based on memoirs by the revolutionaries themselves and other writers," and invited Columbia scholars to participate in the project. Since, only the day before, he had ridiculed the director of Columbia's Russian Institute, Marshall Shulman, by name in his New York speech, and had let it be known privately that he regarded the Columbia faculty as leftists and fellow-travellers, out of touch with Soviet reality, his proposal did not meet with much enthusiasm. Nor was his cause helped by his failure to find time to meet the couple of dozen students of Russian who had waited for four to five hours to meet him.[22]

The preceding year, when reproached by Walter Cronkite with having

---

*The texts that appear in Russian in the Collected Works are slightly different from what was distributed by the AFL-CIO in English. I have used the AFL-CIO texts, since these represent what listeners actually heard at the time.

"nothing good" to say about America, Solzhenitsyn had protested that he couldn't judge America until he had been there personally and even lived there for about a year. He still hadn't lived there, but at a ceremony in New York, at which he was presented with a key to the city by Mayor Beame, he did have some warm things to say about his drive across America from California. New York and Washington, he said, expressing his familiar dislike of large cities, "are no more representative of your country than Moscow or the old St Petersburg of ours." He had formed some fond impressions of the places where "American history had emerged" and had been impressed by the strength and firmness of the Middle West and by the freedom and vitality of the country as a whole. He could now understand, he said, some of America's reluctance to face up to the great problems of the outside world: "Sometimes while I am here, I almost forget them myself."[23]

A few days later, Solzhenitsyn repeated these sentiments on NBC television's "Meet the Press," where he was questioned by four American journalists. It was a much briefer and tidier session than his rambling marathon on French television, less controversial, and had infinitely less impact. His answers, especially to some pointed questions from Norman Cousins and Peter Lisagor, were evasive and added nothing to what he had said in his speeches, but he did try to clarify his ideas on Western democracy in response to a comment about his *Letter to the Leaders*. He did not, said Solzhenitsyn, regard Western democracy as in decline, and he cited Switzerland as a shining example of a democracy that functioned beautifully. But he was concerned about the future. "What I did say was that there is a decline in the will and self-confidence of the democracies, and my purpose is somehow to inspire them, inspire their will, make their will firmer and more self-confident."[24]

It was an interesting illustration of Solzhenitsyn's present view of his personal mission. Formerly, his mission had been to document and to inform the world of the monstrosities of Gulag and the deformities of the state that had created it. Subsequently, he had taken upon himself the mission—primarily in his literary works but also in his journalism—to explain the origins and nature of the Russian Revolution and to reinterpret modern Russian history. Now, finding himself in the West and dismayed by what he saw as the West's indifference to the Soviet menace, he had apparently taken upon himself this new task of awakening the West to the danger and also, as it were, of interpreting the West's history to itself. It stemmed, perhaps, from a noble impulse and a sense of duty, but where Solzhenitsyn seemed to have the power and talent to measure up to his Russian missions, in the West he appeared to be overreaching himself, and among those not swayed by his charm, authority, and charisma, a sense of disillusionment began to be perceptible.

A good example was Norman Cousins. Noting, after his appearance with him on television, Solzhenitsyn's commanding presence and the zest and power of his words, Cousins nonetheless regretted that Solzhenitsyn's persuasiveness seemed to rest more on personal conviction than on a command of historical perspective or concrete data. "In the Soviet Union," wrote Cousins, "his dissent was majestic, but it is the fact of that dissent even more than its substance that gives him his claim on history. The man has become more important than his platform. The symbolism supersedes the message."[25] Cousins was apparently surprised to discover that Solzhenitsyn was not in the tradition of Milton, Paine, Mill, Jefferson, and "not even" of Edmund Burke.*

Similar misgivings were being voiced in Washington, to which Solzhenitsyn was due to return from New York. Critics wondered whether the Soviet government hadn't been exceptionally clever in allowing Solzhenitsyn to come to the West. Speaking and writing from inside the Soviet Union, he had possessed an unchallenged (and virtually unchallengeable) authority, but his words now, coming from a free man in no immediate danger, seemed to have lost much of their power. He was perceived by many as a "cold warrior," a stick-in-the-mud conservative with mystical leanings, a crony of George Meany and the conservative hardhats of organized labour, and no different in his opinions from the hundreds of thousands of other embittered exiles from Eastern Europe whom many Americans regarded as defenders of obscurantism and reaction.

These critics might have damaged Solzhenitsyn's reputation irreversibly in the political circles he hoped to influence, had he not been inadvertently saved by the blunderings of President Gerald Ford. Ford had informally indicated, soon after Solzhenitsyn's arrival in the United States, that he would be amenable to a meeting with him if Solzhenitsyn should go to Washington. But on 2 July he had announced that he would not meet Solzhenitsyn, "on the advice of the National Security Council." When pressed to elaborate, some aides of the president disclosed that questions had been raised about Solzhenitsyn's mental stability, and someone had suggested that since Solzhenitsyn was in the United States "to promote his books," the president should not get mixed up in such commercial enterprises[26] (having posed with "the cotton queen" on the White House lawn the week before and with Pelé, the Brazilian soccer player, a few days later). The president had declined an invitation to the AFL-CIO banquet, as had Vice-President Rockefeller, Secretary of State Henry Kissinger, and the leaders of both the Senate and the House of Representatives (Secretary of Defense Schlesinger and Secretary of Labor Dunlop had gone in the end, along with the U.S. ambassador to the United Nations, Daniel Moynihan).

It was Solzhenitsyn's views on *détente* that made him so unpopular with the Ford administration. In the very week that Solzhenitsyn returned to Washington, American and Soviet astronauts were due to link up in space, symbolizing what was to be a new era of friendship and co-operation between the two superpowers. The U.S. government was anxious not to spoil the

---

*Among foreign critics of the American speeches were two former staunch supporters of Solzhenitsyn, Raymond Aron and Milovan Djilas.

atmosphere, which was why Solzhenitsyn's presence was so inopportune. Some of Ford's political opponents, however, notably Senators Jesse Helms, Henry Jackson (co-author of the Jackson amendment), and Clifford Case, seized on this opportunity to embarrass the president by inviting Solzhenitsyn to Washington to address a group of members from both houses of Congress. Almost immediately, on the eve of Solzhenitsyn's television appearance, Ford back-pedalled and let it be known that if Solzhenitsyn was to seek a meeting with him, he would be happy to see him. But now Solzhenitsyn had the satisfaction of declining in his turn. "I am not here as the guest of the American government," he told his television audience, "but of the AFL-CIO. My purpose is to appeal not to the government but to the American people as a whole."[27]

It was a fitting response, but there can be little doubt that Solzhenitsyn was disappointed. Nor could he miss the irony that after having failed to meet (as he had hoped) the Soviet leaders in Moscow, he had now been spurned by the American leaders in Washington as well.

Perhaps for this reason he was at pains to emphasize, in his remarks to the congressmen, how pleased he was to be speaking for the first time to "participants in your country's legislative process, whose influence in recent years has spread well beyond the limits of American history alone," and he was particularly corrosive in his denunciation of the "loathsome and repulsive" system with which America was hoping to come to terms. He equated *détente* with "diplomatic shovels" ready to "bury and pack down bodies still breathing in a common grave" and described himself as a messenger from the voiceless millions of the Soviet camps, sent to break through "that calamitous wall of ignorance or of unconcerned arrogance" that he had found in America. He appealed to the members present to rise above the narrow concerns of party and state and see themselves as leaders "on whom depends whether the course of world history will tend to tragedy or salvation." He had done his best to warn and prepare them but was unsure whether he had succeeded. "I have done what I was bound to do, and what I could. So much the worse if the justice of my warning becomes evident only some years hence."[28]

The pantomime of the presidential invitation, however, was not over yet. In the course of the two weeks since President Ford's original refusal to meet Solzhenitsyn, White House spokesmen had twice changed the official reason for the snub. First it was said that the president's timetable was too crowded for him to fit Solzhenitsyn in, and then that the president, not knowing what he was supposed to discuss with Solzhenitsyn, had seen no point in a meeting "without substance." Most commentators concluded, even when they disagreed with Solzhenitsyn's views, that it had been a crass blunder on President Ford's part not to see him, and a political and personal gaffe that reflected more on President Ford than on the author (the president's mail on the subject was said to be unusually voluminous and unusually hostile). The debate rumbled on for the rest of the month, during which it emerged that Henry Kissinger was the person responsible for having advised the president against the meeting. In a speech defending his position, Kissinger declared that there was "no alternative" to *détente* and said that while Solzhenitsyn was a great writer whose suffering entitled him to be heard, he was convinced that if Solzhenitsyn's views were adopted as the American national policy, "we would be confronting a considerable threat of military conflict."[29] It was also suggested in the press that after changing his original decision, President Ford had sent numerous messages to Solzhenitsyn via Senators Helms and Jackson to visit him, but that Solzhenitsyn had insisted on a written invitation before he would accept. Solzhenitsyn later denied this story but did make it clear that what he had wanted with the president was not a "symbolic" meeting but a discussion of the issue of *détente*, and this had been the final stumbling-block. From Alexandra Tolstoy's farm in upstate New York, where he released this information, he denounced President Ford for agreeing to journey to Europe to sign the Helsinki Final Act, which had just been concluded by the thirty-five nations participating in the European Security Conference in Finland. Ford was going, said Solzhenitsyn, "to sign . . . the betrayal of Eastern Europe, to acknowledge officially its slavery forever."[30]

In the final analysis it was a moral victory for Solzhenitsyn against the odds. Just as in Moscow he had failed to meet the "leaders" but had broadcast his views to the world through the world's press, so now in Washington he had profited from the American government's blunders to get double the publicity and attention his visit might otherwise have merited. His charisma and his single-mindedness had again proved spectacularly (if misleadingly) effective, and Solzhenitsyn could be forgiven for thinking that his mission to the West had not been undertaken in vain.

Solzhenitsyn's last port of call in the United States was Vermont. After spending three days in seclusion in a quiet inn in the western part of the state, he travelled to Northfield to spend a further three days at Norwich University, at the invitation of the Russian department there, headed by Nikolai Pervushin. While on campus, he took the opportunity to play a rare game of tennis, and at the end of his stay he complimented Norwich on its "efforts to preserve Russian culture without the Soviet imprint." He was reported to be impressed with both the climate and the countryside of Vermont, and news that he had retained a prominent Vermont lawyer to act for him provoked speculation that he was thinking of settling there.[31] Certainly, Vermont had all the advantages of Canada, in addition to belonging to a political superpower. It would be possible to be both physically isolated and yet close to the centres of real influence if the need arose.

During his stay in Vermont, Solzhenitsyn spent a part of his time writing a long article about his impressions of the two American branches of the Russian Orthodox church,* which was to involve him in yet another controversy with his fellow Russians, a controversy that threw a great deal of light

---

*The Orthodox Church in America (OCA) is autocephalous but maintains relations with the church in Moscow, whereas the Russian Orthodox Church Abroad does not recognize any other Russian church. In Paris the Russian Orthodox church is under the authority of the patriarchate of Constantinople. It recognizes both Moscow and the OCA.

on his current assumptions and intellectual processes. The article appeared in no. 116 of the Paris *Vestnik* as "Letter from America," and in it Solzhenitsyn criticized the two branches for their mutual hostility and for their inability to unite with the Ukrainian Orthodox church. Among other things, he reversed his position on the Orthodox Church in America and now berated it for having established relations with the Moscow patriarchate, for accepting orders from it, and, in effect, for making a deal with the Soviet Communist regime. The Russian Orthodox Church Abroad, on the other hand, which was separate from the Orthodox Church in America, was noteworthy for its "implacable hatred of Bolshevism" and its attachment to pre-revolutionary Russian traditions, a stand that Solzhenitsyn now found infinitely preferable to the posture of the other church.

Solzhenitsyn did not stop there, however. According to him, "all three" branches of the Russian Orthodox church outside the Soviet Union (the two churches in America and the church based in Paris)* were guilty of gradually moving away from and forgetting the Orthodox population of Russia, and the resulting split, if it took place, could be catastrophic not just for Russia but for the whole world.

> In the year and a half of my exile, I have become more convinced than ever that sufficiently powerful hands and sufficiently stout hearts simply do not exist in the West: everyone here is so enfeebled by prosperity and so preoccupied with increasing it that either the world will soon perish or else the hands to battle hell will be found only in the enslaved East. For the world history of the twentieth century, Russia is the key country. . . . That is why a preoccupation with Russian problems is not so very narrow after all, but of universal significance.

It was the duty of the Russian churches abroad to preserve their links with Russia and to carry the message of Russian Orthodoxy to the rest of the world. But to do that they had to be worthy of Russia, to make a spiritual sacrifice, to atone for the sins of the past. The primal sin of the Orthodox church was the great schism of the seventeenth century, when the Old Believers had been driven from the church and persecuted. He himself had visited the Old Believers in their settlements in America and had been overwhelmed by their piety, their courage, their stamina, their fierce devotion to the old traditions, and their Russianness. Similarly, in Alaska he had been astonished by the tenacity of the faithful: "One has got to admit that the culture brought to them from 'backward' Russia has proved to be spiritually superior to that 'better' televisio-technico-consumer culture offered them by today's United States." It was the duty of the Russian churches in exile to repent and take two major steps: one, to refuse to have any dealings with the satanic Communist regime and, two, to heal the schism with the Old Believers and welcome them back into the fold. For the Old Believers had much to teach the

---

*Technically speaking, there are not "three branches." See note p. 919.

other churches, and "in the Russia of the Old Believers the Leninist revolution would have been impossible."[32]

It may seem that this obscure debate (if we do not take Solzhenitsyn's assertions of its global significance at their face value) about the fate of the Russian Orthodox church abroad would not be of much interest, but as the responses showed, it revealed, in a particularly clear way, some of the preoccupations and methods that Solzhenitsyn was bringing to his polemical declarations on both politics and religion, as well as some of the problems those preoccupations and methods posed. Solzhenitsyn's apocalyptic view that the world was on the brink of a major crisis, for instance, had been voiced in both Washington (we face "a threat to the world") and New York ("We are approaching a major turning-point in world history, in the history of civilization"), and in the latter he had repeated his view that the world faced a turning-point similar to that dividing the Middle Ages from the modern era. In his speech to the congressmen, he had elaborated on this in speaking about "the oncoming combination of a world political crisis with a shift in the spiritual values of a humanity exhausted and choked by the existing false hierarchy of values," and in his television remarks he had hinted at what was now fully spelled out—namely, that it was the mission of Russia, which "has been forced to undergo such spiritual experiences, such spiritual burdens, and has had to undergo such growth that it has now, I think, more experience than any other country in the world" to speak to the West as "a voice from the future" and ultimately to save it from perdition.

Responses to Solzhenitsyn's letter came from his two most faithful and fervent supporters in the West, Nikita Struve, editor of the *Vestnik* (and a director of the YMCA Press, Solzhenitsyn's Russian-language publisher), and Father Alexander Schmemann, Solzhenitsyn's favourite preacher in America and the man who had once pronounced him a living literary classic and a prophet. Both men asserted that Solzhenitsyn had got many of his facts wrong, had exaggerated the seriousness of the squabbles between the churches, and had overestimated the virtue of the Old Believers. Struve pointed out that the Russian Orthodox Church Abroad had much in common with the Old Believers, for in both, hostility to evil tended to turn into intolerance of fellow believers and steadfastness into bitterness, while a total rejection of the modern world had led to an immoderate idealization of the past, and especially of tsarist Russia (the fact that this also described Solzhenitsyn's position was not spelled out by Struve). Father Schmemann put his finger even more fearlessly on what was wrong with Solzhenitsyn's letter in the eyes of a convinced admirer. What saddened and perplexed him, he wrote, was Solzhenitsyn's failure to check his facts, his willingness to repeat malicious gossip, the unfoundedness of his accusations, and above all the letter's inexplicable tone of exasperation. Schmemann charitably ascribed this asperity to some delusion on Solzhenitsyn's part and to his having inadvertently adopted the usual, condescending tone of Russian intellectuals whenever they discussed church matters. He could not refrain from pointing out, however, that the Solzhenitsyn of *The Gulag Archipelago* and *August 1914* was completely different from the Solzhenitsyn of the letter. In the former he had done his homework, mastered the facts, and written with a "creative conscience," none of which was in evidence in the letter.

This increasingly common view of Solzhenitsyn's strengths and weaknesses carried all the more weight in coming from one of his most dedicated champions, but Schmemann went much further than that. It was clear, he wrote, that Solzhenitsyn's obsession with the Old Believers and their schism from the main church was not fortuitous, but occupied a key position in his thinking, and this was because Solzhenitsyn was convinced that the great schism of the seventeenth century had been the reason for Russia's downfall and had led inexorably to the disaster (and second great schism) of the Revolution. Schmemann was inclined to agree with Solzhenitsyn, but for quite the opposite reasons. Solzhenitsyn's call for repentance and reunion, wrote Schmemann, could be divided into two parts. With one of the parts—repentance for the harsh persecution of the Old Believers once the split had taken place—everyone could agree, and Schmemann pointed out that, contrary to Solzhenitsyn's self-righteous assumption that he was preaching something new, it was the consensus among Orthodox believers and had become official church policy. The second part of Solzhenitsyn's appeal, calling for repentance because the Old Believers had been right and were closer to the true faith, was unacceptable to Schmemann, and in his view turned the truth on its head. The Old Believers had not been the innocent victims of revolutionary zeal on the part of the main church. On the contrary, it was they who were the revolutionaries, who had rebelled against the church in the name of a false utopia, and who had been the first in Russian history to succumb to the temptation of ideology. It was the first time that the Russian consciousness had given in to certain characteristic temptations—a love of false absolutisms, a tendency to splits and alienation, an inclination to "escape" from history into apocalyptic fears and utopias.

For Schmemann, "ideologism," as he called it, was the chief fruit of the great schism, and ideologism inexorably led to "the absolutization of a single historiosophical schema, which, taken as an absolute truth, is no longer subject to verification by reality, but on the contrary, itself becomes the sole criterion for reality's understanding and evaluation." It was obsession with ideology that had captured and torn Russia apart, and this was the result of the psychological temptations and "ambiguous maximalism" spawned by the schism. This explained the attraction of the Old Believers for radicals of both the right and the left. "One day it will finally be admitted as a self-evident truth that all ideologies, whether they be of the 'left' or the 'right,' directed towards either the past or the future, give birth to the same type of person: someone who is above all blind to reality, although he appears to be addressing it, for the sake of radically changing it, with all his will and with the totality of his ideological faith."[33]

Schmemann stopped there. As he pointed out at the end of his article,

Russian literature had generally avoided the temptations of ideologization, and that was one of the keys to its greatness. Solzhenitsyn was a part of Russian literature (indeed, Solzhenitsyn's was the loudest contemporary voice warning against the dangers of ideology). But although Schmemann drew no conclusions, it was hard not to find certain parallels between the vehement ecclesiastical maximalist blinded by his utopian visions and the thundering political prophet of the Washington and New York speeches, or not to see a Solzhenitsyn who was both a part of Russian literature and a roistering preacher who quoted his opponents out of context and spoke with an accumulation of rancour and resentment that did not appear justified by the facts. The second Solzhenitsyn was not against ideology as such, but only against one type of ideology. "Those who do not have a full democracy," as he delicately described some right-wing regimes in his Washington speech, "should be protected by the USA from Marxism," for "that which is against communism is for humanity." In other words, "My enemy's enemy is my friend." Was this not Marxist ideology turned inside out, and equally an ideology of its own?

Simultaneously with this seemingly esoteric dispute, Solzhenitsyn was enveloped in a controversy of a more personal and literary nature. His literary memoir, *The Oak and the Calf*, had been in circulation for some months now, had been read by almost the entire *émigré* community, and, more importantly, had had time to filter back to the Soviet Union and be read there. On one plane the book was an intensely personal memoir of Solzhenitsyn's literary career in his homeland and a blow-by-blow account of his epic struggle against the authorities, ending with his expulsion in 1974. The book gained enormously from being in a quasi-diary form, from the freshness with which Solzhenitsyn had been able to set down his impressions, and from the zest and gusto with which he had confided his thoughts, prejudices, hopes, and fears to paper, apparently for himself alone (although, as emerged later, he had always had eventual publication in mind).

The high points in the book described the climaxes of Solzhenitsyn's career: the publication of *Ivan Denisovich*, his letter to the Writers' Congress, the award of the Nobel Prize, and his expulsion, but there were other notable features as well, above all his portrayal of the *Novy Mir* editor, Alexander Tvardovsky, and their stormy friendship. There was also the question of style. In its mixture of high-flown literary rhetoric, cool analysis, colloquial asides, and salty comment, it came closest to some of the racier parts of *The Gulag Archipelago* in the rest of Solzhenitsyn's *oeuvre*, but was unique in terms of its personal and autobiographical content and its certain element of gossipy immediacy. It was stimulating and exciting to read and must be accounted one of Solzhenitsyn's very best books.

However, from the beginning there was also a persistent note of unease in Russian readers' responses to the book, a substratum of discomfort that was expressed only verbally to begin with but that eventually surfaced in print. The grounds for the criticisms naturally varied, but they can be summarized more or less as follows. First, there was Solzhenitsyn's by now ingrained propensity to have his cake and to eat it. Characteristic was his introduction, where he managed both to disparage the whole idea of literary memoirs, which he called "secondary" literature of little moment (perhaps with his own earlier detraction of Ehrenburg and Paustovsky in mind) and to pave the way for five hundred pages of explanation of his motives and actions from 1962 to 1974. Secondly, there was the outsize egotism of the narrative. Solzhenitsyn had placed himself squarely at the centre of the literary and political universe of the sixties and seventies, and the entire world was described as rotating around his axis. There was a certain grandeur in this defiant fidelity to what were clearly Solzhenitsyn's true feelings about himself, but it lent itself too easily to hypocrisy and bathos to sit comfortably on the autobiographical narrator throughout 500 pages. Passages like the ones in which he solemnly described himself, without irony, as "a sword in God's hand" sent to smite His enemies, and numerous other sentiments of that nature, were difficult to bring off in the mid-twentieth century. There were also the all-pervading military metaphors. "They were lined up in battle array, but before they could sound the charge, I gave them a 144-gun salvo and meekly resumed my seat in the hanging smoke,"[34] was how he described his initial statement at the Writers' Union secretariat meeting to discuss *Cancer Ward*. If he could not be Samsonov in real life, it seemed, he would be the Samsonov of the Writers' Union.

But the aspect of the book that provoked most criticism was the consequent disparagement of almost everyone else with whom Solzhenitsyn came into contact, and above all of Tvardovsky. Solzhenitsyn's portrait of Tvardovsky will remain one of the finest things in Russian memoir literature ("I raised a monument to him," he protested as the tide of criticism began to rise),[35] but it is also a prejudiced portrait in which Tvardovsky's weaknesses are exaggerated at the expense of his strengths, while Solzhenitsyn's picture of himself is exactly the reverse. Thus, in many parts of the narrative a drunken, unstable, erratic Tvardovsky, by turns arrogant and submissive, a Party grandee at the mercy of his political masters and without the courage of his convictions, is contrasted with a heroic, all-seeing, all-knowing (but cunning) Solzhenitsyn, hampered by the weaknesses of his friend and ally. This tone was carried over into most of the other portraits in the book. Friends were for the most part referred to neutrally or in words of faint praise, whereas enemies were pinioned and dispatched with merciless vigour. Among former friends and allies to suffer retrospective condemnation were Zhores Medvedev and, of course, his former wife Natalia Reshetovskaya, whose role during his last few years in the Soviet Union was depicted as part of a sinister political manoeuvre rather than the desperate flailings of an abandoned woman. Others to come under the lash were Valeri Chalidze, who was accused, in so many words, of making a deal with the KGB; Veniamin Teush and Ilya Zilberberg, for criminal negligence in mishandling his literary archive; Vladimir Lakshin, for influencing Tvardovsky in the direction of Party orthodoxy; and most of the rest of *Novy Mir*'s editorial staff, for putting their magazine before Solzhenitsyn's contributions to it. Even Sakharov, whom Solzhenitsyn handled, on the whole, with kid gloves, was condescended to and allotted a peripheral role in the struggle for human rights.

The responses came in a pained and not very coherent letter from Tvardovsky's daughter, Valentina Tvardovskaya, a much sharper and more penetrating article by Roy Medvedev, a long and detailed rebuttal by Vladimir Lakshin of Solzhenitsyn's description of Tvardovsky and *Novy Mir*, and eventually a whole book by Ilya Zilberberg chronicling the events surrounding the confiscation of Solzhenitsyn's papers in 1965. The first three maintained that Solzhenitsyn's portrait of Tvardovsky was a travesty. To the extent that some of their indignation was provoked by the "naturalism" of Solzhenitsyn's portrayal, particularly in the now-notorious scene of Tvardovsky's drunken reading of *The First Circle* in Ryazan, it can perhaps be ascribed to the overall prudishness of Russian literary taste. Nadezhda Mandelstam had provoked similar outrage with the frankness of some of her descriptions of writers in the second volume of her memoirs—Russians like their writers on a pedestal. But the weightier objections were to Solzhenitsyn's depiction of Tvardovsky as a powerless lightweight, and of *Novy Mir* as a Party journal not much different, in principle, from the reactionary *Oktyabr*.

Tvardovskaya pointed out that in Solzhenitsyn's memoirs, he and Tvardovsky were made to represent opposed principles: Solzhenitsyn was the wise, far-seeing hero who understood everything, while Tvardovsky was blinded by his Party membership and doomed to vacillate. But in reality, she wrote, the opposition was of a different nature. It was Solzhenitsyn who was doctrinaire, who "craved simple solutions and unambiguous formulae," for whom a negation of the entire Soviet system was sufficient, whereas Tvardovsky was a complex thinker, highly dissatisfied with the life he saw around him, but not content just to dismiss it and throw out the baby with the bath-water. Tvardovsky had been aware of Solzhenitsyn's simplistic notions and extreme nationalism and had often had to exercise great self-discipline not to quarrel with him, wrote Tvardovskaya. She made many other points about her father and *Novy Mir*, but her most telling accusation was that of hypocrisy. "While asserting the supremacy of morality over politics," she wrote, "you deem it possible . . . to overstep all rightful limits. You allow yourself the unscrupulous use of things you have heard or seen through keyholes and of third-hand rumours. . . . While inviting people to 'live not by lies,' you relate with unbridled cynicism, though not without a certain coquetry, how you made deceit a rule in your dealings not only with those you considered your enemies but also with those who held out a helping hand to you, who trusted you and supported you when times were hard."[36]

Roy Medvedev took a similar line but concentrated, in his article, on *Novy Mir*'s political position. It was a travesty, he wrote, to describe *Novy Mir* as akin to conservative journals like *Oktyabr* or *Ogonyok*. It was never "on its knees," as Solzhenitsyn had alleged, nor did it blindly follow the Party line. On the contrary, it persistently pushed against the limits and was frequently successful, as in the case of Solzhenitsyn himself. In all this Tvardovsky's had been the leading role. "From my conversations with Tvardovsky," wrote Medvedev, "I gathered that by defending Solzhenitsyn before the highest authorities, he was exposing himself to danger, but he also liked Solzhenitsyn and felt hurt when he was unjustly attacked by critics or his behaviour was worrisome." Medvedev pointed out, as had Tvardovskaya, how anxious Solzhenitsyn had been to receive the Lenin Prize, despite his protestations in *The Oak and the Calf* to the contrary, and how in conversation with other writers he had praised Lenin and the early days of the October Revolution.[37]

Of a rather different order of authority was Vladimir Lakshin's extended essay "Solzhenitsyn, Tvardovsky, and *Novy Mir*." If Solzhenitsyn's memoir was in part the case for the prosecution against Tvardovsky and *Novy Mir*, Lakshin's was the case for the defence. He had been impelled to pick up his pen, he wrote, because he had been one of the main actors in the drama unfolded by Solzhenitsyn, and the closest witness to Tvardovsky's motives and actions. In his book Solzhenitsyn had "insulted the memory of a man who was very dear to me, whom I regarded as a second father," he had "offended" many of Lakshin's colleagues, but above all he had "poured arrogant scorn on the journal which was the very cradle of his own literary career" and had "besmirched the cause of that journal which, in the eyes of millions of people . . . was a worthwhile and honourable cause."[38]

Lakshin's defence of Tvardovsky was more or less along the lines of those mounted by Tvardovsky's daughter and Medvedev, but he was able to furnish it with a wealth of illustration and of inside knowledge about the relations between Tvardovsky and Solzhenitsyn that were beyond the reach of the others, and, by analysing many of the episodes in Solzhenitsyn's book in minute detail, he was able to demonstrate quite convincingly the ways in which Solzhenitsyn had misunderstood the editor's character or misread simple gestures and phrases.

But unlike his predecessors, Lakshin also went over to the attack. He had once considered, he wrote, that what Solzhenitsyn had said as a writer was far more important to men of goodwill than his "ill-considered interviews and improvised tirades on some burning political topic of the moment," and he had therefore thought it wrong to criticize him, but now it was time to speak out frankly and without restraint. *The Oak and the Calf* was "neither memoir nor history," because Solzhenitsyn preferred not to mention a great many things that had occurred, and described others in misleading terms. Many of the personages in his book were nothing more than "lampoons bearing the names of real people." As for Solzhenitsyn's three main charges against Tvardovsky—of cowardice, drunkenness, and pride—Lakshin wrote, "I declare that everything said about Tvardovsky in this vein is either a blatant untruth, rooted in Solzhenitsyn's hopelessly obtuse incomprehension of Tvardovsky's nature and character, or is that nasty, slimy, slanderous kind of half-truth that is worse than a conscious lie." Solzhenitsyn had violated all the canons of decency and good taste in his portrait of Tvardovsky. Therefore, wrote

Lakshin, "I shall be rude, too: supposing someone, in the role of virtuous moralist, were to start discussing the ins and outs of the personal life of the 'calf' himself and to expose what is known about him from hearsay? Or started collecting stories of his meanness and ingratitude from people who have helped him or are close to his family?"

It should not be ignored that Lakshin, too, had been criticized in *The Oak and the Calf*, albeit less harshly than many others, and therefore had his own scores to settle. For the most part he declined to discuss these criticisms in detail but maintained that many of them stemmed from a failure of psychological insight on Solzhenitsyn's part and from Solzhenitsyn's insincerity in personal relations. Whereas Tvardovsky, according to Lakshin, had been direct and sincere, Solzhenitsyn was devious and cunning. "For a long time, in my heart of hearts, I discounted the nagging feelings of distaste which Solzhenitsyn's behaviour evoked in me, and I tried to explain away his tactlessness as 'the foibles of genius,' eccentricities whose meaning I preferred not to examine too closely in order not to be disillusioned." Solzhenitsyn, however, brooked no half-measures: either one agreed with him and followed him unquestioningly or else one was beyond the pale. "That is why I think that, with all his tremendous gifts of artistic insight, he is doomed to be perpetually disappointed in other people, to live in a world of illusions and phantoms, and to be hopelessly prone to error in his judgement of broader political perspectives, because his criteria derive only from himself and his immediate circumstances."*

What Lakshin was describing was the classical disposition of the creative writer guided above all by his intuition. In that sense, perhaps, this last criticism was not necessarily so grave, though it did have a bearing on Solzhenitsyn's claims to political insight, and it identified a point of political difference that was not irrelevant to the larger debate about Solzhenitsyn's memoir. For Tvardovskaya, Medvedev, and Lakshin could all be identified as belonging to a particular "party"—the "party," if one may put it that way, of the loyal opposition and of *Novy Mir*. Whatever the merits of their criticisms of Solzhenitsyn's behaviour and his handling of the facts (and they were not all fair), there stood behind these criticisms the larger issue of political belief.† A clue to their attitude could be found in Lakshin's charge that Solzhenitsyn had besmirched "the cause" of *Novy Mir*—the cause, in brief, of democratic socialism. What Lakshin, Medvedev, and Tvardovsky's daughter (and Tvardovsky himself) had in common was that "we believed in socialism as a noble ideal of justice, we believed in a socialism that was human through

---

*Solzhenitsyn replied to many of Lakshin's criticisms in his "Sixth Supplement to *The Oak and the Calf*," published in *Vestnik RKhD*, no. 137 (1982), where he accused Lakshin of quoting him out of context, of not understanding the point of *The Oak and the Calf*, and of being too bound by his loyalty to socialism to be honest and open in his criticisms.

†Other former friends of Solzhenitsyn who more or less shared these views and had begun to move away from him included Boris Mozhayev, Efim Etkind, and, most notably, Lev Kopelev, who had taken great exception to Solzhenitsyn's *Letter to the Leaders* and also found fault with *The Gulag Archipelago*.

and through, and not just with a human face." Since they had once believed that Solzhenitsyn shared these views (he had indeed once shared them), his "apostasy" in their eyes was all the greater and more painful, especially since his authority was so high. And now their differences with him about his interpretations of the past were also part of a debate about what Russia's future should be.

Somewhat apart from these responses to *The Oak and the Calf* stood Ilya Zilberberg's book *A Necessary Conversation with Solzhenitsyn*. Zilberberg, a former Zionist activist in the Soviet Union, had emigrated to Israel in 1971 and then moved to England, where he found work as a lecturer. Zilberberg was impelled to write his book by a sense of outrage over Solzhenitsyn's distorted, as he saw it, account of the confiscation of his papers and over his slighting of his friend (and Zilberberg's mentor) Veniamin Teush. The book was far from a diatribe, and what made it especially interesting was the view of Solzhenitsyn it offered from the vantage point of a younger generation of human-rights activists. Starting from Solzhenitsyn's own comment to Tvardovksy that, as a writer, he owed "as much to the Russian forced-labour system as to Russian literature," Zilberberg pointed out how important a role the psychology of a son of Gulag had played in the memoirs of the "calf": "extreme caution, secretiveness, distrust of others . . . self-camouflage, time-serving, a willingness and ability to dissimulate and lie, to be cunning and brazen, constant fear, an exaggerated sense of danger and belief in the worst . . . fear of making mistakes," and so on. All this, wrote Zilberberg, was the poison with which Solzhenitsyn had been infected in Stalin's camps and which he had involuntarily brought back with him and imported into his relations with others in the "normal" world of Moscow and Ryazan in the fifties and sixties. It was this camp psychology that had forced him into the military mould in his thinking and his obsession with dividing everyone he met into allies or enemies, helpers or wreckers, fellow spirits or traitors.

Of course, Solzhenitsyn had laboured mightily in his life to find an antidote to these poisons, and his book was the story of his search for such an antidote, yet the poison was still there, and it was just such a poison that the younger human-rights activists had been able to eliminate and transcend thanks to their youth. In this sense, Solzhenitsyn was an anachronism, not because he had nothing to teach the younger generation, but because he had taught them only too well, while remaining incapable of assimilating his own teaching.

> You, an old camp hand who had waited for years for a final struggle with the system of tyranny that you had written an encyclopaedia about and condemned to death—when it came, at last, to the final clinch, before the eyes of the whole world and having the support of millions of living and dead allies, you proved so helpless and bewildered that you stood up at the first command of a representative of the prison system that you had damned. Yet a totally unknown Jew who was struggling for his right to go to Israel yelled down the telephone to a representative of the same system summoning him to the KGB: "To see you? Vol-

untarily? Never! . . . Only when you deliver me in handcuffs!"

What has happened is this: both personally and as a representative of the "terrible past," by your life, your torments, your inexpressible agonies, and then by your works, you have liberated us representatives of "the present" more quickly and successfully than you have liberated yourself.

This "failure" was a tragic personal failure but also the price of Solzhenitsyn's success, the price of his survival, as Solzhenitsyn had demonstrated in *The Oak and the Calf*. For these "sketches of literary life" were sketches of "normal" literary life in the Soviet Union and, as such, "a searing exposure and merciless condemnation of those forces of evil that have seized your country and threaten the world. They are a condemnation of the state order, political system, and ideology that proclaim artistic creation a crime, turn writing into a conspiratorial activity and the writer into an underground plotter, obliged to dissemble, intrigue, lie, go into hiding, fight . . . and almost commit suicide."[39]

Zilberberg's point about the damage to Solzhenitsyn's psychology had been made by Lakshin: he was "the offspring of our terrible century, the prodigy who has absorbed all its inspiration and its degradation. . . . As well as the best and loftiest of human qualities, his psychology also bears the stamp of the concentration camp, of war, of totalitarianism and the atom bomb—the chief features of this age."[40]

Although they came near to it in some of their comments, none of Solzhenitsyn's critics (nor his—less voluble—supporters, for that matter) seems to have grasped the essentially didactic purpose behind Solzhenitsyn's memoir, which was to demonstrate to the whole world, but particularly to his fellow Russians, how it was possible in practice to "live not by lies."* In a sense, Solzhenitsyn was making the supreme sacrifice. In his book he had wholly renounced his own ego, the personal Solzhenitsyn, with wives, friends, and relatives, with private hopes, griefs, and fears, in favour of the public Solzhenitsyn as exemplar, as the knight on a white charger, the searcher after the holy grail. Hence his ability to write about himself virtually in the third person, to describe himself, without blushing, as God's instrument. He was indeed, in his own eyes, only an instrument, and he seems to have taken literally what Lakshin wrote of him in anger: "He is leading us towards the light, and no one is supposed to ask questions—we must *believe* in him. If Solzhenitsyn summons us to humility and repentance, then naturally everyone must repent. . . ." Lakshin added, "except him," and asserted that in spiritual matters, "Solzhenitsyn does not recognize equality,"[41] but the essential point remained. Solzhenitsyn had been writing in the tradition of the old

---

*Ilya Zilberberg perhaps came closest: "Your book is about how, at a certain stage in your life, you were able to struggle free, and therein lies its unique value. Rising from your knees was not easy for you—at times it was sheer agony, for you were whipped to your feet. After each blow you winced with pain and groaned, but you slowly stood up, and after each blow you felt yourself freer, bolder, and stronger. . . ."

saints' lives, but he had taken on more than mere hagiography: the exemplary life was his own.* And the result was a final irony: this in many ways most personal of his books, with its vivid colloquial style and seemingly free expression of his emotions and prejudices, was at the same time rigidly controlled in the service of a practical and spiritual message. Perhaps here lay that extra twist of tension that made it, from the literary point of view, one of his best.

*One is irresistibly reminded of a seventeenth-century predecessor and Russia's first "modern" writer, the archpriest Avvakum, whose *Life Written by Himself* has more than a few similarities with Solzhenitsyn's memoir. Grigori Pomerants, a historian who has circulated many essays in samizdat, has also pointed out in his samidat essay "A Dream of Just Retribution" (later published in *Syntax* [Paris], no. 6 [1980]) that for a million people Christianity began with reading 'Matryona's Place.' A million people (if not more) took the first step towards the light with Solzhenitsyn (and not with Tvardovsky or *Novy Mir*). It is not for Solzhenitsyn to say so, but we can and must: *Gulag* alone means more for the moral development of our country than the whole of *Novy Mir*." Lakshin, writes Pomerants, was more or less correct in his appraisal of Solzhenitsyn the man, and fair to his talent as a writer, but he failed to appreciate the spirit that had spoken through Solzhenitsyn. An American critic, Maurice Friedberg, has indicated another apt parallel with Solzhenitsyn's book: the memoirs of Russian revolutionaries of the turn of the century (which Friedberg compares to medieval saints' lives in form and intention).

50

TALKING TO
THE EUROPEANS

I N OCTOBER 1975 volume 2 of *The Gulag Archipelago* appeared in translation
into a number of languages, including English. After the sensation caused
by volume 1, it was inevitably something of an anticlimax, especially since
volume 2 was longer than the first volume (in English, 712 pages as opposed
to 660) and contained more analysis and less description, with a consequent
loss of immediacy. Understandably, it sold considerably fewer copies than
its predecessor and suffered, in market terms, from having the same title as
volume 1.

Nevertheless, its publication was an event, and it held a particular interest for American readers, so recently exposed to the force of Solzhenitsyn's
personality and rhetoric. Professor Leonard Schapiro in *The New York Review
of Books* remarked that an "intellectual era" had elapsed since the publication
of volume 1, just over a year before. Solzhenitsyn had then been a mystery
to Western readers, an enigma wrapped in the aura of martyrdom created by
his expulsion, and for many months after that a silent hermit in the heart of
Switzerland. But now he had begun to travel and to reveal himself to reporters and the television cameras, had voiced and published a great many opinions, and had become the subject of a vast literature of comment and criticism.
He had also become known as the most vocal, controversial, and perhaps
influential opponent of *détente*, all of which had created a new climate for the
appearance of volume 2 of his master-work.[1]

For some the publication came as a welcome antidote to the dismay and
doubt sown by Solzhenitsyn's American speeches among many of his admirers.
As Patricia Blake (a long-time admirer) put it in *Time*, "The passage from
inquiry to advocacy, from exposition to exhortation, from literature to poli-

tics (or proselytism) has disabled many a Russian writer, including Gogol and Tolstoy. *Gulag Two* comes to us as a reminder of Solzhenitsyn's immutable achievements."[2] For others it was an opportunity to look for clues that would throw light on Solzhenitsyn's present attitudes.

The subject matter of volume 2 was, above all, the pervasive network of labour camps created by Stalin as the basis of a vast and elaborate system of slave labour, intended to hasten the industrialization of the Soviet Union. Solzhenitsyn's exhaustive anatomy of this system, resting partly on oral accounts by ex-prisoners and partly on obscure and hard-to-obtain archival material, was difficult going in parts, but the bill of indictment was formidable. From start to finish the Gulag had claimed 66 million lives, according to Solzhenitsyn's calculations (25,000 perished in the construction of the White Sea–Baltic Canal alone), and in its heyday there were never fewer than 10 to 15 million men, women, and children behind barbed wire. While these figures were high, they did not provoke much dissent among commentators, and most of Solzhenitsyn's documentation was confirmed as generally accurate. But considerable controversy was caused by his underlying thesis that the camps were by no means solely a phenomenon of Stalinism but were implicit (and, in a small way, explicit) in Lenin's political philosophy as well. Stalin was but a blind follower and executor of Lenin's will (who in turn was carrying out Marx's prescriptions) and not at all an originator in this field. Furthermore, those who defended Lenin and heaped all the blame on Stalin were guilty of bad faith, and did so only to save their beloved Marxism from disrepute.

These views had already caused something of a furore among dissident circles in the Soviet Union, especially among those who took the "loyal oppositionist" view of Roy Medvedev and his sympathizers and still spoke of a possible return to "Leninist norms" (Medvedev had already written a well-publicized rebuttal in a review of the Russian edition), and they now provoked further debate in the West. They certainly went a long way towards explaining the vehemence of Solzhenitsyn's present animus against all forces of Marxism and communism and provided a theoretical framework for what had formerly seemed like arbitrary and provocative statements. Equally revealing were Solzhenitsyn's account of how these views had been formed in (and by) the camps, the description of his rites of passage as a loyalist trusty at Novy Ierusalim and Kaluga Gate, the stunning admission of his brief enlistment as an informer at the peak of his conformist period, and the unfolding of his long, slow path to enlightenment in the Marfino *sharashka* and at Ekibastuz.

The picture of Solzhenitsyn that emerged was of an individual who had heard, seen, and suffered much but who had been saved by his religious faith and a return to traditional Russian Christian values. First had come his discovery that "the line separating good from evil passes not through states . . . or between political parties, but through each human heart," then the conviction that the struggle with evil must therefore take place "within each human being," and finally an implacable hostility to all forms of materialism for their falsification of these truths and their location of the moral battlefield not in individuals but in society. It was for this reason that Solzhenitsyn was offering *The Gulag Archipelago* not only as an act of national repentance and contrition but also as a personal confession of guilt and complicity in the larger crime. As in *The Oak and the Calf*, he called on others to emulate this feat of "self-limitation" and contrition.[3]

Gulag Two went a long way towards rehabilitating Solzhenitsyn's reputation with English and American readers, but there were still problems. Even Professor Schapiro, a profound admirer, was obliged to concede that Solzhenitsyn's counsel of "uncompromising perfection" held difficulties for most normal mortals (though he absolved Solzhenitsyn of the charge of hypocrisy). He conceded that Solzhenitsyn's "fanaticism" often led him to exaggeration, especially in the political sphere, that his "extreme intolerance" towards dissidents (not to speak of others) with opinions at variance with his own was calculated to make him more enemies than friends, and that Solzhenitsyn was "not entirely free from the irritating tendency of so many Russian émigrés to dismiss all the work of Western historians of Soviet Russia . . . as little more than a regurgitation of Soviet propaganda"—as one of the better Western historians, Professor Schapiro was sensitive to (and resented) this charge. So long as the debate was restricted to Russian subject matter, however, and to a discussion of Soviet policies and Soviet society, dialogue was possible, for Solzhenitsyn had thought profoundly about these questions and was writing from long and bitter experience.[4]

As if to confute the apologies and exegeses of his admirers, Solzhenitsyn immediately jumped back into the whirlpool of American politics. From his home in Zurich he sent the *New York Times* an article on the dismissal, in November, of the American secretary of defense, James Schlesinger, by President Ford. The article appeared on 1 December and blamed Henry Kissinger for Schlesinger's downfall, alleging that the defense secretary had been sacrificed on the altar of a false *détente*. Solzhenitsyn accused Kissinger of being ignorant of Soviet psychology, of presiding over a policy of "unending concessions," of bringing about the West's "worst diplomatic defeat" in thirty years (in Vietnam), and of arranging at best only a shaky peace in the Middle East. Kissinger was a "capitulator," a loser, a diplomatic simpleton, who was turning the West's "surrender of world positions" into "an avalanche." As for President Ford, he had acted without decency or foresight and should at least have consulted his allies first, for Schlesinger, "a man of steadfast, perceptive, and brilliant mind," had been responsible for the defence of the entire free world. His dismissal, though an event of a different order of magnitude, had caused in America's friends feelings of "pain, bewilderment, and disillusionment" akin to those produced by the assassination of President Kennedy and by the "inability or lack of desire of the American judicial authorities to uncover the assassins and clean up the crime." The bathos, lack of proportion, and clumsiness of Solzhenitsyn's analogy with the Kennedy assassination and the tone of contemptuous dismissal with which Solzhenitsyn discussed the failings of the not necessarily popular Kissinger were resented by most Americans, who found his remarks "naïve," "clumsy," "outrageous," "interfering," and "self-destructive." They consoled themselves with the thought that Russian novelists were not the only ones with a penchant for making crass political statements. Mark Twain, Dos Passos, and Steinbeck (to name only three) had been equally silly in their time,[5] and they were perhaps relieved that the proposal to grant Solzhenitsyn honorary American citizenship had been allowed to lapse by Congress.

In the course of the autumn of 1975 Solzhenitsyn made several statements denying newspaper reports about one or another aspect of his private life, congratulated Sakharov on the award to him of the Nobel Peace Prize, expressed public support for Vladimir Osipov and Igor Shafarevich, and in early December issued an appeal to Russian *émigrés* who were "older than the Revolution" to write to him with their reminiscences of the period 1917–22. Also in December he gave a long and interesting interview on mainly literary and autobiographical topics to Georges Suffert, editor of the Paris-based magazine *Le Point*, which had just made him "man of the year." And in February 1976 he was off on his travels again, first to England, then France, and then Spain.

Solzhenitsyn arrived in England on 19 February and stayed for ten days. His visit was in most respects a rerun of his earlier forays to France and the United States: a prime-time television interview, a radio broadcast, visits to one or two universities, a talk with his publishers, and the rest of his movements shrouded in secrecy. In contrast to his stay in America and Canada, however, there was no travelling, apart from a visit to Oxford and Stratford-upon-Avon, and Solzhenitsyn showed remarkably little curiosity about the country he was visiting. For most of the time, he and his wife stayed in their small hotel in Windsor under false names (later they moved to London for a few days), and except for early morning walks by the Thames, they spent most of their days, when not occupied with official duties, in their room. Indeed, they virtually camped there, refusing to go down to the dining-room for meals, consuming bread and salami that Solzhenitsyn bought in nearby shops, and drinking glasses of tea made with a portable electric element. This element caused a minor crisis at the beginning of their stay, because it was French and wouldn't plug into English sockets; the manager offered to send to Solzhenitsyn's room as much tea as he desired, but Solzhenitsyn would not hear of it: he sometimes drank tea in the middle of the night, he said, and would not dream of troubling the maid (in similar fashion he had insisted on carrying his own suitcases on arrival at Victoria Station).[6]

The English countryside, it appears, did not impress Solzhenitsyn, nor did Stratford-upon-Avon. In Oxford he declined to tour the colleges and spent most of the day closeted with his latest (and best) English translator, Harry Willetts. In Windsor he seemed equally unimpressed with Eton, and in London, when taken to the National Gallery and Trafalgar Square to do some location shots for his television programme, had no time to inspect the gallery's pictures. He did like Windsor Castle, however, and surveying Trafalgar Square from the gallery's steps, proclaimed it fit for an imperial capital. His visit to the gallery led to an incident that also amused him. On being summoned to a side door and informed in reverential tones that "Alexander Solzhenitsyn is here," the gallery's caretaker responded curtly that it was a Sunday, adding, "I don't care if it's God himself, he's not coming in." The caretaker was wrong, of course: television can accomplish many things beyond the power of God, and one of them was to open the National Gallery on a Sunday.[7]

Solzhenitsyn found time to visit the House of Commons during question time, when Prime Minister Harold Wilson and the Tory party leader Margaret Thatcher were debating the best means to help people emigrate from Eastern Europe, and to visit the BBC's Television Centre and Russian Service. At the Television Centre he scandalized the top brass by preferring to watch the end of a videotaped film on Eastern Europe to lunching with them in the executive dining-room upstairs, and at the Russian Service startled the staff by declining wine and requesting Coca-Cola, which no one had thought to provide. At the Russian Service he produced from his pocket a detailed list of criticisms of the way the service was run, together with a correspondingly long list of suggestions for improvement, and read them to the assembled staff.[8]

The high point of his stay was undoubtedly the hour-long television interview broadcast by the BBC's top news and current affairs programme, "Panorama." Solzhenitsyn repeated his conviction that Russia was about "seventy to eighty years" in advance of the West, spiritually speaking, that the West had declined more rapidly and catastrophically in the two years since he had arrived than before, but that he was not "a critic of the West," simply a critic of the West's weaknesses. The West had given up not just "four, five, six countries" in the last two years but "all its world positions" and had done a great deal to strengthen Soviet tyranny. "At the moment the question is not how the Soviet Union will find a way out of totalitarianism but how the West will be able to avoid the same fate." The nuclear-disarmament debate was a side-issue, he said, irrelevant to the main threat. "Nuclear war is not necessary to the Soviet Union. You can be taken simply with bare hands." And *détente* was meaningless without an ideological *détente*. The Soviet Union could reverse its policy of *détente* overnight, and the West would be left floundering, for the West required at least a year or two to make the same change, which made it a very dangerous path to enter upon. Solzhenitsyn attacked the press once more for trivializing and misrepresenting what he had had to say earlier, and in some interesting comments on *The Gulag Archipelago*, he reaffirmed his belief in the power of the seriously written word to affect history. "If today the three volumes of *The Gulag Archipelago* were widely published in the Soviet Union and were freely available to all, then in a very short space of time no Communist ideology would be left. For people who had read and understood all this would simply have no more room in their minds for Communist ideology." He added that, in his view, the Soviet authorities had expelled him out of weakness but that whereas, two years ago, he had hoped to return home "very soon," the Soviet Union had since grown so strong that it would take longer—if they did not assassinate him first.[9]

The response to Solzhenitsyn's interview was astonishing. Bernard Levin in the *Times* printed a breathless account of a prior meeting with Solzhenitsyn at a cocktail party ("There was no need to ask him where he gets such inner strength and integrity; this is a man who walks with God and makes one understand what 'Holy Russia' once meant") and went on to compare Solzhenitsyn's television performance with Martin Luther nailing his manifesto to the doors at Wittenberg (with references to Thor, Dostoyevsky, and Socrates along the way). The *Guardian*'s television critic wrote, "He talked like an angel. You could hear the great whoosh of wings that makes great orators seem to hover a foot or two off the floor." Michael Davie in the *Observer*, perhaps with tongue slightly in cheek, likened Solzhenitsyn to Charlton Heston playing Moses, and the *Sunday Telegraph* wrote that Solzhenitsyn's appearance was an event whose magnitude it was impossible to grasp—those who had heard him would never forget it.[10] The BBC's weekly magazine, the *Listener*, containing extracts from Solzhenitsyn's interview, sold out immediately and had to be reprinted for the first time in its history.* But the improbably theatrical climax was undoubtedly the public resignation from the Labour party of Lord George Brown, formerly foreign secretary and once one of Prime Minister Harold Wilson's closest confidants. For long a sharp critic of the direction his party was moving in, Lord George Brown quoted Solzhenitsyn's interview as the reason for his decision and said he was now ready to join "Solzhenitsyn's army."

In this orgy of masochistic euphoria, which said as much for the low state of British morale and the multiple inferiority complexes engendered by half a century of decline as it did for the truth of Solzhenitsyn's assertions, dissenting voices were slow to make themselves heard. But after ritual obeisances to the novelist's power as an artist and to the keenness of his spiritual insight, a number of critics did indeed begin to question his diagnosis. Specialists on Russian affairs like Edward Crankshaw in the *Observer* and Professor Richard Peace in a letter to the *Times* pointed out that Solzhenitsyn's knowledge of history was weak and that his disillusionment with the West and apocalyptic warnings of doom were in a very Russian tradition that encompassed Herzen, Dostoyevsky, and many other thinkers in the not too distant past. Others pointed out that Solzhenitsyn was essentially in the same millenarian tradition as the hated Marx himself and that his vision of an all-conquering Soviet Union and the onward march of its armies owed more to Soviet propaganda than to Western perceptions of the world. His under-

---

*The interview was later shown on television in America, albeit with rather less success.

standing of the West, and of such concepts as democracy and of freedom under democracy, seemed sketchy at best, though this was hardly surprising given what was known of Solzhenitsyn's life and habits in the West. "A man now committed to working 16–18 hours a day on his historical novel series about Russia, who speaks German but little English or French, and who relies on Russian sources, émigré or otherwise, for his information is not going to be in the best position to pronounce on the fate of the West."[11]

Opinion was thus divided between those who valued his moral and spiritual message and his appeal to higher values above all quibbles about historical accuracy and the daily detail of politics, and those who felt that his inadequacies in these spheres invalidated the main message. But what was incontestable was the impact of Solzhenitsyn's personality and the indubitable charisma he possessed. He had become the very thing he claimed to abhor: a media star, and his Garbo-like games of hide-and-seek with the press only intensified this quality. As the debate about his interview mushroomed—and as the newspapers filled with readers' letters—the BBC capitalized on the interest it had created by devoting the next "Panorama" programme to a discussion of Solzhenitsyn's ideas on détente between a former prime minister, Edward Heath, the Dutch secretary-general of NATO, Dr. Joseph Luns, an American presidential candidate, Hubert Humphrey, and the former defense secretary whom Solzhenitsyn had praised, James Schlesinger. On 24 March the BBC broadcast a radio talk by Solzhenitsyn hastily commissioned during his stay at Windsor (he had sat down in his hotel room and written it), then a radio discussion of the talk by two English professors and a French radio journalist, then the original interview on television again, and finally another television discussion between two journalists (including Bernard Levin), a historian, and the chairman of Amnesty International.

None of this added very much to what had gone before or altered the main lines of the debate, but Solzhenitsyn did introduce a new dimension of invective into his radio broadcast, which was considerably shriller than his television interview. He elaborated on his charge that Britain had "treacherously disarmed and bound" those who had fled Soviet oppression and "had not shrunk from using the butts of your rifles on seventy-year-olds . . . who were being hastily handed over to be murdered."* He excoriated "your free, independent, incorruptible press" and its conspiracy of silence, charged that the democracies were fully capable of using "Fascist techniques" to promote their ends, and in the same breath accused Britain of being unfair to Franco's Fascist Spain. Twice the Russians had helped to save the freedom of Western Europe, "and twice you repaid us by abandoning us to our slavery." Europe was "nothing but a collection of cardboard stage sets, all bargaining with one another to see how little can be spent on defence in order to leave more for the comforts of life." And there was more in a similar vein.[12]

* A reference to the Russian émigrés who were forcibly repatriated after the Second World War.

It is difficult to account for the high-pitched tone of Solzhenitsyn's radio outburst, rising as it did in places to a veritable scream of rage and frustration. It is understandable that, given the high goals he set himself, he must have felt frustrated. In Washington he had failed to alter the course of *détente*. He must have seen and felt himself to be a prophet crying in the wilderness each time he preached his message of repentance, regeneration, and rearmament to apparently deaf ears. The talk had not been his idea anyway; it had been pressed upon him by the BBC; perhaps he had not expected it to come out the way it did. Was it the solitude of his hotel room, the solitude of the studio, and the consequent sense of isolation from his audience, that had caused him to be so extreme? Or could there have been another psychological mechanism at work? The British, after all, had received him with more enthusiasm—and with more modesty and humility—than any other nation. Had this national self-abasement produced the opposite effect to that intended? In the Soviet Union, and often in Russia beforehand, sweet reasonableness and self-effacement have all too frequently invited bullying and humiliation. Had Solzhenitsyn, almost without realizing it, yielded to the temptation to kick the up-ended bottoms of his prostrate hosts? One distinguished professor in a letter to the *Times*, suggested that Solzhenitsyn's contempt was in reality a sign of the special favour with which he had earlier regarded Britain and therefore a token of his special disappointment.[13] National masochism could hardly go further.

Solzhenitsyn, meanwhile, had moved on well before his talk was broadcast and well before the debate about his ideas was even half over. Like the Scarlet Pimpernel, he had slipped unnoticed into France, and on 9 March he appeared in another television marathon in the series "Les Dossiers de l'Ecran," in which he answered viewers' questions. The programme proper was preceded by a showing of Caspar Wrede's film of *A Day in the Life of Ivan Denisovich*, which Solzhenitsyn was seeing for the second time. The interview part of the programme was not as exclusively political as most of Solzhenitsyn's previous interviews had been, and perhaps because the questions came directly from the public (though transmitted and translated via intermediaries in the studio), both they and Solzhenitsyn's answers had a directness and freshness that had been lacking in his earlier performances. A great many of the questions were biographical or related to Solzhenitsyn's works, and he was able to answer unaffectedly about the experiences that had inspired him and his intentions in writing this or that particular book. In discussing the political context of *Ivan Denisovich*, he made the somewhat startling claim that Khrushchev had authorized publication as part of his campaign against China (instead of against his opponents in the Party), and added that whereas Khrushchev had been oblivious of the danger the book posed, others in the Politburo had seen it clearly but been powerless to stop it. Another answer dealt with the alleged contradiction between the labour-camp system of slave labour and the Soviet Union's status as an industrialized nation. There was no contradiction, said Solzhenitsyn. "The existence of the Gulag is contrary to ethics and humanity, it affronts the soul and the heart, but it is not in opposition to industrial might." The reason the Soviet authorities had eventually dissolved most of it had nothing to do with ethics; rather, it was the result of a rational calculation that it had outlived its usefulness. Slave labour had been replaced by commerce with the West and by the import of Western technology as the engine of industrial progress.

The rational and relatively unemotional tone of these early exchanges in the programme eventually had a beneficial effect on the more political discussion that came later. In answer to a question about Leonid Plyushch, the recently arrived Soviet dissident who had announced on French television that he was still a Marxist (while detesting the Soviet regime),* Solzhenitsyn was eminently fair. He pointed to certain contradictions between Plyushch's view of Marxism and his negative assessment of the Soviet variety, reminded listeners that Plyushch himself had said he still needed time for study and reflection, and hinted (not without foundation) that Plyushch was being manipulated by the French Left for domestic political purposes. Another subject of dispute was Chile. *Le Monde*, among others, had recently printed a story saying that Solzhenitsyn had either visited or was about to visit Chile at the invitation of General Pinochet, and a viewer wanted to know whether Solzhenitsyn was aware that Chile had its own concentration camps. Solzhenitsyn replied that the story was false. He had never been to Chile and had never been invited. Unfortunately, the question provoked him to mount one of his favourite hobby-horses, and from there on the temperature rose to familiar levels. Not only was the story wrong, exclaimed Solzhenitsyn, it was "a complete lie from beginning to end . . . a journalistic invention." He attacked *Le Monde* for having misrepresented him, and the Western press in general for knowing how to lie "just as skilfully as the Soviet press." On the subject of Chile in general he was reasonably sober, pointing out that it was Chile that had offered to free all its political prisoners if the Soviet Union did the same and that the Soviet Union had refused. He also mentioned the little-known and little-discussed fact that a number of Chilean exiles had emigrated to Rumania, had been appalled by what they found there, and had experienced the greatest difficulty in getting out again and moving to West Berlin. But he could not resist remarking provocatively that he kept hearing the word Chile more often than he heard references to the Berlin Wall or the occupation of Czechoslovakia and that "if Chile hadn't existed, it would have been necessary to invent it." After that, the questions reverted to *détente*, the future of the Soviet Union, the alleged decline of the West, and subjects on which Solzhenitsyn had already voiced his well-known opinions.[14]

The curious result of all this was that, despite the vast difference in tone,

* Plyushch, who arrived in France in 1976, after having been incarcerated in a Soviet psychiatric hospital, was at that time very popular with the French Left as a dissident who was also a Marxist; since then he has moved somewhat away from his earlier views. His book *History's Carnival* (London and New York, 1979) is one of the more interesting and original autobiographies to have been published by a dissident.

and for the most part in substance, between this and Solzhenitsyn's earlier interviews in England and America, the public response was almost identical. Again there were the hyperbolic headlines—"One Man against an Empire"; "Solzhenitsyn, a Saint of Olden Times"; "Is God Russian?"—the extravagant comparisons—to Joan of Arc, to David against Goliath—and the grandiose claims for his powers of prophecy and vision. Once again there was a split between the Left and liberals, on one side, and his conservative supporters on the other. And almost the entire attention of the press was concentrated on the last "political" quarter of Solzhenitsyn's remarks, at the expense of his more ruminative statements earlier in the programme. Matters were made worse, in this respect, by accusations against the French television network (which is fairly closely controlled by the French government) of having chosen the programme date with an eye to the French cantonal elections and by charges made in the course of the programme itself that the whole thing was part of an orchestrated compaign against the Left. The editors of Le Monde were infuriated by Solzhenitsyn's public attack on their newspaper. They had printed a retraction of the Chile story that (contrary to Solzhenitsyn's claim) was longer and more prominently positioned than the original story, they asserted that the other misrepresentation he complained of had not been nearly so bad as alleged and had also been followed by a clarification, and they revealed that Solzhenitsyn had recently instituted legal proceedings against them. Was this not an attempt at censorship, asked Michel Tatu, a former Moscow correspondent of Le Monde who had written favourably about Solzhenitsyn in the past, and was it not a relic of bad old "Soviet" habits? Elsewhere in the same issue Le Monde indicated its views on the matter in the headline to a commentary by Bernard Feron—"From Intransigence to Intolerance"—and later lodged a formal protest with the French Television Service, demanding the right of reply to Solzhenitsyn's "prejudicial" presentation of the case.

One is tempted to pity Solzhenitsyn for the political capital that was made out of his visit and for the way he was inevitably drawn into local political squabbles. Solzhenitsyn had repeatedly emphasized in his interviews and speeches that he was not a politician and not a political thinker. He was an artist and a moralist, he said, appealing to a higher sphere of action, and in a separate interview in Paris, given to Nikita Struve, the editor of the Vestnik, he repeated his astonishment that "everybody who talks to me pushes me in the direction of politics and wants to hear my political opinions. I find it very irritating, but it's so." He claimed that his press interviews took place "almost accidentally."[15] But his television host on "Dossiers de l'Ecran," in explaining why the programme had not been intended to influence the cantonal election, revealed that the date had been set by Solzhenitsyn three months in advance; and Solzhenitsyn himself, in yet another interview (with Jean-Claude Lamy of Le Soir) disclosed that one of his principal aims in agreeing to do the television programme had been to express his views on the new relations recently established between Moscow and foreign

Communist parties (including the French party). In other words, he had intended to intervene in French politics, and he was disappointed, according to Lamy, by the way the programme had gone. He had been softened up, he said, by his viewing of *Ivan Denisovich*. "The memories of my imprisonment came surging back to me. Soon I found myself in a lyrical mood; my soul was vibrating." He had been disoriented by the multiplicity of microphones and blinded by arc lights and had not been able to marshal his thoughts properly.[16] It was this that accounted for the unusually soft and meditative tone of many of his remarks, which Solzhenitsyn now regretted; in discounting them, the French press had correctly divined the author's true intentions.

A last political twist was given to the affair by the Soviet ambassador in Paris, who lodged a formal protest with the French authorities against Solzhenitsyn's television appearance. Solzhenitsyn's views, the note said, "confirm that he is an enemy of *détente* who declares himself in favour of a return to the cold war," and the fact that French television had given him a chance to spread his "hate-filled slander" was incompatible with France's promise to promote mutual understanding. The French government rejected the protest as interference in its internal affairs and revealed that the Soviet embassy had intervened with the television authorities to get the programme banned before it even took place.[17] When news of the Soviet *démarche* was released, it naturally had the opposite effect of that intended and increased sympathy for Solzhenitsyn's case, even among those who basically disagreed with him.

A contributory reason for Solzhenitsyn's choice of early March as the date of his Paris visit was the publication there of the third and final volume of *The Gulag Archipelago* in Russian. His vast chronicle of the "Soviet holocaust" was at last before readers in its entirety, although it would be many months before enough people had read it to debate its merits, and well over a year before its appearance in translation into other languages. Another reason was the publication in French, English, and German of *Lenin in Zurich*, an extract from his series of historical novels. In his interview with Struve, Solzhenitsyn explained how he had involuntarily become "the trusted annalist of the camp world to whom everyone brought their truth" after the appearance of *Ivan Denisovich* and how he had evolved his method of "literary investigation" to deal with the material.

> I had never thought about the form of a literary investigation; it was dictated to me by the material in *The Gulag Archipelago*. A literary investigation is the handling of factual (not transformed) real-life material in such a way that the separate facts and fragments, linked by artistic means, yield a general idea that is totally convincing and in no way inferior to that produced by a scientific investigation.[18]

Work on his camp novels and on *The Gulag Archipelago* had postponed his arrival at his "main theme," the history of the Revolution, but when he eventually got there, he found that the methods evolved for *Gulag* were suitable for his historical novels too, and this had been one of his guiding principles in writing the chapters that made up *Lenin in Zurich*.

In an interview already recorded for the BBC on the subject of *Lenin in Zurich*, Solzhenitsyn expanded on his approach.

> I should say it is a form of creative research. My aim is to reconstruct history in its fullness, in its authenticity, in its complexity, but for this I have to use the artist's vision, because a historian uses only documentary material, much of which has been lost. The historian uses evidence from witnesses, most of whom are no longer alive . . . whereas the artist can see farther and deeper, thanks to the force of perception in the artist's vision. I am not writing a novel. I am using all the artistic means available to me to penetrate as deeply as possible into historical events.[19]

The use of the word "novel" here was in response to a question and did not describe the form of *Lenin in Zurich*. Solzhenitsyn shared the traditional Russian reluctance to be bound by West European concepts of genre (the only one of his works he described as a novel was *The First Circle*), as was shown by his invention of the term "knot" to describe *August 1914* and the volumes planned to follow it. *Lenin in Zurich* was not a "knot" but "fragments of an epic," unified only by its subject—the personality of Lenin—and by its place—Zurich.

Solzhenitsyn's fragments dealt with Lenin's life in Zurich during the First World War and on the eve of the Revolution. It was in most respects a peculiarly empty and frustrating period for Lenin. The war had cut him off from direct communication with Russia, and there was little he could do to exert any influence anywhere. Indeed, according to Solzhenitsyn, Lenin was on the verge of giving up his revolutionary hopes entirely and retiring to America when the opportunity arose for him to return home. Solzhenitsyn described what that life had been like, with its frustrated hopes and extravagant dreams. Lenin was shown experiencing emotional difficulties with his wife, Nadezhda Krupskaya, and longing for the company of his former mistress, Inessa Armand. He was shown as short-tempered with his Swiss and Russian Social Democratic colleagues, intolerant of the opinions of others, incapable of friendship, and addicted to plotting and scheming. The climax of the action came with a meeting between Lenin and another notable revolutionary (more famous than Lenin at the time), Alexander Helphand, alias Parvus, a wealthy Jew who was said to have played a major role (along with Trotsky) in the abortive revolution of 1905 and who had subsequently gone abroad and made his fortune. Helphand was depicted by Solzhenitsyn as Lenin's evil genius, his satanic tempter, and his superior in cunning and foresight. In a scene reminiscent of Ivan Karamazov's vision of the Grand Inquisitor, Helphand offers to help Lenin get to Petrograd by persuading the Germans to give him safe passage in a sealed compartment of a train and to supply him with money. Lenin remains non-committal when the offer is made but later capitulates and accepts it.[20]

As fiction *Lenin in Zurich* showed Solzhenitsyn returning to top form. The best chapters were up to the best in *August 1914*, and if there were *longueurs*, due to the welter of unfamiliar names and mass of historical detail, these were felt by most critics to be a blemish that would fade when the chapters took their place in the complete epic. The book had, in addition, some intriguing features. Solzhenitsyn's portrait of Lenin was highly personal, with autobiographical overtones. The picture of a lonely and unheeded prophet, self-centered, short-tempered, miserly with his time ("a single wasted hour made Lenin ill"), suspicious of others, virtually friendless, cut off from his homeland, and dreaming of leaving his wife for another woman seemed uncannily close to certain biographical details in the life of the author— breathtakingly so to those who knew him well—and there was much comment among Russian readers about Solzhenitsyn's psychological identification with his revolutionary predecessor and ideological opponent.

Solzhenitsyn seems not to have been unduly upset by these speculations, but he vigorously rejected them whenever they were put to him directly. To the BBC interviewer he said he had invented nothing in his portrait of Lenin, had endowed him with no characteristic that Lenin had not possessed in real life. "My aim is to give as little play to the imagination as possible and to re-create as closely as possible what he was really like. The writer's imagination only helps to forge the separate elements into one whole and, by penetrating into the character, to try to explain how these elements interact."[21] On the same occasion, Solzhenitsyn declined to answer the question of whether he admired Lenin or not ("Read the book" was his classic author's answer to the challenge), but the fact of his long preoccupation with Lenin was no secret, and in speaking to Struve he was more explicit about the form his fascination had taken.

> Lenin is one of the central figures in my epic and a central figure in our history. I have been thinking of Lenin from the very moment I conceived the idea of my epic, for forty years already, and have collected every crumb and fragment that is known about him, absolutely everything. . . .
>
> Throughout the years I gradually came to understand him; I even compiled catalogues listing his actions throughout his life according to which characteristics they illustrated. Everything I learned about him I read in his books and in memoirs. . . . I don't use this directly at the moment of writing, but it is all systematized and sorted in my head. Now, when I regard myself as having matured to the point where I can write about Lenin, I am describing his concrete years in Zurich, while retrospectively including events from his private and political life. I have no other task than to describe the living Lenin exactly as he was, abjuring all official embellishments and official legends. And it's absolutely superficial to say that I'm writing him out of myself. I am writing him only out of his own characteristics . . . [but] I cannot describe him without myself having reached a certain level of psychology and experience, without being able to understand another man in his particular circumstances and with his particular aims.[22]

Lenin, of course, was his old hero. Long after his total disillusionment with Stalin, Lenin had remained his idol, the shining knight of the Revolution, and it had taken him a long time before he plucked up the courage to tear him from his pedestal. Stalin was torn down in *The First Circle*. Stalin had been the first father-figure to go (other writers, like Mandelstam, Pasternak, Bulgakov, and Grossman, had tackled Stalin as well), but Lenin was a bigger challenge, and Solzhenitsyn had few predecessors in this particular act of literary regicide. He was quite explicit, however, about his intentions. His aim was to demystify Lenin, to cut him down from his mythic dimensions to human size and to create a counter-myth to the official Soviet legend of the avuncular idealist with the heart of gold and the cares of mankind on his shoulders. He had once thought, he told Struve, of waiting until his entire epic was complete before publishing any part of it, but he couldn't resist starting now, because it was "impossible not to try to influence the thinking of one's contemporaries."[23]

Not surprisingly, Solzhenitsyn's iconoclastic treatment of one of the great heroes of twentieth-century history became a new point of controversy. The principal objections were set out at great length in the French magazine *Est et Ouest* by Boris Souvarine, a founder member of the French Communist party and leading member of the Comintern who later broke with both, became a distinguished historian, wrote a critical biography of Stalin, and eventually came to oppose Leninism as well. Souvarine had known Lenin (and some of the other individuals described in Solzhenitsyn's book) personally, and insisted that Solzhenitsyn had misrepresented Lenin's character and actions. While acknowledging Solzhenitsyn's enormous merits as a novelist, moralist, and chronicler of Gulag, and admitting that "Solzhenitsyn's sincerity was beyond question," Souvarine advanced a variety of charges against him. Solzhenitsyn, he wrote, had been misled by over-exposure to tendentious Communist historiography. As an example, he quote Solzhenitsyn's authorial note on "events . . . which have been carefully concealed from history and which, because of the development of the West, have received little attention." On the contrary, wrote Souvarine, they were the subject of a vast and still-growing literature, with only a part of which Solzhenitsyn had familiarized himself before writing his book. This must have been why Solzhenitsyn had accepted and was promulgating two pernicious myths: that Helphand was a friend and helper of Lenin's (on the contrary, wrote Souvarine, Lenin detested him and repeatedly rejected his help) and that Lenin had accepted German money and had travelled through Germany in a "sealed carriage" in order to return to Russia. There was no evidence at all, according to Souvarine, that Lenin had ever accepted a penny of German money, and the journey by train had been perfectly open and legal, and conducted in such a way that Lenin's compartment (and those of his companions) were officially regarded as "extraterritorial"—formally speaking, Lenin never set foot on enemy territory.

Souvarine deployed a wealth of references and invoked an array of scholars to support his point of view and accused Solzhenitsyn of over-reliance on tainted and discredited sources. Solzhenitsyn was said to be guilty of selective quotation and distortion, and Souvarine drew attention to a passage about

Lenin that had already acquired a certain notoriety among Russian readers: "Just because a quarter of his blood was Russian, fate had hitched him to the ramshackle Russian rattletrap. A quarter of his blood, but nothing in his character, his will, his inclinations, made him kin to that slovenly, slapdash, eternally drunken people." Did this mean, asked Souvarine, that the whole of Russian history should be examined to determine what its chief characters' racial origins were and how much Russian blood ran in their veins? In that case, things would go badly with the entire Russian royal family, not to speak of writers like Pushkin (part Ethiopian), Lermontov (of Scottish descent), Karamzin (of Tartar stock), and dozens of others.[24]

It was to be three years before Solzhenitsyn got around to replying to Souvarine, but it is worth mentioning the main lines of his "defence" here. Souvarine was guilty of forgetting that *Lenin in Zurich* was first of all a work of literature, although Solzhenitsyn wrote that he had endeavoured to make it "historically irreproachable," and Souvarine had not found any factual distortions. Secondly, the book "stood or fell" by its characterization of Lenin as a psychological type, and again Souvarine had not questioned this. As for research and sources, in the end it came down to whom you believed, and he preferred his authorities to the ones Souvarine had cited, just as he firmly believed that Helphand *had* channelled German money to the Bolsheviks and had thereby helped to bring about the October *putsch*. He had not himself used the word "sealed" with reference to the train Lenin had travelled in, but how could Souvarine describe the journey through Germany as "legal" and legitimate? Germany and Russia were at war; Germany had permitted the journey precisely to bring about subversion and collapse in Russia and forward her war aims. Lenin's acceptance of the guarantee of safe passage was treachery (Solzhenitsyn later amended this to "high treason").[25] Finally:

> You can scarcely conceal your admiration for this great villain. Several times you let slip such expressions as "Lenin-denigrators," "Leninophobes," "slanderers," but only virtue can be slandered or denigrated. And how can anyone blacken Lenin's name more than he did himself? . . . What can anyone say about Lenin and Trotsky . . . that would be worse than simply recalling how they created the first and greatest totalitarianism the world has seen and how they devised their methods of mass terror. . . . Your article is morally dangerous in that it seeks to whitewash the crimes of this pair—and with them the Communist system itself—while laying the whole blame on their disciple [Stalin].[26]

As in most such disputes, the two sides were to a certain extent talking past one another. Souvarine (and many other critics, including, in the Soviet Union, Roy Medvedev) was accusing Solzhenitsyn of manipulating the facts and distorting history in the service of a tendentious interpretation of it, while Solzhenitsyn maintained, on the one hand, that he was straightening out an already tendentious version of history and, on the other, that his critics were raising quibbles that did not detract from his essentially correct central interpretation. The dispute continued in the pages of the French and *émigré* press (and in samizdat) for many months more, but nothing essentially new was added by either side.

Long before this debate had got truly under way, Solzhenitsyn had moved on again—this time to Spain. After ten days of travelling around the country incognito came the usual prepared television interview and, later that same day, 20 March 1976, a press conference, at which he spontaneously answered journalists' questions. Both were extremely interesting and among his better performances. In the interview he explained how important a place the Spanish civil war had occupied in Soviet mythology during his youth. "We were passionately . . . caught up in your civil war. Names like Toledo, the university campus in Madrid, the Ebro, Teruel, and Guadalajara were totally familiar to my generation, and if anyone had summoned us and allowed us to go, we would have dropped everything to go and fight for the Republicans." However, that had been long ago. He now realized that, compared with the Russian Civil War, the Spanish war had cost far fewer lives. More importantly, the outcome had been completely different. In Spain "the Christian world view" had triumphed, leading to peace and reconciliation, whereas the triumph of communism in Russia had meant the start of a longer and more bloody war—the war of the state against the population—and this had cost, according to statistics he trusted, sixty-six million lives* (against "a half-million" for Spain).

Solzhenitsyn went on to say that he had heard critics describe contemporary Spain as a "dictatorship" and "totalitarian" but that after travelling around the country, he could say that these critics did not know what the words meant. No Spaniard was tied to his place of residence. Spaniards could travel abroad freely, newspapers and magazines from all over the world were on sale in the kiosks, everyone had free access to photocopying machines, even strikes (with some exceptions) were permitted, and there had recently been a limited amnesty for political prisoners. "If we had such conditions in the Soviet Union today, we would be thunderstruck, we would say this was unprecedented freedom, the sort of freedom we haven't seen in sixty years." It was natural, he said, that progressive circles in Spain should want to have as much freedom as possible and to give their country the status of the other countries of Western Europe, but he wanted to warn them against moving too quickly. The democracies were on the retreat, and it wasn't certain that Spain could avoid the danger of falling into a true totalitarianism in the not too distant future.

He also clarified his view of the way in which Russia's experience held a lesson for the West.

> Russia's social experience has placed her ahead of the rest of the world. I am not saying she has become a leader of nations. No, she has become a nation of slaves

---

* The figure was provided by an *émigré* statistician, Professor I. A. Kurganov, who has tried to calculate Soviet losses from the terror, purges, and other repressions by analyzing the officially provided statistics.

that calls itself the Soviet Union. But we have gone through an experience that nobody in the West has gone through. And we now look with pity on the West. It is a strange feeling, as if we were looking back on the past. And in relation to the West one can say we are looking at you from your future. Everything that is happening here now happened to us along ago.[27]

He wanted to escape, he said, from the tyranny of "left" and "right." Mankind's crisis was not political but spiritual, and the opposition "East-West" was relative. Both communities suffered from the same disease: "the ailment of materialism, the ailment of inadequate moral standards. It was precisely the absence of moral standards that led to the appearance of such a horrible dictatorship as the Soviet one, and of such a greedy consumer society as the West's. On the one hand we get totalitarian socialism, and on the other, indifference to the unhappiness and suffering of others."

He traced the origin of mankind's malaise back to the great leap that man had made from the Middle Ages to the Renaissance. Man had done so as a protest against the impoverishment of his material nature and the exaggeration of the spiritual. But then he had grown more and more materialistic, more and more neglecting his spirituality, ending with the universal triumph of materiality, together with a decline in spiritual life. "The picture today's world presents to the eye strikes me as appalling. I think that if mankind is not doomed to die, it must restore a proper appreciation of values. In other words, spiritual values must again predominate over material values. This does not mean that we should return to the Middle Ages. Every development is enriched by time. I am speaking of new horizons, or so it seems to me."[28]

The thoughtful tone of these and other answers by Solzhenitsyn was greatly at variance with the stridency of the thunderbolts hurled in Washington, Paris, and London, perhaps because he felt he had to shout less loudly away from the centres of power or perhaps because Spain had evoked in him a genuine spontaneity and warmth that informed his whole attitude. At all events his sincerity, his sense of commitment, and his social ease were widely commented on by Spanish journalists who attended the press conference. But it was tactless, to say the least, to lecture the Spaniards so directly on the nature of true dictatorship and to admonish a nation just emerging from a dictatorship (however mild by Soviet standards—and Solzhenitsyn did not know nearly enough to make a true comparison) on the failings and dangers of democracy. Solzhenitsyn was widely perceived as interfering again; and while a few commentators concentrated on the apocalyptic nature of his vision (one newspaper likened him to a mixture of Job and Isaiah), most responses were political. Solzhenitsyn's views were said to have been "gleefully received" by the Spanish Right, up to and including the neo-Nazis, and to have embarrassed Spain's conservative prime minister, Carlos Arias, who was just then seeking a commercial agreement with the Soviet Union. A spokesman of the Left alleged that Solzhenitsyn must "be suffering from a serious mental illness" that had destroyed his political judgement and caused him to allow himself to be "exploited as a figure-head and used by right-wing extremists to attack the cause of social democracy, human rights, and workers' freedom."[29] Perhaps predictably, his words on dictatorship were widely misquoted, most flagrantly by *Le Monde* (still smarting, it seems, from Solzhenitsyn's Paris attack), which carried the headline "Solzhenitsyn Thinks That the Spaniards Live in 'Absolute Freedom.' " A few days later, in Brussels, the International Confederation of Free Trade Unions (to which the AFL-CIO belonged) issued a "strong protest" against Solzhenitsyn's statements on television and announced that in his "exaltation of the Franco regime" he was "abandoning his own cause" of respect for human beings and their right to freedom and democracy.[30] Few commentators had the perspicacity, or temerity, to point out that Solzhenitsyn had, if anything, endorsed the Spanish reforms and had merely cautioned against going too fast.

Interestingly enough, Solzhenitsyn had foreseen some of these reactions in his press conference. One of his questioners had asked whether he did not fear that his attacks on left totalitarianism would give encouragement to supporters of right-wing totalitarianism. After repeating his conviction that there was totalitarianism only of the Left (in his view the dictatorship of right-wing regimes was less than total), Solzhenitsyn replied that a writer could not worry about whether his words pleased someone or not, and emphasized that his allegiance was only to Russia. "I never intended to become a Western writer. I came to the West against my will. I write only for my homeland. . . . I cannot worry about what someone somewhere makes of what I write and if he uses it in his own way." At another point, when asked why he lived in Switzerland, he replied, "I do not live in Switzerland, I live in Russia. All my interests, all the things I care about, are in Russia."[31] Earlier, on television, he had been more explicit about his feelings.

> . . . in the prosperous countries of the West we live like captives. If it were possible for us tomorrow to return to our starving, beggarly country we would all go back like a shot. The Communist press is very fond of speculating about that Solzhenitsyn who went to the West and became a millionaire. When I was starving at home, they didn't write a word. When we were all starving there (and they still are today), they lied that we had full bellies. Yes, of course, I get big royalties here, but the major part of them goes to the Russian Social Fund to help the persecuted in the Soviet Union and their families, and we send this aid by various channels into the Soviet Union.[32]

Just before the end of his press conference, Solzhenitsyn asked to make a little digression and pleaded with reporters either to use his answers in full or to omit certain topics altogether. "I know from . . . experience . . . that newspapers usually take only what they need. They tear some phrase out of context, destroy all proportion, and distort my ideas. . . . Leave the scissors alone, do you understand what I mean?"[33]

His plea was in vain, of course, with the result that his Spanish visit and his Spanish speeches caused, if anything, more scandal than his earlier statements and certainly did more to discredit him with the "established Left" than anything that had gone before. He hardly deserved it, but few cared to make the effort to find out what he had really said. Unfortunately, this all too predictable reaction to his words served only to strengthen Solzhenitsyn's prejudices as well. Both sides of the ideological divide were becoming locked into stereotypical attitudes that not only misrepresented their true positions but were increasingly difficult to break out of.

51

THE SAGE
OF VERMONT

AMONG THE VARIOUS explanations that Solzhenitsyn had given for living in Zurich, the latest (mentioned by him in both Paris and Madrid) was that he had wanted to stay there while writing his chapters on Lenin for his series of historical novels. *Lenin in Zurich* was now out, but on the question of his future plans Solzhenitsyn was evasive, even to good friends. In Paris he had admitted that he did not like Zurich and told Jean-Claude Lamy that he would probably retire to the countryside, while "definitely remaining in Switzerland." But in early May 1976 he surfaced unexpectedly in the United States, and it was announced that he would spend some weeks at the Hoover Institution at Stanford, to carry out historical research. In Spain he had disclosed that the next two novels in the sequence begun by *August 1914— October 1916* and *March 1917*—were already complete, but it seems there were archives at Hoover that he needed to consult before he could consider these works ready for publication.

For three weeks he worked quietly, but on 20 May he suddenly called a press conference to denounce a new Soviet campaign of denigration against him. The Soviet press, under orders, had been more or less silent about him since the propaganda outburst accompanying his expulsion two years beforehand. It appears, however, that his speeches in America, and his latest round of appearances in Britain, France, and Spain, with his persistent attacks on *détente*, had had some effect in Moscow. In mid-March the Soviet press had broken its silence with a series of attacks on Solzhenitsyn's remarks in Spain. Tass and *Pravda* had quoted left-wing circles to the effect that Solzhenitsyn was a total reactionary, and had joyfully picked up the allegation, cited in the English *Guardian*, that Solzhenitsyn was "mentally unbalanced." A week later *Pravda* had carried a round-up of the left-wing Spanish press in which Solzhenitsyn's speeches were indignantly rejected as interfering and Solzhenitsyn himself was denounced as a bourgeois chauvinist and a mystic who opposed every form of progress.[1]

A completely different tack had been taken, also in March, by Boris Danilov in the *Literaturnaya Gazeta*. Solzhenitsyn was alleged to have paid a visit, while in Madrid, to Grand Duke Vladimir Romanov, the senior surviving male of the Russian royal family and thus heir presumptive to the Russian throne. Nothing is known of what passed between them, and Solzhenitsyn's visit is easily explained by his historical interests, but the *Literaturnaya Gazeta* chose to portray him as a convinced monarchist anxious to restore tsarism, and as hoping to recover the estates and property confiscated from his grandparents.[2] It was pathetic stuff, relying on a regurgitation of the *Literaturnaya Gazeta*'s earlier rehash of the *Stern* article, but its general approach, and a side reference to the origin of Solzhenitsyn's scar, indicated that the "biographical line" of attack on Solzhenitsyn was far from exhausted, a fact that emerged even more clearly from Solzhenitsyn's Stanford press conference.

He had decided to call it, he said, after learning that the KGB had forged a letter trying to show that he had been an active informer in the camps and had betrayed his friends. The allegation was not entirely new. A year earlier, the Novosti press agency had prepared a filmed interview with one of Solzhenitsyn's informants for *The Gulag Archipelago*, Mikhail Yakubovich, called "Postscript to the Archipelago," in which Yakubovich had accused Solzhenitsyn of being a "religious hypocrite" for marrying "his own god-daughter" (a reference to Natalia Svetlova)* and of having been an active informer. Yakubovich, an elderly ex-Menshevik and ex-Bolshevik in infirm health, was one of dozens of Solzhenitsyn's sources who had been tracked down, interrogated by the KGB, and subjected to threats, but he was the only one to co-operate, partly as a result of his advanced age and partly because he felt Solzhenitsyn had slighted him.† Yakubovich's allegation was founded on Solzhenitsyn's admission in volume 2 of *The Gulag Archipelago* that he had agreed to become an informer while at Kaluga Gate and on the supposition that this was the reason he had been sent to the *sharashka*. "It is absolutely unlikely that a man who agreed to inform on his fellow prisoners and did not produce any information should be sent to such a special camp. It is out of the question."[3]

Yakubovich's accusation had obviously given the KGB some inspiration, but it had not followed his suggestion slavishly. The forgery was dated

---

* It is not clear how or with whom this rumour originated, but it gained a certain currency in Moscow for a while, although there was no truth in it.

† Apparently, Novosti made another "documentary" film about Solzhenitsyn containing allegations of anti-Semitism and a false version of how he sustained the scar on his forehead. This would suggest that it contained an interview with Simonyan, and perhaps others, but the contents are not clear from the information available to me.

20 January 1952, that is, from the period after the *sharashka* when Solzhenitsyn was at Ekibastuz, and purported to show him betraying the prisoners' rebellion that was to break out there on 22 January (which Solzhenitsyn extols in volume 3 of *The Gulag Archipelago*) by informing the security officer in advance. The words were phrased in such a way as to suggest prejudice on Solzhenitsyn's part against the Ukrainian Banderites involved in the uprising, and also against a Polish colonel, while the proof of his complicity was alleged to be his immediate transfer to the camp hospital (in response to a request that the camp authorities "protect me against the outrages of the criminals who recently troubled me with suspicious questions"). The letter ws signed "Vetrov"—the Kaluga Gate pseudonym Solzhenitsyn had cited in *The Gulag Archipelago*.[4]

Solzhenitsyn did not quote from the letter directly. It was being circulated among foreign correspondents, he said, and a Swiss journalist had sent him a photocopy. The KGB agents must have used the collection of his letters to his first wife, Natalia Reshetovskaya (which they had tried to sell in the West), including letters from Ekibastuz, as a model for their forgery, but it did not stand up to close analysis, neither reproducing his phraseology accurately nor reflecting his mental make-up as it appeared in his account of the rebellion in *The Gulag Archipelago*. The attempt to sow suspicion of him among Ukrainians and Poles was a crude failure. What more pathetic confession of their ridiculous weakness could there be, he added sarcastically, than "this accusation against their mortal enemy that he had collaborated with none other than . . . themselves"? In short, the Soviet authorities would stoop to anything to discredit *The Gulag Archipelago* but had nothing to answer it with, "no facts or arguments . . . only lies."[5]

Four days after his press conference, the Hoover Institution gave a private dinner in Solzhenitsyn's honour at which he spoke on the subject of historical research in the field of Russian and Soviet studies. He did not, as might have been expected, speak about his own research at all, but used the occasion to criticize the work of Western, and above all American, scholars working in the field and to correct what he saw as their misconceptions and errors. The source of many of these errors, he said, lay in the very abnormality of contemporary Russian history. Although the country was very real and existed in the present, to study it was like studying archaeological prehistory: "the spine of its history has been fractured, its memory has failed, it has lost the power of speech." The truth was obscured by a torrent of "programmed lies." Even this might have been surmountable but for two further obstacles. One was that the historian was disoriented by "a hurricane" of propaganda about the Soviet Union whipped up by "committed socialist circles," and the other that revolutionary and opposition-minded *émigrés* from an earlier era had unfairly blackened pre-revolutionary Russia. As a result, a "tendentious generalization" had come into being, according to which the Revolution was a logical continuation of Russian history and owed its origins to "perennial Russian slavery" and "the Asiatic tradition." As a prime example of what he meant, Solzhenitsyn referred to "an American scholar, for many years the director of one of your 'Russian Centres,' " who had published a "pseudo-academic book" that was full of "mistakes, exaggerations, and perhaps premeditated distortions"—premeditated, said Solzhenitsyn, because the book's illustrations included cartoons, although it was supposed to be scholarly.*

Solzhenitsyn's objection to the book was that it postulated a natural continuity between Old Russia and the Soviet Union that was not present. "Soviet development is not an extension of Russian development, but its diversion in a completely new and unnatural direction which is inimical to her people. . . . Not only are the terms 'Russian' and 'Soviet' not interchangeable, not equivalent, and not unilinear—they are irreconcilably contradictory and completely exclude each other." To think otherwise was a "gross mistake" and "scholarly slovenliness" and was disastrous for Western understanding of historical perspective.[6] As antidotes to this kind of misunderstanding, Solzhenitsyn recommended two samizdat works: *What Is Socialism?* by his old friend Igor Shafarevich, to which he had just written a preface for the Russian-language edition and which he hoped to persuade one of his American publishers to bring out,† and a new work by the jailed physicist Yuri Orlov that had just arrived in the West.[7] Shafarevich, said Solzhenitsyn, had demonstrated that socialism was an ancient and supranational system of beliefs that had always existed independently of any one country, and both Shafarevich and Orlov had convincingly shown that consistent socialism could not be anything else than totalitarian and inevitably led to "the total suppression of individuality and the human spirit."

Solzhenitsyn seemed to many onlookers to be tilting at windmills, while the American historian at the centre of his attack went on to become a personal adviser on Soviet affairs to President Reagan, not generally known for his softness on communism or a tendency to bow to the "socialist hurricane." It is true that there were (and are) many historians of Russian and Soviet society who hold views more favourable to the Soviet Union than Solzhenitsyn would wish (or than is perhaps compatible with a sober appreciation of the facts) and that some are sympathetic to socialism (the one position does not always entail the other), but in all the millions of words that have been spilled in the West on the subject of Marxism, Bolshevism, and the Soviet Communist Party, one would be hard put to it to discern a prevailing distortion of the sort espied by Solzhenitsyn.

In a sense, of course, it hardly mattered, for the nature of Solzhenitsyn's dyspepsia was not such as to be dispelled by a mere recital of facts and statistics (he had specifically rejected "meaningless statistics" early on in his address), and he had neither the time nor the inclination to subject Western

---

* The reference was to *Russia under the Old Regime*, a work of historical inquiry by Richard Pipes, formerly director of the Russian Research Center at Harvard, in which Pipes sought to define some enduring characteristics of Russian history.

† The book was eventually published by Harper & Row in 1980 as *The Socialist Phenomenon*.

society and Western codes to anything like the intense scrutiny he was used to training on his own country. This became clear at a second address delivered at the Hoover Institution a week later, in response to the award to him of the American Friendship Medal from the Freedoms Foundation of Valley Forge, Pennsylvania. Having stated his admirable belief that the aim of life was "not to take boundless pleasure in material goods" but for men to leave the world as "better persons" than they entered it—"better than our inherited instincts would have made us"—for which freedom was a necessary, but not a sufficient, condition, Solzhenitsyn went on to draw a startling picture of how Western freedom looked to him.

> Freedom! To fill people's mailboxes, eyes, ears, and brains with commercial rubbish against their will, television programmes that are impossible to watch with a sense of coherence. Freedom! To force information on people, taking no account of their right *not* to accept it or their right to peace of mind. Freedom! To spit in the eyes and souls of passersby with advertisements. Freedom! For publishers and film producers to poison the younger generations with corrupting filth. Freedom! For adolescents of fourteen to eighteen to immerse themselves in idleness and pleasure instead of intensive study and spiritual growth. . . . Freedom! For strikers . . . to deprive all other citizens of a normal life. . . . Freedom! For speeches of exoneration when the lawyer himelf is aware of the guilt of the accused. . . . Freedom! For vulgar, casual pens to slide irresponsibly over the surface of any problem. . . . Freedom! To divulge the defence secrets of one's country for personal political gain. . . .[8]

It was Solzhenitsyn at his demagogic worst again, passing off a bar-room tirade (not that he went into bars himself) as profound comment worthy of respectful attention. At the root of all this evil, as he saw it, was America's devotion to the rule of law, and the elevation of juridical rights over moral rights. In opposition to these, and to the "empty," external freedoms he had inveighed against, he invoked the "inner freedom" granted by God, and implied that the two were incompatible.

After this it may have come as something of a surprise to members of his audience to learn, three months later, that Solzhenitsyn had decided to settle permanently in America—in Vermont, as had been rumoured the preceding year. In fact, he seems hardly to have returned to Switzerland after leaving the Hoover Institution (except for a brief formal visit), for in mid-June he was at Yale University to study the historical archives there, before returning to California, and in mid-July he was booked for speeding (Natalia Svetlova was driving) in Kansas on his way east. He told the patrolman that he and Natalia were on their way to see "Natalia's brother" in Vermont, and the fine was eventually paid from Vermont (though not by Natalia's "brother").

The official announcement came on 8 September from the United States immigration authorities. Typically, Solzhenitsyn was already in residence, having quietly moved in on 30 July with no fanfare. The house found for him had been the summer residence of an American businessman (recently deceased); it was situated outside the sleepy small town of Cavendish, in the south-eastern corner of Vermont, near the New Hampshire border. A young architect named Alexis Vinogradov had purchased the house on Solzhenitsyn's behalf the preceding autumn (the sale was completed on 31 October 1975), together with fifty acres of land surrounding it,* and since then had supervised a renovation and rebuilding programme estimated to have cost about a quarter of a million dollars (the house and land had cost a hundred and fifty thousand dollars). Undoubtedly, the most controversial feature of the property was the eight-foot chain-link fence topped with a single strand of barbed wire that surrounded the entire property. Fences are unusual in Vermont, and usually unwelcome, for they obstruct hunters, used to ranging more or less where they wish, and get in the way of the snowmobiles that have become the almost universal mode of cross-country transport in snow-bound Vermont in winter.

The accepted explanation for the fence was that it was part of Solzhenitsyn's security arrangements against incursions by the KGB. Some Swiss newspapers writing about his departure reported that Solzhenitsyn had been increasingly concerned about KGB spying and harassment in Zurich and had recently received another threatening letter posted from Bern. He had allegedly asked for police protection, but not been granted it. Whatever the true reason, or combination of reasons, the fence quickly proved its worth in another direction. The announcement of Solzhenitsyn's move immediately brought crowds of reporters to the picturesquely named Windy Hill Road, where the house was situated. Alexis Vinogradov, inveigled reluctantly to the main gate, denied all knowledge of Solzhenitsyn's whereabouts, and insisted that the house belonged to him. He had no plans to transfer the house to Solzhenitsyn, he said, and even if he had, "I would give you the same answer." Since the main gate was about half a mile from the house down a winding drive, and since bulldozers had pushed up high mounds behind the fence to block any view of the house from open ground, the reporters were totally frustrated and had to content themselves with the cryptic descriptions of the few locals who had been inside.[9]

That security against reporters was more or less the true purpose of the fence was admitted by Solzhenitsyn when he attended the annual Cavendish town meeting the following February to explain himself and confirm for the first time that he was actually living there. By now his main gate had been equipped with an electric-eye alarm device and closed-circuit television cameras that could be monitored in the main house, and he was aware that these Citizen Kane–type precautions had caused some concern to his tight-lipped but free-spirited neighbours. Revealing that death threats had already been slipped under his gate since his arrival in Vermont, he conceded that there was "no doubt the fence cannot protect me against Soviet agents," and added, "but it keeps away people who just want to see me." In Zurich he had been

* It appears that Solzhenitsyn did not even bother to look at it before buying it. Vinogradov sent photographs to Switzerland, and Solzhenitsyn said yes from there.

inundated with unwanted visits from Soviet agents, journalists, and sight-seers. "Anybody and everybody could come there. . . . In those two years there was a real procession: hundreds of people came, people I didn't know, people of different nations. They came without invitations and without warning. . . . And so for hundreds of hours I talked to hundreds of people, and my work was ruined." His only interest, he said, was work, and the character of his work did not permit interruptions. "Sometimes there is a five-minute interruption, and the whole day is lost."

Solzhenitsyn apologized for any inconvenience he was causing his neighbours. He had chosen to live in Cavendish, he said, because of "the simple way of life of the people, the countryside, and the long winters with the snow, which remind me of Russia." He liked it there, and he did not want his presence to upset others. "My fence prevents your snowmobiles and hunters from going on their way—I am sorry for that and ask you to forgive me, but I had to protect myself from certain types of disturbances." He also invited their sympathy with an account of his difficulties in the Soviet Union, saying that "I shall soon be sixty, but in all my life before, I have never had a permanent home." The Soviet authorities had chased him from one place to another until they threw him out. "God has determined that everyone should live in the country where his roots are. . . . As a growing tree sometimes dies when transplanted, the spirit of a human being is also stunted when it is removed from the place of its roots. It is a very bitter fate to think and look back at one's own country. What is perfectly normal for those who live there is strange for one who is exiled."

Solzhenitsyn did not let this opportunity slip to attack the Soviet Union once more and repeated his admonition at the Hoover Institution not to con-fuse "Russian" with "Soviet," and his warning that the "sickness" of com-munism might spread to America. "The Russian people dream of the day when they can be liberated from the Soviet system," he said, "and when that day comes, I will thank you very much for being good friends and neigh-bours and will go home."[10]

Solzhenitsyn spoke for about twenty minutes (his words were translated by his newly acquired secretary, Irina Alberti) and was greeted with loud applause. His eloquence had been more than enough to win over the dour Vermont townsfolk, even those who had grumbled about the fence and threatened to make holes in it. After shaking a few hands, he left the meeting, which was perhaps a pity: Cavendish was well known for its spirit of local independence. Its annual town meeting was an excellent example of tradi-tional, grass-roots American democracy in action, and as in Switzerland, all business was transacted by voice vote from the floor. Had Solzhenitsyn stayed, he would have seen something to remind him of Appenzell, would have increased his understanding of the land he had come to and perhaps modified his gloomy, media-fed view of America's stumbling democracy. As it was, his visit to the meeting was not as spontaneous as the rest of the proceedings, or as improvised as it had seemed. It had been arranged in advance by the governor of Vermont, Richard Snelling, and the town manager, Quentin Phelan. Once Solzhenitsyn had stated his case, he was too busy to stay on and listen to the rest of the meeting.

The people of Cavendish were pleased that he had come, however, and with their conservative ways and belief in each man's minding his own business, vere quite happy to have this ultra-recluse as a neighbour. In the next few years there were no complaints of substance against him. Solzhenitsyn had chosen the perfect place in which to disappear into the landscape.

But if he was invisible locally, Solzhenitsyn was still highly visible in international affairs, and the peace of Vermont was not matched by any lessening in the intensity with which the Soviet authorities continued to follow his activities. At the beginning of February 1977 the *Literaturnaya Gazeta* published a long article by a known prison-camp informer, Alexander Petrov, attacking some of the better-known dissidents, including Yuri Orlov and Sakharov's wife, Elena Bonner, and in particular accusing Alexander Ginzburg of illegal currency transactions. Ginzburg had been singled out because of his work for the Russian Social Fund, which Solzhenitsyn was supporting with the royalties from *The Gulag Archipelago*, and the article revealed that Ginzburg's flat had been raided and 5,000 rubles confiscated, along with various documents and lists, and allegedly some foreign currency.[11] Ginzburg responded by calling an impromptu news conference in his flat, at which he revealed, for the first time, the dimensions of the fund. Since April 1974, when Solzhenitsyn had set it up in its new form, the fund had helped 120 political prisoners or their families in the first year, 720 in the second year, and 630 in the third. About 270,000 rubles (equivalent to $360,000) had been expended during that time, of which just over a quarter had been raised inside the Soviet Union and the rest supplied by Solzhenitsyn. The Solzhenitsyn funds had been sent legally in the beginning, with the Soviet government siphoning off a third in taxes, but when the authorities had discovered the purpose of the money, they had blocked further payments, and after that it had been sent in through unofficial channels.[12]

The raid on Ginzburg's flat was obviously an attempt to prevent the fund from continuing its work. This was confirmed by other prominent dissidents who attended the Ginzburg press conference, such as General Grigorenko and Valentin Turchin, chairman of the unofficial Moscow group of Amnesty International. They revealed that there had been growing police pressure on the families of political prisoners not to accept aid from the fund, and Turchin said that he himself had been summoned for interrogation the following day. Later that day, 3 February, Ginzburg was arrested. Solzhenitsyn, who kept in close touch with Ginzburg and the activities of the fund as a matter of course (Natalia Svetlova was the fund's president), at once issued a protest and characteristically—if exaggeratedly—linked the arrest with the fate of the West. "This act of violence concerns Western people more than can be imagined at first glance. It is an essential link in the unflinching total preparation of the Soviet home front so that it should not in any way hinder the external offensive conducted so successfully during these years, and which will yet be broadened, against the strength, the spirit, and the very existence of the West."[13] A week or two later he announced that he was retaining the prominent American lawyer Edward Bennett Williams to take on the legal defence of Ginzburg, and declared that he was in a position to affirm that Ginzburg had had no dealings with foreign currency and that the currency allegedly found in Ginzburg's flat had been planted there by KGB agents. "I believe that legal counselling in the Ginzburg case will open up a new world even to a lawyer with your vast experience and world prestige," he wrote to Williams, and expressed himself ready to supply the lawyer with all the facts necessary for undertaking the case.[14]

Unfortunately, sanctions against the fund continued throughout the spring and summer of 1976. Ginzburg's place as administrator of the fund in Moscow was taken partly by his wife, Irina Zholkovskaya, and partly by two less prominent dissidents, Tatyana Khodorovich and Malva Landa, to whom Solzhenitsyn sent a message of support in May. In June, Khodorovich revealed in an interview that the campaign against supporters of the fund was unprecedented and that she was appealing to President Carter to save the fund from "annihilation." Meanwhile, Solzhenitsyn himself was not neglected. At the beginning of April the Supreme Soviet of the USSR announced that Natalia Svetlova had been stripped of her Soviet citizenship by a decree passed the preceding October, and news came of a new attack on Solzhenitsyn by his old school friend Kirill Simonyan.

It appears that, having escaped Vitkevich's fate of being obliged to give interviews and appear on television after Solzhenitsyn's expulsion in 1974, Simonyan had nonetheless agreed to co-operate with the authorities and was now keeping his side of the bargain. The co-operation took the form of a twenty-three-page pamphlet published, for some unfathomable reason, in Danish by an obscure left-wing publishing house called Melbyhus in the small provincial town of Skaerbaek. Its title was *Who Is Solzhenitsyn?* and in it Simonyan concentrated on what he regarded as three crucial incidents in Solzhenitsyn's life. One was the episode of the scar acquired at school, which Simonyan described as a consequence of Solzhenitsyn's anti-Semitism. The second was Solzhenitsyn's arrest, which according to Simonyan had been engineered by Solzhenitsyn himself out of cowardice to avoid further fighting at the front. And the third was the incident of 1952, when Simonyan had been called in for questioning by the KGB and shown Solzhenitsyn's interrogation record. There was also a reference to Solzhenitsyn's later letter to him and the futile attempt to renew their friendship in 1967, and an allegation that Solzhenitsyn's mother had once told him that her husband, Isaaki, had committed suicide in 1918 in a funk over the victory of the Reds.[15]

The story of how the pamphlet got to Denmark is a mystery, and the director of the publishing house refused to divulge his source when questioned on the subject. The fact that it was never translated into any other language may indeed indicate that not even the KGB felt comfortable with these charges, although they were to surface in a somewhat modified guise in later "exposures" of Solzhenitsyn's early life. Perhaps fortunately for Simonyan, he did not live to see his essay in print. He died of a heart attack in the summer of 1976, shortly before its publication.

Attacks on Solzhenitsyn by the Soviet authorities or their surrogates were not surprising, nor were the objections raised to some of his political views by prominent dissidents such as Roy Medvedev, Sakharov, Litvinov, and others, or the criticisms of his handling of history in *August 1914* and *Lenin in Zurich*. But in the summer of 1977 fresh currency was given to a disquieting question that had first been raised in 1972 and that had been discussed on and off ever since: Was Solzhenitsyn an anti-Semite? The immediate occasion this time was the publication of volume 2 of *The Gulag Archipelago*, in which Solzhenitsyn had included six photographs of six notable scoundrels responsible for some of the worst excesses of the Gulag administration. Illustrations in *The Gulag Archipelago* were very rare, so that the photographs stood out starkly in that vast expanse of text, but what particularly caught the eye of Russian readers (ever sensitive to such niceties) was that all six villains happened to be Jews. Solzhenitsyn later explained that these were the only photographs available and that these bloodthirsty Jewish executioners really had existed. He was only telling the truth. Sceptical readers pointed out that there were many more purely Russian administrators in the Gulag than Jewish ones, that they were not a whit less cruel or sadistic than their Jewish colleagues, and that it could hardly be a coincidence that Solzhenitsyn had laid so much emphasis on the Jews, not only in his photographs, but also in his text. The question was, Did Solzhenitsyn do it deliberately, had it come about unconsciously, or had he been "fed" this information and fallen into a trap?

The question was naturally bound up with other aspects of Solzhenitsyn's known views. His nationalism, for instance, was obviously founded on a deep and passionate love of the Russian people. But did not this passion, carried to its logical conclusion (as Solzhenitsyn was all too prone to do), imply either exclusion or at least second-class status for non-Russians in the Russian state? Solzhenitsyn had repeatedly expressed his support for the right of Jews to emigrate to the Jewish state and seemed to approve of such emigration (as opposed to the emigration of Russians), but what about assimilationist Jews who felt themselves to be more Russian than Jewish and did not wish to emigrate, not to speak of the Jews who wished to stay without being assimilated? Then there was the religious question. In a country in which Russian Orthodoxy guided all moral and spiritual life (and perhaps more than that, for moral and spiritual questions transcended political ones in Solzhenitsyn's view), what was to be the status of the Jews? In the pre-revolutionary Russia that Solzhenitsyn admired, their status had been difficult and in many respects pitiful. Solzhenitsyn had rarely mentioned this, or the existence of pogroms, in his literary works and statements.

These and similar concerns led critics back to Solzhenitsyn's works, and in the summer of 1977 a translation appeared in the United States of the case against him by a Jewish scientist who had recently emigrated from the Soviet Union to Israel named Mark Perakh.* Perakh analysed Solzhenitsyn's entire output from *A Day in the Life of Ivan Denisovich* up to and including *Lenin in Zurich*, and came to some negative conclusions. In *Ivan Denisovich* and *Cancer Ward*, there were no Jewish characters of note and the Jewish question was entirely missing, he wrote, but that very omission, in a writer as uncompromising in his search for truth as Solzhenitsyn, was surprising. It was common knowledge that everyday anti-Semitism was rife in the camps, that the word "Yid" was a universal term of abuse not reserved exclusively for Jews, and that such a word would have sounded entirely natural in the mouth of Ivan Denisovich, particularly when Solzhenitsyn had allowed him to use obscenities. In Central Asia, where *Cancer Ward* was set, there had been a big purge of Jewish doctors just two years before the time of the novel's action, and again it was inconceivable that this had not left its mark on the life of the hospital, yet there was only one fleeting reference to it in the entire book.

As for the rest of Solzhenitsyn's works, where either Jews or the Jewish question appeared in some form or other, Perakh wrote that Solzhenitsyn's portraits of individual Jews were generally fair and that in describing them, Solzhenitsyn had brought all his great powers of observation and his ability to depict character into play, for they were vivid and lifelike. However, when one scrutinized their role in Solzhenitsyn's works, no matter how sympathetic they seemed individually, it was always negative. In *The First Circle*, for instance, there were three main Jewish characters: Lev Rubin and Isaak Kagan among the prisoners, and Adam Roitman among the administrators, and all three were in one way or another the defenders of evil. The larger phenomenon of anti-Semitism was certainly discussed and denounced at some length in *The First Circle*, but it was also treated as a purely Stalinist manifestation, hence as a product of the Communist system and not linked to deeper Russian attitudes.

It was in certain of Solzhenitsyn's other works, however, that Perakh found the most to criticize, notably in Solzhenitsyn's early play *The Tenderfoot and the Tart*. Again the three Jews in the play—Arnold Gurvich, Boris Khomich, and the bookkeeper named Solomon—were all representatives of evil, but this time grossly and disgustingly so, and Solomon was the very

---

*The debate about Solzhenitsyn's alleged anti-Semitism had begun with an article in the *Jerusalem Post* in 1972 by the newly arrived Soviet *émigré* Mikhail Grobman. Grobman's charges were answered by three prominent Jewish dissidents still in the Soviet Union (one of them was Mikhail Agursky), and at greater length by Roman Rutman in *Soviet Jewish Affairs* (London) in 1974. In 1976 the same magazine published another defence of Solzhenitsyn by the American scholar Edith Rogovin Frankel, and in 1977 more allegations of anti-Semitism by the Soviet *émigré* critic Simon Markish. All these articles, except Frankel's, had appeared in Russian first. Perakh's article, a kind of *summa* of those that had gone before, had appeared in Russian in the *émigré* magazine *Vremia i My* (Time and We) in February 1976 before being published in English in *Midstream*.

incarnation of the greedy, crafty, influential "court Jew," manipulating the "simple" Russian camp commandant and oozing guile and corruption. As it happened, Solomon was modelled on the real-life prototype of Isaak Bershader, whom Solzhenitsyn had met at Kaluga Gate and later described at length in volume 3 of *The Gulag Archipelago*, and Perakh dwelt on this description too. It was not that the facts were necessarily false (though Perakh found the lip-smacking portrait of the dirty, fat, and greedy Bershader definitely excessive), but that the naming of only Bershader among the numerous members of the camp elite who were allowed to choose mistresses from among the prisoners made it seem like a generalization and certainly left the reader with that impression. It was noteworthy that both in Solzhenitsyn's play and in *The Gulag Archipelago*, "most" of the Jews portrayed were negative characters and "most" of the heroes were Russians, which certainly did not match reality, and Perakh made a damning comparison of *Gulag* with Robert Conquest's *The Great Terror*, which dealt with much of the same material. Though far behind Solzhenitsyn's book in artistic forcefulness, wrote Perakh, Conquest's was infinitely more impartial in its dealings with Russians and Jews and made no attempt to single out one nation at the expense of the other.

Finally, Perakh turned his attention to *August 1914* and *Lenin in Zurich*. *August* was notable for avoiding the Jewish theme altogether, although it also had a "completely positive" portrait of the Jewish engineer, Ilya Arkhangorodsky, the only one of its kind in Solzhenitsyn's entire *oeuvre*. Perakh hazarded a guess (correctly) that this character must have been based on someone Solzhenitsyn knew. In *Lenin in Zurich*, on the other hand, he found that Bershader-Solomon had surfaced again in the person of the fat Jewish businessman and Lenin's evil genius, Israil Lazarevich Helphand (Parvus): "There he stood—such as he was, in his flesh and blood: with an immense gut, an extended dome-shaped head, fleshy bulldog-like physiognomy, with a wedged beard . . . ," with a taste for "openly cavorting with plump blondes" (i.e., Aryans). Not only did Helphand manipulate others from the shadows, like Bershader and "Solomon," but it was he who stood behind Lenin and exploited him to bring about his main goal—the collapse of the Russia he hated.[16]

Perakh did not deny that Solzhenitsyn was the "greatest contemporary Russian writer" and that *The Gulag Archipelago* was "a superb book;" an impressive work whose "enormous impact" would be felt far beyond Russia, and he conceded that Solzhenitsyn might have selected his heroes and villains "subconsciously," with no overt intention to distort reality. He also conceded that there were problems with what some might call a "percentual approach"— simply adding up the positive and negative Jews portrayed in Solzhenitsyn's works and drawing crude conclusions. Nevertheless, he felt that his analysis had gone beyond percentages and that it was possible to express "enthusiasm and respect for Solzhenitsyn both as a creator and as a champion of truth and justice," while regretting the encouragement (perhaps unconscious) of anti-Semitic attitudes generated by many of his works.

Perakh was not alone in harbouring such sentiments, nor was he the first to voice them in print, but he was the most thorough, and was followed by other commentators. But Solzhenitsyn also had his defenders, not least among the Jews, and allegations of anti-Semitism were met with counter-arguments. Representative of these was an article by Roman Rutman, a Jewish physicist then living in Israel. Rutman wrote some three years before Perakh and was taking issue with some rather crude articles accusing Solzhenitsyn of anti-Semitism that had appeared in the *Jerusalem Post* as early as 1972 and 1973* (he also revealed that he had been asked many questions on the same subject when lecturing to Soviet Jewish *émigrés* in the United States in 1972).

Unfortunately, Rutman's article was not as detailed as that of Perakh and notably avoided dealing at any length with *The Gulag Archipelago*, although volume 1 was out by then. Rutman's case was that Solzhenitsyn could be made out to be an anti-Semite only if one took as one's starting point the uniqueness of the suffering of the Jews (especially in the twentieth century) and the necessity of stressing this fact and demonstrating one's desire for atonement at every possible opportunity. In the Russian context this meant accepting three propositions: that the extraordinary fate of the Jewish people had made them the symbol of the suffering of mankind, that the Jews in Russia had always been the victims of one-sided persecution, and that Russian society was in debt to the Jewish people. Rutman had little difficulty in demonstrating that Solzhenitsyn accepted none of these propositions. Solzhenitsyn had written of the Second World War in *The Gulag Archipelago* that "in general, this war had revealed to us that the worst thing in the world was to be a Russian." In his *Letter to the Leaders*, he had written of "the incomparable sufferings of our people," and elsewhere in *Gulag* he had described the horrors of collectivization as a precedent for Hitler and the Holocaust. In other words, Solzhenitsyn did not accept that any one people had a monopoly of suffering; he maintained that in the twentieth century Russians had suffered as much as Jews. With regard to the second proposition, that the Jews in Russia had endured extraordinary persecution, Rutman found that Solzhenitsyn had resolved the problem by concentrating on the sufferings of *all* the people in the Soviet Union, absorbing the trials of Soviet Jewry into the greater ordeal of the entire population. And on the question of whether the Russians owed a debt to the Jews, Rutman concluded that the proposition was too shallow and that those Russians who had publicly embraced this position (such as Gorky or Evtushenko) were guilty of hypocrisy.

Rutman's essential argument was that Solzhenitsyn was too "big" to be encompassed by the pro- or anti-Jewish label and that to take the statistical approach to the Jewish characters in his works was to adopt a new "party line" and show how influenced Russian readers had been by the official and censored Soviet press. This, wrote Rutman, made all allegations based on the virtual absence of Jewish characters and the Jewish theme from *Ivan*

*See note to p. 960.

Denisovich and *Cancer Ward* meaningless. Nevertheless, he did agree to play the game in part by dwelling on the glowing portrait of Arkhangorodsky in *August 1914* and praising the characterizations of Lev Rubin and Adam Roitman in *The First Circle*. The portrait of Roitman was particularly important for Rutman because it was sympathetic to one of Solzhenitsyn's natural enemies, yet did not hesitate to condemn Roitman for being misled by his Party loyalties. It was a complex and true-to-life picture, whereas an author guided by "the Jewish question" would have been less objective and thereby have falsified reality.

In conclusion Rutman dealt with the argument that the "logical extension" of Solzhenitsyn's Russian patriotism and love of patriarchal custom was anti-Semitism. He quoted the example of the nineteenth-century Russian Orthodox philosopher Vladimir Solovyov to show that a deep and almost mystical love of Orthodoxy and Russia was not incompatible with love of the Jews, and he referred to recent statements in support of Solzhenitsyn by the Jewish samizdat writer Mikhail Agursky and the Jewish literary critic Grigori Svirski, both of whom felt that to draw such conclusions was unwarranted.[17] Svirski, indeed, later elaborated his views on this point (and criticized Rutman for the inadequacy of his defence) in his *History of Post-war Soviet Writing*, published in Russian in 1979 (and in English in 1981). It was true that Solzhenitsyn had been silent, he wrote, on many outstanding Soviet acts of persecution of the Jews. But Tolstoy had written that "every writer has his sore point," and Solzhenitsyn's sore point was the sufferings of the Russian people, which hurt him more than the sufferings of the Jews. It was a question of selection and personal preference, and perhaps the main problem was that there was "only one Solzhenitsyn." Everybody wanted to have him on their side and have him write about their sufferings with the same eloquence and vividness that he had brought to the sufferings of the Russians.[18]

Meanwhile, in Vermont, Solzhenitsyn was gradually getting his new estate in order. Despite newspaper speculation about the kind of luxury that could be bought for a quarter of a million dollars (a modest enough sum, in truth, by American standards), a very large part of the money had been spent not on the house but on the construction of a modern and well-equipped annex to house Solzhenitsyn's personal papers and literary archive as well as an independent library. In September 1977 Solzhenitsyn announced the establishment of the All-Russian Memoir Library, to be financed by him and situated on his estate. It was to be an extension of the Russian Social Fund and would have as its aim the collection of all possible material, but mainly personal memoirs, pertaining to Russian history of the twentieth century. It was another reflection of Solzhenitsyn's desire to rescue the national memory of the Russian people before it was too late. He appealed to those who had written their memoirs, no matter how brief, modest, or unliterary they might be, to send him copies. The library would accept *all* materials, even those of two to three pages, and would attempt to publish some of the longer and more interesting ones (Solzhenitsyn already had a functioning type-setting

machine on the premises, so he was in an excellent position to fulfil his promise). He would ensure that all materials were catalogued and filed systematically and in time made available to scholars who desired to consult them, and
he emphasized that photographs, letters, and other *memorabilia* were equally
of interest to him. "I call upon my fellow countrymen to sit down at once
and write their recollections and send them to me—so that our grief does not
vanish with them, leaving no trace, but is preserved for Russia's memory as
a warning to the future." He solemnly promised that his heirs would take
over the duty of preservation even after he was gone and that as soon as a
favourable moment arrived, the entire contents of the library would be transferred to "one of the cities of central Russia," where it would be merged with
similar archives written by people still inside the Soviet Union to form "a
concentrate of our national memory and experience."[19]

Curiously enough, Solzhenitsyn's obsession with national history and
his emphasis on the need for every nation to examine its past and repent of
its misdeeds was just about to find another echo in England. Of all the countries he had visited in the past year and a half, England had greeted him with
the greatest enthusiasm and had responded the most generously to his calls
for self-examination and contrition. Already in 1974 Nicholas Bethell had
published a short book, *The Last Secret* (whose title was taken from a phrase
in *The Gulag Archipelago*), about the British role in the forced repatriation to
the Soviet Union after the Second World War of innocent *émigrés* and refugees from communism, along with Russian troops who had fought for the
Germans.[20] Bethell's book had sparked off a debate about both the ethics and
the politics of British policy at the time (Bethell had suggested that the principal villain of the piece was Britain's then–foreign secretary, Anthony Eden,
and stressed the *realpolitik* behind the minister's actions), which had later died
down, but it was revived all the more fiercely in the first months of 1978 by
the publication of a second and much longer book, *Victims of Yalta*, by Nikolai Tolstoy (a distant descendant of the great novelist but born and bred in
Britain). Tolstoy demonstrated at great length the full consequences for
hundreds of thousands of Russian *émigrés* and refugees of the agreement reached
at Yalta to repatriate them to the Soviet Union, and he described in harrowing detail the violence inflicted on them by Allied (primarily British) troops.[21]
Publication of his book led to calls for a public inquiry, and for a whole week
the *Times* carried out its own investigation, while its correspondence columns
were filled with anguished letters for or against.

Solzhenitsyn's name rarely figured in this second debate, yet his figure,
and above all his monumental book, loomed in the background and clearly
set the tone for many of the participants. Nicholas Bethell summed up the
case for an inquiry in almost Solzhenitsynian terms. "In 1944 the British
government took a decision which cost many lives. It killed not only war
criminals and traitors, but also innocent prisoners-of-war, displaced persons,
forced labourers, women and children. Was it really necessary?

"Perhaps a fuller and franker account from those personally involved would convince the nation and quieten a growing sense of collective guilt. Alternatively, it might show that . . . we were accomplices in a massive crime. . . . In either case, the nation now needs *all* the available evidence."[22]

Solzhenitsyn had likewise been an invisible presence in Washington. When he had received the Freedoms Foundation award at Stanford in 1976, President Ford had sought to make slight amends for his Washington snub by sending a personal telegram to the foundation congratulating it on its decision. Later that year, there was an open struggle at the Republican National Convention in Kansas between the pro-Reagan faction and the pro-Ford faction over whether to endorse Solzhenitsyn's views as part of the Party's official election platform. In the end, the pro-Reagan faction won, and Solzhenitsyn was extolled as a "great beacon of human courage and morality,"[23] though not before Henry Kissinger had reputedly threatened to resign. The election was won by Carter, and a few months later, ex-President Ford publicly admitted that he had made a mistake in refusing to see Solzhenitsyn. "It is regrettable that the meeting did not take place," he told a gathering of history students and professors at Yale University in February 1977. "If history were ever rewritten, it would take place."[24] The newly victorious President Carter had had no mention of Solzhenitsyn in his platform at all, but after his election he had been pressed by Malcolm Mabry, a Mississippi state representative, to say whether he would meet the Russian novelist or not, and in a note to Mabry had written that he would. More than that, the president had said it was his "intention" to meet Solzhenitsyn, and in the course of 1977 was publicly pressed to do so by journalists and political figures, just as his predecessor had been.

Like President Ford, however, Carter was quickly caught up in the contradictions of *détente* and never got around to issuing an invitation. But in 1978 the opportunity arose for Solzhenitsyn himself to take the initiative again—not by securing an invitation to the White House but by putting his views before the American nation from a nationally respected platform. He was asked whether he would accept an honorary degree from Harvard University and make the annual commencement address in early June. The commencement address was traditionally used as the occasion for important speeches, and not for the first time was to be carried on nation-wide television. It was Solzhenitsyn's first opportunity to address, in effect, the entire American nation since his AFL-CIO speeches three years earlier and since becoming an American resident. In conditions of the usual secrecy he accepted the invitation, and the announcement of his participation was not made public until two days before the speech was scheduled to take place.

This secretiveness about the speaker, though not unusual for Harvard commencement addresses, naturally created an air of expectancy, and the announcement of Solzhenitsyn's name guaranteed that a large crowd would assemble to listen to his speech (it turned out to be a record 22,000 people). With television carrying the entire address live, it is fair to say that the atmosphere was one of considerable excitement. Solzhenitsyn could hardly have had more favourable circumstances in which to express his ideas.

The speech he delivered proved to be a kind of summation of the things he had been saying virtually since the day of his arrival in the West. Entitled "A World Split Apart," it consisted of an introduction and fifteen short sections whose headings summarized his main themes: Contemporary Worlds; Convergence; The Collapse of Courage; Prosperity; Juridical Life; The Direction of Freedom; The Direction of the Press; Fashions in Thought; Socialism; Not a Model; Short-sightedness; Loss of Will; Humanism and Its Consequences; Unlikely Bedfellows; At the Turning-point. An interesting aspect of the title, which did not emerge from the official English translation, was that it expressed Solzhenitsyn's preoccupation with the phenomenon of schism. The Russian word for "split apart" *(raskoloty)* is the adjective derived from the Russian word for "schism" *(raskol)*, and a better translation would have been "The World in Schism."* In a sense, the whole speech could be read as an impassioned plea against schism of any kind, an appeal for unity, and Solzhenitsyn began and ended with this idea, although it was not carried through with any consistency—indeed, many of the ideas contained in the body of the speech could just as easily be interpreted as serving to widen splits instead of to heal them. Nevertheless, some sort of vision of unity undoubtedly underlay Solzhenitsyn's often harsh and wounding formulations, and his intention (or his hope) was clearly to foster the elimination of schisms of one kind or another.

The speech contained few surprises. Again it consisted of variations on the Spenglerian theme of the decline of the West. He pointed out that the world was split not just into East and West but into multiple, self-sufficient "worlds" or civilizations, such as China, India, Africa, and the Islamic world. He added that to these, despite the misconceptions of Western "specialists," belonged Russia, which possessed a cultural identity of its own, separate and different from the West. The West had once been monolithic and all-conquering, and in the period of colonization had seemed about to take over the entire world, but now the tide had receded and the West was in retreat. Therefore, it was an illusion that where the West led, all other countries had to follow, and that the Western way of doing things was best. That was why the theory of "convergence," among others, was a false one.

From there Solzhenitsyn proceeded to his familiar litany of the West's failings. The "collapse of courage" was particularly noticeable among Western intellectuals and the ruling circles. The preoccupation with prosperity was a result of the fact that the "modern" states of the West (these apparently included France, England, Germany, Italy, and Spain, all of which in one way or another were considerably older than Russia, but Solzhenitsyn did not specify) had been founded on the principle of the government's serving the people and had set the pursuit of happiness as one of their goals (in, for example, the American Declaration of Independence). But this happiness

* In his Russian text Solzhenitsyn wrote the word for "peace"—*mir*—with an old-style Russian *i*, since in the modern orthography *mir* also means "peace."

was deceptive, for the faces of many people in the West showed how worried and oppressed they were by the fierce struggle to possess more goods, "even though it was considered proper to try to conceal these expressions." "Juridical life" in the West was a cold and formal system that could not satisfy people's deeper desires or prove strong enough to withstand the strains that lay ahead. By placing law above all other values, this system was actively detrimental. "Having passed all my life under communism, I will say that a society in which there are no impartial judicial scales is abominable. But a society in which there are no scales other than the judicial is also little worthy of man."*

In his section on freedom Solzhenitsyn expressed the exact nature of his charge against the West with his first sentence: "In today's Western society there has opened up a disequilibrium between the freedom to do good deeds and the freedom to do bad." One consequence of this was that "a truly outstanding, great man with extraordinary, surprising policies cannot make his influence felt—he will be tripped up a dozen times before he can even get started," while statesmen were hamstrung by "thousands of hasty and irresponsible critics and the constant intervention of press and parliament." Another consequence was the corruption of youth by pornographic films and an inevitable growth in crime. "It is a strange thing, but in the West, where the very best social conditions have been created, there is . . . much more crime than in the impoverished and lawless Soviet Union." In the case of the press, this freedom had simply degenerated into licence. The press had the chance to "simulate" public opinion and corrupt it, and was a product of the main "mental illness of the twentieth century—haste and superficiality." It was indicative that the longest of all Solzhenitsyn's sections was devoted to his old *bête noire*, the press, and this because of his conviction that "the press has become the strongest of all forces in Western states, exceeding the powers of the executive, legislative, and judicial branches. And yet . . . who elects them and to whom are they responsible?"

From here it was a short step to a consideration of the dominance of fashion in intellectual matters and the tyranny of the consensus. And this consensus, according to Solzhenitsyn, was far too favourable to socialism, which the academician Shafarevich had already exposed in his "brilliantly argued book." There was also the West's "short-sightedness," demonstrated by its attraction to the ideas of *détente* and disarmament as instanced in the writings of George Kennan, and its "loss of will," demonstrated by the American

*Compare Tocqueville: "But if you think it profitable to turn man's intellectual and moral activity towards the necessities of physical life and use them to produce well-being, if you think that reason is more use to men than genius, if your object is not to create heroic virtues but rather tranquil habits, if you would rather contemplate vices than crimes and prefer fewer transgressions at the cost of fewer splendid deeds, if in place of a brilliant society you are content to live in one that is prosperous, and finally, if in your view the main object of government is not to achieve the greatest strength or glory for the nation as a whole but to provide for every individual therein the utmost well-being, protecting him as far as possible from all afflictions, then it is good to make conditions equal and to establish a democratic government."

capitulation in Vietnam and the diplomatic manoeuvres of those who engineered it (a swipe at Kissinger, although the former secretary of state was
not mentioned by name). The West had become conservative and wedded to
the status quo, but no matter how well armed it might be, it could never
prevail without its people's willingness to die for a cause. Preference for the
status quo was a sure sign of decline and impending collapse.

For all those reasons Solzhenitsyn declared that he "could not recommend today's West as a model" for his countrymen. Eastern Europe was
spiritually far ahead of the West. "The complex and deadly pressures bearing
upon our lives have developed characters that are stronger and more profound and interesting than those developed by the prosperous, ordered life
of the West." For the East to become like the West would be for it to lose
more than it gained.

Solzhenitsyn did not say what he *would* recommend, but neither did he
stop there. The whole crisis of mankind, he said, could be traced back to the
heritage of the Renaissance and the Enlightenment. The spirit of rationalism
had led man to reject God and place himself at the centre of the universe,
and this was why he no longer understood the nature of good and evil. In
this context, the "unlikely bedfellows" were communism and capitalism, for
they were both logical products of the development of humanism and materialism. But since it seemed to be a social law that the radical always won out
over the liberal and that political movement was always to the left, communism was in the ascendant. But this was not necessarily the end of the story.
Whether a military catastrophe was imminent Solzhenitsyn could not say,
but the demise of irreligious, humanist consciousness was already at hand,
and mankind was at a turning-point. Both East and West were sick of the
same disease, and the values of the Renaissance no longer had any efficacy.
We were at a "turning-point" analogous to the turn from the Middle Ages to
the Renaissance. There was no question of going back to the Middle Ages,
but we should seek to unite the best that the Middle Ages had given us in
the spiritual sphere with the best that the Renaissance had brought in the
human and physical sphere and rise to a higher plane. There was nowhere
else to go but up.[25]

Solzhenitsyn's speech was greeted, as on so many occasions in the past,
by a standing ovation. Not everyone in the audience applauded, and it is not
clear how much the ardour of the general response had to do with Solzhenitsyn's personal magnetism and the passion with which he spoke (which, as
usual, passed the barrier of simultaneous translation). But it was in a sense a
sort of apotheosis. Harvard was a more distinguished and more elevated forum
than the Hilton Hotel in Washington, the audience was more influential,
more representative, and less partisan than that provided by the AFL-CIO,
and television carried the speech to all sections of the population who cared
to watch, on a scale vaster than anything since the Cronkite interview. Whatever his difficulties with the political establishment, Solzhenitsyn had succeeded in getting his message across to the American people as never before.

He would have much preferred, of course, to be speaking to his own people, and it was poorly understood for a while that his words had indeed been directed as much to them as to his listeners in America. But he had done his best, as he saw it, for both, and was able to retire in triumph to Vermont to savour the impact of his words.

That he was not indifferent to that impact is attested by a friend who visited him soon afterwards and found him "intensely interested" in the public reactions to his speech. Of the thousands of letters he was said to have received, the majority were said to be "overwhelmingly favourable;" but that still left the newspapers and magazines to which, despite his professed contempt, Solzhenitsyn as usual paid close attention. The consensus here was not favourable at all, though some endorsed his speech almost without reservation. The conservative *National Review* perceived that the true drift of 'Solzhenitsyn's message was "antimodern" but found in him not someone who was hostile to the West but rather "the greatest living representative of the West, an avatar of the West's most ancient and honourable principles," because he was appealing for a return to the "almost forgotten alternative to modernity: classical and early Christian political philosophy."[26] The Catholic magazine *Commonweal* found more to quarrel with in Solzhenitsyn's detailed exposition of his views but still supported his overall plea for more room for spirituality and morality in daily life and rejected the idea (put forward by some) that Solzhenitsyn favoured an authoritarian political system and censorship of the press.[27]

The balance of press and published opinion, however, was decidedly against Solzhenitsyn. The *New York Times* saw Solzhenitsyn participating in an argument that was as old as the American Republic itself—between religious enthusiasts sure of their interpretation of the divine will and men of the Enlightenment trusting in the rationality of mankind. Solzhenitsyn's role in forcing the West to understand the full brutality of the Soviet regime had been beneficial, but his crusade against communism bespoke "an obsession that we are happy to forgo in this nation's leaders." James Reston, in the same newspaper, wondered whether Solzhenitsyn's exaltation of Russian spirituality as being far in advance of the West did not indicate the wanderings of "a mind split apart," despite the many brilliant passages elsewhere in his speech. The *Washington Post* explained his view as "very Russian," arising from "particular religious and political strains remote from modern Western experience." Solzhenitsyn, wrote the *Post*, was bent on summoning Americans to a crusade and speaking on behalf of a "boundless cold war." The *Christian Science Monitor*, while praising Solzhenitsyn's call for a return to spirituality, found his claims for Russian spiritual superiority preposterous and his ignorance of America and American ways deplorable, and a columnist in the same newspaper found him squarely in the tradition of earlier foreign visitors who had come and denounced what they found in America, such as Dickens and Alexis de Tocqueville.[28]

It was the more serious commentators who had the most to say, however. Arthur Schlesinger, the liberal historian once associated with President Kennedy, likened Solzhenitsyn to early generations of Harvard men, whose fundamentalist Christianity had led them to thunder from the Harvard rostrum in tones, and even in words, remarkably similar to Solzhenitsyn's (Schlesinger quoted a few to drive his point home). Solzhenitsyn's charges against America were familiar, many would have no difficulty in agreeing with his strictures against American excesses, and his "challenge to American smugness and hedonism, to the mediocrity of our mass culture, to the decline of self-discipline and civic spirit," was "bracing and valuable." To this extent Solzhenitsyn was at one with America's Puritan founding fathers. But Solzhenitsyn's faith was suffused by the "other-worldly mysticism of the Russian church" and by a strain of quietism and passivity that was entirely alien to America. "Even the New England ministry had to temper its conviction of divine sovereignty with concessions to the rough democracy of a nonprescriptive society where men made their way in life through their own labor." The two traditions were divergent and alien to one another. Solzhenitsyn had remarked at Harvard that the West has "never understood Russia." One could respond that Solzhenitsyn had never understood America. All he knew was what he had learned from television, the newspapers, and gazing through a car window; he did not know enough to recognize television's "depressing parody of American life" for what it was. If prophecy was one human virtue, humility was another. "Knowing the crimes committed in the name of a single Truth, Americans prefer to keep their ears open to a multitude of competing lower-case truths." While they welcomed Solzhenitsyn in their midst and honoured his presence, the message of his Harvard address was irrelevant to them.[29]

Notable among the many other critics of Solzhenitsyn's speech was the once Marxist and now right-wing political philosopher Sidney Hook, a professor emeritus of New York University and research fellow at the Hoover Institution. Hook found far more in Solzhenitsyn's speech to agree with than had the liberal Schlesinger but, he, too, felt that the "profound truths" Solzhenitsyn had uttered were likely to be cancelled out by his equally profound errors. Hook agreed with Solzhenitsyn's warnings against an ever more powerful East and the vacillating weakness of the West and with his analysis of the degradation of Western society. He also agreed with Solzhenitsyn's notions of the importance of morality and the need to balance various freedoms, but he felt that Solzhenitsyn was "profoundly wrong" to identify the sickness of the West with the heritage of the Renaissance and the Enlightenment and a loss of belief in God. Belief in a Supreme Being was entirely compatible with the worst excesses and atrocities—the history of organized religion was too full of examples for there to be a need to enumerate them. Nor was such a belief a necessary foundation of morality. It was Dostoyevsky who had propagated that idea, but more eminent thinkers such as St Augustine, Kierkegaard, and the unknown authors of the Book of Job had shown that morality was logically independent of religion. Solzhenitsyn also misunderstood the nature of freedom, for freedom of choice meant the freedom to err, yet Solzhenitsyn could not bear the consequences of error.

Hook made one further point in his capacity as one of those "who have for many decades beeen fighting the monstrous evil of totalitarianism, even before Solzhenitsyn himself discovered its true nature," and that was the potential divisiveness of Solzhenitsyn's attempt to lay down a "party line" for those engaged in this fight. "There are legitimate grounds for fear that any attempt to base the broad struggle against the growing menace of Communism on one special doctrine or premise will result in demoralizing the common effort. It may convert the contenders into warring, ineffectual sects. . . . The principles of morality are more truly universal and more generally considered valid than any religious principle. . . . They can serve more readily as a unifying bond than any parochial conceit about first and last things." Hook, like many before and after him, cited Sakharov as a more unifying figure than Solzhenitsyn in the opposition to communism.[30]

Hook was accusing Solzhenitsyn of doing, in effect, the opposite of what he had set out to do, of being responsible for splits and causing his own particular schism in the ranks of dissidents and others opposed to Soviet communism, and his words were prophetic. *Letter to the Leaders*, *The Oak and the Calf*, *From under the Rubble*, and Solzhenitsyn's speeches in the West had already created the beginnings of a schism, which until now had remained muted or indirect, out of respect for Solzhenitsyn's reputation and his colossal achievements. From now on, however, dissent from his views was destined to grow louder and stronger, until it broke out into charges that Solzhenitsyn wished to become "the Russian Ayatollah" and to impose his own form of theocracy on a future Russia.* Meanwhile, his own attacks, both in private and public, on other members of the emigration and on a variety of *émigré* journals that had sprung up since the early seventies ensured that the split would widen and deepen until it was virtually unbridgeable, resulting in a new version of the philosophy that "he who is not with us is against us."

There were many precedents in Russian history for Solzhenitsyn's attitude to the West. The superiority of Russian over Western ways had been a theme in Russian thought ever since Peter the Great's forcible Westernization of Russia at the beginning of the eighteenth century, and an essential strand of the Slavophiles' thinking in the nineteenth century had been the view that the West was in decline. Some Slavophiles, while aware of the

---

*The comparison of Solzhenitsyn's views with those of Ayatollah Khomeini first occurred in a long article by Valery Chalidze in the New York newspaper *Novoye Russkoye Slovo* (New Russian Word) in October 1979. In the body of the article, Chalidze was reasonably circumspect, but the newspaper provided it with a sensational headline—"Khomeinism or National Communism"—that stirred up a lot of bad feeling. Chalidze's article was reprinted in *Kontinent* no. 10 (under a different title) and answered by Bukovsky in *Kontinent* no. 11. Meanwhile, Efim Etkind entered the argument on Chalidze's side, in an article that was published in *L'Express* and *Die Zeit*, and Solzhenitsyn published his rebuttal of these charges in *L'Express* and *Novoye Russkoye Slovo* in November 1979.

rising power and vigour of the United States, had nonetheless assimilated that country to the general decline of western Europe, and had unfavourably contrasted American materialism and legalism with the higher spiritual qualities allegedly to be found in Russia.* But distaste for the coldness and emptiness of European life had not been limited to the Slavophiles. Gogol, Dostoyevsky, and Tolstoy had all been repelled in differing degrees by western Europe, and even such a pronounced Westernizer as the socialist Alexander Herzen had been reduced to despair by his experiences there. Indeed, Herzen's responses had been strikingly similar to Solzhenitsyn's a hundred years later.

> I do not know who could find in Europe today happiness or rest. . . . You saw sadness expressed in every line of my letters; life here is very hard, venomous malignity mingles with love, bile with tears, feverish anxiety infects the whole organism, the time of former illusions and hopes has passed. I believe in nothing here, except in a handful of people, a few ideas, and the fact that one cannot arrest the movement. I see the inevitable doom of old Europe and feel no pity for anything that now exists, neither the peaks of its culture nor its institutions. And I stay . . . stay to suffer doubly, to suffer my own personal anguish and that of this world; which will perish, perhaps, to the sound of thunder and destruction towards which it is racing at full steam.[31]

Some of this was pointed out in a perceptive essay on Solzhenitsyn's Harvard speech by the French writer Alain Besançon, who also drew attention to the parallels with Herzen. But Solzhenitsyn, felt Besançon, did not fully share the pessimism about the West of Herzen and other nineteenth-century thinkers, for he still had some hope, as was evidenced by his very willingness to make such speeches and to continue to exhort the West to improve itself. Solzhenitsyn's essential intention was not to construct a theory about Russia and the West—he was more practical than that—but to warn the West of the unprecedented dangers of communism. In Solzhenitsyn's view, communism was not something particularly Russian, nor was it external to the West: it was inherent in the civilization common to both Russia and the West. Solzhenitsyn's message, according to Besançon, was that communism had triumphed in Russia because Russia was more vulnerable, but that it had not been born in Russia. The forces that had brought communism to power there were the same ones that had racked Europe in the nineteenth century and that were still at work all over the world. If the West did not heed the warnings of Solzhenitsyn and others, it, too, would be devoured by this anti-life and change its very nature. The decision as to whether this would happen or not lay in the West's own hands.[32]

The debate about Solzhenitsyn's Harvard address continued for a long time, both in America and in Europe (and, most interestingly, in Japan). As

---

*There is an interesting discussion of the history of this concept in an article by Dale E. Peterson, "Solzhenitsyn's Image of America: The Survival of a Slavophile Idea," in the *Massachusetts Review* (Spring 1978).

late as the winter of 1980, an entire book was published on the subject,[33] and the speech has continued to be regarded as Solzhenitsyn's most authoritative word on these matters and as a major contribution to the debate about American foreign policy and *détente*.*

Whatever the individual views expressed about the speech (an enormous variety of opinion emerged in the usual flood of comment and letters to the press), one thing was undeniable: Solzhenitsyn had again fulfilled his self-chosen function of drawing attention to the subjects and ideas that preoccupied him and putting them on the public agenda. Since the day when *Ivan Denisovich* was published, that agenda had steadily widened: Stalin's labour camps, the Soviet labour-camp system in general, Soviet history, the history of the Revolution, Russian history before the Revolution, the nature of Soviet society, and now the nature of Western society and the conflict (and also the similarities) between the two. He may have been overreaching himself, his voice may have been growing shriller and less convincing as he tried to extend his range further, but the sheer nerve, the sheer courage, and the sheer ambition of the man commanded attention and admiration. They had made him what he was. There was to be no changing him, and no going back. He would continue to proclaim his vision from the roof-tops come what may, and because of his fanatical dedication, the immense strength of his will, and, above all, the magnitude of his past achievements, the world would continue to listen.

*One consequence of the address was that it ruined Solzhenitsyn's chances of visiting the White House. Two weeks later, in a speech to the National Press Club in Washington, Rosalynn Carter went out of her way to reject Solzhenitsyn's allegations that America was "weak, cowardly, and spiritually exhausted" and gave a long list of reasons why she regarded him as wrong. The "intention" to invite Solzhenitsyn to a talk with President Carter was quietly forgotten.

52

EPILOGUE

THERE CAN BE no end to the biography of a living man. The Harvard address would seem an appropriate moment at which to interrupt this chronicle of an extraordinary and unfinished life. Yet there is still something missing, and that is a sense of the domestic life of Solzhenitsyn and his family in their new habitat; and certain loose ends should perhaps be secured before letting the story go.

One might start with Vermont. The journey up to Solzhenitsyn's house through New England is very beautiful and gives one a sense of how successfully the spot was chosen. Leaving Boston, the road passes through a landscape that is characteristically urban American—freeways, shopping plazas, filling stations, motels, a riot of billboards and shrieking neon signs—not the sort of thing to appeal to Solzhenitsyn (or anyone in his right mind). But after a while the asphalt and concrete begin to thin out, green woods and fields appear, and the countryside gets hillier. Wisps of cloud cling to the highest hills, and the light grows soft and luminous—one can see why it reminded the early settlers of England.

Along the striking valley of the Connecticut River, the changes grow more pronounced. The houses are poorer and smaller, the filling stations are down to two pumps standing in the open air, and the farms behind them are fewer and farther apart. The hills get higher, until they turn into thickly wooded mountains with swift, rocky rivers rushing between them. After the ugly regional centre of Ludlow comes Cavendish, which seems idyllic by comparison—a modest village of neat clapboard houses, some white and some in soft hues of red and green, scattered along the shallow valley of the Black River.

Solzhenitsyn's house is situated about four miles past Cavendish, up a narrow, winding road that runs beside a swift mountain stream. The road is paved at first but soon gives way to gravel. There are a few scattered houses and farms, a graveyard clings to a hill above the road to the left, a few local people wave when the Solzhenitsyn family car drives past. Then the road narrows and runs through dense, darkening woods. The undergrowth is tangled; dead trees lie where they have fallen. At the top of the rise, one comes to a single steel gate covered in wire mesh, with a modest sign that says "No Trespassing." Away to either side stretches the chain-link fence about six to eight feet high—a real barrier, but hardly formidable. High above the gate is a television monitor, and just in front of it an electronic box mounted on a pillar, as at the entrance to car-parks. One inserts a card into the box, and the gate opens automatically with a loud buzzing sound. Inside there is another electronic box to reset the mechanism—the gate has already shut itself automatically again.

A narrow dirt track winds up between densely crowded trees and round a sharp bend. Down to the left is a small stream dammed to form a large pond and a waterfall, and beside it is a kind of rustic summer-house. At last one comes to the main house, a two-storey, smoothly boarded rectangular structure with modern windows somewhat in the Swiss or German style, with two wings added in the same material. Inside, the house is as simple as it looks from outside. The entire shell and some of the rooms have been lined with foot-wide cedar boards polished to a tawny reddish brown. The floors are covered with worsted cord carpet in plain solid colours, and the furniture is unobtrusively modern.

Having been completely remodelled, the house has a feeling of light and spaciousness about it. The centre-piece is an enormous lounge from which the ceiling has been removed to allow the room to rise to the roof—the former upstairs landing has been turned into an open gallery that links the two new wings. At one end of this lounge is a wide brick chimney running its full height, with an open hearth facing into the room, and a picture window gives a view of the Vermont mountains. The simple furnishings include a couple of modern couches, a piano in one corner, a photocopier in another, and some bookshelves containing, among other things, foreign editions of Solzhenitsyn's works in Russian. From yet another corner a spiral staircase rises to the gallery. The only problem with this spacious room is that it neither looks nor feels lived in. It is a space, comfortable but impersonal, for receiving visitors, rather like the one the Solzhenitsyns had in Zurich, but more elegant and spacious than the rented accommodation there.

In 1977, when I paid my one and only visit to Vermont, the real life of the house proceeded elsewhere, and first of all in the big, modern American kitchen, where the family meals were taken at a long table with a view of the garden through the picture window. Then there were the study of Solzhenitsyn's secretary and the children's class-room, where they were taught variously by a Russian tutor, by Solzhenitsyn himself, and by his wife, Natalia.

Natalia also had, her work-room in the house, and there was a separate little room near the secretary's study where the television monitor and intercom were situated. Every time it buzzed or crackled, someone (usually the secretary) had to go and answer it.

This was about a year before the Harvard speech, when nine people were living permanently in the house. The noisiest and most visible were Solzhenitsyn's three young children: Ermolai, Ignat, and Stepan (Ermosha, Igonya, and Styopa, to the family). Ermolai was then seven, Ignat five, and Stepan only three. The day for them began with breakfast with their grandmother at seven-thirty, which was preceded by a long Orthodox prayer, recited in unison to the accompaniment of much fervent crossing of the heart and ending with a plea for Russia to be saved from her oppressors. To a non-Russian the prayer had a slightly archaic flavour; given the unchanging (and unchanged) nature of Orthodox ritual, it was probably the same prayer that Solzhenitsyn himself had recited as a child in Kislovodsk. From eight-thirty to ten-thirty for the two younger boys, and for Ermolai during the holidays, there were lessons with a young Russian tutor in the schoolroom (Ermolai had already started at the local school, and since then the other two have started as well). With the tutor they studied reading, writing, arithmetic, history, and geography. As they grew older, Solzhenitsyn himself began giving lessons in elementary mathematics and physics (he remains an excellent teacher), and Natalia taught them Russian literature. The aim was to keep them in a purely Russian atmosphere for as long as possible and to give them a thorough grounding in Russian culture before they started attending American schools—to prepare them, as Natalia put it, for an eventual return to Russia. The children also had a spacious nursery downstairs, a sand-pit, swings, and a heap of rocks to play on outside—and fifty acres of woodland to roam through when they felt like it.

During the holidays a fourth child was in the house—Natalia's son by her first marriage, Dmitri Tiurin. By 1977, when he was fifteen, Dmitri had grown into a broad-shouldered, dark, and handsome boy about six feet tall, with his mother's prominent Russian cheek-bones and broad forehead. During the school year he was away at boarding-school, as a result of which his English was fluent and idiomatic. When at home, he liked to spend most of his days down the road, driving tractors, diggers, and bulldozers for the neighbouring contractor who had done much of the work on Solzhenitsyn's estate (as is the way in Vermont, the contractor was also a farmer and supplied the Solzhenitsyns daily with fresh milk from his small herd of cows).

In addition to Natalia and the children's tutor, two other women were in the house. Solzhenitsyn's secretary (Solzhenitsyn had conceded the need for a secretary only after his move to America—to a large extent, it seems, because he felt less comfortable with English than with German and needed a reliable interpreter) was Irina Alberti, a middle-aged Russian lady, the daughter of Russian *émigrés* of the first emigration (her father had been a Don Cossack and a lawyer, her mother the daughter of a Russian general), and the widow of an Italian diplomat. As a result of her diplomatic peregrinations Mrs Alberti was reputed to speak nine languages, a tremendous help for Solzhenitsyn with his world-wide contacts and correspondence, and she had considerable experience as a journalist. She was, moreover, a devout Russian patriot, deeply devoted to her native land (though born herself in Belgrade) and to Solzhenitsyn himself.

The fourth woman was Ekaterina Svetlova, Natalia's mother, who had taken charge, as in Moscow, of most of the domestic arrangements and was the linchpin that held all its disparate elements together. With her quick intelligence and genius for practical matters, Ekaterina had soon picked up English, learned the ways of American life, and got the household functioning efficiently. She did most of the driving and shopping, the fetching and carrying, and saw to it that the others were able to go about their jobs without worrying too much about daily details.

As for Natalia, she had the most difficult job of all. Apart from her normal duties as wife and mother, which she took very seriously, she acted as a confidential secretary to her husband. She was (and is) the only person in the world he trusts completely, and for that reason was constantly on call for consultations, reading and writing letters, or simply seeing to his physical well-being. Natalia also carried an enormous burden as chairman of the Russian Social Fund, particularly after the arrest of Ginzburg, when she initiated and carried through an international campaign for his release, travelling to a variety of countries and appearing on public platforms in his defence. On these and many other occasions, she acted as Solzhenitsyn's personal representative and ambassador and often attended hearings and committees to testify on dissident matters that Solzhenitsyn considered important. Not least among her duties was that of literary assistant and adviser. She was personally charged with setting and proof-reading the entire nine-volume edition of Solzhenitsyn's Collected Works that he had begun to prepare soon after arriving in Vermont, and she performed similar duties on much else that he wrote.* Finally, she had to deal with Solzhenitsyn's social engagements and many visitors, and ensure that his work programme ran smoothly and was not interrupted by unwelcome intrusions.

At the centre of this professional and domestic web was Solzhenitsyn, yet there was a symbolic appropriateness in the fact that for two-thirds of the year he was physically removed from the house and spent most of his waking hours in the little summer-house beside the pond. It was an exceedingly pretty spot. A footpath wound down from the main house through a dense coppice of birch, sycamore, and pine trees. In the summer, wild flowers grew on the edges of the coppice, and the scent of the blossoms, mingled

---

* The works have since grown to twelve volumes, with more to come. Meanwhile, since the children have grown older, they too have begun to assist with Solzhenitsyn's literary chores. In 1983, at the age of twelve, Ermolai began using Solzhenitsyn's IBM composer and set the type for a volume of memoirs that was due to appear as part of Solzhenitsyn's All-Russian Memoir Library.

with that of the pine needles, was overpowering, particularly towards evening. A wooden foot-bridge traversed the rushing stream that fed the pond. The waterfall was never still, in contrast to the stillness of the pond, whose mirrorlike surface reflected the trees that crowded to the shore on three of its four sides. On the fourth side was the summer-house, a simple creosoted wooden cabin with a tin roof, two windows overlooking the pond, and a small terrace in front of it, on which stood a rustic wooden bench and table. From a small landing-stage jutting into the pond, Solzhenitsyn liked to swim every morning, even in early spring and late into the autumn. His love of the cold, and ability to withstand it, remained undiminished by the years. In the summer the children swam in the pond too.

It is amusing that much play has been made in the press about the alleged luxury of Solzhenitsyn's surroundings and the extravagance of his domestic arrangements, such as the supposed existence of a secret tunnel from the house to his study. Such speculation was fed by Solzhenitsyn's reclusiveness and inaccessibility, but it also rested on a total misunderstanding of his character. Solzhenitsyn detests formality, luxury, elaborateness of any kind. He genuinely prefers the simple life not only on principle but also as a matter of practical comfort and convenience. It is what he has always been accustomed to. There were (and probably still are) no servants in the house, not even a cleaning woman. The four women* did everything themselves in addition to their other duties. As for Solzhenitsyn, he was perfectly capable of taking care of his own domestic needs, and actively preferred to do so. The summer-house was equipped with an ancient refrigerator and a hotplate. He had the food for most of his meals brought to him, so that he could prepare it himself. There was also a high old-fashioned bed and a modest bathroom, making it convenient for him to stay the night in his summer-house. In short, he retained many of his bachelor ways, and his style of life was hardly different from what it once had been in Kok Terek, and then again in his various hide-outs in Solotcha, Rozhdestvo, Rostropovich's and Chukovsky's dachas, and his mountain retreat in Sternenberg.

There was one sense, however, in which the popular myth was accurate. The picture of the former Gulag prisoner surrounding himself with a fence of his own making and shutting himself in behind tight security expressed an essential psychological truth. In his interview with Nikita Struve in 1976, Solzhenitsyn had attributed his choice of closed institutions for the action of most of his novels—the labour camp for *Ivan Denisovich*, the *sharashka* for *The First Circle*, the cancer clinic for the *Cancer Ward*—not only to a psychological quirk but also to the fact that he had spent so much of his life in confinement himself. Whatever the primal source of his behaviour, his retreat to the tiny cabin by the lake inside his stockade only confirmed this deep-seated tendency. Wherever he found himself, it seems, even in the bosom of his family safe from intruders, he felt obliged to retreat still further to peace and soli-

---

*Irina Alberti left Solzhenitsyn's service in 1980. Since then his secretaries have been men.

tude. The spacious house up the hill, with its comfortable armchairs, carpets on the floors, an ultra-modern kitchen stocked with every kind of food, and well-appointed bedrooms and bathrooms, was as nothing to him compared with this draughty summer-house without curtains, with bare tiles on the floor, an oilcloth-covered table to eat from, and a chipped enamel basin and shower cubicle for his ablutions.

These monkish conditions enabled him to concentrate to the fullest on his work and to stick to his preferred routine. Rising between five and six, he would take a dip in the pond, eat breakfast alone, and do domestic chores or read until eight o'clock, when his writing day began. He would then work uninterruptedly until five,* except for short breaks for lunch and to give the children their lesson, after which another break was taken for dinner. If guests were present, Solzhenitsyn would often go up to the house for the evening meal, but not invariably. The evenings would be given over to correspondence, consultations with Natalia and with guests if their business could be put off until that time, and to extra background reading. If he needed to do research that could be carried out at home, he could repair to the modern annex beside the house that held his papers and library and the beginnings of the Russian Memoir Library. This modernist structure, consisting of a cluster of cubes of unequal height and featuring ingeniously angled skylights and an air-conditioned interior, was at the opposite pole from the cabin in its conveniences and was intended to provide space for one or two permanent archivists, as well as for visiting scholars. But whatever his evening occupation, Solzhenitsyn strove to be in bed by ten o'clock. He was a man of strict and rigid habits, and hated disrupting his timetable.

There were, however, one or two physical relaxations (besides swimming) he indulged in occasionally. One of these was tennis, and the one luxury he had permitted himself was the construction of a tennis court in a clearing in the pine woods. It had been an old childhood dream of his to play, yet he had never found an opportunity until his arrival in Vermont. He acknowledged that it was something of an absurdity to start learning at the age of sixty, but he was determined to try. The problem was that he had no regular partners. Ekaterina, his mother-in-law, would play occasionally, and he tried to press Natalia to do the same. In her youth she had represented the Soviet Union in sculling and had been a talented basketball player, but now she practised no sports and would rarely play. Occasionally, she teased her husband that it was "a bourgeois game" that he had no business playing, but mainly she was simply too loaded down with work. "It's not that I don't want to play," she said one day; "I just don't have the time. He doesn't realize how frantically busy I am, and when I have a bit of time to spare, especially with him, I don't want to spend it playing tennis." Solzhenitsyn was graceful on the tennis court but slow and inexpert. He had put on some weight over

*Owing to the sciatica from which he had suffered since the mid-sixties, Solzhenitsyn had taken to doing much of his writing standing up—at a kind of lectern he had had specially constructed for himself—which made the long hours he worked an even more impressive feat of endurance.

the years and this impeded him. He was also impatient, considering a quarter of an hour plenty of time for practice.

He also continued to enjoy certain kinds of physical labour. The one that he invariably permitted himself to be photographed at was sawing logs, sometimes with the children, but he also persisted with the scything that he had learnt at Rozhdestvo. A stainless-steel scythe leaned against the rear wall of his cabin—not for Solzhenitsyn were the noisy, stinking motor mowers of his Vermont neighbours.

For almost all the rest of the time Solzhenitsyn worked, as did everyone else in the house, which gave an aura of seriousness to the whole establishment. There was no solemnity. Indeed, the atmosphere was an appealing blend of the informal and the formal. Meals and mealtimes, except for the evening meal, were entirely informal. Each person pursued his or her timetable at whatever pace was preferred, ate whenever necessary, and washed the dishes afterwards. At the same time, great punctiliousness and formality were observed in arranging meetings or consultations between any two or more people, and punctuality was obligatory. Everyone knocked on doors before entering (except the communal rooms, of course) and waited to be invited in. The central purpose of these arrangements was clearly to protect Solzhenitsyn's working hours as much as possible and to see that not a minute of his time was wasted, and it seemed to work surprisingly well. It also lent a sense of purposefulness and order to the entire household, which had the cohesiveness of a kind of informal monastery, each individual working away for the common good—a situation that Solzhenitsyn emphatically approved of and encouraged.

At the same time there was a slight but noticeable air of suppressed mystery about the place. It was not that Solzhenitsyn's well-known love of secrecy and conspiratorial relations made the atmosphere oppressive (though it may have had this effect in the long run), but there was a general awareness of boundaries and limits. For instance, nearly all visits to the house had to be made in secret, and extensive precautions were taken to see that each visitor concealed from the outside world the very fact of his having been there. Solzhenitsyn's rationale for this was that so many people were clamouring to visit him that he didn't wish to upset those who were refused or to cause undue jealousy among his less fortunate friends and admirers. There was a certain sense in this, but the real reason seems to have been Solzhenitsyn's twin obsessions of maintaining absolute privacy and of controlling everything that had to do with his life and career. One of the simplest ways of exercising that control was to ensure that his various friends, helpers, and advisers never got together, since they did not know who the others were. Another feature was that certain conversations on Russian themes would suddenly run into an evasion or a silence, and it would be suggested that further discussion of that theme was unwise or unwelcome. Then there were the comings and goings of members of the household, especially Natalia, leading to whispered huddles and sometimes the sudden breaking off of one activity to deal with some urgent matter that had just arisen elsewhere. Finally, there were the robot-like humming of the closed-circuit television monitor in its little room, the periodic explosions of the loud buzzer announcing that someone was at the gate, and the crackling of the intercom as the visitor was interrogated. All this created a certain air of excitement that enhanced one's sense of participating in an enterprise of great moment, something that was purposeful, relevant, and perhaps of great importance to the outside world.

The main point of that enterprise was (and still is) Solzhenitsyn's series of novels. *August 1914* had been completed in 1970 and published in 1971. In the six years since then, apart from the essays in *From under the Rubble*, his memoir, *The Oak and the Calf* (most of which had been written by 1973), and *Lenin in Zurich* (also partly written before Solzhenitsyn's expulsion), there had been only speeches and interviews. It was not a great deal in terms of literature, and Solzhenitsyn was aware of it, for he had not forgotten where his true vocation lay. He had felt drawn in the other direction by duty, but his real work was still literature, as he made clear in 1977.

> I was obliged to take an interest in [politics] owing to the appalling circumstances of our life. But I would much prefer not to. . . . Whenever I am attacked, my opponents always insist on regarding me in political terms, under this or that political classification, completely missing the point that this is not my frame-work, not my task, and not my dimension. I cannot be regarded in political terms. A writer's view of the world differs in kind from that of the politician or the philosopher. A politician chooses a political system for himself—"I will accept such and such a party"—and off he goes. A writer chooses above all his language, that is, his people's language. And language is such a mighty, living thing that it subjugates one even more. That is, through language the writer is bound to the tradition of his people. . . . There cannot be a writer who is indifferent to his nationality or to his country. And there cannot be a writer indifferent to his tradition. When I say this, they call me a reactionary and a nationalist. A writer is necessarily bound to his tradition and his nation; it cannot be otherwise. And it is simply impossible to cast a writer in political terms—to say he belongs here or there. It's the wrong way of going about things, a pointless occupation and a waste of time.

Solzhenitsyn elaborated on this theme on the same occasion as follows:

> My critics in the West are constantly saying, "But what is he offering us in exchange?" Well, I could offer plenty if I wanted, but I'm not obliged to. It's not my job. . . . The writer's ultimate task is to restore the memory of his murdered people. Is that not enough for a single writer? . . . They murdered my people and destroyed its memory. And I'm dragging it into the light of day all on my own. Of course, there are hundreds like me back there who could drag it out too. Well, it didn't fall to them; it fell to me. And I'm doing the work of a hundred men, and that's all there is to it. . . . I'm no philosopher, I'm no politician, I get mixed up in this politics, but I loathe it. . . .[1]

There was an element of disingenuousness in these protestations. Sol-zhenitsyn was right about himself insofar as he was describing the Solzhenitsyn of the novels, of *The Gulag Archipelago*, and even of his memoir, but the very genre of the press conference, the newspaper article, the polemical essay, and the public speech seemed to preclude, in his case, the sensitivity that informed his literary works and to bring out the worst in him. It was not that there were "two Solzhenitsyns" with two different philosophies but that the crudity and coarseness of his journalism failed to convince because it lacked the complexity and integrity of his literary prose. These statements were "political" in the sense that was ascribed to them, and Solzhenitsyn could have avoided them had he so wished, and chosen to appear before his public only as a "writer." He did not, however, and perhaps could not, for he returned to the genre of the polemical article again and again, and always with the same dismal results. It was like an addiction that he could not throw off and that was slowly killing not him but his reputation.

It is possible that Solzhenitsyn had got more mixed up in politics since his expulsion not only out of a sense of compulsion but also as a subconscious escape from some of the problems he was encountering in his historical novels. The flood of new information available to him in the West had seemed like a godsend at first, but integrating it into the largely written volumes 2 and 3 of his series was proving to be very difficult, and new light had been thrown on the events depicted in volume 1, *August 1914*. A further problem was connected with the development of one of his principal fictional person-ages, Lenartovich. The figure of this Marxist pro-Bolshevik, once intended to be the hero of the epic (identified with Solzhenitsyn himself) and now cast as a negative character, was destined to play a major role in volume 3, *March 1917*, and Solzhenitsyn was wrestling with the task of depicting him sym-pathetically enough to make him convincing, while not concealing his nega-tive evaluation of Lenartovich's opinions and actions. In doing so, he was engaged in a kind of re-evaluation of his own youth, a process that appears to have caused Solzhenitsyn considerable difficulties.

There was also perhaps the larger question, which Solzhenitsyn has nowhere touched on, of the appropriateness of the whole enterprise. Solzhe-nitsyn has freely admitted that the example of Tolstoy was decisive in lead-ing him to undertake his historical epic. "This is the meaning of literary tradition," he said in 1977, but he implied that he would have come to this form sooner or later even without Tolstoy and even if he had been less steeped in purely Russian literature (and correspondingly better versed in foreign literatures). But the question remains whether the genre of the historical epic has the same meaning and the same validity in the second half of the twen-tieth century that it had in the nineteenth—and whether Solzhenitsyn has been wise to cling so faithfully to a concept first evolved in the thirties, when he was still young. Apart from the century that has elapsed since *War and Peace*, the nearly fifty years since 1936 have been among the most turbulent and exigent of modern times. Solzhenitsyn has rarely admitted to writing difficulties, but it would seem that the transition from East to West, with all its attendant complexities, caused him more problems of this kind than he had ever experienced before.

One sign of it was his decision to add a second volume to *August 1914* and to rewrite parts of the existing volume. He had learned that certain of the domestic details of the Tomchak family (based on his mother's family) were wrong, owing to his too ready acceptance of certain family legends; and he also wished to incorporate many of the criticisms that discerning readers had made of the first volume and passed on to him in letters. It seems that by 1978 the task was finished and that he was also well advanced on the revision of *October 1916* and *March 1917*, regarding parts of them as complete, for in that year he started publishing individual chapters of historical analysis from the former (which he called "survey chapters") in the *Vestnik* and let it be known that the overall title of the series of novels was now to be *The Red Wheel*.* In the same year, he began to publish, through the YMCA Press, a collected edition of his works to date, beginning with the full ninety-six-chapter version of the *The First Circle*, the text of which he had personally checked and revised.

One should not, perhaps, make too much of Solzhenitsyn's delay in publishing the succeeding volumes to *August 1914*, for there were practical difficulties in the way of bringing out more books very quickly. Owing to the chaotic way in which the texts of *The First Circle* and *Cancer Ward* had reached the West, incorporating many errors and deviations from the originals, Solzhenitsyn was anxious to have accurate texts on record. He also wanted to have a complete and accurate text of *The Gulag Archipelago* in print (when the new edition came out, he had added some new notes based on fresh information, and it was copyrighted to the Russian Social Fund instead of to Solzhenitsyn personally). Finally, he was anxious to publish his early plays and screenplay, written while in exile, and accurate versions of *Candle in the Wind* and *The Tenderfoot and the Tart*. All this constituted a backlog that he felt he had to clear before publishing his newer works (even if they were ready), and the position was complicated by an additional backlog in the translations into other languages. Volume 3 of *The Gulag Archipelago*, for instance, did not appear in English until June 1978, just after the Harvard address, and it was to be 1980 before the English and American publication of *The Oak and the Calf*.

There were no financial pressures on Solzhenitsyn to publish. He was one of the world's best-selling authors, and his income was commensurate. In 1976, when *Publishers Weekly* published an informal investigation into Solzhenitsyn's sales, it found that approximately thirty million copies of his books has been sold throughout the world in upwards of thirty languages. The first volume of *The Gulag Archipelago* alone had sold eight to ten million copies, and the three volumes were expected to sell in the region of fifteen million altogether. Volume 1 had sold about two and a half million copies in the United States alone, just over a million in Germany, and just under a million each in Britain, France, and Japan. Sales of the early novels were

*The title was taken from one of the cinematic scenes in *August 1914* in which Solzhenitsyn portrayed a detached carriage wheel revolving in flames, a symbol of a collapsing Russia out of control and on the path to destruction.

almost impossible to compute because of their piecemeal publication, but there had been a distinct drop in Solzhenitsyn's sales after volume 1 of *Gulag*. Volume 2 had sold about a quarter as many as volume 1, and volume 3 fewer than that. *August 1914* and *The Oak and the Calf* had both achieved best-seller status on the continent of Europe, but *August 1914* had done less well in Britain and America, and *The Oak and the Calf* was destined to do likewise.[2] Meanwhile, according to UNESCO's 1976 guide to translations, the *Index Translationum* (which was four years behind with its figures), Solzhenitsyn had "tied with Shakespeare" in 1972 for the number of languages into which his works had been translated, which means that by 1976 the number was probably higher. Solzhenitsyn was outperformed in the matter of translations only by Marx, Engels, Dostoyevsky, Tolstoy, Jules Verne, Gorky, Pearl Buck, and Balzac.[3] When one stops to consider that the figures for the two classics of Marxism and the Russians on the list were certainly inflated by the inclusion of figures for translations into and between the various languages of the USSR (which may well have accounted for the high positions of Jules Verne, Pearl Buck, and Balzac too), and that Solzhenitsyn, on the contrary (unlike Shakespeare), suffered from an absolute absence of such translations, it was a remarkable tribute to his popularity.

The financial consequences were obvious, but since Solzhenitsyn was generally as guarded about his financial affairs as about other aspects of his private life, the figures could only be guessed at. One of the penalties of life in the West, however, was that income-tax statements were open to public scrutiny, and in June 1977 a Zurich newspaper—"insulted," it claimed, by Solzhenitsyn's "arrogant" description of Switzerland in *Lenin in Zurich* as a "republic of lackeys" (these words were Lenin's, not the narrator's)—revealed that in 1974, the year of his exile, Solzhenitsyn had declared earnings of $320,000 and savings of $1.8 million.* Two years later his income was said to have halved to $155,000 and his savings gone down slightly to $1.4 million, but they were still very substantial.[4]

The reason for these disclosures became apparent a few months later, when it was reported that the Swiss tax authorities were investigating Solzhenitsyn's wealth with a view to claiming a large sum in back taxes. The sum mentioned varied from $1.8 million to $2.5 million according to which source one consulted, and word got out because someone in the Swiss Central Taxation Office had leaked confidential documents to the left-wing Zurich newspaper *Tages-Anzeiger*.[5]

The sum at issue related to money deposited by Solzhenitsyn in the Russian Social Fund and consisted mainly of royalties from the sale of *The Gulag Archipelago*. Since the fund was charitable, Solzhenitsyn and his lawyers maintained that no income tax was payable on it, whereas the Swiss tax authorities were questioning this fact. The *Tages-Anzeiger*, which had long been hostile to Solzhenitsyn, exploited the leak to run a whole campaign on

---

*The *New York Times* put it at $401,000 and $2–$3 million, respectively, but the margin of uncertainty indicates how little is known about Solzhenitsyn's real income and financial worth.

the issue, leading some critics of the paper's conduct to conclude that the KGB was behind the leak and that it was all part of that same Moscow campaign to crush the Social Fund which had led to the arrest of Ginzburg. There were suggestions that a host of KGB agents were operating in Switzerland to unearth details about the workings of the fund and the names of the beneficiaries, and one of Solzhenitsyn's Swiss lawyers, Hans-Rudolf Staiger, was said to have received threatening telephone calls demanding to know whom the fund was helping.[6]

It is not clear whether the KGB was truly involved (though it could only have been pleased by the outcry, and there was some publicity about it in the Soviet press). According to Mayor Widmer, there was no investigation. The Swiss authorities had simply reacted to a request from the American tax authorities for clarification of the fund's status and had automatically put a block on any withdrawal of money from the fund until its status had been determined.[7] The other point was that, unlike American law, Swiss law limited the amount of donations that could be considered tax free, and it appeared that Solzhenitsyn, or his advisers, had overlooked this fact when calculating his income. When the dust finally settled, Solzhenitsyn was found to owe about $90,000 in back taxes and was cleared of any imputation of bad faith.[8] Meanwhile, the editor and five reporters of the *Tages-Anzeiger* were charged by the Zurich cantonal authorities with "aiding and abetting the prevention of criminal proceedings" by refusing to hand over the leaked documents, and were subjected to modest fines when found guilty.[9]

Money had a lot to do with the next controversy to burst over Solzhenitsyn's head as well. In June 1978 Olga Carlisle published a short book detailing her relations with Solzhenitsyn and her efforts to ensure the publication of *The First Circle* and *The Gulag Archipelago* in the West. It was a defence against his charge, made without naming names, in *The Oak and the Calf*, that she and her husband had been responsible for delaying the publication of *The Gulag Archipelago* in America and thereby, indirectly, for his expulsion ("two or three soulless, mercenary products of a Western upbringing made a mess of everything that I had sent out at the Feast of Trinity in 1968. The American edition would be six months late and would not help me to hoist myself over the abyss").[10] The wording, as usual in Solzhenitsyn's memoir, was gratuitously sharp, and the generalization about a "Western education" simply shallow (it was a gibe at Olga Carlisle as a Westernized Russian, implying an unfavourable contrast with her Russian parents), nor was it self-evident that his fate would have been different had the American edition of *The Gulag Archipelago* appeared on time. Nevertheless, his basic charge of procrastination seemed unassailable: he (or in this case his lawyer) had not received a publishable text of *Gulag* five years after having delivered it for translation. Olga Carlisle's answer to this was that she (and to a lesser extent her husband) had spent seven years working selflessly on Solzhenitsyn's behalf, that she had cut herself off from "the land of her parentage" as a result, and that her marriage had been "strained by the pressure." Solzhenitsyn's charge was therefore black ingratitude. As to whether the work of editing *The Gulag Archipelago* had been done or not, she maintained that she had offered Dr Heeb a finished version of volume 1 but that Heeb had preferred to take Thomas Whitney's unpolished rough translation instead.

Carlisle derived a good deal of sympathy from the fact of Solzhenitsyn's well-known irascibility and unpredictability,* and this was strengthened when Solzhenitsyn added a footnote to the English-language edition of *The Oak and the Calf*, adducing an additional reason for his criticism. For her "services, expenses, sacrifices, losses, sleepless nights, and those of her husband and their lawyer" described in her book, wrote Solzhenitsyn, Carlisle had taken payments equal to "about half the royalties from the world-wide sale" of *The First Circle*.† "That's the way it always happens: those who perform the main task are not the ones who seek glory. The selfless Western people who aided me in substantial ways in my struggle, who assured the steady flow of my publications in the West . . . are all modestly silent to this day."[11]

The Carlisles responded to this footnote by filing a $2 million lawsuit (for "exemplary and punitive damages") against Solzhenitsyn, charging him and his American publishers (Harper & Row) with libel and invasion of privacy. They maintained that the payments made to them had been "entirely reasonable," that they had "worked expeditiously" in preparing *The Gulag Archipelago* for publication, and that Solzhenitsyn's description of them had "injured their good names and employment prospects and caused them humiliation and anguish." It seemed to confirm Solzhenitsyn's worst suspicions about Westerners and their obsession with invoking the law, but the law in fact vindicated itself. The action was dismissed by a San Francisco judge on the grounds that, even if what Solzhenitsyn had written about the Carlisles had been false, the matter was not actionable because the material complained of constituted an expression of opinion and not allegations of misconduct.[12]

Long before the lawsuit had run its full course, Solzhenitsyn was obliged to deal with some new sallies from his old friends at the KGB. Least disturbing was the publication by the small Hamburg journal *Neue Politik* in February 1978 of the allegations that he had been an informer in Ekibastuz, complete with a photocopy of the letter he was supposed to have written and signed as "Vetrov." The publication was accompanied by a circumstantial account of the supposed investigation of this matter in Moscow by a recently deceased Swiss journalist called Walter Arnau. The account of Arnau's "sensational" discoveries was so swathed in mystery and ambiguity that it added little to what Solzhenitsyn had already divulged himself, and it sank with hardly a ripple.[13]

---

*Some of this sympathy was overdone. Advance publicity described Olga Carlisle as someone who had "risked her life smuggling Solzhenitsyn's works out of the Soviet Union." It is true that Carlisle herself did not write this in her book, but out of an understandable concern for her father, who was still alive at the time, she did not describe his role in the affair as fully as she might, and many readers were left with the impression that the danger to herself had been great.
† The amount charged to Solzhenitsyn was $169,000, of which $50,000 was for lawyers' fees.

Potentially more damaging was the re-emergence of the Czech writer Tomáš Řezáč into the public eye. After returning to Czechoslovakia from Zurich, Řezáč had made a public recantation on Czech television. He had then been taken up by Novosti and "encouraged" to write a Soviet-style biography of Solzhenitsyn. The book appeared first in Italian, published by Teti (the specialists in anti-Solzhenitsyn literature), and soon thereafter in Russian, entitled *The Spiral of Solzhenitsyn's Betrayal.*[14] Řezáč had been afforded every assistance by the Novosti press agency to visit the Soviet Union, travel to the places of Solzhenitsyn's birth and schooldays, and interview former friends and acquaintances. Judging by the list of people mentioned in the book, the overwhelming majority must have refused to have anything to do with Řezáč. He did, however, manage to get a few words with Alexander Kagan, the boy Solzhenitsyn had tussled with at school, and predictably met the thoroughly frightened Vitkevich and Simonyan, although they added little to what they had said already. Řezáč had also called on Natalia Reshetovskaya under the pretext of being the Czech translator of her book, later passing off his question-and-answer session with her (on the subject of her book) as an independent interview, and claimed to have interviewed a friend of Solzhenitsyn's referred to as "L.K."—a transparent reference to Lev Kopelev. Kopelev categorically denied ever having spoken to Řezáč and affirmed in an open letter that every word attributed to him in the book was a fabrication.[15]

The book was published in Russian in the spring of 1978 (on 1 April, to be precise, an appropriate date) by the Progress publishing house in Moscow, and was billed as a translation from the original Czech. The publisher claimed in a foreword that Řezáč had belonged to the "inner circle of Solzhenitsyn's friends" while in Zurich, that his book was "strictly objective," that it "exposed the image of Solzhenitsyn . . . assiduously propagated by contemporary bourgeois propaganda" and constituted, among other things, "a powerful polemic with Solzhenitsyn's most feted publication in the West, *The Gulag Archipelago.*"[16]

Řezáč's book was a predictable tissue of innuendoes, quotations out of context, invented dialogue, and unfounded speculation whose tone can be gauged from the author's opening statement that he had written "not the biography of a writer but an autopsy of the corpse of a traitor." Řezáč's "case" against Solzhenitsyn was a shakily cobbled together patchwork of earlier statements by Vitkevich and Simonyan, the shadier parts of Reshetovskaya's memoirs (mostly interpolations by Novosti), some new allegations by Burkovsky (the prototype of Buinovsky in *Ivan Denisovich*), the resentful Yakubovich, and the terrified Samutin, and a mass of fantastic speculation and invention presumably by Řezáč himself. According to this picture, Solzhenitsyn had been a cunning dodger at school, a coward in the army, an informer in the camps, a lecher in exile, a thief after his rehabilitation, a betrayer of his friends, a committer of incest with his second wife, a talentless hack who had not even mastered the Russian language, a traitor to his country, and a warmonger in the West.

It seems not to have occurred to Řezáč that this "portrait" may have struck its readers as a shade exaggerated. On the other hand, it was difficult to say who its readers were, for the Progress edition was very small, being given only a restricted circulation among senior Party members (even such a relentlessly black picture of Solzhenitsyn as this could be trusted only to a handful of loyalists), and there were no translations into languages other than the Italian. Nevertheless, it seems to have touched a sensitive nerve in Solzhenitsyn. Just before the book's appearance, Natalia Svetlova gave an interview to the German newspaper *Bild am Sonntag* in which she denied that Solzhenitsyn had ever met Řezáč. She also claimed that the Holub couple, who had been Řezáč's friends, had soon been exposed to Solzhenitsyn. as Soviet agents, but Solzhenitsyn, "at the request of the Swiss police," had concealed his knowledge of the fact and fed them disinformation.[17] In early 1979 Solzhenitsyn published an entire booklet, *Skvoz' chad* (Through the Fumes), about Řezáč's book, in which he, too, denied having met Řezáč or having spoken to him.[18]

The booklet was described as a sequel to, or continuation of, *The Oak and the Calf*. Solzhenitsyn had subtitled it "the sixth supplement" (the fifth supplement evidently described Solzhenitsyn's first few months in the West and Svetlova's feat in smuggling out his archives under the noses of the KGB), and it marked a departure from his former practice of not answering attacks. He explained his reasons for this as follows.

> Goodness knows how many have written against me all these years, but I never replied; I kept doing my own work. And that same Novosti agency distributed two collections of slanders against me free of charge in a variety of languages, and I didn't reply. But put yourself in the place of our countrymen now: anyone who wants to find out the truth about me in the Soviet Union can't lay his hands on either *Gulag* or the *Calf*, but only the Progress publication. And when I die, lots more will sink without a trace or simply die away, and [the slander] will stick all the more. And who is behind the slanders? The mightiest power in the modern world, with excellent chances of expanding further.[19]

Solzhenitsyn appears to have been particularly stung by the fact that Řezáč was slandering not only himself but also his parents and family and that, unlike most of the other attacks on him, this one was intended for circulation inside the Soviet Union (and perhaps among Russian *émigrés*). He was ultra-sensitive to his reputation with the Russian people.

It was to be two years before another major attack on Solzhenitsyn was launched by the Soviet authorities; it is worth mentioning, however, not only for the indication of a complete change of tack but also for one unexpected consequence. The change of tack was simply from personal to more general political scurrility. Whereas Řezáč's muck-raking effort had concentrated on depicting Solzhenitsyn as a moral degenerate, a new book, published at the beginning of 1980, tried to show that Solzhenitsyn had been an active CIA agent since before the publication of his first story. The subject of the book was indeed the wider one of the insidious influence of the CIA on the Soviet dissident movement. Written by Solzhenitsyn's old adversary Professor Nikolai Yakovlev and entitled *The CIA against the USSR*,[20] the book was a cold-war manual purporting to show that all the unrest in the Soviet Union since 1957 and all the unofficial art and literature produced during that time were the fruit of CIA infiltration and manipulation. About fifty pages of the book were devoted to Solzhenitsyn, and the tract was meant to serve as a warning to Soviet citizens not to get involved in protest or the reading and distribution of samizdat. Those who did so were the willing (or unwilling) dupes of the CIA and traitors to their country.

One seemingly unlikely outcome of the book's publication was the reappearance on the public scene in Moscow of Natalia Reshetovskaya. Since Solzhenitsyn's expulsion she had dropped out of sight; the publication of her book and the threatened publication of Solzhenitsyn's letters to her had been handled mostly by Novosti, without her direct participation. But in April 1980 she released a blistering attack on Yakovlev (a friend passed it to the *Los Angeles Times*, explaining that Reshetovskaya was afraid to meet Western corresondents herself), accusing him of having produced "a pack of lies" that travestied Solzhenitsyn's life and career, completely distorted the meaning of Solzhenitsyn's works, and hopelessly misjudged Solzhenitsyn's character. Her detailed refutation of some of Yakovlev's cruder arguments could not affect the Soviet publishers, since the purpose of the book was not truth but propaganda, and Reshetovskaya's unfeigned indignation merely demonstrated yet again her naïvety in the face of the cynical manoeuvring of the Soviet authorities (according to the *Los Angeles Times*, Reshetovskaya had personally delivered a copy of her nine-page letter to a startled and embarrassed Yakovlev at his home). The letter also demonstrated her deep and continuing interest in the affairs of her ex-husband, and a surprising willingness to defend him in view of the damaging nature of her own earlier book and the harsh things Solzhenitsyn had had to say about her since.[21]

In fact, her attitude had for some time been ambiguous. She had begun rewriting and expanding her memoirs, and the very process of rereading Solzhenitsyn's early letters to her and of recalling their life together seem to have somewhat softened her bitterness. On the other hand, she had been deeply upset by his comments about her in *The Oak and the Calf* (particularly the allegation that she had been sent to meet him at the Kazan Station by the KGB and that she had published her memoirs with KGB help) and even more by his remarks in *Through the Fumes*, where Solzhenitsyn had again accused her of aiding and abetting the KGB and of helping its agents to fake the "Vetrov" letter. As a result, she had sent Solzhenitsyn a letter in 1979 in the form of a chapter from her new memoirs, in which she denied any connection with the KGB and described some of the problems that she herself had had with Novosti over the preparation and publication of her book. This letter had been given to an American newspaper correspondent in the spring of 1980 and was apparently sent on to Solzhenitsyn via New York.[22]

According to what Reshetovskaya wrote there and elsewhere, she had refrained from protesting about her problems with Novosti out of regard for her friend Konstantin Semyonov and because of her depressed condition in the aftermath of the divorce and Solzhenitsyn's expulsion. She had not realized how badly her book was being mutilated and manipulated by the Novosti editors until she received a copy of the Teti edition in Italian, published in Milan in 1974 (predating the Russian edition). When she saw that her manuscript had been cut by a quarter and its sense distorted in many places, she had written Teti a complaint (in November 1974), and six months later had followed it with an even stronger letter to Novosti. She revealed that she had been prevented from reading either the final typescript sent to Teti or the proofs of the Russian-language edition, on the preposterous grounds that they were "secret," and accused the agency of a variety of sharp practices, ranging from handing out the foreign rights to her book without consulting her to pocketing the royalties and failing to furnish her with accounts. After a considerable struggle she had, it seems, succeeded in getting some of the distortions eliminated and had been able to introduce a number of improvements into the American and French editions of her book. She also asserted that the idea of publishing a collection of Solzhenitsyn's letters had been Semyonov's, not Father Shpiller's, as Solzhenitsyn had alleged, but that she herself had refused. Finally, she disclosed that Tomas Řezáč had been to see her only once—instead of many times, as he had insinuated—and that they had discussed only the contents of her book, nothing more. When she had read Řezáč's final text, she had been absolutely disgusted and had protested energetically to Progress Publishers, demanding that it be withdrawn from circulation.

It is not clear whether Solzhenitsyn received Reshetovskaya's chapter. In any case, it came too late to modify the harsh remarks published in *Through the Fumes*, and it seems unlikely that Solzhenitsyn would have withdrawn them publicly, in the light of his previous comments in *The Oak and the Calf* (and of his known reluctance to recant or apologize). Reshetovskaya suggested another reason why that was unlikely: Solzhenitsyn needed to paint her in black colours and to assign her a negative *political* role, in order to justify his behaviour towards her and assuage a bad conscience. If it was in the name of the "cause," his conduct was easier to justify.

There are indications that she was not, perhaps, too wide of the mark. Just as she, alone in Moscow—or especially on her summer visits to the cabin at Rozhdestvo—recalled the past and grieved over the irrevocable wrong turns and mistakes, so did Solzhenitsyn, in his Vermont seclusion, meditate on that same past and regret the painful dissolution of his marriage. As he remarked in 1977:

> As always, every family story is incredibly complicated and confused. Each side can marshal a thousand arguments, and each person is unavoidably guilty—it's always that way. That's why it is the sort of thing that doesn't allow of a simple solution or a simple paraphrase. All that can be said in the most general terms,

when you take a bird's-eye view of it . . . is that we were both wrong to get married, especially the second time; we should never have done it twice. . . . But of course, so many feelings and memories are invested in any joint life together. And it's terribly painful when it breaks up. . . .

Natalia . . . and I would never have parted if we hadn't had such an awful life the last five years. . . . I was ready for any sort of peaceful coexistence, but she wouldn't have it, she couldn't imagine the seriousness of the danger, she was sure we would never split up.

And when he was obliged to give reasons, his words more or less confirmed Reshetovskaya's fears.

Yes . . . it is a great pity she took the line she did. If only she had taken up a position of non-resistance in the course of our family breakdown, if only she had said, all right, we'll live apart, I would never have done it. But she immediately declared war on me, and in a big way. Well, to wage war against me in almost the same way I waged war against the state, the way I describe it in the *Calf*, is also pretty hopeless. You see, she literally . . . sent word that she would get her revenge, that she would find Solzhenitsyn's enemies, and it's well known who Solzhenitsyn's enemies are. And it's true that if she hadn't chosen that path, we would have simply stayed on good terms, and it's possible we would never have separated. But she immediately started that way, grabbed my papers, and started using them against me, using my letters and in general entering into battle against me. Well, doing battle against me is a waste of time; it's bound to end badly. But if she had simply said, if she had behaved, so to speak, like a wounded bird, I would never have thrown her over; it would have been impossible. I understand that it's wrong to abandon women at that age, I know it. It's terrible, absolutely terrible. It's a weight that will be with you till the end of your days; you'll never have a clear conscience again. It will always be here inside . . . and it's very hard. . . . But it's easier, too, because she went to the KGB—when she co-operates with the KGB and publishes her book, it makes it easier for me. . . . Then I no longer feel that remorse, that awful remorse. . . .[23]

At times like these Solzhenitsyn was apt to grow gloomy and view the world in dark colours. After discussing his difficult relationship with Reshetovskaya and the breakdown of their marriage, he remarked on the way a man's sins catch up with him as he grows older: "In our Orthodox religion the old men are always furiously trying to pray away their sins, because old age has caught up with them and is beginning to strangle them. There is a wonderful Russian proverb: You are born in a clear field, but you die in a dark wood."[24]

For Solzhenitsyn, both the Orthodox religion and the Russian proverbs were a form of consolation, and it would be difficult to say that one was more important than the other. Religion was certainly important to him. Everyone in the house in Vermont wore a cross. Lent was rigorously observed, Easter was more important than Christmas, and the children's saints' day were celebrated as enthusiastically as their birthdays. There was also an Orthodox chapel in the library annex, and services were said there whenever a priest came to the house. But, according to a priest who knew Solzhenitsyn well, it would be a mistake to call him devout. The nearest Orthodox church was only fifteen miles away, in nearby Claremont, and was in the charge of an acquaintance of Solzhenitsyn's (Father Tregubov), yet Solzhenitsyn never went there and would wait for the priest to come to the house to see him (despite the fact that other members of the family attended church regularly). Religion for him, it seems, is not an essential part of his being, but a contingent tool and even a weapon. The sentimental picture of him as a pious man of God is false. Solzhenitsyn certainly believes in God, though it is not always clear whether it is a Christian God, but he experiences insuperable difficulties in humbling himself. He is a deist and does not understand mysticism or the life of the church.*

There is also a sense in which the Orthodox church appears to Solzhenitsyn as just another attribute of Russia. On one occasion he informed an American priest of Russian origin that he should stop his pastoral work and serve Russia, and was taken aback when the priest replied that it was his duty to serve God, not Russia.[25] Solzhenitsyn's love of Russia is passionate and profound, the deepest emotion of his life, and Vermont, if anything, given its superficial resemblances to his homeland, only intensifies his nostalgia. What he misses most is the enveloping warmth of human relations in Russia. "Absolutely everybody lives badly in our country," he said on one occasion, "but you only have to call for help if you need it. I, for example, was helped by dozens of people absolutely disinterestedly. And I never had to ask myself; Can I pay?" In the West, on the other hand, he feels that everything has to be done for money. It is a different style of relations, which is why Russians feel uncomfortable here. "Why else do we all strain to go back? There are lots of other countries that are very good. But it's a different atmosphere, and when you're with your own kind, that's a different atmosphere again."[26]

So strong is his yearning that at one point he suggested he would have made a deal with the Soviet authorities in order to be able to stay. All he wanted was to live peacefully in his own country. "I would have come to an agreement with them . . . you don't touch me and I won't touch you. Just let me work. But they wouldn't let me go anywhere—not to the library, not to the reading-room. They stole my papers, followed me everywhere, and arrested my friends. How can you come to an agreement with people like that? It's impossible, isn't it?"[27]

A consolation is his relationship with Natalia Svetlova. Whatever the true nature of his marriage to Reshetovskaya, this second marriage has every appearance of being a love-match. Svetlova has all the qualities he was look-

---

*This reading of Solzhenitsyn's attitude to religion comes extremely close to some of the reproaches levelled at Solzhenitsyn by Panin in the sixties. Another well-placed source assures me that Solzhenitsyn has taken the criticisms of certain Orthodox friends to heart and has wrestled mightily to bend his will to that of the church.

ing for in a helpmate. She is intelligent, quick-witted, energetic, physically strong, and capable of carrying an enormous work-load. She is devoted body and soul to her husband's cause, and she is warm and physically attractive, capable of providing a solace that was beyond the powers of the elderly, and now ailing, Reshetovskaya. But beyond that she seems truly in love with her husband, and he with her. He is inevitably strict and demanding, but he also shows her great tenderness, calling her by her pet name of "Alya," or "my little girl," when called upon to offer sympathy and consolation.

She also shares his patriotism and his yearning for Russia. Their entire life in Vermont has been organized with a view to getting the maximum amount of work done, but also in such a way that they are ready to abandon everything and return to Russia at a moment's notice. They regard themselves as only temporary visitors to the West. Solzhenitsyn is even sure that this is so.

> I am firmly convinced . . . that I will return, that I will be in time for this business. You know, I feel so optimistic that it seems to me it is only a matter of a few years before I return to Russia. . . . I have no proof of it, but I have a premonition, a feeling. And I have very often had these accurate feelings, prophetic feelings, when I know in advance what is going to happen, how things will turn out, and that's the way it is. I think—I am sure—that I will return to Russia and still have a chance to live there.[28]

Meanwhile he watches and waits—and is still watching and waiting. And working on his great epic. In 1982 the impending publication of the second volume of *August 1914* was announced,* to be followed fairly soon by *October 1916* and *March 1917*, with further volumes in the pipeline. When they appear, they will mark a new period in Solzhenitsyn's long and productive career, a period that in a sense is only just beginning. Readers are waiting to know whether this will represent a falling off from the achievements of the past or, as everyone hopes, a step farther and higher. He regards it as his last and most important task in life. "I am writing a kind of 'Gulag Archipelago' of 1917. If I can do it, I require no more of life. And nothing more can be demanded of a writer."[29]

One thing seems reasonably certain. If he himself does not return to Russia, his books undoubtedly will.

---

* It was published in 1983, together with a revised version of volume 1.

NOTES

These notes are intended as a guide to the sources employed in the composition of this biography, and there are three points that should be borne in mind by readers using them.

The first is that certain individuals, some of whom are inside and some outside the Soviet Union, provided me with information on the express understanding that their names not be revealed. In such instances, I have listed the source as "private information," but in every case I know the identity of the person concerned.

The second point concerns translations. In quoting from Russian originals, I have adopted a policy that some may regard as idiosyncratic. Where no translation into English exists, I have simply made my own. Where the translations into English exist and are accurate (e.g., in the Nobel lecture, *The Oak and the Calf*, and a few other items), I have quoted them verbatim. In most other cases I have made my own translations from the Russian but have referred to existing English-language versions for the convenience of readers. There is, however, a category of translations in which the English version is generally accurate but in which a key word or phrase has been rendered in such a way as to obscure its precise meaning or nuance for the biographer. In these cases I have taken the liberty of amending the relevant words or phrases to bring out the point that needed making (specialists may easily check this procedure by comparing the text with the original Russian).

Thirdly, I should point out that whereas in some notes a reference is made to page numbers, in others the reference is to a chapter. This is because I am often dealing with a text that exists in several versions, and in particular because these notes are meant to serve both English and American readers.

Since the paginations in British and U.S. editions of the books in question rarely coincide, it seemed more satisfactory to indicate chapters than to give preference to a particular set of editions.

Chapter 1

1. *August*, chap. 2. Solzhenitsyn has confirmed to the author that the opening chapters of the novel (and other chapters dealing with the Tomchak family) contain a true account of his ancestry. Some of this information was repeated and enlarged upon in his Mar. 1972 interview with the two American correspondents Robert Kaiser and Hedrick Smith. For the fullest text of the interview see appendix 22 to *Oak*.

2. Leo Tolstoy, *The Cossacks*, trans. Louise and Aylmer Maude, in *Collected Works*, vol. 4 (Oxford, 1932), 281. Tolstoy's journey this way is recorded in N. N. Gusev, *Letopis' zhizni i tvorchestva L'va Nikolaevicha Tolstogo* (Chronicle of the Life and Works of Lev Nikolayevich Tolstoy) (Moscow, 1958), 45.

3. Information about the names and ages of Solzhenitsyn's grandparents and aunts and uncles in this and the next paragraph was provided by Solzhenitsyn in an interview with the author in Vermont in June 1977 (hereafter referred to as Solzhenitsyn interview).

4. Ibid.

5. Ibid.

6. Ibid.

7. Solzhenitsyn referred to the manner of his father's death in his interview with Smith and Kaiser and has mentioned it obliquely in a number of other interviews. The circumstantial account given here is based on Solzhenitsyn's description of it to the author.

8. Dieter Steiner, "Eine Familie von Flegeln" (A Family of Boors), *Stern*, 21 Nov. 1971, pp. 105–10. This tendentious article, based in part on Irina's memoirs, is not very reliable on the whole, but does contain some accurate information on Solzhenitsyn's mother's side of the family (see my discussion of the circumstances in which the article was written, in chap. 41.

9. Nikolai Zernov, *Na perelome* (At the Breaking-point) (Paris, 1970), 286.

10. Ibid., 286–88.

11. Ibid., 289; and A. D. Shkuro, *Zapiski belogo partizana* (Memoirs of a White Partisan) (Buenos Aires, 1961), 62, 64, 66, 71, 74, 76.

12. Solzhenitsyn interview.

13. Shkuro, 55, 67–77.

14. Information on the political and military situation in the North Caucasus incorporated into the remainder of this chapter and into Chapter 2 is drawn from the following sources (in addition to Zernov and Shkuro): J. F. N. Bradley, *Civil War in Russia, 1917–1920* (London, 1975); David Footman, *Civil War in Russia* (New York, 1961); M. Philips Price, *War and Revolution in Asiatic Russia* (London, 1918) and *My Reminiscences of the Russian Revolution* (London, 1921); W. H. Chamberlin, *The Russian Revolution, 1917–1921*, 2 vols. (New York, 1965); E. H. Carr, *The Bolshevik Revolution, 1917–1923*, vol. 1 (London, 1950); V. I. Kuznetsov, ed., *Istoria Dona* (A History of the Don) (Rostov, 1967); I. Borisenko, *Sovetskie respubliki na severnom Kavkaze v 1918 godu* (Soviet Republics in the North Caucasus) (Rostov, 1930); *Dvadtsat' let osvobozhdenia Stavropol'ia ot Belykh* (The Twentieth Anniversary of the Liberation of Stavropol from the Whites); Philip Longworth, *The Cossacks* (London and New York, 1969).
1969).

15. Zernov, 289–90.

16. Shkuro, 192.

Chapter 2

1. Zernov, 322.

2. Solzhenitsyn interview.

3. H. N. H. Williamson, *Farewell to the Don* (London, 1971), 166.

4. Ibid., 250.

5. Solzhenitsyn interview.

6. Ibid.

7. Georges Suffert, "Solzhenitsyn in Zurich: An Interview," *Encounter*, Apr. 1976, pp. 9–15.

8. Information for this and the two preceding paragraphs is taken from my interview with Solzhenitsyn.

9. Ibid.

10. *Gulag*, vol. 3, pt. 5, chap. 2.

11. Stephen Graham, *Changing Russia* (London, 1915), 25–26.

12. Rhoda Power, *Under Cossack and Bolshevik* (London, 1919), 19.

13. *The Way* (unpublished), chap. 1. This poem is also known by its original title, *Volunteers' Highway*.

14. *August*, chap. 59.

15. Solzhenitsyn interview.

16. *August*, chap. 59.

17. Information on Taissia's situation in Rostov is taken from my interview with Solzhenitsyn.

18. Conversation with Anna Voloshina, 17 Apr. 1983.

19. Solzhenitsyn interview.

20. Pavel Ličko, "Jedného dňa u Alexandra Isajeviča Solženicyna" (One Day with Alexander Isayevich Solzhenitsyn), in *Kulturni Život* (Cultural Life) (Bratislava), 31 Mar. 1967. A partial translation is in Leopold Labedz, ed., *Solzhenitsyn: A Documentary Record*, enl. ed. (Bloomington, Ind., 1973), 32–38.

21. Solzhenitsyn interview.

22. Ibid.

23. *August*, chap. 3. The description of the Shcherbak family is based on chaps. 3 and 9 of this novel (one-volume edition).

24. Ibid., chap. 9.

25. *The Way*, chap. 1; and Solzhenitsyn interview.

26. *Gulag*, vol. 1, pt. 1, chap. 5.

27. Solzhenitsyn interview.

28. Ibid.

Chapter 3

1. *Gulag*, vol. 1, pt. 1, chap. 5.

2. Solzhenitsyn interview; private information; and Solzhenitsyn's extract from the "sixth supplement to *The Oak and the Calf*," published in Russian as a separate pamphlet, *Skvoz' chad* (Through the Fumes) (Paris, 1979).

3. Solzhenitsyn interview.

4. Ibid.

5. Vladimir Bukovsky, *To Build a Castle*, trans. Michael Scammell (London, 1978), 95.

6. *Skvoz' chad*, 22.

7. Ibid., 29.

8. *First Circle*, chap. 68. Unless otherwise indicated, all references to *First Circle* are to the shorter, 87-chapter version, which was translated into English.

9. Solzhenitsyn interview.

10. *Skvoz' chad*, 29–30.

11. Solzhenitsyn interview.

12. Ibid.

13. This story of Zakhar's last days and death was told to me by Solzhenitsyn. It is also briefly referred to in *The Way*.

14. *The Way*, chap. 1.

15. *Gulag*, vol. 1, pt. 1, chap. 1.

16. *Encounter*, Apr. 1976, pp. 9–15; and Solzhenitsyn interview.

17. *The Way*, chap. 3.

18. *Gulag*, vol. 1, pt. 1, chap. 1.

19. Solzhenitsyn interview; and *The Way*, chap. 3.

Chapter 4

1. Conversation with Lev Kopelev, 15 May 1970.

2. *Encounter*, Apr. 1976, pp. 9–15.

3. Robert Conquest, *The Great Terror* (London, 1968), 22.

4. *Times* (London), 21 Feb. 1976.

5. Conversation with Bayara Aroutunova, 11 June 1977.

6. Solzhenitsyn interview.

7. *Skvoz' chad*, 41; Solzhenitsyn interview; conversation with Natalia Svetlova, 17 June 1977; and unpublished letter to the author from Natalia Reshetovskaya, 16 May 1982.

8. *Skvoz' chad*, 41–42.

9. *First Circle*, chap. 24.

10. Natalia Reshetovskaya, *Sanya: My Life with Alexander Solzhenitsyn*, trans. Elena Ivanoff (Indianapolis, 1975), 19.

11. *Skvoz' chad*, 42–43.

12. Unpublished letter to the author from Natalia Reshetovskaya, 16 May 1982.

13. *Skvoz' chad*, 42–43.

14. This discussion of Solzhenitsyn's early works is based on the author's examination of them in June 1977.

15. Solzhenitsyn interview.

16. *Prussian Nights*, trans. Robert Conquest (London and New York, 1977), 26–27. This long poem originally formed chap. 9 of *The Way*.

17. *Gulag*, vol. 1, pt. 1, chap. 5.

18. Solzhenitsyn interview.

19. Unpublished letter to the author from Natalia Reshetovskaya, 31 Oct. 1982; and conversation with Anna Voloshina.

20. Solzhenitsyn interview.

21. Ibid.
22. *Encounter*, Apr. 1976, pp. 9–15.
23. Ibid.
24. *Gulag*, vol. 3, pt. 6, chap. 7.
25. Solzhenitsyn interview.
26. Ibid.; and *Gulag*, vol. 1, pt. 1, chap. 2.
27. Ibid.
28. *Encounter*, Apr. 1976, pp. 9–15.
29. *First Circle*, chap. 34.
30. *Gulag*, vol. 1, pt. 1, chap. 4.
31. Ibid.

Chapter 5

1. *The Way*, chap. 1.
2. *First Circle*, chap. 61.
3. Solzhenitsyn interview.
4. *The Way*, chap. 1.
5. Solzhenitsyn interview.
6. Reshetovskaya, 1.
7. Ibid., 5–6.
8. Ibid., 7.
9. Unpublished letter to the author from Natalia Reshetovskaya, 16 May 1982.
10. Ibid.
11. Solzhenitsyn interview.
12. Reshetovskaya, 6.
13. Ibid., 8.
14. Solzhenitsyn interview.
15. Reshetovskaya, 8–9; and Solzhenitsyn interview.
16. Solzhenitsyn interview.
17. Reshetovskaya, 9.
18. Conversation with Veronica Stein, 11 Sept. 1976.
19. *The Way*, chap. 2.
20. *Ibid.*
21. Solzhenitsyn interview; and Reshetovskaya, 10.
22. *The Way*, chap. 2.
23. Reshetovskaya, 11; part of the quotation appears only in the Russian edition, *V spore so vremenem* (In Dispute with Time) (Moscow, 1975), 15.
24. Solzhenitsyn interview.
25. Reshetovskaya, 59; and Solzhenitsyn interview.
26. Reshetovskaya, 12.
27. Solzhenitsyn interview.
28. Ibid.
29. Ibid.
30. *Gulag*, vol. 1, pt. 1, chap. 5.

31. *The Way*, chap. 2.
32. *Gulag*, vol. 3, pt. 5, chap. 1.
33. Ibid.; and Reshetovskaya, 36–37, 40.
34. Reshetovskaya, 21.

Chapter 6

1. *First Circle*, chap. 61.
2. Reshetovskaya, 23. The English translation contains a mistake: "inappropriate" should read "appropriate."
3. Solzhenitsyn interview.
4. "Incident at Krechetovka Station," in Alexander Solzhenitsyn, *Stories and Prose Poems*, trans. Michael Glenny (London and New York, 1971), 171–73.
5. Ibid., 173.
6. Solzhenitsyn interview.
7. *Gulag*, vol. 1, pt. 1, chap. 4.
8. Ibid.
9. Reshetovskaya, 34.
10. Ibid., 33–34.
11. Ibid.
12. Natalia Reshetovskaya, Russian edition, 26. This phrase does not appear in the English translation.
13. Reshetovskaya, 36–37. Additional information from Reshetovskaya, Russian edition, 27–29; and Solzhenitsyn interview.
14. Reshetovskaya, Russian edition, 26.
15. *The Way*, chap. 5.
16. Ibid., chap. 8.
17. Solzhenitsyn interview.
18. Reshetovskaya, 37.
19. Quoted in Alexander Werth, *Russia at War: 1941–1945* (New York, 1964), 682.
20. Solzhenitsyn interview.
21. Reshetovskaya, 55–56.

Chapter 7

1. Reshetovskaya, 26, 44, 53, 96.
2. Ibid., 45.
3. Ibid., 45–46.
4. Solzhenitsyn interview.
5. Reshetovskaya, 50.
6. Ibid., 50; and Russian edition, p. 39.
7. *Skvoz' chad*, 24–25; Solzhenitsyn interview; and unpublished letter to the author from Natalia Reshetovskaya, 16 May 1982.
8. Solzhenitsyn interview.
9. Unpublished letter to the author from Natalia Reshetovskaya, 31 Oct. 1982.
10. Solzhenitsyn interview.

11. Reshetovskaya, 56; and unpublished letter to the author from Natalia Reshetovskaya, 16 May 1982.

12. Reshetovskaya, 55.

13. *Gulag*, vol. 3, pt. 5, chap. 1.

14. *The Way*, chap. 5.

15. *Gulag*, vol. 1, pt. 1, chap. 6.

16. Quoted in Labedz, 23.

17. *Gulag*, vol. 1, pt. 1, chap. 4.

18. Ibid.

19. Reshetovskaya, 59–60.

20. Ibid., 60–61.

21. Ibid., 61.

22. Unpublished footnote to *Gulag*, vol. 1, made available to the author by Solzhenitsyn.

23. Solzhenitsyn interview.

24. Reshetovskaya, 58–59.

25. Quoted by Solzhenitsyn in *The Way*, chap. 8.

26. Ibid.

27. Reshetovskaya, 62. The comment about the listening-posts appears only in the Russian edition, 47.

28. Ibid., 63.

29. This account of Solzhenitsyn's adventure in East Prussia is taken from *Skvoz' chad*, 34–39.

30. *Prussian Nights*, 22–27.

31. *Gulag*, vol. 1, pt. 1, chap. 6.

32. Reshetovskaya, 63–64.

33. Solzhenitsyn interview.

34. Reshetovskaya, 64.

35. This account of Solzhenitsyn's arrest is based on *Gulag*, vol. 1, pt. 1, chap. 1, and the author's interview with Solzhenitsyn. After the publication of *Ivan Denisovich* had made him famous, Solzhenitsyn had a cordial reunion with Travkin, who was by then a general in retirement.

Chapter 8

1. *Kulturni Život*, 31 Mar. 1967.

2. Solzhenitsyn interview, and *The Way*, chap. 10.

3. *Gulag*, vol. 1, pt. 1, chap. 1; and Solzhenitsyn interview.

4. Solzhenitsyn interview.

5. *The Way*, chap. 11.

6. Solzhenitsyn interview.

7. I have it on Solzhenitsyn's authority that the description of Volodin's induction into the Lubyanka is based literally on what happened to him. I have therefore utilized his description in chronicling his own first days in the prison.

8. *First Circle*, chap. 83.

9. Ibid.

10. James Allan, *No Citation* (London, 1955).

11. Solzhenitsyn interview.

12. *Gulag*, vol. 1, pt. 1, chap. 5. The entire following description of Solzhenitsyn's first cell is taken from that chapter.

13. Ibid.

14. Ibid.

Chapter 9

1. *Gulag*, vol. 1, pt. 1, chap. 5.

2. Ibid.

3. Ibid.

4. Ibid.

5. Ibid.

6. Ibid.

7. Solzhenitsyn interview.

8. *Gulag*, vol. 1, pt. 1, chap. 3.

9. Solzhenitsyn interview.

10. Reshetovskaya, 84.

11. *Gulag*, vol. 1, pt. 1, chap. 3.

12. Solzhenitsyn interview.

13. Werth, 969.

14. *Gulag*, vol. 1, pt. 1, chap. 3.

15. Ibid.

16. Ibid.

17. Ibid., chap. 6.

18. Ibid.

19. Ibid.

20. Ibid., chap. 7.

Chapter 10

1. The Special Board was evidently abolished in 1953, soon after Stalin's death, but it is characteristic that the news of its abolition emerged only three years later. For my account of the Special Board, I have drawn on Conquest, *Great Terror;* Ivo Lapenna, *Soviet Penal Policy* (London and Chester Springs, Pa., 1968); David Dallin and Boris Nicolaevsky, *Forced Labor in Soviet Russia* (New Haven, 1947); and *Gulag*, vol. 1.

2. *Gulag*, vol. 1, pt. 1, chap. 7.

3. Ibid., pt. 2, chap. 4.

4. Ibid.

5. Ibid.

6. Reshetovskaya, 65–66.

7. Ibid., 66.
8. Ibid., 68.
9. Ibid., 86–88; and conversation with Veronica Stein.
10. Ibid., 91.
11. *Gulag*, vol. 1, pt. 2, chap. 2.
12. Ibid.
13. Ibid.
14. Ibid.
15. Ibid.
16. Ibid.
17. Reshetovskaya, 78–79; and Russian edition, 66–67.
18. *First Circle*, chap. 34.
19. Reshetovskaya, 93.

Chapter 11

1. *Gulag*, vol. 1, pt. 2, chap. 2.
2. Ibid.
3. Reshetovskaya, 92–93.
4. *First Circle*, chap. 35.
5. Reshetovskaya, 94.
6. *Gulag*, vol. 2, pt. 3, chap. 6.
7. Ibid.
8. Ibid.
9. Ibid.
10. Ibid.
11. Ibid.
12. Ibid.
13. Reshetovskaya, 100.
14. *Gulag*, vol. 2, pt. 3, chap. 6.
15. Reshetovskaya, 95.
16. *Gulag*, vol. 2, pt. 3, chap. 6.
17. Ibid.
18. Ibid.
19. Ibid.

Chapter 12

1. *Gulag*, vol. 2, pt. 3, chap. 9.
2. Ibid.
3. Ibid.
4. *First Circle*, chap. 35.
5. Reshetovskaya, 96.
6. *First Circle*, chap. 35.
7. *Gulag*, vol. 2, pt. 3, chap. 9.
8. Reshetovskaya, 100–101.
9. *Gulag*, vol. 2, pt. 3, chap. 12. I have followed the rest of this chapter for my description of Solzhenitsyn's recruitment as an informer.
10. Ibid., chap. 8.
11. Ibid., chap. 9.

12. Ibid., chap. 18.
13. Ibid.
14. Ibid.
15. Unpublished letter to the author from Natalia Reshetovskaya, 31 Oct. 1982.
16. *Gulag*, vol. 1, pt. 2, chap. 4.

Chapter 13

1. *Gulag*, vol. 1, pt. 2, chap. 4.
2. Ibid.
3. Ibid.
4. Ibid.
5. Ibid.
6. Zhores Medvedev, *Soviet Science* (New York, 1978), 32–41.
7. Reshetovskaya, 107–8.
8. Solzhenitsyn interview.
9. *First Circle*, chap. 5.
10. Lev Kopelev has described the conversion in vol. 3 of his memoirs, *Ease My Sorrows*, trans. Antonina W. Bouis (New York, 1983), 3–9.
11. Dimitri Panin, *The Notebooks of Sologdin*, trans. John Moore (London, 1976), 262–63.
12. Ibid., 259.
13. Ibid., 258.
14. *First Circle*, chap. 3.
15. Kopelev, 8.
16. Reshetovskaya, 101.
17. Kopelev, 20.
18. Ibid., 11.
19. *First Circle*, chap. 31.
20. Panin, 265.
21. Kopelev, 12.
22. Conversation with Peretz Hertzenberg, 24 May 1980.
23. Kopelev, 12–13.
24. Ibid., 14.
25. Ibid., 17.
26. Ibid., 18–19.
27. Reshetovskaya, 110.
28. Kopelev, 5.

Chapter 14

1. Kopelev, 9, 22, 25–26.
2. *First Circle*, chap. 34.
3. Kopelev, 113; and Reshetovskaya, 118–19.
4. Reshetovskaya, 116.
5. Conversation with Veronica Stein.
6. Ibid.

7. Reshetovskaya, 116–17, 124–29.
8. Ibid., 131, 133.
9. Ibid., 116–17.
10. Ibid., 117.
11. Solzhenitsyn interview.
12. Ibid.
13. Ibid.
14. Ibid.
15. Conversation with Peretz Hertzenberg.
16. Kopelev, 93–94.
17. Panin, 284.
18. *First Circle*, chap. 53.
19. Kopelev, 3, 12, 18–19; and *First Circle*, chaps. 24, 61, 62.
20. Reshetovskaya, 107.
21. Ibid.
22. Kopelev, 16–17.
23. Solzhenitsyn interview.
24. Ibid.
25. Kopelev, 24.
26. *First Circle*, chap. 5.
27. Reshetovskaya, 114–15.
28. Kopelev, 23.
29. *First Circle*, chap. 37.
30. Reshetovskaya, 132.
31. Ibid., 136.
32. *First Circle*, chap. 42. The two sentences beginning with "What did the state . . ." and ending with "matter" were omitted from the shorter version of the novel that circulated in samizdat and was translated into foreign languages. They appear in the longer version—96 chapters instead of 87—that was published in Russian in Paris in 1978 (chap. 46 in *Sobranie sochinenii*, vol. 1, p. 362). There is as yet no English translation of the full version of the novel.
33. Reshetovskaya, 132–33.
34. Ibid., 134.
35. Ibid., 136.

Chapter 15

1. Kopelev, 34–35; and conversation with Peretz Hertzenberg.
2. Kopelev, 37–38.
3. *First Circle*, chap. 14.
4. Kopelev, 38; and conversation with Peretz Hertzenberg.
5. Kopelev, 59, 83–84; and conversation with Peretz Hertzenberg.
6. Kopelev, 47–49, 67–68.
7. *First Circle*, chaps. 43 and 74; Kopelev,
88–89; and conversation with Peretz Hertzenberg.
8. Kopelev, 44.
9. Ibid., 39–45; and conversation with Peretz Hertzenberg.
10. Conversation with Veronica Stein; and Reshetovskaya, 137.
11. Reshetovskaya, 139.
12. Ibid., 143.
13. Kopelev, 72–76.
14. Panin, 270–73.
15. Kopelev, 59.
16. Ibid., 90–92.
17. Solzhenitsyn interview.
18. *First Circle*, chap. 26.
19. Reshetovskaya, 116.
20. *First Circle*, chap. 5.
21. Reshetovskaya, 148.
22. Ibid.
23. This detailed account is largely based on information provided by Lev Kopelev in *Ease My Sorrows*, 88–92, and on a conversation with Kopelev.
24. Kopelev, 91.
25. Panin, 273–74; Kopelev, 90–92; *First Circle*, chap. 87; and conversation with Peretz Hertzenberg.

Chapter 16

1. *Gulag*, vol. 1, pt. 2, chap. 4.
2. *First Circle*, chap. 85.
3. Anatoly Marchenko, *My Testimony*, trans. Michael Scammell (London, 1969), 15–16.
4. *First Circle*, chap. 85.
5. *Gulag*, vol. 3, pt. 5, chap. 2.
6. Ibid.; and Panin, 290–91.
7. *Gulag*, vol. 3, pt. 5, chap. 2.
8. Ibid.
9. Ibid., vol. 1, pt. 2, chap. 2.
10. Quoted in Leonid Grossman, *Dostoevsky: A Biography*, trans. Mary Mackler (Indianapolis and New York, 1975), 173.
11. *Gulag*, vol. 3, pt. 5, chap. 2.
12. Ibid.
13. Panin, 293.
14. *Gulag*, vol. 3, pt. 5, chap. 2. The description of Ekibastuz and of Solzhenitsyn's first days there is taken from chaps. 2 and 3 of vol. 3, pt. 5.
15. Ibid., chap. 3.
16. Ibid. (the translation has been slightly adjusted).

17. Reshetovskaya, 150.

18. *Gulag*, vol. 2, pt. 3, chap. 9.

19. Ibid., vol. 3, pt. 5, chap. 3.

20. S. P. Shevchenko, *Ekibastuz* (Alma-Ata, 1982), 41.

21. Reshetovskaya, 154.

22. *Gulag*, vol. 3, pt. 5, chap 5.

23. Ibid.

24. Ibid.

25. Ibid.

26. Ibid.

27. Ibid.

28. Panin, 296.

29. Conversation with Dimitri Panin, 10 Dec. 1980.

30. *Gulag*, vol. 2, pt. 3, chap. 5.

Chapter 17

1. *Gulag*, vol. 3, pt. 5, chap. 5.

2. Ibid.

3. Ibid.

4. The story of Tenno's escapes is found ibid.

5. Ibid.; and Panin, 297–317.

6. Panin, 310–11.

7. *Gulag*, vol. 3, pt. 5, chap. 11.

8. Panin, 314.

9. Ibid.

10. *Gulag*, vol. 3, pt. 5, chap. 11.

11. Ibid.

12. Ibid.

13. Panin, 315–17; and conversation with Dimitri Panin.

14. *Gulag*, vol. 2, pt. 4, chap. 1; and *Cancer Ward*, chap. 6.

15. *Gulag*, vol. 2, pt. 4, chap. 1.

16. Reshetovskaya, 150 and 152, and unpublished letter to the author, 16 May 1982.

17. *Gulag*, vol. 2, pt. 4, chap. 1.

18. Ibid.

19. Ibid.

20. Unpublished letter to the author from Natalia Reshetovskaya, 16 May 1982.

21. *Gulag*, vol. 2, pt. 4, chap. 1.

22. Ibid.

23. Ibid.

24. Reshetovskaya, 166.

25. Ibid., 167.

26. *The Love-Girl and the Innocent*, trans. Nicholas Bethell and David Burg (London, 1969), 23.

27. Reshetovskaya, 156–57, and unpublished letter to the author, 16 May 1982.

28. Reshetovskaya, 160.

29. Unpublished letter to the author from Natalia Reshetovskaya, 16 May 1982.

30. Ibid. The following account of Natalia's relationship with Vsevolod and of their subsequent marriage is based partly on her unpublished letter to the author of 16 May 1982 and partly on her memoirs.

31. Reshetovskaya, 169.

32. Unpublished letter to the author from Natalia Reshetovskaya, 16 May 1982.

33. Reshetovskaya, 161.

34. Ibid., 167.

35. Notably a former friend and colleague of Simonyan's who prefers not to be identified at present.

36. Both the poem and the extract from *The Way* are in *Vestnik RKhD*, no. 117 (1976).

37. *Gulag*, vol. 3, pt. 6, chap. 7.

Chapter 18

1. *Gulag*, vol. 3, pt. 6, chap. 5.

2. Ibid.

3. Ibid.

4. Ibid.

5. *Cancer Ward*, chap. 20.

6. Solzhenitsyn interview.

7. *Leninskaya Smena*, 10 Jan. 1965.

8. Solzhenitsyn interview.

9. *Gulag*, vol. 3, pt. 6, chap. 6.

10. *Leninskaya Smena*, 10 Jan. 1965.

11. Solzhenitsyn interview.

12. *Gulag*, vol. 3, pt. 6, chap. 5.

13. Ibid.

14. Ibid.

15. Solzhenitsyn interview.

16. Ibid.

17. Ibid.

18. Dimitri Panin, *Zapiski Sologdina* (The Memoirs of Sologdin) (Frankfurt, 1973), 479.

19. *Index on Censorship* (London), 1, no. 2 (1972), 149–51.

20. *Oak*, 66.

21. Solzhenitsyn interview.

22. Anna Akhmatova, *Sochineniia* (Works), vol. 2 (Munich, 1968), 343.

23. In English translation, *Victory Celebrations*, trans. Helen Rapp and Nancy Thomas (London, 1983), 31.

24. Ibid., 79.

25. Solzhenitsyn interview; and unpublished letter to the author from Natalia Reshetovskaya, 1 Dec. 1982.

26. Part of the poem's preface was quoted by Veniamin Teush in his article "A. Solzhenitsyn and the Writer's Spiritual Mission." The translation appeared in *Index on Censorship*, 1, no. 2 (1972), 149–51.

27. Reshetovskaya, 175.

28. *Gulag*, vol. 3, pt. 6, chap. 6.

29. Solzhenitsyn interview.

30. Reshetovskaya, 176–77.

31. Shown to the author by Solzhenitsyn. Its accuracy has been confirmed by Natalia Reshetovskaya.

Chapter 19

1. Solzhenitsyn interview. Solzhenitsyn later introduced the root and the story of his excursion into the plot of *Cancer Ward*.

2. *Gulag*, vol. 2, pt. 4, chap. 3.

3. Unpublished letter to the author from Natalia Reshetovskaya, May 1983.

4. *Cancer Ward*, chap. 3.

5. Unpublished letter to the author from Natalia Reshetovskaya, May 1983.

6. *Oak*, 3–4.

7. Solzhenitsyn interview.

8. *Cancer Ward*, chap. 6; and William A. Knaus, *Inside Russian Medicine* (New York, 1981), chap. 14.

9. Reshetovskaya, 179.

10. *Cancer Ward*, chap. 6.

11. "The Right Hand," in *Stories and Prose Poems*.

12. *Cancer Ward*, chap. 22.

13. Ibid., chap. 11.

14. Ibid., chap. 35.

15. *Oak*, 4.

16. Solzhenitsyn interview.

17. *Leninskaya Smena*, 10 Jan. 1965.

18. Ibid.

19. Ibid.

20. *Oak*, 4.

21. Solzhenitsyn interview.

22. Ibid.

23. Ibid.

24. Ibid.

25. Ibid.; and Reshetovskaya, 183.

26. Conversation with Lev Kopelev.

27. Solzhenitsyn interview.

28. Conversation with Veronica Stein.

29. *Oak*, 29.

30. Quoted in the unpublished samizdat magazine *Veche* (Assembly), no. 5 (25 May 1972). *Veche* published two chapters from Reshetovskaya's original draft of her memoirs before they were edited by the Novosti news agency. They are much fuller than the published version. *Veche*, no. 5, can be found, in Russian, in *Arkhiv Samizdata* (Samizdat Archive), Document no. AS1230 (18 May 1973), distributed by Radio Liberty in Munich.

31. *Gulag*, vol. 3, pt. 5, chap. 11.

32. Unpublished letter to the author from Natalia Reshetovskaya, 1 Jan. 1983.

33. Solzhenitsyn interview.

34. *Gulag*, vol. 3, pt. 6, chap. 6.

35. Solzhenitsyn interview.

36. Ibid.; and unpublished letter to the author from Natalia Reshetovskaya.

37. Reshetovskaya, 185.

38. Solzhenitsyn interview.

Chapter 20

1. Solzhenitsyn interview; and conversations with Dimitri Panin and with Lev Kopelev.

2. *Stories and Prose Poems*, 4.

3. Solzhenitsyn interview.

4. *Gulag*, vol. 3, pt. 6, chap. 6.

5. Unpublished letter to the author from Natalia Reshetovskaya, 16 May 1982.

6. Ibid.

7. Reshetovskaya, 186.

8. Ibid., 187.

9. Solzhenitsyn interview.

10. Ibid.

11. Ibid.; and conversation with Galina Nekrasova, 11 Dec. 1980.

12. Solzhenitsyn interview; and unpublished letter to the author from Natalia Reshetovskaya, 1 Dec. 1982.

13. Solzhenitsyn interview; private information; and unpublished letter to the author from Natalia Reshetovskaya, 16 May 1982.

14. This account of Solzhenitsyn's arrival is based on his fictional reworking of it in "Matryona's Place."

15. Solzhenitsyn interview.

16. Reshetovskaya, 188.

17. Unpublished letter to the author from Natalia Reshetovskaya, 1 Jan. 1983.

18. Ibid.

19. Reshetovskaya, 192.

20. Solzhenitsyn interview.

21. Unpublished letter to the author from Natalia Reshetovskaya, 31 Oct. 1982.

22. Ibid.
23. Labedz, 22.
24. Conversation with Veronica Stein.
25. Reshetovskaya, 193–94, 198.
26. Conversation with Veronica Stein.
27. Reshetovskaya, 196.
28. *Stories and Prose Poems*, 243.

Chapter 21

1. *Gulag*, vol. 2, pt. 3, chap. 11.
2. Solzhenitsyn interview.
3. *Uchitel'skaya Gazeta* (Teachers' Gazette), 1 Dec. 1962.
4. *Literaturnaya Rossia*, 25 Jan. 1963; and *Sovetskaya Kirgizia* (Soviet Kirgizia), 30 and 31 Jan. 1963.
5. Reshetovskaya, 199–200.
6. Unpublished letter to the author from Natalia Reshetovskaya, 1 Dec. 1982.
7. Panin, 285.
8. *Oak*, 6.
9. *Gulag*, vol. 3, pt. 6, chap. 7.
10. Ibid.; and conversation with Veronica Stein.
11. *Gulag*, vol. 2, pt. 3, chap. 9.
12. Ibid., vol. 3, pt. 6, chap. 7.
13. Reshetovskaya, 207–8; and unpublished letter to the author from Natalia Reshetovskaya.
14. Reshetovskaya, 209–10.
15. *One Day in the Life of Ivan Denisovich*, trans. Max Hayward and Ronald Hingley (New York, 1963), 98.
16. Solzhenitsyn interview.
17. Reshetovskaya, 225.
18. *Oak*, 6.
19. Reshetovskaya, 225.
20. Ibid., 211.
21. "Panorama" interview with Alexander Solzhenitsyn, BBC Television, London, 1 Mar. 1976, transcript, p. 5.
22. Ličko.
23. "Panorama" interview transcript, p. 8.
24. Ibid.
25. Reshetovskaya, 211–12.
26. Conversation with Veronica Stein.
27. *Veche*, no. 5, p. 81.
28. Reshetovskaya, 213.
29. Ibid., 219.
30. Ibid., 220–22, 224.
31. Ibid., 224.
32. Ibid., 226.

33. Ibid., 224–25.
34. Ibid.
35. Ibid., 226.
36. *Oak*, 12.

Chapter 22

1. Reshetovskaya, 222.
2. Solzhenitsyn interview.
3. Reshetovskaya, 222.
4. Ibid.
5. "Matryona's House," in *Stories and Prose Poems*.
6. Ibid.
7. Ličko.
8. *Oak*, 12–13.
9. Conversation with Veronica Stein.
10. Reshetovskaya, 232–33.
11. Conversation with Ilya Zilberberg, 7 Mar. 1976.
12. Ilya Zilberberg, *Neobkhodimy razgovor s Solzhenitsynym* (A Necessary Talk with Solzhenitsyn) (Sussex, Eng., 1976), 50.

13. *Oak*, 10.
14. Quoted in Marc Slonim, *Soviet Russian Literature: Writers and Problems* (New York, 1964), 299.
15. The speech was printed in *Pravda*, 28 Aug. 1957, and in many other Soviet newspapers.
16. Robert Conquest, *Courage of Genius* (London, 1961), 138.
17. Ibid., 42.
18. Ibid., 160.
19. Ibid., 133–35, 164, 169.
20. Autobiographical note to the Nobel committee, quoted in Labedz, 28.
21. *XXII s'ezd kommunisticheskoi partii Sovetskogo Soyuza* (22nd Congress of the Communist Party of the Soviet Union) (17–31 Oct. 1961), stenographic record (Moscow, 1962), vol. 2, p. 584.
22. Ibid., 531–32.
23. *Oak*, 14.
24. Conversation with Lev Kopelev, 22 June 1982.
25. Unpublished letter to the author from Lev Kopelev, 31 Aug. 1981. Kopelev's wife, Raisa Orlova, has since confirmed most of these details in her book *Vospominania o neproshedshem vremeni* (Recollection of Time Not Past) (Ann Arbor, 1983), chap. 21.
26. *Oak*, 16–17.

Chapter 23

1. The account given in this chapter draws on all the well-known published sources, on conversations with the Kopelevs, Victor Nekrasov, 11 Dec. 1980., and Veronica Stein, and especially on Reshetovskaya's two unpublished chapters that appeared in Russian in *Veche*, no. 5.

2. Details are given by Efim Etkind in his introduction to the Russian edition of the novel published in Switzerland some twenty years later. See Vasily Grossman, *Zhizn' i sud'ba* (Life and Fate) (Lausanne, 1980), v.

3. Conversation with Lev Kopelev.

4. *Oak*, 20.

5. *Veche*, no. 5, p. 85.

6. Conversation with Victor Nekrasov.

7. *Veche*, no. 5, p. 97.

8. Victor Nekrasov, *Isaichu* . . . (To Isaich), in *Kontinent*, no. 18 (1978), *Spetsial'noye prilozheniye* (Special Supplement), 3–5.

9. *Veche*, no. 5, p. 97.

10. Ibid., 85–86.

11. Ibid.

12. Ibid., 87–88.

13. Ibid., 89; and *Oak*, 22.

14. *Veche*, no. 5, p. 87.

15. *Oak*, 26.

16. *Veche*, no. 5, pp. 90–92.

17. *Oak*, 35.

18. Ibid.

19. *Veche*, no. 5, p. 93.

20. Ibid.

21. *Oak*, 30.

22. Ibid.

23. Ibid.

24. *Veche*, no. 5, p. 95.

25. Ibid., 96.

26. Ibid.

27. Reshetovskaya, 232.

28. *Veche*, no. 5, pp. 97–99; and Lydia Chukovskaya, *Zapiski ob Anne Akhmatove* (Notes on Anna Akhmatova) (Paris, 1980), vol. 2, pp. 608–9.

29. *Veche*, no. 5, pp. 97–99.

30. Ibid., 95–97.

31. Ibid.

32. *Oak*, 34.

33. *Veche*, no. 5, p. 98.

Chapter 24

1. *Veche*, no. 5, p. 100.

2. Ibid.

3. Ibid., 101.

4. Ibid.

5. *Oak*, 38.

6. *Veche*, no. 5, p. 102.

7. *Oak*, 38.

8. *Veche*, no. 5, p. 102.

9. Ibid.

10. Ibid., 103.

11. Conversation with Victor Nekrasov.

12. *Veche*, no. 5, p. 106.

13. Ibid.

14. Ibid.

15. Ibid., 108.

16. Ibid.

17. Ibid., 110.

18. Michel Tatu, *Power in the Kremlin*, trans. Helen Katel (New York, 1967), 248.

19. Peter Benno, "The Political Aspect," in Max Hayward and Edward L. Crowley, eds., *Soviet Literature in the Sixties* (London, 1965), 191.

20. *Oak*, 41.

21. *Time*, 27 Sept. 1968.

22. Benno, 191.

23. *Veche*, no. 5, p. 110.

24. *Oak*, 42.

25. Zhores A. Medvedev, *Ten Years after Ivan Denisovich*, trans. Hilary Sternberg (London, 1973), 17.

26. Ibid.

27. *Veche*, no. 5, p. 111.

28. Ibid.

29. Ibid., 113.

30. Ibid., 111.

31. Ibid.

32. Chukovskaya, *Zapiski*, 449–54. An English translation can be found in *Solzhenitsyn Studies* 1 (1980), 177–78.

33. *Gulag*, vol. 1, pt. 1, chap. 7.

34. *Oak*, 9.

35. Ibid., 11n.

36. *Veche*, no. 5, pp. 115–16.

37. Ibid.

38. Ibid.

39. Ibid., 118–19; and *Oak*, 44–45.

40. *Veche*, no. 5, pp. 119–20; and *Oak*, 45–46.

41. *Oak*, 46.

42. *Veche*, no. 5, pp. 121–22.

43. Ibid.

44. Ibid.

45. Ibid., 117–18.

46. *Gulag*, vol. 3, pt. 7, chap. 3, in Russian edition only.

47. Reshetovskaya, 255–56.
48. Ibid.
49. Chukovskaya, *Zapiski*, 474n; and *Solzhenitsyn Studies* 1 (1980), 178.
50. *Oak*, 46.
51. Labedz, 38.
52. Ibid., 41–42.
53. Ibid.

Chapter 25

1. These and the other Soviet reviews quoted in this chapter have been collected in a samizdat anthology devoted to Solzhenitsyn's career and entitled *Slovo probivaet sebe dorogu* (The Word Hews a Path for Itself), which exists in Russian only. All quotations are from *Slovo* unless otherwise indicated.
2. Benno, 192.
3. Priscilla Johnson, *Khrushchev and the Arts* (Cambridge, Mass., 1965), 102–3.
4. Quoted in David Burg and George Feifer, *Solzhenitsyn* (London, 1972), 195–96.
5. *Oak*, 53.
6. Ibid.
7. Conversation with Victor Nekrasov.
8. *Oak*, 53.
9. Ibid., 50–51.
10. Ibid., 52.
11. *Literaturnaya Rossia*, 25 Jan. 1963; and *Sovetskaya Kirgizia*, 30 and 31 Jan. 1963.
12. Conversation with Andrei Sinyavsky, 8 Dec. 1980.
13. Ibid.
14. Both articles are reproduced in *Slovo*.
15. *Oak*, 61.
16. Johnson, 102–3.
17. Ibid., 117.
18. Ibid., 121.
19. Conversation with Evgenia Ginzburg, 15 May 1970.

Chapter 26

1. *Slovo*, 36.
2. Ibid., 36–37.
3. *Oak*, 62.
4. Johnson, 140. This account of the March meeting is based on Johnson, 140–81.
5. Quoted in Burton Rubin, "Highlights of the 1962–1963 Thaw," in Hayward and Crowley, *Soviet Literature in the Sixties*, 94–95.
6. *Slovo*, 153–54.
7. *Oak*, 60.
8. Ibid., 64.

9. *Stories and Prose Poems*, 114.
10. *Gulag*, vol. 1, pt. 1, chap. 7.
11. Ibid., chap. 4.
12. *Oak*, 58.
13. Conversation with Andrei Sinyavsky.
14. The author of this appreciation still lives in the Soviet Union and prefers not to be identified.
15. *Oak*, 49.
16. Ibid.
17. Ibid., 66–67.
18. Ibid., 68.
19. Conversation with Victor Nekrasov.
20. Johnson, 240–71.
21. *Oak*, 68–69.
22. *Slovo*, 192.
23. Johnson, 71.
24. Medvedev, *Ten Years*, 20–21; and *Literaturnaya Gazeta*, 26 Dec. 1963.

Chapter 27

1. *Oak*, 69.
2. Reshetovskaya, 256.
3. *Oak*, 70.
4. Johnson, 75.
5. *Slovo*, 225–26.
6. *Novy Mir*, 40, no. 1 (Jan. 1964).
7. *Slovo*, 226–28.
8. Labedz, 79.
9. D. Blagov (pseudonym of Veniamin Teush), *A. Solzhenitsyn i dukhovnaya missia pisatelya* (A. Solzhenitsyn and the Writer's Spiritual Mission), in Alexander Solzhenitsyn, *Sobranie sochinenii* (Collected Works) (Frankfurt, 1969–70), vol. 6, pp. 483–551 (in Russian).
10. Ibid.
11. *Gulag*, vol. 3, pt. 7, chap. 2.
12. Ibid.
13. Ibid.
14. Solzhenitsyn interview.
15. *Index on Censorship*, 1, no. 2 (1972). For some reason this prose poem did not find its way into the standard English edition, *Stories and Prose Poems*, but appears (in Russian) in *Sobranie sochinenii* (Collected Works) (Paris, 1978–83), vol. 3, p. 174.
16. Reshetovskaya, 261–62.
17. Conversation with Efim Etkind, 10 Dec. 1980.
18. Reshetovskaya, 251–52.
19. Ibid., 250.
20. Ibid., 268.

21. Ibid., 268–74.
22. Ibid.
23. Ibid., 276.
24. Ibid., 278.
25. Medvedev, *Ten Years*, 25.
26. *Oak*, 72.
27. Johnson, 76.
28. Medvedev, *Ten Years*, 26. I have relied on Medvedev for the rest of this account of the Lenin Prize committee's meeting.

Chapter 28

1. *Oak*, 72.
2. Reshetovskaya, 259–60; and unpublished letter to the author from Raisa Orlova, 31 Aug. 1981.
3. Reshetovskaya, 259–60.
4. This unpublished letter was shown to the author by Lev Kopelev.
5. Panin, 274; and conversation with Dimitri Panin.
6. *Oak*, 73–79.
7. Conversation with Ilya Zilberberg.
8. *Oak*, 80–84.
9. Ibid., 86–87.
10. *Literaturnaya Gazeta*, 12 May 1964; *Literaturnaya Rossia*, 29 May 1964; *Literaturnaya Gazeta*, 4 June 1964; and *Moskva*, July 1964 (cited in Medvedev, *Ten Years*, 30).
11. Conversation with Veronica Stein.
12. *Oak*, 73.
13. *Grani* (Facets), no. 56 (Oct. 1964).
14. Conversation with Zhores Medvedev, 2 Dec. 1981.
15. Private information.
16. Olga Carlisle, *Solzhenitsyn and the Secret Circle* (New York, 1978), 23–24.
17. *Gulag*, vol. 3, pt. 7, chap. 1.
18. Reshetovskaya, 247.
19. Medvedev, *Ten Years*, 2–3.
20. Ibid., 5.
21. *Oak*, 59.
22. Conversation with Zhores Medvedev.
23. *Oak*, 91.
24. Ibid., 95.
25. Ibid., 96–97.

Chapter 29

1. *Oak*, 202.
2. Solzhenitsyn interview.
3. Ibid.
4. *First Circle*, chap. 55.
5. Ibid.

6. This passage does not appear in the shorter, 87-chapter version that was translated into English. It can be found, in Russian, in chap. 60 of the longer version, published in the Collected Works (Paris), vol. 2, pp. 73–74.
7. *First Circle*, chap 55.
8. Solzhenitsyn interview.
9. Collected Works (Paris), vol. 2, chap. 61 (in Russian).
10. *First Circle*, chap. 55.
11. *Oak*, 1–2.
12. Conversation with Ilya Zilberberg.
13. *Oak*, 97–99.
14. Ibid., 99–102.
15. Conversation with Veronica Stein.
16. *Solzhenitsyn: A Pictorial Record* (London, 1974), 60.
17. *Oak*, 105–6.
18. Ibid.; and conversation with Veronica Stein.

Chapter 30

1. *Oak*, 103–4.
2. *Gulag*, vol. 2, pt. 4, chap. 1.
3. *Oak*, 104–5.
4. Ibid., 110.
5. Ibid., 108–9.
6. This account is taken from Medvedev, *Ten Years*, 39–42.
7. Private information.
8. Ibid.
9. Conversation with Zhores Medvedev.
10. Conversation with Efim Etkind.
11. *Oak*, 111–12.
12. This is the version that Solzhenitsyn told to Zhores Medvedev and that Medvedev incorporated into the initial text of his book *Ten Years after Ivan Denisovich*. After meeting Zilberberg in London in 1973, Medvedev slightly modified his text and added a cautionary footnote but allowed Solzhenitsyn's theory to stand.
13. *Oak*, 101–2.
14. Zilberberg.
15. Ibid., 75.
16. Ibid., 80.
17. *Oak*, 101–2.
18. Conversation with Veronica Stein.
19. Private information.
20. *Oak*, 118.

Chapter 31

1. *Oak*, 114.
2. Blagov, 511.

3. *Oak*, 113–14.

4. *Literaturnaya Gazeta*, 4 Nov. 1965.

5. Solzhenitsyn did not publish this story until 1978, when it was included in vol. 3 of his Collected Works (Paris). It has not so far been translated into English.

6. *Oak*, 122.

7. Ibid.

8. Private information.

9. *Oak*, 126–27.

10. Quoted in Bukovsky, 192–95.

11. Quoted in *Russia's Other Poets*, ed. Janis Sapiets (London, 1969), xx.

12. These events are described in Bukovsky, 160–63, 234–41, 249–56.

13. A detailed account of the trial and of the defendants' speeches can be found in *On Trial*, ed. and trans. Max Hayward (New York and London, 1967).

14. Conversation with Mark Bonham Carter, of Collins in London, 17 June 1982. It was Bonham Carter who flew to Stockholm.

15. Medvedev, *Ten Years*, 60–61; and unpublished chapters from Reshetovskaya's memoirs made available to the author.

16. Solzhenitsyn interview.

17. Hans Björkegren, *Aleksandr Solzhenitsyn: A Biography*, trans. Kaarina Eneberg (New York, 1972), 80–81.

18. *On Trial*, 290–91.

19. Conversation with Maria Rozanova, 8 Dec. 1980.

20. *Oak*, 98, 128.

21. Ibid., 119n; and Simone de Beauvoir, *All Said and Done*, trans. Patrick O'Brian (New York, 1974), 321.

22. Vladimir Lakshin, *Solzhenitsyn, Tvardovsky, and "Novy Mir,"* trans. and ed. Michael Glenny (Cambridge, Mass., 1980), 51–52.

23. Grigori Svirski, *A History of Post-war Soviet Writing*, trans. and ed. Robert Dessaix and Michael Ulman (Ann Arbor, 1981), 172, 175.

24. *Gulag*, vol. 2, pt. 3, chap. 3.

25. "Panorama" interview transcript, p. 14.

26. Quoted by Natalia Reshetovskaya in a statement to the press, 9 Apr. 1980. Parts of Reshetovskaya's statement appeared in the *Los Angeles Times*, 22 May 1980. A full translation appears in *Russia* (New York), 1, no. 2 (1981).

27. Ibid.

Chapter 32

1. *Oak*, 135.

2. Ibid., 137.

3. Ibid., 139.

4. *Slovo*, 297; and *Oak*, 141n.

5. *Oak*, 306; and Labedz, 87–90. A translation of the proceedings is in Labedz, 83–105.

6. Labedz, 98–101; additional details from A. V. Belinkov, "Delo Solzhenitsyna" (The Solzhenitsyn Case), in *Novy Zhurnal* (New Journal) (New York), no. 93 (1968).

7. *Slovo*, 359–67; and Labedz, 102 (abridged text).

8. Labedz, 104.

9. *Slovo*, 366–67.

10. *Oak*, 146–49.

11. Ibid., 458.

12. Conversation with Veronica Stein.

13. *Oak*, 142–45.

14. Ibid., 144–45.

15. Ibid.

16. Solzhenitsyn interview.

17. Reshetovskaya, unpublished chapters.

18. Pavel Litvinov, ed., *The Demonstration in Pushkin Square*, trans. Manya Harari (London, 1969), 1–7, 13–49. For an account of the Galanskov-Ginzburg trial, see Pavel Litvinov, ed., *The Trial of the Four*, trans. Janis Sapiets, Hilary Sternberg, and Daniel Weissbort (London and New York, 1972).

19. *Oak*, 151.

20. Ibid., 156.

21. Ibid., 156–58.

22. Ibid., 155; and Ličko interview with BBC Television, 14 Mar. 1969.

23. *Kulturni Život*, 31 Mar. 1967.

24. Ličko affidavit to the Bodley Head, 5 Sept. 1968.

25. Carlisle, 18–19.

26. Reshetovskaya, unpublished chapters.

27. Ibid.

28. *Oak*, 164–65, and notes; and Reshetovskaya, unpublished chapters.

Chapter 33

1. Medvedev, *Ten Years*, 68–69.

2. *Pravda*, 26 May 1967.

3. The full text of the letter can be found in *Oak*, 458–62, and in Labedz, 106–12.

4. Reshetovskaya, unpublished chapters.

5. Ibid.

6. Medvedev, *Ten Years*, 70; and *Chetverty vse-soyuzny s'ezd sovetskikh pisatelei* (Fourth All-Union Congress of Soviet Writers), stenographic record (Moscow, 1968), 197–98.

7. Labedz, 112–13.

8. *Oak*, 164.

9. Conversation with Efim Etkind.

10. Private information.

11. Reshetovskaya, unpublished chapters.

12. *Oak*, 164.

13. Ibid., 165–66; and Reshetovskaya, unpublished chapters.

14. *Oak*, 169–74.

15. Ibid., 174–76.

16. Reshetovskaya, unpublished chapters.

17. Ibid.

18. Ibid.

19. *Gulag*, vol. 1, pt. 1, chap. 3 note; *Skvoz' chad*, 50; Simonyan, 14–15; and private information.

20. Carlisle, 72.

21. *Oak*, 463.

22. Ibid., 181. The following account of the secretariat meeting is based on Solzhenitsyn's transcript of it, which appears in the appendix to *Oak*, 463–80.

23. Ibid., 183–85.

24. Ibid., 186.

25. Reshetovskaya, unpublished chapters.

26. *Oak*, 186, 475–76.

27. Labedz, 152–53.

28. Litvinov, *Demonstration*, 125, 127.

29. Ibid., 137–38.

30. Reshetovskaya, unpublished chapters.

31. Ibid.

32. Labedz, 151.

33. *Oak*, 186.

34. Reshetovskaya, unpublished chapters; and Solzhenitsyn interview.

35. Ibid.

36. Conversation with Victor Nekrasov.

37. Reshetovskaya, unpublished chapters.

38. Ibid.

39. This account of Solzhenitsyn's movements and decisions during this crucial episode is based on Reshetovskaya's description in her unpublished chapters.

40. *Oak*, 200–201.

41. The full text of Tvardovsky's letter appears in Labedz, 155–67.

42. *Oak*, 203; and Reshetovskaya, unpublished chapters.

Chapter 34

1. *Oak*, 7, 196.

2. Letter to Zhores Medevedev from Praeger, date unknown.

3. Karel van het Reve in *Observer* (London), 29 Mar. 1970.

4. Litvinov, *Trial*, 219–20.

5. Ibid., 227.

6. Ibid.

7. Ibid., 289.

8. Ibid., 302–3.

9. Conversation with Pavel Litvinov, 10 Dec. 1981.

10. *Oak*, 405–6.

11. A translation is available in Labedz, 44–62.

12. *Oak*, 482.

13. Ibid., 206.

14. Ibid., 206–9, 483.

15. Ibid., 483–84.

16. *Time*, 27 Sept. 1968.

17. Private information.

18. *Oak*, 204.

19. A copy of this letter was shown to the author in 1968.

20. *Oak*, 213–16.

21. Ibid., 214, 218.

22. Ibid., 219.

Chapter 35

1. Labedz, 189–92.

2. Ibid., 192–96.

3. Ibid., 199.

4. Medvedev, *Ten Years*, 94.

5. Quoted in *Slovo*, 443–44.

6. *Oak*, 227.

7. Ibid., 239.

8. *Chronicle of Current Events*, no. 3 (30 Aug. 1968).

9. The full story is given in Natalia Gorbanevskaya, *Red Square at Noon*, trans. Alexander Lieven (New York and London, 1972).

10. *Oak*, 220.

11. Ibid., 222.

12. Ibid., 370.

13. Unpublished letter to the author from Natalia Reshetovskaya, undated [Feb. 1983].

14. Medvedev, *Ten Years*, 97.

15. *International Herald Tribune*, 17 Mar. 1969; reprinted in Labedz, 181.

16. *Oak*, 240.

17. The text appears in the Collected Works (Paris), vol. 8, pp. 519–89. There is as yet no English translation.

18. Solzhenitsyn interview.

19. *Oak*, 223.

20. Carlisle, 126.

21. Medvedev, *Ten Years*, 98.

22. *Oak*, 224–25.

23. Conversation with Veronica Stein.

24. Medvedev, *Ten Years*, 112–16.

25. *Oak*, 225, 484.

26. Ibid., 272.

27. *Vozrozhdenie* (Rebirth), no. 205 (Jan. 1969).

Chapter 36

1. Conversation with Veronica Stein.

2. Reshetovskaya, p. 251.

3. Ličko interview, BBC Television, 14 Mar. 1969.

4. Solzhenitsyn interview.

5. Private information.

6. Conversation with Dimitri Panin.

7. Conversation with Veronica Stein.

8. Private information.

9. Solzhenitsyn interview.

10. Conversation with Veronica Stein.

11. Reshetovskaya, unpublished chapters.

12. Solzhenitsyn interview.

13. Conversation with Natalia Svetlova.

14. Abraham Brumberg, ed., *In Quest of Justice* (London, 1970), 137–38.

15. Solzhenitsyn interview.

16. Private information.

17. Conversations with Lev Kopelev and Veronica Stein.

18. Conversation with Veronica Stein.

19. Letter to the author from Irina Alberti (formerly Solzhenitsyn's secretary), 25 Oct. 1978.

20. Petro Grigorenko, *V podpol'ye mozhno vstretit' tol'ko krys . . .* (In the Underground You Meet Only Rats . . .) (New York, 1981).

21. Medvedev, *Ten Years*, 100–101.

22. Ibid., 99–100.

23. Ibid., 102.

24. Quoted by Max Hayward in his introd. to the English-language edition of

Alexander Solzhenitsyn et al., *From under the Rubble*, trans. A. M. Brock et al. under the supervision of Michael Scammell (Boston, 1975), vi.

25. *From under the Rubble*, 4, 12, 18–19.

26. *Oak*, 232.

27. *Molodaya Gvardia*, nos. 3 and 9 (1968).

28. *Oak*, 294.

29. Ibid., 406.

30. Andrei Amalrik, "An Open Letter to Kuznetsov," in Andrei Amalrik, *Will the Soviet Union Survive until 1984?* rev. and enl. ed., trans. Peter Reddaway, ed. Hilary Sternberg (London, 1980), 64–74.

31. *Oak*, 294.

32. Ibid., 273, 293–94.

33. Medvedev, *Ten Years*, 110.

34. Quoted from Solzhenitsyn's transcript of the meeting. A translation appears in the appendix to *Oak*, 484–93, from which the following account is taken.

35. Medvedev, *Ten Years*, 107.

36. *Chronicle of Current Events*, no. 12 (28 Feb. 1970).

37. *Oak*, 493–94.

Chapter 37

1. Unpublished letter to the author from Natalia Reshetovskaya, 31 Oct. 1982.

2. Conversation with Veronica Stein.

3. Unpublished letter to the author from Natalia Reshetovskaya, 31 Oct. 1982.

4. *Oak*, 269.

5. Quoted in Labedz, 217–18.

6. *Oak*, 494.

7. Medvedev, *Ten Years*, 107–8.

8. *Oak*, 267.

9. *Chronicle of Current Events*, no. 11 (31 Dec. 1969).

10. *Oak*, 272.

11. Ibid.

12. Medvedev, *Ten Years*, 109–10.

13. Labedz, 221–24.

14. Medvedev, *Ten Years*, 109.

15. Labedz, 225.

16. Ibid., 225–26.

17. Quoted in Medvedev, *Ten Years*, 122–23.

18. Ibid., 124–25.

19. *Oak*, 275.

20. Ibid., 275–77.

21. Ibid., 278–89.

22. Ibid., 121–22, 282.

23. *Chronicle of Current Events*, no. 15 (31 Aug. 1970).

24. Ibid.

25. Ibid.

26. Medvedev, *Ten Years*, 130.

27. The whole affair was later described in great detail by the Medvedev brothers. See Roy Medvedev and Zhores Medvedev, *A Question of Madness*, trans. Ellen de Kadt (London, 1971).

28. *Oak*, 298.

29. Ibid., 494–95.

30. Medvedev and Medvedev, *Question of Madness*, 30, 43–49, 155–57.

31. *Oak*, 325.

32. Medvedev, *Ten Years*, 128.

33. *New York Times Magazine*, 12 Apr. 1970.

34. Conversation with Per Hegge, June 1976.

35. Carlisle, 155–56.

36. *Oak*, 324.

37. *Times* (London), 14 Apr. 1970.

Chapter 38

1. Amalrik, 91–92.

2. Andrei Sakharov, *Sakharov Speaks* (New York, 1974), 116–34.

3. *Chronicle of Current Events*, no. 14 (30 June 1970).

4. *Oak*, 298–99.

5. *New York Times Magazine*, 12 Apr. 1970.

6. *Oak*, 290–92.

7. Labedz, 141.

8. *Oak*, 285.

9. Medvedev, *Ten Years*, 131.

10. Per Egil Hegge, *Mellommann i Moskva* (Middleman in Moscow) (Oslo, 1971). An extract appears in Labedz, 298–99.

11. *Oak*, 300.

12. Labedz, 299.

13. Ibid., 240.

14. Ibid., 241.

15. Ibid., 242.

16. Medvedev, *Ten Years*, 136–38; *Literaturnaya Gazeta*, 14, 21, 28 Oct. 1970; and *Pravda*, 21 Oct. 1970. Medvedev sums up the arguments of the Soviet press very well but slightly confuses the dates on which the various articles appeared.

17. Medvedev, *Ten Years*, 135.

18. Labdedz, 244.

19. *Oak*, 307.

20. Ibid., 495–96.

21. Ibid., 303.

22. Conversation with Veronica Stein.

23. Unpublished letter to the author from Natalia Reshetovskaya, 1 Jan. 1983.

24. Ibid.

25. Ibid.; and conversation with Veronica Stein.

26. Ibid.

27. Conversation with Veronica Stein.

28. Solzhenitsyn interview.

29. Conversation with Veronica Stein.

30. Unpublished letter to the author from Natalia Reshetovskaya, 1 Jan. 1983.

31. Conversation with Veronica Stein.

32. *Daily Telegraph* (London), 12 Oct. 1970.

33. Unpublished letter to the author from Natalia Reshetovskaya, 1 Jan. 1983; and conversations with Veronica Stein and Lev Kopelev.

34. Unpublished letter to the author from Natalia Reshetovskaya, Jan. 1983.

35. Conversation with Veronica Stein.

36. Ibid.; and unpublished letter to the author from Natalia Reshetovskaya, 1 Jan. 1983.

37. *Oak*, 293.

38. Ibid., 295–96.

39. Ibid., 304.

40. Conversation with Per Hegge.

41. Ibid.; and Labedz, 301.

42. Conversation with Per Hegge.

43. *Oak*, 306.

44. Ibid., 496.

45. Ibid., 497.

Chapter 39

1. *New York Times*, 11 Dec. 1970.

2. Conversation with Victor Sparre, 6 June 1979.

3. *Observer* (London), 13 Dec. 1970.

4. *Times* (London), 13 Nov. 1970.

5. *New York Times*, 10 Dec. 1970.

6. Conversation with Zhores Medvedev.

7. Conversation with Natalia Svetlova.

8. *Oak*, 305; and Medvedev, *Ten Years*, 138.

9. *Oak*, 285.

10. Ibid., 317.

11. Ibid., 311.

12. *International Herald Tribune*, 27 Mar. 1971.

13. *Oak*, 338.

14. Unpublished letter to the author from Natalia Reshetovskaya, 1 Jan. 1983.

15. Ibid.

16. Ibid.

17. *Oak*, 310–11.

18. Ibid., 321.

19. Ibid., 313–14.

20. Ibid., 320, and note; Carlisle, 159–60, 164–67; and letter to the author from Irina Alberti, 25 Oct. 1978.

21. *New York Times*, 14 Apr. 1971.

22. "Panorama" interview transcript.

23. Conversation with Maria Rozanova.

24. *Oak*, 315.

25. *Newsweek*, 19 July 1976; and *Die Zeit*, 29 Oct. 1971.

26. Conversation with Per Hegge; and *Times* (London), 13 Oct. 1971.

27. Conversation with Michael Glenny.

28. *Neue Zürcher Zeitung*, 22 Sept. 1971.

29. *August*, afterword to the Russian edition (Paris, 1971). An English translation can be found in Labedz, 260–61.

Chapter 40

1. Conversation with Veronica Stein.

2. Ibid.; and A. M. Gorlov, *Sluchai na dache* (Dacha Incident) (Paris, 1977), 9.

3. Gorlov, 12. The following story of Gorlov's adventures is based on his book.

4. *Oak*, 497–98.

5. Gorlov, 24–25.

6. Ibid., 43.

7. *Oak*, 339.

8. Labedz, 300–302; Medvedev, *Ten Years*, 152; and conversation with Per Hegge.

9. *New York Times*, 17 Sept. 1971.

10. *Oak*, 500.

11. *Times* (London), 20 Oct. 1971.

12. Ibid.; and *Oak*, 328.

13. *Oak*, 500–502.

14. Medvedev, *Ten Years*, 161–63.

15. Ibid., 163–66.

16. Lakshin, 84–85.

17. *Oak*, 499.

18. Medvedev, *Ten Years*, 169.

Chapter 41

1. Unpublished letter to the author from Natalia Reshetovskaya, 1 Jan. 1983.

2. Ibid.

3. Solzhenitsyn interview.

4. Ibid.

5. Ibid.

6. *Stern*, 21 Nov. 1971.

7. *Literaturnaya Gazeta*, 12 Jan. 1972.

8. Conversation with Dieter Steiner, 18 May 1977; and Steiner letter to *Die Zeit*, 1 Sept. 1972.

9. Medvedev, *Ten Years*, 173.

10. Conversation with Solzhenitsyn.

11. *Oak*, 508.

12. Zhores Medvedev in the *New York Review of Books*, 19 July 1973.

13. *Die Zeit*, 24 Dec. 1971. It is also quoted, in English, in the introduction to Burg and Feifer, 9–10.

14. The following account is based on *Oak*, 331, 503–14; Hedrick Smith, *The Russians* (New York, 1976), 418–24; Robert Kaiser, *Russia* (New York, 1976 and 1977), 428–33; *New York Times*, 3 Apr. 1972; and *Washington Post*, 3 Apr. 1972.

15. Smith, 421.

16. Kaiser, 432.

17. All excerpts from the interview are quoted from the *New York Times*, 3 Apr. 1972.

18. Smith, 424.

19. Kaiser, 435.

20. *Oak*, 513.

21. Ibid., 332.

22. Medvedev, *Ten Years*, 179.

23. *Stern*, 21 Nov. 1971.

24. *Literaturnaya Gazeta*, 12 Jan. 1972.

25. Ibid., 23 Feb. 1972.

26. *Oak*, 329.

27. Ibid., 327.

28. Ibid., 329–30.

29. "To Patriarch Pimen of Russia," trans. Alexis Klimoff, in John Dunlop et al., eds., *Aleksandr Solzhenitsyn: Critical Essays and Documentary Materials* (Belmont, Mass., 1973), 472–78.

30. *Vestnik RSKhD* (YMCA Herald) (Paris), no. 103 (1972).

31. Ibid.

32. Ibid., no. 98 (1970).

33. "Letter to a Friend," in *Novoye Russkoye Slovo* (New Russian Word) (New York), 9 Aug. 1972.

34. *Vestnik RSKhD*, no. 103 (1972), 150.

35. *Novoye Russkoye Slovo*, 9 Aug. 1972.

36. *Oak*, 349, 356, 367, 379.

Chapter 42

1. *Oak*, 330, 334.

2. "Nobel Lecture," trans. Alexis Klimoff, in *Aleksandr Solzhenitsyn: Critical Essays*, 483–97.

3. *Oak*, 332.

4. Ibid., 515.

5. Ibid., 333.

6. *Trud* (Labour), 7 Apr. 1972; and *Literaturnaya Rossia*, 7 Apr. 1972.

7. Medvedev, *Ten Years*, 182–89.

8. *Literaturnaya Gazeta*, 12 Apr. 1972.

9. Ibid., 19 Apr. 1972.

10. Medvedev, *Ten Years*, 187–88.

11. *Veche*, no. 2 (19 May 1971), reproduced in *Samizdat Archive*, no. AS1020 (12 Jan. 1972).

12. *Veche*, no. 1 (Jan. 1971), in *Samizdat Archive*, no. AS1013 (11 Sept. 1972).

13. Quoted in Mikhail Heifetz, *Vremia i mesto* (A Time and a Place), unpublished chapters.

14. Ibid.

15. *Veche*, no. 4 (31 Jan. 1972), in *Samizdat Archive*, no. AS1140 (28 Mar. 1973).

16. Ibid.

17. Heifetz.

18. *Veche*, no. 5 (25 May 1972), in *Samizdat Archive*, no. AS1230 (18 May 1973).

19. Smith and Kaiser did not reproduce this comment in their newspaper articles or books, but Solzhenitsyn sent his own text of the interview to the West and later reprinted it in the appendix to *Oak*, 512.

20. Conversation with Dimitri Panin.

21. Conversation with Veronica Stein; and Medvedev in *New York Review of Books*, 17 May and 19 July 1973.

22. *Russkaya Mysl'* (Russian Thought) (Paris), 3 Aug. 1972. An abridged translation was published in the *New York Times Book Review*, 17 Sept. 1972.

23. *New York Times*, 3 Apr. 1972.

24. Ibid., 11 Dec. 1972.

25. Ibid., 21 Dec. 1972.

26. Ibid., 18 Dec. 1972.

27. Ibid., 21 Dec. 1972.

28. Ibid., 8 Jan. 1973.

29. Ibid., 26 Feb. 1973.

30. Ibid., 9 Mar. 1973.

31. Ibid., 28 Mar. 1973.

32. Unpublished letter to the author from Natalia Reshetovskaya, 1 Dec. 1982.

33. Ibid.

34. Ibid.

Chapter 43

1. *Avgust chetyrnadtsatogo chitayut na rodine* (Reading *August 1914* in the Homeland) (Paris, 1973), 8.

2. Ibid., 43–48.

3. Medvedev, *Ten Years*, 157.

4. Ibid.

5. "Panorama" interview transcript, p. 12.

6. Medvedev, *Ten Years*, 156.

7. *Oak*, 327.

8. Michael Glenny quoted in the *New York Times Book Review*, 24 Sept. 1972.

9. Bernard Williams in *Guardian* (London), 21 Sept. 1972.

10. *New York Times*, 6 Sept. 1972.

11. *World* (New York), 26 Sept. 1972.

12. *Saturday Review*, 16 Sept. 1972.

13. Conversation with Vladimir Maximov, 16 Dec. 1980.

14. *Oak*, 371–73.

15. See Edward Kuznetsov, *Prison Diaries*, trans. Howard Spier (London and New York, 1975), for a detailed account of the Leningrad "hijacking" and its consequences.

16. Joshua Rubenstein, *Soviet Dissidents* (Boston, 1980), 174.

17. *New York Times*, 9 Feb. 1972; and Medvedev, *Ten Years*, 170.

18. Rubenstein, 187–88.

19. *The Press on Solzhenitsyn* (Moscow, 1972).

20. *Chronicle of Current Events*, no. 29 (31 July 1973).

21. *Oak*, 373.

22. Ibid., 373–75.

23. Ibid., 335.

24. Ibid., 336, 339–40.

25. Ibid., 340–41.

26. Kaiser, 426.

27. *Oak*, 515.

28. Kaiser, 437.

29. The text of the letter was never published. It was shown to the author by Maximov in Dec. 1980.

30. *Oak*, 343.

31. Ibid., 521.

32. Conversation with Andrei Sinyavsky.

33. Interview with AP and *Le Monde*, 23 Aug. 1973. Reprinted in *Oak*, 521.

34. Ibid., 342, 406.
35. Sakharov, *Sakharov Speaks*, 166–78.
36. Ibid., 191.
37. Ibid., 204–5.
38. *Oak*, 515.
39. Ibid., 345.
40. Ibid., 517–27.
41. Ibid., 529.
42. Rubenstein, 142–45.
43. *Oak*, 522.
44. *New York Times*, 31 Aug. 1973.
45. Smith, 372.
46. Ibid., 309–10.
47. Ibid., 451.
48. Ibid., 452.
49. Ibid., 451.
50. *Oak*, 354; and *Index on Censorship*, 1, no. 4 (Winter 1973).
51. *Oak*, 524.
52. Ibid., 342.
53. *Christian Science Monitor*, 13 Sept. 1973.
54. *Times* (London), 22 Sept. 1973.
55. *First Circle*, chap. 57.

Chapter 44

1. *Oak*, 312–14.
2. Carlisle, 173.
3. Ibid., 176–78.
4. *Oak*, 320n.
5. Carlisle, 179.
6. *Oak*, 530.
7. Ibid., 348; *Skvoz' chad*, 59–60; and conversation with Efim Etkind.
8. *Skvoz' chad*, 59–60.
9. *Oak*, 349.
10. Ibid.
11. *August*, chap. 25.
12. *Oak*, 360.
13. Ibid., 360–61.
14. Ibid., 363–66.
15. Reshetovskaya, unpublished chapters, and unpublished letter to the author, 16 May 1982.
16. Unpublished letter to the author from Natalia Reshetovskaya, 16 May 1982.
17. Lydia Chukovskaya, *Protsess isklyuchenia* (Process of Exclusion) (Paris, 1979), 133.
18. Ibid., 134.
19. Private information.
20. *Oak*, 403.
21. Ibid., 530.
22. Ibid., 375–77.
23. Chukovskaya, *Protsess*, 135.
24. *Oak*, 383–84.

25. Ibid., 386–87.
26. Ibid., 530–31.
27. *Times* (London), 29 Dec. 1973.
28. Quoted in *Oak*, 389.
29. *Times* (London), 3 and 4 Jan. 1974.
30. Chukovskaya, *Protsess*, 140.
31. Ibid., 141–43.
32. Ibid., 170.
33. *New York Times*, 11 and 14 Jan. 1974.

Chapter 45

1. *Literaturnaya Gazeta*, 16 Jan. 1974.
2. *Washington Post*, 16 Jan. 1974.
3. *Oak*, 390–91.
4. Ibid., 532–34.
5. *Times* (London); and *New York Times*, 25 Jan. 1974.
6. *Times* (London), 25 Jan. and 10 Feb. 1974; and *Oak*, 535.
7. Private information.
8. Unpublished letter to the author from Natalia Reshetovskaya, 16 May 1982.
9. *New York Times*, 4 Feb. 1974.
10. *Christian Science Monitor*, 31 Jan. 1974.
11. Unpublished letter to the author from Natalia Reshetovskaya, 16 May 1982.
12. *Oak*, 536.
13. *Le Figaro*, 5 Feb. 1974.
14. Reshetovskaya, unpublished chapters.
15. *Oak*, 396.
16. Ibid., 537–38.
17. *Times* (London), 13 Feb. 1974.
18. *Letter to the Soviet Leaders*, trans. Hilary Sternberg (London, 1975). A copy of the original, unaltered text is in the author's possession.
19. *Oak*, 409. This account of Solzhenitsyn's arrest follows the one he has given himself ibid., 409–43.
20. *Pravda*, 14 Feb. 1974.
21. *Oak*, 538.
22. *New York Times*, 14 Feb. 1974.
23. *Washington Post*, 14 Feb. 1974.
24. Ibid.; and *New York Times*, 14 Feb. 1974.
25. *New York Times*, 14 Feb. 1974.
26. *Der Spiegel*, 12 Feb. 1974; and conversation with Heinrich Böll 3 Jan. 1976.
27. *La Fiera Letteraria*, 24 Feb. 1974.

Chapter 46

1. *New York Times* and *Washington Post*, 14 Feb. 1974.

2. Conversation with Heinrich Böll.

3. Conversation with Per Hegge.

4. Conversation with Janis Sapiets, 26 Nov. 1982.

5. Kaiser, 434.

6. *Oak*, 451.

7. Conversation with Dr Heeb.

8. Press conference in Stockholm, 12 Dec. 1974, trans. Christopher Barnes and Constantin Olgin (Radio Liberty Research Supplement, 3 June 1975).

9. *Times* (London), 17 Feb. 1974.

10. *Baltimore Sun*, 19 Feb. 1974; and *Russkaya Mysl'*, 28 Feb. 1974.

11. Reuter dispatch, 19 Feb. 1974.

12. Conversation with Nikita Struve, 9 Dec. 1980.

13. Conversation with Victor Sparre.

14. Victor Sparre, *The Flame in the Darkness*, trans. Alwyn and Dermot McKay (London, 1979), 36–37.

15. Conversations with Per Hegge and with Victor Sparre.

16. Sparre, 42.

17. Press conference in Stockholm.

18. Conversation with Victor Sparre.

19. Conversation with Sigmund Widmer, 2 May 1980.

20. *New York Times*, 28 Mar. 1974.

21. Ibid., 30 Mar. 1974.

22. *Times* (London), 30 Mar. 1974.

23. *Washington Post* and *Baltimore Sun*, 15 Feb. 1974.

24. *New York Times*, 16 Feb. 1974.

25. *Golos rodiny* (Voice of the Motherland) (Moscow), no. 13 (Feb. 1974). An abridged version appeared in the *Literaturnaya Gazeta*, 20 Feb. 1974.

26. *Krokodil* (Crocodile) (Moscow), 7 Mar. 1974.

27. *Baltimore Sun*, 15 Feb. 1974.

28. Chukovskaya, *Protsess*, 170.

29. *New York Times*, 18 Feb. 1974; and *Zhit' ne po lzhi* (Live Not by Lies) (Paris, 1974), 160–65.

30. *Yunost* (Youth) (Moscow), 18 Feb. 1974.

31. *Zhit' ne po lzhi*, 103.

32. Ibid., 194–98.

Chapter 47

1. *Zhit' ne po l'zhi*, 174 and 192.

2. Sparre, 49.

3. *Letter to the Soviet Leaders*.

4. *New York Times*, 4 Mar. 1974.

5. Solzhenitsyn's preface was restored in later editions of the *Letter*.

6. *Washington Post*, 2 Apr. 1974.

7. Available in the English-language anthology *Kontinent* (Garden City, N.Y., 1976).

8. *New York Times*, 15 Mar. 1974.

9. *Christian Science Monitor*, 8 Mar. 1974.

10. *New York Times*, 15 Mar. 1974.

11. Carlisle, 195–97.

12. Solzhenitsyn interview with Walter Cronkite, "CBS News Special Report: Solzhenitsyn," 24 June 1974.

13. *Times* (London), 6 Apr. 1974.

14. *Baltimore Sun*, 27 Apr. 1974.

15. *Washington Post*, 28 Apr. 1974.

16. Cronkite interview.

17. See Stephen F. Cohen in *New York Times Book Review*, 16 June 1974.

18. Edward Crankshaw in *Observer* (London), 30 June 1974.

19. *New York Review of Books*, 21 Mar. 1974.

20. *Sunday Times* (London), 17 Feb. 1974.

21. Conversation with Nikita Struve.

22. Sparre, 41–42.

23. *Der Spiegel*, 12 Feb. 1974.

24. *La Fiera Letteraria*, 24 Feb. 1974.

25. *Russkaya Mysl'*, 18 Apr. 1974.

26. These impressions are based on the author's first visit to the Stapferstrasse, in Sept. 1974.

27. Conversation with Natalia Svetlova.

Chapter 48

1. Conversation with Sigmund Widmer.

2. Unpublished article by Alan Levy.

3. Cronkite interview.

4. Levy, 12–13.

5. Alexander Solzhenitsyn, "Otryvki iz vtorogo toma 'Ocherkov iz literaturnoi zhizni' " (Extracts from the Second Volume of "Memoirs of Literary Life"), in *Vestnik RKbD*, no. 137 (1982), 120–30. I.e., a continuation of *Oak*.

6. Conversation with Sigmund Widmer.

7. Conversation with Petr Pašek, 28 Apr. 1980.

8. *New York Times*, 17 Feb. 1974.

9. Conversation with Oskar Krause, 26 Apr. 1980.

10. Ibid.

11. A. Lidin, *Trpaslík na houpačce* (Dwarf on a Swing) (Cologne, 1973). Lidin was a *nom de plume*.

12. Conversation with Oskar Krause.

13. Conversation with Petr Pašek.

14. Conversations with Oskar Krause and with Petr Pašek.

15. Cronkite interview.

16. *Time*, 27 May 1974.

17. *New York Times*, 17 Mar. 1974.

18. *Chronicle of Current Events*, nos. 34 (31 Dec. 1974) and 35 (Mar. 1975).

19. Heifetz.

20. *The Last Circle* (Moscow, 1974), 32–34.

21. Reshetovskaya, 84.

22. Ibid.

23. Solzhenitsyn interview.

24. Cronkite interview.

25. Conversation with Vladimir Maximov.

26. *Kontinent* (Paris), no. 1 (1974).

27. *Vestnik RKhD*, nos. 112–3 (1974).

28. Conversation with Dimitri Panin.

29. Conversation with Zhores Medvedev.

30. *Russkaya Mysl'*, 26 Sept. 1974.

31. Conversation with Natalia Svetlova.

32. Roy Medvedev, quoted in *Washington Post*, 24 Sept. 1974.

33. Abram Tertz, "Literaturny protsess v Rossii," in *Kontinent*, no. 1 (1974). Translated as "The Literary Process in Russia," in the English-language anthology *Kontinent*.

34. *Dve press-konferentsii: k sborniku "Iz-pod glyb"* (Two Press Conferences: The Anthology *From under the Rubble*) (Paris, 1975).

35. Ibid.

36. *Gulag*, vol. 1, pt. 1, chap. 2.

37. Janis Sapiets, "Conversation with Solzhenitsyn on 17 November 1974," BBC External Services, *CARIS Report*, no. 16/74; reprinted in *Encounter*, Mar. 1975, pp. 67–72.

38. Ibid.

39. Igor Shafarevich, "Does Russia Have a Future?" in *From under the Rubble*, 294. Solzhenitsyn was paraphrasing rather than quoting directly.

40. *Washington Post*, 11 Dec. 1974.

41. Solzhenitsyn interview.

42. Stockholm Press Conference.

Chapter 49

1. Alexander Solzhenitsyn, "Interviu na literaturniye temy s N. A. Struve" (Interview on Literary Topics with N. A. Struve) (Mar. 1976), in *Vestnik RKhD*, no. 120 (1977).

2. Conversation with Paul Fritz, 30 Apr. 1980.

3. Ibid.

4. Conversation with Dr Heeb, 29 Apr. 1980.

5. Alexander Solzhenitsyn, "Iz press-konferentsii A. I. Solzhenitsyna korrespondentam Madridskikh gazet" (From A. I. Solzhenitsyn's Press Conference with Madrid Correspondents) (20 Mar. 1976), in *Kontinent*, no. 11 (1976).

6. Conversation with Natalia Svetlova.

7. Unpublished article by Alan Levy.

8. *Le Monde*, 12 Apr. 1975.

9. *Chronicle of Current Events*, no. 35 (35 Mar. 1975), p. 150.

10. *Novoye Russkoye Slovo*, 6 Mar. 1975. An abridged version of the letter appeared in *New York Times*, 6 Mar. 1975.

11. *Vestnik RKhD*, no. 114 (1974). An incomplete summary of these letters appeared in *Le Monde*, 12 Apr. 1975.

12. *Encounter*, Sept. 1975.

13. *Montreal Gazette*, 5 May 1975.

14. Conversation with Raissa Scriabine, 8 Feb. 1980.

15. *Washington Post*, 7 June 1975.

16. Ibid.

17. *New York Times*, 17 June 1975.

18. Boris Shragin in the *New York Review of Books*, 26 June 1975.

19. AFL-CIO transcript of Solzhenitsyn's Washington speech, 30 June 1975. Reprinted in Alexander Solzhenitsyn, *Warning to the West* (New York, 1976).

20. AFL-CIO transcript of Solzhenitsyn's New York speech, 9 July 1975. Reprinted in *Warning to the West*.

21. Conversation with Raissa Scriabine.

22. *New York Times*, 11 July 1975.

23. Ibid., 10 July 1975.

24. NBC transcript of "Meet the Press," vol. 19, no. 28.

25. *Saturday Review*, 23 Aug. 1975.

26. *New York Times*, 3 July 1975.

27. "Meet the Press" transcript.

28. *Congressional Record*, 94th Cong., 1st sess., 16 July 1975, p. 22959.

29. *New York Times*, 17 July 1975.

30. Ibid., 22 July 1975.

31. *Christian Science Monitor* and *New York Times*, 1 Aug. 1975.

32. *Vestnik RKhD*, no. 116 (1975).

33. Ibid., no. 117 (1976).

34. *Oak*, 182.

35. Solzhenitsyn interview.

36. Valentina Tvardovskaya, "Open Letter to Solzhenitsyn," printed in *Foreign Broadcast Information Service*, 16 July 1975.

37. Roy Medvedev, *Political Essays* (Nottingham, 1976), 110–20.

38. All Lakshin quotations are from Lakshin, *Solzhenitsyn, Tvardovsky, and "Novy Mir,"* 10–11, 15, 20, 27, 58, 66.

39. Zilberberg, 165–83.

40. Lakshin, 75.

41. Ibid., 58.

Chapter 50

1. Leonard Schapiro in *New York Review of Books*, 13 Nov. 1975.

2. Patricia Blake in *Time*, 26 Oct. 1975.

3. *Gulag*, vol. 2, pt. 4, chap. 1.

4. Schapiro.

5. *Washington Post*, 6 Dec. 1975; and *New York Times*, 10 Dec. 1975.

6. Conversation with Janis Sapiets.

7. Ibid.; and *Observer*, 29 Feb. 1976.

8. Conversation with Janis Sapiets.

9. "Panorama" interview transcript.

10. *Times* and *Guardian*, 2 Mar. 1976; *Observer*, 29 Feb. 1976; *Sunday Telegraph*, 7 Mar. 1976.

11. *New Society*, 11 Mar. 1976.

12. Untitled speech, BBC Radio 3, 24 Mar. 1976; reprinted in *Warning to the West*.

13. *Times*, 29 Mar. 1976.

14. "Les Dossiers de l'Ecran," ORTF, 9 Mar. 1976, transcript; and *Le Monde*, 11 Mar. 1976.

15. *Vestnik RKhD*, no. 120 (1977).

16. *Le Soir*, 12 Mar. 1976.

17. *Baltimore Sun*, 12 Mar. 1976.

18. *Vestnik RKhD*, no. 120 (1977).

19. "The Book Programme," BBC TV, "Interview with Solzhenitsyn," 27 Apr. 1976, transcript.

20. *Lenin in Zurich*, trans. H. T. Willets (London, 1976), 178–85.

21. "Book Programme" interview transcript.

22. *Vestnik RKhD*, no. 120 (1977).

23. Ibid.

24. *Est et Ouest*, no. 570 (Apr. 1976). An abridged version was published in English in *Dissent*, no. 108 (Summer 1977).

25. Alexander Solzhenitsyn, "O fragmentakh g. Suvarina" (On Mr Souvarine's Fragments), *Vestnik RKhD*, no. 132 (1980).

26. Alexander Solzhenitsyn, "Pis'mo Borisu Suvarinu" (A Letter to Boris Souvarine), *Vestnik RKhD*, no. 131 (1980).

27. Alexander Solzhenitsyn, "Ispanskoye interv'iu" (Spanish Interview), *Kontinent*, no. 8 (1976), 429–40.

28. Alexander Solzhenitsyn, "Ispanskiye rechi" (Spanish Speeches), *Kontinent*, no. 11 (1977), *Spetsial'noye prilozheniye* (Special Supplement), 19–28.

29. *Guardian*, 21 Mar. 1976.

30. International Confederation of Free Trade Unions, press release, 25 Mar. 1976.

31. *Kontinent*, no. 11 (1976), 19–28.

32. Ibid., no. 8 (1976), 429–40.

33. Ibid., no. 11 (1976), 19–28.

Chapter 51

1. *Pravda*, 24 and 30 Mar. 1976.

2. *Literaturnaya Gazeta*, 17 Mar. 1976.

3. *International Herald Tribune*, 8–9 Mar. 1975.

4. A photocopy of this letter was later published in facsimile in *Neue Politik* (Hamburg), 15 Feb. 1978.

5. *Washington Post*, 20 May 1976; and *Novoye Russkoye Slovo*, 23 May 1976.

6. *Solzhenitsyn Speaks at the Hoover Institution* (24 May and 1 June 1976) (brochure published by the Hoover Institution, Stanford, 1976). The first speech was published in *Russian Review* 36, no. 2 (Apr. 1977).

7. It is not clear which book Solzhenitsyn had in mind. It was probably Orlov's essay *Vozmozhen li netotalitarny sotsializm?* (Is a Nontotalitarian Socialism Possible?) (New York, 1976).

8. *Solzhenitsyn Speaks at the Hoover Institution.*

9. *Washington Post*, 18 Sept. 1976.

10. *Rutland Herald*, 1 Mar. 1977.

11. Reported in the *New York Times*, 3 Feb. 1977.

12. Ibid.

13. *Christian Science Monitor*, 7 Feb. 1977.

14. *Washington Post*, 1 Mar. 1977.

15. *Hvem er Solsjenitsyn?*

16. *Midstream* (New York), no. 6 (June–July 1977).

17. Roman Rutman, "Solzhenitsyn and the Jewish Question," in *Soviet Jewish Affairs* 4, no. 2 (1974).

18. Svirski, 180–81.

19. *New York Times*, 23 Jan. 1977.

20. Nicholas Bethell, *The Last Secret* (London and New York, 1974).

21. Nikolai Tolstoy, *Victims of Yalta* (London, 1977). Published in America as *The Secret Betrayal* (New York, 1978).

22. *Times* (London), 19 Mar. 1978.

23. *Washington Post*, 2 Sept. 1976.

24. *New York Daily News*, 8 Feb. 1977.

25. Alexander Solzhenitsyn, *A World Split Apart*, trans. Irina Alberti (New York, 1978).

26. *National Review*, 15 Sept. 1978.

27. *Commonweal*, 1 Sept. 1978.

28. *New York Times*, 11 and 13 June 1978; *Washington Post*, 11 June 1978; *Christian Science Monitor*, 12 June and 25 July 1978.

29. *Washington Post*, 25 June 1978.

30. *Humanist* (Schenectady), Nov.–Dec. 1978.

31. Alexander Herzen, *From the Other Shore*, trans. Moura Budberg (London, 1956). Quoted by Alain Besançon in *Commentaire* (Paris), no. 4 (Winter 1978–79); reprinted as "Solzhenitsyn at Harvard," in *Survey*, no. 106 (Winter 1979), 133–44.

32. Ibid.

33. *Solzhenitsyn at Harvard: The Address, Twelve Early Responses, and Six Reflections* (Washington, D.C., 1980).

Chapter 52

1. Solzhenitsyn interview.

2. Conversation with Claude Durand, 15 Dec. 1980.

3. *New York Times*, 5 Mar. 1976.

4. Ibid., 4 June 1977.

5. Conversation with Sigmund Widmer.

6. *Times* (London), 22 Feb. 1978.

7. Conversation with Sigmund Widmer.

8. *Washington Post*, 19 Sept. 1978.

9. AP news agency dispatch.

10. *Oak*, 394.

11. Ibid., 320n.

12. *New York Times*, 25 Oct. 1980; and *Publishers Weekly*, 21 Nov. 1980.

13. *Neue Politik*, 15 Feb. 1978.

14. Tomáš Řezáč, *Spiral' izmeny Solzhenitsyna* (The Spiral of Solzhenitsyn's Betrayal) (Moscow, 1978).

15. *Russkaya Mysl'*, 26 Oct. 1978.

16. Řezáč, 3–4.

17. *Bild am Sonntag*, 2 Apr. 1978.

18. *Skvoz' chad.*

19. Ibid.

20. N. N. Yakovlev, *TsRU protiv SSSR* (The CIA against the USSR) (Moscow, 1980).

21. *Los Angeles Times*, 22 May 1980 (extracts); reprinted in full in *Russia*, 1, no. 2 (1981). (1981).

22. Unpublished letter to the author from Natalia Reshetovskaya, 19 May 1982.

23. Solzhenitsyn interview.

24. Ibid.

25. Private information.

26. Solzhenitsyn interview.

27. Ibid.

28. Ibid.

29. Ibid.

SELECT

BIBLIOGRAPHY

No attempt has been made here to be comprehensive. Apart from Solzhenitsyn's collected works in Russian, all the books listed are in English. For fuller information, including a listing of articles and of sources in other languages, readers should consult Donald Fiene's *Alexander Solzhenitsyn: An International Bibliography of Writings by and about Him* (Ann Arbor: Ardis, 1973). An update of this material can be found in Michael Nicholson's "Solzhenitsyn in 1976: A Bibliographical Reorientation," in the *Russian Literature Triquarterly*, no. 143 (Winter 1976), 462–82. Since 1980, Nicholson has been bringing out a quarterly survey of literature by and about Solzhenitsyn, *Solzhenitsyn Studies*, which is currently published by the University of Lancaster, England.

Works by Alexander Solzhenitsyn

Sobranie sochinenii (Collected Works) (in Russian). 11 vols. Paris: YMCA Press, 1978–83. The most up-to-date and complete collection of Solzhenitsyn's works in print, checked and approved by the author. A further four volumes have been announced for 1985–86.

August 1914. Translated by Michael Glenny. London: Bodley Head; New York: Farrar, Straus & Giroux, 1972. This is a translation of the original text of the novel. In 1983 Solzhenitsyn reissued it in Russian in two volumes instead of one (vols. 10 and 11 of the Collected Works). The new version has not yet appeared in English.

Cancer Ward. Translated by Nicholas Bethell and David Burg. 2 vols. London: Bodley Head, 1968–69; New York: Farrar, Straus & Giroux, 1969.

The Cancer Ward. Translated by Rebecca Frank. New York: Dial Press, 1968.

Candle in the Wind. Translated by Keith Armes, with Arthur Hudgins. Minneapolis: University of Minnesota; London: Bodley Head, 1973.

Decembrists without December. Translated by Helen Rapp and Nancy Thomas. London: Bodley Head, 1983.

The First Circle. Translated by Thomas Whitney. New York: Harper & Row, 1968.

————. Translated by Michael Guybon. London: Collins/Harvill, 1968. Both translations are of the original, 87-chapter version of the novel. A translation of the longer, 96-chapter version is said to be in preparation.

The Gulag Archipelago. Vol. 1. Translated by Thomas Whitney. New York: Harper & Row; London: Collins, 1974.

————. Vol. 2. Translated by Thomas Whitney. New York: Harper & Row; London: Collins, 1975.

————. Vol. 3. Translated by Harry Willetts. New York: Harper & Row; London: Collins, 1978.

Lenin in Zurich. Translated by H. T. Willetts. London: Bodley Head; New York: Farrar, Straus & Giroux, 1976.

A Lenten Letter to Pimen, Patriarch of All Russia. Translated by Keith Armes. Minneapolis: Burgess, 1972.

Letter to the Soviet Leaders. Translated by Hilary Sternberg. London: Index on Censorship/Fontana; New York: Index on Censorship/Harper & Row, 1975.

The Love-Girl and the Innocent. Translated by Nicholas Bethell and David Burg. London: Bodley Head; New York: Farrar, Straus & Giroux, 1969. This is the play referred to throughout this book as *The Tenderfoot and the Tart*.

The Mortal Danger: How Misconceptions about Russia Imperil America. Translated by Alexis Klimoff and Michael Nicholson. New York: Harper & Row, 1980. Contains Solzhenitsyn's article in the spring 1980 issue of *Foreign Affairs* and his reply to critics of that article.

The Oak and the Calf. Translated by Harry Willetts. London: Collins; New York: Harper & Row, 1979.

One Day in the Life of Ivan Denisovich. Translated by Max Hayward and Ronald Hingley. New York: Praeger, 1963.

————. Translated by Ralph Parker. London: Gollancz; New York: Dutton, 1963. These are the two first and best-known translations. At least two others have been made since.

Prussian Nights. Translated by Robert Conquest. London: Collins/Harvill; New York: Farrar, Straus & Giroux, 1977.

Stories and Prose Poems. Translated by Michael Glenny. London: Bodley Head; New York: Farrar, Straus & Giroux, 1971. Contains all Solzhenitsyn's shorter prose works with the exception of two prose poems. There are many alternative translations of "Matryona's Place" and at least one alternative for each of the other stories.

Victory Celebrations. Translated by Helen Rapp and Nancy Thomas. London: Bodley Head, 1983. Better known under its alternative title of *Feast of the Conquerors*.

Warning to the West. New York: Farrar, Straus & Giroux, 1976. Includes Solzhenitsyn's speeches to the AFL-CIO in Washington and New York in 1975.

A World Split Apart. Translated by Irina Alberti. New York: Harper & Row, 1978. The text of Solzhenitsyn's Harvard address.

(With Mikhail Agursky, A.B., Evgeny Barabanov, Vadim Borisov, F. Korsakov, and Igor Shafarevich). *From under the Rubble*. Translated by A. M. Brock, Milada Haigh, Marita Sapiets, Hilary Sternberg, and Harry Willetts, under the direction of Michael Scammell. Boston: Little, Brown; London: Collins, 1975.

BIOGRAPHICAL WORKS

Björkegren, Hans. *Aleksandr Solzhenitsyn: A Biography*. Translated from the Swedish by Kaarina Eneberg. New York: Third Press, 1972. A slender and not very informative essay published while Solzhenitsyn was still in the Soviet Union. Quite good on the literary politics of the period.

Burg, David, and George Feifer. *Solzhenitsyn*. London: Hodder & Stoughton; New York: Stein & Day, 1972. The first full-length biography of Solzhenitsyn and the best so far. Because

Solzhenitsyn was still in the Soviet Union when it was written, it suffers from an understandable shortage of facts but is accurate as far as it goes.

Carlisle, Olga. *Solzhenitsyn and the Secret Circle*. New York: Holt, Rinehart & Winston, 1978. An essay about the author's involvement with Solzhenitsyn and intended to refute Solzhenitsyn's charges of incompetence and material greed. Good on the conspiratorial side of Solzhenitsyn's character.

Grazzini, Giovanni. *Solzhenitsyn*. Translated from the Italian by Eric Mosbacher. London: Michael Joseph, 1973. A biographical sketch.

Kopelev, Lev. *Ease My Sorrows*. Translated by Antonina W. Bouis. New York: Random House, 1983. Volume 3 of Kopelev's memoirs, dealing mainly with his imprisonment in the Marfino *sharashka* and containing much valuable information about Solzhenitsyn's stay there and his friendship with Kopelev.

Lakshin, Vladimir. *Solzhenitsyn, Tvardovsky, and "Novy Mir."* Translated and edited by Michael Glenny. Cambridge, Mass.: MIT Press, 1980. A translation of Lakshin's critique of *Oak*, with some additional information on Tvardovsky and *Novy Mir* by Linda Aldwinckle and Mary Chaffin.

Medvedev, Zhores. *Ten Years after Ivan Denisovich*. Translated by Hilary Sternberg. London: Macmillan, 1973; New York: Knopf, 1974. A sympathetic account of Solzhenitsyn's trials and tribulations in the Soviet Union from 1963 to 1973 by an insider personally acquainted with most of the protagonists.

Panin, Dimitri. *The Notebooks of Sologdin*. Translated by John Moore. London: Hutchinson; New York: Harcourt Brace Jovanovich, 1976. Panin's reminiscences of his life in Soviet prisons and camps, including the time he spent with Solzhenitsyn in the *sharashka* and at Ekibastuz.

Reshetovskaya, Natalia. *Sanya: My Life with Alexander Solzhenitsyn*. Translated by Elena Ivanoff. Indianapolis: Bobbs-Merrill, 1975; London: Hart-Davis, 1977. The heavily cut and tendentiously edited memoirs of Solzhenitsyn's first wife, which nevertheless contain a lot of interesting detail about Solzhenitsyn's domestic and personal affairs.

Solzhenitsyn: A Pictorial Record. London: Bodley Head, 1974. *Solzhenitsyn: A Pictorial Autobiography*. New York: Farrar, Straus & Giroux, 1974. An album of photographs of Solzhenitsyn from childhood to the time of his second marriage, selected by the author.

LITERARY AND SPECIALIST STUDIES

Barker, Francis. *Solzhenitsyn: Politics and Form*. London: Macmillan; New York: Barnes & Noble, 1977.

Carter, Stephen. *The Politics of Solzhenitsyn*. New York: Holmes & Meier; London: Macmillan, 1977.

Dunlop, John, Richard Haugh, and Alexis Klimoff, eds. *Aleksandr Solzhenitsyn: Critical Essays and Documentary Materials*. 2d ed. New York: Macmillan; London: Collier Macmillan, 1975.

Ericson, Edward E. *Solzhenitsyn: The Moral Vision*. Grand Rapids: Eerdmans, 1980.

Feuer, Kathryn, ed. *Solzhenitsyn: A Collection of Critical Essays*. Englewood Cliffs, N.J.: Prentice-Hall, 1976.

Kodjak, Andrej. *Alexander Solzhenitsyn*. Boston: Twayne, 1978. A short critical study of Solzhenitsyn's main literary works.

Krasnov, Vladislav. *Solzhenitsyn and Dostoevsky: A Study in the Polyphonic Novel*. Athens: University of Georgia Press, 1980.

Labedz, Leopold, ed. *Solzhenitsyn: A Documentary Record*. Enl. ed. Bloomington: Indiana University Press, 1973; Harmondsworth: Penguin Books, 1974.

Lukács, Georg. *Solzhenitsyn*. Translated from the German by William David Graf. London: Merlin Press, 1970; Cambridge, Mass.: MIT Press, 1971. Two critical essays on Solzhenitsyn's relation to socialist realism.

Moody, Christopher. *Solzhenitsyn*. 2d ed. rev. Edinburgh: Oliver & Boyd; New York: Barnes & Noble, 1976. A short critical study of Solzhenitsyn's literary works up to *August 1914*, the best to date.

Nielsen, Niels Christian. *Solzhenitsyn's Religion*. Nashville: Thomas Nelson, 1975; London: Mowbray, 1976.

Rothberg, Abraham. *Aleksandr Solzhenitsyn: The Major Novels*. Ithaca: Cornell University Press, 1971. A superficial examination of *Ivan Denisovich*, *Cancer Ward*, and *First Circle*.

Rzhevsky, Leonid. *Solzhenitsyn: Creator and Heroic Deed*. Translated by Sonja Miller. University: University of Alabama Press, 1978. An interesting study of Solzhenitsyn's literary works by a Russian critic living in the United States.

Berman, Ronald, et al. *Solzhenitsyn at Harvard: The Address, Twelve Early Responses, and Six Later Reflections*. Washington, D.C.: Ethics and Public Policy Center, 1980.

GENERAL BACKGROUND

Allan, James. *No Citation*. London: Angus & Robertson, 1955. Absorbing account of an Englishman's incarceration in the Lubyanka during the Second World War on suspicion of being a spy.

Amalrik, Andrei. *Notes of a Revolutionary*. Translated by Guy Daniels. New York: Knopf; London: Weidenfeld & Nicolson, 1982.

————. *Will the Soviet Union Survive until 1984?* Rev. and enl. ed. Translated by Peter Reddaway, edited by Hilary Sternberg. London: Pelican Books, 1980; New York: Harper & Row, 1981.

Brumberg, Abraham, ed. *In Quest of Justice*. New York: Praeger; London: Pall Mall, 1970.

Bukovsky, Vladimir. *To Build a Castle*. Translated by Michael Scammell. London: Deutsch; New York: Viking Press, 1978.

Chamberlin, W. H. *The Russian Revolution*. 2 vols. New York: Grossett & Dunlap, 1965.

Conquest, Robert. *Courage of Genius*. London: Collins/Harvill, 1961. A history of the "Pasternak affair."

————. *The Great Terror*. London and New York: Macmillan, 1968.

Dallin, David, and Boris Nicolaevsky. *Forced Labor in Soviet Russia*. New Haven: Yale University Press, 1947.

Etkind, Efim. *Notes of a Non-conspirator*. Translated by Peter France. Oxford and New York: Oxford University Press, 1978.

Gorbanevskaya, Natalia. *Red Square at Noon*. Translated by Alexander Lieven. London: Deutsch; New York: Holt, Rinehart & Winston, 1972.

Grigorenko, Petr. *The Grigorenko Papers*. Translated by A. Knight, Marita Sapiets, and Peter Reddaway. Boulder, Colo.: Westview Press, 1976.

Hayward, Max, ed. and trans. *On Trial*. London: Harvill; New York: Harper & Row, 1967. A translation of Alexander Ginzburg's "White Book" on the 1966 trial of Daniel and Sinyavsky.

Hayward, Max, and Edward L. Crowley, eds. *Soviet Literature in the Sixties*. New York: Praeger, 1964; London: Methuen, 1965.

Johnson, Priscilla. *Khrushchev and the Arts*. Cambridge, Mass.: MIT Press, 1965.

Kaiser, Robert. *Russia*. New York: Atheneum, 1976; London: Secker & Warburg, 1977.

Kuznetsov, Edward. *Prison Diaries*. Translated by Howard Spier. London: Vallentine, Mitchell; New York: Stein & Day, 1975.

Lapenna, Ivo. *Soviet Penal Policy*. London: Bodley Head; Chester Springs, Pa.: Dufour, 1968.

Litvinov, Pavel, ed. *The Demonstration in Pushkin Square*. Translated by Manya Harari. London: Harvill; Boston: Gambit, 1969.

————, ed. *The Trial of the Four*. Translated by Janis Sapiets, Hilary Sternberg, and Daniel Weissbort. [London]: Longman; New York: Viking Press, 1972.

Marchenko, Anatoly. *My Testimony*. Translated by Michael Scammell. London: Pall Mall; New York: Dutton, 1969.

Medvedev, Roy. *Let History Judge*. Translated by Colleen Taylor. London: Macmillan; New York: Knopf, 1971.

Medvedev, Roy, and Zhores Medvedev. *A Question of Madness*. Translated by Ellen de Kadt. London: Macmillan; New York: Knopf, 1971.

Medvedev, Zhores. *The Medvedev Papers*. Translated by Vera Rich. London: Macmillan, 1971.

Reddaway, Peter, ed. and trans. *Uncensored Russia*. London: Cape; New York: American Heritage Press, 1972. Based on nos. 1–11 of the *Chronicle of Current Events*.

Rubenstein, Joshua. *Soviet Dissidents*. Boston: Beacon Press, 1980.

Sakharov, Andrei D. *Progress, Coexistence, and Intellectual Freedom*. Translated by the *New York Times*. London: Deutsch; New York: Norton, 1968.

———. *Sakharov Speaks*. Translated by Guy Daniels et al. New York: Knopf; London: Collins/Harvill, 1974.

Smith, Hedrick. *The Russians*. New York: Quadrangle Books; London: Times Books, 1976.

Svirski, Grigori. *A History of Post-war Soviet Writing*. Translated and edited by Robert Dessaix and Michael Ulman. Ann Arbor: Ardis, 1981.

Tatu, Michel. *Power in the Kremlin*. Translated from the French by Helen Katel. New York: Viking Press, 1969.

For a detailed account of how censorship has been exercised and how civil and human rights have been suppressed in the Soviet Union from 1968 to the present day, readers may like to consult the incomparable *Chronicle of Current Events* (Khronika tekushchikh sobytii). Issues 1–11 (covering the years 1968–69) form the substance of Peter Reddaway's book *Uncensored Russia* (see above). Issues 12–64 (the latest to appear to date) have been published in full in an English translation by Amnesty International, London (1 Easton Street, London WC1X 8DJ).

Other publications used as sources for this biography will be found in the numbered notes to each chapter.

INDEX

Politics in Paladin Books

Aneurin Bevan (Vols 1 & 2)　　　　　　　　　£2.95　☐
Michael Foot　　　　　　　　　　　　　　　　　　each
The classic political biography of post-war politics.

Karl Marx: His Life and Thought　　　　　　　£3.95　☐
David McLellan
A major biography by Britain's leading Marxist historian. Marx is shown in his private and family life as well as in his political contexts.

The Strange Death of Liberal England　　　　　£2.95　☐
George Dangerfield
This brilliant and persuasive book examines the forces responsible for the breakdown of Liberal Society in England. At once an exposition of the causes for the dissolution of a great period in English history and a reluctant threnody for the age of purpose and order. 'A brilliant analysis.' *The Times*.

War Plan UK　　　　　　　　　　　　　　　　£2.95　☐
Duncan Campbell
The secret truth about Britain's civil defence. The result of more than five years' research, the book reveals the incredible history of how one government after another has planned to protect itself and survive. 'An unprecedented break in the secrecy surrounding civil defence planning.' *The Observer*. Fully illustrated.

The Plutonium Business　　　　　　　　　　　£2.95　☐
Walter C. Patterson
Concerned by the rarity of uranium at the dawn of the nuclear age, physicists came up with a compelling concept – the fast breeder reactor. But uranium is no longer scarce and a great vision has gone sour. In this searching analysis, Patterson argues that the plutonium people must be stopped – for the sake of all humanity.

To order direct from the publisher just tick the titles you want and fill in the order form.　　　　　　　　　**PAL7482**

History in Paladin Books

Europe's Inner Demons £1.75 ☐
Norman Cohn
The history of the vilification of minority groups as scapegoats, by the author of *The Pursuit of the Millennium*.

In Time of War £4.95 ☐
Robert Fisk
In this exciting and brilliantly vivid narrative, Robert Fisk brings to life the little-known history of Ireland during the Second World War. Illustrated.

A History of the Great War 1914-1918 £3.95 ☐
C R M F Cruttwell
An intelligent and graphically readable account of the campaignings and battles of the 1914-18 War presented here for the general reader along with sympathetic portraits of the leaders and generals of all the countries involved. Scrupulously fair, praising and blaming friend and enemy as circumstances demand, it has become established as the classic acocunt of the first world-wide war. Illustrated.

Anatomy of the SS State £2.50 ☐
Helmut Krausnick and Martin Broszat
The inside story of the concentration camps, 'probably the most impressive work on the Nazi period ever to appear'. *Times Educational Supplement*.

Blind Eye to Murder £3.95 ☐
Tom Bower
A dispassionate but shocking indictment of Allied postwar policy. Bower dispels once and for all the myth that important Nazi criminals were removed from power. 'Devastating'. *Max Hastings*. Illustrated.

To order direct from the publisher just tick the titles you want and fill in the order form. PAL7182

Biography in Paladin Books

Mussolini   £2.95 ☐
Denis Mack Smith
'Will be remembered . . . for the exceptional clarity and brilliance of
the writing. His portrait of Mussolini the man is the best we have.'
Times Literary Supplement.

Karl Marx: His Life and Thought   £3.95 ☐
David McLellan
A major biography by Britain's leading Marxist historian. Marx is
shown in his private and family life as well as in his political
contexts.

Miles Davis   £3.95 ☐
Ian Carr
'For more than a quarter-century Miles Davis has personified the
modern jazz artist. Mr Carr's biography is in a class by itself. He
knows his music and his Miles' *New York Times Book Review*

The Life of William Blake   £1.95 ☐
Mona Wilson
Poet, printer, prophet, philosopher – the importance and influence of
William Blake's extraordinary vision continue to grow. Originally
published in 1927, this is still the most authoritative biography
available.

Freud: The Man and the Cause   £3.95 ☐
Ronald W Clark
With great objectivity, Ronald Clark provides a new, human and
revealing portrait of the physician who changed man's image of
himself. He also gives a clear and balanced account of the medical
world of Freud's early professional years; the conception of
psychoanalysis; Freud's struggle for recognition; and how his
achievement can be viewed in the light of contemporary knowledge.
Illustrated.

To order direct from the publisher just tick the titles you want
and fill in the order form.   **PAL4182**

All these books are available at your local bookshop or newsagent, or can be ordered direct from the publisher.

To order direct from the publishers just tick the titles you want and fill in the form below.

Name _____

Address _____

_____

Send to:
Paladin Cash Sales
PO Box 11, Falmouth, Cornwall TR10 9EN.

Please enclose remittance to the value of the cover price plus:

UK 45p for the first book, 20p for the second book plus 14p per copy for each additional book ordered to a maximum charge of £1.63.

BFPO and Eire 45p for the first book, 20p for the second book plus 14p per copy for the next 7 books, thereafter 8p per book.

Overseas 75p for the first book and 21p for each additional book.

Paladin Books reserve the right to show new retail prices on covers, which may differ from those previously advertised in the text or elsewhere.